Trademark Law
and Policy

Trademark Law and Policy

Second Edition

Kenneth L. Port
PROFESSOR OF LAW AND
DIRECTOR, INTELLECTUAL PROPERTY INSTITUTE
WILLIAM MITCHELL COLLEGE OF LAW

CAROLINA ACADEMIC PRESS
Durham, North Carolina

ISBN 978-1-59460-547-5
LCCN: 2008924394

Carolina Academic Press
700 Kent Street
Durham, North Carolina 27701
Telephone (919) 489-7486
Fax (919) 493-5668
www.cap-press.com

Printed in the United States of America

Summary of Contents

Prelude   xxxix

Chapter I: Introduction   3
  A. Source of American Trademark Law   3
  B. Natural Rights or Positive Rights?   7
  C. Comparison: Civil Law vs. Common Law   20

Chapter II: Why Protect Trademarks?   29
  A. Competition   29
  B. Economic Justification of Protecting Trademarks   30
  C. Social Justification of Protecting Trademarks   32
  D. Justification in Light of the First Amendment   33

Chapter III: Subject Matter   49
  A. Word Marks   49
  B. Trade Dress   55
  C. Scent Marks   63
  D. Sound   66
  E. Color   69

Chapter IV: Infringement of the Trademark Right   77
  A. Likelihood of Confusion   77
  B. Relevant Consuming Public   93
  C. Initial Interest Confusion   101
  D. Reverse Confusion   103
  E. Contributory Infringement   107
  F. Vicarious Liability   110
  G. Defenses   115

Chapter V: Requirements of a Trademark   141
  A. Distinctiveness   141
  B. Secondary Meaning in Trademarks   147

Chapter VI: Acquisition of Trademark Rights   165
  A. Adoption and Use   165
  B. Priority   180
  C. Concurrent Use   193
  D. Intent to Use   200

Chapter VII: Trademark Registration   219
    A. Registration Process   219
    B. Advantages of Registration   222
    C. Statutory Bars to Registration   224
    D. Trademark Searches   303

Chapter VIII: Incontestability   305

Chapter IX: Loss of Trademark Rights   325
    A. Genericism   325
    B. Abandonment   357

Chapter X: Section 43(a)   385
    A. Unregistered "Marks"   385
    B. Inherently Distinctive Trade Dress 394
    C. Functional Trade Dress   401
    D. False Advertising   416
    E. Outer Limits of Claims under §43(a) 432
    F. Section 43(b)   441

Chapter XI: Dilution (Section 43(c))   449
    A. Background   449
    B. State Law Incorporation   455
    C. FTDA   465

Chapter XII: Domain Names (Section 43(d))   497
    A. The Problem: Cybersquatting   497
    B. Introduction to the Current Domain Name System 499
    C. The Domain Name Registration Process 505
    D. Legal Protections of Domain Names   509
    E. Dilution   515
    F. Anticybersquatting Consumer Protection Act (ACPA) 521
    G. Administrative Dispute Resolution of Domain Names:
        The Uniform Domain Name Dispute Resolution Policy (UDRP) 550
    H. Other Cybersquatting Issues   562
    I. Relationship between the ACPA and the UDRP 592
    J. Nominative Use (Meta Tags)   598
    K. Pop-Up Advertising   602
    L. "Key Word Density"   609

Chapter XIII: International Influences and Harmonization 615
    A. Paris Convention   615
    B. TRIPs Agreement   619
    C. Madrid Protocol   629
    D. Extraterritoriality   634

Chapter XIV: Remedies   645
    A. Injunctions   645
    B. Disclaimers   650

   C. Recalls and Destruction   654
   D. Monetary Relief   657

Appendix: Lanham Act, U.S.C. §15   679

Index   723

Detailed Table of Contents

Table of Primary Cases   xxi

Table of Secondary Sources   xxv

Table of Graphs, Charts and Images   xxxiii

Acknowledgments   xxxv

Editorial Note   xxxvii

Prelude   xxxix

Chapter I: Introduction   3
  A. Source of American Trademark Law   3
    The Trademark Cases   4
    United Drug Co. v. Theodore Rectanus Co.   6
  B. Natural Rights or Positive Rights?   7
    INS v. AP   7
    The National Basketball Association v. Motorola, Inc. and
      Sports Team Analysis and Tracking Systems, Inc.   14
    Cheney Bros. v. Doris Silk Corporation   17
    Order of Job's Daughters v. Lindeburg & Co.   19
  C. Comparison: Civil Law vs. Common Law   20
    McDonald's Co. (Japan), Ltd. v. K.K. Marushin Foods   20
      Notes   23

Chapter II: Why Protect Trademarks?   29
  A. Competition   29
    Restatement of the Law (Third), Unfair Competition—
      Chapter 1. The Freedom to Compete   29
  B. Economic Justification of Protecting Trademarks   30
    Kenneth L. Port, The Congressional Expansion of American
      Trademark Law: A Civil Law System in the Making   30
  C. Social Justification of Protecting Trademarks   32
    Kenneth L. Port, The Congressional Expansion of American
      Trademark Law: A Civil Law System in the Making   32
      Notes   33

D. Justification in Light of the First Amendment   33
   Dallas Cowboy Cheerleaders Inc. v. Pussycat Cinema, Inc.   34
   L.L. Bean, Inc. v. Drake Publishers, Inc.   35
   Mattel, Inc. v. MCA Records   41
        Notes   45

Chapter III: Subject Matter   49
  A. Word Marks   49
    1. Trademarks   49
   Coca-Cola Co. v. Koke Co. of America   49
    2. Service Marks   51
   15 U.S.C. §1127, Lanham Act §45   51
   In re Dr Pepper Co.   51
        Notes   55
  B. Trade Dress   55
    1. Product Packaging   55
   Fun-Damental Too v. Gemmy Indus. Corp.   55
    2. Product Configuration   59
   Ashley Furniture Industries v. Sangiacomo N.A.   59
        Note   61
    3. The "Tertium Quid"   62
   Two Pesos, Inc. v. Taco Cabana, Inc.   62
        Notes   62
  C. Scent Marks   63
   In re Celia Clarke   63
        Notes   65
  D. Sound   66
   In re General Electric Broadcasting Company, Inc.   66
        Notes   68
  E. Color   69
   Qualitex Co. v. Jacobson Products Co. Inc.   69
        Notes   74

Chapter IV: Infringement of the Trademark Right   77
  A. Likelihood of Confusion   77
   15 U.S.C. §1114 (Lanham Act §32)   77
   Polaroid Corp. v. Polarad Elects. Corp.   77
   Duluth News-Tribune v. Mesabi Publ. Co.   80
        Note   85
   Vitarroz Corp. v. Borden, Inc.   85
   Borinquen Biscuit Corp. v. M. V. Trading Corp.   89
        Notes   91
  B. Relevant Consuming Public   93
   Mastercrafters Clock& Radio Co. v.
      Vacheron & Constantin—Le Coultre Watches, Inc.   93
   Munsingwear, Inc. v. Jockey International   95
  C. Initial Interest Confusion   101
   Australian Gold, Inc. v. Hatfield   101
  D. Reverse Confusion   103

Sands, Taylor & Wood Co. v. Quaker Oats Co. 103
    Notes 106
E. Contributory Infringement 107
Restatement (Third) of Unfair Competition §26 107
Inwood Labs., Inc. v. Ives Labs., Inc. 107
    Note 110
F. Vicarious Liability 110
Lockheed Martin Corp. v. Network Solutions, Inc. 111
    Note 115
G. Defenses 115
  1. Fair Use 115
United States Shoe Corp. v. Brown Group Inc. 115
KP Permanent Make-Up, Inc. v. Lasting Impression I, Inc. 119
    Notes 124
  2. Nominative Fair Use 124
Brother Records v. Jardine 124
Century 21 Real Estate Corp. v. Lendingtree. Inc. 127
    Notes 132
  3. Laches/Acquiescence 133
Menendez v. Holt 133
What-a-Burger of Virginia, Inc. v.
    Whataburger, Inc., of Corpus Christi, Texas 136
    Notes 139

Chapter V: Requirements of a Trademark 141
A. Distinctiveness 141
Abercrombie & Fitch Co. v. Hunting World, Inc. 141
    Notes 146
B. Secondary Meaning in Trademarks 147
International Kennel Club of Chicago, Inc. v. Mighty Star, Inc. .. 147
Zatarains, Inc. v. Oak Grove Smokehouse, Inc. 153
Foamation, Inc. v. Wedeward Enterprises, Inc. 157
    Notes 162

Chapter VI: Acquisition of Trademark Rights 165
A. Adoption and Use 165
15 U.S.C. §1127, Lanham Act §45 165
Proctor & Gamble Company v. Johnson & Johnson, Inc. 166
Larry Harmon Pictures Corp. v. Williams Restaurant Corp. 172
Int'l Bancorp, LLC v. Societe Des Bains De Mer et
    du Cercle Des Etrangers a Monaco 175
    Notes 179
B. Priority 180
Blue Bell, Inc. v. Farah Mfg. Co. 180
Bell v. Streetwise Records, Ltd. 185
Maryland Stadium Authority v. Becker 189
    Notes 192
C. Concurrent Use 193
Burger King of Florida, Inc. v. Hoots 193

Dawn Donut Co. v. Hart's Food Stores, Inc.   196
        Notes   199
D. Intent to Use   200
    15 U.S.C. §1051, Lanham Act §1   200
    15 U.S.C. §1057, Lanham Act §7   200
    Introduction to the ITU System   201
    Zirco Corp. v. American Telephone & Telegraph Co.   202
    Fila Sport, S.P.A. v. Diadora America, Inc.   205
    Eastman Kodak Co. v.
        Bell & Howell Document Management Products Co.   210
        Notes   216

Chapter VII: Trademark Registration   219
A. Registration Process   219
B. Advantages of Registration   222
C. Statutory Bars to Registration   224
    1. Section 2(a): Scandalous Marks   224
    15 U.S.C. §1052, Lanham Act §2   224
    In re Old Glory Condom Corp.   225
    Pro-Football, Inc. v. Harjo   229
        Notes   239
    2. Section 2(b): Flag or Coat of Arms   243
    15 U.S.C. §1052, Lanham Act. §2   243
    In re United States Dept. of the Interior   244
        Note   245
    3. Section 2(c): Names, Portrait, Signatures   246
    15 U.S.C. §1052, Lanham Act §2   246
    In re Steak and Ale Restaurants of America   246
        Note   248
    4. Section 2(d): Confusion   248
    15 U.S.C. §1052, Lanham Act §2   248
    In re Majestic Distilling Co.   248
    Marshall Field & Company v. Mrs. Fields Cookies   254
        Notes   262
    5(a). Section 2(e)(1): Merely Descriptive   262
    15 U.S.C. §1052, Lanham Act §2   262
    In re Bed & Breakfast Registry   262
    5(b). Section 2(e)(1): Deceptively Misdescriptive   264
    Steinberg Brothers, Inc. v. New England-Overall Co., Inc.   264
    Glendale Int'l Corp. v. PTO   265
    5(c). Section 2(e)(2): Primarily Geographically Descriptive   268
    15 U.S.C. §1052, Lanham Act §2   268
    In re Compagnie Generale Maritime   268
    5(d). Section 2(e)(3): Primarily Geographically Deceptively Misdescriptive 270
    15 U.S.C. §1052, Lanham Act §2   270
    In re Cal. Innovations, Inc.   270
    Japan Telecom, Inc. v. Japan Telecom America Inc.   275
    In re Wada   277
    Daesang Corp. v. Rhee Bros., Inc.   280
        Notes   283

5(e). Section 2(e)(4): Primarily Merely a Surname 285
15 U.S.C. §1052, Lanham Act §2 285
In re Kahan & Weisz Jewelry Mfg. 285
Taylor Wine Company, Inc. v. Bully Hill Vineyards, Inc. 286
5(f). Section 2(e)(5): Functionality 290
15 U.S.C. §1052, Lanham Act §2 290
In re Morton-Norwich Products, Inc. 290
   Notes 298
6. Section 2(f): Statutory Secondary Meaning 299
15 U.S.C. §1052, Lanham Act §2 299
Yamaha International Corporation v. Hoshino Gakki Co., Ltd. 299
D. Trademark Searches 303

Chapter VIII: Incontestability 305
15 U.S.C. §1064, Lanham Act §14 305
15 U.S.C. §1065, Lanham Act §15 305
15 U.S.C. §1115, Lanham Act §33 306
Park 'N Fly, Inc. v. Dollar Park and Fly, Inc. 311
Munters Corporation v. Matsui America Inc. 319
Dieter v. B & H Industries, Inc. 321
   Notes 323

Chapter IX: Loss of Trademark Rights 325
A. Genericism 325
15 U.S.C. §1064, Lanham Act §14 325
Kellogg Co. v. National Biscuit Co. 325
Bayer Co. v. United Drug 330
King-Seeley Thermos Co. v. Aladdin Industries, Inc. 335
Anti-Monopoly, Inc. v. General Mills Fun Group, Inc. 338
Yellow Cab Co. of Sacramento v. Yellow Cab of Elk Grove, Inc. 345
   Notes 346
   Special Note on Surveys 347
Schering Corp. v. Pfizer Inc. 347
B. Abandonment 357
1. Non-Use 357
Silverman v. CBS, Inc. 357
University Bookstore v. Wisconsin Board of Regents 361
Birch Publications, Inc., et al. v. RMZ of St. Cloud, Inc. 367
   Notes 370
2. Inappropriate Use 371
  a. Assignment in Gross 371
Marshak v. Green 371
   Note 374
  b. Naked Licenses/Lack of Quality Control 374
Clark Yocum v. Warren Covington 374
Kentucky Fried Chicken Corp. v. Diversified Packaging Corp. 380
   Note 383
  c. Failure to Police 383
Wallpaper Mfrs., Ltd. v. Crown Wallcovering Corp. 383
   Note 384

Chapter X: Section 43(a)   385
  A. Unregistered "Marks"   385
    15 U.S.C. §1125, Lanham Act §43   385
    Two Pesos, Inc. v. Taco Cabana, Inc.   386
        Note   394
  B. Inherently Distinctive Trade Dress   394
    Wal-Mart Stores, Inc. v. Samara Brothers, Inc.   394
    In re Joanne Slokevag   398
        Notes   400
  C. Functional Trade Dress   401
    TrafFix Devices, Inc. v. Marketing Displays, Inc.   401
    Tie Tech, Inc. v. Kinedyne Corporation   406
    Global Mfg. Group, LLC v. Gadget Universe.com   411
        Notes   414
  D. False Advertising   416
    15 U.S.C. §1125, Lanham Act §43   416
    Coors Brewing Company v. Anheuser-Busch Companies, Inc. 417
    Surdyk's Liquor, Inc. v. MGM Liquor Stores, Inc.   425
        Note   432
  E. Outer Limits of Claims under §43(a)   432
    Dastar Corp. v. Twentieth Century Fox Film Corp.   432
    ETW Corp. v. Jireh Publ.   438
        Notes   440
  F. Section 43(b)   441
    15 U.S.C. §1125, Lanham Act §43   441
    Ross Cosmetics Distribution Ctrs. v. United States   441

Chapter XI: Dilution (Section 43(c))   449
  A. Background   449
    Frank Schecter, The Rational Basis of Trademark Protection 449
  B. State Law Incorporation   455
    Allied Maintenance Corporation v. Allied Mechanical Trades, Inc. 455
        Notes   460
    Mead Data Central, Inc. v. Toyota Motor Sales, U.S.A., Inc. 460
  C. FTDA   465
    1. Cause of Action   465
    15 U.S.C. §1125 (c)(1)   465
      a. Dilution by Blurring   465
      15 U.S.C. §1125 (c)(2)(B)   465
      Louis Vuitton Malletier v. Haute Diggity Dog, LLC 466
      b. Dilution by Tarnishment   472
      15 U.S.C. §1125 (c)(2)(C)   472
      Louis Vuitton Malletier v. Haute Diggity Dog, LLC 472
      Diane Von Furstenberg Studio v. Snyder   472
        Notes   474
    2. Dilution of Trade Dress   474
    I.P. Lund Trading ApS and Kroin Inc. v. Kohler Co.   474
    3. The Supreme Court's View on Dilution   478
    Moseley v. V Secret Catalogue, Inc.   478
        Note   485

Note on Dilution 485
4. Academic View of Dilution 488
Robert G. Bone, A Skeptical View of the
    Trademark Dilution Revision Act 488
        Notes 495

Chapter XII: Domain Names (Section 43(d)) 497
A. The Problem: Cybersquatting 497
    Dan L. Burk, Trademarks along the Infobahn:
        A First Look at the Emerging Law of Cybermarks 497
            Notes 499
B. Introduction to the Current Domain Name System 499
    Image Online Design, Inc. v. Core Association and Ken Stubbs 499
    Wayde Brooks, Wrestling over the World Wide Web: ICANN's
        Uniform Dispute Resolution Policy for Domain Name Disputes 501
            Notes 505
C. The Domain Name Registration Process 505
    ICANN Information 505
        Notes 507
D. Legal Protections of Domain Names 509
    1. Infringement 509
    Intermatic v. Toeppen 509
        Notes 514
E. Dilution 515
    Panavision, Int'l, L.P. v. Toeppen 515
    Bosley Medical Institute, Inc. v. Kremer 518
        Notes 521
F. Anticybersquatting Consumer Protection Act (ACPA) 521
    1. Cause of Action 521
    15 U.S.C. §1125, Lanham Act §43 521
    Sporty's Farm L.L.C. v. Sportsman's Market, Inc. 524
        Note 528
    2. Bad Faith 529
    15 U.S.C. §1125 (d)(l)(B)(i) 529
    Virtual Works, Inc. v. Volkswagen of America, Inc. 529
    Coca-Cola Company v. Purdy 534
    Nissan Motor Co. v. Nissan Computer Corporation 537
        Notes 539
    3. In Rem Jurisdiction: 15 U.S.C. §1125(d)(2)(A) 540
    Harrods Limited v. Sixty Internet Domain Names 540
    Caesars World, Inc. v. Caesars-palace.com 543
        Notes 545
    4. Statutory Damages under the ACPA 546
    15 U.S.C. §1117, Lanham Act §35 546
    E. & J. Gallo Winery v. Spider Webs, Ltd. 547
        Notes 549
G. Administrative Dispute Resolution of
    Domain Names: The Uniform Domain Name
    Dispute Resolution Policy (UDRP) 550

Telstra Corporation Limited v. Nuclear Marshmallows   552
    Notes   555
    1. Identical or Confusingly Similar Mark: UDRP §4(a)(i)   556
Motorola, Inc. v. Newgate Internet, Inc.   556
    Note   557
    2. Legitimate Interests: UDRP §4(a)(ii)   557
Volvo Trademark Holding AD v. e-motordealer Ltd.   558
    3. Registration and Use in Bad Faith: UDRP §4(a)(iii) and §4(b)   560
Recordati S.Pa. v. Domain Name Clearing Company   560
    Notes   562
H. Other Cybersquatting Issues   562
    1. Typosquatting   562
Disney Enterprises, Inc. v. John Zuccarini, Cupcake City and Cupcake Patrol 562
    Notes   567
    2. Reverse Domain Name Hijacking   567
Goldline International, Inc. v. Gold Line   567
    Note   569
    3. John Jacob Jingle Heimer Schmidt, His Name Is
      My Domain Name, Too: Using One's Own "Famous Name"   569
Bruce Springsteen v. Jeff Burgar and Bruce Springsteen Club   569
Gordon Sumner, p/k/a Sting v. Michael Urvan   575
    Notes   581
    4. Your Trademark Sucks.com: Free Speech or Bad Faith?   581
Wal-Mart Stores, Inc. v. Walsucks and Walmarket Puerto Rico   581
Wal-Mart Stores, Inc. v.
    Wallmartcanadasucks.com and Kenneth J. Harvey   588
    Note   592
I. Relationship between the ACPA and the UDRP   592
Sallen v. Corinthians Licenciamentos Ltda   592
    Note   597
J. Nominative Use (Meta Tags)   598
Playboy Enterprises v. Welles   598
Promatek Indus., Ltd v. Equitrac Corp.   601
    Note   602
K. Pop-Up Advertising   602
U-Haul International, Inc. v. WhenU.com, Inc.   602
1-800 Contacts, Inc., v. WhenU.Com, Inc.   605
    Note   609
L. "Key Word Density"   609
J.K. Harris & Co., LLC v. Kassel   609
    Note   612

Chapter XIII: International Influences and Harmonization   615
A. Paris Convention   615
SCM Corp. v. Langis Foods, Ltd.   615
B. TRIPs Agreement   619
J.H. Reichman, Universal Minimum Standards of Intellectual Property
    Protection under the TRIPS Component of the WTO Agreement   619

Kenneth L. Port, Trademark Harmonization:
    Norms, Names and Nonsense   624
        Note   629
C. Madrid Protocol   629
    Experience with the Madrid Protocol   631
D. Extraterritoriality   634
    Steele v. Bulova Watch Co.   634
    Cecil McBee v. Delica Co., Ltd.   638
        Notes   642

Chapter XIV: Remedies   645
A. Injunctions   645
    15 U.S.C. §1116, Lanham Act §34   645
    Firma Melodiya v. ZYX Music GmbH   645
        Note   650
B. Disclaimers   650
    Home Box Office, Inc. v. Showtime/The Movie Channel Inc.   650
C. Recalls and Destruction   654
    Kiki Undies Corp. v. Promenade Hosiery Mills, Inc.   654
D. Monetary Relief   657
    15 U.S.C. §1117, Lanham Act §35   657
    1. Recovery of Defendant's Profits (Accounting)   657
    George Basch Co. v. Blue Coral, Inc.   657
    2. Recovery of Plaintiff's Actual Damages   664
    Brunswick v. Spinit   664
        Note   665
    3. Punitive Damages   666
    15 U.S.C. §1117(a), Lanham Act §35(a)   666
    Getty Petroleum Corp. v. Bartco Petroleum Corp.   666
        Notes   671
    4. Attorneys' Fees   672
    15 U.S.C. §1117(a), Lanham Act §35(a)   672
    Quaker State Oil Refining Corp. v. Kooltone, Inc.   672
    WSM, Inc. v. Wheeler Media Services, Inc.   673
        Notes   676

Appendix: Lanham Act, U.S.C. §15   679

Index   723

Table of Primary Cases

Abercrombie & Fitch Co. v. Hunting World, Inc., 69, 141, 312, 395

Allied Maintenance Corporation v. Allied Mechanical Trades, Inc., 455

Anti-Monopoly, Inc. v. General Mills Fun Group, Inc., 338

Ashley Furniture Industries v. Sangiacomo N.A., 59

Australian Gold, Inc. v. Hatfield, 101

Bayer Co. v. United Drug, 42, 330

Bed & Breakfast Registry, In re, 262

Bell v. Streetwise Records, Ltd., 185

Birch Publications, Inc., et al. v. RMZ of St. Cloud, Inc., 367

Blue Bell, Inc. v. Farah Mfg. Co., 180

Borinquen Biscuit Corp. v. M. V. Trading Corp., 89

Bosley Medical Institute, Inc. v. Kremer, 518

Brother Records v. Jardine, 124

Bruce Springsteen v. Jeff Burgar and Bruce Springsteen Club, 569

Brunswick v. Spinit, 664

Burger King of Florida, Inc. v. Hoots, 193

Caesars World, Inc. v. Caesarspalace.com, 543

Cecil McBee v. Delica Co., Ltd., 638, 643

Celia Clarke, In re, 63

Century 21 Real Estate Corp. v. Lendingtree. Inc., 127

Cheney Bros. v. Doris Silk Corporation, 17

Clark Yocum v. Warren Covington, 374

Coca-Cola Co. v. Koke Co. of America, 49, 73

Coca-Cola Company v. Purdy, 534

Compagnie Generale Maritime, In re, 268

Coors Brewing Company v. Anheuser-Busch Companies, Inc., 417

Daesang Corp. v. Rhee Bros., Inc., 280, 285

Dallas Cowboy Cheerleaders Inc. v. Pussycat Cinema, Inc., 34

Dastar Corp. v. Twentieth Century Fox Film Corp., 432

Dawn Donut Co. v. Hart's Food Stores, Inc., 196

Diane Von Furstenberg Studio v. Snyder, 472

Dieter v. B & H Industries, Inc., 321

Disney Enterprises, Inc. v. John Zuccarini, Cupcake City and Cupcake Patrol, 562

Dr Pepper Co., In re, 51

Duluth News-Tribune v. Mesabi Publ. Co., 80

E. & J. Gallo Winery v. Spider Webs, Ltd., 547

Eastman Kodak Co. v. Bell & Howell Document Management Products Co., 210

ETW Corp. v. Jireh Publ., 438

Fila Sport, S.P.A. v. Diadora America, Inc., 205

Firma Melodiya v. ZYX Music GmbH, 645

Foamation, Inc. v. Wedeward Enterprises, Inc., 157

Fun-Damental Too v. Gemmy Indus. Corp., 55

General Electric Broadcasting Company, Inc., In re, 66

George Basch Co. v. Blue Coral, Inc., 657

Getty Petroleum Corp. v. Bartco Petroleum Corp., 666

Glendale Int'l Corp. v. PTO, 265

Global Mfg. Group, LLC v. Gadget Universe.com, 411

Goldline International, Inc. v. Gold Line, 567

Gordon Sumner, p/k/a Sting v Michael Urvan, 575

Harrods Limited v. Sixty Internet Domain Names, 540

Home Box Office, Inc. v. Showtime/The Movie Channel Inc., 650

I.P. Lund Trading ApS and Kroin Inc. v. Kohler Co., 474

Image Online Design, Inc. v. Core Association and Ken Stubbs, 499

Int'l Bancorp, LLC v. Societe Des Bains De Mer et du Cercle Des Etrangers a Monaco, 175

Intermatic v. Toeppen, 509, 521

International Kennel Club of Chicago, Inc. v. Mighty Star, Inc., 147

Inwood Labs., Inc. v. Ives Labs., Inc., 107

J.K. Harris & Co., LLC v. Kassel, 609

Japan Telecom, Inc. v. Japan Telecom America Inc., 275

Joanne Slokevag, In re, 398, 401

Kahan & Weisz Jewelry Mfg., In re, 285

Kellogg Co. v. National Biscuit Co., 156, 325, 435

Kentucky Fried Chicken Corp. v. Diversified Packaging Corp., 380

Kiki Undies Corp. v. Promenade Hosiery Mills, Inc., 654

King-Seeley Thermos Co. v. Aladdin Industries, Inc., 335, 342

KP Permanent Make-Up, Inc. v. Lasting Impression I, Inc., 119, 128

L.L. Bean, Inc. v. Drake Publishers, Inc., 42, 463

Larry Harmon Pictures Corp. v. Williams Restaurant Corp., 172

Lockheed Martin Corp. v. Network Solutions, Inc., 111

Louis Vuitton Malletier v. Haute Diggity Dog, LLC, 466, 472

Majestic Distilling Co.,In re, 248

Marshak v. Green, 371, 373

Marshall Field & Company v. Mrs. Fields Cookies, 254

Maryland Stadium Authority v. Becker, 189

Mastercrafters Clock& Radio Co. v. Vacheron & Constantin-Le Coultre Watches, Inc., 93

Mattel, Inc. v. MCA Records, 41, 519

McDonald's Co. (Japan), Ltd. v. K.K. Marushin Foods, 20

Mead Data Central, Inc. v. Toyota Motor Sales, U.S.A., Inc., 460, 476

Menendez v. Holt, 133

Morton-Norwich Products, Inc., In re, 290

Moseley v. V Secret Catalogue, Inc., 478, 488

Motorola, Inc. v. Newgate Internet, Inc., 556

Munsingwear, Inc. v. Jockey International, 95

Munters Corporation v. Matsui America Inc., 319

Nissan Motor Co. v. Nissan Computer Corporation, 537

Old Glory Condom Corp., In re, 225, 228

1-800 Contacts, Inc., v. WhenU.Com, Inc., 605

Order of Job's Daughters v. Lindeburg & Co., 19

Panavision, Int'l, L.P. v. Toeppen, 515

Park 'N Fly, Inc. v. Dollar Park and Fly, Inc., 311, 320, 666

Pebble Beach Co. v. Tour 18 Limited, xxxiii

Playboy Enterprises v. Welles, 598

Polaroid Corp. v. Polarad Elects. Corp., 77

Proctor & Gamble Company v. Johnson & Johnson, Inc., 166

Promatek Indus., Ltd v. Equitrac Corp., 601

Quaker State Oil Refining Corp. v. Kooltone, Inc., 672

Qualitex Co. v. Jacobson Products Co. Inc., 69

Recordati S.Pa. v. Domain Name Clearing Company, 560

Ross Cosmetics Distribution Ctrs. v. United States, 441

Sallen v. Corinthians Licenciamentos Ltda, 592

Sands, Taylor & Wood Co. v. Quaker Oats Co., 103

Schering Corp. v. Pfizer Inc., 347

SCM Corp. v. Langis Foods, Ltd., 209, 615

Silverman v. CBS, Inc., 357

Sporty's Farm L.L.C. v. Sportsman's Market, Inc., 524, 530

Steak and Ale Restaurants of America, In re, 246

Steele v. Bulova Watch Co., 519, 634, 638

Steinberg Brothers, Inc. v. New England-Overall Co., Inc., 264

Surdyk's Liquor, Inc. v. MGM Liquor Stores, Inc., 425

Taylor Wine Company, Inc. v. Bully Hill Vineyards, Inc., 286

Telstra Corporation Limited v. Nuclear Marshmallows, 552, 561, 580

The National Basketball Association v. Motorola, Inc. and Sports Team Analysis and Tracking Systems, Inc., 14

The Trademark Cases, 4, 23

Tie Tech, Inc. v. Kinedyne Corporation, 406

TrafFix Devices, Inc. v. Marketing Displays, Inc., 401, 412, 435

Two Pesos, Inc. v. Taco Cabana, Inc., 58, 61, 69, 222, 386, 403, 412, 439

U-Haul International, Inc. v. WhenU.com, Inc., 602, 606

United Drug Co. v. Theodore Rectanus Co., 6, 24, 167, 177, 182

United States Dept. of the Interior, In re, 244

United States Shoe Corp. v. Brown Group Inc., 115

University Bookstore v. Wisconsin Board of Regents, 361

Virtual Works, Inc. v. Volkswagen of America, Inc., 529

Vitarroz Corp. v. Borden, Inc., 85

Volvo Trademark Holding AD v. e-motordealer Ltd., 558

Wada, In re, 277

Wallpaper Mfrs., Ltd. v. Crown Wallcovering Corp., 383

Wal-Mart Stores, Inc. v. Samara Brothers, Inc., 394, 403, 436

Wal-Mart Stores, Inc. v. Wallmart-canadasucks.com and Kenneth J. Harvey, 588

Wal-Mart Stores, Inc. v. Walsucks and Walmarket Puerto Rico, 557, 581, 591

What-a-Burger of Virginia, Inc. v. Whataburger, Inc., of Corpus Christi, Texas, 136

WSM, Inc. v. Wheeler Media Services, Inc., 673

Yamaha International Corporation v. Hoshino Gakki Co., Ltd., 299

Yellow Cab Co. of Sacramento v. Yellow Cab of Elk Grove, Inc., 345

Zatarains, Inc. v. Oak Grove Smokehouse, Inc., 146, 153

Zirco Corp. v. American Telephone & Telegraph Co., 202

Table of Secondary Sources

Todd Anten, Note, *Self-Disparaging Trademarks and Social Change: Factoring the Reappropriation of Slurs into Section 2(a) of the Lanham Act*, 106 Colum. L. Rev. 288 (2006), 242.

Orion Armon, *Is This as Good as It Gets? An Appraisal of ICANN's Uniform Domain Name Resolution Policy (UDRP) Three Years After Implementation*, 22 Rev. Litig. 99 (2003), 555.

Maury Audet, *Native American Tribal Names as Monikers and Logos: Will These Registrations Withstand Cancellation Under Lanham Act § 2(b) After the Trademark Study on Official Insignia of Native American Tribes?*, 2 J. Intell. Prop. 4 (2000), 246.

Douglas Baird, *Common Law Intellectual Property and the Legacy of* International News Service v. Associated Press, 50 U. Chi. L. Rev. 411, 428 (1983), 23.

Barton Beebe, *A Defense of the New Federal Trademark Antidilution Law*, 16 Fordham Intell. Prop., Media & Ent. L.J. 1143, 1144 (2006), 495.

Ingrida Karins Berzins, *The Emerging Circuit Split Over Secondary Meaning in Trade Dress Law*, 152 U. Pa. L. Rev. 1661 (2004), 400.

Robert G. Bone, *A Skeptical View of the Trademark Dilution Revision Act*, 11 Intell. Prop. L. Bull. 187 (2007), 488.

Steven A. Bowers, *Location, Location, Location: The Case Against Extending Geographical Indiction Protection Under the TRIPs Agreement*, 31 AIPLA Q. 129 (2003), 243.

Robert Brauneis & Roger E. Schechter, *Geographic Trademarks and the Protection of Competitor Communication*, 96 Trademark Rep. 782, 786 (2006), 284.

Michael J. Breslin, Note: ETW Corp. v. Jireh Publishing, Inc: *Turning an Athlete's Publicity Over to the Public*, 11 J. Intell. Prop. L. 369 (2004), 441.

Wayde Brooks, *Wrestling over the World Wide Web: ICANN's Uniform Dispute Resolution Policy for Domain Name Disputes*, 22 Hamline J. Pub. L. & Pol'y 297 (2001), 501.

Clifford W. Browning, Traffix *Revisited: Exposing the Design Flaw in the Functionality Doctrine*, 94 Trademark Rep. 1059 (2004), 415.

W.W. BUCKLAND, A TEXT-BOOK OF ROMAN LAW FROM AUGUSTUS TO JUSTINIAN (1990), 25.

J. Taylor Buckley, *The Bike That Roared: Can Harley's Sound Be Trademarked?*, USA TODAY, Jan. 8, 1996, 68.

Dan L. Burk, *Trademarks along the Infobahn: A First Look at the Emerging Law of Cybermarks,* 1 Rich. J. L. & Tech. 1 (1995), 497.

Irene Calboli, *Trademark Assignment "With Goodwill": A Concept whose Time has Gone*, 57 Fla. L. Rev. 771 (2005), 374.

Rudolph Callmann, The Law of Unfair Competition, Trademarks, and Monopolies § 21.12 (3d ed. 1969), 25.

Rudolph Callmann, *Unfair Competition Without Competition?: The Importance of the Property Concept in the Law of Trade-Marks*, 95 U.Pa. L.Rev. 443, 467 (1947), 25, 324.

Pamela C. Chalk, *The True Value of Trademarks: Influencing Who We Are and Who We Want to Be*, 12 J. Contemp. Legal Issues 20 (2001), 33.

Douglas D. Churovich, *Policy Considerations from a Practitioner's Perspective: Scents, Sense or Cents? Something Stinks in the Lanham Act Scientific Obstacles to Scent Marks*, 20 St. Louis U. Pub. L. Rev. 293 (2001), 65.

Christopher C. Colson, Note, Pizza Hut, Inc. v. Papa John's International, Inc.-*Creating Conflict and Uncertainty in Lanham Act False Advertising Claims*, 41 Brandeis L. J. 333 (2002), 432.

Rosemary J. Coombe, The Cultural Life of Intellectual Properties: Authorship, Appropriation, and the Law (1998), 33.

Rosemary J. Coombe, *Interdisciplinary Approaches to International Economic Law: The Cultural Life of Things: Anthropological Approaches to Law and Society in Conditions of Globalization*, 69 Tex. L.

Rev. 1853 (1991), 33.

Rosemary J. Coombe, *New Direction: Critical Cultural Legal Studies*, 10 Yale J.L. & Human. 463 (1998), 33.

Rosemary J. Coombe, *Objects of Property and Subjects of Politics: Intellectual Property Laws and Democratic Dialogue*, 13 Yale J.L. & Human. 451 (2001), 33.

Cowgirls Calendar at http://www.dallascowboys.com/cheerleaders/home.cfm, 45.

Cybersquatting Remains on the Rise with further Risk to Trademarks from New Registration Practices, htttp://www.wipo.int /pressroom/en/aticles/2007/article_0014.html, 555.

Sanjeev Dave, *Trademark Law Lost in Cyberspace: Had Progress Been Made?*,12 J. Contmp. Legal Issues 506 (2001), 545.

Benjamin G. Davis, *Une Magouille Planetaire: The UDRP Is an International Scam*, 72 Miss. L.J. 815 (2002), 555.

"Debbie Does Dallas," video cover at http://www.xratedcollection.com/gallery/xrated/20738.html, 45.

Robert C. Denicola, *Trademarks as Speech: Constitutional Implications of the Emerging Rationales for the Protection of Trade Symbols*, 1982 Wis. L. Rev. 158, 46.

Deven R. Desai & Sandra L. Rierson, *Confronting the Genericism Conundrum*, 28 Cardozo L. Rev. 1789 (2007), 384.

Shahar J. Dilbary, *Famous Trademarks and Rational Basis for Protecting "Irrational Beliefs,"* 14 Geo. Mason L. Rev. 605 (2007), 496.

Joan L. Dillon & Michael Landau, Two Pesos v. Taco Cabana: *Still More Interesting for What it Did Not Decide*, 94 Trademark Rep. 944 (2004), 394.

Graeme B. Dinwoodie, *Trademarks and Territory: Detaching Trademark Law from the Nation-state*, 41 Hous. L. Rev. 885, 973 (2004), 180.

Graeme B. Dinwoodie & Mark D. Janis, *Dilution's (Still) Uncertain Future*, 105 Mich. L. Rev. First Impressions 98 (2006), 495.

Stacy L. Dogan & Mark A. Lemley, *Grounding Trademark Law through Trademark Use*, 92 Iowa L. Rev. 1669 (2007), 602.

Daniel Domenico, Note, *"Mark Madness": How Brent Musberger and the Miracle Bra May have Led to a More Equitable and Efficient Understanding of the Reverse Confusion Doctrine in Trademark Law*, 86 VA. L. Rev. 597 (2000), 107.

Rochelle Cooper Dreyfuss, *Expressive Genericity: Trademarks as Language in the Pepsi Generation*, 65 Notre Dame L. Rev. 397 (1990), 46.

Kenneth Sutherlin Dueker, *Trademark Law Lost in Cyberspace: Trademark Protection for Internet Addresses,* 9 Harv. J.L. & Tech. 483, 511 (1996), 545.

Tracy-Gene G. Durkin & Julie D. Shirk, *Design Patents and Trade Dress Protection: Are the Two Mutually Exclusive?*, 87 J. Pat. & Trademark Off. Soc'y 770 (2005), 415.

Bettina Elias, *Do Scents Signify Source? An Argument Against Trademark Protection For Fragrances*, 82 Trademark Rep. 475, 509, (1992), 65.

Gary Feldon, Comment, *The Antitrust Model of Extraterritorial Trademark Jurisdiction: Analysis and Predictions after F. Hoffmann-LA Rouch*, 20 Emory Int'l L. Rev. 651 (2006), 642.

Joseph J. Ferretti, *Product Design Trade Dress Hits the Wall … Mart:* Wal-Mart v. Samara Bros., 42 Idea 417, 450 (2002), 400.

Jason Fortenberry, International Bancorp, LLC v. Soiete Des Bains De Mer Et Du Cercle Des Estrangers A Monaco: *The Supreme Court's Silence Speaks Louder than Words*, 25 Miss. College L. Rev. 183, 220 (2006), 180.

Michelle S. Friedman, *Naked Trademark Licenses in Business Format Franchising: The Quality Control Requirement and the Role of Local Culture,* 10 J. Tech. L. & Pol'y, 354, 376 (2005), 383.

Michael G. Frey, Note, *Is It Fair to Confuse? An Examination of Trademark Protection, the Fair Use Defense, and the First Amendment*, 65 U. Cin. L. Rev. 1255 (1997), 132.

Beth Fulkerson, *Theft By Territorialism: A Case For Revising TRIPS To Protect Trademarks From National Market Foreclosure*, 17 Mich. J. Int'l L. 801, 823 (1996), 193.

Brian Gardiner, Comment, *Squatters' Rights And Adverse Possession: A Search for Equitable Application of Property Laws*, 8 Ind. Int'l & Comp. L. Rev. 119 (1997), 499.

H. David Gold, *Legal Strategies to Address the Misrepresentation of Vermont Maple Syrup*, 59 Food & Drug L. J. 93 (2004), 283.

Andrew J. Grotto, *Due Process and In Rem Jurisdiction Under the Anti-Cybersquatting Consumer Protection Act,* 2 Colum. Sci. & Tech. L. Rev. 3 (2001), 545.

Sheldon Halpern, *A High Likelihood of Confusion:* Wal-Mart, Traffix, Moseley, *and* Dastart-*The Supreme Court's New Trademark Jurisprudence*, 61 N.Y.U. Ann. Surv. Am. L. 237 (2005), 415.

Faye M. Hammersley, *The Smell of Success: Trade Dress Protection For Scent Marks,* 2 Marq. Intell. Prop. L. Rev. 105, 156 (1998), 65.

Milton Handler & Charles Pickett, *Trade-Marks and Trade Name—An Analysis and Synthesis: II*, 30 Colum. L. Rev. 759, 767 (1930), 216.

Frank Z. Hellwig, *The Trademark Law Revision Act of 1988: The 100th Congress Leaves Its Mark*, 79 TMR 287 (1989), 204.

Jesse A. Hofrichter, Note, *Tool of the Trademark: Brand Criticism and Free Speech Problems with the Trademark Dilution Revision Act of 2006*, 28 Cardozo L. Rev. 1923 (2007), 474.

Justin Hughes, *The Philosophy of Intellectual Property*, 77 Geo. L. J. 287 (1988), 26.

ICANN Information: http://www.icann.org/general/, 505.

ICANN, "Second Staff Report on Implementation Documents for the Uniform Dispute Resolution Policy," October 24, 1999 at http://www. icann.org/udrp/udrp-second-staff-report-24oct99, 562.

Jacob Jacoby, *Experimental Design and the Selection of Controls in Trademark and Deceptive Advertising Surveys*, 92 Trademark Rep. 890 (2002), 496.

Jacob Jacoby, *The Psychological Foundations of Trademark Law: Secondary Meaning, Genericism, Fame, Confusion and Dilution*, 91 Trademark Rep. 1013 (2001), 496.

Jacob Jacoby & Robert Lloyd Raskopf, *Disclaimers in Trademark Infringement Litigation: More Trouble Than They Are Worth?*, 76 TRADEMARK REP. 35 (1986), 92.

Jacob Jacoby & Maureen Mon-in, *"Not Manufactured or Authorized By ...": Recent Federal Cases Involving Trademark Disclaimers*, 17 J. Pub. Pol'y & Marketing 97 (1998), 92.

ADAM B. JAFFE & JOSH LERNER, INNOVATION AND ITS DISCONTENTS (2004), 416.

H.F. JOLOWICZ, HISTORICAL INTRODUCTION TO THE STUDY OF ROMAN LAW (1952), 25.

Alex Kozinski, *Trademarks Unplugged*, 68 N.Y.U. L. Rev. 960, 974 (1993), 33.

Robert N. Kravitz, *Trademarks, Speech, and the Gay Olympics Case*, 69 B.U.L. Rev. 131 (1989), 45.

Rudolph J. Kuss, *The Naked Licensing Doctrine Exposed: How Courts Interpret the Lanham Act to Require Licensors to Police their Licensees and Why this Requirement Conflicts with Modern Licensing Realities and the Goals of Trademark Law*, 9 Marq. Intell. Prop. L. Rev. 361 (2005), 383.

Mary LaFrance, *Innovations Palpatations: The Confusing Status of Geographically Misdescriptive*

Trademarks, *12 J. Intell. Prop. L. 125, 148-49 (2004), 284.*

Henry W. Leeds, *Intent To Use—Its Time Has Come*, 79 TMR 269 (1989), 204.

Jeffrey Lefstin, Note, *Does the First Amendment Bar Cancellation of REDSKINS?*, 52 Stan. L. Rev. 665 (2000), 241.

Jason K. Levine, *Contesting the Incontestable: Reforming Trademark's Descriptive Mark Protection Scheme*, 41 Gonz. L. Rev. 29 (2006), 324.

Marc C. Levy, *From Genericism to Trademark Significance: Deconstructing the De Facto Secondary Meaning Doctrine*, 95 Trademark Rep. 1197 (2005), 347.

Leigh Ann Lindquist, *Champagne or Champagne? An Examination of U.S. Failure to Comply with the Geographical Provisions of the TRIPS Agreement*, 27 Ga. J. Int'l & Comp. L. 309 (1999), 243.

Courtney Liotti, *The Registrability of Primarily Geographically Deceptively Misdescriptive Marks: The Development of Section 1052(e)(3)*, 22 Touro L. Rev. 511, 573 (2006), 284.

Adam Liptak, *Welcome to Our Law School, Young Man. We'll See You in Court*, N.Y. Times, May 6, 2002, at A12, 529.

JOHN LOCKE, TWO TREATISES ON GOVERNMENT (Peter Laslett ed., 3d ed. 1988), 25.

John Magee, *Domain Name Disputes: An Assessment of the UDRP as Against Traditional Litigation*, 2003 U. Ill J.L. Tech & Pol'y 203 (2003), 555.

Mattoon, Illinois—The Original "Burger King": http://www.roadsideamerica.com/tips/get Attraction.php3?tip_AttractionNo==8105, 200.

J. THOMAS McCARTHY, McCARTHY ON TRADEMARKS AND UNFAIR COMPETITION § 29:4 (4th ed. 2002), 193.

Steve Meleen, et al., *Recent Developments in Trademark Law: Elusive Dilution and Sorting the Resulting Confusion*, 11 Tex. Intell. Prop. L. J. 351 (2003), 486.

GAVIN MENZIES, 1421: THE YEAR CHINA DISCOVERED AMERICA (2003), 4.

Christopher T. Micheletti, *Preventing Loss of Trademark Rights: Quantitative and Qualitative Assessments of "Use" and their Impact on Abandonment Determinations*, 94 Trademark Rep. 634 (2004), 370.

Sue Ann Momta, Case Note, *Victor's Little Secret Prevails (For Now) over Victoria's Secret: The Supreme Court Requires Proof of Actual Dilution under the FTDA*, 19 Santa Clara Comp. & High Tech. L. J. 551 (2003), 486.

Xuan-Thao N. Nguyen, *The Digital Trademark Right: A Troubling New Extraterritorial Reach of United States Law*, 81 N.C.L. Rev. 483 (2003), 642.

Xuan-Thao N. Nguyen, *Nationalizing Trademarks: A New International Trademark Jurisprudence?*, 39 Wake Forest L. Rev. 729, 781 (2004), 284.

Robert T. Neufeld, *Closing Federalism's Loophole in Intellectual Property Rights*, 17 Berkeley Tech. L.J. 1295 (2002), 140.

Robert Nup, *Concurrent Use of Trademarks on the Internet: Reconciling the Concept of Geographically*

Delimited Trademarks with the Reality of the Internet, *64 Ohio St. L. J. 617 (2003), 200.*

A. Samuel Oddi, *The Functions of "Functionality" in Trademark Law*, 22 Hous. L. Rev. 925, 963 (1985), 414.

SHOEN ONO, SHOHYOHO (*TRADEMARK LAW*) 22 (1994), 4.

Kimberly A. Pace, *The Washington Redskins Case and The Doctrine of Disparagement: How Politically Correct Must a Trademark Be?*, 22 Pepp. L. Rev. 7 (1994), 241.

Vincent N. Palladino, *Trade Dress Functionality after* TrafFix: *The Lower Courts Split Again*, 93 Trademark Rep. 1219 (2003), 415.

Jason Parent, Comment, *Federal Trademark Law—A Roadblock to Small Business Success?*, 6 Barry L. Rev. 105 (2006), 179.

Mark V.B. Partridge, *Trademark Parody and the First Amendment: Humor in the Eye of the Beholder*, 29 J. Marshall L. Rev. 877, 890 (1996), 46.

Justin Pats, *Conditioning Functionality: Untangling the Divergent Strands of Argument Evidenced by Recent Case Law and Commentary*, 10 Marq. Intell. Prop. L. Rev. 515 (2006), 298.

Beverly W. Pattishall, *Dawning Acceptance of the Dilution Rationale for Trademark-Trade Identity Protection*, 74 Trademark Rep. 289, 309 (1984), 25.

Beverly W. Pattishall, D. Hilliard, & J. Welch, TRADEMARK AND UNFAIR COMPETITION 2 (4th ed. 2000), 3.

Jeffery R. Peterson, *What's the Use? Establishing Mark Rights in the Modern Economy*, 5 Hous. Bus. & Tax. L. J. 450 (2005), 180.

Andrew Pickett, *The Death of Genericide? A Call for a Return to the Text of the Lanham Act*, 9 Tul. J. Tech. & Intell. Prop. 329 (2007), 347.

Kenneth A. Plevan, *Daubert's Impact on Survey Experts in Lanham Act Litigation*, 95 Trademark Rep. 596, 600 (2005), 347.

Kenneth L. Port, *The Congressional Expansion of American Trademark Law: A Civil Law System in the Making*, 35 Wake Forest L. Rev. 827 (2000), 30-32, 32-33, 201, 486.

Kenneth L. Port, *The Illegitimacy of Trademark Incontestability*, 26 Ind. L. Rev. 519 (1993), 324.

Kenneth L. Port, *Learned Hand's Trademark Jurisprudence: Legal Positivism and the Myth of the Prophet,* 27 Pacific Law Journal 221, 238 (1996), 23, 26.

Kenneth L. Port, *Trademark Dilution Law in Japan,* 4 NW. J. Tech. & Intell. Prop. 228 (2006), 496.

Kenneth L. Port, *Trademark Harmonization: Norms, Names and Nonsense* 2 Marq. Intell. Prop. L. Rev. 33 (1998), 624.

Kenneth L. Port, Trademark Law and Policy in Japan: Japanese Trademark Jurisprudence 19 (2007), 4.

Kenneth L. Port, *Trademark Monopolies in the Blue Nowhere,* 28 Wm. Mitchell L. Rev. 1091 (2002), 499.

Kenneth L. Port, *The Unnatural Expansion of Trademark Rights: Is a Federal Dilution Statute Necessary?,* 18 Seton Hall Leg. J. 433 (1994), 486.

J.H. Reichman, *Universal Minimum Standards of Intellectual Property Protection under the TRIPS Component of the WTO Agreement,* 29 Int'l. Law. 345 (1995), 619.

John R. Renaud, *Can't Get There From Here: How NAFTA and GATT Have Reduced Protection for Geographical Trademarks,* 26 Brooklyn J. Int'l L. 1097 (2001), 242.

Restatement (Third) of Unfair Competition, § 1, 29-30.

Restatement (Third) of Unfair Competition § 26, 107.

Frank I. Schechter, The Historical Foundations of the Law Relating to Trademarks 150-52 (1925), 24.

Frank I. Schechter, *The Rational Basis of Trademark Protection,* 40 Harv. L. Rev. 813 (1927), 449.

Roger E. Schechter, *The Case for Limited Extraterritorial Reach of the Lanham Act,* 37 Va. J. Int'l L. 619 (1997), 642.

Scott Shipman, Comment: *Trademark and Unfair Competition in Cyberspace: Can These Laws Deter "Baiting" Practices on Web Sites?,* 39 Santa Clara L. Rev. 245 (1998), 92.

Michael Sloan, Note, *Too Famous for the Right of Publicity: ETW Corp. And the Trend Towards*

Diminished Protection for Top Celebrities, *22 Cardozo Arts & Ent. L. J. 903 (2005),* 441.

Lars Smith, *Trade Distinctiveness: Solving Scalia's Tertium Quid Trade Dress Conundrum,* Mich. St. L. Rev. 243 (2005), 401.

S. Lloyd Smith, Wal-Mart v. Samara Brothers *and its Progeny,* 94 Trademark Rep. 1037 (2004), 401.

Regan Smith, *Trademark Law and Free Speech: Protection for Scandalous and Disparaging Marks,* 42 Harv. Civil Rights-Civil Liberties L. Rev. 451 (2007), 242.

Rudolph Sohm, The Institutes: A Textbook of the History and System of Roman Private Law (1970), 25.

Barbara Solomon, *Can the Lanham Act Protect Tiger Woods? An Analysis of Whether the Lanham Act is a Proper Substitute for a Federal Right of Publicity*, 94 Trademark Rep. 1202 (2004), 441.

Keith M. Stolte, *How Early Did Anglo-American Trademark Law Begin? An Answer to Schechter's Conundrum*, 8 Fordham I.P, Media & Ent. L. J. 505 (1998), 3.

Robert H. Thornburg, *Trademark Survey Evidence: Review of Current Trends in the Ninth Circuit*, 21 Santa Clara Computer & High Tech. L. J. 715 (2005), 347.

Elizabeth Thrornburg, *Fast, Cheap, and Out of Control: Lessons from the ICANN Dispute Resolution Process*, 6 J. Small & Emerging Bus. L. 191, 196 (2002), 555.

Mark A. Thurmon, *Ending the Seventh Amendment Confusion: A Critical Analysis of the Right to a Jury Trial in Trademark Cases*, 11 Tex. Intell. Prop. L. J. 1 (2002), 549, 665.

Mark A. Thurmon, *The Rise and Fall of Trademark Law's Functionality Doctrine*, 56 Fla. L. Rev. 243 (2004), 298, 415.

Molly Torsen, *Apples and Oranges (and Wine): Why the International Conversation Regarding Geographic Indications is at a Standstill*, 87 J. Pat. & Trademark Off. Soc'y 31, 61 (2005), 243.

Trademark cases in district courts: http://www.uscourts.gov/caseload2002/tables/c04mar02.pdf, 650.

Trademark Dilution Revision Act, 109 P.L. 312, 120 Stat. 1730 (2006), 488.

Trademark Remedy Clarification Act, Pub. L. No. 102-542 (1992) (codified at 15 U.S.C. 1122 (2000)), 140.

Uniform Domain Name Dispute Resolution Policy: Purpose, Representations, Cancellations, Transfers and Changes, UDRP Paragraphs 1-4 http://www.icann.org//udrp/policy.htm, 550.

United Sstates' territories: http://www.lib.uconn.edu/online/research/govtinfo/ConnState/territ.html, 91.

United States Trademark Association Trademark Review Commission Report and Recommendations

to USTA President and Board of Directors, 77 TMR 375 (1987), 204.

Shashank Upadhye, *Trademark Surveys: Identifying the Relevant Universe of Confused Consumers*, 8 Fordham Intell. Prop. Media & Ent. L.J. 549, 568 (1998), 107.

Andrew P. Vance, *Can't Get There From Here: How NAFTA and GATT Have Reduced Protection for Geographical Trademarks*, 26 Brook. J. Int'l L. 1097 (2001), 284.

Eugene Volokh & Mark Lemley, *Freedom of Speech and Injunctions in Intellectual Property Cases*, 48 Duke L. J. 147 (1998), 133.

Webster's Encyclopedic Unabridged Dictionary of the English Language 1466 (1996), 62.

Harold R. Weinberg, *Trademark Law, Functional Design Features, and the Trouble with TrafFix*, 9 J. Intell. Prop. L. 1, 60 (2001), 415.

Alexis Weissberger, *Is Fame Alone Sufficient to Create Priority Rights: An International Perspective on the Viability of the Famous/Well-known Marks Doctrine*, 24 Cardozo Arts & Ent. L. J. 739 (2006), 193.

David Welkowitz, Trademark Dilution: Federal, State, and International Law (2002), 474, 485.

Uli Widmaier, *Use, Liability and the Structure of Trademark Law*, 33 Hoftsra L. Rev. 603, 709 (2004), 546.

Steven Wilf, *Who Authors Trademarks?*, 17 Cardozo Arts & Ent. L.J. 1, 29 (1999), 33.

Ashley H. Wilkes, In Re Gucci: *The Lack of Goodwill in Matters Regarding Bankruptcy, Trademarks, and High Fashion*, 23 Emory Bankr. Dev. J. 647 (2007), 371.

Mitchell M. Wong, *The Aesthetic Functionality Doctrine and the Law of Trade Dress Protection*, 83 Cornell L. Rev. 1116 (1998), 415.

David Yan, Note, *Virtual Reality: Can We Ride Trademark Law to Surf Cyberspace?*, 10 Fordham I. P., Media & Ent. L. J. 773, 775 (2000), 499.

Table of Graphs, Charts, and Images

McDonald's Trademarks		22
Marushin's Trademarks		23
Figure 1.1	Federal Intellectual Property Law Summary	27
Picture 4.1	Jaeger-LeCoultre Atmos Clock	94
	Trademark Continuum	146
Picture 5.1	Zatarain's Fish-Fri	154
Picture 5.2	Cheesehead	158
Picture 6.1	Burger King of Mattoon, IL	194
Table 7.1	Application and Registration Statistics	220
Table 7.2	Use-Based Trademark Application Process	221
Table 7.3	Intent-to-Use Based Trademark Application Process	222
Table 7.4	Application Process Under the Madrid Protocol	223
	Old Glory Condom Corp.	225
	Percentage of People Finding Indicated Terms Offensive	239
	National Park Service Logo	244
	Mrs. Fields Logo	255
French Line Trademark		268
Picture 9.1	Anti-Monopoly	338
Picture 9.2	"Bucky Badger"	362
Picture 10.1	Taco Cabana Restaurant	387
Picture 10.2	Two Pesos Restaurant	387
	Madrid Applications Report	633
	Completed Trademark Cases in U.S. District Courts FY1997–FY2002	650

Acknowledgments

I am especially indebted to a core of very good research assistants at William Mitchell College of Law who made this project much better and much more fun to do. Specifically, Stephanie Budge and Paul Godfread did the research for the Second Edition. Joshua Jones copyedited the entire manuscript. Steve Hickman volunteered the "Hickman Report," a generous critique of the entire manuscript. Meg Daniel and Cal Bonde provided expert support for the project. General comments on the first edition were provided by Sheldon Helpern, David Welkowitz, Marshall Leaffer, and Niels Schaumann. Needless to say, any and all mistakes that remain are mine alone.

Editorial Note

For the sake of simplicity, many footnotes in cases as well as excerpted law review articles have been deleted without any indication. Those footnotes that remain have been renumbered.

Prelude

Pebble Beach Co. v. Tour 18 Limited

155 F. 3d 526 (5th Cir. 1998)

King, C.J.:

Defendant Tour 18 I, Ltd. appeals the district court's judgment that it infringed and diluted the plaintiffs' service marks and one of the three golf-hole designs at issue, and it challenges the district court's injunction as vague, punitive, and overly broad. Plaintiffs Pebble Beach Co.; Resorts of Pinehurst, Inc.; and Sea Pines Co., Inc. cross-appeal, arguing that (1) the district court erroneously held that two of the three golf-hole designs at issue were not infringed or diluted, (2) its injunction is inadequate to bar future infringement, and (3) its denial of an accounting of profits and an award of attorneys' fees was erroneous. We affirm the district court's judgment as modified below.

I. BACKGROUND

Defendant-appellant-cross-appellee Tour 18 I, Ltd. (Tour 18) owns and operates a public golf course in Humble, Texas named "Tour 18." Tour 18 began life as a limited partnership that subsequently merged into Tour 18, Inc., which also owns and operates a "Tour 18" public golf course in Flower Mound, Texas. Tour 18 has created these two golf courses exclusively of golf holes copied from famous golf courses across the country. The Tour 18 course in Humble, Texas has three golf holes that are copies of golf holes from golf courses owned and operated by plaintiffs-appellees-cross-appellants Pebble Beach Co. (Pebble Beach); Resorts of Pinehurst, Inc. (Pinehurst); and Sea Pines Co., Inc. (Sea Pines) (collectively, the Plaintiffs).

C. District Court Proceedings

The Plaintiffs filed suit against Tour 18 asserting federal claims under the Lanham Act, 15 U.S.C. §§ 1051-1127, for service-mark and trade-dress infringement, unfair competition, and false advertising. See Pebble Beach, 942 F. Supp. at 1526. Under Texas law, the Plaintiffs asserted claims for common-law unfair competition, conversion, and civil conspiracy and for service-mark and trade-dress dilution under the Texas anti-dilution statute, see TEX. BUS. & COM. CODE ANN. § 16.29 (Vernon Supp. 1998). Pebble Beach also asserted a claim for copyright infringement based upon maps used by Tour 18. Tour 18 counterclaimed under Texas common law for unfair competition, interference with existing and prospective business relations, and civil conspiracy. See id.

After a bench trial, the district court issued an excellent opinion and entered judgment for the Plaintiffs on their infringement, dilution, and unfair competition claims in relation to Tour 18's use of their names and the image of the lighthouse, and the court entered judgment for Sea Pines in relation to Tour 18's copying of its golf-hole design. The district court entered judgment for Tour 18 on the remainder of the Plaintiffs' claims and entered judgment for the Plaintiffs on all of Tour 18's counterclaims. The district court denied the Plaintiffs' requests for damages, an accounting of profits, and attorneys' fees, but it entered an injunction against Tour 18 requiring it to (1) cease using Pebble Beach and Pinehurst's marks, except to inform the public of the golf holes it copied; (2) cease using Sea Pines' marks and images of the lighthouse, without any exceptions; (3) remove the replicas of Sea Pines' lighthouse from both of its courses; (4) include a conspicuous disclaimer in all advertisements, promotional material, and informational guides; (5) maintain the disclaimers on the course; and (6) make no claims of use of original blue-prints, maps, or other data in the construction of the course without a disclaimer. The district court has partially stayed the injunction pending appeal in relation to the re-quirement of removing the replica lighthouses. Tour 18 and the Plaintiffs now appeal.

II. DISCUSSION

Tour 18 appeals the district court's judgment that it infringed and diluted the Plain-tiffs' service marks and Sea Pines' trade dress and that it competed unfairly. Tour 18 also appeals the district court's injunction, claiming that it is overly broad, punitive, and vague. The Plaintiffs cross-appeal the district court's judgment that Tour 18 did not infringe or dilute Pebble Beach and Pinehurst's trade dress, its injunction as providing inadequate re-lief, and its denial of an accounting of profits and an award of attorneys' fees. We con-sider each issue in turn.

A. Infringement

For the Plaintiffs to prevail on their service-mark and trade-dress infringement claims, they must show (1) that the mark or trade dress, as the case may be, qualifies for protection and (2) that Tour 18's use of the mark or trade dress creates a likelihood of confusion in the minds of potential consumers. A trademark or service mark is "any word, name, symbol, or device or combination thereof" used by a person to "identify and distinguish his or her goods [or services], including a unique product [or service]," from the goods or services of another and "to indicate the source of the goods [or services], even if that source is unknown." 15 U.S.C. § 1127. "'Trade dress' refers to the total image and overall appearance of a product" and "may include features such as the size, shape, color, color combinations, textures, graphics, and even sales techniques that characterize a particular product." Sunbeam Prods., Inc. v. West Bend Co., 123 F.3d 246, 251 & n.3 (5th Cir.), cert. denied, 140 L. Ed. 2d 936, 118 S. Ct. 1795 (1997). With trade dress, the question is whether the "combination of features creates a distinctive visual impression, identifying the source of the product." Id. at 251 n.3.

The same tests apply to both trademarks and trade dress to determine whether they are protectible and whether they have been infringed, regardless of whether they are reg-istered or unregistered. Both are protectible if they are inherently distinctive or have achieved secondary meaning in the public's mind—i.e., if the trade dress or mark "'has come through use to be uniquely associated with a specific source.'" Sunbeam Prods., 123 F.3d at 253 (quoting Two Pesos, 505 U.S. at 766 n.4). However, trade dress is not protectible and cannot be distinctive if it is functional—i.e, if the design "is one of a lim-ited number of equally efficient options available to competitors and free competition would be unduly hindered by according the design trademark protection." Two Pesos, 505 U.S. at 775. Once a plaintiff's mark or trade dress is found to be protectible, liabil-ity for trademark and trade-dress infringement hinges upon whether a likelihood of con-fusion exists in the minds of potential consumers as to the source, affiliation, or sponsorship of the defendant's product or service due to the use of the allegedly infringing marks or trade dress.

* * *

2. Protectible marks and trade dress

The district court considered the Plaintiffs' marks, "Pebble Beach," "Pinehurst," and "Harbour Town," and the image of the lighthouse and found them to be protectible. In the case of the design of the three golf holes, the district court determined that the configuration of a golf hole is nonfunctional, but it found that only Sea Pines' golf-hole design was protectible. Tour 18 challenges only the district court's findings that the Sea Pines' golf-hole design is protectible and that Sea Pines has protectible rights in the lighthouse. Tour 18 does not challenge the district court's finding that the Plaintiffs' other marks are protectible. The Plaintiffs challenge the district court's finding that Pebble Beach and Pinehurst's golf-hole designs are not protectible. We consider the golf-hole designs and the lighthouse in turn.

a. golf-hole designs

Turning first to the district court's traditional trade-dress analysis of Tour 18's challenge to the protectibility of the designs of the Plaintiffs' golf holes, Tour 18 attacks the district court's findings that a golf-hole design is nonfunctional and that Sea Pines' golf-hole design is protectible in that it is inherently distinctive or alternatively has acquired secondary meaning. The Plaintiffs challenge the district court's findings that Pebble Beach and Pinehurst's golf holes are not inherently distinctive and are therefore unprotectible, but they do not challenge its finding that neither golf-hole design has acquired secondary meaning.

i. functionality

The Lanham Act protects only nonfunctional distinctive trade dress; this limitation "serves to assure that competition will not be stifled by the exhaustion of a limited number of trade dresses." Two Pesos, 505 U.S. at 775. "[A] design is legally functional, and thus unprotectible, if it is one of a limited number of equally efficient options available to competitors and free competition would be unduly hindered by according the design trademark protection." Id. (citing Sicilia Di R. Biebow, 732 F.2d at 426); ... A collection of functional features in a product design does not necessarily make the combination of those features functional and therefore unprotectible. Where the trade dress of a product consists of a particular configuration of features, the functionality of the design turns on "whether its design as a whole is superior to other designs, not on whether its component features viewed individually each have a function." Vaughan Mfg. Co. v. Brikam Int'l, Inc., 814 F.2d 346, 350 (7th Cir. 1987) (emphasis added). In determining whether competition would be stifled, we have considered whether the feature or combination of features is "superior or optimal in terms of engineering, economy of manufacture, accommodation of utilitarian function or performance." Sicilia Di R. Biebow, 732 F.2d at 429; ... The Supreme Court has stated the question more generally as whether the trade dress is "'essential to the use or purpose of the article or if it affects the cost or quality of the article,' that is, if exclusive use of the feature would put competitors at a significant non-reputation-related disadvantage." Qualitex Co. v. Jacobson Prods. Co., 514 U.S. 159, 165, 131 L. Ed. 2d 248, 115 S. Ct. 1300 (1995) (quoting Inwood Lab., Inc. v. Ives Lab., Inc., 456 U.S. 844, 850 n.10, 72 L. Ed. 2d 606, 102 S. Ct. 2182 (1982)).

The district court determined that the golf-hole designs at issue here are nonfunctional, noting that there is an "unlimited number of alternative designs" to the Plaintiffs' golf-hole designs and that no evidence indicated that the Plaintiffs' designs are superior to the many available alternatives. In finding that competition would not be hindered by protecting the Plaintiffs' golf-hole designs, the district court noted that one of Tour 18's experts testified that protecting the design of the golf holes from copying would not unduly injure competition and that Tour 18's director of marketing testified that a golf course need not copy golf-hole designs in order to be competitive in the Houston market. See id.

Tour 18 first attacks the district court's finding that golf holes are nonfunctional by defining its product as a golf course that provides replicas of famous golf holes. It claims that such a product requires that it be able to copy famous golf holes in order to have any commercial success in delivering its product: a course copying famous golf holes. While Tour 18's product may be a golf course the commercial success of which has been based upon copying golf holes, it nevertheless is still just a collection of golf holes. Features that contribute to the commercial success of a product are not thereby necessarily classed as functional. In Sicilia Di R. Biebow, this court rejected the argument that functionality should be defined in terms of commercial success or marketing effectiveness because such a definition would allow a second comer to copy the protectible trade dress of a product whenever the product became successful and preferred by consumers. Tour 18 argues that in Qualitex the Supreme Court overruled this holding with its citation of Justice White's concurrence in Inwood Laboratories, which stated that "[a] functional characteristic is an important ingredient in the commercial success of the product." See Qualitex, 514 U.S. at 165 (internal quotation marks omitted) (quoting Inwood Lab., 456 U.S. at 863 (White, J., concurring in the result)). However, these two statements are not inconsistent. Justice White's statement is merely an acknowledgment that a functional feature is by definition important to the commercial success of a product because without the functional feature a viable, competitive product could not be produced and because competition would be injured if such a feature were protectible by trademark law. The converse, however, is not true. To define functionality based upon commercial success would allow the second comer to trade on the first comer's goodwill, purely because it would be easier to market his product and not because he could not produce a viable, competitive product. Such a rule does not promote innovation, nor does it promote competition, leaving no reason to narrow trademark protection. The logical extension of this argument would practically obliterate trademark protection for product design because a defendant could always argue that its innovative product is a widget that provides a replica of the most popular or most prestigious widget on the market, thus requiring that the defendant be allowed without further analysis to copy the plaintiff's widget.

Tour 18 then argues that every feature of a golf hole and how it is configured affects how the hole plays, making any golf-hole design functional. Without citing any authority, Tour 18 urges a rule that a feature or configuration of features is functional unless "a specific design can be made another way without affecting use, purpose, cost, quality or commercial desirability." This rule is much broader than any applied in this circuit or by the Supreme Court and could conceivably render any design functional because any change would undoubtedly somehow affect cost, use, or commercial desirability. Additionally, the Supreme Court limited its statement that trade dress is functional if the trade dress is essential to the use or purpose of the product or affects the cost or quality of the product with the following language: "that is, if exclusive use of the features [or combination of features] would put competitors at a significant non-reputation-related disadvantage." Qualitex, 514 U.S. at 165. This language makes it clear that any effect must be great enough to significantly disadvantage competitors in ways other than consumer preference for a particular source.

Next, Tour 18 contends that Qualitex imposes as a threshold inquiry in the functionality analysis the question of whether the trade dress serves "any other significant function." See 514 U.S. at 166. It argues that this question must be considered before concerns of competition and available alternative designs can be addressed. This is a misreading of Qualitex, which held that, in certain circumstances, color can be a registerable trademark. See id..Where the Supreme Court uses the language "without serving any other significant function," it is stating that color alone may sometimes meet the basic legal requirements for use as a trademark. This language in Qualitex, as supported by its accompanying citations, is just another way of stating that functionality, with its consideration of the needs of competition, bars Lanham Act protection to functional features and configurations, which by definition serve a significant function other than source-identification. As noted earlier, functionality takes into account whether protecting a particular feature or combination of features would "hinder competition or impinge upon the rights of others to compete effectively." See Sunbeam Prods., 123 F.3d at 255 (internal quotation marks omitted). Therefore, Qualitex does not create a threshold inquiry in the functionality analysis. Additionally, we have held that nonfunctional trade dress may still have some utility—i.e., serve a function other than source-identification—and still be legally nonfunctional. See Sicilia Di R. Biebow, 732 F.2d at 429.

Having rejected Tour 18's challenges to the district court's analysis, and after reviewing the evidence, we find that the district court did not clearly err in finding that the Plaintiffs' golf-hole designs are nonfunctional.

ii. distinctiveness

Trademarks and trade dress are distinctive and protectible if they serve as indicators of source. Trademarks and trade dress are classified into the following categories: (1) generic, (2) descriptive, (3) suggestive, (4) arbitrary, or (5) fanciful. The last three categories—suggestive, arbitrary, and fanciful—are inherently distinctive, requiring no additional showing to be protectible, "'because their intrinsic nature serves to identify a particular source of a product.'" Sunbeam Prods., 123 F.3d at 252 (quoting Two Pesos, 505 U.S. at 768). A mark or trade dress is descriptive if it "identifies a characteristic or quality of an article or service, such as its color, odor, function, dimensions, or ingredients." Zatarains, Inc. v. Oak Grove Smokehouse, Inc., 698 F.2d 786, 790 (5th Cir. 1983) (citations and internal quotation marks omitted). A descriptive mark or trade dress is protectible only when it has "acquired a secondary meaning in the minds of the consuming public." Id. A generic mark or trade dress is never protectible because it connotes "a particular genus or class of which an individual [product] or service is but a member . . . , rather than the more individualized characteristics of a particular product." Id. (citations and internal quotation marks omitted).

The district court found that Pebble Beach and Pinehurst's golf-hole designs were not inherently distinctive because they were variations on commonplace themes in the design of golf holes..Sea Pines' golf-hole design, however, is inherently distinctive according to the district court because the incorporation of the lighthouse adds an "arbitrary source-identifying feature[]." Additionally, the district court determined that Sea Pines' golf-hole design had acquired secondary meaning in the public's mind. As to Pebble Beach and Pinehurst's golf-hole designs, the district court found no evidence to support a conclusion that either design had acquired secondary meaning.

The Plaintiffs argue that the district court should have found Pebble Beach and Pinehurst's golf holes to be inherently distinctive. However, Pebble Beach and Pinehurst's golf-hole designs do not fall into any of the three inherently distinctive classifications. Arbitrary and fanciful marks or trade dress "bear no relationship to the products or services to which they are applied." Zatarains, 698 F.2d at 791. The trade dress of Pebble

Beach and Pinehurst's golf holes is a configuration of commonplace features of a golf hole and therefore does bear a relationship to the product, a golf hole. A suggestive mark or trade dress "suggests, rather than describes, some particular characteristic of the goods or services to which it applies and requires the consumer to exercise the imagination in order to draw a conclusion as to the nature of the goods and services." Id. The configurations of the features in Pebble Beach and Pinehurst's golf-hole designs create golf holes and nothing more. They require no exercise of one's imagination to realize that one is viewing a golf hole. Therefore, the district court did not clearly err in finding that Pebble Beach and Pinehurst's golf-hole designs were not inherently distinctive.

Tour 18 argues that Sea Pines' golf-hole design is not protectible because a golf hole's trade dress is generic and because, even if it is descriptive, the Plaintiffs failed to present evidence that demonstrates that Sea Pines' trade dress has acquired secondary meaning. In general, a golf hole's trade dress may be generic, but Sea Pines' inclusion of the distinctive lighthouse in the design of the golf hole takes it out of the generic classification because it emphasizes the "individualized characteristics" of this particular golf-hole design rather than connoting golf holes in general. Therefore, the district court did not clearly err in finding that Sea Pines' golf-hole design was not generic.

As Sea Pines' golf-hole design is not generic, it is protectible if it has acquired secondary meaning. That a particular mark or trade dress has acquired secondary meaning can be proven by a consideration of the following evidence: (1) length and manner of use of the mark or trade dress, (2) volume of sales, (3) amount and manner of advertising, (4) nature of use of the mark or trade dress in newspapers and magazines, (5) consumer-survey evidence, (6) direct consumer testimony, and (7) the defendant's intent in copying the trade dress. See RESTATEMENT, supra, § 13 cmt. e; … While each of these types of evidence alone may not prove secondary meaning, in combination they may indicate that consumers consider the mark or trade dress to be an indicator of source. In considering this evidence, the focus is on how it demonstrates that the meaning of the mark or trade dress has been altered in the minds of consumers. See id. For example, in the case of advertising, spending substantial amounts of money does not of itself cause a mark or trade dress to acquire secondary meaning, but advertisements may emphasize "the source significance of the designation through prominent use of the [mark or trade dress]" and are therefore likely to alter the meaning of the mark or trade dress in the minds of consumers. See RESTATEMENT, supra, § 13 cmt. c, at 110.

The district court based its finding of secondary meaning upon Sea Pines' extensive advertising; unsolicited publicity of the trade dress of Sea Pines' golf hole, including the lighthouse, in golf publications; and Tour 18's intent to copy and use the trade dress prominently in its advertising. Tour 18 argues that the district court erred in relying upon the advertising and publicity because they touted the design of the golf hole for its playing qualities and not as a designation of source. While some of Sea Pines' advertising and publicity does promote the playability of the golf hole, the trade dress of Sea Pines' golf hole, including the lighthouse, is prominently used in the advertising and the publicity of the Harbour Town Golf Links in a manner other than simply to promote the playing qualities of the golf hole. Therefore, the district court did not clearly err in finding that Sea Pines' trade dress had acquired secondary meaning.

b. the lighthouse

Tour 18 does not challenge the protectibility of depictions of the lighthouse; rather, it challenges Sea Pines' rights in the lighthouse. Tour 18 argues that Sea Pines no longer has any rights in the lighthouse because (1) it does not own the lighthouse and (2) by its course of conduct, it has abandoned the lighthouse as a mark. In response to the first argument, we adopt the reasoning of the district court:

> The Lanham Act does not require a party to "own" a word, symbol, or other identifying mark before it may be granted protection from infringement. Rather, all that is required is that a party "use" the mark in commerce to identify its services and distinguish them from the services of others. 15 U.S.C. § 1127 ...

Tour 18 styles its argument as attacking Sea Pines' interest in the structure of the lighthouse itself and not in the image of the lighthouse, arguing that the only connection between the golf course and the lighthouse is that the lighthouse can be seen from the course. However, Harbour Town Golf Links was built by the same entity that constructed the lighthouse and the evidence demonstrates that the placement and design of the course and the lighthouse were specifically designed to create the relationship between the course and the lighthouse. This is not a case where the only connection is the coincidence of proximity or location. The connection between the course and the lighthouse is much greater and dates back to the conception of both. Sea Pines has used depictions of the lighthouse in relation to golfing services since 1969, and the district court did not clearly err in finding that the lighthouse has achieved secondary meaning in relation to golfing services in the minds of consumers. The sale of the lighthouse to Fogelman's predecessor, while reserving trademark rights in depictions of the lighthouse, does not alter this finding.

In relation to abandonment, Tour 18 argues that Sea Pines' failure to police third-party uses of the lighthouse as a mark has caused the mark "to lose its significance as a mark," thus constituting abandonment under 15 U.S.C. § 1127. As Tour 18 argues, this form of abandonment does not require any intent to abandon on the part of Sea Pines. However, the evidence shows, as the district court discussed, that Sea Pines has not failed to police third-party uses of depictions of the lighthouse; rather, it has aggressively policed third-party uses. Additionally, the district court's finding of secondary meaning in the lighthouse mark for golfing services shows that the lighthouse has not lost its significance as a mark for golfing services, despite the third-party uses in relation to other products and services. Those third-party uses are only relevant to the strength of the mark in this case and do not evidence abandonment.

3. Likelihood of confusion

Next we turn to whether Tour 18's use of the Plaintiffs' marks and trade dress infringed the Plaintiffs' rights. The touchstone of infringement is whether the use creates a likelihood of confusion as to the "source, affiliation, or sponsorship" of Tour 18's golf course. Likelihood of confusion is synonymous with a probability of confusion, which is more than a mere possibility of confusion. In determining whether a likelihood of confusion exists, this court considers the following nonexhaustive list of factors: (1) the type of mark allegedly infringed, (2) the similarity between the two marks, (3) the similarity of the products or services, (4) the identity of the retail outlets and purchasers, (5) the identity of the advertising media used, (6) the defendant's intent, and (7) any evidence of actual confusion. No single factor is dispositive, and a finding of a likelihood of confusion does not require a positive finding on a majority of these "digits of confusion."

While noting that no golfer will stand on the tee at Tour 18 and believe that he or she is playing at Pebble Beach, Pinehurst, or Harbour Town, in considering Tour 18's use of the Plaintiffs' marks and depictions of the lighthouse, the district court found that all seven digits of confusion weighed in favor of a likelihood of confusion as to whether the courses are otherwise affiliated. In reaching this determination, the district court considered Tour 18's use of disclaimers and found them to be inadequate where present and to be absent from the majority of advertisements and promotional material. In relation to Sea Pines' trade dress, the district court also found that the digits of confusion weighed in favor of a likelihood of confusion, partially relying upon its analysis of the likelihood of confusion in relation to the marks and upon the same actual confusion evidence as used in relation to the marks.

Tour 18 attacks the district court's finding of a likelihood of confusion based upon its consideration of evidence of actual confusion that consumers believed that Tour 18 had obtained "permission" to use the Plaintiffs' marks and to copy their golf holes. Tour 18 argues that "permission" does not include a connotation of control and therefore does not express a relationship that is relevant to confusion as to source, affiliation, sponsorship, or approval. We disagree.

Permission is synonymous with approval and suggests some connection between the parties. The idea that one party has given permission to another implies a form of approval of the other's activities. See WEBSTER'S THIRD NEW INTERNATIONAL DICTIONARY 1683 (Philip Babcock Gove ed., 1963) (defining "permission" as "the act of permitting : formal consent : AUTHORIZATION" and "permit" as "to consent to expressly or formally"); WILLIAM C. BURTON, LEGAL THESAURUS 30, 383 (2d ed. 1992) (including "consent to" among synonyms of "approve," "permit" among synonyms of "approval," and "approval" among synonyms of "permission"); see also ROGET'S DESK THESAURUS 30, 397 (Joyce O'Connor ed., 1995) (same). For a party to suggest to the public, through its use of another's mark or a similar mark, that it has received permission to use the mark on its goods or services suggests approval, and even endorsement, of the party's product or service and is a kind of confusion the Lanham Act prohibits. Therefore, confusion as to permission is relevant confusion under the Lanham Act.

The Plaintiffs' survey was conducted among golfers who had played a round of golf at Tour 18. Tour 18 argues that the survey was flawed because, by relying upon "permission," it created the possibility that those surveyed believed that permission was required, thereby skewing the result. But the survey asked whether Tour 18 "did get" or "did not get" permission to use the Plaintiffs' marks or to copy the Plaintiffs' golf holes. This question asks what message Tour 18's use of the Plaintiffs' marks and trade dress conveyed, rather than whether Tour 18 needed to get permission, which would focus on what those surveyed believed to be required. Although, this latter form is more problematic because it allows for the consumer's misunderstanding of the law, rather than the defendant's use the marks, to be the basis for his belief, it has been accepted by other courts as probative as to confusion. Therefore, the district court did not improperly rely upon the Plaintiffs' survey.

In addition to the survey evidence, the district court relied upon the testimony of the witnesses that, before actually playing the course, they thought Tour 18 had obtained permission to use the Plaintiffs' marks and trade dress; most notably, two witnesses testified that Tour 18's advertising in particular caused their confusion. This confusion was relevant even if it was obviated by playing the course and viewing the holes and disclaimers on the golf course signs. Moreover, those disclaimers and signs did not necessarily obviate the confusion as evidenced by the findings of the Plaintiffs' survey of golfers who had played Tour 18 and had been exposed to all of Tour 18's disclaimers on the course. Additionally, "evidence of actual confusion is not necessary to a finding of a likelihood of confusion." Elvis Presley Enters., 141 F.3d at 203-04 (citing Amstar, 615 F.2d at 263). After reviewing the record, we cannot say that the district court committed clear error in finding actual confusion and in finding a likelihood of confusion based partially upon that actual confusion, resulting from Tour 18's use of the Plaintiffs' marks and trade dress.

4. Nominative use

Tour 18 asserts that it has used the Plaintiffs' marks only to identify the Plaintiffs' golf holes that it copied and that such use, as a matter of law, does not create a likelihood of confusion. The district court treated this argument by Tour 18 as a species of the fair-use defense and considered it after finding a likelihood of confusion. While a claim that the use was to identify the markholder's goods or services is analogous to the statutory fair-use defense, it is in actuality a claim that the use is noninfringing and thus creates no likelihood of confusion.

Courts have long recognized that one who has lawfully copied another's product can tell the public what he has copied. Likewise, one can use another's mark truthfully to identify another's goods or services in order to describe or compare its product to the markholder's product. This right to use a mark to identify the markholder's products—a nominative use—however, is limited in that the use cannot be one that creates a likelihood of confusion as to source, sponsorship, affiliation, or approval.

As the Ninth Circuit has recognized, where a nominative use of a mark occurs without any implication of affiliation, sponsorship, or endorsement—i.e., a likelihood of confusion—the use "lies outside the strictures of trademark law." New Kids on the Block, 971 F.2d at 308. In order to avail itself of the shield of nominative use, the defendant (1) may only use so much of the mark as necessary to identify the product or service and (2) may not do anything that suggests affiliation, sponsorship, or endorsement by the markholder. By definition, the defendant cannot use the mark to identify its goods because this would not be a nominative use, and it would also suggest affiliation, sponsorship, or endorsement.

The district court found that Tour 18 used the Plaintiffs' marks as service marks to name its own products and to distinguish them from those offered by other golf courses. Based upon the prominent use of the Plaintiffs' marks in its advertising and promotional material, use of the marks on its menu, and use of the marks on signs directing players to each tee, Tour 18 has used the marks in ways suggesting affiliation, sponsorship, or approval. Therefore, the district court did not clearly err in finding that Tour 18 had used the Plaintiffs' marks in a service-mark context on its own products and services and did not err in denying Tour 18 the shield of nominative use.

In addition, Tour 18 argues that, because the allowable use of a mark in comparative advertising (a nominative use) will normally result in a positive finding among a majority of the digits of confusion, the traditional likelihood-of-confusion analysis cannot be applied. However, implicit in this argument is a misunderstanding of the likelihood-of-confusion analysis. The digits of confusion "are not an end in themselves, and all are not of equal significance. The [digits] serve only as guides on the analytical route to the ultimate determination of whether confusion is likely to result." Champions Golf Club, 78 F.3d at 1122; see also Falcon Rice Mill, Inc. v. Community Rice Mill, Inc., 725 F.2d 336, 345 n.9 (5th Cir. 1984) ("It is clear that some factors are more important than others and that they may have different weight in different cases."). Additionally, a court is not limited to considering only the standard digits of confusion and should consider other relevant factors in its analysis. Furthermore, as noted earlier, a positive finding on a majority of the digits of confusion does not require a court to find a likelihood of confusion. Therefore, the traditional likelihood-of-confusion analysis is applicable in a comparative-advertising situation, but the court should usually consider the nominative-use claim in conjunction with its likelihood-of-confusion analysis to avoid lowering the standard of confusion. Because Tour 18 used the Plaintiffs' marks in more than a merely nominative sense, a different approach would not have altered the result.

5. Effect of Sears-Compco

In addition to its attack on the district court's traditional trade-dress analysis, Tour 18 contends that it has the unfettered right to copy the Plaintiffs' golf-hole designs and lighthouse under the Intellectual Property Clause of the Constitution. See U.S. Const. art. I, § 8, cl. 8. Tour 18 points to Sears, Roebuck & Co. v. Stiffel Co., 376 U.S. 225, 11 L. Ed. 2d 661, 84 S. Ct. 784 (1964), and Compco Corp. v. Day-Brite Lighting, Inc., 376 U.S. 234, 11 L. Ed. 2d 669, 84 S. Ct. 779 (1964), to demonstrate that unfair-competition law cannot protect product designs or configurations to which no current, valid patent applies. We disagree.

First, Sears and Compco, both decided the same day, concerned the preemption of state trade-dress protection by federal patent law and barred the use of state unfair-competition laws to prohibit the copying of products that are not protected by federal patents. See Sears, 376 U.S. at 231-32 (copying of a lamp); Compco, 376 U.S. at 237-38 (copying of a reflector for a fluorescent light fixture). This bar to state prohibitions on copying includes nonfunctional designs and designs that have achieved secondary meaning. See Compco, 376 U.S. at 238. However, the Supreme Court noted that "other federal statutory protection," in addition to the patent laws, may bar copying of a product. See id. at 238. In Bonito Boats, Inc. v. Thunder Craft Boats, Inc., 489 U.S. 141, 103 L. Ed. 2d 118, 109 S. Ct. 971 (1989), the Supreme Court reaffirmed its Sears-Compco holdings that limit state protection of product designs and noted that the application of Sears-Compco to nonfunctional product design must take into account competing federal policies as evidenced by the Lanham Act. Thus, federal trademark protection is not limited by the preemption holdings in Sears-Compco.

Second, the federal trademark laws are "other federal statutory protection," and their protection of product designs and configurations does not conflict with the federal patent laws or the Intellectual Property Clause. The patent laws and the trademark laws have two entirely different and consistent purposes, addressing entirely different concerns. The patent laws serve (1) "to foster and reward invention," (2) "to promote[] disclosure of inventions to stimulate further innovation and to permit the public to practice the invention once the patent expires," and (3) "to assure that ideas in the public domain remain there for the free use of the public." Aronson v. Quick Point Pencil Co., 440 U.S. 257, 262, 59 L. Ed. 2d 296, 99 S. Ct. 1096 (1979); see also Duraco Prods., 40 F.3d at 1446 (noting that the policy of encouraging innovative designs is the province of the patent and copyright laws). The principal purposes of the trademark laws are to avoid consumer confusion and to protect the goodwill of the trademark owner's business. While the federal trademark laws provide a trademark or trade-dress owner indefinite protection unlike the limited-duration protection provided by the patent laws, traditional trade-dress analysis limits the scope of product designs or configurations that can be protected to avoid conflict between the two areas of law.

Third, in the more than thirty years since Sears-Compco, Congress and the courts have recognized that federal unfair-competition law provides protection to product designs and configurations consistent with the patent laws. The Supreme Court found in Qualitex that the reenactment of this language—along with its legislative history explicitly referring to the Trademark Commission's recommendation that the terms "symbol, or device" be left unchanged to allow registrations of color, shape, smell, sound, or configuration that function as a mark—undercut restrictive trademark precedent. Thus, Congress and the Court have embraced a broad reading of the Lanham Act and its protections, which can encompass product designs and configurations.

For the above reasons, the Intellectual Property Clause, the federal patent laws, and the Sears-Compco-line of cases do not preclude federal trademark protection for product designs and configurations. Under our jurisprudence today, the result of North Shore Laboratories alternative holding would be the same because the color of the tire-patch material was functional and lacked secondary meaning, each independently barring protection under the Lanham Act.

Finally, if the acid test of any theory is how it works in practice, we note that the application of traditional trade-dress analysis under the Lanham Act to the product configurations at issue here, the design of the Plaintiffs' golf holes, has effectively left intact Tour 18's right to copy the Plaintiffs' golf holes, barring only its copying of the lighthouse.

* * *

III. CONCLUSION

For the foregoing reasons, we AFFIRM the district court's judgment as modified. Each party shall bear its own costs on appeal.

———————

Notes

1. Keep in mind as you read these materials whether or not the court's opinion in *Tour 18* regarding trade dress is still good law, in light of Wal-Mart Stores, Inc. v. Samara Bros., 529 U.S. 205 (2000).

2. In *Tour 18,* the court described a potential conflict between federal and state law and whether the Lanham Act preempts state common law of trademarks. Citing *Bonito Boats, Sears*, and *Compco*, the court concluded that there is no preemption. In Sears, Roebuck & Co. v. Stiffel Co., 376 U.S. 225 (1964), and Compo Corp. v. Day-Brite Lighting, Inc., 376 U.S. 234 (1964), the Supreme Court held that state trademark statutes were not pre-empted by the Lanham Act. Later, the Supreme Court clarified this decision in *Bonito Boats* as follows:

> [T]he States may not offer patent-like protection to intellectual creations which would otherwise remain unprotected as a matter of federal law. Both the novelty and the nonobviousness requirements of federal patent law are grounded in the notion that concepts within the public grasp, or those so obvious that they readily could be, are the tools of creation available to all. They provide the baseline of free competition upon which the patent system's incentive to creative effort depends. A state law that substantially interferes with the enjoyment of an unpatented utilitarian or design conception which has been freely disclosed by its author to the public at large impermissibly contravenes the ultimate goal of public disclosure and use which is the centerpiece of federal patent policy. Moreover, through the creation of patent-like rights, the States could essentially redirect inventive efforts away from the careful criteria of patentablility developed by Congress over the last 200 years. We understand this to be the reasoning at the core of our decisions in *Sears* and *Compco*, and we reaffirm that reasoning today.

Bonito Boats, Inc. v. Thunder Craft Boats, Inc., 489 U.S. 141 (1989).

Is there ever a time when state trademark law would be pre-empted by the Lanham Act? If we are to have one federal system of trademark law, what is the value of not preempting state trademark statutes? Both the federal Copyright Act and the Patent Act are said to preempt the state laws of copyright and trademark. In that case, why not preempt state trademark statutes as well?

Trademark Law
and Policy

Chapter I

Introduction

A. Source of American Trademark Law

The Congress shall have power to …

Regulate Commerce with foreign nations, and among the several states, and with the Indian tribes;

…

Promote the progress of science and useful arts, by securing for limited times to authors and inventors the exclusive right to their respective writings and discoveries.

U.S. Constitution, Article I, §8 cl. 3 & 8.

The term "trademark" includes any word, name, symbol, or device, or any combination thereof—

(1) used by a person, or

(2) which a person has a bona fide intention to use in commerce and applies to register on the principal register established by this Act,

to identify and distinguish his or her goods, including a unique product, from those manufactured or sold by others and to indicate the source of the goods, even if that source is unknown.

15 U.S.C. 1127 (2003) (The Lanham Act).

The original source of United States trademark law is the broader law of unfair competition, which is rooted in the English Common Law. *Moseley v. Victoria's Secret*, 537 U.S. 418 (2003). The United States adopted the unfair competition and trademark laws of England and made them their own. B. Pattishall, D. Hilliard, & J. Welch, Trademark and Unfair Competition 2 (4th ed. 2000). As such, one cannot ignore the common law origins of the American trademark right. This, in fact, is the cornerstone to both understanding the American trademark right and to these materials.

The notion of protecting marks as an appellation of source has developed over centuries of time. The first use of a mark to identify source started more than 3,500 years ago when potters made scratchings on the bottom of their works. William Henry Browne, A Treatise on the Law of Trademarks 8–9 (1885). The first common law judicial recognition of the trademark right was probably in Sandforth's Case in 1584. Cory's Entries, BLMS. Hargrave 123, fo. 168 (1584). For a full analysis of the case and its significance, see Keith M. Stolte, *How Early Did Anglo-American Trademark Law Begin? An Answer to Schechter's Conundrum*, 8 Fordham I.P, Media & Ent. L. J. 505 (1998). In this case, the trademark owner was protected from economic loss due to the deceit of another. There was no statute in existence regarding this concept and therefore the judge in Sandforth's Case created a new right to protect a mark claimant. To be sure, Sandforth's Case is not the earliest such case in the world. Medieval England was culturally, technologically, and legally far behind the development of such norms in Asia, particularly China. *See, e.g.,* Gavin Menzies, 1421: The Year China Discovered America (2003). More specifically, the first judicial recognition of the trademark right in Japan occurred in 1478 when one manufacturer of sake was enjoined from using the mark ROKUSEIMON on its sake containers because another manufacturer had previously used it as such. *See* Kenneth L. Port, Trademark Law and Policy in Japan Japanese Trademark Jurisprudence 19 (2007). The first state-sponsored recognition of appellations of source in Japan was at least as early as 701 A.D. when family heraldry was mandated on flags or coats of arms. *See* Shoen Ono, Shohyoho (*Trademark Law*) 22 (1994).

As this brief overview demonstrates, although the United States has a long and rich trademark jurisprudential history, it is certainly not as long as other countries'. More importantly, the trademark right in the United States is created by using a mark in commerce, not registering the mark with a central patent office as in most Civil Law jurisdictions. Consider the following cases.

The Trademark Cases
100 U.S. 82 (1879)

Miller, J.

The three cases whose titles stand at the head of this opinion [raise the same principal question:] namely, are the acts of Congress on the subject of trade-marks founded on any rightful authority in the Constitution of the United States?

The entire legislation of Congress in regard to trade-marks is of very recent origin. It is first seen in sects. 77 to 84, inclusive, of the act of July 8, 1870, entitled "An Act to revise, consolidate, and amend the statutes relating to patents and copyrights." 16 Stat. 198. The part of this act relating to trade-marks is embodied in chap. 2, tit. 60, sects. 4937 to 4947, of the Revised Statutes.

It is sufficient at present to say that they provide for the registration in the Patent Office of any device in the nature of a trade-mark to which any person has by usage established an exclusive right, or which the person so registering intends to appropriate by that act to his exclusive use; and they make the wrongful use of a trade-mark, so registered, by any other person, without the owner's permission, a cause of action in a civil suit for damages. Six years later we have the act of Aug. 14, 1876 (19 Stat. 141), punishing by fine and imprisonment the fraudulent use, sale, and counterfeiting of Trademarks registered in pursuance of the statutes of the United States, on which the informations and indictments are founded in the cases before us.

The right to adopt and use a symbol or a device to distinguish the goods or property made or sold by the person whose mark it is, to the exclusion of use by all other persons, has been long recognized by the common law and the chancery courts of England and of this country, and by the statutes of some of the States. It is a property right for the violation of which damages may be recovered in an action at law, and the continued violation of it will be enjoined by a court of equity, with compensation for past infringement.

This exclusive right was not created by the act of Congress, and does not now depend upon it for its enforcement. The whole system of trade-mark property and the civil remedies for its protection existed long anterior to that act, and have remained in full force since its passage.

These propositions are so well understood as to require neither the citation of authorities nor an elaborate argument to prove them.

As the property in trade-marks and the right to their exclusive use rest on the laws of the States, and, like the great body of the rights of person and of property, depend on them for security and protection, the power of Congress to legislate on the subject, to establish the conditions on which these rights shall be enjoyed and exercised, the period of their duration, and the legal remedies for their enforcement, if such power exist at all, must be found in the Constitution of the United States, which is the source of all the powers that Congress can lawfully exercise.

In the argument of these cases this seems to be conceded, and the advocates for the validity of the acts of Congress on this subject point to two clauses of the Constitution, in one or in both of which, as they assert, sufficient warrant may be found for this legislation.

The first of these is the eighth clause of sect. 8 of the first article. That section, manifestly intended to be an enumeration of the powers expressly granted to Congress, and closing with the declaration of a rule for the ascertainment of such powers as are necessary by way of implication to carry into efficient operation those expressly given, authorizes Congress, by the clause referred to, "to promote the progress of science and useful arts, by securing for limited times, to authors and inventors, the exclusive right to their respective writings and discoveries."

As the first and only attempt by Congress to regulate the Right of trade-marks is to be found in the act of July 8, 1870, to which we have referred, entitled "An Act to revise, consolidate, and amend the statutes relating to Patents and Copyrights," terms which have long since become technical, as referring, the one to inventions and the other to the writings of authors, it is a reasonable inference that this part of the statute also was, in the opinion of Congress, an exercise of the power found in that clause of the Constitution. It may also be safely assumed that until a critical examination of the subject in the courts became necessary, it was mainly if not wholly to this clause that the advocates of the law looked for its support.

Any attempt, however, to identify the essential characteristics of a trade-mark with inventions and discoveries in the arts and sciences, or with the writings of authors, will show that the effort is surrounded with insurmountable difficulties.

The ordinary trade-mark has no necessary relation to invention or discovery. The trade-mark recognized by the common law is generally the growth of a considerable period of use, rather than a sudden invention. It is often the result of accident rather than design, and when under the act of Congress it is sought to establish it by registration, neither originality, invention, discovery, science, nor art is in any way essential to the right conferred by that act. If we should endeavor to classify it under the head of writings of authors, the objections are equally strong. In this, as in regard to inventions, originality is required. And while the word writings may be liberally construed, as it has been, to include original designs for engravings, prints, etc., it is only such as are original, and are founded in the creative powers of the mind. The writings which are to be protected are the fruits of intellectual labor, embodied in the form of books, prints, engravings and the like.

The trade-mark may be, and generally is, the adoption of something already in existence as the distinctive symbol of the party using it. At common law the exclusive right to it grows out of its use, and not its mere adoption. By the act of Congress this exclusive right attaches upon registration. *But in neither case does it depend upon novelty, invention, discovery, or any work of the brain. It requires no fancy or imagination, no genius, no laborious thought. It is simply founded on priority of appropriation.* [Italics not in original—Ed.] We look in vain in the statute for any other qualification or condition. If the symbol, however plain, simple, old, or well-known, has been first appropriated by the claimant as his distinctive trade-mark, he may by registration secure the right to its exclusive use. While such legislation may be a judicious aid to the common law on the subject of trade-marks, and may be within the competency of legislatures whose general powers embrace that class of subjects, we are unable to see any such power in the constitutional provision concerning authors and inventors, and their writings and discoveries.

* * *

United Drug Co. v. Theodore Rectanus Co.
248 U.S. 90 (1918)

PITNEY, J.

There is no such thing as property in a trade-mark except as a right appurtenant to an established business or trade in connection with which the mark is employed. The law of trade-marks is but a part of the broader law of unfair competition; the right to a particular mark grows out of its use, not its mere adoption; its function is simply to designate the goods as the product of a particular trader and to protect his good will against the sale of another's product as his; and it is not the subject of property except in connection with an existing business. *Hanover Milling Co.* v. *Metcalf*, 240 U.S. 403, 412–414.

The owner of a trade-mark may not, like the proprietor of a patented invention, make a negative and merely prohibitive use of it as a monopoly. See *United States* v. *Bell Telephone Co.*, 167 U.S. 224, 250; *Bement* v. *National Harrow Co.*, 186 U.S. 70, 90; *Paper Bag Patent Case*, 210 U.S. 405, 424.

In truth, a trade-mark confers no monopoly whatever in a proper sense, but is merely a convenient means for facilitating the protection of one's good-will in trade by placing a distinguishing mark or symbol—a commercial signature—upon the merchandise or the package in which it is sold.

It results that the adoption of a trade-mark does not, at least in the absence of some valid legislation enacted for the purpose, project the right of protection in advance of the extension of the trade, or operate as a claim of territorial rights over areas into which it thereafter may be deemed desirable to extend the trade. And the expression, sometimes met with, that a trade-mark right is not limited in its enjoyment by territorial bounds, is true only in the sense that wherever the trade goes, attended by the use of the mark, the right of the trader to be protected against the sale by others of their wares in the place of his wares will be sustained.

* * *

B. Natural Rights or Positive Rights?

INS v. AP

248 U.S. 215 (1918)

PITNEY, J.

The parties are competitors in the gathering and distribution of news and its publication for profit in newspapers throughout the United States. The Associated Press, which was complainant in the District Court, is a cooperative organization, incorporated under the Membership Corporations Law of the State of New York, its members being individuals who are either proprietors or representatives of about 950 daily newspapers published in all parts of the United States. Complainant gathers in all parts of the world, by means of various instrumentalities of its own, by exchange with its members, and by other appropriate means, news and intelligence of current and recent events of interest to newspaper readers and distributes it daily to its members for publication in their newspapers. The cost of the service, amounting approximately to $3,500,000 per annum, is assessed upon the members and becomes a part of their costs of operation, to be recouped, presumably with profit, through the publication of their several newspapers. Under complainant's by-laws each member agrees upon assuming membership that news received through complainant's service is received exclusively for publication in a particular newspaper, language, and place specified in the certificate of membership, that no other use of it shall be permitted, and that no member shall furnish or permit anyone in his employ or connected with his newspaper to furnish any of complainant's news in advance of publication to any person not a member. And each member is required to gather the local news of his district and supply it to the Associated Press and to no one else.

Defendant is a corporation organized under the laws of the State of New Jersey, whose business is the gathering and selling of news to its customers and clients, consisting of newspapers published throughout the United States, under contracts by which they pay certain amounts at stated times for defendant's service. It has wide-spread news-gathering agencies; the cost of its operations amounts, it is said, to more than $2,000,000 per annum; and it serves about 400 newspapers located in the various cities of the United States and abroad, a few of which are represented, also, in the membership of the Associated Press.

The parties are in the keenest competition between themselves in the distribution of news throughout the United States; and so, as a rule, are the newspapers that they serve, in their several districts.

Complainant in its bill, defendant in its answer, have set forth in almost identical terms the rather obvious circumstances and conditions under which their business is conducted. The value of the service, and of the news furnished, depends upon the promptness of transmission, as well as upon the accuracy and impartiality of the news; it being essential that the news be transmitted to members or subscribers as early or earlier than similar information can be furnished to competing newspapers by other news services, and that the news furnished by each agency shall not be furnished to newspapers which do not contribute to the expense of gathering it. And further, to quote from the answer: "Prompt knowledge and publication of world-wide news is essential to the conduct of a modern newspaper, and by reason of the enormous expense incident to the gathering and distribution of such news, the only practical way in which a proprietor of a newspaper can obtain the same is, either through cooperation with a considerable number of other newspaper proprietors in the work of collecting and distributing such news, and the equitable division with them of the expenses thereof, or by the purchase of such news from some existing agency engaged in that business."

The bill was filed to restrain the pirating of complainant's news by defendant in three ways: First, by bribing employees of newspapers published by complainant's members to furnish Associated Press news to defendant before publication, for transmission by telegraph and telephone to defendant's clients for publication by them; Second, by inducing Associated Press members to violate its by-laws and permit defendant to obtain news before publication; and Third, by copying news from bulletin boards and from early editions of complainant's newspapers and selling this, either bodily or after rewriting it, to defendant's customers.

The District Court, upon consideration of the bill and answer, with voluminous affidavits on both sides, granted a preliminary injunction under the first and second heads; but refused at that stage to restrain the systematic practice admittedly pursued by defendant, of taking news bodily from the bulletin boards and early editions of complainant's newspapers and selling it as its own. The court expressed itself as satisfied that this practice amounted to unfair trade, but as the legal question was one of first impression it considered that the allowance of an injunction should await the outcome of an appeal. 240 Fed. Rep. 983, 996. Both parties having appealed, the Circuit Court of Appeals sustained the injunction order so far as it went, and upon complainant's appeal modified it and remanded the cause with directions to issue an injunction also against any bodily taking of the words or substance of complainant's news until its commercial value as news had passed away. The present writ of certiorari was then allowed.

The only matter that has been argued before us is whether defendant may lawfully be restrained from appropriating news taken from bulletins issued by complainant or any of its members, or from newspapers published by them, for the purpose of selling it to defendant's clients. Complainant asserts that defendant's admitted course of conduct in this regard both violates complainant's property right in the news and constitutes unfair competition in business. And notwithstanding the case has proceeded only to the stage of a preliminary injunction, we have deemed it proper to consider the underlying questions, since they go to the very merits of the action and are presented upon facts that are not in dispute. As presented in argument, these questions are: 1. Whether there is any property in news; 2. Whether, if there be property in news collected for the purpose of being published, it survives the instant of its publication in the first newspaper to which it is communicated by the news-gatherer; and 3. Whether defendant's admitted course of conduct in appropriating for commercial use matter taken from bulletins or early editions of Associated Press publications constitutes unfair competition in trade.

The federal jurisdiction was invoked because of diversity of citizenship, not upon the ground that the suit arose under the copyright or other laws of the United States. Complainant's news matter is not copyrighted. It is said that it could not, in practice, be copyrighted, because of the large number of dispatches that are sent daily; and, according to complainant's contention, news is not within the operation of the copyright act. Defendant, while apparently conceding this, nevertheless invokes the analogies of the law of literary property and copyright, insisting as its principal contention that, assuming complainant has a right of property in its news, it can be maintained (unless the copyright act be complied with) only by being kept secret and confidential, and that upon the publication with complainant's consent of uncopyrighted news by any of complainant's members in a newspaper or upon a bulletin board, the right of property is lost, and the subsequent use of the news by the public or by defendant for any purpose whatever becomes lawful.

* * *

In considering the general question of property in news matter, it is necessary to recognize its dual character, distinguishing between the substance of the information and the particular form or collocation of words in which the writer has communicated it.

No doubt news articles often possess a literary quality, and are the subject of literary property at the common law; nor do we question that such an article, as a literary production, is the subject of copyright by the terms of the act as it now stands. In an early case at the circuit Mr. Justice Thompson held in effect that a newspaper was not within the protection of the copyright acts of 1790 and 1802 (*Clayton* v. *Stone*, 2 Paine, 382; 5 Fed. Cas. No. 2872). But the present act is broader; it provides that the works for which copyright may be secured shall include "all the writings of an author," and specifically mentions "periodicals, including newspapers." Act of March 4, 1909, c. 320, §§4 and 5, 35 Stat. 1075, 1076. Evidently this admits to copyright a contribution to a newspaper, notwithstanding it also may convey news; and such is the practice of the copyright office, as the newspapers of the day bear witness. See Copyright Office Bulletin No. 15 (1917), pp. 7, 14, 16–17.

But the news element—the information respecting current events contained in the literary production—is not the creation of the writer, but is a report of matters that ordinarily are *publici juris*; it is the history of the day. It is not to be supposed that the framers of the Constitution, when they empowered Congress "to promote the progress of science and useful arts, by securing for limited times to authors and inventors the exclusive right to their respective writings and discoveries" (Const., Art I, §8, par. 8), intended to confer upon one who might happen to be the first to report a historic event the exclusive right for any period to spread the knowledge of it.

We need spend no time, however, upon the general question of property in news matter at common law, or the application of the copyright act, since it seems to us the case must turn upon the question of unfair competition in business. And, in our opinion, this does not depend upon any general right of property analogous to the common-law right of the proprietor of an unpublished work to prevent its publication without his consent; nor is it foreclosed by showing that the benefits of the copyright act have been waived. We are dealing here not with restrictions upon publication but with the very facilities and processes of publication. The peculiar value of news is in the spreading of it while it is fresh; and it is evident that a valuable property interest in the news, as news, cannot be maintained by keeping it secret. Besides, except for matters improperly disclosed, or published in breach of trust or confidence, or in violation of law, none of which is involved in this branch of the case, the news of current events may be regarded as common property. What we are concerned with is the business of making it known to the world, in which both parties to the present suit are engaged. That business consists in maintaining a prompt, sure, steady, and reliable service designed to place the daily events of the world at the breakfast table of the millions at a price that, while of trifling moment to each reader, is sufficient in the aggregate to afford compensation for the cost of gathering and distributing it, with the added profit so necessary as an incentive to effective action in the commercial world. The service thus performed for newspaper readers is not only innocent but extremely useful in itself, and indubitably constitutes a legitimate business. The parties are competitors in this field; and, on fundamental principles, applicable here as elsewhere, when the rights or privileges of the one are liable to conflict with those of the other, each party is under a duty so to conduct its own business as not un-necessarily or unfairly to injure that of the other.

Obviously, the question of what is unfair competition in business must be determined with particular reference to the character and circumstances of the business. The question here is not so much the rights of either party as against the public but their rights as between themselves. See *Morison* v. *Moat*, 9 Hare, 241, 258. And although we may and do assume that neither party has any remaining property interest as against the public in uncopyrighted news matter after the moment of its first publication, it by no means follows that there is no remaining property interest in it as between themselves. For, to both of them alike, news matter, however little susceptible of ownership or dominion in the absolute sense, is stock in trade, to be gathered at the cost of enterprise, organization, skill, labor, and money, and to be distributed and sold to those who will pay money for it, as for any other merchandise. Regarding the news, therefore, as but the material out of which both parties are seeking to make profits at the same time and in the same field, we hardly can fail to recognize that for this purpose, and as between them, it must be regarded as *quasi* property, irrespective of the rights of either as against the public.

In order to sustain the jurisdiction of equity over the controversy, we need not affirm any general and absolute property in the news as such. The rule that a court of equity concerns itself only in the protection of property rights treats any civil right of a pecuniary nature as a property right (*In re Sawyer*, 124 U.S. 200, 210; *In re Debs*, 158 U.S. 564, 593); and the right to acquire property by honest labor or the conduct of a lawful business is as much entitled to protection as the right to guard property already acquired. It is this right that furnishes the basis of the jurisdiction in the ordinary case of unfair competition.

The question, whether one who has gathered general information or news at pains and expense for the purpose of subsequent publication through the press has such an interest in its publication as may be protected from interference, has been raised many times, although never, perhaps, in the precise form in which it is now presented.

* * *

Not only do the acquisition and transmission of news require elaborate organization and a large expenditure of money, skill, and effort; not only has it an exchange value to the gatherer, dependent chiefly upon its novelty and freshness, the regularity of the service, its reputed reliability and thoroughness, and its adaptability to the public needs; but also, as is evident, the news has an exchange value to one who can misappropriate it.

The peculiar features of the case arise from the fact that, while novelty and freshness form so important an element in the success of the business, the very processes of distribution and publication necessarily occupy a good deal of time. Complainant's service, as well as defendant's, is a daily service to daily newspapers; most of the foreign news reaches this country at the Atlantic seaboard, principally at the City of New York, and because of this, and of time differentials due to the earth's rotation, the distribution of news matter throughout the country is principally from east to west; and, since in speed the telegraph and telephone easily outstrip the rotation of the earth, it is a simple matter for defendant to take complainant's news from bulletins or early editions of complainant's members in the eastern cities and at the mere cost of telegraphic transmission cause it to be published in western papers issued at least as early as those served by complainant. Besides this, and irrespective of time differentials, irregularities in telegraphic transmission on different lines, and the normal consumption of time in printing and distributing the newspaper, result in permitting pirated news to be placed in the hands of defendant's readers sometimes simultaneously with the service of competing Associated Press papers, occasionally even earlier.

Defendant insists that when, with the sanction and approval of complainant, and as the result of the use of its news for the very purpose for which it is distributed, a portion of complainant's members communicate it to the general public by posting it upon bulletin boards so that all may read, or by issuing it to newspapers and distributing it indiscriminately, complainant no longer has the right to control the use to be made of it; that when it thus reaches the light of day it becomes the common possession of all to whom it is accessible; and that any purchaser of a newspaper has the right to communicate the intelligence which it contains to anybody and for any purpose, even for the purpose of selling it for profit to newspapers published for profit in competition with complainant's members.

The fault in the reasoning lies in applying as a test the right of the complainant as against the public, instead of considering the rights of complainant and defendant, competitors in business, as between themselves. The right of the purchaser of a single newspaper to spread knowledge of its contents gratuitously, for any legitimate purpose not unreasonably interfering with complainant's right to make merchandise of it, may be admitted; but to transmit that news for commercial use, in competition with complainant—which is what defendant has done and seeks to justify—is a very different matter. In doing this defendant, by its very act, admits that it is taking material that has been acquired by complainant as the result of organization and the expenditure of labor, skill, and money, and which is salable by complainant for money, and that defendant in appropriating it and selling it as its own is endeavoring to reap where it has not sown, and by disposing of it to newspapers that are competitors of complainant's members is appropriating to itself the harvest of those who have sown. Stripped of all disguises, the process amounts to an unauthorized interference with the normal operation of complainant's legitimate business precisely at the point where the profit is to be reaped, in order to divert a material portion of the profit from those who have earned it to those who have not; with special advantage to defendant in the competition because of the fact that it is not burdened with any part of the expense of gathering the news. The transaction speaks for itself, and a court of equity ought not to hesitate long in characterizing it as unfair competition in business.

The underlying principle is much the same as that which lies at the base of the equitable theory of consideration in the law of trusts—that he who has fairly paid the price should have the beneficial use of the property. Pom. Eq. Jur., §981. It is no answer to say that complainant spends its money for that which is too fugitive or evanescent to be the subject of property. That might, and for the purposes of the discussion we are assuming that it would, furnish an answer in a common-law controversy. But in a court of equity, where the question is one of unfair competition, if that which complainant has acquired fairly at substantial cost may be sold fairly at substantial profit, a competitor who is misappropriating it for the purpose of disposing of it to his own profit and to the disadvantage of complainant cannot be heard to say that it is too fugitive or evanescent to be regarded as property. It has all the attributes of property necessary for determining that a misappropriation of it by a competitor is unfair competition because contrary to good conscience.

The contention that the news is abandoned to the public for all purposes when published in the first newspaper is untenable. Abandonment is a question of intent, and the entire organization of the Associated Press negatives such a purpose. The cost of the service would be prohibitive if the reward were to be so limited. No single newspaper, no small group of newspapers, could sustain the expenditure. Indeed, it is one of the most obvious results of defendant's theory that, by permitting indiscriminate publication by anybody and everybody for purposes of profit in competition with the news-gatherer, it would render publication profitless, or so little profitable as in effect to cut off the service by rendering the cost prohibitive in comparison with the return. The practical needs and requirements of the business are reflected in complainant's by-laws which have been referred to. Their effect is that publication by each member must be deemed not by any means an abandonment of the news to the world for any and all purposes, but a publication for limited purposes; for the benefit of the readers of the bulletin or the newspaper as such; not for the purpose of making merchandise of it as news, with the result of depriving complainant's other members of their reasonable opportunity to obtain just returns for their expenditures.

It is to be observed that the view we adopt does not result in giving to complainant the right to monopolize either the gathering or the distribution of the news, or, without complying with the copyright act, to prevent the reproduction of its news articles; but only postpones participation by complainant's competitor in the processes of distribution and reproduction of news that it has not gathered, and only to the extent necessary to prevent that competitor from reaping the fruits of complainant's efforts and expenditure, to the partial exclusion of complainant, and in violation of the principle that underlies the maxim *sic utere tuo*, etc.

It is said that the elements of unfair competition are lacking because there is no attempt by defendant to palm off its goods as those of the complainant, characteristic of the most familiar, if not the most typical, cases of unfair competition. *Howe Scale Co. v. Wyckoff, Seamans & Benedict*, 198 U.S. 118, 140. But we cannot concede that the right to equitable relief is confined to that class of cases. In the present case the fraud upon complainant's rights is more direct and obvious. Regarding news matter as the mere material from which these two competing parties are endeavoring to make money, and treating it, therefore, as *quasi* property for the purposes of their business because they are both selling it as such, defendant's conduct differs from the ordinary case of unfair competition in trade principally in this that, instead of selling its own goods as those of complainant, it substitutes misappropriation in the place of misrepresentation, and sells complainant's goods as its own.

Besides the misappropriation, there are elements of imitation, of false pretense, in defendant's practices. The device of rewriting complainant's news articles, frequently resorted to, carries its own comment. The habitual failure to give credit to complainant for that which is taken is significant. Indeed, the entire system of appropriating complainant's news and transmitting it as a commercial product to defendant's clients and patrons amounts to a false representation to them and to their newspaper readers that the news transmitted is the result of defendant's own investigation in the field. But these elements, although accentuating the wrong, are not the essence of it. It is something more than the advantage of celebrity of which complainant is being deprived.

* * *

There is some criticism of the injunction that was directed by the District Court upon the going down of the mandate from the Circuit Court of Appeals. In brief, it restrains any taking or gainfully using of the complainant's news, either bodily or in substance, from bulletins issued by the complainant or any of its members, or from editions of their newspapers, "*until its commercial value as news to the complainant and all of its members has passed away.*" The part complained of is the clause we have italicized; but if this be indefinite, it is no more so than the criticism. Perhaps it would be better that the terms of the injunction be made specific, and so framed as to confine the restraint to an extent consistent with the reasonable protection of complainant's newspapers, each in its own area and for a specified time after its publication, against the competitive use of pirated news by defendant's customers. But the case presents practical difficulties; and we have not the materials, either in the way of a definite suggestion of amendment, or in the way of proofs, upon which to frame a specific injunction; hence, while not expressing approval of the form adopted by the District Court, we decline to modify it at this preliminary stage of the case, and will leave that court to deal with the matter upon appropriate application made to it for the purpose.

The decree of the Circuit Court of Appeals will be

Affirmed.

Mr. Justice Clarke took no part in the consideration or decision of this case.

CONCUR: Mr. Justice Holmes:

When an uncopyrighted combination of words is published there is no general right to forbid other people repeating them—in other words there is no property in the combination or in the thoughts or facts that the words express. Property, a creation of law, does not arise from value, although exchangeable—a matter of fact. Many exchangeable values may be destroyed intentionally without compensation. Property depends upon exclusion by law from interference, and a person is not excluded from using any combination of words merely because someone has used it before, even if it took labor and genius to make it. If a given person is to be prohibited from making the use of words that his neighbors are free to make some other ground must be found. One such ground is vaguely expressed in the phrase unfair trade. This means that the words are repeated by a competitor in business in such a way as to convey a misrepresentation that materially injures the person who first used them, by appropriating credit of some kind which the first user has earned. The ordinary case is a representation by device, appearance, or other indirection that the defendant's goods come from the plaintiff. But the only reason why it is actionable to make such a representation is that it tends to give the defendant an advantage in his competition with the plaintiff and that it is thought undesirable that an advantage should be gained in that way. Apart from that the defendant may use such unpatented devices and uncopyrighted combinations of words as he likes. The ordinary case, I say, is palming off the defendant's product as the plaintiff's, but the same evil may follow from the opposite falsehood—from saying, whether in words or by implication, that the plaintiff's product is the defendant's, and that, it seems to me, is what has happened here.

Fresh news is got only by enterprise and expense. To produce such news as it is produced by the defendant represents by implication that it has been acquired by the defendant's enterprise and at its expense. When it comes from one of the great news-collecting agencies like the Associated Press, the source generally is indicated, plainly importing that credit; and that such a representation is implied may be inferred with some confidence from the unwillingness of the defendant to give the credit and tell the truth. If the plaintiff produces the news at the same time that the defendant does, the defendant's presentation impliedly denies to the plaintiff the credit of collecting the facts and assumes that credit to the defendant. If the plaintiff is later in western cities it naturally will be supposed to have obtained its information from the defendant. The falsehood is a little more subtle, the injury a little more indirect, than in ordinary cases of unfair trade, but I think that the principle that condemns the one condemns the other. It is a question of how strong an infusion of fraud is necessary to turn a flavor into a poison. The [sic] does seems to me strong enough here to need a remedy from the law. But as, in my view, the only ground of complaint that can be recognized without legislation is the implied misstatement, it can be corrected by stating the truth; and a suitable acknowledgment of the source is all that the plaintiff can require. I think that within the limits recognized by the decision of the Court the defendant should be enjoined from publishing news obtained from the Associated Press for hours after publication by the plaintiff unless it gives express credit to the Associated Press; the number of hours and the form of acknowledgment to be settled by the District Court.

* * *

The National Basketball Association v. Motorola, Inc. and Sports Team Analysis and Tracking Systems, Inc.
105 F.3d 841 (2d Cir. 1997)

WINTER, CIRCUIT JUDGE:

Motorola, Inc. and Sports Team Analysis and Tracking Systems ("STATS") appeal from a permanent injunction entered by Judge Preska. The injunction concerns a handheld pager sold by Motorola and marketed under the name "SportsTrax," which displays updated information of professional basketball games in progress. The injunction prohibits appellants, absent authorization from the National Basketball Association and NBA Properties, Inc. (collectively the "NBA"), from transmitting scores or other data about NBA games in progress via the pagers, STATS's site on America On-Line's computer dial-up service, or "any equivalent means."

The crux of the dispute concerns the extent to which a state law "hot-news" misappropriation claim based on *International News Service v. Associated Press*, 248 U.S. 215, 63 L. Ed. 211, 39 S. Ct. 68 (1918) ("INS"), survives preemption by the federal Copyright Act and whether the NBA's claim fits within the surviving INS-type claims. We hold that a narrow "hot-news" exception does survive preemption. However, we also hold that appellants' transmission of "real-time" NBA game scores and information tabulated from television and radio broadcasts of games in progress does not constitute a misappropriation of "hot news" that is the property of the NBA.

I. BACKGROUND

The facts are largely undisputed. Motorola manufactures and markets the SportsTrax paging device while STATS supplies the game information that is transmitted to the pagers. The product became available to the public in January 1996, at a retail price of about $200. SportsTrax's pager has an inch-and-a-half by inch-and-a-half screen and operates in four basic modes: "current," "statistics," "final scores" and "demonstration." It is the "current" mode that gives rise to the present dispute. In that mode, SportsTrax displays the following information on NBA games in progress: (i) the teams playing; (ii) score changes; (iii) the team in possession of the ball; (iv) whether the team is in the free-throw bonus; (v) the quarter of the game; and (vi) time remaining in the quarter. The information is updated every two to three minutes, with more frequent updates near the end of the first half and the end of the game. There is a lag of approximately two or three minutes between events in the game itself and when the information appears on the pager screen.

SportsTrax's operation relies on a "data feed" supplied by STATS reporters who watch the games on television or listen to them on the radio. The reporters key into a personal computer changes in the score and other information such as successful and missed shots, fouls, and clock updates. The information is relayed by modem to STATS's host computer, which compiles, analyzes, and formats the data for retransmission. The information is then sent to a common carrier, which then sends it via satellite to various local FM radio networks that in turn emit the signal received by the individual SportsTrax pagers.

The NBA's complaint asserted six claims for relief: (i) state law unfair competition by misappropriation; (ii) false advertising under Section 43(a) of the Lanham Act, 15 U.S.C. §1125(a); (iii) false representation of origin under Section 43(a) of the Lanham Act; (iv) state and common law unfair competition by false advertising and false designation of origin; (v) federal copyright infringement; and (vi) unlawful interception of communications under the Communications Act of 1934, 47 U.S.C. §605. Motorola counterclaimed, alleging that the NBA unlawfully interfered with Motorola's contractual relations with four individual NBA teams that had agreed to sponsor and advertise SportsTrax.

The district court dismissed all of the NBA's claims except the first—misappropriation under New York law. The court also dismissed Motorola's counterclaim. Finding Motorola and STATS liable for misappropriation, Judge Preska entered the permanent injunction, reserved the calculation of damages for subsequent proceedings, and stayed execution of the injunction pending appeal. Motorola and STATS appeal from the injunction, while NBA cross-appeals from the district court's dismissal of its Lanham Act false-advertising claim. The issues before us, therefore, are the state law misappropriation and Lanham Act claims.

II. THE STATE LAW MISAPPROPRIATION CLAIM
A. Summary of Ruling

Because our disposition of the state law misappropriation claim rests in large part on preemption by the Copyright Act, our discussion necessarily goes beyond the elements of a misappropriation claim under New York law, and a summary of our ruling here will perhaps render that discussion—or at least the need for it—more understandable.

The issues before us are ones that have arisen in various forms over the course of this century as technology has steadily increased the speed and quantity of information transmission. Today, individuals at home, at work, or elsewhere, can use a computer, pager, or other device to obtain highly selective kinds of information virtually at will. *International News Service v. Associated Press*, 248 U.S. 215, 63 L. Ed. 211, 39 S. Ct. 68 (1918) ("INS") was one of the first cases to address the issues raised by these technological advances, although the technology involved in that case was primitive by contemporary standards. *INS* involved two wire services, the Associated Press ("AP") and International News Service ("INS"), that transmitted news stories by wire to member newspapers. *Id.* INS would lift factual stories from AP bulletins and send them by wire to INS papers. *Id.* at 231. INS would also take factual stories from east coast AP papers and wire them to INS papers on the west coast that had yet to publish because of time differentials. *Id.* at 238. The Supreme Court held that INS's conduct was a common-law misappropriation of AP's property. *Id.* at 242.

With the advance of technology, radio stations began "live" broadcasts of events such as baseball games and operas, and various entrepreneurs began to use the transmissions of others in one way or another for their own profit. In response, New York courts created a body of misappropriation law, loosely based on *INS*, that sought to apply ethical standards to the use by one party of another's transmissions of events.

Federal copyright law played little active role in this area until 1976. Before then, it appears to have been the general understanding—there being no caselaw of consequence—that live events such as baseball games were not copyrightable. Moreover, doubt existed even as to whether a recorded broadcast or videotape of such an event was copyrightable. In 1976, however, Congress passed legislation expressly affording copyright protection to simultaneously-recorded broadcasts of live performances such as sports events. See 17 U.S.C. §101. Such protection was not extended to the underlying events.

The 1976 amendments also contained provisions preempting state law claims that enforced rights "equivalent" to exclusive copyright protections when the work to which the state claim was being applied fell within the area of copyright protection. See 17 U.S.C. §301. Based on legislative history of the 1976 amendments, it is generally agreed that a "hot-news" *INS*-like claim survives preemption. H.R. No. 94-1476 at 132 (1976), reprinted in 1976 U.S.C.C.A.N. 5659, 5748. However, much of New York misappropriation law after *INS* goes well beyond "hot-news" claims and is preempted.

We hold that the surviving "hot-news" INS-like claim is limited to cases where: (i) a plaintiff generates or gathers information at a cost; (ii) the information is time-sensitive; (iii) a defendant's use of the information constitutes free-riding on the plaintiff's efforts; (iv) the defendant is in direct competition with a product or service offered by the plaintiffs; and (v) the ability of other parties to free-ride on the efforts of the plaintiff or others would so reduce the incentive to produce the product or service that its existence or quality would be substantially threatened. We conclude that SportsTrax does not meet that test.

* * *

2. The Legality of SportsTrax

We conclude that Motorola and STATS have not engaged in unlawful misappropriation under the "hot-news" test set out above. To be sure, some of the elements of a "hot-news" INS-claim are met. The information transmitted to SportsTrax is not precisely contemporaneous, but it is nevertheless time-sensitive. Also, the NBA does provide, or will shortly do so, information like that available through SportsTrax. It now offers a service called "Gamestats" that provides official play-by-play game sheets and half-time and final box scores within each arena. It also provides such information to the media in each arena. In the future, the NBA plans to enhance Gamestats so that it will be networked between the various arenas and will support a pager product analogous to SportsTrax. SportsTrax will of course directly compete with an enhanced Gamestats.

However, there are critical elements missing in the NBA's attempt to assert a "hot-news" INS-type claim. As framed by the NBA, their claim compresses and confuses three different informational products. The first product is generating the information by playing the games; the second product is transmitting live, full descriptions of those games; and the third product is collecting and retransmitting strictly factual information about the games. The first and second products are the NBA's primary business: producing basketball games for live attendance and licensing copyrighted broadcasts of those games. The collection and retransmission of strictly factual material about the games is a different product: e.g., box-scores in newspapers, summaries of statistics on television sports news, and real-time facts to be transmitted to pagers. In our view, the NBA has failed to show any competitive effect whatsoever from SportsTrax on the first and second products and a lack of any free-riding by SportsTrax on the third.

With regard to the NBA's primary products — producing basketball games with live attendance and licensing copyrighted broadcasts of those games — there is no evidence that anyone regards SportsTrax or the AOL site as a substitute for attending NBA games or watching them on television. In fact, Motorola markets SportsTrax as being designed "for those times when you cannot be at the arena, watch the game on TV, or listen to the radio …"

The NBA argues that the pager market is also relevant to a "hot-news" INS-type claim and that SportsTrax's future competition with Gamestats satisfies any missing element. We agree that there is a separate market for the real-time transmission of factual information to pagers or similar devices, such as STATS's AOL site. However, we disagree that SportsTrax is in any sense free-riding off Gamestats.

An indispensable element of an INS "hot-news" claim is free-riding by a defendant on a plaintiff's product, enabling the defendant to produce a directly competitive product for less money because it has lower costs. SportsTrax is not such a product. The use of pagers to transmit real-time information about NBA games requires: (i) the collecting of facts about the games; (ii) the transmission of these facts on a network; (iii) the assembling of them by the particular service; and (iv) the transmission of them to pagers or an on-line computer site. Appellants are in no way free-riding on Gamestats. Motorola and STATS expend their own resources to collect purely factual information generated in NBA games to transmit to SportsTrax pagers. They have their own network and assemble and transmit data themselves.

To be sure, if appellants in the future were to collect facts from an enhanced Gamestats pager to retransmit them to SportsTrax pagers, that would constitute free-riding and might well cause Gamestats to be unprofitable because it had to bear costs to collect facts that SportsTrax did not. If the appropriation of facts from one pager to another pager service were allowed, transmission of current information on NBA games to pagers or similar devices would be substantially deterred because any potential transmitter would know that the first entrant would quickly encounter a lower cost competitor free-riding on the originator's transmissions.

However, that is not the case in the instant matter. SportsTrax and Gamestats are each bearing their own costs of collecting factual information on NBA games, and, if one produces a product that is cheaper or otherwise superior to the other, that producer will prevail in the marketplace. This is obviously not the situation against which INS was intended to prevent: the potential lack of any such product or service because of the anticipation of free-riding.

For the foregoing reasons, the NBA has not shown any damage to any of its products based on free-riding by Motorola and STATS, and the NBA's misappropriation claim based on New York law is preempted.

———————

Cheney Bros. v. Doris Silk Corporation
35 F.2d 279 (2d Cir. 1929)

L. Hand, Circuit Judge.

The plaintiff, a corporation is a manufacturer of silks, which puts out each season many new patterns, designed to attract purchasers by their novelty and beauty. Most of these fail in that purpose, so that not much more than a fifth catch the public fancy.

Moreover, they have only a short life, for the most part no more than a single season of eight or nine months. It is in practice impossible, and it would be very onerous if it were not, to secure design patents upon all of these; it would also be impossible to know in advance which would sell well, and patent only those. Besides, it is probable that for the most part they have no such originality as would support a design patent. Again, it is impossible to copyright them under the Copyright Act (17 USCA §§1 et seq.), or at least so the authorities of the Copyright Office hold. So it is easy for any one to copy such as prove successful, and the plaintiff, which is put to much ingenuity and expense in fabricating them, finds itself without protection of any sort for its pains.

Taking advantage of this situation, the defendant copied one of the popular designs in the season beginning in October, 1928, and undercut the plaintiff's price. This is the injury of which it complains. The defendant, though it duplicated the design in question, denies that it knew it to be the plaintiff's, and there thus arises an issue which might be an answer to the motion. However, the parties wish a decision upon the equity of the bill, and, since it is within our power to dismiss it, we shall accept its allegation, and charge the defendant with knowledge.

The plaintiff asks for protection only during the season, and needs no more, for the designs are all ephemeral. It seeks in this way to disguise the extent of the proposed innovation, and to persuade us that, if we interfere only a little, the solecism, if there be one, may be pardonable. But the reasoning which would justify any interposition at all demands that it cover the whole extent of the injury. A man whose designs come to harvest in two years, or in five, has prima facie as good right to protection as one who deals only in annuals. Nor could we consistently stop at designs; processes, machines, and secrets have an equal claim. The upshot must be that, whenever any one has contrived any of these, others may be forbidden to copy it. That is not the law. In the absence of some recognized right at common law, or under the statutes—and the plaintiff claims neither the statutes—and the plaintiff claims neither—a man's property is limited to the chattels which embody his invention. Others may imitate these at their pleasure. This is confirmed by the doctrine of "nonfunctional" features, under which it is held that to imitate these is to impute to the copy the same authorship as the original. These decisions imply that, except as to these elements, any one may copy the original at will. Unless, therefore, there has been some controlling authority to the contrary, the bill at bar stands upon no legal right and must fail.

Of the cases on which the plaintiff relies, the chief is *International News Service v. Associated Press*, 248 U. S. 215, 39 S. Ct. 68, 63 L. Ed. 211, 2 A. L. R. 293. Although that concerned another subject-matter—printed news dispatches—we agree that, if it meant to lay down a general doctrine, it would cover this case; at least, the language of the majority opinion goes so far. We do not believe that it did. While it is of course true that law ordinarily speaks in general terms, there are cases where the occasion is at once the justification for, and the limit of, what is decided. This appears to us such an instance; we think that no more was covered than situations substantially similar to those then at bar. The difficulties of understanding it otherwise are insuperable. We are to suppose that the court meant to create a sort of common-law patent or copyright for reasons of justice. Either would flagrantly conflict with the scheme which Congress has for more than a century devised to cover the subject-matter.

Qua patent, we should at least have to decide, as tabula rasa, whether the design or machine was new and required invention; further, we must ignore the Patent Office whose action has always been a condition upon the creation of this kind of property. Qua copyright, although it would be simpler to decide upon the merits, we should equally be obliged to dispense with the conditions imposed upon the creation of the right. Nor, if we went so far, should we know whether the property so recognized should be limited to the periods prescribed in the statutes, or should extend as long as the author's grievance. It appears to us incredible that the Supreme Court should have had in mind any such consequences. To exclude others from the enjoyment of a chattel is one thing; to prevent any imitation of it, to set up a monopoly in the plan of its structure, gives the author a power which the Constitution allows only Congress to create.

True, it would seem as though the plaintiff had suffered a grievance for which there should be a remedy, perhaps by an amendment of the Copyright Law, assuming that this does not already cover the case, which is not urged here. It seems a lame answer in such a case to turn the injured party out of court, but there are larger issues at stake than his redress. Judges have only a limited power to amend the law; when the subject has been confided to a Legislature, they must stand aside, even though there be an hiatus in completed justice. An omission in such cases must be taken to have been as deliberate as though it were express, certainly after long-standing action on the subject-matter. Indeed, were are not in any position to pass upon the questions involved, as Brandeis, J., observed in *International News Service v. Associated Press*. We must judge upon records prepared by litigants, which do not contain all that may be relevant to the issues, for they cannot disclose the conditions of this industry, or of the others which may be involved. Congress might see its way to create some sort of temporary right, or it might not. Its decision would certainly be preceded by some examination of the result upon the other interests affected. Whether these would prove paramount we have no means of saying; it is not for us to decide. Our vision is inevitably contracted, and the whole horizon may contain much which will compose a very different picture.

The order is affirmed, and as the bill cannot in any event succeed, it may be dismissed, if the defendant so desires.

————————

Order of Job's Daughters v. Lindeburg & Co.
633 F.2d 912 (9th Cir. 1980)

[Order of Job's Daughters was a fraternal organization that adopted an insignia to identify the Order. Defendants had sold jewelry bearing that insignia without a license.]

Job's Daughters relies on *Boston Professional Hockey Ass'n, Inc. v. Dallas Cap & Emblem Mfg., Inc.*, 510 F.2d 1004 (5th Cir.), *cert. denied*, 423 U.S. 868, 96 S. Ct. 132, 46 L. Ed. 2d 98 (1975), in which the Boston Bruins and other National Hockey League clubs brought a trademark infringement suit against a company that sold replicas of the NHL team emblems. The Fifth Circuit, applying the Lanham Act infringement test and focusing on the "likelihood of confusion," found infringement:

> The confusion or deceit requirement is met by the fact that the defendant duplicated the protected trademarks and sold them to the public knowing that the public would identify them as being the teams' trademarks. The certain knowledge of the buyer that the source and origin of the trademark symbols were the plaintiff's satisfies the requirement of the act. The argument that confusion must be as to the source of the manufacture of the emblem itself is unpersuasive, where the trademark, originated by the team, is the triggering mechanism for the sale of the emblem.

510 F.2d at 1012.

Job's Daughters asserts that *Boston Hockey* supports its contention that even purely functional use of a trademark violates the Lanham Act. We reject the reasoning of *Boston Hockey*.

Interpreted expansively, *Boston Hockey* holds that a trademark's owner has a complete monopoly over its use, including its functional use, in commercial merchandising. But our reading of the Lanham Act and its legislative history reveals no congressional design to bestow such broad property rights on trademark owners. Its scope is much narrower: to protect consumers against deceptive designations of the origin of goods and, conversely, to enable producers to differentiate their products from those of others. The *Boston Hockey* decision transmogrifies this narrow protection into a broad monopoly. It does so by injecting its evaluation of the equities between the parties and of the desirability of bestowing broad property rights on trademark owners. A trademark is, of course, a form of business property. But the "property right" or protection accorded a trademark owner can only be understood in the context of trademark law and its purposes. A trademark owner has a property right only insofar as is necessary to prevent consumer confusion as to who produced the goods and to facilitate differentiation of the trademark owner's goods. The *Boston Hockey* court decided that broader protection was desirable. In our view, this extends the protection beyond that intended by Congress and beyond that accorded by any other court.

We express no opinion about whether *Job's Daughters* could prevent Lindeburg from using its name and emblem under federal patent law, federal copyright law, or state unfair competition law.

Indeed, the court in *Boston Hockey* admitted that its decision "may slightly tilt the trademark laws from the purpose of protecting the public to the protection of the business interests of plaintiffs." 510 F.2d at 1011. We think that this tilt was not slight but an extraordinary extension of the protection heretofore afforded trademark owners. It is an extension we cannot endorse. Instead, we agree with Judge Waterman of the Second Circuit, who recently said that under the Lanham Act "one can capitalize on a market or fad created by another provided that it is not accomplished by confusing the public into mistakenly purchasing the product in the belief that the product is the product of the competitor." *American Footwear Corp. v. General Footwear Co. Ltd.*, 609 F.2d 655, 662 (2d Cir. 1979), *cert. denied*, 445 U.S. 951, 100 S. Ct. 1601, 63 L. Ed. 2d 787 (1980) (finding that the manufacturer of a "Bionic Boot" did not infringe the trademark of the producers of the "Bionic Woman" television program).

C. Comparison: Civil Law vs. Common Law

McDonald's Co. (Japan), Ltd. v. K.K. Marushin Foods
10 Mutai Zaisan Hanreishu 478 (October 25, 1978)
Tokyo High Court

[In 1966, before McDonald's established a formal presence in Japan, the name "McDonald's" became known as the name of an American restaurant. In July of 1969 as the name McDonald's become widely recognized in Japan, K.K. Marushin Foods first acquired the mark BAGA (a transliteration of the Japanese word for "burger") and then filed trademark registrations for a variety of marks which were identical with or closely similar to the marks used by McDonald's. In January of 1971, McDonald's announced its intention to open restaurants in Japan and on July 20th of 1971 its first store opened at the Mitsukoshi department store in Ginza, Tokyo. In May of 1972, after receiving other trademark registrations, K.K. Marushin Foods started selling hamburgers from vending machines using the marks listed below as "Appellees's Trademarks." McDonald's sued under the Trademark Act and under the Unfair Competition Prevention Act. McDonald's demanded an order restraining the defendants from using any of the Appellee's Trademarks and damages in the amount of 30 million yen (about $300,000) or 5% of sales from February 23, 1974. McDonald's argued that its trademarks listed below (Nos. 2 through 8) were "well-known" marks under the Unfair Competition Prevention Act and therefore, even though K.K. Marushin Foods registered similar marks first, McDonald's should still prevail in preventing K.K. Marushin Foods from using their marks. The Tokyo District Court dismissed McDonald's cause of action and ordered McDonald's to pay costs. The Tokyo District Court held that the "well-known" mark exception applied only to marks that were truly well-known in Japan, not in any other parts of the world. *See McDonald's Co. (Japan), Ltd. v. Mac Sangyo K.K.*, Tokyo District Court, July 21, 1975.]

LAWS AT ISSUE:

Unfair Competition Prevention Law, Arts. 1 and 6.

Trademark Law, Arts. 25, 36, and 37.

FORMAL JUDGEMENT

I. The judgement below shall be amended as follows:

1. The Appellees shall not use either Appellees' Mark (2) or (3) [listed below] on hamburger products it manufactures and sells in vending machines and will not sell hamburger products bearing these Marks.

2. The Appellee Mac Sangyo K.K. shall destroy all containers and packaging it owns that bear either of the Marks above and Appellee K.K. Marushin Foods shall remove these Marks from the automatic vending machines it owns and in which it sells hamburger products.

3. The Appellant's remaining demands are dismissed.

II. The costs of both this appeal and the costs at trial shall be added together and divided by three. The Appellant shall be responsible for the first one third of the costs and the Appellees shall be responsible for the remainder.

* * *

REASONING

I. Appellant's demand for the cessation of use of Appellees' Mark (1)

This court concurs with the opinion below that [Appellant's] demand that [Appellee] cease use of that mark is groundless. [The court cited a vague portion of the lower court's opinion where that court concluded that a side-by-side comparison of the two marks showed significant differences and that no consumer would be confused. Marushin actually ceased use of its Mark No. 1 below, rendering that part of the matter moot.]

II. Appellant's demand for the cessation of use of Appellees' Marks (2) and (3)

A. Appellant's marks and the degree to which they are well-known

* * *

- In light of the facts articulated above, this court concludes that the Appellant's Marks (1)–(6) and Mark (8) have become well-known marks within Japan since July of 1971 as indications of Appellant's [hamburger products and business].

B. Appellees' marks and their manner of use

- There is no dispute that Appellee K.K. Marushin Foods has manufactured hamburger products and that Appellee Mac Sangyo has been packaging and selling hamburger products since May of 1972 on automatic vending machines … Originally, all of the Appellees' Trademarks as listed below were used on or in connection with the sale of hamburgers or hamburger products on automatic vending machines. However, since June of 1973, Appellees ceased use of Appellees' Mark (1) and has been using only Appellees' Marks (2) and (3).

* * *

IV. Confusion of Goods

* * *

In light of the facts herein, this court concludes that Appellees' Marks (2) and (3) used in the sale of hamburger products are likely to confuse and deceive purchasers into believing that Appellees' products actually come from Appellant. The fact that the systems by which the respective goods are sold—Appellees by vending machines and Appellant via over-the-counter shops—does not mitigate this likely confusion.

V. Assertion of the Trademark Right

* * *

One may conclude that most of Appellant's marks are conceptually included in Appellees' Marks (2) and (3) [and therefore the prior registration of these marks by Appellee should result in a dismissal for the Appellant as the lower court concluded]. However, although a trademark owner does have the right to exclude the use of another's mark that is within the scope of similarity of the registered mark, that trademark owner has no absolute right to use that registered mark. Using a [registered] mark [in light of a similar, well-known mark] is not an exercise of the trademark right as provided in Article 6 of the Unfair Competition Prevention Act. Therefore, Appellees' claim that its use of Appellees' Marks (2) and (3) because it had previously registered Appellees' is appropriate cannot be recognized.

McDONALD'S TRADEMARKS

McDonald's

McDonald's

マクドナルド

ビッグマック

Mac

マックフライポテト

マック

マックシェイク

MARUSHIN'S TRADEMARKS

———

Notes

1. In the first portion of *The Trademark Cases, supra*, Justice Miller states that advocates for the constitutionality of the Trademark Act of 1870 point to two clauses that support their argument. The excerpt focuses on whether or not trademarks could conceivably be regulated under the Patent and Copyright Clause (Art. I, §8 cl. 8). The other clause the proponents of the Act pointed to was the Commerce Clause (Art. I, §8 cl. 3). This is the clause upon which the Lanham Act, the current trademark statute, rests its constitutional legitimacy. Why does the Commerce Clause provide constitutional justification today, but it did not in 1879?

2. Justice Pitney issued the opinion in the *INS* case, *supra*, 14 days after he issued the opinion in the *United Drug* case, *supra*. What were Justice Pitney's real views of the property rights in intellectual property? Are the two cases consistent on this point?

3. Can the holding in *Doris Silk*, *supra*, be justified in light of the Supreme Court's ruling in *INS*? Learned Hand, who wrote the opinion in *Doris Silk*, was deeply troubled by this problem. In fact, in a memorandum to the other judges on the panel in this case, Hand wrote as follows:

> I confess that the Associated Press Case is somewhat of a stumbling block, but I do not believe that the five justices who united in Pitney, J's opinion meant to lay down a general rule that a man is entitled to "property" in the form of whatever he makes with his labor and money, so as to prevent others from copying it. To do so would be to short-circuit the Patent Office and throw upon courts the winnowing out of all such designs that might be presented. While I agree that on principle it is hard to distinguish, and that the language applies, I cannot suppose that any principle of such far-reaching consequence was intended. It will make patent cases an exception; it will give to State courts jurisdiction over inventions; it will overthrow the practice of centuries.

Memorandum from L. Hand to Manton and Swan (Oct. 8, 1929), *quoted in* Kenneth L. Port, *Learned Hand's Trademark Jurisprudence: Legal Positivism and the Myth of the Prophet*, 27 Pacific Law Journal 221, 238 (1996) (pointing out that Hand's opinion in *Doris Silk* does not seem particularly bothered by *INS*, but that Hand was actually quite concerned about the apparent disregard for Supreme Court precedent). In the end, did Learned Hand ignore his responsibilities under *stare decisis*?

4. The *INS* case is one of the more controversial cases in intellectual property law. What is the specific holding in that case? On what grounds does Justice Pitney base the misappropriation of information? If information cannot be owned via copyright or patent, how can it be misappropriated? This case has spawned an entire genre of scholarship. One of the more commonly cited articles is Douglas Baird, *Common Law Intellectual Property and the Legacy of International News Service v. Associated Press*, 50 U. Chi. L. Rev. 411, 428 (1983) ("The major virtue of allowing common law judges to discover intellectual property rights in the tradition of *INS* may also be its major vice. Discovering new intellectual property rights forces a judge to confront and reassess first principles. As in *INS*, a judge may not be forced to choose decisively between a natural rights theory or an economic incentive theory, but this is not to say that the balance is standardless or without subtlety. The common law judge reasons by analogy, and when a new kind of intellectual property dispute confronts him, he must search for analogies in a legal universe that, like all universes in which first principles dot the landscape, is so primitive and so unformed that it is hard to identify clear landmarks.").

5. Given the above, should infringement of the trademark right sound in trespass or in tort? Consider the following:

> The law of unfair competition has its roots in the common-law tort of deceit: its general concern is with protecting consumers from confusion as to source. While that concern may result in the creation of "quasi-property rights" in communicative symbols, the focus is on the protection of consumers, not the protection of producers as an incentive to product innovation.

Bonito Boats, Inc. v. Thunder Craft Boats, Inc., 489 U.S. 141, 157 (1989)

Thus, trademark protection is justified as a tort intended to prevent the consumer from being deceived, not a trespass on the trademark itself.

In fact, the quotation above is neither a novel nor unique expression of the common law of trademarks. The Supreme Court has continuously held that the trademark right is "not in gross," *Prestonettes, Inc. v. Coty*, 264 U.S. 359, 360 (1924); *United Drug Co. v. Theodore Rectanus Co.*, 248 U.S. 90, 97 (1918); *Hanover Star Milling Co. v. Metcalf*, 240 U.S. 403, 413–15 (1916), and not a copyright or a patent, but that any rights to trademarks are appurtenant to the related business. The purpose of trademark law is to exclude others from confusing usages, not to grant a monopoly in the mark in gross.

Trademark law developed from unfair competition; unfair competition developed from the tort of fraud and deceit. English courts first invoked the notion of unfair competition in 1803, using the words "passing off" or "palming off." *Hogg v. Kirby*, 32 Eng. Rep. 336 (1803). The justification of this tort was that one should not pass off one's goods as those of another and thereby profit from the deception.

The confusion regarding whether trademark sounds in tort or in trespass stems from the old English rule in equity that an injunction would not issue unless a property right was at stake. Frank I. Schechter, The Historical Foundations of the Law Relating to Trademarks 150–52 (1925). However, the court in *Millington v. Fox*, 40 Eng. Rep. 956 (Ch. 1838), granted an injunction in equity for trademark infringement and held that proof of defendant's intent to defraud and knowledge of plaintiff's rights in and to the mark were not necessary for the plaintiff to prevail. Based upon this case, some commentators have come to the conclusion that a trademark was subject to property ownership and that infringement constituted a trespass, not a tort. *See, e.g.*, Beverly W. Pattishall, *Dawning Acceptance of the Dilution Rationale for Trademark-Trade Identity Protection*, 74 TRADEMARK REP. 289, 309 (1984), 3 Rudolph Callmann, THE LAW OF UNFAIR COMPETITION, TRADEMARKS, AND MONOPOLIES §21.12 (3d ed. 1969).

Most specifically, Callmann has argued that the Lanham Act "gives this property right a legislative standing it had not had before by declaring trademarks incontestable.... This development should effectively put to rest all arguments advanced by opponents of the property right theory." Rudolph Callmann, *Unfair Competition Without Competition?: The Importance of the Property Concept in the Law of Trade-Marks*, 95 U. PA. L. REV. 443, 467 (1947).

Not only has the ancient notion that specific legal rules can be deduced from general principles been largely discredited and discarded, but the momentary fixation that American courts had on claiming trademark as property has also rightfully passed. Today, when courts refer to trademarks as property, they are referring to the limited right of exclusion that constitutes the trademark right. Undoubtedly, this right of exclusion is a property right because it exhibits all normal incidents of ownership. However, no courts have recognized property rights to the mark itself.

6. The outcome in *INS v. AP*, *supra*, can be understood as a manifestation of the natural rights concept of property (here specifically applied to intellectual property). The concept of "natural rights" originated with the Romans. *See generally* W.W. Buckland, A TEXT-BOOK OF ROMAN LAW FROM AUGUSTUS TO JUSTINIAN (1990); Rudolph Sohm, THE INSTITUTES: A TEXTBOOK OF THE HISTORY AND SYSTEM OF ROMAN PRIVATE LAW(1970); H.F. Jolowicz, HISTORICAL INTRODUCTION TO THE STUDY OF ROMAN LAW (1952). According to the Romans, the principal manner of acquiring property rights in objects was occupancy. The first person to possess an object was said to have a natural right to own that object, providing it was not owned by someone else and was actually capable of ownership. The Romans defined things such as air, water, the sea, etc. as common to all and not subject to ownership by any single entity. Therefore, the first person to physically possess a wild animal, for example, was said to own the wild animal provided that possession was continuous. However, because of the doctrine of *ferae naturae*, wild animals are considered to be inherently free, and once a wild animal escaped, it subsequently belonged only to the next person to physically possess it. This approach to natural rights, as applied to intellectual property, would render even ideas themselves physically owned and, therefore, subject those ideas to property ownership by the first individual to conceive of them. The title granted would have to be in the idea itself, however manifested or not manifested, because the inventor/author was the first to conceive of the idea and, therefore, the first to possess it.

Trademarks traditionally act like wild animals under Roman law—free for all to use except to the extent others have actually "captured" them and used them on products.

One popular expression of the natural rights theory of property can be found in John Locke's Two TREATISES ON GOVERNMENT(Peter Laslett ed., 3d ed. 1988). Some use this justification for property to justify intellectual property akin to the understanding as expressed by the majority in *INS v. AP*.

According to Locke, recognizing property rights is not justified by an empty reap/sow rhetoric, nor on the basis of merely the first to occupy (by thinking of) an idea. Rather, according to Locke, all things are a grant from God and held in common by all people. However, in this stage they are not useful to anyone. Therefore, an individual exerts labor upon the object and transforms it into something useful and worthy of property ownership. Because the individual exerted labor upon the thing, he or she should own it because without his or her labor, no one would be able to benefit from it. *See* Justin Hughes, *The Philosophy of Intellectual Property*, 77 Geo. L. J. 287 (1988).

The enticing part of Locke's theory is not merely a reap/sow logic where the object upon which work is exerted is only meaningful to one person. Rather, the normative aspect of Locke's theory is that property should be granted to the one who exerted labor upon the thing and to reward that person, thereby encouraging work and disclosure so that all can put the idea to use.

This is better known as the bargain theory or the reward theory. The theory is that if rights to an invention are not granted, people would cease to invent (or at least not invent as much) and more importantly, they would cease to disclose because to disclose would be to lose control of the invention. Therefore, without this reward, society would suffer.

By protecting trademarks, society derives two major benefits: accurate information and less expensive products. Consumers benefit by not being deceived as to the source of a good or service. Consumers also financially benefit because manufacturers can charge less for their products if manufacturers can use one, well-recognized trademark, rather than re-educating the consumer every time the consumer goes shopping for a product. That is, it is far more efficient for manufacturers to use the shorthand of a trademark, say Tidy brand laundry detergent, than to attempt to communicate all of Tidy's attributes (removes stains, non-allergenic, etc.) afresh with each new transaction. *See infra* Chapter II.B. Therefore, to provide some incentives to manufacturers to create trademarks does not appear to be a normatively negative concept.

It appears that Justice Pitney followed a natural rights notion of intellectual property when writing his opinion in *INS v. AP.*

As alluded to above, Learned Hand appears to have rejected this notion in *Doris Silk*. It is possible that Learned Hand had a much more positivist perspective of intellectual property and this perspective guided his view of whether or not the design of scarves should be protectable trade dress.

At its core, legal positivism is the notion that all law is the product of the will of the state and that law is divorced from morals. *See* H.L.A. Hart, The Concept of Law 181–207 (1961). In other words, a legal positivist is mostly concerned with what the law is in order to determine the will of the state. The legal positivist is not concerned with whether the moral propositions upon which the laws are based are normatively true or false.

Legal positivism began as an English philosophical response to the natural law proponents and was the first modern attempt at a coherent theory of law. In response to natural law proponents such as John Locke, John Austin, a disciple of Jeremy Bentham, proposed a detailed theory of the law of a nation-state. Both Bentham and Austin—generally considered the founders of legal positivism—were concerned that if the natural law proponents' concepts were put into effect, chaos would result. Therefore, both Bentham and Austin clearly delineated that what the law *is* was distinct from what the law *ought to be*. Whereas natural rights theorists purported that only those laws that conformed to morality were binding, legal positivists held that laws, as an expression of the will of the state, were binding whether or not they comported with morality.

It could be that the different outcomes in INS v. AP and Doris Silk can be explained on the basis that Justice Pitney recognized natural rights on one hand and Learned Hand was a strict positivist on the other. See Kenneth L. Port, *Learned Hand's Trademark Jurisprudence: Legal Positivism and the Myth of the Prophet*, 27 Pacific L. J. 221 (1996).

7. Is an economic incentive theory a subset of natural rights? If not codified, is wealth maximization an idea grounded in a natural rights view of property rather than a positivist view of property rights? Are trademark rights created or found?

8. Perhaps the clearest statement of the scope of trademark rights in the United States was put this way: "[O]nly active use allows consumers to associate a mark with a particular good and notifies other firms that the mark is so associated." Zazu Designs v. L'Oreal, S.A. 979 F. 2d 499, 503 (7th Cir. 1992).

9. The Japanese Supreme Court affirmed the Tokyo High Court's decision in the *McDonald's Case. McDonald's Co. (Japan) Ltd. v. KK Marushin Foods*, 35 Saikosaibansho Minjihanreishu 1129, 1020 Hanrei Jiho 15 (Supreme Court October 13, 1981). This case shows the importance of the distinction between first-to-use systems like the United States and first-to-register systems like Japan.

10. The potential significance of a first to file system remains enormous. It took McDonald's a decade and significant legal fees to ascertain the status of its trademarks in Japan. As a result, McDonald's was very slow in developing in the Japanese market. Today McDonald's has thousands of stores all across Japan; however, it is unclear how much the uncertainty over their trademark delayed their market entrance and what sales were lost in Japan while McDonald's ascertained the status of their trademark.

Figure 1.1   Federal Intellectual Property Law Summary

	Patent	Copyright	Trademark
Source of Authority	Constitution: Art. 1 § 8 Cl. 8 "Patent and Copyright Clause"	Constitution: Art. 1 § 8 Cl. 8 "Patent and Copyright Clause"	Constitution: Art.1 § 8 Cl. 3 "Commerce Clause"
Purpose	"Promote Invention and Discovery" by creating a limited monopoly	"Promote Invention and Discovery" by protecting "original works of authorship"	Protect consumers from confusion, protect the merchant's goodwill, and protect 3rd parties' ability to compete
Length of Protection	20 years from application date for utility patents; 14 years from date of application for design patents	Life + 70 years	10-year renewable term of registration if in continuous use
Scope of Protection	Define in claims in letters patent	Protects against copying if "substantially similar"	Same or similar goods or services
Protection Begins	Date of issuance of letters patent	The moment original expression is fixed in a tangible medium	Used in commerce

Chapter II

Why Protect Trademarks?

A. Competition

Restatement of the Law (Third), Unfair Competition — Chapter 1. The Freedom to Compete

§1. General Principles

One who causes harm to the commercial relations of another by engaging in a business or trade is not subject to liability to the other for such harm unless:

(a) the harm results from acts or practices of the actor actionable by the other under the rules of this Restatement relating to:

(1) deceptive marketing, as specified in Chapter Two;

(2) infringement of trademarks and other indicia of identification, as specified in Chapter Three;

(3) appropriation of intangible trade values including trade secrets and the right of publicity, as specified in Chapter Four;

or from other acts or practices of the actor determined to be actionable as an unfair method of competition, taking into account the nature of the conduct and its likely effect on both the person seeking relief and the public; or

(b) the acts or practices of the actor are actionable by the other under federal or state statutes, international agreements, or general principles of common law apart from those considered in this Restatement.

Comment:

a. The freedom to compete. The freedom to engage in business and to compete for the patronage of prospective customers is a fundamental premise of the free enterprise system. Competition in the marketing of goods and services creates incentives to offer quality products at reasonable prices and fosters the general welfare by promoting the efficient allocation of economic resources. The freedom to compete necessarily contemplates the probability of harm to the commercial relations of other participants in the market. The fundamental rule stated in the introductory clause of this Section promotes competition by insuring that neither new entrants nor existing competitors will be subject to liability for harm resulting solely from the fact of their participation in the market.

The freedom to compete implies a right to induce prospective customers to do business with the actor rather than with the actor's competitors. This Section permits a seller to seek to divert business not only from competitors generally, but also from a particular competitor. This Section is applicable to harm incurred by persons with whom the actor directly competes and to harm incurred by other persons affected by the actor's decision to enter or continue in business. Thus, the actor is not subject to liability to indirect competitors or to employees or suppliers of others who may be harmed by the actor's presence in the market. Liability is imposed under this Section, and under this Restatement generally, only in connection with harm resulting from particular methods of competition determined to be unfair.

The principle embodied in this Section is often loosely described as a "privilege" to compete. That characterization, however, is sometimes taken to imply that any intentional interference in the commercial relations of another is prima facie tortious, with the burden on the actor to establish an applicable privilege as an affirmative defense. There is as yet no consensus with respect to the allocation of the burdens of pleading and proof under the general tort of intentional interference with prospective economic relations. See Restatement, Second, Torts §767, Comment k. However, in the case of harm resulting from competition in the marketplace, the privilege rationale appears inconsistent with the basic premise of our free enterprise system. Rather than adopting the view that such harm is prima facie tortious subject to a competitive privilege, this Restatement rejects the privilege rationale in favor of a general principle of non-liability. A person alleging injury through competition must therefore establish facts sufficient to subject the actor to liability under one or more of the rules enumerated in this Section.

This Section does not preclude the imposition of liability when the actor's participation in the market is itself unlawful. One who engages in a particular business or trade in violation of a statute prohibiting such activity, either absolutely or without prescribed permission, may be subject to liability to others engaged in the business or trade if one of the purposes of the enactment is to protect the others against unauthorized competition and the recognition of a private right of action is not inconsistent with the legislative intent. This result is an application of the general principles relating to the imposition of tort liability for violations of legislative enactments that do not explicitly authorize a private cause of action.

———————

B. Economic Justification of Protecting Trademarks

Kenneth L. Port, *The Congressional Expansion of American Trademark Law: A Civil Law System in the Making*
35 Wake Forest L. Rev. 827 (2000)

* * *

The economic rationale of intellectual property, in general, it is claimed, stems from the lauded Coase Theorem. The Coase Theorem predicts that in a world of zero transactions costs, it will be irrelevant which party to a conflicting situation is given legal rights because those parties will reach a mutual, wealth maximizing bargain. Transaction costs include information costs, negotiation costs, policing and enforcement costs, and costs of free riders. As such, legal rules should not add to transaction costs between any two private parties. Legal rules should be formulated as to reduce transaction costs. In its most basic form, the economic rationale of trademark protection is to reduce consumer search costs. Landes and Posner call this the "essential economic function of trademarks." The conclusion of this part of this Article is that the legislative expansion described above will add to the transaction costs involved in the overall scheme of trademark protection and, as such, is not desirable.

That is, the economic value of trademarks is to reduce the specific knowledge consumers must master before making purchases. If consumers were required to master the contents and ingredients of products and required to be able to chemically or physically distinguish which aspect of any given product manifests their desired characteristics, the search costs might become so astronomical that the purchaser would either not buy the product or would buy an undesired one.

Take laundry detergent for example. Hypothetically, let us presume that Tidy brand detergent is desirable because it gets Emily's clothes clean while Aller brand detergent is not because although it gets Emily's clothes clean, it also makes her break out in a rash if she wears clothes washed in Aller brand detergent. The economic function of trademarks in this setting is realized because Emily can make a quick and inexpensive choice between Tidy and Aller in the grocery store. Although she knows they each share the quality function of getting her clothes clean, they also do not share the quality function of being non-allergenic because one makes her break out in a rash and the other does not. As such, Emily can rely on the trademarks to identify one consistent product emanating from one consistent source, even if that source is not specifically known by Emily.

On the other hand, if Emily cannot rely on the source and quality functions of trademarks, she will be forced to research the chemical compositions of Tidy and Aller and determine precisely which chemical or combination of chemicals irritate her skin. She will then be required to read each package of detergent and study the ingredients to determine which box of detergent contains the undesirable characteristics. Consequently, Emily will incur a significantly higher total cost in purchasing the box of detergent if she cannot rely on trademarks to identify the information she desires about laundry detergent.

However, the accepted view of the economics of trademark law is presented by Landes and Posner. It is rather clear that Landes and Posner do not accept the application of the Coase Theorem to the economic justification of trademark law. In fact, Landes and Posner dismiss the Coase Theorem as applied to trademarks because there are simply too many transaction costs involved in a complex commercial setting to keep track of them all.

Both the static and the dynamic benefits of property rights presuppose that there are too many potential users of property for transactions with all of them to be economical. When transaction costs (which, in general, though not always, are a positive function of the number of contracting parties) are low, the Coase Theorem implies that enforceable contract rights are all that are needed to achieve optimal use and investment.

That is, in the setting of trademark law, more is needed than just private bargained contractual relationships to divide the right of exclusion to words which may also have a societal as well as a competitive value in addition to their value as indicia of source.

Landes and Posner represent Emily's predicament above as follows: $[pi] = P + H(T;Y;W)$. This formula predicts that the full price ($[pi]$) of a good (X) will be the money costs paid for X (P) plus the consumer search costs (H). However, H will be affected by several variables. These variables include the distinctive capabilities of the trademark itself (T) which includes all information communicated by the trademark to prospective purchasers including the quality guarantee function, the consistent source function and the consistent product function. Y represents, among other things, the variable of competition. The more competition exists, the more the consumer will spend searching between the various sources to be sure he has chosen the desired product with the desired characteristics. The last variable in the Landes and Posner model is W, which represents the index of all available terms and symbols that may be used as trademarks.

Two other indicia that are used in the Landes and Posner model are R and Z. R represents the cost to the corporation of producing one unit of T. Z denotes the words used in common with other producers — that is, generic terms used as part of a language needed to sell specific products.

C. Social Justification of Protecting Trademarks

Kenneth L. Port, *The Congressional Expansion of American Trademark Law: A Civil Law System in the Making*
35 Wake Forest L. Rev. 827 (2000)

* * *

The social function of trademarks recognizes that in some instances, trademarks or other trade symbols come to have a second life in the society in which they are used. Not only do they identify source or origin for one particular manufacturer, they also have iconic value for the society itself. In such an instance, such trademarks as "Batman" or "Superman" become cultural properties. As cultural property, these icons have an existence separate from any source identifying function. The question becomes, to whom does the benefit of such marks inure, the manufacturer or society at large?

I am not the first to recognize that, as trademark protection for the trademark owner expands, the room left over for the cultural dimension or iconic dimension correspondingly decreases. In fact, the social function of trademarks posits that society as a whole, not individual consumers, not producers, and not third party competitors, has an interest in retaining access to a social icon that ought to be owned by all.

Ralph Brown's "original prescription" of the social function of trademarks seems to still hold today even fifty years after it was first posited. As Jessica Litman articulates, "legal protection for trade symbols, in the absence of confusion, disserves competition and thus the consumer. It arrogates to the producer the entire value of cultural icons that we should more appropriately treat as collectively owned."

That is, although the well settled doctrine states that a trademark holder ought to enjoy the right of excluding others from using even an iconic trademark to prevent confusion, mistake, or deception as to the source or origin of the goods or services on which it uses the trademark, where no confusion is likely, protecting the trademark holder likely gives the holder a monopoly right in uses of that iconic mark that should rightfully be shared by all.

It should be shared by all, of course, because society at large played a large role in making it a cultural icon. The popularity of the icon was not exclusively created by the manufacturer. Society at large responded to the icon by purchasing the initial goods associated with the mark. At some point, the notion of "Batman" or "Superman" has an existence separate from its source-identifying existence. This existence is generated by each individual's concept of the mark in the abstract. How, and more importantly why, should the manufacturer lay claim to trademarks that have become cultural icons even as they exist in the abstract in each individual's mind, especially when there is no likelihood of confusion as to source?

Therefore, as Congress expands trademark protection to allow the trademark holder to prevent confusing as well as non-confusing uses of an iconic mark by another, the social function of trademarks is undermined.

———

Notes

1. Professor Rosemary Coombe has created an impressive body of literature regarding the cultural and social ramifications and justifications for protecting a variety of intellectual property including trademarks. *See, e.g.*, THE CULTURAL LIFE OF INTELLECTUAL PROPERTIES: AUTHORSHIP, APPROPRIATION, AND THE LAW (1998); Rosemary J. Coombe, *Interdisciplinary Approaches to International Economic Law: The Cultural Life of Things: Anthropological Approaches to Law and Society in Conditions of Globalilzation*, 69 TEX. L. REV. 1853 (1991); *New Direction: Critical Cultural Legal Studies*, 10 YALE J.L. & HUMAN. 463 (1998); *Objects of Property and Subjects of Politics: Intellectual Property Laws and Democratic Dialogue*,13 YALE J.L. & HUMAN. 451 (2001).

2. Can anyone claim to be the "author" of trademarks? *See* Steven Wilf, *Who Authors Trademarks?*, 17 CARDOZO ARTS & ENT. L.J. 1, 29 (1999) ("Language is different than real property because its appropriation always demands consent.").

3. *Strong protection or weak?* Those who argue for strong trademark protection claim that such protection will encourage innovation by preventing consumer confusion and provide a stable and predictable return on their investment. Those that argue for weaker protection fear that trademark owners will constrain us in the manner in which we express ourselves. Which view do you find most sympathetic? For an excellent review of these positions, see Pamela C. Chalk, *The True Value of Trademarks: Influencing Who We Are and Who We Want to Be*, 12 J. CONTEMP. LEGAL ISSUES 20 (2001).

4. One commentator points out that any property rights given to words or symbols must be carefully weighed against the communicative function those words might serve. "Words and images do not worm their way into our discourse by accident; they're generally thrust there by well-orchestrated campaigns intended to burn them into our collective consciousness." Alex Kozinski, *Trademarks Unplugged*, 68 N.Y.U. L. Rev. 960, 974 (1993). Should individual purchasers somehow share in the value of the trademark because they recognize the mark as such?

———

D. Justification in Light of the First Amendment

Nothing in this title shall affect any defense available to a defendant ... or a person's right of free speech or expression under the first amendment of the United States Constitution.

113 Stat. 1536, 1501A-551, (1999).

Dallas Cowboy Cheerleaders Inc. v. Pussycat Cinema, Inc.
604 F.2d 200 (2d Cir. 1976)

GRAAFEILAND, J.

This is an appeal from orders of the United States District Court for the Southern District of New York granting plaintiff's motions for a preliminary injunction prohibiting Pussycat Cinema, Ltd., and Michael Zaffarano from distributing or exhibiting the motion picture "Debbie Does Dallas." On March 14 this Court granted defendants' motion to stay the injunction and ordered an expedited appeal. The case was argued before us on April 6, following which we dissolved the stay and reinstated the preliminary injunction. We now affirm the orders of the district court.

Plaintiff in this trademark infringement action is Dallas Cowboys Cheerleaders, Inc., a wholly owned subsidiary of the Dallas Cowboys Football Club, Inc. Plaintiff employs thirty-six women who perform dance and cheerleading routines at Dallas Cowboys football games. The cheerleaders have appeared frequently on television programs and make commercial appearances at such public events as sporting goods shows and shopping center openings. In addition, plaintiff licenses others to manufacture and distribute posters, calendars, T-shirts, and the like depicting Dallas Cowboys Cheerleaders in their uniforms. These products have enjoyed nationwide commercial success, due largely to the national exposure the Dallas Cowboys Cheerleaders have received through the news and entertainment media. Moreover, plaintiff has expended large amounts of money to acquaint the public with its uniformed cheerleaders and earns substantial revenue from their commercial appearances.

At all the football games and public events where plaintiff's cheerleaders appear and on all commercial items depicting the cheerleaders, the women are clad in plaintiff's distinctive uniform. The familiar outfit consists of white vinyl boots, white shorts, a white belt decorated with blue stars, a blue bolero blouse, and a white vest decorated with three blue stars on each side of the front and a white fringe around the bottom. In this action plaintiff asserts that it has a trademark in its uniform and that defendants have infringed and diluted that trademark in advertising and exhibiting "Debbie Does Dallas."

Pussycat Cinema, Ltd., is a New York corporation which owns a movie theatre in New York City; Zaffarano is the corporation's sole stockholder. In November 1978 the Pussycat Cinema began to show "Debbie Does Dallas," a gross and revolting sex film whose plot, to the extent that there is one, involves a cheerleader at a fictional high school, Debbie, who has been selected to become a "Texas Cowgirl." In order to raise enough money to send Debbie, and eventually the entire squad, to Dallas, the cheerleaders perform sexual services for a fee. The movie consists largely of a series of scenes graphically depicting the sexual escapades of the "actors". In the movie's final scene Debbie dons a uniform strikingly similar to that worn by the Dallas Cowboys Cheerleaders and for approximately twelve minutes of film footage engages in various sex acts while clad or partially clad in the uniform. Defendants advertised the movie with marquee posters depicting Debbie in the allegedly infringing uniform and containing such captions as "Starring Ex Dallas Cowgirl Cheerleader Bambi Woods" and "You'll do more than cheer for this X Dallas Cheerleader." Similar advertisements appeared in the newspapers.

Plaintiff brought this action alleging trademark infringement under section 43(a) of the Lanham Act (15 U.S.C. §1125(a)), unfair competition, and dilution of trademark in violation of section 368-d of the New York General Business Law. The district court, in its oral opinion of February 13, 1979, found that "plaintiff ha(d) succeeded in proving by overwhelming evidence the merits of each one of its contentions." Defendants challenge the validity of all three claims.

* * *

[The court found the words Dallas Cowboy Cheerleaders and the cheerleaders' uniform to be valid trademarks.]

... [The] first amendment doctrine [does not] protect defendants' infringement of plaintiff's trademark. That defendants' movie may convey a barely discernible message[1] does not entitle them to appropriate plaintiff's trademark in the process of conveying that message.

For similar reasons, the preliminary injunction did not constitute an unconstitutional "prior restraint". This is not a case of government censorship, but a private plaintiff's attempt to protect its property rights. The propriety of a preliminary injunction where such relief is sought is so clear that courts have often issued an injunction without even mentioning the first amendment. The prohibition of the Lanham Act is content neutral, and therefore does not arouse the fears that trigger the application of constitutional "prior restraint" principles.

Accordingly, we affirm the orders of the district court.

Affirmed.

A side-by-side comparison of the Dallas Cheerleaders with the Debbie Does Dallas video cover might make the case against the film more convincing. See the current Cowgirls Calendar at http://www.dallascowboys.com/cheerleaders/home.cfm and the Debbie video cover at http://www.xratedcollection.com/gallery/xrated/20738.html.

L.L. Bean, Inc. v. Drake Publishers, Inc.
811 F.2d 26 (1st Cir. 1987)

BOWNES, C. J.

Imitation may be the highest form of flattery, but plaintiff-appellee L.L. Bean, Inc., was neither flattered nor amused when *High Society* magazine published a prurient parody of Bean's famous catalog. Defendant-appellant Drake Publishers, Inc., owns *High Society*, a monthly periodical featuring adult erotic entertainment. Its October 1984 issue contained a two-page article entitled "L.L. Beam's Back-To-School-Sex-Catalog." (Emphasis added.) The article was labelled on the magazine's contents page as "humor" and "parody." The article displayed a facsimile of Bean's trademark and featured pictures of nude models in sexually explicit positions using "products" that were described in a crudely humorous fashion.

L.L. Bean sought a temporary restraining order to remove the October 1984 issue from circulation. The complaint alleged trademark infringement, unfair competition, trademark dilution, deceptive trade practices, interference with prospective business advantage and trade libel. The United States District Court for the District of Maine denied Bean's

---

1. The question whether "Debbie Does Dallas" is obscene is not before us.

request for a temporary restraining order. Thereafter, both parties sought summary judgment. The district court granted summary judgment in favor of Drake on the claims for trade libel and interference with prospective business advantage. It denied summary judgment to both parties on Bean's claims for trademark infringement, unfair competition and deceptive trade practices, leaving the factual question of "likelihood of confusion" for resolution at trial. *L.L. Bean, Inc. v. Drake Publishers, Inc.*, 625 F. Supp. 1531 (D. Me. 1986).

* * *

Since the district court rejected defendant's position that a trademark parody constituted a defense to a claim based on the anti-dilution statute, we assume, as we must for purposes of this appeal, that the article is a trademark parody.

Parody is a humorous form of social commentary and literary criticism that dates back as far as Greek antiquity. "The rhapsodists who strolled from town to town to chant the poems of Homer," wrote Issac D'Israeli, "were immediately followed by another set of strollers—buffoons who made the audiences merry by the burlesque turn which they gave to the solemn strains." I. D'Israeli, *Curiosities of Literature, quoted in* D. MacDonald, *Parodies: An Anthology from Chaucer to Beerbohm—and After* 562 (1960). The Oxford English Dictionary defines parody as "[a] composition in which the characteristic turns of thought and phrase of an author are mimicked to appear ridiculous, especially by applying them to ludicrously inappropriate subjects." Chaucer, Shakespeare, Pope, Voltaire, Fielding, Hemingway and Faulkner are among the myriad of authors who have written parodies. Since parody seeks to ridicule sacred verities and prevailing mores, it inevitably offends others, as evinced by the shock which Chaucer's *Canterbury Tales* and Voltaire's *Candide* provoked among their contemporaries.

* * *

The ridicule conveyed by parody inevitably conflicts with one of the underlying purposes of the Maine anti-dilution statute, which is to protect against the tarnishment of the goodwill and reputation associated with a particular trademark. *Pignons, S.A. de Mecanique de Precision v. Polaroid Corp.*, 657 F.2d 482, 494–95 (1st Cir. 1981). The court below invoked this purpose as the basis for its decision to issue an injunction. The issue before us is whether enjoining the publication of appellant's parody violates the first amendment guarantees of freedom of expression.

II.

The district court disposed of the first amendment concerns raised in this matter by relying on the approach taken in *Dallas Cowboys Cheerleaders, Inc. v. Pussycat Cinema, Ltd.*, 604 F.2d 200 (2d Cir. 1979). In rejecting Drake's claim that the first amendment protects the unauthorized use of another's trademark in the process of conveying a message, the district court cited the following language from *Dallas Cowboys Cheerleaders*:

> "Plaintiff's trademark is in the nature of a property right, ... and as such it need not 'yield to the exercise of First Amendment rights under circumstances where adequate alternative avenues of communication exist.' Lloyd Corp. v. Tanner, 407 U.S. 551 (1972)."

L.L. Bean v. Drake, 625 F. Supp. at 1537 (quoting *Dallas Cowboys Cheerleaders*, 604 F.2d at 206).

We do not believe that the first amendment concerns raised here can be resolved as easily as was done in *Dallas Cowboys Cheerleaders*. *Cf.* Dorsen, *Satiric Appropriation*, 65 B.U. L. Rev. at 951; Denicola, *Trademarks As Speech: Constitutional Implications of the*

Emerging Rationales for the Protection of Trade Symbols, 1982 Wis. L. Rev. 158, 206 ("the sweeping rejection of the defendant's first amendment claim in *Dallas Cowboys Cheerleaders* is dangerously simplistic."). Aside from our doubts about whether there are alternative means of parodying plaintiff's catalog, we do not think the court fully assessed the nature of a trademark owner's property rights.

A trademark is a form of intellectual property; the Supreme Court case, *Lloyd Corp. v. Tanner*, 407 U.S. 551, 33 L. Ed. 2d 131, 92 S. Ct. 2219 (1972), relied upon by the *Dallas Cowboys Cheerleaders* court involved a shopping center. The first amendment issues involved in this case cannot be disposed of by equating the rights of a trademark owner with the rights of an owner of real property:

> *Trademark is not property in the ordinary sense* but only a word or symbol indicating the origin of a commercial product. The owner of the mark acquires the right to prevent the goods to which the mark is applied from being confused with those of others and to prevent his own trade from being diverted to competitors through their use of misleading marks.

Power Test Petroleum Distributors v. Calcu Gas, 754 F.2d 91, 97 (2d Cir. 1985) (emphasis added) (quoting *Industrial Rayon Corp. v. Dutchess Underwear Corp.*, 92 F.2d 33, 35 (2d Cir. 1937), *cert. denied*, 303 U.S. 640, 82 L. Ed. 1100, 58 S. Ct. 610 (1938)). *Accord Dresser Industries, Inc. v. Heraeus Engelhard Vacuum, Inc.*, 395 F.2d 457 (3d Cir.), *cert. denied*, 393 U.S. 934, 89 S. Ct. 293, 21 L. Ed. 2d 270, 159 U.S.P.Q. (BNA) 799 (1968); *Lucasfilm Ltd. v. High Frontier*, 622 F. Supp. 931 (D.D.C. 1985).

The limits on the scope of a trademark owner's property rights was considered recently in *Lucasfilm Ltd. v. High Frontier, supra*. In that case, the owners of the trademark "Star Wars" alleged injury from public interest groups that used the term in commercial advertisements presenting their views on President Reagan's Strategic Defense Initiative. Judge Gesell stressed that the sweep of a trademark owner's rights extends only to injurious, unauthorized *commercial uses* of the mark by another. 622 F. Supp. at 933–35. Trademark rights do not entitle the owner to quash an unauthorized use of the mark by another who is communicating ideas or expressing points of view. *Id.* As Justice Holmes observed while sitting on the Supreme Judicial Court of Massachusetts, "When the common law developed the doctrine of trademarks and trade-names, it was not creating a property in advertisements more absolute than it would have allowed the author of *Paradise Lost*." *Chadwick v. Covell*, 151 Mass. 190, 193, 23 N.E. 1068, 1069 (1890).

The limits imposed on a trademark owner's property rights demonstrate that the constitutional issue raised here cannot be dispensed with by simply asserting that Bean's property right need not yield to the exercise of first amendment rights. *L.L. Bean v. Drake*, 625 F. Supp. at 1537. We turn now to an examination of whether the Constitution prohibits the application of Maine's anti-dilution statute as construed by the district court to the instant case.

* * *

The district court believed that if a noncommercial parody "would result in images of impurity in the minds of [consumers] ... such connotations would obviously tarnish the affirmative associations the mark had come to convey." *L.L. Bean v. Drake Publishers*, 625 F. Supp. at 1536. It thus read the anti-dilution statute as granting a trademark owner the unfettered right to suppress the use of its name in any context, commercial or noncommercial, found to be offensive, negative or unwholesome. As one commentator has pointed out, there are serious first amendment implications involved in applying anti-dilution statutes to cover noncommercial uses of a trademark:

Famous trademarks offer a particularly powerful means of conjuring up the image of their owners, and thus become an important, perhaps at times indispensable, part of the public vocabulary. Rules restricting the use of well-known trademarks may therefore restrict the communication of ideas.... If the defendant's speech is particularly unflattering, it is also possible to argue that the trademark has been tarnished by the defendant's use. The constitutional implications of extending the misappropriation or tarnishment rationales to such cases, however, may often be intolerable. Since a trademark may frequently be the most effective means of focusing attention on the trademark owner or its product, the recognition of exclusive rights encompassing such use would permit the stifling of unwelcome discussion.

Denicola, *Trademarks As Speech*, 1982 Wis. L. Rev. at 195–96.

The district court's opinion suggests that tarnishment may be found when a trademark is used without authorization in a context which diminishes the positive associations with the mark. Neither the strictures of the first amendment nor the history and theory of anti-dilution law permit a finding of tarnishment based solely on the presence of an unwholesome or negative context in which a trademark is used without authorization. Such a reading of the anti-dilution statute unhinges it from its origins in the marketplace. A trademark is tarnished when consumer capacity to associate it with the appropriate products or services has been diminished. The threat of tarnishment arises when the goodwill and reputation of a plaintiff's trademark is linked to products which are of shoddy quality or which conjure associations that clash with the associations generated by the owner's lawful use of the mark:

> The risk may be that of detracting from the plaintiff's good will by the possibility that a defendant's use of plaintiff's unique mark will tarnish plaintiff's trade name by reason of public dissatisfaction with defendant's *product* and a resultant holding of this dissatisfaction against plaintiff.

> An alternative to this ... risk is the danger of public identification of plaintiff's trade name or mark with a *product or service* of a type incompatible with the quality and prestige previously attached by the public to the plaintiff's product.

Tiffany & Co. v. Boston Club, Inc., 231 F. Supp. 836, 844 (D. Mass. 1964) (emphasis added).

As indicated by Judge Caffrey in *Tiffany*, the dilution injury stems from an unauthorized effort to market incompatible products or services by trading on another's trademark. The Constitution is not offended when the anti-dilution statute is applied to prevent a defendant from using a trademark without permission in order to merchandise dissimilar products or services. Any residual effect on first amendment freedoms should be balanced against the need to fulfill the legitimate purpose of the anti-dilution statute. *See Friedman v. Rogers*, 440 U.S. 1, 15–16, 59 L. Ed. 2d 100, 99 S.Ct. 887 (1979). The law of trademark dilution has developed to combat an unauthorized and harmful appropriation of a trademark by another for the purpose of identifying, manufacturing, merchandising or promoting dissimilar products or services. The harm occurs when a trademark's identity and integrity—its capacity to command respect in the market—is undermined due to its inappropriate and unauthorized use by other market actors. When presented with such circumstances, courts have found that trademark owners have suffered harm despite the fact that redressing such harm entailed some residual impact on the rights of expression of commercial actors. *See, e.g.,*

Dallas Cowboys Cheerleaders v. Pussycat Cinema, Ltd., 604 F.2d 200 (plaintiff's mark damaged by unauthorized use in content and promotion of a pornographic film); *Chemical Corp. of America v. Anheuser-Busch, Inc.*, 306 F.2d 433 (5th Cir. 1962), *cert. denied*, 372 U.S. 965, 83 S. Ct. 1089, 10 L. Ed. 2d 129, 137 U.S.P.Q. (BNA) 913 (1963) (floor wax and insecticide maker's slogan, "Where there's life, there's bugs," harmed strength of defendant's slogan, "Where there's life, there's Bud."); *Original Appalachian Artworks, Inc. v. Topps Chewing Gum*, 642 F. Supp. 1031 (N.D. Ga. 1986) (merchandiser of "Garbage Pail Kids" stickers and products injured owner of Cabbage Patch Kids mark); *D.C. Comics, Inc. v. Unlimited Monkey Business*, 598 F. Supp. 110 (N.D. Ga. 1984) (holder of Superman and Wonder Woman trademarks damaged by unauthorized use of marks by singing telegram franchisor); *General Electric Co. v. Alumpa Coal Co.*, 205 U.S.P.Q. (BNA) 1036 (D. Mass. 1979) ("Genital Electric" monogram on underpants and T-shirts harmful to plaintiff's trademark); *Gucci Shops, Inc. v. R.H. Macy & Co.*, 446 F. Supp. 838 (S.D.N.Y. 1977) (defendant's diaper bag labelled "Gucchi Goo" held to injure Gucci's mark); *Coca-Cola Co. v. Gemini Rising, Inc.*, 346 F. Supp. 1183 (E.D.N.Y. 1972) (enjoining the merchandise of "Enjoy Cocaine" posters bearing logo similar to plaintiff's mark).

While the cases cited above might appear at first glance to be factually analogous to the instant one, they are distinguishable for two reasons. First, they all involved unauthorized commercial uses of another's trademark. Second, none of those cases involved a defendant using a plaintiff's trademark as a vehicle for an editorial or artistic parody. In contrast to the cases cited, the instant defendant used plaintiff's mark solely for noncommercial purposes. Appellant's parody constitutes an editorial or artistic, rather than a commercial, use of plaintiff's mark. The article was labelled as "humor" and "parody" in the magazine's table of contents section; it took up two pages in a one-hundred-page issue; neither the article nor appellant's trademark was featured on the front or back cover of the magazine. Drake did not use Bean's mark to identify or promote goods or services to consumers; it never intended to market the "products" displayed in the parody.

We think the Constitution tolerates an incidental impact on rights of expression of commercial actors in order to prevent a defendant from unauthorizedly merchandising his products with another's trademark. In such circumstances, application of the anti-dilution statute constitutes a legitimate regulation of commercial speech, which the Supreme Court has defined as "expression related solely to the economic interests of the speaker and its audience." *Central Hudson Gas & Elec. v. Public Serv. Comm'n*, 447 U.S. 557, 561, 65 L. Ed. 2d 341, 100 S. Ct. 2343 (1980). It offends the Constitution, however, to invoke the anti-dilution statute as a basis for enjoining the noncommercial use of a trademark by a defendant engaged in a protected form of expression:

> The failure to distinguish between commercial and non-commercial speech "could invite dilution, simply by a leveling process, of the force of the" First "Amendment's guarantee with respect to the latter kind of speech."

Id. at 563 n.5 (quoting *Ohralik v. Ohio State Bar Ass'n*, 436 U.S. 447, 456, 56 L. Ed. 2d 444, 98 S. Ct. 1912 (1978)).

If the anti-dilution statute were construed as permitting a trademark owner to enjoin the use of his mark in a noncommercial context found to be negative or offensive, then a corporation could shield itself from criticism by forbidding the use of its name in commentaries critical of its conduct. The legitimate aim of the anti-dilution statute is to prohibit the unauthorized use of another's trademark in order to market incompatible products or services. The Constitution does not, however, permit the range of the anti-dilution statute to encompass the unauthorized use of a trademark in a noncommercial setting such as an editorial or artistic context.

The district court's application of the Maine anti-dilution statute to appellant's noncommercial parody cannot withstand constitutional scrutiny. Drake has not used Bean's mark to identify or market goods or services; it has used the mark solely to identify Bean as the object of its parody. The reading of the anti-dilution provision advanced by the district court would improperly expand the scope of the anti-dilution statute far beyond the frontiers of commerce and deep into the realm of expression. "Courts obviously cannot regulate the type of descriptive, non-trade use involved here without becoming the monitors of the spoken or written English language." *Lucasfilm Ltd. v. High Frontier*, 622 F. Supp. at 935.

Our reluctance to apply the anti-dilution statute to the instant case also stems from a recognition of the vital importance of parody. Although, as we have noted, parody is often offensive, it is nevertheless "deserving of substantial freedom — both as entertainment and as a form of social and literary criticism." *Berlin v. E.C. Publications, Inc.*, 329 F.2d 541 (2d Cir.), *cert. denied*, 379 U.S. 822, 143 U.S.P.Q. (BNA) 464, 13 L. Ed. 2d 33, 85 S. Ct. 46 (1964). *Accord Fisher v. Dees*, 794 F.2d 432, 437–38 (9th Cir. 1986) ("'Destructive' parodies play an important role in social and literary criticism and thus merit protection even though they may discourage or discredit an original author."); *Pring v. Penthouse International, Ltd.*, 695 F.2d 438 (10th Cir. 1982), cert. denied, 462 U.S. 1132, 77 L. Ed. 2d 1367, 103 S. Ct. 3112 (1983) (defendants' bawdy "spoof" and "ridicule" of Miss America pageant entitled to full range of first amendment protection); *Groucho Marx Productions v. Day and Night Co.*, 689 F.2d 317, 319 n.2 (2d Cir. 1982) (noting "the broad scope permitted parody in first First Amendment law."); *Elsmere Music v. National Broadcasting Co.*, 623 F.2d 252, 253 (2d Cir. 1980) ("in today's world of unrelieved solemnity, copyright law should be hospitable to the humor of parody...."). It would be anomalous to diminish the protection afforded parody solely because a parodist chooses a famous trade name, rather than a famous personality, author or creative work, as its object.

The district court's injunction falls not only because it trammels upon a protected form of expression, but also because it depends upon an untoward judicial evaluation of the offensiveness or unwholesomeness of the appellant's materials. The Supreme Court has recognized the threat to free speech inherent in sanctioning such evaluations. *Cohen v. California*, 403 U.S. 15, 25, 29 L. Ed. 2d 284, 91 S. Ct. 1780 (1971). Nevertheless, the district court was swayed by evidence suggesting that the "coarseness and baseness" of *High Society* would ineluctably damage Bean's mark. *L.L. Bean v. Drake*, 625 F. Supp. at 1536–37. The first amendment, however, does not warrant inquiry into "measures of distress or offensiveness, depending on the reader, listener or viewer." *United States v. Guarino*, 729 F.2d 864, 867 (1st Cir. 1984) (en banc). While appellant's article is coarse and vulgar, "sexually explicit but nonobscene materials,[2] however distasteful, are entitled to no less protection than other forms of expression." *Fantasy Book Shop, Inc. v. City of Boston*, 652 F.2d 1115, 1126 (1st Cir. 1981).

Reversed and remanded.

---

2. The question of the obscenity of the article or the entire magazine has not been raised.

Mattel, Inc. v. MCA Records

296 F.3d 894 (9th Cir. 2002)

KOZINSKI, CIRCUIT JUDGE:

If this were a sci-fi melodrama, it might be called Speech-Zilla meets Trademark Kong.

I

Barbie was born in Germany in the 1950s as an adult collector's item. Over the years, Mattel transformed her from a doll that resembled a "German street walker," as she originally appeared, into a glamorous, long-legged blonde. Barbie has been labeled both the ideal American woman and a bimbo. She has survived attacks both psychic (from feminists critical of her fictitious figure) and physical (more than 500 professional makeovers). She remains a symbol of American girlhood, a public figure who graces the aisles of toy stores throughout the country and beyond. With Barbie, Mattel created not just a toy but a cultural icon.

With fame often comes unwanted attention. Aqua is a Danish band that has, as yet, only dreamed of attaining Barbie-like status. In 1997, Aqua produced the song Barbie Girl on the album *Aquarium*. In the song, one bandmember impersonates Barbie, singing in a high-pitched, doll-like voice; another bandmember, calling himself Ken, entices Barbie to "go party." (The lyrics are in the Appendix.) Barbie Girl singles sold well and, to Mattel's dismay, the song made it onto Top 40 music charts.

Mattel brought this lawsuit against the music companies who produced, marketed and sold Barbie Girl: MCA Records, Inc., Universal Music International Ltd., Universal Music A/S, Universal Music & Video Distribution, Inc. and MCA Music Scandinavia AB (collectively, "MCA"). MCA in turn challenged the district court's jurisdiction under the Lanham Act and its personal jurisdiction over the foreign defendants, Universal Music International Ltd., Universal Music A/S and MCA Music Scandinavia AB (hereinafter "foreign defendants"); MCA also brought a defamation claim against Mattel for statements Mattel made about MCA while this lawsuit was pending. The district court concluded it had jurisdiction over the foreign defendants and under the Lanham Act, and granted MCA's motion for summary judgment on Mattel's federal and state-law claims for trademark infringement and dilution. The district court also granted Mattel's motion for summary judgment on MCA's defamation claim.

Mattel appeals the district court's ruling that Barbie Girl is a parody of Barbie and a nominative fair use; that MCA's use of the term Barbie is not likely to confuse consumers as to Mattel's affiliation with Barbie Girl or dilute the Barbie mark; and that Mattel cannot assert an unfair competition claim under the Paris Convention for the Protection of Industrial Property. MCA cross-appeals the grant of summary judgment on its defamation claim as well as the district court's jurisdictional holdings.

II

A. All three foreign defendants are affiliated members of Universal Music Group and have an active relationship with each other and with domestic members of the Group. Defendants entered into cross-licensing agreements and developed a coordinated plan to distribute the Barbie Girl song in the United States (including California), and sent promotional copies of the Barbie Girl single and the *Aquarium* album to the United States (including California). This conduct was expressly aimed at, and allegedly caused harm in, California, Mattel's principal place of business. *See Panavision Int'l, L.P. v.*

Toeppen, 141 F.3d 1316, 1321 (9th Cir. 1998). Mattel's trademark claims would not have arisen "but for" the conduct foreign defendants purposefully directed toward California, and jurisdiction over the foreign defendants, who are represented by the same counsel and closely associated with the domestic defendants, is reasonable. *See id.* at 1321–22. The district court did not err in asserting specific personal jurisdiction over the foreign defendants.

B. Sales of the *Aquarium* album worldwide had a sufficient effect on American foreign commerce, and Mattel suffered monetary injury in the United States from those sales. *See Ocean Garden, Inc. v. Marktrade Co.*, 953 F.2d 500, 503 (9th Cir. 1991). Moreover, Mattel's claim is more closely tied to interests of American foreign commerce than it is to the commercial interests of other nations: Mattel's principal place of business is in California, the foreign defendants are closely related to the domestic defendants, and Mattel sought relief only for defendants' sales in the United States. *See Star-Kist Foods, Inc. v. P.J. Rhodes & Co.*, 769 F.2d 1393, 1395–96 (9th Cir. 1985). The district court properly exercised extraterritorial jurisdiction under the Lanham Act.

III

A. A trademark is a word, phrase or symbol that is used to identify a manufacturer or sponsor of a good or the provider of a service. *See New Kids on the Block v. News Am. Publ'g, Inc.*, 971 F.2d 302, 305 (9th Cir. 1992). It's the owner's way of preventing others from duping consumers into buying a product they mistakenly believe is sponsored by the trademark owner. A trademark "informs people that trademarked products come from the same source." *Id.* at 305 n.2. Limited to this core purpose—avoiding confusion in the marketplace—a trademark owner's property rights play well with the First Amendment. "Whatever first amendment rights you may have in calling the brew you make in your bathtub 'Pepsi' are easily outweighed by the buyer's interest in not being fooled into buying it." *Trademarks Unplugged*, 68 N.Y.U.L. Rev. 960, 973 (1993).

The problem arises when trademarks transcend their identifying purpose. Some trademarks enter our public discourse and become an integral part of our vocabulary. How else do you say that something's "the Rolls Royce of its class?" What else is a quick fix, but a Band-Aid? Does the average consumer know to ask for aspirin as "acetyl salicylic acid?" *See Bayer Co. v. United Drug Co.*, 272 F. 505, 510 (S.D.N.Y. 1921). Trademarks often fill in gaps in our vocabulary and add a contemporary flavor to our expressions. Once imbued with such expressive value, the trademark becomes a word in our language and assumes a role outside the bounds of trademark law.

Our likelihood-of-confusion test, see *AMF Inc. v. Sleekcraft Boats*, 599 F.2d 341, 348–49 (9th Cir. 1979), generally strikes a comfortable balance between the trademark owner's property rights and the public's expressive interests. But when a trademark owner asserts a right to control how we express ourselves—when we'd find it difficult to describe the product any other way (as in the case of aspirin), or when the mark (like Rolls Royce) has taken on an expressive meaning apart from its source-identifying function—applying the traditional test fails to account for the full weight of the public's interest in free expression.

The First Amendment may offer little protection for a competitor who labels its commercial good with a confusingly similar mark, but "trademark rights do not entitle the owner to quash an unauthorized use of the mark by another who is communicating ideas or expressing points of view." *L.L. Bean, Inc. v. Drake Publishers, Inc.*, 811 F.2d 26, 29 (1st Cir. 1987). Were we to ignore the expressive value that some marks assume, trademark rights would grow to encroach upon the zone protected by the First Amendment.

When unauthorized use of another's mark is part of a communicative message and not a source identifier, the First Amendment is implicated in opposition to the trademark right."). Simply put, the trademark owner does not have the right to control public discourse whenever the public imbues his mark with a meaning beyond its source-identifying function. *See Anti-Monopoly, Inc. v. Gen. Mills Fun Group*, 611 F.2d 296, 301 (9th Cir. 1979) ("It is the source-denoting function which trademark laws protect, and nothing more.").

B. There is no doubt that MCA uses Mattel's mark: Barbie is one half of Barbie Girl. But Barbie Girl is the title of a song about Barbie and Ken, a reference that—at least today—can only be to Mattel's famous couple. We expect a title to describe the underlying work, not to identify the producer, and Barbie Girl does just that.

The Barbie Girl title presages a song about Barbie, or at least a girl like Barbie. The title conveys a message to consumers about what they can expect to discover in the song itself; it's a quick glimpse of Aqua's take on their own song. The lyrics confirm this: The female singer, who calls herself Barbie, is "a Barbie girl, in [her] Barbie world." She tells her male counterpart (named Ken), "Life in plastic, it's fantastic. You can brush my hair, undress me everywhere/Imagination, life is your creation." And off they go to "party." The song pokes fun at Barbie and the values that Aqua contends she represents. *See Cliffs Notes, Inc. v. Bantam Doubleday Dell Publ'g Group*, 886 F.2d 490, 495–96 (2d Cir. 1989). The female singer explains, "I'm a blond bimbo girl, in a fantasy world/Dress me up, make it tight, I'm your dolly."

The song does not rely on the Barbie mark to poke fun at another subject but targets Barbie herself. *See Campbell v. Acuff-Rose Music, Inc.*, 510 U.S. 569, 580, 127 L. Ed. 2d 500, 114 S. Ct. 1164 (1994); *see also Dr. Seuss Ents., L.P. v. Penguin Books USA, Inc.*, 109 F.3d 1394, 1400 (9th Cir. 1997). This case is therefore distinguishable from *Dr. Seuss*, where we held that the book *The Cat NOT in the Hat!* borrowed Dr. Seuss's trademarks and lyrics to get attention rather than to mock *The Cat in the Hat!* The defendant's use of the Dr. Seuss trademarks and copyrighted works had "no critical bearing on the substance or style of" *The Cat in the Hat!*, and therefore could not claim First Amendment protection. *Id.* at 1401. *Dr. Seuss* recognized that, where an artistic work targets the original and does not merely borrow another's property to get attention, First Amendment interests weigh more heavily in the balance. *See id.* at 1400–02; *see also Harley-Davidson, Inc. v. Grottanelli*, 164 F.3d 806, 812–13 (2d Cir. 1999) (a parodist whose expressive work aims its parodic commentary at a trademark is given considerable leeway, but a claimed parodic use that makes no comment on the mark is not a permitted trademark parody use).

The Second Circuit has held that "in general the [Lanham] Act should be construed to apply to artistic works only where the public interest in avoiding consumer confusion outweighs the public interest in free expression." *Rogers v. Grimaldi*, 875 F.2d 994, 999 (2d Cir. 1989); *see also Cliffs Notes*, 886 F.2d at 494 (quoting *Rogers*, 875 F.2d at 999). *Rogers* considered a challenge by the actress Ginger Rogers to the film *Ginger and Fred*. The movie told the story of two Italian cabaret performers who made a living by imitating Ginger Rogers and Fred Astaire. Rogers argued that the film's title created the false impression that she was associated with it.

At first glance, Rogers certainly had a point. Ginger was her name, and Fred was her dancing partner. If a pair of dancing shoes had been labeled Ginger and Fred, a dancer might have suspected that Rogers was associated with the shoes (or at least one of them), just as Michael Jordan has endorsed Nike sneakers that claim to make you fly through the air. But Ginger and Fred was not a brand of shoe; it was the title of a movie and, for the reasons explained by the Second Circuit, deserved to be treated differently.

A title is designed to catch the eye and to promote the value of the underlying work. Consumers expect a title to communicate a message about the book or movie, but they do not expect it to identify the publisher or producer. *See Application of Cooper*, 45 C.C.P.A. 923, 254 F.2d 611, 615–16 (C.C.P.A. 1958) (A "title ... identifies a specific literary work, ... and is not associated in the public mind with the ... manufacturer." (internal quotation marks omitted)). If we see a painting titled "Campbell's Chicken Noodle Soup," we're unlikely to believe that Campbell's has branched into the art business. Nor, upon hearing Janis Joplin croon "Oh Lord, won't you buy me a Mercedes-Benz?," would we suspect that she and the carmaker had entered into a joint venture. A title tells us something about the underlying work but seldom speaks to its origin:

> Though consumers frequently look to the title of a work to determine what it is about, they do not regard titles of artistic works in the same way as the names of ordinary commercial products. Since consumers expect an ordinary product to be what the name says it is, we apply the Lanham Act with some rigor to prohibit names that misdescribe such goods. But most consumers are well aware that they cannot judge a book solely by its title any more than by its cover.

Rogers, 875 F.2d at 1000 (citations omitted).

Rogers concluded that literary titles do not violate the Lanham Act "unless the title has no artistic relevance to the underlying work whatsoever, or, if it has some artistic relevance, unless the title explicitly misleads as to the source or the content of the work." *Id.* at 999 (footnote omitted). We agree with the Second Circuit's analysis and adopt the *Rogers* standard as our own.

Applying *Rogers* to our case, we conclude that MCA's use of Barbie is not an infringement of Mattel's trademark. Under the first prong of *Rogers*, the use of Barbie in the song title clearly is relevant to the underlying work, namely, the song itself. As noted, the song is about Barbie and the values Aqua claims she represents. The song title does not explicitly mislead as to the source of the work; it does not, explicitly or otherwise, suggest that it was produced by Mattel. The *only* indication that Mattel might be associated with the song is the use of Barbie in the title; if this were enough to satisfy this prong of the *Rogers* test, it would render *Rogers* a nullity. We therefore agree with the district court that MCA was entitled to summary judgment on this ground. We need not consider whether the district court was correct in holding that MCA was also entitled to summary judgment because its use of Barbie was a nominative fair use.

Appendix:
Barbie Girl by Aqua

-Hiya Barbie!
-Hi Ken!
You wanna go for a ride?
-Sure, Ken!
-Jump in!
-Ha ha ha ha!
(CHORUS:)
I'm a Barbie girl, in my Barbie world
Life in plastic, it's fantastic
You can brush my hair, undress me everywhere

Imagination, life is your creation
Come on Barbie, let's go party!
(CHORUS)
I'm a blonde bimbo girl, in a fantasy world
Dress me up, make it tight, I'm your dolly
You're my doll, rock and roll, feel the glamour in pink
Kiss me here, touch me there, hanky-panky
You can touch, you can play
If you say "I'm always yours," ooh ooh
(CHORUS)
(BRIDGE:)
Come on, Barbie, let's go party, ah ah ah yeah
Come on, Barbie, let's go party, ooh ooh, ooh ooh
Come on, Barbie, let's go party, ah ah ah yeah
Come on, Barbie, let's go party, ooh ooh, ooh ooh
Make me walk, make me talk, do whatever you please
I can act like a star, I can beg on my knees
Come jump in, be my friend, let us do it again
Hit the town, fool around, let's go party
You can touch, you can play
You can say "I'm always yours"
You can touch, you can play
You can say "I'm always yours"
(BRIDGE)
(CHORUS x2)
(BRIDGE)
-Oh, I'm having so much fun!
-Well, Barbie, we're just getting started!

Notes

1. Other interesting and noteworthy cases regarding the first amendment defense to a claim of trademark infringement include *Bally Total Fitness Holding Corp. v. Faber*, 29 F. Supp. 2d 1161 (C.D. Cal. 1998).

2. So-called "cybergriping" or "complaint" sites on the Internet have been held to be protected speech. Some people adopt a "sucks.com" domain name to complain about a company. They place the company's name before the "sucks.com" portion of the URL and register that as their domain name. The company name that precedes the "sucks.com" is, of course, a trademark. One such trademark owner sued to enjoin such use but did not prevail on the ground that such cybergriping was protected speech. *Taubman Co. v. Webfeats*, 319 F.3d 770 (6th Cir. 2003); *see also infra* Chapter XII.

3. For the argument that courts usually deny the first amendment defense to trademark infringement and that *LL Bean, supra*, is a rare case, see Robert N Kravitz, *Trademarks, Speech, and the Gay Olympics Case*, 69 B.U.L. Rev. 131 (1989). In *San Francisco Arts & Athletics, Inc. v. United States Olympic Committee*, 107 S. Ct. 2971 (1987), the Supreme Court held that the interests of protecting the Olympic trademark outweighed the restrictions placed on homsexual activists who had adopted the mark "Gay Olympics" for their use. The Court stated:

This Court has recognized that words are not always fungible, and that the suppression of particular words "runs a substantial risk of suppressing ideas in the process." ... Yet this recognition always has been balanced against the principle that when a word acquires value "as the result of organization and the expenditure of labor, skill, and money" by an entity, that entity constitutionally may obtain a limited property right in the word.

Id. at 532.

Why wouldn't or shouldn't a court be more demanding of a trademark holder to show how its claimed rights do not infringe on the First Amendment?

4. Perhaps the seminal work in this regard is Robert C. Denicola, *Trademarks as Speech: Constitutional Implications of the Emerging Rationales for the Protection of Trade Symbols*, 1982 Wis. L. Rev. 158 ("Judicial antipathy toward the enrichment that flows to the copyist has carried trademark owners to a series of triumphs over competing contentions. At some point, however, extensions of the trademark monopoly must be tempered by the realization that unlimited control over the use of trade symbols will at times interfere with the exercise of basic first amendment rights."). More than 20 years later, Professor Denicola's argument seems even more appropriate. Can you see why? *See also* Rochelle Cooper Dreyfuss, *Expressive Genericity: Trademarks as Language in the Pepsi Generation*, 65 Notre Dame L. Rev. 397 (1990) (some trademarks should be considered expressively generic when used in certain contexts to allow free use and expression which happens to include words that are also considered trademarks). Why are Professors Denicola and Dreyfuss so concerned?

5. One prominent trademark practitioner in Chicago describes the state of the law of parody of trademarks as follows: "In practice, it seems a plaintiff is most likely to succeed against a trademark parody when the parody is disparaging or offensive, the parody is identical or closely similar to the original trademark, and the interest of the public in avoiding confusion is strong." Mark V.B. Partridge, *Trademark Parody and the First Amendment: Humor in the Eye of the Beholder*, 29 J. Marshall L. Rev. 877, 890 (1996). If one is making a joke about some trademark, why should the trademark holder be concerned at all?

6. Other entertaining examples of unsuccessful claims of parody of well-known trademarks include the following:

MUTANT OF OMAHA for T-shirts, caps and mugs protesting nuclear arms. *Mut. of Omaha Ins. Co. v. Novak*, 775 F.2d 247 (8th Cir. 1985);

WHERE THERE'S LIFE THERE'S BUGS for floor wax insecticide. *Chem Corp. of Am. v. Anheuser-Busch, Inc.*, 306 F.2d 433 (5th Cir. 1962), *cert. denied*, 372 U.S. 965 (1963).

7. Other entertaining examples of successful claims of parody of well-known trademarks include the following:

Poster of a pregnant Girl Scout with the caption BE PREPARED. *Girl Scouts of United States v. Personality Posters Mfg. Co.*, 304 F. Supp 1228 (S.D.N.Y. 1969);

ENERGIZER BUNNY as played by Leslie Nielsen with rabbit ears on an advertisement for COORS beer. *Eveready Battery Co. v. Adolph Coors Co.*, 765 F. Supp. 440 (N.D. Ill. 1991).

8. Why did the Dallas Cowboys sue a movie theater rather than the producer of the film? Did the court's ruling prevent showing or distributing the film? The original movie ap-

parently has had several sequels, spin-offs and even a Broadway musical. One wonders what the subject of the songs might be.

9. Examples of allowed cybergriping:

www.oreilly-sucks.com (Complaining of talk-show host Bill O'Reilly).

www.peta-sucks.com (Site complaining about People for the Ethical Treatment of Animals.)

Chapter III

Subject Matter

The Lanham Act defines trademarks as "any word, name, symbol, or device or any combination thereof … used … To indicate the source of the goods …" 15 U.S.C. §1127 (2004). U.S. courts have been giving this statement an increasingly literal interpretation. Therefore, if "any" aspect of a product indicates the source or origin of that product, courts today in the United States are very likely to recognize it as a trademark. Hence, the scope of trademark protection is theoretically unlimited, confined only by the requirement that the mark act to identify source (and otherwise not be in violation of the Lanham Act). Thus, the inside of a restaurant might be distinctive enough to warrant trademark protection,[1] the color alone of a product or a feature of a product,[2] or even the sound a motorcycle makes when idling might warrant protection if it has come to identify a consistent source of that product.[3]

A trademark serves to identify the source of goods or services. The source itself need not be known; rather, to act as a trademark, it is important that the relevant consuming public recognizes and associates the source with a particular good or service.

A. Word Marks

1. Trademarks

Coca-Cola Co. v. Koke Co. of America
254 U.S. 143 (1920)

HOLMES, J.

This is a bill in equity brought by the Coca-Cola Company to prevent the infringement of its trade-mark Coca-Cola and unfair competition with it in its business of making and selling the beverage for which the trade-mark is used. The District Court gave the plaintiff a decree. 235 Fed. Rep. 408. This was reversed by the Circuit Court of Appeals. 255 Fed. Rep. 894. Subsequently a writ of certiorari was granted by this Court. 250 U.S. 637.

It appears that after the plaintiff's predecessors in title had used the mark for some years it was registered under the Act of Congress of March 3, 1881, c. 138, 21 Stat. 502, and again under the Act of February 20, 1905, c. 592, 33 Stat. 724. Both the Courts below agree that subject to the one question to be considered the plaintiff has a right to equi-

---

1. Two Pesos, Inc. v. Taco Cabana Int'l, Inc., 505 U.S. 763 (1992).
2. Qualitex Co. v. Jacobson Prod. Co., 514 U.S. 159 (1995).
3. See Application Serial No. 74/485,223, on file with the United States Patent and Trademark Office (since abandoned).

table relief. Whatever may have been its original weakness, the mark for years has acquired a secondary significance and has indicated the plaintiff's product alone. It is found that defendant's mixture is made and sold in imitation of the plaintiff's and that the word Koke was chosen for the purpose of reaping the benefit of the advertising done by the plaintiff and of selling the imitation as and for the plaintiff's goods. The only obstacle found by the Circuit Court of Appeals in the way of continuing the injunction granted below was its opinion that the trade-mark in itself and the advertisements accompanying it made such fraudulent representations to the public that the plaintiff had lost its claim to any help from the Court. That is the question upon which the writ of certiorari was granted and the main one that we shall discuss.

Of course a man is not to be protected in the use of a device the very purpose and effect of which is to swindle the public. But the defects of a plaintiff do not offer a very broad ground for allowing another to swindle him. The defence relied on here should be scrutinized with a critical eye. The main point is this: Before 1900 the beginning of the good will was more or less helped by the presence of cocaine, a drug that, like alcohol or caffeine or opium, may be described as a deadly poison or as a valuable item of the pharmacopoea according to the rhetorical purposes in view. The amount seems to have been very small, but it may have been enough to begin a bad habit and after the Food and Drug Act of June 30, 1906, c. 3915, 34 Stat. 768, if not earlier, long before this suit was brought, it was eliminated from the plaintiff's compound. Coca leaves still are used, to be sure, but after they have been subjected to a drastic process that removes from them every characteristic substance except a little tannin and still less chlorophyll. The cola nut, at best, on its side furnishes but a very small portion of the caffeine, which now is the only element that has appreciable effect. That comes mainly from other sources. It is argued that the continued use of the name imports a representation that has ceased to be true and that the representation is reinforced by a picture of coca leaves and cola nuts upon the label and by advertisements, which however were many years before this suit was brought, that the drink is an "ideal nerve tonic and stimulant," etc., and that thus the very thing sought to be protected is used as a fraud.

The argument does not satisfy us. We are dealing here with a popular drink not with a medicine, and although what has been said might suggest that its attraction lay in producing the expectation of a toxic effect the facts point to a different conclusion. Since 1900 the sales have increased at a very great rate corresponding to a like increase in advertising. The name now characterizes a beverage to be had at almost any soda fountain. It means a single thing coming from a single source, and well known to the community. It hardly would be too much to say that the drink characterizes the name as much as the name the drink. In other words Coca-Cola probably means to most persons the plaintiff's familiar product to be had everywhere rather than a compound of particular substances. Although the fact did not appear in *United States v. Coca Cola Co.*, 241 U.S. 265, 289, we see no reason to doubt that, as we have said, it has acquired a secondary meaning in which perhaps the product is more emphasized than the producer but to which the producer is entitled. The coca leaves and whatever of cola nut is employed may be used to justify the continuance of the name or they may affect the flavor as the plaintiff contends, but before this suit was brought the plaintiff had advertised to the public that it must not expect and would not find cocaine, and had eliminated everything tending to suggest cocaine effects except the name and the picture of the leaves and nuts, which probably conveyed little or nothing to most who saw it. It appears to us that it would be going too far to deny the plaintiff relief against a palpable fraud because possibly here and there an ignorant person might call for the drink with the hope for incipient cocaine intoxication. The plaintiff's position must be judged by the facts as they were when the suit was begun, not by the facts of a different condition and an earlier time.

The decree of the District Court restrains the defendant from using the word Dope. [The District Court had enjoined the defendant from even using the word "Dope" on or in connection with its goods. Ed.] The plaintiff illustrated in a very striking way the fact that the word is one of the most featureless known even to the language of those who are incapable of discriminating speech. In some places it would be used to call for Coca-Cola. It equally would have been used to call for anything else having about it a faint aureole of poison. It does not suggest Coca-Cola by similarity and whatever objections there may be to its use, objections which the plaintiff equally makes to its application to Coca-Cola, we see no ground on which the plaintiff can claim a personal right to exclude the defendant from using it.

The product including the coloring matter is free to all who can make it if no extrinsic deceiving element is present. The injunction should be modified also in this respect.

---

2. Service Marks

15 U.S.C. §1127, Lanham Act §45

The term "service mark" means any word, name, symbol, or device, or any combination thereof—

(1) used by a person, or

(2) which a person has a bona fide intention to use in commerce and applies to register on the principal register established by this chapter,

to identify and distinguish the services of one person, including a unique service, from the services of others and to indicate the source of the services, even if that source is unknown. Titles, character names, and other distinctive features of radio or television programs may be registered as service marks notwithstanding that they, or the programs, may advertise the goods of the sponsor.

In re Dr Pepper Co.
836 F.2d 508 (CAFC 1987)

Nies, Circuit Judge.

Dr Pepper Company appeals from the decision of the Patent and Trademark Office Trademark Trial and Appeal Board, 1 U.S.P.Q.2d 1421 (TTAB 1986), affirming the examining attorney's refusal to register the mark PEPPER MAN as a service mark on the ground that applicant's asserted service of sponsoring and operating a particular contest to promote its soft drinks was not a service within the contemplation of sections 3 and 45 of the Trademark Act of 1946, 15 U.S.C. §§1053 and 1127 (1982 & Supp. III 1985). We affirm.

I

Appellant filed an application, Serial No. 477,600, seeking registration of PEPPER MAN which it asserts is its "service mark for sponsorship and operation of contest services." To promote its DR PEPPER soft drinks, appellant conducts a promotional contest in which cash prizes are awarded to households found to have on hand certain specified quantities of unopened cans or bottles of DR PEPPER soft drinks, or certain coupons called "I'M A PEPPER" cards, which can be obtained free of charge from Dr. Pepper or its bottlers. Appellant displays the name PEPPER MAN on promotional pieces for the contest.

The examining attorney refused registration, and the board affirmed, on the ground that applicant was not rendering a service within the contemplation of the Act. The crux of the board's reasoning is that

> where, as here, an activity claimed to be a service is incidental to the sale of goods, the activity cannot be separately recognizable as a service unless it is shown that the activity constitutes something clearly different from, or over and above, any activity normally involved in promoting the sale of such goods. The running of a contest to advertise and promote the sale of one's goods is not a service over and above, or materially different from, what would normally be expected from one engaged in the sale of goods.

1 U.S.P.Q.2d at 1422 (citations omitted).

II

The sole issue raised on appeal is whether conducting a contest to promote the sale of one's own goods is a "service" within the meaning of sections 3 and 45 of the Trademark Act of 1946, 15 U.S.C. §§1053, 1127 (1982). Appellant maintains that sponsorship and operation of a promotional contest is a "service" to the public because some of them will receive the benefit of cash prizes. Thus, it maintains that the name it uses in promoting the contest is registrable as its service mark.

While this court and its predecessor have stated that "services" is a term of "broad scope" under the Lanham Act, *In re Advertising & Mktg. Dev., Inc.*, 821 F.2d 614, 618, 2 U.S.P.Q.2d 2010, 2013 (Fed. Cir. 1987), some business activities which may be described in terms of a "service" to the public do not constitute a service within the intendment of the Act. Appellant does not challenge that general proposition, but urges that contest activities to promote one's products should not be placed in that category, particularly when denominated by a name different from the trademark for the product.

The Act itself provides no definition of a "service" and the legislative history gives no guidance beyond the general principle that, for the first time, marks of businesses engaged in rendering services, such as laundries, were made registrable. Further refinement was left to the administrative agency, now the Patent and Trademark Office, and to the courts.

Through a series of decisions it has become a settled principle that the rendering of a service which is normally "expected or routine" in connection with the sale of one's own goods is not a registrable service whether denominated by the same or a different name from the trademark for its product. This interpretation is a refinement of the basic principle that the service for which registration is sought must be rendered *to others*. Merely advertising one's own goods, while, in a sense, an "informational" or in some instances an "entertainment" service to others, was early held not to be a "service" within the purview of sections 3 and 45.

The interpretation that a company's promotional activities are not services to others under the Act was subsequently endorsed in judicial decisions of our predecessor, the Court of Customs and Patent Appeals. *In re Radio Corp. of Am.*, 40 C.C.P.A. 1025, 205

F.2d 180, 182, 98 U.S.P.Q. 157, 158 (CCPA 1953) (supplying radio stations with pack-aged radio programs of records is mere advertising of record company, not a "service" to consumers). *See also In re Orion Research Inc.*, 523 F.2d 1398, 1400, 187 U.S.P.Q. 485, 487 (CCPA 1975) (*Orion I*) (the repair or replacement of one's own merchandise or "guar-anteeing" same held not a registrable "service" because it is normally expected by pur-chasers from the purveyor of goods); *In re Orion Research Inc.*, 669 F.2d 689, 691, 205 U.S.P.Q. 688, 690 (CCPA 1980) (*Orion II*) (same). Thus, our precedent has drawn the line in connection with promotional activities that those which are "ordinary or routine" are not registrable services, despite some extra benefit to the public beyond the existence of the goods themselves. The public does not, per our precedent, perceive such activity as a service to the public but as mere sales activity by and for the benefit of the offerer of the goods.

In several decisions the board has specifically addressed the registrability of the name for a contest promoting the goods of the company conducting the contest. In *In re John-son Publishing Co.*, 130 U.S.P.Q. 185 (TTAB 1961), the board held that the publisher of a magazine which offered prizes to readers who submitted at least one paid subscription and solved a puzzle was not providing a registrable service. This interpretation was fol-lowed and reaffirmed in *In re Loew's Theatres, Inc.*, 179 U.S.P.Q. 126, 127 (TTAB 1973), where the board stated:

> The lottery type contest, as conducted by applicant, is incidental to the sale of goods, and it is not a service over and above that normally involved in the pro-motion and sale of its goods. It is directly related to and tied to applicant's "KENT" cigarettes, and it is nothing more and would not be recognized as any-thing more than a promotional gimmick or device used to advertise and foster the sale of these cigarettes. Benefits do accrue to winners of the contest, but this is true generally of all promotional devices, but this fact alone cannot serve to obfuscate the true nature and character of applicant's contest.

While the interpretations of the statute by the board are not binding on this court, under general principles of administrative law, deference should be given by a court to the interpretation by the agency charged with its administration. *United States v. Riverside Bayview Homes, Inc.*, 474 U.S. 121, 131, 88 L. Ed. 2d 419, 106 S. Ct. 455 (1985) ("An agency's construction of a statute it is charged with enforcing is entitled to deference if it is reasonable and not in conflict with the expressed intent of Congress."). We conclude that the board reasonably has treated promotional contests as "routine" sales activity for a producer's goods.

Acknowledging that "routine and ordinary" sales activities have not been registrable ser-vices in the past, appellant argues that the board adopted a more "modern" standard with respect to what constitutes a registrable service in *In re Landmark Communications, Inc.*, 204 U.S.P.Q. 692, 696 (TTAB 1979), and urges that we endorse that new standard. In *Landmark*, the board found that the publisher of a newspaper was not entitled to regis-ter the name of a section of its newspaper for "educational and entertainment services," stating that for a service to be registrable, an "activity must be qualitatively different from anything *necessarily done* in connection with the sale of goods." 204 U.S.P.Q. at 695 (em-phasis added).

Focusing on the word "necessarily," appellant asserts that because its contest is not *nec-essary* to the sale of its goods, the conduct of its contest must be held to constitute a reg-istrable service under the *Landmark* test. A closer reading of *Landmark* in the light of prior case law, however, dispels this facial inconsistency. First, it must be noted that neither this panel nor the board can depart from the above precedent of this court which holds that ordinary or routine promotional activities of one's own goods do not constitute a registrable service. *South Corp. v. United States*, 690 F.2d 1368, 1369, 215 U.S.P.Q. 657, 657 (Fed. Cir. 1982). Equally important, the board's decision in *Landmark* addresses a somewhat different facet of the problem.

Some purported services by a seller of goods simply are inherent in the goods. The service of "designing," "manufacturing," "packaging," or "distribution" of one's own goods or, as in *Landmark*, the collation of articles and features for a newspaper, are "necessarily done" to have goods to sell. Such activities are clearly performed for one's self, not offered to others. Advertising and other promotional activities are not "necessary" in the sense that the goods would not exist without them. Thus, the goods and associated promotional activities can more easily be seen as separable, and, depending on the nature of the activity, some degree of service may be rendered to the public, not merely to one's self. Thus, while "routine and ordinary" activities are not "necessary," activities which are "necessarily done" in connection with the sale of one's goods are the quintessential "routine or ordinary" activities associated with the sale of one's goods. Thus, the *Landmark* "necessarily done" standard and the *Orion* "routine or ordinary" standard mesh harmoniously. With this understanding, the *Landmark* standard does not conflict with the test applied by the board here, nor is it a more "modern" standard.

Appellant argues that the exclusion of services ordinarily or routinely rendered in connection with the sale of goods will preclude registration of marks for a vast array of activities currently recognized as services under the Act, such as those provided by retail department stores, mail order companies, and gasoline stations. Contrary to appellant's view, this consequence does not follow. Appellant leaves out the key element which is that the activities being questioned here relate to promotion of *its own goods*. Department stores and gasoline stations are service businesses and provide precisely the types of services intended to be brought under the Act. Indeed, advertising agency services as well as the service of conducting contests *for others* are within the Act. A parallel nonregistrability situation with a service business would be a refusal to register an asserted service of offering "free" glassware to customers who have made a certain level of purchases at a gasoline station, the service of providing "free" bags for purchasers at a grocery store, or a lottery contest by a new shopping mall. Registration of the marks identifying the services of service businesses is not endangered by continuing to apply the principle that services which are ordinary or routine in the sale of goods (or services), such as promotional activities for one's own business, are not services within the meaning of the Act. As stated by Professor McCarthy:

> The point is that a manufacturer or merchant cannot proliferate registrations by obtaining a trademark registration along with a whole raft of service mark registrations covering each and every "service" which every other competitor also provides as an adjunct to the sale of goods....

> Thus, even though a given term may function as both a trademark and a service mark, the service must constitute more than mere promotion and advertising of one's own goods. The difference lies between those services which are mandatory or common in promoting the sale of this type of merchandise, and those services which are not so mandatory or common.

1 J. McCarthy, *Trademarks and Unfair Competition* §§19.30, at 940 (2d ed. 1984) (footnotes omitted). Such proliferation of registrations by devising ways to describe a sale-of-goods situation as a service has been held not to be within the intendment of the Act. We adhere to that precedent.

Alternatively, appellant seeks to elevate its promotional contest to a service under the Act on the ground that its contest is different from a routine advertising contest in that persons who have not purchased its goods may be contacted. However, it admits that only persons who have full containers for its soft drink or have obtained promotional coupons can win. We see nothing which takes this contest out of the ordinary advertising contest.

III

For the foregoing reasons, we affirm the board's decision refusing registration on the ground that appellant is not rendering a service within the meaning of the Act.

Notes

1. What is the difference between a service mark and a trademark? Are these distinctions meaningful?

2. Notice that although Congress provided a definition in the Lanham Act for a "service mark," it did not provide a definition for a "service." The Federal Circuit has filled in a working definition: "[t]he performance of labor for the benefit of another." *In re Adver. and Mktg. Dev., Inc.* 821 F. 2d 614, 618 (Fed. Cir. 1987). The definition has been significantly broadened by the Second Circuit. That court determined that the service provider does not have to intend to benefit another from the service. The only requirement is that someone, in fact, benefitted from the service. *Morningside Group Ltd. v. Morningside Capital Group, LLC,* 182 F. 3d 133 (2d Cir. 1999). Why has Congress failed to provide a definition of "services"? Perhaps the outer parameter was set in *In re Canadian Pac. Ltd.,* 754 F.2d 992 (Fed. Cir. 1985). There the court found that the offering of shares of stock to current shareholders was not offering a service to the public and therefore affirmed the refusal to register the mark.

B. Trade Dress

1. Product Packaging

Fun-Damental Too v. Gemmy Indus. Corp.
111 F.3d 993 (2d Cir. 1997)

CARDOMONE, CIRCUIT JUDGE:

This is an appeal in a trade dress infringement case. For the purpose of legal analysis, trade dress is generally broken down into two categories: product configuration, which relates to the design of a product distinct from the package in which it is sold, and product packaging. Among the several issues we have to resolve is whether it is appropriate—when evaluating the inherent distinctiveness of the packaging—to consider also the product itself, which is quite visible in an open-style box. Another difficult issue is the significance—when considering the likelihood of confusion between two products' packaging—

of the junior user's copying the senior user's trade dress. Imitation may well be the sincerest form of flattery, but copying another's trade dress poses vexing legal problems.

Plaintiff Fun-Damental Too, Ltd. (plaintiff or Fun-Damental) brought suit in the United States District Court for the Southern District of New York (Mukasey, J.) against defendants Gemmy Industries Corp. and Kay-Bee Toy & Hobby Shops, Inc. (defendants, appellants, or Gemmy and Kay-Bee) for trade dress infringement under the Lanham Act, 15 U.S.C. §1125(a), as well as for claims alleging injury to its business under New York law. According to Fun-Damental's complaint, Gemmy copied the packaging of plaintiff's "Toilet Bank," a retail novelty item, for use with defendant's similar product, the "Currency Can" (photographs of the two products as packaged are reproduced as an appendix to this opinion). Pending resolution of Fun-Damental's claims, Judge Mukasey granted a preliminary injunction prohibiting Kay-Bee and Gemmy from manufacturing, selling or distributing the Currency Can in its present packaging or in any other packaging similar to plaintiff's. The injunction further directs Gemmy to bring all finished products from its Chinese factory to the United States and retain them here.

BACKGROUND
A. Facts

Fun-Damental is a Pennsylvania limited partnership that develops and sells novelty toys and gifts, most of which feature some mechanism for producing sound. These products are known in the toy industry as "impulse items," because they are purchased based on a consumer's quick decision made while in the store, without comparison shopping or investigation. Fun-Damental sells its line of products through large chains such as Walgreen's, Service Merchandise and Toys 'R' Us, and through gift shops, hardware stores, college bookstores and other small retail outlets.

In 1992 plaintiff began developing the Toilet Bank, a toy coin bank closely resembling the familiar white tank toilet. An important feature of this product is its ability to simulate the flushing sound of a toilet when its handle is depressed. "Flushing" the Toilet Bank also enables coins placed in the toilet bowl to drop into the bank's base. When development was completed in 1994, Fun-Damental began promoting its novelty coin bank through its catalogs and at trade shows. Consumers have since purchased more than 860,000 of these items at a retail price of $15 to $20 each.

In May 1995 defendant Kay-Bee, a major toy and novelty retailer, expressed interest in buying the Toilet Bank. But after examining a sample, Kay-Bee decided against carrying the product because of its high cost relative to other impulse items. In September 1995 Fun-Damental's sales manager visited Kay-Bee and noticed a toilet-shaped bank resembling the Toilet Bank on a shelf in the office of Kay-Bee's purchasing agent in charge of impulse items. The sales manager's request to examine the item more closely was turned down. In October Fun-Damental sent Kay-Bee a product notice requesting to examine a sample of the observed product for possible infringement. No sample was sent.

It turned out that defendant Gemmy, a novelty manufacturer, had approached Kay-Bee and supplied it with toilet-shaped coin banks similar to Fun-Damental's. Kay-Bee was able to purchase Gemmy's Currency Cans at a lower wholesale price than the Toilet Bank, and was therefore able to retail Gemmy's product at $9.99 each. The record reveals that when Gemmy's vice-president learned of Fun-Damental's Toilet Bank, he contacted his company's Chinese factory in May 1995 and asked it to design a similar product. In the design phase of the Currency Can, a sample of Fun-Damental's Toilet Bank was sent to Gemmy's Chinese manufacturer. The Gemmy official testified that the Currency Can was designed with dimensions virtually identical to those of the Toilet Bank in order to compete effectively with it.

B. Trade Dress

Plaintiff's product is displayed in stores in a royal blue triangular-shaped box. The Toilet Bank itself is visible within the open-style box, which allows a consumer access to the toilet handle so that the flushing sound may be tested. The toy's bowl is covered with a clear plastic cover that includes a raised three-dimensional circle to which is affixed a gray sticker depicting a coin. The bank is held in place in its box by a 1/4 inch strap running up one side of the toilet bowl, through the plastic cover, and down the other side.

The product name "TOILET BANK" appears in yellow letters on the royal blue box's lower front panel. The four inch-high upper rear panel is decorated with the product name and two pictures demonstrating how to use the product. The top picture shows a hand holding a coin over the toilet bowl, and the bottom one shows an index finger depressing the handle with the message "REAL FLUSHING SOUND" in white letters on a red bubble. In the upper right hand corner of this panel is a yellow starburst with the words "REAL FLUSHING SOUND" in red letters. Below it is a yellow arrow pointing down toward the handle with the legend in red: "TRY ME" and in smaller letters: "PRESS HANDLE." The same message appears on a red arrow sticker, affixed to the toilet tank, pointing diagonally towards the silver handle.

Gemmy's Currency Can is packaged in a box identical in its configuration and dimensions to Fun-Damental's box, including the various tabs and slots used to assemble each. Gemmy has used two different color schemes on its boxes. The first version featured a yellow background with powder blue squares in a "bathroom tile" design. At the behest of Kay-Bee's purchasing agent, who preferred a brighter color scheme, the second and more widely-used design features a deeper blue background with bright yellow "bathroom tile" squares. In the center of their upper panels, both of Gemmy's boxes include a starburst with yellow lettering: "A BANK WITH A REAL FLUSHING SOUND!" Both also include, at the right of the upper panel, an arrow pointing down toward the silver handle with "PRESS HANDLE" in small yellow lettering followed by "TRY ME!" in large white letters. A similar red arrow is affixed to the tank of the toilet and angled toward the toilet's handle. Gemmy's Currency Can also has a flat plastic cover over the toilet bowl opening on which a gray coin-like sticker is affixed.

C. Prior Legal Proceedings

Fun-Damental filed its complaint against Gemmy and Kay-Bee on February 13, 1996, alleging trade dress infringement in violation of §43(a) of the Lanham Act, injury to business reputation under N.Y. Gen. Bus. L. §368-d, and unfair competition and tortious interference with contractual relations under New York common law. Plaintiff also sought a preliminary injunction and an order of impoundment. After a hearing, the district court granted the preliminary injunction in a March 18, 1996 Memorandum and Order which was subsequently amended on March 20. Kay-Bee was ordered to remove Currency Can units from its retail shelves and place them in storage during the pendency of the injunction. The district court ordered Gemmy to acquire all units of the Currency Can (packaged in the allegedly infringing trade dress) located outside the United States and ship them to its warehouse in this country for storage, along with all units presently in its possession. From the issuance of this preliminary injunction, defendants appeal. We affirm.

DISCUSSION
I. The Lanham Act in General

The Lanham Act is designed to protect trademarks for the benefit of both the consumer and business. Congress recognized that a trademark aids competition in the marketplace because it helps a consumer distinguish among competing products. S. Rep. No. 79-1333 (1946), reprinted in 1946 U.S.C.C.A.N. 1274, 1275. Trademarks also encourage producers to maintain a high quality product by assuring that any goodwill associated with their products is not misappropriated by competitors. Id.

> Section 43(a) of the Lanham Act provides a private cause of action against any person who in connection with any goods ... or any container for goods, uses in commerce any word, term, name, symbol, or device, or any combination thereof ... which ... is likely to cause confusion, or to cause mistake, or to deceive ... as to the origin, sponsorship, or approval of his or her goods ... by another person....

15 U.S.C. §1125(a).

The statutory protection of unregistered trademarks extends to trade dress. *See Two Pesos, Inc. v. Taco Cabana, Inc.*, 505 U.S. 763, 773, 120 L. Ed. 2d 615, 112 S. Ct. 2753 (1992) ("§43(a) provides no basis for distinguishing between trademark and trade dress."). The concept of trade dress encompasses the design and appearance of the product together with all the elements making up the overall image that serves to identify the product presented to the consumer. *Jeffrey Milstein, Inc. v. Greger, Lawlor, Roth, Inc.*, 58 F.3d 27, 31 (2d Cir. 1995). These other elements include "the appearance of labels, wrappers, and containers used in packaging a product as well as displays and other materials used in presenting the product to prospective purchasers." Restatement (Third) of Unfair Competition §16 cmt. a (1995).

"Trade dress today encompasses a broad concept of how a product presented to the public looks, including its color, design, container, and all the elements that make up its total appearance." *Mana*, 65 F.3d at 1069.

This "total look" approach is the only workable way to consider such elements of the trade dress as the arrow sticker that is affixed to the Toilet Bank's tank. Because the box is open in order to display the product, it was proper to analyze Fun-Damental's trade dress as seen by consumers—including the Toilet Bank product. Further, there is no risk of "spillover" protection for the Toilet Bank as a product here since the injunction is limited to the sale of a similar product in a particular package, rather than an absolute ban on the sale of the Currency Can in an open-style box. In sum, we conclude that looking at the product itself in the context of its packaging is a proper method of analyzing open-style packaging for trade dress protection.

* * *

The finding that Gemmy intentionally copied Fun-Damental's packaging was based on the trial court's observation that the unfolded pattern of Gemmy's box is identical to that of Fun-Damental and departed from the pattern of the open-style boxes Gemmy had previously used. Additional proof presented could support the inference that Gemmy and Kay-Bee intended to mislead consumers by appearing to mark down prices on the Currency Can. Although the product always sold for $9.99, its price sticker listed an "original price" which was subsequently crossed out. This pricing system created the confusing impression that the higher priced product produced by plaintiff, which the consumer may have seen on an earlier occasion, is being sold now for less. Hence, the finding of bad faith was amply supported.

* * *

In sum, the preliminary injunction against Gemmy and Kay-Bee was properly issued. The district court did not abuse its discretion by finding that Fun-Damental is likely to succeed on the merits of its claim that the Toilet Bank's trade dress is inherently distinctive, that it is nonfunctional, and that there is a substantial likelihood of confusion between the Toilet Bank and the Currency Can, as presently packaged. Because all parties subject to the injunction are American corporations and the regulated conduct has a substantial effect on United States commerce, the injunction's reach over the extraterritorial conduct of these parties is properly within the power of the district court under the Lanham Act.

Affirmed.

---

2. Product Configuration

Ashley Furniture Industries v. Sangiacomo N.A.
187 F.3d 363 (4th Cir. 1999)

Motz, Circuit Judge:

This case requires us to determine under what circumstances the configuration of a product can constitute inherently distinctive trade dress that is protectable under federal law. Because we conclude that a product's configuration qualifies as inherently distinctive trade dress if it is capable of functioning as a designator of an individual source of the product, we reverse the contrary ruling of the district court and remand for further proceedings.

I.

Ashley Furniture Industries, Inc., and SanGiacomo N.A. Ltd. manufacture home furniture. In this action, Ashley alleges that SanGiacomo copied the design of one of Ashley's bedroom suites, in violation of federal trade dress law and an oral contract between the parties.

Both companies market furniture in the mid-level price range and sell numerous lines of furniture nationwide. Between them, for example, the two companies produce over thirty different bedroom suites. Ashley and SanGiacomo sell their furniture to retailers, who display the furniture of various manufacturers and fill consumers' orders either from inventory or by ordering from the wholesaler.

Generally, those seeking to buy this sort of furniture cannot determine the manufacturer of a piece or set of furniture simply by looking at it. Manufacturers in this market do not carve or emboss their names or trademarks on the exterior of their furniture; instead they rely on hang tags and emblems inside drawers to identify their goods. Often, retailers do not identify the manufacturer or the name of the design to the consumer, refusing even to use the hang tags. Retailers provide pictures of the furniture they offer in flyers, newspapers, and on television, but again these advertisements may not include any reference to the manufacturer.

Ashley and SanGiacomo aggressively compete for customers, and their rivalry has previously led to litigation. In that action, filed in 1993, the parties' roles were reversed: SanGiacomo sued Ashley charging that it had infringed the trade dress of SanGiacomo's bedroom furniture and seeking a declaratory judgment that a design patent obtained by Ashley was invalid as a matter of law. The parties settled the claims during a one-on-one, closed-door negotiation between Carlo Bargagli-Stoffi, the chief executive of SanGiacomo, and Ronald Wanek, the chairman and chief executive of Ashley. Wanek and Bar-gagli-Stoffi agreed that both sides would walk away from the suit, and that neither company would, in the future, copy the other's furniture designs. Bargagli-Stoffi characterizes this deal as a "gentlemen's agreement" that they would not make any "Polaroid copies" of the other's designs. Although the parties then entered into a written settlement agreement drawn up by counsel, that formal agreement contains no reference to any mutual covenant not to copy.

Approximately one year after that settlement, in the fall of 1995, Ashley introduced a neo-classical bedroom suite under the trade name "Sommerset." The suite consists of a headboard, two night stands, an armoire, and a dresser with a mirror. The design of the Sommerset suite combines a "modern" high-gloss polyester look and feel with "classical" elements including a finish that suggests marble or travertine, fluted columns, arches, and entablatures.

According to Ashley's witnesses, the design and overall appearance of the Sommerset suite were unique and unlike any other bedroom furniture ever sold. For example, one Ashley industry expert, a retired home furniture retailer with 25 years of experience, explained:

> Based on my experience, the common high gloss polyester finish in all the pieces of the Sommerset suite, in either the Carmelstone or lighter Goatskin finish, combined with the off white moldings and classic columns and flutings, pro vide a unique and unusual appearance for the Ashley Sommerset bedroom suite. The combination of features provides both a traditional and contemporary appearance. Although these individual features have been used in other bedroom suites, I do not recall seeing the combination of such features in a single bedroom suite. Therefore, the Ashley Sommerset has a unique appearance in the furniture industry ... [that] distinguishes it from other bedroom suites in either the contemporary or the traditional furniture markets.

Another expert opined that "the overall appearance of Ashley's Sommerset bedroom suite is not a common design in the bedroom furniture market" but rather is "different and distinct from every other bedroom suite on the market or that had previously been on the market" in his 17-year retail home furniture experience. SanGiacomo offered no contradictory evidence.

Retail sales of the Sommerset suite began in March 1996, and it quickly became one of Ashley's best-selling bedroom designs.

In December 1996 or January 1997, SanGiacomo began selling a line of bedroom furniture under the name "La Dolce Vita." This bedroom set, like the Sommerset suite, consists of a headboard, two night stands, an armoire, and a dresser with a mirror. Also like Ashley's Sommerset, SanGiacomo's La Dolce Vita includes a high-gloss marble-like finish, fluted columns, arches, and entablatures. The entire Sommerset suite retails for approximately $2,500; the La Dolce Vita suite retails for approximately $1,800. Ashley asserts that the materials and craftsmanship used in making SanGiacomo's La Dolce Vita furniture are far inferior to those used in making its own Sommerset furniture. In the months that followed introduction of the La Dolce Vita collection, it displaced sales of Ashley's Sommerset suite at many retailers.

Ashley maintains that SanGiacomo's marketing of the La Dolce Vita design infringes upon its rights in the Sommerset design. Accordingly, it filed this action asserting a violation of federal trade dress law, breach of the parties' alleged oral agreement not to copy, and other state law claims. After discovery, Ashley moved for summary judgment on its breach of contract claim and on the issue of whether SanGiacomo copied the Sommerset design. SanGiacomo, in turn, moved for summary judgment on Ashley's trade dress claim. The district court denied Ashley's motion and granted SanGiacomo's. Ashley appeals, asserting that summary judgment should not have been granted on either the trade dress or contract claim.

II.

The trade dress of a product consists of its "total image and overall appearance," including its "size, shape, color or color combinations, texture, graphics, or even particular sales techniques." *Two Pesos, Inc. v. Taco Cabana, Inc.*, 505 U.S. 763, 764 n.1, 120 L. Ed. 2d 615, 112 S. Ct. 2753 (1992) (quoting district court instruction); *Tools USA & Equip. Co. v. Champ Frame Straightening Equip., Inc.*, 87 F.3d 654, 657 (4th Cir. 1996) (quoting *Two Pesos*).

In addition to protecting registered trademarks, the Lanham Act protects unregistered marks and trade dress. Specifically, §43 of the Lanham Act provides that

> any person who, on or in connection with any goods or services ... uses in commerce any word, term, name, symbol, or device, or any combination thereof ... which ... is likely to cause confusion, or to cause mistake, or to deceive as to the affiliation, connection, or association of such per son with another person, or as to the origin ... of his or her goods ... shall be liable in a civil action by any person who believes that he or she is or is likely to be damaged by such act.

15 U.S.C.A. §§1125(a) (West 1998).

The Supreme Court has explained that "protection of trade dress, no less than of trademarks, serves the Act's purpose." *Two Pesos*, 505 U.S. at 774. That purpose is two-fold: §43(a) seeks (1) "to secure to the owner of the mark the goodwill of his business" and (2) "to protect the ability of consumers to distinguish among competing producers." *Id.* (quoting *Park 'N Fly, Inc. v. Dollar Park & Fly, Inc.*, 469 U.S. 189, 198, 83 L. Ed. 2d 582, 105 S. Ct. 658 (1985)).

Thus, §43 does not prohibit copying per se. Rather, the statute only prohibits a copy that can be passed off as the product of the originator, thereby confusing the consumer and interfering with the originator's rights in the goodwill of its business. *See Bonito Boats, Inc. v. Thunder Craft Boats, Inc.*, 489 U.S. 141, 157, 103 L. Ed. 2d 118, 109 S. Ct. 971 (1989) (citing *Crescent Tool Co. v. Kilborn & Bishop Co.*, 247 F. 299, 301 (2d Cir. 1917) (Hand, J.)). By prohibiting copying just in this narrow class of circumstances, the statute protects the substantial public interest in free imitation. "Imitation is the life blood of competition" and only the ready "availability of substantially equivalent units ... yields the fair price society" seeks. *American Safety Table Co. v. Schreiber*, 269 F.2d 255, 272 (2d Cir. 1959).

[The court reversed the trial court's finding of invalidity of the bedroom furniture and found the trade dress worthy of protection if it was capable of functioning as a designator of the source of the product.]

———————

Note

1. In *Wal-Mart Stores, Inc. v. Samara Bros.*, 529 U.S. 205 (2000), *infra*, Chapter 10, the Supreme Court determined that product configuration trade dress could never be inherently distinctive. In light of this holding, is *Ashley Furniture* still good law?

———————

3. The "Tertium Quid"

Two Pesos, Inc. v. Taco Cabana, Inc.
505 U.S. 763 (1992)

JUSTICE WHITE delivered the opinion of the Court.

The issue in this case is whether the trade dress of a restaurant may be protected under §43(a) of the Trademark Act of 1946 (Lanham Act), 60 Stat. 441, 15 U.S.C. §1125(a) (1982 ed.), based on a finding of inherent distinctiveness, without proof that the trade dress has secondary meaning.

I

Respondent Taco Cabana, Inc., operates a chain of fast-food restaurants in Texas. The restaurants serve Mexican food. The first Taco Cabana restaurant was opened in San Antonio in September 1978, and five more restaurants had been opened in San Antonio by 1985. Taco Cabana describes its Mexican trade dress as

> a festive eating atmosphere having interior dining and patio areas decorated with artifacts, bright colors, paintings and murals. The patio includes interior and exterior areas with the interior patio capable of being sealed off from the outside patio by overhead garage doors. The stepped exterior of the building is a festive and vivid color scheme using top border paint and neon stripes. Bright awnings and umbrellas continue the theme.

932 F.2d 1113, 1117 (CA5 1991).

[The Court found this trade dress or overall commercial impression protectable.]

* * *

Notes

1. After almost a decade of relying on *Two Pesos* as the principal case regarding the Supreme Court's position on trade dress, in *Wal-Mart Stores, Inc. v. Samara Bros.*, 529 U.S. 205 (2000), *infra*, Justice Scalia dismissed *Two Pesos* as neither a case regarding product configuration nor product packaging but "some *tertium quid* that is akin to product packaging and has no bearing on [product configuration analysis]." *Id.* at 215.

2. What is a "tertium quid"? It is defined as "something related in some way to two things, but distinct from both." Webster's Encyclopedic Unabridged Dictionary of the English Language 1466 (1996). Why did the Supreme Court elect to create a new form of trade dress, the tertium quid, rather than just overruling *Two Pesos*? What does that tell you about the Supreme Court's view of trademark rights?

C. Scent Marks

In re Celia Clarke
17 U.S.P.Q.2D (BNA) 1238 (TTAB 1990)

SIMMS, MEMBER.

Applicant, Celia Clarke, doing business as Clarke's OSEWEZ, has appealed from the final refusal of the Trademark Examining Attorney to register applicant's asserted mark for "sewing thread and embroidery yarn."[4] Applicant has described her mark in the "drawing" filed with her application as follows: "The mark is a high impact, fresh, floral fragrance reminiscent of Plumeria blossoms."

The Examining Attorney has refused registration on the ground that applicant's asserted mark does not function as a trademark because it does not identify or distinguish applicant's goods from those of others. In the initial refusal, the Examining Attorney observed that applicant's fragrance mark is analogous to other forms of product ornamentation in that it is not the type of matter which consumers would tend to perceive as an indication of origin. The Examining Attorney also refused registration on the basis that applicant's alleged mark was de jure functional, assertedly because of the competitive need for free access to pleasant scents or fragrances. In his appeal brief, the Examining Attorney withdrew the de jure functionality refusal.

In support of her attempt to register this fragrance mark, counsel for applicant submitted a declaration of applicant attesting to the fact that, to the best of her knowledge, no other company has ever offered any scented embroidery yarn or thread; that she has placed advertisements stressing the fact that her company is the source of sweet-scented embroidery products, known in the trade as Russian embroidery or punch embroidery; and that due to the success of her products, applicant is now a major source of yarn and thread and supplies dealers and distributors throughout the United States. Applicant also states that her company has received a great number of favorable and positive responses to her unique product and that, to the best of her knowledge, customers, dealers and distributors throughout the embroidery field recognize applicant as the source of scented embroidery yarn and thread. While maintaining that her fragrance is registrable as a mark because it is inherently distinctive of yarns and threads, no other manufacturer having sold such goods, applicant nevertheless argues that she has presented sufficient evidence of recognition of her asserted mark. Applicant concludes, brief, 13:

Others are free to adopt any other scent for their yarns and threads, including floral scents such as that of a lily of the valley, a carnation or a rose to give but three examples. Surely people have come [to] distinguish these floral scents from one another, just as they can distinguish the color pink (for fiberglass insulation) from other warm colors such as red, orange, and yellow. Just as the registration of the color pink for fiberglass insulation has been held to not present a significant obstacle for competitors wishing to produce fiberglass insulation, so does the applicant's particular fragrance not present a significant obstacle to competitors wishing to offer scented yarns.

Applicant has made of record a complete sealed kit containing scented yarn and thread for making a scented skunk.

---

4. Serial No. 758,429, filed October 18, 1988, claiming use since October 6, 1988.

Expressing unawareness of any precedent dealing with the registrability of an arbitrary, nonfunctional scent, the Examining Attorney states that the most closely analogous determinations appear to be those dealing with colors as trademarks. The Examining Attorney concedes that there is no inherent bar to the registrability of an arbitrary, nonfunctional scent or fragrance and that this record discloses that the scent applicant has added to her product is not a natural or inherent feature of the goods and does not provide any utilitarian advantage. The Examining Attorney adds that, presumably, if applicant's scent does function to indicate origin, potential consumers may readily be able to distinguish among the vast array of scents in identifying competing sources of goods.

In support of his argument that applicant's fragrance mark is not of a character usually recognized by potential consumers as an indication of origin, he requests the Board to take judicial notice of the fact that there are pleasant, arbitrary and nonfunctional scents in a wide variety of products, including cosmetics and cleaning products, which have the sole purpose of making the use of those products more pleasant or attractive. Therefore, while applicant is the only source of scented yarn and thread, the Examining Attorney argues that potential consumers are unlikely to regard scent in any product as an indication of exclusive origin in view of their conditioning in the consumer product marketplace. The rarity of usage of fragrance as a feature of applicant's goods weighs against registration, according to the Examining Attorney. Rather, it is much more likely that consumers will regard the scent as a pleasant feature of the goods.

While the Examining Attorney concedes that the asserted fragrance may be registrable upon a convincing showing of trademark function, he maintains that applicant has not specifically promoted the particular scent as an indication of origin. Applicant's advertising makes reference to "Clarke's Distinctive Sof-Scented Yarns," but no reference is made to a specific fragrance. Nor does the advertising make any attempt, according to the Examining Attorney, to draw attention to the scent as an indicator of origin.

Upon careful review of this record, we believe that applicant has demonstrated that its scented fragrance does function as a trademark for her thread and embroidery yarn. Under the circumstances of this case, we see no reason why a fragrance is not capable of serving as a trademark to identify and distinguish a certain type of product. It is clear from the record that applicant is the only person who has marketed yarns and threads with a fragrance.[5] That is to say, fragrance is not an inherent attribute or natural characteristic of applicant's goods but is rather a feature supplied by applicant. Moreover, applicant has emphasized this characteristic of her goods in advertising, promoting the scented feature of her goods. Applicant has demonstrated that customers, dealers and distributors of her scented yarns and threads have come to recognize applicant as the source of these goods. In view of the unique nature of applicant's product, we do not believe that the failure of applicant to indicate in her promotional materials the specific scent or fragrance of her yarn (admittedly difficult to describe except in the manner that applicant has done so) is significant. In her advertisements and at craft fairs, applicant has promoted her products as having a scented nature. We believe that applicant has presented a prima facie case of distinctiveness of her fragrance mark. *Compare In re Star*

5. It should be noted that we are not here talking about the registrability of scents or fragrances of products which are noted for those features, such as perfumes, colognes or scented household products. Nor is this a case involving the question of descriptiveness of a term which identifies a particular fragrance of a product. In such cases it has been held that a term is unregistrable under Section 2(e)(1) of the Act if it merely describes an odor or other significant feature of the product. See In re Gyulay, 820 F.2d 1216, 3 USPQ2d 1009 (Fed. Cir. 1987) (APPLE PIE held merely descriptive since the term described the scent released by potpourri simmered in water).

Pharmaceuticals, Inc., 225 U.S.P.Q. 209 (TTAB 1985) (where applicant failed to demonstrate that the features (colors) sought to be registered had been promoted as a source indicator).[6]

Decision: The refusal of registration is reversed.[7]

———————

Notes

1. Apparently corporate America has not caught on to the registration of scent marks. There are still very few scent marks registered on the Principal Registry in the United States but there are far more scent marks in the United Kingdom. *See* Faye M. Hammersley, *The Smell of Success: Trade Dress Protection For Scent Marks,* 2 Marq. Intell. Prop. L. Rev. 105, 156 (1998) (encouraging U.S. trademark owners to apply for more scent marks and predicting success in light of *In re Clarke*).

2. On the other hand, one commentator argues strenuously that scent marks are inherently inappropriate for protection under the Lanham Act. *See* Douglas D. Churovich, *Policy Considerations from a Practitioner's Perspective: Scents, Sense or Cents? Something Stinks in the Lanham Act Scientific Obstacles to Scent Marks*, 20 St. Louis U. Pub. L. Rev. 293 (2001) (arguing that scent was not originally contemplated as protectable under the Lanham Act, the very nature of scents make them inherently confusing and functional, and any advantage to protection and registration is heavily outweighed by the administrative burdens of regulation and enforcement). *See also* Bettina Elias, *Do Scents Signify Source? An Argument Against Trademark Protection For Fragrances*, 82 Trademark Rep. 475, 509 (1992).

3. Are scent marks normatively protectable as appellations of source or not? Should they be?

4. Ms. Clarke was represented in front of the TTAB by James Hawes, one of the leading trademark treatise authors. However, after triumphing at the TTAB, the Clarke registration was canceled on September 29, 1997 for failure to file a Section 8 affidavit alleging continued use of the mark. Ms. Clarke continues to sell sewing supplies, however she seems to have left the scents behind.

5. Your client comes to you with what he says is a magnificent idea. He wants to know if he will be likely to claim trademark rights to the scent of motor oil. He is a purveyor of motor oil and sponsors a stock car that runs in the Nascar circuit. One of many competitive advantages that cars attempt to get over one another is using the correct grade motor oil for the right weather conditions. As all pit crews are closely assembled on pit row, it is difficult to conceal what grade motor oil a car is using. Your client had an idea to fix that. He pours the three most popular choices into generically marked containers. The

———————

6. We note that the Trademark Review Commission of the United States Trademark Association, in its review of the Trademark Act of 1946, determined that the terms "symbol, or device" should not be deleted or narrowed to preclude registration of such things as a color, shape, smell, sound, or configuration which functions as a mark. The United States Trademark Association Trademark Review Commission Report and Recommendations to USTA President and Board of Directors, 77 TMR 375, 421 (Sept.–Oct. 1987). See also Moon-Ki Chai, "Protection of Fragrances under the Post-Sale Confusion Doctrine," 80 TMR 368, 371–72 (July–Aug. 1990).

7. The description of applicant's mark noted above will appear on the certificate of registration as applicant's mark. Although advances are continually being made in Office operations and practices, the era of "scratch and sniff" registrations is not yet upon us.

heaviest grade he scents with the smell of cherries. The middle grade he scents with the smell of pineapple. The lightest grade oil he scents with the smell of apple. Will your client be able to claim trademark rights to these scents? What else will you need to know to give him a clear answer?

———————

D. Sound

In re General Electric Broadcasting Company, Inc.
199 U.S.P.Q. 560 (BNA) (TTAB 1978)

LEFKOWITZ, MEMBER.

An application has been filed by General Electric Broadcasting Company, Inc. to register a mark consisting of the sound made by a Ship's Bell Clock as a service mark for radio broadcasting services. The mark is claimed to have been first used in a modified form on September 15, 1967 and in its present form on July 4, 1975 by radio station WJIB of Boston, Massachusetts, a station wholly owned and operated by applicant.

The mark is described in the application as comprising

> … a series of bells tolled during four, hour sequences, beginning with one ring at approximately a first half hour and increasing in number by one ring at approximately each half hour thereafter.

As provided for in Rule 2.58(b), specimens filed with the application comprise tape recordings which, when played at the appropriate speed, reproduce the mark as used in connection with applicant's radio broadcasting services.

Registration has been refused on the ground that the sequential sounds sought to be registered do not and cannot constitute a mark serving to identify applicant's services in commerce.

Applicant has appealed.

It is the Examiner's position that "… the scheme of bell ringing described in the application is not a service mark. Applicant is doing no more than telling its listeners the time by broadcasting the traditional maritime bells ringing in the traditional maritime sequence. The Examiner contends that this system of telling time is in the public domain and is not subject to exclusive appropriation by applicant."

In essence, the Examiner's point is that telling time on radio by means of tolling bells in the traditional maritime sequence is not and cannot be considered to be a service mark.

According to applicant, the mark comprising a series of ship's clock sounds is consonant with the nautical nature of the radio station call letters "WJIB" incorporating the term "JIB", which is generally defined as a triangular sail set in front of the forward mast; the mark sought to be registered is a distinctive sound in a distinctive form which is neither descriptive nor deceptively misdescriptive of the services rendered by applicant (the sound generated to form the mark essentially originated from the bell on the USS Constitution); the telling of time by announcement through speech emanating at a radio station is unlike the use of applicant's mark, namely,

The station primarily broadcasts music and does not make a station break at exact hour or half hour intervals for purposes of identification. It is customary at the time of tolling the bells for the announcer at the station to give the exact time to the listening audience. Thus, in actual use, the bells may be tolled at times which are between two minutes before to two minutes after the actual hour or half-hour", and it is clear that applicant does not seek to vest in itself the sole right to tell time over radio, but rather to identify its broadcasting services through use of the mark it seeks to register.

A service mark is defined in Section 45 of the Statute as "... a mark used in the sale or advertising of services to identify the services of one person and distinguish them from the services of others. Titles, character names, and other distinctive features of radio and television programs may be registered as service marks notwithstanding that they, or the programs may advertise the goods of the sponsor."

Apart from the reference to "titles" and "character" names of radio and television pro-grams, the framers of the Lanham Act did not define the term "services" or indicate what constitutes a "service mark." It appears that no attempt was made in this direction be-cause of the innumerable services that are being rendered in all aspects of society and the various different types of marks, devices, symbols, and the like that are and may be used to identify services rendered in commerce. The salient question provided for in the def-inition is whether what is sought to be registered serves "to identify the services of one person and distinguish them from the services of others" without regard as to the nature of the mark in question. The difficulty of attempting to delineate what specific forms a service mark or, in fact, a trademark should assume is recognized in the preamble of Sec-tion 2 which provides, in part, that:

> No trademark by which the goods of the applicant may be distinguished from the goods of others shall be refused registration on the principal register on ac-count of its nature ...

Thus, the nature of a mark is no basis for refusing to register it either as a service mark or as a trademark if it performs as an indication of source and does not fall within the prohibitions of subsections (a) through (e) of Section 2 which, in essence, comprise a codification of basic principles of common law that preclude the establishment of pro-prietary rights in a trademark that may be in derogation of an equal or superior right that another may possess therein.

In view of this flexible approach toward the concept of what constitutes a service mark or a trademark, a flexibility that is required in order to keep up with the ever-changing ramifications brought about by the changing technology that accompanies the growth of a nation and creates goods, services, and concepts unheard of in the past, the Patent and Trademark Office has recognized that a mark need not be confined to a graphic form. That is, sounds may, under certain conditions, at least as far as services are concerned where the traditional concept of affixation of a trademark has not been ingrained or, in fact, is not practical or possible, likewise function as source indicators in those situations where they assume a definitive shape or arrangement and are used in such a manner so as to create in the hearer's mind an association of the sound with a service. *See*, T.M.E.P. 1301.07 [§§] (a) and (b). This practice has manifested itself in the registration of such sound marks as a series of musical chimes (Reg. No. 916,522, issued July 13, 1971), the ringing of the Liberty Bell (Reg. No. 548,458, issued September 18, 1951), the sound of a creak-ing door (Reg. No. 556,780, issued November 25, 1952), the audio and visual represen-tation of a coin spinning on a hard surface (Reg. No. 641,872 issued February 19, 1957), a sound consisting of three short pulses followed by a longer pulse (Reg. No. 922,585, issued October 19, 1971), and the musical notes, E flat, B flat, G, C, F, electrically reproduced (Reg. No. 928,479, issued February 1, 1972).

However, it is believed that the criteria for the registration of sound marks must be somewhat different from those applied to the average trademark notwithstanding that more often than not, they do not fall within any of the proscriptions set forth in Section 2(a) through (e). That is, unlike the case of a trademark which is applied to the goods in such a manner as to create a visual and lasting impression upon a purchaser or prospective purchaser encountering the mark in the marketplace, a sound mark depends upon aural perception of the listener which may be as fleeting as the sound itself unless, of course, the sound is so inherently different or distinctive that it attaches to the subliminal mind of the listener to be awakened when heard and to be associated with the source or event with which it is struck. Thus, a distinction must be made between unique, different, or distinctive sounds and those that resemble or imitate "commonplace" sounds or those to which listeners have been exposed under different circumstances. This does not mean that sounds that fall within the latter group, when applied outside of the common environment, cannot function as marks for the services in connection with which they are used. But, whereas the arbitrary, unique or distinctive marks are registrable as such on the Principal Register without supportive evidence, those that fall within the second category must be supported by evidence to show that purchasers, prospective purchasers and listeners do recognize and associate the sound with services offered and/or rendered exclusively with a single, albeit anonymous, source.

Thus, in the instant case, the fact that applicant's sound mark is a play on the traditional ship's bell clock sounds does not mean that in the environment of radio broadcasting services, it is incapable of functioning as a mark to identify such services. This is manifestly a question of fact and, in view of the experience of the average person with ship's bells, whether as a member of the armed forces or otherwise, evidence in such a situation is necessary to establish that the ship's bell sounds have become distinctive of applicant's services and do, in fact, identify and distinguish applicant's broadcasting services to those exposed to such services. That is, the sounds ring a bell for the listener.

It is therefore concluded that the record herein is insufficient to establish that the mark sought to be registered performs a service mark function.

Decision

The refusal of registration is affirmed only to the extent indicated.

Notes

1. In 1994, Harley Davidson received a significant amount of publicity when it applied to register as a trademark the sound of the Harley Engine." *See* J. Taylor Buckley, *The Bike That Roared: Can Harley's Sound Be Trademarked?*, USA TODAY, Jan. 8, 1996. Harley described its engine's sound as similar to that produced by rapidly repeating the word "potato." Other motorcycle manufacturers opposed the registration and it was finally abandoned. If you were the Trademark Examiner, would you grant the registration?

The sound as claimed in the application can be found at:

http://www.bc.edu/bc_org/avp/law/st_org/iptf/articles/content/1998101101.html

2. Some representative sounds of various famous registered trademarks can be found at:

http://www.uspto.gov/go/kids/kidsound.html

E. Color

Qualitex Co. v. Jacobson Products Co. Inc.
514 U.S. 159 (1995)

Justice Breyer delivered the opinion of the Court.

The question in this case is whether the Trademark Act of 1946 (Lanham Act), 15 U.S.C. §§1051–1127 (1988 ed. and Supp. V), permits the registration of a trademark that consists, purely and simply, of a color. We conclude that, sometimes, a color will meet ordinary legal trademark requirements. And, when it does so, no special legal rule prevents color alone from serving as a trademark.

I

The case before us grows out of petitioner Qualitex Company's use (since the 1950's) of a special shade of green-gold color on the pads that it makes and sells to dry cleaning firms for use on dry cleaning presses. In 1989, respondent Jacobson Products (a Qualitex rival) began to sell its own press pads to dry cleaning firms; and it colored those pads a similar green-gold. In 1991, Qualitex registered the special green-gold color on press pads with the Patent and Trademark Office as a trademark. Registration No. 1,633,711 (Feb. 5, 1991). Qualitex subsequently added a trademark infringement count, 15 U.S.C. §1114(1), to an unfair competition claim, §1125(a), in a lawsuit it had already filed challenging Jacobson's use of the green-gold color.

Qualitex won the lawsuit in the District Court. 21 U.S.P.Q.2D (BNA) 1457 (CD Cal. 1991). But, the Court of Appeals for the Ninth Circuit set aside the judgment in Qualitex's favor on the trademark infringement claim because, in that Circuit's view, the Lanham Act does not permit Qualitex, or anyone else, to register "color alone" as a trademark. 13 F.3d 1297, 1300, 1302 (1994).

The Courts of Appeals have differed as to whether or not the law recognizes the use of color alone as a trademark. Compare *NutraSweet Co. v. Stadt Corp.*, 917 F.2d 1024, 1028 (CA7 1990) (absolute prohibition against protection of color alone), with *In re Owens-Corning Fiberglas Corp.*, 774 F.2d 1116, 1128 (CA Fed. 1985) (allowing registration of color pink for fiberglass insulation), and *Master Distributors, Inc. v. Pako Corp.*, 986 F.2d 219, 224 (CA8 1993) (declining to establish *per se* prohibition against protecting color alone as a trademark). Therefore, this Court granted certiorari. 512 U.S. 1287 (1994). We now hold that there is no rule absolutely barring the use of color alone, and we reverse the judgment of the Ninth Circuit.

II

* * *

True, a product's color is unlike "fanciful," "arbitrary," or "suggestive" words or designs, which almost automatically tell a customer that they refer to a brand. *Abercrombie & Fitch Co. v. Hunting World, Inc.*, 537 F.2d 4, 9–10 (CA2 1976) (Friendly, J.); *see Two Pesos, Inc. v. Taco Cabana, Inc.*, 505 U.S. 763, 768, 120 L. Ed. 2d 615, 112 S. Ct. 2753 (1992). The imaginary word "Suntost," or the words "Suntost Marmalade," on a jar of orange jam immediately would signal a brand or a product "source"; the jam's orange color does not do so. But, over time, customers may come to treat a particular color on a product or its packaging (say, a color that in context seems unusual, such as pink on a firm's insulating material or red on the head of a large industrial bolt) as signifying a brand. And, if so, that color would have come to identify and distinguish the goods—*i.e.*, "to indicate" their "source"—much in the way that descriptive words on a product (say, "Trim" on nail clippers or "Car-Freshner" on deodorizer) can come to indicate a product's origin. *See, e. g., J. Wiss & Sons Co. v. W. E. Bassett Co.*, 59 C.C.P.A. 1269, 1271, 462 F.2d 567 (Pat.), 462 F.2d 567, 569 (1972); *Car-Freshner Corp. v. Turtle Wax, Inc.*, 268 F. Supp. 162, 164 (SDNY 1967). In this circumstance, trademark law says that the word (e. g., "Trim"), although not inherently distinctive, has developed "secondary meaning." *See Inwood Laboratories, Inc. v. Ives Laboratories, Inc.*, 456 U.S. 844, 851, n. 11, 72 L. Ed. 2d 606, 102 S. Ct. 2182 (1982).

"Secondary meaning" is acquired when "in the minds of the public, the primary significance of a product feature ... is to identify the source of the product rather than the product itself"). Again, one might ask, if trademark law permits a descriptive word with secondary meaning to act as a mark, why would it not permit a color, under similar circumstances, to do the same?

We cannot find in the basic objectives of trademark law any obvious theoretical objection to the use of color alone as a trademark, where that color has attained "secondary meaning" and therefore identifies and distinguishes a particular brand (and thus indicates its "source"). In principle, trademark law, by preventing others from copying a source-identifying mark, "reduce[s] the customer's costs of shopping and making purchasing decisions," 1 J. McCarthy, McCarthy on Trademarks and Unfair Competition §2.01[2], p. 2–3 (3d ed. 1994) (hereinafter McCarthy), for it quickly and easily assures a potential customer that *this* item—the item with this mark—is made by the same producer as other similarly marked items that he or she liked (or disliked) in the past. At the same time, the law helps assure a producer that it (and not an imitating competitor) will reap the financial, reputation-related rewards associated with a desirable product. The law thereby "encourage[s] the production of quality products," *ibid.*, and simultaneously discourages those who hope to sell inferior products by capitalizing on a consumer's inability quickly to evaluate the quality of an item offered for sale. *See, e. g.*, 3 L. Altman, Callmann on Unfair Competition, Trademarks and Monopolies §17.03 (4th ed. 1983); Landes & Posner, The Economics of Trademark Law, 78 T. M. Rep. 267, 271–272 (1988); *Park 'N Fly, Inc. v. Dollar Park & Fly, Inc.*, 469 U.S. 189, 198, 83 L. Ed. 2d 582, 105 S. Ct. 658 (1985); S. Rep. No. 100-515, p. 4 (1988).

* * *

It would seem, then, that color alone, at least sometimes, can meet the basic legal requirements for use as a trademark. It can act as a symbol that distinguishes a firm's goods and identifies their source, without serving any other significant function. See U.S. Dept. of Commerce, Patent and Trademark Office, Trademark Manual of Examining Procedure §1202.04(e), p. 1202–13 (2d ed. May, 1993) (hereinafter PTO Manual) (approving trademark registration of color alone where it "has become distinctive of the applicant's goods in commerce," provided that "there is [no] competitive need for colors to remain available in the industry" and the color is not "functional"); see also 1 McCarthy §3.01[1], 7.26, pp. 3-2, 7-113.

("The requirements for qualification of a word or symbol as a trademark" are that it be (1) a "symbol," (2) "used ... as a mark," (3) "to identify and distinguish the seller's goods from goods made or sold by others," but that it not be "functional"). Indeed, the District Court, in this case, entered findings (accepted by the Ninth Circuit) that show Qualitex's green-gold press pad color has met these requirements. The green-gold color acts as a symbol. Having developed secondary meaning (for customers identified the green-gold color as Qualitex's), it identifies the press pads' source. And, the green-gold color serves no other function. (Although it is important to use *some* color on press pads to avoid noticeable stains, the court found "no competitive need in the press pad industry for the green-gold color, since other colors are equally usable." 21 U.S.P.Q.2D (BNA) at 1460.) Accordingly, unless there is some special reason that convincingly militates against the use of color alone as a trademark, trademark law would protect Qualitex's use of the green-gold color on its press pads.

III

Respondent Jacobson Products says that there are four special reasons why the law should forbid the use of color alone as a trademark. We shall explain, in turn, why we, ultimately, find them unpersuasive.

First, Jacobson says that, if the law permits the use of color as a trademark, it will produce uncertainty and unresolvable court disputes about what shades of a color a competitor may lawfully use. Because lighting (morning sun, twilight mist) will affect perceptions of protected color, competitors and courts will suffer from "shade confusion" as they try to decide whether use of a similar color on a similar product does, or does not, confuse customers and thereby infringe a trademark. Jacobson adds that the "shade confusion" problem is "more difficult" and "far different from" the "determination of the similarity of words or symbols." Brief for Respondent 22.

We do not believe, however, that color, in this respect, is special. Courts traditionally decide quite difficult questions about whether two words or phrases or symbols are sufficiently similar, in context, to confuse buyers.

* * *

We do not see why courts could not apply those standards to a color, replicating, if necessary, lighting conditions under which a colored product is normally sold. *See* Ebert, Trademark Protection in *Color: Do It By the Numbers!*, 84 T. M. Rep. 379, 405 (1994). Indeed, courts already have done so in cases where a trademark consists of a color plus a design, *i. e.*, a colored symbol such as a gold stripe (around a sewer pipe), a yellow strand of wire rope, or a "brilliant yellow" band (on ampules). *See, e. g., Youngstown Sheet & Tube Co. v. Tallman Conduit Co.*, 149 U.S.P.Q. (BNA) 656, 657 (TTAB 1966); *Amsted Industries, Inc. v. West Coast Wire Rope & Rigging Inc.*, 2 U.S.P.Q.2D (BNA) 1755, 1760 (TTAB 1987); *In re Hodes-Lange Corp.*, 167 U.S.P.Q. (BNA) 255, 256 (TTAB 1970).

Second, Jacobson argues, as have others, that colors are in limited supply. *See, e. g., NutraSweet Co.*, 917 F.2d at 1028; *Campbell Soup Co. v. Armour & Co.*, 175 F.2d 795, 798 (CA3 1949). Jacobson claims that, if one of many competitors can appropriate a particular color for use as a trademark, and each competitor then tries to do the same, the supply of colors will soon be depleted. Put in its strongest form, this argument would concede that "hundreds of color pigments are manufactured and thousands of colors can be obtained by mixing." L. Cheskin, Colors: What They Can Do For You 47 (1947). But, it would add that, in the context of a particular product, only some colors are usable. By the time one discards colors that, say, for reasons of customer appeal, are not usable, and adds the shades that competitors cannot use lest they risk infringing a similar, registered shade, then one is left with only a handful of possible colors. And, under these circumstances, to permit one, or a few, producers to use colors as trademarks will "deplete" the supply of usable colors to the point where a competitor's inability to find a suitable color will put that competitor at a significant disadvantage.

This argument is unpersuasive, however, largely because it relies on an occasional problem to justify a blanket prohibition. When a color serves as a mark, normally alternative colors will likely be available for similar use by others. *See, e. g., Owens-Corning*, 774 F.2d at 1121 (pink insulation). Moreover, if that is not so—if a "color depletion" or "color scarcity" problem does arise—the trademark doctrine of "functionality" normally would seem available to prevent the anticompetitive consequences that Jacobson's argument posits, thereby minimizing that argument's practical force.

The functionality doctrine, as we have said, forbids the use of a product's feature as a trademark where doing so will put a competitor at a significant disadvantage because the feature is "essential to the use or purpose of the article" or "affects [its] cost or quality." *Inwood Laboratories, Inc.*, 456 U.S. at 850, n. 10. The functionality doctrine thus protects competitors against a disadvantage (unrelated to recognition or reputation) that trademark protection might otherwise impose, namely their inability reasonably to replicate important non-reputation-related product features. For example, this Court has written that competitors might be free to copy the color of a medical pill where that color serves to identify the kind of medication (*e.g.*, a type of blood medicine) in addition to its source. And, the federal courts have demonstrated that they can apply this doctrine in a careful and reasoned manner, with sensitivity to the effect on competition. Although we need not comment on the merits of specific cases, we note that lower courts have permitted competitors to copy the green color of farm machinery (because customers wanted their farm equipment to match) and have barred the use of black as a trademark on outboard boat motors (because black has the special functional attributes of decreasing the apparent size of the motor and ensuring compatibility with many different boat colors) [citations omitted]. The Restatement (Third) of Unfair Competition adds that, if a design's "aesthetic value" lies in its ability to "confer a significant benefit that cannot practically be duplicated by the use of alternative designs," then the design is "functional." Restatement (Third) of Unfair Competition §17, Comment *c*, pp. 175–176 (1993). The "ultimate test of aesthetic functionality," it explains, "is whether the recognition of trademark rights would significantly hinder competition." *Id.*, at 176.

The upshot is that, where a color serves a significant nontrademark function—whether to distinguish a heart pill from a digestive medicine or to satisfy the "noble instinct for giving the right touch of beauty to common and necessary things," G. Chesterton, Simplicity and Tolstoy 61 (1912)—courts will examine whether its use as a mark would permit one competitor (or a group) to interfere with legitimate (nontrademark-related) competition through actual or potential exclusive use of an important product ingredient. That examination should not discourage firms from creating esthetically pleasing mark designs, for it is open to their competitors to do the same. *See, e. g., W. T. Rogers Co. v. Keene*, 778 F.2d 334, 343 (CA7 1985) (Posner, J.). But, ordinarily, it should prevent the anticompetitive consequences of Jacobson's hypothetical "color depletion" argument, when, and if, the circumstances of a particular case threaten "color depletion."

Third, Jacobson points to many older cases—including Supreme Court cases—in support of its position. In 1878, this Court described the common-law definition of trademark rather broadly to "consist of a name, symbol, figure, letter, form, or device, if adopted and used by a manufacturer or merchant in order to designate the goods he manufactures or sells to distinguish the same from those manufactured or sold by another." *McLean. v. Fleming*, 96 U.S. 245, 254, 24 L. Ed. 828. Yet, in interpreting the Trademark

Acts of 1881 and 1905, 21 Stat. 502, 33 Stat. 724, which retained that common-law definition, the Court questioned "whether mere color can constitute a valid trade-mark," *A. Leschen & Sons Rope Co. v. Broderick & Bascom Rope Co.*, 201 U.S. 166, 171, 50 L. Ed. 710, 26 S. Ct. 425 (1906), and suggested that the "product including the coloring matter is free to all who make it," *Coca-Cola Co. v. Koke Co. of America*, 254 U.S. 143, 147, 65 L. Ed. 189, 41 S. Ct. 113 (1920). Even though these statements amounted to dicta, lower courts interpreted them as forbidding protection for color alone. *See, e. g., Campbell Soup Co.*, 175 F.2d at 798, and n. 9; *Life Savers Corp. v. Curtiss Candy Co.*, 182 F.2d 4, 9 (CA7 1950) (*Campbell Soup, supra*, at 798).

These Supreme Court cases, however, interpreted trademark law as it existed *before* 1946, when Congress enacted the Lanham Act. The Lanham Act significantly changed and liberalized the common law to "dispense with mere technical prohibitions," S. Rep. No. 1333, 79th Cong., 2d Sess., 3 (1946), most notably, by permitting trademark registration of descriptive words (say, "U-Build-It" model airplanes) where they had acquired "secondary meaning." See *Abercrombie & Fitch Co.*, 537 F.2d at 9 (Friendly, J.). The Lanham Act extended protection to descriptive marks by making clear that (with certain explicit exceptions not relevant here) nothing ... shall prevent the registration of a mark used by the applicant which has become distinctive of the applicant's goods in commerce." 15 U.S.C. §1052(f) (1988 ed., Supp. V).

This language permits an ordinary word, normally used for a nontrademark purpose (*e.g.*, description), to act as a trademark where it has gained "secondary meaning." Its logic would appear to apply to color as well. Indeed, in 1985, the Federal Circuit considered the significance of the Lanham Act's changes as they related to color and held that trademark protection for color was consistent with the jurisprudence under the Lanham Act developed in accordance with the statutory principle that if a mark is capable of being or becoming distinctive of [the] applicant's goods in commerce, then it is capable of serving as a trademark." *Owens-Corning*, 774 F.2d at 1120.

In 1988, Congress amended the Lanham Act, revising portions of the definitional language, but left unchanged the language here relevant. §134, 102 Stat. 3946, 15 U.S.C. §1127. It enacted these amendments against the following background: (1) the Federal Circuit had decided Owens-Corning; (2) the Patent and Trademark Office had adopted a clear policy (which it still maintains) permitting registration of color as a trademark, see PTO Manual §1202.04(e) (at p. 1200-12 of the January 1986 edition and p. 1202-13 of the May 1993 edition); and (3) the Trademark Commission had written a report, which recommended that "the terms 'symbol, or device'... not be deleted or narrowed to preclude registration of such things as a color, shape, smell, sound, or configuration which functions as a mark," The United States Trademark Association Trademark Review Commission Report and Recommendations to USTA President and Board of Directors, 77 T. M. Rep. 375, 421 (1987); see also 133 Cong. Rec. 32812 (1987) (statement of Sen. DeConcini) ("The bill I am introducing today is based on the Commission's report and recommendations"). This background strongly suggests that the language "any word, name, symbol, or device," 15 U.S.C. §1127, had come to include color. And, when it amended the statute, Congress retained these terms. Indeed, the Senate Report accompanying the Lanham Act revision explicitly referred to this background understanding, in saying that the "revised definition intentionally retains ... the words 'symbol or device' so as not to preclude the registration of colors, shapes, sounds or configurations where they function as trademarks." S. Rep. No. 100-515, at 44. (In addition, the statute retained language providing that no trademark by which the goods of the applicant may be distinguished from the goods of others shall be refused registration ... on account of its nature" (except for certain specified reasons not relevant here). 15 U.S.C. §1052 (1988 ed., Supp. V).

This history undercuts the authority of the precedent on which Jacobson relies. Much of the pre-1985 case law rested on statements in Supreme Court opinions that interpreted pre-Lanham Act trademark law and were not directly related to the holdings in those cases. Moreover, we believe the Federal Circuit was right in 1985 when it found that the 1946 Lanham Act embodied crucial legal changes that liberalized the law to permit the use of color alone as a trademark (under appropriate circumstances). At a minimum, the Lanham Act's changes left the courts free to reevaluate the preexisting legal precedent which had absolutely forbidden the use of color alone as a trademark. Finally, when Congress reenacted the terms "word, name, symbol, or device" in 1988, it did so against a legal background in which those terms had come to include color, and its statutory revision embraced that understanding.

Fourth, *Jacobson* argues that there is no need to permit color alone to function as a trademark because a firm already may use color as part of a trademark, say, as a colored circle or colored letter or colored word, and may rely upon "trade dress" protection, under §43(a) of the Lanham Act, if a competitor copies its color and thereby causes consumer confusion regarding the overall appearance of the competing products or their packaging, see 15 U.S.C. §1125(a) (1988 ed., Supp. V). The first part of this argument begs the question. One can understand why a firm might find it difficult to place a usable symbol or word on a product (say, a large industrial bolt that customers normally see from a distance); and, in such instances, a firm might want to use color, pure and simple, instead of color as part of a design. Neither is the second portion of the argument convincing. Trademark law helps the holder of a mark in many ways that "trade dress" protection does not. See 15 U.S.C. §1124 (ability to prevent importation of confusingly similar goods); §1072 (constructive notice of ownership); §1065 (incontestible status); §1057(b) (prima facie evidence of validity and ownership). Thus, one can easily find reasons why the law might provide trademark protection in addition to trade dress protection.

IV

Having determined that a color may sometimes meet the basic legal requirements for use as a trademark and that respondent Jacobson's arguments do not justify a special legal rule preventing color alone from serving as a trademark (and, in light of the District Court's here undisputed findings that Qualitex's use of the green-gold color on its press pads meets the basic trademark requirements), we conclude that the Ninth Circuit erred in barring Qualitex's use of color as a trademark. For these reasons, the judgment of the Ninth Circuit is

Reversed.

Notes

1. The *Qualitex* decision seems to have finally put to rest whether or not color alone could act as an appellation of source. Prior to 1995, there was substantial disagreement among commentators and courts regarding this issue.

2. Austria joined the United States in 1997 in protecting color alone as trademarks even though the statute there has no provision for the registration of color trademarks. *See Manz'sche Verlags v. Linde Verlag, Entscheidungen des Handelsgerichtes* [HG Wien] [Court of Appeal] HS 4 R 185/97y (1997).

3. The Lance Armstrong Foundation sued a pet supply company for trademark infringement claiming that Armstrong had created trademark rights in a yellow band and words formed from the derivative "strong." Therefore, the Foundation claims that a yellow collar with "barkstrong" written on it or another yellow collar with "purrstrong" written on it is confusingly similar to the Foundation's yellow wrist bands which bear the words "Livestrong." Is the Foundation likely to prevail in its claim that yellow is a protectable color for bands (be they around the wrist or around a pet's neck)? What about Steven Cobert's creation of yellow "Wriststrong" bracelets? Would such use be considered parody as in *MCA v. Mattel* or *L.L. Bean v. Drake*? *See* Plaintiff's Original Complaint, *Lance Armstrong Found. v. Ohman*, No. A07CA-769SS (W.D. Tex. Sept. 11, 2007).

4. What is the outer limit of the scope of trademark protection in the United States? As long as an indicator of source identifies a producer, is there one? Should there be one? *See, In Re N.V. Organon*, 79 U.S.P.Q.2d 1639 (TTAB 2006) (Board rejects claims to orange flavoring for antidepressant medication tablet because the orange flavor performs a "functional part of our lives" and could never operate as a trademark). *See also*, Michael D. Hobbs, Jr., Orange Flavor is no Trademark: Trademark Trial and Appeal Board Finds it Functional; mark for Taste has yet to be Registered, National Law Journal, April 23, 2007, S1, col. 1.

Chapter IV

Infringement of the Trademark Right

A. Likelihood of Confusion

15 U.S.C. §1114 (Lanham Act §32)

(1) Any person who shall, without the consent of the registrant—

(a) use in commerce any reproduction, counterfeit, copy or colorable imitation of a registered mark in connection with the sale, ... shall be liable in a civil action by the registrant for the remedies hereinafter provided.

———————

The owner of a trademark has the exclusive right to use the mark in commerce. This right includes the right to use the mark itself on or in connection with identified goods or services as well as the right to license this right to third parties. The trademark holder, registrant, or first user may claim infringement when another individual or party attempts to use the mark or a similar mark without first procuring permission or a license.

In order to prevail under Section 32 of the Lanham Act and, for unregistered marks, under Section 43(a), the plaintiff must show there is a likelihood that the consumer will be confused, misled, or deceived regarding the source or origin of the goods or services. That is, the plaintiff must show only a *likelihood* of confusion and need not establish actual confusion. Likelihood of confusion is the central requirement in actions both at common law and under the federal trademark statute. While each circuit has adopted its own list of elements and tests for determining likelihood of confusion, they are remarkably similar. The Second Circuit's version, set out in 1961 in the *Polaroid* case excerpted below, is perhaps the most comprehensive and the most popular.

———————

Polaroid Corp. v. Polarad Elects. Corp.
287 F.2d 492 (2d Cir. 1961), cert. denied 368 US. 820 (1961)

FRIENDLY, CIRCUIT JUDGE.

Plaintiff, Polaroid Corporation, a Delaware corporation, owner of the trademark Polaroid and holder of 22 United States registrations thereof granted between 1936 and 1956 and of a New York registration granted in 1950, brought this action in the Eastern District of New York, alleging that defendant's use of the name Polarad as a trademark and as part of defendant's corporate title infringed plaintiff's Federal and state trademarks and constituted unfair competition. It sought a broad injunction and an accounting.

Defendant's answer, in addition to denying the allegations of the complaint, sought a declaratory judgment establishing defendant's right to use Polarad in the business in which defendant was engaged, an injunction against plaintiff's use of Polaroid in the television and electronics fields, and other relief. Judge Rayfiel, in an opinion reported in D.C. 1960, 182 F. Supp. 350, dismissed both the claim and the counterclaims, concluding that neither plaintiff nor defendant had made an adequate showing with respect to confusion and that both had been guilty of laches. Both parties appealed but defendant has withdrawn its cross-appeal. We find it unnecessary to pass upon Judge Rayfiel's conclusion that defendant's use of Polarad does not violate any of plaintiff's rights. For we agree that plaintiff's delay in proceeding against defendant bars plaintiff from relief so long as defendant's use of Polarad remains as far removed from plaintiff's primary fields of activity as it has been and still is.

The name Polaroid was first adopted by plaintiff's predecessor in 1935. It has been held to be a valid trademark as a coined or invented symbol and not to have lost its right to protection by becoming generic or descriptive, *Marks v. Polaroid Corp.*, D.C.D.Mass.1955, 129 F.Supp. 243. Polaroid had become a well known name as applied to sheet polarizing material and products made therefrom, as well as to optical desk lamps, stereoscopic viewers, etc., long before defendant was organized in 1944. During World War II, plaintiff's business greatly expanded, from $1,032,000 of gross sales in 1941 to $16,752,000 in 1945, due in large part to government contracts. Included in this government business were three sorts on which plaintiff particularly relies, the sale of Schmidt corrector plates, an optical lens used in television; research and development contracts for guided missiles and a machine gun trainer, both involving the application of electronics; and other research and development contracts for what plaintiff characterizes as 'electro-optical devices employing electronic circuitry in combination with optical apparatus.' In 1947 and 1948 plaintiff's sales declined to little more than their pre-war level; the tremendous expansion of plaintiff's business, reaching sales of $65,271,000 in 1958, came after the development of the Land camera in 1948.

Defendant was organized in December, 1944. Originally a partnership called Polarad Electronics Co., it was converted in 1948 into a New York corporation bearing the name Polarad Television Corp., which was changed a year later to Polarad Electronics Corp. Its principal business has been the sale of microwave generating, receiving and measuring devices and of television studio equipment. Defendant claimed it had arrived at the name Polarad by taking the first letters of the first and last names of its founder, Paul Odessey, and the first two letters of the first name of his friend and anticipated partner, Larry Jaffe, and adding the suffix 'rad,' intended to signify radio; however, Odessey admitted that at the time he had 'some knowledge' of plaintiff's use of the name Polaroid, although only as applied to glasses and polarizing filters and not as to electronics. As early as November, 1945, plaintiff learned of defendant; it drew a credit report and had one of its attorneys visit defendant's quarters, then two small rooms; plaintiff made no protest. By June, 1946, defendant was advertising television equipment in 'Electronics'—a trade journal. These advertisements and other notices with respect to defendant came to the attention of plaintiff's officers; still plaintiff did nothing. In 1950, a New York Attorney who represented plaintiff in foreign patent matters came upon a trade show display of defendant's television products under the name Polarad and informed plaintiff's house counsel; the latter advised plaintiff's president, Dr. Land, that 'the time had come when he thought we ought to think seriously about the problem.' However, nothing was done save to draw a further credit report on defendant, although defendant's sales had grown from a nominal amount to a rate of several hundred thousand dollars a year, and the report related, as had the previous one, that defendant was engaged 'in developing and manufacturing equipment for radio, television and electronic manufacturers throughout the United States.' In October, 1951, defendant, under its letterhead, forwarded to plaintiff a letter addressed to 'Polarad Electronics Corp.' at defendant's Brooklyn address, inquiring in regard to 'polaroid material designed for night driving'; there was no protest by plaintiff. In 1953, defendant applied to the United States Patent Office for registration of its trademark Polarad for radio and television units and other electronic devices; in August, 1955, when this application was published in the Official Gazette of the Patent Office, plaintiff for the first time took action by filing a notice of opposition, which was overruled by the Examiner in April, 1957. Still plaintiff delayed bringing suit until late 1956. Through all this period defendant was expending considerable sums for advertising and its business was growing—employees increasing from eight in the calendar year 1945 to 530 in the year ended June 30, 1956, fixed assets from $2,300 to $371,800, inventories from $3,000 to $1,547,400, and sales from $12,000 to $6,048,000.

Conceding that the bulk of its business is in optics and photography, lines not pursued by defendant, plaintiff nevertheless claims to be entitled to protection of its distinctive mark in at least certain portions of the large field of electronics. Plaintiff relies on its sales of Schmidt corrector plates, used in certain types of television systems, first under government contracts beginning in 1943 and to industry commencing in 1945; on its sale, since 1946, of polarizing television filters, which serve the same function as the color filters that defendant supplies as a part of the television apparatus sold by it; and, particularly, on the research and development contracts with the government referred to above. Plaintiff relies also on certain instances of confusion, predominantly communications intended for defendant but directed to plaintiff. Against this, defendant asserts that its business is the sale of complex electronics equipment to a relatively few customers; that this does not compete in any significant way with plaintiff's business, the bulk of which is now in articles destined for the ultimate consumer; that plaintiff's excursions into electronics are insignificant in the light of the size of the field; that the instances of confusion are minimal; that there is no evidence that plaintiff has suffered either through loss of customers or injury to reputation, since defendant has conducted its business with high standards; and that the very nature of defendant's business, sales to experienced industrial users and the government, precludes any substantial possibility of confusion. Defendant also asserts plaintiff's laches to be a bar.

The problem of determining how far a valid trademark shall be protected with respect to goods other than those to which its owner has applied it, has long been vexing and does not become easier of solution with the years. Neither of our recent decisions so heavily relied upon by the parties, *Harold F. Ritchie, Inc. v. Chesebrough-Pond's, Inc.*, 2 Cir., 1960, 281 F.2d 755, by plaintiff, and *Avon Shoe Co., Inc. v. David Crystal, Inc.*, 2 Cir., 1960, 279 F.2d 607 by defendant, affords much assistance, since in the Ritchie case there was confusion as to the identical product and the defendant in the *Avon* case had adopted its mark 'without knowledge of the plaintiff's prior use,' at page 611. Where the products are different, the prior owner's chance of success is a function of many variables: the strength of his mark, the degree of similarity between the two marks, the proximity of the products, the likelihood that the prior owner will bridge the gap, actual confusion, and the reciprocal of defendant's good faith in adopting its own mark, the quality of defendant's product, and the sophistication of the buyers. Even this extensive catalogue does not exhaust the possibilities—the court may have to take still other variables into account. American Law Institute, Restatement of Torts, §§729, 730,

731. Here plaintiff's mark is a strong one and the similarity between the two names is great, but the evidence of actual confusion, when analyzed, is not impressive. The filter seems to be the only case where defendant has sold, but not manufactured, a product serving a function similar to any of plaintiff's, and plaintiff's sales of this item have been highly irregular, varying, e.g., from $2,300 in 1953 to $303,000 in 1955, and $48,000 in 1956.[1]

If defendant's sole business were the manufacture and sale of microwave equipment, we should have little difficulty in approving the District Court's conclusion that there was no such likelihood of confusion as to bring into play either the Lanham Act, 15 U.S.C.A. §1114(1), or New York General Business Law, §368-b, or to make out a case of unfair competition under New York decisional law, *see Avon Shoe Co. v. David Crystal, Inc., id.,* at page 614, footnote 11. What gives us some pause is defendant's heavy involvement in a phase of electronics that lies closer to plaintiff's business, namely, television. Defendant makes must [sic] of the testimony of plaintiff's executive vice president that plaintiff's normal business is 'the interaction of light and matter.' Yet, although television lies predominantly in the area of electronics, it begins and ends with light waves. The record tells us that certain television uses were among the factors that first stimulated Dr. Land's interest in polarization, *see Marks v. Polaroid Corporation, id.,* 129 F.Supp. at page 246, plaintiff has manufactured and sold at least two products for use in television systems, and defendant's second counterclaim itself asserts likelihood of confusion in the television field. We are thus by no means sure that, under the views with respect to trademark protection announced by this Court in such cases as *Yale Electric Corp. v. Robertson,* 2 Cir., 1928, 26 F.2d 972 (locks vs. flashlights); *L.E. Waterman Co. v. Gordon,* 2 Cir., 1934, 72 F.2d 272 (mechanical pens and pencils vs. razor blades); *Triangle Publications, Inc. v. Rohrlich,* 2 Cir., 1948, 167 F.2d 969, 972 (magazines vs. girdles); and *Admiral Corp. v. Penco, Inc.,* 2 Cir., 1953, 203 F.2d 517 (radios, electric ranges and refrigerators vs. sewing machines and vacuum cleaners), plaintiff would not have been entitled to at least some injunctive relief if it had moved with reasonable promptness. However, we are not required to decide this since we uphold the District Court's conclusion with respect to laches.

[*The court affirmed the district court opinion.*]

Duluth News-Tribune v. Mesabi Publ. Co.
84 F.3d 1093 (8th Cir. 1996)

WOLLMAN, CIRCUIT JUDGE.

Duluth News-Tribune, a division of Northwest Publications, Inc., filed this trademark infringement action against Mesabi Publishing Company (Mesabi) and Hibbing Tribune Company, Inc., (Hibbing) under section 43(a) of the Lanham Trademark Act, 15 U.S.C. §1125(a) (1995) and under Minnesota Stat. §325.165 (1995). After considering cross-motions for summary judgment, the district court granted judgment in favor of defendants on all claims. We affirm.

---

1. Even the high figure, in 1955, amounted to little more than 1% Of plaintiff's business. Plaintiff also cites defendant's sale of bicycle headlights and other consumer products and defendant's patents for a radio automatic vehicle guidance system and an electronic auto headlight dimmer. However, the former business, conducted through a separate division, has been abandoned, and exploitation of the patents has not been instituted. Our decision is not to be understood as dealing with plaintiff's rights if defendant should resume, or begin, activity along any of these lines.

I. Background

For more than 100 years plaintiff has circulated a daily newspaper, the Duluth News-Tribune, in the Northeast region of Minnesota, which includes the distinct geographic area known as the Iron Range. Although the paper has always provided both national and regional news coverage, in 1992 plaintiff expanded the Iron Range edition to provide more local coverage.

From 1946 to the present, defendant Mesabi has published a daily newspaper, the "Mesabi Daily News," in Virginia, Minnesota, which is located in the eastern region of the Iron Range. Since 1899 defendant Hibbing has published a paper Sunday through Friday in Hibbing, Minnesota, in the western Iron Range. That paper, previously entitled the "Hibbing Daily Tribune," is now entitled simply the "Daily Tribune."

This controversy began when Mesabi and Hibbing, both subsidiaries of the Murphy Publishing Company, began a joint publication of a Saturday newspaper entitled the "Saturday Daily News Tribune," which they distributed throughout the Iron Range. On July 9, 1994, in response to plaintiff's complaints about the similarity in names between plaintiff's paper and the new Saturday paper, defendants added an ampersand between the words "News" and "Tribune."

Duluth News-Tribune, unsatisfied with this change, filed suit claiming trademark infringement under the Lanham Act ... The district court denied plaintiff's motion for a preliminary injunction and granted summary judgment in defendant's favor on all counts.

II. The Summary Judgment Standard

Summary judgment is proper when, after reviewing the facts in the light most favorable to the nonmovant and giving that party the benefit of all reasonable inferences to be drawn from the facts, the court finds that no genuine issue of material fact exists and that the moving party is entitled to judgment as a matter of law. On appeal we apply this standard de novo.

III. The Lanham Act: Likelihood of Confusion

To prevail under the Lanham Act, plaintiff must prove that defendants' use of the name "Saturday Daily News & Tribune" creates a likelihood of confusion, deception, or mistake among an appreciable number of ordinary buyers as to the source of or association between the two papers.

In determining whether a likelihood of confusion exists, we consider the following factors:1) the strength of the trademark; 2) the similarity between the parties' marks; 3) the competitive proximity of the parties' products; 4) the alleged infringer's intent to confuse; 5) evidence of actual confusion; and 6) the degree of care reasonably expected of potential customers. *Anheuser-Busch, Inc. v. Balducci Publications*, 28 F.3d 769, 774 (8th Cir. 1994), *cert. denied*, 130 L. Ed. 2d 787, 115 S. Ct. 903 (1995). These factors do not operate in a mathematically precise formula; rather, we use them at the summary judgment stage as a guide to determine whether a reasonable jury could find a likelihood of confusion. Factual disputes regarding a single factor are insufficient to support the reversal of summary judgment unless they tilt the entire balance in favor of such a finding. *See Squirtco v. Seven-Up Co.*, 628 F.2d 1086, 1091 (8th Cir. 1980) ("Resolution of [the likelihood of confusion] issue does not hinge on a single factor"). Accordingly, we will separately examine each factor with its corresponding relevant facts.

A. The Strength of the Trademark

As a preliminary matter, we must determine whether plaintiff's mark is strong enough to merit trademark protection. To do this, we must classify the mark, "Duluth News-Tribune," into one of four categories: 1) arbitrary or fanciful, 2) suggestive, 3) descriptive, or 4) generic. An arbitrary or fanciful trademark is the strongest type of mark and is afforded the highest level of protection. *Id.* at 486. At the other end of the spectrum, a generic term is one that is used by the general public to identify a category of goods, and as such merits no trademark protection. *See Miller Brewing Co. v. G. Heileman Brewing Co.*, 561 F.2d 75, 79–81 (7th Cir. 1977) (holding "Lite Beer" to be generic), *cert. denied*, 434 U.S. 1025, 54 L. Ed. 2d 772, 98 S. Ct. 751 (1978). Suggestive and descriptive marks fall somewhere in between. A suggestive mark is one that requires some measure of imagination to reach a conclusion regarding the nature of the product. *See American Home Products Corp. v. Johnson Chemical Co. Inc.*, 589 F.2d 103, 106 (2d Cir. 1978) (holding the mark "Roach Motel" to be suggestive because "while roaches may live in some motels against the will of the owners, motels are surely not built for roaches to live in"). A descriptive mark, on the other hand, immediately conveys the nature or function of the product and is entitled to protection only if it has become distinctive by acquiring a secondary meaning. *See 20th Century Wear, Inc. v. Sanmark-Stardust Inc.*, 747 F.2d 81, 87–88 (2d Cir. 1984) (finding "Cozy Warm ENERGY-SAVERS" to be descriptive), *cert. denied*, 470 U.S. 1052, 84 L. Ed. 2d 818, 105 S. Ct.1755 (1985).

We find that the district court properly classified plaintiff's mark, "Duluth News-Tribune," as descriptive. The words convey meaning too directly to be suggestive, yet are too specific to be generic. The name "Duluth News-Tribune" notifies the reader that the product is a Duluth newspaper, but is too specific to describe all newspapers, or even all Duluth newspapers. Viewing the facts in plaintiff's favor, we will also assume that the mark "Duluth News-Tribune" has acquired secondary meaning meriting trademark protection.[2]

Plaintiff attempts, however, to extend this protection beyond "Duluth News-Tribune," to the term "News-Tribune," on the theory that customers in the Iron Range refer to plaintiff's paper in shorthand form as the "News-Tribune." Plaintiff has offered no evidence sufficient to substantiate this claim. The only direct evidence of a customer's shorthand reference to the Duluth News-Tribune is from a customer who refers to the paper as "Duluth News." Moreover, the widespread use of the words "news" and "tribune" throughout the newspaper industry precludes plaintiff from claiming exclusive privilege to use these words. Thus, although the mark "Duluth News-Tribune" merits some level of protection, the shorthand "News-Tribune" merits none.

B. The Similarity between the Parties' Marks

Having determined that the relevant protected mark is "Duluth News-Tribune," we must consider the similarity between that mark and defendants' mark, "Saturday Daily News & Tribune." The use of dominant identical words in common does not mean that two marks are similar. *General Mills*, 824 F.2d at 627. Rather than consider the similarities between the component parts of the marks, we must evaluate the impression that each mark in its entirety is likely to have on a purchaser exercising the attention usually given by purchasers of such products. *Id.*

Although the marks are aurally similar, when pronounced in their entirety the word "Saturday" and the ampersand in defendants' paper make the two distinguishable. More-

---

2. We take judicial notice of plaintiff's recent registration of the trademark "Duluth News-Tribune."

over, several significant visual distinctions distinguish the two marks. First, in defendants' paper the words "news" and "tribune" appear on different lines; in plaintiff's paper the words "news" and "tribune"appear on the same line. Second, defendants' title appears in two colors, i.e., red and black; plaintiff's title appears all in black. In addition, the size and style of type used by the two papers differs. *Cf. Esquire, Inc. v. Esquire Slipper Manuf. Co., Inc.*, 243 F.2d 540, 542 (1st Cir. 1957) (giving weight to distinctive script in avoiding likelihood of confusion).

The most significant distinction, however, is the defendants' placement of a blue banner reading, "Publication of the Mesabi Daily News, Virginia and Daily Tribune, Hibbing" beneath the title. These distinctions appear to be sufficient to notify an ordinary customer that the papers originate from two different publishers.

C. The Competitive Proximity of the Parties' Products

Neither party contests that both papers provide regional and local news coverage and that they directly compete in the Iron Range; thus we need not further examine this factor.

D. The Alleged Infringer's Intent to Confuse

Plaintiff alleges bad faith on the part of defendants, pointing specifically to defendants' adoption of the mark "Saturday Daily News & Tribune" and simultaneous decision to expand the Saturday edition to provide regional news coverage shortly after plaintiff's paper extended regional coverage in its Iron Range edition. Plaintiff also points to the absence of a written agreement between Hibbing and Mesabi as evidence that defendants' "joint venture" explanation for the use of the words "Daily News & Tribune" is simply an excuse to infringe on plaintiff's mark.

We find these bare allegations to be unsupported by the record. The name "Saturday Daily News & Tribune" is a logical merger of the names "Daily News" and "Daily Tribune." The identification of defendants' paper as a joint publication appears on each individual paper. The paper's sales extend to cover both the area served by the Mesabi paper and that served by the Hibbing paper. The paper is sold in newsstands identified as belonging to either Hibbing or Mesabi,and through subscriptions to the Mesabi or Hibbing paper. Likewise, defendants announced the formation of the joint Saturday edition in each of their respective papers, clearly identifying the source of the Saturday edition. Moreover, after plaintiff's initial letter protesting the paper's name, defendants contacted the Minnesota Newspaper Association and accepted the Association's recommendation that defendants add an ampersand between the words "news" and "tribune." The record, then, reveals no evidence of bad faith on the part of defendants, leaving no genuine factual dispute regarding defendants' intent.

E. Evidence of Actual Confusion

"When determining whether there exists a likelihood of confusion, weight is given to the number and extent of instances of actual confusion." Life Technologies, Inc. v. Gibbco Scientific,Inc., 826 F.2d 775, 777 (8th Cir. 1987). Plaintiff points to the following incidents of actual confusion: 1) plaintiff's receipt of defendants' mail and phone calls; 2) a reporter who alleges that he routinely identifies himself as working for the News-Tribune, and that on a particular occasion he was asked, "which News-Tribune?"; 3) plaintiff's receipt of phone calls asking whether the two newspapers are associated; 4) plaintiff's receipt of a subscription form for defendants' paper; and 5) plaintiff's receipt of a reader's letter proposing corrections to an article that appeared in defendants' paper.

In evaluating the evidence at the summary judgment stage, we consider only those responses that are supported by admissible evidence. Applying this standard, we find that plaintiff's claim of actual confusion through misdirected mail and phone calls fails to raise a genuine factual dispute for two reasons. First, the vague evidence of misdirected phone calls and mail is hearsay of a particularly unreliable nature given the lack of an opportunity for cross-examination of the caller or sender regarding the reason for the "confusion." Second, we find such evidence to be de minimis and to show inattentiveness on the part of the caller or sender rather than actual confusion.

The question to the reporter who was asked to specify which News-Tribune he worked for indicates a distinction in the mind of the questioner, rather than confusion. The nature of the question demonstrates an understanding that at least two newspapers contain the words "news" and "tribune." Likewise, the calls questioning whether the two papers were associated demonstrate that potential customers do not automatically associate the words "news" and "tribune" with "Duluth News-Tribune."

Plaintiff next points to its receipt of a subscription form for defendants' paper. This evidence is of little value to plaintiff, as upon defendants' inquiry the sender clarified that she subscribed to both papers and had inadvertently placed the subscription forms in the wrong envelopes. Moreover, the fact that her check was made out to "Duluth News" cuts against plaintiff's claim of actual confusion.

Plaintiff offers one incident of actual confusion — a letter from a reader offering plaintiff editorial suggestions regarding an article that appeared in defendants' paper. Although this incident provides some support for plaintiff's claim of likelihood of confusion, even several isolated incidents of actual confusion that occur initially upon the creation of a potentially confusing mark are insufficient to establish a genuine issue of material fact as to the likelihood of confusion. Rather, we look to whether an appreciable number of ordinary purchasers are likely to be so misled, and here the record before us compels an answer in the negative.

F. The Degree of Care Reasonably Expected of Potential Customers

In evaluating this factor, we look to the degree of care expected of an ordinary purchaser. Plaintiff argues that because of the low cost of newspapers, ordinary buyers will exercise only minimal care in selecting one. Although plaintiff's argument is not without some force when applied to the customer who makes a quick stop at a convenience store to buy a paper, plaintiff ignores the reality of defendants' distribution methods. Approximately ninety-two percent of defendants' papers are sold through home subscriptions. Customers who spend the money and effort to subscribe to a newspaper are likely to know which paper they are buying, and to complain if they get the wrong one. Moreover, an additional two percent are sold through newspaper racks that clearly identify defendants as the paper's publication source. This leaves only six percent of papers sold as potential candidates for buyer confusion, a number too small to create a genuine issue of fact regarding the likelihood that an appreciable number of customers will be confused.

IV. The Appropriateness of Summary Judgment in this Case

When, as in this case, a trademark dispute centers on the proper interpretation to be given to the facts, rather than on the facts themselves, summary disposition is appropriate.

Our evaluation of the foregoing six factors leads us to conclude that no factual dispute exists the resolution of which would allow a reasonable jury to find a likelihood of confusion. Plaintiff's trademark, though deserving of some protection, is relatively weak.

Although the newspapers themselves compete directly and provide similar news coverage, the titles, as they appear on the two papers, are sufficiently distinct to allow an ordinary purchaser to distinguish between them. Moreover, the remaining factors balance in defendants' favor. We find no evidence that defendants chose their mark with the intent to infringe on plaintiff's goodwill. The evidence of actual confusion is de minimis and insufficient to establish a genuine issue of material fact. Finally, and most decisive, defendants' distribution methods ensure that the vast majority of ordinary purchasers will not be confused. Thus we affirm the district court's grant of summary judgment on the Lanham Act claims.

Note

1. What factors did the court in *Polaroid* choose *not* to include in its analysis? Why would it not consider them?

Vitarroz Corp. v. Borden, Inc.
644 F.2d 960 (2d Cir. 1981)

NEWMAN, J.

This is an appeal from a judgment of the District Court for the Southern District of New York (Gerard L. Goettel, Judge), dismissing after a bench trial a suit for trademark infringement. The issue on the merits is whether the District Court properly denied the plaintiff's request for an injunction, even though the marks of the plaintiff and defendant are virtually identical and their products share at least some competing uses. We conclude that the District Court was entitled to deny injunctive relief upon its consideration of all the relevant factors, including the balance of equities.

Facts

Plaintiff-appellant Vitarroz Corporation sells food products primarily in the New York-New Jersey metropolitan area to approximately 4,000 retail stores, one-half of which are small bodegas catering to a Spanish-speaking clientele. Vitarroz conducts its advertising in Spanish, and its name is well known in the Hispanic market. Its present volume of sales is approximately $17 million per year, 70–75% of which derives from the sale of rice.

In July 1976, Vitarroz decided to add an "all purpose cracker" to its line of food products under the name BRAVO'S. After selecting this name, Vitarroz conducted a trademark search for the name BRAVO. The search disclosed reported uses of BRAVO for a wide variety of food products, including macaroni, olives, spaghetti sauces, corned beef, roast beef, and cheese; state registrations of BRAVO for food and food ingredients, vegetable oil, olive oil, olives, and alcoholic beverages; and federal registrations of BRAVO for canned meat, vegetables, fish, spaghetti sauce, alimentary paste, powders for making soft drinks, and wines. Vitarroz previously had registered eight marks for some of its other products, but it did not file an application to register BRAVO'S for its crackers.

Vitarroz introduced its BRAVO'S crackers in November 1976. The crackers look and taste like Ritz crackers. They may be eaten plain, topped with a variety of spreads, served with hors d'oeuvres, or used as a scoop for dips. The crackers are packaged in a box. The

VITARROZ mark appears at the top of the face of the box in large letters. The BRAVO'S mark appears below the VITARROZ mark in smaller letters. The remainder of the face of the box is devoted to a realistic depiction of the crackers.

Vitarroz's expenses in introducing the crackers were approximately $13,000, a substantial part of which was spent on Spanish-language radio advertising during the period November 24, 1976, to February 27, 1977. Vitarroz has not advertised the product since February 1977. Its total sales of the product during the three and one-half years preceding the trial of this action were about $136,000.

Defendant-appellee Borden, Inc. is a New Jersey corporation having its principal places of business in Columbus, Ohio, and New York City. Borden's Snack Foods Group sells snack foods under the WISE trademark to independent distributors for resale to supermarkets and grocery stores throughout the Eastern United States. The Wise products usually are displayed in what was referred to as a store's "salty, crunchy snack food" section, often in a rack holding only Wise products.

Sometime in 1978, Borden decided to add a round tortilla chip to its line of Wise products under the name BRAVOS. Borden chose the name BRAVOS because of its suggestive meaning of approval and because it has a Mexican flavor, like the chips themselves. Before adopting the name, Borden conducted a trademark search, which disclosed essentially the same information turned up by Vitarroz, but did not disclose Vitarroz's unregistered BRAVO'S mark for crackers.

Borden introduced its BRAVOS tortilla chips in 1979. The tortilla chips resemble ordinary potato chips, though appearing to be slightly thicker. They may be eaten plain or used as a scoop for dips. The chips are packaged in a colorful cellophane bag through which they may be readily seen by the shopper. The bag is dominated by the name BRAVOS appearing at the top, with the BORDEN and WISE marks appearing less prominently, though still boldly, at the bottom. Like other Wise products, the chips usually are stocked in a store's "salty, crunchy snack food" section, often in the Wise rack. In some small stores, however, including some of the bodegas that carry Vitarroz's products, the chips may be found near Vitarroz's crackers.

Vitarroz became aware of the marketing of Borden's BRAVOS chips sometime prior to March 1979. In that month, it filed an application in the United States Patent and Trademark Office to register the BRAVO'S mark for crackers. This application and a similar application filed with New York State authorities were rejected due to federal and state registrations of BRAVO for a variety of other food products.

In May 1979, Vitarroz informed Borden of its use of the BRAVO'S mark on crackers, and proposed that Borden adopt a different mark. Borden replied that it already had spent in excess of $1.3 million in developing good will for its BRAVOS chips, without knowledge of Vitarroz's prior use of the BRAVO'S mark. Borden did not believe that the risk of consumer confusion was sufficiently grave to justify wasting this investment.

Since Borden's receipt of Vitarroz's objection, Borden has continuously advertised and promoted its BRAVOS chips. In 1979, its advertising and promotion costs exceeded.$2.5 million. In 1980, its marketing outlays rose to approximately $2.8 million. Borden's total sales of the product from the date of introduction to the time of trial were approximately $9 million.

Vitarroz commenced this suit in New York State Supreme Court for injunctive relief, claiming trademark infringement and unfair competition. The complaint did not specify whether these claims were based on state or federal law. A bench trial ensued.

The District Court first considered jurisdiction and concluded that jurisdiction existed because the suit could have been brought as an original action in federal court under §43(a) of the Lanham Act, 15 U.S.C. §1125(a) (1976). Proceeding to the merits, the Court recognized that the issue was whether Vitarroz had demonstrated a "likelihood" that, as a result of Borden's use of the name BRAVOS, "an appreciable number of ordinarily prudent purchasers are likely to be misled, or indeed simply confused, as to the source of the goods in question." Analyzing the likelihood of confusion in light of the factors enumerated in Polaroid Corporation v. Polarad Electronics Corp., 287 F.2d 492 (2d Cit.), cert. denied, 368 U.S. 820, 82 S. Ct. 36, 7 L. Ed. 2d 25 (1961), the Court found that Vitarroz's BRAVO'S mark is suggestive and has acquired no secondary meaning; that the BRAVO'S and BRAVOS marks, though nearly identical, are presented in different contexts; that"there is some proximity of the goods," in that they share "some areas of competing use"; that "probably no more than 10,000 persons" have purchased Vitarroz's BRAVO'S crackers, and probably "only half of them" purchased the crackers in stores that also stock the defendant's product; and that no actual consumer confusion had been shown. The Court also found that Vitarroz has no interest in bridging the gap and selling its own chips; that Borden's chips are of a very high quality; that Borden adopted the name BRAVOS in good faith, failing, after reasonable effort, to discover Vitarroz's prior use of the BRAVO'S mark only because Vitarroz had failed to register it; and that a grant of the requested injunction would cause Borden to lose most of its multi-million dollar investment in developing good will for its product.

In light of these findings, the District Court concluded that there is no likelihood of confusion as to the source of the goods, and that Borden's use of the name BRAVOS would, if anything, redound to Vitarroz's benefit. Weighing, on the one hand, the slight risk of harm to Vitarroz, and, on the other, Borden's good faith and substantial investment, the Court decided that the balance of equities tipped decidedly in Borden's favor. It therefore declined to enjoin Borden from using the BRAVOS name and dismissed the complaint.

Discussion

* * *

2. Turning to the merits of the infringement claim, we are confronted at the outset with Vitarroz's claim that, as the senior user of the BRAVO'S mark for its crackers, it was entitled as a matter of law to an injunction against Borden's use of the virtually identical name BRAVOS for its chips. Vitarroz concedes that this approach is contrary to the "now classic" analysis based on the Polaroid factors, *McGregor-Doniger Inc. v. Drizzle Inc.*, 599 F.2d 1126, 1130 (2d Cir. 1979), which calls for consideration of, among other things, the balance of equities. It contends, however, that consideration of the Polaroid factors is proper only when the products do not compete, on the theory that when products compete, failure to enjoin the junior user is tantamount to depriving the senior user of a property right without compensation.

The issue raised by Vitarroz's argument is not whether the Polaroid factors should be ignored entirely, as Vitarroz urges, for the Polaroid factors include the similarity of the marks and the "proximity" of the products, the very factors on which Vitarroz bases its asserted right to relief. *See* 287 F.2d at 495. The issue, rather, is whether we should confine our attention to these two factors, and take no account of the others, such as the strength of Vitarroz's BRAVO'S mark, the presence or absence of any evidence of actual confusion, the likelihood that Vitarroz will bridge whatever gap currently exists between the products, the defendant's good faith in adopting the name BRAVOS, and the balance of interests. Or, to put it another way, we must decide whether the full range of Polaroid-type factors may be considered when virtually identical marks are used on products that compete to some extent.

Equitable relief historically has not been available as a matter of right, but has been awarded in the court's discretion only upon consideration of all the facts and circumstances, *Hecht Co. v. Bowles*, 321 U.S. 321, 64 S. Ct. 587, 88 L. Ed. 754 (1944). Nevertheless, in the trademark context some support can be found for Vitarroz's argument that a plaintiff must prevail when it shows virtually identical marks used for competing products. In *Avon Shoe Co. v. David Crystal, Inc.*, 279 F.2d 607 (2d Cir.), *cert. denied*, 364 U.S. 909, 81 S. Ct. 271, 5 L. Ed. 2d 224 (1960), a case decided before Polaroid, we stated in dictum that when a junior user's product is "in competition" with a senior user's product, the senior user "may" have a right to "automatically enjoin" the junior user, even though the junior user has acted in good faith. 279 F.2d at 613. *See also Yale Electric Corp. v. Robertson*, 26 F.2d 972 (2d Cir. 1928). When Polaroid articulated a range of factors for determining a senior user's right to injunctive relief, it pointedly noted that such an approach was to be used "(w)here the products are different." 287 F.2d at 495 (emphasis added). In applying the Polaroid factors, we have consistently noted that they apply when the products are "non-competing." Our cases demonstrate, moreover, that the likelihood of confusion, the "crucial" issue in a case such as this often depends on the similarity of the marks and the proximity of the products. Thus, when a junior user has affixed a senior user's mark to "substantially identical products directed at the same market and sold through the same outlets," *id.*, we have found a likelihood of confusion as a matter of law.

In no case, however, have we determined a senior user's right to injunctive relief solely on the basis of the similarity of the marks and the proximity of the products. Our statement in the Avon case raising the possibility of such a restricted analysis rested on citation of *La Touraine Coffee Co. v. Lorraine Coffee Co.*, 157 F.2d 115 (2d Cir.), *cert. denied*, 329 U.S. 771, 67 S. Ct. 189, 91 L. Ed. 663 (1946), but in that case the majority weighed the defendant's interest in avoiding an injunction, 157 F.2d at 119, and stressed the defendant's bad faith, *id.* at 118. Such a flexible approach also is evident in our other pre-Polaroid decisions. Even in Avon the Court considered the balance of equities in concluding that the senior user was not entitled to relief. *See* 279 F.2d at 614.

Since the Polaroid decision, we have consistently considered all the Polaroid factors, including the junior user's good faith, despite the similarity of the marks and the close proximity of the products.

Vitarroz argues that the products in this case are more closely related than the products in our prior cases. It is difficult to see, however, how crackers and chips are more closely related than two different brands of insect traps, or men's cream hair dressings, or coffees. Nor do they appear to be more closely related than women's footwear and sportswear, or pantyhose and tights. Analysis of the proximity of the products demonstrates, moreover, that the competitive gap between them is not so narrow as to leave no room for consideration of other factors.

In assessing product proximity, we have considered the nature of the products themselves and the structure of the relevant market. Taking these criteria in turn, we note that the products in this case differ in ways that may be deemed material to consumers. Although both are snack foods that can be eaten plain or used as a scoop for dips, only the crackers are ordinarily buttered or served with hors d'oeuvres. In addition, the ingredients of the products are markedly different. The crackers are flour-based and essentially bland, while the chips are corn-based, heavily salted, and spicy. The products also differ in the ways they are prepared; the crackers are baked, but the chips are fried.

With regard to the structure of the market, both products are eventually sold to consumers in retail stores. However, since "modern marketing methods tend to unify widely different types of products in the same retail outlets or distribution networks," *Continental Connector Corp. v. Continental Specialties Corp., Id.*, 492 F. Supp. at 1096, this factor is not of overriding importance. Within retail food stores, the record shows that the products are shelved in different sections whenever space permits, the crackers in the "cookies and crackers" section, and the chips in the section for "salty, crunchy snacks." More important, the record shows that Vitarroz targets its product at a distinct group of consumers, who shop for the Vitarroz name in specialty stores, many of which do not carry Borden's chips. This factor is entitled to some weight, just like the analogous factor of the sophistication of the relevant purchasers.

The plaintiff's per se rule based on the similarity of the marks and the competition between the products could be justified only if we could say with reasonable certainty that injury to the plaintiff is inevitable. The Lanham Act protects the plaintiff against three types of injury: loss of patronage, loss of reputation, and limitation on business expansion. Injury of this kind might be inevitable when the marks and products are practically identical and the products are interchangeable for all or at least all significant uses. But that is not this case. When, as here, the products differ in non-trivial respects and share only "some areas of competing use," and the trier has found no significant risk of injury to the senior user, the merits may be "close" and "vexing," *Mushroom Makers, Inc. v. R. G. Barry Corp., id.*, 580 F.2d at 48, but that circumstance only underscores the need for comprehensive analysis of all the relevant facts and circumstances.

We therefore agree with the District Court's comprehensive approach [and affirm.]

Judgment affirmed.

Borinquen Biscuit Corp. v. M. V. Trading Corp.
443 F.3d 112 (1st Cir 2006)

SEYLA, J.

I. BACKGROUND

Borinquen is a manufacturer and distributor of "galletas." "Galleta" (or, in the plural, "galletas") encompasses all types of crackers, cookies, and biscuits. Since 1976, Borinquen has sold a round, yellowish, semi-sweet galleta in Puerto Rico under the federally registered trademark "RICA." The federal registration states that "the Spanish word 'Rica' may be translated as 'rich.'"

Borinquen's "RICA" has always borne a logo that consists of a red circle encompassing the white-lettered phrase "Galletas RICA Sunland." Borinquen registered both the mark "RICA" and the product's logo with the Puerto Rico Department of State in 2000. It currently sells the product in predominately red-and-white packaging, with the circular logo centered against a background consisting of rows of the galletas.

The tectonic plates shifted in April of 2003, when M.V. began selling a round, yellowish, salty galleta bearing the name "Nestle Ricas." The product logo consists of a white oval with the name "Ricas" centered in red letters and with a red square in the upper right-hand corner of the oval bearing the white-lettered brand name "Nestle." M.V.'s packaging is mostly red and white, albeit with some yellow and blue design. The logo is centered in the upper half of the box against a background of scattered galletas.

In or around the summer of 2004, Borinquen learned that M.V. was marketing Nestle Ricas in earnest. Since both parties' galletas were being sold in Puerto Rican supermarkets and convenience stores, this was a matter of considerable concern. Borinquen informed M.V. that it believed M.V.'s distribution of galletas under the name "Ricas" infringed its registered trademark and asked M.V. to cease and desist.

II. ANALYSIS
B. Likelihood of Success.

2. Consumer Confusion. M.V.'s remaining assignment of error attacks the district court's determination that its use of the "Nestle Ricas" mark was likely to cause consumer confusion. This court has enumerated eight factors to guide the inquiry into likelihood of confusion:

> (1) the similarity of the marks; (2) the similarity of the goods; (3) the relationship between the parties' channels of trade; (4) the relationship between the parties' advertising;(5) the classes of prospective purchasers; (6) evidence of actual confusion; (7) the defendant's intent in adopting its mark; and (8) the strength of the plaintiff's mark.

Astra Pharm. Prods., Inc. v. Beckman Instruments, Inc., 718 F.2d 1201, 1205 (1st Cir. 1983); accord *Pignons S.A. de Mecanique de Precision v. Polaroid Corp.*, 657 F.2d 482, 487 (1st Cir. 1981). A proper analysis takes cognizance of all eight factors but assigns no single factor dispositive weight. *Keds*, 888 F.2d at 222; *Volkswagenwerk*, 814 F.2d at 817. Because likelihood of confusion is a fact bound inquiry, appellate review of a trial-level finding on that issue is for clear error. *Keds*, 888 F.2d at 222.

The court below applied the eight-factor screen and concluded that, on the whole, the evidence preponderated in favor of a finding that M.V.'s use of its mark in Puerto Rico was likely to result in consumer confusion. This conclusion was predicated on a measured view of the evidence. On the one hand, the court noted that the parties' goods were dissimilar, that no actual confusion had been shown, and that no evidence existed that M.V. intended to mislead consumers. On the other hand, the court found that the remaining factors all tended to favor a likelihood of confusion. The court then performed the necessary balancing and determined that the latter points outweighed the former.

M.V. assails this determination, arguing that the court misapplied the eight-factor test in two principal ways: by underestimating the significance of Borinquen's failure to present a consumer survey designed to show actual confusion and by deeming "RICA" a strong mark. After careful perscrutation of the record, we reject both arguments.

To begin, a trademark holder's burden is to show likelihood of confusion, not actual confusion. While evidence of actual confusion is "often deemed the best evidence of possible future confusion," *Attrezzi, LLC v. Maytag Corp.*, 436 F.3d 32, 40 (1st Cir. 2006), proof of actual confusion is not essential to finding likelihood of confusion. *See Volkswagenwerk*, 814 F.2d at 818; *see also Pignons*, 657 F.2d at 490.

Historically, we have attached substantial weight to a trademark holder's failure to prove actual confusion only in instances in which the relevant products have coexisted on the market for a long period of time. *See, e.g., Aktiebolaget Electrolux v. Armatron Int'l, Inc.*, 999 F.2d 1, 4 (1st Cir. 1993). This is not such a case: M.V.'s product was introduced to the Puerto Rican market in April of 2003, and M.V.'s own evidence suggests that sales did not proliferate until the summer of 2004. This corresponds to the time frame in which Borinquen discovered the presence of Nestle Ricas and took action to protect its mark. Since the preliminary injunction issued just over a year later, there was no protracted period of product coexistence. Nor is there any other compelling reason why, in this case, survey evidence should be required at the preliminary injunction stage. We hold, therefore, that while survey evidence would have been helpful, it was not indispensable to a finding of likelihood of confusion. *See id.*; *see also Volkswagenwerk*, 814 F.2d at 818.

In much the same vein, the court did not clearly err in determining that "RICA" is a relatively strong mark. Various factors are relevant in ascertaining the strength of a trademark, including the length of time the mark has been used, the trademark holder's renown in the industry, the potency of the mark in the product field (as measured by the number of similar registered marks),and the trademark holder's efforts to promote and protect the mark. *See Boston Athletic Ass 'n*, 867 F.2d at 32; *see also Keds*, 888 F.2d at 222. In assessing the strength of Borinquen's mark, the district court found that the mark had been registered for more than three decades; that Borinquen's "RICA" was the only cookie, cracker, or biscuit trademarked under that name in the United States; and that Borinquen's efforts in promoting and protecting its mark were in conformance with industry standards. These three findings, all of which are supported by substantial evidence in the record, furnish ample grounding for the court's conclusion that "RICA" should be considered a strong mark.

To say more on this issue would be supererogatory. The short of it is that we discern no clear error in the findings of fact underlying the district court's determination that Borinquen has a better-than-even chance of succeeding in establishing a likelihood of consumer confusion.

Notes

1. Notice that this dispute occurred in Puerto Rico. Section 1127 defines the United States as "include[ing] and embrac[ing] all territory which is under its jurisdiction and control." 15 USC §1127. Puerto Rico is one of the United States territories, as are American Samoa, Federal States of Micronesia, Guam, US Virgin Islands, and several others. For a complete list of US territories, *see* http://www.lib.uconn.edu/online/research/govtinfo/ConnState/territ.html.

2. The Lanham Act does not set out the exact parameters of "infringement." The test for infringement, therefore, is a judicial construction. As such, although all circuit courts of appeal use the term "likelihood of confusion" and follow a test rather similar to the one articulated above in the Polaroid case, the circuits use inconsistent language when describing the factors that should be considered in determining a likelihood of confusion. The unanswered question is to what extent this inconsistent language leads to inconsistent results when adjudicating infringement claims.

The Polaroid case sets out the following eight, non-exclusive factors:

1. The strength of the plaintiff's mark;
2. The degree of similarity between the plaintiff's and the defendant's marks;
3. The proximity of the products or services;
4. The likelihood that the plaintiff will bridge the gap;

5. Evidence of actual confusion;

6. Defendant's good faith in adopting the mark;

7. The quality of defendant's goods or services;

8. The sophistication of the buyers.

Although "the Polaroid test" is technically only applicable in the Second Circuit, it has gained fame as the most popular test nation-wide. All other circuits use a multi-factor test to determine if infringement has occurred; however, each circuit's wording of the test differs slightly in terms but not in meaning. Furthermore, the Polaroid analysis is not a "mechanical measurement.... [the] court should focus on the ultimate question of whether consumers are likely to be confused." *Nora Beverages, Inc. v. Perrier Group of Am., Inc.*, 269 F.3d 114, 119 (2d Cir. 2001). That being said, some courts find it error if the district court does not consider any of the factors in analyzing infringement. *See, e.g., Acme Pad Corp. v. Warm Prods.*, Inc. 26 Fed. Appx. 271(4th Cir. 2002) (unpublished opinion).

3. Prior to the amendments of the Lanham Act that took effect on January 1, 1996, the term "likelihood of confusion" did not appear in the Act whatsoever. In the two places the term was added(in Section 43(c) regarding dilution and in Section 45 in a definition section regarding cyber squatting), the Lanham Act only refers to infringement as a matter of fact without providing any definition. Why would Congress leave such an important element of the Act to judicial construction?

4. In the *News-Tribune* case, the court implies that when the defendant adds the words "Publication of the Mesabi Daily News, Virginia and Daily Tribune, Hibbing" in a banner on top of its newspaper, consumers would be less likely to be confused; this is known as a "disclaimer." Disclaimers come up throughout these materials in a variety of settings. Some courts and scholars find disclaimers to be effective; some do not. *See, e.g.,* Jacob Jacoby & Robert Lloyd Raskopf, *Disclaimers in Trademark Infringement Litigation: More Trouble Than They Are Worth?*, 76 TRADEMARK REP. 35 (1986) (arguing that disclaimer ineffective to guard against consumer confusion); Jacob Jacoby & Maureen Mon-in, *"Not Manufactured or Authorized By ...": Recent Federal Cases Involving Trademark Disclaimers,* 17 J. PUB. POL'Y & MARKETING 97 (1998); Scott Shipman, Comment: *Trademark and Unfair Competition in Cyberspace: Can These Laws Deter "Baiting" Practices on Web Sites?,* 39 SANTA CLARA L. REV. 245 (1998) (arguing that disclaimers can be effective). Is the disclaimer in *News-Tribune* effective? Could it be improved? Should the court order that its opinion is contingent upon the continued use of the disclaimer? If you drafted the disclaimer in this case, how would it read?

5. *Disclaimers.* Disclaimers are often used in trademark litigation. In a typical disclaimer, the defendant agrees to place language on the product indicating that the good does not emanate from the plaintiff. Disclaimers are covered in some detail in Chapter 14 B under remedies.

6. *Initial interest confusion.* Initial interest confusion occurs in a "bait and switch" type of situation where the defendant intentionally uses the plaintiff's mark or a similar mark even though, once the consumer is in the store, it becomes obvious that the plaintiff and the defendant are not related. Initial interest confusion is now a popular consideration in domain name cases. *See infra* Chapter 12. However, initial interest confusion is most often only applied when the competitors are directly or very closely interrelated. *See Checkpoint SYS., Inc. v. Check Point Software Tech., Inc.*, 269F.3d 270 (3d Cir. 2001).

B. Relevant Consuming Public

Mastercrafters Clock& Radio Co. v.
Vacheron & Constantin — Le Coultre Watches, Inc.
221 F.2d 464 (2d Cir.), cert denied, 350 US. 832 (1955)

FRANK, CIRCUIT JUDGE.

Mastercrafters Clock & Radio Co., the plaintiff below, is an American manufacturer of electric clocks. Vacheron & Constantin-Le Coultre Watches, Inc. (hereinafter referred to as 'Vacheron'), defendant-counter claimant, is an American importer and distributor of Swiss watches.Jaeger-Le Coultre, S.A., intervenor-counter claimant, is a Swiss corporation engaged in selling Swiss-manufactured watches.

In 1952, when Mastercrafters launched the production and distribution of its Model 308 clock, Vacheron wired Mastercrafters and many of its customers-distributors that Model 308 was a counterfeit of the distinctive appearance and configuration of the Atmos clock, distributed by Vacheron, and that Vacheron would commence legal action if necessary. Following these telegrams, Vacheron started state-court suits against several of Mastercrafters' distributors for damages and an injunction. Mastercrafters, faced with a cancellation of orders for its Model 308 from distributors being sued in the state courts, countered by bringing the present action seeking a declaratory judgment that its Model 308 does not unfairly compete with Vacheron, and asking damages allegedly resulting from Vacheron's suits against Mastercrafters' distributors and an injunction to restrain further prosecution of those suits. Vacheron counterclaimed for damages from alleged unfair competition and for an injunction restraining the manufacture and distribution of Model 308. Jaeger-Le Coultre was permitted to intervene and join in Vacheron's counterclaim. The facts are more fully stated in the opinion of the trial judge, reported in 119 F.Supp. 209. Pursuant to that opinion, he entered an order in favor of plaintiff and dismissing the counterclaims. From this order, defendant and the intervenor have appealed. After a further hearing as to the amount of plaintiff's damage, he subsequently entered a judgment granting plaintiff damages in the amount of $4,844. From this judgment plaintiff has appealed, complaining of the insufficiency of the amount of damages awarded.

The judge found that, before plaintiff began production of its Model 308, the Atmos clock 'was readily distinguishable from all other clocks then on the market by virtue of its appearance'; that plaintiff's Model 308 copied that appearance; that plaintiff 'undoubtedly intended to, and did, avail itself of an eye-catching design and hoped to cater to the price-conscious purchaser who desires to own a copy of a luxury design clock regardless of mechanism or source'; that the Atmos clock sold for not less than $175, while plaintiff's sold for $30 or $40; that on 'two or three occasions Model 308 has been described as "a copy of Atmos," once by a representative of plaintiff at an exhibit in Chicago, on the other occasions by distributors of plaintiff's clock; that 'since the introduction of the Model 308, Vacheron's salesmen have encountered considerable sales resistance and its sales have "fallen off"; and that these facts undoubtedly prove 'the uniqueness and even the aesthetic qualities of the Atmos clock. He further found that three customers inquired as to "the lower priced Atmos" and that others said they knew where they "could get a clock for $30 or $40 just like the Atmos." But he held there was no unfair competition by plaintiff because (a) more than one person lawfully distributed the Atmos clock and therefore there was no single source, (b) there was no evidence to show that the public cared

Picture 4.1   Jaeger-Le Coultre Atmos Clock
[Copyright 1999. Used by permission of Mark Headuck,
http://www.geocites.comlCapeCanaverallHall/3934/lecoultre.html, figure 22.]

what was the ultimate source, and (c) plaintiff's clock was plainly marked and advertised as plaintiff's.

Absent a design patent or a secondary meaning, of course there would be no actionable harm by plaintiff. But the existence of a secondary meaning, attaching to the unique appearance of the Atmos clock, is not precluded by the mere fact that more than one person distributed that clock in the same area. The actionable harm, in a secondary-meaning case, may result either from the likelihood (a) of loss of customers or (b) of loss of reputation, or (c) of both. Such loss can result from the customer's belief that the competing article derives from the same source as that of the party complaining; and it matters not whether the customers know just who is the source. The ultimate source here was the Swiss manufacturer, while the intermediate sources, in this country, were the defendant and Cartier. All three had actionable claims against plaintiff, if its conduct did or was likely to injure the reputation of the ultimate source of the Atmos clock, for all three legitimately enjoyed the benefits of that reputation.

True, a customer examining plaintiff's clock would see from the electric cord, that it was not an 'atmospheric' clock. But, as the judge found, plaintiff copied the design of the Atmos clock because plaintiff intended to, and did, attract purchasers who wanted a "luxury design" clock. This goes to show at least that some customers would buy plaintiff's cheaper clock for the purpose of acquiring the prestige gained by displaying what many visitors at the customers' homes would regard as a prestigious article. Plaintiff's wrong thus consisted of the fact that such a visitor would be likely to assume that the clock was an Atmos clock. Neither the electric cord attached to, nor the plaintiff's name on, its clock would be likely to come to the attention of such a visitor; the likelihood of such confusion suffices to render plaintiff's conduct actionable.

Plaintiff's intention thus to reap financial benefits from poaching on the reputation of the Atmos clock is of major importance. Of course, where there is no likelihood of confusion—as, e.g., where the alleged infringing article is not in a sufficiently adjacent field—then an alleged infringer's intent becomes irrelevant, since an intent to do a wrong cannot transmute a lawful into an unlawful act. But where the copying is unlawful, if only there is a likelihood of confusion, then the intent of the copier becomes decidedly relevant: It gives rise to a powerful inference that confusion is likely, and puts on the alleged infringer the burden of going forward with proof that it is not. Here the plaintiff's intent is unmistakable; accordingly, plaintiff had the burden of going forward with proof showing an absence of such likelihood; and that burden plaintiff did not discharge. Consequently, we do not accept the judge's findings as to the absence of unfair competition by plaintiff.

It would seem that the Swiss manufacturer was not an indispensable party; but, even if it was, plaintiff waived its absence as a party by not asserting that fact as a defense. We reject plaintiff's argument that it will be unfair to plaintiff to hold it liable here, because it may be subjected to a subsequent suit by Cartier: Defendant and the intervenor are entitled to an injunction, and also to the damages they have suffered; we need not now decide whether Cartier can also later collect damages for the harm done to it.

Since plaintiff was guilty of unfair competition, the judgment against defendant must be reversed. We remand with directions to dismiss plaintiff's complaint and, on the counterclaim, to grant an injunction against plaintiff, and to ascertain the damages to defendant and the intervenor.

The trial judge should determine whether defendant should also be awarded a sum equal to plaintiff's profits from sales of the infringing clock. We do not now decide that such an amount should be awarded but leave that matter to be decided, in the first instance at any rate, by the trial judge.

Reversed and remanded.

Munsingwear, Inc. v. Jockey International

31 U. S. P. Q. 2d 1146 (D. Minn.), aff'd, 39 F. 3d 1184 (8th Cir. 1994)

DOTY, DISTRICT JUDGE.

This matter is before the court on plaintiff Munsingwear's motion for a preliminary injunction and defendant Jockey's motion for summary judgment. Based on a review of the file, record, and proceedings herein, the court grants Jockey's motion and denies Munsingwear' s motion.

BACKGROUND

This matter involves the marketing of a horizontal-fly version of mens' underwear by Jockey. Jockey first introduced its horizontal-fly[3] briefs under the "Jockey Pouch" ("Pouch") name in June 1992. The Pouch line consisted of briefs with the horizontal-fly and the "JOCKEY" trademark woven into the waistband. They were sold through Jockey's standard lines of commerce. The packaging consisted of standard cellophane wrapped around the brief with the "JOCKEY" trademark and Jockey Design trademark on both the front and back of the packaging.

Munsingwear instituted this action against Jockey claiming trademark infringement under §43(a) of the Lanham Act, common law trademark infringement, and deceptive trade practices. Munsingwear based these claims on its alleged preexisting trademark rights in the horizontal-fly (or H-FLY) mark. While not having actual federal registration of the H-FLY, Munsingwear claims it is entitled to protection based upon its continuous use of the design since 1946, reinforced by millions of dollars of advertising.

----

3. A horizontal-fly is exactly as it is described. Rather than running vertical, or parallel with the leg, the horizontal-fly is perpendicular to the leg and looks generally like a pocket.

Munsingwear now moves for a preliminary injunction to prevent Jockey from manufacturing, distributing and selling Pouch underwear. Jockey moves for summary judgment claiming that there is no likelihood of confusion between the two manufacturers' underwear as a matter of law.

DISCUSSION
1. Jockey's Motion for Summary Judgment

* * *

To ultimately prevail, Munsingwear must show that its "H-Fly": (1) is nonfunctional; (2) is either inherently distinctive or has acquired a secondary meaning; and (3) Jockey's product is likely to be confused with Munsingwear's product by members of the consuming public. Two Pesos, 112 S. Ct. at 2758. In its motion for summary judgment, Jockey does not contest Munsingwear's claims as to the first and second elements but only contests the third element claiming that there is no likelihood of confusion between the competing products.

Likelihood of confusion is a material fact, an essential element of a §43(a) infringement action. Woodsmith Pub. Co. v. Meredith Corp., 904 F.2d 1244, 1248 (8th Cir. 1990). Any legal conclusion is usually based on underlying findings of fact. Olde Tyme Foods, Inc. v. Roundy's Inc., 961 F.2d 200, 202 (Fed. Cir. 1992). While there is no litmus test that can provide a ready guide to all cases, Application of E.I. DuPont De Nemours & Co., 476 F.2d 1357, 1361 (Cust. & Pat. App. 1973), ultimately the court must be satisfied that substantial numbers of customers are likely to be confused. General Mills, Inc. v. Kellogg Co., 824 F.2d 622, 626 (8th Cir. 1987). Such a determination is based on examination of "all pertinent factors" including both the characteristics of the mark and also the distinguishing differences or indistinguishable similarities of the goods themselves. These differences or similarities include the form, composition, texture and quality and the manner in which the products are advertised, displayed, sold and used. Mutual of Omaha Ins. Co. v. Novak, 836 F.2d 397, 399 n.3 (8th Cir. 1987).

The Eighth Circuit has established a six factor analysis to test the likelihood of customer confusion in Squirtco v. Seven-Up Co., 628 F.2d 1086 (8th Cir. 1980). The six factors are: (1) product similarity; (2) competitive proximity; (3) intent to pass off; (4) actual confusion; (5) survey evidence; and (6) cost and conditions of purchase. Squirtco, 628 F.2d at 1090–91. In deciding whether there is a likelihood of confusion, "each factor must be considered and excessive weight should not be given to any one factor at the exclusion of others." Life Technologies, Inc. v. Gibbco Scientific, Inc., 826 F.2d 775, 776 (8th Cir. 1987). The decision as to infringement in each case turns on its own unique facts. ConAgra, 990 F.2d at 371.

Before undertaking the six factor Squirtco analysis, the court must initially determine which products are to be compared. In this action two alternatives exist, either the pre-sale or post-sale product. The pre-sale product consists of the underwear as packaged and sold to the consuming public, seen in Figures 1 and 2 of Jockey's motion for summary judgment. The post-sale product consists of the actual individual briefs themselves, seen in Figures 1 and 2 of Munsingwear's motion for preliminary injunction. Determination of which products are to be compared is made by referring to how consumers[4]

---

4. "In applying the principles of trademark law, courts often refer to 'the consumer,' much like the reference to 'the reasonable person' in resolving questions of tort law." Calvin Klein Cosmetics Corp. v. Parfums de Coeur, 824 F.2d 665, 669 (8th Cir. 1987).

will encounter the two products. *Lindy Pen Co., Inc. v. Bic Pen Corp.*, 725 F.2d 1240 (9th Cir. 1984) (Similarity of marks considered in light of the way they are encountered in the marketplace and the circumstances surrounding their purchase.)

Jockey contends that the overall combination and arrangement of the package design elements, the pre-sale product, should serve as the basis of analysis. Evidence submitted in support of that contention shows that underwear is purchased in single or multi-unit cellophane wrapped packages that indicate source and style information.

Munsingwear claims that, while the products are purchased as packaged, consumers base their buying decision on other factors. Among those cited are the consumer's desire for certain styles and purchase place exposure to the product while it is on mannequins. Munsingwear contends that the combination of the two factors often leads to the subsequent purchasing decision and thus likelihood of customer confusion. Munsingwear equates this display technique to post-sale exposure which serves as the basis for its argument that consumers will be confused.

The courts that have decided the question have split as to whether pre-sale products or post-sale product provide the proper basis for analysis. The Eighth Circuit has not yet ruled on this issue. On the facts of this case, the argument for pre-sale exposure is stronger because any relevant consumer confusion will likely occur prior to sale, if at all. As customarily worn, underwear is concealed by other articles of clothing. The general public does not ordinarily see underwear in the same manner and to the extent that it views outerwear. Thus, the potential for customer confusion is not as great as it could be for other articles of clothing. *Lois Sportswear, U.S.A., Inc. v. Levi Strauss & Co.*, 631 F. Supp. 735, 228 U.S.P.Q. 648 (S.D.N.Y. 1985), aff'd, 799 F.2d 867, 872–73(2d Cir. 1986). In *Levi* the Second Circuit held that potential confusion may exist in consumers seeing appellant's jeans worn outside the retail store absent any identifying labels that may be attached at the time of purchase. *Id.* The inherently concealed nature of worn underwear diminishes the concern for post-sale confusion noted by the *Levi* court. Thus Munsingwear's reliance on *Levi* is misplaced. The lack of post-sale exposure of the product to the general public reduces the risk that any customers will be confused as to source.

In addition to the lack of post-sale exposure, the underwear is embroidered with "JOCKEY" or "MUNSINGWEAR" around the waistband. This permanently stitched manufacturer's name in the waistband helps reduce any serious possibility of customer confusion. The presence of permanent labeling has been generally recognized to make post-sale customer confusion unlikely. *L.A. Gear v. Tom McAn Shoe Co.*, 988 F.2d 1117, 1134 (Fed. Cir. 1993), *cert. denied*, 114 S. Ct. 219; *Bose Corp. v. Linear Design Labs, Inc.*, 467 F.2d 304 (2d Cir. 1972). Therefore, the court finds that the pre-sale or packaged underwear serves as the basis for customer decision making, and accordingly, will be the products examined under the *Squirtco* analysis.

a. Similarity

The first step in the Squirtco analysis is to compare the two products as they are encountered by the consuming public. Examination of the two product packages reveals that they are not similar.The Jockey package consists of a cardboard insert that has a picture of a man wearing the style of underwear the package contains. The "JOCKEY POUCH" label is written across the top with the "JOCKEY" and Jockey logo trademarks. Finally, the material makeup of the underwear is also listed as well as the size and manufacturer's barcodes. The Munsingwear package does not have a cardboard insert but rather consists of a "band and medallion" through the middle of the package. The medallion has the kangaroo design with "MUNSINGWEAR KANGAROO BRIEF" encircling the drawing. Under the band is the Munsingwear trade mark. The Munsingwear package also lists sizes. When viewed side by side, it is obvious which package is produced by which manufacturer. Thus, the court finds that there is no substantial similarity between the two products.

b. Proximity

While competitive proximity is not controlled by the two manufactures, both products are sold in the men's department of stores. Munsingwear cites an individual instance where the two products were sold side-by-side; Jockey contends that this is not the usual course of business and is unusual. However, whether Munsingwear and Jockey are sold side-by-side becomes irrelevant when the market is viewed. In a market controlled by only a few producers it is inevitable that one brand will be located near another. Efficiency and customer assistance dictate that many stores will display and sell all similar products in relatively close proximity. Thus, the court finds that due to the nature of the product, it is highly likely that the two products will be sold in relatively close proximity, but that this is a function of market decisions made by individual stores rather than by the litigants.

c. Intent to Pass-Off

Munsingwear next argues that Jockey formed a specific intent to pass-off its "Pouch" underwear as Munsingwear's "H-Fly" underwear. Jockey contends that the existing strength of its trademark and the amount spent in advertising indicate that this is not the case. Jockey claims that its marketing of Pouch underwear is a form of competition for market share rather than an attempt to pass-off its underwear as that of Munsingwear.

Viewing the two packages together, the court finds that it is evident that there is no intent to pass off. First, the two packages prominently indicate who the manufacturer is. Second, the individual pieces of underwear have the manufacturer's name permanently stitched into the waistband. Based upon these factors, the court finds that Jockey has no intent to pass off its underwear as that of Munsingwear.

d. Actual Confusion

Munsingwear next argues that actual confusion has in fact occurred based upon customer letters received by Jockey. Evidence of actual confusion, while possibly the single best evidence of likelihood of confusion, is not conclusive of its existence. *Calvin Klein Cosmetics Corp. v. Parfumsde Coeur*, 824 F.2d 665, 668–69 (8th Cir. 1987) (proof of actual confusion while highly probative on the issue of likely confusion, is not dispositive in finding trademark infringement); *A-Veda Corp.v. Aura Inc.*, 19 U.S.P.Q. 1864, 1867 (D. Minn. 1991) (production of affidavits from distributors and sellers of plaintiff's products does not overcome the court's conclusion that customer confusion is not likely in an appreciable number of cases). In fact, the court may find such evidence insufficient to establish the existence of a genuine issue of material fact regarding likelihood of confusion. *Id.* Munsingwear submits two letters that Jockey received from its customers to demonstrate actual confusion. In these letters the customers state that they were confused as to whether Jockey now owned Munsingwear or was just licensing the right to produce horizontal flies. While letters are enlightening as to customers' beliefs, two letters standing alone are insufficient to establish a genuine issue of actual confusion. *Alpha Indus., Inc. v. Alpha Steel Tube & Shapes, Inc.*, 616 F.2d 440, 445 (9th Cir. 1980). Actual confusion requires more than de minimis proof.

Furthermore, Jockey argues that these letters indicate that, while the customer may have been misled or confused as to source, they understood that the product that they had purchased was made by Jockey. While the customer may have been confused as to the ownership of Munsingwear, they were not confused as to who made the underwear they purchased. Jockey also submitted several letters from customers indicating their ability to differentiate between the two products. The ability of consumers to differentiate between two products indicates that there is no likelihood of confusion. *Woodsmith Pub. Co. v. Meredith Corp.*, 904 F.2d 1244, 1249 (8th Cir. 1990). The court finds that the customer letters are insufficient to demonstrate that there has been any significant instances of actual consumer confusion.

e. Survey Evidence

In Lanham Act cases, survey evidence is often introduced on the issue of likelihood of confusion. While surveys are a valuable method to demonstrate actual confusion, they are not required to prove likelihood of confusion. Although surveys are probably the most accurate evidence of actual confusion, the absence of a consumer survey was not fatal to a request for a preliminary injunction where likelihood of confusion was the issue, since the plaintiff's burden was slight at that state of the proceedings. In its motion for a preliminary injunction, Munsingwear has not brought forward any surveys to demonstrate likelihood of confusion. Therefore, this factor is not analyzed and will not be construed in favor of either party.

f. Costs and Conditions of Purchase

Finally, the court must consider the costs and conditions surrounding the purchase of the two products. Generally, the more sophisticated the average consumer of a product is, the less likely it is that similarities in trade dress and trademarks will result in confusion concerning the source or sponsorship of the product. In this action, both parties suggest that its products are purchased in a retail setting and that the costs are similar and relatively inexpensive. The purchasers of relatively inexpensive goods are held to a lesser standard of purchasing care and do not give much thought to the purchase of such inexpensive goods. Therefore, due to the inexpensive nature of the products, the court finds that the relevant consumer is not generally sophisticated and gives little thought to the purchasing decision.

Upon review of the facts in this case, and applying the Squirtco analysis, the court finds that the dissimilarity between the two products in their pre-sale condition, the lack of an intent to pass off by Jockey and the lack of actual customer confusion all weigh heavily in Jockey's favor. The relatively close proximity of the two products during retail sale, the unsophisticated decision making process of the average consumer and the lack of a survey to establish or disprove actual confusion weigh in favor of neither party. Therefore, the court finds that Jockey has established that no likelihood of confusion exists between the two products.

2. Munsingwear's Motion For A Preliminary Injunction

The court considers four factors in determining whether to grant the plaintiff's Rule 65 motion for a preliminary injunction:

> 1. Is there a substantial threat that the plaintiff will suffer irreparable harm if relief is not granted;
>
> 2. Does the irreparable harm to the plaintiff outweigh any potential harm that granting a preliminary injunction may cause the defendant;

3. Is there a substantial probability that the plaintiff will prevail on the merits; and

4. The public interest.

Dataphase SYS., Inc. v. C L SYS., Inc., 640 F.2d 109, 114 (8th Cir. 1981) (en banc). The court balances the four factors to determine whether a preliminary injunction is warranted. *Id.* at *113;West Publishing Co. v. Mead Data Cent. Inc.*, 799 F.2d 1219, 1222 (8th Cir. 1986). The plaintiff bears the burden of proof concerning the four factors. *Gelco Corp. v. Coniston Partners*, 811 F.2d 414, 418 (8th Cir. 1987).

a. The Threat of Irreparable Harm

To satisfy the element of threat of irreparable harm, plaintiff must prove that harm will result without injunctive relief and the harm will not be compensable by money damages. Possible or speculative harm is not enough. The absence of such a showing alone is sufficient to deny a preliminary injunction. *Gelco*, 811 F.2d at 420; *Roberts v. Van Buren Pub. Sch.*, 731 F.2d 523, 526 (8th Cir. 1984). The court finds that if Munsingwear were to lose its market share based on unlawful infringement of its trademark it will have suffered irreparable harm to its ability to compete. Thus, this factor weighs in favor of Munsingwear.

b. Balance of Harm

The court must balance the potential harm to both the parties in deciding whether to grant injunctive relief. *Dataphase*, 640 F.2d at 114. The balance of harm must tip decidedly toward the plaintiffs to justify issuing a preliminary injunction. Both parties have a right to compete fairly in a free market place. Jockey, just as Munsingwear, has an interest in selling its product. Enjoining Jockey's marketing has the potential of decreasing its profits, just as issuing an injunction will likely increase Munsingwear's sales. Consumers now accustomed to purchasing Jockey's horizontal-fly underwear may be confused as to why the product is not available and may switch brands. Thus, the court finds that the balance of harms does not weigh decidedly in either party's favor. As result, because the balance must tip decidedly in the plaintiff's favor in order to justify granting an injunction, this factor weighs against granting an injunction.

c. The Likelihood of Success on the Merits

In order for the court to grant plaintiff's motion for a preliminary injunction, it must demonstrate a likelihood of success on the merits. The court has already analyzed the likelihood of success on the merits in its discussion of Jockey's motion for summary judgment. The finding that Jockey is not infringing on Munsingwear's trademark is dispositive of the question of Munsingwear's likelihood of success on the merits here. This factor thus weighs heavily in Jockey's favor.

d. The Public Interest

The final *Dataphase* factor to consider in deciding whether to grant a preliminary injunction is that of the public interest apart from the interests of the litigants themselves. The court finds that consumers have an interest in free and fair competition in the market place. Competition will have the natural effect of controlling prices and encouraging the introduction of new and improved products. Preventing Jockey from competing for a share in the market will work against that public interest. Therefore, the court finds that it is in the public interest to not grant Munsingwear the requested injunction.

Taken together, the four *Dataphase* factors weigh heavily in Jockey's favor. The court therefore finds that Munsingwear's motion for a preliminary injunction should be denied.

CONCLUSION

Munsingwear commenced this action to stop Jockey's sale of horizontal-fly underwear claiming common law trademark infringement, unfair competition and violation of §43(a) of the Lanham Act. Munsingwear filed a motion for a preliminary injunction and Jockey filed a motion for summary judgment based on a lack of customer confusion. Upon a review of the competing products in light of the criteria set forth by the Eighth Circuit in Squirtco, the court finds that no likelihood of confusion exists between the two products and no genuine issue of material fact exists that would allow a reasonable jury to conclude otherwise. Likelihood of consumer confusion is one of three indispensable elements in a prima facie case of trademark or trade dress infringement. *Woodsmith*, 904 F.2d at 1248. Thus, the court concludes that because Munsingwear cannot sustain each element of a prima facie case, Jockey's motion for summary judgment should be granted. *Celotex*, 477 U.S. at 322–23. The court further finds that under the Dataphase four factor analysis Munsingwear's motion for a preliminary injunction should be denied.

Accordingly, IT IS HEREBY ORDERED that defendant Jockey International, Inc.'s motion for summary judgment is granted and plaintiff Munsingwear, Inc.'s motion for a preliminary injunction is denied.

————————

C. Initial Interest Confusion

Australian Gold, Inc. v. Hatfield
436 F.3d 1228 (10th Cir 2006)

EBEL, CIRCUIT JUDGE.

BACKGROUND

[Australian Gold are three related tanning lotion businesses that manufacture and distribute these items to tanning salons. Australian Gold owns all trademarks to the brand and is the sole distributor of such lotions. However, Australian Gold contracts with independent distributors to sell the products to the tanning salons.

Hatfield resells Australian Gold's products over the internet without the permission of Australian Gold. Hatfield knew of the contractual agreements Australian Gold had with their distributors, but they ignored it. Hatfield concealed their activities by using fictitious names to sell Australian Gold products.]

DISCUSSION
III. Lanham Act Claims

Defendants argue that the district court erred in denying Defendants' motion for judgment as a matter of law on Plaintiffs' Lanham Act claims because Plaintiffs did not present evidence of a likelihood of consumer confusion, Defendants' activities were shielded by the first sale doctrine, and Plaintiffs did not present evidence of damages sufficient to support their Lanham Act claims. Defendants' arguments are without merit.

A. Likelihood of Confusion

"The unauthorized use of 'any reproduction, counterfeit, copy, or colorable imitation' of a registered trademark in a way that 'is likely to cause confusion' in the marketplace concerning the source of the different products constitutes trademark infringement under the Lanham Act." *Universal Money Ctrs., Inc. v. AT&T Co.*, 22 F.3d 1527, 1529 (10th Cir. 1994); *see* 15 U.S.C. § 1114(1)(a)-(b). The party alleging infringement has the burden of proving likelihood of confusion. *See Universal Money Ctrs.*, 22 F.3d at 1530. Ordinarily, to prevail on a trademark infringement claim, a plaintiff must demonstrate that a defendant's use of the trademark is likely to cause consumers to believe either that the plaintiff is the source of the defendant's products or services (direct confusion), or alternatively, that the defendant is the source of the plaintiff's products or services (reverse confusion). *See id.*

In this case, we recognize another variant of potential confusion: "initial interest confusion." Initial interest confusion results when a consumer seeks a particular trademark holder's product and instead is lured to the product of a competitor by the competitor's use of the same or a similar mark. *See Buckman*, 183 A.L.R. Fed. 553. Even though the consumer eventually may realize that the product is not the one originally sought, he or she may stay with the competitor. *Id.* In that way, the competitor has captured the trademark holder's potential visitors or customers. *Id.*

Even if the consumer eventually becomes aware of the source's actual identity, or where no actual sale results, there is nonetheless damage to the trademark. This damage can manifest itself in three ways: (1) the original diversion of the prospective customer's interest to a source that he or she erroneously believes is authorized; (2) the potential consequent effect of that diversion on the customer's ultimate decision whether to purchase caused by an erroneous impression that two sources of a product may be associated; and (3) the initial credibility that the would-be buyer may accord to the infringer's products— customer consideration that otherwise may be unwarranted and that may be built on the strength of the protected mark, reputation and goodwill. *See BigStar Entm't, Inc. v. Next Big Star, Inc.*, 105 F. Supp. 2d 185 (S.D.N.Y. 2000).

The federal courts, though not using the phrase "initial interest confusion," have acknowledged the potential for such confusion for decades. *See, e.g., Grotrian, Helfferich, Schulz, Th. Steinweg Nachf v. Steinway & Sons*, 523 F.2d 1331 (2d Cir. 1975). Initial interest confusion in the internet context derives from the unauthorized use of trademarks to divert internet traffic, thereby capitalizing on a trademark holder's goodwill. *See Nissan Motor Co. v. Nissan Computer Corp.*, 378 F.3d 1002, 1018 (9th Cir. 2004), *cert. denied*, 544 US. 974, 161 L. Ed. 2d 723, 125 S. Ct. 1825 (2005).

In this case, as noted above, Defendants used Plaintiffs' trademarks on Defendants' Web sites. Defendants also placed Plaintiffs' trademarks in the metatags of Defendants' Web sites. Further, Defendants paid Overture.com to list Defendants in a preferred position whenever a computer user searched for Plaintiffs' trademarks. All of these actions were attempts to divert traffic to Defendants' Web sites. While viewing Defendants' Web sites, consumers had the opportunity to purchase Products, but also to purchase lotions from Plaintiffs' competitors. Moreover, Defendants continued to use the trademarks to divert internet traffic to their Web sites even when they were not selling Products. Thus, Defendants used the goodwill associated with Plaintiffs' trademarks in such a way that consumers might be lured to the lotions from Plaintiffs' competitors. This is a violation of the Lanham Act.

We evaluate Plaintiffs' claim for initial interest confusion according to the six-prong test we announced in *Sally Beauty Co. v. Beautyco, Inc.*, 304 F.3d 964 (10th Cir. 2002). We look at (1) the degree of similarity between the marks; (2) the intent of the alleged infringer in adopting the mark; (3) evidence of actual confusion; (4) similarity of products and manner of marketing; (5)the degree of care likely to be exercised by purchasers; and (6) the strength or weakness of the marks. *Id.* at 972. No one factor is dispositive, and likelihood of confusion is a question of fact. *Id.* at 972.

In this case, the degree of similarity of the marks weighed heavily in favor of Plaintiffs, since the trademarked terms were identical to the terms used by Defendants. The intent of the infringer in adopting the mark also weighed in favor of Plaintiffs. Here the Hatfields deliberately used the trademarks to drive internet traffic to their own Web sites, where they sold both Products and lotions from Plaintiffs' competitors.

Moreover, the similarity of products and manner of marketing weighed in favor of Plaintiffs. The trademarked terms were tanning-related, just like the products offered on Defendants' website were. Further, the degree of care likely to be exercised in purchasing Products weighed in favor of Plaintiffs because Plaintiffs' low-cost products were subject to impulse purchases. *See id.* at 975.

Finally, the strength of the trademarks weighed in favor of Plaintiffs. Approximately fifty to sixty percent of the tanning salons in the United States carry Plaintiffs' trademarked Products. The substantial volume of sales of Products, both through Defendants' Web sites and through traditional salons, speaks to the strength of the trademarks.

However, Plaintiffs did not offer any direct evidence of actual confusion, so that factor weighs in favor of Defendants. Moreover, Defendants attempted to prevent actual confusion by placing disclaimers on their Web sites — though because these disclaimers do not tie particular trademarks to particular holders, the disclaimers are inadequate. More importantly, "a defendant's website disclaimer, proclaiming its real source and disavowing any connection with its competitor, cannot prevent the damage of initial interest confusion, which will already have been done by the misdirection of consumers looking for the plaintiff's websites." *Buckman*, 183 A.L.R. Fed. 553. In any event, even if this one factor does weigh in favor of Defendants, one factor alone is not dispositive of the likelihood of confusion. *See Sally Beauty Co.*, 304 F.3d at 972.

Because the evidence at trial on likelihood of confusion did not point only in favor of Defendants, the district court did not err in denying Defendants' motion for judgment as a matter of law.

D. Reverse Confusion

Sands, Taylor & Wood Co. v. Quaker Oats Co.
978 F.2d 947 (7th Cir. 1992)

CUDAHY, CIRCUIT JUDGE.

Sands, Taylor & Wood Company (STW) brought this action against The Quaker Oats Company (Quaker) for federal trademark infringement and related state-law claims, alleging that Quaker's use of the words "Thirst Aid" in its advertising slogan "Gatorade is Thirst Aid" infringed STW's registered trademark for THIRST-AID. The district court agreed, and entered judgment for STW in the amount of $42,629,399.09, including prejudgment interest and attorney's fees. The court also permanently enjoined Quaker from using the words "Thirst Aid." Not surprisingly, Quaker appeals.

I.

Plaintiff STW is a small, Vermont-based company that for the past 180 years has sold bagged flour at retail under the brand name "King Arthur Flour." In 1973, STW acquired Joseph Middleby, Jr., Inc. (Middleby), a manufacturer of soft drinks, soda fountain syrups and ice cream toppings. STW thereby became the owner of three trademarks registered to Middleby: (1) THIRST-AID "First Aid for Your Thirst," issued October 10, 1950, for use on "nonalcoholic maltless beverages, sold as soft drinks, and syrups therefor"; (2) THIRST-AID, issued August 26, 1952, for use on various ice cream toppings as well as "fruits and sauces used in the making of ice cream"; and (3) THIRST-AID, issued March 24, 1953, for use on "soda fountain syrups used in the preparation of maltless soft drinks."

From 1921 to 1973, Middleby used the THIRST-AID mark on a wide variety of beverage products and syrups that it sold to soda fountains, ice cream parlors and food service outlets. Middleby also supplied its THIRST-AID customers with various items displaying the name THIRST-AID, including streamers, banners, glasses and pitchers, for in-store advertising and promotion. STW continued these activities after it acquired Middleby, which it operated as a wholly-owned subsidiary.

In the late 1970s sales of THIRST-AID soft drinks declined as consumers turned increasingly to bottles and cans rather than soda fountains and ice cream parlors for their soft drinks. In addition, between 1979 and 1983 STW underwent a period of severe economic hardship during which its annual gross revenues dropped from $40 million to approximately $3.1 million. In the spring of 1980, Pet, Inc. (Pet), negotiated with STW a nationwide license to use the name THIRST-AID on a new isotonic beverage intended to compete with the very popular Gatorade brand isotonic beverage manufactured by Stokely Van Camp Company (Stokely). Pet began test-marketing the product in twenty stores in Columbia, South Carolina in June of 1980. Pet's THIRST-AID was advertised through the same media as Gatorade, and was sold through the same channels of trade (grocery stores) to the same customers. During the five-month period of the test, Pet's THIRST-AID captured approximately 25% of the isotonic beverage market in the test area. Nevertheless, for reasons that are not important here, Pet decided not to enter the market with the new product and in June of 1981 its license to use the name THIRST-AID expired.

In December of 1981, STW sold the assets of Middleby (now renamed Johnson-Middleby)to L. Karp & Sons (Karp), a distributor of bakery products. As part of the sale, STW assigned to Karp all of the registered THIRST-AID trademarks. STW obtained a simultaneous exclusive license back for retail use of the trademark on certain "Products" defined as "jams, jellies, pie fillings" and various other bakery supplies.

In August of 1983, Stokely, the manufacturer of Gatorade, was acquired by Quaker. Shortly thereafter, Quaker solicited proposals for a new advertising campaign intended to educate consumers about Gatorade's ability to quench thirst and replace fluids and minerals lost by the human body through strenuous exercise. One of the candidates was the slogan "Gatorade is Thirst Aid for That Deep Down Body Thirst."

Pursuant to Quaker's regular practice, the proposed "Thirst Aid" campaign was submitted to the legal department for approval in February or March of 1984. Quaker's inhouse counsel, Charles Lannin, concluded that the words "Thirst Aid" did not raise any trademark problems because they were used to describe an attribute of the product rather than as a designation of source or affiliation. Lannin therefore did not conduct a trademark search for the term "Thirst Aid" at this time.

Shortly thereafter, an employee of Quaker's research and development division telephoned Lannin and informed him that Pet had previously test-marketed an isotonic beverage called THIRST-AID. Lannin contacted Pet and was told that Pet had discontinued its isotonic beverage a few years before. Some weeks later, another Quaker employee informed Lannin that he thought a "Thirst Aid" beverage was being marketed in Florida. At this point, on May 2, 1984, Lannin obtained a trademark search of the phrase "Thirst Aid." The search revealed the three THIRST-AID registrations by Middleby as well as the sale of the marks to Karp. Lannin directed a trademark paralegal employed by Quaker to contact Karp in order to determine what products it was selling under the THIRST-AID name; the Karp employee to whom the paralegal spoke stated that "they [sic] didn't think they marketed anything under that name."

On May 12, 1984, the first "Gatorade is Thirst Aid" commercials ran on television. On May 31, 1984, Karp's lawyer, Russell Hattis, called Quaker regarding Quaker's use of "Thirst Aid." Hattis claimed that Quaker was infringing Karp's trademarks, to which Lannin responded that there was no infringement because Quaker was using the words "Thirst Aid" descriptively. In a subsequent meeting between the two, Lannin learned from Hattis that the THIRST-AID mark had not been used on soft drinks or beverages since the Pet test-market. On June 2, Quaker sought an opinion from outside trademark counsel, Robert Newbury, who essentially agreed with Lannin that there was no infringement because Quaker was using the words "Thirst Aid" descriptively rather than as a trademark.

On June 4, Lannin was contacted by Frank Sands, the president of STW, who stated that STW owned the rights to use the THIRST-AID mark at retail under a license-back agreement with Karp. Sands claimed that Quaker was infringing those rights, although he acknowledged that STW did not sell any THIRST-AID products at that time.

Quaker did not hear from either Karp or STW again until the commencement of this litigation. In the interim, STW entered into a written agreement with Karp under which STW paid Karp $1 for an assignment of Karp's trademark registrations. Sands filed suit one week later, alleging that the slogan "Gatorade is Thirst Aid for That Deep Down Body Thirst" infringed its registrations and constituted unfair competition under the Lanham Act, 15 U.S.C. §1051 et seq., state common law and various state statutes. After granting summary judgment in favor of STW on Quaker's fair use defense, the district court held a bench trial on the remaining issues. On December 18, 1990, the court issued its opinion holding that Quaker had infringed STW's trademark and awarding STW 10% of Quaker's pre-tax profits on Gatorade for the period during which Quaker used "Thirst Aid" in its advertising. *Sands, Taylor & Wood v. The Quaker Oats Co.*, 1990 U.S. Dist. LEXIS 17342, 18 U.S.P.Q.2D (BNA) 1457 (N.D. Ill. 1990). The court also awarded STW attorney's fees and costs as well as prejudgment interest. Gatorade appeals.

* * *

A. Reverse Confusion

The "keystone" of trademark infringement is "likelihood of confusion" as to source, affiliation, connection or sponsorship of goods or services among the relevant class of customers and potential customers. 2 McCarthy, *id.* §23:1, at 42–43, 46–47. Usually, the confusion alleged is "forward confusion," which occurs "when customers mistakenly think that the junior user's goods or services are from the same source as or are connected with the senior user's goods or services." *Id.* at 48. In such a case, the junior user attempts to capitalize on the senior user's good will and established reputation by suggesting that his product comes from the same source as does the senior user's product. *Big 0 Tire Dealers v. Goodyear Tire & Rubber Co.*, 561 F.2d 1365 (10th Cir. 1977); 2 McCarthy, *id.* §23:1, at 48.

In this case, however, STW relies not on classic forward confusion but on the doctrine of "reverse confusion." Reverse confusion occurs when a large junior user saturates the market with a trademark similar or identical to that of a smaller, senior user. In such a case, the junior user does not seek to profit from the good will associated with the senior user's mark. Nonetheless, the senior user is injured because

> the public comes to assume that the senior user's products are really the junior user's or that the former has become somehow connected to the latter. The result is that the senior user loses the value of the trademark — its product identity, corporate identity, control over its goodwill and reputation, and ability to move into new markets.

Ameritech, Inc. v. American Information Technologies Corp., 811 F.2d 960, 964 (6th Cir. 1987); *see also Banff, Ltd.*, 841 F.2d at 490–91; *Big 0 Tire Dealers*, 561 F.2d at 1372. Although this court has not previously recognized reverse confusion as the basis for a claim under the Lanham Act, several other circuits have endorsed the concept. We agree with those courts that "the objectives of the Lanham Act — to protect an owner's interest in its trademark by keeping the public free from confusion as to the source of goods and ensuring fair competition — are as important in a case of reverse confusion as in typical trademark infringement." *Banff, Ltd.*, 841 F.2d at 490. We therefore hold that reverse confusion is a redressable injury under the Lanham Act.

* * *

[On remand, STW ultimately was awarded $10,328,411 in total damages.]

Notes

1. Why is reverse confusion actionable in the first place? In reverse confusion, the first-comer (plaintiff) benefits to the extent consumers are exposed to the trademark through advertising and other promotional activities. Why should Sands, Taylor & Woods receive a money award for the promotional activities of Quaker Oats?

2. While announcing a 1982 basketball game, then CBS broadcaster Brent Musburger inadvertently coined the term "March Madness" to refer to the nationwide, National Collegiate Athletic Association's (NCAA) annual college basketball tournament that is held starting in March of each year. As a result, the media widely adopted MARCH MADNESS to refer to the NCAA tournament. By 1993, NCAA began licensing the mark MARCH MADNESS to apparel manufacturers to take advantage of the popularity of the name. NCAA even licensed a video game with the MARCH MADNESS designation. Apparently unknown to either CBS or NCAA, the Illinois High School Association (IHSA) had used the term MARCH MADNESS to refer to its annual March basketball tournament. The IHSA tournament had become a premier high school basketball tournament in Illinois. IHSA had begun using the mark in the 1940s. *See Ill. High Sch. Ass'n v. GTE Vantage, Inc.*, 99 F.3d 244 (7th Cir. 1996), *cert. denied*, 117 S. Ct. 1083 (1997) (dismissing IHSA's motion for preliminary injunction because MARCH MADNESS was coined by a reporter, and not by the NCAA; therefore, it had a "dual-use," one of protected First Amendment speech and another designating source). If the "dual-use" exception were

wide-spread, would it obviate the reverse confusion cause of action? *See also,* Daniel Domenico, Note, "Mark Madness": How Brent Musberger and the Miracle Bra May have Led to a More Equitable and Efficient Understanding of the Reverse Confusion Doctrine in Trademark Law, 86 VA. L. Rev. 597 (2000).

3. Generally, there is an "inverse relationship between the degree of care exercised and the likelihood of confusion." Shashank Upadhye, Trademark Surveys: Identifying the Relevant Universe of Confused Consumers, 8 FORDHAM INTELL. PROP. MEDIA & ENT. L.J. 549, 568 (1998). Is this perspective still valid in reverse confusion cases?

E. Contributory Infringement

Restatement (Third) of Unfair Competition §26

[Liability for contributory infringement should be imposed when] (a) the actor intentionally induces the third person to engage in the infringing conduct; or (b) the actor fails to take reasonable precautions against the occurrence of the third person's infringing conduct in circumstances in which the infringing conduct can be reasonably anticipated.

Inwood Labs., Inc. v. Ives Labs., Inc.
456 U.S. 844 (1982)

JUSTICE O'CONNOR delivered the opinion of the Court:

This action requires us to consider the circumstances under which a manufacturer of a generic drug, designed to duplicate the appearance of a similar drug marketed by a competitor under a registered trademark, can be held vicariously liable for infringement of that trademark by pharmacists who dispense the generic drug.

I

In 1955, respondent Ives Laboratories, Inc. (Ives), received a patent on the drug cyclandelate, a vasodilator used in long-term therapy for peripheral and cerebral vascular diseases. Until its patent expired in 1972, Ives retained the exclusive right to make and sell the drug, which it did under the registered trademark CYCLOSPASMOL. Ives marketed the drug, a white powder, to wholesalers, retail pharmacists, and hospitals in colored gelatin capsules. Ives arbitrarily selected a blue capsule, imprinted with "Ives 4124," for its 200 mg dosage and a combination blue-red capsule, imprinted with "Ives 4148," for its 400 mg dosage.

After Ives' patent expired, several generic drug manufacturers, including petitioners Premo Pharmaceutical Laboratories, Inc., Inwood Laboratories, Inc., and MD Pharmaceutical Co., Inc. (collectively the generic manufacturers), began marketing cyclandelate.[5]

----

5. The generic manufacturers purchase cyclandelate and empty capsules and assemble the product for sale to wholesalers and hospitals. The petitioner wholesalers, Darby Drug Co., Inc., Rugby Laboratories, Inc., and Sherry Pharmaceutical Co., Inc., in turn, sell to other wholesalers, physicians, and pharmacies.

They intentionally copied the appearance of the CYCLOSPASMOL capsules, selling cyclandelate in 200 mg and 400 mg capsules in colors identical to those selected by Ives.

The marketing methods used by Ives reflect normal industry practice. Because cyclandelate can be obtained only by prescription, Ives does not direct its advertising to the ultimate consumer. Instead, Ives' representatives pay personal visits to physicians, to whom they distribute product literature and "starter samples." Ives initially directed these efforts toward convincing physicians that CYCLOSPASMOL is superior to other vasodilators. Now that its patent has expired and generic manufacturers have entered the market, Ives concentrates on convincing physicians to indicate on prescriptions that a generic drug cannot be substituted for CYCLOSPASMOL.

The generic manufacturers also follow a normal industry practice by promoting their products primarily by distribution of catalogs to wholesalers, hospitals, and retail pharmacies, rather than by contacting physicians directly. The catalogs truthfully describe generic cyclandelate as "equivalent" or "comparable" to CYCLOSPASMOL. In addition, some of the catalogs include price comparisons of the generic drug and CYCLOSPASMOL and some refer to the color of the generic capsules. The generic products reach wholesalers, hospitals, and pharmacists in bulk containers which correctly indicate the manufacturer of the product contained therein.

A pharmacist, regardless of whether he is dispensing CYCLOSPASMOL or a generic drug, removes the capsules from the container in which he receives them and dispenses them to the consumer in the pharmacist's own bottle with his own label attached. Hence, the final consumer sees no identifying marks other than those on the capsules themselves.

II
A

Ives instituted this action in the United States District Court for the Eastern District of New York under §§32 and 43(a) of the Trademark Act of 1946 (Lanham Act), 60 Stat. 427, as amended,15 U. S. C. §1051 *et seq.*, and under New York's unfair competition law, N. Y. Gen. Bus. Law §368-d (McKinney 1968).

Ives' claim under §32, 60 Stat. 437, as amended, 15 U. S. C. §1114, derived from its allegation that some pharmacists had dispensed generic drugs mislabeled as CYCLOSPASMOL. Ives contended that the generic manufacturers' use of look alike capsules and of catalog entries comparing prices and revealing the colors of the generic capsules induced pharmacists illegally to substitute a generic drug for CYCLOSPASMOL and to mislabel the substitute drug CYCLOSPASMOL. Although Ives did not allege that the petitioners themselves applied the Ives trademark to the drug products they produced and distributed, it did allege that the petitioners contributed to the infringing activities of pharmacists who mislabeled generic cyclandelate.

Ives' claim under §43(a), 60 Stat. 441, 15 U. S. C. §1125(a), alleged that the petitioners falsely designated the origin of their products by copying the capsule colors used by Ives and by promoting the generic products as equivalent to CYCLOSPASMOL. In support of its claim, Ives argued that the colors of its capsules were not functional and that they had developed a secondary meaning for the consumers.

Contending that pharmacists would continue to mislabel generic drugs as CYCLOSPASMOL so long as imitative products were available, Ives asked that the court enjoin the petitioners from marketing cyclandelate capsules in the same colors and form as Ives uses for CYCLOSPASMOL. In addition, Ives sought damages pursuant to §35 of the Lanham Act, 60 Stat. 439, as amended, 15 U. S. C. §1117.

B

The District Court denied Ives' request for an order preliminarily enjoining the petitioners from selling generic drugs identical in appearance to those produced by *Ives*. 455 F.Supp. 939 (1978). Referring to the claim based upon §32, the District Court stated that, while the "knowing and deliberate instigation" by the petitioners of mislabeling by pharmacists would justify holding the petitioners as well as the pharmacists liable for trademark infringement, Ives had made no showing sufficiently to justify preliminary relief. *Id.*, at 945. Ives had not established that the petitioners conspired with the pharmacists or suggested that they disregard physicians' prescriptions.

The Court of Appeals for the Second Circuit affirmed. 601 F.2d 631 (1979). To assist the District Court in the upcoming trial on the merits, the appellate court defined the elements of a claim based upon §32 in some detail. Relying primarily upon *Coca-Cola Co. v. Snow Crest Beverages, Inc.*, 64 F.Supp. 980 (Mass. 1946), *aff'd*, 162 F.2d 280 (CAl), *cert. denied*, 332 U.S. 809 (1947), the court stated that the petitioners would be liable under §32 either if they suggested, even by implication, that retailers fill bottles with generic cyclandelate and label the bottle with Ives' trademark or if the petitioners continued to sell cyclandelate to retailers whom they knew or had reason to know were engaging in infringing practices. 601 F.2d, at 636.

C

After a bench trial on remand, the District Court entered judgment for the petitioners. 488 F.Supp. 394 (1980). Applying the test approved by the Court of Appeals to the claim based upon §32, the District Court found that the petitioners had not suggested, even by implication, that pharmacists should dispense generic drugs incorrectly identified as CYCLOSPASMOL.

In reaching that conclusion, the court first looked for direct evidence that the petitioners intentionally induced trademark infringement. Since the petitioners' representatives do not make personal visits to physicians and pharmacists, the petitioners were not in a position directly to suggest improper drug substitutions. Therefore, the court concluded, improper suggestions, if any, must have come from catalogs and promotional materials. The court determined, however, that those materials could not "fairly be read" to suggest trademark infringement. 488 F.Supp., at 397.

The trial court next considered evidence of actual instances of mislabeling by pharmacists, since frequent improper substitutions of a generic drug for CYCLOSPASMOL could provide circumstantial evidence that the petitioners, merely by making available imitative drugs in conjunction with comparative price advertising, implicitly had suggested that pharmacists substitute improperly. After reviewing the evidence of incidents of mislabeling, the District Court concluded that such incidents occurred too infrequently to justify the inference that the petitioners' catalogs and use of imitative colors had "impliedly invited" druggists to mislabel. *Ibid.* Moreover, to the extent mislabeling had occurred, the court found it resulted from pharmacists' misunderstanding of the requirements of the New York Drug Substitution Law, rather than from deliberate attempts to pass off generic cyclandelate as CYCLOSPASMOL. *Ibid.*

The District Court also found that Ives failed to establish its claim based upon §43(a). In reaching its conclusion, the court found that the blue and blue-red colors were functional to patients as well as to doctors and hospitals: many elderly patients associate color with therapeutic effect; some patients commingle medications in a container and rely on color to differentiate one from another; colors are of some, if limited, help in identifying drugs in emergency situations; and use of the same color for brand name drugs and their generic equivalents helps avoid confusion on the part of those responsible for dispensing drugs. *Id.,* at 398–399. In addition, because Ives had failed to show that the colors indicated the drug's origin, the court found that the colors had not acquired a secondary meaning. *Id.,* at 399.

Without expressly stating that the District Court's findings were clearly erroneous, and for reasons which we discuss below, the Court of Appeals concluded that the petitioners violated §32. 638 F.2d 538 (1981). The Court of Appeals did not reach Ives' other claims. We granted certiorari, 454 U.S. 891 (1981), and now reverse the judgment of the Court of Appeals.

III
A

As the lower courts correctly discerned, liability for trademark infringement can extend beyond those who actually mislabel goods with the mark of another. Even if a manufacturer does not directly control others in the chain of distribution, it can be held responsible for their infringing activities under certain circumstances. Thus, if a manufacturer or distributor intentionally induces another to infringe a trademark, or if it continues to supply its product to one whom it knows or has reason to know is engaging in trademark infringement, the manufacturer or distributor is contributorially responsible for any harm done as a result of the deceit. *See William R. Warner & Co. v. Eli Lilly & Co., id.; Coca-Cola Co. v. Snow Crest Beverages, Inc., id.*

It is undisputed that those pharmacists who mislabeled generic drugs with Ives' registered trademark violated §32. However, whether these petitioners were liable for the pharmacists' infringing acts depended upon whether, in fact, the petitioners intentionally induced the pharmacists to mislabel generic drugs or, in fact, continued to supply cyclandelate to pharmacists whom the petitioners knew were mislabeling generic drugs. The District Court concluded that Ives made neither of those factual showings.

[The court reversed and remanded the Circuit Court finding no contributory infringement.]

———————

Note

1. In *Fonovisa, Inc. v. Cherry Auction, Inc.,* 76 F.3d 259 (9th Cir. 1996), cited by the court in *Inwood Labs,* the court found a sponsor of a "flea market" liable for contributory trademark infringement by "supplying the necessary marketplace" for the sale of, in this case, record albums. Given this, prior to becoming a legitimate music sharing service, was Napster guilty of contributory trademark infringement as well as contributory copyright infringement?

———————

F. Vicarious Liability

Vicarious liability for trademark infringement is imposed on defendants who are considered to be legally responsible for the actions of others. Courts often use agency law to analyze liability in this context. *See, e.g., AT&T v. Winback & Conserve Program, Inc.*, 42 F. 3d 1421 (3d Cir. 1994). Consider the following case.

———————

Lockheed Martin Corp. v. Network Solutions, Inc.
194 F.3d 980 (9th Cir. 1999)

Trott, Circuit Judge:

Plaintiff Lockheed Martin Corp. ("Lockheed") appeals summary judgment in favor of Defendant Network Solutions, Inc. ("NSI") on Lockheed's action for trademark infringement, unfair competition, dilution, and contributory infringement under the Lanham Trademark Act of 1946, 15 U.S.C. §§1051–1127 (1994 & Supp. I 1995), as amended (the "Lanham Act"). The district court published its decision granting summary judgment to NSI and refusing to grant Lockheed's motion or leave to amend its complaint. 985 F. Supp. 949 (C.D. Cal. 1997). Lockheed contends that (1) genuine issues of material fact remain on its contributory infringement claim, (2) the district court erred in holding that 15 U.S.C. §1114(2) did not create an independent basis for liability, and (3) the district court should have permitted Lockheed to amend the complaint to add a cause of action for contributory dilution. We have jurisdiction under 28 U.S.C. §1291 (1994), and we affirm the judgment of the district court.

I

This appeal concerns the NSI registration scheme for domain-name combinations, which we discussed in our recent *Avery Dennison Corp. v. Sumpton*, 189 F.3d 868, 1999 U.S. App. LEXIS 19954 (9th Cir. 1999), decision. An interested reader may wish to review the district court's in-depth discussion of the Internet technology that forms the basis of this cause of action. 985 F. Supp. at 951–53.

When a third party seeks to maintain an Internet web site, that party must reserve a location, called an Internet Protocol ("IP") Address, and do the necessary programming. When an Internet user accesses the third party's web site, the user enters the domain-name combination that corresponds to the IP Address and is routed to the host computer. An industry of surrogate hosts has developed, where an Internet Service Provider licenses space on its computers to a third-party web-site operator, permitting the operator to maintain a web site without keeping his or her computer continually connected to the Internet. The Internet Service Providers do not provide the translation service from an entered domain-name combination to the appropriate IP Address. A separate organization has the responsibility to perform the translation function.

A

At all relevant times, NSI was the sole National Science Foundation contractor in charge of registering domain-name combinations for the top-level domains <.gov>, <.edu>, <.com>, <.org>, and <.net>. (For clarity, we set off Internet-related character strings with the caret symbols ("< >").) After registration, NSI entered the combination and the corresponding IP Address in its database, permitting automatic translation when an Internet user entered a domain-name combination. NSI is no longer the exclusive registrar. Since oral argument on this appeal, a new competitive scheme has been implemented. *See* Jeri Clausing, 3-Week Delay in Opening Up Internet Name Registration, N.Y. Times, June 28, 1999, at C1.

When registering with NSI to receive a domain-name combination, an applicant submits NSI's "template" electronically over the Internet. On approval, NSI puts the domain-name combination in its database in conjunction with the correct IP Address. NSI then routes Internet users who enter a certain domain-name combination to the registrant's computer. At the time of argument on this appeal, NSI was receiving approximately 130,000 registrations per month, although evidence indicates that the number of monthly registrations has been increasing steadily and is possibly much larger today. Ninety percent of templates are processed electronically, and the entire registration process for each application requires between a few minutes and a few hours. Ten percent of the time, an employee of NSI reviews the application. Human intervention might occur because of an error in filling out the form or because the applied-for domain name includes a "prohibited" character string—such as specific variations on the words Olympic, Red Cross, or NASA, and certain "obscene" words. NSI also performs a conflict check on all applications, which compares an application to other registered domain-name combinations. However, NSI does not consult third parties during the registration process, check for a registrant's right to use a particular word in a domain-name combination, or monitor the use of a combination once registered. NSI is also not an Internet Service Provider. It performs none of the "hosting" functions for a web site.

NSI does maintain a post-registration dispute-resolution procedure. Anyone who feels that his or her rights are violated by the domain-name combination maintained by a registrant can submit a certified copy of a trademark registration to NSI. NSI then requires the registrant to obtain a declaratory judgment of the right to maintain the domain-name combination. If the registrant fails to do so, its registration is terminated.

B

Lockheed owns and operates "The Skunk Works," an aircraft design and construction laboratory. Since 1943, The Skunk Works has developed prototypes of this country's first jet fighter, the U-2 and SR-71 spy planes, and the F-117 and F-22 fighter planes. The Skunk Works is currently involved in designing a possible replacement for the space shuttle. "Skunk Works" is a registered and incontestable service mark.

II

Third parties, not involved in this litigation, have registered domain-name combinations with NSI which are variations on the phrase "skunk works." These include:

> <skunkworks.com>, <skunkworks.net>, <skunkwrks.corn>, <skunkwerks.com>, <skunkworx.com>, <theskunkworks.com>, <skunkworks1.com>, <skunkworks.org>, <skunkwear.coin,> <the-skunkwerks.com>, <skunkwurks.com>, and <theencryptedskunkworks.com>.

Lockheed alleges that many of these registrations infringe and dilute its "Skunk Works" service mark.

Lockheed sent two letters, on May 7 and June 18, 1996, bringing the <skunk works.com> and <skunkworks.net> registrations to NSI's attention. Lockheed's letters informed NSI of its belief that the third-party registrants were infringing or diluting Lockheed's service mark. Lockheed requested that NSI cancel the allegedly offending registrations. Lockheed also requested that NSI cease registering domain-name combinations that included "Skunk Works" or variations on the phrase and report to Lockheed all such domain-name combinations contained in its registry. NSI took no action on Lockheed's requests, informing Lockheed by letter that Lockheed had failed to comply with the terms of NSI's dispute resolution policy. Due to Lockheed's dealings with the third-party registrants, <skunkworks.com> and <skunkworks.net> ceased being used, but NSI did not immediately cancel the registrations and later permitted a new registrant to register <skunkworks.com>.

Lockheed sued NSI on October 22, 1996, claiming contributory service mark infringement, infringement, unfair competition, and service mark dilution, all in violation of the Lanham Act, and also seeking declaratory relief. The complaint alleged that four specific domain-name registrations infringed or diluted Lockheed's "Skunk Works" service mark. The parties stipulated to April 1, 1997, as the cut-off date for motions to amend the pleadings. Lockheed later proposed, over NSI's objection, that the cutoff date be moved to July 7, 1997. NSI moved for summary judgment. On August 19, 1997, Lockheed moved to amend its complaint to add a cause of action for contributory dilution and to allege several additional domain-name combinations registered with NSI. The district court denied the motion to amend and granted summary judgment to NSI.

* * *

IV

Contributory infringement occurs when the defendant either intentionally induces a third party to infringe the plaintiff's mark or supplies a product to a third party with actual or constructive knowledge that the product is being used to infringe the service mark. *Inwood Lab., Inc. v. Ives Lab., Inc.*, 456 U.S. 844, 853–54, 72 L. Ed. 2d 606, 102 S. Ct. 2182 (1982). Lockheed alleges only the latter basis for contributory infringement liability and therefore must prove that NSI supplies a product to third parties with actual or constructive knowledge that its product is being used to infringe "Skunk Works." *Id.* at 854.

The district court assumed for purposes of summary judgment that third parties were infringing Lockheed's "Skunk Works" service mark, and NSI does not ask us to affirm on the alternate ground that no genuine issue of material fact exists as to infringement. We are thus left to consider two issues on Lockheed's contributory infringement cause of action: (1) whether NSI supplied a product to third parties and (2) whether NSI had actual or constructive knowledge of any infringement. Because we accept the district court's excellent analysis on the first question, *see* 985F. Supp. at 960–62, we affirm summary judgment without reaching the second.

A

Under the plain language of the *Inwood Lab.* formulation, to be liable for contributory infringement, NSI must supply a "product" to a third party with which the third party infringes Lockheed's service mark. 456 U.S. at 854. In *Inwood Lab.,* the Supreme Court considered an action against a manufacturer of generic pharmaceuticals. *Id.* at 847. Nonparty pharmacists packaged the defendant's less-expensive generic pills, but labeled them with the plaintiff's brand name. *Id.* at 850. The plaintiff stated a cause of action for contributory infringement by alleging that the defendant "continued to supply [the product] to pharmacists whom the petitioners knew were mislabeling generic drugs." *Id.* at 855.

Inwood Lab. has been applied in the broader context of renting booth space at a flea market. *See Hard Rock Cafe Licensing Corp. v. Concession Servs., Inc.*, 955 F.2d 1143, 1148–49 (7th Cir. 1992). In *Hard Rock,* the Seventh Circuit explicitly addressed the distinction between a product and a service, noting that while the pharmaceutical company in *Inwood Lab.* clearly supplied a product to the third-party pharmacists, a "temporary help service … might not be liable if it furnished [to the defendant] the workers he employed to erect his stand." *Hard Rock,* 955 F.2d at 1148. The court then held that space at a flea market was more comparable to pharmaceuticals than to manpower, in part because of the close comparison between the legal duty owed by a landlord to control illegal activities on his or her premises and by a manufacturer to control illegal use of his or her product. *Id.* at 1149. We adopted the *Hard Rock* analysis in *Fonovisa, Inc. v. Cherry Auction, Inc.,* 76 F.3d 259 (9th Cir. 1996), holding that a flea market could be liable for contributory infringement if it "supplied the necessary marketplace" for the sale of infringing products. *Id.* at 265 (citing *Hard Rock,* 955 F.2d at 1149).

Hard Rock and *Fonovisa* teach us that when measuring and weighing a fact pattern in the contributory infringement context without the convenient "product" mold dealt with *Inwood Lab.,* we consider the extent of control exercised by the defendant over the third party's means of infringement. *Hard Rock,* 955 F.2d at 1148–49 (noting the common-law responsibilities of a landlord regarding illegal activity on a rented premises); *see Fonovisa,* 76 F.3d at 265 (adopting *Hard Rock's* analysis). Direct control and monitoring of the instrumentality used by a third party to infringe the plaintiff's mark permits the expansion of *Inwood Lab.'s* "supplies a product" requirement for contributory infringement.

B

The case at bench involves a fact pattern squarely on the "service" side of the product/service distinction suggested by *Inwood Lab* and its offspring. All evidence in the record indicates that NSI's role differs little from that of the United States Postal Service: when an Internet user enters a domain-name combination, NSI translates the domain-name combination to the registrant's IP Address and routes the information or command to the corresponding computer. Although NSI's routing service is only available to a registrant who has paid NSI's fee, NSI does not supply the domain-name combination any-more than the Postal Service supplies a street address by performing the routine service of routing mail. As the district court correctly observed,

> Where domain names are used to infringe, the infringement does not result from NSI's publication of the domain name list, but from the registrant's use of the name on a web site or other Internet form of communication in connection with goods or services.... NSI's involvement with the use of domain names does not extend beyond registration.

985 F. Supp. at 958.

The "direct control and monitoring" rule established by *Hard Rock* and *Fonovisa* likewise fails to reach the instant situation. The district court correctly recognized that NSI's rote translation service does not entail the kind of direct control and monitoring required to justify an extension of the "supplies a product" requirement. *See* 985 F. Supp. at 962 ("While the landlord of a flea market might reasonably be expected to monitor the merchandise sold on his premises, NSI cannot reasonably be expected to monitor the Internet."). Such a stretch would reach well beyond the contemplation of *Inwood Lab.* and its progeny.

In an attempt to fit under *Fonovisa's* umbrella, Lockheed characterizes NSI's service as a licensing arrangement with alleged third-party infringers. Although we accept Lockheed's argument that NSI licenses its routing service to domain-name registrants, the routing service is just that—a service. In *Fonovisa* and *Hard Rock,* by contrast, the defendants licensed real estate, with the consequent direct control over the activity that the third-party alleged infringers engaged in on the premises. *Hard Rock,* 955 F.2d at 1149; *see Fonovisa,* 76 F.3d at 265.

* * *

VIII

NSI is not liable for contributory infringement as a matter of law. Lockheed does not appeal the district court's decision on its infringement, unfair competition, and dilution claims against NSI, and the district court did not abuse its discretion in refusing leave to amend the complaint. We have also considered Lockheed's request for judicial notice and motion to strike and deny both.

AFFIRMED.

_____

Note

1. The Uniform Dispute Resolution Policy (UDRP) provides immunity for the Registrars of domain names. *See infra* Chapter XII. Should there be blanket immunity for trademark liability for all Internet Service Providers (ISPs)? *See Gucci* America, Inc. v. Hall & Associates, 135 F. Supp. 2d 409 (S.D.N.Y. 2001) (blanket immunity not warranted). What policy considerations are there for granting or not granting such immunity?

_____

G. Defenses

There are multiple defenses available in an infringement case. Any affirmative defense not raised in the answer is considered waived; therefore, it is important to consider all available defenses at the outset of any infringement action.

1. Fair Use

If the mark is not generic, another popular defense is that the mark was used "fairly." The fair use defense typically arises when the plaintiff's mark is descriptive in nature (not fanciful or a coined term) and the defendant uses it in a way to describe its goods or services and not to identify source.

_____

United States Shoe Corp. v. Brown Group Inc.
740 F. Supp. 196 (2d Cir. 1990)

Legal, D.J.

Plaintiff United States Shoe Corp. ("U.S. Shoe"), asserts trademark violation and unfair competition against Brown Group, Inc., in connection with the advertising and sale of women's dress shoes. Plaintiff advertises its women's dress pumps under the slogan and musical jingle, "Looks Like a Pump, Feels Like a Sneaker." Defendant has launched an advertising campaign that compares its pump to a sneaker and asserts that it "feels like a sneaker." Plaintiff seeks a preliminary injunction barring defendant from using the phrase. An evidentiary hearing was held on submission.

Background

The facts are largely undisputed. In August 1987, the plaintiff began to sell walking shoes under the Easy Spirit trademark. In or around October 1988, the plaintiff introduced under the same trademark a line of "comfortable women's dress pumps" which were intended to incorporate design and comfort elements of the plaintiff's walking shoes. Since that time, Easy Spirit pumps have been promoted and advertised by associating them with sneakers, and in particular by using the slogan or tag line, "Looks Like a Pump, Feels Like a Sneaker." This slogan has been prominently featured in plaintiff's print ads, point of purchase displays, catalog sheets and promotional brochures. Exhibits 1–6 to Hepting Affidavit. It has also been used in a widely distributed television commercial, in which the slogan is sung while women are pictured playing basketball in Easy Spirit dress shoes. The plaintiff spent more than nine million dollars on advertising including the slogan in 1988 and 1989. During this time, sales increased dramatically. Sales of Easy Spirit pumps increased between 56% and 133% in the relevant market in the several weeks following runs of plaintiff's television commercial.

The defendant is the manufacturer and distributor of the Natural Sport line of walking shoes, and also of the Townwalker, a comfortable women's dress pump considered to be one of the key competitors of the Easy Spirit dress pump. In mid-1988, defendant retained the advertising agency D'Arcy, Masius, Benton & Bowles ("D'Arcy") to develop an ad campaign for the Townwalker and other NaturalSport shoes. D'Arcy recommended a campaign to communicate the basic product concept of the Townwalker: "a sneaker in a pump." D'Arcy submitted several proposed print ads for the Townwalker to the defendant, including some which used the slogan, "The pump that feels like a sneaker." The defendant rejected these ads, in part because of their similarity to plaintiff's advertising slogan, "Looks Like a Pump, Feels Like a Sneaker," of which defendant was aware.

The print advertisement ultimately selected by defendant features a photograph of a women's pump with the headline, "Think Of It As A Sneaker With No Strings Attached." The text of the ad includes the phrase, "And when we say it feels like a sneaker, we're not just stringing you along." The ad includes the NaturalSport logo, the slogan, "Walk Our Way" and the words "From Naturalizer," which defendant uses to advertise other styles of shoe in the NaturalSport line.

Plaintiff contends that the Townwalker ad's statement "And when we say it feels like a sneaker" is deliberately meant to mislead consumers into believing the Townwalker is the brand previously advertised by the slogan, "Looks Like a Pump, Feels Like a Sneaker," and thus cause consumers to purchase defendant's pump rather than plaintiff's. Plaintiff alleges that this constitutes a violation of the Lanham Act, as well as unfair competition and trademark violation under state common law.

Discussion

In order for a movant to prevail on its motion for a preliminary injunction, it must demonstrate both "(a) irreparable harm and (b) either a likelihood of success on the merits or sufficiently serious questions going to the merits to make them a fair ground for litigation and a balance of hardships tipping decidedly in the movant's favor." *Home Box Office, Inc. v. Showtime/The Movie Channel Inc.*, 832 F.2d 1311, 1314 (2d Cir. 1987).

A. Likelihood of Success on the Merits

To prove infringement, a trademark owner must demonstrate that the alleged infringer's use of the mark is likely to cause confusion or mistake as to the origin of the two products. When a mark is made of descriptive terms, the alleged infringer may defend his use of the terms by demonstrating that he used them in good faith in their descriptive sense and not as a trademark, thus making "fair use" of descriptive terms, as codified in Section 33(b)(4) of the Lanham Act. 15 U.S.C. § 1115(b)(4).

For the purposes of plaintiff's motion, I will assume that U.S. Shoe through heavy advertising has succeeded in establishing an association in the minds of the public between its descriptive slogan and its product. Nonetheless, I conclude that defendant's advertising claim that the Townwalker shoe"feels like a sneaker" does not infringe plaintiff's trademark.

Defendant's use of the words "feels like a sneaker" falls squarely within the "fair use" defense codified in Section 33(b)(4) of the Lanham Act. The fair use doctrine provides a statutory defense to a trademark infringement claim when "the use of the name, term, or device charged to bean infringement is a use, otherwise than as a trade or service mark, ... of a term or device which is *descriptive of and used fairly and in good faith only to describe* to users the goods or services of such party, or their geographic origin." 15 U.S.C. § 1115(b)(4) (emphasis added). The purpose of the defense is to prevent the trademark rights of one party from being extended to preclude another party from the description of his product to the public. *See Eli Lilly & Co. v. Revlon, Inc.,* 577 F. Supp. 477, 486 (1983). When the plaintiff chooses a mark with descriptive qualities, the fair use doctrine recognizes that "he cannot altogether exclude some kinds of competing uses," particularly those which use words in their primary descriptive and non-trademark sense.

An understanding of statutory fair use doctrine depends on the purposes and justifications of the trademark law. In general, the law disfavors the grant of exclusive monopoly rights. Exceptions exist, however, where the grant of monopoly rights results in substantial benefits to society. Because of the benefits to society resulting from the ability easily to recognize the goods or services of a purveyor or manufacturer, the trademark law grants the exclusive right to employ an identifying mark. A reciprocal benefit results. The merchant is thereby permitted to profit from a well earned reputation; the public is thereby enabled to choose the products produced by those who have satisfied them in the past, avoid those that have disappointed and recognize an unknown quantity as exactly that. The benefits are great, and because potential identifying marks exist in virtually inexhaustible supply, the cost of the monopoly to society is minimal.

The cost-free aspect of the trademark depends, however, on the exclusivity being practiced only over identifiers that are not needed by others for trade communication. If only one manufacturer of candy were permitted to call the product "candy"; if only one were permitted to say that it is "lemon flavored," then society would not be enriched but impoverished. Society would be deprived of useful information about competing products, and one supplier would receive an unfair and unjustified advantage over competitors. Thus the trademark law presumptively forbids the establishment of rights over "generic" or "descriptive" marks—marks that define or describe the product. An exception was permitted, however, to a user of a descriptive mark who over time had built up a customer recognition (secondary meaning) in the mark. It would be unfair to permit competitors to piggyback on the reputation earned by such a merchant. Thus a showing of acquired secondary meaning would overcome the presumptive ineligibility of descriptive words to exclusive reservation.

A user of a descriptive word may acquire the exclusive right to use that descriptive word *as an identifier* of the product or source. This, however, does not justify barring others from using the words in good faith *for descriptive purposes* pertinent to their products. Returning to the example of the candy manufacturers, the fact that one might acquire trademark rights over a descriptive identifier like "chewy" or "lemon flavored" cannot deprive society of the opportunity to be advised by other manufacturers that their candy is chewy or lemon flavored. Therefore, notwithstanding the establishment of trademark rights over a descriptive term by a showing that it has acquired secondary meaning, the statute preserves in others the right to the use of such terms "fairly and in good faith only to describe [and not to designate] the goods or services." 15 U.S.C. §1115(b)(4). The purpose of this provision is to ensure that the according of monopoly trademark rights over descriptive marks (upon a showing of acquired secondary meaning) will not over-broadly deprive society of the use of those terms in their descriptive sense in commercial communication.

In this case, the defendant uses the phrase "feels like a sneaker" in a descriptive sense, claiming a virtue of the product. It essentially restates the key selling claim of defendant's product — that the Townwalker shoe was designed specifically to incorporate the comfort of athletic shoes.

Moreover, defendant is not using the phrase as an identifier or trademark to indicate origin or source. That function is performed in defendant's ad by the NaturalSport logo, which is prominently displayed, and by the slogan, "Walk our Way … From Naturalizer." Defendant's use of the words "feels like a sneaker" is not even as a caption or slogan, but as a fragment of a sentence in small print. In short, defendant uses the words "otherwise than as a trade or service mark, … fairly and in good faith only to describe to users the goods" marketed by defendant. 15 U.S.C. §1115(b)(4). Under the fair use doctrine, such a use is not an infringement. There is no justification for permitting plaintiff to monopolize an essentially descriptive phrase which claims virtues, simply because plaintiff may have been the first to employ it in widely distributed advertisements.

Plaintiff, furthermore, has not demonstrated a sufficient likelihood of confusion as to source to justify a finding of infringement. Descriptive advertising claiming a product's virtues is likely to be understood as such rather than as an identifier of source. No confusion should be presumed from the defendant's use of descriptive words similar to plaintiff's, because the consumer is likely to understand that it is the claimed features of both products that are being discussed, and not their origin. Notwithstanding that plaintiff may have built up consumer recognition in its slogan and musical jingle, there is no reason to suppose that consumers will assume that any manufacturer who claims his shoes feel like a sneaker is the plaintiff. This is a standard descriptive approach to a claim of comfort and is unlikely to be understood as an identifier. Plaintiff has not met its burden of demonstrating that defendant's ad is likely to confuse consumers as to the source of defendant's product.

Plaintiff submits a consumer survey, designed by an experienced survey researcher, which demonstrates that defendant's print advertisement reminds consumers of plaintiff's advertisements more than do the ads of other brands. *See* Affidavit of Dr. Michael Rappeport at 3. To say that defendant's ads remind consumers of plaintiff's ads is very different from saying that they confuse consumers as to the source. Ads may be reminiscent of one another if they focus on similar claims about the products. It does not follow that they create confusion about the sources.

The fact that defendant's print advertisement includes prominent references to its own distinctive brand name makes it even less likely that consumers will confuse defendant's ad as coming from the same source as plaintiff's advertisements. Defendant's ad contains a fairly large reproduction of the NaturalSport logo (which is quite different from plaintiff's logo), and the slogan,"Walk Our Way ... From Naturalizer." Defendant's advertisement is distinguished from that of plaintiff in other ways. Whereas the caption in plaintiff's ad is its slogan, "Looks Like a Pump, Feels Like a Sneaker," defendant's bold print caption reads, "Think of It as a Sneaker With No Strings Attached." The "feels like a sneaker" phrase in defendant's ad is not in the caption, but in smaller print below, and appears not as a separate slogan but as a fragment of a sentence in a paragraph of text.

In short, defendant's advertisement is not designed to, nor is it likely to, cause confusion between plaintiff and defendant in the consumer's mind. It simply advances defendant's message that its shoes have the comfort of sneakers, using language which is essentially descriptive. The fact that the plaintiff used similar language in describing a similar product does not entitle it to exclusivity in claiming virtues of the product. The purpose of trademark law is not to give any promoter or seller an exclusive opportunity to make advertising claims about its product. It seeks only to permit clear brand recognition for the mutual benefit of the merchant and the consuming public.

* * *

Conclusion

For the numerous reasons stated above, plaintiff's motion for a preliminary injunction is hereby denied.

───────────

KP Permanent Make-Up, Inc. v. Lasting Impression I, Inc.

543 U.S. 111 (2004)

JUSTICE SOUTER delivered the opinion of the Court.

The question here is whether a party raising the statutory affirmative defense of fair use to a claim of trademark infringement, 15 U.S.C. §1115(b)(4), has a burden to negate any likelihood that the practice complained of will confuse consumers about the origin of the goods or services affected. We hold it does not.

[The 9th Circuit described the facts in this case in the following terms: KP and Lasting are direct competitors in the permanent makeup industry. To better understand the nature of the term "micro color," a brief description of permanent makeup and the permanent makeup industry is of use. Permanent makeup is similar to a tattoo, in that both are created by injecting pigment into the skin. Permanent makeup has both cosmetic and medical uses. For example, it may be used to create permanent eye liner and to enhance eyebrows, or it may be used in scar revision or in cases of pigmentary disorder. Permanent makeup is also known as micropigmentation.

The pigments used for permanent makeup are sold in small bottles for use by trained professionals. Both KP and Lasting have a separate line of pigments for use in the permanent makeup process. These pigments are sold in various colors. Further, both KP and Lasting sell their pigments to the same end users, such as beauty salons.

Lasting began using "micro colors" commercially as a trademark for its line of permanent makeup pigments in April 1992. The mark was registered on the Principal Register of the United States Patent and Trademark Office on May 11, 1993, as Reg. No. 1,769,592. The mark is registered as a design and word mark and consists of a solid black rectangle, with the words "micro" and "colors" in reverse white lettering. The word "micro" appears directly over the word "colors," and the two are separated by a green horizontal bar. In 1999, Lasting's mark, as registered, became incontestable. An illustration of the registered trademark is shown in Appendix A.

KP used the term "micro color" on its flyers beginning in 1990 and has continued to use the term on its pigment bottles since 1991. KP's use of the term "micro color" on its bottle labels consists of the word in full capitals before the actual color of the pigment in the bottle. For example, KP's use of the word on a bottle containing black pigment would appear as: "MICROCOLOR: BLACK."

In 1999, KP adopted a new use of the term "micro color." Rather than using it only on its bottles, KP began using the term in its marketing brochures. The brochures display the term "microcolor" in a stylized format. "Micro color" sits directly over the word "pigment," and a vial with pigment flowing out of it is depicted to the side of the word display. Additionally, under both the vial and the phrase "micro color pigment" is the word "chart." Both the words "pigment" and "chart" appear in a smaller size type than the term "micro color," making the term the most dominant feature of the image. The brochure on which this image appears contains a chart displaying all the various colors in which KP's pigments are available. 328 F.3d 1061(9th Cir. 2002)]

I

We granted KP's petition for certiorari, 540 US. 1099, 540 US. 1099, 157 L. Ed. 2d 811, 124 S. Ct. 981 (2004), to address a disagreement among the Courts of Appeals on the significance of likely confusion for a fair use defense to a trademark infringement claim, and the obligation of a party defending on that ground to show that its use is unlikely to cause consumer confusion. *Compare* 328 F.3d at 1072 (likelihood of confusion bars the fair use defense); *PACCAR Inc. v. TeleScan Technologies, L. L. C.*, 319 F.3d 243, 256 (CA6 2003) ("[A] finding of a likelihood of confusion forecloses a fair use defense"); and *Zatarains, Inc. v. Oak Grove Smokehouse*, 698 F.2d 786, 796 (CA5 1983) (alleged infringers were free to use words contained in a trademark "in their ordinary, descriptive sense, so long as such use [did] not tend to confuse customers as to the source of the goods"), with Cosmetically Sealed Industries, Inc. v. Chesebrough Pond 's USA Co., 125 F.3d 28, 30–31 (CA2 1997) (the fair use defense may succeed even if there is likelihood of confusion); *Shakespeare Co. v. Silstar Corp. of Am.*, 110 F.3d 234, 243 (CA4 1997) ("[A] determination of likely confusion [does not] preclude] considering the fairness of use"); *Sunmark, Inc. v. Ocean Spray Cranberries, Inc.*, 64 F.3d 1055, 1059 (CA71995) (finding that likelihood of confusion did not preclude the fair use defense). We now vacate the judgment of the Court of Appeals.

II

A

The Trademark Act of 1946, known for its principal proponent as the Lanham Act, 60 Stat 427, as amended, 15 U.S.C. §1051 et seq., provides the user of a trade or service mark with the opportunity to register it with the PTO, §§1051, 1053. If the registrant then satisfies further conditions including continuous use for five consecutive years, "the right … to use such registered mark in commerce" to designate the origin of the goods specified in the registration "shall be incontestable" outside certain listed exceptions. §1065.

The holder of a registered mark (incontestable or not) has a civil action against anyone employing an imitation of it in commerce when "such use is likely to cause confusion, or to cause mistake, or to deceive." §1114(1). Although an incontestable registration is "conclusive evidence … of the registrant's exclusive right to use the … mark in commerce," §1115(b), the plaintiff's success is still subject to "proof of infringement as defined in section 1114," §1115(b). And that, as just noted, requires a showing that the defendant's actual practice is likely to produce confusion in the minds of consumers about the origin of the goods or services in question. This plaintiff's burden has to be kept in mind when reading the relevant portion of the further provision for an affirmative defense of fair use, available to a party whose

> "use of the name, term, or device charged to be an infringement is a use, otherwise than as a mark, ... of a term or device which is descriptive of and used fairly and in good faith only to describe the goods or services of such party, or their geographic origin...." §1115(b)(4).

Two points are evident. Section 1115(b) places a burden of proving likelihood of confusion (that is, infringement) on the party charging infringement even when relying on an incontestable registration. And Congress said nothing about likelihood of confusion in setting out the elements of the fair use defense in §1115(b)(4).

Starting from these textual fixed points, it takes a long stretch to claim that a defense of fair use entails any burden to negate confusion. It is just not plausible that Congress would have used the descriptive phrase "likely to cause confusion, or to cause mistake, or to deceive" in §1114 to describe the requirement that a markholder show likelihood of consumer confusion, but would have relied on the phrase "used fairly" in §1115(b)(4) in a fit of terse drafting meant to place a defendant under a burden to negate confusion. "'[W]here Congress includes particular language in one section of a statute but omits it in another section of the same Act, it is generally presumed that Congress acts intentionally and purposely in the disparate inclusion or exclusion.'" *Russello v. United States*, 464 US. 16, 23, 78 L. Ed. 2d 17, 104 S. Ct. 296 (1983) (quoting *United States v. Wong Kim Bo*, 472 F.2d 720, 722 (CA5 1972)) (alteration in original).[6] Nor do we find much force in Lasting's suggestion that "used fairly" in §1115(b)(4) is an oblique incorporation of a likelihood-of-confusion test developed in the common law of unfair competition. Lasting is certainly correct that some unfair competition cases would stress that use of a term by another in conducting its trade went too far in sowing confusion, and would either enjoin the use or order the defendant to include a disclaimer. *See, e.g., Baglin v. Cusenier Co.*, 221 US. 580, 602, 55 L. Ed. 863, 31 S. Ct. 669, 1911 Dec. Comm 'r Pat. 552 (1911) ("[W]e are unable to escape the conclusion that such use, in the manner shown, was to serve the purpose of simulation ..."); *Herring-Hall-Marvin Safe Co. v. Hall's Safe Co.*, 208 US. 554, 559, 52 L. Ed. 616, 28 S. Ct. 350, 6 Ohio L. Rep. 367 (1908) ("[T]he rights of the two parties have been reconciled by allowing the use, provided that an explanation is attached"). But the common law of unfair competition also tolerated some degree of confusion from a descriptive use of words contained in another person's trademark. *See, e.g., William R. Warner & Co. v. Eli Lilly & Co.*, 265 US. 526, 528, 68 L. Ed. 1161, 44 S. Ct. 615, 1925 Dec. Comm 'r Pat. 420 (1924) (as to plaintiff's trademark claim, "[t]he use of a similar name by another to truthfully describe his own product does not constitute a legal or moral wrong, even if its effect be to cause the public to mistake the origin or ownership of the product"); *Canal Co. v. Clark*, 80 US. 311, 13 Wall. 311, 327, 20 L. Ed. 581 (1872) ("Purchasers may be mistaken, but they are not deceived by false representations, and equity

---

6. Not only that, but the failure to say anything about a defendant's burden on this point was almost certainly not an oversight, not after the House Subcommittee on Trademarks declined to forward a proposal to provide expressly as an element of the defense that a descriptive use be "'[un]likely to deceive the public.' Hearings on H. R. 102 et al. before the Subcommittee on Trade-Marks of the House Committee on Patents, 77th Cong., 1st Sess., 167–168 (1941) (hereinafter Hearings) (testimony of Prof. Milton Handler).

will not enjoin against telling the truth"); *see also* 3 L. Altman, Callmann on Unfair Competition, Trademarks and Monopolies § 18:2, pp 18-8 to 18-9, n 1 (4th ed. 2004) (citing cases). While these cases are consistent with taking account of the likelihood of consumer confusion as one consideration in deciding whether a use is fair, they do not stand for the proposition that an assessment of confusion alone may be dispositive. Certainly one cannot get out of them any defense burden to negate it entirely.

Finally, a look at the typical course of litigation in an infringement action points up the incoherence of placing a burden to show nonconfusion on a defendant. If a plaintiff succeeds in making out a prima facie case of trademark infringement, including the element of likelihood of consumer confusion, the defendant may offer rebutting evidence to undercut the force of the plaintiff's evidence on this (or any) element, or raise an affirmative defense to bar relief even if the prima facie case is sound, or do both. But it would make no sense to give the defendant a defense of showing affirmatively that the plaintiff cannot succeed in proving some element (like confusion); all the defendant needs to do is to leave the factfinder unpersuaded that the plaintiff has carried its own burden on that point. A defendant has no need of a court's true belief when agnosticism will do. Put another way, it is only when a plaintiff has shown likely confusion by a preponderance of the evidence that a defendant could have any need of an affirmative defense, but under Lasting's theory the defense would be foreclosed in such a case. "[I]t defies logic to argue that a defense may not be asserted in the only situation where it even becomes relevant." *Shakespeare Co. v. Silstar Corp.*, 110 F.3d at 243. Nor would it make sense to provide an affirmative defense of no confusion plus good faith, when merely rebutting the plaintiff's case on confusion would entitle the defendant to judgment, good faith or not.

Lasting tries to extenuate the anomaly of this conception of the affirmative defense by arguing that the oddity reflects the "vestigial" character of the fair use defense as a historical matter. Lasting argues that, because it was only in 1988 that Congress added the express provision that an incontestable markholder's right to exclude is "subject to proof of infringement," Trademark Law Revision Act of 1988, § 128(b)(1), 102 Stat. 3944, there was no requirement prior to 1988 that a markholder prove likelihood of confusion. Before 1988, the argument goes, it was sensible to get at the issue of likely confusion by requiring a defendant to prove its absence when defending on the ground of fair use. When the 1988 Act saddled the markholder with the obligation to prove confusion likely, § 1115(b), the revision simply failed to relieve the fair use defendant of the suddenly strange burden to prove absence of the very confusion that a plaintiff had a new burden to show in the first place.

But the explanation does not work. It is not merely that it would be highly suspect in leaving the claimed element of 1115(b)(4) redundant and pointless. *Hibbs v. Winn*, 542 US. 88, 159 L. Ed. 2d 172, 124 S. Ct. 2276 (2004)). The main problem of the argument is its false premise: Lasting's assumption that holders of incontestable marks had no need to prove likelihood of confusion prior to 1988 is wrong. *See, e.g., Beer Nuts, Inc. v. Clover Club Foods Co.*, 805 F.2d 920, 924–925 (CA101986) (requiring proof of likelihood of confusion in action by holder of incontestable mark); 5 J. McCarthy, Trademarks and Unfair Competition § 32:154, p 32-247 (4th ed. 2004) ("Before the 1988 Trademark Law Revision Act, the majority of courts held that while incontestability grants a conclusive presumption of the 'exclusive right to use' the registered mark, this did not relieve the registrant of proving likelihood of confusion").

B

Since the burden of proving likelihood of confusion rests with the plaintiff, and the fair use defendant has no free-standing need to show confusion unlikely, it follows (contrary to the Court of Appeals's view) that some possibility of consumer confusion must be compatible with fair use, and so it is. The common law's tolerance of a certain degree of confusion on the part of consumers followed from the very fact that in cases like this one an originally descriptive term was selected to be used as a mark, not to mention the undesirability of allowing anyone to obtain a complete monopoly on use of a descriptive term simply by grabbing it first. *Canal Co. v. Clark, id.*, at 323–324, 327, 20 L. Ed. 581. The Lanham Act adopts a similar leniency, there being no indication that the statute was meant to deprive commercial speakers of the ordinary utility of descriptive words. "If any confusion results, that is a risk the plaintiff accepted when it decided to identify its product with a mark that uses a well known descriptive phrase." *Cosmetically Sealed Industries, Inc. v. Chesebrough Pond's USA Co.*, 125 F.3d at 30.[7] This right to describe is the reason that descriptive terms qualify for registration as trademarks only after taking on secondary meaning as "distinctive of the applicant's goods," 15 U.S.0 §10520, with the registrant getting an exclusive right not in the original, descriptive sense, but only in the secondary one associated with the markholder's goods, 2 McCarthy, *id.*, §11:45 ("The only aspect of the mark which is given legal protection is that penumbra or fringe of secondary meaning which surrounds the old descriptive word").

While we thus recognize that mere risk of confusion will not rule out fair use, we think it would be improvident to go further in this case, for deciding anything more would take us beyond the Ninth Circuit's consideration of the subject. It suffices to realize that our holding that fair use can occur along with some degree of confusion does not foreclose the relevance of the extent of any likely consumer confusion in assessing whether a defendant's use is objectively fair. Two Courts of Appeals have found it relevant to consider such scope, and commentators and *amici* here have urged us to say that the degree of likely consumer confusion bears not only on the fairness of using a term, but even on the further question whether an originally descriptive term has become so identified as a mark that a defendant's use of it cannot realistically be called descriptive. *See Shakespeare Co. v. Silstar Corp., id.*, at 243 ("[T]o the degree that confusion is likely, a use is less likely to be found fair …" (emphasis omitted)); *Sunmark, Inc. v. Ocean Spray Cranberries, Inc.*, 64 F.3d at 1059; Restatement (Third) of Unfair Competition, §28.

Since we do not rule out the pertinence of the degree of consumer confusion under the fair use defense, we likewise do not pass upon the position of the United States, as *amicus*, that the "used fairly" requirement in §1115(b)(4) demands only that the descriptive term describe the goods accurately. Accuracy of course has to be a consideration in assessing fair use, but the proceedings in this case so far raise no occasion to evaluate some other concerns that courts might pick as relevant, quite apart from attention to confusion. The Restatement raises possibilities like commercial justification and the strength of the plaintiff's mark. Restatement §28. As to them, it is enough to say here that the door is not closed.

III

In sum, a plaintiff claiming infringement of an incontestable mark must show likelihood of consumer confusion as part of the prima facie case, 15 U.S.C. §1115(b), while the defendant has no independent burden to negate the likelihood of any confusion in raising the affirmative defense that a term is used descriptively, not as a mark, fairly, and in good faith, §1115(b)(4).

---

7. *See also* Hearings 72 (testimony of Wallace Martin, Chairman, American Bar Association Committee on Trade-Mark Legislation) ("Everybody has got a right to the use of the English language and has got a right to assume that nobody is going to take that English language away from him").

Because we read the Court of Appeals as requiring KP to shoulder a burden on the issue of confusion, we vacate the judgment and remand the case for further proceedings consistent with this opinion.

It is so ordered.

Notes

1. How did the Supreme Court's decision change the way the fair use defense is supposed to be addressed today? Do you think that the Supreme Court fully addressed the discrepancy between the Circuits regarding fair use?

2. Other examples where fair use was found include the following:

> Use of the terms "camel safari," "hippo safari," and "chukka safari" on boots did not infringe the trademark SAFARI. *Abercrombie & Fitch v. Hunting World, Inc.*, 537 F.2d 4 (2d Cir. 1976); Use of the term "honeycomb" to describe desiccant wheels in dehumidifying equipment did not infringe the registered trademark HONEY COMBE for the same goods. *Munters Corp. v. Matsui Am. Inc.*, 909 F. 2d 250 (7th Cir.), *cert. denied*, 498 U.S. 1016 (1990).

3. Other examples where fair use was not found include the following:

> Use of the term "auditor's fine point" infringed the trademark AUDITOR for use on ball-point pens. Lindy Pen Co. v. Bic Pen Corp. 725 F.2d 1240 (9th Cir. 1984), cert. denied, 469 U.S. 1188 (1985).

> Use of the term "brew nuts" infringed the trademark BEER NUTS as used on sweetened and salted peanuts. Beer Nuts, Inc. v. Clover Club Foods Co., 711 F.2d 934 (10th Cir. 1983).

---

2. Nominative Fair Use

Brother Records v. Jardine
318 F. 3d 900 (9th Cir. 2003)

TASHIMA, CIRCUIT JUDGE:

Alan Jardine appeals the district court's grant of summary judgment in favor of Brother Records, Inc. ("BRI"), on BRI's Lanham Act, 15 U.S.C. §§1051–1129, trademark infringement action alleging that Jardine infringed BRI's "The Beach Boys" trademark. We have jurisdiction under 28 U.S.C. §1291, and we affirm.

BACKGROUND

In 1961, Al Jardine, Mike Love, Brian Wilson, Carl Wilson, and Dennis Wilson formed The Beach Boys. The band shortly thereafter achieved huge commercial success, producing numerous hit songs and touring to huge audiences throughout the country. In 1967, the members of the Beach Boys incorporated BRI to hold and administer the intellectual property rights for The Beach Boys. Currently, BRI is equally owned by four shareholders, who are also its directors: Al Jardine, Mike Love, Brian Wilson, and the estate of Carl Wilson. BRI is the registered owner of "The Beach Boys" trademark.

Over the years, personal difficulties arose between some of the members, and some members of the band decided to not tour full time, or at all. In 1991, the members of the Beach Boys incorporated Brother Tours, Inc., which handled their touring and distributed their touring income. In 1993, the directors of BRI agreed to devote a certain percentage of the touring income to the corporation for use of the trademark and designated a larger percentage of the income to those members who actually toured. By 1998, Carl Wilson had died, Love and Jardine no longer wanted to tour together, and Brian Wilson did not want to tour at all. Love began negotiating with BRI the terms of a license to use "The Beach Boys" trademark in connection with his own band.

BRI's directors met on July 14, 1998, to discuss how the trademark should be used. The representative of Carl Wilson's estate suggested that BRI issue non-exclusive licenses to each shareholder on the same terms and conditions as the license that was being negotiated with Love, thus giving each member an equal right to tour. Three of the four board members, including Jardine, voted to grant each Beach Boy a non-exclusive license. On October 1, 1998, BRI executed a non-exclusive license agreement with Love (the "Love license"). The Love license contained clauses designed to protect the value of the trademark, requiring the licensee to preserve The Beach Boys style and to choose from a list of approved booking agencies and managers.

The parties dispute whether BRI and Jardine entered into a non-exclusive license agreement. After the July 1998 BRI board meeting, Jardine began touring with his own band, using a booking agent and manager that were not included in the list approved by the Love license. On October 25, 1998, Jardine's attorney sent BRI a letter saying that Jardine would be performing as "Beach Boys Family and Friends," and that therefore, "a license from BRI [was] unnecessary." On October 28,1998, BRI told Jardine that his unlicensed use of the trademark would be an infringement.

Jardine then proposed a license that included terms different from those included in the Love license. Jardine's proposal contemplated only a five-percent royalty to BRI on the first $1 million of gross receipts and a 17.5 percent royalty thereafter. BRI proposed a 17.5 percent royalty across the board. Love's license required a royalty of 20 percent of the first $1 million and 17.5 percent of receipts thereafter. Also, Jardine wanted to use a booking agent and manager that were not on the approved list. Jardine stated that, whether or not BRI accepted the proposal, he would continue performing as the "Beach Boys Family and Friends."

The BRI board scheduled another meeting for November 24, 1998 to discuss Jardine's proposal. Before the meeting, Jardine's attorney sent a letter to the board with a proposed license agreement signed by Jardine. At the meeting, the BRI board voted to reject Jardine's proposal. In the months following the meeting, Jardine both attempted to negotiate an agreement and claimed he had a license.

Jardine and his band continued to perform using names that included "The Beach Boys" trademark. The performances were promoted under names such as: Al Jardine of the Beach Boys and Family & Friends; The Beach Boys "Family and Friends"; Beach Boys Family & Friends; The Beach Boys, Family & Friends; Beach Boys and Family; as well as, simply, The Beach Boys. Jardine and his band performed in locations and on dates close to Love's "The Beach Boys" shows. With two bands touring as The Beach Boys or as a similar-sounding combination, show organizers sometimes were confused about what exactly they were getting when they booked Jardine's band. A number of show organizers booked Jar-dine's band thinking they would get The Beach Boys along with special added guests, but subsequently canceled the booking when they discovered that Jardine's band was not what they thought it was. Numerous people who attended one of Jardine's shows said that they had been confused about who was performing. During this time period, BRI sent Jardine cease and desist letters objecting to Jardine's use of the trademark.

On April 9, 1999, BRI filed its complaint in the district court alleging that Jardine was infringing its trademark. Jardine answered, asserting the defenses of fair use, laches, estoppel, and unclean hands, and counterclaimed for breach of employment agreement, breach of license agreement, and for a declaratory judgment that Jardine could tour as the "Beach Boys Family and Friends." On March 28, 2000, the district court issued the preliminary injunction prohibiting Jardine from using "The Beach Boys," "The Beach Boys Family and Friends," and other similar combinations, but still allowing Jardine to refer to his past membership in the band "in a descriptive fashion."

On March 19, 2001, two weeks before the close of discovery, Jardine moved for leave to amend his pleading to add third-party claims against the shareholders and directors of BRI and an additional counterclaim against BRI for breach of fiduciary duty. The district court denied the motion. On June 4, 2001, BRI moved for summary judgment on its trademark infringement claim and Jardine's counterclaims. The district court granted summary judgment in favor of BRI and issued a permanent injunction against Jardine's use of the trademark. This timely appeal followed.

* * *

Where the defendant uses the trademark not in its primary, descriptive sense, but rather in its secondary, trademark sense, the nominative fair use analysis applies. *See New Kids*, 971 F.2d at 308. The nominative fair use defense acknowledges that "it is often virtually impossible to refer to a particular product for purposes of comparison, criticism, point of reference or any other such purpose without using the mark." *Id.* at 306. Still, the "core element" of trademark infringement law is "whether an alleged trademark infringer's use of a mark creates a likelihood that the consuming public will be confused as to who makes what product." *Thane Int'l*, 305 F.3d at 901 (internal quotation marks omitted). Therefore, the nominative fair use defense is available only if "the use of the trademark does not attempt to capitalize on consumer confusion or to appropriate the cachet of one product for a different one." *New Kids*, 971 F.2d at 307–308.

In *New Kids*, we articulated the three requirements of the nominative fair use defense:

> First, the product or service in question must be one not readily identifiable without use of the trademark; second, only so much of the mark or marks may be used as is reasonably necessary to identify the product or service; and third, the user must do nothing that would, in conjunction with the mark, suggest sponsorship or endorsement by the trademark holder.

Id. at 308. Just as it is virtually impossible to refer to the New Kids on the Block, the Chicago Bulls, Volkswagens, or the Boston Marathon without using the trademarked names, so too is it virtually impossible to refer to the Beach Boys without using the trademark, and Jardine therefore meets the first requirement. Also, BRI does not allege that Jardine uses any distinctive logo "or anything else that isn't needed" to identify the Beach Boys, and Jardine therefore satisfies the second requirement.

Jardine fails, however, to meet the third requirement. Jardine's promotional materials display "The Beach Boys" more prominently and boldly than "Family and Friends," suggesting sponsorship by the Beach Boys. *Cf. Kassbaum v. Steppenwolf Prods., Inc.*, 236 F.3d 487, 493 (9th Cir. 2000) (reasoning that promotional materials reduced likelihood of confusion by minimizing references to trademarked name "Steppenwolf"). Also, there is evidence that Jardine uses "The Beach Boys" trademark to suggest that his band is in fact sponsored by the Beach Boys, as Jardine's management testified that they recommended including the trademark "The Beach Boys" in the name of Jardine's band in order to create or enhance marquee value. Finally, Jardine's use of the trademark caused actual consumer confusion, as both event organizers that booked Jardine's band and people who attended Jardine's shows submitted declarations expressing confusion about who was performing.

Because Jardine's use of the trademark suggested sponsorship or endorsement by the trademark holder, Jardine's nominative fair use argument fails.[8] The plain language of Rule 56(c) mandates the entry of summary judgment ... against a party who fails to make a showing sufficient to establish the existence of an element essential to that party's case, and on which that party will bear the burden of proof at trial." *Celotex Corp. v. Catrett*, 477 U.S. 317, 322, 91 L. Ed. 2d 265, 106 S. Ct. 2548 (1986). The district court did not err in concluding that Jardine's use of the Beach Boys' trademark was an infringement. No genuine issue of material fact exists regarding Jardine's suggestion of sponsorship or endorsement by BRI. We therefore affirm the district court's grant of summary judgment in favor of BRI on BRI's trademark infringement claim.

Century 21 Real Estate Corp. v. Lendingtree. Inc.
425 F.3d 211 (3 Cir 2005)

RENDELL, CIRCUIT JUDGE.

I. Factual and Procedural Background

Appellees Century 21 and ERA have each been in business for over 30 years. Coldwell Banker has been in business for almost 100 years. Each of these real estate companies oversees a system of franchisees. Franchise agreements permit those brokerage companies to provide realty services under trademarks held by Cendant Corporation. Every franchisee is granted a license to use its franchisor's trademark only in connection with its "d/b/a" name.

Appellant LendingTree ("LT") ... has a real estate referral service that consumers can access by visiting its website and inputting the location and characteristics of the house they are seeking to buy or sell. LT then selects and transmits information about up to four real estate companies participating in LT's referral network that service that community.

The alleged infringement here is based on the following uses of CCE's marks:

(1) Coldwell Banker "For Sale" sign with a woman, on which the blue and white Coldwell Banker logo was somewhat obscured by the word "SOLD." LT's phone number was at the bottom. This scene was depicted at the bottom of LT's homepage on its website.

(2) A statement by LT on its "Find a Realtor" homepage stating that LT will "give you access to a national network of brokers representing the country's leading real estate companies, including Coldwell Banker, ERA and Century 21." The marks on those pages were in block letter format.

---

8. In reaching this conclusion, we note that the third requirement of the nominative fair use defense—the lack of anything that suggests sponsor-ship or endorsement—is merely the other side of the likelihood-of-confusion coin.

(3) LT's statement on its website's Help Center that LT is "represented by large independent real estate companies and members of major franchises—Coldwell Banker, Century 21, Prudential, ERA, ReMAX, GMAC (formerly Better Homes & Gardens), and Realty Executives."

(4) LT's use of printed marketing materials that stated that "LT is affiliated with more than 700 certified brokers such as Coldwell Banker, Century 21, Prudential, ERA and RE/MAX."

In January 2003, Kathryn Geib, in-house counsel for CCE's parent company, wrote to LT to demand that it stop using CCE's "marks" on its website in any manner in the operation of its business. At that time, LT was using CCE's logos on its website. After receipt of the letter, LT stopped using the logos (or any other of CCE's marks) on that webpage, but continued to use CCE's marks in block letter form on other webpages. In May 2003, CCE discovered that LT was using CCE's marks, but in block letters, on its webpage. Geib again wrote, asking LT to stop such use.

* * *

IV. Fair Use

It must be recognized at the outset that "fair use" presents a fact pattern different from that of a normal infringement suit. But the fair use defense, by reason of the circumstances giving rise to its applicability, alters the premise somewhat. The defendant is not purporting to be selling goods or services that the plaintiff has trademarked, but, rather, is using plaintiff's mark in order to refer to defendant's own goods or to the goods of the trademark owner in a way that might confuse the public as to the relationship between the two. *See Cairns v. Franklin Mint Co.*, 292 F.3d 1139, 1151 (9th Cir. 2002). Accordingly, the legal framework still involves a showing that A's reference to B's mark will likely confuse the public, but the analysis does not end there, for the use may nonetheless be permissible if it is "fair."

In *KP Permanent Make-Up, Inc. v. Lasting Impression I, Inc.*, 543 US. 111, 125 S. Ct. 542, 545–46, 160 L. Ed. 2d 440 (2004), the Supreme Court rejected the notion that, in the context of classic fair use, the party asserting the fair use defense to a claim of trademark infringement had any burden to negate the likelihood that the practice complained of will confuse consumers about the origin of the services or goods affected. Instead, plaintiff has the exclusive burden to demonstrate likelihood of confusion, and then defendant's burden is only to show the affirmative defense of fair use. The Supreme Court stated, "since the burden of proving likelihood of confusion rests with the plaintiff, and the fair use defendant has no free-standing need to show confusion unlikely ... it follows that some possibility of consumer confusion must be compatible with fair use...." *Id.* at 550. Thus, consumer confusion and fair use are not mutually exclusive. The latter will in essence rebut or excuse the former so that the use is permissible.

Few other courts have spoken on the precise issue of how nominative fair use is successfully invoked. Indeed, it seems that only the Second, Fifth, and Sixth Circuits have referenced the nominative fair use defense by name and even on these occasions have done so only to refer to what district courts had done with the issue or to decline to adopt the Ninth Circuit's test as a whole.

While we agree with the Ninth Circuit Court of Appeals that a distinct analysis is needed for nominative fair use cases, we do not accept the legal basis or advisability of supplanting the likelihood of confusion test entirely. First, we do not see nominative fair use as so different from classic fair use as to warrant such different treatment. The Ninth Circuit Court of Appeals believed that the two types of fair use could be distinguished on the basis that nominative fair use makes it clear to consumers that the plaintiff, not the defendant, is the source of the trademarked product or service, while classic fair use does not. Thus, the Ninth Circuit Court of Appeals believed that a different analysis was appropriate for nominative fair use and that it could abandon the need for proof of confusion in these circumstances. *New Kids On The Block*, 971 F.2d at 307–08. Yet, it is clear to us that even a defendant's nominative use has the potential of confusing consumers with respect to its products or services. Since the defendant ultimately uses the plaintiff's mark in a nominative case in order to describe its own product or services, *Cairns*, 292 F.3d at 1151 & n.8, even an accurate nominative use could potentially confuse consumers about the plaintiff's endorsement or sponsorship of the defendant's products or services. Thus, we disagree with the fundamental distinction the Ninth Circuit Court of Appeals drew between classic and nominative fair use.

In addition, the approach of the Court of Appeals for the Ninth Circuit would relieve the plaintiff of the burden of proving the key element of a trademark infringement case — likelihood of confusion — as a precondition to a defendant's even having to assert and demonstrate its entitlement to a nominative fair use defense. The Supreme Court in KP Permanent Make-Up clearly established that it was plaintiff's burden in a classic fair use case to prove likelihood of confusion. [O]nce the plaintiff proves likelihood of confusion, defendant only had to show that defendant's use, even if confusing, was "fair."

This view finds support not only in the Supreme Court's recent opinion, but also in the relevant statutory framework. The very language of the Lanham Act leads us to conclude that likelihood of confusion is an essential indicator of whether or not trademark infringement has occurred. Both §§ 32 and 43(a) of the Lanham Act, allegedly violated in this case, forbid use of words or marks in a way which is likely to cause confusion as to the origin, sponsorship, or approval of goods or services. Surely the plaintiff's success in its claim must rely on a finding in this regard. Given this, we decline to read this requirement out of a case alleging trademark infringement.

V. The Proper Analytical Approach for Nominative Fair Use Cases
A. Overview

Today we adopt a two-step approach in nominative fair use cases. The plaintiff must first prove that confusion is likely due to the defendant's use of plaintiff's mark. Once plaintiff has met its burden of proving that confusion is likely, the burden then shifts to defendant to show that its nominative use of plaintiff's mark is nonetheless fair. To demonstrate fairness, a defendant must show: (1) that the use of plaintiff's mark is necessary to describe both the plaintiff's product or service and the defendant's product or service; (2) that the defendant uses only so much of the plaintiff's mark as is necessary to describe plaintiff's product; and (3) that the defendant's conduct or language reflect the true and accurate relationship between plaintiff and defendant's products or services.

If the factors for determining fairness were incorporated into the likelihood of confusion test, a plaintiff's showing of confusion might well overwhelm a defendant's showing of fair use. This would essentially force a defendant asserting nominative fair use to negate all likelihood of confusion to succeed, a proposition that the Supreme Court rejected in KP Permanent Make-Up. Under our approach, the defendant has no duty to negate confusion, but rather must merely show that its use of the plaintiff's mark is fair, a burden which, by contrast, is not cumbersome. Thus, it is our view that the bifurcated approach is ultimately less burdensome to a nominative use defendant.

Finally, we believe that the bifurcated approach that we adopt today is more workable than a unified confusion/fairness test. We leave the now familiar test for likelihood of confusion largely intact and in the form in which district courts are accustomed to applying it. Our test for nominative fair use considers distinct factors that are readily susceptible to judicial inquiry. Because confusion and fairness are separate and distinct concepts that can co-exist, blending them together into one test is, to our mind, a much less manageable approach.

* * *

C. The Affirmative Defense of Nominative Fair Use

Under the nominative fair use test adopted by the Court of Appeals for the Ninth Circuit, a defendant must prove: (1) that the product or service in question is one not readily identifiable without use of the trademark; (2) that only so much of the mark or marks is used as is reasonably necessary to identify the product or service; and (3) that the user did nothing that would, in conjunction with the mark, suggest sponsorship or endorsement by the trademark holder. *New Kids on the Block*, 971 F.2d at 308. In the Ninth Circuit, if these elements are proven, the use is "fair" and defendant will prevail. Further, this nominative fair use test, as discussed above, replaces the likelihood of confusion test in the Court of Appeals for the Ninth Circuit. We must decide the extent to which we should adopt this test as our own, mindful that we will employ it as an affirmative defense to be proven by defendant after likelihood of confusion has been demonstrated by the plaintiff.

We are tempted to use the three-pronged Ninth Circuit test outright, as it has withstood the test of time, has been tinkered with in no less than seven opinions. The Supreme Court's rejection of its view of how the fair use defense works in a classic fair use case emboldens us to examine the elements of the Ninth Circuit Court of Appeals' nominative fair use test a bit more closely.

In so doing, we conclude that the test as written suffers from a lack of clarity. This is evident, in the contortions that the Ninth Circuit Court of Appeals itself has gone through in applying it, the confusion that the District Court here encountered in its application, and in our conviction that a modified inquiry would aid in reaching the right result. We will adjust the test to include a slightly different set of considerations:

1. Is the use of plaintiff's mark necessary to describe (1) plaintiff's product or service and (2) defendant's product or service?

2. Is only so much of the plaintiff's mark used as is necessary to describe plaintiff's products or services?

3. Does the defendant's conduct or language reflect the true and accurate relationship between plaintiff and defendant's products or services?

The following discussion explains how these factors should be applied.

1. First Prong

The first element of the Ninth Circuit Court of Appeals' test involved an inquiry only into the necessity of using plaintiff's trademark to describe plaintiff's product. The first prong of New Kids On The Block is at best confusing and at worst incomplete. While it should be asked whether plaintiff's product needs to be described by reference to its mark, should it not also be examined whether defendant's use of it, at all, is necessary to accurately describe what defendant does or sells, or whether its reference to plaintiff's mark is actually gratuitous? The District Court's inquiry into the latter aspect was not called for under the New Kids On The Block test, but it actually seems entirely appropriate.

The focus on the necessity of the mark in order for defendant to describe plaintiff's product makes sense in the context of nominative fair use, where the plaintiff's mark is being used because it identifies the plaintiff's product. We further note that the court need not find that the use of the mark is indispensable in order to find this factor fulfilled. For, as we have stated before, "the Lanham Act does not compel a competitor to resort to second-best communication." G.D. Searle & Co., 715 F.2d 837 at 842.

Therefore, the court need only be satisfied that the identification by the defendant of plaintiff's product or service would be rendered significantly more difficult without use of the mark.

Additionally, we believe that it is important for a court to understand how necessary the use of the mark is to the identification of defendant's product.

2. Second Prong

Here again, the *New Kids On The Block* test focuses on the "amount" of plaintiff's mark that is used, asking whether only so much is used as is necessary to describe plaintiff's product.

But the proper focus under this prong is on whether only so much of plaintiff's mark as is reasonably necessary to identify plaintiff's product or service has been used by defendant. Consideration should be given at this stage to the manner in which the mark is portrayed. For example, did the defendant use plaintiff's distinctive lettering when using the plaintiff's mark or did the defendant, as in this case, simply use block letters to spell out plaintiff's names?

3. Third Prong

The *New Kids* test at this stage asks whether the user did anything that would, in conjunction with the mark, suggest sponsorship or endorsement by the trademark holder. However, we believe the appropriate question should be a bit broader: does the defendant's conduct or language reflect the true and accurate relationship between plaintiff and defendant's products or services? A defendant's purposeful portrayal of plaintiff's endorsement of its product through defendant's conduct or language does not necessarily render the use unfair, as long as the depiction of the endorsement is accurate. In addition, our version suggests that we can consider the defendant's failure to state or explain some aspect of the relationship, whereas the New Kids version focuses on affirmative acts, i.e., what the defendant did to suggest sponsorship.

The mere presence or use of the mark does not suggest unfairness under this prong. Here, LT added a disclaimer, the significance of which the District Court downplayed, stating that "LendingTree is not sponsored by or affiliated with the parent franchisor companies of any of the participating members of its network." Far from unimportant, such a disclaimer must be considered in determining whether the alleged infringer accurately portrayed the relationship that existed between plaintiff and defendant.

The Ninth Circuit's test for nominative fair use does not explicitly include accuracy within the analysis, but the Supreme Court has recognized that "accuracy of course has to be a consideration in assessing fair use." *KP Permanent Make-Up, Inc.*, 125 S. Ct. at 551. In examining the conduct of the defendant to determine whether the defendant has done anything to affirmatively cause consumer confusion, it is only reasonable to consider the precision with which the defendant has described its relationship with plaintiff. In this case, the evaluation of accuracy would necessarily include consideration of LT's characterization of the nature and extent of its relationship with CCE and its agents. This would include the District Court's consideration of LT's reference to its affiliation with CCE brokers in general, rather than referencing each more accurately by their "d/b/a/" title and whether this rendered the use inaccurate or was somehow misleading as to any endorsement or relationship.

Notes

1. Is the decision in this case consistent with the Supreme Court's decision in KP Permanent Makeup? If it is, how so?

2. The decision in this case states "we believe that the bifurcated approach that we adopt today is more workable than a unified confusion/fairness test." What is this bifurcated approach? What tests does this court implement to analyze fair use?

3. Fair use is another area of some dispute in trademark jurisprudence. Should fair use be an affirmative defense to otherwise infringing conduct, or should fair use be used only to allow non-trademark use of a term otherwise subject to trademark protection? Here, too, we see the strong tension between the protection of trademarks and the concept of freedom of expression. One commentator recommends adopting a balancing approach. When the defendant raises a fair use defense, the inquiry ought to be whether such use was primarily to inform or to confuse. To the extent the use was to inform, the fair use defense ought to be an affirmative defense to otherwise infringing conduct. *See* Michael G. Frey, Note, *Is It Fair to Confuse? An Examination of Trademark Protection, the Fair Use Defense, and the First Amendment,* 65 U. Cin. L. Rev. 1255 (1997). When should the fair use defense be appropriate?

4. The fair use doctrine usually applies to the use of descriptive marks in a descriptive way. That is, strong marks would not usually be subject to fair use by others. The nominative fair use doctrine was created to allow some use of famous marks and restrict the scope of the trademark. What would be the result if the nominative fair use doctrine had not been established?

5. If a third party uses a trademark with intent to criticize and does so publicly on the internet, should such use be considered "fair"? In *Bally Total Fitness v. Faber*, 29 F. Supp. 2d 1161 (C.D. Cal. 1998), the court held that appending the word "sucks" after the trademark "Bally" to create a web page called "ballysucks" was fair because it was devoted to critical commentary regarding Bally and the defendant had no commercial purpose in creating and maintaining the site. That is, in Frey's terms from Note 1, *id.*, the primary purpose of the use was to inform and not to confuse. This issue is raised again in these materials in the context of "___sucks.com" web sites. *See infra* Chapter XII.

6. Fair use examples, like so many trademark cases, tend to be rather entertaining. In *Packman v. Chicago Tribune Co.*, 267 F.3d 628 (7th Cir. 2001), the famous Chicago newspaper began using the appellation "The Joy of Six" in a front page headline (and on some products) to describe the city of Chicago's feelings of happiness regarding the six championships the Chicago Bulls professional basketball team had won and to poke fun at the book titled "The Joy of Sex." The plaintiff owned a registration for THE JOY OF SIX for entertainment services in the nature of basketball games. The court found fair use because of the nature of the mark and the fact that the phrase is widely used to describe the joy of six of anything.

7. Fair use is a counterweight to a monopoly. Without fair use, trademark holders would have wide powers over words, phrases and expressions. Many trademark infringement cases are concluded at the preliminary injunction stage. Does a preliminary injunction forbidding the use of a mark have implications for free speech? Is it a prior restraint and therefore unconstitutional? *See* Eugene Volokh & Mark Lemley, Freedom of Speech and Injunctions in Intellectual Property Cases, 48 Duke L. J. 147 (1998).

----

3. Laches/Acquiescence

Menendez v. Holt

128 U S. 514 (1888)

Mr. Chief Justice Fuller, after stating the case, delivered the opinion of the court.

A reversal of the decree in this case is asked on the grounds that the words "La Favorita," as used by the complainants, cannot be protected as a trade-mark; that there has been no infringement; that the words had been used as a brand before being used by Holt & Co.; that the title of Holt & Co. was not superior to that of S. O. Ryder; and that whatever rights complainants may once have had been forfeited by laches.

The fact that Holt & Co. were not the actual manufacturers of the flour upon which they had for years placed the brand in question, does not deprive them of the right to be protected in the use of that brand as a trade-mark.

They used the words "La Favorita" to designate flour selected by them, in the exercise of their best judgment, as equal to a certain standard. The brand did not indicate by whom the flour was manufactured, but it did indicate the origin of its selection and classification. It was equivalent to the signature of Holt & Co. to a certificate that the flour was the genuine article which had been determined by them to possess a certain degree of excellence. It did not, of course, in itself, indicate quality, for it was merely a fancy name and in a foreign language, but it evidenced, that the skill, knowledge and judgment of Holt & Co. had been exercised in ascertaining that the particular flour so marked was possessed of a merit rendered definite by their examination and of a uniformity rendered certain by their selection. The case clearly does not fall within the rule announced in *Manufacturing Co. v. Trainer*, 101 U.S. 51, 55, that "letters or figures which, by the custom of traders, or the declaration of the manufacturer of the goods to which they are attached, are only used to denote quality, are incapable of exclusive appropriation, but are open to use by any one, like the adjectives of the language;" or in *Raggett v. Findlater*, L.R. 17 Eq. 29, where an injunction to restrain the use upon a trade label of the term "nourishing shout" was refused on the obvious ground that "nourishing" was a mere English word denoting quality. And the fact that flour so marked acquired an extensive sale, because the public had discovered that it might be relied on as of a uniformly meritorious quality, demonstrates that the brand deserves protection rather than that it should be debarred therefrom, on the ground, as argued, of being indicative of quality only.

Holt & Co., then, having acquired the exclusive right to the words "La Favorita," as applied to this particular vendible commodity, it is no answer to their action to say that there was no invasion of that right because the name of S. O. Ryder accompanied the brand upon flour sold by appellants, instead of the name of Holt & Co. That is an aggravation and not a justification, for it is openly trading in the name of another upon the reputation acquired by the device of the true proprietor.

These views dispose of two of the defences specifically urged on behalf of appellants, and we do not regard that of prior public use, even if it could be properly considered under the pleadings, as entitled to any greater weight. Evidence was given to the effect that from 1857 to 1860 the words "La Favorita" were occasionally used in St. Louis by Sears & Co., then manufacturing in that city, as designating a particular flour, but the witnesses were not able to testify that any had been on sale there under that brand (unless it were that of Holt & Co.) for upwards of twenty years. The use thus proven was so casual and such little importance apparently attached to it, that it is doubtful whether Sears & Co. could at any time have successfully claimed the words as a trade-mark, and at all events, such use was discontinued before Holt & Co. appropriated the words to identify their own flour, and there was no attempt to resume it.

It is argued, however, that the title of Holt & Co. to the use of the mark was not superior to that of S. O. Ryder, because it is said that Ryder, upon leaving the firm, took with him his share of the good-will of the business, and consequently of the trade-marks, and hence that the defendants below rightfully sold flour under the brand "La Favorita," when selected by Ryder and so marked by him.

Good-will was defined by Lord Eldon, in *Cruttwell v. Lye*, 17 Ves. 335, 346, to be "nothing more than the probability that the old customers will resort to the old place;" but Vice Chancellor Wood, in *Churton v. Douglas, Johnson*, V.C. 174, 118, says it would be taking too narrow a view of what is there laid down by Lord Eldon, to confine it to that, but that it must mean every positive advantage that has been acquired by the old firm in the progress of its business, whether connected with the premises in which the business was previously carried on, or with the name of the late firm, or with any other matter carrying with it the benefit of the business.

It may be that where a firm is dissolved and ceases to exist under the old name, each of the former partners would be allowed to obtain "his share" in the good-will, so far as that might consist in the use of trade-marks, by continuing such use in the absence of stipulation to the contrary; but when a partner retires from a firm, assenting to or acquiescing in the retention by the other partners of possession of the old place of business and the future conduct of the business by them under the old name, the good-will remains with the latter as of course.

Holt & Co. commenced business in 1845, and had had an uninterrupted existence under that name since 1855; the trade-mark in question was adopted by the senior member of the firm in 1861,and had been thereafter in continuous use; Ryder became a partner in 1861, and retired February 1, 1869, when a circular was issued, in which he participated, announcing the dissolution by his retirement, the continuance of the business by the other partners under the same firm name, and the formation of another partnership by Ryder with one Rowland, to transact the flour and commission business at another place, under the name of Rowland & Ryder.

In addition to these facts it is established by the preponderance of evidence, that it was verbally agreed, at the time Ryder retired, that he surrendered all interest in the brands belonging to Holt & Co. Ryder attempts to deny this, but his denial is so qualified as to render it unreliable as against the direct and positive character of the evidence to the contrary. Indeed, when asked why the brands were not made the subject of appraisement when he went out, as it was conceded all the other property of the firm was, he says that it was because he "gave up all right, title and interest to those valuable brands to Robert

S. Holt out of friendship, so there was no occasion for it." In our judgment, Ryder's claim to any interest in the good-will of the business of Holt & Co., including the firm's trademarks, ended with his withdrawal from that firm.

Counsel in conclusion earnestly contends that whatever rights appellees may have had were lost by laches; and the desire is intimated that we should reconsider *McLean v. Fleming*, 96 U.S. 245, so far as it was therein stated that even though a complainant were guilty of such delay in seeking relief upon infringement as to preclude him from obtaining an account of gains and profits, yet, if he were otherwise so entitled, an injunction against future infringement might properly be awarded. We see no reason to modify this general proposition, and we do not find in the facts as disclosed by the record before us anything to justify us in treating this case as an exception.

The intentional use of another's trade-mark is a fraud; and when the excuse is that the owner permitted such use, that excuse is disposed of by affirmative action to put a stop to it. Persistence then in the use is not innocent; and the wrong is a continuing one, demanding restraint by judicial interposition when properly invoked. Mere delay or acquiescence cannot defeat the remedy by injunction in support of the legal right, unless it has been continued so long and under such circumstances as to defeat the right itself. Hence, upon an application to stay waste, relief will not be refused on the ground that, as the defendant had been allowed to cut down half of the trees upon the complainant's land, he had acquired, by that negligence, the right to cut down the remainder, *Attorney General v. Eastlake*, 11 Hare, 205; nor will the issue of an injunction against the infringement of a trade-mark be denied on the ground that mere procrastination in seeking redress for depredations had deprived the true proprietor of his legal right. *Fullwood v. Fullwood*, 9 Ch. D. 176. Acquiescence to avail must be such as to create a new right in the defendant. *Rodgers v. Nowill*, 3 De G., M. & G. 614. Where consent by the owner to the use of his trade-mark by another is to be inferred from his knowledge and silence merely, "it lasts no longer than the silence from which it springs; it is, in reality, no more than a revocable license." *Duer, J., Amoskeag Mfg. Co. v. Spear*, 2 Sandford (N.Y.) 599; *Julian v. Hoosier Drill Co.*, 78 Indiana, 408; *Taylor v. Carpenter*, 3 Story, 458; S.C. 2 Woodb. & Min. 1.

So far as the act complained of is completed, acquiescence may defeat the remedy on the principle applicable when action is taken on the strength of encouragement to do it, but so far as the act is in progress and lies in the future, the right to the intervention of equity is not generally lost by previous delay, in respect to which the elements of an estoppel could rarely arise. At the same time, as it is in the exercise of discretionary jurisdiction that the doctrine of reasonable diligence is applied, and those who seek equity must do it, a court might hesitate as to the measure of relief, where the use, by others, for a long period, under assumed permission of the owner, had largely enhanced the reputation of a particular brand.

But there is nothing here in the nature of an estoppel, nothing which renders it inequitable to arrest at this stage any further invasion of complainants' rights. There is no pretence of abandonment. That would require proof of non-user by the owner or general surrender of the use to the public. The evidence is positive that Holt & Co. continuously used the trade-mark, always asserted their exclusive right to it, and never admitted that of any other firm or person, and, in the instance of every party, including Ryder, who used this brand on flour not of Holt & Co.'s selection, that use, when it came to their knowledge, was objected to by the latter, and personal notice given, while publication was also made in the newspapers, circulating where the flour was usually marketed, containing a statement of Holt & Co.'s rights and warning against imitations. It is idle to talk of acquiescence in view of these facts. Delay in bringing suit there was, and such delay as to preclude recovery of damages for prior infringement, but there was neither conduct nor negligence which could be held to destroy the right to prevention of further injury.

The decree of the Circuit Court will, therefore, be

Affirmed.

What-a-Burger of Virginia, Inc. v.
Whataburger, Inc., of Corpus Christi, Texas
357 F.3d 441 (4th Cir 2004)

TRAXLER, CIRCUIT JUDGE:

I.

On September 24, 1957, Harmon Dobson, founder of the Whataburger (Texas WAB) restaurant chain in Texas, was issued a certificate of registration for the word mark WHATABURGER in connection with hamburgers. Texas WAB [was granted] the exclusive right to use and control the WHATABURGER (R) mark. Neither Texas WAB nor any of its predecessors in interest have ever opened or operated a Whataburger restaurant in Virginia.

What-A-Burger of Virginia (Virginia W-A-B) claims that Jack Branch opened a restaurant using the name "What-A-Burger" in Newport News, Virginia, prior to August 1, 1957. Branch moved to Richmond in 1958, where he opened another What-A-Burger restaurant, at which point his brother Paul became the proprietor of the Newport News location. From 1958 until 1989, Branch opened several additional What-A-Burger restaurants in various Virginia locations.

Virginia W-A-B and Texas WAB first became aware of each other in 1970. A representative of Texas WAB was traveling in Virginia and, noticing the What-A-Burger sign, stopped in one of the restaurants and mentioned the possibility of the Branches running the restaurant as a franchise of Texas WAB. The record contains a June 24, 1970, letter to Paul Branch from George Garrison, an officer of Texas WAB, referring to the meeting and indicating that Texas WAB held the name WHATABURGER (R) as a registered trademark. Garrison suggested that Texas WAB might be willing to license Virginia W-A-B to use its trademark. The record contains a second letter, dated July 7, 1970, from Sam Main, General Manager for Texas WAB, suggesting that he meet with Paul Branch the following week in Richmond to discuss the issues raised in the Garrison letter.

The record does not reflect any further contact between these businesses until 2002, more than thirty years later. In a letter dated January 25, 2002, an attorney representing Texas WAB indicated that Virginia W-A-B's use of the name What-A-Burger might be an infringement of Texas WAB's registered trademark.

In an effort to settle the issue of whether it could continue using the What-A-Burger name, Virginia W-A-B filed this declaratory judgment action seeking an order declaring that Virginia W-A-B is "the rightful owner[]of the trademark or trade name What-A-Burger in the State of Virginia" and therefore enjoys the right to "the exclusive use of [the] trademark ... in the market areas of Richmond, Virginia; Chester, Virginia; Petersburg, Virginia; Newport News, Virginia; and Colonial Heights, Virginia."

II.

A. Laches

The primary obstacle to the application of laches here is that there was never any infringing use of the mark by Virginia W-A-B to which Texas WAB was required to respond. Estoppel by laches generally applies in a trademark infringement action to preclude relief for an owner of a mark who has unreasonably slept on his rights. *See Brittingham v. Jenkins*, 914 F.2d 447, 456 (4th Cir. 1990). "Courts may apply the doctrine of estoppel by laches to deny relief to a plaintiff who, though having knowledge of an infringement, has, to the detriment of the defendant, unreasonably delayed in seeking redress." *Sara Lee Corp. v. Kayser-Roth Corp.*, 81 F.3d 455, 461 (4th Cir. 1996) (emphasis added). Thus, a court's consideration of laches in the trademark context should encompass at least these questions: "(1) whether the owner of the mark knew of the infringing use; (2) whether the owner's delay in challenging the infringement of the mark was inexcusable or unreasonable; and (3) whether the infringing user was unduly prejudiced by the owner's delay." *Brittingham*, 914 F.2d at 456. Because the Lanham Act does not include a limitations period, courts use the doctrine of laches to address the inequities created by a trademark owner who, despite having a colorable infringement claim, allows a competitor to develop its products around the mark and expand its business, only then to lower the litigation boom.

The key question, for purposes of estoppel by laches, is not simply whether there has been some delay, but whether that delay was unreasonable. Logic dictates that "unreasonable delay" does not include any period of time before the owner is able to pursue a claim for infringement — otherwise, a trademark owner could be punished for not bringing a claim he had no right to bring. For this reason, we have recognized that laches "assumes the existence of an infringement for an extended period prior to the commencement of litigation." *See Sara Lee*, 81 F.3d at 462.

Thus, regardless of when the trademark owner initially discovers the use of a similar mark, action against the infringing user is not necessary until, in light of the circumstances, the "right to protection has clearly ripened." *Id.*; *see* 5 McCarthy at § 31: 19 ("One cannot be guilty of laches until his right ripens into one entitled to protection. For only then can his torpor be deemed inexcusable." (internal quotation marks omitted) (alteration in original)). Instead of focusing on when the trademark owner first knew that another party was using its mark, the court should be trying to determine the time at which the use became infringing and the time at which the owner should have known it: "To the extent that a plaintiff's prior knowledge may give rise to the defense of estoppel by laches, such knowledge must be of a pre-existing, infringing use of a mark." *Sara Lee*, 81 F.3d at 462; *see Brittingham*, 914 F.2d at 456 (explaining that, in determining whether laches applies, a court should ordinarily consider "whether the owner of the mark knew of the infringing use" (emphasis added)). Accordingly, "unreasonable delay" begins at "the time at which the [trademark owner] knows or should know she has a provable claim for infringement." *Kason Indus.*, 120 F.3d at 1206; *see Kellogg Co. v. Exxon Corp.*, 209 F.3d 562, 569 (6th Cir. 2000) ("Implicit in a finding of laches … is the presumption that an underlying claim for infringement existed at the time at which we begin to measure the plaintiff'ss delay."). The owner's mere knowledge that he might have an infringement claim at some future date is not sufficient to trigger the period of unreasonable delay required for estoppel by laches. *See Profitness Phys. Therapy Ctr. v. Pro-Fit Orthopedic & Sports Phys. Therapy*, 314 F.3d 62, 70 (2d Cir. 2002).

The district court, therefore, mistakenly measured the period of delay from Texas WAB's first knowledge of Virginia W-A-B's use of the mark without considering whether such use of the mark was an infringing use that required action by Texas WAB. Mere use of a mark that is similar or even identical to a registered trademark does not a fortiori establish infringement. The"keystone of infringement" is "the likelihood of confusion." *Sara Lee*, 81 F.3d at 462 (internal quotation marks omitted); *see* 15 U.S.C.A. § 1114(1)(a) and (b) (West 1997 & Supp. 2003). Although the district court observed that "the use of the names What-A-Burger and Whataburger is confusing," 256 F. Supp. 2d at 484, similarity of the conflicting names is but one of many factors relevant to a determination of whether the concurrent use of the marks creates a likelihood of confusion. An informed analysis of whether the likelihood of confusion exists cannot rest solely upon a "side-by-side" comparison of the marks without regard to the marketplace in which they are used. *Meridian Mut. Ins. Co. v. Meridian Ins. Group, Inc.*, 128 F.3d 1111, 1115 (7th Cir. 1997). Usually, a court should consider a number of factors relating to the way in which the competing marks operate in the workplace. For example, courts have considered "the similarity in scope of the parties' geographic markets" in deciding whether a likelihood of confusion exists. Kellogg, 209 F.3d at 572; *see Profitness Therapy*, 314 F.3d at 69–70; *Thomas & Betts Corp. v. Panduit Corp.*, 138 F.3d 277, 296 (7th Cir. 1998). Another consideration when "the goods or services are sold in different territories" is "the extent to which the senior user's designation is known in the junior user's territory." 3 McCarthy at § 23: 19. The fact that Texas WAB and Virginia W-A-B operate in separate territorial markets—and that Texas WAB professes no plans to enter the Virginia market—raises significant doubt that Virginia W-A-B's use of the mark creates the "likelihood of confusion" required for infringement.

The question in such a case is this: at what point does the defendant's expansion create a sufficient likelihood of confusion to trigger the registered owner's obligation to sue? In the progressive encroachment context, a requirement obligating the owner to sue at the first sign of a potentially infringing use "would foster meritless litigation." *Profitness Therapy*, 314 F.3d at 70. The owner would likely be "rushed immediately into litigation ... [with] little or no evidence of actual confusion and real commercial damage." *Sara Lee*, 81 F.3d at 462 (internal quotation marks omitted).

In this case, of course, if anyone is expanding the scope of its operations, it is the registered owner rather than the junior user. The principles underlying our decision in Sara Lee, however, are controlling here: (1) delay is measured from the time at which the owner knew of an infringing use sufficient to require legal action; and (2) legal action is not required until there is a real likelihood of confusion. Even if Texas WAB sought to enjoin Virginia W-A-B from operating its establishments in Virginia under the name What-A-Burger, it would not be able to do so on this record. Although "a senior federal registrant has superior priority" which extends nationwide, "there is no likely confusion for a court to enjoin unless and until the senior user shows a likelihood of entry into the junior user's trade territory." 4 McCarthy at § 26: 33. "The injunctive remedy does not ripen until the registrant shows a likelihood of entry" into the territory in question. *Lone Star Steakhouse & Saloon, Inc. v. Alpha of Va., Inc.*, 43 F.3d 922, 932 (4th Cir. 1995) (second emphasis added); *see Armand's Subway, Inc. v. Doctor's Assocs., Inc.*, 604 F.2d 849, 849–50 (4th Cir. 1979) (explaining that even though the owner of a registered trademark has an exclusive right of use that enjoys nationwide protection, "the protection is only potential in areas where the registrant in fact does not do business" and that "[a] competing user could use the mark there until the registrant extended its business to the area"). In such a scenario, "a likelihood of confusion flows directly from the proof of likelihood of entry by the registrant." 4 McCarthy at § 26:34.

There is nothing in this case to indicate a likelihood of entry into the local Virginia market by Texas WAB (in fact, Texas WAB specifically disavows any such intention) or that the likelihood of confusion otherwise looms large, triggering the obligation for Texas WAB to initiate an action for trademark infringement. And, of course, the district court made no finding of an infringing use upon which to base its application of laches. Accordingly, we conclude that there was no unreasonable delay that would prevent Texas WAB from asserting its counterclaim for declaratory relief, and the application of laches was inappropriate

---

Notes

1. Perhaps the most common defense to an action for trademark infringement is the claim that the plaintiff's mark is invalid. The rationale for these claims of invalidity track Section 2 of the Lanham Act. This text addresses "bars to registration" in a subsequent chapter. *See infra* Chapter XII.

2. Although often times (as in these materials) the terms "acquiescence" and "laches" are used together and sometimes interchangeably, they are, of course, separate concepts in trademark law. To show acquiescence, the defendant needs to prove that the plaintiff intentionally delayed in pursuing litigation and that the defendant was materially prejudiced by the delay. Laches, on the other hand, is the negligent and unintentional failure to protect trademark rights. The element of intent is the primary difference. *See Induct-o-matic Corp. v. Inductotherm Corp.*, 747 F.2d 358, 367(6th Cir. 1984) (quoting *United States v. Weintraub*, 613 F.2d 612, 619 (6th Cir. 1979)). *See also Kellogg Co. v. Exxon Corp.*, 209 F.3d 562 (6th Cir. 2000). Nonetheless, the outcome is the same: unreasonable delay can forfeit the ability to enforce trademark rights.

3. What, then, is "unreasonable delay"? Does a trademark owner have to enforce its trademark rights against each and every alleged infringer it detects? Laches is a bar to any relief when a plaintiff delays for a significant period of time. *Hot Wax, Inc. v. Turtle Wax, Inc.*, 191 F.3d 813 (7th Cir. 1999) (delay of 20 years); *Saratoga Vichy Spring Co. v. Lehman*, 625 F. 2d 1037 (2d Cir. 1980) (delay of 69 years). On the other hand, a dely of only a few years will rarely provide the infringer with the defense of laches. *AmBrit, Inc. v. Kraft, Inc.*, 812 F.2d 1531 (11th Cir. 1986).

4. Sovereign Immunity. In 1999 the United States Supreme Court created a bit of a surprise for intellectual property owners. In *Coll. Sav. Bank v. Fla. Prepaid Post secondary Educ. Expense Bd.*, 527 U.S. 666 (1999), the Court held that Florida's sovereign immunity was neither validly abrogated by the Trademark Remedy Clarification Act, nor was it voluntarily waived when the state engaged in activities in interstate commerce. That is, after Coll. Sav. Bank, states do not have to recognize the trademark rights of private parties-states can infringe with impunity and recognize no legal consequences.

The problem is the Eleventh Amendment to the United States Constitution. The Eleventh Amendment states that "the Judicial power of the United States shall not be construed to extend to any suit in law or equity, commenced or prosecuted against one of the United States by Citizens of another State, or by Citizens or Subjects of any Foreign State." U.S. CONST. amend. XI.

In *Atascadero State Hosp. v. Scanlon*, 473 U.S. 234 (1985), the Court held that Congress' abrogation must be clear and unmistakable to invalidate a state's immunity from suit by a private party. When appellate courts started applying Scanlon to intellectual property law cases and finding in favor of the states, Congress, in 1990 and 1992 amended the Lanham Act to specifically and clearly abrogate states' Eleventh Amendment right to sovereign immunity. Trademark Remedy Clarification Act, Pub. L. No. 102-542 (1992) (codified at 15 U.S.C. 1122 (2000)). In College Savings Bank, the Court held that Congress could not use Article I enumerated powers (the Commerce Clause or the Patent and Copyright Clause) to abrogate states' rights. Therefore, the attempted abrogation in §40 of the Lanham Act was invalid.

This has most recently been applied again to allow a state to be free of liability for its otherwise infringing conduct. *Hapco Farms, Inc. v. Idaho Potato Comm'n*, 238 F.3d 468 (2d Cir. 2001) (Idaho Potato Commission is a state agency and therefore immune from suit).

As one might guess, trademark owners are not too amused with this situation. The proposed law to rectify the situation is referred to as the Intellectual Property Protection Restoration Act (IPPRA). It was proposed in the Senate as Senate Bill 2031 of 2002. No action was taken on the bill last Congress. Submission of this Bill or other similar legislation has occurred without adoption in every Congress since the College Savings Bank decision. It is rather safe to presume that other legislation will be submitted, debated, and perhaps adopted during the shelf-life of this book.

For an excellent review of the history of this issue and a very helpful review of the IPPRA, *see* Robert T. Neufeld Closing Federalism's Loophole in Intellectual Property Rights,17 BERKELEY TECH. L.J. 1295 (2002).

5. *Insurance coverage.* Most companies have a general insurance plan known as a comprehensive general liability plan (or CGL) to cover things such as "advertising injury." Naturally, when an insured allegedly commits trademark infringement, the insurance companies sometimes challenge the notion that their "advertising injury" clause (or some other equivalent) covers trademark infringement. Some courts seem slow to recognize the duty of insurance companies to cover trademark infringement. *See, e.g., Older Darby & Darby, P.C. v. VSI Int'l, Inc.*, 739 N.E.2d 744 (N.Y. 2000) (law firm had no duty to inform client of potential coverage by insurance company for patent infringement when states at that time did not recognize such duty in insurer); *Sport Supply Group, Inc. v. Columbia Cas. Co.*, 335 F.3d 453 (5th Cir. 2003) (denying insurer's duty to defend because use of a trademark did not constitute an "advertising injury"). Today, most courts now recognize that CGLs include paying the expenses an insured encounters when defending a trademark infringement cause of action especially when the policy is vague and the insured had a reasonable expectation that trademark infringement was part of the CGL policy. *See, e.g., Arnette Optic Illusions, Inc. v. ITT Hartford Group*, 43 F. Supp. 2d 1088 (C.D. Cal. 1998).

Chapter V

Requirements of a Trademark

A. Distinctiveness

The first consideration in determining whether a trademark is protectable in the United States is to determine whether or not the mark is distinctive of the products or services on which the mark is used. Distinctiveness is either "inherent" in the trademark itself or acquired through secondary meaning. A trademark that merely describes the product or service it is used on is not distinctive but merely descriptive. Marks that are inherently distinctive may be immediately registered on the Principal Register provided they do not violate any of the prohibitions provided in Section 2 of the Lanham Act.

Abercrombie & Fitch Co. v. Hunting World, Inc.
537 F.2d 4 (2d Cir. 1976)

FRIENDLY, CIRCUIT JUDGE:

This action in the District Court for the Southern District of New York by Abercrombie & Fitch Company (A&F), owner of well-known stores at Madison Avenue and 45th Street in New York City and seven places in other states, against Hunting World, Incorporated (HW), operator of a competing store on East 53rd Street, is for infringement of some of A&F's registered trademarks using the word 'Safari'. It has had a long and, for A&F, an unhappy history. On this appeal from a judgment which not only dismissed the complaint but canceled all of A&F's 'Safari' registrations, including several that were not in suit, we relieve A&F of some of its unhappiness but not of all.

The complaint, filed in January, 1970, after describing the general nature of A&F's business, reflecting its motto, "The Greatest Sporting Goods Store in the World," alleged as follows: For many years A&F has used the mark 'Safari' on articles "exclusively offered and sold by it." Since 1936 it has used the mark on a variety of men's and women's outer garments. Its United States trademark registrations include:

Trademark	Number	Issued	Goods
Safari	358781	14086	Men's and Women's outer garments, including hats
Safari Mills	125531	43604	Cotton Piece goods
Safari	652098	21086	Men's and Women's outer garments, including shoes
Safari	703279	22150	Woven cloth, sporting-goods, apparel, etc.

A&F has spent large sums of money in advertising and promoting products identified with its mark 'Safari' and in policing its right in the mark, including the successful conduct of trademark infringement suits. HW, the complaint continued, has engaged in the retail marketing of sporting apparel including hats and shoes, some identified by use of 'Safari' alone or by expressions such as 'Minisafari' and 'Safariland'. Continuation of HW's acts would confuse and deceive the public and impair "the distinct and unique quality of the plaintiff's trademark." A&F sought an injunction against infringement and an accounting for damages and profits.

HW filed an answer and counterclaim. This alleged, *inter alia*, that "the word 'safari' is an ordinary, common, descriptive, geographic, and generic word" which "is commonly used and understood by the public to mean and refer to a journey or expedition, especially for hunting or exploring in East Africa, and to the hunters, guides, men, animals, and equipment forming such an expedition" and is not subject to exclusive appropriation as a trademark. HW sought cancellation of all of A&F's registrations using the word 'Safari' on the ground that A&F had fraudulently failed to disclose the true nature of the term to the Patent Office.

HW having moved for summary judgment, Judge Lasker granted this only in part, 327 F. Supp. 657 (S.D.N.Y. 1971). He held, 327 F. Supp. at 662, that:

> Although "safari" is a generic word, a genuine issue of fact exists as to whether the plaintiff has created a secondary meaning in its use of the word "identifying the source" and showing that "purchasers are moved to buy it because of its source."

On the other hand, he concluded that A&F had no right to prevent HW from using the word 'Safari' to describe its business as distinguished from use in the sale of a particular product—a conclusion we do not understand to be disputed; that HW had not infringed A&F's registered mark using the word 'Safari' under its brand name on a "classical safari hat" or in advertising this as "The Hat for Safari" since such use was purely descriptive, 327 F. Supp. at 664; that HW had also not infringed by using the term 'Minisafari' as a name for its narrower brimmed safari hats, and that HW was entitled to use the word 'Safariland' as the description of an area within its shop and as the name of a corporation engaged in the wholesale distribution of products imported from East Africa by an affiliate, Lee Expeditions, Ltd., and in the "Safariland News," a newsletter issued by HW and Lee Expeditions, 327 F. Supp. at 664–65. With respect to shoes he concluded that both parties had used the word 'Safari' in a fanciful rather than a descriptive sense and hence that plaintiff might have a valid infringement claim if it could establish a secondary meaning, 327 F. Supp. at 665.

On A&F's appeal this court reversed and remanded for trial, 461 F.2d 1040 (2 Cir. 1972). Most of Judge Thomsen's opinion for the court concerned the issue of appealability, as did most of Judge Timbers' concurring opinion and all of Judge Feinberg's dissent. Intimating no opinion on the ultimate merits, this court concluded "that genuine issues of fact exist which made it improper to enter a summary judgment finally denying even in part the injunctive relief sought by plaintiff." *Id.* at 1042.

Judge Ryan, before whom the action was tried on remand, ruled broadly in HW's favor. He found there was frequent use of the word 'Safari' in connection with wearing apparel, that A&F's policing efforts thus had evidently been unsuccessful, and that A&F had itself used the term in a descriptive sense not covered by its registration, e. g., in urging customers to make a "Christmas Gift Safari" to the A&F store. After referring to statements by Judge Lasker that 'Safari' was a "weak" mark, 327 F. Supp. at 663, the judge found the mark to be invalid. 'Safari', the court held, "is merely descriptive and does not serve to distinguish plaintiff's goods as listed on the registration from anybody else's"; while such terms are afforded protection by the Lanham Act if they come to identify the company merchandising the product, rather than the product itself, A&F had failed to establish that this had become the situation with respect to 'Safari'. The opinion did not discuss A&F's assertion that some of its marks had become incontestable under §15 of the Lanham Act, 15 U.S.C. §1065. The court entered a judgment which dismissed the complaint and canceled not only the four registered trademarks in suit but all A&F's other registered 'Safari' trademarks. A&F has appealed.

II.

It will be useful at the outset to restate some basic principles of trademark law, which, although they should be familiar, tend to become lost in a welter of adjectives.

The cases, and in some instances the Lanham Act, identify four different categories of terms with respect to trademark protection. Arrayed in an ascending order which roughly reflects their eligibility to trademark status and the degree of protection accorded, these classes are (1) **generic**, (2) **descriptive**, (3) **suggestive**, and (4) **arbitrary or fanciful**. The lines of demarcation, however, are not always bright. Moreover, the difficulties are compounded because a term that is in one category for a particular product may be in quite a different one for another,[1] because a term may shift from one category to another in light of differences in usage through time,[2] because a term may have one meaning to one group of users and a different one to others, and because the same term may be put to different uses with respect to a single product. In various ways, all of these complications are involved in the instant case.

A generic term is one that refers, or has come to be understood as referring, to the genus of which the particular product is a species. At common law neither those terms which were generic nor those which were merely descriptive could become valid trademarks, *see Delaware & Hudson Canal Co. v. Clark*, 80 U.S. (13 Wall.) 311, 323, 20 L. Ed. 581 (1872) ("Nor can a generic name, or a name merely descriptive of an article or its qualities, ingredients, or characteristics, be employed as a trademark and the exclusive use of it be entitled to legal protection"). The same was true under the Trademark Act of 1905, *Standard Paint Co. v. Trinidad Asphalt Mfg. Co.*, 220 U.S. 446, 55 L. Ed. 536, 31 S. Ct. 456 (1911), except for marks which had been the subject of exclusive use for ten years prior to its enactment, 33 Stat. 726. While, as we shall see, p. 10 *infra*, the Lanham Act makes an important exception with respect to those merely descriptive terms which have acquired secondary meaning, see §2(f), 15 U.S.C. §1052(f), it offers no such exception for generic

---

1. To take a familiar example "Ivory" would be generic when used to describe a product made from the tusks of elephants but arbitrary as applied to soap.

2. See, e.g., Haughton Elevator Co. v. Seeberger, 85 U.S.P.Q. 80 (1950), in which the coined word 'Escalator', originally fanciful, or at the very least suggestive, was held to have become generic.

marks. The Act provides for the cancellation of a registered mark if at any time it "becomes the common descriptive name of an article or substance," §14(c).[3] This means that even proof of secondary meaning, by virtue of which some "merely descriptive" marks may be registered, cannot transform a generic term into a subject for trademark. As explained in J. Kohnstam, Ltd. v. Louis Mark and Company, 47 C.C.P.A. 1080, 280 F.2d 437, 440 (C.C.P.A. 1960), no matter how much money and effort the user of a generic term has poured into promoting the sale of its merchandise and what success it has achieved in securing public identification, it cannot deprive competing manufacturers of the product of the right to call an article by its name. We have recently had occasion to apply this doctrine of the impossibility of achieving trademark protection for a generic term, *CES Publishing Corp. v. St. Regis Publications, Inc.*, 531 F.2d 11 (1975). The pervasiveness of the principle is illustrated by a series of well known cases holding that when a suggestive or fanciful term has become generic as a result of a manufacturer's own advertising efforts, trademark protection will be denied save for those markets where the term still has not become generic and a secondary meaning has been shown to continue. A term may thus be generic in one market and descriptive or suggestive or fanciful in another.

The term which is descriptive but not generic[4] stands on a better basis. Although §2(e) of the Lanham Act, 15 U.S.C. §1052, forbids the registration of a mark which, when applied to the goods of the applicant, is "merely descriptive, "§2(f) removes a considerable part of the sting by providing that "except as expressly excluded in paragraphs (a)–(d) of this section, nothing in this chapter shall prevent the registration of a mark used by the applicant which has become distinctive of the applicant's goods in commerce" and that the Commissioner may accept, as prima facie evidence that the mark has become distinctive, proof of substantially exclusive and continuous use of the mark applied to the applicant's goods for five years preceding the application. As indicated in the cases cited in the discussion of the unregistrability of generic terms, "common descriptive name," as used in §14(c) and 15(4), refers to generic terms applied to products and not to terms that are "merely descriptive." In the former case any claim to an exclusive right must be denied since this in effect would confer a monopoly not only of the mark but of the product by rendering a competitor unable effectively to name what it was endeavoring to sell. In the latter case the law strikes the balance, with respect to registration, between the hardships to a competitor in hampering the use of an appropriate word and those to the owner who, having invested money and energy to endow a word with the good will adhering to his enterprise, would be deprived of the fruits of his efforts.

The category of "suggestive" marks was spawned by the felt need to accord protection to marks that were neither exactly descriptive on the one hand nor truly fanciful on the other—a need that was particularly acute because of the bar in the Trademark Act of 1905, 33 Stat. 724, 726, (with an exceedingly limited exception noted above) on the registration of merely descriptive marks regardless of proof of secondary meaning. See Or-

---

3. [Editor's Note: The Trademark Law Amendment Act of 1988 changed the phrase "becomes the common descriptive name of an article or substance" to "becomes the generic name for the goods or services."]

4. See, e.g., W. E. Bassett Co. v. Revlon, Inc., 435 F.2d 656 (2 Cir. 1970). A commentator has illuminated the distinction with an example of the "Deep Bowl Spoon":

"Deep Bowl" identifies a significant characteristic of the article. It is "merely descriptive" of the goods, because it informs one that they are deep in the bowl portion.... It is not, however, "the common descriptive name" of the article [since] the implement is not a deep bowl, it is a spoon...."Spoon" is not merely descriptive of the article—it identifies the article—[and therefore] the term is generic. Fletcher, Actual Confusion as to Incontestability of Descriptive Marks, 64 Trademark Rep. 252, 260 (1974). On the other hand, "Deep Bowl" would be generic as to a deep bowl.

ange Crush Co. v. California Crushed Fruit Co., 54 App. D.C. 313, 297 F. 892 (1924). Having created the category the courts have had great difficulty in defining it. Judge Learned Hand made the not very helpful statement:

It is quite impossible to get any rule out of the cases beyond this: That the validity of the mark ends where suggestion ends and description begins.

Franklin Knitting Mills, Inc. v. Fashionit Sweater Mills, Inc., 297 F. 247, 248 (S.D.N.Y. 1923), aff'd *per curiam*, 4 F.2d 1018 (2d Cir. 1925)—a statement amply confirmed by comparing the list of terms held suggestive with those held merely descriptive in 3 Callmann, Unfair Competition, Trademarks and Monopolies §71.2 (3d ed.). Another court has observed, somewhat more usefully, that:

A term is suggestive if it requires imagination, thought and perception to reach a conclusion as to the nature of goods. A term is descriptive if it forthwith conveys an immediate idea of the ingredients, qualities or characteristics of the goods.

Stix Products, Inc. v. United Merchants & Manufacturers Inc., 295 F. Supp. 479, 488 (S.D.N.Y. 1968)—a formulation deriving from *General Shoe Corp. v. Rosen*, 111 F.2d 95, 98 (4th Cir. 1940). Also useful is the approach taken by this court in *Aluminum Fabricating Co. of Pittsburgh v. Season-All Window Corp.*, 259 F.2d 314 (2d Cir. 1958), that the reason for restricting the protection accorded descriptive terms, namely the undesirability of preventing an entrant from using a descriptive term for his product, is much less forceful when the trademark is a suggestive word since, as Judge Lumbard wrote, 259 F.2d at 317:

The English language has a wealth of synonyms and related words with which to describe the qualities which manufacturers may wish to claim for their products and the ingenuity of the public relations profession supplies new words and slogans as they are needed.

If a term is suggestive, it is entitled to registration without proof of secondary meaning. Moreover, as held in the *Season-All* case, the decision of the Patent Office to register a mark without requiring proof of secondary meaning affords a rebuttable presumption that the mark is suggestive or arbitrary or fanciful rather than merely descriptive.

It need hardly be added that fanciful or arbitrary terms[5] enjoy all the rights accorded to suggestive terms as marks—without the need of debating whether the term is "merely descriptive" and with ease of establishing infringement.

In the light of these principles we must proceed to a decision of this case.

III.

We turn first to an analysis of A&F's trademarks to determine the scope of protection to which they are entitled. We have reached the following conclusions: (1) applied to specific types of clothing 'safari' has become a generic term and 'minisafari' may be used for a smaller brim hat; (2) 'safari' has not, however, become a generic term for boots or shoes; it is either "suggestive" or "merely descriptive" and is a valid ...

* * *

---

5. As terms of art, the distinctions between suggestive terms and fanciful or arbitrary terms may seem needlessly artificial. Of course, a common word may be used in a fanciful sense; indeed one might say that only a common word can be so used, since a coined word cannot first be put to a bizarre use. Nevertheless, the term 'fanciful', as a classifying concept, is usually applied to words invented solely for their use as trademarks. When the same legal consequences attach to a common word, i.e., when it is applied in an unfamiliar way, the use is called "arbitrary."

Notes

1. *Abecrombie* may be the most often cited American trademark case. The continuum *Abercrombie* contemplates may be depicted as follows:

The Trademark Continuum

[handwritten annotations: suggest desirable characteristic of a product like "Ivory"; Apple; made-up name; Xerox; Kodak]

Generic	Descriptive	Descriptive with Secondary Meaning	Suggestive	Arbitrary/ Fanciful

| | **Invalid Trademark** | **Valid Trademark** | |

Inherently distinctive

Virtually all courts in America use this continuum to judge the strength of the trademark at issue. All marks are said to fit somewhere on this continuum from generic words to arbitrary and fanciful marks. Where a trademark falls on this continuum, at any given point in time, will dictate the strength the mark is afforded. Unfortunately, placing a mark on the continuum is, itself, an inherently difficult task and has an element of subjectivity to it. In the end, determining where a mark falls on the continuum is simply a question of whether a mark deserves much protection. "These categories, like the tones in a spectrum, tend to blur at the edges and merge together. The labels are more advisory than definitive, more guidelines than pigeon holes. Not surprisingly, they are somewhat difficult to articulate and apply." *Zatarains, Inc. v. Oak Grove Smokehouse, Inc.*, 698 F.2d 786 (5th Cir. 1983).

2. There has been much judicial consternation, however, regarding whether or not *Abercrombie* should be applied to trade dress as well as trade marks. The tension is focused around the strongest trademarks, inherently distinctive marks. Under what circumstances can trade dress be considered to be inherently distinctive? Can all trade dress be inherently distinctive just like trademarks? What about sensory marks such as sound or scent? What justifies any distinction? *See infra* Chapter X.

3. *Abercrombie* provides clear incentives to producers to choose more distinctive trademarks. Marketing departments sometimes clash with legal departments in corporations because it is clearly more expensive to adopt a fanciful or arbitrary term for use as a mark. Descriptive terms require little or no advertising to establish mark/goods association in the minds of the relevant consumers. The more arbitrary or coined a word is, the more it will cost in advertising to establish that same association. Trademark lawyers, however, cringe at the notion of creating complete mark/goods association, for when the mark primarily stands for the good or service and not the source, it becomes generic. *See infra* Chapter IX.

4. Some examples of generic marks include the following:

LITE for use on low-calorie beer. *Miller Brewing Co. v. G. Heileman Brewing Co.*, 561 F.2d 75 (7th Cir. 1977), *cert. denied*, 434 U.S. 1025 (1978);

SUPER GLUE for use on strong-bonding, fast-setting glue. *Loctite Corp. v. Nat'l Starch & Chem. Corp.*, 516 F. Supp. 190 (S.D.N.Y. 1981);

YELLOW CAB for use on a taxi cab service. *Yellow Cab. Co. of Sacramento v. Yellow Cab Co. of Elk Grove*, In. 266 F. Supp. 2d 1199 (E.D. Cal. 2003);

ICE for use on beer. *Anheuser-Busch, Inc. v. John Labatt Ltd.*, 89 F.3d 1339 (8th Cir. 1996), *cert. denied*, 519 U.S. 1109 (1997).

B. Secondary Meaning in Trademarks

Descriptive marks may qualify for registration under the Lanham Act if they have acquired secondary meaning. Secondary meaning may take two forms. One is statutory secondary meaning. Secondary meaning is presumptively created if a mark is in continuous and exclusive use for a period of five years. 15 U.S.C. §1052(f) (Lanham Act §2). Common law secondary meaning is created through use of a mark in commerce in a manner where observers of the mark come to think of it as an appellation of source instead of the primary meaning of the term. In this case, secondary meaning may be created and the mark protected and made registrable without the passage of five years.

International Kennel Club of Chicago, Inc. v. Mighty Star, Inc.
846 F.2d 1079 (7th Cir. 1988)

COFFEY, CIRCUIT JUDGE.

Plaintiff-appellee International Kennel Club of Chicago, Inc. ("IKC"), brought this action against the defendants-appellants Mighty Star, Inc. ("Mighty Star") and DCN Industries, Inc. ("DCN"), alleging that the defendants' use of the plaintiff's "International Kennel Club" name violates section 43(a) of the Lanham Act, 15 U.S.C. §1125(a), as well as state statutory and common law. The district court granted the plaintiff's motion for a preliminary injunction against the defendants' use of the name. The defendants appeal. We affirm in part, reverse in part, and remand.

I.
A. Plaintiff's use of the "International Kennel Club" name

The IKC is an Illinois business corporation that sponsors dog shows in Chicago, and is a "show giving member club" of the American Kennel Club ("AKC"), a nationwide organization devoted to furthering the "sport" of showing purebred dogs. In addition to giving dog shows, the IKC serves as an information source for AKC activities in Chicago and provides assistance in the pedigree registration of purebred dogs with the AKC. The

IKC also sponsors seminars and contributes funds for animal medical research, the Dog Museum of America, and 4-H programs.

The IKC sponsors two major dog shows each year, with the annual spring show having an attendance of between 20,000 to 30,000 people. An average of 1,500 to 2,000 dogs are entered in plaintiff's shows, and for the spring 1986 show, entries came from 36 different states and various Canadian provinces. Persons who attend the plaintiff's shows are often interested in canine-related paraphernalia. While the IKC does not sell such items, private vendors rent booth space at plaintiff's shows at prices ranging from $600 to $800 per booth and sell dog-related items, including stuffed dogs. In 1985 and 1986, the annual revenue from the rental of booth space averaged $60,000.

In an effort to promote its activities, the IKC spent approximately $60,000 of its total revenue of $231,226 for fiscal year 1986 to hire a full-time staff person to handle the advertising of the dog shows and public relations. The paid advertising of the IKC, consisting of advertisements in magazines with a nationwide circulation such as the *American Kennel Club Gazette* and *Dog World Magazine*, as well as advertisements in the Chicago-area media, is primarily designed to reach canine enthusiasts (the dog "fancy"[6] in trade parlance). The activities of the IKC have also been covered in a variety of national and local publications.[7]

B. Defendant's decision to market toy dogs under the name "International Kennel Club"

For almost three decades, defendants DCN and its wholly-owned subsidiary Mighty Star have sold stuffed toys in the United States, Canada, England, Australia and Asia. For many years, defendants used the trademark "Polar Puff" to refer to their top of the line products and prominently displayed the trademark on their products and in their advertisements. In the later part of 1985, the defendants decided to add to their product line of stuffed animals a line of stuffed "pedigree" dogs representing different breeds. The defendants state that at the time they had never heard of the plaintiff, and that they chose the name "International Kennel Club" in part because of the international scope of their business, and also because the products were toy dogs. The defendants utilized a marketing strategy whereby purchasers could "register" their dogs with the "International Kennel Club" and receive an "official International Kennel Club membership and pedigree certificate." Part of the defendants' registration strategy was to emphasize that the stuffed canines represent breeds "sanctioned by the International Kennel Club." Although the defendants' International Kennel Club collection of dogs was marketed in conjunction with their "24K Polar Puff" line of toy animals, the advertising for the stuffed dogs did not always use this second name along with the International Kennel Club name. Defendants' in-store advertising included plaques, buttons and counter displays, all of which

---

6. Webster's Third New International Dictionary defines "fancy" as "persons who pursue or are enthusiastic over some particular art, practice, or amusement: as ... (3): fanciers of animals (the bulldog)."

7. For instance, the IKC points to a poll conducted by *Kennel Review Magazine*, listing the International Kennel Club's show as one of the best in the country. A review of the plaintiff's activities between 1938 and 1984 in *Kennel Review Magazine* concluded that: "The International Kennel Club, after forty-five years, still remains a show of prestige and education and still follows the original premise—that is to provide a showcase for the best of purebred dogs." The editor of *Kennel Review* also commented that "the International Kennel Club has long been a prestigious event, but in the last few years it has really put forth effort to become one of the most important events of the year."

referred to the "International Kennel Club Center," the "International Kennel Club," or the "IKC" without also referring to the defendants' "Polar Puff" trademark.

After choosing the IKC name for its line of toy dogs, Mighty Star's counsel conducted a search of trade directories in major cities as well as a search of federally registered trademarks. The search disclosed two telephone directory listings in Chicago-one for "International Kennel" and one for the "International Kennel Club of Chicago." Nevertheless, counsel advised the defendants that the use of the International Kennel Club name would not infringe upon the plaintiff's name given the local scope of the plaintiff's operations and the fact that the plaintiff did not directly compete with Mighty Star or DCN. Thus, the defendants proceeded to market their line of stuffed dogs under that name without contacting the plaintiff to determine if the use of the International Kennel Club name would present a problem of infringement.

C. Evidence of confusion allegedly caused by the marketing of the defendants' toy dogs under the "International Kennel Club" name

In late March 1986—six months after learning of the plaintiff's existence—the defendants placed a full-page advertisement for their line of stuffed dogs in the April edition of the *Good Housekeeping* magazine. This advertisement was followed by ads in the June issues of *Better Homes and Gardens, Vogue*, and *Cosmopolitan* magazines that reached the public in mid-May. Following the publication of these ads, IKC officials began receiving telephone calls (at a rate of about one per day), letters, and personal inquiries from people expressing confusion as to the plaintiff's relationship to the International Kennel Club stuffed dogs. Prior to the plaintiff's spring 1986 dog show, the IKC's public relations officer, Ms. Johnson, received telephone calls asking to purchase "International Kennel Club stuffed dogs." Ms. Johnson testified that she thought the callers were referring to the stuffed dogs sold by vendors at the plaintiff's shows, and told the callers that the toy dogs would continue to be sold at the show.

The IKC learned of the defendants' line of International Kennel Club toys at the plaintiff's spring dog show on March 29 through 30, 1986. Mr. Auslander, the Secretary and Treasurer of the IKC, testified that a vendor at the show brought one of the defendants' ads to his attention, and asked "why I was involved or why our club was involved in a venture of that type." Thereafter, in early April, the IKC began to receive letters of inquiry concerning the defendants' toy canines. Eight letters requested information on purchasing the dogs, and another from a vendor expressed concern about the IKC's apparent competition. The latter wrote that "we are concerned as vendors that this practice [the plaintiff's apparent selling of toy dogs] conflicts with the stated aims of your involvement as a purebred dog club." The defendants' Executive Vice-President Sheldon Bernstein testified that neither Mighty Star nor DCN received any letters indicating confusion as to their relationship with the plaintiff.

After the plaintiff's spring 1986 dog show, Mr. Auslander attended between 15 and 20 other dog shows throughout the country during 1986. Auslander testified that at about half of these shows—including the shows in Florida, Wisconsin, Nebraska, Colorado, Massachusetts, California and Illinois—he was questioned about the relationship between the IKC and Mighty Star's toy dogs. Auslander further recounted that members of the board of directors of the American Kennel Club consulted him, expressing concern that the International Kennel Club might be involved in their sale. According to Auslander's testimony, the President of the American Kennel Club reported to Auslander that it had received questions about whether the toys were a fundraising effort for the Dog Museum of America or the American Kennel Club. Thereafter, at the request of the American Kennel Club, the plaintiff placed an ad disclaiming any relationship to the defendants' toys in the July issue of the *American Kennel Club Gazette*.

D. Plaintiff files suit and moves for a preliminary injunction

Confronted with the complaints and inquiries noted above, the IKC filed the instant trademark infringement action on May 23, 1986, and simultaneously filed a motion to preliminarily enjoin Mighty Star and DCN's use of the International Kennel Club name. In response to the lawsuit, the defendants cancelled almost all of their advertising of the products bearing the plaintiff's name. One of the defendants' advertisements—placed in the September issue of *Good Housekeeping*—used the International Kennel Club name but contained a disclaimer of any relationship to the plaintiff's dog shows. This was the last advertisement that DCN and Mighty Star placed for their line of toy canines.

On July 14–16, 1986, the trial court held a hearing on the plaintiff's motion for injunctive relief and on July 21, 1986, ruled from the bench that the plaintiff was entitled to a preliminary injunction. In so ruling, the court found:

> "I believe that the preliminary injunction in this case which is sought by the plaintiff should be granted. ... it seems to me the thing that the parties should do is this: I think a plan should be worked out between the plaintiff and the defendant under which the defendant is given an opportunity to find a new name in a reasonable period of time, but during—and then to start advertising under its new name, but during the interim that they work out a system where, with disclaimer or otherwise, the defendant can gradually shift over from its present business enterprise and use of the name to some other name without undue disruption of its business. I think the parties in good faith can do that."

Despite the court's directions that the parties attempt to work out a plan that would allow the defendant to gradually shift to using a new name for its toy dogs, the parties failed to agree on the terms of such a plan. After a hearing on the terms of the injunction, the court entered an order preliminarily enjoining the defendants' use of the "International Kennel Club" name. Specifically, the order: (1) required defendants to immediately choose a new name which would not be "confusingly similar" to International Kennel Club, but which could have the initials "IKC"; (2) prohibited defendants from placing any more advertising in any North American publication using the name "International Kennel Club" to identify their stuffed dogs; (3) ordered the defendants to withdraw—where possible—unpublished advertising containing the name "International Kennel Club"; and (4) ordered the defendants to begin as soon as commercially practicable, but no later than January 31, 1987, to cease selling stuffed dogs under the "International Kennel Club" name. The order further required the defendants to pay into an escrow account a licensing fee of fifty cents per dog sold under the plaintiff's name subsequent to October 15, 1986 (calculated to be a 3 1/3% royalty). This fund was to serve as a bond for the plaintiff on appeal.

Subsequently, the defendants filed a motion to require the plaintiff to post security and to modify and stay the injunction. The court refused to modify the injunction, but stated that to avoid a stay of the injunction order, the plaintiff would have to post a bond pending appeal in addition to the escrow money provided for in the initial injunction. However, when plaintiff's counsel represented to the court that the plaintiff could not afford a bond, the court found that "to force you to post a bond would be basically to destroy your little operation." Consequently, rather than ordering the plaintiff to post a bond, the court granted the defendants' motion to stay the preliminary injunction order pending appeal.

II.

* * *

A. Likelihood of success on the merits

In order to prevail in its action under section 43(a) of the Lanham Act, the IKC must establish: (1) that it has a protectible trademark, and (2) a "likelihood of confusion" as to the origin of the defendant's product. *A.J. Canfield*, 796 F.2d at 906; *McGraw-Edison Company v. Walt Disney Productions*, 787 F.2d 1163, 1167 (7th Cir. 1986). At the preliminary injunction stage, however, a plaintiff need only demonstrate that he or she has a "better than negligible" chance of succeeding on the merits to justify injunctive relief. *Curtis*, 840 F.2d at 1296; *Brunswick Corp.*, 784 F.2d at 275 ("Although the plaintiff must demonstrate some probability of success on the merits, 'the threshold is low. It is enough that the plaintiff's chances are better than negligible …'") (quoting *Roland Machinery*, 749 F.2d at 387). We therefore analyze not whether the plaintiff will or will not prevail on the merits, but whether the plaintiff has demonstrated a better than negligible chance of establishing the "trademark" and "likelihood of confusion" prongs under section 43(a). *Hyatt Corp.*, 736 F.2d at 1156.

The first step in determining whether an unregistered mark or name is entitled to the protection of the trademark laws is to categorize the name according to the nature of the term itself. Trademarks that are fanciful, arbitrary [i.e. made-up terms like "Kodak"] or suggestive are fully protected, while "descriptive words (e.g. "bubbly" champagne) may be trademarked only if they have acquired *secondary meaning*, that is, only if most consumers have come to think of the word not as descriptive at all but as the name of the product." *Blau Plumbing, Inc. v. SOS Fix-It, Inc.*, 781 F.2d 604, 609 (7th Cir. 1986). In *Blau*, the court explained that:

> "The goal of trademark protection is to allow a firm to affix an identifying mark to its product (or service) offering that will, because it is distinctive and no competitor may use a confusingly similar designation, enable the consumer to discover in the least possible amount of time and with the least possible amount of head scratching whether a particular brand is that firm's brand or a competitor's brand…. *To allow a firm to use as a trademark a generic word, or a descriptive word still understood by the consuming public to describe, would make it difficult for competitors to market their own brands of the same product.* Imagine being forbidden to describe a Chevrolet as a 'car' or an 'automobile' because Ford or Chrysler or Volvo had trademarked these generic words, or an after-shave lotion as 'bracing' because the maker of one brand of after-shave lotion had trademarked this descriptive word."

(Emphasis added, citations omitted). Hence, although a term's "primary" meaning is merely descriptive, if through use the public has come to identify the term with a plaintiff's product or service, the words have acquired a "secondary meaning" and would become a protectible trademark. *Gimix, Inc. v. J S & A Group, Inc.*, 699 F.2d 901, 907 (7th Cir. 1983); *Miller Brewing Co. v. G. Heileman Brewing Co.*, 561 F.2d 75, 79 (7th Cir. 1977), *cert. denied*, 434 U.S. 1025, 54 L. Ed. 2d 772, 98 S. Ct. 751 (1978). In other words, "'secondary meaning' denotes an association in the mind of the consumer between the trade dress [or name] of a product and a particular producer." *Vaughan Manufacturing Co. v. Brikam Intern., Inc.*, 814 F.2d 346, 348 (7th Cir. 1987). We agree with the district court that the phrase "International Kennel Club" fits within the category of descriptive words in that it "specifically describes a characteristic or ingredient of an article [or service]." *Miller*

Brewing Co., 561 F.2d at 79. Thus, the "International Kennel Club" name is entitled to trademark protection only if the name has acquired "secondary meaning," i.e. has become distinctive of the plaintiff's goods and/or services.

The defendants claim that the plaintiff's evidence introduced at the preliminary injunction hearing is insufficient to demonstrate that the plaintiff has better than a negligible chance of establishing that the "International Kennel Club" name acquired secondary meaning among the consuming public. "The factors which this court has indicated it will consider on the issue of secondary meaning include 'the amount and manner of advertising, volume of sales, the length and manner of use, direct consumer testimony, and consumer surveys.'" *Gimix, Inc.*, 699 F.2d at 907 (quoting *Union Carbide Corp. v. Everready, Inc.*, 531 F.2d 366, 380 (7th Cir.), cert. denied, 429 U.S. 830, 50 L. Ed. 2d 94, 97 S. Ct. 91 (1976)). "Consumer testimony and consumer surveys are the only direct evidence on this question ... the other factors are relevant in a more circumstantial fashion." *Id.* Not surprisingly, the defendants attack the absence of a consumer survey in the evidence produced by the plaintiff at the preliminary injunction hearing.

Despite this attack, we are not persuaded that the absence of a consumer survey is *per se* fatal to the plaintiff's request for a preliminary injunction. As noted previously, the trial court merely granted a *preliminary* injunction; it did not decide the case on the merits after allowing for full discovery. *See Hyatt Corp.*, 736 F.2d at 1156. The IKC may be in a better position to produce a survey at a full trial on the merits. Thus, while the lack of survey evidence fails to support the plaintiff's request for preliminary relief, we are convinced that it does not necessarily destroy the plaintiff's entitlement to that relief: the existence of a survey is only one of the variety of factors outlined in *Gimix* as being relevant to the issue of secondary meaning, and the plaintiff may resort to evidence other than a survey in attempting to demonstrate a "better than negligible" chance of establishing secondary meaning. Moreover, *Gimix* was decided at the summary judgment stage, after the parties had completed their discovery. In contrast, the plaintiff's motion in this case was decided under the time pressures characteristic of preliminary injunction hearings and without the benefit of extensive discovery. For these reasons, the plaintiff's burden at the preliminary injunction stage is slight, and on two separate occasions this court has declined to mandate a consumer survey at this preliminary stage. *See A.J. Canfield*, 796 F.2d at 908 ("Although Canfield [the plaintiff] did not introduce its own survey, it was not required to do so in order to prevail on a preliminary injunction motion."); *Vaughan Manufacturing Co.*, 814 F.2d at 346.

The remaining factors articulated in *Gimix* as material to the issue of secondary meaning weigh in favor of the trial court's conclusion that the International Kennel Club of Chicago "has acquired a secondary meaning like that among a small but very well-defined group of people in Chicago and elsewhere." In particular, the "amount and manner of advertising" and the "length and manner of use" of the International Kennel Club name yields a better than negligible chance of establishing secondary meaning. With respect to advertising, the plaintiff introduced evidence supporting the inference that the International Kennel Club has developed and maintained its reputation among canine enthusiasts through advertising carefully targeted to reach persons interested in the sport of showing purebred dogs. It has advertised in publications with a continent-wide circulation that are of interest to dog fanciers, including the *American Kennel Club Gazette, Kennel Review*, and *Dog World*. And because its shows are held in Chicago, the plaintiff advertises in regional publications of a more general appeal, including the major Chicago newspapers and magazines, as well as various local periodicals. Moreover, the plaintiff mails out as many as 15,000 "premium lists" prior to each show to persons on its mailing lists, and also employs a full-time public relations professional. In its most recent fiscal year, these advertising and public relations expenses have amounted to almost $60,000, or more than 42 percent of the club's total administrative and operating expenses. Viewed another way, these expenses come to more than 25 percent of the club's total revenues; further, the club's activities are often given extensive free publicity. As an example, both major Chicago newspapers have highlighted the plaintiff's dog shows and have designed and promoted special advertising supplements around those columns.

As evidence of secondary meaning, the International Kennel Club also introduced evidence that the club received a number and a variety of letters and phone calls asking about the defendants' toy dogs. In *A.J. Canfield*, the court found similar evidence — letters and phone calls to Canfield "all searching for the elusive diet chocolate fudge drink" (after a competitor advertised its own "Chocolate Fudge" drink) — "sufficient to show that when consumers think of diet chocolate fudge soda they think of Canfield." 796 F.2d at 907. Likewise, the correspondence directed to the plaintiff provides support for the inference that when dog fanciers see the "International Kennel Club" name, they think of the plaintiff. Finally, the plaintiff has operated under and advertised the "International Kennel Club" name continuously for over 50 years. In our view, the club's half-century use of the name, combined with their advertising, substantial free publicity, and wide-ranging activities in support of dog groups, clearly renders the plaintiff's chances of establishing that the International Kennel Club name has acquired secondary meaning better than negligible. *See* A.J. Canfield, 796 F.2d at 907 (Plaintiff's use of the label "chocolate fudge" for 13 years, combined with substantial advertising and free publicity, is sufficient to establish a likelihood of secondary meaning); *Vaughan Manufacturing Company*, 814 F.2d at 349 (plaintiff's use of its "trade dress" for over 14 years, combined with extensive advertising and evidence of copying, is sufficient to demonstrate a likelihood of secondary meaning).

[The court found IKC's mark had secondary meaning and was protectable.]

Zatarains, Inc. v. Oak Grove Smokehouse, Inc.
698 F.2d 786 (5th Cir. 1983)

GOLDBERG, CIRCUIT JUDGE.

This appeal of a trademark dispute presents us with a menu of edible delights sure to tempt connoisseurs of fish and fowl alike. At issue is the alleged infringement of two trademarks, "Fish-Fri" and "Chick-Fri," held by appellant Zatarain's, Inc. ("Zatarain's"). The district court held that the alleged infringers had a "fair use" defense to any asserted infringement of the term "Fish-Fri" and that the registration of the term "Chick-Fri" should be cancelled. We affirm.

I. FACTS AND PROCEEDINGS BELOW
A. THE TALE OF THE TOWN FRIER

Zatarain's is the manufacturer and distributor of a line of over one hundred food products. Two of these products, "Fish-Fri" and "Chick-Fri," are coatings or batter mixes used to fry foods. These marks serve as the entree in the present litigation.

Zatarain's "Fish-Fri" consists of 100% corn flour and is used to fry fish and other seafood. "Fish-Fri" is packaged in rectangular cardboard boxes containing twelve or twenty-four ounces of coating mix. The legend "Wonderful FISH-FRI (R)" is displayed

Picture 5.1   Zatarains Fish-Fri
[Copyright 2004. Used by permission of Zatarain Corp.]

prominently on the front panel, along with the block Z used to identify all Zatarain's products. The term "Fish-Fri" has been used by Zatarain's or its predecessor since 1950 and has been registered as a trademark since 1962.

Zatarain's "Chick-Fri" is a seasoned corn flour batter mix used for frying chicken and other foods. The "Chick-Fri" package, which is very similar to that used for "Fish-Fri," is a rectangular cardboard container labelled "Wonderful CHICK-FRI." Zatarain's began to use the term "Chick-Fri" in 1968 and registered the term as a trademark in 1976.

Zatarain's products are not alone in the marketplace. At least four other companies market coatings for fried foods that are denominated "fish fry" or "chicken fry." Two of these competing companies are the appellees here, and therein hangs this fish tale.

Appellee Oak Grove Smokehouse, Inc. ("Oak Grove") began marketing a "fish fry" and a "chicken fry" in March 1979. Both products are packaged in clear glassine packets that contain a quantity of coating mix sufficient to fry enough food for one meal. The packets are labelled with Oak Grove's name and emblem, along with the words "FISH FRY" OR "CHICKEN FRY." Oak Grove's "FISH FRY" has a corn flour base seasoned with various spices; Oak Grove's "CHICKEN FRY" is a seasoned coating with a wheat flour base.

Appellee Visko's Fish Fry, Inc. ("Visko's") entered the batter mix market in March 1980 with its "fish fry." Visko's product is packed in a cylindrical eighteen-ounce container with a resealable plastic lid. The words "Visko's FISH FRY" appear on the label along with a photograph of a platter of fried fish. Visko's coating mix contains corn flour and added spices.

Other food manufacturing concerns also market coating mixes. Boochelle's Spice Co. ("Boochelle's"), originally a defendant in this lawsuit, at one time manufactured a seasoned "FISH FRY" packaged in twelve-ounce vinyl plastic packets. Pursuant to a settlement between Boochelle's and Zatarain's, Boochelle's product is now labelled "FISH AND VEGETABLE FRY." Another batter mix, "YOGI Brand (R) OYSTER SHRIMP and FISH FRY," is also available. Arnaud Coffee Corporation ("Arnaud") has manufactured and marketed "YOGI Brand" for ten to twenty years, but was never made a party to this litigation. A product called "Golden Dipt Old South Fish Fry" has recently entered the market as well.

B. OUT OF THE FRYING PAN, INTO THE FIRE

Zatarain's first claimed foul play in its original complaint filed against Oak Grove on June 19, 1979, in the United States District Court for the Eastern District of Louisiana. The complaint alleged trademark infringement and unfair competition under the Lanham Act §32(1), 43(a) ...

The case was tried to the court without a jury. Treating the trademark claims first, the district court classified the term "Fish-Fri" as a descriptive term identifying a function of the product being sold. The court found further that the term "Fish-Fri" had acquired a secondary meaning in the New Orleans geographical area and therefore was entitled to trademark protection, but concluded that the defendants were entitled fair use of the term "fish fry" to describe characteristics of their goods. Accordingly, the court held that Oak Grove and Visko's had not infringed Zatarain's trademark "Fish-Fri."

With respect to the alleged infringement of the term "Chick-Fri," the court found that "Chick-Fri" was a descriptive term that had not acquired a secondary meaning in the minds of consumers. Consequently, the court held that Zatarain's claim for infringement of its trademark "Chick-Fri" failed and ordered that the trademark registration of "Chick-Fri" should be cancelled.

Turning to Zatarain's unfair competition claims, the court observed that the evidence showed no likelihood of or actual confusion on the part of the buying public. Additionally, the court noted that the dissimilarities in trade dress of Zatarain's, Oak Grove's, and Visko's products diminished any possibility of buyer confusion. For these reasons, the court found no violations of federal or state unfair competition laws.

Finally, the court addressed the counter-claims asserted by Oak Grove and Visko's. Because no evidence was introduced to support the defendants' allegations of monopolistic behavior, fraud, and bad faith on the part of Zatarain's, the court dismissed the federal and state antitrust and unfair trade practices counterclaims. The court also dismissed the counterclaim based on Zatarain's allegedly improper product identity labeling. Both sides now appeal to this court.

II. ISSUES ON APPEAL

The district court found that Zatarain's trademark "Fish-Fri" was a descriptive term with an established secondary meaning, but held that Oak Grove and Visko's had a "fair use" defense to their asserted infringement of the mark. The court further found that Zatarain's trademark "Chick-Fri" was a descriptive term that lacked secondary meaning, and accordingly ordered the trademark registration cancelled. Additionally, the court concluded that Zatarain's had produced no evidence in support of its claims of unfair competition on the part of Oak Grove and Visko's. Finally, the court dismissed Oak Grove's and Visko's counterclaims for antitrust violations, unfair trade practices, misbranding of food products, and miscellaneous damages.

Battered, but not fried, Zatarain's appeals from the adverse judgment on several grounds. First, Zatarain's argues that its trademark "Fish-Fri" is a suggestive term and therefore not subject to the "fair use" defense. Second, Zatarain's asserts that even if the "fair use" defense is applicable in this case, appellees cannot invoke the doctrine because their use of Zatarain's trademarks is not a good faith attempt to describe their products. Third, Zatarain's urges that the district court erred in cancelling the trademark registration for the term "Chick-Fri" because Zatarain's presented sufficient evidence to establish a secondary meaning for the term. For these reasons, Zatarain's argues that the district court should be reversed.

Oak Grove and Visko's also present an appeal to this court, contending that the district court erred in dismissing their counterclaims against Zatarain's. In particular, Oak Grove and Visko's again urge that Zatarain's conduct has violated the Sherman Act, the Lanham Act, the federal regulations governing product identity labeling, and Louisiana law prohibiting restraint of trade; Oak Grove and Visko's also pray for an award of attorneys' fees. We now turn to an appraisal of these issues.

III. THE TRADEMARK CLAIMS
A. BASIC PRINCIPLES

* * *

2. *Secondary Meaning*

As noted earlier, descriptive terms are ordinarily not protectable as trademarks. They may be protected, however, if they have acquired a secondary meaning for the consuming public. The concept of secondary meaning recognizes that words with an ordinary and primary meaning of their own "may by long use with a particular product, come to be known by the public as specifically designating that product." *Volkswagenwerk Aktiengesellschaft v. Rickard*, 492 F.2d 474, 477 (5th Cir.1974). In order to establish a secondary meaning for a term, a plaintiff "must show that the primary significance of the term in the minds of the consuming public is not the product but the producer." *Kellogg Co. v. National Biscuit Co.*, 305 U.S. 111, 118, 59 S. Ct. 109, 113, 83 L. Ed. 73 (1938). The burden of proof to establish secondary meaning rests at all times with the plaintiff; this burden is not an easy one to satisfy, for "'[a] high degree of proof is necessary to establish secondary meaning for a descriptive term.'" *Vision Center*, 596 F.2d at 118 (quoting 3 R. Callman, *supra*, §77.3, at 359). Proof of secondary meaning is an issue only with respect to descriptive marks; suggestive and arbitrary or fanciful marks are automatically protected upon registration, and generic terms are unprotectable even if they have acquired secondary meaning. *See Soweco*, 617 F.2d at 1185.

* * *

Descriptive terms are not protectable by trademark absent a showing of secondary meaning in the minds of the consuming public. To prevail in its trademark infringement action, therefore, Zatarain's must prove that its mark "Fish-Fri" has acquired a secondary meaning and thus warrants trademark protection. The district court found that Zatarain's evidence established a secondary meaning for the term "Fish-Fri" in the New Orleans area. We affirm.

The existence of secondary meaning presents a question for the trier of fact, and a district court's finding on the issue will not be disturbed unless clearly erroneous. *American Heritage*, 494 F.2d at 13; *Volkswagenwerk*, 492 F.2d at 477. The burden of proof rests with the party seeking to establish legal protection for the mark—the plaintiff in an infringement suit. *Vision Center*, 596 F.2d at 118. The evidentiary burden necessary to establish secondary meaning for a descriptive term is substantial. *Id.; American Heritage*, 494 F.2d at 12; 3 R. CALLMAN, *supra*, §77.3, at 359.

In assessing a claim of secondary meaning, the major inquiry is the consumer's attitude toward the mark. The mark must denote to the consumer "a single thing coming from a single source," *Coca-Cola Co. v. Koke Co.*, 254 U.S. 143, 146, 41 S. Ct. 113, 114, 65 L. Ed. 189 (1920); *Aloe Creme Laboratories*, 423 F.2d at 849, to support a finding of secondary meaning. Both direct and circumstantial evidence may be relevant and persuasive on the issue.

Factors such as amount and manner of advertising, volume of sales, and length and manner of use may serve as circumstantial evidence relevant to the issue of secondary meaning. While none of these factors alone will prove secondary meaning, in combination they may establish the necessary link in the minds of consumers between a product and its source. It must be remembered, however, that "the question is not the *extent* of the promotional efforts, but their *effectiveness* in altering the meaning of [the term] to the consuming public." *Aloe Creme Laboratories*, 423 F.2d at 850.

Since 1950, Zatarain's and its predecessor have continuously used the term "Fish-Fri" to identify this particular batter mix. Through the expenditure of over $400,000 for advertising during the period from 1976 through 1981, Zatarain's has promoted its name and its product to the buying public. Sales of twelve-ounce boxes of "Fish-Fri" increased from 37,265 cases in 1969 to 59,439 cases in 1979. From 1964 through 1979, Zatarain's sold a total of 916,385 cases of "Fish-Fri." The district court considered this circumstantial evidence of secondary meaning to weigh heavily in Zatarain's favor.

In addition to these circumstantial factors, Zatarain's introduced at trial two surveys conducted by its expert witness, Allen Rosenzweig. In one survey, telephone interviewers questioned 100 women in the New Orleans area who fry fish or other seafood three or more times per month. Of the women surveyed, twenty-three percent specified *Zatarain's* "Fish-Fri" as a product they "would buy at the grocery to use as a coating" or a "product on the market that is especially made for frying fish." In a similar survey conducted in person at a New Orleans area mall, twenty-eight of the 100 respondents answered "*Zatarain's* 'Fish-Fri'" to the same questions.[8]

The authorities are in agreement that survey evidence is the most direct and persuasive way of establishing secondary meaning. The district court believed that the survey evidence produced by Zatarain's, when coupled with the circumstantial evidence of advertising and usage, tipped the scales in favor of a finding of secondary meaning. Were we considering the question of secondary meaning *de novo*, we might reach a different conclusion than did the district court, for the issue is close. Mindful, however, that there is evidence in the record to support the finding below, we cannot say that the district court's conclusion was clearly erroneous. Accordingly, the finding of secondary meaning in the New Orleans area for Zatarain's descriptive term "Fish-Fri" must be affirmed.

[The Court found the mark Chicken Fri to be generic and ordered its registration cancelled. The Court also found that although Fish Fri had secondary meaning, it was subject to the fair use defense so that competitors could use the term "fish fry" to describe their products.]

Foamation, Inc. v. Wedeward Enterprises, Inc.
970 F. Supp. 676 (E.D. Wisc. 1997)

CALLAHAN, UNITED STATES MAGISTRATE JUDGE

* * *

---

8. The telephone survey also included this question: "When you mentioned 'fish fry,' did you have a specific product in mind or did you use that term to mean any kind of coating used to fry fish?" To this inartfully worded question, 77% of the New Orleans respondents answered "specific product" and 23% answered "any kind of coating." Unfortunately, Rosenzweig did not ask the logical follow-up question that seemingly would have ended the inquiry conclusively: "Who makes the specific product you have in mind?" Had he but done so, our task would have been much simpler.

Foamation, Inc. ("Foamation") is a Wisconsin corporation with its principal place of business at 2018 South 1st Street, Milwaukee, Wisconsin, 53201. Wedeward Enterprises, Inc. ("Wedeward") is a Wisconsin corporation with a principal place of business at N91 W17174 Appleton Avenue, Menomonee Falls, Wisconsin, 53051, and is doing business in Wisconsin and this judicial district.

Thomas Wedeward and Rose Wedeward are residents of this judicial district, are President and Vice-President of Wedeward Enterprises, Inc., are sole shareholders of Wedeward Enterprises, Inc., and are directly responsible for the activities of Wedeward Enterprises, Inc.

Ralph Bruno ("Bruno") made his first wedge shaped cheese hat out of foam no later than May 1987. When he created his first foam cheese hat, Bruno was employed by S&R Model & Pattern ("S&R"), a partnership comprised of Bruno and Scott Papke ("Papke").

Picture 5.2   Cheesehead
[Photo courtesy of Ralph Bruno.]

The foam cheese hats initially sold by S&R were identified by means of an S&R return address label that was embedded in the foam in the crown of the hat. The return address label did not make any reference to copyright or include the © symbol. At least 1,500 foam cheese wedge hats were sold by S&R without any copyright notice. The foam cheese hats continued to be sold under the S&R Model & Pattern name until some time in late 1988 when the name "Foamation" was adopted for S&R's foam products business activities.

When the Foamation name was adopted, Bruno and Papke began affixing labels with the name Foamation to the hats. The Foamation labels did not make any reference to copyright or to the © symbol.

The partnership between Bruno and Papke was dissolved effective June 2, 1989. The partnership Dissolution Agreement specifically addressed the disposition of certain tangible assets of the partnership, such as the real property and machinery and materials used by the partnership, but did not address the disposition of any intangible assets of the partnership such as copyright, trademark, or other intellectual property rights.

After the partnership was dissolved, Bruno continued the foam product manufacturing business, including the manufacture of cheese wedge hats as a sole proprietorship under the name Foamation. Bruno did not place any copyright notice in hats manufactured by Foamation, a sole proprietorship, until at least some time in 1989 when he acquired new machinery that simplified the process of imprinting identification information directly into the hat itself.

The Plaintiff's Claims

Foamation's complaint alleges three claims: "copyright infringement"; "federal unfair competition"; and, "Wisconsin state trademark infringement". Wedeward's motion seeks dismissal of Foamation's complaint in its entirety.

Foamation's first claim is based on its assertion that it has a copyright in a "Novelty Hat", which "… consists of a wearable sculpture in the form of a cheese wedge, typically molded from polyurethane foam."

In its second claim, Foamation asserts that, "since at least 1987, Foamation has extensively marketed its unique and distinctive 'novelty hat'" and that "as a result of Foamation's efforts its novelty hats have acquired an exceedingly valuable goodwill owned by Foamation and have become widely and favorably known throughout the United States as an indication of source and origin in Foamation." Foamation claims that Wedeward's hat is copied from Foamation's and that Wedeward's conduct in copying Foamation's novelty hat was intended to cause, and is likely to cause, confusion or mistake, or to deceive as to source, origin, sponsorship, authorization and quality, and is likely to mislead the public into believing that Wedeward's products emanate from Foamation, all in violation of 15 U.S.C. §1125(a).

Foamation's third claim asserts that Foamation is the owner of a Wisconsin state trademark registration issued on May 22, 1996, covering the mark "consisting of the actual configuration of the goods—a pie shaped configuration in a yellow/orange color, and used as a novelty hat, design of a novelty hat." Foamation claims that Wedeward's manufacture and distribution of its own novelty hat infringes on Foamation's trademark pursuant to Chapter 132 of the Wisconsin Statutes and the common law of Wisconsin.

* * *

Federal Unfair Competition

Foamation's second claim is one for federal unfair competition. It is based on 15 U.S.C. §1125(a) (§43(a) of the Lanham Act).

* * *

Reduced to its essence, Foamation's claim is that its cheese wedge hat is entitled to trade dress protection. Wedeward argues that it is entitled to summary judgment dismissing this claim because Foamation cannot prove that its cheese wedge hat is entitled to trade dress protection.

* * *

Have Foamation's Cheese Wedge Hats Acquired "Secondary Meaning"?

On the one hand, trademark law allows the producer to prohibit the copying of a product feature which serves as a signifier of choice in order to preserve his reputation and the goodwill consumers have for his brand. On the other hand, effective competition and the penumbra of the patent laws require that competitors be able to slavishly copy the design of a successful product. *Thomas & Betts Corp.*, 65 F.3d at 658.

To police this distinction, courts require as a prerequisite to protection that trade dress which is not inherently distinctive have acquired secondary meaning. Secondary meaning is acquired when "in the minds of the public, the primary significance of a product feature ... is to identify the source of the product rather than the product itself." *Id.*, citing *Qualitex Co. v. Jacobson Products Company, Inc.*, 514 U.S. 159, 115 S. Ct. 1300, 1303, 131 L. Ed. 2d 248 (1995). "It is not enough, however, that the consumers associate the form of the product with the particular producer. Such an association is inevitable when the first comer is the exclusive producer under [for example] a patent. Consumers must also *care* that the product comes from a particular producer (though they need not be able to identify him) and must *desire* the product with the particular feature *because* it signifies the producer." *Thomas & Betts Corp.*, 65 F.3d at 658–59. (Emphasis provided). To establish secondary meaning, the plaintiff must show that the design is a "mark of distinction identifying the source of the article and that purchasers are moved to buy it because of its source." *Blisscraft of Hollywood v. United Plastics Co.*, 294 F.2d 694, 697 (2d Cir. 1961).

In the instant action, Foamation argues that its hats have acquired secondary meaning because its customers "... recognize Foamation as the source of origin for wedge-shaped cheese hats and ... acknowledge that the media has given Foamation considerable publicity as the originator of the 'Cheesehead' hat." In support of this argument, Foamation relies on certain statements attached to the Declaration of Chris Becker.

First of all, the statements attached to Mr. Becker's Declaration are unsworn. As such, they are hearsay. Rule 56(e), Fed. R. Civ. P., states that "when a motion for summary judgment is made and supported as provided in this rule, an adverse party may not rest upon the mere allegations or denials of the adverse party's pleading, but the adverse party's response, by affidavits or otherwise as provided in this rule, must set forth specific facts showing that there is a genuine issue for trial ..." That rule further requires that "supporting and opposing affidavits shall be made on personal knowledge, shall set forth such facts as would be admissible in evidence, and shall show affirmatively that the affiant is competent to testify to the matters stated therein."

As mentioned above, the statements attached to Chris Becker's Declaration are unsworn. Furthermore, Mr. Becker has no first hand knowledge of the information the purported customers make in such unsworn statements. To be sure, Mr. Becker avers that "Foamation intends to accumulate such evidence and introduce the same at trial either through live testimony or deposition transcript as evidence of inherent distinctiveness and/or secondary meaning." But, the time for presenting sworn affidavits raising genuine issues of fact is now, not at some future trial, and Foamation has not done so. Again, it is important to remember that Foamation bears the burden of proof on its claims and "the plain language of Rule 56(c) mandates the entry of summary judgment, after adequate time for discovery and upon motion, against a party who fails to make a showing sufficient to establish the existence of an element essential to that party's case, and on which that party will bear the burden of proof at trial." *Celotex*, 477 U.S. at 322. Foamation has not made the showing required by Rule 56(c). For this reason alone the entry of summary judgment dismissing its federal unfair competition claim is appropriate.

But, even if the court were to consider the customer statements, summary judgment in favor of Wedeward would nevertheless be appropriate. All of the statements attached to Chris Becker's Declaration are on Foamation, Inc. letterhead. The text of each of them reads as follows:

February 28, 1997

These statements are made to the best of my knowledge and belief.

I am in the business of buying and selling products, including Cheesehead TM hats which I purchase from Foamation, Inc. of Milwaukee, Wisconsin.

In the business, I am familiar with the hat which is wedge shaped, like a piece of pie cut from a circular pie and it is yellow/gold in color, and it has pock marks which are circular or oval shaped depressions on its surface.

This hat has been outstandingly poplar [sic] in my sales and it is known by me and my customers to originate from Foamation, Inc. I have been selling this hat for several years and I have sold thousands of them.

The hat has received extensive news type publicity from both the print and electronic (T.V.) media, and Foamation's name is included in that publicity, which is unsolicited by Foamation, Inc. or myself.

Throughout the above activities, it is the configuration of the hat that is involved, and that, I believe, is the identifying feature of the hat.

First of all, each of these statements conclude with the observation that "... it is the configuration of the hat that is involved, and that, I believe, is the identifying feature of the hat." Even assuming that were true, and that the particular signator could testify to such fact, that would not raise an issue of material fact with regard to secondary meaning.

The issue in trade dress product configuration cases, such as this, is not the primary meaning to consumers of a particular signifier. Rather, it is whether a product feature's primary significance to consumers is as an identifier of source as opposed to an element which contributes to the inherent appeal of the product. If the latter, then it is not protectable trade dress. It was for this reason that the court denied trademark protection to "pillow shape" shredded wheat: "a form in which the public has become accustomed to see the article and which, in the minds of the public, is primarily associated with the article rather than a particular producer." *See, Kellogg*, 305 U.S. at 120, 59 S. Ct. at 114.

To be sure, the configuration of the cheese wedge hat is the identifying feature of the hat. And, even assuming, as asserted in the statements, that the hat has been outstandingly popular, and is known by [the particular] individual signing the statement, and their customers, to originate from Foamation, Inc., this is not enough to demonstrate secondary meaning. Once again, as the Seventh Circuit held in Thomas & Betts Corp., supra:

> It is not enough that the consumers associate the form of the product with a particular producer.... Consumers must also care that the product comes from a *particular* producer ... and must *desire* the product with the particular feature *because it signifies that producer.*

Thomas & Betts Corp., 65 F.3d at 658–59. (Emphasis provided).

Nowhere in the statements attached to Chris Becker's Declaration do the signators state, or even suggest, that it is because Foamation, Inc. produces the cheese wedge hats that the particular signator to such statements purchased such hats. To the contrary, that the statements indicate it is the configuration of the hat that is important would suggest its producer, i.e., its manufacturer, is not all that important.

Moreover, that Foamation's "hat has received extensive news type publicity from both the print and electronic (T.V.) media, and Foamation's name is included in that publicity ..." adds nothing to the analysis. "Such evidence may not provide the basis for an inference of secondary meaning because something other than the secondary meaning of the trade dress may have been responsible for the success of the product. Success of a product is not among the types of evidence described by the [Patent and Trademark Office] as useful in establishing secondary meaning." *Aromatique, Inc. v. Gold Seal, Inc.*, 28 F.3d 863, 873 (8th Cir. 1994).

This principle would appear to be particularly applicable here where, as the defendants point out in their reply brief, "… several of Foamation's statements demonstrate that its cheese hat is desirable as an identifiable badge of support for the Green Bay Packers and the State of Wisconsin. For example, the videotape excerpts submitted by Foamation as an exhibit to Chris Becker's declaration are proof that cheese wedge hats are desirable to Green Bay football fans as a badge of support. Similarly, the representation that Foamation cheese hats were 'badly needed' at the January, 1997, Super Bowl site is an acknowledgement that purchases are driven by Packer support rather than loyalty to Foamation. Moreover, Foamation touts the cheese wedge hat as 'synonymous with America's dairyland' and 'a national symbol representing Wisconsinites'.

In order to establish that its product feature, i.e., the wedge shape of its pock marked hat, possesses secondary meaning, Foamation must be able to prove that in the minds of consumers **the primary** significance of the wedge shaped pock marked hat is to identify the hat as a Foamation product. The materials submitted by Foamation have not demonstrated that Foamation can meet that burden. Because of such failure, summary judgment in favor of Wedeward dismissing Foamation's claim of federal unfair competition, i.e., trade dress infringement, is appropriate. *See, Mana Products, Inc. v. Columbia Cosmetics Mfg.*, 65 F.3d 1063 (2d Cir. 1995) [Court granted summary judgment dismissing the plaintiff's claims under §43 of the Lanham Act on the grounds that the plaintiff had failed to raise a material issue of fact regarding either the issue of inherent distinctiveness or acquired secondary meaning.]; *See also, Petersen Manufacturing Company v. Central Purchasing*, 740 F.2d 1541 (Fed. Cir. 1984) [Summary judgment is appropriate given the lack of proof of secondary meaning. "The non-movant is not entitled to a full trial if he proffers no 'significant probative evidence tending to support the complaint.'" *Peterson Manufacturing Company*, 740 F.2d at 1551.]

For the reasons stated above, Foamation has failed in its effort to demonstrate a genuine issue of material fact on the question of secondary meaning. Accordingly, summary judgment dismissing its state trademark claim is appropriate.

Therefore, for the reasons expressed above,

IT IS ORDERED that the defendants' motion for summary judgment is GRANTED and the plaintiff's complaint is DISMISSED.

Notes

1. In the secondary meaning cases, *supra*, the courts analyzed various factors to determine if a given mark had obtained secondary meaning. However, in secondary meaning analysis, the true question is not how hard the trademark claimant worked to establish secondary meaning. The true question is did the use of the mark have the effect of creating a word, symbol, or device that identified the source or origin of some good or service in the minds of the relevant consuming public. That is, no matter how hard the trademark claimant tries to create trademark rights, the real question is whether it was successful.

2. Secondary meaning should not be confused with the term "de facto secondary meaning." De facto secondary meaning describes a setting where a term was from its adoption generic or, through use, has become generic but still is perceived by the public as identi-

fying source. There are said to be two types of de facto secondary meaning. The first is a situation where the consuming public does not perceive the mark to be a brand name but still believes there is one source of the goods or services on or in connection with which it is used. The second form of de facto secondary meaning is where a business adopts a word in the English language that is already generic and through advertising and use eventually establishes real secondary meaning in the mark. The result, however is the same: no trademark protection for either. *See, e.g., AOL v. AT&T*, 243 F. 3d 812 (4th Cir. 2001). Genericism is the subject of Chapter 9, *infra*.

3. Whether or not a mark has secondary meaning is measured by its effect on the consuming public. Regardless of how much money a producer spends on promoting a mark as used on or in connection with some goods or services, the effect on the consumer is the key. Therefore, in trademark law, we often say, "Money can buy you love, but it can't buy you secondary meaning." This, however, clearly has not stopped producers from trying, essentially, to buy secondary meaning.

4. Foamation is still in business. It's goods can be found at www.cheesehead.com.

————————

Chapter VI

Acquisition of Trademark Rights

A. Adoption and Use

15 U.S.C. §1127, Lanham Act §45

The term "use in commerce" means the bona fide use of a mark in the ordinary course of trade, and not merely to reserve a right in a mark.

———————

Federal trademark rights in the United States are premised upon the adoption and use of the mark in interstate commerce. 15 U.S.C. §1051(a) (Lanham Act §1(a)). Priority of rights is determined by first use, not who registered the trademark first as in Civil Law countries (intent to use is a limited exception to this rule discussed in detail. *See infra* Part E). Therefore, the first party to use a mark in the ordinary course of trade will have priority over others who may want to use that same or similar mark on the same or similar goods or services. If a mark is not registered, concurrent use is possible in remote geographic locations where no consumers will be confused. The federal registration system is considered to be a codification of those rights obtained via the common law through priority of adoption and use.

In order to gain priority in a mark, use of the mark must be "sufficient" to confer rights. For sales to constitute the necessary use, they must be at "arm's length," meaning that the sale is actually one representing a commercial transaction and not merely an internal business deal.

Sale of a product to which the mark is attached may or may not be sufficient depending upon the purpose and circumstances of the sale. A minimal number of sales spread over a long period of time are not necessarily sufficient to confer priority. *Sweetarts v. Sunline, Inc.*, 380 F.2d 923 (8th Cir. 1967). Initial sales of a product in an effort to establish a market for the good may be adequate to acquire rights if that use is in the ordinary course of trade. *International Tel. Tel. Corp. v. Int'l. Mobil Mach. Corp.*, 800 F.2d 1118 (Fed. Cir. 1986). A transaction undertaken only to get the mark before the public, but not an actual sale, will not be enough to confer rights.

bona fide sale

———————

Proctor & Gamble Company v. Johnson & Johnson, Inc.
485 F.Supp. 1185 (S.D.N.Y.), aff'd, 636 F.2d 1203 (2d Cir. 1980)

LEVAL, DIST. JUDGE

I. Introduction.

This is an action for trademark infringement, false designation of origin, unfair competition and trademark dilution. The plaintiff, Procter & Gamble Co. ("P&G"), an Ohio corporation, is one of the country's largest manufacturers of household and personal use products. The defendants are Johnson & Johnson Incorporated ("J&J") and its wholly-owned subsidiary Personal Products Company ("PPC"), both New Jersey corporations. PPC is the leading manufacturer of women's external menstrual protection products. The case raises interesting questions.

The defendants' trademarks which are alleged to infringe rights of the plaintiff are "Assure!" as used on a woman's menstrual tampon, and "Sure & Natural", as used on an external menstrual protection shield.

The plaintiff's marks alleged to be infringed are "Sure" for an underarm anti-perspirant deodorant and for a woman's tampon, and "Assure" for a mouthwash and a shampoo.

* * *

II. Facts.

The history of the development of the controversy is as follows.

a. P&G'S Establishment of its Marks.

In 1964 P&G acquired the trademark "Sure" for a personal deodorant from a prior owner. At the time P&G considered using the mark on two different products which it had in development. One was an anti-perspirant underarm deodorant which eventually entered test market in 1972 bearing the name "Sure" and which has since established itself as one of the best selling anti-perspirants in the country. The other was a woman's tampon which was to be P&G's first entry into the woman's sanitary protection field. Accordingly, P&G applied in 1964 for a federal trademark registration for "Sure" for tampons. As a deodorant mark, "Sure" was already registered by the predecessor.

P&G encountered clouds and potential obstacles to its use of the mark. Litigation with one adverse claimant was settled in 1968, following which the registration of "Sure" for tampons was granted by the patent office. In 1970, P&G succeeded in removing another potential cloud by buying from its owner the mark "Assure" which was registered for use on a mouthwash and a shampoo.

Also in 1970, P&G won a favorable resolution of a lawsuit brought by the manufacturer of a competing deodorant Arrid which sought to prevent P&G's use of "Sure" on the deodorant by reason of trademark rights in Arrid's advertising slogan "Use Arrid, to be sure". *Carter-Wallace, Inc. v. Procter & Gamble Co.*, 434 F.2d 794 (9 Cir. 1970).

The anti-perspirant was ready for test marketing far in advance of the tampon. It was given the name Sure Anti-perspirant Deodorant and entered test market in 1972; it went national in 1973. Since it was introduced, over 300 million units have been sold bringing revenues to P&G of approximately $300,000,000. P&G has spent approximately $100,000,000 on the promotion of the product.

In 1974, P&G's tampon was ready to enter test market. The name Sure was not adopted. The name chosen was Rely. The marketing of Rely has expanded from year to year to the point that it is now sold in approximately two-thirds of the United States, including substantially all but the northeast.

Sure for tampons, since 1964, and Assure for mouthwash and shampoo, since 1970, have been carried by P&G in its "minor brands program". The minor brands program is designed by P&G to establish and maintain ownership rights over trademarks which have not been assigned by P&G to any commercially marketed product. One of the most hotly contested issues in this lawsuit is the legal effectiveness of this program to maintain ownership rights in the Assure and Sure-for-tampon marks for ten and sixteen years respectively.

* * *

III. The Contentions

Plaintiff asserts that the Assure and the Sure & Natural marks infringe, compete unfairly with and dilute plaintiff's marks and that defendants' use of the marks would involve a false designation of origin.

Defendants contend insofar as plaintiff's claims are made on behalf of its Sure deodorant mark, that there is (1) no substantial likelihood of consumer confusion as to a common source of the products at issue; (2) no likelihood that P&G will use the Sure mark on a menstrual protection product; and (3) no threat to P&G's business reputation or to the strength of the Sure deodorant mark. Thus, defendants contend that no infringement, unfair competition, false designation of origin or unfair competition has been shown.

Insofar as plaintiff's claims are made on behalf of the minor brands, defendants contend that P&G has not established the right to trademark protection because it has not used the marks in commerce. Defendants seek an order directing the cancellation of these registrations.

I find that the defendants have thoroughly and convincingly demonstrated the validity of their contentions.

* * *

(b) P&G's Minor Brands.

P&G's action is premised in part upon its registered ownership of the brands Sure for tampons and Assure for mouthwash and deodorant. PPC rebuts this part of plaintiff's claim by contending that P&G owns no rights in these marks, having failed to utilize them in commerce. In language of the Supreme Court dating from 1916:

> "There is no such thing as property in a trade-mark except as a right appurtenant to an established business or trade in connection with which the mark is employed. The law of trade-marks is but a part of the broader law of unfair competition; the right to a particular mark grows out of its use, not its mere adoption; its function is simply to designate the goods as the product of a particular trader and to protect his good will against the sale of another's product as his; and it is not the subject of property except in connection with an existing business."

United Drug Co. v. Theodore Rectanus Co., 248 U.S. 90, 97, 39 S. Ct. 48, 51, 63 L. Ed. 141 (1918); *Hanover Star Milling Co. v. Metcalf*, 240 U.S. 403, 36 S. Ct. 357, 60 L. Ed. 713 (1916).

The defendant relies on Judge Friendly's landmark opinion in *La Societe Anonyme des Parfums Le Galion v. Jean Patou, Inc.*, 495 F.2d 1265 (2 Cir. 1974) (the "Snob" case) to the effect that usage which is sporadic, nominal and intended solely for trademark maintenance is insufficient to establish and maintain trademark rights.

Broad statements of principle, however, will not answer for a particular case since "determining what constitutes sufficient use ... (is) a case-by-case task ... (and) the balance of the equities plays an important role in deciding whether defendant's use is sufficient...." *Snob*, 495 F.2d at 1274 n. 11; *Pab Produits v. Satinine Societa*, 570 F.2d 328, 334 (C.C.P.A.1978). Upon detailed review of all the pertinent facts, I have concluded that P&G does not own a protectable interest in the marks in question.

Most of the facts here are not in dispute, although there is some dispute concerning P&G's intentions and motives.

For many years P&G has maintained a formal program for the purpose of protecting its ownership rights in brand names which were not being actively used in commerce on its products. This program was entitled the "Minor Brands Program". In 1974 P&G's office of legal counsel circulated a memorandum institutionalizing the procedures to be followed for this brand maintenance program. The memorandum was revised in 1976 and was received in evidence at the trial. (Exhibit D-74) The memorandum begins by stating that the failure to use a trademark for two consecutive years may result in its loss. "The Minor Brands Sales Program is intended", it states, "to rebut any such inference of abandonment and thus maintain the company's ability to subsequently use the marks on goods in question as major brands." The memorandum directs that the trademark section of the legal division will annually prepare a list of every mark owned by the company. The list will be divided into three categories, to be designated as Major Brand, Minor Brand and No Value. A major brand is one which is currently marketed on a day to day basis. "A 'No Value' mark is one in which there is no current commercial interest ... All others automatically fall into the Minor Brand category." The memorandum goes on to state that each year the list will be reviewed with each division. "A diligent assessment will be made each year to place any marks which are in the Minor Brand category but which are unlikely to be selected for Major Brand usage within a reasonable period of time into the No Value category so as to keep Minor Brands to a minimum." The memorandum further instructs that when the list of minor brands has been reviewed each year, the trademark coordinator will pack 50 units of each product in the Minor Brand category and ship the 50 units to at least 10 states with a recommendation of alternation of states in succeeding years so as to achieve wide distribution. The shipments are made to normal customers for each type of product.

The evidence showed that the system functioned as follows. The distribution of goods in the Minor Brands Program is not handled by persons normally involved in P&G's merchandising operation. Indeed few employees at any level of P&G are even aware of the minor brands' existence. In each division of the company, one employee is charged with the distribution of minor brands. This "Minor Brands Coordinator" causes labels to be made and simple packages to be prepared for each minor brand. He then ships in accordance with the standing written instructions from trademark counsel. For all items in the Minor Brands Program regardless of size, cost or any other feature, the price billed is $2 per case.

As there are no products of P&G covered by these minor brands, the coordinator takes some other P&G product in the brand category to be shipped under the minor brand's label. P&G's Prell Shampoo is bottled under 13 different minor brand labels for annual shipment at $2 a case. P&G's Scope Mouthwash is bottled under 7 different minor brand la-bels for annual shipment. The situation as to tampons is particularly curious. Prior to 1974 when Rely was introduced, P&G had no such product. Accordingly, it was the prac-tice to buy the tampons of other manufacturers and to repackage them under P&G's var-ious minor brand tampon labels. PPC learned through documents produced at the trial that in the 1960's, its own Modess tampons had been purchased by P&G and repackaged and shipped under a "Sure" Tampon label. In recent years for its minor brand tampons, P&G has been purchasing and shipping Tampax. Although since 1974 P&G has had a tam-pon product of its own, the Minor Brands Coordinator for the paper goods division has continued to ship Tampax rather than P&G's own product, apparently through oversight.

None of P&G's catalogues, price lists or other published materials make any refer-ence to the minor brands. Indeed it appears that virtually none of P& G's personnel is aware of their existence. No steps are taken to see whether these goods are actually sold by the recipients of the shipments. The only evidence received in the trial concerning any such resale was to the effect that once in 1977 the president of PPC had seen some P&G minor brands including Sure Tampons on the shelves of a store in Milwaukee and had bought a box.

* * *

P&G has claimed rights to the Sure Tampon brand since 1964. P&G contends that since it was in litigation over the right to use the name Sure from 1964 to 1968, it is not reasonably chargeable with failure to use the name during that period. Taking the facts in the light most favorable to P&G, the Sure Tampon brand has resided in the Minor Brands Program for nearly 12 years, with approximately 50 cases being shipped once a year. The total revenues which P&G has realized from the sale of Sure Tampons are $874.70. During those years P&G has introduced one tampon product into the commercial market. It did not receive the name Sure. P&G personnel testified that the company now has four or five catamenial products under development and five tampon names in the Minor Brands Program. P&G's personnel testified that they intend to use each of the minor brand names on a product to be introduced. But Sure has not been assigned to any of the products. While there may well be persons at P&G who would like to use the Sure name on a tampon to be marketed in the future, for the reasons indicated in my discussion of the likelihood of P&G's bridging the gap I find it most unlikely that the Sure name will be assigned to a tampon while P&G's uses that name on an anti-perspirant.

P&G has owned the Assure mark for shampoo and mouthwash since 1970. The sham-poo mark has been maintained as a minor brand since 1970 bringing in total revenues of $491.30. The mouthwash brand has been in the program for only three years bringing in total revenues of $161.50; apparently for the first six years the Assure mouth wash brand was not utilized at all. P&G has introduced a new mouthwash and a shampoo into test markets without selecting the name Assure.

Applying to these facts the reasoning of the Court of Appeals in the Snob case, I find that P&G "has never put (these brands) on the market in any meaningful way; indeed, it has given no indication (which I would regard as convincing) that it has any current plans to do so." "Trademark rights are not created by sporadic, casual, and nominal shipments of goods bearing a mark. There must a trade in the goods sold under the mark or at least an active and public attempt to establish such a trade" 495 F.2d at 1272–74, citing *Clairol, Inc. v. Holland Hall Products, Inc.*, 165 U.S.P.Q. 214 (Trademark Trial & App.Bd.1970).

While P&G's annual shipment of 50 cases for periods of nine to twelve years may not be sporadic or casual, it is certainly nominal and does not represent a bona fide attempt to establish a trade in any meaningful way. As the Snob opinion further points out "(a) trademark maintenance program obviously cannot in itself justify a minimal sales effort, or the requirement of good faith commercial use would be read out of trademark law altogether." 495 F.2d at 1273 n. 10; *See Blue Bell, Inc. v. Jaymar-Ruby, Inc.*, 497 F.2d 433, 437 (2 Cir. 1974).

I recognize that P&G's minor brands program might well be legally effective in other circumstances, as where a brand is reserved in connection with reasonably well-formulated plans to use it on a particular product under development, especially if the artificial maintenance does not continue for an unreasonably long time. *See PAB Produits*, 570 F.2d at 334 n. 10. But there must be a "present intent … to market the trademarked product," *Snob*, 495 F.2d at 1272. P&G's vague, remote and almost abstract intentions for the Sure and Assure marks are not satisfactory. P&G's personnel testified, for example, as to each of its 13 minor shampoo brands (including Assure), that it held a present intention to utilize them on a commercially marketed product. At present, P&G offers only 3 shampoos on the commercial market. While there are several shampoos under development, I find no firm intention to use Assure on any of these. Intentions which are so vague and remote and so unlikely to come to fruition within a reasonable near future are not sufficient to meet the test.

* * *

I conclude nonetheless that P&G owns no enforceable rights in Sure tampon brand or in the Assure mark and that its action on behalf of those interests must fail. P&G has failed to show that it established trademark rights through bona fide commercial use.

* * *

IV. Observations on Current Brand Selection Standards.

The evidence in this case of brand selection practices by today's major marketing companies raises some concern as to whether the benefits of the federal trademark law are being diverted to uses for which they were never intended. The trademark law confers a legally protected monopoly on the brand owner. The origin and purpose of this monopoly is to permit manufacturers and distributors to identify their goods to the public and distinguish them from goods manufactured or sold by others. *See* 15 U.S.C. §1127 (defining "trade-mark"); 3 Callmann §65. It permits the manufacturer to benefit from the goodwill that he has earned by distributing satisfactory products in the past. To a like extent it protects the consuming public, by offering it an opportunity to select the goods of dependable manufacturers and to avoid the goods of those who have disappointed them in the past. It prevents charlatans from trading on reputations earned by others.

The monopoly conferred is justified by those very considerable advantages which it offers to all legitimate interests. At the same time such a monopoly is virtually without cost to society. Where all that has been conferred under exclusive title is the right to use a unique identifying mark or word to identify one's goods, society has been deprived of nothing by the giving of exclusive rights to each user. Distinctive marks are plentiful almost without limit, as long as people possess imaginations to create them. The monopoly therefore has double justification, both from the benefits the practice confers and from the lack of any significant cost or sacrifice to society.

In conferring its monopoly rights, it was never the purpose of the trademark laws to give any producer of goods an exclusive right to claim benefits of a product through the name. It is identification that justifies the system. Thus the body of trademark law has developed its spectrum of strength and weakness, according to which generic and descriptive names are generally not entitled to protection, the strongest protection being reserved for marks which are arbitrary or fanciful.

The evidence in this case suggests that major marketers today are selecting brand names according to principles which are not only inconsistent with the policies and justifications of the trademark laws but almost contrary to them. The evidence suggests that names are no longer being selected for identification. They are being selected rather for the purpose of building into the name descriptions or praises of the product's claimed benefits.

One of the nation's leading advertising executives described it as follows. "The name is a crucial part, because eventually the name selected has to reflect the claims you are talking about." A new product development manager for a major manufacturer of consumer products testified on brand name selection, "Tell her what it's going to do for her; tell her how it is going to make her feel and try to give her a reason to believe that all at the same time." Endless testimony was received to the effect that the value of names like Sure, Rely, and Assure lay in their capacity to inspire the confidence of the consumer.

The testimony of both companies as to the potential brand names which have received their most serious attention for menstrual protection products confirms these indications. At P&G the company's first named tampon was given the name Rely. The five names held in reserve for use of future such products are Soft Shape, Soft and Certain, Sure, Merit and Always. At J&J's Personal Products subsidiary, two years after the introduction of P&G's Rely tampon, an internal memo noted "We continue to search for a Rely type handle." Among the names receiving prime consideration were Assurance Plus, Protection Plus, Surity, Assure, Feel Free, Free 'n Easy. When PPC came in 1978 to the naming of its new thin "Maxishield," the leading candidates were Natural Comfort, Sure Comfort, Protection Plus, Surity, Sure & Natural, Feel Free and Thin 'n Sure.

It seems perfectly clear that major marketers today are seeking to appropriate to their exclusive use names which convey as much of the essential advertising message for their product as the trademark laws will tolerate.

The practice seems worthy of mention because the justifications for the lawful monopoly granted by the trademark laws are scarcely present when trademarks are selected in this fashion. Looking first at the social costs, it is highly doubtful whether a single entity in commerce should be granted the exclusive right to use a name consisting of common English words which describe or evaluate the claimed virtues of the product. There are only a few familiar words in the language which say what is said by "Rely" and "Assure". It is quite difficult to justify a grant of a monopoly over the use of those words in their primary senses.

The practice also undermines the principal purpose of the trademark laws which is to avoid confusion in the marketplace. As the practice becomes more widespread, the products of competitors come to be identified by increasingly similar names. Since such trademarks are inherently weak, their exclusivity being limited to the narrow area in which the name is being used, other companies may come in and use the same or similar names on other products. The marketplace becomes a jumble of similar, non-distinctive adjectival or laudatory brand names. And when the "Sure's" have been exhausted, the marketers will turn to the "Sure & Naturals". As the two word combinations become exhausted they will go to three, or to inverted combinations.

For two reasons, court judgments are not best suited to redress this tendency: first, only a tiny number of trademark selections are reviewed in court. Secondly, when a dispute comes to court, the litigant has generally made a major investment or built significant goodwill around the brand name. A court is understandably reluctant to reach judgments which will have harsh effects, will destroy good faith expectations, and often reward unworthy imitators. The more effective and fairer exercise of controls would be at the earliest stages upon application to register.

If, as the evidence in this case suggests, the marketing industry is crowding closer and closer against the line which separates the unregistrable descriptive mark from the suggestive, I raise the question whether the Patent and Trademark office ought to adopt interpretations which raise the standard and require higher quotients of fancy, imagination or arbitrariness in order to qualify.

* * *

————

Larry Harmon Pictures Corp. v. Williams Restaurant Corp.
929 F.2d 662 (Fed. Cir. cert. denied, 502 U.S. 823 (1991)

ARCHER, CIRCUIT JUDGE

This is an appeal from the grant of a summary judgment by the United States Patent and Trademark Office Trademark Trial and Appeal Board (board), Opposition No. 73,217 (January 13, 1989), dismissing the opposition of Larry Harmon Pictures Corporation (Harmon) to the application for registration by The Williams Restaurant Corporation (Williams) of the service mark BOZO'S for restaurant services. On the sole issue raised by Harmon's opposition, the board held that Williams "satisfied the use in commerce requirement of Section 3" of the Lanham Trademark Act of 1946, 15 U.S.C. §1053 (1988). We affirm.

I

The board found the following facts to be undisputed. Williams has operated BOZO'S pit barbecue restaurant in Mason, Tennessee, since 1932. Mason is about a 50 or 60 minute drive from Memphis, Tennessee, which is a large city and a major commercial center for the Mid-South region. The Memphis metropolitan statistical area comprises not only a portion of Tennessee, but also portions of Mississippi and Arkansas. As conceded by Harmon before the board, BOZO'S "restaurant is obviously popular with Memphis residents ... It is close enough (50–60 minutes) to make a pleasant outing from the city. Articles ... from Memphis newspapers and magazines also refer to the restaurant's popularity with Memphis residents." In addition, BOZO'S restaurant has been at least mentioned in publications originating in New York, New York; Washington, D.C.; Dallas, Texas; Gila Bend, Arizona; and Palm Beach, Florida. Further, according to the board's opinion, "there is no dispute that BOZO'S restaurant services are rendered to interstate travelers" and Harmon "acknowledges that applicant's restaurant ... serves some interstate travelers."

The board concluded on the basis of these "undisputed facts" that Williams had made use of its service mark BOZO'S in a manner sufficient to satisfy the use in commerce requirement of Section 3 of the Lanham Act. The board, therefore, granted Williams' motion for summary judgment and dismissed Harmon's opposition. In doing so it stated that it "resolve[d] all factual disputes in favor of [Harmon]" and "construe[d] all inferences to be drawn from established facts in the light most favorable to [Harmon]." The proper standard for considering a summary judgment motion was therefore applied. *Anderson v. Liberty Lobby, Inc.*, 477 U.S. 242, 255, 91 L. Ed. 2d 202, 106 S. Ct. 2505 (1986)

("The evidence of the non-movant is to be believed, and all justifiable inferences are to be drawn in his favor.").[1]

II

The only issue in this appeal is whether the board correctly concluded that the "use in commerce" requirement set forth in Section 3 of the Lanham Act is satisfied by the service in a single-location restaurant of interstate customers. Harmon argues that the use in commerce requirement of Section 3 cannot be satisfied by a single-location restaurant, such as BOZO'S, that serves only a minimal number of interstate travelers. In support of its argument, Harmon relies on *In re Bookbinder's Restaurant, Inc.*, 44 C.C.P.A. 731, 240 F.2d 365, 112 U.S.P.Q. (BNA) 326 (1957), in which a single-location restaurant in Philadelphia was not permitted to register its service mark. Harmon further contends that if the *Bookbinder's* rule — which it interprets to be that single-location restaurants, not located on an interstate highway, cannot be considered as rendering services in commerce — seems too restrictive, this court should adopt the test that a single-location restaurant is not entitled to register its service mark unless (1) it is located on an interstate highway, (2) at least 50% of its meals are served to interstate travelers, or (3) it regularly advertises in out-of-state media. We decline to circumscribe the statute in the manner suggested.

Section 1 of the Lanham Act provides that the "owner of a trade-mark *used in commerce* may apply to register his trade-mark under this chapter." 15 U.S.C. §1051 (1988) (emphasis added). Section 3 of the Act states that "service marks shall be registrable, in the same manner and with the same effect as are trade-marks." 15 U.S.C. §1053 (1988). In general, therefore, service marks must be "used in commerce" before they may be registered.

Section 45 of the Lanham Act provides the following definitions for the word "commerce" and the phrase "use in commerce:"

> The word "commerce" means *all commerce which may lawfully be regulated by Congress.*
>
> ....
>
> For purposes of this chapter a mark shall be deemed to be in use in commerce ... on services when it is used or displayed in the sale or advertising of services and the services are rendered in commerce, or the services are rendered in more than one State or in the United States and a foreign country and the person rendering the services is engaged in commerce in connection with the services.

---

1. In the proceedings below, Miss Williams' affidavit estimated "that 15% of BOZO's business each year is with customers from other states. This has been true for many years including prior to October 28, 1982." Supporting the fact that restaurant services were rendered to interstate travellers, the board also had before it the stipulated pages from the visitor's register maintained by BOZO's restaurant for a period subsequent to the application filing date and a number of affidavits and letters from persons out of state who had patronized BOZO's at various times prior to the application filing date. The only contrary evidence before the board was that Harmon's representative visited the restaurant from 11:00 a.m. to 1:00 p.m. on June 29, 1987, and "did not see a single customer who seemed to be from out-of-state or a single out-of-state car in the restaurant's parking lot." The board's holding implicitly recognized that this evidence was not adequate to raise a genuine issue of material fact. *See* Fed. R. Civ. Proc. 56(c). Harmon argues that Miss Williams' affidavit is "biased and self serving" and "suspect for many reasons." The arguments of Harmon's counsel are insufficient to raise a genuine issue of material fact where there is an absence of probative evidence conflicting with the evidence presented by Williams. *Anderson v. Liberty Lobby, Inc.*, 477 U.S. at 249 ("If the [non-movant's] evidence is merely colorable ... or is not significantly probative ... summary judgment may be granted.").

15 U.S.C. §1127 (1988) (emphasis added).

Congress has broad powers under the commerce clause of the United States Constitution, Art. 1, §8, to regulate interstate commerce. In *In re Silenus Wines, Inc.*, 557 F.2d 806, 194 U.S.P.Q. (BNA) 261 (CCPA 1977), this court's predecessor observed that the Lanham Act represented a change in the scope of federal trademark jurisdiction and that in making the change "Rep. Lanham and his subcommittee," and presumably the Congress, were "mindful of the broad scope of Congressional regulatory powers which the Supreme Court has sanctioned." *Id.* at 810, 194 U.S.P.Q. at 265. The CCPA stated:

> In the Lanham Act, Congress set out what appears to be an unambiguous statement of the scope of federal trademark jurisdiction, namely, "all commerce which may lawfully be regulated by Congress." 15 USC 1127 (1976). This language represents an obvious change from the phrasing of the former trademark acts, which phrasing expressly limited trademark jurisdiction to interstate and foreign commerce and commerce with Indians. [Footnote omitted.] The change clearly involves a broadening of jurisdiction.

Silenus Wines, 557 F.2d at 809, 194 U.S.P.Q. at 264–65.

Harmon's position is based primarily on *In re Bookbinder's*, but in that case the court's decision reflects clearly the failure to prove *any* use in commerce. The court observed that "the record indicates that appellant operates a single restaurant in Philadelphia, Pennsylvania, and the services relied on are rendered in that city," and that "there are no affidavits or testimony of record and the application states merely that the mark is used 'for restaurant, catering and banquet services.'" 240 F.2d at 366, 368, 112 U.S.P.Q. at 326, 328. The court also discounted as not probative the "unverified statement [by the applicant's attorney] that the services were offered to customers and prospective customers in states adjoining Pennsylvania." 240 F.2d at 368, 112 U.S.P.Q. at 328.

In *In re Gastown, Inc.*, 51 C.C.P.A. 876, 326 F.2d 780, 140 U.S.P.Q. (BNA) 216 (1964), decided seven years after *Bookbinder's*, the CCPA again discussed the "use in commerce" requirement set forth in Section 3 of the Lanham Act. In *Gastown*, the appellant operated a chain of automobile and truck service stations, some of which were located on federal highways. Although the services rendered by the appellant were confined to the State of Ohio, some of appellant's customers had their legal situs in other states, were engaged in interstate commerce when served by appellant in Ohio, and were extended credit and billed in their respective domiciliary states. The court held that those circumstances established that the services had a direct effect on interstate commerce and were sufficient to show that applicant's mark was used in commerce within the meaning of Sections 3 and 45 of the Lanham Act.

The *Bookbinder's* and *Gastown* decisions are distinguishable from each other on the basis of the underlying evidence before the board in each case. *See Gastown*, 326 F.2d at 784, 140 U.S.P.Q. at 218 (noting the deficiency in proof of interstate commerce in *Bookbinder's* and stating that "no weight ... was given to those unverified statements"). In *Bookbinder's*, the evidence of record indicated that the applicant's services were not "rendered in commerce" within the meaning of the Act. In *Gastown*, the opposite was true. 326 F.2d at 782, 140 U.S.P.Q. at 217.

While the facts supporting Williams' contention that its service mark is used in commerce are not as extensive, or as persuasive, as those in *Gastown*, we are convinced they are sufficient to satisfy the statutory requirement for registration. In *Gastown*, the court approved the Fifth Circuit's observation that in enacting the Lanham Act "it would seem that ... Congress intended to regulate interstate and foreign commerce to the full extent of its constitutional powers," *Gastown*, 326 F.2d at 784, 140 U.S.P.Q. at 218 (quoting the Fifth Circuit's decision in *Bulova Watch Co. v. Steele*, 194 F.2d 567, 571, 92 U.S.P.Q. (BNA) 266, 269 (5th Cir.), *aff'd*, 344 U.S. 280, 97 L. Ed. 319, 73 S. Ct. 252 (1952)).

* * *

The record here established that the BOZO'S mark has been used in connection with services rendered to customers traveling across state boundaries. It is not required that such services be rendered in more than one state to satisfy the use in commerce requirement. *See Gastown*, 326 F.2d at 782–84, 140 U.S.P.Q. at 217–18; *see also In re Smith Oil Corp.*, 156 U.S.P.Q. (BNA) 62, 63 (TTAB 1967); 1 J. McCarthy, *Trademarks and Unfair Competition*, §19:36.A at page 960 (2d ed. 1984). Harmon does not dispute that there has been some use in commerce of Williams' mark. It contends only that the volume of such activity was less than Williams' affidavit would indicate. Harmon, however, has produced no evidence to counter the proof of interstate activity by Williams, and its reliance on attorney arguments is similar to the situation in *Bookbinder's* where such arguments were given no weight. *See Bookbinder's*, 240 F.2d at 368, 112 U.S.P.Q. at 216; *Gastown*, 326 F.2d at 784, 140 U.S.P.Q. at 218.

We therefore reject Harmon's argument that a certain increased threshold level of interstate activity is required before registration of the mark used by a single-location restaurant may be granted. The Lanham Act by its terms extends to all commerce which Congress may regulate. This court does not have the power to narrow or restrict the unambiguous language of the statute. Accordingly, we affirm the decision of the board.

AFFIRMED.

Int'l Bancorp, LLC v. Societe Des Bains De Mer et du Cercle Des Etrangers a Monaco
329 F.3d 359 (4th Cir. 2003)

LUTTIG, CIRCUIT JUDGE:

Plaintiff companies appeal from the district court's summary judgment that their registration and use of forty-three domain addresses infringe a foreign corporation's rights under the Lanham Act and violate the Anticybersquatting Act, where the foreign corporation advertised its trademark domestically, but only rendered services under it abroad. We conclude that the district court's judgment, although not its reasoning, was correct, and therefore affirm.

I.

Appellee, Societe des Bains de Mer et du Cercle des Etrangers a Monaco ("SBM"), owns and operates historic properties in Monte Carlo, Monaco, including resort and casino facilities. One of its properties, a casino, has operated under the "Casino de Monte Carlo" trademark since 1863. The mark is registered in Monaco, but not in the United States. SBM promotes this casino, along with its other properties, around the world. For 18 years, SBM has promoted its properties from a New York office staffed with four employees. SBM's promotions within the United States, funded with $ 1 million annually, include trade show participation, advertising campaigns, charity partnerships, direct mail solicitation, telephone marketing, and solicitation of media coverage.

Appellants, the plaintiff companies, are five companies formed and controlled by a French national, which operate more than 150 web sites devoted to online gambling. Included in this roster are 53 web sites whose domain addresses incorporate some portion of the term "Casino de Monte Carlo." These web sites, along with the gambling software they employ, also exhibit pictures of *the* Casino de Monte Carlo's exterior and interior, contain renderings that are strikingly similar to the Casino de Monte Carlo's interior, and make allusion to the geographic location of Monte Carlo, implying that they offer online gambling as an alternative to *their* Monaco-based casino, though they operate no such facility.

When SBM learned of the plaintiff companies' web sites and their uses of the "Casino de Monte Carlo" mark, it challenged them in the World Intellectual Property Organization (WIPO). A WIPO panel ruled against the plaintiff companies and ordered the transfer of the 53 domain addresses to SBM. To escape this judgment, the plaintiff companies brought suit in federal court against SBM seeking declaratory judgment, pursuant to 28 U.S.C. §2201(a), that they are entitled to the disputed domain names. SBM counterclaimed under the Lanham Act (15 U.S.C. §1111 *et seq.*) for trademark infringement under section 1125(a); trademark dilution under section 1125(c); cybersquatting under section 1125(d)(1); and unfair competition in violation of section 1126(h). The district court ruled against SBM on its section 1125(c) trademark dilution claim, because SBM had not shown actual economic harm, and on its section 1126(h) unfair competition claim. But the court ruled in favor of SBM on its trademark infringement claim and on its cybersquatting claim, awarding SBM $ 51,000 in statutory damages and transfer of 43 of the 53 contested domain addresses. The plaintiff companies now appeal from that adverse judgment.

This circuit requires that an *unregistered* trademark satisfy two requirements if its owner is to have a protectible interest in the trademark: The mark must be used in commerce, *see* 15 U.S.C. §1051 (only trademarks "used in commerce," or which a person has a bona fide intention to use in commerce, can be registered, signaling Lanham Act protectibility); *see also Larsen* v. *Terk Technologies Corp.*, 151 F.3d 140, 146 (4th Cir. 1998) ("to receive protection under [1125(a)] a trademark ... must be "in use" in commerce"), and it must be distinctive, *see Sara Lee Corp.* v. *Kayser-Roth Corp.*, 81 F.3d 455, 464 (4th Cir. 1996) (noting that the degree of protection a mark may receive is directly related to its distinctiveness). The plaintiff companies argue that the district court erred in concluding that SBM met these two requirements. We address both arguments in turn.

A.

Both parties have agreed, in their briefs and at oral argument, that the critical question in assessing whether SBM "used its mark in commerce" is whether the *services* SBM provided under the "Casino de Monte Carlo" mark were *rendered in commerce*. As shown below, the Lanham Act's plain language makes this conclusion unavoidable and the parties' agreement unsurprising.

We must first contend with a threshold matter, however. This circuit has never directly addressed the scope of the term "commerce" within the Lanham Act. Because of the clarity of the Act's own definition of the term, *see* 15 U.S.C. §1127 (defining "commerce" as "all commerce which may lawfully be regulated by Congress"), we now hold that "commerce" under the Act is coterminous with that commerce that Congress may regulate under the Commerce Clause of the United States Constitution. The other circuits to address this question have concluded the same. Of course, Article I of the Constitution provides that, the Congress shall have Power … to regulate Commerce with foreign nations, and among the several States, and with the Indian Tribes[.]

U.S. Const. art. I, §8, cl. 3. Consequently, "commerce" under the Lanham Act necessarily includes all the explicitly identified variants of interstate commerce, foreign trade, and Indian commerce.

Understanding commerce under the Act to be coterminous with that commerce Congress may regulate under the Commerce Clause, we turn next to the determination of what constitutes "*use in* commerce" under the Act. Again we rely on section 1127, which provides, of particular relevance here, a specific definition of that term as it relates to servicemarks, which the "Casino de Monte Carlo" mark unquestionably is:

> The term "*use in commerce*" means the *bona fide use of a mark in the ordinary course of trade, and not made merely to reserve a right in a mark.* For purposes of this chapter, a mark shall be deemed to be used in commerce—
>
> …
>
> (2) *on services* when it is used or displayed in the sale or advertising of services *and the services are rendered in commerce,* or the services are rendered in more than one State or in the United States and a foreign country and the person rendering the services is engaged in commerce in connection with the services.

15 U.S.C. §1127 (emphasis added).

Consistent with this definition of the statutory "use in commerce" requirement, the Supreme Court has said that "there is no such thing as property in a trade-mark except as a right appurtenant to an established business or trade in connection with which the mark is employed…. The right to a particular mark grows out of its use, not its mere adoption;" *United Drug Co.* v. *Theodore Rectanus, Co.*, 248 U.S. 90, 97, 63 L. Ed. 141, 39 S. Ct. 48, 1918 Dec. Comm'r Pat. 369 (1918). Because a mark is used in commerce only if it accompanies services rendered in commerce, *i.e.*, it is employed appurtenant to an established business or trade that is in commerce, "mere advertising" of that mark does not establish its protectibility, though advertising is itself commerce that Congress may regulate.

With these principles in clear view, we proceed to address whether the "Casino de Monte Carlo" mark was used in commerce. In their briefs and before the court below, the parties debate principally whether the activities of SBM's New York office conducted under the "Casino de Monte Carlo" mark constitute services rendered in interstate commerce. SBM, for its part, contends that the office's booking of reservations is a rendered service, and that its maintenance of the office, its advertising in this country, and its promotional web page attach the "Casino de Monte Carlo" mark for sales and advertising purposes to this interstate service, thereby satisfying the "use in commerce" requirement. The plaintiff companies argue, to the contrary, that there is no evidence in the record that the New York office books reservations to the casino, and that, as a result, the office engages in no activity beyond "mere advertising." They argue further that the casino gambling services are the only established business to which the trademark applies, and that *that* service, being rendered in Monaco, is not rendered in commerce that Congress may regulate. The district court, accepting SBM's arguments, concluded as follows:

> It is clear from the undisputed record that SBM's New York office was one of SBM's many international sales offices from which customers could book reservations. Thus, the record shows that in this respect, SBM "services are rendered" in the United States.

Int'l Bancorp v. *SBM*, 192 F. Supp. 2d 467, 479–80 (E.D. Va. 2002) [*Summary Judgment*].

SBM's argument and the district court's reasoning are in error because the New York-office bookings on which they rely do not relate to the casino in question, but, rather, to SBM's resort facilities. As became evident at oral argument and upon our review of the record, SBM's assertion that the record contains evidence that its New York office booked reservations to the casino is unsubstantiated. The plaintiff companies correctly point out that since the "Casino de Monte Carlo" mark only pertains to the casino and its gambling services, any guest reservations SBM's New York office and web site book for SBM's various resorts, which reservation services the record does disclose, are irrelevant to the analysis. And the other operations of SBM's New York office, at least as they appear in the record, are merely promotional in nature. The Lanham Act and the Supreme Court, as shown above, make clear that a mark's protection may not be based on "mere advertising."

Because SBM presented no record evidence that the New York office did anything other than advertise the "Casino de Monte Carlo" mark, if its case rested on this alone, the plaintiff companies would have the better of the argument. When they appeared before the court, however, we asked the parties to address themselves to the question of whether the casino services at issue were rendered in foreign trade, and the plaintiff companies conceded that the record contained evidence that United States citizens went to and gambled at the casino. This concession, when taken together with the undisputed fact that the Casino de Monte Carlo is a subject of a foreign nation, makes unavoidable the legal conclusion that foreign trade was present here, and that as such, so also was "commerce" under the Lanham Act.

Since the nineteenth century, it has been well established that the Commerce Clause reaches to foreign trade. And, for the same length of time, the Supreme Court has defined foreign trade as trade between subjects of the United States and subjects of a foreign nation. And, of course, commerce does not solely apply "to traffic, to buying and selling, or the interchange of commodities … Commerce, undoubtedly, is traffic, but it is something more: it is [commercial] intercourse." *Gibbons* v. *Ogden*, 22 U.S. 1, 189, 6 L. Ed. 23 (1824) (C.J. Marshall). Service transactions are clearly commercial intercourse, and by extension can clearly constitute foreign trade. Thus, while SBM's promotions within the United States do not on their own constitute a use in commerce of the "Casino de Monte Carlo" mark, the mark is nonetheless used in commerce because United States citizens purchase casino services sold by a subject of a foreign nation, which purchases constitute trade with a foreign nation that Congress may regulate under the Commerce Clause. And SBM's promotions "use[ ] or display[ ] [the mark] in the sale or advertising of [these] services … rendered in commerce."

At oral argument, the plaintiff companies objected to this straightforward reasoning. They argued first that any trade that United States citizens engaged in at the casino was not subject to regulation by Congress since it did not occur in the United States.

COURT: Commerce [*i.e.*, commerce within Congress' regulatory ambit, and thus equally commerce under the Lanham Act] includes services with a foreign country doesn't it?

Appellant: Not unless they're rendered in the United States.

COURT: Unless the Supreme Court has held otherwise?

Appellant: Unless the Supreme Court has held otherwise, of course.

* * *

Notes

1. Compare Proctor & Gamble's minor brand program with the restaurant services in the *Harmon* case. What is the precise distinction?

2. *Definition of "use in commerce."* Notice that the date of the *Proctor & Gamble* case is 1980. Effective November 16, 1989, the Trademark Law Amendment Act of 1988 changed the definition of "use." For registration purposes, prior to the effective date of this Act, token use was acceptable. That is, one manufacturer could package a small amount of goods, mail it to a related party across state lines, and claim "interstate commerce" for purposes of registering a trademark. This practice was curtailed in the 1988 Act. Today, as is indicated at the top of this sub-chapter, the term "use in commerce" means the bona fide use of a mark in the ordinary course of trade, and not made merely to reserve a right in a mark. 15 U.S.C. §1127. Notice that *Proctor & Gamble* was decided a decade before this amendment took effect. At that time, some of the sales in the minor brand program would have been sufficient to establish token use to support a trademark registration. In fact, Proctor & Gamble's conduct was not unlike the conduct of many other manufacturers. Why did the court, 30 plus years after implementation of the Lanham Act, choose this case to chart new ground? The previous language of the Lanham Act as it became applied to "token use" read as follows:

> For purposes of this chapter a mark shall be deemed to be used in commerce (a) on goods when it is placed in any manner on the goods or their containers or the displays associated therewith or on the tags or labels affixed thereto and the goods are sold or transported in commerce ...

15 U.S.C. §1127 (1987).

3. The Lanham Act is said to be a statute that codifies the common law without creating new rights. The legislative history of the Act makes it clear that this was Congress' intent. *See* 92 Cong. Rec. 7524 (1946). Unlike some other meaningful amendments to the Lanham Act (which will be studied in detail, *infra*), the amendment to the definition of use in commerce followed the intended course. First, the concept and validity of token use was narrowed in the case law, and a new definition of use emerged. Only then was the Act amended to include the new notion of bona fide use. That is, the statute did not change the common law-common law changed, and that change was codified. This is the evolution that the Lanham Act contemplates. Reversing this order raises constitutional questions, as we will see *infra*.

4. Some courts have defined use in commerce to include merely transporting the goods but not actually selling them. *General Healthcare Ltd. v. Isam Qashat*, 364 F.3d 332 (1st Cir 2004). Is it wise to define use so broadly? Is it constitutional?

5. One commentator claims that federal trademark registration which allows for nation-wide priority is a huge wet blanket for small businesses. Jason Parent, *COMMENT: Federal Trademark Law—A Roadblock to Small Business Success?*, 6 Barry L. Rev. 105 (2006). "Through federal registration, a large business can effectively destroy any chance of small business growth, confining small businesses to their local market prisons." *Id.* at 118. Do you agree?

6. *Domain names and "use in commerce."* This area of the law is evolving. Of course, registering a known trademark of another as a domain name is "cybersquatting." *See,*

infra Chapter XII. However, at what point is that trademark deemed "used in commerce"? Although some courts differ, the general understanding by courts today is that the mere registration of the mark as a domain name is not "use in commerce" but the marketing of domain names for sale is. *See* Jeffery R. Peterson, *What's the Use? Establishing Mark Rights in the Modern Economy*, 5 Hous. Bus. & Tax. L. J. 450 (2005).

7. *Territoriality.* The world basically operates under the territoriality principle regarding trademark rights. Under this notion, each country determines what is required for trademark protection. The creation of trademark rights in one nation confers no trademark rights whatsoever in any other nation (although some nations recognize famous marks from other countries). Therefore, a foreign automobile manufacturer that did not sell its cars in the United States cannot be said to have used the mark "in commerce" to be recognized under United States law. *Maruti.com v. Maruit Udyog Ltd.*, 447 F. Supp. 2d 494 (D.Md. 2006).

8. What is the effect of *International Bancorp*? Does it "create a tool for acquiring United States rights of an American user by establishing only a minimal presence in the United States"? *See*, Jason Fortenberry, *International Bancorp, LLC v. Soiete Des Bains De Mer Et Du Cercle Des Estrangers A Monaco: The Supreme Court's Silence Speaks Louder than Words*, 25 Miss. College L. Rev. 183, 220 (2006). *See also*, Graeme B. Dinwoodie, Trademarks and Territory: Detaching Trademark Law from the Nation-state, 41 Hous. L. Rev. 885, 973 (2004) ("[Trademark law] is informed by both intrinsic and pragmatic notions of territoriality. Ironically, although both International Bancorp and the developments in the protection of well-known marks appear to be motivated by a desire to reflect the realities of global markets and to facilitate the ready acquisition of rights on a broader geographic basis, they may in fact impede global commerce").

B. Priority

Because the United States trademark system is based upon use, it is important to establish priority in the use of a mark in order to obtain and enforce trademark rights. The first to use requirement is strict. Prior common law rights, based on prior use, will not be defeated by subsequent federal registrations. Use sufficient to establish priority for purposes of the Lanham Act requires that the use be in the ordinary course of trade, 15 U.S.C. §1127 (2004) (Lanham Act §45), and not to merely secure or maintain trademark rights. Merely picking out or thinking up a mark, without actually using it in commerce, is not enough to acquire use-based rights in and to that mark.

As we shall see, however, constructive first use will be conferred upon the successful applicant of an intent to use application. 15 U.S.C. §1057(c) (Lanham Act §7(c)).

Blue Bell, Inc. v. Farah Mfg. Co.
508 F.2d 1260 (5th Cir. 1975)

Gewin, Circuit Judge:

In the spring and summer of 1973, two prominent manufacturers of men's clothing created identical trademarks for goods substantially identical in appearance. Though the record offers no indication of bad faith in the design and adoption of the labels, both Farah Manufacturing Company (Farah) and Blue Bell, Inc. (Blue Bell) devised the mark "Time Out" for new lines of men's slacks and shirts. Both parties market their goods on a national scale, so they agree that joint utilization of the same trademark would confuse the buying public. Thus, the only question presented for our review is which party established prior use of the mark in trade. A response to that seemingly innocuous inquiry, however, requires us to define the chameleonic term "use" as it has developed in trademark law.

After a full development of the facts in the district court both parties moved for summary judgment. The motion of Farah was granted and that of Blue Bell denied. It is not claimed that summary judgment procedure was inappropriate; the controversy presented relates to the application of the proper legal principles to undisputed facts. A permanent injunction was granted in favor of Farah but no damages were awarded, and Blue Bell was allowed to fill all orders for garments bearing the Time Out label received by it as of the close of business on December 5, 1973. For the reasons hereinafter stated,we affirm.

Farah conceived of the Time Out mark on May 16, after screening several possible titles for its new stretch menswear. Two days later the firm adopted an hourglass logo and authorized an extensive advertising campaign bearing the new insignia. Farah presented its fall line of clothing, including Time Out slacks, to sales personnel on June 5. In the meantime, patent counsel had given clearance for use of the mark after scrutiny of current federal registrations then on file. One of Farah's top executives demonstrated samples of the Time Out garments to large customers in Washington, D.C. and New York, though labels were not attached to the slacks at that time. Tags containing the new design were completed June 27. With favorable evaluations of marketing potential from all sides, Farah sent one pair of slacks bearing the Time Out mark to each of its twelve regional sales managers on July 3. Sales personnel paid for the pants, and the garments became their property in case of loss.

Following the July 3 shipment, regional managers showed the goods to customers the following week. Farah received several orders and production began. Further shipments of sample garments were mailed to the rest of the sales force on July 11 and 14. Merchandising efforts were fully operative by the end of the month. The first shipments to customers, however, occurred in September.

Blue Bell, on the other hand, was concerned with creating an entire new division of men's clothing, as an avenue to reaching the "upstairs" market. Though initially to be housed at the Hicks-Ponder plant in El Paso, the new division would eventually enjoy separate headquarters. On June 18 Blue Bell management arrived at the name Time Out to identify both its new division and its new line of men's sportswear. Like Farah, it received clearance for use of the mark from counsel. Like Farah, it inaugurated an advertising campaign. Unlike Farah, however, Blue Bell did not ship a dozen marked articles of the new line to its sales personnel. Instead, Blue Bell authorized the manufacture of several hundred labels bearing the words Time Out and its logo shaped like a referee's hands forming a T. When the labels were completed on June 29, the head of the embryonic division flew them to El Paso. He instructed shipping personnel to affix the new Time Out labels to slacks that already bore the "Mr. Hicks" trademark. The new tags, of varying sizes and colors, were randomly attached to the left hip pocket button of slacks and the left hip pocket of jeans. Thus, although no change occurred in the design or manufacture of the pants, on July 5 several hundred pair left El Paso with two tags.

Blue Bell made intermittent shipments of the doubly-labeled slacks thereafter, though the out-of-state customers who received the goods had ordered clothing of the Mr. Hicks variety. Production of the new Time Out merchandise began in the latter part of August, and Blue Bell held a sales meeting to present its fall designs from September 4–6. Sales personnel solicited numerous orders, though shipments of the garments were not scheduled until October.

By the end of October Farah had received orders for 204,403 items of Time Out sportswear, representing a retail sales value of over $2,750,000. Blue Bell had received orders for 154,200 garments valued at over $900,000. Both parties had commenced extensive advertising campaigns for their respective Time Out sportswear.

Soon after discovering the similarity of their marks, Blue Bell sued Farah for common law trademark infringement and unfair competition, seeking to enjoin use of the Time Out trademark on men's clothing. Farah counter-claimed for similar injunctive relief. The district court found that Farah's July 3 shipment and sale constituted a valid use in trade, while Blue Bell's July 5 shipment was a mere "token" use insufficient at law to create trademark rights. While we affirm the result reached by the trial court as to Farah's priority of use, the legal grounds upon which we base our decision are somewhat different from those undergirding the district court's judgment.

Federal jurisdiction is predicated upon diversity of citizenship, since neither party has registered the mark pursuant to the Lanham Act. Given the operative facts surrounding manufacture and shipment from El Paso, the parties agree the Texas law of trademarks controls. In 1967 the state legislature enacted a Trademark Statute. Section 16.02 of the Act explains that a mark is "used" when it is affixed to the goods and "the goods are sold, displayed for sale, or otherwise publicly distributed." Thus the question whether Blue Bell or Farah established priority of trademark use depends upon interpretation of the cited provision. Unfortunately, there are no Texas cases construing §16.02. This court must therefore determine what principles the highest state court would utilize in deciding such a question. In view of the statute's stated purpose to preserve common law rights, we conclude the Texas Supreme Court would apply the statutory provision in light of general principles of trademark law.

A trademark is a symbol (word, name, device or combination thereof) adopted and used by a merchant to identify his goods and distinguish them from articles produced by others. Lanham Act §45, 15 U.S.C. §1127; *Clairol, Inc. v. Gillette Co.*, 270 F. Supp. 371 (E.D.N.Y.1967); *see* Vernon's Tex.Code Ann., Bus. & Comm. §16.01(5) (1968). Ownership of a mark requires a combination of both appropriation and use in trade, *United Drug Co. v. Theodore Rectanus Co.*, 248 U.S. 90, 39 S. Ct. 48, 63 L. Ed. 141 (1918). Thus, neither conception of the mark, nor advertising alone establishes trademark rights at common law. Rather, ownership of a trademark accrues when goods bearing the mark are placed on the market.

The exclusive right to a trademark belongs to one who first uses it in connection with specified goods. Such use need not have gained wide public recognition, and even a single use in trade may sustain trademark rights if followed by continuous commercial utilization.

The initial question presented for review is whether Farah's sale and shipment of slacks to twelve regional managers constitutes a valid first use of the Time Out mark. Blue Bell claims the July 3 sale was merely an internal transaction insufficiently public to secure trademark ownership. After consideration of pertinent authorities, we agree.

Secret, undisclosed internal shipments are generally inadequate to support the denomination "use." Trademark claims based upon shipments from a producer's plant to its sales office, and vice versa, have often been disallowed. Though none of the cited cases dealt with *sales* to intra-corporate personnel, we perceive that fact to be a distinction without a difference. The sales were not made to customers, but served as an accounting device to charge the salesmen with their cost in case of loss. The fact that some sales managers actively solicited accounts bolsters the good faith of Farah's intended use, but does not meet our essential objection: that the "sales" were not made to the public.

The primary, perhaps singular purpose of a trademark is to provide a means for the consumer to separate or distinguish one manufacturer's goods from those of another. Personnel within a corporation can identify an item by style number or other unique code. A trademark aids the public in selecting particular goods. As stated by the First Circuit:

> But to hold that a sale or sales are the *sine qua non* of a use sufficient to amount to an appropriation would be to read an unwarranted limitation into the statute, for so construed registration would have to be denied to any manufacturer who adopted a mark to distinguish or identify his product, and perhaps applied it thereon for years, if he should in practice lease his goods rather than sell them, as many manufacturers of machinery do. It seems to us that although evidence of sales is highly persuasive, the question of use adequate to establish appropriation remains one to be decided on the facts of each case, and that evidence showing, first, adoption, and, second, *use in a way sufficiently public to identify or distinguish the marked goods in an appropriate segment of the public mind as those of the adopter of the mark*, is competent to establish ownership....

New England Duplicating Co. v. Mendes, 190 F.2d 415, 418 (1st Cir. 1951) (Emphasis added). Similarly, the Trademark Trial and Appeal Board has reasoned:

> To acquire trademark rights there has to be an "open" use, that is to say, a use has to be made to the relevant class of purchasers or prospective purchasers since a trademark is intended to identify goods and distinguish those goods from those manufactured or sold by others. There was no such "open" use rather the use can be said to be an "internal" use, which cannot give rise to trademark rights.

incorrect

Sterling Drug, Inc. v. Knoll A. G. Chemische Fabriken, supra at 631.

Farah nonetheless contends that a recent decision of the Board so undermines all prior cases relating to internal use that they should be ignored. In *Standard Pressed Steel Co. v. Midwest Chrome Process Co.*, 183 U.S.P.Q. 758 (TTAB 1974) the agency held that internal shipment of marked goods from a producer's manufacturing plant to its sales office constitutes a valid "use in commerce" for registration purposes.

An axiom of trademark law has been that the right to register a mark is conditioned upon its actual use in trade. Theoretically, then, common law use in trade should precede the use in commerce upon which Lanham Act registration is predicated. Arguably, since only a trademark owner can apply for registration, any activity adequate to create registrable rights must perforce also create trademark rights. A close examination of the Board's decision, however, dispels so mechanical a view. The tribunal took meticulous care to point out that its conclusion related solely to registration use rather than ownership use.

> It has been recognized and especially so in the last few years that, in view of the expenditures involved in introducing a new product on the market generally and the attendant risk involved therein prior to the screening process involved in re-sorting to the federal registration system and in the absence of an "intent to use" statute, a token sale or a single shipment in commerce *may be sufficient to support an application to register a trademark* in the Patent Office notwithstanding that the evidence may not show what disposition was made of the product so

shipped. That is, the fact that a sale or a shipment of goods bearing a trademark was *designed primarily to lay a foundation for the filing of an application for registration* does not, per se, invalidate any such application or subsequent registration issued thereon.

* * *

Inasmuch as it is our belief that a most liberal policy should be followed in a situation of this kind [*in which dispute as to priority of use and ownership of a mark is not involved*], applicant's initial shipment of fasteners, although an intra-company transaction in that it was to a company sales representative, was a bona fide shipment....

Standard Pressed Steel Co. v. Midwest Chrome Process Co., supra at 764–65 (Emphasis added).

Priority of use and ownership of the Time Out mark are the only issues before this court. The language fashioned by the Board clearly indicates a desire to leave the common law of trademark ownership intact. The decision may demonstrate a reversal of the presumption that ownership rights precede registration rights, but it does not affect our analysis of common law use in trade. Farah had undertaken substantial preliminary steps toward marketing the Time Out garments, but it did not establish ownership of the mark by means of the July 3 shipment to its sales managers. The gist of trademark rights is actual use in trade. Though technically a "sale", the July 3 shipment was not "publicly distributed" within the purview of the Texas statute.

Blue Bell's July 5 shipment similarly failed to satisfy the prerequisites of a bona fide use in trade. Elementary tenets of trademark law require that labels or designs be affixed to the merchandise actually intended to bear the mark in commercial transactions. Furthermore, courts have recognized that the usefulness of a mark derives not only from its capacity to identify a certain manufacturer, but also from its ability to differentiate between different classes of goods produced by a single manufacturer. Here customers had ordered slacks of the Mr. Hicks species, and Mr. Hicks was the fanciful mark distinguishing these slacks from all others. Blue Bell intended to use the Time Out mark on an entirely new line of men's sportswear, unique in style and cut, though none of the garments had yet been produced.

While goods may be identified by more than one trademark, the use of each mark must be bona fide. Mere adoption of a mark without bona fide use, in an attempt to reserve it for the future, will not create trademark rights. In the instant case Blue Bell's attachment of a secondary label to an older line of goods manifests a bad faith attempt to reserve a mark. We cannot countenance such activities as a valid use in trade. Blue Bell therefore did not acquire trademark rights by virtue of its July 5 shipment.

We thus hold that neither Farah's July 3 shipment nor Blue Bell's July 5 shipment sufficed to create rights in the Time Out mark. Based on a desire to secure ownership of the mark and superiority over a competitor, both claims of alleged use were chronologically premature. Essentially, they took a time out to litigate their differences too early in the game. The question thus becomes whether we should continue to stop the clock for a remand or make a final call from the appellate bench. While a remand to the district court for further factual development would not be improper in these circumstances, we believe the interests of judicial economy and the parties' desire to terminate the litigation demand that we decide, if possible, which manufacturer first used the mark in trade.

Careful examination of the record discloses that Farah shipped its first order of Time Out clothing to customers in September of 1973. Blue Bell, approximately one month behind its competitor at other relevant stages of development, did not mail its Time Out garments until at least October. Though sales to customers are not the *sine qua non* of trademark use, *see New England Duplicating Co. v. Mendes, supra*, they are determinative in the instant case. These sales constituted the first point at which the public had a chance to associate Time Out with a particular line of sportswear. Therefore, Farah established priority of trademark use; it is entitled to a decree permanently enjoining Blue Bell from utilization of the Time Out trademark on men's garments.

The judgment of the trial court is affirmed.

———————

Bell v. Streetwise Records, Ltd.

640 F. Supp. 575 (Dist. Ct. Mass. 1986)

ZOBEL, D. J.

Plaintiffs Bell, Bivins, Brown, DeVoe and Tresvant, members of a singing group, are known to teenagers across the nation and around the world by the name "New Edition." Together with their present recording company, MCA Records, Inc. ("MCA"), they seek to establish their exclusive right to appear, perform and record under that mark. Defendants and counter-claimants (hereinafter "defendants"), Boston International Music, Inc. ("BIM"), and Streetwise Records, Ltd. ("Streetwise") produced, recorded and marketed the first New Edition long-playing album, "Candy Girl," as well as the singles from that album. Defendants claim that they employed the five individual plaintiffs to serve as a public front for a "concept" which they developed, and to promote musical recordings embodying that "concept." Because the mark New Edition allegedly identifies those recordings, and not the group members, defendants assert that they are its rightful owners. Each side has asked that this court enjoin the other from using the mark.

The amended complaint charges defendants with violations of §43(a) of the Lanham Act, …

FINDINGS OF FACT AND RULINGS OF LAW

Background

The five plaintiffs, calling themselves New Edition, form one of the hottest song-and-dance acts on the entertainment scene today. They have released four albums, numerous singles and several videos. They have performed throughout this country, filling major concert halls. They have toured Britain and Germany, and have plans for an upcoming trip to Japan. They have appeared on television shows, at charity events, and—the crowning sign of success—they have even been featured in a COKE commercial.

The group got its start in 1981 when four of the five current members[2] performed in a talent show at Roscoe's Lounge, in Boston. They were each about thirteen years old at the time and they called themselves New Edition.[3] Travis Gresham, who knew Bell and Tresvant from the marching band he directed, saw the show and thought they had potential. Within a week or two he became their manager and Brook Payne, who had collaborated with Bell, Bivins and Brown on an earlier endeavor, became their choreographer.

———————

2. Ronald DeVoe joined the group several months later.
3. The name was first used in 1978 when Bell, Bivins, Brown and two others formed a group under the direction of Mr. Brook Payne. Payne thought up the name. They performed for a couple of months and disbanded.

Gresham booked a series of performances for the group. Their sixth engagement, on November 15, 1981, was the "Hollywood Talent Night" at the Strand Theatre, where the group performed a medley of songs made famous by the Jackson Five. First prize and plaintiffs' goal for the night was a recording contract with Maurice Starr, president of defendant BIM, who originated and organized the event. New Edition came in second but Starr, who had an agenda of his own, decided to work with them anyway.

Maurice Starr, who partly from his "Hollywood Talent Nights" had become something of a local celebrity, had been in the music business for a long time.[4] Starr—originally Larry Johnson—performed with his five brothers in a rock band in the early seventies. Modelled after the Jackson Five, whom they sought to emulate, Starr and his brothers called themselves the Johnson Six. They achieved moderate success but broke up in the mid-seventies when they became too mature for the image.

It was around this time that Starr began developing the "concept," which, in its final form, he dubbed "black bubble gum music of the eighties." The concept is essentially the Jackson Five updated by the addition of modern elements like synthesizers (electronic instrumentation) and rap (speaking parts). As early as 1972, Starr began to search for the right kids to act out his concept. In November 1981, when he first encountered Bell, Bivins, Brown and Tresvant, he was still looking.

Although he decided to work with them, Starr believed plaintiffs were short on talent. They had no training to speak of; none could read or write music. Nevertheless, he used the four boys to create a demonstration tape of a song he had composed earlier, entitled Candy Girl. Starr played all the instruments, sang background vocals and did the arranging and mixing. He had to teach the thirteen-year-old group members everything, and while it is disputed whether lead singer Ralph Tresvant had to record his part bar-by-bar or note-by-note, it is clear Starr ran the show in the sound studio.

The tape was completed in the winter of 1982, and Starr expended considerable effort attempting to sell it to a recording company. He finally connected with Streetwise in the following fall. In the meantime, under the supervision of Gresham and Payne, plaintiffs continued to rehearse their dance routines and to perform locally. Starr played little if any role in these activities.

During this period Starr and the group members had three disagreements, all stemming from Starr's desire to make the group more like the Jackson Five. First, Starr insisted they acquire a fifth member. The boys resisted, but Starr prevailed. Plaintiffs selected Ronnie DeVoe, a nephew of Brook Payne, whom Starr approved. Second, he wanted the group to grow "afros." They refused. Third, and perhaps most significant, he wanted the newly expanded group to change its name to the MaJic Five [sic]; the upper case "J," not surprisingly, to evoke "Jackson." Plaintiffs were adamantly opposed and remained New Edition.

In November and December of 1982, Streetwise entered into separate recording contracts with each of the five plaintiffs, who were at the time approximately age fourteen. Each contract granted to Streetwise the exclusive right to use the name. Each, except Tresvant's, confirmed that the name "The New Edition" was wholly owned by BIM.[5]

---

4. It is not disputed here that Starr is a man of extensive and varied talents. Producer, engineer, songwriter, Starr testified that he plays "every instrument there is." He even created a literary version of the "concept"—a play called *Harmony*—about five kids trying to make it in the entertainment world.

5. Defendants have conceded that plaintiffs' disaffirmance of these contracts, because of their minority at the time of signing, is, for purposes of this proceeding, legally valid. Their claim to ownership of the mark is therefore based exclusively on the law of trademarks and unfair competition.

Streetwise released the "Candy Girl" single in February 1983. The long-playing album—containing ten songs selected, produced, and for the most part written by Starr—came out the following June. Streetwise launched an unusually extensive and elaborate promotional campaign, placing advertisements in print and on radio, and producing three videos. After the single was released, plaintiffs—high school students at the time—performed every weekend night, in Massachusetts and beyond. At first they "lip-synched" to a recorded track; later they sang to a live band. For a period of time Starr accompanied them on these tours, announcing the group, playing instruments (four simultaneously, he testified), and performing background vocals. The records and the group were smash hits.

Sometime in the summer of 1983 plaintiffs began to perform without Starr. In August, they fired Gresham and Payne. That same month they performed in Britain and Germany. In September they acquired new management and in November they disaffirmed their contracts with Streetwise. After defendants revealed plans to issue New Edition records featuring five different young singers, and after they sought federal registration of the New Edition mark, plaintiffs commenced this lawsuit.

One postscript completes the evidentiary picture before the court. In January of 1984, Jheryl Busby, a senior vice president at MCA, was dragged by his fourteen-year-old son to see a performance of New Edition. None too impressed, he left to meet a friend at a nearby hotel. Young girls had swarmed the place. When he asked his friend what was going on he was told, "that group, New Edition, is staying here and those little girls have been looking for them all night." Busby signed the group.

Discussion

In order to prevail on the merits, plaintiffs or defendants must establish that the mark is valid and protectable, that they own the mark, and that use of the mark by the opposing party is likely to confuse the public.

Both sides concede that New Edition is a distinctive mark, protectable under state and federal law; it is accordingly unnecessary to pass on that issue. They also concede, and the opinion of the Court of Appeals assumes, that use of the mark by both plaintiffs and defendants will lead to public confusion. Thus this court must decide the sole remaining issue: who owns the mark.

I.

It is settled law that ownership of a mark is established by priority of appropriation. Priority is established not by conception but by bona fide usage. The claimant "must demonstrate that his use of the mark has been deliberate and continuous, not sporadic, casual or transitory." *La Societe Anonyme des Parfums LeGalion v. Jean Patou, Inc.*, 495 F.2d 1265, 1272 (2d Cir. 1974) (citing 3 Callmann, Unfair Competition, Trademarks & Monopolies §76.2(d) (1969)). While it is not required that a product be an instant success the moment it hits the market, its usage must be consistent with a "present plan of commercial exploitation." *Id.* at 1273. Finally, while the Lanham Act is invoked only through use in interstate commerce, common law rights can be acquired through interstate or intrastate usage.

A great deal of testimony was offered at the December 1985 hearing concerning the circumstances of the signings. That evidence is irrelevant to this case as I now view the issues before me. Any unconscionability on the part of defendants, even if proven, would have no bearing on their ownership of the mark had they acquired it by means not contractual.

With these principles in mind, I make the following findings of fact. First, on the basis of testimony by Mr. Busby and by defendants' expert, Thomas Silverman, I find that there is only one relevant market at issue here: the entertainment market. Second, I find that as of the release of "Candy Girl" in February 1983 — the first use in commerce — plaintiffs, calling themselves New Edition, had publicly performed in the local entertainment market on at least twenty occasions. Those performances (for which they frequently received compensation; albeit in nominal amounts), the promotional efforts by Travis Gresham on their behalf, their regular rehearsals with Gresham and Payne, their attempt to win a recording contract, and their hard work with Maurice Starr to further their career, all evidence a "present plan of commercial exploitation."

I accordingly conclude that plaintiffs have acquired legal rights to the mark New Edition through their prior use in intrastate commerce. Even if defendants' use had been the first in interstate commerce, they used the name simultaneously in Massachusetts, where plaintiffs had already appropriated it. And while it is well recognized that a junior user may occasionally acquire superior rights to a mark it used in good faith and in a different market, that was obviously not the case here. On this basis alone, plaintiffs own the mark.

II.

Even assuming there was no prior appropriation by the plaintiffs, however, they nonetheless own the mark under the controlling standard of law. Defendants correctly state that in the case of joint endeavors, where prior ownership by one of several claimants cannot be established, the legal task is to determine which party "controls or determines the nature and quality of the goods which have been marketed under the mark in question." *See In re Polar Music International AB*, 714 F.2d 1567 (Fed. Cir. 1983). The difficulty in performing that task in this case, however, is in deciding what the "goods" are. The parties have given the court little guidance in how to go about making that determination. Rather, each side baldly asserts the result that leads most logically to a decision in its favor. Defendants claim the goods are the recordings; plaintiffs claim they are the entertainment services of Bell, Bivins, Brown, DeVoe and Tresvant.

The role of "public association" in determining ownership has been much disputed in this case. Defendants have argued, and the Court of Appeals has confirmed, that the "finding that the public associate[s] the name NEW EDITION with the plaintiffs [does not compel] the conclusion that the name belong[s] to the plaintiffs." *Bell, supra*, 761 F.2d at 76. But defendants are wrong when they say that public association plays no part in determining ownership. It is crucial in establishing just what the mark has come to identify, i.e., what the "goods" are.

In order to determine ownership in a case of this kind, a court must first identify that quality or characteristic for which the group is known by the public. It then may proceed to the second step of the ownership inquiry, namely, who controls that quality or characteristic.

As a preliminary matter, I find that the norm in the music industry is that an artist or group generally owns its own name. This case does not fit into one of the clearer exceptions to this rule. The name New Edition has not been assigned, transferred, or sold. Nor is New Edition a "concept group," whose name belongs to the person or entity that conceived both concept and name

With respect to defendants, although Maurice Starr's contribution to the "Candy Girl" records was substantial, I find that all the functions he performed were consistent with the duties of a producer. He was credited and compensated separately for each role. Similarly, while Streetwise's promotional work was unusually extensive, and though it proceeded at considerable risk, marketing—or "educating your label," as one witness put it—is a normal function of a recording company.

With respect to the plaintiffs themselves, as noted elsewhere in this opinion, they existed and performed as New Edition long before defendants released "Candy Girl." They had already used songs of the Jackson Five. Their membership has been essentially constant; they were not, as defendants contend, replaceable actors in a play written by Maurice Starr. (*Compare Rick v. Buchansky, supra*, where the four-person "Vito and the Salutations" had had twenty-two different members, including ten different "Vitos," to its one manager, Rick—who was found to own the name.) They were individual persons that the public came to know as such. While defendants would have us believe this is only the result of their successful promoting, I find that it was personality, not marketing, that led to the public's intimacy with plaintiffs. The "magic" that sold New Edition, and which "New Edition" has come to signify, is these five young men.

Based on the totality of the evidence, I conclude that the quality which the mark New Edition identified was first and foremost the five plaintiffs with their distinctive personalities and style as performers. The "goods" therefore are the entertainment services they provide. They and no one else controlled the quality of those services. They own the mark.

Maryland Stadium Authority v. Becker

806 F. Supp. 1236 (D.Md. 1992), aff'd, 36 F.3d 1093 (4th Cir. 1994)

Motz, District Judge

The Maryland Stadium Authority ("MSA") has brought this action against Roy G. Becker, asserting claims under Section 43(a) of the Lanham Act, 15 U.S.C. §1125(a), and for unfair competition under Maryland common law. MSA, the owner of the baseball park in which the Baltimore Orioles play, alleges that Becker has wrongfully used the mark "Camden Yards" in connection with the sale of tee shirts and several other items of clothing. Discovery has been completed, and the parties have filed cross-motions for summary judgment.

I.

MSA is a public corporation created in 1986 by the Maryland General Assembly to plan, build and operate a sports complex, including a baseball park and, possibly, a football stadium (in the event that Baltimore is again awarded a franchise by the National Football League). Md. Fin. Inst. Code Ann., §13-702 (1992 Supp.). In 1987 the General Assembly approved MSA's recommendation that the sports complex be constructed at Camden Yards, an area which for over a century had been a center of operations for the Baltimore & Ohio Railroad in downtown Baltimore.

In 1989 demolition of old buildings at the site commenced, and in early 1991 the superstructure of the new park began to rise from the ground. The park was scheduled to be completed for the start of the 1992 season, and throughout the summer of 1991, as public excitement grew, there was extensive public debate as to what it should be called. The two names most prominently mentioned were "Camden Yards" and "Oriole Park." In October 1991 the debate ended in compromise with the announcement that the name "Oriole Park at Camden Yards" had been chosen.

Construction proceeded apace during the long winter months, and on a cold but glorious afternoon in early April, 1992, the park was first opened for an exhibition game between the Baltimore Orioles and the New York Mets (a team last seen, unhappily, in Baltimore in the 1969 World Series). The following day the Orioles' official season began with a game against the Cleveland Indians (who, even more unhappily, had beaten the Orioles 19 out of 21 times in 1954 when Memorial Stadium, the Birds' former park, had been opened).

In the meantime, in July 1991, Becker had begun selling tee shirts outside Memorial Stadium. These tee shirts bore the lettering "Camden Yards means baseball," "Baltimore, Maryland," and "1992," and displayed a design including an oriole, crossed baseball bats and a baseball diamond. Becker continued his street vendoring until the last day of the 1991 baseball season. He also sold his shirts by direct mail, through sports bars and stores, and by advertising in a local publication known as the "Penny Saver."

On August 22, 1991, MSA wrote to Becker demanding that he cease use of the name Camden Yards. Becker did not respond to the letter, and MSA filed this suit on September 23, 1991.

II.

Section 43(a) of the 1947 Lanham Act creates a federal claim for unfair competition by prohibiting the use in interstate commerce of any "false designation of origin, or any false description or representation, including words or other symbols tending falsely to describe or represent the same...." 15 U.S.C. §1125(a) (1988). This provision protects against trademark, service mark, trade dress and trade name infringement even though the mark or name in question has not been federally registered. *Perini Corp. v. Perini Constr., Inc.*, 915 F.2d 121, 124 (4th Cir. 1990).[6]

The two basic elements necessary to establish infringement of an unregistered mark are "(1) the adoption and use of a mark and [the] entitlement to enforce it, and (2) the adoption and use by a junior user of a mark that is likely to cause confusion that goods or services emanate from the senior owner." *Quality Inns Int'l, Inc. v. McDonald's Corp.*, 695 F. Supp. 198, 209 (D. Md. 1988); *see also Yarmuth-Dion, Inc. v. D'ion Furs, Inc.*, 835 F.2d 990, 992–93 (2d Cir. 1987). Thus, "the gist of a claim for trademark infringement ... is a sanction against one who trades by confusion on the goodwill or reputation of another, whether by intention or not." *Perini*, 915 F.2d at 124 (quoting *Quality Inns Int'l, Inc.*, 695 F. Supp. at 209).

"Word marks" are classified into four categories: generic, descriptive, suggestive, and arbitrary or fanciful. Perini, 915 F.2d at 124. Geographic locations are considered descriptive word marks.[7] *See American Waltham Watch Co. v. United States Watch Co.*, 173 Mass. 85, 53 N.E. 141 (1899) (Holmes, J.). To obtain trademark rights in a descriptive word mark and satisfy the first element of infringement, MSA must prove that: (a) it adopted and used the mark, and (b) the mark acquired secondary meaning. *Perini*, 915 F.2d at 124.

---

6. For purposes of this case, distinctions between the types of marks are irrelevant. *See Accuride Int'l, Inc. v. Accuride Corp.*, 871 F.2d 1531, 1534–35 (9th Cir. 1989) ("As a practical matter, courts are rarely called upon to distinguish between trade names, trademarks, and service marks."); *Nutri/System, Inc. v. Con-Stan Indus.*, Inc., 809 F.2d 601, 604 (9th Cir. 1987) (identical standards govern trademark and service mark infringements).

7. MSA contends that Camden Yards is not a geographically descriptive mark on the ground that Camden Yards is a specific location which it now exclusively owns and at which only one service is provided. *See* 1 J.T. Mccarthy, Trademarks and Unfair Competition, 14:1 at 621 (2d ed. 1984). I need not decide this issue in light of my ruling that the name has acquired a secondary meaning.

III.

As a threshold matter, Becker argues that MSA's use of the name Camden Yards as the name of the sports complex was insufficient to create trademark rights prior to July 1991 because MCA had not sold goods or services with the Camden Yards mark by that time. The argument is without merit. Although the sale or shipment of goods in commerce is necessary as part of a valid trademark application, *see In Re Cedar Point, Inc.*, 220 U.S.P.Q. 533, 535–36 (TTAB 1983), the sale of goods or services using an unregistered mark is not necessary to establish use of the mark. *See New England Duplicating Co. v. Mendes*, 190 F.2d 415, 418 (1st Cir. 1951). Advertising and promotion is sufficient to obtain rights in a mark as long as they occur "within a commercially reasonable time prior to the actual rendition of service…, *Kinark Corp. v. Camelot, Inc.*, 548 F. Supp. 429, 442 (D.N.J. 1982), and as long as the totality of acts "create[s] association of the goods or services and the mark with the user thereof." *New West Corp. v. NYM Co. of California, Inc.*, 595 F.2d 1194, 1200 (9th Cir. 1979) (citing *Hotel Corp. of America v. Inn America, Inc.*, 153 U.S.P.Q. (BNA) 574, 576 (1967)); *see also Selfway, Inc. v. Travelers Petroleum, Inc.*, 579 F.2d 75, 79 (C.C.P.A. 1978). Therefore, the questions which must be resolved are (1) whether MSA had adopted and used the Camden Yards mark prior to July, 1991, (2) whether the mark had obtained secondary meaning and (3) whether Becker's use of the mark creates a likelihood of confusion. As will be seen, the latter two questions merge.

A. Adoption and Use of the Mark

The name Camden Yards first became associated with the proposed sports complex in 1987 when the Maryland General Assembly approved MSA's recommendation that the complex be constructed at the location of B&O's former railroad yard in Baltimore City. The General Assembly specifically defined the site as "85 acres in Baltimore City in the area bounded by Camden Street on the north, Russell Street on the west, Osten Street on the south, and Howard Street and Interstate 395 on the east." Md. Fin. Inst. Code Ann. §13-709(f) (1992 Supp.).

MSA, itself, has referred to the project as the Camden Yards sports complex for many years. In November 1988 it formulated a "Camden Yards Sports Complex Development Plan" for "a major professional sports complex accommodating both a baseball park and a football stadium in the area of Camden Yards." This plan was disseminated to both the public and the press. Beginning in July 1989, MSA published a bi-monthly baseball newsletter that contained such phrases as "ball park at Camden Yards," "Camden Yards site," and "Camden Yards industrial area." The newsletter (as well as other brochures and pamphlets making reference to Camden Yards) was distributed to the press, to 2,500 readers and to members of the public who made inquiries about the new sports complex. Beginning in September 1989, MSA distributed to the press and sold to the public photographic renditions of the sports complex and baseball park, entitling them "Camden Yards Sports Complex" or "Camden Yards Ball Park." It also published drawings entitled "Camden Yards stadium properties" depicting the area where the sports complex was to be built. Likewise, its 1990 annual report, distributed to the Governor's office, members of the Maryland General Assembly, the news media and the Pratt Library, specifically referred to the Camden Yards sports complex.

MSA held a number of promotional events at Camden Yards which included media briefings and photo opportunities. At the "Wrecking Ball" and "Grand Slam" in June and November 1989, over 4,000 members of the public watched the demolition of various buildings which had been standing in the Camden Yards area. In February 1990, Pete Harnisch, Elrod Hendricks and Randy Milligan came to pitch, catch and hit the first balls thrown over the actual location of home plate at the new stadium. In April 1990, MSA began conducting regular tours of the Camden Yards sports complex. The name Camden Yards was used in publicizing all of these events.

MSA also generated public interest in the historical qualities of Camden Yards. In January 1990, it sponsored an "Archeological Open House" during which 1,000 people toured the location of the saloon once managed by George Herman Ruth, Sr., father of Babe Ruth. On March 27 and 28, 1990, it sponsored "Student Press Days" in which 200 middle and high school students studied the archeology of the area. It prepared a pamphlet detailing Camden Yards' archeological significance and distributed it to the Governor's Office, to the General Assembly, at locations visited by a mobile publicity van, to the Babe Ruth Museum and to members of the public who asked about the complex. MSA even designed a continuing education course, given at the University of Maryland, Baltimore County, entitled "The Camden Yards Ballpark — Baltimore's New Stadium," which covered various aspects of the sports complex, including the area's history and archeology.

Baltimore's 1991 baseball season was a remarkable one. While the team's performance on the field was rather dismal, attendance figures soared. Nostalgic and sentimental by nature, Oriole fans flocked to old Memorial Stadium to see a baseball game there just one more time. On the final day of the season, poignant closing ceremonies were held during which waves of Orioles from different eras streamed onto the field to say goodbye to the old ballpark on 33rd Street. But just as those ceremonies dramatically culminated in digging up home plate, transporting it by limousine and placing it at its new downtown home, so too throughout Memorial Stadium's last baseball season talk about the new ballpark had constantly been in the air. It represented the hope of the future and was on the mind and in the heart of every true Oriole fan. What would it be called? Oriole Park or Camden Yards? Controversy raged, from bar room to living room, from State House to penthouse. When it appeared that perhaps an impasse had been reached, such bland alternatives as "Harbor Stadium" crept into discussion. But one thing was certain: by the summer of 1991, whatever the official name of the ballpark might end up to be, Camden Yards had, as Becker's own tee shirts proclaimed, come to "mean baseball."

In short, at the time that Becker started his business, MSA's promotional efforts had already borne fruit. For any reasonable person to have made any association other than baseball with the Camden Yards name would have been as unlikely as Boog Powell hitting an inside-the-park home run, Paul Blair playing too deep, Brooks Robinson dropping a pop-up, Frank Robinson not running out a ground ball, Jim Palmer giving up a grand slam home run, Don Stanhouse pitching an easy 1-2-3 inning, or Cal Ripken, Jr., missing a game because of a cold. It is of such stuff that summary judgment is made.

Notes

1. *On "ownership" of trademarks.* Do you really "own" a trademark or just the right to exclude others? What is the difference? What would be the effect if a trademark user actually "owned" the trademark itself?

2. Should priority mean only who used a trademark first in the United States, or should it mean first use anywhere in the world? The general rule is that priority means the first use within the United States. This is one manifestation of what is known of as the territoriality principle. That is, all trademark laws in the world are determined by each country's domestic laws. The laws do not usually extend outside of each country's physical

jurisdiction. One interesting exception to this occurred in *Grupo Gigante S.A. de C.V. v. Dallo Co., Inc.*, 119 F. Supp.2d 1083 (C.D. Cal. 2003). In that case, the court held that use of the plaintiff's trademark in Mexico established sufficient distinctiveness to warrant protection of the mark in San Diego. The court stated: "If a mark used only on products or services sold abroad is so famous that its reputation is known in the United States, then that mark should be legally recognized in the United States." *Id.* at 1089, *quoting* 4 J. Thomas McCarthy, McCARTHY ON TRADEMARKS AND UNFAIR COMPETITION§29:4 (4th ed. 2002).

3. *Famous marks.* Whether the United States courts will recognize the famous marks doctrine is unsettled. The basic notion of the famous marks doctrine is that countries should recognize the famous marks of other countries if that mark has gained secondary meaning, not through use but through general knowledge. There is currently a split among courts on how to resolve such claims. Some recognize the famous marks doctrine and some do not. For an overview of this issue, *see* Alexis Weissberger, Is Fame Alone Sufficient to Create Priority Rights: An International Perspective on the Viability of the Famous/Well-known Marks Doctrine, 24 CARDOZO ARTS & ENT. L. J. 739 (2006). Some claim that the doctrine ought to be abandoned and that rights should be created solely through the laws of each nation, or not. *See*, Beth Fulkerson, *Theft By Territorialism: A Case For Revising TRIPS To Protect Trademarks From National Market Foreclosure*, 17 MICH. J. INT'L L. 801, 823 (1996).

C. Concurrent Use

Burger King of Florida, Inc. v. Hoots
403 F.2d 904 (7th Cir. 1968)

KILEY, CIRCUIT JUDGE.

Defendants' appeal presents a conflict between plaintiffs' right to use the trade mark "Burger King," which plaintiffs have registered under the Federal Trade Mark Act, and defendants' right to use the same trade mark which defendants have registered under the Illinois Trade Mark Act. The district court resolved the conflict in favor of plaintiffs in this case of first impression in this Circuit. We affirm the judgment restraining the defendants from using the name "Burger King" in any part of Illinois except in their Mattoon, Illinois, market, and restraining plaintiffs from using their trade mark in the market area of Mattoon, Illinois.[8]

Defendants do not challenge the district court's findings of fact and have not included testimony of witnesses at the trial in the record on appeal.

Plaintiff Burger King of Florida, Inc. opened the first "Burger King" restaurant in Jacksonville, Florida, in 1953. By 1955, fifteen of these restaurants were in operation in Florida, Georgia and Tennessee; in 1956 the number operating in Alabama, Kentucky and Virginia was twenty-nine; by 1957, in these states, thirty-eight restaurants were in operation.

---

8. The district court defined the Mattoon market area as a circle having a radius of twenty miles and a center located at the defendants' place of business in Mattoon, Illinois.

Picture 6.1   Burger King of Mattoon, IL

In July, 1961, plaintiffs opened their first Illinois "Burger King" restaurant in Skokie, and at that time had notice of the defendants' prior registration of the same mark under the Illinois Trade Mark Act. Thereafter, on October 3, 1961, plaintiffs' certificate of federal registration of the mark was issued. Subsequently, plaintiffs opened a restaurant in Champaign, Illinois, and at the time of the trial in November, 1967, were operating more than fifty "Burger King" restaurants in the state of Illinois.

In 1957 the defendants, who had been operating an ice cream business in Mattoon, Illinois, opened a "Burger King" restaurant there. In July, 1959, they registered that name under Illinois law as their trade mark, without notice of plaintiffs' prior use of the same mark. On September 26, 1962, the defendants, with constructive knowledge of plaintiffs' federal trade mark, opened a second similar restaurant, in Charleston, Illinois.

Both parties have used the trade mark prominently, and in 1962 they exchanged charges of infringement in Illinois. After plaintiffs opened a restaurant in Champaign, Illinois, defendants sued in the state court to restrain plaintiffs' use of the mark in Illinois. Plaintiffs then brought the federal suit, now before us, and the defendants counter-claimed for an injunction, charging plaintiffs with infringement of their Illinois trade mark.

The district court concluded, from the unchallenged findings, that plaintiffs' federal registration is prima facie evidence of the validity of the registration and ownership of the mark; that plaintiffs have both a common-law and a federal right in the mark superior to defendants' in the area of natural expansion of plaintiffs' enterprise which "logically included" all of Illinois, except where defendants had actually adopted and used the mark, innocently, i.e., without notice and in good faith; and that the defendants had adopted and continuously used the mark in the Mattoon area innocently and were entitled to protection in that market.

We hold that the district court properly decided that plaintiffs' federal registration of the trade mark "Burger King" gave them the exclusive right to use the mark in Illinois except in the Mattoon market area in Illinois where the defendants, without knowledge of plaintiffs' prior use, actually used the mark before plaintiffs' federal registration. The defendants did not acquire the exclusive right they would have acquired by their Illinois registration had they actually used the mark throughout Illinois prior to the plaintiffs' federal registration.

We think our holding is clear from the terms of the Federal Trade Mark Act. Under 15 U.S.C. §1065 of the Act, plaintiffs, owners of the federally registered trade mark "Burger King," have the "incontestable" right to use the mark in commerce, except to the extent that such use infringes what valid right the defendants have acquired by their continuous use of the same mark prior to plaintiffs' federal registration.

Under 15 U.S.C. §1115(b), the federal certificate of registration is "conclusive evidence" of plaintiffs' "exclusive right" to use the mark. This Section, however, also provides a defense to an exclusive right to use a trade mark: If a trade mark was adopted without knowledge of the federal registrant's prior use, and has been continuously used, then such use "shall" constitute a defense to infringement, provided that this defense applies only for the area in which such continuous prior use is proved. Since the defendants have established that they had adopted the mark "Burger King" without knowledge of plaintiffs' prior use and that they had continuously used the mark from a date prior to plaintiffs' federal registration of the mark, they are entitled to protection in the area which that use appropriated to them.

Plaintiffs agree that the defendants as prior good faith users are to be protected in the area that they had appropriated. Thus, the question narrows to what area in Illinois the defendants have appropriated by virtue of their Illinois registration.

At common law, defendants were entitled to protection in the Mattoon market area because of the innocent use of the mark prior to plaintiffs' federal registration. They argue that the Illinois Trade Mark Act was designed to give more protection than they already had at common law, and that various provisions of the Illinois Act indicate an intention to afford Illinois registrants exclusive rights to use trade marks throughout the state, regardless of whether they actually used the marks throughout the state or not. However, the Act itself does not express any such intention. And no case has been cited to us, nor has our research disclosed any case in the Illinois courts deciding whether a registrant is entitled to statewide protection even if he has used the mark only in a small geographical area.

Two decisions of this court, however, shed light on the defendants' argument. In *Philco Corp. v. Phillips Mfg. Co.*, 133 F.2d 663, 148 A.L.R. 125 (7th Cir. 1943), this court, through Judge Kerner, discussed the 1905 and 1920 Trade Mark Acts, and decided that Congress had the constitutional power to legislate on "merits of trade mark questions," *supra* at 670 of 133 F.2d. It then stated that the policy of the Acts, to provide protection of federally registered marks used in interstate commerce, "may not be defeated or obstructed by State law" and that if state law conflicts with the policy it "must yield to the superior federal law." The court held that Philco's federal-registration rendered all questions of use and protection in interstate commerce questions of federal law, not state law. And in *John Morrell & Co. v. Reliable Packing Co.*, 295 F.2d 314 (7th Cir. 1961), Judge Duffy states, at 317, "However, the Illinois registration carries no presumption of validity" — thus attributing greater value to a federal registration because of its "incontestability" feature, which is prima facie evidence of exclusivity in interstate commerce. *See also Hot Shoppes, Inc. v. Hot Shoppe, Inc.*, 203 F. Supp. 777, 781–782. (M.D.N.C.1962).

The competing federal and state statutes confirm the correctness of this court's statements. Under 15 U.S.C. §1115(b) of the Lanham Act, the federal certificate can be "conclusive evidence" of registrant's "exclusive right." And 15 U.S.C. §1127 of the Act provides that "The intent of this chapter is . . . to protect registered marks used in such commerce from interference by State . . . legislation." The Illinois Act, however, provides only that a certificate of registration "shall be admissible . . . evidence as competent and sufficient proof of the registration . . ." Ill.Rev.Stat. Ch. 140, §11 (1967).

Moreover, we think that whether or not Illinois intended to enlarge the common law with respect to a right of exclusivity in that state, the Illinois Act does not enlarge its right in the area where the federal mark has priority. *See Hot Shoppes, supra*, 782. Congress expanded the common law, however, by granting an exclusive right in commerce to federal registrants in areas where there has been no offsetting use of the mark. Congress intended the Lanham Act to afford nation-wide protection to federally-registered marks, and that once the certificate has issued, no person can acquire any additional rights superior to those obtained by the federal registrant. Cases cited by the defendants in support of their claim to exclusive right in Illinois do not help them. *ABC Stores v. T. S. Richey & Co.*, 280 S.W. 177, (Tex.Com.App.1926) is a pre-Lanham Act case involving a Texas trade mark dispute between Texas corporations involving intrastate commerce. *Hotel Sherman, Inc. v. Harlow et al.*, 186 F. Supp. 618 (S.D.Cal.1960), concerning the mark "Pump Room" did not, apparently, involve a dispute between federal and state registrants. However, we note that the court there in a mode similar to the district court judgment before us allocated territory to each of the parties. And in *Nielsen v. American Oil Co.*, 203 F. Supp. 473 (D.Utah 1962), the district court held that American Oil Co. by virtue of its prior use of its mark "within the State of Utah and Cache County" was entitled under Utah law to the exclusive intrastate use of the mark. However, the opinion also states that as early as 1932 defendant used its mark in sales at Bonneville Salt Flats, and starting in 1953 made annually a few interstate sales in Utah, and beginning in 1960 used the mark throughout Utah.

We conclude that if we were to accept the defendants' argument we would be fostering, in clear opposition to the express terms of the Lanham Act, an interference with plaintiffs' exclusive right in interstate commerce to use its federal mark.

The undisputed continuous market for the defendants' "Burger King" products was confined to a twenty mile radius of Mattoon. There is no evidence before us of any intention or hope for their use of their Illinois mark beyond that market. Yet they seek to exclude plaintiffs from expanding the scope of their national exclusive right, and from operating fifty enterprises already begun in Illinois. This result would clearly burden interstate commerce.

The defendants argue also that unless they are given the right to exclusive use throughout Illinois, many persons from all parts of Illinois in our current mobile society will come in contact with the defendants' business and will become confused as to whether they are getting the defendants' product, as they intended.

We are not persuaded by this argument. Defendants have not shown that the Illinois public is likely to confuse the products furnished by plaintiffs and by defendants. *John R. Thompson Co. v. Holloway*, 366 F.2d 108 (5th Cir. 1966), and cases cited therein. We are asked to infer that confusion will exist from the mere fact that both trade marks co-exist in the state of Illinois. However, the district court found that the defendants' market area was limited to within twenty miles of their place of business. The court's decision restricted the use of the mark by plaintiffs and defendants to sufficiently distinct and geographically separate markets so that public confusion would be reduced to a minimum. The mere fact that some people will travel from one market area to the other does not, of itself, establish that confusion will result. Since the defendants have failed to establish on the record any likelihood of confusion or any actual confusion, they are not entitled to an inference that confusion will result.

For the reasons given, the judgment of the district court is affirmed.

Dawn Donut Co. v. Hart's Food Stores, Inc.
267 F.2d 358 (2d Cir. 1959)

LUMBARD, CIRCUIT JUDGE

The principal question is whether the plaintiff, a wholesale distributor of doughnuts and other baked goods under its federally registered trademarks 'Dawn' and 'Dawn Donut,' is entitled under the provisions of the Lanham Trade-Mark Act to enjoin the defendant from using the mark 'Dawn' in connection with the retail sale of doughnuts and baked goods entirely within a six county area of New York State surrounding the city of Rochester. The primary difficulty arises from the fact that although plaintiff licenses purchasers of its mixes to use its trademarks in connection with the retail sales of food products made from the mixes, it has not licensed or otherwise exploited the mark at the retail level in defendant's market area for some thirty years.

We hold that because no likelihood of public confusion arises from the concurrent use of the mark in connection with retail sales of doughnuts and other baked goods in separate trading areas, and because there is no present likelihood that plaintiff will expand its retail use of the mark into defendant's market area, plaintiff is not now entitled to any relief under the Lanham Act, 15 U.S.C.A. §1114. Accordingly, we affirm the district court's dismissal of plaintiff's complaint.

This is not to say that the defendant has acquired any permanent right to use the mark in its trading area. On the contrary, we hold that because of the effect of the constructive notice provision of the Lanham Act, should the plaintiff expand its retail activities into the six county area, upon a proper application and showing to the district court, it may enjoin defendant's use of the mark.

* * *

Plaintiff, Dawn Donut Co., Inc., of Jackson, Michigan since June 1, 1922 has continuously used the trademark 'Dawn' upon 25 to 100 pound bags of doughnut mix which it sells to bakers in various states, including New York, and since 1935 it has similarly marketed a line of sweet dough mixes for use in the baking of coffee cakes, cinnamon rolls and oven goods in general under that mark. In 1950 cake mixes were added to the company's line of products. Dawn's sales representatives call upon bakers to solicit orders for mixes and the orders obtained are filled by shipment to the purchaser either directly from plaintiff's Jackson, Michigan plant, where the mixes are manufactured, or from a local warehouse within the customer's state. For some years plaintiff maintained a warehouse in Jamestown, New York, from which shipments were made, but sometime prior to the commencement of this suit in 1954 it discontinued this warehouse and has since then shipped its mixes to its New York customers directly from Michigan.

Plaintiff furnishes certain buyers of its mixes, principally those who agree to become exclusive Dawn Donut Shops, with advertising and packaging material bearing the trademark 'Dawn' and permits these bakers to sell goods made from the mixes to the consuming public under that trademark. These display materials are supplied either as a courtesy or at a moderate price apparently to stimulate and promote the sale of plaintiff's mixes.

The district court found that with the exception of one Dawn Donut Shop operated in the city of Rochester, New York during 1926–27, plaintiff's licensing of its mark in connection with the retail sale of doughnuts in the state of New York has been confined to areas not less than 60 miles from defendant's trading area. The court also found that for the past eighteen years plaintiff's present New York state representative has, without interruption, made regular calls upon bakers in the city of Rochester, N.Y., and in neighboring towns and cities, soliciting orders for plaintiff's mixes and that throughout this period orders have been filled and shipments made of plaintiff's mixes from Jackson, Michigan into the city of Rochester. But it does not appear that any of these purchasers of plaintiff's mixes employed the plaintiff's mark in connection with retail sales.

The defendant, Hart Food Stores, Inc., owns and operates a retail grocery chain within the New York counties of Monroe, Wayne, Livingston, Genesee, Ontario and Wyoming. The products of defendant's bakery, Starhart Bakeries, Inc., a New York corporation of which it is the sole stockholder, are distributed through these stores, thus confining the distribution of defendant's product to an area within a 45 mile radius of Rochester. Its advertising of doughnuts and other baked products over television and radio and in newspapers is also limited to this area. Defendant's bakery corporation was formed on April 13, 1951 and first used the imprint 'Dawn' in packaging its products on August 30, 1951. The district court found that the defendant adopted the mark 'Dawn' without any actual knowledge of plaintiff's use or federal registration of the mark, selecting it largely because of a slogan 'Baked at midnight, delivered at Dawn' which was originated by defendant's president and used by defendant in its bakery operations from 1929 to 1935. Defendant's president testified, however, that no investigation was made prior to the adoption of the mark to see if anyone else was employing it. Plaintiff's marks were registered federally in 1927, and their registration was renewed in 1947. Therefore by virtue of the Lanham Act, 15 U.S.C.A. §1072, the defendant had constructive notice of plaintiff's marks as of July 5, 1947, the effective date of the Act.

Defendant's principal contention is that because plaintiff has failed to exploit the mark 'Dawn' for some thirty years at the retail level in the Rochester trading area, plaintiff should not be accorded the exclusive right to use the mark in this area.

We reject this contention as inconsistent with the scope of protection afforded a federal registrant by the Lanham Act.

Prior to the passage of the Lanham Act courts generally held that the owner of a registered trademark could not sustain an action for infringement against another who, without knowledge of the registration, used the mark in a different trading area from that exploited by the registrant so that public confusion was unlikely. By being the first to adopt a mark in an area without knowledge of its prior registration, a junior user of a mark could gain the right to exploit the mark exclusively in that market.

But the Lanham Act, 15 U.S.C.A. §1072, provides that registration of a trademark on the principal register is constructive notice of the registrant's claim of ownership. Thus, by eliminating the defense of good faith and lack of knowledge, §1072 affords nationwide protection to registered marks, regardless of the areas in which the registrant actually uses the mark.

That such is the purpose of Congress is further evidenced by 15 U.S.C.A. §1115(a) and (b) which make the certificate of registration evidence of the registrant's 'exclusive right to use the . . . mark in commerce.' 'Commerce' is defined in 15 U.S.C.A. 1127 to include all the commerce which may lawfully be regulated by Congress. These two provisions of the Lanham Act make it plain that the fact that the defendant employed the mark 'Dawn,' without actual knowledge of plaintiff's registration, at the retail level in a limited geographical area of New York state before the plaintiff used the mark in that market, does not entitle it either to exclude the plaintiff from using the mark in that area or to use the mark concurrently once the plaintiff licenses the mark or otherwise exploits it in connection with retail sales in the area.

Plaintiff's failure to license its trademarks in defendant's trading area during the thirty odd years that have elapsed since it licensed them to a Rochester baker does not work an abandonment of the rights in that area. We hold that 15 U.S.C.A. §1127, which provides for abandonment in certain cases of non-use, applies only when the registrant fails to use his mark, within the meaning of §1127, anywhere in the nation. Since the Lanham Act affords a registrant nationwide protection, a contrary holding would create an insoluble problem of measuring the geographical extent of the abandonment. Even prior to the passage of the Lanham Act, when trademark protection flowed from state law and therefore depended on use within the state, no case, as far as we have been able to ascertain, held that a trademark owner abandoned his rights within only part of a state because of his failure to use the mark in that part of the state.

Accordingly, since plaintiff has used its trademark continuously at the retail level, it has not abandoned its federal registration rights even in defendant's trading area.

* * *

Accordingly, we turn to the question of whether on this record plaintiff has made a sufficient showing to warrant the issuance of an injunction against defendant's use of the mark 'Dawn' in a trading area in which the plaintiff has for thirty years failed to employ its registered mark.

* * *

Accordingly, because plaintiff and defendant use the mark in connection with retail sales in distinct and separate markets and because there is no present prospect that plaintiff will expand its use of the mark at the retail level into defendant's trading area, we conclude that there is no likelihood of public confusion arising from the concurrent use of the marks and therefore the issuance of an injunction is not warranted. A fortiori plaintiff is not entitled to any accounting or damages. However, because of the effect we have attributed to the constructive notice provision of the Lanham Act, the plaintiff may later, upon a proper showing of an intent to use the mark at the retail level in defendant's market area, be entitled to enjoin defendant's use of the mark.

[The court affirmed the district court's finding of no likelihood of confusion.]

————————

Notes

1. Thrifty Rent-a-Car began using the term THRIFTY on rental car services on March 3, 1958. Use was confined to the Tulsa, Oklahoma area. Interstate commerce commenced on July 30, 1962, after the business was purchased and moved to Houston, Texas. Thrifty received a federal trademark registration for THRIFTY RENTAL CAR SYSTEM in July of 1964. Thrift Cars, Inc. began rental car services in October of 1962. At first this business was a small business conducted out of the home of its owner in East Tauton, Massachusetts. Thrift's business was focused in Massachusetts. Thrift delivered cars to Logan Airport, Cape Cod, and Nantucket. In 1970 Thrift began larger scale rental car services out of the Nantucket airport. Thrifty sued Thrift for trademark infringement. What result? *See Thrifty Rent-a-Car Sys. v. Thrift Cars, Inc.*, 831 F. 2d 1177 (1st Cir. 1987).

2. Section 33(b)(5) (15 U.S.C. §1115(b)(5)) of the Lanham Act, relied upon in *Burger King*, was designed to address common law trademark rights that had developed prior to the effective date of the Lanham Act (July 5, 1947). As we will see in Chapter 8, *infra*, a trademark registration becomes incontestable after at least five years of continuous use and when the registrant files a Section 15 Affidavit with the PTO. Although the court in *Burger King* is not clear on this filing, it must have been done, since the court refers to Burger King's registration becoming incontestable under 15 U.S.C. §1065 (Lanham Act §15).

3. It appears that one can still purchase a "Hooter Burger" from the Burger King in Mattoon, Illinois. *See Mattoon, Illinois—The Original "Burger King,"* ROADSIDEAMER-ICA.COM: YOUR ONLINE GUIDE TO OFFBEAT ATTRACTIONS, *at* http://www.roadsideamer-ica.com/tips/getAttraction.php3?tip_AttractionNo==8105.

4. If someone opened a BURGERQUEEN restaurant in 1950 in Skokie, Illinois, how would she have fared against attacks from Hoots in 1957? From Burger King of Florida in 1961? What if BURGERQUEEN first opened in Skokie, Illinois, in 1958? If BURG-ERQUEEN only sold supplies to restaurants? Or if BURGERQUEEN opened in Noam, Alaska in 1950?

5. *Concurrent use and the Internet.* How should courts delimit geographical boundaries for purposes of concurrent use when the use takes place on the Internet? Is all Internet use, by definition, nation-wide use? Should geographically specific Top Level Domain Names (TLDs) be created to recreate concurrent use? NOTE: Robert Nup, Concurrent Use of Trademarks on the Internet: Reconciling the Concept of Geographically Delimited Trademarks with the Reality of the Internet, 64 OHIO ST. L. J. 617 (2003).

D. Intent to Use

15 U.S.C. §1051, Lanham Act §1

(b) (1) A person who has a bona fide intention, under circumstances showing the good faith of such person, to use a trademark in commerce may request registration of its trademark on the principal register hereby established by paying the prescribed fee and filing in the Patent and Trademark Office an application and a verified statement, in such form as may be prescribed by the Director.

15 U.S.C. §1057, Lanham Act §7

(c) Application to register mark considered constructive use. Contingent on the registration of a mark on the principal register provided by this Act, the filing of the application to register such mark shall constitute constructive use of the mark, conferring a right of priority, nationwide in effect, on or in connection with the goods or services specified in the registration against any other person except for a person whose mark has not been abandoned and who, prior to such filing—

(1) has used the mark;

(2) has filed an application to register the mark which is pending or has resulted in registration of the mark; or

(3) has filed a foreign application to register the mark on the basis of which he or she has acquired a right of priority, and timely files an application under section 44(d) [15 USCS §1126(d)] to register the mark which is pending or has resulted in registration of the mark.

Introduction to the ITU System[9]

In 1988, one of the most significant changes to United States trademark law took place. Almost exclusively at the urging of the United States Trademark Association ("USTA"), the United States Congress amended the Lanham Act to allow for the federal recognition of trademark rights prior to their actual use in commerce. Under these new provisions, trademark owners are now allowed to file and preserve their intention to use a mark on or in connection with specific goods or services. This amendment is known as the ITU provision. This change was, in fact, rather significant because, as we have seen in these materials, all rights in trademarks are conferred through use of the marks, not through registration. Prior to November 16, 1989, the effective date of the amendment, if a trademark owner had not used its mark in interstate commerce, no prior rights could have been claimed and that claimant could not prevent the use of the exact same mark on precisely the same goods by a third party.

The ITU application is similar to the actual use application described in the next chapter. All of the information required in the use application is also required in the ITU application, except that the dates for first use and first use in commerce are omitted. Instead, the applicant must state a "bona fide intention to use the mark in U.S. interstate or foreign commerce." Naturally, because no actual use has occurred, the applicant may also not be able to provide a specimen of use.

If actual use occurs before any action on the application by an examiner (usually within three months of the actual filing date), the applicant may file an amendment to the ITU application claiming that actual use has taken place and convert the application to a standard use-based application. As will be seen in the cases, *infra*, descriptive marks, which may lack secondary meaning, actually using and converting to a use-based application too early in the process may be a bad idea.

The PTO examines and publishes all ITU applications in the same manner as actual use applications and, if there is no successful opposition, issues a Notice of Allowance rather than a Certificate of Registration.

Within six months of the date of the Notice of Allowance, the applicant must file either an affidavit claiming actual use (known as a Statement of Use) or file a Request for an Extension of Time in which to file a Statement of Use. This time period can be extended for an additional six months without showing cause and an additional aggregate of twenty-four months by showing cause (for a total of thirty-six months) if the Requests for Extension of Time are timely filed. Upon completion of the review process, all ITU applications are also published in the Official Gazette and are, at that point, open for opposition by parties who believe they will be harmed by the registration.

Perhaps the most crucial element of the ITU system is the nationwide constructive first use doctrine. When Congress created the ITU system, it provided in section 7(c) of the Lanham Act as follows:

> Contingent on the registration of a mark on the principal register provided by this Act, the filing of the application to register such mark shall constitute constructive use of the mark, conferring a right of priority, nationwide in effect, on or in connection with the goods or services specified in the registration....

15 U.S.C. §1057(c), Lanham Act §7(c).

---

9. Adapted from Kenneth L. Port, *The Congressional Expansion of American Trademark Law: A Civil Law System in the Making*, 35 Wake Forest L. Rev. 827 (2000).

That is, once an actual Certificate of Registration issues, the registrant enjoys a nationwide first use date as of the date of the ITU application. Although some argue that no rights are created upon the filing of the ITU application because of this contingency language in section 7(c), while reading the cases, *infra*, you should consider whether or not this is true. If not, rights are actually created. You might ask yourself why are more than half of all applications with the PTO today ITU, and not use, applications?

When it created the ITU system, Congress had several express intentions in mind. One intent was to provide certainty for trademark claimants so that they could consider trademarks for products, test market, gear up for actual sales, etc., resting assured that after they invested much time, money, and energy in the marks, the marks would still be available to them when they were actually ready to use them. That is, under the pre-1988 system, an interloper could obtain prior trademark rights by using the mark in commerce first, even though another party conceived of and planned to use the mark on the same or similar goods or services.

Although true and somewhat meritorious, certainty for trademark claimants has been the unimaginative, banal explanation of congressional intent behind the ITU system. The more interesting intentions were focused on protecting the American trademark owner from perceived unfair competition from foreigners.

Of course, the ITU amendments could easily have been described in terms of international trademark harmonization as the ITU system brings United States trademark law closer to the regimes of trademark protection in civil law countries. In fact, in the entire record, there is only one fleeting reference to the goal of harmonization.

Rather, the ITU system was necessary, Congress and its supporters concluded, because section 44(d) of the Lanham Act allows applicants of trademark registrations in certain foreign countries to be given the priority date of their foreign application, provided that the U.S. application is filed within six months of the foreign application date. That is, trademark applicants in some foreign countries have the ability to use their foreign application to claim priority and register a mark in the United States without ever having used the mark in the United States. If the original jurisdiction was a civil law country where rights in trademarks are generally granted upon registration and not conferred only after use, such a trademark owner could obtain a federal registration under the Lanham Act without ever using the mark anywhere. This put United States trademark owners at an insurmountable competitive disadvantage. From the United States trademark owners' perspective, the imbalance of fairness regarding section 44 was the primary motivation for an ITU system.

Therefore, the intent of the ITU system was twofold: first, to avoid common law interlopers and protect the investment trademark claimants were making in marks prior to filing applications and second, to even the playing field with foreign competitors. When reading the cases, *infra*, ask yourself if these objectives seem to be satisfied or if ITU claimants are using the system for other purposes.

Zirco Corp. v. American Telephone & Telegraph Co.
21 U.S.P.Q.2d 1542 (TTAB 1991)

By the Board,

Opposer, on April 23, 1991, filed a notice of opposition to the registration of applicant's mark DATACEL for a portable cellular data transmission and reception system comprising a cellular transceiver integrated with a cellular protocol modem, which is the subject of an intent-to-use application filed on January 11, 1990. [Serial No. 74/018,298]. In its notice of opposition, opposer alleges, inter alia, that opposer has been the user of the mark DATACELL for a cellular adapter allowing linkage of substantially any and all telephone equipment to any cellular telephone since about April 15, 1990; that opposer has perfected its common law rights in its mark throughout the United States; that applicant's use of its mark in commerce, if any, is well after the first use date of opposer's mark; that opposer had no actual knowledge of applicant's intent-to-use application prior to its adoption and use of its mark; and that because of the similarities between opposer's and applicant's marks and because of the related nature of the goods provided by opposer under its mark and the goods proposed to by sold by applicant under its mark, there is a likelihood of confusion on the part of the trade and purchasing public.

Applicant, on July 1, 1991, has filed a motion to dismiss the opposition pursuant to Fed. R. Civ. P.12(b)(6) for failure to state a claim upon which relief may be granted. Applicant asserts that under Section 7(c) of the Trademark Act (15 US.C. §1057(c)), as amended, the filing of its intent-to-use application constitutes constructive use of its mark since the filing date of January 11, 1990 and thus opposer's allegations of first use of its mark on or about April 15, 1990, even if true, do not afford it a basis for relief, in that opposer, as a subsequent user, cannot be damaged.

Opposer has filed its opposition to the motion, arguing that it is clear from Section 7(c) that constructive use does not come into play until the mark has been registered and issued; that, accordingly, applicant does not have conferred upon it a nationwide right of priority of January 11, 1990 until it uses the mark and registration is completed; that since applicant has not perfected constructive use of its mark, it cannot prevent opposer from acquiring common law rights in its mark; that opposer can exert these common law rights against parties which are junior to it, until the issuance of a dominating registration; and that since under Section 18 (15 U.S.C. §1068), as amended, no judgment shall be entered in favor of an intent-to-use applicant before the mark is registered, if that applicant cannot prevail without establishing constructive use pursuant to Section 7(c),[10] no judgment can be made final herein in favor of applicant and thus the motion to dismiss must be denied. Opposer further contends that Section 7(c) is in violation of the commerce clause of the Constitution and as such can confer no rights on applicant.

Applicant has filed a reply, contending that opposer's position would require that an intent-to-use applicant make use of its mark before it could assert constructive use priority to prevail in an opposition and accordingly would defeat the purpose of the intent-to-use provisions of the Trademark Revision Act. Applicant argues that opposer cannot rely upon the acquisition of common law rights after the filing date of applicant's application; that the conditional language of Section 7(c) and Section 18 does not affect applicant's right to assert constructive use priority in this opposition, only the entry of final judgment in applicant's favor would be suspended pending issuance of a registration; and that the legislative history of the Trademark Law Revision Act reveals that the constitutionality of the intent-to-use provisions was thoroughly scrutinized and determined to be satisfactory.

Section 7(c) was added to the Lanham Act by the Trademark Law Revision Act of 1988 in order to provide constructive use, dating from the filing date of an application for reg-

---

10. Section 18, in pertinent part, reads:
    … no final judgment shall be entered in favor of an applicant under section 1(b) before the mark is registered if such applicant cannot prevail without establishing constructive use pursuant to section 7(c).

istration on the principal register, for a mark registered on that register. As a review of the legislative history shows, the provision is intended to fix a registrant's nationwide priority rights in its mark from the filing date of its application whether the application is based on use or intent-to-use. This right of priority is to have legal effect comparable to the earliest use of a mark at common law. Senate Judiciary Committee Report on S.1883, Senate Report No. 100-515 (September 15, 1988).

While constructive use is applicable to applications based on use as well as intent-to-use, the provision is considered to be essential to the intent-to-use system. Without this provision, an intent-to-use applicant would be vulnerable to theft of its mark or to innocent use of the mark by anyone after the filing of its application. *See* Frank Z. Hellwig, The Trademark Law Revision Act of 1988: The 100th Congress Leaves Its Mark, 79 TMR 287, 299 (1989). Moreover, by according conditional rights to those who publicly disclose their marks, constructive use encourages the early filing of applications and the searching of trademark records prior to the adoption and investment in new marks. Senate Judiciary Committee Report on S. 1883, *supra*.

Opposer's major contention is that under Section 7(c), constructive use is conditional upon registration of the mark and thus applicant, having neither used its mark nor having been issued a registration, is not entitled to assert any priority rights as of the filing date of its application in this opposition.

It is true that a reading of Section 7(c) alone, specifically of that portion which reads "[c]ontingent on the registration of a mark..., the filing of the application to register such mark shall constitute constructive use of the mark ...", might be construed to limit an applicant's right to rely upon the constructive use date as the first use date of its mark to post-registration actions. But the Board does not believe that such a literal interpretation of Section 7(c) can be adopted. Instead this section must be read in conjunction with Sections 13 and 18 of the Trademark Act. Under Section 13, an opposition may be filed against any application for registration of a mark on the principal register, regardless of whether the application is based on use or intent-to-use. Under Section 18 the Board may render a decision on the opposition; it is only the entry of final judgment in favor of an intent-to-use applicant which must be deferred until the mark is registered, if that applicant cannot prevail without establishing constructive use pursuant to Section 7(c). If an intent-to-use applicant were not allowed to rely upon the constructive use date prior to actual use and registration of its mark, it would be rendered defenseless in any opposition against the registration of its mark based on likelihood of confusion. Constructive use would only function as a sword in affirmative actions by an intent-to-use applicant and only after the registration of its mark, never as a shield in actions against that applicant prior to the registration of its mark.

Accordingly, the Board finds that on its face the Lanham Act, as amended by the Trademark Law Revision Act, cannot be interpreted to limit an intent-to-use applicant's entitlement to rely upon the constructive use provision of Section 7(c) to the time after which it has used its mark and has been issued a registration. If the legislative history and the commentaries[11] on the revised statute are taken into consideration, it is readily apparent that the constructive use provision was intended to foster the filing of intent-to use applications, to give an intent-to-use applicant a superior right over anyone adopting a

---

11. *See* United States Trademark Association Trademark Review Commission Report and Recommendations to USTA President and Board of Directors, 77 TMR 375 (1987); Henry W. Leeds, Intent To Use—Its Time Has Come, 79 TMR 269 (1989); Frank Z. Hellwig, The Trademark Law Revision Act of 1988: The 100th Congress Leaves Its Mark, 79 TMR 287 (1989).

mark after applicant's filing date (providing the applicant's mark is ultimately used and registered) and to prevent a third party from acquiring common law rights in a mark after the filing date of the intent-to-use application. With these being the aims of the constructive use provision, there can be no doubt but that the right to rely upon the constructive use date comes into existence with the filing of the intent-to-use application and that an intent-to-use applicant can rely upon this date in an opposition brought by a third party asserting common law rights. Whether this provision violates the commerce clause of the Constitution is not a matter falling within the jurisdiction of the Board.

In view thereof, applicant's motion to dismiss the opposition under Fed. R. Civ. P. 12(b)(6) is well taken. Opposer's allegations of common law rights in its mark as of April 15, 1990, a date subsequent to applicant's constructive use date, are inadequate to support the ground of priority of use and likelihood of confusion and accordingly opposer has failed to set forth a claim upon which it can prevail.

Judgment in favor of applicant dismissing the opposition is hereby entered, subject to applicant's establishment of constructive use. The time for filing an appeal or for commencing a civil action will run from the date of the present decision. *See* Trademark Rules 2.129(d) and 2.145. When applicant's mark has been registered or the application becomes abandoned, applicant should inform the Board, so that appropriate action may be taken to terminate this proceeding.

Fila Sport, S.P.A. v. Diadora America, Inc.

21 U.S.P.Q. 2d 1063 (N.D. Ill. 1991)

GUZMAN, MAGISTRATE JUDGE

Defendant, DIADORA AMERICA, Inc. ("Diadora") has filed its Motion to Dismiss the complaint of FILA SPORT, S.p.A. ("Fila") pursuant to Federal Rules of Civil Procedure 12(b)(1) and 12(b)(6). Diadora also has requested that sanctions be imposed against Fila pursuant to Rule 11 of the Federal Rules of Civil Procedure.

BACKGROUND FACTS

Fila, formerly known as "Maglificio Biellese Fratelli," is a corporation organized and existing under the laws of Italy, having its principal place of business at Viale Cesare Battisti 26, 13051 Biella, Italy. Fila manufactures and distributes, and selectively licenses others to manufacture and distribute, their sportswear and sporting goods, including sport shoes. These items bear the Fila "F" logo.

Since March of 1974, Fila has sold sportswear bearing the Fila trademarks through its wholly-owned California subsidiary, Fila Sports, Inc., in the United States and elsewhere. Further, Fila has had famous athletes promote its products and has sponsored major sports events, many of which are broadcast worldwide on television. As a result of these promotions and sales, Fila's trademarks have become assets of importance to Fila and have become associated in the minds of the trade and the general public with Fila.

In the spring of 1989, Fila conceived, designed, manufactured and patented a new athletic shoe which allows the wearer to absorb the shock produced by the impact of the foot on the ground and then transfers to the wearer a portion of the energy resulting from the shock. In connection with these shoes, Fila has two trademarks, "Fila 2 Actions 2A," and "Fila Double Action."

On November 27, 1989, Fila registered the trademark "Fila 2 Actions 2A" for footwear in Italy and a second trademark applicable to the entirety of Europe. On June 15, 1990, Fila filed an Intent to Use Trademark Application under the name "Fila Double Action" in the United States pursuant to 15 U.S.C. §1051(b), for "footwear and t-shirts," No. 74/069315.

In its complaint, Fila states that on December 28, 1989, more than a month after Fila filed in Italy for trademark protection under the "2 Actions" mark, Diadora's Italian parent corporation, Diadora-Calzatorificio Fratelli Danielli, S.p.A. ("Diadora Italy") applied for a trade mark in Italy under the name "Double Action." Fila has commenced litigation against Diadora in Italy challenging its application for a "Double Action" or "2 Actions."

Fila states that a major international trade show was held in Chicago, Illinois beginning approximately July 30, 1990. At the Chicago trade show, Diadora maintained a booth where it displayed footwear prominently bearing the name "Double Action," and distributed brochures promoting the sale of "Double Action" shoes. On information and belief, Diadora offered and sold at the Chicago trade show "Double Action" shoes to distributors and retailers from throughout the United States, including, without limitation, the Northern District of Illinois.

Fila further states that use of the "Double Action" trademark by Diadora is likely to cause confusion and mistake in the minds of wholesalers, retailers, and the purchasing public, and, in particular, falsely creates the impression that the goods manufactured, distributed and sold by defendants are authorized, sponsored or approved by Fila, when, in fact, they are not.

DISCUSSION

When ruling on a motion to dismiss pursuant to Rule 12(b)(6), "the factual allegations contained in plaintiff's complaint must be taken as true and must be viewed, along with all reasonable inferences to be drawn therefrom, in the light most favorable to the plaintiff." *Meriwether v. Faulkner*, 821 F.2d 408, 410 (7th Cir. 1987), *cert. denied* 484 U.S. 935, 98 L. Ed. 2d 269, 108 S. Ct. 311 (1987). A complaint should be dismissed only when "it appears beyond doubt that the plaintiff can prove no set of facts that would entitle him to relief." *Rutan v. Republican Party of Illinois*, 868 F.2d 943, 954 (7th Cir. 1989,) *cert. granted*, 497 U.S. 62, 110 S. Ct. 2729, 111 L. Ed. 2d 52 (1989), modified on other grounds.

Once the existence of subject matter jurisdiction is challenged in a motion to dismiss under Fed.R.Civ.P. 12(b)(1), the burden of establishing such jurisdiction shifts to the party asserting the same. The burden always rests on the party asserting jurisdiction. If the motion to dismiss challenges the truth of the jurisdictional facts in the complaint, the court may receive evidentiary materials such as affidavits, deposition testimony and the like in order to decide the factual issues.

Diadora asserts that both counts of Fila's complaint lack subject matter jurisdiction pursuant to Rule 12(b)(1) and fail to state a claim upon which relief can be granted pursuant to Rule 12(b)(6). In particular, Diadora argues that Fila must have a valid federal trademark registration to assert a claim for infringement, and have used its mark in commerce to assert a claim for unfair competition. Because Fila has only filed an application to register under the "intent to use" statute and has not used its mark in United States commerce, defendant argues there is no jurisdictional basis either for the Count I allegation of infringement, or the Count II allegation of unfair competition and the complaint must be dismissed. Fila's complaint clearly alleges that it has actually "registered" the trademarks in question. However Diadora directly refutes this in its motion and attaches evidentiary material, including certified copies of the official files of plaintiff's applications, showing that the applications remain in the preliminary stages and have not yet resulted in registrations. I find from these materials and from the lack of any contrary submissions by Fila in its response to the motion, that Fila has failed to establish actual registration in the U.S. of either of its two marks.

Fila, in opposition to Diadora's motion to dismiss, contends that Diadora's lack of jurisdiction argument is not the relevant argument but contends, however, that this case presents the question of whether a party who files an "intent to use" trademark application, and thereby discloses valuable trade secret information regarding its future product and marketing plans, is left unprotected when a competitor decides to saturate the market with competing goods under the same or a confusingly similar name before the party filing the intent to use applications is ready to sell its product. Fila argues that the relevant issue is not one of jurisdiction, but whether a party's stated intent to use a mark is bona fide. This issue, Fila claims, is not susceptible to determination on a motion to dismiss.

Diadora cites 15 USC §1051 of the recently Amended Lanham Act to support its claim of dismissal. This recently amended section of the Lanham Act is commonly referred to as the "intent to use" provision and states as follows:

15 U.S.C. §1051(b)

A person who has a bona fide intention, under circumstances showing good faith of such persons, to use a trademark in commerce may apply to register the trademark under this chapter [15 U.S.C. §1051 et. seq.] on the principal register hereby established: (1) By filing in the Patent and Trademark Office — (A) a written application ... specifying applicant's ... bona fide intention to use the mark in commerce....

15 U.S.C. §1051(c)

A any time during examination of the an application filed under subsection (b) of this section, an applicant who has made use of the mark in commerce may claim the benefits of such use for purposes of this chapter, by amending his or her application to bring it into conformity with the requirements of subsection (a) of this section.

15 U.S.C. §1051(d)(1)

Within six months after the date on which the notice of allowance with respect to a mark is issued under section 1063(b)(2) of this title to an applicant under subsection (b) of this section, the applicant shall file in the Patent and Trademark Office, ... a verified statement that the mark is in use in commerce and specifying the date of the applicant's first use of the mark in commerce.... Subject to examination and acceptance of the statement of use, the mark shall be registered in the Patent and Trademark Office, a certificate of registration shall be issued for those goods or services recited in the statement for use for which the mark is entitled to registration, and notice of registration shall be published in the Official Gazette of the Patent and Trademark Office.

As can be seen, the amended statute, at subsection "(d)", provides that the applicant has six months after its "intent to use" filing to verify actual use in commerce before the mark is actually registered. The applicant also has the option of amending the application to one which verifies actual use as opposed to intended use. The difference between a mere application and actual registration has not been abrogated by the "intent to use" amendments. These new statutory sections merely change the law as to when an "application" for registration may first be filed. There is no change as to when registration, which triggers federal jurisdiction, takes place.

The above provision for the first time allows parties to apply for registration of a mark without ever having used the mark in interstate commerce. As the Senate Judiciary Committee report on the Amended Act recognized, in certain industries it may be impossible to make use of a mark before a business makes a significant financial investment in the goods or services to which the mark will apply. Senate Report No. 100-515, September 15, 1988.

Diadora's point is that despite this markedly new amendment, the provisions of the Lanham Act concerning jurisdiction were not amended and that the grant of original jurisdiction to the federal district court in an infringement action is solely where the infringed mark is the subject of an United States Registration. Diadora relies on 15 U.S.C. §§1114(1)(a), 1116 and 1125(a). These sections provide as follows:

§1114. Remedies; infringement; innocent infringement by printers and publishers.

(1) Any person who shall, without the consent of the registrant—

(a) use in commerce any reproduction, counterfeit, copy, or colorable imitation of a registered mark in connection with the sale, offering for sale, distribution, or advertising of any goods or services or in connection with which such use is likely to cause confusion, or to cause mistake, or to deceive; or

....

§1116. Injunctions; enforcement; notice to Commissioner

The several courts vested with jurisdiction of civil actions arising under this chapter shall have power to grant injunctions, according to the principles of equity and upon such terms as the court may deem reasonable, to prevent the violation of any right of the registrant of a mark registered in the Patent and Trademark Office.

....

§1125. False designations of origin and false descriptions forbidden.

(a) Any person who shall affix, apply or annex, or use in connection with any goods or services, or any container or containers for goods, a false designation of origin, or any false description or representation, including words or other symbols tending falsely to describe or represent the same, and shall causes such goods or services to enter into commerce, and any person who shall with knowledge of the falsity of such designation of origin or description or representation cause or procure the same to be transported or used in commerce or deliver the same to any carrier to be transported or used, shall be liable to a civil action by any person doing business in the locality falsely indicated as that of origin or in the region in which said locality is situated, or by any person who believes that he is or is likely to be damaged by the use of any such false description or representation.

Diadora argues that the records of the Patent and Trademark Office unequivocally show that Fila has no effective registrations. Rather, Fila has only a pending "intent to use" application and that Fila as yet has not used these two marks in United States commerce. Diadora also argues that Congress did not intend for "intent to use" applicants to have access to the federal courts prior to registration. *See* H.R. Rep. No. 1028, 100th Cong., 2d Sess. 4 (1988). The above quoted sections of the statute seem to support this argument.

It is clear from these sections that application and the granting of actual registration are two separate things. It is also clear that the actual registration of the mark will not take place until there is a verification of actual use, or an amendment of the application to allege actual use. There is no statement in that statute to indicate that mere application under this new (intent to use) section will suffice to grant the applicant rights of access to the federal court before the registration is granted.

Traditionally, Section 1338(a) of the Judicial Code conferred upon the district courts jurisdiction of any civil action arising under any Act of Congress relating to patents, copyrights, and trademarks. 28 U.S.C.A. §1338(a) citing Wright, Miller and Cooper, Federal Practice, §3582, p. 298 (2d ed. 1988) This general grant of jurisdiction, however, has been somewhat limited in trademark cases. Wright, Miller and Cooper, Federal Practice, §3582, (2d ed. 1988) at 312. While the Constitution gives Congress express powers to enact patent and copyright laws, Congress must rely on its general powers to regulate interstate and foreign commerce in order to regulate trademarks. *Id.* at 312. Since only trademarks used in interstate commerce may be registered under federal law, and since, in the absence of diversity, the district courts have no jurisdiction over common law trademarks or other trademarks not registered under federal law, an action for trademark infringement must involve interstate commerce for a district court to have jurisdiction. *Id.* at 315.

Further, certain provisions of the Lanham Act were specifically designed to provide protection to trademarks registered elsewhere by foreign nationals, and 15 U.S.C. §1126(d) provides that a trademark registration application filed by a foreign national "shall be accorded the same force and effect as would be accorded to the same application if filed in the United States on the same date in which the application was first filed in (the) foreign country." However, 15 U.S.C. §1126(d)(4) requires that nothing in this subsection (d) shall entitle the owner of a registration granted under this section to sue for acts committed prior to the date on which his mark was registered in this country unless the registration is based on use in commerce.

In the case at bar, in the spring of 1989, Fila conceived, designed, manufactured and patented the new athletic shoe which is the subject of the registrations. Further, on May 24, 1990, Fila filed an intent to use application for registration of its name "Fila 2 Actions 2A" in the United States for footwear pursuant to, 15 U.S.C. 1051(b). Fila's pending application clearly states that they are asserting a claim of priority based upon this foreign application in accordance with 15 U.S.C. 1126(d) as amended with respect to the footwear.

The above statute clearly affords protection to applicants such as Fila and permits qualified foreign applicants who own a registered mark in their country of origin to obtain a United States trademark registration without alleging actual use in United States commerce as long as the United States application is filed within six months of the filing of the foreign application. *See SCM Corp. v. Langis Foods, Ltd.*, 176 U.S. App. D.C. 194, 539 F.2d 196, 199 (1976). However, this statute only affects the when, how and why of filing the application. It does not grant federal jurisdiction independent of that existing for applications based upon actual use or upon actual registration. So that the Statute makes it easier and more convenient for a foreign trademark bolder to file for trademark registration in the U.S., but it does not grant that foreign trademark holder any right to sue in federal court absent actual use in the U.S. or final actual registration in this country. It does not grant the same rights to applicants as exist for actual registrants. Fila is at this point only an applicant. Absent a valid actual registration of its mark, Fila must allege either diversity jurisdiction, or use in interstate commerce. Although Fila has alleged actual registration, this has been challenged by Diadora and I have found that Fila has failed to establish any such registration. The record is also clear that there is no use of the mark in interstate commerce and diversity ju-risdiction, though it appears to be a possibility, has not been alleged or argued by Fila.

Therefore, it is recommended that defendant's motion to dismiss Count I (trademark infringement) and Count II (unfair competition) for lack of subject matter jurisdiction be sustained.

Having recommended the dismissal of both counts of plaintiff's complaint for lack of jurisdiction, it becomes necessary to take up the movant's request for Rule 11 sanctions against plaintiff and its attorneys. I note that Diadora's "brief" in support of this request consists of one paragraph without a single citation to supporting authority of any kind. My discussion will be just as brief. I am bothered by Fila's allegations of ownership of federal registrations for its trademarks when in fact it has been awarded no such registrations. However, the "intent to use" section of the statute is very new, and the precise issue of whether or not its passage was also meant to give an applicant rights of enforcement has not been ruled upon in this Circuit. At least no such case has been cited to me. I therefore do not believe that Fila's attempt to obtain such a ruling or interpretation ought to be sanctioned. I do believe that Fila's attorneys unnecessarily put their client in jeopardy of such a rul-ing by claiming ownership of a registration, rather than asserting rights under this new application procedure. The claim of ownership however, can be viewed as merely a ve-hicle for asserting rights of protection under the new application procedure, and as such, I believe, would not be sanctionable.

CONCLUSION

For the reasons set forth herein, it is recommended that defendant's motions to dis-miss be sustained as to both counts, but defendant's motion for sanctions be denied.

Eastman Kodak Co. v.
Bell & Howell Document Management Products Co.
994 F.2d 1569 (Fed. Cir. 1993)

MICHEL, CIRCUIT JUDGE.

Eastman Kodak Company (Kodak) appeals from the decision of the Trademark Trial and Appeal Board (Board) of the Patent and Trademark Office (PTO) in an intent-to-use application proceeding under the Lanham Act, as amended by the Trademark Law Revision Act of 1988, 15 U.S.C. §§1051–1127 (1992), *Eastman Kodak Co. v. Bell & Howell Document Management Prods. Co.*, Nos. 86,083, 86,093, and 86,101 (TTAB June 8, 1992). In its decision, the Board denied Kodak's motion for summary judgment, grant-ing summary judgment for Bell & Howell Document Management Products Company (B&H) on the issue of descriptiveness, and dismissing the oppositions "without preju-dice to the filing of a petition to cancel the registration issued after a statement of use has been filed," *id.*, slip op. at 6. Because we hold that, in the circumstances of an in-tent-to-use application proceeding, the Board's actions are permissible under the statute, we affirm.

BACKGROUND

On October 12, 1990, B&H filed intent-to-use applications, under 15 U.S.C. §1051(b), to register the numbers "6200," "6800" and "8100" on the Principal Register as trademarks for microfilm reader/printers. After initial examination of the applications, the trademark examining attorney approved the applications for publication in the PTO's Official Gazette.

Section 1051(b) allows an applicant who alleges a bona fide intent to use a mark to file an application seeking registration on the Principal Register. If, upon examination, the mark appears registrable, the PTO publishes it for opposition. 15 U.S.C. §1062(a). If no opposer is successful, the PTO issues a notice of allowance. *Id.* §1063(b)(2). The applicant then has six months in which to file a statement that verifies that the mark is in use in commerce, the date of first use in commerce, the goods and services in connection with the mark are used in commerce, and the manner in which the mark is being used. *Id.* §1051(d)(1). The statement of use is then subject to another examination, in which the PTO considers how the mark is used and, if it is still satisfied that, as used, the mark is registrable, issues a certificate of registration. *Id.*

Kodak, a competitor of B&H in the manufacture and marketing of business equipment products, including microfilm reader/printers, timely filed a notice of opposition to registration of each of the three marks. Kodak alleged that the marks would be used solely as model designators for the reader/printers and therefore would be merely descriptive. Kodak argued that B&H had not shown that the marks had acquired secondary meaning and that, therefore, registration of the marks would be improper. The three opposition proceedings were consolidated before the Board.

B&H moved for summary judgment on the grounds that there were no genuine issues of material fact regarding the alleged mere descriptiveness of its applied-for number marks and, alternatively, that Kodak had no standing to oppose B&H's applications. Kodak filed a cross-motion for summary Judgment. The Board determined that Kodak did have standing to oppose and that conclusion is not contested in this appeal.

On the issue of mere descriptiveness, the Board stated that it "believes that it is possible for a numerical designation, which functions only in part to designate a model or grade, to be inherently distinctive and registrable without a showing of secondary meaning." *Eastman Kodak*, slip op. at 5 (citing *Neapco Inc. v. Dana Corp.*, 1989 TTAB LEXIS 43, 12 U.S.P.Q.2D (BNA) 1746, 1748 (TTAB 1989)). Due to the nature of intent-to-use applications, the number marks at issue had not been used at the time of the opposition proceeding. Accordingly, the Board held that it could not determine whether the numerical designations "are merely descriptive or if they are registrable without a showing of secondary meaning." *Id.* The Board concluded that in such situations, where the descriptiveness issue could not be resolved until use had begun, the opposition should be dismissed without prejudice to the initiation of a cancellation proceeding against the mark if the mark is registered after the statement of use is filed. Consequently, the Board denied Kodak's motion for summary judgment, granted B&H summary judgment on the descriptiveness issue, and dismissed the oppositions without prejudice. As a result, B&H received a notice of allowance.

DISCUSSION

The principal issue in this case is whether the Board's implied creation of a presumption in favor of the applicant for a numerical mark intended for use as more than a model designator is a reasonable interpretation of the Board's authority under the Lanham Act. We hold that it is.

Under the *Chevron* doctrine, established in *Chevron U.S.A. Inc. v. Natural Resources Defense Council, Inc.*, 467 U.S. 837, 81 L. Ed. 2d 694, 104 S. Ct. 2778 (1984), "when a court reviews an [administrative] agency's construction of the statute which it administers, it is confronted with two questions." *Id.* at 842. The first is whether Congress has directly addressed the precise question at issue. If so, then the agency "must give effect to the unambiguously expressed intent of Congress," *id.* at 843, and the court must, of course, review the agency's interpretation accordingly. If, however, "the statute is silent or ambiguous with respect to the specific issue, the question for the court is whether the agency's answer is based on a permissible construction of the statute." *Id.* (emphasis added). In order to uphold the agency's interpretation, the court need not conclude that it was the only permissible construction or even the construction the court would have reached on its own reading of the statute. *Id.* n.11. The agency's interpretation must merely be "reasonable."

In the instant case, the Board's decision to grant B&H summary judgment and dismiss Kodak's opposition without prejudice, necessarily involved the Board's concluding that numerical designators are presumptively not merely descriptive under Lanham Act section 2(e), 15 U.S.C. §1052 (e), when applied for in an intent-to-use application under section 1(b), 15 U.S.C. §1051(b). Section 1(b) sets forth the requirements for filing an intent-to-use application. *See* 15 U.S.C. §1051(b). Section 2(e) precludes registration of a trademark on the Principal Register that, inter alia, "consists of a mark which, ... when used on or in connection with the goods of the applicant is merely descriptive or deceptively misdescriptive of them." *Id.* §1052(e). The statute on its face neither requires nor precludes the Board's interpretation.

Nor does the legislative history of the Trademark Law Revision Act of 1988 speak directly to this issue. The legislative history does demonstrate that Congress intended most marks applied for in an intent-to-use application (intent-to-use mark) to be reviewed for descriptiveness in the initial examination/pre-use stage of the intent-to-use application process. For example, Senate Report 515 states that "the absence of specimens at the time the application is filed will not affect examination on numerous fundamental issues of registrability (that is, descriptiveness, geographic or surname significance, or confusing similarity)." S. Rep. No. 515, 100th Cong., 2d Sess. 32 (1988), reprinted in 1988 U.S.C.C.A.N. 5577, 5595. With respect to the examination of the statement of use, which is filed after a notice of allowance has been issued, the Report states:

> The Patent and Trademark Office's examination of the statement of use will be only for the purpose of determining issues that could not have been fully considered during the initial examination of the application, that is, whether the person filing the statement of use is the applicant, whether the mark as used corresponds to the drawing submitted with the application, whether the goods or services were identified in the application and not subsequently deleted, and whether the mark, as displayed in the specimens or facsimiles, functions as a mark.

Id. at 34, 1988 U.S.C.C.A.N. at 5596 (emphasis added). As the highlighted phrase shows, Congress did intend the PTO to confirm, after the filing of the statement of use, that the intent-to-use mark, as displayed and used, actually "functions as a mark." Indeed, the statute provides: "Subject to examination and acceptance of the statement of use, the mark shall be registered.... Such examination may include an examination of the factors set forth in subsections (a) through (e) of section 1052." 15 U.S.C. §1051(d)(1) (emphasis added). And the legislative history itself emphasized that "this provision [of the statute] permits the [PTO] to raise issues of registrability that might not be evident until the applicant makes available specimens showing the mark as used and/or clarifying the nature of the goods or services involved." H.R. Rep. No. 1028, 100th Cong., 2d Sess. 9 (1988).

Thus, the statute and legislative history provide for the situation where, as here, the question of mere descriptiveness cannot be answered until after use has begun.

Furthermore, it is clear from the legislative history that Congress, for policy reasons, chose to sequence the opposition process before the use of an intent-to-use mark had commenced. *See* S. Rep. No. 515 at 32, 1988 U.S.C.C.A.N. at 5595 ("Subjecting an intent-to-use application to the opposition process before the applicant makes use of its mark is essential if the system is to achieve its goal of reducing uncertainty before the applicant invests in commercial use of the mark."). Accordingly, Congress knew that some issues of registrability could not be decided in opposition proceedings and would therefore have to be addressed in the post-use PTO examination or challenged in a cancellation proceeding after the mark was registered.

Thus, under step one of our inquiry under the Chevron doctrine, the Board's interpretation does not contravene any clear and unambiguous statutory meaning.

II.

We further conclude, under step two of the Chevron doctrine, that the Board's construction is a reasonable interpretation of the Lanham Act.

Kodak argues, however, that the Board's interpretation is unreasonable because it would preclude asserting mere descriptiveness as a basis for denying registration of both word and number marks in intent-to-use applications. This argument is unavailing for several reasons. First, there are words and phrases that, as applied to certain goods, the examining attorney in the initial examination could certainly find to be prima facie merely descriptive. For example, an examining attorney could easily find that the term "reader/printer" applied to the microfilm reader/printers at issue here would be merely descriptive or that the term "slow-cooker" was merely descriptive of a Dutch oven. Furthermore, the examining attorney may also find numbers that are intended for use solely as model designators to be prima facie merely descriptive. *Cf. J.M. Huber Corp. v. Lowery Wellheads, Inc.*, 778 F.2d 1467, 1469, 228 U.S.P.Q. (BNA) 206, 207 (10th Cir. 1985) (common law trademark infringement action in district court).

Second, Kodak's argument must assume that under circumstances such as these, after a notice of allowance is issued, intent-to-use marks will automatically be passed to registration. However, the statute provides for another examination of the mark after the statement of use is filed. 15 U.S.C. §l051(d)(1) ("Subject to examination and acceptance of the statement of use, the mark shall be registered in the Patent and Trademark Office...."). Moreover, the statute contemplates the need, in certain circumstances, for a complete reexamination: "such examination may include an examination of the factors set forth in subsections (a) through (e) of section 1052." *Id.* In addition, the trademark regulations, promulgated by the PTO pursuant to authority granted by statute, *see id.* §1123, provide that "[a] timely filed statement of use which meets the minimum requirements specified in paragraph (e) of this section will be examined in accordance with §§2.61 through 2.69." 37 C.F.R. §2.88(f) (emphasis added). Thus, once the examining attorney establishes that the statement of use has met the minimum requirements set forth in 37 C.F.R. §2.88(e) (the prescribed fee, at least one specimen of use, and a declaration by the applicant that the mark is in use in commerce), the regulation requires that the examining attorney reexamine the mark under the standards of the initial examination (37 C.F.R. §§2.61–2.69).

Furthermore, the Trademark Examination Guide 3-89 (TEG) sets forth a standard for this examination of the statement of use: "The [PTO] will not issue any requirements or refusals concerning matters which could have or should have been raised during initial examination, unless the failure to do so in initial examination constitutes a clear error." TEG §A.9.b. The TEG defines "clear error" as "an error which, if not corrected, would result in issuance of a registration in violation of the Act." *Id.* Thus, the examining attorney's examination standard is for legal error and is not the deferential clearly erroneous standard due, for example, fact-findings of a district court. Accordingly, the examining attorney essentially must make a de novo determination on any issue that would affect the legal correctness of registration.

The descriptiveness of the manner of use of numerical designators, such as the marks challenged in these oppositions, is such an issue. This is so even though the TEG singles out descriptiveness in its discussion of the extent of reexamination of the mark: "The examining attorney may not issue a refusal under Trademark Act Section 2(e)(1), 15 U.S.C. Section 1052(e)(1), unless the refusal is dictated by changed circumstances from the time of initial examination or the failure to issue such a refusal would constitute clear error." *Id.* (emphasis added). In a case such as this, however, as the Board acknowledged, the issue of whether the numerical marks are merely descriptive cannot be resolved until they have been used, because it is the manner in which the numerical marks are used that renders them merely descriptive (solely model designators) or not. Thus, the situation delineated in the TEG of when "evidence that the mark is merely descriptive was available during initial examination," *id.*, is not present here. The use of the mark may constitute "changed circumstances" from the information which the examining attorney could analyze in the initial examination. But even if the circumstances are not considered changed, unless the applicant originally claims use of the mark as purely a model designator, the examining attorney can make a determination of descriptiveness of numerical designators only after the statement of use has been filed. If, upon such further examination, the examining attorney determines that the mark is used in a merely descriptive manner, then the examining attorney must refuse registration because registration of a merely descriptive mark on the Principal Register would constitute "issuance of a registration in violation of the Act," *id.*—the TEG's definition of "clear error," *id.*

There is a serious question of whether the presumption created by the Board in favor of numerical designators would be lawful if the examining attorney, after the statement of use and specimens are filed, were to approve the mark for registration without serious inquiry as to whether, as used, the mark functions as a trademark under the provisions of section 2. Such a de novo determination under section 2 appears to be the only way the practical presumption created by the Board could be sustainable under Chevron. Therefore, any other interpretation of the applicable procedure would be of questionable validity as long as the Board maintains this presumption.

Furthermore, Kodak's contention that the Board's interpretation of the statute "in effect eliminates Lanham Act §2(e) as a basis for rejecting an intent-to-use application," is unavailing because Kodak's analysis would eliminate the use of intent-to-use applications for any numerical mark that could possibly be used as a model designator, in whole or in part. However, the statute does not exclude from intent-to-use applications any type of mark. Because Kodak is incorrect that the Board's decision precludes the use of descriptiveness as a basis for rejecting intent-to-use applications and because Kodak's interpretation would preclude use of intent-to-use applications for such numerical marks in direct contravention of the statute, certainly the Board's failure to adopt such an interpretation is not unreasonable.

Kodak further asserts that the Board's interpretation is unreasonable because it allegedly creates a different standard for registrability for intent-to-use applications from use-based applications with regard to descriptiveness, contrary to statutory design. Kodak is correct that the statute provides for the same substantive requirements to be met for intent-to-use and use-based applications. *Compare* 15 U.S.C.§ 1051(a) (requirements for use-based applications) with *id.* §§1051(b)–(d) (requirements for intent-to-use applications). However, Kodak's argument misunderstands the character of the Board's action. The Board merely adopted a presumption that a numerical mark, which may be used at least in part as a model designator, is not merely descriptive in the absence of evidence of how it is actually used. Once B&H files its statement of use with specimens of actual use, the PTO will refuse registration if the marks are, indeed, used in a merely descriptive fashion, just as the PTO would deny such a mark registration in a use-based application. *See* 37 C.F.R. §2.88(f) ("A timely filed statement of use which meets the minimum requirements specified in paragraph (e) of this section will be examined in accordance with §§2.61 through 2.69."); TEG §A.9.e. ("The same standards applied in use applications in determining whether the specimens support use of the applied-for mark apply to specimens in intent-to-use applications."); *id.* §A.9.f. ("The examining attorney should issue requirements and refusals, as appropriate, based on the examination of the specimens, subject to the same standards which govern the examination of specimens in any other phase of examination."). Thus, the standard that the PTO applies in either case is the same — only the timing of such review is different. Accordingly, the Board's interpretation is not unreasonable under this analysis.

Kodak contends that the difference in timing is sufficiently prejudicial to render the Board's interpretation unreasonable. Kodak argues particularly that the Board's decision relegates such questions of mere descriptiveness to a post-registration cancellation proceeding. Kodak maintains that the delay is prejudicial to it because in a cancellation proceeding, the registration at issue enjoys a presumption of validity. Kodak's argument is misplaced because, although the registration is considered prima facie valid, the challenger's burden of proof in both opposition and cancellation proceedings is a preponderance of the evidence. 2 J. Thomas McCarthy, Mccarthy on Trademarks and Unfair Competition §20.16 (3d ed. 1992).

* * *

Because the Board's interpretation is consistent with the language and purposes of the statute, we hold that it is reasonable.

III.

Kodak argues that the Board erred in denying it summary judgment because Kodak believes that B&H's intent-to-use marks will be used as model designators, rendering them merely descriptive and therefore not registrable without a showing of secondary meaning. Kodak further asserts that it submitted evidence to the Board supporting this contention. Even if we assume that Kodak's evidence proves that B&H's numerical marks will be used as model designators, this conclusion is not dispositive of the descriptiveness issue as Kodak claims. In order for B&H's marks to be found merely descriptive, they must be used solely as model designators and not in any source-indicating function. As part of its intent-to-use application, B&H necessarily must have asserted a bona fide intent to use each number as a trademark, *see* 15 U.S.C. §1051(b)(1), and not, therefore, solely as model designators. And prevailing Board authority establishes that "depending upon the nature and manner of use, it is possible for an alphanumeric designation, which functions only in part to designate model or grade, to be inherently distinctive, and hence not require a showing of secondary meaning in order to be protected as a trademark." *Neapco*, 12 U.S.P.Q.2D (BNA) at 1748 (citing *In re Clairol Inc.*, 59 C.C.P.A. 918, 457 F.2d

509, 510, 173 U.S.P.Q. (BNA) 355, 356 (CCPA 1972)) (emphasis added). Thus, even if Kodak is correct that the intent-to-use marks will be used as model designators, the law does not support Kodak's ultimate conclusion that therefore the marks will necessarily be merely descriptive. Indeed, the PTO has already granted B&H registration of one numerical (7500) and one alphanumeric mark (4000R), used in connection with microfilm reader/printers, without proof of secondary meaning. *Eastman Kodak*, slip op. at 4.

CONCLUSION

Based on the foregoing, the Board's decision is

AFFIRMED.

Notes

1. Return to the initial question asked at the beginning of this subchapter: Is it true that absolutely no rights are created when the Notice of Allowance issues? If your answer is that some rights seem to be created, what is the significance of this?

2. When do ITU rights vest?

3. *Eastman Kodak Co. v. Bell & Howell Document Mgmt. Prods. Co.*, *supra*, may be the broadest application of the ITU system. There the court held that marks that lacked secondary meaning at the time an ITU application was filed were not per se barred because, once the marks were used, they may obtain secondary meaning. That is, if one attempts to register a use-based mark that is descriptive and lacks sufficient secondary meaning, it will be denied registration. However, if one makes that same application based on an ITU, the mere fact that it lacks secondary meaning will not in and of itself be grounds for refusal to grant the applicant a Notice of Allowance.

It appears that Judge Michel in *Kodak* adopts a notion of secondary meaning in the making that has been thoroughly rejected for use-based marks. How can we rationalize rejecting secondary meaning in the making for use-based marks while we not only recognize it but strongly encourage applicants to rely on it for ITU marks?

The secondary meaning in the making doctrine recognized that, when a defendant purposefully and willfully trades off the goodwill of a trademark owner, that defendant's conduct should not be condoned merely because the plaintiff's mark has not yet become recognized in the minds of the consumer as indicating source or origin. *Metra Kane Imps., Ltd. v. Federated Dept. Stores, Inc.*, 625 F. Supp. 313, 316 (S.D.N.Y. 1985). This doctrine was first articulated by Handler & Pickett as follows:

> [Although descriptive terms must possess secondary meaning to be protected,] we would make an exception, however, where defendant willfully appropriates the brand when it is on the verge of attaining a secondary meaning, in which case we think the mark should be protected.... Piracy should no more be tolerated in the earlier stages of the development of good will than in the later.

Milton Handler & Charles Pickett, *Trade-Marks and Trade Name—An Analysis and Synthesis: II*, 30 Colum. L. Rev. 759, 767 (1930).

Although some commentators may have once supported this rationale, today it is difficult to find any that do. After all, the justification of trademark protection only arises when a mark comes to indicate origin. If the plaintiff cannot show that its mark has risen to that level, it owns nothing in the abstract that warrants protection. For this reason, the Second Circuit has rather definitively renounced the secondary meaning in the making doctrine. *Laureyssens v. Idea Group, Inc.*, 964 F.2d 131, 139 (2nd Cir. 1992).

After all, "the doctrine, if taken literally, is inimical to the purpose of the secondary meaning requirement." RESTATEMENT (THIRD) OF UNFAIR COMPETITION §13 Comment (e) (1995). Secondary meaning is required to ensure that the trademark owner possesses some right worth protecting.

That all being said, does Judge Michel resurrect the secondary meaning in the making doctrine for ITU marks? If so, what is the significance of that?

4. In Civil Law jurisdictions, it is possible to "bank" a trademark. That is, one registers a mark in use in another country and simply waits until that trademark claimant uses that mark in the banked country. This is possible because of the territoriality principle discussed above and because trademark rights in Civil Law countries subsist upon registration, not upon use. Trademark banking is not allowed in the United States. *Custom Vehicles, Inc. v. Forest River, Inc.*, 476 F.3d 481 (7th Cir. 2007).

Chapter VII

Trademark Registration

A. Registration Process

The Patent and Trademark Office is charged with receiving, reviewing, and ultimately registering all federal trademarks in the United States. Each state in the United States also maintains trademark registration services; however, these state services do not engage in any review or analysis of "registrability." These state services only check to determine if an identical trademark is already registered. If not, the state registration issues.

The federal system is different. The federal system, governed by the Lanham Act, allows for review and analysis of trademark applications. This analysis is conducted by Trademark Examiners, employees of the PTO. Trademark Examiners, unlike Patent Examiners, are all attorneys. Unlike other countries, like Japan, where Examiners are some of the most experienced employees of the relevant patent office, in the United States, Trademark Examiners are sometimes the least experienced. To be sure, Examiners go through intensive training and in the first years of being on the job their work is reviewed by an experienced Examiner; however, the position of Trademark Examiner is an entry level job with the United States PTO.

The PTO claims that its relationship with applicants is not a contentious one. The PTO's policy is to facilitate the registration of trademarks. The PTO's policy is to encourage registration of trademarks because the consumers and competitors alike benefit from the registration of marks.

The PTO's work load changes with the economy: a more robust economy means there will be more trademark applications; a recession means fewer. Table 7.1 below shows clearly how the number of applications for registration tracks the strength of the United States economy.

The PTO has long claimed that they follow a 3/13 policy. That is, within three months of the initial application, the applicant should receive notice that its trademark application was received and assigned a serial number. This serial number is critical because that is the way an applicant can track its application through the process.

Within 13 months of the application date, the PTO's policy is to complete initial review of the application and either inform the applicant in the form of an "Office Action" that the application is insufficient, inappropriate, or inconsistent with the Lanham Act, or issue the application to be published for opposition.

Table 7.1   Application and Registration Statistics

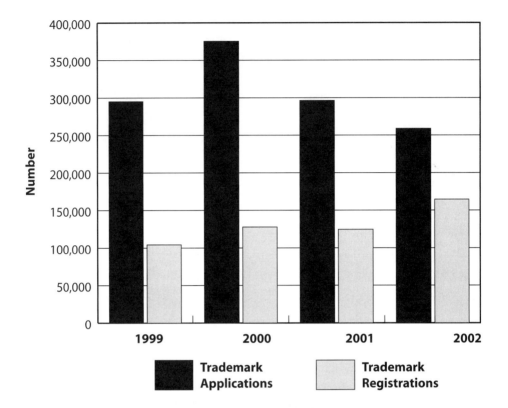

Applicants are allowed six months to respond to Office Actions. Therefore, it is not un-common for the entire process to take two years or more.

Once the trademark application is published for opposition, the PTO's work is complete. The mark is published in the Official Gazette. Third parties who feel they will be harmed if the registration issues can oppose this application. Oppositions are brought before the Trademark Trial and Appeal Board (TTAB).

If either the opposition is unsuccessful or there is no opposition, three months after the mark is published, a trademark registration issues. This trademark registration must be maintained or it will be cancelled by the PTO. During the fifth anniversary year of registration, a Section 8 Affidavit must be filed with the PTO (with the appropriate fee) claiming that the Registrant has continuously used the mark in commerce for those five years and intends to continue to do so. Any time after the fifth anniversary of registration (most Registrants do this at the same time as their Section 8 Affidavit filing), the Registrant may also file a Section 15 Affidavit claiming that the mark has become "incontestable." *See* Chapter VIII, *infra*.

Section 8 Affidavits now have to be also filed in the 9th year, the 19th year, the 29th year, etc. for as long as the mark is used. Section 9 Affidavits (applications to renew the mark) can be filed every ten years.

Failure to file either a Section 8 Affidavit in a timely fashion or failure to apply to renew a registration every 10 years will result in the cancellation of the trademark registration.

Table 7.2 depicts the flow of the application process for use-based registration. Table 7.3 shows the same process for ITU registration.

Table 7.2   Use-Based Trademark Application Process

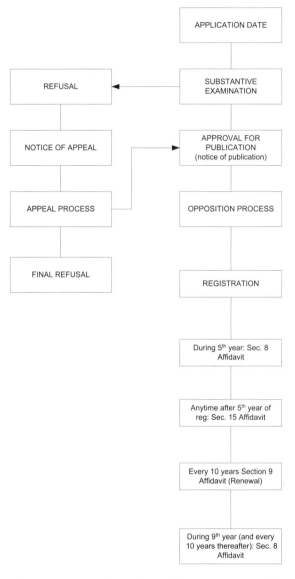

Effective November 2, 2003, trademark applicants can now take advantage of the Madrid Protocol in the United States. *See infra* Chapter XIII for a detailed description of the policy ramifications of the Madrid Protocol.

Although often called an "international" system of trademark registration, it is important to understand that the international registration obtained under the Protocol is not effective without specific examination in each designated country as demonstrated in Table 7.4. That is, once the international registration is obtained, the application is then forwarded to each designated country where it undergoes examination anew. Some countries, such as France, appear to give great weight to the international registration and do not appear to engage in a "re-examination" of the application. Other countries, such as the United States, appear to give the international registration almost no deference.

Table 7.3   Intent-to-Use Based Trademark Application Process

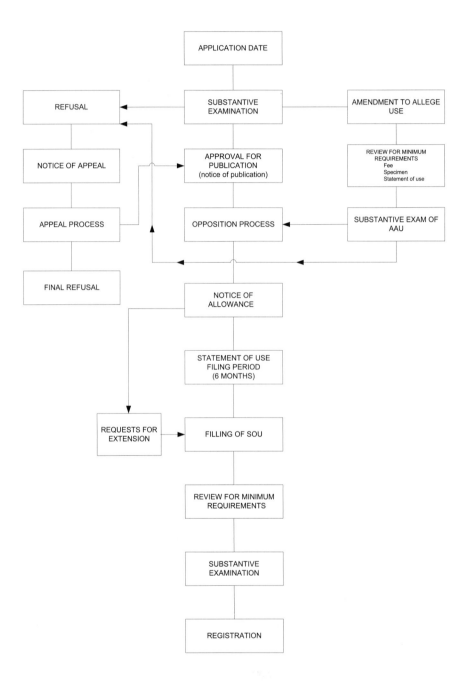

B. Advantages of Registration

The United States is a common law jurisdiction where all trademark rights are based upon use, not upon registration. Registration is not a prerequisite for bringing an infringement cause of action. *Two Pesos, Inc. v. Taco Cabana, Inc.*, 505 U.S. 763, 768 (1992).

Table 7.4 Application Process Under the Madrid Protocol

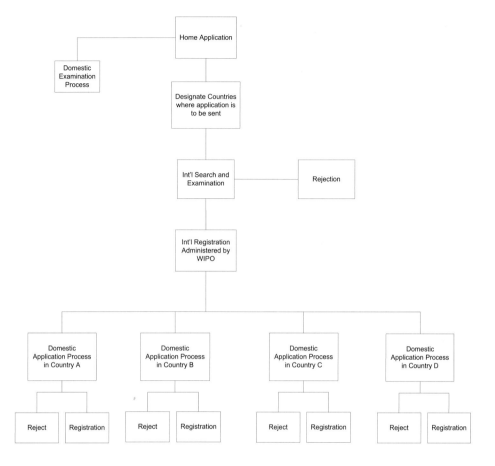

Nevertheless, there are still numerous reasons why a rational user of trademarks would elect, in addition to merely using the mark, to also seek federal registration for that mark. Some of these reasons include the following.

1. **Notice.** Perhaps one of the most significant reasons to register a trademark regards notice of rights. Section 22 (15 U.S.C. §1072) provides for constructive notice of claimed rights under the Lanham Act. That is, once a trademark is registered, all would-be infringers are charged with knowledge of the registration and the benefits derived thereunder. In litigation, this could have a significant impact on the outcome of any given case.

2. **Deterrence.** Closely related to the notice function, trademark registration owners can claim use of the (r) symbol on goods or services. Although not precisely documented as such, it is thought that use of the (r) symbol provides some deterrence to infringers.

3. **National protection.** Once a trademark is registered, the owner of that registration can claim national priority. If this registration is based on an intent to use a mark, that priority date reverts back to the actual application date of the registration.

4. **Incontestability.** Once a registered trademark is used for five consecutive years, the owner of that registration can claim the registration has become "incon-

testable" under Section 15 of the Lanham Act. As will be seen, this, too, can provide many positive consequences for the plaintiff/trademark registration owner.

5. **Cybersquatting.** It is far easier to establish a bona fide commercial interest in a registered trademark for purposes of both the Uniform Dispute Resolution Policy (governing the transfer of domain names) and the Anti-cybersquatting Consumer Protection Act (governing the same but in an Article III-style court of law). Bringing a cause of action under either of these provisions based on a registered trademark substantially minimizes the burden of proving the complainant or plaintiff had a commercial interest in the mark. Furthermore, if a trademark is registered, it makes it exceedingly difficult (especially under the UDRP) to make the requisite showing that subsequently registering that trademark as a domain name was done in bad faith.

6. **Evidentiary advantages.** Section 33(b) (15 U.S.C. §1115) provides, in relevant part, as follows:

    To the extent that the right to use the registered mark has become incontestable…, the registration shall be *conclusive evidence* of the validity of the registered mark and of the registration of the mark, of the registrant's ownership of the mark, and of the registrant's exclusive right to use the registered mark in commerce….

    (Emphasis added.) That is, incontestable status provides the owner with "conclusive evidence" of the validity of the mark and other advantages. This, too, in a close call in a litigation setting has the potential of dictating outcomes.

7. There are many other advantages to registration, including barring infringing goods by evoking part of Customs law to certain advantages regarding counterfeiting. Although significant in their own right, neither of these topics plays a significant role in these materials.

C. Statutory Bars to Registration

1. Section 2(a): Scandalous Marks

15 U.S.C. §1052, Lanham Act §2

No trademark by which the goods of the applicant may be distinguished from the goods of others shall be refused registration on the principal register on account of its nature unless it—

(a) Consists of or comprises immoral, deceptive, or scandalous matter; or matter which may disparage or falsely suggest a connection with persons, living or dead, institutions, beliefs, or national symbols, or bring them into contempt, or disrepute….

In re Old Glory Condom Corp.
26 U.S.P.Q.2d 1216 (TTAB 1993)

SAMS, MEMBER

Old Glory Condom Corp. has appealed from the examining attorney's final refusal to register its mark "OLD GLORY CONDOM CORP" (and design), as shown below, for "prophylactics (condoms)." The design feature of applicant's mark consists of a pictorial representation of a condom decorated with stars and stripes in a manner to suggest the American flag.

The drawing of the mark is lined for the colors red and blue.

OLD GLORY CONDOM CORP.

The examining attorney refused registration, under section 2(a) of the Trademark act, on the grounds that the mark consists of immoral or scandalous matter. In particular, the examining attorney found that the use of the American flag as part of applicant's mark for condoms was scandalous because it was likely to offend "a substantial composite of the general public."

Applicant's Use of Its Mark

The record on appeal shows that applicant corporation was formed after Jay Kritchley, applicant's president, participated in an exhibition at the List Visual Arts Center of the Massachusetts Institute of Technology (M.I.T.) in Cambridge, Massachusetts. The exhibition, held in October 1989, was entitled "Trouble in Paradise" and focused on artists' responses to contemporary social and political issues. Mr. Kritchley's exhibit was an adaptation of the symbols of American patriotism to focus attention on the AIDS epidemic and, in particular, to emphasize that Americans have a patriotic duty to fight the AIDS epidemic and other sexually transmitted diseases. Applicant states that, when the exhibition received widespread critical acclaim, Mr. Kritchley decided to turn his theoretical concepts into a corporate enterprise, which now markets condoms under the mark applicant is seeking to register.

While the American flag design appears as a feature of applicant's trademark for condoms, the flag design is not applied to the condoms themselves. Applicant states that on the back of each condom package is the "Old Glory Pledge":

> We believe it is patriotic to protect and save lives. We offer only the highest quality condoms. Join us in promoting safer sex. Help eliminate AIDS. A portion of Old Glory profits will be donated to AIDS related services.

The Refusal of Registration

In refusing registration of applicant's mark, the examining attorney argues that a majority of the American public would be offended by the use of American flag imagery to promote products associated with sexual activity. She argues that the flag is a sacrosanct symbol whose association with condoms would necessarily give offense.

Applicant characterizes the issue on appeal as one of first impression: whether a trademark may be refused registration as scandalous solely on the basis of its political content. Applicant argues that the Patent and Trademark Office has registered more than a thousand marks for condoms, many of them sexually suggestive and many that might be considered vulgar. Applicant goes on to argue that the Patent and Trademark Office has registered more than one thousand marks in which an image of the American flag appears. Applicant emphasizes that its mark is expressly designed not to offend but to redefine patriotism to include the fight against sexually-transmitted diseases, including AIDS. Applicant points to its exhibit at M.I.T., which employed a frank sense of humor about both condoms and patriotism to encourage people to overcome an aversion to the use of condoms.

In this record, the only direct evidence of the impact of applicant's mark on the public is that described by applicant in its response to the first office action in this case. Applicant alluded to a "marketing study commissioned by applicant from the Simmons College Graduate School of Management." About this study, applicant noted:

> The study, which was made completely independent of applicant, which took three months to complete, and which was undertaken by Simmons College without cost to applicant (due to the College's recognition of the pressing social need to encourage the use of condoms), found that there was a negative public reaction of under 5% of those polled to applicant's use of the subject mark with regard to condoms. [emphasis in original]

We do not know the details of the survey, because applicant did not submit a copy for the record (nor, indeed, did applicant mention the survey in its appeal brief). On the other hand, the examining attorney did not request that applicant submit a copy of the survey, nor did she challenge applicant's summary of the survey results.

"Scandalous" Marks under Section 2(a)

There is relatively little published precedent to guide us in deciding whether a mark is "scandalous" within the meaning of Section 2(a) of the Trademark Act. The examining attorney places principal reliance on *In re McGinley*, 211 U.S.P.Q. 668 (CCPA 1981), the most recent decision in which the Board's reviewing court has interpreted the section of the Trademark Act here at issue. In *McGinley*, the Court was asked to decide the registrability of a mark comprising a photograph of a man and woman kissing and embracing in a manner appearing to expose the man's genitalia. In deciding whether the mark presented for registration was "scandalous" under Section 2(a), the Court first noted that whether a mark is scandalous is to be determined from the standpoint of a substantial composite of the general public. *Id.*, 211 U.S.P.Q. at 673, citing *In re Riverbank Canning Co.*, 95 F.2d 327, 37 U.S.P.Q. 268, 270 (CCPA 1938). To define "scandalous," under Section 2(a), the Court looked to the "ordinary and common meaning" of the term, which meaning could be established, according to the Court, by reference to Court and Board decisions and to dictionary definitions. The Court went on to cite dictionary definitions of "scandalous" as "shocking to the sense of … propriety," "[that which gives] offense to the conscience or moral feelings" and "giving offense to the conscience or moral feelings; exciting reprobation, calling out condemnation … disgraceful to reputation.…" [Webster's New International Dictionary (2d ed. 1942)] and "shocking to the sense of truth, decency, or propriety; disgraceful, offensive; disreputable.…" [Funk & Wagnalls New Standard Dictionary (1945)]. In an attempt to put these provisions of Section 2(a) in context, the Court expressed its opinion that this section of the Trademark Act represents not "... an attempt to legislate morality, but, rather a judgment by the Congress that such marks not occupy the time, services, and use of funds of the federal government." Having set forth its opinion as to the underpinnings of this portion of Section 2(a) of the Trademark Act, the Court (one judge dissenting) concluded that the mark for which registration was sought (i.e., the pictorial representation of an embracing nude couple with exposed male genitalia) was scandalous and, therefore, unregistrable.

In the more than ten years since the *McGinley* decision, this Board has decided only four cases involving the issue of whether marks were "scandalous" under Section 2(a). The first of these cases, *In re Tinseltown, Inc.*, 212 U.S.P.Q. 863 (TTAB 1981), involved the mark "BULLSHIT" for attache cases, handbags, purses, belts, and wallets. The Board allowed that the registrability of a profane word was a case of first impression and found that "BULLSHIT," the profane word at issue, was scandalous, within the meaning of Section 2(a), and, therefore, unregistrable. In finding the mark unregistrable, the Board relied on the McGinley case and, in particular, two of the dictionary definitions of "scandalous" cited by the Court in that case: "[g]iving offense to the conscience or moral feelings ..." and "shocking to the sense of ... decency or propriety...."

In re Hershey, 6 U.S.P.Q.2d 1470 (TTAB 1988) involved the mark "BIG PECKER BRAND" for T-shirts. The mark had been refused registration, as scandalous, on the grounds that "pecker" was a vulgar expression for "penis" and that the mark as a whole, therefore, was offensive or shocking to a substantial composite of the general public. The Board reversed the refusal of registration, finding the evidence unpersuasive to demonstrate the vulgarity of the word "pecker" and noted that the specimens of record were labels showing a design of a bird in conjunction with the word mark "BIG PECKER BRAND." The Board concluded that, in view of the context of the mark's use, the mark neither offended morality nor raised a scandal.

In *Greyhound Corp. v. Both Worlds Inc.*, 6 U.S.P.Q.2d 1635 (TTAB 1988), the Board determined that a design consisting of the silhouette of a defecating dog, as a mark for polo shirts and T-shirts, was scandalous. Citing the definitions of "scandalous" relied on by the Court in McGinley and by the Board in Tinseltown, the Board found applicant's design mark "vulgar", and, therefore, scandalous. The Board noted in particular the depiction of feces as part of the mark.

The most recent case in which the Board considered whether a mark was "scandalous under Section 2(a) was *In re In Over Our Heads Inc.*, 16 U.S.P.Q.2d 1653 (TTAB 1990). In that case, the mark involved was "MOONIES" (and a design feature) for dolls. The particular dolls to which the mark was applied were novelty items which, upon the squeezing of an attached collapsible bulb, dropped their pants to reveal buttocks (an action known as "mooning"). The examining attorney had contended that the mark was lacking in taste and was an affront to an organized religious group, namely, the Unification Church, whose members were sometimes referred to as "Moonies." The Board reversed the refusal of registration, finding that purchasers were more likely to view the mark as an allusion to "mooning" than as a reference to members of the Unification Church. In discussing the Section 2(a) issue presented, the Board noted that the standards for determining whether a mark is scandalous are somewhat vague and the determination of the issue necessarily highly subjective. In view of the subjective nature of the decision, the Board determined that any doubts about whether a mark was scandalous should be resolved in favor of allowing the mark to be published, to permit any party who believes it would be damaged by registration of the mark to file an opposition to registration.

Registrability of Applicant's Mark

Applicant's argument for reversing the refusal to register in this case is essentially two-fold. First, applicant argues that, when viewed in the light of the legal precedent of the Board and the Board's reviewing court, its mark is not scandalous. Second, applicant makes a Constitutional argument that the Board is obligated to apply the provisions of Section 2(a) in a Constitutional manner and that denial of the benefits of registration to applicant's mark because of its political content, even assuming (we presume) the political content of the mark would give offense, would violate the First and Fifth Amendments to the Constitution. Because we are in agreement with applicant's first line of argument, we need not consider the second line of argument in order to allow registration of the mark in this case.

Taking as our starting point the definitions of "scandalous" to which the Board has in previous cases looked for assistance in applying Section 2(a), we have considered whether "OLD GLORY CONDOM CORP" (and flag design) can be characterized as "[g]iving offense to the conscience or moral feelings" or "shocking to the sense of decency or propriety." If any pattern can be discerned from the most recent cases, previously discussed, where the Board or its reviewing court found marks to be scandalous [viz., a mark comprising a photograph of a man and woman kissing and embracing in a manner appearing to expose the man's genitalia, for newsletters (*McGinley, supra*), "BULLSHIT," for handbags, wallets, etc. (*Tinseltown, supra*), and the design of a defecating dog, for shirts (*Greyhound Corp. v. Both Worlds Inc., supra*)], that pattern seems to describe marks that convey, in words or in pictures, vulgar imagery.

As applicant has asserted (and as the examining attorney seems to concede), this Office has registered many trademarks and service marks that include imagery of the American flag. While we realize that there may be citizens of this country who disapprove of any commercial use of the American flag or American flag imagery, such uses have been sufficiently common that there can be no justification for refusing registration of applicant's mark simply on the basis of the presence in that mark of flag imagery. Nor do we find any evidence in this case that convinces us that a mark containing a pictorial representation of a condom should, simply because of that fact, be refused registration as scandalous. The particular pictorial presentation featured in applicant's composite mark was not found by the examining attorney to be vulgar, nor do we find it so. The examining attorney's objection to applicant's mark seems to be directed to the mark's linking of flag imagery and a pictorial representation of a condom, each of which, in itself, she apparently finds unobjectionable. Precisely why this combination of images is scandalous the examining attorney fails to articulate.

Moreover, the examining attorney offers very little evidence in support of her refusal of registration in this case. Her position is supported mainly by an expression of opinion that a substantial composite of the public would be offended by applicant's mark, which opinion is, in turn, supported by her opinion that the American flag is a "sacrosanct" symbol. To bolster the latter opinion, she alluded to an unsuccessful proposed amendment to the U.S. Constitution to prohibit flag burning and to a comment by Chief Justice Rehnquist in his dissent in *Texas v. Johnson*, 491 U.S. 397, 428 (1989) that many Americans have an "almost mystical reverence" for the American flag. The examining attorney also made of record printouts, from Mead Data's NEXIS data base, of several news stories referring to a video public service announcement promoting voter registration. The video in question showed rock star Madonna, scantily clad and wrapped in an American flag. The news stories made mention of the disapproval in some quarters of the video's use of the American flag. We are not willing, based solely on the examining attorney's opinion, the evidence of the reaction to the Madonna video, and the unsuccessful effort to amend the U.S. Constitution to prohibit the burning of the flag, to presume that the flag imagery of applicant's mark would give offense in a manner that must be deemed "scandalous" under Section 2(a).

Moreover, whether applicant's mark would be likely to offend must be judged not in isolation but in the entire context of the mark's use. The Board has in other cases looked to the entire context of the use in determining whether the mark in question was scandalous. *See* In re Hershey, *supra* ["BIG PECKER BRAND" applied to T-shirts with labels bearing both the trademark and the design of a bird]; *In re Leo Quan Inc.*, 200 U.S.P.Q. 370 (TTAB 1978) ["BADASS" for bridges for stringed musical instruments found not scandalous, the Board noting that the mark was an acronym derived from the words "Bettencourt Acoustically Designed Audio Sound Systems"]. Here, applicant markets its condoms in packaging which emphasizes applicant's commitment to the sale of high quality condoms as a means of promoting safer sex and eliminating AIDS and its belief that the use of condoms is a patriotic act. Although we know that not everyone would share applicant's view that the use of condoms is a patriotic act, the seriousness of purpose surrounding the use of applicant's mark — a seriousness of purpose made manifest to purchasers on the packaging for applicant's goods — is a factor to be taken into account in assessing whether the mark is offensive or shocking. When we consider that factor, along with the others we have discussed, we find that applicant's mark can in no way be considered "scandalous" under Section 2(a).

Decision: The refusal to register is reversed.

Pro-Football, Inc. v. Harjo

284 F.Supp. 2d 96 (D.D.C. 2003)

KOLLAR-KOTELLY, UNITED STATES DISTRICT JUDGE

* * *

5. The TTAB's Finding of Disparagement

The Court concludes that the TTAB's finding that the marks at issue [Redskins as used on or in connection with a professional football team] "may disparage" Native Americans is unsupported by substantial evidence, is logically flawed, and fails to apply the correct legal standard to its own findings of fact. With no material facts in dispute, the Court finds that Defendants' motion for summary judgment must be denied, and that Pro-Football's motion must be granted as to the Counts I and II of the Complaint. The Court will first turn to the TTAB's discussion of the "meaning of the matter in question," and then will focus on the TTAB's decision that the matter "may disparage" Native Americans.[1]

---

1. It is important to point out that the TTAB rejected the Defendants' argument that the use of Native American references or imagery by non-Native Americans is *per se* disparaging to Native Americans. Harjo II, 50 U.S.P.Q.2d at 1743. This decision has not been appealed. In addition, because the evidence below tended to revolve exclusively around the disparaging nature of the term "redksin(s)," there was "very little evidence or argument" related to the portrait of a Native American or the Native American spear in Pro-Football's trademarks. *Id.* Given this lack of evidence, the TTAB concluded that the Defendants' had not established that the picture of the Native American and the Native American spear "may disparage" Native Americans. *Id.* This finding has also not been appealed

a. Meaning of the Matter In Question

The Court concludes that substantial evidence exists in the record to support the TTAB's finding that "when considered in relation to the other matter comprising at least two of the subject marks and as used in connection with [Pro-Football]'s services, 'Redskins' clearly both refers to respondent's professional football team and carries the allusion to Native Americans inherent in the original definition of that word." *Id.* at 1742 (noting that this conclusion is equally applicable to the time periods encompassing 1967, 1974, 1978 and 1990, as well as to the present time"). The TTAB began its analysis by focusing on the word "redskin(s)" as it appears in each of the six challenged trademarks. *Id.* at 1741. The TTAB observed that one denotive meaning of the word was a Native American person. *Id.* The TTAB observed that dictionary definitions and articles that refer to the word "redskin(s)" in connection with Native Americans indicate the term has remained a denotive term for Native Americans from the 1960's to the present. *Id.; see also id.* n.109. The TTAB, however, also agreed with Pro-Football that "there is a substantial amount of evidence in the record establishing that, since at least the 1960's and continuing to the present, the term 'Redskins' has been used widely in print and other media to identify [Pro-Football's] professional football team and its entertainment services." *Id.* at 1741.

Nevertheless, the TTAB observed that, in focusing on the manner in which Pro-Football's trademarks were actually used in the marketplace, the Washington Redskins football club used Native American imagery throughout its logos and team imagery. *Id.* at 1741–42. The TTAB found that although the record disclosed that the vast majority of the use of the term "redskin(s)" in the media and press since the 1960's refers to the Washington football club, "it would be both factually incomplete and disingenuous to ignore the substantial evidence of Native American imagery used by [Pro-Football], as well as by [Pro-Football's] fans, in connection with [Pro-Football's] football team and its entertainment services." *Id.* at 1742. Indeed, the TTAB noted that two of the registered marks include a portrait of the profile of a Native American and what presumably is a Native American spear. *Id.* Given this situation the TTAB remarked:

> This is not a case where, through usage, the word "redskin(s)" has lost its meaning, in the field of professional football, as a reference to Native Americans in favor of an entirely independent meaning as the name of a professional football team. Rather, when considered in relation to the other matter comprising at least two of the subject marks and as used in connection with respondent's services, "Redskins" clearly both refers to respondent's professional football team and carries the allusion to Native Americans inherent in the original definition of that word.

Id. Based on the record before the TTAB, the Court finds that this conclusion is supported by substantial evidence.

b. Whether the Matter in Question May Disparage Native Americans

The Court determines that the TTAB's conclusion that the six trademarks may disparage Native Americans is not supported by substantial evidence. The Board began by correctly articulating the question before it as "whether the word 'redskin(s)' may be disparaging of and to Native Americans, as that word appears in the marks in the subject registrations, in connection with the identified services, and during the relevant time periods." *Id.* at 1743. In answering this question and rendering its opinion, the Board made a number of initial statements that are problematic.

In rendering its decision, the TTAB stated that "we consider the broad range of evidence in this record as relevant to this question either *directly* or by inference." *Id.* (emphasis added). The difficulty with this statement is transparent. Even a cursory review of the TTAB's findings of fact reveals that there is no *direct* evidence in the findings that answers the legal question posed by the TTAB. None of the findings of fact made by the TTAB tend to prove or disprove that the marks at issue "may disparage" Native Americans, during the relevant time frame, especially when used in the context of Pro-Football's entertainment services. For example, none of the findings of fact related to the linguistic testimony tended to directly prove that the marks at issue "may disparage" Native Americans as used in connection with Pro-Football's football club during the relevant times at issue. Indeed, the TTAB said it was unable to resolve the dispute between the linguists related to the connotation of the word "redskin(s)" as used in Pro-Football's team name. *Id.* at 1731. Moreover, even if the Court considers all of the findings of fact related to the survey evidence, the survey is not directly dispositive of the legal question before the TTAB because it asked participants for views about the word "redskin(s)" as a reference for Native Americans in 1996. The survey did not test the participants' view of the term "redskin(s)" in the context of Pro-Football's services and it did not measure the attitudes of the survey participants as they were held during the relevant time periods. While the TTAB noted that such information would have been "extremely relevant," *id.* at 1743, the fact remains that the TTAB did not have what would be considered "direct" or circumstantial evidence before it, or evidence from which it could draw reasonable inferences for such a conclusion.

Second, in finding that the trademarks "may disparage" Native Americans, the TTAB stated that "no single item of evidence or testimony alone brings us to this conclusion; rather, we reach our conclusion *based on the cumulative effect of the entire record.*" *Id.* at 1743 (emphasis added). The troubling aspect of this statement is that the Board made findings of fact in only two very specific areas; and many of these findings of fact simply summarized undisputed testimony. As a result, many of the TTAB's findings of fact never involved weighing conflicting evidence or addressing criticisms of some of the evidence. The TTAB compounded this problem by declining to make specific findings of fact in key areas. The result of this approach is that the TTAB reached its decision to cancel the trademarks inferentially, by piecing together bits of limited, undisputed evidence from the record. Even though the Court defers to the TTAB's inferences under the rubric of a substantial evidence review, the TTAB's approach is flawed because as will be demonstrated *infra*, the inferences are predicated on assumptions that are not contained anywhere in the record.

As the Court explains *infra*, the decision of the TTAB cannot withstand even the deferential level of judicial scrutiny provided by the substantial evidence test. While a *de novo* test to the TTAB's findings of fact might have led to an immediate reversal, due to the paucity of actual findings of fact, the substantial evidence test counsels otherwise and requires that the Court not substitute its judgment for that of the TTAB. Instead, the Court reviews point-by-point whether "substantial evidence" supports the TTAB's disparagement finding.

(1) Equating the Views of the General Public with Those of Native Americans

In rendering its decision, the TTAB stated that "we have considered the perceptions of both the general public and Native Americans to be probative [to determining if the marks at issue 'may disparage']." *Id.* at 1743. The TTAB went on to state:

> For example, we have found that the evidence supports the conclusion that a substantial composite of the general public finds the word "redskin(s)" to be a derogatory term of reference for Native Americans. *Thus, in the absence of evidence to the contrary, it is reasonable to infer that a substantial composite of Na-*

tive Americans would similarly perceive the word. This is consistent with the testimony of the petitioners.

Id. at 1743–44 (emphasis added). The problem with this approach is manifest.

First, and most importantly, the Ross survey indicates that the views of the general populace and the Native American population are distinct. *Harjo II,* 50 U.S.P.Q.2d at 1733 (36.6% of Native Americans view the term "redskin" offensive as a term of reference for Native Americans, compared to 46.2% for the general population). Thus, the evidence before the TTAB indicated that the views of the Native Americans on this issue were not congruent with that of the population as a whole.

Second, the legal question before the TTAB only pertained to whether a "substantial composite" of Native Americans would conclude that the term "redskin(s)" may disparage. As the Board itself stated only five pages earlier in its opinion, "it is only logical that, in deciding whether the matter may be disparaging, *we look, not to American society as a whole,* as determined by a substantial composite of the general population, but to the views of the referenced group." *Id.* at 1739 (emphasis added); *id.* (quoting *Hines,* 31 U.S.P.Q.2d at 1688) ("'In determining whether or not a mark is disparaging, *the perceptions of the general public are irrelevant.*'") (emphasis added). By concluding that the views of the general public were probative, the TTAB erred. By focusing on the general public and inferring that the Native Americans would simply agree with those views, the TTAB made a decision unsupported by substantial evidence.

Third, outside the testimony of the seven Native Americans who brought suit, the TTAB cited no independent or additional evidence to support its conclusion. Defendants clearly do not constitute a "substantial composite" of Native Americans. From this testimony it was impossible for the Board to reasonably corroborate its decision to equate the views of the American public with the views of the Native American population.

Fourth, the TTAB reached this conclusion only because there was an "absence of evidence to the contrary," *Harjo II,* 50 U.S.P.Q.2d at 1744, thus, completely shifting the burden of proof in the wrong direction. This is not a case of the TTAB simply crediting unrebutted evidence. Indeed, the Ross survey and other evidence clearly demonstrates that the views of Native Americans do not necessarily correlate with the views of the general population. At the very least, there was other evidence in the record that the TTAB ignored in making this finding.[2] Since Defendants had the burden of proving their case by a preponderance of the evidence in the proceeding below, the TTAB, by making this statement, impermissibly shifted the burden to Pro-Football. Consequently, the Court is unable to conclude that this finding is supported by substantial evidence.

---

2. The statement by the TTAB that there was no evidence to the contrary is belied by the fact that Pro-Football had introduced two news articles as evidence in the proceeding below that Native Americans use the term "redskin(s)" interchangeably with the term "Indian" as a reference for Native Americans. Pl.'s Opp'n at 32 (citing Pl.'s Stmt. PP 273, 287). The TTAB did not indicate in its opinion that it was not crediting this evidence. Although not considered by the TTAB in the record below, it certainly is not fair to say that there was no evidence in the record to support a contrary view. While the Defendants object to these news articles on reliability and hearsay grounds, *see* Def.'s Opp'n Stmt. PP 273, 287, and in the case of one of the articles on the ground that the writer was being "sarcastic," *id.* P 273, these articles certainly could have been considered by the Board according to the Defendants' own arguments. Indeed, it is the Defendants who vociferously argue that "the Federal Rules of Evidence do not apply to agency proceedings," Defs.' Opp'n at 7, in seeking to persuade the Court that even evidence inadmissible under the federal rules can be considered "substantial evidence." Thus, under the Defendants' own logic the Board could have considered this evidence and it was error for the Board to say that there was no evidence to the contrary on this point without addressing this evidence in some manner.

(2) The Derogatory Nature of the Word "redskin(s)"

The TTAB began by discussing the term "redskin(s)," decoupled from Pro-Football's entertainment services. Putting aside the relevance of this sojourn into linguistics, the Board concluded that "the word 'redskin(s)' has been considered by a substantial composite of the general population, *including by inference Native Americans*, a derogatory term of reference for Native Americans during the time period of relevance herein." *Id.* at 1746 (emphasis added). As the Court has already explained, the TTAB's decision to conflate the views of the general population with those of Native Americans cannot be supported by substantial evidence. Nevertheless, even a review of the evidence that supports this conclusion leads the Court to conclude that the TTAB's finding on this point was not supported by substantial evidence. The Court examines this evidence in turn.

(a) Dictionary Evidence

In support of the proposition that the term "redskin(s)" was a derogatory term for Native Americans, the TTAB first turned its attention to the dictionary definitions that were in evidence. As discussed *supra*, the TTAB had refused to make findings about the expert testimony surrounding the definitions and therefore only had the dictionary definitions, themselves, to consider. The TTAB observed that half of the dictionaries in the record contained a usage label indicating, for example, that the word "redskin(s)" is "often offensive," "informal," or "offensive slang." Half of the dictionaries did not have any usage labels. Based solely on this evidence, the TTAB wrote that "from the fact that usage labels appear in approximately half of the dictionaries of record at any point in the time period covered, we can conclude that a not insignificant number of Americans have understood 'redskin(s)' to be an offensive reference to Native Americans since at least 1966." *Id.* at 1744.

There are a number of concerns that the Court has with this conclusion. First, the TTAB expressly found that it would not make findings on the conflicting linguistic expert testimony that related to the "significance to be attached to the usage labels, or the lack thereof." *Id.* at 1732. Even though it made this statement, the TTAB still made a finding about the significance to be attached to the usage labels in the dictionary. The TTAB's conclusion is without any basis because there is no evidence in the record that was credited as to the purpose and methodology for including or not including usage labels in dictionaries or an explanation as to the basis for their conclusion. There are no findings of fact to support the TTAB's conclusion; rather, it is mere speculation on the part of the TTAB that this is the case.

Second, the fact that a "not insignificant number of Americans have understood "redskin(s)" to be an offensive reference to Native Americans," has nothing to do with whether Native Americans, themselves, consider the term "offensive," which would obviously be more probative or relevant. Third, the dictionary evidence only states that the term "redskin(s)" is "often offensive," which, as Pro-Football observes, means that in certain contexts the term "redskin(s)" was not considered offensive. Pl.'s Mot. at 27. In fact, the TTAB concluded that the term "redskin(s)" means both a Native American and the Washington-area professional football team. The fact that it is usually offensive may mean the term is only offensive in one of these contexts. There is not a discussion of this possibility in the TTAB's opinion. Moreover, as Defendants' own expert observed, "disparaging and offensive are two different words and mean two different things." Pl.'s Stmt. P 124.

Finally, the dictionary evidence was, at best, equivocal. The TTAB observed in a footnote that:

> In view of the contradictory testimony of the parties' linguistics experts regarding the significance of a lack of usage label for a dictionary entry, we can-

not conclude that the lack of such labels in the other excerpts of record establishes that the word "redskin(s)" was *not* considered offensive during the relevant time period.

Harjo II, 50 U.S.P.Q.2d at 1744 n.114 (emphasis in original). By the same token, however,
the conflicting linguist expert testimony should not necessarily lead to a finding that usage
labels establish that the term "redskin(s)" was necessarily considered offensive by the
American public. Accordingly, the Court finds that the TTAB's findings related to the significance of the dictionary evidence are not supported by substantial evidence.

(b) Historical Evidence

The TTAB next deviated into a lengthy discussion of the history of the term "red-
skin(s)." The TTAB observed that it had found that during the late 1800's and early 1900's
that the vast majority of evidence which included the word "redskin(s)" as a reference for
Native Americans, portrayed Native Americans in a "derogatory manner." *Id.* at 1744.
The TTAB then observed that the evidence demonstrates that by the 1930's through the
late 1940's the word "redskin(s)" as a reference for Native Americans "reflected a slightly
less disdainful, but still condescending, view of Native Americans." *Id.* at 1745. However,
the TTAB then states that "from the 1950's forward, the evidence shows, and neither party
disputes, that there are minimal examples of uses of the word 'redskin(s)' as a reference
to Native Americans." *Id.* During this same time period the TTAB noted that the record
reflects "significant occurrences of the word 'redskin(s)' as a reference to [Pro-Football's]
football team." *Id.* From this latter evidence, the TTAB stated:

> We conclude from the evidence of record that the word "redskin(s)" does not
> appear during the second half of this century in written or spoken language, for-
> mal or informal, as a synonym for "Indian" or "Native American" because it is,
> and has been since at least the 1960's, perceived by the general population, which
> includes Native Americans, as a pejorative term for Native Americans.

Id. The Court determines that this finding is also not supported by substantial evidence
because no concrete evidence supports this conclusion.

First, the TTAB agreed with Pro-Football, that "the pejorative nature of 'redskin(s)' in the
early historical writings of record comes from the overall negative viewpoints of the writings." *Id.* Despite this finding, the TTAB merely assumed that because the term "redskin(s)"
dropped out of use as a term for Native Americans it must have been because the term was
derogatory. There is no evidence in the record to support this finding one way or the other.
Concerned with adopting witness testimony that reached the ultimate legal question, the TTAB
did not make findings regarding the significance of the use of the word from the 1960's on-
ward. *Id.* at 1731. However, the ultimate legal inquiry is whether the six trademarks at issue
may disparage Native Americans when used in connection with Pro-Football's services and
during the relevant time frame. The ultimate legal inquiry is not whether the term "red-
skin(s)" is a pejorative term for Native Americans. Accordingly, the TTAB's reluctance to
make findings in this area deprives the Court of meaningful review. There is no evidence
to support the conclusion that the drop-off of the use of the term "redskin(s)" as a reference
for Native Americans is correlative with a finding that the term is pejorative. Accordingly,
the Court finds that this finding is unsupported by substantial evidence.

(c) Survey Evidence

As discussed earlier, the Court found the TTAB's conclusion that the survey could be
extrapolated to the Native American population as a whole to be unsupported by substantial

evidence. Nevertheless, to the extent that the survey would be even included in the calculus, the Court determines that it does not support the TTAB's decision that the word "redskin(s)" was viewed by a substantial composite of Native Americans to be a derogatory term of reference for Native Americans from the mid-1960's to 1990. The survey measures attitudes of Native Americans about their perceptions of the term "redskin" as used as a reference to Native Americans in *1996*. The survey, therefore, is entirely irrelevant to the question before the Board.

As the TTAB itself observed, "neither [the fact that the survey measured the views of individuals not alive at the time of registration of certain of the trademarks or the fact that the survey did not consider participants' views of the word 'redskin(s)' as used in connection with Pro-Football's entertainment services] diminishes the value of petitioners' survey for what it is—a survey of *current* attitudes towards the word "redskin(s)" as a reference to Native Americans." *Id.* at 1734 (emphasis added). The TTAB has no evidence, therefore, to draw a conclusion that during the relevant time periods, i.e. 1967, 1974, 1978, and 1990, the term Native Americans [sic, court means "Redskins"] was a pejorative term for Native Americans.[3] Putting aside the fact that the survey results have no bearing on Native Americans perceptions of the term "redskin(s)" as used in connection with the Pro-Football's professional sports team, the survey tells us nothing about the relevant time frame.[4] Accordingly, it fails to support with substantial evidence the TTAB's finding that the term "redskin(s)" is viewed by a substantial composite of Native Americans as a derogatory term for Native Americans.[5]

(3) The Word "redskin(s)" as a Term of Disparagement

The TTAB next turned to the ultimate inquiry before the Board and found that "within the relevant time periods, the derogatory connotation of the word 'redskin(s)' in connection with Native Americans extends to the term 'Redskin(s)' as used in [Pro-Football's] marks in connection with the identified services, such that [Pro-Football's] marks

---

3. Indeed, during this time frame, several different PTO examiners reviewed the Redskins marks and none came to the conclusion that the trade marks were disparaging. *See* 15 U.S.C. §1052(a); Pl.'s Opp'n at 32–33.

4. For example, while a word like "redskin(s)" may have been accepted as an informal term for a Native American in 1967, by 1996, attitudes of people may have changed as Native American culture became increasingly accepted and respected. The TTAB addressed this argument in a footnote stating that Pro-Football "has presented no evidence suggesting that, as a term identifying Native Americans, the perception of the derogatory nature of the word 'redskin(s)' by any segment of the general population, including Native Americans changed significantly during this time period." *Harjo II*, 50 U.S.P.Q.2d at 1746 n.121 (observing that the evidence in the record supports the conclusion that the term "redskin(s)" has been viewed by Native Americans a derogatory word since at least the 1960s). The difficulty with the TTAB's statement is that, as the Court has discussed at length in this section, there is no evidence or findings of fact made by the TTAB that a substantial composite of Native Americans view the term "redskin(s)" as derogatory as a reference for Native Americans. Hence, it is not as if the TTAB was crediting some unrebutted testimony in making this finding.

5. The survey evidence, that Native Americans find the term "redskin(s)" offensive as a term for Native Americans, does not even represent a majority of Native Americans polled. Indeed only 36.6 of Native Americans agreed with that statement. While the TTAB found that 36.6 was a substantial composite, *Harjo II*, 50 U.S.P.Q.2d at 1746 n.120 (quoting McCarthy, *supra*, §32.185) (noting that in cases dealing with likelihood of confusion, "an appreciable number of customers" may be less than a majority), the Court finds that conclusion difficult to support in the context of this case. The survey only found that 131 out of the 358 participants agreed that this term was offensive when used as a reference to Native Americans. This Court, accordingly, finds that the survey results do not demonstrate that a "substantial composite" of Native Americans found the term offensive as a reference for Native Americans.

may be disparaging of Native Americans to a substantial composite of this group of people." *Id.* at 1748. The crux of the TTAB's conclusion, therefore, is that the "derogatory
connotation of the word 'redskin(s)'" extends to the term "Redskin(s)" as used in connection
with Pro-Football's entertainment services. This finding is not supported by substantial
evidence.

To reach its conclusion that the trademarks may disparage Native Americans, the TTAB
essentially determined that because the *word* "redskin(s)" may be viewed by Native Americans as derogatory when used as a reference for Native Americans, the trademarks are
disparaging because they use that word. The result of this analysis is that there is very little discussion of the use of the mark in connection with Pro-Football's product or services. Unlike in the *Doughboy* case, where the Examiner-in-Chief of the Patent Office stated
that use of the term "Doughboy"—a reference for a World War I soldier—was disparaging when used to sell an anti-venereal prophylactic, *Doughboy*, 88 U.S.P.Q. at 228, in this
case the TTAB did very little analysis of *how* the use of the trademarks in connection with
Pro-Football's services disparages Native Americans. The Board was content with stating
that because it found the name to be pejorative, the marks must be disparaging.[6]

First, the TTAB observed that "as we move through the 1960's to the present, the evidence shows increasingly respectful portrayal of Native Americans." *Id.* at 1746. The
TTAB then noted that "*the evidence herein shows a parallel development of [Pro-Football's]
portrayal of Native Americans.*" *Id.* (emphasis added). What the TTAB found therefore,
was that during the relevant time periods, the use of the term "redskin(s)" in connection
with Pro-Football's marks was used in a respectful manner. Nevertheless, despite this
stunning observation—that during the relevant time frame Pro-Football used Native
American imagery in a respectful manner as connected to its entertainment services—
the Board still concluded that the use of the term "redskin(s)" was disparaging when used
in the context of Pro-Football's professional football club.

The TTAB apparently premised this conclusion on a number of factors. First, the
TTAB discussed the fact that the media has used Native American imagery in connection with Pro-Football's football team, throughout the entire period, "in a manner that
often portrays Native Americans as aggressive savages or buffoons." *Id.* at 1747 (noting
newspaper headlines referring to Washington Redskins team, players or managers scalp-
ing opponents, seeking revenge on the warpath, holding pow wows, or using pidgin
English). In addition, newspaper and video excerpts of games were presented showing
Washington Redskins fans dressed "in costumes and engaging in antics that clearly poke
fun at Native American culture and portrays [sic] Native Americans as savages and buffoons." *Id.* While the TTAB stated that it agreed with Pro-Football that it was not responsible for the actions of the media or its fans, the TTAB, nevertheless, found "the actions
of the media and fans … probative of *the general public's* perception of the word 'red-
skin(s)' as it appears in respondent's marks herein." *Id.* (emphasis added). From this
evidence, the TTAB concluded that the term "redskin(s)" "retains its derogatory character as part of the subject marks and as used in connection with respondent's football
team." *Id.*

---

6. The Board's reasoning reflects the views of Defendants in this case, as the following statement
from Defendant Harjo at her deposition makes clear:
   Q: Have any actions been taken by the Washington Redskins football team that you believe
   disparage Native Americans other than the use of the name?
   A: The use of their name, the use of that term, colors all their actions in my estimation.
   And so I find everything disparaging.

The problem with this reasoning is twofold. First, the perceptions of the general public are irrelevant to determining if the marks are disparaging to Native Americans. In other words, this evidence is simply not relevant to the legal question in the case. Second, and most importantly, this finding is logically flawed. At best, this evidence demonstrates that Pro-Football's fans and the media continue to equate the Washington Redskins with Native Americans and not always in a respectful manner. However, the evidence does not automatically lead the Court to conclude that the word "redskin(s)" as used in Pro-Football's marks is derogatory in character. Under the broad sweep of the TTAB's logic, no professional sports team that uses Native American imagery would be permitted to keep their trademarks if the team's fans or the media took any action or made any remark that could be construed as insulting to Native Americans. The Court cannot accept such an expansive doctrine; particularly when premised on a finding that is not supported by any substantial evidence.

Clearly, the evidence relating to the media and fans has no bearing on whether a substantial composite of Native Americans finds the term "redskin(s)" to be disparaging when used in connection with Pro-Football's marks. In this regard, the evidence the TTAB put forward comes nowhere close to meeting the substantial evidence test. First, the TTAB noted that the record contained the testimony of the Defendants who stated that they were "seriously offended" by Pro-Football's use of the term in connection with its services. *Id.* This testimony, however, is a reflection of their individual viewpoints and there is no evidence that Defendants' views are a reasonable proxy for a substantial composite of the entire Native American population. As Pro-Football's counsel stated at the July 23, 2003, motions hearing, "Do these seven petitioners strongly believe that our famous football team mark Washington Redskins is disparaging? Apparently. That's fine. They have an opinion, but they are representing themselves and no one else. There are 2.41 million Native Americans in this country, Your Honor. There are over 500 Native American tribes. So I ask, can petitioner's opinions, no matter how stridently held, be extrapolated to even one additional Native American by some method acceptable in a courtroom? The answer is, of course, not at all."

To corroborate its ultimate conclusion, the TTAB cites to other evidence which this Court views as irrelevant because it has no correlation to the relevant time frame at issue and it does not add exponentially to the requirement that the marks, when used in connection with Pro-Football's services, are considered disparaging by a substantial composite of Native Americans. The TTAB noted that the record includes Resolutions indicating a present objection to the use of the word "redskin(s)" in connection with Pro-Football's services, from the National Congress of American Indians ("NCAI"), "a broad-based organization of Native American tribes and individuals" from the Oneida tribe, and from Unity 94, "an organization including Native Americans." All of these resolutions were made after the relevant time frame, with no explanation by the TTAB as to how they "shed light" on the relevant time period, and thus, are irrelevant to the calculus. *See* Pl.'s Mot. at 23. Indeed, all of these resolutions were adopted after Defendants filed their Petition to Cancel. *Id.* at 24. Moreover, the TTAB made no findings of fact about the strength of this evidence. For example, only two Native Americans voted for the Unity '94 resolution. Pl.'s Stmt. P 212.

In addition, the TTAB relies on "news articles," which appeared at various times from 1969 to 1992, describing Native American objections to the team name. *Harjo II*, 50 U.S.P.Q.2d at 1747. The TTAB does not describe the contents of these news articles and it is impossible to determine if they would represent a substantial composite of Native Americans. Moreover, these articles were only introduced to demonstrate "the existence of a controversy spanning over a long period of time." *Id.* Again, the existence of a controversy does not inform the Court as to whether the trademarks at issue are perceived of as disparaging by a substantial composite of Native Americans.

Finally, the TTAB relied on a letter written by Harold Gross in 1972 to Edward Bennett Williams, the then-team owner urging the team name be changed. *Id.* at 1747. The record also indicates that Mr. Gross and seven other colleagues from Native American organizations met with Mr. Williams to discuss the disparaging nature of the team's name. *Id.*; *see also* Pl.'s Stmt. P 202. Again, this evidence does not represent a "substantial composite" of Native Americans.

The TTAB concluded that "the evidence of record establishes that, within the relevant time periods, the derogatory connotation of the words "redskin(s)" in connection with Native Americans extends to the term "Redskins," as used in [Pro-Football's] marks in connection with the identified services, such that [Pro-Football's] marks may be disparaging of Native Americans to a substantial composite of this group of people." *Harjo II*, 50 U.S.P.Q.2d at 1748. The Court determines that this decision is not supported by substantial evidence.[7] As such, the decision of the TTAB must be reversed.

* * *

V. SUMMARY OF ANALYSIS

The Court's decision today only focuses on the evidence supporting the TTAB's decision and Defendants' delay in bringing this proceeding. This opinion should not be read as a making any statement on the appropriateness of Native American imagery for team names. The Board premised its disparagement conclusion on a paucity of actual findings of fact that were linked together through inferential arguments that had no basis in the record. Contrary to the TTAB's ruling, this Court finds that Defendants did not carry their burden of proof in the TTAB proceeding. The evidentiary findings of the TTAB did not rise to the level of "substantial evidence" to support their ultimate conclusion that the six trademarks at issue were disparaging to a substantial composite of Native Americans.

The legal question before the TTAB was whether the six trademarks, when used in connection with Pro-Football's entertainment services, "may disparage" a substantial composite of Native Americans at the time the marks were registered starting in 1967. The findings do not come close to shedding any light on the legal inquiry. There is no evidence in the record that addresses whether the use of the term "redskin(s)" in the context of a football team and related entertainment services would be viewed by a substantial composite of Native Americans, in the relevant time frame, as disparaging. In addition, none of the TTAB's findings related to the linguists' expert testimony help explain whether the term "redskins," when used in connection with the "Washington Redskins" football team, disparaged Native Americans during the relevant time frame.

The only other findings of fact that the TTAB made involved the Ross survey. The TTAB found that the survey methodology was sound, that the survey was nothing more than a survey of attitudes as of the time the poll was conducted in 1996, and that the survey adequately represents the views of the two populations sampled. This survey, aside from its extrapolation flaws, says nothing about whether the term "redskin(s)" when used

---

7. Moreover, it is undisputed that the six marks at issue were published and registered without opposition from Native Americans or anyone else on *twelve* different occasions. This fact would appear, at least, to work against the TTAB's inferential conclusion that the marks, when used in connection with Pro-Football's entertainment services may disparage Native Americans.

in connection with Pro-Football's football team disparages Native Americans. Furthermore, the survey provides no information about the relevant time periods. The survey is completely irrelevant to the analysis.

Besides making findings of fact that did not address the legal conclusion, the TTAB did not hear live testimony; instead the TTAB predicated its decision on a cold factual record. With the reasoning laid entirely out in front of it, the TTAB rarely credited one side's evidence at the expense of another or provided an explanation as to why it accepted the evidence or the weight it gave the evidence. In this case, the TTAB could have easily articulated its reasoning based on the substance of the record before it. Ultimately, the evidence in the case does not answer the legal question of whether the trademarks, in the context of their use during the relevant time frames, may have disparaged Native Americans. The evidence chips away at the sides of this legal question but never helps answer it directly.

This is undoubtedly a "test case" that seeks to use federal trademark litigation to obtain social goals. The problem, however, with this case is evidentiary. The Lanham Act has been on the books for many years and was in effect in 1967 when the trademarks were registered. By waiting so long to exercise their rights, Defendants make it difficult for any fact-finder to affirmatively state that in 1967 the trademarks were disparaging.

Notes

1. Survey results in proceeding before the TTAB were as follows:

Percentage of People Finding Indicated Terms Offensive

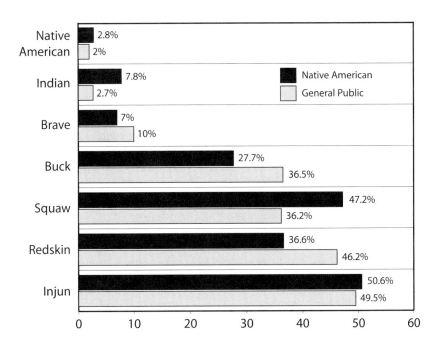

2. 15 U.S.C. §1071(b), §21 of the Lanham Act, allows parties dissatisfied with the outcome of proceedings before the TTAB to appeal directly to the Court of Appeals for the

Federal Circuit. In the alternative, the non-prevailing party may bring a civil action against the prevailing party in any district court in the United States that would have personal jurisdiction over the parties. In *Harjo*, rather than appealing the TTAB's decision to the Court of Appeals for the Federal Circuit, Pro-Football brought a lawsuit against Harjo, et al., before the D.C. District Court. Why would they do that?

3. As *Harjo* indicates, there are very distinct practice rules parties must follow when appealing to the TTAB. Some of these rules mirror the Federal Rules of Civil Procedure. Some of them are unique to the TTAB. *See generally*, TBMP § 101 et seq. (2004), GPO Access, *available at* http://www.uspto.gov/web/offices/dcom/ttab/tbmp/index.html. However, the TTAB manual does not give specific timetables which administrative judges at the TTAB must follow. It took the TTAB seven years to come to a final decision in *Harjo*.

4. In *Dickenson v. Zirco*, 527 U.S. 150 (1999), the Supreme Court concluded that appellate courts must give deference to PTO decisions and that the Administrative Procedures Act (5 U.S.C. §706) applied to the review of PTO decisions. As such, federal courts must accept PTO determinations unless they are unsupported by substantial evidence. Does this explain why Pro-Football filed a new case against Harjo instead of appealing to the Court of Appeals for the Federal Circuit? One court recently summarized this situation as follows:

> We first determine which standard of review applies to a district court's review of a TTAB decision, and we then evaluate whether the district court applied that standard in this case. As described above, the Lanham Act provides two avenues for review of TTAB decisions: review by the Federal Circuit on the closed record of the TTAB proceedings, *see* 15 U.S.C. §1071(a)(4); or review by the district court with the option of presenting additional evidence and raising additional claims … In the latter scenario, the district court sits in a dual capacity. It is an appellate reviewer of facts found by the TTAB and is also a fact-finder based on new evidence introduced to the court. Although the district court's review of the TTAB's decision is considered de novo when the parties present new evidence and assert additional claims, the district court also must afford deference to the fact findings of the TTAB.
>
> The degree of deference that the district court must afford the TTAB's findings of fact is a matter that recently has come under scrutiny. Before 1999, a majority of courts, including this one, followed the thorough conviction standard … [that] the TTAB's determination "must be accepted as controlling upon a finding of fact about confusing similarity of trademarks, unless the contrary is established by testimony which in character and amount carries thorough conviction…."
>
> In 1999, however, the Supreme Court held in *Dickinson v. Zurko*, 527 U.S. 150, 144 L. Ed. 2d 143, 119 S. Ct. 1816 (1999), that the proper standard of judicial review of findings of fact made by the PTO is not the stricter "clearly erroneous" standard but rather the slightly more deferential standard of the Administrative Procedure Act ("APA"), 5 U.S.C. §706. Section 706 of the APA sets forth the standards governing the scope of judicial review of agency factfinding: The reviewing court shall—
>
> … (2) hold unlawful and set aside agency … findings … found to be—
>
> (A) arbitrary, capricious, [or] an abuse of discretion, or …
>
> …
>
> (E) unsupported by substantial evidence in a case subject to sections 556 and 557 of this title or otherwise reviewed on the record of an agency hearing provided by statute….

In making the foregoing determinations, the court shall review the whole record or those parts of it cited by a party....

5 U.S.C. §706. Although the Court left open the question of which APA standard applied — "arbitrary, capricious, or abuse of discretion" under §706(2)(A) or "substantial evidence" under §706(2)(E) — the Federal Circuit has concluded that, after *Zurko,* it will review TTAB findings of fact for substantial evidence. "Substantial evidence is more than a mere scintilla. It means such relevant evidence as a reasonable mind might accept as adequate to support a conclusion." *Consol. Edison Co. v. NLRB,* 305 U.S. 197, 229, 83 L. Ed. 126, 59 S. Ct. 206 (1938).

CAE, Inc. v. Clean Air Engineering, Inc., 267 F.3d 660, 664–67 (7th Cir. 2001).

5. Jack Kent Cooke, the longtime and colorful owner of the Redskins, died in 1997. The estate of Jack Kent Cooke sold the Washington Redskins to Daniel M. Snyder Ownership Group in 1999 for $800 million. Do you suspect the controversy over the mark affected the market value of the team? In January of 1999, a month before the TTAB ruling, the NFL, which owns a veto right over the sale price of football teams, rejected a bid for $800 million. Four months after the TTAB decision came out, they accepted a bid for the same $800 million. Now that the District Court has, in effect, reinstated the trademark registration, do you suppose the market value of the Redskins franchise has gone up? Do you suppose this fact, if true, influenced the judge at the district court? Should it?

6. *First amendment and 2(a).* Commercial speech is generally protected speech. To determine if the commercial speech ought to be protected, courts generally apply the following test. Currently, courts apply "intermediate scrutiny" to determine if restrictions on commercial speech are constitutional. Courts inquire generally as follows: (1) does the speech concern lawful activity and is not misleading? (2) is the governmental interest served by restricting commercial speech substantial? (3) does the regulation directly advance the asserted government interest? and (4) is the regulation more extensive than is necessary to serve that interest? *See generally,* Va. Bd. of Pharmacy v. Va. Citizens Consumer Council, Inc., 425 U.S. 748 (1976). Courts have also determined that a trademark is a form of commercial speech. Friedman v. Rogers, 440 U.S. 1, 11 (1979). Some argue that the government does not have a substantial interest in restricting the type of speech involved in the REDSKINS case and therefore the application of Section 2(a) in that instance should be deemed unconstitutional. Jeffrey Lefstin, *Note, Does the First Amendment Bar Cancellation of REDSKINS?,* 52 Stan. L. Rev. 665 (2000). Is Section 2(a) constitutional? In *Harjo, supra,* the court held in favor of the NFL and therefore found its constitutional attack moot. Section 2(a) has been upheld by other courts as constitutional because the cancellation or refusal to register a mark does not affect the claimant's right to use the mark in commerce. *See, e.g., In re Mavety Media Group, Ltd.,* 33 F.3d 1367, 1374 (Fed. Cir. 1994); *In re McGinley,* 660 F.2d 481, 484 (C.C.P.A. 1981) ("With respect to [the applicant's] First Amendment rights, it is clear that the PTO's refusal to register [the mark] does not affect his right to use it.... No conduct is proscribed, and no tangible form of expression is suppressed. Consequently, [the applicant's] First Amendment rights would not be abridged by the refusal to register his mark."). Others have argued, however, that although the refusal to register a mark does not affect the claimant's right to use the mark, the economic consequences to a refusal to register implicate the First Amendment. Kimberly A. Pace, *The Washington Redskins Case and The Doctrine of Disparagement: How Politically Correct Must a Trademark Be?,* 22 Pepp. L. Rev. 7 (1994).

7. Should self-disparaging trademarks, such as DYKES ON BIKES be treated any differently than a mark that disparages others? *See* McDermott v. San Francisco Women's Motorcycle Contingent, 240 Fed Appx. 865 (CAFC 2007), cert. denied, 2008 Lexis 299 (January 7, 2008). In this case, a group of lesbian motorcycle riders in San Francisco applied to register the mark DYKES ON BIKES. The mark was opposed by McDermott, a male. The CAFC ruled that McDermott lacked standing to claim it disparaged him because the mark addresses females, not males. Why does a man lack standing to claim that a mark disparages women? Is chivalry that dead? *See generally*, Todd Anten, NOTE, *Self-Disparaging Trademarks and Social Change: Factoring the Reappropriation of Slurs into Section 2(a) of the Lanham Act*, 106 COLUM. L. REV. 288 (2006); Regan Smith, Trademark Law and Free Speech: Protection for Scandalous and Disparaging Marks, 42 Harv. Civil Rights-Civil Liberties L. Rev. 451 (2007).

8. *Section 2(a) and O.J.* Within five weeks of the brutal murder of his wife in 1994 which brought notoriety to the name O.J. Simpson, Simpson filed several ITU trademark applications for a variety of goods, including clothing, toys, etc. *See, e.g.*, Application Serial Number 74551770 (filed July 21, 1994). One concerned citizen (a Patent attorney in Concord, New Hampshire) thought this was inconsistent with his Christian values and that the marks were "synonymous with a wife-beater and wife-murderer." As such, he opposed the registration of Simpson's marks on grounds that they were scandalous, disparaging and immoral. The TTAB ruled that he did not have standing to sue, but the CAFC reversed. *See* Ritchie v. Simpson, 41 U.S.P.Q.2d 1859 (T.T.A.B. 1996), *rev'd*, 170 F.3d 1092 (Fed. Cir. 1999). Simpson mooted the opposition by abandoning the applications in April of 2000. If you were a TTAB administrative judge faced with this opposition, how would you rule and why?

9. Section 2(a) cases are sometimes difficult to accord with one another. In *In re Mavety Media Group, Ltd.*, *supra*, the court held that BLACK TAIL was not scandalous for use on or in connection with a pornographic magazine featuring African American women. However, in *In re Boulevard Entm't Inc*, 334 F.3d 1336 (2003), the same court held that "Jack-Off" was in violation of Section 2(a) and upheld the Examiner's rejection to registration. The stated reasoning was that BLACK TAIL was a double entendre whereas JACK-OFF had but one meaning in many dictionaries and that meaning was a scandalous term meaning masturbation. Compare these two cases and determine if there are other reasons to distinguish these two marks. Do you accept the court's stated rationale?

10. In all Section 2(a) cases, there is a risk of Examiners applying their subjective sensitivities to any given mark. How would you change the Lanham Act to prevent the possibility that Examiners legislate morality? Should they be allowed to impose morality as they see fit?

11. Much has been made in the trademark literature about "geographical indications." *See, e.g.*, John R. Renaud, *Can't Get There From Here: How NAFTA and GATT Have Reduced Protection for Geographical Trademarks*, 26 BROOKLYN J. INT'L L. 1097 (2001). Section 2(a) of the Lanham Act was, in fact, amended pursuant to the terms of NAFTA to allow for some geographical indicators to be registered. Section 2(a) now reads in relevant part as follows:

> No trademark by which the goods of the applicant may be distinguished from the goods of others shall be refused registration on the principal register on account of its nature unless it—
>
> (a) Consists of or comprises ... a geographical indication which, when used on or in connection with wines or spirits, identifies a place other than the origin of

the goods and is first used on or in connection with wines or spirits by the applicant on or after one year after the date on which the WTO Agreement (as defined in section 2(9) of the Uruguay Round Agreements Act [19 USCS §3501(9)]) enters into force with respect to the United States.

15 U.S.C. §1052(a), Lanham Act §2.

Additionally, the TRIPs Agreement (*See infra* Chapter XIII), defines geographical indications as follows:

> ... indications which identify a good as originating in the territory of a Member, or a region of locality in that territory, where a given quality, reputation or other characteristic of the good is essentially attributable to its geographical origin.

TRIPs Agreement, Article 22.1.

As will be discussed in Chapter 13, the TRIPs Agreement made intellectual property law an issue enforced under the World Trade Organization (WTO). As such, member nations must meet the provisions of TRIPs or suffer a complaint brought against them before the WTO that could result in real sanctions against that offending State.

The United States is a member of the TRIPs Agreement and its laws, through Section 2(a) of the Lanham Act, apparently comports with TRIPs.

Geographical indications play a more important role in trademark law in France, for example, than in the United States. After all the fuss about geographical indications, to date, there are no reported cases under United States law where a geographical indication, as contemplated by TRIPs was squarely at issue. Why?

For an excellent review of the state of the law, *see* Steven A. Bowers, *Location, Location, Location: The Case Against Extending Geographical Indiction Protection Under the TRIPs Agreement*, 31 AIPLA Q. 129 (2003). For the view that the United States has failed to meet its obligations regarding geographical indications, *see* Leigh Ann Lindquist, *Champagne or Champagne? An Examination of U.S. Failure to Comply with the Geographical Provisions of the TRIPS Agreement*, 27 GA. J. INT'L & COMP. L. 309 (1999). Geographical indications continues to attract the attention of many scholars. Why is it so controversial? Molly Torsen, *Apples and Oranges (and Wine): Why the International Conversation Regarding Geographic Indications is at a Standstill*, 87 J. PAT. & TRADEMARK OFF. SOC'Y 31, 61 (2005) ("Individual domestic GI schemes must be studied and understood by WTO members so that individual countries are not talking "apples and oranges," but are capable of reaching a consensus on what a GI means and what kind of legal system might be feasible on the international scale. GIs need not be lost in the shuffle of trade discussions that focus on other intellectual property protection; they simply need to be given their due recognition as an intellectual property right with an erratic past but a promising future").

---

2. Section 2(b): Flag or Coat of Arms

15 U.S.C. §1052, Lanham Act. §2

No trademark by which the goods of the applicant may be distinguished from the goods of others shall be refused registration on the principal register on account of its nature unless it—

   ...

(b) Consists of or comprises the flag or coat of arms or other insignia of the United States, or of any State or municipality, or of any foreign nation, or any simulation thereof.

––––––––––

In re United States Dept. of the Interior
142 U.S.P.Q. 506 (TTAB 1964)

SHYROCK, MEMBER.

An application has been filed by The United States Department of the Interior to register as a service mark the matter reproduced below for the service of "(1) operation and maintenance of recreational and educational facilities in connection with parks, monuments, camp sites, trails, museums and similar institutions, and (2) Making available to the public publications and other informational material in connection with the activities of (1)." In its application, applicant alleges use of the service mark since April, 1952.

Registration has been refused on the grounds that (a) an agency of the United States government is not a "juristic person" and therefore not a proper applicant within the meaning of Section 1 of the Trademark Act and (b) the matter sought to be registered consists of an insignia of the United States, which is precluded registration under the express provisions of Section 2(b) of the Act.

Applicant has appealed.

As to (a), Section 45 of the Act states, in part, that:

> "The term 'juristic person' includes a firm, corporation, union association, or other organization capable of suing and being sued in a court of law."

It is well established that the United States Government, or an official department thereof, is an organization capable of suing or being sued (albeit with its consent) in a court of law. The United States Department of the Interior is therefore a proper applicant within the meaning of the Trademark Act. Moreover, the granting of trademark and service mark registrations to state and governmental agencies does not appear to be contrary to the established policy of the Patent Office, as shown by the registry.

As to (b), Section 2 of the Act reads, in part, as follows:

> "No trademark by which the goods of the applicant may be distinguished from the goods of others shall be refused registration on the principal register on account of its nature unless it—
>
> (b) consists of or comprises the flag or coat of arms or other insignia of the United States, or of any State or municipality, or of any foreign nation, or any simulation thereof;"

The above quoted language from Section 2 of the Act makes it clear that the Examiner of Trademarks is relying, in his refusal to register, on the wording "other insignia of the United States." The question for determination, therefore, is whether the insignia of the "National Park Service," here sought to be registered, falls within the category of "or other insignia" prohibited by Section 2(b). In making this determination, it is believed, as urged by applicant, that the "ejusdem generis" rule of construction is applicable in construing this general language of the Statute. This rule is stated in "American Jurispurdence" as follows:

> "General and specific words in a statute which are associated together, and which are capable of an analogous meaning, take color from each other, so that the general words are restricted to a sense analogous to the less general. Under this rule, general terms in a statute may be regarded as limited by subsequent more specific terms. Similarly, in accordance with what is commonly known as the rule of ejusdem generis, where, in a statute, general words follow a designation of particular subjects or classes of persons, the meaning of the general words will ordinarily be presumed to be, and construed as, restricted by the particular designation and as including only things or persons of the same kind, class, character, or nature as those specifically enumerated. The general words are deemed to have been used, not to the wide extent which they might bear if standing alone, but as related to words of more definite and particular meaning with which they are associated. In accordance with the rule of ejusdem generis such terms as 'other' 'other thing,' 'other persons,' 'others' 'otherwise' or 'any other,' when preceded by a specific enumeration, are commonly given a restricted meaning and limited to articles of the same nature as those previously described."

While this rule is inapplicable in cases where it is clear that it was the legislative intention to go beyond the class specifically designated, we are unaware of any such intention here, nor has the Examiner of Trademarks suggested any. Under the circumstances, we can see no reason for applying a broad dictionary definition of "insignia" as relied upon by the examiner in his refusal to register.

When the rule of "ejusdem generis" is applied to the general language or Section 2(b), the wording "or other insignia of the United States" must be restricted in its application to insignia of the same general class as "the flag or coats of arms" of the United States. Since both the flag and coat or arms are emblems of national authority it seems evident that other insignia of national authority such as the Great Seal of the United States, the Presidential Seal, and seals of government departments would be equally prohibited registration under Section 2(b). On the other hand, it appears equally evident that department insignia which are merely used to idetnify a service or facility of the Government are not insignia of national authority and that they therefore do not fall within the general prohibitions of this section of the Statute.

Decision

The refusal to register is overruled.

———————

Note

1. Does §2(b) provide even more grounds for the cancellation of trademarks of sports teams such as the "Illini" or the "Seminoles"? As Native American tribes are gaining more

independence and are recognized in more official capacities as sovereign in some ways, could they ever be considered a "simulation" of the nation/states contemplated by §2(b)? Of course, proof ought to be easier for a challenger to a registration on 2(b) grounds because there is no need to show some appreciable portion of the public was offended in any way by the use of the insignia. Section 2(b) is an absolute bar. *See* TMEP, §1204 (2004). *See also*, Maury Audet, *Native American Tribal Names as Monikers and Logos: Will These Registrations Withstand Cancellation Under Lanham Act §2(b) After the Trademark Study on Official Insignia of Native American Tribes?*, 2 J. INTELL. PROP. 4 (2000) (arguing that although there is some merit to this argument, no such outcome should be expected any time soon).

————————

3. Section 2(c): Names, Portrait, Signatures

15 U.S.C. §1052, Lanham Act §2

No trademark by which the goods of the applicant may be distinguished from the goods of others shall be refused registration on the principal register on account of its nature unless it—

...

(c) Consists of or comprises a name, portrait, or signature identifying a particular living individual except by his written consent, or the name, signature, or portrait of a deceased President of the United States during the life of his widow, if any, except by the written consent of the widow.

————————

In re Steak and Ale Restaurants of America
185 U.S.P.Q. 447 (TTAB 1975)

LEFKOWITZ, MEMBER.

An application has been filed by Steak and Ale Restaurants of America, Inc. to register the notation "PRINCE CHARLES" as a trademark for fresh and cooked meat, use of the mark since as early as February 1966 being claimed.

Registration has been refused under Section 2(c) of the statute on the ground that "PRINCE CHARLES" consists of or comprises a name identifying a particular living individual whose consent is not of record. Specifically, it is the examiner's position that "PRINCE CHARLES" is the name of the well-known member of the current English royal family.

Applicant has appealed.

It is applicant's argument that (A) "PRINCE CHARLES" is a title associated with more than one living individual and, as such, it does not identify a name of a particular living individual [there are, according to applicant, at least two individuals that are named "PRINCE CHARLES", a member of the English royal family referred to by the examiner, Charles Philip Arthur George, and a member of Swedish royalty, Karl (Charles) Gustav;] (B) "PRINCE CHARLES" is an arbitrary usage of a historical title and does not identify a name of a particular living individual [applicant has made of record specific pages from the Encyclopaedia Britannica (1973) and from Webster's New Collegiate Dictionary, Second Edition, 1953, which detail and contain references to the historical use of "CHARLES" to designate members of royalty of various countries]; and (C) "PRINCE CHARLES" is a royal title and not a name [applicant has offered in evidence dictionary definitions of both the word "prince" and "title"].

As to (A), applicant's interpretation of Section 2(c) is not well founded. Even accepting the existence of more than one living "PRINCE CHARLES", it does not follow that each is not a particular living individual. Apropos thereto, there are possibly a great many individuals possessing the same name such as John Smith and the like, but this does not make any one of them any less of a particular living individual. It is apparent under the restrictive provision of Section 2(c) that, if a party were to seek to register "JOHN SMITH" as a trademark, and it could be shown that this name is, in fact, the name of a living John Smith as distinguished from the name of a fictitious individual, registration would be withheld pending receipt of a consent to use and registration by the individual in question. *Cf. Ex parte Dallioux*, 83 U.S.P.Q. 262 (Comr., 1949); *Brand v. Fairchester Packing Co.*, 84 U.S.P.Q. 97 (Comr., 1950); *Reed & Bakers Engineering & Equipment Company*, 100 U.S.P.Q. 196 (Comr., 1954); and *Armour et al. v. Commissioner of Internal Revenue*, 101 U.S.P.Q. 257 (U.S. Tax Ct., 1954).

With regard to (B), applicant's listings of historical figures of the past known and identified by "CHARLES" or even "PRINCE CHARLES" are without any probative value herein if for no other reason than that the pertinent portion of Section 2(c) relates to a "particular living individual". Thus, the existence in the past of one or more individuals with a name or a combination of a title and a name such as that herein involved cannot negate the proposition that a contemporary with the same or a similar name or title is a particular living individual.

Turning finally to (C), namely, "The term 'Prince Charles' is a royal title and not a name …", there is no dispute but that the word "PRINCE", per se, or when linked with a geographical designation, may constitute nothing more than a title where royalty is concerned, but the addition of a given name or a surname to the word "PRINCE" could well serve as a name or "nickname" for a particular living individual who could be identified and referred to in the various walks of life with this appellation. It is noted in this regard that the Commissioner in Reed v. Bakers Engineering & Equipment Company, *supra*, stated that:

> " … the statute uses the words 'a name' and not the words 'the name'. Hence 'name' in section 2(c) is not restricted to the full name of an individual but refers to any name regardless of whether it is a full name or a surname or given name, or even a nickname, which identifies a particular living individual…."

Attention is also directed to Ex parte Martha Maid Manufacturing Company, 37 U.S.P.Q. 156 (Comr., 1938), in which "QUEEN MARY" was denied registration as a trademark for various items of women's underwear on the grounds that "QUEEN MARY", being the name of the then Dowager Queen of England, was scandalous and "shocking to the sense of propriety"; and that, moreover, "within the meaning of Section 5 of the Trademark Act of 1905 the mark as presented 'consists merely in the name of an individual' not distinctively displayed…. Although this decision was rendered under the Act of 1905, it is believed that the reasoning behind the refusal of registrability of "QUEEN MARY" has equal applicability to the registration of "PRINCE CHARLES" in view of the proscription of Section 2(c) of the Act of 1946.

Decision

The refusal of registration is affirmed.

Note

Although admittedly used in rather obscure circumstances, this provision of the Lanham Act can have important consequences. In *Hot Stuff Foods, L.L.C. v. Mean Gene's Enterprises, Inc.* 468 F. Supp. 2d 1078 (D. S. D. 2006), a "celebrity" named Mean Gene was able to get Hot Stuff Foods' trademark cancelled for violating this precise provision. For purposes of this provision, "a measure of celebrity as the voice of professional wrestling" was enough. *Id.* at 1091.

4. Section 2(d): Confusion

15 U.S.C. §1052, Lanham Act §2

(d) Consists of or comprises a mark which so resembles a mark registered in the Patent and Trademark Office, or a mark or trade name previously used in the United States by another and not abandoned, as to be likely, when used on or in connection with the goods of the applicant, to cause confusion, or to cause mistake, or to deceive ...

In re Majestic Distilling Co.

315 F.3d 1311 (Fed. Cir. 2003)

Lourie, Circuit Judge.

Majestic Distilling Company, Inc. appeals from the decision of the United States Patent and Trademark Office ("PTO") Trademark Trial and Appeal Board ("TTAB" or "Board") affirming the examining attorney's refusal to register the mark "RED BULL" for tequila. In re Majestic Distilling Co., Serial No. 74/622,781, Paper No. 22 (TTAB Nov. 29, 2001). The Board held that the examining attorney correctly refused registration on the basis of likelihood of confusion with previously registered "RED BULL" marks for malt liquor. We affirm.

BACKGROUND

Majestic seeks to register the mark "RED BULL" for tequila. Despite having asserted use in commerce since November 1, 1984, Majestic did not file its application for registration until January 18, 1995. In a first Office Action mailed August 10, 1995, the examining attorney refused registration of the mark under§2(d) of the Lanham Act, 15 U.S.C. §1052(d) (2000), on the ground of likelihood of confusion with Registration No. 1,071,580 ("RED BULL" for Scotch whiskey), issued August 16, 1977, to George Willsher & Co., Ltd.; Registration No. 1,542,792 ("RED BULL A SCHLITZ MALT LIQUOR BRAND" for malt liquor), issued June 6, 1989, to The Stroh Brewery Company; and Registration No. 1,541,794 (stylized "RED BULL" for malt liquor), issued May 30, 1989, also to Stroh. Office Action, Serial No. 74/622,781 (Aug. 10, 1995). The examining attorney also cited four of Stroh's pending applications for registration, Serial Nos. 74/541,371, 74/541,372, 74/589,654, and 74/589,656, against Majestic's application. *Id.*

After petitioning to cancel Willsher's mark for Scotch whiskey on the ground of abandonment, Majestic responded to the Office Action. Finding Majestic's response unpersuasive, however, the examining attorney made his refusal final. Office Action, Serial No. 74/622,781 (June 6, 1996). Majestic then appealed to the Board. *In re Majestic Distilling Co.*, Serial No. 74/622,781 (TTAB Apr. 15, 1997).

While Majestic's appeal was pending, Willsher's mark was canceled and Stroh's four pending applications matured into registrations. At the examining attorney's request, the Board remanded the case to him. *Id.*, slip op. at 1. He then issued another non-final Office Action, in which he refused registration of Majestic's mark not only over the '580, '792, and '794 registrations, but also over Stroh's newly matured registrations: Registration No. 1,923,974 ("RED BULL" with design for malt liquor), issued from Serial No. 74/589,656 on October 3, 1995; Registration No. 1,935,272 ("RED BULL" for malt liquor), issued from Serial No. 74/589,654 on November 14, 1995; Registration No. 2,046,277 ("RED BULL REPRESENTIN' THE REAL" for brewed malt liquor), issued from Serial No. 74/541,371 on March 18, 1997; and Registration No. 2,046,278 ("RED BULL REPRESENTIN'" for brewed malt liquor), issued from Serial No. 74/541,372 on March 18, 1997. Office Action, Serial No. 74/622,781 (Apr. 23, 1997).

Majestic made several unsuccessful attempts to traverse the examining attorney's refusal to register its mark, but the examining attorney again made his refusal final. Office Action, Serial No. 74/622,781 (Mar. 15, 2000). Majestic again appealed to the Board, which affirmed the examining attorney's second final refusal. In re Majestic Distilling Co., Serial No. 74/622,781 (TTAB Nov. 29, 2001). Majestic now appeals to this court. We have jurisdiction pursuant to 15 U.S.C. §1071 and 28 U.S.C. §1295(a)(4)(B).

DISCUSSION

Under §2(d) of the Lanham Act, the PTO may refuse to register a trademark if it "so resembles" a previously registered mark "as to be likely, when used on or in connection with the goods of the applicant, to cause confusion, or to cause mistake, or to deceive." 15 U.S.C. §1052(d) (2000). We review a determination of likelihood of confusion as a question of law based on findings of relevant underlying facts. *Specialty Brands, Inc. v. Coffee Bean Distribs., Inc.*, 748 F.2d 669, 671, 223 U.S.P.Q. 1281, 1282 (Fed. Cir. 1984). Although we review the Board's ultimate legal conclusion de novo, *In re Int'l Flavors & Fragrances, Inc.*, 183 F.3d 1361, 1365, 51 U.S.P.Q.2d 1513, 1515 (Fed. Cir. 1999), we review the Board's underlying findings of fact under the substantial evidence standard. *On-Line Careline Inc. v. Am. Online Inc.*, 229 F.3d 1080, 1085, 56 U.S.P.Q.2d 1471, 1474 (Fed. Cir. 2000). Thus, we ask whether a reasonable person might find that the evidentiary record supports the Board's conclusion. *Id.* at 1085, 56 U.S.P.Q.2d at 1475. When reviewing for substantial evidence, we take the entire record into account, including evidence that detracts from an agency's finding as well as evidence that justifies it. *Id.* at 1086, 56 U.S.P.Q.2d at 1475. The possibility that inconsistent conclusions may be drawn from the same record does not render a Board's finding unsupported by substantial evidence. *Id.*; *In re Gartside*, 203 F.3d 1305, 1312, 53 U.S.P.Q.2d 1769, 1773 (Fed. Cir. 2000).

We determine likelihood of confusion by focusing on the question whether the purchasing public would mistakenly assume that the applicant's goods originate from the same source as, or are associated with, the goods in the cited registrations. *Paula Payne Prods. Co. v. Johnson Publ'g Co.*, 473 F.2d 901, 902, 177 U.S.P.Q. 76, 77 (CCPA 1973). We make that determination on a case-by-case basis, *On-Line Careline*, 229 F.3d at 1084, 56 U.S.P.Q.2d at 1474, aided by the application of the factors set out in *In re E.I. du Pont de Nemours & Co.*, 476 F.2d 1357, 177 U.S.P.Q. 563 (CCPA 1973). Those factors are:

(1) The similarity or dissimilarity of the marks in their entireties as to appearance, sound, connotation, and commercial impression.

(2) The similarity or dissimilarity and nature of the goods ... described in an application or registration or in connection with which a prior mark is in use.

(3) The similarity or dissimilarity of established, likely-to-continue trade channels.

(4) The conditions under which and buyers to whom sales are made, i.e. "impulse" vs. careful, sophisticated purchasing.

(5) The fame of the prior mark....

(6) The number and nature of similar marks in use on similar goods.

(7) The nature and extent of any actual confusion.

(8) The length of time during and the conditions under which there has been concurrent use without evidence of actual confusion.

(9) The variety of goods on which a mark is or is not used....

(10) The market interface between the applicant and the owner of a prior mark....

(11) The extent to which applicant has a right to exclude others from use of its mark on its goods.

(12) The extent of potential confusion....

(13) Any other established fact probative of the effect of use.

Id. at 1361, 177 U.S.P.Q. at 567. Not all of the DuPont factors may be relevant or of equal weight in a given case, and "any one of the factors may control a particular case," *In re Dixie Rests., Inc.*, 105 F.3d 1405, 1406–07, 41 U.S.P.Q.2d 1531, 1533 (Fed. Cir. 1997).

Both the examining attorney and the Board applied the relevant DuPont factors to the facts of the present case. With regard to the first factor, they found that one of Stroh's registered marks, Reg. No. 1,935,272, is identical to Majestic's applied-for mark. They also found that a second registration, Reg. No. 1,541,794, is almost identical to Majestic's mark, but for the use of stylized lettering in the former. As pointed out by the examining attorney, because the drawing for Majestic's mark is in typed format and hence can potentially be represented in any manner, that stylized lettering does not provide a significant difference between the marks. We have previously held that, when word marks are identical but neither suggestive nor descriptive of the goods associated with them, the first DuPont factor weighs heavily against the applicant, *In re Martin's Famous Pastry Shoppe, Inc.*, 748 F.2d 1565, 1566, 223 U.S.P.Q. 1289, 1290 (Fed. Cir. 1984), and "even when goods or services are not competitive or intrinsically related, the use of identical marks can lead to the assumption that there is a common source," *In re Shell Oil Co.*, 992 F.2d 1204, 1207, 26 U.S.P.Q.2d 1687, 1689 (Fed. Cir. 1993).

The Board found that, if marketed under the identical mark, consumers would be likely to believe that malt liquor and tequila emanate from, or are sponsored or endorsed by, the same entity. Majestic argues against the Board's finding, asserting that malt liquor and tequila are unrelated. First, Majestic argues, malt liquor is a brewed product, whereas tequila is distilled. Secondly, the PTO's evidence of a relationship between malt liquor and tequila consists only of (1) articles demonstrating that malt liquor and tequila are occasionally found in some of the same places and (2) articles relating to Anheuser-Busch's Tequiza, a tequila-flavored beer.

The PTO responds, and we agree, that malt liquor and tequila are similar by virtue of the fact that both are alcoholic beverages that are marketed in many of the same channels of trade to many of the same consumers. Although the PTO apparently found no evidence of any manufacturer who both brews malt liquor and distills tequila, Majestic has not shown that the PTO's lack of evidence in that regard is relevant. Unless consumers are aware of the fact, if it is one, that no brewer also manufactures distilled spirits, that fact is not dispositive. The DuPont factors require us to consider only "trade channels," which may be, but are by no means necessarily, synonymous with manufacturing channels. In this case, Majestic has not demonstrated that consumers distinguish alcoholic beverages by manufacturer rather than brand name. Because substantial evidence supports the Board's conclusions that malt liquor and tequila are similar goods and are sold in many of the same established and likely-to-continue trade channels, we conclude that the second and third DuPont factors, respectively, weigh against Majestic, as well as the first.

The fourth DuPont factor seems to us to be a close question. On the one hand, the Board found that malt liquor and tequila are both relatively inexpensive products that are likely to be purchased on impulse rather than selected with careful, studied consideration and sophistication. As we have held in the past, "when the products are relatively low-priced and subject to impulse buying, the risk of likelihood of confusion is increased because purchasers of such products are held to a lesser standard of purchasing care." *Recot Inc. v. M.C. Becton*, 214 F.3d 1322, 1329, 54 U.S.P.Q.2d 1894, 1899 (Fed. Cir. 2000). On the other hand, Majestic's response that common experience suggests that "beer drinkers and drinkers of distilled spirits are extremely, and often fiercely, brand-conscious and discriminating" also has some merit. Still, Majestic has provided no survey data or evidence other than Stroh's identification of consumers of its products as "reasonably intelligent and discerning" to support its argument, and it is unclear in any event that evidence of such brand-consciousness would even favor Majestic. First, even if Majestic were correct that "common experience" shows that consumers sometimes become attached to a particular brand of beer or spirits after purchasing and consuming that brand at least once, that would say little, if anything, about whether the consumer's initial selection of that brand was based on studied consideration and sophistication or, alternatively, on impulse. Secondly, it appears to us that brand-consciousness not only can be expected to lead a consumer who already has a favorite brand of tequila to be loyal to that brand, but it also should compel a consumer who enjoys "RED BULL"-brand malt liquor but has not yet developed a taste for a particular brand of tequila to purchase "RED BULL"-brand tequila in the mistaken belief that it is manufactured or sponsored by the same entity. It seems to us that that is precisely the mistake that §2(d) of the Lanham Act seeks to prevent. To be sure, a side-by-side comparison of the two products' labels would probably dispel the mistake for most consumers. It is doubtful, however, that such a comparison would be undertaken prior to purchase of these relatively inexpensive products.

Thus, we can hardly say that the PTO's finding with respect to the fourth factor is lacking in substantial evidence. We will not upset the Board's conclusion, based on its balancing of the evidence, that these goods are more likely than not purchased on impulse.

Although the Board did not evaluate the fifth DuPont factor, Majestic argues that Stroh's "RED BULL" marks for malt liquor are not famous marks with decades of prior use, and that the present case can accordingly be distinguished from cases such as *Schlieffelin & Co. v. Molson Cos.*, 1989 TTAB LEXIS 1, 9 U.S.P.Q.2d 2069 (TTAB 1989); *In re Leslie Hennessy, Jr.*, 226 U.S.P.Q. 274 (TTAB 1985); and *Fleischmann Distilling Corp. v. Maier Brewing Co.*, 314 F.2d 149, 136 U.S.P.Q. 508 (9th Cir. 1963), which were cited by the Board. However, we find no evidence in the record to substantiate Majestic's counsel's argument that Stroh's marks are not famous. Even if such evidence were of record, though, it would have little probative value. Although we have previously held that the fame of a registered mark is relevant to likelihood of confusion, *DuPont*, 476 F.2d at 1361, 177 U.S.P.Q. at 567 (factor five), we decline to establish the converse rule that likelihood of confusion is precluded by a registered mark's not being famous.

With regard to the seventh *DuPont* factor, we agree with the Board that Majestic's uncorroborated statements of no known instances of actual confusion are of little evidentiary value. *See In re Bissett-Berman Corp.*, 476 F.2d 640, 642, 177 U.S.P.Q. 528, 529 (CCPA 1973) (stating that self-serving testimony of appellant's corporate president's unawareness of instances of actual confusion was not conclusive that actual confusion did not exist or that there was no likelihood of confusion). A showing of actual confusion would of course be highly probative, if not conclusive, of a high likelihood of confusion. The opposite is not true, however. The lack of evidence of actual confusion carries little weight, *J.C. Hall Co. v. Hallmark Cards, Inc.*, 52 C.C.P.A. 981, 340 F.2d 960, 964, 144 U.S.P.Q. 435, 438 (CCPA 1965), especially in an ex parte context.

Majestic's principal challenge appears to focus on the sixth, eighth, and tenth *DuPont* factors. First, Majestic asserts that other companies have marketed distilled spirits under the trade name "RED BULL" without any incidents of actual confusion over the course of the sixteen years that it has been selling its "RED BULL" tequila. Secondly, Majestic points to evidence showing that, over a twelve-year period, Stroh not only argued before the PTO that the "RED BULL" mark can be used concurrently for its malt liquor and others' distilled spirits without creating confusion, but also entered into agreements with George Willsher & Co., Ltd., which, as noted above, had registered "RED BULL" for Scotch whiskey, and Red Bull GmbH, which Majestic alleges manufactures "RED BULL" gin, vodka, brandy spirits, and wine. According to Majestic, the Board and the examining attorney improperly discredited the objective evidentiary value of the agreements among Stroh, Willsher, and Red Bull GmbH, as those agreements reflect the opinions of persons most familiar with the actual trade and marketing practices surrounding the goods and marks at issue, and "decisions of men who stand to lose if wrong are normally more reliable than those of examiners and judges." (quoting *DuPont*, 476 F.2d at 1363, 177 U.S.P.Q. at 569).

As the Board and the examining attorney have pointed out, however, there has been no consent agreement executed between Majestic and Stroh, only between Stroh and third parties. The record appears to be silent as to whether Majestic ever attempted to negotiate an agreement with Stroh, but, in any event, we agree that no presumption can be made that Stroh consents to Majestic's use of the mark or that Stroh has determined or admits that confusion of the public by Majestic's concurrent use of the mark is unlikely. Moreover, the Stroh agreements with Willsher and Red Bull GmbH are several years old and may not reflect current views. For example, Stroh may now have knowledge of incidents of actual confusion, and may no longer hold the same view with respect to likelihood of confusion as it did when it executed those third-party agreements or when it argued to the PTO that there was no likelihood of confusion. Moreover, the consent agreements between Stroh and the third parties contain express limitations; in particular, the Willsher-Stroh agreement prohibits Stroh's use or registration of "BLACK BULL" or "THE MAGNIFICENT BULL" for brewed malt liquor, beer, or ale, even though Willsher apparently uses those marks only on Scotch whiskey.

Majestic invited the PTO to simply pass its mark to publication so that Stroh could oppose the mark if it saw fit to do so. The PTO properly turned down Majestic's request. The appellant in Dixie Restaurants raised essentially the same argument, 105 F.3d at 1408, 41 U.S.P.Q.2d at 1535, and we held in that case that:

> It is the duty of the PTO and this court to determine whether there is a likelihood
> of confusion between two marks. *In re Apparel, Inc.*, 54 C.C.P.A. 733, 366 F.2d

1022, 1023, 151 U.S.P.Q. 353, 354 (CCPA 1966). It is also our duty "to afford rights to registrants without constantly subjecting them to the financial and other burdens of opposition proceedings." *Id.*; *see also In re Clorox Co.*, 578 F.2d 305, 308, 198 U.S.P.Q. 337, 341 (CCPA 1978); McCarthy, [McCarthy on Trademarks and Unfair Competition] §23.24[1][d] (where PTO rejects an application under section 1052(d), "it is no answer for the applicant to ask that the application be passed to publication to see whether the owner of the cited mark will oppose the registration"). Otherwise protecting their rights under the Lanham Act would be an onerous burden for registrants.

Id.

Majestic also argues that it is the senior user and, as such, its "decision ... not to petition to cancel Stroh's registrations, or to sue Stroh to stop its use of the RED BULL trademark, is significant evidence that confusion is not likely." In support of its position, Majestic cites *Bongrain International (American) Corp. v. Delice de France, Inc.*, 811 F.2d 1479, 1 U.S.P.Q.2d 1775 (Fed. Cir. 1987), for the proposition that "conduct of a prior user in not objecting to subsequent use of a similar mark by another is objective evidence to be considered when determining likelihood of confusion." It is unclear where Majestic derived that paraphrase, because the only statement in *Bongrain* that relates to objections raised by a prior user is: "As the prior user, Delice would be the one to object to the use and registration of Bongrain's mark. It has never objected to the use and, notwithstanding this cancellation proceeding, it has not seriously objected to its registration." *Id.* at 1485, 1 U.S.P.Q.2d at 1779. That statement merely shows that Delice's actions were consistent with a belief that no likelihood of confusion existed. Neither that statement nor any other in Bongrain, however, suggests to us that the inaction of a prior user is "objective evidence to be considered when determining likelihood of confusion."

In any event, the Board's decision in the present case is not in conflict with our decision in *Bongrain*, for there are at least three critical distinctions that can be drawn between the facts in *Bongrain* and those in this case. First, unlike in the present case, there was an agreement executed between the parties to the suit in *Bongrain*, governing the uses of the respective marks. *Id.* at 1482, 1 U.S.P.Q.2d at 1776. Secondly, the products in connection with which the marks at issue in *Bongrain* were to be used were significantly different from each other (i.e., milk and cheese on one hand, and baked goods on the other). *Id.* at 1481, 1 U.S.P.Q.2d at 1776. Third, the court in *Bongrain* distinguished *DuPont*, which, as here, involved identical marks, on the basis that the marks (i.e., "DELICE DE FRANCE" and "LE PETIT DELICE DE FRANCE"), although similar, were not identical. *Id.* at 1483, 1 U.S.P.Q.2d at 1777. Thus, whereas in *Bongrain* we held that it was "not necessary, in view of cumulative differences between the marks and the goods enumerated, to hold that confusion is likely," we hold that, in view of the similarities between the marks and the goods enumerated in the present case, we see no error in the Board's conclusion that confusion is likely.

We also agree with the Board that Majestic's decision not to avail itself of the statutory provisions for opposition and cancellation before Stroh's marks became incontestable could have been made for any number of business reasons unrelated to the likelihood of confusion between the marks, and is not entitled to any significant weight. Although prior use can be relevant to the questions whether a party can enjoin another's use of a mark, whether and where a party has a right to use a mark after the same mark is registered by another party for use in connection with the same goods or services, and whether a party can successfully oppose or petition to cancel another party's registration, it is not one of the *DuPont* factors and does not directly bear on likelihood of confusion. Several of the *DuPont* factors contain the phrase "the prior mark," but it is clear from their context that that phrase refers to a prior registered mark and not simply to a prior used mark. In any event, vindication of Majestic's asserted position of priority is more appropriately raised in proceedings designed to evaluate such a position.

Neither the Board nor either party has raised arguments that relate to any of the ninth, eleventh, twelfth, and thirteenth *DuPont* factors, and we therefore do not discuss them.

In summary, we find no fault in the Board's affirmance of the examining attorney's refusal to register Majestic's mark. The Board found, on the basis of substantial evidence, that Majestic's mark is identical to at least one of the previously registered marks, that malt liquor and tequila are related as alcoholic goods sold through the same trade channels to many of the same consumers, and that malt liquor and tequila are both fairly inexpensive and likely to be purchased on impulse. Although Majestic's principal arguments are not without merit, analysis under DuPont requires a balancing of the relevant factors, and we find the balance in this case tilts towards a likelihood of confusion. *See Dixie Rests.*, 105 F.3d at 1407, 41 U.S.P.Q.2d at 1533 ("We see no error in the board's decision to focus on the DuPont factors it deemed dispositive.").

We have considered Majestic's other arguments and find them unpersuasive.

CONCLUSION

Substantial evidence supports the Board's findings. On the basis of those findings, we agree with the Board's conclusion that consumers who are aware of Stroh's "RED BULL" malt liquor and who then encounter Majestic's "RED BULL" tequila are likely to mistakenly believe that both come from or are sponsored or licensed by the same entity. Accordingly, the Board's decision is

AFFIRMED.

Marshall Field & Company v. Mrs. Fields Cookies
25 U.S.P.Q.2d (BNA) 1321 (TTAB 1992)

OPINION BY ROONEY, MEMBER:

An application was filed by Mrs. Fields Cookies to register the mark MRS. FIELDS on the principal register under Section 2(f) for bakery goods, namely, cookies and brownies. Use since November 15, 1981 was alleged.

Registration has been opposed by Marshall Field & Company on the ground that applicant's mark so resembles the mark FIELD'S previously used and registered by opposer for retail department store services and the mark MARSHALL FIELD'S previously used and registered by opposer for baked goods and other foods and for retail department store services, as to be likely to cause confusion, mistake or deception.

Applicant admitted that opposer is the "purported" owner of the pleaded registrations; that applicant is engaged in the baking, advertising, distributing and selling of baked goods and other foods, including but not limited to chocolate chip cookies, brownies and candies and in rendering retail food services; and that it adopted and began use of the mark MRS. FIELDS in script form after opposer's first use of its pleaded marks. The remaining allegations were denied. Applicant affirmatively pleaded laches, acquiescence and estoppel.

Subsequently, Marshall Field & Company (opposer above) filed a petition to cancel the registrations of the marks MRS. FIELD'S COOKIES in the design.... (the word, "cook-

ies" disclaimed) for retail bakery store services; MRS. FIELD'S COOKIES in the same de-sign with the same disclaimer for bakery goods, namely, cookies and brownies; and MRS. FIELDS, for retail bakery store services.

The grounds for cancellation are that petitioner has, for many years prior to respon-dent's date of first use, been engaged in the production and sale of baked goods and other foods and in rendering retail food and department store services; that, as early as 1865, petitioner adopted and was known by the mark FIELD'S in association with retail de-partment stores and the sale of a wide variety of goods therein; that as early as 1881, pe-titioner adopted and was known by the mark MARSHALL FIELD'S in connection with retail department stores and the sale of goods therein; that as early as 1946, petitioner adopted and was known by the mark MARSHALL FIELD'S in connection with retail food store and department store services and the sale of food items, particularly cookies and brownies; that petitioner has registered FIELD'S for retail department store services, and MARSHALL FIELD'S (in script form, for baked goods and other foods, and for retail de-partment store services; and that respondent's marks, as applied to its bakery goods and retail bakery store services, so resemble petitioner's marks as to be likely to cause confu-sion, mistake or deception.

* * *

Turning now to the merits of these proceedings, the facts revealed by the record show that petitioner has 26 department stores in the United States. In addition to the usual re-tail store services, the company issues catalogs and sells through mail and telephone or-ders. The main products in MARSHALL FIELD'S stores are apparel, housewares and furniture. In addition, MARSHALL FIELD'S stores contain restaurants and sell candy and bakery products. The first in-store restaurant was opened in 1890. There are 41 restaurants in 21 stores. There is a group of restaurants called Greener Fields and another group all having names of trees, such as, the Walnut Room and the Linden Room. Cer-tain dishes on the menus of petitioner's restaurants are referred to by the name FIELD'S, such as, FIELD'S Special Sandwich and FIELD'S Covered Apple Pie. When this practice started is not quite clear, although there is testimony that it occurred at least as early as 1970. The bakeries use the name MARSHALL FIELD'S or MARSHALL FIELD'S GOURMET on their packaging, and those bakery goods which are considered MAR-SHALL FIELD'S specialties are sometimes, at the discretion of the department manager, labeled as FIELD'S, such as, Field's Pecan Pie. When this practice was initiated has not been established.

There has been a full-line bakery operating on the 13th floor of the Chicago store since 1920 producing breads, pies, cakes, tortes, cookies, muffins and wedding cakes which are baked fresh daily and are sold in the in-store bakeries or in the restaurants. There are five stores which have free-standing bakery counters and there are five bakeries that are outside of, but adjacent to, restaurants in MARSHALL FIELD'S stores. In 1988, petitioner had sales of just over a billion dollars. In the same year, petitioner's sales of baked goods amounted to $3 million.

Petitioner issues several mail order catalogs each year and has done so since the 1920's. These are mailed to over 800,000 charge account customers and are available in the retail department stores. Since the 1940's petitioner has issued a catalog for packaged food items and includes packaged food items in its Christmas catalog. Petitioner makes candy which is sold in its retail stores and is also available through mail and telephone order catalogs. Petitioner's goods are packaged in bags, boxes and other packaging bearing its marks either in block print or in a distinctive script.

Petitioner employs various media for its advertising, i.e., radio, television, print and in-store distributed brochures. The evidence illustrates that petitioner's stores are often referred to as FIELD'S in newspaper and magazine articles as well as in books. Certain of the departments in the retail operations use the term FIELD'S, i.e., FIELD'S AFAR is a gift department, FIELD'S CHOICE, FIELD GEAR and FIELD MANOR are apparel departments, and there is also a FIELD'S FASHION SERVICE which is a shopping service for customers.

Petitioner owns registrations for the marks, MARSHALL FIELD'S for baked goods and other foods; MARSHALL FIELD'S for retail department store services; MARSHALL FIELD'S GOURMET and design for baked goods and other foods; FIELD'S for retail department store services; MARSHALL FIELD'S GOURMET for retail grocery store, mail and telephone order food services and restaurant services, FIELD GEAR for men's, women's and children's clothing; FIELD SPORT for men's and women's clothing; FIELD'S CHOICE for women's clothing; FIELD'S AFAR for clothing and retail department store services; and MARSHALL FIELD'S EXPRESSED for mail and telephone order services.

Respondent's business came into being in 1977 when Mrs. Debra Fields opened a cookie shop called MRS. FIELDS CHOCOLATE CHIPPERY in Palo Alto, California. By 1981, there were 23 MRS. FIELDS CHOCOLATE CHIPPERY stores. The mark was used in the stores and on the packaging for the cookies. During this period, some of the stores carried only the name MRS. FIELDS because of size constraints or because of landlord specifications. In 1981, respondent began use of the marks MRS. FIELDS in script form and MRS. FIELDS COOKIES in script form on a polka dot background and began use of a red and white motif which was, and is, used in the stores on signs and uniforms and on the packaging. There are currently more than 400 MRS. FIELDS stores in the country. Respondent does not use FIELDS alone, although there were one or two instances, noted in publications, of references to respondent as FIELDS by third parties. However, in these instances this was the author's shorthand method of referring back to MRS. FIELDS, which had been previously mentioned.

* * *

The persona of Debra Fields is central to all of respondent's advertising and she has made and continues to make frequent public appearances at lectures, meetings, on television, etc. In addition, the company uses other methods of advertising such as television, radio, print and in-store point of purchase materials. Debra Fields estimated that about 5% of annual sales are spent on advertising. A great many articles have been written about the company and about Debra Fields in newspapers and magazines.

* * *

Turning to the question of likelihood of confusion, petitioner's evidence of its ownership of valid and subsisting registrations of its pleaded marks make it unnecessary for us to examine the question of priority with respect to petitioner's registered marks for the goods and services listed in the registrations. Apart therefrom, there is ample evidence of use of the marks MARSHALL FIELD'S for retail department store services for a very long period of time before the date of first use by respondent. There is also evidence that petitioner has used the mark FIELD'S as well for department store services, and that the public has come to recognize the mark FIELD'S in connection with the famous department store since before respondent's first use of its marks. There is further evidence that FIELD'S has been used to designate certain foods, including baked goods, on menus in petitioner's restaurants since at least 1970 and that at some time FIELD'S came to be used to designate certain specialty items in petitioner's bakeries.

Petitioner argues that respondent's marks are nearly identical to petitioner's marks, FIELD'S and MARSHALL FIELD'S; that the evidence of record of petitioner's and the public's use of the nickname or abbreviation FIELD'S to refer to petitioner and the goods sold and services rendered by petitioner supports its ownership of the mark FIELD'S; that respondent's marks are MRS. FIELDS and MRS. FIELDS COOKIES; that respondent has abandoned the earlier version of its mark, MRS. FIELDS' CHOCOLATE CHIPPERY, and has essentially stopped using MRS. FIELDS COOKIES; that the dominant portion of both parties' marks is FIELD'S; and that purchasers familiar with petitioner's marks are likely to assume, upon encountering respondent's advertising or packaging bearing the marks MRS. FIELDS or MRS. FIELDS COOKIES that those marks are mere variations of petitioner's marks and that there is a business association or connection between the parties. It is asserted that the other portions of respondent's mark merely add to the commercial impression the idea that a relative of a person named FIELD or FIELDS is selling similar goods. It is also petitioner's position that respondent has increased the likelihood of confusion between its mark and petitioner's since its initial use of MRS. FIELDS' CHOCOLATE CHIPPERY in connection with the sale of cookies and brownies; that it now seeks to register and to maintain registrations for marks which are nearly identical to petitioner's marks, particularly petitioner's FIELD'S mark with the marks presented in a similar signature script, while at the same time expanding the types of goods sold by respondent and the channels of trade through which its goods are sold so that they are more similar to those through which the goods of petitioner are sold than was previously so.

With respect to the services of these parties, it is noted that respondent's application and one of its registrations are for "bakery goods, namely, cookies and brownies" while the other two registrations are for retail bakery store services. Petitioner uses its marks FIELD'S and MARSHALL FIELD'S in relation to retail department store services. Petitioner has a number of bakeries and restaurants within its department stores and respondent has sold its bakery products in major department stores, i.e., Bloomingdale's and Macy's. We would have to conclude that there is a relationship between the parties' goods and services such that the use of the same or confusingly similar marks is likely to cause confusion, mistake or deception. The question to be resolved is whether the marks of these parties are so similar as to be likely to cause this confusion.

It is noted initially that petitioner's Chairman Miller has testified that it was only because of the evolution of respondent's marks from MRS. FIELDS CHOCOLATE CHIPPERY to MRS. FIELDS COOKIES to MRS. FIELDS and the change from block letters to script that petitioner has come to believe that respondent's marks have become progressively closer to its own marks, thereby increasing the likelihood of confusion.

We would not have a problem with Mrs. Fields using her name in conjunction with cookies and baked goods products if it were not conflicting in design and color with Marshall Field's traditional signature and our use of color.

Introduced during Mr. Miller's testimony was a newspaper article dated January 31, 1988 from the Sun Times in which a MARSHALL FIELD'S employee was quoted as saying much the same thing, i.e., that petitioner does not oppose respondent's using the name for bakery goods, but that the evolution of the name to its current use is at the root of the dispute. Mr. Miller stated that he did not disagree with that statement.

With that in mind, we turn to the question of likelihood of confusion of the parties' marks. As to the mark MARSHALL FIELD'S, it is used in connection with all of the department store services performed by petitioner. There is no doubt that, for petitioner's department store services, the mark MARSHALL FIELD's is extremely well known. There is also evidence that this mark is used in connection with petitioner's in-store bakeries and restaurants. For the most part, petitioner uses the mark MARSHALL FIELD'S GOURMET and design and MARSHALL FIELD'S on the packaging used in the bakeries and for those carry-out items sold in its restaurants.

Petitioner has argued that FIELD'S is the dominant part of the mark MARSHALL FIELD'S and that the purchasing public will assume upon seeing MRS. FIELDS on baked goods that there is a connection between the MRS. FIELDS bakeries and MARSHALL FIELD'S department stores. With respect to that argument, we note that Field(s) is a common surname as shown by a number of telephone directories and in two dictionaries of surnames, American Surnames, 1969, Chilton Book Company and A Dictionary of Surnames, 1989, Oxford University Press, submitted by respondent. In addition, respondent has also introduced a number of third-party registrations of marks having as a component thereof the name FIELD(S) and its variations as well as deposition testimony of nine individuals involved in retail sales who use the name FIELD(S) in connection therewith.

It is duly noted that, except in the case of the deposition evidence, the remaining third-party evidence is subject to the objection that this material does not prove use of FIELD(S) by third parties. However, we do not have to find proof of use of FIELD(S) as a trade or service mark in order to conclude that this is a common surname easily recognized as such and that purchasers are accustomed to distinguishing between such common surnames by whatever slight differences may exist in the marks as a whole. In this case, the question is whether the addition of FIELD(S) of, on the one hand, the given name MARSHALL and, on the other, the title MRS., is enough of a difference to enable purchasers to make that distinction. We believe that, given the fame of MARSHALL FIELD'S for department store services and the fame shown to have been afforded to MRS. FIELDS for its bakery services and goods, the public will readily recognize the differences in the marks as used on the respective goods and services and are not likely to be confused as to the sources of the goods and services offered thereunder.

We recognize that MARSHALL FIELD'S is a famous mark and that famous marks are normally afforded a wide scope of protection. However, in this case we are faced with a situation in which the respondent's mark has also achieved a significant degree of fame in the marketplace. It is because both marks are famous that we believe the public will easily recognize the differences in the marks and distinguish between them. It might have been a closer question had there been some evidence that MARSHALL FIELD'S used other familial terms with FIELD'S such as MISS FIELD'S, MR. FIELD'S or even GRANDMA FIELD'S. But the combining forms used by petitioner have altogether different connotations, such as, FIELD'S AFAR, FIELD'S CHOICE, FIELD GEAR, FIELD'S MANOR and FIELD'S FASHION SERVICE. Rather than causing an association to be assumed between MRS. FIELDS and MARSHALL FIELD'S, these combined terms are more likely to have the opposite effect.

As to whether the script form of respondent's mark enhances the likelihood of confusion, the two marks are shown below.

It appears to the Board that the script used in each mark is different enough that, combined with the differences in the words, purchasers are not likely to confuse the source of the goods or services offered thereunder because of the script forms in which they are presented. As for petitioner's arguments relative to trade dress, it is recognized that trade dress may have some effect as well in the public's perception of a mark. *See* Kenner Parker Toys, Inc., *supra.* However, we do not believe the trade dress used by these parties would foster a likelihood of confusion between these marks. Respondent uses the colors red and white on its packaging and signs while petitioner has frequently referred to its own color scheme as MARSHALL FIELD'S green. The only time respondent uses any green in its packaging is during the Christmas and St. Patrick's Day holidays, at which time the colors will be perceived as holiday decorations. We do not think that the parties' color schemes are likely to foster any confusion in the minds of purchasers.

There are a number of additional reasons which lead us to this conclusion. While there is abundant evidence of the fame of the mark MARSHALL FIELD'S, as used in connection with department store services, we are not convinced that MARSHALL FIELD'S is equally famous for bakery goods and services, except to the extent that they are sold within its department stores. That is to say, the evidence is clear that the restaurant and bakery store services of petitioner have always been confined to its own premises so that customers of petitioner would not expect to find a bakery belonging to petitioner standing alone in a shopping mall or on a city street. When they purchase baked goods in either the in-store bakeries or restaurants, customers know they are dealing with MARSHALL FIELD'S department store. As to those MRS. FIELDS bakeries located in Bloomingdale's and Macy's, it is unlikely that a bakery found in a competing department store would be attributed to petitioner.

Turning to petitioner's mark FIELD'S, the record shows that in addition to use as a service mark for department store services, FIELD'S is sometimes used to identify bakery products, such as, FIELD'S cheese cake, in bakery counter displays and is used to identify specialty items on menus in petitioner's restaurants, as in FIELD'S Famous Specialties, The FIELD'S Special or FIELD'S Fruit Cake. Although petitioner has achieved secondary meaning for the mark FIELD'S alone, as illustrated by petitioner's catalogs and the numerous publications referring to petitioner by that name, we agree with respondent that the secondary meaning of that mark is limited to department store services and does not extend to restaurant and bakery store services. The evidence strongly suggests that use of the mark FIELD'S in catalogs and in the stores is intended to be and is recognized as a shorthand reference to MARSHALL FIELD'S. As petitioner itself has suggested, companies are frequently called by shortened names, such as, Penney's for J.C. Penney's, Sears for Sears and Roebuck (even before it officially changed its name to Sears alone), Ward's for Montgomery Ward's, and Bloomies for Bloomingdale's. Moreover, we believe that FIELD'S for petitioner's services may be readily distinguished from MRS. FIELD'S for respondent's goods and services in the same way that KING'S for candy was held to be distinguishable from MISS KING'S for cakes. *See King Candy Company v. Eunice King's Kitchen, Inc.,* 182 U.S.P.Q. 108 (CCPA 1974).

In reaching our conclusion on the likelihood of confusion, we have taken into consideration the survey introduced by petitioner. In June of 1988, petitioner engaged the services of Dr. Ivan Ross, Professor of Marketing at the University of Minnesota, to design and supervise a mall intercept survey to determine whether there is a likelihood of confusion between the marks of these parties. The interviews were conducted by trained market research interviewers under the direction of Dr. Leon Kaplan of Princeton Research and Consulting of Princeton, New Jersey.

The study took place in shopping malls in Chicago, Milwaukee and Houston. The cities were selected because both parties had retail stores in those markets, but the particular malls at which the interviews were conducted were selected to exclude any in which the parties' stores were located. The respondents were adults of 18 years or older who did not work at any of the stores in that particular mall. A total of 450 persons were interviewed.

The survey featured three cells. Cell 1 involved the MRS. FIELDS CHOCOLATE CHIPPERY bag and a MARSHALL FIELD'S (green) bag. Cell 2 involved the MRS. FIELDS' COOKIES bag and the same MARSHALL FIELD'S (green) bag. Cell 3 involved the MRS. FIELDS MACADAMIA ROYALES chocolate covered nuts box and MARSHALL FIELD'S (green) bag. The last comparison was changed in Houston and Milwaukee where a MARSHALL FIELD'S Frango raspberry chocolate box was substituted for the green bag.

Potential interviewees were approached by the interviewer and asked initial screening questions. Following successful screening and agreement to an interview, these individuals were taken to an interview location and assigned randomly to one of the 3 study cells where the first inquiry was as follows.

I'd like you to look at these two bags. (SHOW RESPONDENT TWO Bags marked 12 and 46). Would you say that the store whose things come in this bag (HAND 12 BAG TO RESPONDENT) and the store whose things come in this bag (HAND 46 BAG TO RESPONDENT) have a business connection or a business association with one another, or not?

To those responding affirmatively, the first question was followed by questions as to how the respondent thought they were connected or associated. Respondents who gave a negative answer were asked why they answered as they did, while the interviewees who indicated that they didn't know the answer to the first question were then asked the personal information questions which concluded each participant's interview.

The report on the study indicates that the highest degree of source connection was between the MRS. FIELDS' box for chocolate covered macadamia nuts and the MARSHALL FIELD'S Frango raspberry chocolate box (27.5% +/- 10% at .95 confidence level) and the smallest between the MRS. FIELDS' macadamia box and the MARSHALL FIELD'S bag (6% with sample size 50, not significantly greater than zero). Intermediate levels of 8.4 to 11.7% (+/- 7/5 at the .95 confidence level) source connection was seen between MRS. FIELDS' bags and MARSHALL FIELD'S green bag. Following a discussion of the responses, it was concluded by Dr. Ross that "a significant number of consumers in geographically dispersed markets in which MARSHALL FIELD'S and MRS. FIELDS compete erroneously believe that there is a business connection or association between these two stores because of their names."

Respondent argues, based on the testimony of its witness, Dr. Sorensen, who found a number of flaws in the design, implementation and interpretation of the survey, that the findings of the survey are based on leading questions, side-by-side comparisons, irrelevant stimuli, an absence of control questions and a design incongruous with the marketplace.

Survey evidence is often controversial, if only because there are so many factors to be considered in determining the weight to be given to this type of evidence. We frankly confess that we are not experts in this area. However, we tend to agree with Dr. Sorensen on several of the points he made. It appears to us that the initial inquiry to the respondents was indeed a leading question in that it clearly indicated the direction that the responses would be expected to go. We do not think that it can be seriously disputed that this is a leading question from the emphasis intended to be given to certain words and the formation of the question, which introduces nothing more than the idea that a business association indeed exists right up to the final two words. This question tends to deliberately plant in the respondent's mind the idea that there is a connection between the stores from which the two packages come. Such a question is certainly highly prejudicial to the results.

The presentation of the packages side-by-side also appears to us to be prejudicial inasmuch as they are unlikely to be seen in this mode in an actual encounter in the marketplace. This type of presentation introduces additional features, such as the trade dress of the packages, which are not directly involved in a determination of the likelihood of confusion between the marks. We agree also that the use of a bag showing the MRS. FIELDS CHOCOLATE CHIPPERY mark is not helpful to our present determination of likelihood of confusion inasmuch as that mark had been discontinued almost a decade before the survey was conducted. Another objection that we find to be of merit is to the question concerning the parties' boxes for candies, goods which are not involved in this proceeding.

For these reasons, we find the survey to be seriously flawed and the results to be of little probative value.

Finally, we are convinced that respondent's mark was not selected with any motive of trading on petitioner's good will. Nor do we believe that the selection of the sites for MRS. FIELDS cookie stores were made with any such intent. Rather, the evidence supports the contention that the site selections were made in accordance with the requirements discussed by Mr. Murphy during his deposition and that these requirements involved questions of traffic patterns, visibility, accessibility and opportunity. As to those stores in locations close to petitioner's stores, there appears to be no reason to believe that respondent located any of its stores near a MARSHALL FIELD'S store in order to trade on petitioner's good will.

As for the purported instances of actual confusion, we have previously indicated that Mr. Rozak's testimony to the effect that he had spoken to at least three persons, known to him, who asked him whether MRS. FIELDS is a part of, or a franchise of, MARSHALL FIELD'S does not convince us that there has been actual confusion. This is because the inquiries indicate that these persons were aware that MARSHALL FIELD'S and MRS. FIELDS were two different entities. Another reason we find this testimony unpersuasive is because none of these persons was called as a witness and questioned as to the reasons for his inquiries. The same is true with respect to similar testimony from Mr. Miller, petitioner's Chairman. Nor can we say that actual confusion was expressed by respondent's attorney in referring to MARSHALL FIELD'S when he meant MRS. FIELDS during the course of deposing a witness. It is obvious that respondent's attorney was quite aware of the differences between the two and that what occurred was nothing more than a slip of the tongue under the pressure of conducting the interrogation.

* * *

In view of the foregoing, the petitions for cancellation are denied, the opposition is dismissed and the counterclaim for cancellation is dismissed.

Notes

1. *Use analogous to trademark use.* Refusals contemplated under Section 2(d) of the Lanham Act arise when a third party uses the same or similar mark on the same or similar goods prior to the applicant. However, in rare cases "use" sufficient to oppose a trademark application under Section 2(d) need not be the same level of "use" that generates actual trademark rights in the prior user. That is, "use analogous to trademark use" might be sufficient to oppose a registration but not sufficient to actually obtain a registration for the prior user. Use analogous to trademark use means "use of a nature and extent such as to create an association of the term with the user's goods." *Malcolm Nicol & Co. v. Witco Corp.*, 881 F.2d 1063, 1065 (Fed. Cir. 1989) (*quoting* 3 McCarthy §20:16, at 20–35 to 20–36). That is, one does not have to claim actual use in the normal course of trade to establish rights to oppose a trademark application. Prior advertising or use in product literature, for example, would not be sufficient use to obtain a registration but it would be sufficient use to oppose the application of another.

2. In a move stunning in its disregard for an overwhelming loyal customer base, in 2005 Federated Department Stores acquired the Marshall Field's line and in 2006 discontinued the use of that ubiquitous household trademark. Generations of young would-be shoppers grew up going to the downtown Chicago flag-ship store, shopping with their parents, eating lunch at the Walnut Room, and generally sensing that Marshall Field's was a cultural icon as well as a well-anointed department store. In 2006, the stores were renamed Macy's. The loyal Marshal Field shoppers are now convinced that Macy's is a lesser mark and many will now not step foot inside a Macy's store. Why would Macy's engage in what can only be described as self-destructive conduct and eliminate the Marshall Field's brand. What can they hope to accomplish?

5(a). Section 2(e)(1): Merely Descriptive

15 U.S.C. §1052, Lanham Act §2

(e) Consists of a mark which

(1) when used on or in connection with the goods of the applicant is merely descriptive or deceptively misdescriptive of them

In re Bed & Breakfast Registry
791 F.2d 157 (CAFC 1986)

Newman, J.

The U.S. Patent and Trademark Office (PTO) refused registration on the Principal Register of the service mark BED & BREAKFAST REGISTRY for "making lodging reservations for others in private homes." The Trademark Trial and Appeal Board (the "Board") upheld the refusal on two grounds: first, that applicant's mark so resembles the service mark BED & BREAKFAST INTERNATIONAL for "room booking agency services" as to be likely to cause confusion under 15 U.S.C. §1052(d) (section 2(d) of the Lanham Act); and second, the applicant's mark as applied to its services is merely descriptive of those services in terms of 15 U.S.C. §1052(e)(1) (section 2(e)(1) of the Lanham Act). We reverse the rejection under section 2(d) and affirm the rejection under section 2(e)(1).

Descriptiveness

A mark is "merely descriptive", in terms of section 2(e)(1) of the Lanham Act, if it "would immediately convey to one seeing or hearing it the thought of appellant's services." *In re American Society of Clinical Pathologists, Inc.*, 58 C.C.P.A. 1240, 442 F.2d 1404, 1407, 169 U.S.P.Q. (BNA) 800, 801 (CCPA 1971). Whether a mark is merely descriptive is a question of fact, determined from the viewpoint of the relevant purchasing public. Evidence of the purchasing public's understanding of the term may be obtained from any competent source, such as dictionaries, newspapers, or surveys. *See In re Northland Aluminum Products, Inc.*, 777 F.2d 1556, 1559, 227 U.S.P.Q. (BNA) 961, 963 (Fed. Cir. 1985); *In re Abcor Development Corp.*, 588 F.2d 811, 814, 200 U.S.P.Q. (BNA) 215, 218 (CCPA 1978). The public's understanding of the term may also change with time.

Although the phrase "bed and breakfast" is descriptive, applicant argues that the mark BED & BREAKFAST REGISTRY is not merely descriptive as applied to its services. This issue turns on the meaning of the word "registry" in the context of the mark in its entirety.

The parties have analyzed the dictionary definitions of "registry" in great detail, these definitions including: registration, enrollment, a ship's nationality, an official record, and an entry in a register. Applicant points out that it does not keep a register of lodgings for public use, and argues that "registry" requires an official record. Applicant asserts that it provides a reservation service, and that this service is independent of whether it chooses to maintain a private list of lodgings. The Board found that applicant's registry "is nonetheless clearly a part of its services and in fact it is so essential a part that without it the services could not be conducted".

In *American Society of Clinical Pathologists*, a majority of the Court of Customs and Patent Appeals held that the mark REGISTRY OF MEDICAL TECHNOLOGISTS was merely descriptive as applied to its services, which included examining and certifying medical technologists. That court viewed the maintenance of a roster or registry of medical technologists as part of the certification services, and concluded that the mark was descriptive of the services to which it was applied. 442 F.2d at 1406–07, 169 U.S.P.Q. at 801.

The Board was not persuaded by applicant's argument that *American Society of Clinical Pathologists* equates "registry" with an official record book. Before the Board were the results of the examining attorney's "Nexis" search which contained excerpts from two 1983 newspaper articles, one in the Washington Post and one syndicated by United Press International (UPI), which reported a bed and breakfast registry offered in Maryland by Sharp-Adams, Inc. The UPI article stated that the idea resulted from the founders' "reading a newspaper article about bed-and-breakfast registries in California and New England". The descriptive use of the word "registry" by others weighs against the applicant's argument that its own use is not descriptive of similar services.

The Board concluded that BED & BREAKFAST REGISTRY, in its common and dictionary meaning, would be understood to describe a register of bed and breakfast lodgings, and may convey the related thought of registering at a bed and breakfast lodging. On the record adduced, the Board did not err in finding applicant's mark merely descriptive of the services to which it is applied. We affirm the refusal of registration under section 2(e)(1).

The denial of registration is affirmed.

AFFIRMED

5(b). Section 2(e)(1): Deceptively Misdescriptive

Steinberg Brothers, Inc. v. New England-Overall Co., Inc.
377 F.2d 1004 (CCPA 1967)

ALMOND, J.

This is an appeal from the decision of the Trademark Trial and Appeal Board dismissing appellant's opposition to appellee's application to register NUHIDE for "dungarees."

Appellant is engaged in the tanning of animal hides into leather, and the sale of such leather, which is used, inter alia, in making cowboys' chaps, which are leather leggings resembling trousers without a seat and worn over regular pants as a leg protection. Appellee's dungarees, on the other hand, are not made of, nor do they contain, leather.

Appellant contends that NUHIDE is the phonetic equivalent of either "new hide" or "gnu hide," a gnu being a type of antelope, and that, as applied to dungarees, the mark sought to be registered by appellee is deceptive and/or deceptively misdescriptive of the goods under sections 2(a) and 2(e)(1) of the Trademark Act of 1946, 15 USC 1052(a), (e)(1), since the term NUHIDE would indicate to purchasers thereof that the goods contain, or are made of, leather or hide, whereas such is not in fact the case. In support of these contentions appellant cites the decisions of this court in R. Neumann & Co. v. Bon-Ton Auto Upholstery, Inc., 51 CCPA 934, 326 F.2d 799, 140 U.S.P.Q. 245 (1964) and R. Neumann & Co. v. Overseas Shipments, Inc., 51 CCPA 946, 326 F.2d 786, 140 U.S.P.Q. 276 (1964).

The former case involved the term VYNAHYDE for non-leather plastic film which could be made to simulate leather, and for plastic film made into furniture slip covers used to cover various types of upholstery, including leather. The latter case involved the term DURA-HYDE for plastic material of leatherlike appearance made into shoes, the uppers thereof being made to simulate both the grain appearance and the color of tanned leather. With regard to these and other precedents relied upon by appellant-opposer, we think the board correctly and appropriately stated that:

In each of the cases relied upon by opposer, however, the goods in question were either leather substitutes or products made of leather substitutes, whereas such is not the case with respect to the goods of the instant applicant; and none of the cited cases otherwise stand for the proposition advanced by opposer, i.e. the use of leather terms for any and all non-leather products is per se deceptive and deceptively misdescriptive.

We likewise agree with the following analysis by the board of the particular facts and circumstances of the case at bar:

It thus appears, and it is a matter of common knowledge, that dungarees are a particular type of garment made exclusively from a particular type of cotton fabric, as it likewise is that chaps are a distinctly different type of garment made exclusively of leather. Under these circumstances, it is our opinion that the purchasing public is not at all likely to be deceived, misled or induced by applicant's use of "NUHIDE" into buying applicant's dungarees in the mistaken belief that they are made in whole or in part of leather or into buying applicant's dungarees in the mistaken belief that they are chaps.

Appellant's arguments are largely based on the fact that dungarees, e.g. bluejeans, are one type of work pants, a class of goods which might also include cowboys' chaps. Therefore, according to appellant, the goods of the parties are competing. This argument seems to ignore the fact that chaps, which have no seat, would only be worn in conjunction with regular work pants, such as dungarees. Thus the parties' goods are not competing. Also, the description of goods in appellee's application is limited to "dungarees," not work pants broadly, and the specimen label for the goods describes them as "A COMPLETELY WASHABLE Western Dungaree." While the label also apparently misdescribes the dungarees as "CHAPS," as noted by the board, we do not consider this to be deceptively misdescriptive under the circumstances of this case, especially since seatless chaps may be worn in conjunction with, but not as a substitute for, dungarees.

Having found no reversible error in the decision of the board dismissing appellant's opposition, we affirm that decision.

WORLEY, C.J., did not participate.

DISSENT: KIRKPATRICK, JUDGE, DISSENTING.

As noted by the majority, this court in *R. Neumann & Co. v. Bon-Ton Auto Upholstery, Inc.*, 51 CCPA 934, 326 F.2d 799, 140 U.S.P.Q. 245, held that "VYNAHYDE" was both deceptive and deceptively misdescriptive of plastic films and plastic films made into furniture slipcovers, because it gave the erroneous impression that they were made of leather. In the present case the majority holds that "NUHIDE" is not deceptive or deceptively misdescriptive when applied to a type of pants known as dungarees. The fact that dungarees are made from a certain type of cloth does not in my view prevent a purchaser from assuming that the same style of pants is made from a different material, the word "dungarees" being regarded as a style designation. Under these circumstances I think that the word "NUHIDE" would convey to the prospective purchaser that he would be obtaining a pair of leather pants styled as blue jeans or dungarees are now styled. It seems to me that the majority's reasoning might lead to a conclusion that a trademark such as "LEATHER DUNGAREES" would not be deceptive or deceptively misdescriptive, presumably because no one ought to believe the statement. It is also of some significance that the specimen label misdescribes the goods in question as chaps which are normally made of leather.

I would, therefore, reverse the decision of the board.

Glendale Int'l Corp. v. PTO

374 F. Supp. 2d 479 (E.D. VA 2005)

T. S. ELLIS, III, DISTRICT JUDGE

Plaintiff Glendale International Corp. is a Canadian corporation that markets recreational vehicles under the trademark "TITANIUM." In November 2000, plaintiff began its multi-year quest to register the TITANIUM mark in the United States by filing an intent-to-use application with the U.S. Patent & Trademark Office ("PTO"). In its application, plaintiff identified the goods that would bear the TITANIUM mark only as "recreational vehicles." Approximately five months later, in April 2001, the PTO Examining Attorney reviewing plaintiff's application refused registration of the TITANIUM mark on the ground that it was "merely descriptive" of plaintiff's recreational vehicles and therefore non-registrable pursuant to §2(e)(1) of the Trademark Act. As part of her refusal letter, the Examining Attorney attached a definition of titanium taken from The American Heritage Dictionary—"[a] strong, low-density, highly corrosion-resistant, lustrous white metallic element that … is used to alloy aircraft metals for low weight, strength, and high-temperature stability"—and explained that "absent any limitations in the identification of goods, it is presumed that the applicant's recreational vehicles are made wholly or in part of titanium," noting in addition a 1996 news article from Tooling & Production magazine that mentions the use of titanium in recreational vehicles. The Examining Attorney also stated, however, that the refusal was not a final action, and invited plaintiff to submit additional evidence and arguments bearing on registrability, including a more detailed description of the goods in issue.

In June 2001, in response to the refusal, plaintiff submitted an amendment to its application clarifying that "applicant's product does not contain any titanium." The amendment also added considerably greater detail to the identification of goods, describing them as:

Recreational vehicles, namely, a vehicular type unit primarily designed as temporary living quarters for recreational camping, travel, or seasonal use that either has its own motive power or is mounted on, or towed by, another vehicle, namely, camping trailers, fifth wheel trailers, motor homes, travel trailers, and truck campers …

Based on these changes, plaintiff contended that the TITANIUM mark was not "merely descriptive" of its goods, and asked that the refusal of registration be withdrawn. In an apparent attempt to preempt refusal on different grounds, plaintiff also contended that the TITANIUM mark was not "[deceptively] misdescriptive" of its goods, explaining that the mark was unlikely to cause consumers to believe mistakenly that plaintiff's vehicles were made of titanium.

The TTAB concluded that "consumers familiar with the benefits of titanium would conclude … that [plaintiff's] vehicles contain titanium," and that "this belief would be reinforced by applicant's own promotional brochure, which emphasizes the advanced composite materials used in its products and the lighter weight of its materials." The TTAB reasoned that "the fact that applicant's TITANIUM recreational vehicles are expensive is more likely, rather than less likely, to cause consumers to believe that such products do, in fact, contain titanium."

II.

In the typical case, the district court's task at the summary judgment stage is "to determine whether there is a genuine issue for trial" after reviewing the parties' evidence in the light most favorable to the non-moving party. *See Anderson v. Liberty Lobby, Inc.*, 477 U.S. 242, 249, 91 L. Ed. 2d 202, 106 S. Ct. 2505 (1986); *Walton v. Greenbrier Ford*, 370 F.3d 446, 449 (4th Cir. 2004). Here, however, this familiar formulation inaccurately describes the judicial task at hand. In cases brought pursuant to 15 U.S.C. §1071(b), the district court "sits in a dual capacity, "serving on one hand as the finder of fact with respect to new evidence presented by the parties, and on the other as an appellate reviewer of facts found by the TTAB. *See CAE, Inc. v. Clean Air Eng'g, Inc.*, 267 F.3d 660, 674 (7th Cir. 2001); *Skippy, Inc. v. Lipton Invs., Inc.*, 345 F. Supp. 2d 585, 586 (E.D. Va. 2002). Here, as previously noted, no new evidence has been introduced, and the parties have submitted the matter for decision solely on the basis of the administrative record. In the circumstances, therefore, no fact-finding in required and the judicial function in this case is limited to the exercise of the appellate review.

As both the Examining Attorney and the TTAB correctly noted, the test for deceptive misdescriptiveness has two prongs: (i) whether the mark misdescribes the goods to which it applies; and (ii) whether consumers are likely to believe the misdescription. *See In re Automatic Radio Mfg. Co., Inc.*, 404 F.2d 1391, 1396, 56 C.C.P.A. 817 (C.C.P.A. 1969); *Gold Seal Co. v. Weeks*, 129 F. Supp. 928, 935 (D.D.C. 1955); *In re Phillips-Van Heusen Corp.*, 63 USPQ2d 1047 (TTAB 2002); Quady Winery, 221 USPQ at 1214. Importantly, the misdescription need not be material to the consumer's decision to purchase the goods, nor result in consumer confusion as to the source of the goods. Here, plaintiff concedes that the TITANIUM mark misdescribes its recreational vehicles, and thus only the second prong is in issue. Thus, the question presented is whether the administrative record reflects substantial evidence that consumers will likely believe that TITANIUM recreational vehicles are, in fact, made of titanium.

When evaluating the evidence set forth by the PTO in an ex parte trademark prosecution case, it is incumbent on courts to be "mindful that the PTO has limited resources for acquiring evidence," and "cannot ... be expected to conduct a survey of the marketplace or obtain consumer affidavits" as a means of measuring popular perceptions of a particular trademark. *In re Budge Mfg. Co., Inc.*, 857 F.2d 773, 775 (Fed. Cir. 1988). Instead, the PTO must rely, as it did here, on sources of publicly-available information likely to reflect such perceptions and, of course, common sense. The record reflects that when confronted with the TITANIUM mark, the Examining Attorney and the TTAB turned first to The American Heritage Dictionary, which defines "titanium" as a "metallic element" that is "used to alloy aircraft metals" and is characterized by its "low weight, strength, and high-temperature stability." Because "titanium" is not a particularly esoteric word, this definition, by any reasonable measure, suffices to establish a common baseline understanding of titanium as a metal with industrial uses.

The Examining Attorney, however, did not end her analysis with the dictionary definition, but instead proceeded, over the course nearly two years, to assemble a collection of more than twenty-five news articles. The record reflects, in fact, that the idea of using titanium in automobiles was regularly in circulation, perhaps even growing in popularity, during the time that plaintiff's application was pending. From these articles, the Examining Attorney sensibly reasoned that because consumers were regularly exposed to the idea of titanium in different types of vehicles, it would not be "a leap in logic" for consumers to assume that a towed or mounted vehicle like plaintiff's might also be made with titanium, particularly when it is advertised—in boldface no less—as possessing one of titanium's principal characteristics, namely light weight.

Faced with this prima facie case against registrability, plaintiff had the burden to come forward with evidence indicating a lack of consumer awareness of the industrial uses of titanium. *See Budge*, 857 F.2d at 776. It produced none. Instead, plaintiff now offers a number of arguments against the sufficiency of the PTO's administrative record, all of which are meritless. Contrary to plaintiff's claims, it is irrelevant whether or not any non-motorized recreational vehicles are, in fact, made with titanium. The proper test for the likelihood of consumer belief in a misdescription is plausibility, not reality. *See Humanetics Corp. v. Neways, Inc.*, 2004 TTAB LEXIS 215 at 22 (March 31, 2004). For the same reason, it is also irrelevant that only one of the articles cited by the Examining Attorney referred specifically to the use of titanium in "recreational vehicles," and that some of the articles—by no means all—referred to the potential rather than the actual use of titanium in vehicles.

In sum, the record reflects that the TTAB relied on substantial evidence of consumer familiarity with the use of titanium in the automotive industry when it found that consumers would likely believe that recreational vehicles bearing the TITANIUM mark were, in fact, made from titanium. Accordingly, the TTAB's conclusion that the TITANIUM mark is deceptively misdescriptive of plaintiff's goods is supported by substantial evidence. For these reasons, plaintiff's claim that registration of the TITANIUM mark was wrongly refused must fail.

5(c). Section 2(e)(2): Primarily Geographically Descriptive

15 U.S.C. §1052, Lanham Act §2

(e) Consists of a mark which

(2) when used on or in connection with the goods of the applicant is primarily geographically descriptive of them, except as indications of regional origin may be registrable under section 4 [15 USCS §1054]

In re Compagnie Generale Maritime
993 F.2d 841 (CAFC 1993)

MICHEL, CIRCUIT JUDE.

Compagnie Generale Maritime (CGM) appeals from the September 28, 1990 decision of the Trademark Trial and Appeal Board (Board), In re Compagnie Generale Maritime, Nos. 584,002, 647,509, 647,512 & 739,620 (TTAB September 28, 1990) (In re CGM), refusing registration for the mark FRENCH LINE for all of the myriad goods and services applied for by CGM. Because we hold that the Board's subsidiary fact findings and resolutions of the questions of ultimate fact regarding geographic descriptiveness and deceptive misdescriptiveness are not clearly erroneous, we affirm.

BACKGROUND

CGM, a French corporation, sought registrations, under section 44(e) of the Lanham Act (the "Act"), 15 U.S.C. §1126(e) (1982), of the mark FRENCH LINE in stylized design shown below:

for a wide variety of goods and services in a multitude of classes covered by several applications, which were consolidated by the Board at CGM's request. The applications were based on French registrations and, in accordance with the statute as interpreted in Board precedent in effect at the time of application, no specimens or affidavits of actual use were required or were submitted therewith. The Examining Attorney for the Patent and Trademark Office (PTO) refused registration under section 2(e) of the Act, 5 U.S.C. § 1052(e), on the alternative grounds, as interpreted by the Board, that CGM's mark was either merely descriptive or primarily geographically descriptive.

Before the Board, the Trademark Examining Attorney relied only on the primarily geographically descriptiveness ground, arguing that the primary significance of the words "FRENCH LINE" is geographical and a goods/place association exists or can be presumed to exist between the mark and the goods and services covered by the application. CGM, however, contended that its mark, FRENCH LINE, is not primarily geographically descriptive because the words "bring to mind applicant's transatlantic luxury steamship passenger service and 'applicant's world famous fleet of transatlantic luxury ocean liners,'" In re CGM, slip op. at 6–7, even though CGM no longer owns or operates any luxury liners.

The Board recognized that in order to establish a prima facie case of primary geographic descriptiveness, the PTO "must establish that the public associates the goods with the place named in the mark," id. at 8. The Board found that because France is "a major manufacturing and commercial nation," id., the applied-for goods and services would be associated with the country. The Board further found that the words "FRENCH LINE" are primarily geographic. Thus, the Board found that a potential purchaser of goods or services under the mark "FRENCH LINE" would believe that the products or services came from France, rendering CGM's mark primarily geographically descriptive if the goods and services actually come from France or primarily geographically deceptively misdescriptive if the goods and services do not come from France.

[GGM represented that its goods do not emanate from France.]

Furthermore, upon consideration of CGM's other contentions on appeal, the Board similarly affirmed refusal of registration. The Board concluded that CGM proffered no evidence to support its contention that "purchasers may associate the mark with applicant's former luxury passenger service rather than with the geographic source," id. at 9 — CGM had provided no evidence with its application of any actual use or any public reaction thereto. The Board also determined that the mark was not registrable even with CGM's disclaimer as to the words "French" and "Line" apart from the stylized mark because the stylization was minimal.

ANALYSIS

We review the Board's findings under the deferential clearly erroneous standard. Whether a mark is primarily geographically descriptive or deceptively misdescriptive is a question of fact. Likewise, "the issue of acquired distinctiveness is a question of fact." While we might perhaps have reached a different outcome with respect to some of the goods or services in question had we conducted de novo review, we cannot say that CGM has shown that the Board was clearly erroneous in its findings here.

For example, with regard to clothing, the Board took into account evidence presented by the Trademark Examining Attorney in the form of newspaper clippings discussing, inter alia, party dresses from France, children's fashions from France, and French designer clothes, respectively, as "French line[s]." Moreover, the Board noted that the mark, "THE AMERICAN LINE," for clothing was registered on the Supplemental Register. In addition, one clipping referred to a certain brand of cosmetics from France as a "French line of cosmetics." On such bases, the Board found that the mark is primarily geographical. No clear error is seen in this determination.

We likewise hold that the Board did not clearly err in finding that "France, a major manufacturing and commercial nation, would be perceived as the source of the numerous goods and services listed in the applications if the mark is primarily geographical." *In re CGM*, slip op. at 8. Certainly, all of the goods and services would either originate in France or should be considered as if they did because they are sold by a French company. The Board's associational finding is not clearly erroneous.

Because CGM provided no specimens of actual use of its mark or evidence on what associations purchasers made with respect to the mark, we hold that the Board did not clearly err in finding that CGM did not carry its burden of proof that its mark had become distinctive for any of the applied-for goods and services. In any event, CGM never sought registration based on distinctiveness.

In short, the Board's decision rests entirely on findings or determinations of fact, none of which have been shown to be clearly erroneous. Therefore, the decision of the Board upholding the refusal of registration is

AFFIRMED.

––––––––

5(d). Section 2(e)(3): Primarily Geographically Deceptively Misdescriptive

15 U.S.C. §1052, Lanham Act §2

(e) Consists of a mark which

(3) when used on or in connection with the goods of the applicant is primarily geographically deceptively misdescriptive of them

––––––––

In re Cal. Innovations, Inc.
329 F.3d 1334 (CAFC 2003)

RADER, CIRCUIT JUDGE

California Innovations, Inc. (CA Innovations), a Canadian-based corporation, appeals the Trademark Trial and Appeal Board's refusal to register its mark—CALIFORNIA INNOVATIONS. Citing section 2(e)(3) of the Lanham Act, 15 U.S.C. § 1052(e)(3) (2000), the Board concluded that the mark was primarily geographically deceptively misdescriptive. Because the Board applied an outdated standard in its analysis under § 1052(e)(3), this court vacates the Board's decision and remands.

I.

CA Innovations filed an intent-to-use trademark application, Serial No. 74/650,703, on March 23, 1995, for the composite mark CALIFORNIA INNOVATIONS and Design. The application sought registration for [automobile visor organizers an other automobile accessories.]

[After initially refusing the mark under 2(d) of the Lanham Act,] the PTO issued a notice of publication. The mark was published for opposition on September 29, 1998. No opposition was ever filed.

In July 1999, the PTO reasserted jurisdiction over the application under 37 C.F.R. §2.84(a) and refused registration under §1052(e)(3), concluding that the mark was primarily geographically deceptively misdescriptive. Applicant filed a timely notice for reconsideration with the PTO and a notice of appeal to the Board in November 2000. After the PTO refused to reconsider its decision, CA Innovations renewed its appeal to the Board. On February 20, 2002, the Board upheld the PTO's refusal to register applicant's mark and concluded that the mark was **primarily geographically deceptively misdescriptive**.

II.

The Lanham Act addresses geographical marks in three categories. The first category, §1052(a), identifies geographically deceptive marks:

> No trademark by which the goods of the applicant may be distinguished from the goods of others shall be refused registration on the principal register on account of its nature unless it—(a) Consists of or comprises immoral, *deceptive*, or scandalous matter; or matter which may disparage or falsely suggest a connection with persons, living or dead, institutions, beliefs, or national symbols, or bring them into contempt, or disrepute.

15 U.S.C. §1052(a) (2000) (emphasis added).

Although not expressly addressing geographical marks, §1052(a) has traditionally been used to reject geographic marks that materially deceive the public. A mark found to be deceptive under §1052(a)cannot receive protection under the Lanham Act. To deny a geographic mark protection under §1052(a), the PTO must establish that (1) the mark misrepresents or misdescribes the goods, (2) the public would likely believe the misrepresentation, and (3) the misrepresentation would materially affect the public's decision to purchase the goods. This test's central point of analysis is materiality because that finding shows that the misdescription deceived the consumer.

The other two categories of geographic marks are (1) "primarily geographically descriptive" marks and (2) "primarily geographically deceptively misdescriptive" marks under §1052(e). The North American Free Trade Agreement [NAFTA] has recently changed these two categories. Before the NAFTA changes, §1052(e) and (f) stated:

> No trademark by which the goods of the applicant may be distinguished from the goods of others shall be refused registration on the principal register on account of its nature unless it—
>
> (e) Consists of a mark which ...
>
> (2) when used on or in connection with the goods of the applicant is primarily geographically descriptive or deceptively misdescriptive of them.
>
> ⋆ ⋆ ⋆
>
> (f) Except as expressly excluded in paragraphs (a)–(d) of this section, nothing in this chapter shall prevent the registration of a mark used by the applicant which has become distinctive of the applicant's goods in commerce.

15 U.S.C. §1052(e)(2) and (f) (1988). The law treated these two categories of geographic marks identically. Specifically, the PTO generally placed a "primarily geographically descriptive" or "deceptively misdescriptive" mark on the supplemental register. Upon a showing of acquired distinctiveness, these marks could qualify for the principal register.

Thus, in contrast to the permanent loss of registration rights imposed on deceptive marks under §1052(a), pre-NAFTA §1052(e)(2) only required a temporary denial of registration on the principal register. Upon a showing of distinctiveness, these marks could acquire a place on the principal register. As permitted by pre-NAFTA § 1052(f), a mark could acquire distinctiveness or "secondary meaning" by showing that "in the minds of the public, the primary significance of a product feature or term is to identify the source of the product rather than the product itself." *Inwood Labs., Inc. v. Ives Labs.*, 456 U.S. 844, 851 n.11, 72 L. Ed. 2d 606, 102 S. Ct. 2182 (1982).

In the pre-NAFTA era, the focus on distinctiveness overshadowed the deceptiveness aspect of §1052(e)(2) and made it quite easy for the PTO to deny registration on the principal register to geographically deceptively misdescriptive marks under § 1052(e)(2). On the other hand, the deception requirement of § 1052(a) protected against fraud and could not be overlooked. Therefore, the PTO had significantly more difficulty denying registration based on that higher standard.

Before NAFTA, in *In re Nantucket*, 209 USPQ 868, 870 (TTAB 1981), the Board used a three-prong test to detect either primarily geographically descriptive or deceptively misdescriptive marks. Under the Board's test, the only substantive inquiry was whether the mark conveyed primarily a geographical connotation. On appeal in *In re Nantucket*, this court's predecessor rejected that test:

> The board's test rests mechanistically on the one question of whether the mark is recognizable, at least to some large segment of the public, as the name of a geographical area. NANTUCKET is such. That ends the board's test. Once it is found that the mark is the name of a known place, i.e., that it has "a readily recognizable geographic meaning," the next question, whether applicant's goods do or do not come from that place, becomes irrelevant under the board's test, for if they do, the mark is "primarily geographically descriptive"; if they don't, the mark is "primarily geographically deceptively misdescriptive." Either way, the result is the same, for the mark must be denied registration on the principal register unless resort can be had to § 2(f).

In re Nantucket, Inc., 677 F.2d 95, 97–98 (CCPA 1982). Thus *In re Nantucket*, for the first time, set forth a goods-place association requirement. *Id.* at 99–100. In other words, this court required a geographically deceptively misdescriptive mark to have more than merely a primary geographic connotation. Specifically, the public must also associate the goods in question with the place identified by the mark—the goods-place association requirement. However, this court did not require a showing that the goods-place association was material to the consumer's decision before rejection under § 1052(e).

In *In re Loew's Theatres, Inc.*, 769 F.2d 764, 767–69 (Fed. Cir. 1985), this court expressly permitted a goods-place association without any showing that the place is "well-known" or "noted" for the goods in question. The *Loew's* court explained: "If the place is noted for the particular goods, a mark for such goods which do not originate there is likely to be deceptive under § 2(a) and not registrable under any circumstances." *Id.* at 768, n.6. Clarifying that pre-NAFTA § 1052(e)(2) does not require a "well-known" place, this court noted:

> The PTO's burden is simply to establish that there is a reasonable predicate for its conclusion that the public would be likely to make the particular goods/place association on which it relies.... The issue is not the fame or exclusivity of the place name, but the likelihood that a particular place will be associated with particular goods.

Id.

As noted, the Lanham Act itself does not expressly require different tests for geographically misleading marks. In order to implement the Lanham Act prior to the NAFTA amendments, the PTO used a low standard to reject marks for geographically deceptive misdescriptiveness under pre-NAFTA § 1052(e), which was relatively simple to meet. In contrast, the PTO required a much more demanding finding to reject for geographical deception under § 1052(a). This distinction was justified because rejection under subsection (a) was final, while rejection under pre-NAFTA subsection (e)(2) was only temporary, until the applicant could show that the mark had become distinctive. The more drastic consequence establishes the propriety of the elevated materiality test in the context of a permanent ban on registration under § 1052(a).

NAFTA and its implementing legislation obliterated the distinction between geographically deceptive marks and primarily geographically deceptively misdescriptive marks. Article 1712 of NAFTA provides:

> 1. Each party [United States, Mexico, Canada] shall provide, in respect of geographical indications, the legal means for interested persons to prevent:
>
> (a) the use of any means in the designation or presentation of a good that indicates or suggests that the good in question originates in a territory, region or locality other than the true place of origin, in a manner that misleads the public as to the geographical origin of the good....

See NAFTA, Dec. 17, 1992, art. 1712, 32 I.L.M. 605, 698. This treaty shifts the emphasis for geographically descriptive marks to prevention of any public deception. Accordingly, the NAFTA Act amended § 1052(e) to read:

No trademark by which the goods of the applicant may be distinguished from the goods of others shall be refused registration on the principal register on account of its nature unless it—

> (e) Consists of a mark which (1) when used on or in connection with the goods of the applicant is merely descriptive or deceptively misdescriptive of them, (2) when used on or in connection with the goods of the applicant is primarily geographically descriptive of them, except as indications of regional origin may be registrable under section 4 [15 USCS § 1054], (3) when used on or in connection with the goods of the applicant is primarily geographically deceptively misdescriptive of them, (4) is primarily merely a surname, or (5) comprises any matter that, as a whole, is functional.
>
> (f) Except as expressly excluded in subsections (a), (b), (c), (d), (e)(3), and (e)(5) of this section, nothing herein shall prevent the registration of a mark used by the applicant which has become distinctive of the applicant's goods in commerce.

15 U.S.C. § 1052(e)-(f) (2000).

Recognizing the new emphasis on prevention of public deception, the NAFTA amendments split the categories of geographically descriptive and geographically deceptively misdescriptive into two subsections (**subsections (e)(2) and (e)(3) respectively**). Under the amended Lanham Act, subsection (e)(3)—geographically deceptive misdescription— could no longer acquire distinctiveness under subsection (f). Accordingly, marks determined to be primarily geographically deceptively misdescriptive are permanently denied registration, as are deceptive marks under § 1052(a).

Thus, § 1052 no longer treats geographically deceptively misdescriptive marks differently from geographically deceptive marks. Like geographically deceptive marks, the analysis for primarily geographically deceptively misdescriptive marks under § 1052(e)(3) focuses on deception of, or fraud on, the consumer. The classifications under the new § 1052 clarify that these two deceptive categories both receive permanent rejection. Accordingly, the test for rejecting a deceptively misdescriptive mark is no longer simple lack of distinctiveness, but the higher showing of deceptiveness.

The amended Lanham Act gives geographically deceptively misdescriptive marks the same treatment as geographically deceptive marks under § 1052(a). Because both of these categories are subject to permanent denial of registration, the PTO may not simply rely on lack of distinctiveness to deny registration, but must make the more difficult showing of public deception. In other words, by placing geographically deceptively misdescriptive marks under subsection (e)(3) in the same fatal circumstances as deceptive marks under subsection (a), the NAFTA Act also elevated the standards for identifying those deceptive marks.

Before NAFTA, the PTO identified and denied registration to a primarily geographically deceptively misdescriptive mark with a showing that (1) the primary significance of the mark was a generally known geographic location, and (2) "the public was likely to believe the mark identified the place from which the goods originate and that the goods did not come from there." *In re Loew's*, 769 F.2d at 768. The second prong of the test represents the "goods-place association" between the mark and the goods at issue. This test raised an inference of deception based on the likelihood of a goods-place association that did not reflect the actual origin of the goods. A mere inference, however, is not enough to establish the deceptiveness that brings the harsh consequence of non-registrability under the amended Lanham Act. As noted, NAFTA and the amended Lanham Act place an emphasis on actual misleading of the public.

Therefore, the relatively easy burden of showing a naked goods-place association without proof that the association is material to the consumer's decision is no longer justified, because marks rejected under § 1052(e)(3) can no longer obtain registration through acquired distinctiveness under § 1052(f). To ensure a showing of deceptiveness and misleading before imposing the penalty of non-registrability, the PTO may not deny registration without a showing that the goods-place association made by the consumer is material to the consumer's decision to purchase those goods. This addition of a materiality inquiry equates this test with the elevated standard applied under § 1052(a). *See House of Windsor*, 221 USPQ at 56–57 (establishing "a 'materiality' test to distinguish marks that fall within the proscription of Section 2(e)(2) from those that fall also within the proscription of Section 2(a)"). This also properly reflects the presence of the deceptiveness criterion often overlooked in the "primarily geographically *deceptively* misdescriptive" provision of the statute.

The shift in emphasis in the standard to identify primarily geographically deceptively misdescriptive marks under § 1052(e)(3) will bring that section into harmony with § 1052(a). Both sections involve proof of deception with the consequence of non-registrability. The adherence to the pre-NAFTA standard designed to focus on distinctiveness would almost read the term "deceptively" out of § 1052(e)(3), which is the term that the NAFTA amendments to the Lanham Act has reemphasized. Accordingly, under the amended Lanham Act, both subsection (a) and subsection (e)(3) share a similar legal standard.

As a result of the NAFTA changes to the Lanham Act, geographic deception is specifically dealt with in subsection (e)(3), while deception in general continues to be addressed under subsection (a). Consequently, this court anticipates that the PTO will usually address geographically deceptive marks under subsection (e)(3) of the amended Lanham Act rather than subsection (a). While there are identical legal standards for deception in each section, subsection (e)(3) specifically involves deception involving geographic marks.

[Because the materiality test was not applied by the Board, this case was reversed and remanded.]

———————

Japan Telecom, Inc. v. Japan Telecom America Inc.
287 F.3d 866 (9th Cir. 2002)

KOZINSKI, CIRCUIT JUDGE.

Japan Telecom, Inc. ("Japan Telecom") sells and installs telephone and computer networking equipment in the Los Angeles area. Japan Telecom is a California corporation, and a subsidiary of Hasegawa Company, Ltd., a small Japanese corporation. After Japan Telecom had been in business for fourteen years, a new kid on the block showed up: Japan Telecom America, Inc. ("Japan Telecom America"). Japan Telecom America is the United States subsidiary of Japan Telecom Company, Ltd., the third-largest telecommunications company in Japan. While Japan Telecom's business mostly involves the installation of telephone and computer networks, Japan Telecom America sells telecommunications transmission services, including both long-distance telephone and data.

Japan Telecom sued Japan Telecom America in federal court, alleging that Japan Telecom America's use of the "Japan Telecom" name constituted trademark infringement and unfair competition. Later, Japan Telecom sued Japan Telecom America in California state court for unfair competition and trade name infringement on the same theory. Japan Telecom America removed the state suit to federal court, and the district court consolidated the two actions. Japan Telecom's consolidated complaint alleges trade name infringement and unfair competition under the Lanham Act, unfair competition under California law, and "trade name violation under state law."

The district court granted Japan Telecom America's motion for summary judgment on all claims, holding that Japan Telecom had unclean hands. Japan Telecom appeals.

* * *

The district court erred in finding that Japan Telecom's trade name is primarily geographically deceptively misdescriptive. "Whether a mark is primarily geographically deceptively misdescriptive is a question of fact." *In re Save Venice New York, Inc.*, 259 F.3d 1346, 1351 (Fed. Cir. 2001). It may only be resolved on summary judgment if the evidence presented by both sides would permit the trier of fact to come to only one conclusion.

A mark is primarily geographically deceptively misdescriptive if "(1) the mark's primary significance is a generally known geographic location; and (2) consumers would reasonably believe the [marked] goods are connected with the geographic location in the mark, when in fact they are not." *In re Save Venice New York, Inc.*, 259 F.3d at 1352.

The parties dispute whether the name "Japan Telecom, Inc." refers to a geographic location. While it is tempting to conclude that "Japan" means "Japan, the country," we cannot examine a trademark or trade name's individual words in isolation. *See Filipino Yellow Pages, Inc. v. Asian Journal Publ'ns, Inc.*, 198 F.3d 1143, 1147–51 (9th Cir. 1999). Using the name of a country in a trade name does not automatically make the trade name geographically descriptive; instead, we must look to whether consumers would reasonably believe that the term is being used geographically. *See In re Save Venice New York, Inc.,* 259 F.3d at 1352.

The district court erred by ignoring Japan Telecom's evidence that consumers might understand the word "Japan" in its name as referring to a specific ethnic community, rather than the country. Japan Telecom argues that customers seeing its advertising are familiar with a convention of using the word "Japan" in a business' name to indicate that the business caters to Japanese-speaking customers. Japan Telecom offered an affidavit from Chieko Mori, the president of a company that publishes a telephone directory of businesses catering to the "local Japanese community in California." Mori stated that over eighty companies with the word "Japan" in their name—including "Japan Pilot Club," "Japan Landscaping, Inc.," and "Japan Printing Service"—advertise in Mori's directory, but only a few of those are affiliated with companies in Japan.

Japan Telecom America offered evidence that there is a pattern in the telecommunications industry of using the word "Telecom" after a country's name to signify geographic origin—such as "Deutsche Telecom," "China Telecom," and "British Telecom." Without any evidence of widespread knowledge of this pattern of naming countries, this does not establish that consumers would reasonably believe that Japan Telecom was connected with Japan. At best, it only raises an inference that Japan Telecom's trademark may have confused customers. On summary judgment, the district court must draw all inferences in the non-movant's favor. *Clicks Billiards Inc. v. Sixshooters Inc.,* 251 F.3d 1252, 1257 (9th Cir. 2001). Japan Telecom presented contrary evidence on this point, and therefore created a triable issue of fact.

Japan Telecom America did not meet its burden of showing that customers "would reasonably believe [Japan Telecom's services] are connected with" Japan for yet another reason. *In re Save Venice New York, Inc.,* 259 F.3d at 1352. Japan Telecom's business is primarily service-related: It installs and maintains telephone and computer networking equipment. Japan Telecom also acts as a sales agent for MCI, a well-known American long distance company. Incident to its services, Japan Telecom sells goods (like telephones and network routers), but there is no evidence that Japan Telecom marks those goods with "Japan Telecom." When services are performed on a customer's site, the customer is unlikely to associate the service with any geographic region other than where the services are performed. Because Japan Telecom can only perform its services in person and on customer premises, it is hard to see how a reasonable customer could conclude that the technician installing his new phone wiring just came off a jet from Tokyo, equipped with the very latest in Japanese wiring know-how.

The district court found that Japan Telecom's use of the word "Japan" played on a popular notion that Japan excels in telecommunications and electronics. But the court did not cite to any evidence that customers have such a favorable impression of Japan's telecommunications industry. Even if there were such evidence, it would hardly follow that the use of the name "Japan Telecom" misled consumers into inferring that Japan Telecom was affiliated with Japan. Our examination of the record reveals at best a disputed issue of fact on this question. We also find no evidence that the consumers Japan Telecom targets would be more likely to hold these views.

[The court affirmed summary judgement for JTA because JT's mark had no secondary meaning.]

* * *

Affirmed

In re Wada

194 F. 3d 1297 (CAFC 1999)

GARJARSA, CIRCUIT JUDGE.

DECISION

Hiromichi Wada appeals from a decision of the U.S. Patent and Trademark Office Trademark Trial and Appeal Board ("the Board") affirming the final rejection of Application Serial No. 74/657,464, seeking to register the mark NEW YORK WAYS GALLERY. Because we find that the Board did not err in refusing to register the mark, we affirm.

BACKGROUND

In 1995, Hiromichi Wada filed an intent-to-use application for the mark NEW YORK WAYS GALLERY. The goods identified in the trademark application included various kinds of leather bags, luggage, back packs, wallets, tote bags, and the like. Wada disclaimed any exclusive rights to the term NEW YORK apart from its use within the composite mark, NEW YORK WAYS GALLERY.

The examining attorney refused registration of the mark under 15 U.S.C. §1052(e)(3) (1994), finding that it was primarily geographically deceptively misdescriptive for the goods identified. The examiner noted that Wada, a Japanese citizen and Michigan resident, had failed to demonstrate any connection between the goods identified and the city or state of New York. The examiner found that the primary significance of the term NEW YORK was geographical, and determined, based upon evidence that hand bags and luggage are designed and manufactured in New York, that the public associates the identified goods with New York. Because Wada failed to refute the goods/place association between New York and the identified goods, the examiner refused registration of the mark in a final rejection. Wada appealed this rejection to the Board.

The Board affirmed the examiner's refusal to register the mark. *See In re Wada*, 1998 TTAB LEXIS 379, 48 U.S.P.Q.2D (BNA) 1689 (TTAB Oct. 9, 1998). The Board found that the evidence established that the mark was primarily geographically deceptively misdescriptive. *See* 48 U.S.P.Q.2D (BNA) at 1692. In particular, the Board pointed to evidence that showed 1) New York is a well-known geographic place and 2) New York is well-known as a place where leather goods and handbags are designed and manufactured. *See id.* at 1690. It rejected Wada's assertion that the mark is intended to evoke a "New York style," and thus is not primarily geographic. *See id.* at 1691–92. The Board found that the addition of the words WAYS GALLERY to NEW YORK did not detract from the primary geographic significance of the mark, particularly since Wada could point to no evidence that there was a "New York style" of the products at issue. *See id.* at 1691.

Further, the Board rejected Wada's argument that the disclaimer of NEW YORK allowed the mark as a whole to be registered. The Board recognized that prior to the implementation of the NAFTA amendments to the Lanham Act, primarily geographically deceptively misdescriptive marks could be registered with a disclaimer of the geographic terms. *See id.* at 1692. However, the Board found that because of the NAFTA amendments, the disclaimer of geographic terms no longer salvages registrability of such marks. *See id.* This appeal followed.

DISCUSSION

* * *

B. The Mark is Primarily Geographically Deceptively Misdescriptive.

The Board found that the mark NEW YORK WAYS GALLERY was primarily geographically deceptively misdescriptive when applied to the goods in Wada's application. For a mark to be primarily geographically deceptively misdescriptive, the mark must (1) have as its primary significance a generally known geographic place, and (2) identify products that purchasers are likely to believe mistakenly are connected with that location. *See Institut National Des Appellations D'Origine v. Vinters Int'l Co.*, 958 F.2d 1574, 1580, 22 U.S.P.Q.2D (BNA) 1190, 1195 (Fed. Cir. 1992). A mark is not primarily geographic where the geographic meaning is obscure, minor, remote, or not likely to be connected with the goods. *See In re Nantucket, Inc.*, 677 F.2d 95, 99, 213 U.S.P.Q. (BNA) 889, 892 (CCPA 1982). Thus, a mark with a geographic term used fancifully or arbitrarily may be registered like any other fanciful or arbitrary mark. *See In re Loew's Theatres, Inc.*, 769 F.2d 764, 767, 226 U.S.P.Q. (BNA) 865, 867 (Fed. Cir. 1985).

In this case, Wada argues that the primary significance of the mark is not geographic. Instead, Wada claims that the mark evokes a gallery that features New York "ways" or "styles." Since New York Ways Gallery is a fictitious location, Wada argues that the primary significance of the mark is fanciful or arbitrary. The Board, however, found that NEW YORK is not an obscure geographical term and that it is known as a place where the goods at issue here are designed, manufactured, and sold. It found that primary geographic significance is not lost by the addition of WAYS GALLERY to NEW YORK. In making its determination, the Board pointed to evidence such as manufacturer listings and NEXIS excerpts showing that various leather goods and handbag manufacturers are located in New York. The Board also pointed out that Wada had not brought forth any evidence showing a "New York style" of the goods at issue here. Given our deferential standard of review, we see no reason to disturb the Board's factual findings on this issue.

To satisfy the second part of the test, it must be shown that the public is likely to believe mistakenly that the mark identifies a place connected with the goods—a goods/place association. *See Nantucket*, 677 F.2d at 99. The Board found it likely that the public, upon encountering goods bearing the mark NEW YORK WAYS GALLERY, would believe that the goods have some connection to New York. *See Wada*, 48 U.S.P.Q.2D (BNA) at 1691. Wada contends that consumers would not view the mark as identifying a place connected with the goods, but rather would see the mark as evoking an aura of status or prestige. The Board refuted Wada's argument by pointing to evidence that New York is a world renowned fashion center and is well-known as a place where goods of this kind are designed, manufactured, or sold. *See id.* Thus, the Board concluded that there is a goods/place association between the goods identified in Wada's application and New York. Once again, we see no reason to disturb the Board's factual findings on this issue. The Board's determination that the mark NEW YORK WAYS GALLERY is primarily geographically deceptively misdescriptive rests upon factual determinations which have not been shown to be arbitrary, capricious, an abuse of discretion, or unsupported by substantial evidence. *See Loew's Theatres*, 769 F.2d at 768 (approving the use of directories to establish a goods/place association).

C. Disclaimer of NEW YORK Does Not Permit
Registration of the Mark as a Whole.

Wada argues that even if we affirm the Board's conclusion that NEW YORK WAYS GALLERY is primarily geographically deceptively misdescriptive, the disclaimer of NEW YORK should permit registration of the mark as a whole. We disagree.

Prior to the implementation of the NAFTA amendments to the Lanham Act, marks that were primarily geographically deceptively misdescriptive could be registered if they had acquired secondary meaning. Additionally, even if the mark had not acquired secondary meaning, the mark could be registered with a disclaimer of the primarily geographically deceptively misdescriptive terms. By disclaiming such terms, the applicant could not claim exclusive rights to the disclaimed portions apart from their use in the mark as a whole. However, with the incorporation of the NAFTA amendments into the Lanham Act in 1993, primarily geographically deceptively misdescriptive marks were precluded from registration under all circumstances, even with a showing of secondary meaning. *See* 15 U.S.C. §1052(f) (1994). Neither the statute nor the legislative history address the practice of disclaiming primarily geographically deceptively misdescriptive terms. In response to the statutory amendments, the PTO issued an Official Gazette notice stating "[a] mark that is … primarily geographically deceptively misdescriptive … will not be rendered registrable by a disclaimer of the geographically deceptively misdescriptive component." U.S. Patent and Trademark Office, 1162 Official Gazette 15 (May 3, 1994); *see also* Trademark Manual of Examining Procedure §1210.06 (1993) (containing identical language).

The Commissioner is given broad flexibility in implementing disclaimer policies. Here, the Commissioner has adopted a policy that use of a disclaimer will not be permitted to salvage a mark that is primarily geographically deceptively misdescriptive. This policy is consistent with the NAFTA amendments to the Lanham Act, that eliminated the ability to register primarily geographically deceptively misdescriptive marks that have acquired secondary meaning. It also complies with Article 1712 of NAFTA, which prohibits the registration of marks that may mislead the public as to the geographical origin of goods. This policy treats primarily geographically deceptively misdescriptive marks the same as deceptive marks, which are not registrable under any circumstances. *See* 15 U.S.C. §1052(f). A disclaimer of deceptive terms does not permit registrability of a mark that is deceptive.

Wada argues that since the statute and its legislative history are silent on the matter, the Lanham Act amendments should not change the disclaimer policy regarding primarily geographically deceptively misdescriptive marks. Wada points out that unregistrability under §1052(f) does not necessarily mean that disclaimer is improper. For example, while generic terms are unregistrable under any circumstances, marks containing generic terms can be registered with disclaimer of such terms. However, generic terms are unregistrable because registration would preclude others from using terms that truthfully describe their products. Disclaimer of generic terms in composite marks allows marks containing generic terms to be registered as a whole while preventing any exclusive rights in the generic terms themselves.

Primarily geographically deceptively misdescriptive marks, like deceptive marks, mislead the public even with a disclaimer. This similarity between primarily geographically deceptively misdescriptive marks and deceptive marks justifies similar treatment with respect to disclaimers. If Wada were permitted to use the mark NEW YORK WAYS GALLERY with NEW YORK disclaimed, the public will still be likely to believe mistakenly that products bearing the mark are connected with New York. In other words, "it would be anomalous to prohibit registration [of a] primarily geographically deceptively misdescriptive

[mark], but allow registration of the same geographically deceptively misdescriptive mark with a mere disclaimer of the geographic element." *Wada*, 48 U.S.P.Q.2D (BNA) at 1692.

CONCLUSION

The Board's finding that the mark NEW YORK WAYS GALLERY is primarily geographically deceptively misdescriptive is a finding of fact that is not arbitrary, capricious, an abuse of discretion, or unsupported by substantial evidence. Additionally, the Board's conclusion that disclaimer of NEW YORK does not salvage registrability is correct in light of the NAFTA amendments to the Lanham Act and the subsequent change in PTO policy regarding disclaimers of primarily geographically deceptively misdescriptive marks. The Board's refusal to register the mark NEW YORK WAYS GALLERY, therefore, is

AFFIRMED.

Daesang Corp. v. Rhee Bros., Inc.
77 U.S.P.Q.2D (D. MD 2005)

ANDRE M. DAVIS, DISTRICT JUDGE

I. FINDINGS OF FACT

"Gochujang" (also written as "gochuchang," "go choo chang," "kochujang" or "kochujang") is a Korean condiment or sauce commonly known in English as "hot pepper paste" or "hot bean paste." Gochujang is a very popular food among Koreans. By a wide margin, the primary purchasers of gochujang in the United States are persons of Korean origin.

The Soon Chang province of South Korea has been well known for and associated with producing high quality gochujang for centuries. Most Koreans and Korean Americans are, and have long been, familiar with the goods-place association between Soon Chang and gochujang; Rhee Bros.' contention that knowledge of the goods-place association between Soon Chang and gochujang is a result of recent efforts by, if not an invention of, the Korean government or the local Soon Chang government, is rejected.

One of the famous products in Soon Chang is gochujang. It is believed that the water here created today's "Soonchang Gochuchang" not to mention the culinary technique.... From ancient times high government officials who toured this district received a gochuchang jar as a gift and noble individuals who left this district received a gochuchang jar (as a souvenir).

Consequently, numerous companies located in Soon Chang make gochujang and other sauces. Saying "Soon Chang gochujang" to people familiar with Korean culture is similar to saying "Idaho potatoes" or "Maine lobsters" to an American; each such term implies quality and authenticity.

. . .

In 1978, Rhee Bros. began selling gochujang using the term "Soon Chang" in its brand name. *Tr. at 158.* On July 2, 1986, Rhee Bros. filed Application Serial No. 73/607565 for the mark. *Rhee Dec. PP 31,36.* In the 1986 application, Rhee Bros. represented to the Patent and Trademark Office ("PTO") that Soon Chang meant "pure spear." *Plf. Exh. 28.* Rhee Bros. made no mention in the 1986 application that there is a region of South Korea known as Soon Chang or that the region is famous for high quality gochujang in spite of Rhee Bros.' knowledge of the fact. *Id.*

Although the mark literally translates in the Korean alphabet to the separate words "pure" and "spear," there is no association in the Korean alphabet or Korean culture between the words "pure" and "spear" that would make "pure spear" a plausible interpretation of the phrase …

…

Daesang is a Korean corporation, which maintains a place of business at 52-I Kayang-dong, Kangseo-ku, Seoul, Korea. *Yu Dec. P 1.* Daesang sells a variety of food products in the United States, including gochujang. *Yu Dec. P 1.* Daesang's gochujang is made in the Soon Change province of South Korea. *Yu Dec. P 3.* To indicate the geographical origin of the products, the gochujang labels display the Korean characters that transliterate to Soon Chang. *Yu Dec. PP 5–7.*

…

In 2001, Rhee Bros. filed a trademark infringement suit in this court to challenge the use of the term "Soon Chang" by Daesang's customer, the Korean grocery store chain Han Ah Reum. *Rhee Dep. at 110–11.*

II. CONCLUSIONS OF LAW
1. Rhee Bros. Fraudulently Obtained its Trademark Containing the Term "Soon Chang"

A trademark is any word, name, symbol, or device that identifies and distinguishes the goods of one manufacturer or merchant from those of others. *See 15 U.S.C. § 1127.* A geographically descriptive term is one in which the primary significance attached to the term is a generally known geographic location. *See Burke-Parsons-Bowlby Corp. v. Appalachian Log Homes, Inc.*, 871 F.2d 590, 595 (6th Cir. 1989). A geographically descriptive term is not inherently distinctive, and thus cannot receive trademark protection unless it has achieved secondary meaning. *Id.*

Secondary meaning exists when the public no longer associates the goods with a particular place, but rather with a particular source. *Resorts of Pinehurst, Inc. v. Pinehurst Nat'l Corp.*, 148 F.3d 417, 421 (4th Cir. 1998); *Boston Beer Co. Ltd. P'ship v. Slesar Bros. Brewing Co., Inc.*, 9 F.3d 175, 181 (1st Cir. 1993) (rejecting a claim of secondary meaning for Boston beer' because most consumers connected the term with beer brewed in Boston). Therefore, if a geographically descriptive term that lacks secondary meaning is trademarked as a result of the applicant's failure to reveal the geographical description to the PTO, or if the applicant makes a material misrepresentation of the term's definition, the trademark registration has been procured by fraud and may be canceled at any time.

It is well established that an applicant for a registration of a trademark has a duty of candor in his communications with the PTO. *T.A.D. Avanti, Inc. v. Phone-Mate, Inc.*, 199 U.S.P.Q. 648, 655 (C.D. Cal. 1978). Consequently, there is no presumption of validity attached to a PTO registration where pertinent information is not presented to the PTO. *T.A.D. Avanti*, 199 U.S.P.Q. at 655. Fraud arises, therefore, not only where the applicant makes false statements, which is clear with respect to Rhee Bros.' 1987 trademark registration, but also where the applicant fails to make full disclosure of all material facts, which is clear with respect to the later registration.

In its first trademark application in 1986, Rhee Bros. did not inform the PTO of Soon Chang's geographical identity nor did it mention Soon Chang's association with high quality gochujang. Instead, Rhee Bros. represented that Soon Chang meant "pure spear." Daesang's unrebutted expert witness testimony, fully credited here, and Mr. Rhee's demonstrated knowledge at the time, of Soon Chang's fame for high quality gochujang, make clear that "pure spear" is not only grammatically and syntactically incorrect, but also affirmatively misleading as to Soon Chang's goods-place association with gochujang. Although Rhee Bros.' 1987 trademark registration, which was canceled in 1994 due to Rhee Bros.' failure to file a Section 8 affidavit, is not the trademark at issue in the instant case, the context in which it was obtained is highly probative of the fraudulent circumstances surrounding the registration of the instant trademark.

It is clear from the evidence presented at trial that Soon Chang is, and has been for centuries, famous for its high quality gochujang among Korean consumers, and that Rhee Bros. knew this at all relevant times. The primary purchasers of gochujang in the United States, by orders of magnitude, are persons of Korean origin, and as far back as 1978, Rhee Bros. had knowledge of Soon Chang's fame for high quality gochujang.

Mr. Rhee's testimony lacks credibility with regard to his alleged ignorance of Soon Chang's fame for high quality gochujang at the time he applied for the instant trademark in 1996. The fact that Rhee Bros. filed a letter of protest in September 1996 with the PTO in connection with Daesang's trademark applications for a mark with the term "Soon Chang" establishes Rhee Bros.' knowledge of the goods-place association between Soon Chang and gochujang. The letter claimed that Daesang's mark was not only identical to the mark Rhee Bros. was attempting to register, but that the term Soon Chang is geographically descriptive and "the public association with Soon Chang is presumed." Rhee Bros.' September 1996 letter of protest was filed a full year prior to the Ahn application, in which Rhee Bros. admitted that Soon Chang is the name of a town in Korea and thereby materially omitted disclosure of the goods-place association between Soon Chang and gochujang. It is at best disingenuous for Rhee Bros. to admit this material information in connection with its challenge to a competitor's attempts at trademarking Soon Chang, only to claim ignorance of the fact as to Soon Chang's geographical descriptiveness in its own trademark application.

Rhee Bros. did indeed have knowledge of Soon Chang's geographical descriptiveness at the time of its initial application with the PTO in August 1996 for the mark *sub judice*. Furthermore, Mr. Rhee was cognizant of his lawyers' representations in the trademark applications. The Amberly application filed in 1994 made absolutely no mention of Soon Chang's geographical identity as a province in South Korea or of the goods-place association between Soon Chang and high quality gochujang until September 1997, when Amberly stated that Soon Chang is a region in South Korea that is famous for sauces. However, Amberly affirmatively stated that there is no goods-place association for the mark in the U.S. despite the fact that a majority of U.S. consumers are of Korean origin and indeed are familiar with Soon Chang's reputation for gochujang.

The Ahn application, which resulted in the instant mark, stated in July 1997 that Soon Chang is the name of a town located in Korea, but did not mention Soon Chang's fame for high quality gochujang. This material omission, in combination with all the evidence in the record, points to Rhee Bros.' fraudulent intent in concealing this highly relevant information from the PTO. *See Aromatique, 28 F.3d at 877–78.* In this case there was no "mere error."

Given the plethora of evidence establishing Soon Chang's fame for high quality gochujang and Rhee Bros.' knowledge of such, Rhee Bros.' duty of candor with regard to the instant trademark clearly included a duty to disclose the goods-place association between Soon Chang and gochujang. Merely stating that Soon Chang is a town in Korea is simply insufficient to satisfy Rhee Bros.' duty to make a full disclosure as to all relevant facts of which it had knowledge bearing on the PTO's decision to grant the registration. *See T.A.D.*, 199 U.S.P.Q. at 656.

...

III. CONCLUSION

On the basis of the findings and conclusions set forth above, an Order shall issue declaring: Rhee Bros. has never established any trademark or exclusive rights in the geographical name Soon Chang (its alleged mark) because as this name is used by Rhee Bros., (a) it is deceptive and thus barred from protection under *15 U.S.C. § 1052(a)*; *(b)* it is primarily geographically deceptively misdescriptive and thus barred from protection under *15 U.S.C. § 1052(e)(3).*

_____

Notes

1. In a most heartfelt comment, H. David Gold, *Legal Strategies to Address the Misrepresentation of Vermont Maple Syrup*, 59 Food & Drug L. J. 93 (2004), claims that the Vermont maple syrup industry has been harmed by attempts to imitate. When others use the word "vermont" on or in connection with the sale of goods that do not meet the specifications of the certification mark for VERMONT, that association is harmed. He claims this is similar to the following uses that have been stopped:

> "WisPride" on cheese spread not from Wisconsin, but made in Kentucky by a French company with headquarters in New Jersey;

> "Kona" on coffee not from Hawaii, but from South America;

> "Florida Style" on citrus punch not from Florida, but manufactured in California, Georgia, Indiana, New Jersey, and Texas; and

> "Omaha" on steaks not from Nebraska, but sold by a California corporation.

Is it? Or is VERMONT the name of a state from which maple syrup happens to emanate but it is not the only state in which maple trees grow that produce the sap that is the source of the syrup. Furthermore, maple syrup from Vermont has no special features that distinguish it from maple syrup from New Hampshire, for example. Is this relevant to the analysis?

2. Mary LaFrance has argued the following:

> In *California Innovations*, the Federal Circuit unnecessarily introduced a dramatically new interpretation of what it means for a geographic mark to be "deceptively misdescriptive." In so doing, the court failed to observe the most basic canons of statutory construction, rendering section 2(e)(3) of the Lanham Act superfluous and the last sentence of section 2(f) arguably inoperative. Furthermore, nothing in the legislative history of this statutory language supports the court's interpretation.

> There is a simpler and more logical way to interpret the NAFTA amendments to section 2: Congress simply retained the familiar two-part test for identifying primarily geographically deceptively misdescriptive marks, but chose to impose a conclusive ban on registration of such marks, just as it imposes a conclusive ban on, inter alia, deceptive, scandalous, immoral, disparaging, or functional marks. In so doing, rather than upset settled pre-NAFTA expectations, it grandfathered any primarily geographically deceptively misdescriptive marks (unless also de-

ceptive under section 2(a)) that had already achieved distinctiveness under the
pre-NAFTA trademark regime, which for several decades had permitted such
marks to be registered once they acquired distinctiveness. Moreover, Congress
retained the older, more flexible standard (i.e., the presumptive registration ban,
defeasible under section 2(f) through acquired distinctiveness) for deceptively
misdescriptive nongeographic marks, because it intended to subject inaccurate
geographic marks to more rigorous standards than inaccurate nongeographic
marks, which were not a concern of NAFTA. This interpretation is consistent
with the Federal Circuit's earliest interpretations of the NAFTA amendments in
In re Wada and In re Save Venice, notwithstanding the court's revisionist rein-
terpretation of those decisions in California Innovations. And it is the only interpretation under which section 2(e)(3) and section 2(f) are fully operative
provisions.

Under this more logical interpretation, it would indeed be more difficult to
register a false geographic mark in the post-NAFTA regime. And Congress may
indeed have imposed an unnecessarily harsh consequence when it made that
choice. It may have erred in believing that Article 1712 of NAFTA mandated this
change in policy. But this is the only reading of the NAFTA amendments that
makes sense and conforms to the fundamental rules of statutory construction.

Ironically, when the Federal Circuit chose to adopt a strained interpretation of
the plain language of section 2(e)(3) in California Innovations and Les Halles,
its holding made it easier to register geographically confusing marks than other
types of confusing marks. Yet there is no indication in the NAFTA amendments,
or their legislative history, that Congress intended such disparate results. The
more logical inference is that Congress intended to make geographically confusing marks impossible to register, even where the misleading nature of the mark
is immaterial to the purchasing decision, based on the belief that Article 1712 requires NAFTA members to ban registration of all geographically confusing marks.

If Congress erred in the choices it made in 1993, the Federal Circuit's aggressive recasting of section 2(e)(3) is merely a second wrong that compounds,
rather than corrects, this legislative error. The court should reconsider its holdings in California Innovations, and leave Congress to reconsider the wisdom of
the NAFTA amendments.

Mary LaFrance, *Innovations Palpatations: The Confusing Status of Geographically Misdescriptive Trademarks*, 12 J. INTELL. PROP. L. 125, 148–49 (2004). Is Mary LaFrance correct in claiming that the CAFC has made matters worse? *See, also*, Andrew P. Vance, *Can't
Get There From Here: How NAFTA and GATT Have Reduced Protection for Geographical
Trademarks*, 26 BROOK. J. INT'L L. 1097 (2001). *See also*, Courtney Liotti, *The Registrability of Primarily Geographically Deceptively Misdescriptive Marks: The Development of
Section 1052(e)(3)*, 22 TOURO L. REV. 511, 573 (2006) ("[T]he most drastic consequence
of the development of [primarily geographically deceptively misdescriptive] marks is the
negative consumer impact, which results from increased consumer deception thought
the immediate registration of non-arbitrary geographically false marks); Robert Brauneis
and Roger E. Schechter, *Geographic Trademarks and the Protection of Competitor Communication*, 96 TRADEMARK REP. 782, 786 (2006) ("[T]he crucial issues for trademark protection are whether a demonstration of secondary meaning will be required, and if so
how and when that demonstration can be made"). *But c.f.*, Xuan-Thao N. Nguyen, *Nationalizing Trademarks: A New International Trademark Jurisprudence?*, 39 WAKE FOREST
L. Rev. 729, 781 (2004) ("The EU is lobbying for a new international law that would pro-

hibit countries from using generic names within their own borders to identify the names of products. Under such law, no country would be able to use generic names to sell or market products for export." Also, claiming that the EU has created regulations that grant it the exclusive right to use the word "sardine", a generic name of a fish in the United States. Claiming also that the EU is demanding that all members of WIPO stop using 41 other generic names including "parmesan", "romano", "feta", "chablis", and others). Who is right? Should geographical indications be protected to the extent that the EU is demanding? Under current US law, is that possible?

3. Do you think that there should have been an allegation of fraud against the USPTO in *Daesang Corp. v. Rhee Bros., Inc.*? It is clear from the facts and the court's decision that Rhee Bros. clearly knew of their actions but did not disclose their knowledge to the PTO. Why doesn't this rise to fraud before the PTO? *See Robi v. Five Platters, Inc.*, 918 F.2d 1439 (9th Cir. 1990) (affirming the district court's finding that defendant had submitted a false and misleading trademark application, resulting in the cancellation of the trademark based on fraud in the procurement).

5(e). Section 2(e)(4): Primarily Merely a Surname

15 U.S.C. §1052, Lanham Act §2

(e) Consists of a mark which

(4) is primarily merely a surname

In re Kahan & Weisz Jewelry Mfg.

508 F.2d 831 (1975)

BALDWIN, J.

This appeal is from the decision of the Trademark Trial and Appeal Board affirming the examiner's refusal to register the mark DUCHARME as a trademark for watches on the Principal Register. We reverse.

The examiner refused registration under the Lanham Act, section 2(e)(3) (15 USC 1052(e)(3)) on the ground that DUCHARME is primarily merely a surname. The board affirmed the refusal to register while adding, "[moreover], 'DUCHARME' is admittedly a surname and while it may well be, as applicant in substance contends, a rare surname, Section 2(e)(3) of the Statute makes no distinction between rare or commonplace surnames." Further, the board quoted from the examiner's answer:

The name Ducharme is listed in various telephone directories as a surname just as applicant has disclosed in its amendment on June 16, 1971.

Opinion

The sole issue here is whether the mark sought to be registered, DUCHARME, was properly refused registration under section 2(e)(3) of the Lanham Act as being primarily merely a surname.

It is clear that the burden is on the Patent Office to prove that the trademark is primarily merely a surname.

This court has recognized that section 2(e)(3) is difficult to apply in determining whether a mark is primarily merely a surname. However, we are of the opinion that a correct resolution of the issue can be made only after the primary significance of the mark to the purchasing public is determined, as suggested by Ex parte Rivera Watch Corp., 106 U.S.P.Q. 145, 149 (Com'r Pat. 1955).

A trademark is a trademark only if it is used in trade. When it is used in trade it must have some impact upon the purchasing public, and it is that impact or impression which should be evaluated in determining whether or not the primary significance of a word when applied to a product is a surname significance. If it is, and it is only that, then it is primarily merely a surname.

The board held that in view of the lack of any established secondary meaning of appellant's mark, the mark would only have the significance of a surname to purchasers. Thus, the board, in essence, shifted the burden of proof to appellant without first establishing that DUCHARME is primarily merely a surname. As stated previously, the Patent Office has the burden to show that DUCHARME is primarily merely a surname and unless it meets its burden, appellant need not demonstrate non-surname significance of its mark.

The examiner stated that DUCHARME is listed in various telephone directories as a surname. In fact, in answer to the examiner's refusal to register, appellant referred to the Manhattan telephone directory in New York City noting that it lists six names similar to applicant's mark.[8] Although the board did not specifically state that it adopted such an approach as establishing that DUCHARME is primarily merely a surname, the telephone directory is the only evidence produced by the examiner as a basis for his refusal to register DUCHARME on the Principal Register.

Although the use of a telephone directory may be considered a factor in determining whether a mark is primarily merely a surname, we do not find this, standing alone, to be determinative of the issue. This is particularly true here where the Patent Office only relied upon six listings in the Manhattan telephone directory supplied by appellant. Such a showing does not establish that the primary significance of DUCHARME to the purchasing public is that of a surname.

Therefore, the decision of the board is reversed.

REVERSED

Taylor Wine Company, Inc. v. Bully Hill Vineyards, Inc.
569 F.2d 731 (2d Cir. 1978)

GURFEIN, CIRCUIT JUDGE

Bully Hill Vineyards, Inc. appeals from a preliminary injunction order issued by the U.S. District Court of the Western District of New York, Burke, J., on August 10, 1977, enjoining it from using and infringing the trademarks owned by the plaintiff, the Taylor Wine Company, Inc., and from engaging in acts of unfair competition. There was no trial below. The injunction was granted on findings of fact and conclusions of law based upon the affidavits submitted.

The broad order enjoined Bully Hill from using the word "Taylor" or any colorable imitation thereof in connection with any labeling, packaging materials, advertising, or

---

8. The six names are written in three different forms: du Charme, Du Charme, and Ducharme.

promotional materials for any of its products, from infringing plaintiff's trademarks, and from continuing to engage in acts of unfair competition.

The plaintiff, Taylor Wine Company, Inc., has marketed wine from the Finger Lakes region of New York under the Taylor name since 1880, and since 1927 has registered thirteen Taylor trademarks in the U.S. Patent Office, and used them in commerce. It has spent almost ten million dollars in advertising its wine products under the Taylor name in the last ten years. The District Court found that the Taylor trademarks have come to be accepted by the consuming public as identifying the distinctive product of the Taylor Wine Company.

Walter S. Taylor owns the defendant company, Bully Hill Vineyards, Inc. He is the grandson of Walter Taylor who, in 1878, started a winery on Bully Hill. The defendant company was established in 1970, selling its products under the brand name of Bully Hill. At some time before May, 1977, the defendant began to market a new line of wines under a brand name "Walter S. Taylor."

"Walter S. Taylor" appears in large print on the front, back or both of labels of defendant's wines. The word "Original" is displayed in large print or otherwise given prominence. At various places, the name "Walter S. Taylor" is used with the statement "Owner of the Estate" or "Owner of the Taylor Family Estate." Bully Hill has also stated on labels and in its advertising that it was founded in 1878. In fact, the grandfather of the present Taylor with some partners, formed a partnership whose assets were later conveyed in the lifetime of Walter S. Taylor's father to the plaintiff company. Whatever trademark use of the name "Taylor" inhered in the partnership was transferred with the wine business to the plaintiff corporation. Bully Hill, the vineyard, itself did not stay in the Taylor family but was sold to strangers. Walter S. Taylor bought it in 1958. Thus, neither the use of "Taylor" as a trademark nor the vineyards at Bully Hill devolved upon Walter S. Taylor, the grandson, by descent.

Appellant contends that its use of "Taylor" as a trademark does not infringe the appellee's trademarks because the appellant's wines are better and are not in actual competition with appellee's wines. It also urges us to say that the injunction is too broad, in any case, and that it would be enough if we made Bully Hill add some distinguishing words if it chooses to use Walter S. Taylor's own surname as a trademark.

This is not a case where a first comer seeks to save himself a place in a new market he has not yet entered by denying to a man the use of his own name in exploiting that market. The wines of defendant and plaintiff compete in the same general market. It is a truism that every product has its own separate threshold for confusion of origin. Wine is a product whose quality is accepted by many simply on faith in the maker. They can perhaps identify the vintner better than the wine.

It is doubtless true that some wartime soldiers did bring back from Europe an inchoate taste for wine and for some of its nuances, and that other Americans have acquired a similar taste. Yet, the average American who drinks wine on occasion can hardly pass for a connoisseur of wines. He remains an easy mark for an infringer. Whether appellant's or appellee's wines are better is not the issue. Trespass upon the secondary meaning of the Taylor brand name, developed at great cost over the years, cannot be forgiven on the ground that subtlety of taste will avoid the confusion inherent in the overlapping labels and representations of origin.

We do not doubt that Walter S. Taylor, a former employee of the plaintiff, knew well the customer appeal of the Taylor name, nor that he chose to capitalize on the name as if his grandfather had left it to him as an inheritance. The only serious question we must meet is whether the injunction is too broad.

The conflict between a first comer who has given a secondary meaning (as well as trademark registration) to a family name, and a later comer who wishes to use his own true family name as a trademark in the same industry has been one of the more interesting issues in the law of trademark infringement. The problem is made more difficult when the second comer has his own background of experience in the particular industry, and is not simply a newcomer. *See John T. Lloyd Laboratories, Inc. v. Lloyd Brothers Pharmacists, Inc,* 131 F.2d 703 (6th Cir. 1942).

In the nineteenth and earlier twentieth centuries, both the state and federal courts tended to be highly solicitous of an individual's personal right to use his name in trade.

With the passage of the Federal Trade-Mark Act of 1905, 33 Stat. 742, and an increasing commercial reliance on marketing techniques to create name recognition and goodwill, the courts adopted a more flexible approach to the conflicting property interests involved in surname trademark infringement cases. By 1908, the Supreme Court was willing to enjoin the use of a surname unless accompanied by a disclaimer. *Herring-Hall-Marvin Safe Co. v. Hall's Safe Co.,* 208 U.S. 554, 559–60, 28 S. Ct. 350, 52 L. Ed. 616 (1908). Shortly thereafter, in *Thaddeus Davids Co. v. Davids,* 233 U.S. 461, 58 L. Ed. 1046, 34 S. Ct. 648 (1914) and *L. E. Waterman Co. v. Modern Pen Co.,* 235 U.S. 88, 59 L. Ed. 142, 35 S. Ct. 91 (1914), the Supreme Court established what has since become a guiding principle in trademark surname cases. Once an individual's name has acquired a secondary meaning in the marketplace, a later competitor who seeks to use the same or similar name must take "reasonable precautions to prevent the mistake." *L. E. Waterman Co., supra,* at 94.

It is, however, difficult to distill general principles as to what are "reasonable precautions" from the Supreme Court's decisions in *Thaddeus Davids* and *Waterman.* In *Davids, supra,* the Court affirmed without modification a lower court decree enjoining entirely the use of the words "Davids" or "Davids Mfg. Co." in connection with the manufacturing and sale of inks. 233 U.S. at 472. In *Waterman, supra,* on the other hand, the Supreme Court affirmed without modification a lower court's injunction which simply prescribed the use of a full first name instead of an initial, and required a notice of disclaimer.

Since the field is one that does not lend itself to strict application of the rule of stare decisis because the fact patterns are so varied, we must try to identify the elements that have influenced decisions on the adequacy of the remedy.

For example, the fact that an alleged infringer has previously sold his business with its goodwill to the plaintiff makes a sweeping injunction more tolerable. So, too, if an individual enters a particular line of trade for no apparent reason other than to use a conveniently confusing surname to his advantage, the injunction is likely to be unlimited.

If, however, the second comer owns the company himself and evinces a genuine interest in establishing an enterprise in which his own skill or knowledge can be made known to the public, that argues in favor of allowing him to use his own name in some restricted fashion. As this court said in *Societe Vinicole de Champagne de Mumm,* 143 F.2d 240, 241 (2d Cir. 1944), to prohibit an individual from using his true family surname is to "take away his identity: without it he cannot make known who he is to those who may wish to deal with him; and that is so grievous an injury that courts will avoid imposing it, if they possibly can." When confusion is likely, however, there must obviously be some limitation on an individual's unrestricted use of his own name. Thus, a second comer may not use any name, mark or advertisement indicating that he is the successor of another corporation or that his goods are the products of that corporation. *Donnell v. Herring-Hall-Marvin Safe Co.,* 208 U.S. 267, 52 L. Ed. 481, 28 S. Ct.

288 (1908). Yet, he may retain a limited use of the family name even though goodwill has been conveyed to the plaintiff. *Herring-Hall-Marvin Safe Co. v. Hall's Safe Co.*, 208 U.S. 554, 558, 28 S. Ct. 350, 52 L. Ed. 616 (1908). As Justice Holmes commented in *Herring-Hall*:

> "The name of a person or a town may have become so associated with a partic-
> ular product that the mere attaching of that name to a similar product without
> more would have all the effect of a falsehood.... An absolute prohibition against
> using the name would carry trade-marks too far. Therefore the rights of the two
> parties have been reconciled by allowing the use, provided that an explanation
> is attached.... Of course, the explanation must accompany the use, so as to give
> the antidote with the bane," 208 U.S. at 559 [citations omitted].

The injunction issued in *Herring-Hall* prohibited use of the name Hall unless it was stated that the defendant was not the original Hall's Safe and Lock Company or its successor, and that defendant's products were not those of that company. Significantly, the Court not only permitted the defendants to use the Hall name with such a distinguishing explanation, but also to "show that they are sons of the first Hall and brought up in their business by him, and otherwise state the facts." 208 U.S. at 560.

Speaking generally, when the defendant demonstrates a genuine desire to build a business under his own name, courts have been reluctant to proscribe all surname use whatever even though the defendant's conduct has been less than exemplary. In *L. E. Waterman Co. v. Modern Pen Co., supra*, the Court declined to order an absolute prohibition although it was clear that the defendant *intended* to use his surname to garner benefits from the plaintiff's successful exploitation of the same name. 235 U.S. at 94–96. Particularly when the infringer is a son or grandson, as in Hall, *supra*; *National Distillers Products Corp. v. K. Taylor Distilling Co.*, 31 F. Supp. 611, 615 (E.D. Ky. 1940), and *Friend v. H. A. Friend & Co.*, 416 F.2d 526, 534 (9th Cir. 1969) *cert. denied*, 397 U.S. 914, 25 L. Ed. 2d 94, 90 S. Ct. 916 (1970), the courts have given qualified relief which reflects "a judicious balancing of the countervailing interests of protecting an individual's use of his own name and the avoiding of confusion." 416 F.2d at 534.

* * *

We do not doubt the necessity for an injunction in this case, but we think that its provisions were too broad. Walter S. Taylor is apparently a scholar of enology and a commentator on wines. He runs a wine museum in the Finger Lakes District, and seems to be a person sincerely concerned with the art of wine-growing. Yet, in granting him the right to let people know that he is personally a grower and distributor of regional wines, the public must be assured that he does not by his "estate bottled" nomenclature and his claims to being the "original" Taylor, confuse the public into believing that his product originates from the Taylor Wine Company which is so well-known.

We have concluded that neither Bully Hill nor Walter S. Taylor should use the "Taylor" name as a trademark, but that the defendant may show Walter's personal connection with Bully Hill. He may use his signature on a Bully Hill label or advertisement if he chooses, but only with appropriate disclaimer that he is not connected with, or a successor to, the Taylor Wine Company. He must also be restrained from using such words as "Original" or "Owner of the Taylor Family Estate." He must, in short, not pretend that his grandfather or his father passed anything on to him as a vintner. To the extent that Walter S. Taylor can exploit his own knowledge and techniques as a person, he may do so with the limitations noted, if he refrains from trading on the goodwill of the plaintiff company by competing unfairly.

Since these matters will require careful delineation, we remand to the District Court with a suggestion that it request the submission of appropriate proposed orders from the parties and that it enter an order in the light of this opinion in language adequate to make possible a contempt proceeding if its decree is violated.

The order is affirmed in part, modified in part, and remanded for further proceedings in accordance with this opinion

5(f). Section 2(e)(5): Functionality

15 U.S.C. §1052, Lanham Act §2

(e) Consists of a mark which

(5) comprises any matter that, as a whole, is functional

In re Morton-Norwich Products, Inc.

671 F.2d 1332 (CCPA 1982)

RICH, JUDGE.

This appeal is from the ex parte decision of the United States Patent and Trademark Office (PTO) Trademark Trial and Appeal Board (board), 209 U.S.P.Q. 437 (TTAB 1980), in application serial No. 123,548, filed April 21, 1977, sustaining the examiner's refusal to register appellant's container configuration on the principal register. We reverse the holding on "functionality" and remand for a determination of distinctiveness.

Background

Appellant's application seeks to register the following container configuration as a trademark for spray starch, soil and stain removers, spray cleaners for household use, liquid household cleaners and general grease removers, and insecticides:

Appellant owns U.S. Design Patent 238,655, issued Feb. 3, 1976, on the above configuration, and U.S. Patent 3,749,290, issued July 31, 1973, directed to the mechanism in the spray top.

The above-named goods constitute a family of products which appellant sells under the word-marks FANTASTIK, GLASS PLUS, SPRAY 'N WASH, GREASE RELIEF, WOOD PLUS, and MIRAKILL. Each of these items is marketed in a container of the same configuration but appellant varies the color of the body of the container according to the product. Appellant manufactures its own containers and stated in its application (amendment of April 25, 1979) that:

Since such first use [March 31, 1974] the applicant has enjoyed substantially exclusive and continuous use of the trademark [i.e., the container] which has become distinctive of the applicant's goods in commerce.

The PTO Trademark Attorney (examiner), through a series of four office actions, maintained an unshakable position that the design sought to be registered as a trademark is not distinctive, that there is no evidence that it has become distinctive or has acquired a secondary meaning, that it is "merely functional," "essentially utilitarian," and non-arbitrary, wherefore it cannot function as a trademark. In the second action she requested applicant to "amplify the description of the mark with such particularity that any portion of the alleged mark considered to be non functional [sic] is incorporated in the description." She said, "The Examiner sees none." Having already furnished two affidavits to the effect that consumers spontaneously associate the package design with appellant's products, which had been sold in the container to the number of 132,502,000 by 1978, appellant responded to the examiner's request by pointing out, in effect, that it is the overall configuration of the container rather than any particular feature of it which is distinctive and that it was intentionally designed to be so, supplying several pieces of evidence showing several other containers of different appearance which perform the same functions. Appellant also produced the results of a survey conducted by an independent market research firm which had been made in response to the examiner's demand for evidence of distinctiveness. The examiner dismissed all of the evidence as "not persuasive" and commented that there had "still not been one iota of evidence offered that the subject matter of this application has been promoted as a trademark," which she seemed to consider a necessary element of proof. She adhered to her view that the design "is no more than a non-distinctive purely functional container for the goods plus a purely functional spray trigger controlled closure * * * essentially utilitarian and non-arbitrary * * *."

Appellant responded to the final rejection with a simultaneously filed notice of appeal to the board and a request for reconsideration, submitting more exhibits in support of its position that its container design was not "purely functional." The examiner held fast to all of her views and forwarded the appeal, repeating the substance of her rejections in her Answer to appellant's appeal brief. An oral hearing was held before the board.

Board Opinion

The board, citing three cases, stated it to be "well-settled" that the configuration of a container "may be registrable for the particular contents thereof if the shape is non-functional in character, and is, in fact, inherently distinctive, or has acquired secondary meaning as an indication of origin for such goods." In discussing the "utilitarian nature" of the alleged trademark, the board took note of photographs of appellant's containers for FANTASTIC spray cleaner and GREASE RELIEF degreaser, the labels of which bore the words, respectively, "adjustable easy sprayer," and "NEW! Trigger Control Top," commenting that "the advertising pertaining to applicant's goods promotes the word marks of the various products and the desirable functional features of the containers."

In light of the above, and after detailed review of appellant's survey evidence without any specific comment on it, the board concluded its opinion as follows:

After a careful review of the evidence in the case before us, we cannot escape the conclusion that the container for applicant's products, the configuration of which it seeks to register, is dictated primarily by functional (utilitarian) considerations, and is therefore unregistrable despite any de facto secondary meaning which applicant's survey and other evidence of record might indicate. As stated in the case of *In re Deister Concentrator Company, Inc.* [48 CCPA 952, 289 F.2d 496, 129 U.S.P.Q. 314 (1961)], "not every word or configuration that has a de facto secondary meaning is protected as a trademark."

Issues

The parties do not see the issues in the same light. Appellant and the solicitor agree that the primary issue before us is whether the subject matter sought to be registered—the configuration of the container—is "functional."

Appellant states a second issue to be whether the configuration has the capacity to and does distinguish its goods in the marketplace from the goods of others.

The solicitor contends that it would be "premature" for us to decide the second issue if we disagree with the PTO on the first issue and have to reach it, and that we should, in that event, remand the case so the board can "consider" it. Whether to remand is, therefore, an issue.

OPINION

As would be expected, the arguments made in this court are, except for the remand question, essentially the same as they were below. The question is not new and in various forms we have been over the ground before: is the design sought to be registered "functional"? There is a plethora of case law on this subject and it becomes a question of which precedents to follow here — and why. In our view, it would be useful to review the development of the principles which we must apply in order to better understand them. In doing so, it should be borne in mind that this is not a "configuration of goods" case but a "configuration of the container for the goods" case. One question is whether the law permits, on the facts before us, exclusive appropriation of the precise configuration described in the application to register. Another facet of the case is whether that configuration in fact functions as a trademark so as to be entitled to registration. We turn first to a consideration of the development of the law on "functionality."

A trademark is defined as "any work, name, symbol, or device or any combination thereof adopted and used by a manufacturer or merchant to identify his goods and distinguish them from those manufactured or sold by others" (emphasis ours). 15 USC 1127 (1976). Thus, it was long the rule that a trademark must be something other than, and separate from, the merchandise to which it is applied.

Aside from the trademark/product "separateness" rationale for not recognizing the bare design of an article or its container as a trademark, it was theorized that all such designs would soon be appropriated, leaving nothing for use by would-be competitors. One court, for example, feared that "The forms and materials of packages to contain articles of merchandise * * * would be rapidly taken up and appropriated by dealers, until some one, bolder than the others, might go to the very root of things, and claim for his goods the primitive brown paper and tow string, as a peculiar property." *Harrington v. Libby*, 11 F. Cas. 605, 606 (C.C.S.D.N.Y. 1877) (No. 6,107). *Accord, Diamond Match Co. v. Saginaw Match Co.*, 142 F. 727, 729–30 (6th Cir. 1906).

This limitation of permissible trademark subject matter later gave way to assertions that one or more features of a product or package design could legally function as a trademark. E.g., *Alan Wood Steel Co. v. Watson*, 150 F. Supp. 861, 863, 113 U.S.P.Q. 311, 312 (D.D.C. 1957); *Capewell Horse Nail Co. v. Mooney, supra.* It was eventually held that the entire design of an article (or its container) could, without other means of identification, function to identify the source of the article and be protected as a trademark. E.g., *In re Minnesota Mining and Manufacturing Co.*, 51 CCPA 1546, 1547–48, 335 F.2d 836, 837, 142 U.S.P.Q. 366, 367 (1964).

That protection was limited, however, to those designs of articles and containers, or features thereof, which were "nonfunctional." It has as its genesis the judicial theory that there exists a fundamental right to compete through imitation of a competitor's product, which right can only be temporarily denied by the patent or copyright laws:

If one manufacturer should make an advance in effectiveness of operation, or in simplicity of form, or in utility of color; and if that advance did not entitle him to a monopoly by means of a machine or process or a product or a design patent; and if by means of unfair trade suits he could shut out other manufacturers who plainly intended to share in the benefits of unpatented utilities * * * he would be given gratuitously a monopoly more effective than that of the unobtainable patent in the ratio of eternity to seventeen years.

An exception to the right to copy exists, however, where the product or package design under consideration is "nonfunctional" and serves to identify its manufacturer or seller, and the exception exists even though the design is not temporarily protectible through acquisition of patent or copyright. Thus, when a design is "nonfunctional," the right to compete through imitation gives way, presumably upon balance of that right with the originator's right to prevent others from infringing upon an established symbol of trade identification.

This preliminary discussion leads to the heart of the matter—how do we define the concept of "functionality," and what role does the above balancing of interests play in that definitional process?

I. Functionality Defined

Many courts speak of the protectability as trademarks of product and package configurations in terms of whether a particular design is "functional" or "nonfunctional." Without proper definition, however, such a distinction is useless for determining whether such design is registrable or protectable as a trademark, for the label "functional" has dual significance. It has been used, on the one hand, in lay fashion to indicate "the normal or characteristic action of anything," and, on the other hand, it has been used to denote a legal conclusion. *Compare, In re Penthouse International Ltd.*, 565 F.2d 679, 681, 195 U.S.P.Q. 698, 699–700 (CCPA 1977) (If the product configuration "has a non-trademark function, the inquiry is not at an end; possession of a function and of a capability of indicating origin are not in every case mutually exclusive."), with *In re Mogen David Wine Corp.*, *supra* at 1270, 328 F.2d at 933, 140 U.S.P.Q. at 582 (Rich, J., concurring) ("The Restatement appears to use the terms 'functional' and 'non-functional' as labels to denote the legal consequence: if the former, the public may copy; and if the latter, it may not. This is the way the 'law' has been but it is not of much help in deciding cases.").

Accordingly, it has been noted that one of the "distinct questions" involved in "functionality" reasoning is, "In what way is [the] subject matter functional or utilitarian, factually or legally?" *In re Honeywell, Inc.*, 497 F.2d 1344, 1350, 181 U.S.P.Q. 821, 826 (CCPA 1974) (Rich, J., concurring). This definitional decision, noted in "truism" (4) in *Deister*, leads to the resolution that if the designation "functional" is to be utilized to denote the legal consequence, we must speak in terms of de facto functionality and de jure functionality, the former being the use of "functional" in the lay sense, indicating that although the design of a product, a container, or a feature of either is directed to performance of a function, it may be legally recognized as an indication of source. De jure functionality, of course, would be used to indicate the opposite—such a design may not be protected as a trademark.

This is only the beginning, however, for further definition is required to explain how a determination of whether a design is de jure functional is to be approached. We start with an inquiry into "utility."

A. "Functional" means "utilitarian"

From the earliest cases, "functionality" has been expressed in terms of "utility." In 1930, this court stated it to be "well settled that the configuration of an article having utility is not the subject of trade-mark protection." (Emphasis ours.) *In re Dennison Mfg. Co.*, 17 CCPA 987, 988, 39 F.2d 720, 721, 5 U.S.P.Q. 316, 317 (1930) (Arbitrary urn or vase-like shape of reinforcing patch on a tag.). *Accord, Sparklets Corp. v. Walter Kidde Sales Co.*, 26 CCPA 1342, 1345, 104 F.2d 396, 399, 42 U.S.P.Q. 73, 76 (1939); *In re National Stone-Tile Corp.*, 19 CCPA 1101, 1102, 57 F.2d 382, 383, 13 U.S.P.Q. 11, 12 (1932). This broad statement of the "law", that the design of an article "having utility" cannot be a trademark, is incorrect and inconsistent with later pronouncements.

We wish to make it clear — in fact, we wish to characterize it as the first addition to the *Deister* "truisms" — that a discussion of "functionality" is always in reference to the design of the thing under consideration (in the sense of its appearance) and not the thing itself. One court, for example, paraphrasing Gertrude Stein, commented that "a dish is a dish is a dish." *Hygienic Specialties Co. v. H. G. Salzman, Inc.*, 302 F.2d 614, 621, 133 U.S.P.Q. 96, 103 (2d Cir. 1962). No doubt, by definition, a dish always functions as a dish and has its utility, but it is the appearance of the dish which is important in a case such as this, as will become clear.

Assuming the *Dennison* court intended that its statement reference an article whose configuration "has utility," its statement is still too broad. Under that reasoning, the design of a particular article would be protectable as a trademark only where the design was useless, that is, wholly unrelated to the function of the article. For example, where a merchant sought to register on the supplemental register the overall configuration of a triangular chemical cake for use in a process of metal plating, this court stated that the shape was capable of becoming a trademark because it "is entirely arbitrary and, except for its solidity (all shapes being solid), has no functional significance whatever." *In re Minnesota Mining and Mfg. Co.*, supra at 1551, 335 F.2d at 840, 142 U.S.P.Q. at 369.

Most designs, however, result in the production of articles, containers, or features thereof which are indeed utilitarian, and examination into the possibility of trademark protection is not to the mere existence of utility, but to the degree of design utility. The ore concentrating and coal cleaning table shape in *Deister*, for example, was refused registration as a trademark because its shape was "in essence utilitarian," *supra* at 968, 289 F.2d at 506, 129 U.S.P.Q. at 322. Likewise, the design of a cast aluminum fitting for joining lengths of tubing together was denied registration because it was held to be "in essence utilitarian or functional." *In re Hollaender Mfg. Co.*, 511 F.2d 1186, 1189, 185 U.S.P.Q. 101, 103 (CCPA 1975). The configuration of a thermostat cover was also refused registration because a round cover was "probably * * * the most utilitarian" design which could have been selected for a round mechanism. *In re Honeywell, Inc.*, 532 F.2d 180, 182, 189 U.S.P.Q. 343, 344 (CCPA 1976).

Thus, it is the "utilitarian" design of a "utilitarian" object with which we are concerned, and the manner of use of the term "utilitarian" must be examined at each occurrence. The latter occurrence is, of course, consistent with the lay meaning of the term. But the former is being used to denote a legal consequence (it being synonymous with "functional"), and it therefore requires further explication.

B. "Utilitarian" means "superior in function (de facto) or economy of manufacture," which "superiority" is determined in light of competitive necessity to copy

Some courts have stated this proposition in the negative. In *American-Marietta Co. v. Krigsman*, 275 F.2d 287, 289, 124 U.S.P.Q. 320, 322 (2d Cir. 1960), the court stated that "those features of the original goods that are not in any way essential to their use" may be termed "nonfunctional." But what does this statement mean? In the case at bar, for example, we cannot say that it means that the subject design is "functional" merely because a hollow body, a handhold, and a pump sprayer are "essential to its use." What this phrase must mean is not that the generic parts of the article or package are essential, but, as noted above, that the particular design of the whole assembly of those parts must be essential. This, of course, leaves us to define "essential to its use," which is also the starting place for those courts which have set forth in positive fashion the reasons they believe that some product or package designs are not protectable as trademarks and thus not registrable.

* * *

Thus, it is clear that courts in the past have considered the public policy involved in this area of the law as, not the right to slavishly copy articles which are not protected by patent or copyright, but the need to copy those articles, which is more properly termed the right to compete effectively. Even the earliest cases, which discussed protectibility in terms of exhaustion of possible packaging forms, recognized that the real issue was whether "the effect would be to gradually throttle trade." *Harrington v. Libby*, *supra* at 606.

More recent cases also discuss "functionality" in light of competition. One court noted that the "question in each case is whether protection against imitation will hinder the competitor in competition." *Truck Equipment Service Co. v. Fruehauf Corp.*, 536 F.2d 1210, 1218, 191 U.S.P.Q. 79, 85 (8th Cir. 1976). Another court, upon suit for trademark infringement (the alleged trademark being plaintiff's building design), stated that "enjoining others from using the building design [would not] inhibit competition in any way." *Fotomat Corp. v. Cochran*, 437 F. Supp. 1231, 1235, 194 U.S.P.Q. 128, 131 (D. Kan. 1977). This court has also referenced "hinderance of competition" in a number of the "functionality" cases which have been argued before it.

The Restatement of Torts, §742, designates a design of goods as "functional" if it "affects their purpose, action or performance, or the facility or economy of processing, handling or using them * * *." (Emphasis ours.) To ensure that use of the word "affects" was clear, Comment a to that section indicates that a "feature" may be found "functional" if it "contributes to" the utility, durability, effectiveness or ease of use, or the efficiency or economy of manufacture of that "feature." Excusing the fact that the design of the "feature" is not referenced, and equating "feature" with "design," this seems to take us back to where we started—with those cases that deny trademark protection to those articles "having utility." Further, it appears to us that "affects" and "contributes to" are both so broad as to be meaningless, for every design "affects" or "contributes to" the utility of the article in which it is embodied. "Affects" is broad enough to include a design which reduces the utility or the economy of manufacture.

Although the Restatement appears to ignore the policies which created the law of "functionality," it is noted at the end of the first paragraph of Comment a to §742, in accord with the cases previously discussed, that we should examine whether prohibition of imitation by others will "deprive them of something which will substantially hinder them in competition."

Given, then, that we must strike a balance between the "right to copy" and the right to protect one's method of trade identification, *In re Mogen David Wine Corp.*, *supra* at 1270, 328 F.2d at 933, 140 U.S.P.Q. at 582 (Rich, J., concurring); *In re Deister Concentrator Co.*, *supra* at 966, 289 F.2d at 504, 129 U.S.P.Q. at 322, what weights do we set upon each side of the scale? That is, given that "functionality" is a question of fact, what facts do we look to in determining whether the "consuming public has an interest in making use of [one's design], superior to [one's] interest in being [its] sole vendor"? *Vaughan Novelty*

Mfg. Co. v. G. G. Greene Mfg. Corp., 202 F.2d 172, 176, 96 U.S.P.Q. 277, 280 (3d Cir.), *cert. denied*, 346 U.S. 820, 99 U.S.P.Q. 491 (1953).

II. Determining "Functionality"
A. In general

Keeping in mind, as shown by the foregoing review, that "functionality" is determined in light of "utility," which is determined in light of "superiority of design," and rests upon the foundation "essential to effective competition," *Ives Laboratories, Inc. v. Darby Drug Co.*, 601 F.2d 631, 643, 202 U.S.P.Q. 548, 558 (2d Cir. 1979), and cases cited *supra*, there exist a number of factors, both positive and negative, which aid in that determination.

Previous opinions of this court have discussed what evidence is useful to demonstrate that a particular design is "superior." In *In re Shenango Ceramics, Inc.*, 53 CCPA 1268, 1273, 362 F.2d 287, 291, 150 U.S.P.Q. 115, 119 (1966), the court noted that the existence of an expired utility patent which disclosed the utilitarian advantage of the design sought to be registered as a trademark was evidence that it was "functional." Since the effect upon competition "is really the crux of the matter," it is, of course, significant that there are other alternatives available.

It is also significant that a particular design results from a comparatively simple or cheap method of manufacturing the article. In *Schwinn Bicycle Co. v. Murray Ohio Mfg. Co.*, 339 F. Supp. 973, 980, 172 U.S.P.Q. 14, 19 (M.D. Tenn. 1971), *aff'd*, 470 F.2d 975, 176 U.S.P.Q. 161 (6th Cir. 1972), the court stated its reason for refusing to recognize the plaintiff's bicycle rim surface design as a trademark:

> The evidence is uncontradicted that the various manufacturers of bicycle rims in the United States consider it commercially necessary to mask, hide or camouflage the roughened and charred appearance resulting from welding the tubular rim sections together. The evidence represented indicates that the only other process used by bicycle rim manufacturers in the United States is the more complex and more expensive process of grinding and polishing.

B. The case at bar
1. The evidence of functionality

We come now to the task of applying to the facts of this case the distilled essence of the body of law on "functionality" above discussed. The question is whether appellant's plastic spray bottle is de jure functional; is it the best or one of a few superior designs available? We hold, on the basis of the evidence before the board, that it is not.

The board thought otherwise but did not state a single supporting reason. In spite of her strong convictions about it, neither did the examiner. Each expressed mere opinions and it is not clear to us what either had in mind in using the terms "functional" and "utilitarian." Of course, the spray bottle is highly useful and performs its intended functions in an admirable way, but that is not enough to render the design of the spray bottle—which is all that matters here—functional.

As the examiner appreciated, the spray bottle consists of two major parts, a bottle and a trigger-operated, sprayproducing pump mechanism which also serves as a closure. We shall call the latter the spray top. In the first place, a molded plastic bottle can have an infinite variety of forms or designs and still function to hold liquid. No one form is necessary or appears to be "superior." Many bottles have necks, to be grasped for pouring or holding, and the necks likewise can be in a variety of forms. The PTO has not produced one iota of evidence to show that the shape of appellant's bottle was required to be as it is for any de facto functional reason, which might lead to an affirmative determination of de jure functionality. The evidence, consisting of competitor's molded plastic bottles for similar products, demonstrates that the same functions can be performed by a variety of other shapes with no sacrifice of any functional advantage. There is no necessity to copy appellant's trade dress to enjoy any of the functions of a spray-top container.

As to the appearance of the spray top, the evidence of record shows that it too can take a number of diverse forms, all of which are equally suitable as housings for the pump and spray mechanisms. Appellant acquired a patent on the pump mechanism (No. 3,749,290) the drawings of which show it embodied in a structure which bears not the slightest resemblance to the appearance of appellant's spray top. The pictures of the competition's spray bottles further illustrate that no particular housing design is necessary to have a pump-type sprayer. Appellant's spray top, seen from the side, is rhomboidal, roughly speaking, a design which bears no relation to the shape of the pump mechanism housed within it and is an arbitrary decoration — no more de jure functional than is the grille of an automobile with respect to its under-the-hood power plant. The evidence shows that even the shapes of pump triggers can and do vary while performing the same function.

What is sought to be registered, however, is no single design feature or component but the overall composite design comprising both bottle and spray top. While that design must be accommodated to the functions performed, we see no evidence that it was dictated by them and resulted in a functionally or economically superior design of such a container.

Applying the legal principles discussed above, we do not see that allowing appellant to exclude others (upon proof of distinctiveness) from using his trade dress will hinder competition or impinge upon the rights of others to compete effectively in the sale of the goods named in the application, even to the extent of marketing them in functionally identical spray containers. The fact is that many others are doing so. Competitors have apparently had no need to simulate appellant's trade dress, in whole or in part, in order to enjoy all of the functional aspects of a spray top container. Upon expiration of any patent protection appellant may now be enjoying on its spray and pump mechanism, competitors may even copy and enjoy all of its functions without copying the external appearance of appellant's spray top.

If the functions of appellant's bottle can be performed equally well by containers of innumerable designs and, thus, no one is injured in competition, why did the board state that appellant's design is functional and for that reason not registrable?

2. The relationship between "functionality" and distinctiveness

One who seeks to register (or protect) a product or container configuration as a trademark must demonstrate that its design is "nonfunctional," as discussed above, and that the design functions as an indication of source, whether inherently so, because of its distinctive nature, *In re McIlhenny*, 47 CCPA 985, 989, 278 F.2d 953, 955, 126 U.S.P.Q. 138, 141 (1960); *In re International Playtex Corp.*, 153 U.S.P.Q. 377, 378 (TTAB 1967), or through acquisition of secondary meaning. These two requirements must, however, be kept separate from one another.

The issues of distinctiveness and functionality may have been somewhat intermixed by the board. The design in issue appears to us to be relatively simple and plain, and the board, although not ruling upon appellant's contention that its design has acquired secondary meaning, discussed only distinctiveness before reaching its conclusion that the design was "functional." The unexpressed (and perhaps unconscious) thought may have been that if something is not inherently distinctive (appellant admits that its design is not), perhaps even austere, then, since it does not at a particular time function as a legally recognized indication of source, it probably never will. And since it is so plain that one may believe it is not and never will be a trademark, it will be perceived—not that the design is not inherently distinctive—but that it is "functional," without analysis of why it is believed to be "functional." The sole criterion seems to have been that the design is ordinary.

We have refrained from using phrases such as "essentially functional," "primarily functional," and "dictated primarily by functional considerations" to denote the legal consequence, all of which use the word "functional" in the lay sense of the term. If, in the legal sense, a particular design is functional, such adverbs as "essentially" and "primarily" are without meaning. Either a design is functional (de jure) or it is not.

While it is certainly arguable that lack of distinctiveness may, where appropriate, permit an inference that a design was created primarily with an eye toward the utility of the article, that fact is by no means conclusive as to the "functionality" of the design of that article. Whether in fact the design is "functional" requires closer and more careful scrutiny. We cannot say that there exists an inverse proportional relationship in all cases between distinctiveness of design and functionality (de facto or de jure).

This relationship—that a nondistinctive design does not necessarily equal a "functional" design—we will term the second addition to the Deister "truisms."

This court's past opinions which indicate that a particular design is "nonfunctional" because it is "arbitrary" are not to be construed as contrary to this additional truism. In this situation, "arbitrary" is not used in the typical trademark (distinctiveness) sense of the word. It is used to indicate a design which may have been selected without complete deference to utility and, thus, is most likely "nonfunctional." That is, it is used to indicate the opposite side of the "functional" coin, since a design can be inherently distinctive (the usual trademark law meaning of the word "arbitrary") and still be "functional."

* * *

The decision of the board on is reversed and the case is remanded for further proceedings consistent with this opinion.

REVERSED AND REMANDED

Notes

1. Note that the *Fantastic Bottle* case, *supra*, pre-dated the amendment to the Lanham Act adding Section 2(e)(5). However, this case is considered the mainstay of cases regarding the functionality doctrine.

2. The functionality doctrine is quickly becoming recognized as an important brake to the ever-expanding trademark right in the United States. Although it is recognized as an important brake, the precise standards for a "functional" mark differ depending upon the various attributes of a product or color, etc. This is certainly an area of trademark jurisprudence that is under development. *See, e.g.*, Mark Alen Thurmon, *The Rise and Fall of Trademark Law's Functionality Doctrine*, 56 Fla. L. Rev. 243 (2004); Justin Pats, *Conditioning Functionality: Untangling the Divergent Strands of Argument Evidenced by Recent Case Law and Commentary*, 10 Marq. Intell. Prop. L. Rev. 515 (2006).

6. Section 2(f): Statutory Secondary Meaning

15 U.S.C. §1052, Lanham Act §2

(f) Except as expressly excluded in subsections (a), (b), (c), (d), (e)(3), and (e)(5) of this section, nothing herein shall prevent the registration of a mark used by the applicant which has become distinctive of the applicant's goods in commerce. The Director may accept as prima facie evidence that the mark has become distinctive, as used on or in connection with the applicant's goods in commerce, proof of substantially exclusive and continuous use thereof as a mark by the applicant in commerce for the five years before the date on which the claim of distinctiveness is made ...

Yamaha International Corporation v. Hoshino Gakki Co., Ltd.

840 F.2d 1572 (CAFC 1988)

Bennett, J.

[Defendant had applied to register two guitar peg head configurations for use on or in connection with the sale of electric and acoustic guitars. Defendant amended its application to apply for registration under Section 2(f) of the Lanham Act. Plaintiff opposed.]

* * *

II. Opposer's Burden for Prima Facie Case under Section 2(f)

Hoshino, seeking to register its configurations/designs under Section 2(f), bore the burden of establishing acquired distinctiveness in ex parte proceedings before the PTO. When registration is sought under Section 2(f), the board publishes the mark for opposition when it is satisfied that the applicant has presented a prima facie case of acquired distinctiveness. If no opposition is filed following publication, the proposed mark will be registered. 37 C.F.R. §2.81.

However, in the opposition proceeding at issue here, Yamaha argues the board erred in requiring it, as the opposer, to prove that Hoshino's marks had not acquired distinctiveness. We agree with Yamaha that the sole issue in this opposition is whether Hoshino did or did not prove acquired distinctiveness. Although the distinction between the two "burdens" was not clearly outlined by the board in its opinion, we do not believe that the board required Yamaha to "prove" a lack of acquired distinctiveness. Whatever may be said of "burdens," it appears to us that one opposing a Section 2(f) registration published for opposition on the basis of that section must have at least the initial burden of challenging or rebutting the applicant's evidence of distinctiveness made of record during prosecution which led to publication of the proposed mark.

An opposer to an application submitted under Section 2(f) sufficiently meets its initial burden if it produces sufficient evidence or argument whereby, on the entire record then before the board, the board could conclude that the applicant has not met its ultimate burden of showing acquired distinctiveness. *Cf. Sanyo Watch Co. v. Sanyo Electric Co.*, 691 F.2d 1019, 1022, 215 U.S.P.Q. 833, 834 (Fed. Cir. 1982) (opposer's prima facie case requires "facts from which the board might reasonably conclude" that applicant was not entitled to the registration sought). Thus, the board's requirement that Yamaha establish a prima facie case of no acquired distinctiveness does not require Yamaha to "prove" anything, but simply requires Yamaha to present sufficient evidence or argument on which the board could reasonably conclude that Hoshino had not proven at least one of the elements necessary to obtain a trademark registration.

Nevertheless, citing *R.J. Reynolds Tobacco Co. v. Philip Morris Inc.*, 210 U.S.P.Q. 34, 41 (TTAB 1981), *Anchor Hocking Glass Corp. v. Corning Glass Works*, 162 U.S.P.Q. 288, 291 (TTAB 1969), and *Federal Glass Co. v. Corning Glass Works*, 162 U.S.P.Q. 279, 283 (TTAB 1969), Yamaha argues that its burden was only to establish a lack of inherent distinctiveness. But an opposer's burden of establishing no inherent distinctiveness, or of showing that the mark is "merely descriptive" under Section 2(e), exists only where an applicant seeks registration on the basis of inherent distinctiveness, as was the case in the *Corning Glass* cases.

Where, as here, an applicant seeks a registration based on acquired distinctiveness under Section 2(f), the *statute* accepts a lack of inherent distinctiveness as an established fact. When registration is sought under Section 2(f), therefore, it is idle to continue to speak of an opposer's burden to establish that fact, or to say that the applicant "conceded" that fact. Similarly, in cases where registration was initially sought on the basis of distinctiveness, subsequent reliance by the applicant on Section 2(f) assumes that the mark has been shown or conceded to be merely descriptive. Whether in ex parte proceedings under Section 2(f), *In re McIlhenny Co.*, 47 C.C.P.A. 985, 278 F.2d 953, 957, 126 U.S.P.Q. 138, 141 (1960), *General Foods Corp. v. MGD Partners*, 224 U.S.P.Q. 479, 485 (TTAB 1984), *Sunbeam Corp. v. Battle Creek Equipment Co.*, 216 U.S.P.Q. 1101, 1102 (TTAB 1982), or in subsequent oppositions, neither party bears any burden on inherent distinctiveness, as it is a nonissue under that subsection of the statute. The only remaining issue under Section 2(f) relating to the proposed mark itself is acquired distinctiveness. To prevent the immediate registration of the mark, the opposer has the initial burden to establish prima facie that the applicant did not satisfy the acquired distinctiveness requirement of Section 2(f). If opposer does not provide sufficient grounds to at least place the matter in issue, the situation is indistinguishable from one in which no opposition was filed. Under such circumstances, there is insufficient basis in the record to indicate that the applicant's mark, contrary to the examiner's prior determination, has *not* "become distinctive of the applicant's goods in commerce." 15 U.S.C. §1052(f).

If the opposer does present its prima facie case challenging the sufficiency of applicant's proof of acquired distinctiveness, the applicant may then find it necessary to present additional evidence and argument to rebut or overcome the opposer's showing and to establish that the mark has acquired distinctiveness. To accept Yamaha's argument that an opposer bears no burden of establishing even a prima facie case as to the sufficiency of applicant's prior proof would make a mere filing of a naked opposition the sole basis for delaying registration and prompting an applicant to reestablish acquired distinctiveness to the satisfaction of the PTO in the face of insufficient evidence or argument by the opposer. We conclude, therefore, that the board was not incorrect in stating that Yamaha, as opposer of a Section 2(f) registration, had the burden to establish a prima facie case, the principal facet of which is showing that Hoshino did not establish acquired distinctiveness.

On the other hand, we believe that the board unnecessarily addressed the issue of whether the prima facie case had indeed been established by Yamaha. As noted above, the PTO rules governing the procedure in oppositions are designed to approximate the proceedings in a courtroom trial. Thus, whether a prima facie case has been made by the opposer only would be relevant to the resolution of a summary judgment motion filed by the applicant following the close of the opposer's testimony period. In *Sanyo*, 691 F.2d at 1022, 215 U.S.P.Q. at 834, this court addressed the requirements of a prima facie case where the board had dismissed the opposition following failure of opposer to present any evidence during its testimony period. Yet here, unlike the situation in *Sanyo*, no motion was made and no judgment was entered after the opposer's testimony period.

Since we are reviewing the entire proceeding in the PTO in which both sides presented all their evidence, filed briefs, and made closing arguments, the only relevant issue before this court on appeal, as it should have been before the board, is which party should prevail on the entire record. At this stage, evaluation of the entire record, not of the prima facie showings previously made by the respective parties, is the only issue relevant to the outcome. Therefore, we do not address or adopt any of the board's discussion relating to whether, under the facts of the present case, Yamaha's showing was sufficient to place Hoshino's showing of acquired distinctiveness at issue. We review instead the board's alternative holding that Hoshino had established, on the entire record, the requisite acquired distinctiveness to support registration of its marks.

III. The Ultimate Burden of Persuasion under Section 2(f)

Yamaha strenuously asserts in its brief on appeal that the ultimate burden of persuasion under Section 2(f) on the issue of acquired distinctiveness is on Hoshino as applicant. We completely agree. "The burden of proving secondary meaning is on the party asserting it, whether he is the plaintiff in an infringement action or the applicant for federal trademark registration." 1 Gilson, *Trademark Protection and Practice* §2.09, at 2–72 (1987). As one of our predecessor courts stated in *In re Hollywood Brands, Inc.*, 41 C.C.P.A. 1001, 214 F.2d 139, 140, 102 U.S.P.Q. 294, 295 (1954), when reviewing the refusal of a registration sought under Section 2(f), "there is no doubt that Congress intended that the burden of proof [under Section 2(f)] should rest upon the applicant for registration." As this court observed while reviewing an opposition proceeding in *Levi Strauss & Co. v. Genesco, Inc.*, 742 F.2d 1401, 1405, 222 U.S.P.Q. 939, 942 (Fed. Cir. 1984), the "one seeking to register [the proposed trademark] bears the burden of showing secondary meaning under Section 2(f)."

However, seizing upon the board's statement that Yamaha had not met its "burden of proof," 231 U.S.P.Q. at 935, Yamaha nevertheless asserts that the board improperly transferred the "burden" of persuasion from applicant to opposer. We disagree. In our view, as indicated above, the board only placed on Yamaha a "burden" of going forward with evidence as the opposer. In any event, once that burden was assumed by the board in the alternative to have been carried by Yamaha, the final "burden," that of going forward with evidence to overcome the opposer's prima facie case and establish acquired distinctiveness by at least a preponderance of the evidence, was properly placed by the board upon the applicant Hoshino. Thus, in making its alternative holding, the board did exactly what Yamaha asserts it should have: placed the ultimate burden of showing acquired distinctiveness on Hoshino.

Admittedly, we do not find it altogether surprising that some of the language used by the board in its opinion is capable of being misinterpreted. At the outset of its discussion, the board observed that "the burden of proof in an inter partes proceeding rests on the plaintiff party." The board then cited *Clinton Detergent Co. v. Procter & Gamble Co.*, 49 C.C.P.A. 1146, 302 F.2d 745, 747, 133 U.S.P.Q. 520, 522 (1962), for the proposition that the "opposer ... has the burden of proof to establish that applicant does not have the right to register its mark." *Id.* (also citing *Wilson v. Delaunay*, 44 C.C.P.A. 1019, 245 F.2d 877, 880, 114 U.S.P.Q. 339, 342 (1957)). However, the board failed to appreciate that the opposer in *Clinton* was asserting likelihood of confusion with its own previously registered mark and that the opposer in *Wilson* was asserting prior use of the mark, issues unrelated to acquired distinctiveness and carrying distinct burdens in accordance with the rules of evidence.

It is beyond question that an opposer alleging likelihood of confusion under Section 2(d) "has the burden of proof to establish that applicant does not have the right to register its mark." *Clinton*, 302 F.2d at 747, 133 U.S.P.Q. at 522. In fact, an opposer alleging likelihood of confusion "bears the burden of proof which encompasses not only the ultimate burden of persuasion, but also the obligation of going forward with sufficient proof of the material allegations of the Notice of Opposition, which, if not countered, negates [applicant's] right to a registration." *Sanyo*, 691 F.2d at 1022, 215 U.S.P.Q. at 834. Since 15 U.S.C. §1052(d) provides that no trademark shall be refused *unless* it is shown that there is a likelihood of confusion with another mark, the requirement that the opposer both establish a prima facie case of likelihood of confusion and carry the ultimate burden of persuasion on that issue is proper in light of Congress's wording of the statute.

However, Section 2(f) applies to registrations for marks which are not inherently distinctive, or which would not otherwise qualify for registration in the face of the provisions of Section 2(e). *See* 37 C.F.R. §2.41(a). Thus, unlike the first five sections of 15 U.S.C. §1052 which define the grounds upon which a trademark registration is to be refused, Section 2(f) serves as an exception to a rejection under the provisions of one of the other sections, Section 2(e). *See In re Loew's Theatres, Inc.*, 769 F.2d 764, 766 n.4, 226 U.S.P.Q. 865, 867 n.4 (Fed. Cir. 1985). Section 2(f) permits registration of marks that, despite not qualifying for registration in light of Section 2(e), have nevertheless "become distinctive of the applicant's goods in commerce." Thus, "Section 2(f) is not a provision on which registration can be refused," *In re Capital Formation Counselors, Inc.*, 219 U.S.P.Q. 916, 917 n.2 (TTAB 1983), but is a provision under which an applicant has a chance to prove that he is entitled to a federal trademark registration which would otherwise be refused.

Thus, seeking registration under Section 2(f) is not unlike an affirmative defense to a showing by the opposer (or a concession by the applicant) that the applicant otherwise is not entitled to a trademark for one of the reasons listed under Section 2(e). Affirmative defenses are to be proved by the party asserting them. Neither *Clinton*, *Wilson*, nor any other opposition proceeding not involving Section 2(f) should be viewed as placing the ultimate burden of persuasion on the opposer in oppositions where acquired distinctiveness under Section 2(f) is at issue. In contrast to the opposer's ultimate burden in oppositions involving Sections 2(a)–(e), the ultimate burden when registration is sought under Section 2(f) is properly placed on the applicant. Furthermore, the applicant has the ultimate burden of showing acquired distinctiveness regardless of whether the lack of inherent distinctiveness or the applicability of Section 2(e) was shown by the opposer during the opposition or conceded by the applicant prior to the opposition. To conclude otherwise would give the applicant for a trademark the rebuttable presumption of validity that properly follows only the registration of the mark, not the publication of the proposed mark prior to its registration. *See* 15 U.S.C. §1057(b) ("[a] certificate of registration of a mark upon the principal register ... shall be prima facie evidence of the validity of the registration, registrant's ownership of the mark, and of registrant's exclusive right to use the mark in commerce").

D. Trademark Searches

Trademark searching is an integral component to an overall trademark strategy. Trademark searching allows the trademark user to know if others are using or have registered its proposed mark.

The usual sequence of trademark searching and clearance flows as follows:

1. The client (corporation or other entity) proposes one to five trademarks for use on or in connection with some specific good or service. The better trademark attorney attempts to involve him/herself at this stage. It is called "naming" or the very earliest phase of choosing a trademark. If the trademark attorney is involved at this stage, many obviously bad trademarks can be avoided.

2. Once the client has determined the one to five trademarks that ought to be searched, the trademark attorney attempts to do a "knock-out" search. This is usually done using online services for no charge. The most appropriate site for this is www.uspto.gov. At this site, one can search all trademark registrations and applications. This is a most efficient and cost effective way to do easy knock-out searches. This search will most often turn up marks with which there would be a clear conflict.

3. The next step is to engage one of many commercial trademark search companies such as Thomson & Thomson or many others. The vendor chosen will produce a "Trademark Research Report" upon which the trademark attorney will base his or her determination regarding whether the mark is available for use and registration.

4. Next, the Trademark Research Report is reviewed by the attorney. The Report will typically include a federal section, a state section, a common law section, a domain name section, and other sections. Each of these needs to be read closely to determine if there are any conflicting prior registrations or uses.

5. Explicitly based on the Trademark Research Report, the trademark attorney next prepares an opinion letter. This letter is extremely important in the process because it is where potential attorney liability for malpractice attaches. Thus, great care should be given to avoid giving inappropriate advice. Absolute statements regarding a mark's availability should be avoided. The Trademark Research Report will only be some 98% accurate. As human beings are involved in the process of compiling the Report, mistakes are possible. As the opinion letter relies on the Report, if there are mistakes in the Report, these mistakes could be passed on in the form of a formal opinion. Therefore, the better opinion letter gives several parameters as follows:

    a. The opinion letter should make it clear to the client that it relies on the Report. To the extent the Report changes, the opinion could change accordingly.

    b. The opinion letter should clearly express the validity dates given in the Report. The Report will disclose the exact dates on which the search was done, on what dates applications were available for searching by the PTO, and what dates the Official Gazette was searched. These dates should be made clear to the client.

    c. The opinion should clearly state any and all trademarks that might provide some obstacle to use and registration of the client's mark. Clearly stating all marks that might pose an obstacle allows the client to make an informed decision about use and registration of the mark.

6. In the end, the final decision regarding use and registration should be made by the client, not the trademark attorney. For this reason, the opinion letter ought to only state whether use and registration of a mark would amount to an "average business risk" or an "above average business risk." Final determination of use and registration should be left to the client.

Once the search is accomplished, a determination can be made regarding availability. Without the search, an informed decision is quite impossible. For this reason, trademark search plays a prominent role in the process of trademark clearance.

———————

Chapter VIII

Incontestability

15 U.S.C. §1064, Lanham Act §14

A petition to cancel a registration of a mark,[may be filed:]

(1) Within five years from the date of the registration of the mark under this Act.

...

(3) At any time if the registered mark becomes the generic name for the goods or services, or a portion thereof, for which it is registered, or is functional, or has been abandoned, or its registration was obtained fraudulently or contrary to the provisions of section 4 or of subsection (a), (b), or (c) of section 2 for a registration under this Act, or contrary to similar prohibitory provisions of such prior Acts for a registration under such Acts, or if the registered mark is being used by, or with the permission of, the registrant so as to misrepresent the source of the goods or services on or in connection with which the mark is used.

...

15 U.S.C. §1065, Lanham Act §15

Except on a ground for which application to cancel may be filed at any time under paragraphs (3) and (5) of section 14 of this Act, ... the right of the registrant to use such registered mark in commerce for the goods or services on or in connection with which such registered mark has been in continuous use for five consecutive years subsequent to the date of such registration and is still in use in commerce, shall be incontestable: Provided, That—

(1) there has been no final decision adverse to registrant's claim of ownership of such mark for such goods or services, or to registrant's right to register the same or to keep the same on the register; and

(2) there is no proceeding involving said rights pending in the Patent and Trademark Office or in a court and not finally disposed of; and

(3) an affidavit is filed with the Director within one year after the expiration of any such five-year period setting forth those goods or services stated in the registration on or in connection with which such mark has been in continuous use for such five consecutive years and is still in use in commerce, and the other matters specified in paragraphs (1) and (2) of this section; and

(4) no incontestable right shall be acquired in a mark which is the generic name for the goods or services or a portion thereof, for which it is registered.

15 U.S.C. §1115, Lanham Act §33

. . .

(b) Incontestability; defenses. To the extent that the right to use the registered mark has become incontestable under section 15, the registration shall be conclusive evidence of the validity of the registered mark and of the registration of the mark, of the registrant's ownership of the mark, and of the registrant's exclusive right to use the registered mark in commerce. Such conclusive evidence shall relate to the exclusive right to use the mark on or in connection with the goods or services specified in the affidavit filed under the provisions of section 15, or in the renewal application filed under the provisions of section 9 if the goods or services specified in the renewal are fewer in number, subject to any conditions or limitations in the registration or in such affidavit or renewal application. Such conclusive evidence of the right to use the registered mark shall be subject to proof of infringement as defined in section 32, and shall be subject to the following defenses or defects:

(1) That the registration or the incontestable right to use the mark was obtained fraudulently; or

(2) That the mark has been abandoned by the registrant; or

(3) That the registered mark is being used, by or with the permission of the registrant or a person in privity with the registrant, so as to misrepresent the source of the goods or services on or in connection with which the mark is used; or

(4) That the use of the name, term, or device charged to be an infringement is a use, otherwise than as a mark, of the party's individual name in his own business, or of the individual name of anyone in privity with such party, or of a term or device which is descriptive of and used fairly and in good faith only to describe the goods or services of such party, or their geographic origin; or

(5) That the mark whose use by a party is charged as an infringement was adopted without knowledge of the registrant's prior use and has been continuously used by such party or those in privity with him from a date prior to (A) the date of constructive use of the mark established pursuant to section 7(c), (B) the registration of the mark under this Act if the application for registration is filed before the effective date of the Trademark Law Revision Act of 1988, or (C) publication of the registered mark under subsection (c) of section 12 of this Act: Provided, however, That this defense or defect shall apply only for the area in which such continuous prior use is proved; or

(6) That the mark whose use is charged as an infringement was registered and used prior to the registration under this Act or publication under subsection (c) of section 12 of this Act of the registered mark of the registrant, and not abandoned: Provided, however, That this defense or defect shall apply only for the area in which the mark was used prior to such registration or such publication of the registrant's mark; or

(7) That the mark has been or is being used to violate the antitrust laws of the United States; or

(8) That the mark is functional; or

(9) That equitable principles, including laches, estoppel, and acquiescence, are applicable.

The standard explanation for "incontestability" under the Lanham Act is that it is premised on the notion that at some point, trademark owners ought to be able essentially to quiet title and rely on the registration as proof that no other party has superior right in or to the relevant trademark. When reading these materials, pay close attention to whether that analogy to property law helps or hurts understanding and enforcement of the concept.

Incontestability[1] under the Lanham Act is a statutory right with no common law counterpart. When the Lanham Act was drafted, it was added to give extra incentive for trademark users to register their marks.

A registration becomes "incontestable" after five years of continuous use and the satisfaction of certain formalistic procedures. Once a trademark registration becomes incontestable, the validity of the mark, the validity of the owner's ownership of the mark, and the owner's exclusive right to use the mark on designated goods may be challenged only on eight enumerated grounds. That is, incontestable doesn't mean completely beyond contest. Acquisition of incontestable status is an amazingly simple procedure in light of the profound advantages the registrant receives. Merely by filing what is known as a Section 15 Affidavit stating the mark has been in use for five consecutive years, and by complying with other minimal requirements, a registration becomes incontestable. There is no substantive review procedure by the Patent and Trademark Office, and no other proof of such five-year use is required.

Once a Section 15 Affidavit is filed and accepted by the Patent and Trademark Office, the mark is considered incontestable and the owner can take advantage of section 33(b) of the Lanham Act. Although the term "incontestable" has been criticized as being misleading given the numerous exceptions stated in section 33(b), incontestable status provides powerful evidentiary advantages in trademark litigation because an incontestable registration is "conclusive evidence of the validity of the registered mark and of the registration of the mark, of the registrant's ownership of the mark, and the registrant's exclusive right to use the registered mark in commerce."

The actual application of the concept of incontestability involves the simultaneous application of three sections of the Lanham Act—sections 14, 15, and 33. Section 14 addresses when and how marks can be canceled. First, Section 14 lists five instances when a petition to cancel a registration of a mark may be filed by a person who believes that they have been or will be damaged by the registration:

1. Within five years from the date of the registration.

2. Within five years of the date of publication under §1062(c) of the Lanham Act of a mark registered under prior trademark laws.

3. At any time if the mark becomes generic, has become abandoned, its registration was obtained by fraud or was contrary to §1052 (a)-(c) of the Lanham Act.

4. At any time if the mark registered under prior acts is not published according to the Lanham Act.

5. At any time if the mark is a certification mark and either the registrant fails to control the mark, the registrant engages in the production or marketing of any goods or services to which the certification mark is applied, the registrant permits use of the mark other than to certify, or the registrant discriminately refuses to certify anyone who maintains appropriate standards.

1. Adapted from Kenneth L. Port, *The Illegitmacy of Trademark Incontestability*, 26 IND. L. REV. 519 (1993).

This provision constitutes what has become known as "incontestability in the Patent and Trademark Office." That is, the clear directive of Section 14(1) is that after the mark has been registered for five years, a petition to cancel the registration will not be accepted by the Patent and Trademark Office, even if the registrant has failed to file affidavits with the Patent and Trademark Office.

This is the first step of the incontestability analysis. Once a mark is registered for five years, potentially harmed third parties may not file to cancel it. A third party may sue for infringement, but that third party may not petition the Patent and Trademark Office to cancel the registration.

The main import of Section 15, the next step of incontestability application, is to clarify the meaning of incontestability (to the extent it can be clarified). Incontestability refers to the "right of the registrant to use such registered mark in commerce for the goods or services on or in connection with which such registered mark has been in continuous use for five consecutive years ... and is still in use in commerce." This also is the source of the Section 15 Affidavit that the Patent and Trademark Office requires before acknowledging statutory incontestability.

Section 15 largely applies to prior users of the same mark on similar goods. Section 15 is meant to protect third parties who were using a mark before the registrant. That is, granting a registrant incontestable status in its mark is subject to the four conditions set forth in Section 15. These include the following:

1. There are no final decisions of any court adverse to the registrant's interests.

2. There is no proceeding pending before the Patent and Trademark Office involving the rights of the registrant.

3. A Section 15 Affidavit is filed with the Patent and Trademark Office.

4. The mark has not become generic.

Section 15 also specifies the scope of incontestable rights. The first sentence of Section 15 has been interpreted to mean that incontestability is limited to those goods on which the mark has been used for the requisite five-year period.

Section 15 specifies the substance of incontestability. It is not the trademark itself that becomes incontestable, as some courts mistakenly articulate. Rather, the registrant's right to use the mark on the goods on its Section 15 Affidavit becomes incontestable. In other words, the registration becomes incontestable, not the mark itself.

Finally, Section 33 is the "cutting edge of incontestability." Section 33(a) applies to registrations that have not become incontestable. Section 33(b) applies to registrations that have become incontestable. Section 33(a) states that a trademark registration shall be prima facie evidence of the validity of the mark, the validity of the registration of the mark, the registrant's ownership of the mark, and of the owner's exclusive right to use the registered mark on the goods or services specified in the registration. Section 33(b) states that an incontestable registration shall be conclusive evidence of the validity of the mark, the validity of the registration of the mark, the registrant's ownership of the mark, and of the owner's exclusive right to use the registered mark on the goods or services specified in the registration. The key distinction between 33(a) and 33(b)—between non-incontestable and incontestable registrations—is that 33(a) grants prima facie evidence while 33(b) grants conclusive evidence of trademark rights.

Once a registration has attained incontestable status, it may not be challenged except for the eight enumerated reasons set forth in Section 33 of the Lanham Act. Once a mark becomes incontestable, it is subject only to the following defects or defenses:

1.   The registration was obtained fraudulently;

2.   The mark was abandoned by the registrant;

3.   The mark is being misused and no longer indicates the registrant as the source of the goods on which it is used;

4.   The mark is being used otherwise than as a trademark to describe a good or service;

5.   The registrant registered the mark subsequent to a regional user although the registrant has prior use nationally;

6.   The alleged infringing mark was registered and used first;

7.   The mark is or has been used to violate the antitrust laws of the United States;

8.   The mark is functional; or

9.   The registrant has violated common law rules of equity such as laches.

Incontestability is a substantive change to the common law of trademarks. Prior to passage of the Lanham Act, trademark registration was considered to be only procedural. Trademark registration granted no new substantive rights to an owner. In fact, the common law notion of trademark rights was that the trademark existed independent of any statute and only arose out of prior exclusive appropriation and use. Most significantly, in *E.F. Prichard Co. v. Consumers Brewing Co.*, 136 F.2d 512, 518 (6th Cir. 1943), *cert. denied*, 321 U.S. 763 (1944), the court stated that the title to a trademark is independent of its registration. Prior to the Lanham Act, trademark registration had little, if any, meaning in the courts.

When the Lanham Act was being discussed in committee, several Senators and other witnesses testified that the Act was intended to codify existing common law and not change substantive trademark law. In fact, the first draft of one section — Section 34 — stated that nothing in the Act was meant to change the existing common law of trademarks. However, when it was pointed out to the committee that the proposed Section 34 would be inconsistent with the Lanham Act's provisions regarding incontestability, Section 34 was promptly deleted.

Courts, however, have refused to recognize the changes brought about by incontestability. Several courts since the enactment of the Lanham Act have acted as if nothing, in fact, had changed. This is peculiar because Section 33 asserts that an incontestable registration shall be conclusive proof of the validity and ownership of the owner's right to use the mark. This has not stopped some courts from stating that trademark registration is only a method of recording ownership for purposes of serving notice of a claim of ownership and informing the public of that claim of ownership.

Even the United States Supreme Court appeared to be unaware of the potential import of a passing statement it made in *Park 'N Fly*. In her majority opinion, Justice O'Connor stated that incontestability was "[a]mong the new protections created by the Lanham Act." *Park 'N Fly, Inc. v. Dollar Park & Fly, Inc.*, 469 U.S. 189, 193 (1985). This statement by the Supreme Court is completely at odds with the express legislative intent of Congress when it enacted the Lanham Act. The Lanham Act was meant to codify common law and not to add new rights. The Supreme Court went a long way in its simple statement to recognize that the Lanham Act, especially through the incontestability provisions, substantively changed the existing common law of trademarks.

Not all courts have accepted this, as is evident in the confusion that arises whenever courts are called upon to adjudicate an issue regarding incontestability. This confusion results from two competing directives: legislative history and common law on one side and the language of the statute on the other. When both legislative history and the common law tell the courts that there is nothing new in the Lanham Act, when in actuality there is, courts as well as students are very likely to be confused.

Incontestability in the Lanham Act was premised on the British system. The legislative history of the Lanham Act indicates that Congress's rationale for including an incontestability provision was to make a certain date after which trademark rights would vest. After that date, other trademark users would be on notice that an incontestable registration was subject only to certain defenses or defects. This was thought to be similar to the concept of adverse possession or quieting title. That is, at some point in time, it should be clear who owns the trademark, because the alternative would be chaos and confusion. Giving trademark owners a certain date after which their rights would become incontestable would provide clarity and predictability in the law, so the argument goes.

Simply stated, the effects of an incontestable trademark registration may be summarized as follows:

1. Plaintiff and holder of an incontestable registration does not have to prove secondary meaning for a weak mark that may otherwise be invalid and undefensible;

2. Defendant non-holder of an incontestable mark is restricted to the eight enumerated attacks or defenses in Section 33(b);

3. Some courts equate an incontestable registration with a "strong mark;" and

4. Plaintiff holders of descriptive marks are statutorily protected from attacks on the validity of their marks.

The life of the incontestability doctrine in trademark law has been quite confused in a variety of respects. For the first forty or so years of the existence of the incontestability doctrine, courts and scholars were not able to agree on whether incontestability could be used only as a defense to a challenge to the validity of a mark, or if it also could be used offensively to obviate the general requirement that the plaintiff show secondary meaning in a trademark infringement action.

The confusion started in 1955 when Assistant Commissioner of Patents and Trademarks Leeds announced his position regarding the effect of incontestability: "The effect of 'incontestability' is a defensive and not an offensive effect. To put it another way, when the right to use a given mark has become incontestable, the owner's rights in the mark are in no wise broadened...." *Rand McNally & Co. v. Christmas Club*, 105 U.S.P.Q. 499, 500–501 (Comm'r Pts. 1955), *aff'd on other grounds*, 242 F.2d 766 (C.C.P.A. 1957). Based upon this distinction, a split in the circuits developed surrounding the effect of incontestability. Some circuits concluded that an incontestable mark could be used only as a procedural, defensive mechanism to counter challenges to the validity of the mark. That is, incontestability could only be used defensively to prevent cancellation of the mark.

Other courts concluded that incontestability could also be used offensively to preclude a defendant from arguing that the plaintiff's mark was descriptive.

The offensive/defensive distinction controversy arose not only over Leeds's "opinion," but also over the precise interpretation of the Lanham Act. Superficially, the offensive/defensive argument has some appeal. After all, Section 33(b), the primary incontestability provision of the Lanham Act, is titled "Incontestability; defenses." At first blush, it would appear that those items which appear in Section 33(b) only apply to defensive uses of an incontestable mark. This was the reasoning of the Ninth Circuit in rejecting plaintiff's claims of trademark infringement in its opinion in *Park 'N Fly*. According to the Ninth

Circuit, the Lanham Act did not allow a trademark registrant to use the incontestable status of its mark in an offensive manner, especially when the mark was merely descriptive. The incontestability provisions of the Lanham Act, the court argued, only applied as defenses to claims that the mark was invalid; incontestability did not apply when the plaintiff was seeking to enforce the mark against others.

This is the background to the *Park 'N Fly* decision below.

Park 'N Fly, Inc. v. Dollar Park and Fly, Inc.

469 U.S. 189 (1985)

O'CONNOR, J.

In this case we consider whether an action to enjoin the infringement of an incontestable trade or service mark may be defended on the grounds that the mark is merely descriptive. We conclude that neither the language of the relevant statutes nor the legislative history supports such a defense.

I

Petitioner operates long-term parking lots near airports. After starting business in St. Louis in 1967, petitioner subsequently opened facilities in Cleveland, Houston, Boston, Memphis, and San Francisco. Petitioner applied in 1969 to the United States Patent and Trademark Office (Patent Office) to register a service mark consisting of the logo of an airplane and the words "Park 'N Fly." The registration issued in August 1971. Nearly six years later, petitioner filed an affidavit with the Patent Office to establish the incontestable status of the mark. As required by §15 of the Trademark Act of 1946 (Lanham Act), 60 Stat. 433, as amended, 15 U. S. C. §1065, the affidavit stated that the mark had been registered and in continuous use for five consecutive years, that there had been no final adverse decision to petitioner's claim of ownership or right to registration, and that no proceedings involving such rights were pending. Incontestable status provides, subject to the provisions of §15 and §33(b) of the Lanham Act, "conclusive evidence of the registrant's exclusive right to use the registered mark...." §33(b), 15 U. S. C. §1115(b).

Respondent also provides long-term airport parking services, but only has operations in Portland, Oregon. Respondent calls its business "Dollar Park and Fly." Petitioner filed this infringement action in 1978 in the United States District Court for the District of Oregon and requested the court permanently to enjoin respondent from using the words "Park and Fly" in connection with its business. Respondent counterclaimed and sought cancellation of petitioner's mark on the grounds that it is a generic term. See §14(c), 15 U. S. C. §1064(c). Respondent also argued that petitioner's mark is unenforceable because it is merely descriptive. See §2(e), 15 U. S. C. §§1052(e). As two additional defenses, respondent maintained that it is in privity with a Seattle corporation that has used the expression "Park and Fly" since a date prior to the registration of petitioner's mark, see §33(b)(5), 15 U. S. C. §1115(b)(5), and that it has not infringed because there is no likelihood of confusion. See §32(1), 15 U. S. C. §1114(1).

After a bench trial, the District Court found that petitioner's mark is not generic and observed that an incontestable mark cannot be challenged on the grounds that it is merely descriptive. The District Court also concluded that there was no evidence of privity between respondent and the Seattle corporation. Finally, the District Court found sufficient evidence of likelihood of confusion. The District Court permanently enjoined respondent from using the words "Park and Fly" and any other mark confusingly similar to "Park 'N Fly."

The Court of Appeals for the Ninth Circuit reversed. 718 F.2d 327 (1983). The District Court did not err, the Court of Appeals held, in refusing to invalidate petitioner's mark. *Id.*, at 331. The Court of Appeals noted, however, that it previously had held that incontestability provides a defense against the cancellation of a mark, but it may not be used offensively to enjoin another's use. *Ibid.* Petitioner, under this analysis, could obtain an injunction only if its mark would be entitled to continued registration without regard to its incontestable status. Thus, respondent could defend the infringement action by showing that the mark was merely descriptive. Based on its own examination of the record, the Court of Appeals then determined that petitioner's mark is in fact merely descriptive, and therefore respondent should not be enjoined from using the name "Park and Fly." *Ibid.*

The decision below is in direct conflict with the decision of the Court of Appeals for the Seventh Circuit in *Union Carbide Corp.* v. *Ever-Ready, Inc.*, 531 F.2d 366, *cert. denied,* 429 U.S. 830 (1976). We granted certiorari to resolve this conflict, 465 U.S. 1078 (1984), and we now reverse.

II

Congress enacted the Lanham Act in 1946 in order to provide national protection for trademarks used in interstate and foreign commerce. S. Rep. No. 1333, 79th Cong., 2d Sess., 5 (1946). Previous federal legislation, such as the Federal Trademark Act of 1905, 33 Stat. 724, reflected the view that protection of trademarks was a matter of state concern and that the right to a mark depended solely on the common law. S. Rep. No. 1333, at 5. Consequently, rights to trademarks were uncertain and subject to variation in different parts of the country. Because trademarks desirably promote competition and the maintenance of product quality, Congress determined that "a sound public policy requires that trademarks should receive nationally the greatest protection that can be given them." *Id.*, at 6. Among the new protections created by the Lanham Act were the statutory provisions that allow a federally registered mark to become incontestable. §§15, 33(b), 15 U. S. C. §§1065, 1115(b).

The provisions of the Lanham Act concerning registration and incontestability distinguish a mark that is "the common descriptive name of an article or substance" from a mark that is "merely descriptive." §§2(e), 14(c), 15 U. S. C. §§1052(e), 1064(c). Marks that constitute a common descriptive name are referred to as generic. A generic term is one that refers to the genus of which the particular product is a species. *Abercrombie & Fitch Co.* v. *Hunting World, Inc.*, 537 F.2d 4, 9 (CA2 1976). Generic terms are not registrable, and a registered mark may be canceled at any time on the grounds that it has become generic. *See* §§2, 14(c), 15 U. S. C. §§1052, 1064(c). A "merely descriptive" mark, in contrast, describes the qualities or characteristics of a good or service, and this type of mark may be registered only if the registrant shows that it has acquired secondary meaning, *i. e.*, it "has become distinctive of the applicant's goods in commerce." §§2(e), (f), 15 U. S. C. §§1052(e), (f).

This case requires us to consider the effect of the incontestability provisions of the Lanham Act in the context of an infringement action defended on the grounds that the mark is merely descriptive. Statutory construction must begin with the language employed by Congress and the assumption that the ordinary meaning of that language accurately expresses the legislative purpose. With respect to incontestable trade or service marks, §33(b) of the Lanham Act states that "registration shall be conclusive evidence of the registrant's exclusive right to use the registered mark" subject to the conditions of §15 and certain enumerated defenses. Section 15 incorporates by reference subsections (c) and (e) of §§14, 15 U. S. C. §1064. An incontestable mark that becomes generic may be canceled at any time pursuant to §14(c). That section also allows cancellation of an incontestable mark at any time if it has been abandoned, if it is being used to misrepresent the source of the goods or services in connection with which it is used, or if it was obtained fraudulently or contrary to the provisions of §4, 15 U. S. C. §§1054, or §§2(a)–(c), 15 U. S. C. §§1052(a)–(c).

One searches the language of the Lanham Act in vain to find any support for the offensive/defensive distinction applied by the Court of Appeals. The statute nowhere distinguishes between a registrant's offensive and defensive use of an incontestable mark. On the contrary, §33(b)'s declaration that the registrant has an "exclusive right" to use the mark indicates that incontestable status may be used to enjoin infringement by others. A conclusion that such infringement cannot be enjoined renders meaningless the "exclusive right" recognized by the statute. Moreover, the language in three of the defenses enumerated in §33(b) clearly contemplates the use of incontestability in infringement actions by plaintiffs. See §§33 (b)(4)–(6), 15 U. S. C. §§1115(b)(4)–(6).

The language of the Lanham Act also refutes any conclusion that an incontestable mark may be challenged as merely descriptive. A mark that is merely descriptive of an applicant's goods or services is not registrable unless the mark has secondary meaning. Before a mark achieves incontestable status, registration provides prima facie evidence of the registrant's exclusive right to use the mark in commerce. §33(a), 15 U. S. C. §1115(a). The Lanham Act expressly provides that before a mark becomes incontestable an opposing party may prove any legal or equitable defense which might have been asserted if the mark had not been registered. *Ibid.* Thus, §33(a) would have allowed respondent to challenge petitioner's mark as merely descriptive if the mark had not become incontestable. With respect to incontestable marks, however, §33(b) provides that registration is *conclusive* evidence of the registrant's exclusive right to use the mark, subject to the conditions of §15 and the seven defenses enumerated in §§33(b) itself. Mere descriptiveness is not recognized by either §15 or §33(b) as a basis for challenging an incontestable mark.

The statutory provisions that prohibit registration of a merely descriptive mark but do not allow an incontestable mark to be challenged on this ground cannot be attributed to inadvertence by Congress. The Conference Committee rejected an amendment that would have denied registration to any descriptive mark, and instead retained the provisions allowing registration of a merely descriptive mark that has acquired secondary meaning. See H. R. Conf. Rep. No. 2322, 79th Cong., 2d Sess., 4 (1946) (explanatory statement of House managers). The Conference Committee agreed to an amendment providing that no incontestable right can be acquired in a mark that is a common descriptive, *i. e.,* generic, term. *Id.,* at 5. Congress could easily have denied incontestability to merely descriptive marks as well as to generic marks had that been its intention.

The Court of Appeals in discussing the offensive/defensive distinction observed that incontestability protects a registrant against cancellation of his mark. 718 F.2d, at 331. This observation is incorrect with respect to marks that become generic or which otherwise may be canceled at any time pursuant to §§14(c) and (e). Moreover, as applied to marks that are merely descriptive, the approach of the Court of Appeals makes incontestable status superfluous. Without regard to its incontestable status, a mark that has been registered five years is protected from cancellation except on the grounds stated in §§14(c) and (e). Pursuant to §14, a mark may be canceled on the grounds that it is merely descriptive only if the petition to cancel is filed within five years of the date of registration. §14(a), 15 U. S. C. §1064(a). The approach adopted by the Court of Appeals implies that incontestability adds nothing to the protections against cancellation already provided in §14. The decision below not only lacks support in the words of the statute; it effectively emasculates §33(b) under the circumstances of this case.

III

Nothing in the legislative history of the Lanham Act supports a departure from the plain language of the statutory provisions concerning incontestability. Indeed, a conclusion that incontestable status can provide the basis for enforcement of the registrant's exclusive right to use a trade or service mark promotes the goals of the statute. The Lanham Act provides national protection of trademarks in order to secure to the owner of the mark the goodwill of his business and to protect the ability of consumers to distinguish among competing producers. *See* S. Rep. No. 1333, at 3, 5. National protection of trademarks is desirable, Congress concluded, because trademarks foster competition and the maintenance of quality by securing to the producer the benefits of good reputation. *Id.*, at 4. The incontestability provisions, as the proponents of the Lanham Act emphasized, provide a means for the registrant to quiet title in the ownership of his mark. *See* Hearings on H. R. 82 before the Subcommittee of the Senate Committee on Patents, 78th Cong., 2d Sess., 21 (1944) (remarks of Rep. Lanham); *id.*, at 21, 113 (testimony of Daphne Robert, ABA Committee on Trade Mark Legislation); Hearings on H. R. 102 et al. before the Subcommittee on Trade-Marks of the House Committee on Patents, 77th Cong., 1st Sess., 73 (1941) (remarks of Rep. Lanham). The opportunity to obtain incontestable status by satisfying the requirements of §15 thus encourages producers to cultivate the goodwill associated with a particular mark. This function of the incontestability provisions would be utterly frustrated if the holder of an incontestable mark could not enjoin infringement by others so long as they established that the mark would not be registrable but for its incontestable status.

Respondent argues, however, that enforcing petitioner's mark would conflict with the goals of the Lanham Act because the mark is merely descriptive and should never have been registered in the first place.[2] Representative Lanham, respondent notes, explained that the defenses enumerated in §33(b) were "not intended to enlarge, restrict, amend, or modify the substantive law of trademarks either as set out in other sections of the act or as heretofore applied by the courts under prior laws." 92 Cong. Rec. 7524 (1946). Respondent reasons that because the Lanham Act did not alter the substantive law of trademarks, the incontestability provisions cannot protect petitioner's use of the mark if it were not originally registrable. Moreover, inasmuch as petitioner's mark is merely descriptive, respondent contends that enjoining others from using the mark will not encourage competition by assisting consumers in their ability to distinguish among competing producers.

These arguments are unpersuasive. Representative Lanham's remarks, if read in context, clearly refer to the effect of the *defenses* enumerated in §33(b).[3] There is no question

---

2. The dissent similarly takes the position that the mark was improperly issued because it was descriptive and petitioner failed to prove that it had secondary meaning. *Post*, at 206–207. Neither the District Court nor the Court of Appeals made any finding whether the mark was properly issued in 1971. After the Patent Office denied the initial application for registration in 1970, petitioner filed a request for reconsideration arguing that the mark was not descriptive. App. 54–56. The Patent Office subsequently granted registration without specifying whether the mark had secondary meaning or instead was not descriptive. *Id.*, at 57–59. Unlike the dissent, we decline to determine in the first instance whether the mark improperly issued. Our holding is not affected by the possibility that the mark was or has become merely descriptive.

3. Representative Lanham made his remarks to clarify that the seven defenses enumerated in §33(b) are not substantive rules of law which go to the validity or enforceability of an incontestable

that the Lanham Act altered existing law concerning trademark rights in several respects. For example, §22, 15 U. S. C. §1072, provides for constructive notice of registration and modifies the common-law rule that allowed acquisition of concurrent rights by users in distinct geographic areas if the subsequent user adopted the mark without knowledge of prior use. *See Hanover Star Milling Co.* v. *Metcalf*, 240 U.S. 403, 415–416 (1916) (describing pre-Lanham Act law). Similarly, §14 cuts off certain grounds for cancellation five years after registration and thereby modifies the previous rule that the validity of a trademark could be attacked at any time. *See White House Milk Products Co.* v. *Dwinell-Wright Co.*, 27 C. C. P. A. (Pat.) 1194, 111 F.2d 490 (1940). Most significantly, Representative Lanham himself observed that incontestability was one of "the valuable new rights created by the act." 92 Cong. Rec. 7524 (1946).

Respondent's argument that enforcing petitioner's mark will not promote the goals of the Lanham Act is misdirected. Arguments similar to those now urged by respondent were in fact considered by Congress in hearings on the Lanham Act. For example, the United States Department of Justice opposed the incontestability provisions and expressly noted that a merely descriptive mark might become incontestable. Hearings on H. R. 82, at 59–60 (statement of the U.S. Dept. of Justice). This result, the Department of Justice observed, would "go beyond existing law in conferring unprecedented rights on trade-mark owners," and would undesirably create an exclusive right to use language that is descriptive of a product. *Id.*, at 60; *see also* Hearings on H. R. 102, at 106–107, 109–110 (testimony of Prof. Milton Handler); *id.*, at 107, 175 (testimony of attorney Louis Robertson). These concerns were answered by proponents of the Lanham Act, who noted that a merely descriptive mark cannot be registered unless the Commissioner finds that it has secondary meaning. *Id.*, at 108, 113 (testimony of Karl Pohl, U.S. Trade Mark Assn.). Moreover, a mark can be challenged for five years prior to its attaining incontestable status. *Id.*, at 114 (remarks of Rep. Lanham). The supporters of the incontestability provisions further observed that a generic mark cannot become incontestable and that §33(b)(4) allows the non-trademark use of descriptive terms used in an incontestable mark. *Id.*, at 110–111 (testimony of Wallace Martin, chairman, ABA Committee on Trade Mark Legislation).

The alternative of refusing to provide incontestable status for descriptive marks with secondary meaning was expressly noted in the hearings on the Lanham Act. *Id.*, at 64, 69 (testimony of Robert Byerley, New York Patent Law Assn.); Hearings on S. 895 before the Subcommittee of the Senate Committee on Patents, 77th Cong., 2d Sess., 42 (1942) (testimony of Elliot Moyer, Special Assistant to the Attorney General). Also mentioned was the possibility of including as a defense to infringement of an incontestable mark the "fact that a mark is a descriptive, generic, or geographical term or device." *Id.*, at 45, 47. Congress, however, did not adopt either of these alternatives. Instead, Congress expressly provided in §§33(b) and 15 that an incontestable mark could be challenged on specified grounds, and the grounds identified by Congress do not include mere descriptiveness.

The dissent echoes arguments made by opponents of the Lanham Act that the incontestable status of a descriptive mark might take from the public domain language that is merely descriptive. *Post*, at 214–216. As we have explained, Congress has already addressed concerns to prevent the "commercial monopolization," *post*, at 214, of descrip-

---

mark. 92 Cong. Rec. 7524 (1946). Instead, the defenses affect the evidentiary status of registration where the owner claims the benefit of a mark's incontestable status. If one of the defenses is established, registration constitutes only prima facie and not conclusive evidence of the owner's right to exclusive use of the mark. *Ibid. See also* H. R. Conf. Rep. No. 2322, 79th Cong., 2d Sess., 6 (1946) (explanatory statement of House managers).

tive language. The Lanham Act allows a mark to be challenged at any time if it becomes generic, and, under certain circumstances, permits the nontrademark use of descriptive terms contained in an incontestable mark. Finally, if "monopolization" of an incontestable mark threatens economic competition, §33(b)(7), 15 U. S. C. §1115(b)(7), provides a defense on the grounds that the mark is being used to violate federal antitrust laws. At bottom, the dissent simply disagrees with the balance struck by Congress in determining the protection to be given to incontestable marks.

* * *

VI

We conclude that the holder of a registered mark may rely on incontestability to enjoin infringement and that such an action may not be defended on the grounds that the mark is merely descriptive. Respondent urges that we nevertheless affirm the decision below based on the "prior use" defense recognized by §33(b)(5) of the Lanham Act. Alternatively, respondent argues that there is no likelihood of confusion and therefore no infringement justifying injunctive relief. The District Court rejected each of these arguments, but they were not addressed by the Court of Appeals. 718 F.2d, at 331–332, n. 4. That court may consider them on remand. The judgment of the Court of Appeals is reversed, and the case is remanded for further proceedings consistent with this opinion.

It is so ordered.

JUSTICE STEVENS, DISSENTING.

In trademark law, the term "incontestable" is itself somewhat confusing and misleading because the Lanham Act expressly identifies over 20 situations in which infringement of an allegedly incontestable mark is permitted. Moreover, in §37 of the Act, Congress unambiguously authorized judicial review of the validity of the registration "in any action involving a registered mark." The problem in this case arises because of petitioner's attempt to enforce as "incontestable" a mark that Congress has plainly stated is inherently unregistrable.

The mark "Park 'N Fly" is at best merely descriptive in the context of airport parking. Section 2 of the Lanham Act plainly prohibits the registration of such a mark unless the applicant proves to the Commissioner of the Patent and Trademark Office that the mark "has become distinctive of the applicant's goods in commerce," or to use the accepted shorthand, that it has acquired a "secondary meaning." *See* 15 U. S. C. §§1052(e), (f). Petitioner never submitted any such proof to the Commissioner, or indeed to the District Court in this case. Thus, the registration plainly violated the Act.

The violation of the literal wording of the Act also contravened the central purpose of the entire legislative scheme. Statutory protection for trademarks was granted in order to safeguard the goodwill that is associated with particular enterprises A mark must perform the function of distinguishing the producer or provider of a good or service in order to have any legitimate claim to protection. A merely descriptive mark that has not acquired secondary meaning does not perform that function because it simply "describes the qualities or characteristics of a good or service." *Ante,* at 194. No legislative purpose is served by granting anyone a monopoly in the use of such a mark.

Instead of confronting the question whether an inherently unregistrable mark can provide the basis for an injunction against alleged infringement, the Court treats the case as though it presented the same question as *Union Carbide Corp.* v. *Ever-Ready, Inc.,* 531 F.2d 366 (7th Cir.), *cert. denied,* 429 U.S. 830 (1976), a case in which the merely descriptive mark had an obvious and well-established secondary meaning. In such a case, I would agree with the Court that the descriptive character of the mark does not provide an infringer with a defense. In this case, however, the provisions of the Act dealing with incontestable marks do not support the result the Court has reached. I shall first explain why I agree with the conclusion that the Court of Appeals reached; I shall then comment on each of the three arguments that the Court advances in support of its contrary conclusion.

I

The word "incontestable" is not defined in the Act. Nor, surprisingly, is the concept explained in the Committee Reports on the bill that was enacted in 1946. The word itself implies that it was intended to resolve potential contests between rival claimants to a particular mark. And, indeed, the testimony of the proponents of the concept in the Committee hearings that occurred from time to time during the period when this legislation was being considered reveals that they were primarily concerned with the problem that potential contests over the ownership of registrable marks might present. No one ever suggested that any public purpose would be served by granting incontestable status to a mark that should never have been accepted for registration in the first instance.

In those hearings the witnesses frequently referred to incontestability as comparable to a decree quieting title to real property. Such a decree forecloses any further contest over ownership of the property, but it cannot create the property itself. Similarly the incontestability of a trademark precludes any competitor from contesting the registrant's ownership, but cannot convert unregistrable subject matter into a valid mark. Such a claim would be clearly unenforceable.

The case that petitioner principally urges in support of reversal, *Union Carbide Corp. v. Ever-Ready, Inc., supra,* does not conflict with this simple proposition. The court there was dealing with a contest between two companies over the name "Eveready." There was no question that the name had acquired a well-established secondary meaning, although it was not originally registered under §1052(f). The problem presented in such a case is properly resolved by giving effect to the incontestable language of the Act, but a wholly different question is presented when the record establishes that a mark should not have been registered at all.

The legislative history of the incontestability provisions indicates that Congress did not intend to prevent the use of mere descriptiveness as a substantive defense to a claim of infringement if the mark has not acquired secondary meaning. The testimony in the Committee hearings concerning the public interest in preventing the grant of monopoly privileges in the use of merely descriptive phrases expressly relied on the administrative practice that was incorporated into §2(f), 15 U. S. C. §1052(f), as a protection against the improper registration of merely descriptive marks. Thus, Dr. Karl Pohl testified:

> "On the question of so-called nontechnical trademarks, Professor Handler assumes that they have been improperly registered.

> "Now, where does that idea originate?

> "They have very carefully circumscribed procedure for getting these marks on the register. It will by no means be easy, Mr. Chairman and gentlemen of the committee, it will be exceedingly difficult to get these descriptive words on the register. The Patent Office will, in the first place, reject them, and you will have to submit a substantial body of evidence that these words by long-continued usage, have acquired a secondary meaning, and by that long-continued usage have acquired that special status which entitles them to be protected in their secondary meaning sense.

"Therefore, to call these marks improperly registered trade-marks is, I believe, a misnomer.

"Now, if you look at the problem from that point of view, you will see that the apprehensions of Mr. Handler are more or less obviated. I believe personally that they are completely obviated, but as to nontechnical trademarks and only a very carefully circumscribed number of trade-marks will be entitled to that protection."

The record in this case demonstrates that Professor Handler's concern was justified, and that Dr. Pohl's assurance to the Committee was somewhat misleading; for the "Park 'N Fly" mark issued without any evidence of secondary meaning having been presented to the Patent and Trademark Office. In light of this legislative history, it is apparent that Congress could not have intended that incontestability should preserve a merely descriptive trademark from challenge when the statutory procedure for establishing secondary meaning was not followed and when the record still contains no evidence that the mark has ever acquired a secondary meaning.

If the registrant of a merely descriptive mark complies with the statutory requirement that prima facie evidence of secondary meaning must be submitted to the Patent and Trademark Office, it is entirely consistent with the policy of the Act to accord the mark incontestable status after an additional five years of continued use. For if no rival contests the registration in that period, it is reasonable to presume that the initial prima facie showing of distinctiveness could not be rebutted. But if no proof of secondary meaning is ever presented, either to the Patent and Trademark Office or to a court, there is simply no rational basis for leaping to the conclusion that the passage of time has transformed an inherently defective mark into an incontestable mark.

No matter how dedicated and how competent administrators may be, the possibility of error is always present, especially in nonadversary proceedings. For that reason the Court normally assumes that Congress intended agency action to be subject to judicial review unless the contrary intent is expressed in clear and unambiguous language. In this statute Congress has expressed no such intent. On the contrary, it has given the courts the broadest possible authority to determine the validity of trademark registrations "in any action involving a registered mark." The exercise of that broad power of judicial review should be informed by the legislative purposes that motivated the enactment of the Lanham Act.

Congress enacted the Lanham Act "to secure trade-mark owners in the goodwill which they have built up." But without a showing of secondary meaning, there is no basis upon which to conclude that petitioner has built up any goodwill that is secured by the mark "Park 'N Fly." In fact, without a showing of secondary meaning, we should presume that petitioner's business appears to the consuming public to be just another anonymous, indistinguishable parking lot. When enacting the Lanham Act, Congress also wanted to "protect the public from imposition by the use of counterfeit and imitated marks and false trade descriptions." Upon this record there appears no danger of this occurrence, and as a practical matter, without any showing that the public can specifically identify petitioner's service, it seems difficult to believe that anyone would imitate petitioner's marks, or that such imitation, even if it occurred, would be likely to confuse anybody.

On the basis of the record in this case, it is reasonable to infer that the operators of parking lots in the vicinity of airports may make use of the words "park and fly" simply because those words provide a ready description of their businesses, rather than because of any desire to exploit petitioner's goodwill. There is a well-recognized public interest in prohibiting the commercial monopolization of phrases such as "park and fly." When a business claims the exclusive right to use words or phrases that are a part of our common vocabulary, this Court should not depart from the statutorily mandated authority to "rectify the register," 15 U. S. C. §1119, absent a clear congressional mandate. Language, even in a commercial context, properly belongs to the public unless Congress instructs otherwise. In this case we have no such instruction; in fact, the opposite command guides our actions: Congress' clear insistence that a merely descriptive mark, such as "Park 'N Fly" in the context of airport parking, remain in the public domain unless secondary meaning is proved.

The basic purposes of the Act, the unambiguous congressional command that no merely descriptive mark should be registered without prior proof that it acquired secondary meaning, and the broad power of judicial review granted by §37 combine to persuade me that the registrant of a merely descriptive mark should not be granted an injunction against infringement without ever proving that the mark acquired secondary meaning.

* * *

In sum, if petitioner had complied with §2(f) at the time of its initial registration, or if it had been able to prove secondary meaning in this case, I would agree with the Court's disposition. I cannot, however, subscribe to its conclusion that the holder of a mark which was registered in violation of an unambiguous statutory command "may rely on incontestability to enjoin infringement." Accordingly, I respectfully dissent.

Munters Corporation v. Matsui America Inc.
909 F.2d 250 (7th Cir. 1990)

PER CURIAM

Plaintiff, the Munters Corporation ("Munters"), manufactures and sells industrial and environmental control devices including a dehumidifying apparatus. Defendant Matsui America, Incorporated ("Matsui") is a wholly owned subsidiary of a Japanese corporation. Matsui manufactures and distributes equipment for the plastics industry in the United States, including dehumidifiers for drying plastic resins.

In May 1989, Munters filed a suit against Matsui for trademark infringement and unfair competition. The complaint showed that Munters, through a subsidiary, had registered the trademark "HONEYCOMBE" and used that trademark on its space dehumidifying apparatus containing a honeycomb-shaped desiccant wheel rotor.

In the fall of 1987, Munters learned that Matsui was selling a "Honeycomb Dehumidifying Unit," which also contained a honeycomb-shaped desiccant wheel rotor. This caused counsel for Munters to advise Matsui to stop using "Honeycomb" in connection with its dehumidifiers. As a result, Matsui allegedly agreed to discontinue the use of that term as a trademark in its advertising materials. After its stock of brochures was exhausted, Matsui continued to use the word honeycomb, but only as an adjective to describe its rotor.

Besides charging Matsui with infringement of its registered trademark, Munters' complaint contained seven other counts not involved on this appeal. In its answer, Matsui denied continuing the use of the word honeycomb as a trademark in connection with its dehumidifiers and claimed that its products were sold through different channels of distribution to different classes of customers and for different purposes.

In June 1989, the district court granted a preliminary injunction restraining Matsui from infringing on Munters' trademark "HONEYCOMBE" in connection with the sale of its dehumidifiers. However, after holding an August 1989 hearing to determine whether Munters was entitled to a permanent injunction, the district court determined on October 25, 1989, that the injunction was not warranted. The court's judgment was accompanied by a comprehensive 13-page memorandum opinion reported at 730 F. Supp. 790. We agree with Judge Zagel's reasoning and therefore hold that a permanent injunction was properly denied.

Only one issue merits elaboration. Munters has argued that the district court's analysis of the strength of its mark is in derogation of the Supreme Court's holding in *Park 'N Fly, Inc. v. Dollar Park and Fly, Inc.*, 469 U.S. 189, 83 L. Ed. 2d 582, 105 S. Ct. 658. *Park 'N Fly* holds that an alleged infringement of an incontestable trademark cannot be defended on the ground that the complainant's mark is merely descriptive. A bit of background is necessary to an understanding of Munters' argument.

In order to prevail in an action under Section 43(a) of the Lanham Act, a complainant must show that it has a protectible trademark and that the alleged infringer's use of that trademark is likely to cause confusion among consumers. Most often an analysis of the strength of the complainant's mark is undertaken to determine whether an unregistered trademark is protectible. Here Munters' "HONEYCOMBE" trademark was registered. The district court accordingly found that it was protectible and, because it had been in continuous use for more than five years following its registration, incontestable. Nevertheless, the district court undertook a strength of the mark analysis in evaluating whether Matsui's use of Munters' mark was likely to cause confusion. This is correct practice in the Seventh Circuit, since strength of the mark is one of the factors in this Circuit for evaluating likelihood of confusion. Some other circuits do not include this factor in their likelihood of confusion analysis. Munters has argued that since a strength of the mark analysis includes a discussion of whether the mark is merely descriptive, the district court's discussion of the strength of Munters' mark disregarded the Supreme Court's holding in *Park 'N Fly* that an incontestable mark cannot be challenged on the grounds that it is merely descriptive.

This argument is unpersuasive. The most that can be said by critics is that this Circuit's practice of including a strength of the mark component in its likelihood of confusion analysis is a practice that is, itself, likely to cause confusion. We conclude, however, that it is Munters, and not the district court, that is confused in this case. The district court explicitly noted that Matsui's argument that Munters' mark was merely descriptive was not intended to demonstrate that Munters' mark was not protectible but rather was advanced solely to bolster Matsui's claim that there was no likelihood of confusion. 730 F. Supp. at 795–796. The Supreme Court's holding in *Park 'N Fly* does not address likelihood of confusion. In fact the Court specifically directed the district court to consider the likelihood of confusion argument on remand. 469 U.S. at 205. Therefore *Park 'N Fly* does not preclude consideration of a mark's strength for purposes of determining the likelihood of confusion.

The district court's findings as to likelihood of confusion are findings of fact subject to the clearly erroneous standard of review. We agree with the district court that Matsui's present use of the word honeycomb is not likely to cause confusion among current or potential purchasers of Matsui's and Munters' products.

After denying Munters' motion for a permanent injunction, the district court denied Matsui's motion to amend its answer and counterclaim to challenge the registration status of Munters' trademark on the ground that "HONEYCOMBE" was a generic term that could not become a trademark. As Judge Zagel explained, the mark does not denominate a type of goods nor classify the noun "dehumidifier" or "wheel" to which it is attached by Munters. Instead the term describes the porous configuration of the goods and not a subcategory of wheel or dehumidifier. *See* 730 F. Supp. at 796. Furthermore, as Matsui admits in its reply brief, the district court gave Matsui the opportunity at trial to present evidence that Munters' mark was generic. More was not required.

The judgment of the district court is affirmed. Matsui's motion for sanctions under Rule 38 of the Federal Rules of Appellate Procedure is denied.

Dieter v. B & H Industries, Inc.
880 F.2d 322 (11th Cir. 1989)

Howard, J.

I. BACKGROUND.

This is a trademark infringement action arising out of two southwest Florida shutter vendors' use of the same name and trademark. Appellant Dieter is the president and sole shareholder of appellant Richard A. Dieter General Contractor, Inc., a Florida corporation (collectively referred to as "Dieter"), headquartered in the Tampa Bay area. Dieter sells several types of shutters, some of which it manufactures. Its products include pre-hung wooden shutter assemblies, which are mostly decorative items intended for indoor use. The wooden shutters which Dieter manufactures are labeled with its registered trademark, which is burned into the wood. Those shutters sold but not manufactured by Dieter are labeled with small silver stickers marked with the name "Shutter-World" in plain block letters, hyphenated.

In 1976, Dieter applied for federal trademark registration of a trademark incorporating the name "Shutterworld." The mark consists of the name in script form, superimposed on a large letter "O." The registration states that Dieter first used the mark in 1970, and that it first used the mark in commerce in 1974. In 1983 Dieter supplemented its federal registration with a "combined sections 8 & 15 declaration," filed on Dieter's behalf by Janet E. Hudson as secretary-treasurer. The declaration stated that "Shutterworld, Inc., a Florida corporation" was owner of federal registration number 1,062,778. It stated that the registered mark had been in continuous use in interstate commerce since April 5, 1977 for "pre-hung wooden shutter assemblies," and that the mark was still so used. Dieter has made extensive use of its mark in forms other than the registered design. Dieter has not obtained Florida registration of its mark.

Appellee B & H Industries of Southwest Florida, Inc., ("B & H") is headquartered in Fort Meyers, Florida, approximately 120 miles south of Tampa and Largo. B & H sells exterior "insulated roll-down security shutters," which are designed for exterior use as protection against weather and intruders. B & H obtained Florida registration of a mark consisting of the name "Shutterworld" in "neon sign" typeface, with an oversized letter "O," and with the letters "SW" in three line script on a dark background. B & H was refused federal registration of a mark which used the word "Shutterworld" with a large "O" with the letters "SW" inside the "O," on the grounds that such a mark was likely to be confused with Dieter's registered mark. B & H amended its application with affidavit and pictorial evidence intended to show that there was a lack of confusion between its mark and Dieter's. The mark was then deemed "entitled to registration, "and was published pursuant to statute. Dieter filed an opposition to registration of that mark.

Dieter filed suit against B & H in the Middle District of Florida, alleging trademark infringement. Its complaint included causes of action under the Lanham Act, 15 U.S.C. §§1114, 1125(a); under the Florida common law of unfair competition; and under FLA. STAT. ANN. §495.151 for damage to business reputation. Dieter sought a permanent injunction against B & H's use of the word "Shutterworld," as well as an accounting for profits, treble damages, and attorney's fees. The case was tried to the district court without a jury. At the close of the trial, the court found that Dieter's mark was valid and enforceable, but that there had been no trademark infringement, because the district court concluded that there was no likelihood of confusion. We disagree and reverse.

II. LIKELIHOOD OF CONFUSION.

* * *

After considering all of the facts, the Court finds that there is a substantial likelihood of confusion. Accordingly, the trial court's determination to the contrary was clearly erroneous.

III. INCONTESTABILITY.

Dieter contends on appeal that the trial court imposed a requirement that it prove secondary meaning in a geographic area as a prerequisite to enforcing an incontestable registration against a junior user in the same geographic area, a rule that Dieter points out is not required by controlling law or case authority. Although this Court agrees with Dieter that such a requirement would be contrary to the law of this circuit, we do not find that the trial court imposed such a requirement.

Terms which may be registered as trademarks fall into four categories of strength: (1) generic, (2) descriptive, (3) suggestive, or (4) arbitrary. *American Television v. American Communications*, 810 F.2d 1546, 1548 (11th Cir. 1987); *University of Georgia Athletic Ass'n v. Laite*, 756 F.2d 1535, 1540 (11th Cir. 1985). "Generic" terms are those which name "the genus or class of which an individual article or service is but a member." *Vision Ctr. v. Opticks*, 596 F.2d 111, 115 (5th Cir. 1979), *cert. denied*, 444 U.S. 1016, 100 S. Ct. 668, 62 L. Ed. 2d 646, 204 U.S.P.Q. (BNA) 696 (1980). "Descriptive" terms "identify a characteristic or quality of an article or service." *Id.* "Suggestive" terms suggest characteristics of the goods and services and "require an effort of the imagination by the consumer in order to be understood as descriptive." *Id.* at 115, 116 (citing *General Shoe Corp. v. Rosen*, 111 F.2d 95, 98 (4th Cir. 1940). "Fanciful" or "arbitrary" terms are words or phrases that bear no direct relationship to the product. Vision Ctr., 596 F.2d at 116. Generic terms represent the weaker end of the spectrum, and arbitrary terms represent the stronger.

Generic terms may never be registered as trademarks under the Lanham Act. 15 U.S.C. §1052(e). Descriptive terms may not be registered as trademarks under the Lanham Act, unless the holder shows that the mark has acquired "secondary meaning." Proof of secondary meaning in a trademark requires a showing that the mark has become distinctive of the trademark holder's product. Five years after registering a mark, the holder may file the affidavit required by §1065 and have its mark declared "incontestable." 15 U.S.C. §1065(3). Once a mark has become "incontestable," its validity is presumed, subject to certain enumerated defenses which are not applicable in this action. 15 U.S.C. §1065. Once a mark has achieved "incontestable" status, its validity cannot be challenged on the grounds that it is merely descriptive, even if the challenger can show that the mark was improperly registered initially:

Thus, §33(a) [would allow challenge to a] mark as merely descriptive if the mark had not become incontestable. With respect to incontestable marks, however, §33(b) provides that registration is *conclusive* evidence of the registrant's exclusive right to use the mark, subject to the conditions of §15 and the seven defenses enumerated in §33(b) itself. Mere descriptiveness is not recognized by either §§15 or 33(b) as a basis for challenging an incontestable mark.

Park'N'Fly, Inc. v. Dollar Park and Fly, 469 U.S. 189, 105 S. Ct. 658, 663, 83 L. Ed. 2d 582 (1985). Dieter's mark is incontestable, and therefore valid.

As stated above, a plaintiff seeking to enjoin another's use of a trademark must show, first, that its mark was valid and, second, that defendant's use of the challenged mark created a likelihood of confusion. *Burger King*, 710 F.2d at 1491. The trial court noted that Dieter's mark was incontestable and that Dieter had established the first requirement. The second part of the test, "likelihood of confusion," is determined by reference to the seven factor analysis discussed above. Analysis of the first of the seven factors requires the court to determine the type of mark for which the plaintiff seeks protection. In *Park'N'Fly*, the issue presented to the Supreme Court involved only the validity of the mark. Whether "incontestable" status affects the *strength* of the mark for purposes of "likelihood of confusion" determinations was left open to question by *Park'N'Fly*. This is an issue of first impression in this circuit.

In the instant action, the lower court evaluated the strength of Dieter's mark without reference to its "incontestable" status, and determined that Dieter's mark was merely descriptive. In doing so, the trial court relied on a district court case from Illinois which held that validity and "likelihood of confusion" are distinct and separate inquiries, and that the "incontestable" status of a plaintiff's mark has no bearing on the "likelihood of confusion" issue. *Source Services Corp. v. Chicagoland Jobsource, Inc.*, 643 F. Supp. 1523, 1532 (N.D. Ill. 1986) (relying on *Union Carbide*). Application of this rule by the trial court in Dieter's case did not impose a requirement that Dieter prove secondary meaning in order to enforce its mark. Rather, the trial court, in the absence of controlling precedent, followed the decision of the Illinois district court and concluded that the "incontestable" status of Dieter's mark had no relevance to the likelihood of confusion analysis. After careful consideration of the district court's position, as well as the case law in this circuit, we decline to follow the Illinois district court. We hold that incontestable status is a factor to be taken into consideration in likelihood of confusion analysis. Because Dieter's mark is incontestable, then it is presumed to be at least descriptive with secondary meaning, and therefore a relatively strong mark. Accordingly, the district court's conclusion that Dieter's mark was merely descriptive, and not entitled to strong protection is REVERSED, and the action is REMANDED to the district court for further proceedings consistent with this opinion.

VI. CONCLUSION.

For the foregoing reasons, the judgment of the district court is REVERSED and this action is REMANDED for further proceedings consistent with this opinion.

Notes

1. *Trademarks as property*. The incontestability provisions of the Lanham Act induced one influential trademark law commentator to conclude that "Section 15 of the Trade-Mark

Act demonstrates Congressional willingness to recognize the trade-mark as property right." Rudolph Callmann, *Unfair Competition Without Competition?: The Importance of the Property Concept in the Law of Trade-Marks*, 95 U. Pa. L. Rev. 443, 467 (1947). Courts, however, have not picked up on this change (if a change was intended) and still treat the trademark right as property but do not find the trademark itself subject to property ownership. *See* Kenneth L. Port, *The Illegitimacy of Trademark Incontestability*, 26 Ind. L. Rev. 519 (1993).

2. *Should incontestability be a determinative factor when courts weigh the strength of a mark in infringement?* Circuit courts are divided on this issue. District courts are in chaos over this issue. The Supreme Court denied certiorari in both *Munters* and in *Dieter, supra.* Should incontestability count or not? Why is this such a difficult issue? Since *Munters* and *Dieter* were decided, it appears that the *Dieter* position on the issue ought to be considered the "minority view." More and more courts are holding that an incontestable registration does mean that the validity of the registration cannot be challenged even if the mark is descriptive but they do not make the leap that the *Dieter* court made in finding an incontestable registration meant the underlying mark was presumptively "a relatively strong mark." *See, e.g., Therma-Scan, Inc. v. Thermoscan, Inc.,* 295 F.3d 623 (6th Cir. 2002); *Entrepreneur Media, Inc. v. Smith,* 279 F.3d 1135 (9th Cir. 2002). *See also,* Jason K. Levine, *Contesting the Incontestable: Reforming Trademark's Descriptive Mark Protection Scheme,* 41 Gonz. L. Rev. 29 (2006) (descriptive terms should not be withdrawn from the "linguistic commons").

3. *Forum shopping.* One might expect a significant amount of forum shopping in trademark litigation where a mark is incontestable. However, there appears to be such chaos over this issue and such little predictability that attorneys do not consider one forum or another to be more advantageous to an incontestable mark.

4. *Fraud.* "Fraud on the Patent and Trademark Office is an exception to incontestability and grounds for canceling a registration. Plaintiffs must allege: (1) a false representation regarding a material fact; (2) knowledge or belief that the representation is false; (3) an intention to induce the listener to act or refrain from acting in reliance upon the misrepresentation; (4) reasonable reliance upon the misrepresentation; and (5) damage proximately resulting from such reliance." *Federal Treasury Enterprise Sojuzplodoimport v. Spirits Int'l N.V.,* 425 F. Supp. 2d 458 (S.D.N.Y 2006). Given what's at stake, should fraud before the PTO over incontestability filings be so rigorous to establish?

Chapter IX

Loss of Trademark Rights

It turns out that trademark rights are a bit fragile in nature. Significant misuse or non-use can result in the loss of rights. As we will see, this fact has caused many trademarks to be lost or abandoned.

A. Genericism

15 U.S.C. §1064, Lanham Act §14

A registered mark shall not be deemed to be the generic name of goods or services solely because such mark is also used as a name of or to identify a unique product or service. The primary significance of the registered mark to the relevant public rather than purchaser motivation shall be the test for determining whether the registered mark has become the generic name of goods or services on or in connection with which it has been used.

Kellogg Co. v. National Biscuit Co.
305 U.S. 111 (1938)

Brandeis, Justice

This suit was brought in the federal court for Delaware by National Biscuit Company against Kellogg Company to enjoin alleged unfair competition by the manufacture and sale of the breakfast food commonly known as shredded wheat. The competition was alleged to be unfair mainly because Kellogg Company uses, like the plaintiff, the name shredded wheat and, like the plaintiff, produces its biscuit in pillow-shaped form.

Shredded wheat is a product composed of whole wheat which has been boiled, partially dried, then drawn or pressed out into thin shreds and baked. The shredded wheat biscuit generally known is pillow-shaped in form. It was introduced in 1893 by Henry D. Perky, of Colorado; and he was connected until his death in 1908 with companies formed to make and market the article. Commercial success was not attained until the Natural Food Company built, in 1901, a large factory at Niagara Falls, New York. In 1908, its corporate name was changed to "The Shredded Wheat Company;" and in 1930 its business and goodwill were acquired by National Biscuit Company.

Kellogg Company has been in the business of manufacturing breakfast food cereals since its organization in 1905. For a period commencing in 1912 and ending in 1919 it made a product whose form was somewhat like the product in question, but whose manufacture was different, the wheat being reduced to a dough before being pressed into shreds. For a short period in 1922 it manufactured the article in question. In 1927, it resumed manufacturing the product. In 1928, the plaintiff sued for alleged unfair competition two dealers in Kellogg shredded wheat biscuits. That suit was discontinued by stipulation in 1930. On June 11, 1932, the present suit was brought. Much evidence was introduced; but the determinative facts are relatively few; and as to most of these there is no conflict.

In 1935, the District Court dismissed the bill. It found that the name "Shredded Wheat" is a term describing alike the product of the plaintiff and of the defendant; and that no passing off or deception had been shown. It held that upon the expiration of the Perky patent No. 548,086 issued October 15, 1895, the name of the patented article passed into the public domain. In 1936, the Circuit Court of Appeals affirmed that decree. Upon rehearing, it vacated, in 1937, its own decree and reversed that of the District Court, with direction "to enter a decree enjoining the defendant from the use of the name 'Shredded Wheat' as its trade-name and from advertising or offering for sale its product in the form and shape of plaintiffs biscuit in violation of its trade-mark; and with further directions to order an accounting for damages and profits." In its opinion the court described the trade-mark as "consisting of a dish, containing two biscuits submerged in milk." 91 F.2d 150, 152. We denied Kellogg Company's petition for a writ of certiorari, 302 U.S. 733; and denied rehearing, 302 U.S. 777.

On January 5, 1938, the District Court entered its mandate in the exact language of the order of the Circuit Court of Appeals, and issued a permanent injunction. Shortly thereafter National Biscuit Company petitioned the Circuit Court of Appeals to recall its mandate "for purposes of clarification." It alleged that Kellogg Company was insisting, contrary to the court's intention, that the effect of the mandate and writ of injunction was to forbid it from selling its product only when he trade name "Shredded Wheat" is applied to a biscuit in the form and shape of the plaintiff's biscuit and is accompanied by a representation of a dish with biscuits in it; and that it was not enjoined from making its biscuit in the form and shape of the plaintiff's biscuit, nor from calling it "Shredded Wheat," unless at the same time it uses upon its cartons plaintiff's trade-mark consisting of a dish with two biscuits in it. On May 5, 1938, the Circuit Court of Appeals granted the petition for clarification and directed the District Court to enter a decree enjoining Kellogg Company (96 F.2d 873):

> "(1) from the use of the name 'SHREDDED WHEAT' as its trade name, (2) from advertising or offering for sale its product in the form and shape of plaintiff's biscuit, and (3) from doing either."

Kellogg Company then filed a petition for a writ of certiorari to review the decree as so clarified, and also sought reconsideration of our denial of its petition for certiorari to review the decree as entered in its original form. In support of these petitions it called to our attention the decision of the British Privy Council in *Canadian Shredded Wheat Co. v. Kellogg Co. of Canada*, 55 R.P.C. 125, rendered after our denial of the petition for certiorari earlier in the term. We granted both petitions for certiorari.

The plaintiff concedes that it does not possess the exclusive right to make shredded wheat. But it claims the exclusive right to the trade name "Shredded Wheat" and the exclusive right to make shredded wheat biscuits pillow-shaped. It charges that the defendant, by using the name and shape, and otherwise, is passing off, or enabling others to pass off, Kellogg goods for those of the plaintiff. Kellogg Company denies that the plaintiff is entitled to the exclusive use of the name or of the pillow-shape; denies any passing off;

asserts that it has used every reasonable effort to distinguish its product from that of the plaintiff; and contends that in honestly competing for a part of the market for shredded wheat it is exercising the common right freely to manufacture and sell an article of commerce unprotected by patent.

First. The plaintiff has no exclusive right to the use of the term "Shredded Wheat" as a tradename. For that is the generic term of the article, which describes it with a fair degree of accuracy; and is the term by which the biscuit in pillow-shaped form is generally known by the public. Since the term is generic, the original maker of the product acquired no exclusive right to use it. As Kellogg Company had the right to make the article, it had, also, the right to use the term by which the public knows it. Ever since 1894 the article has been known to the public as shredded wheat. For many years, there was no attempt to use the term "Shredded Wheat" as a trade-mark. When in 1905 plaintiffs predecessor, Natural Food Company, applied for registration of the words "Shredded Whole Wheat" as a trade-mark under the so-called "ten year clause" of the Act of February 20, 1905, c. 592, §5, 33 Stat. 725, William E. Williams gave notice of opposition. Upon the hearing it appeared that Williams had, as early as 1894, built a machine for making shredded wheat, and that he made and sold its product as "Shredded Whole Wheat." The Commissioner of Patents refused registration. The Court of Appeals of the District of Columbia affirmed his decision, holding that "these words accurately and aptly describe an article of food which … has been produced … for more than ten years …" *Natural Food Co. v. Williams,* 30 App. D. C. 348.

Moreover, the name "Shredded Wheat," as well as the product, the process and the machinery employed in making it, has been dedicated to the public. The basic patent for the product and for the process of making it, and many other patents for special machinery to be used in making the article, issued to Perky. In those patents the term "shredded" is repeatedly used as descriptive of the product. The basic patent expired October 15, 1912; the others soon after. Since during the life of the patents "Shredded Wheat" was the general designation of the patented product, there passed to the public upon the expiration of the patent, not only the right to make the article as it was made during the patent period, but also the right to apply thereto the name by which it had become known. As was said in *Singer Mfg. Co. v. June Mfg. Co.,* 163 U.S. 169, 185:

> "It equally follows from the cessation of the monopoly and the falling of the patented device into the domain of things public, that along with the public ownership of the device there must also necessarily pass to the public the generic designation of the thing which has arisen during the monopoly…. To say otherwise would be to hold that, although the public had acquired the device covered by the patent, yet the owner of the patent or the manufacturer of the patented thing had retained the designated name which was essentially necessary to vest the public with the full enjoyment of that which had become theirs by the disappearance of the monopoly."

It is contended that the plaintiff has the exclusive right to the name "Shredded Wheat," because those words acquired the "secondary meaning" of shredded wheat made at Niagara Falls by the plaintiff's predecessor. There is no basis here for applying the doctrine of secondary meaning. The evidence shows only that due to the long period in which the plaintiff or its predecessor was the only manufacturer of the product, many people have come to associate the product, and as a consequence the name by which the product is generally known, with the plaintiff's factory at Niagara Falls. But to establish a trade name in the term "shredded wheat" the plaintiff must show more than a subordinate meaning which applies to it. It must show that the primary significance of the term in the minds of the consuming public is not the product but the producer. This it has not done. The showing which it has made does not entitle it to the exclusive use of the term shredded wheat but merely entitles it to require that the defendant use reasonable care to inform the public of the source of its product.

The plaintiff seems to contend that even if Kellogg Company acquired upon the expiration of the patents the right to use the name shredded wheat, the right was lost by delay. The argument is that Kellogg Company, although the largest producer of breakfast cereals in the country, did not seriously attempt to make shredded wheat, or to challenge plaintiff's right to that name until 1927, and that meanwhile plaintiff's predecessor had expended more than $17,000,000 in making the name a household word and identifying the product with its manufacture. Those facts are without legal significance. Kellogg Company's right was not one dependent upon diligent exercise. Like every other member of the public, it was, and remained, free to make shredded wheat when it chose to do so; and to call the product by its generic name. The only obligation resting upon Kellogg Company was to identify its own product lest it be mistaken for that of the plaintiff.

Second. The plaintiff has not the exclusive right to sell shredded wheat in the form of a pillow-shaped biscuit—the form in which the article became known to the public. That is the form in which shredded wheat was made under the basic patent. The patented machines used were designed to produce only the pillow-shaped biscuits. And a design patent was taken out to cover the pillow-shaped form.[1] Hence, upon expiration of the patents the form, as well as the name, was dedicated to the public. As was said in *Singer Mfg. Co. v. June Mfg. Co., supra,* p. 185:

> "It is self evident that on the expiration of a patent the monopoly granted by it ceases to exist, and the right to make the thing formerly covered by the patent becomes public property. It is upon this condition that the patent is granted. It follows, as a matter of course, that on the termination of the patent there passes to the public the right to make the machine in the form in which it was constructed during the patent. We may, therefore, dismiss without further comment the complaint, as to the form in which the defendant made his machines."

Where an article may be manufactured by all, a particular manufacturer can no more assert exclusive rights in a form in which the public has become accustomed to see the article and which, in the minds of the public, is primarily associated with the article rather than a particular producer, than it can in the case of a name with similar connections in the public mind. Kellogg Company was free to use the pillow-shaped form, subject only to the obligation to identify its product lest it be mistaken for that of the plaintiff.

Third. The question remains whether Kellogg Company in exercising its right to use the name "Shredded Wheat" and the pillow-shaped biscuit, is doing so fairly. Fairness requires that it be done in a manner which reasonably distinguishes its product from that of plaintiff.

Each company sells its biscuits only in cartons. The standard Kellogg carton contains fifteen biscuits; the plaintiff's twelve. The Kellogg cartons are distinctive. They do not re-

---

1. The design patent would have expired by limitations in 1909. In 1908 it was declared invalid by a district judge on the ground that the design had been in public use for more than two years prior to the application for the patent and theretofore had already been dedicated to the public. *Natural Foods Co. v. Bulkley,* No. 28, 530, U.S. Dist. Ct., N. Dist. Ill., East. Div. (1908).

semble those used by the plaintiff either in size, form, or color. And the difference in the labels is striking. The Kellogg cartons bear in bold script the names "Kellogg's Whole Wheat Biscuit" or "Kellogg's Shredded Whole Wheat Biscuit" so sized and spaced as to strike the eye as being a Kellogg product. It is true that on some of its cartons it had a picture of two shredded wheat biscuits in a bowl of milk which was quite similar to one of the plaintiff's registered trade-marks. But the name Kellogg was so prominent on all of the defendant's cartons as to minimize the possibility of confusion.

Some hotels, restaurants, and lunchrooms serve biscuits not in cartons and guests so served may conceivably suppose that a Kellogg biscuit served is one of the plaintiff's make. But no person familiar with plaintiff's product would be misled. The Kellogg biscuit is about two-thirds the size of plaintiff's; and differs from it in appearance. Moreover, the field in which deception could be practiced is negligibly small. Only 2½ percent of the Kellogg biscuits are sold to hotels, restaurants and lunchrooms. Of those so sold 98 per cent are sold in individual cartons containing two biscuits. These cartons are distinctive and bear prominently the Kellogg name. To put upon the individual biscuit some mark which would identify it as the Kellogg product is not commercially possible. Relatively few biscuits will be removed from the individual cartons before they reach the consumer. The obligation resting upon Kellogg Company is not to insure that every purchaser will know it to be the maker but to use every reasonable means to prevent confusion.

It is urged that all possibility of deception or confusion would be removed if Kellogg Company should refrain from using the name "Shredded Wheat" and adopt some form other than the pillow-shape. But the name and form are integral parts of the goodwill of the article. To share fully in the goodwill, it must use the name and the pillow-shape. And in the goodwill Kellogg Company is as free to share as the plaintiff. Compare *William R. Warner & Co. v. Eli Lilly & Co.*, 265 U.S. 526, 528, 530. Moreover, the pillow-shape must be used for another reason. The evidence is persuasive that this form is functional — that the cost of the biscuit would be increased and its high quality lessened if some other form were substituted for the pillow-shape.

Kellogg Company is undoubtedly sharing in the goodwill of the article known as "Shredded Wheat"; and thus is sharing in a market which was created by the skill and judgment of plaintiff's predecessor and has been widely extended by vast expenditures in advertising persistently made. But that is not unfair. Sharing in the goodwill of an article unprotected by patent or trade-mark is the exercise of a right possessed by all — and in the free exercise of which the consuming public is deeply interested. There is no evidence of passing off or deception on the part of the Kellogg Company; and it has taken every reasonable precaution to prevent confusion or the practice of deception in the sale of its product.

Fourth. By its "clarifying" decree, the Circuit Court of Appeals enjoined Kellogg Company from using the picture of the two shredded wheat biscuits in the bowl only in connection with an injunction against manufacturing the pillow-shaped biscuits and the use of the term shredded wheat, on the grounds of unfair competition. The use of this picture was not enjoined on the independent ground of trade-mark infringement. Since the National Biscuit Company did not petition for certiorari, the question whether use of the picture is a violation of that trade-mark although Kellogg Company is free to use the name and the pillow-shaped biscuit is not here for review.

Decrees reversed with direction to dismiss the bill.

Bayer Co. v. United Drug
272 F. 505 (S.D.N.Y. 1921)

HAND, DISTRICT JUDGE.

The issues in this case do not, I think, depend upon the decision is *Singer Mfg. Co. v. June Mfg. Co.*, 163 U.S. 169, 16 Sup. Ct. 1002, 41 L. Ed. 118, so much as the defendant supposes. That case decided no more than that the existence of a patent during the period when the goods became known to the public might be a controlling element in determining whether the name under which they were sold indicated a single source of origin. Since then courts have several times said that the name of goods protected by patent might in fact indicate not only the kind of goods they were, but as well that they emanated from a single source.

So here it might be that the name "Aspirin" in fact had come at once to describe the drug in question and also its origin from a single source. If it did, that would be enough to justify some protection, since the identity of the course need not be known. *Birmingham, etc., Co. v. Powell*, [1897] App. Cas. 710; *Wetherspoon v. Currie*, L.R. 5. H.L. 508. Indeed, the whole law of "secondary meaning" is built upon that presupposition.

The single question, as I view it, in all these cases, is merely one of fact: What do the buyers understand by the word for whose use the parties are contending? If they understand by it only the kind of goods sold, then, I take it, it makes no difference whatever what efforts the plaintiff has made to get them to understand more. He has failed, and he cannot say that, when the defendant uses the word, he is taking away customers who wanted to deal with him, however closely disguised he may be allowed to keep his identity. So here the question is whether the buyers merely understood that the word "Aspirin" meant this kind of drug, or whether it meant that and more than that; i.e., that it came from the same single, though, if one please anonymous, source from which they had got it before. Prima facie I should say, since the word is coined and means nothing by itself, that the defendant must show that it means only the kind of drug to which it applies. The fact that it was patented until 1917 is indeed a material circumstances, but it is not necessarily controlling.

In deciding that issue I cannot, however, approach the question formally, as the plaintiff wishes; as to say that there was a user before the patent, and therefore the patent could not forfeit this property right, or that there was never any intention to abandon the trademark and so it must have continued. No doubt it is convenient for many purposes to treat a trade-mark as property; yet we shall never, I think, keep clear in our ideas on this subject, unless we remember that relief always depends upon the idea that no man shall be allowed to mislead people into supposing that his goods are the plaintiff's, and that there can be no right or remedy until the plaintiff can show that as least presumptively this will result. *Hanover Milling Co. v. Metcalf*, 240 U.S. 403, 36 Sup. Ct. 357, 60L. Ed. 709.

In the case at bar the evidence shows that there is a class of buyers to whom the word "Aspirin" has always signified the plaintiff, more specifically indeed than was necessary for its protection. I refer to manufacturing chemists, to physicians, and probably to retail druggists. From 1899 it flooded the mails with assertions that "Aspirin" meant its own manufacture. This was done in pamphlets, advertisements in trade papers, on the packages and cartons, and by the gratuitous distribution of samples. True, after 1904 it abandoned the phrase "acetyl salicylic acid" for "monoaceticacidester of salicylicacid," but even that extraordinary collocation of letters was intelligible to these classes of buyers who, except possibly the more ignorant of the retail druggists, were measurably versed in the general jargon of pharmaceutical chemistry. Moreover, the drug continued to be generally known by the more tolerable phrase "acetyl salicylic acid," which also adequately described its chemical organization. As to these buyers the plaintiff has therefore, I think, made out a case at least to compel the addition of some distinguishing suffix, even though its monopoly had been more perfect than in fact it was.

The crux of this controversy, however, lies not in the use of the word to these buyers, but to the general consuming public, composed of all sorts of buyers from those somewhat acquainted with pharmaceutical terms to those who knew nothing of them. The only reasonable inference from the evidence is that these did not understand by the word anything more than a kind of drug to which for one reason or another they had become habituated. It is quite clear that while the drug was sold as powder this must have been so. It was dispensed substantially altogether on prescription during this period, and, although physicians appear to have used the terms, "Aspirin" or "acetyl salicylic acid" indifferently, it cannot be that such patients as read their prescriptions attributed to "Aspirin" any other meaning than as an ingredient in a general compound, to which faith and science might impart therapeutic virtue. Nor is there any evidence that such as may have seen both terms identified them as the same drug. I cannot speculate as to how many in fact did so. No packages could possibly have reached the consumer, nor was any advertising addressed to them; their only acquaintance with the word was as the name for a drug in whose curative properties they had got confidence.

In 1904, however, they began to get acquainted with it in a different way, for then all the larger manufacturing chemists began to make tablets, and the trade grew to extraordinary proportions. The consumer, as both sides agree, had long before the autumn of 1915 very largely abandoned consultation with physicians and assumed the right to drug himself as his own prudence and moderation might prescribe. In all cases—omitting for the moment the infringing product—the drug was sold in bottles labeled "Aspirin" with some indication of the name of the tablet maker, but none of the plaintiff. It is probable that by far the greater part of the tablets sold were in dozens or less, and that the bottles so labeled did not generally reach the hands of the consumer, but, even so, a not inconsiderable number of bottles of 100 were sold, and as to the rest they were sold only under the name "Aspirin." The consumer did not know and could not possibly know the manufacturer of the drug which he got, or whether one or more chemists made it in the United States. He never heard the name "acetyl salicylic acid" as applied to it, and without some education could not possibly have kept it in his mind, if he had. So far as any means of information at all were open to him, they indicated that it was made by most large chemists indiscriminately.

This being the situation up to the autumn of 1915, the defendant seems to me to have effectually rebutted any presumption which the coined word might carry. However, the plaintiff argues along with this user large infringing sales of the drug were being made to consumers under the name "acetyl salicylic acid." It has indeed proved that it was unable absolutely to protect the monopoly of the patent, and it is clear that large quantities were piratically sold, though, so far as this record shows, with uniform respect for its trademark. Further, a good many retail druggists swore, with undoubted truth, that their customers got accustomed to the use of the phrase and could either ask for the drug or get it written out on a slip of paper and present that. I think I must accept the record as showing that this went on to a substantial, though obviously to a wholly indeterminate, extent. However, I need not accept, because I do not believe, that all the piratical drug was sold to the consumer under the name "acetyl salicylic acid." This is inherently improbable, and evidence to the contrary was not produced by, and naturally not available to, the plaintiff.

Aside from the fact that there is authority for saying that the inadequacy of the patent wholly to protect the plaintiff is immaterial (*Horlick's Food Co. v. Elgin Milkine Co.*, 120 Fed. 264, 56 C.C.A. 544), this evidence does not appear to me to help the plaintiff at all.

It shows nothing more than that there was a class of buyers who knew a drug going by the name "acetyl salicylic acid," which was useful for some purposes, in fact (though this they did not necessarily know), the same as those for which "Aspirin" was useful. There is no evidence that these buyers knew that his drug was the same as "Aspirin," or that they ever asked for or bought "Aspirin." Nor is there any evidence, as I have already said (and this is the critical point), that with rare exceptions those who asked for and knew "Aspirin" identified it with "acetyl salicylic acid," or supposed that "Aspirin" was that drug, when made by some one in particular. They bought tablets of various manufacture, and if they knew of the different tablet makers, they would, as above stated, have supposed that not only the tablets, but the drug itself, were made by the chemists from whom it apparently emanated. For these reasons I do not regard the sales of "acetyl salicylic acid" by that name as material to the issue between the parties here.

After the autumn of 1915 the plaintiff totally changed its methods, and thereafter no tablets reached the consumer without its own name. But it is significant that even then it used the word "Aspirin" as though it was a general term, although it is true that there was ample notice upon the bottles and boxes that "Aspirin" meant its manufacture. The most striking part of the label real, "Bayer — Tablets of Aspirin." While this did not show any abandonment of the name, which there has never been, it did show how the plaintiff itself recognized the meaning which the word had acquired, because the phrase most properly means that these tablets were Bayer's make of the drug known as "Aspirin." It presupposes that the persons reached were using the word to denote a kind of product. Were it not so, why the addition of "Bayer," and especially why the significant word "of"?

Disregarding this, however, it was too late in the autumn of 1915 to reclaim the word which had already passed into the public domain. If the consuming public had once learned to know "Aspirin" as the accepted name for the drug, perhaps it is true that an extended course of education might have added to it some proprietary meaning, but it would be very difficult to prove that it had been done in 17 months, and in any case the plaintiff does not try to prove it. The issue in this aspect, indeed, becomes whether during that period the word had obtained a secondary meaning, and I do not understand that any such thing is claimed. If it is, I own I cannot find any basis for it in the record. Probably what really happened was that the plaintiff awoke to the fact that on the expiration of the patent its trade-mark would be questioned, and strove to do what it could to relieve it of any doubts. Yet, had it not been indifferent to the results of selling to the consumer, it could have protected itself just as well as the time when consumers began to buy directly as in 1915. Nothing would have been easier than to insist that the tablet makers should market the drug is small tin boxes bearing the plaintiffs name, or to take over the sale just as it did later. Instead of this, they allowed the manufacturing chemists to build up this part of the demand without regard to the trade-mark. Having made that bed, they must be content to lie in it. Hence it appears to me that nothing happening between October, 1915, and March, 1917, will serve to turn the word into a trade-mark.

The plaintiff argues that, if it is to be so treated, it is impossible to get a trade-mark for an "ethical" remedy, which apparently means a remedy not directly advertised or sold to the public. But it must not blow hot and cold. If a manufacturer thinks it undesirable to advertise and sell drugs direct, the inevitable consequence of adhering to that standard is that no trade-mark among consumers can be acquired, because they can know nothing of it. Virtue in such cases must be its own reward, or must realize its material profits in the long cast. Moreover, the plaintiff's complaint comes now with doubtful consistency after some 16 years of sales in one way or another without the intervention of physicians. It can scarcely claim to have been ignorant of the fact that the millions of tablets which were being sold before October, 1915, were in large part sold direct, and that, if it was not itself addressing the consumer, it had become unnecessary to do so. I do not suggest that there was the least impropriety in all this, but it appears to me to leave little ground for asserting that its superior virtue has been the cause of its undoing. Besides, however ever much can be made of this before October, 1915, thereafter the plaintiff certainly felt no compunctions. Now its drug was no different then from itself in 1899; nor was there, I think, any less danger from self-medication. They had, indeed, through their admirable methods of introducing it, given it a good reputation, consonant with their own very high standing, but that seems to me rather an instance of the skill with which their business was conducted, than of scruples, which, in the light of subsequent events, they would, I should say, have always thought over strained. But, however all that may be, they cannot, of course, get a trade-mark conditioned in fact upon directly addressing the consumer, and maintain a reputation based upon never doing so.

There are words, such as "Lactobacilline" (29 Rep. Pat. Cas. 497), "Vaseline" (19 Rep. Pat. Cas. 342), "Argyrol" ([C.C.] 164 Fed. 213), "Valvoline" ([C.C.] 38 Fed. 922), or "Celluloid" ([C.C.] 32 Fed. 94), which may at once mean both the kind of goods and their maker. These will be entitled to a qualified protection. The most striking illustration is perhaps *Singer Mfg. Co. v. June Mfg. Co., supra,* itself, where the putative mark was a proper name. The validity of a trade-mark does not, indeed, rigidly depend upon its meaning only the differential between a genus, defined by the kind of goods, and a species, defined by that kind when emanating from the owner. *Guastavino v. Comerma* (C.C.) 180 Fed. 920. When it means the owner as well as the kind, it will be entitled to a qualified protection; when, as here among the trade, there is another current word, it may be entitled to an absolute protection, patent or not. For a patent gives the public no greater rights than it has without patent. We speak of a dedication of the disclosure, but that is rather for convenience. In fact, the public may be always practice the invention, except as the monopoly interferes, and it gets that right independently of the patent. But when, as here among consumers, a mark does not give even an intimation of the owner, there is no room at all for any protection. *Centaur Co. v. Heinsfurter,* 84 Fed. 955, 28 C.C.A. 581; *Linoleum Mfg. Co. v. Narin,* L.R. 7 Ch. Div. 834. After all presumptions and other procedural advantages have been weighed, the owner must show that his mark means him, else he cannot prevent others from using it. There is no invention in the word, qua word, which he can protect.

The case, therefore, presents a situation in which, ignoring sporadic exceptions, the trade is divided into two classes, separated by vital differences. One, the manufacturing chemists, retail druggists, and physicians, has been educated to understand that "Aspirin" means the plaintiff's manufacture, and has recourse to another and an intelligible name for it, actually in use among them. The other, the consumers, the plaintiff has, consciously I must assume, allowed to acquaint themselves with the drug only by the name "Aspirin," and has not succeeded in advising that the word means the plaintiff at all. If the defendant is allowed to continue the use of the word of the first class, certainly without any condition, there is a chance that it may get customers away from the plaintiff by deception. On the other hand, if the plaintiff is allowed a monopoly of the word as against consumers, it will deprive the defendant, and the trade in general, or the right effectually to dispose of the drug by the only description which will be understood. It appears to me that the relief granted cannot in justice to either party disregard this division; each party has won, and each has lost.

The plaintiff argues that this is an innovation in the law. I think not. In two very recent cases the Supreme Court has taken the very point, though the division chanced to be territorial instead of arising from the facts of the market. In *Hanover Milling Co. v. Metcalf,* 240 U.S. 403, 36 Sup. Ct.357, 60 L. Ed. 713, and *United Drug Co. v. Rectanus,* 248

U.S. 90, 39 Sup. Ct. 48, 63 L. Ed. 141, a trade-mark and a trade-name were refused protection, though valid elsewhere, in parts of the country where the buyers did not know that they signified the owner, and because they did not. Mr. Justice Pitney especially adverted to the basis upon which the whole law rests. "Cessit ratio, cessist lex." If the rule applies to vertical divisions of the demand, it must apply to horizontal. Of course, we must not attempt too fine an application of such divisions, one reason perhaps for Mr. Justice Holmes' concurring opinion in *Hanover Mills v. Metcalf, supra.* For example, in the case at bar it is impossible to provide for such rare retailers as may not, and such rare customers as may, know that"Aspirin" is a trade-mark. We can cut only so fine as our shears permit, and there will be ragged edges on either side.

As to the first class the question arises whether the injunction should be absolute or conditional. A strong case may be made for the defendant's present labels. They all bear the letters "U. D. Co." in juxtaposition with "Aspirin" and of equal size. These letters are universally known by the trade to signify the plaintiff, because the custom is general for manufacturing chemists in this way to mark their goods. I think that the plaintiff would be adequately protected but for the 10 years' history of the tablet trade. However, the fact is that during that time such legends were used to indicate that the manufacturing chemist who signed, as it were, the label, was making the tablets from the plaintiff's powder. Probably at present that belief has largely disappeared, but, since we are dealing with customers who are presumably aware of that history, and who have been repeatedly told that "Aspirin" signifies the plaintiff, I can see no reason for subjecting it to the chance. The phrase "acetyl salicylic acid" to them is intelligible; it means the same drug as "Aspirin" and its use ought not unduly to hamper the trade in its business. Besides, the case in this aspect is one of trade-mark proper. Therefore I will grant an injunction against direct sales of the drug under the name "Aspirin" to manufacturing chemists, physicians, and retail druggists. This will, of course, include invoices and correspondence.

In sales to consumers there need, however, be no suffix or qualification whatever. In so far as customers came to identify the plaintiff with "Aspirin" between October, 1915, and March, 1917, this may do it some injustice, but it is impracticable to give any protection based on that possibility. Among consumers generally the name has gone into the public domain. The defendant, as I understand it, makes no direct sales, and all its transactions will therefore probably fall within the injunction, but the sale of its stockholding retailers will be free, and it may so instruct them. Moreover, I see no reason why the defendant should be compelled to sell in such large bottles or boxes that the retailers must bottle or box tablets for themselves. This is a trade advantage which conceivably may be of capital consequence in competition. True, it must sell to these retailers clearly under the name "acetyl salicylic acid," but the retailers may themselves use the word "Aspirin." So it seems to me that the defendant should be allowed to pack its tablets in bottles or boxes of 50 or less, bearing the name "Aspirin" without more. These must, however, be sold to the retailers as acetyl salicylic acid, and when shipped must be inclosed in a container marked only "acetyl salicylic acid," with the defendant's name on it. I have limited the quantity to 50 because it seems to me that in greater quantities the permission might be a means by which the retailers could sell the drug to physicians as "Aspirin." True, some physicians may buy as little as 50 at a time, just as some consumers in fact buy more. But some compromise must be made. If there are physicians who buy in such small quantities, the plaintiff must rely upon preventing retailers from using these bottles; if there are consumers who wish more, the defendant must submit to the disadvantage that the retailers must sell *2* at a time, or must relabel a bottle of 100.

King-Seeley Thermos Co. v. Aladdin Industries, Inc.
321 F.2d 577 (2d Cir. 1963)

MOORE, CIRCUIT JUDGE

This action by brought by appellant King-Seeley Thermos Co. (King-Seeley) to enjoin the defendant, Aladdin Industries, Incorporated from threatened infringement of eight trademark registrations for the word 'Thermos' owned by appellant. Defendant answered, acknowledging its intention to sell its vacuum-insulated containers as 'thermos bottles,' asserted that the term 'thermos' or 'thermos bottle' is a generic term in the English language, asked that plaintiffs registrations of its trademark 'Thermos' be cancelled and that it be adjudicated that plaintiff have no trademark rights in the word 'thermos' on its vacuum bottles. The trial court held that plaintiff's registrations were valid but that the word 'thermos' had become 'a generic descriptive word in the English language as a synonym for 'vacuum insulated' container.' 207 F.Supp. 9.

The facts are set out at great length in the comprehensive and well-reasoned opinion of the district court and will not be detailed here. In that opinion, the court reviewed King-Seeley's corporate history and its use of the trademark 'Thermos'. He found that from 1907 to 1923, King-Seeley undertook advertising and educational campaigns that tended to make 'thermos' a generic term descriptive of the product rather than of its origin. This consequence flowed from the corporation's attempt to popularize 'Thermos bottle' as the name of that product without including any of the generic terms then used, such as 'Thermos vacuum-insulated bottle'. The court found that by 1923 the word 'thermos' had acquired firm roots as a descriptive or generic word.

At about 1923, because of the suggestion in an opinion of a district court that 'Thermos' might be a descriptive word, King-Seeley adopted the use of the word 'vacuum' or 'vacuum bottle' with the word 'Thermos.' Although 'Thermos' was generally recognized in the trade as a trademark, the corporation did police the trade and notified those using 'thermos' in a descriptive sense that it was a trademark. It failed, however, to take affirmative action to seek out generic uses by non-trade publications and protested only those which happened to come to its attention. Between 1923 and the early 1950's the generic use of 'thermos' had grown to a marked extent in non-trade publications and by the end of this period there was wide-spread use by the unorganized public of 'thermos' as a synonym for 'vacuum insulated.' The court concluded that King-Seeley had failed to use due diligence to rescue 'Thermos' from becoming a descriptive or generic term.

Between 1954 and 1957, plaintiff showed awareness of the widespread generic use of 'thermos' and of the need to educate the public to the word's trademark significance. It diversified its products to include those not directly related to containers designed to keep their contents hot or cold. It changed its name from the American Thermos Bottle Company to The American Thermos Products Company and intensified its policing activities of trade and non-trade publications. The court found, however, that the generic use of 'thermos' had become so firmly impressed as a part of the everyday language of the American public that plaintiff's extraordinary efforts commencing in the mid-1950's came too late to keep 'thermos' from falling into the public domain. The court also held that appellant's trademarks are valid and because there is an appreciable, though minority, segment of the consumer public which knows and recognizes plaintiff's trademarks, it imposed certain restrictions and limitations on the use of the word 'thermos' by defendant.

We affirm the district court's decision that the major significance of the word 'thermos' is generic. No useful purpose would be served by repeating here what is fully documented in the opinion of the court below.

Appellant's primary protest on appeal is directed at the district court's finding that

> The word 'thermos' became a part of the public domain because of the plaintiff's wide dissemination of the word 'thermos' used as a synonym for 'vacuum-insulated' and as an adjectival-noun, 'thermos', through its educational and advertising campaigns and because of the plaintiffs lack of reasonable diligence in asserting and protecting its trademark rights in the word 'Thermos' among the members of the unorganized public, exclusive of those in the trade, from 1907 to the date of this action.

207 F.Supp. at 14.

We are not convinced that the trademark's loss of distinctiveness was the result of some failure on plaintiffs part. Substantial efforts to preserve the trademark significance of the word were made by plaintiff, especially with respect to members of the trade. However, there was little they could do to prevent the public from using 'thermos' in a generic rather than a trademark sense. And whether the appropriation by the public was due to highly successful educational and advertising campaigns or to lack of diligence in policing or not is of no consequence; the fact is that the word 'thermos' had entered the public domain beyond recall. Even as early as 1910 plaintiff itself asserted that 'Thermos had become a household word.'

Judge Anderson found that although a substantial majority of the public knows and uses the word 'thermos', only a small minority of the public knows that this word has trademark significance.

He wrote at 207 F.Supp. 21–22:

> The results of the survey (conducted at the behest of the defendant) were that about 75% of adults in the United States who were familiar with containers that keep the contents hot or cold, call such a container a 'thermos'; about 12% of the adult American public know that 'thermos' has a trade-mark significance, and about 11% Use the term 'vacuum bottle'. This is generally corroborative of the court's conclusions drawn from the other evidence, except that such other evidence indicated that a somewhat larger minority than 12% Was aware of the trade-mark meaning of 'thermos'; and a somewhat larger minority than 11% used the descriptive term 'vacuum' bottle or other container.

[The key questions asked 3,300 interviewees were:

'Are you familiar with the type of container that is used to keep liquids, like soup, coffee, tea and lemonade, hot or cold for a period of time?

'Have you yourself ever used (or filled) such a container—that is, the type to keep liquids cold or hot?

'What was the occasion for using such a container?

'If you were going to buy one of these containers tomorrow—that is, the type that keeps food and beverages hot or cold—what type of store would you select to make your purchase?

'What would you ask for—that is, what would you tell the clerk you wanted?]

The record amply supports these findings.

Appellant argues that the court below misapplied the doctrine of the Aspirin and Cellophane cases. Its primary contention is that in those cases, there was no generic name, such as vacuum bottle, that was suitable for use by the general public. As a result, to protect the use of the only word the identified the product in the mind of the public would give the owners of the trademark an unfair competitive advantage. The rule of those cases, however, does not rest on this factor. Judge Learned Hand stated the sole issue in Aspirin to be: 'What do the buyers understand by the word for whose use the parties are contending? If they understand by it only the kind of goods sold, then, I take it, it makes no difference whatever what efforts the plaintiff has made to get them to understand more.' 272 F. at 509. Of course, it is obvious that the fact that there was no suitable descriptive word for either aspirin or cellophane made it difficult, if not impossible, for the original manufacturers to prevent their trademark from becoming generic. But the test is not what is available as an alternative to the public, but what the public's understanding is of the word that it uses. What has happened here is that the public had become accustomed to calling vacuum bottles by the word 'thermos'. If a buyer walked into a retail store asking for a thermos bottle, meaning any vacuum bottle and not specifically plaintiff's product, the fact that the appellation 'vacuum bottle' was available to him is of no significance. The two terms had become synonymous; in fact, defendant's survey showed that the public was far more inclined to use the word 'thermos' to describe a container that keeps its content shot or cold than the phrase 'vacuum bottle.'

* * *

Since in this case, the primary significance to the public of the word 'thermos' is its indication of the nature and class of an article rather than as an indication of its source, whatever duality of meaning of word still holds for a minority of the public is of little consequence except as a consideration in the framing of a decree. Since the great majority of those members of the public who use the word 'thermos' are not aware of any trademark significance, there is not enough dual use to support King-Seeley's claims to monopoly of the word as a trademark.

No doubt, the Aspirin and Cellophane doctrine can be a harsh one for it places a penalty on the manufacturer who has made skillful use of advertising and has popularized his product. *See 3* Callman, Unfair Competition and Trademarks 1149–50 (2d ed. 1950). However, King-Seeley has enjoyed a commercial monopoly of the word 'thermos' for over fifty years. During that period, despite its efforts to protect the trademark, the public has virtually expropriated it as its own. The word having become part of the public domain, it would be unfair to unduly restrict the right of a competitor of King-Seeley to use the word.

The court below, mindful of the fact that some members of the public and a substantial portion of the trade still recognize and use the word 'thermos' as a trademark, framed an eminently fair decree designed to afford King-Seeley as much future protection as was possible. The decree provides that defendant must invariably precede the use of the word 'thermos' by the possessive of the name 'Aladdin'; that the defendant must confine its use of 'thermos' to the lower-case 't'; and that it may never use the words 'original' or 'genuine' in describing its product. In addition, plaintiff is entitled to retain the exclusive right to all of its present forms of the trademark 'Thermos' without change. These conditions provide a sound and proper balancing of the competitive disadvantage to defendants arising out of plaintiff's exclusive use of the word 'thermos' and the risk that those who recognize 'Thermos' as a trademark will be deceived.

The courts should be ever alert, as the district court said, 'to eliminate confusion and the possibility of deceit.' The purchasing public is entitled to know the source of the ar-

Picture 9.1   Board Game Anti-Monopoly
[Copyright 2004. Reprinted with permission by Prof. Ralph Anspach.]

ticle it desires to purchase. It is not within our province to speculate whether the dire predictions made by appellant in forceful appellate argument will come to pass. Certain it is that the district court made every endeavor in its judgment to give as much protection to plaintiff as possible. The use by defendant of the now generic word 'thermos' was substantially curtailed. Plaintiff's trademark 'thermos' was protected in every style of printing except the lower case 'thermos' and then the use of the word must be preceded by the possessive of defendant's name 'Aladdin' or the possessive of 'Aladdin' plus one of defendant's brand names. Any doubt about plaintiff's position in the field is removed by the prohibition against the use by defendant in labeling, advertising or publication of the words 'genuine' or 'original' in referring to the word 'thermos'. Furthermore, the district court has given both parties the opportunity to apply to it for such orders and directions as may be warranted in the light of changed circumstances and for the enforcement of compliance or for the punishment of violations. In our opinion the trial court has reached a most equitable solution which gives appropriate consideration to the law and the facts.

Affirmed.

Anti-Monopoly, Inc. v. General Mills Fun Group, Inc.

684 F.2d 1316 (9th Cir. 1982)

DUNIWAY, CIRCUIT JUDGE:

This is the second appeal in this case. Our first opinion is reported in *Anti-Monopoly, Inc. v. General Mills Fun Group*, 9 Cir., 1979, 611 F.2d 296 *(Anti-Monopoly I)*. On remand the district court again found that the "Monopoly" trademark was valid and had been infringed by *Anti-Monopoly, Inc. Anti-Monopoly, Inc. v. General Mills Fun Group, Inc.*, N.D.Cal., 1981, 515 F.Supp. 448 *(Anti-Monopoly II)*. We reverse and remand for further proceedings.

I. Prior Proceedings.

General Mills is the successor to Parker Brothers, Inc., which had produced and sold a game it called Monopoly since 1935. Parker Brothers registered "Monopoly" as a trademark in that year. In 1973 Anti-Monopoly, Inc. was established to produce and sell a game it called Anti-Monopoly. General Mills claimed that this infringed its trademark. This action was then brought by Anti-Monopoly, seeking a declaratory judgment that the registered trademark "Monopoly" was invalid, and cancelling its registration. In a counterclaim, General Mills sought declaratory and injunctive relief upholding its trademark, and the dismissal of the action. The case was tried without a jury in 1976. The court entered a judgment for General Mills. We reversed and remanded for further consideration of (i) the validity of the trademark, (ii) infringement of the trademark, if it is valid, by Anti-Monopoly, and (iii) state law claims concerning unfair competition and dilution. We also chose to defer consideration of (iv) Anti-Monopoly's defense that General Mills had unclean hands. On remand, after hearing further evidence, the district court again entered a judgment for General Mills.

* * *

IV. Generic Terms—The Law.

Our opinion in *Anti-Monopoly I* binds both this court and the district court. There, we set out the law about generic terms and explained how it was to be applied to the particular facts of this case. Anti-Monopoly I, 611 F.2d at 300–306. In this opinion, we assume that the reader will be familiar with that opinion. Here, we emphasize what we consider to be its essence. A word used as a trademark is not generic if "the primary significance of the term in the minds of the consuming public is not the product but the producer." *Id.* at 302. "When a trademark primarily denotes a product, not the product's producer, the trademark is lost." *Id.* at 301. A registered mark is to be cancelled if it has become "the common descriptive name of an article," 15 U.S.C. § 1064(c), and no incontestable right can be acquired in such a mark. 15 U.S.C. § 1065(4). We said "Even if only one producer—Parker Brothers—has ever made the MONOPOLY game, so that the public necessarily associates the product with that particular producer, the trademark is invalid unless source indication is its primary significance." *Anti-Monopoly I*, 611 F.2d at 302. "It is the source-denoting function which trademark laws protect, and nothing more." *Id.* at 301. "One competitor will not be permitted to impoverish the language of commerce by preventing his fellows from fairly describing their own goods." *Id.*, quoting *Bada Co. v. Montgomery Ward & Co.*, 9 Cir., 1970, 426 F.2d 8, 11. "When members of the consuming public use a game name to denote the game itself, and not its producer, the trademark is generic and, therefore, invalid." *Id.* at 304.

V. Was the Term "MONOPOLY" Generic at the Time of Registration?

Anti-Monopoly, Inc. claims that the term "Monopoly" was generic at the time when Parker Brothers registered it. On this question, the trial judge made the following findings:

> Plaintiff [Anti-Monopoly] attempted to show at trial that at the time of Parker Brothers' trademark registration, MONOPOLY was already a widely played game known by that name. The evidence introduced to support this contention consists chiefly of isolated and sporadic examples of individuals playing old oilcloth games referred to in some instances as"Monopoly," the "Landlord's Game," or some other variation thereof.

> * * *

> In order to be "generic," the name MONOPOLY, in the minds of the consuming public, must primarily denote product rather than source. It remains unclear how widely played the precursors to modem MONOPOLY were in the 1920s and early '30s. Plaintiff has simply made no showing as to what the public conception of the term was at that juncture or indeed how widely played it

actually was. As Clarence [sic] Darrow, and later his successor, Parker Brothers, popularized a specific game they called MONOPOLY, this court cannot find that the trademark when registered denoted "a game" rather than the "game's producer." Because Anti-Monopoly has the burden of showing genericness by convincing evidence this finding must be for defendant.

515 F. Supp. at 451–452. The district court found also that Darrow was the inventor of the game (*Id.* at 451) and that the game was "created" by Darrow. *Id.* at 452 n.1. (The quotation marks are in the original.)

*   *   *

We agree with the trial judge's conclusion that "Monopoly" had not become generic before Parker Brothers registered it as a trademark.

VI. Has "Monopoly" Become Generic Since It Was Registered?

This question is discussed, and the trial court's findings of fact appear in *Monopoly II*, 515F. Supp. at 452–455. Under the heading "FINDINGS OF FACT," the following appears:

1. The court again finds as fact each fact found in this Opinion as set forth in the foregoing.

2. As a game trademark, MONOPOLY primarily denotes its producer, Parker Brothers, and primarily denoted its producer when registered.

Id. at 455. We consider finding 2 to be one of ultimate fact, and subject to the "clearly erroneous" standard of Rule 52(a). *See Pullman-Standard, supra,* U.S. at, 102 S. Ct. at 1789.

The district court also said "'Primary significance' logically implies a hierarchical priority over a competing alternative." 515 F. Supp. at 454. Dictionary definitions are in accord. Funk & Wagnalls' New Standard Dictionary gives "primary 1. First in ... thought or intention, 2. First in degree, rank or importance, most fundamental, chief...." Webster's New International Dictionary (2d Ed.) gives "1. First in ... intention; 2. First in ... importance; chief, principal...." We are not sure what the district court meant by a "competing alternative." To us, this carries some suggestion of "either, or." Yet it is nearly always the case, as the district court recognized, that a trademark will identify both the product and its producer. *Anti-Monopoly II,* 515 F. Supp. at 454. Indeed, its value lies in its identification of the product with its producer.

In its opinion, the district court supports its finding 2 as follows:

The difficulty in this regard arises due to the public's dual usage of the tradename, denoting both product and source. For example, the mark "Ford" to the average consumer denotes *both* car and motor car company. However, to demonstrate "primary significance" it is necessary to show more than a high percentage of the consuming public who recognize MONOPOLY as a brand name (as defendant has done: 63% of those polled recognized MONOPOLY as a "brand name"). It is necessary to show more than a public awareness that Parker Brothers is the sole manufacturer of MONOPOLY (55% correctly identified Parker Brothers in defendant's survey). "Primary significance" logically implies a hierarchical priority over a competing alternative.

Yet the cumulative weight of the evidence does satisfy this court that the primary significance of MONOPOLY in the public's eye is to denote a "Parker Brothers' Game" (i.e.,source) in contradistinction to that "popular game of MONOPOLY" (product). Parker Brothers has expended substantial time, energy, and money in promoting and policing their trademark, expending over $4 million in advertising expenditures. One result of these diligent efforts has been the extraordinary success Parker Brothers has achieved in creating public source awareness. Over 55% of the American public correctly identified Parker Brothers as the producer of the game. An even more impressive display of the amount of goodwill which Parker Brothers has imbued through its various games — especially MONOPOLY — is *the finding of plaintiff's survey that one out of three MONOPOLY purchasers do so primarily because "they like Parker Brothers' products."* Hence, source attribution is a dominant perceived effect of the MONOPOLY trademark. This court cannot say from the facts before it that it is not the "primary significance" of the mark.

Id. at 454–455 (emphasis in the original).

In considering whether these findings, and finding 2, are clearly erroneous, we have in mind an obvious proposition. The word "Monopoly," while not in its ordinary meaning descriptive of the game "Monopoly," is an ordinary English word, and it does describe the objective of the game. This was recognized in the rules of the game published by Parker Brothers in 1935. They begin with:

BRIEF IDEA OF THE GAME

THE IDEA OF THE GAME is to BUY and RENT or SELL properties so profitably that one becomes the wealthiest player and eventual MONOPOLIST.

A Monopolist has a monopoly. By choosing the word as a trademark, Parker Brothers subjected itself to a considerable risk that the word would become so identified with the game as to be "generic."

In *Anti-Monopoly II* the district court also said this: "Unless the Ninth Circuit standard is meant to foreclose the possibility of trademark protection for any producer of a unique game whose corporate name does not appear in the title of the game (e.g., 'SCRABBLE,' 'TOWER OF BABBLE'), then its test cannot be used here to thwart MONOPOLY's trademark rights." 515 F. Supp. at 455. Nothing in our opinion in *Anti-Monopoly I* even hints at the relevance of whether or not the corporate name of the producer of a game appears in the title of the game, and our opinion does not foreclose the possibility of trademark protection of the name of a game that does not embody the corporate name of its producer. But our opinion does squarely hold as follows: "Even if only one producer — Parker Brothers — has ever made the MONOPOLY game, so that the public necessarily associates the product with that particular producer, the trademark is invalid unless source identification is its primary significance." 611 F.2d at 302.

The district court obviously felt that our opinion in *Anti-Monopoly I* gave Anti-Monopoly an easier task in trying to show that "Monopoly" has become generic than the district court would give. Nevertheless, both we and the district court are bound by our decision in *Anti-Monopoly I.*

We now consider whether finding 2 of the district court is clearly erroneous. We conclude that it is.

As we have seen, the district court relied in part upon the fact that General Mills and its predecessor have spent time, energy, and money in promoting and policing use of the term "Monopoly." That fact, however, is not of itself sufficient to create legally protectable rights. It is not, of itself, enough that over 55% of the public has come to associate the product, and as a consequence the name by which the product is generally known, with Parker Brothers. Even if one third of the members of the public who purchased the game did so because they liked Parker Brothers' products, that fact does not show that "Monopoly" is primarily source indicating. The very survey on which the district court placed emphasis by italicizing its result shows that two thirds of the members of the public who purchased the game wanted "Monopoly" and did not care who made it.

The real question is what did Parker Brothers and General Mills get for their money and efforts? To us, the evidence overwhelmingly shows that they very successfully promoted the game of Monopoly, but that in doing it they so successfully promoted "Monopoly" as "the name of the game," that it became generic in the sense in which we use that term in trademark law. We recognize that "there is evidence to support" the trial court's findings, United States Gypsum Co., *supra, 333* U.S. at *395,* 68 S. Ct. at *542,* but "on the entire evidence [we are] left with the definite and firm conviction that a mistake has been committed." *Id.*

The principal evidence in the case was in the form of consumer surveys, and to these we now turn.

A. The Brand-Name Survey.

General Mills conducted a survey based upon a survey approved by a district court in the "Teflon" case, *E.I. Du Pont de Nemours & Co. v. Yoshida International, Inc.,* E.D.N.Y., 1975, *393* F. Supp. *502.* In the survey conducted by General Mills, people were asked whether "Monopoly" is a "brand-name," and were told: 'By *brand* name, I mean a name like *Chevrolet,* which is made by *one* company; by common name, I mean 'automobile,' which is made by a number of different companies." (Emphasis in the original.) The results of this survey had no relevance to the question in this case. Under the survey definition, "Monopoly" would have to be a "brand name" because it is made by only one company. This tells us nothing at all about the *primary* meaning of "Monopoly" in the minds of consumers.

It is true that the witness through whom the survey was introduced testified on direct examination that as a result of it his opinion was that "Monopoly" primarily denotes source or producer. However, on cross-examination and redirect examination it became clear that this witness had done no more than reduplicate the "Teflon" survey (with appropriate substitutions and slight additions) and had no opinion on the relevance of this survey to any issue in the present case. The brand-name survey is not even some evidence to support finding *2;* it is no evidence to support it.

B. The "Thermos" Survey.

Anti-Monopoly's first survey was based upon that used in the "Thermos" case, *King-Seeley Thermos Co. v. Aladdin Industries, Inc.,* D. Conn., 1962, 207 F. Supp. *9,* 20–21, *aff'd,* 2 Cir., 1963, 321 F.2d *577.* In Anti-Monopoly's survey people were asked the question: "Are you familiar with business board games of the kind in which players buy, sell, mortgage and trade city streets, utilities and railroads, build houses, collect rents and win by bankrupting all other players, or not"? About 53% said they were. Those people were then asked: "If you were going to buy this kind of game, what would you ask for, that is, what would you tell the sales clerk you wanted"? About 80% said:"Monopoly."

The witness through whom this survey was introduced testified that Anti-Monopoly gave his firm the questions used in the "Thermos" survey and asked it to conduct a similar one. Anti-Monopoly provided the wording of the questions in the present survey as well. The research firm was responsible for deciding how to reach a sample that would adequately represent the population of the United States. The witness gave no testimony as to the relevance of the results of the survey to the issues in the case.

In one of its briefs, General Mills points out that the survey used in the "Thermos" case was described as "generally corroborative of the court's conclusions drawn from other evidence," and that the district court which decided the "Teflon" case found a "Thermos"-like survey defective because "the design of the questions more often than not [focused] on supplying the inquirer a 'name,' without regard to whether the principal significance of the name supplied was 'its indication of the nature or class of an article, rather than an indication of its origin,' *King-Seeley Thermos Co., supra,* 321 F.2d at 580." *E.I. Du Pont de Nemours & Co., supra,* 393 F. Supp. at 527. Be that as it may, we think that the results of this survey are compelling evidence of a proposition that is also dictated by common sense: an overwhelming proportion of those who are familiar with the game would ask for it by the name "Monopoly."

C. The Motivation Survey.

After the remand to the district court, Anti-Monopoly commissioned a further survey. This survey was based upon the following language from our opinion in *Anti-Monopoly I*:

> It may be that when a customer enters a game store and asks for MONOPOLY, he means:"I would like Parker Brothers' version of a real estate trading game, because I like Parker Brothers' products. Thus, I am not interested in board games made by Anti-Monopoly, or anyone other than Parker Brothers." On the other hand, the consumer may mean: "I want a 'Monopoly' game. Don't bother showing me Anti-Monopoly, or EASY MONEY, or backgammon. I am interested in playing the game of Monopoly. I don't much care who makes it."

> In the first example, the consumer differentiates between MONOPOLY and other games according to source-particular criteria. In the second example, source is not a consideration. The relevant genus, or product category, varies accordingly. At the urging of Parker Brothers, the district court erred by first defining the genus, and then asking the "primary significance" question about the wrong genus-species dichotomy. The proper mode of analysis is to decide but one question: whether the primary significance of a term is to denote product, or source. In making this determination, the correct genus-species distinction, that is, the correct genericness finding, follows automatically.

611 F.2d at 305–306. The wording of the questions was provided by Dr. Anspach, Anti-Monopoly's president, and by the expert who testified at trial. The expert had studied our first opinion. The survey was designed to ascertain the use of the term "Monopoly" by those who had purchased the game in the past or intended to do so in the near future. It was conducted by telephone. The results were as follows: 92% were aware of "Monopoly," the business board game produced by Parker Brothers. Of that 92%, 62% either had "purchased 'Monopoly' within the last couple of years" or intended to purchase it in the near future. Those people were asked why they had bought or would buy monopoly. The answers exhibited the following pattern: 82% mentioned some aspect of the playing of the game (e.g., that they played it as a kid, it was a family game, it was enjoyable, it was fun to play, it was interesting), 14% mentioned some educational aspect of the game, 7% mentioned the equipment (e.g., saying it was durable) or said they were replacing a set, 1% spoke of price, 34% gave other reasons neutral to the issues in this case (e.g., it was for a gift, the game was a classic, people like the game). The percentages total more than 100 because respondents often gave more than one reason.

The people who said that they had purchased the game within the last couple of years or would purchase it in the near future were then given a choice of two statements and were asked which best expressed their reasons. Sixty-five percent chose: "I want a 'Monopoly' game primarily because I am interested in playing 'Monopoly,' I don't much care who makes it." Thirty-two percent chose: "I would like Parker Brothers' 'Monopoly' game primarily because I like Parker Brothers' products."

A very similar "intercept survey" was conducted by face to face interviews. The results were very close to those of the telephone survey, but the expert did not claim that the intercept study was validly projectable.

The district court indicated its reasons for rejecting this survey. Insofar as these are findings of fact they must be accorded the deference required by Rule 52(a), and, giving them that deference, we hold them to be clearly erroneous. The district court's major objection to the survey was that it sought an explanation of an actual purchaser's motivation in purchasing the game rather than the primary significance of the word. *Anti-Monopoly, Inc.*, 515 F. Supp. at 453. This objection cannot stand. In our earlier opinion we made it clear that what was relevant was the sense in which a purchaser used the word "Monopoly" when asking for the game by that name. The survey was a reasonable effort to find that out and was modeled closely on what we said in our opinion.

The district court thought that the survey was invalidated by the fact that in the first question people were asked if they were "aware of 'Monopoly,' the business board game *produced by Parker Brothers*" (emphasis supplied). It supposed that the presence of the emphasized words somehow inhibited those who might otherwise have responded to later questions that they bought the game because it was produced by Parker Brothers. No evidence or expert opinion was given to support this view and it has no inherent plausibility.

In a footnote the district court said of this survey that "other methodological deficiencies abound." *Id.*, 515 F. Supp. at 453 n.4. One suggested deficiency is that Professor Anspach suggested the language that was used. This is taken to be evidence of "inherent bias." General Mills argues to us that little weight should be given to this survey because it was devised by Dr. Anspach and the survey firm without the mediation of a trademark attorney. We find no merit in these objections.

The district court found that the study was "overwhelmingly prone to errors of subjective grading." *Id.* No doubt it was referring to the process by which responses were categorized as, for example, education, enjoyable, "played it as a kid," or equipment. This process of categorization was not purely mechanical, and did involve some use of human judgment. However, we are not prepared to dismiss every process that includes the operation of human judgment as "overwhelmingly prone to errors of subjective grading." Nor do we find any special reasons to suspect the exercise of judgment in the case of this survey. The categories that were listed strike us as reasonable ones.

Neither the district court nor General Mills claims that there were *in fact* errors of judgment, but only that there might have been. The raw responses to the survey were at one point offered in evidence by Anti-Monopoly, but the offer was withdrawn after General Mills objected, citing F.R. Evidence 705, 1005 and 1006, and the district judge said: "if [counsel for General Mills had] asked for them, he could have received them. If he received them, he could have turned them over to his expert to check them out and see if they give a reliable or non-reliable basis for the opinion. But since he didn't ask for them, I don't think they should go into evidence." Under these circumstances, General Mills cannot now argue that the raw responses were not in fact correctly categorized.

Finally, in the same footnote, the district court suggested that the result that 82% of monopoly purchasers buy for "product related" reasons *cannot be reconciled* with the other result that 32% of actual or potential buyers chose the statement "I would buy Parker

Brothers' 'monopoly' game primarily because I like Parker Brothers' products." This is a misconception of the survey results. The comparable figure to the 32% is the 65% who chose the statement "I want a 'monopoly' game primarily because I am interested in playing 'monopoly,' I don't much care who makes it." The 82% who gave "product related" answers no doubt had both product related and source related reasons for buying, and, with some, enough to reduce 82% to 65%, the source related reason was stronger when the person had to choose. But it is still true that 65% chose product, rather than source.

We conclude that the findings regarding the survey are clearly erroneous, and that it does support the conclusion that the primary significance of "Monopoly" is product rather than source.

D. The Tide Survey.

General Mills introduced a survey that was intended as a *reductio ad absurdum* of the motivation survey. It showed that when asked to supply a reason for buying Tide about 60% of those who might buy it now or in the future said that they would buy Tide because it does a good job. However, when asked "Would you buy Tide primarily because you like Procter and Gamble's products, or primarily because you like Tide detergent?" about 68% indicated the latter reason. There were various respects in which this survey was different from the motivation survey used by Anti-Monopoly, but we shall not suddenly attach great importance to technical considerations. We suspect that these results tend to show that the general public regards "Tide" as the name of a particular detergent, having particular qualities, rather than as one producer's brand name for the same detergent which is available from a variety of sources. We do not know whether the general public thinks this, or if it does, is correct in thinking this, or whether Procter and Gamble intend them to think it. If the general public does think this, and if the test formulated in *Anti-Monopoly I* could be mechanically extended to the very different subject of detergents, then Procter and Gamble might have cause for alarm. The issue is not before us today. The motivation survey conducted by Anti-Monopoly, Inc. was in accordance with the views we expressed *in Anti-Monopoly I.* The results in the Tide Survey are of no relevance to this case.

E. Conclusion.

We hold that Finding 2 is clearly erroneous because, although there is some evidence to support it, our examination of the evidence leaves us with the definite and firm conviction that a mistake has been committed. We hold that, as applied to a board game, the word "Monopoly" has become "generic," and the registration of it as a trademark is no longer valid.

We remand the case. The district court shall enter judgment for Anti-Monopoly, Inc. on the question of trademark validity and take whatever actions are necessary and consistent with this opinion.

———————

Yellow Cab Co. of Sacramento v. Yellow Cab of Elk Grove, Inc.
419 F.3d 925 (9th Cir. 2005)

We have often determined whether a mark is generic using the "who-are-you/what-are-you" test:" A mark answers the buyer's questions 'Who are you?' 'Where do you come from?' 'Who vouches for you?' But the generic name of the product answers the question 'What are you?'" *Filipino Yellow Pages,* 198 F.3d at 1147 (quoting *Official Airline Guides, Inc. v. Goss,* 6 F.3d 1385, 1391 (9th Cir. 1993)) (alterations omitted).

Analyzing the undisputed evidence, we conducted the "who-are-you/what-are-you" test and held that "Filipino yellow pages" answered the "what are you?" question, and was thus a generic term. *Id.* at 1151. We noted in *Filipino Yellow Pages* that if asked, "What are you?" the three competing companies could all answer "a Filipino yellow pages." *Id.*

In the present case, there is a genuine issue of material fact as to the genericness of the term "yellow cab." If one asks "What are you?" to companies called, for example, Checker Cab Co. or City Cab Co., one would expect the response "a taxicab company" or "a cab company." Posing the question: "Could you refer me to a yellow cab company?", one would expect these same companies to point not to themselves, but to a business operating under the name "Yellow Cab." "Yellow cab" thus appears to answer the "who are you?" rather than the "what are you?" question, demonstrating its nongenericness.

Notes

1. *Doctrine of Foreign Equivalents.* At least for the Second Circuit, evidence of genericism in a foreign language and in a foreign country could be evidence of genericism in the United States because "[a]ny Japanese-speaking customers and others who are familiar with the Japanese terminology would be misled to believe that there is only on brand of otokoyama available in the United States ..." *Otokoyama Co. v. Wine of Japan Imp.,* 175 F. 3d 266, 272 (2d Cir. 1999). What is the significance of such a broad interpretation of genericism? Is this in keeping with the territorial justification for trademark law? The extraterritoriality of trademark law?

2. Would simply adding a French article to a generic term for a trademark result in enforceable trademark rights? For example, "La Yogurt"? *In re Johanna Farms Inc.,* 8 U.S.P.Q. 2d1408 (TTAB 1988) ("We believe ... that the use of the French article combined with the English generic changes the commercial impression of the mark as a whole [and therefore the mark is valid]."

3. Courts are not always consistent in their determinations of genericism. Compare *A.J. Canfield Co. v. Honickman,* 808 F.2d 291, 308 (3d Cir. 1986) ("chocolate fudge" generic as to diet soda) with *A.J. Canfield Co. v. Vess Beverages, Inc.,* 796 F.2d 903, 906 (7th Cir. 1986) ("chocolate fudge" descriptive as to diet soda).

4. *Genericide.* In *Stix Products, Inc. v. United Merchants & Mfrs., Inc.,* 295 F. Supp. 479 (S.D.N.Y. 1968), the plaintiff engaged in deliberative conduct to render the defendant's trademark "sterile" or generic and then sued the defendant for a declaratory judgement that its conduct did not infringe. The plaintiff had intentionally misused the word "contact" in relationship to its adhesive paper. Here, the court held that the plaintiff had only succeeded in intentionally infringing, not in making the defendant's mark generic. What if the plaintiff had been successful? Could defendant use genericism for a defense to infringement when it was the defendant's conduct, not the plaintiff's misuse of a trademark, that led to the genericism? That is, in such a circumstance, an objective survey should find the mark generic, but at whose fault? Need it be the trademark owners? Remember, in trademark law, and specifically with respect to secondary meaning, the test is not how hard a trademark owner tried, or how much money it spent, but whether its use of a mark had the effect of creating an appellation of source in the minds of the consumers. Is the

test for genericism different than this "effect" test? Should it be? *See also* Andrew Pickett, *The Death of Genericide? A Call for a Return to the Text of the Lanham Act*, 9 TUL. J. TECH. & INTELL. PROP. 329 (2007) (Some marks act as "discontinuous hybrids" by acting as a generic indicator for some and an appellation of source for others like Coke).

5. Genericism continues to haunt corporations. The marks "kettle" and "kettle chips" were recently found to be a generic indicator of a type of potato and therefore not enforceable trademarks. *See Classic Foods Intern. v. Kettle Foods, Inc.*, 468 F. Supp.2d 1181 (C.D. Cal. 2007).

6. No one is free from at least the claim that its mark has become generic. Microsoft recently succeeded in a challenge that its mark WINDOWS had been generic 20 years ago when the mark was first adopted. *See* Marc C. Levy, *From Genericism to Trademark Significance: Deconstructing the De Facto Secondary Meaning Doctrine*, 95 TRADEMARK REP. 1197 (2005).

7. Would you prefer the court look to legitimate survey evidence when consider whether a mark is generic or the "who-are-you/what-are-you" test articulated by the 9th Circuit, *supra*?

Special Note on Surveys

For lack of better evidence, surveys are now relied on to prove or disprove everything from secondary meaning, to infringement, to genericism, or, as will be developed in Chapter 11, dilution. A significant cottage industry has developed around the trademark survey. Trademark surveys are expensive. Each survey costs at least $10,000 to write, run and analyze. In addition to that, in order to be admissible, the survey is presented by the expert witness who conducted the survey. These experts are also expensive. One question that comes up is the admissibility of surveys. *See*, Robert H. Thornburg, *Trademark Survey Evidence: Review of Current Trends in the Ninth Circuit*, 21 SANTA CLARA COMPUTER & HIGH TECH. L. J. 715 (2005). That all being said, Daubert v. Merrell Dow Pharm. Inc., 509 U.S. 579 (1993) is having a negative impact on getting surveys admitted into evidence. One study shows that in an eight year period preceding 2005, almost 32% of trademark surveys were excluded by the court. Especially in a jury trial, "federal judges in Lanham Act cases are carefully weighing the admissibility of survey evidence, and the trend toward the use of motions to exclude such testimony appears to be on the increase." *See* Kenneth A. Plevan, *Daubert's Impact on Survey Experts in Lanham Act Litigation*, 95 TRADEMARK REP. 596, 600 (2005).

Schering Corp. v. Pfizer Inc.
189 F. 3d 218 (2d Cir. 1999)

* * *

II. Admissibility of Surveys in General

In the first half of this century, surveys were generally regarded as inherently untrustworthy because they contained hearsay, or out-of-court statements offered to prove the truth of the matters asserted. Schering argues, however, that "the modern view is that the hearsay objection is without merit and that any technical deficiencies in survey methodology go to [a survey's] weight as evidence, not to its admissibility." Under the "modern view," according to Schering, surveys should be admitted as a general rule, and their weight should be determined by whether: (1) the "universe" was properly defined, (2) a representative sample of that universe was selected, (3) the questions to be asked of interviewees were framed in a clear, precise and non-leading manner, (4) sound interview procedures were followed by competent interviewers who had no knowledge of the litigation or the purpose for which the survey was conducted, (5) the data gathered was accurately reported, (6) the data was analyzed in accordance with accepted statistical principles and (7) the objectivity of the entire process was ensured. These factors derive from accepted principles of survey methodology and help define when a survey has been properly conducted. There is no doubt that beginning with Judge Wilfred Feinberg's seminal decision in *Zippo Manufacturing Co. v. Rogers Imports, Inc.*, 216 F.Supp. 670 (S.D.N.Y.1963), the general trend has been toward the admission of surveys of various kinds. Surveys are, for example, routinely admitted in trademark and false advertising cases to show actual confusion, genericness of a name or secondary meaning, all of which depend on establishing that certain associations have been drawn in the public mind. Moreover, contrary to Schering's contention, the case law does not support a general rule allowing surveys into evidence for all purposes. A review of the case law suggests that there are, in fact, two ongoing controversies that tend to complicate the question of whether survey evidence should be admitted in a particular case. First, there is a dispute over the proper consequence of a finding of methodological error in a survey. While some courts in this Circuit believe such flaws are proper grounds for exclusion, others view methodological errors as affecting only the weight of the evidence. Courts have, however, rarely articulated their reasons for falling onto one or another side of this divide.

The second dispute reflected in the case law involves the proper rationale for allowing admissible surveys into evidence. As Judge Feinberg explained in *Zippo*:

> Some cases hold that surveys are not hearsay at all; other cases hold that surveys are hearsay but are admissible because they are within the recognized exception to the hearsay rule for statements of present state of mind, attitude, or belief.

216 F.Supp. at 682 We have sometimes suggested that surveys are properly admitted under the residual hearsay rule and the Advisory Committee for the Federal Rules of Evidence has suggested that surveys are sometimes best admitted as bases of expert testimony pursuant to Rule 703, *see, e.g.,* Fed. R. Evid. 703 advisory committee's note ("[Rule 703] offers a more satisfactory basis for ruling upon the admissibility of public opinion poll evidence. Attention is directed to the validity of the techniques employed rather than to relatively fruitless inquiries whether hearsay is involved."). Quite often, courts simply fail to cite a statutory basis for an admission. These confusions in the case law have led at least one prominent commentator to conclude that

> [a] skeptic would classify the survey cases into two categories: a survey is accepted and relied upon when the judge already has his or her mind made up in favor of the survey results; and a survey is rejected and torn apart when the judge subjectively disagrees with the survey results.

This skepticism is unwarranted. Because the Federal Rules of Evidence govern the admissibility of all evidence over a hearsay objection, the question of survey admissibility is ultimately a question of statutory interpretation. As shown in the following two sections, careful attention to the possible statutory grounds for admitting hearsay can help harmonize most of the caselaw. Whether the district court was correct to exclude the five surveys in this case thus merits detailed discussion, with particular attention to the types of statements contained in the surveys, the purposes for which they were offered and the various possible grounds for their admission.

III. The State of Mind Exception: Admissibility to Show What Was Implied

One of the two most common bases for admitting survey evidence is Rule 803(3), which creates an exception to the hearsay rule for statements that express a declarant's state of mind at the time of the utterance. In particular, Rule 803(3) excepts any

> statement of [a] declarant's then existing state of mind, emotion, sensation, or physical condition (such as intent, plan, motive, design, mental feeling, pain, and bodily health), but not including a statement of memory or belief to prove the fact remembered or believed unless it relates to the execution, revocation, identification, or terms of declarant's will.

Fed.R.Evid. 803(3). The great majority of surveys admitted in this Circuit, including those used in Lanham Act cases to establish actual confusion or secondary meaning, fall into this category: they poll individuals about their presently-existing states of mind to establish facts about the group's mental impressions.

It is important for district courts to recognize surveys of this type because their qualification for a traditional hearsay exception obviates the need to examine methodology before overruling a hearsay objection. Regardless of the basis cited for admitting these surveys, errors in methodology thus properly go only to the weight of the evidence—subject, of course, to Rule 403's more general prohibition against evidence that is less probative than prejudicial or confusing. The "modem view"urged by Schering is thus fully applicable to these kinds of surveys.

Schering argues that both the FasTape and Scott Levin surveys fall into this category because they asked physicians to relate the "main messages" conveyed by Zyrtec agents in the detailings. The surveys thereby asked physicians to relate not only what was said in the meetings but the impressions with which they were left. Such impressions are classic states of mind and, as such, fall under Rule 803(3).

The district court did not address directly whether these surveys polled for then-existing states of mind. Instead, the court appears to have viewed evidence of these states as irrelevant to the present litigation. The court explained:

> The Court does not fully concur with Schering's suggestion that the Court need not conclude that the surveys report "what exact words were spoken." While it may not need to know the exact words spoken, the Court must know the exact substance of what was said by the representatives to the physicians, *because it is that substance that violates, or does not violate, the settlement agreement.* To determine that substance requires an effort to determine, as closely as possible, *the exact words that were spoken.*

Schering Corp., 1999 WL 144921, at *4 n. 4 (emphasis added) (citation omitted). We disagree.

The Settlement Agreement states in relevant part that:

> Pfizer and UCB Pharma hereby agree that, in connection with their advertising and promotion of ZYRTEC in the United States, they will not claim *or allow those acting on their behalf to claim,* either expressly *or by implication* that:
>
>   (1) ZYRTEC and/or its active ingredient cetirizine is nonsedating or essentially nonsedating;

(2) ZYRTEC and/or cetirizine is as non-sedating as CLARITIN.... or is comparable to CLARITIN ... or to the "second" generation of antihistamines ... in terms of its somnolence or sedation;

(3) ZYRTEC's and/or cetirizine's discontinuance rate due to somnolence means that ZYRTEC and/or cetirizine is non-sedating or essentially non-sedating;

(4) After a short period of time, ZYRTEC and/or cetirizine users who experience sedation develop tolerance to its sedating effect.

(Settlement Agreement of 4/4/1996, at 3–4 (emphasis added)) The Settlement Agreement thus prohibits not only explicit but also implicit falsehoods. In this sense, the agreement is reminiscent of the Act upon which it was based—i.e., the Lanham Act which prohibits advertisements that are not only literally but also impliedly false.

Cases in the Lanham Act context demonstrate, moreover, that the mental impressions with which an audience is left can be relevant, and sometimes even necessary, to establish what a defendant is implying in a challenged representation. In fact, although plaintiffs seeking to establish a literal falsehood must generally show the substance of what is conveyed, we have held that a "district court *must* rely on extrinsic evidence to support a finding of an implicitly false message." *See Johnson & Johnson * Merck Consumer Pharms. Co. v. Smithkline Beecham Corp.*, 960 F.2d 294, 297 (2d Cir.1992) (emphasis added). This is because plaintiffs alleging a literal falsehood are claiming that a statement, on its face, conflicts with reality, a claim that is best supported by comparing the statement itself with the reality it purports to describe. By contrast, plaintiffs alleging an implied falsehood are claiming that a statement, whatever its literal truth, has left an impression on the listener that conflicts with reality. This latter claim invites a comparison of the impression, rather than the statement, with the truth. *See generally* Jacob Jacoby et al., Survey Evidence in Deceptive Advertising Cases Under the Lanham Act: An Historical Review of Comments from the Bench, 954 PLI/Corp. 83, 87–88 (1996). Given this distinction in the false advertising context, we see no reason to believe that Schering's allegations of breach of the Settlement Agreement by implied falsehood cannot similarly be tested by this type of evidence. Moreover, Schering rested its argument for a preliminary injunction not only on alleged breaches of the Settlement Agreement but also on alleged violations of the Lanham Act.

These considerations persuade us that the FasTape and Scott Levin surveys are relevant to show ongoing violations of both the Settlement Agreement and the Lanham Act, on a theory that Zyrtec agents were making statements that regardless of their veracity, left the physicians with false impressions. Although statements by out-of-court declarants— e.g., the surveyed physicians—relating such impressions are hearsay where, as here, they are offered to establish the existence of the impressions themselves, *see* Fed.R.Evid. 801(c), these declarations are independently admissible under Rule 803(3) as expressions of the declarant physicians' then-existing states of mind. The district court should have thus admitted the FastTape and Scott Levin surveys for the limited purpose of establishing a pattern of implied falsehood.

This ruling concerning admissibility in no way suggests that the district court should give these surveys any particular weight on remand. The fact that the two surveys corroborate one another is certainly a point in their favor, as is the fact that Schering produced independent evidence of Pfizer training manuals, which appear to have recommended misleading promotional practices. Still, Pfizer has offered a series of criticisms concerning the surveys' methodologies and the potentially leading or ambiguous nature of the questions they posed. Schering also has failed to bring even a small subset of the surveyed physicians into court, a process that would have allowed for their cross-examination and would have greatly assisted the court in determining what weight to give the surveys overall. Finally, Pfizer has argued that the FDA does not draw a sharp distinction between "sedating" and "nonsedating" antihistamines, and that Schering fabricated this distinction to generate surveys that would indicate falsehoods when there were none. We therefore leave it to the district court to assess the weight of all the evidence admitted after making more detailed factual findings concerning these and related issues.

IV. The Residual Hearsay Rule: Admissibility to Show What Was Said

The central reason that Schering sought to introduce its five surveys was to establish not that Zyrtec representatives were leaving physicians with false impressions but that the representatives were stating literal falsehoods in violation of the Lanham Act and the Settlement Agreement. Used for this purpose, the surveys can still be characterized as polling then-existing states of mind because they asked the physicians to relate memories of statements made in the detailings, or beliefs about what the sales representatives had said, both of which are technically states of mind. If statements expressing such states are offered to establish not only that the states existed, however, but also the facts thereby recalled or believed, the statements are no longer simply expressions of mental state. In fact, Rule 803(3) explicitly excludes from its purview any "statement of memory or belief to prove the fact[s] remembered or believed." Fed.R.Evid. 803(3). The district court thus correctly refused to admit Schering's surveys under the present state-of-mind exception to establish what Zyrtec agents were literally saying in their promotional activities.

Schering has, however, cited a second common basis for admitting the survey for this purpose: the residual hearsay rule. This rule, presently codified at Rule 807 of the Federal Rules of Evidence, states that:

> A statement not specifically covered by Rule 803 or 804 but having *equivalent circumstantial guarantees of trustworthiness,* is not excluded by the hearsay rule, if the court determines that (A) the statement is offered as evidence of a material fact; (B) the statement is more probative on the point for which it is offered than any other evidence which the proponent can procure through reasonable efforts; and (C) the general purposes of these rules and the interests of justice will best be served by admission of the statement into evidence. However, a statement may not be admitted under this exception unless the proponent of it makes known to the adverse party sufficiently in advance of the trial or hearing to provide the adverse party with a fair opportunity to prepare to meet it, the proponent's intention to offer the statement and the particulars of it, including the name and address of the declarant.

Fed.R.Evid. 807 (emphasis added). "To be admissible under this exception, 'the evidence must [, in other words,] fulfill five requirements: trustworthiness, materiality, probative importance, the interests of justice and notice.'" *United States v. Harwood,* 998 F.2d 91, 98 (2d Cir.1993) (quoting *Parsons v. Honeywell, Inc.,* 929 F.2d 901, 907 (2d Cir.1991) (citations omitted)).

The district court found Schering's surveys inadmissible under the residual hearsay rule to show what Zyrtec representatives were literally saying on three independent grounds: (i) the survey shad insufficient circumstantial guarantees of trustworthiness; (ii) they were not more probative to show what was said in the detailings than any other evidence that Schering could procure through reasonable efforts; and (iii) the general purposes of the Federal Rules of Evidence and the interests of justice would not be best served by admitting the surveys. Schering argues that in reaching each of these conclusions, the district court abused its discretion by relying on an erroneous *per se* rule against the use of out-of-court memory statements to prove the facts remembered. We agree.

i. Trustworthiness of the Surveys

In deciding that the surveys did not have sufficient guarantees of trustworthiness under the residual hearsay rule to help establish what Zyrtec agents were saying, the district court relied heavily on the same fact that made Rule 803(3) inapplicable for this purpose: the surveys elicited memory statements offered to establish the occurrence of the remembered events. The court explained that

> [a]fter speaking of the [Residual Hearsay] Rule's "theory that under appropriate circumstances a hearsay statement may possess circumstantial guarantees of trustworthiness sufficient to justify nonproduction of the declarant in person at the trial even though he may be available," a theory which "finds vast support in the many exceptions to the hearsay rule…," *the [Advisory] Committee went on to say of Rule 803(3)—the closest analogy to the present situation—that "[t]he exclusion of 'statements of memory or belief to prove the fact remembered or believed' is necessary to avoid the virtual destruction of the hearsay rule* which would otherwise result from allowing a state of mind, provable by a hearsay statement, to serve as the basis for an inference of the happening of the event which produced the state of mind."

Schering, 1999 WL 144921, at *4 (emphasis added) (citations omitted). The court thus drew an explicit analogy between the analyses of memory statements under Rule 803(3) and under the residual hearsay rule.

It is, however, incorrect to project this Rule 803(3) limitation into the residual hearsay rule context. Unlike Rule 803(3), which explicitly excludes from its purview memory statements offered to establish the facts remembered, the residual hearsay rule contains no such express limitation. There is a reason for this difference. Almost any statement used to describe events that a speaker has experienced in the past can be characterized as a "memory," which is a presently-existing state of mind when it is conveyed. If such statements were admissible under Rule 803(3) to prove the facts remembered, parties could thus offer hearsay to establish almost any past fact, a result that would indeed mark "the virtual destruction of the hearsay rule." Fed.R.Evid. 803(3) advisory committee's note. The residual hearsay rule, by contrast, escapes this problem by setting forth its own set of requirements, which include necessity and trustworthiness, before it will allow for a statement's admission. These requirements independently ensure that the rule will "be used very rarely, and only in exceptional circumstances." S.Rep. No. 93-1277, at 36 (1974), *reprinted in* 1974 U.S.C.C.A.N.7051, 7062 (quoted with approval in *United States v. Mahler,* 579 F.2d 730, 736 (2d Cir.1978)). Moreover, by allowing for the admission of memory surveys under the residual hearsay rule only when they would be independently admissible under Rule 803(3), the district court effectively read the residual hearsay rule as incompetent to perform any independent work in these circumstances. As Judge Feinberg explained in *Zippo,* however, surveys can be admitted at times even if they do "not fit within th[e] [present state of mind] exception," based upon "the need for the statement at trial and the circumstantial guaranty of trustworthiness surrounding the making of the statement." 216 F.Supp. at 683. The district court thus erred by relying on a *per se* rule against the trustworthiness of memory surveys.

A close examination of the function of the hearsay rule will illuminate the criterion of trustworthiness that the district court should have employed. The hearsay rule is generally said to exclude out-of-court statements offered for the truth of the matter asserted because there are four classes of risk peculiar to this kind of evidence: those of (1) insincerity, (2) faulty perception, (3) faulty memory and (4) faulty narration, each of which decreases the reliability of the inference from the statement made to the conclusion for which it is offered.

The traditional exceptions to the hearsay rule, in turn, provide the benchmark against which the trustworthiness of evidence must be compared in a residual hearsay analysis. *See* Fed.R.Evid. 807 (allowing for admission of hearsay statements not specifically covered by Rules 803 or 804 but having, among other things, "equivalent circumstantial guarantees of trustworthiness"). It is thus important to recognize that the trustworthiness of these exceptions is a function of their ability to minimize some of the four classic hearsay dangers. Statements based on present sense impressions, for example, do not suffer from the risk of faulty memory because they are made at or near the time of impression. These statements also express knowledge based on direct sensory perception. The Federal Rules of Evidence thus make an exception to the hearsay rule for "statement[s] describing or explaining an event or condition made while the declarant was perceiving the event or condition, or immediately thereafter." Fed.R.Evid. 803(1). Similarly, statements falling under Rule 803(3)'s exception for presently-existing states of mind rarely suffer from the risks of faulty memory because they are made when the declarant is in the relevant state, and they bear minimal risk of faulty perception because speakers generally know their own states of mind. Although both of these kinds of statement can suffer from the remaining risks of insincerity and faulty narration, exceptions to the hearsay rule are made for them on "the theory that ... [the statements] possess circumstantial guarantees of trustworthiness sufficient to justify nonproduction of the declarant in person at the trial even though he may be available." Fed.R.Evid. 803 advisory committee's note. It follows that a hearsay statement need not be free from all four categories of risk to be admitted under Rule 807.

Courts deciding whether evidence is sufficiently trustworthy to be admitted under the residual hearsay rule should therefore be aware of these facts and of the relative degree to which the evidence offered is prone to risks like those under discussion. Survey evidence, for example, is susceptible not only to all four classic hearsay dangers but also to an additional class of risk arising from the fact that parties usually offer surveys to support statistical inferences. These inferences can be subject to methodological error and can sometimes be manipulated through artful data collection or presentation.

Proper survey methodology can, however, help ensure the reliability of the statistical inferences for which a survey is offered. Proper survey methodology can also help reduce two of the four classic hearsay dangers. In particular, the risk of insincerity can ordinarily be reduced if the interviewers and those questioned lack knowledge of the litigation and the purpose of the survey. Similarly, surveyors can reduce the risk of faulty narration by framing questions in a clear, precise and non-leading manner. The only risks that proper survey methodology does not tend to mitigate are those of faulty memory and perception. Still, a particular memory survey, which, for example, relates to events that were learned by direct perception and are unlikely to be forgotten, can, if properly conducted, minimize all five of the classes of risks ordinarily associated with survey evidence. Memory surveys can thus, in principle, have even greater circumstantial guarantees of trustworthiness than many of the traditional exceptions to the hearsay rule.

Because the residual hearsay rule requires an initial trustworthiness determination before it will allow for the admission of evidence, all of these considerations, including those of in methodology, will affect not only the weight but also the admissibility of surveys offered in the present circumstances, i.e., when none of the other traditional hearsay exceptions apply. Contrary to Schering's position, courts deciding whether to admit surveys in these circumstances should therefore examine their trustworthiness—and ultimately their weight, if admitted—both in terms of their methodological strengths and in terms of their proneness to faulty memory and perception. A review of the case law suggests that this totality of factors has in fact come into play when determining the use of such surveys.

Thus, in *Keith*, 858 F.2d at 467, the Ninth Circuit affirmed a district court's decision to admit a survey that asked respondents about their race, income and housing preferences. In determining that the survey was trustworthy, the court examined the survey's methodology and never explicitly mentioned the risks of faulty memory or perception. Statements concerning a declarant's race and income are, however, relatively unsusceptible to these two classes of risk, and this fact may have had some bearing on the outcome.

In the present case, the district court did not make any findings concerning the surveys' methodological strengths or weaknesses. Instead, it rejected them on the ground that the surveys seek to recover, from the physicians' memories, what the Pfizer or UCB representatives said to them, during a very brief personal interchange, thus interjecting a layer of uncertainty, because either of understandable inattention or distraction during that interchange or faulty memory [that is not present in state-of-mind surveys].

Four of the five surveys in this case were, however, performed within a day of the detailings, and the remaining one was performed within a week. Additionally, because the record shows that somnolence level was a critical factor in deciding whether to prescribe antihistamines, the physicians polled presumably would have been poised to look for and remember this type of information in a detailing.

ii. Necessity of the Surveys

The district court's second ground for refusing to admit the five surveys under the residual hearsay rule was based on its finding that the surveys were not "more probative on the point for which [they were] offered than any other evidence which [Schering could] procure through reasonable efforts." Fed.R.Evid. 807(B). In this case, Schering introduced its five surveys, which polled a total of approximately 1166 physicians, to establish statistical facts about what Zyrtec representatives were saying to a much larger group of almost 250,000 physicians nationwide. These facts were relevant to establish the type of irreparable injury necessary for a preliminary injunction.

Rule 807(B)'s so-called "necessity" criterion nevertheless requires courts to compare the reliability, or trustworthiness, of a survey with that of other evidence that a proponent might reasonably obtain to establish the same fact. The district court's erroneous belief that memory surveys are *per se* untrustworthy thus logically compelled its finding that the survey evidence in this case was unnecessary. For these reasons, we vacate this finding as an abuse of discretion and remand for reevaluation on the basis of the considerations set forth in this opinion.

Perhaps because the court deemed the surveys *per se* unreliable, it did not rule conclusively as to whether any reasonable alternatives to the survey evidence were available in this case. The court did, however, note "without passing on" three possibilities:

[1] the availability of depositions by telephone, which would minimize inconvenience to the physicians, [2] the fact that the inquiry could reasonably be limited to the physician's recollection of what was said to him during a very brief and recent detailing, and [3] the apparent probability that a scientifically constructed random sample of a much smaller number of persons than 1166, if they could be cross-examined, would be more reliable, i.e.,would have greater circumstantial guarantees of trustworthiness, than hearsay.

Schering, 1999 WL 144921, at *5 (citation omitted). We briefly address these possibilities here because the foregoing analysis is likely to be revisited on remand.

First, although parties can indeed consent to depositions by telephone, the use of deposition testimony would most likely suffer from some of the risks of statistical error that proper survey methodology can help to avoid. In *Zippo,* Judge Feinberg thus noted that:

[t]he alternatives of having a much smaller section of the public testify … or using expert witnesses to testify … are clearly not as valuable because the inferences which can be drawn from such testimony to [the statistical facts sought to be proven] are not as strong or as direct as the justifiable inferences from a scientific survey.

216 F.Supp. at 684. Second, in recommending that Schering obtain evidence limited to a "physician's recollection of what was said to him during a very brief and recent detailing," the district court ignored the fact that most of the surveys were conducted within a day, and one within a week, of these meetings. The district court's criticisms would thus seem inapplicable to many, if not all, of these surveys.

Finally, we are skeptical of the court's suggestion that a smaller number of physicians, if subjected to cross-examination, might be used to prove the same statistical points for which the surveys were offered. To make the alternative of summoning a reduced number of physicians into court reasonable, this number would have to be much smaller than 1166. It is difficult to see how such a small sample would provide more reliable evidence than the surveys, particularly when is not at all clear that the surveys were untrustworthy to begin with in ways that cross-examination could have cured. Assuming the surveys were trustworthy enough to be admitted under the residual hearsay rule, we therefore find nothing in the record to suggest that this evidence was any less necessary than in cases where surveys have been admitted.

iii. General Interests of Justice

The third ground that the district court cited for refusing to admit the five surveys under the residual hearsay rule was that "the general purposes of [the Federal Rules of Evidence] and the interests of justice [would not] best be served by admission of the [physicians'] statement[s] into evidence." Fed.R.Evid. 807(C). In explaining this finding, the court said:

[A]dmission of [Schering's] surveys to prove what was said to the physicians by the Pfizer and UCB representatives would, in the Advisory Committee's phrase, be a step toward "the virtual destruction of the hearsay rule." Such a precedent could well lead towards a rule that the admissibility of hearsay evidence turns on the proponent's convenience, or, perhaps, business sensibilities.

Schering Corp., 1999 WL 144921, at *5 (citation and footnote omitted). As this quotation shows, this finding, like the others, rested on a *per se* rule against admission of memory statements. We have, however, rejected this rule as erroneous.

It is worth noting that we have often admitted surveys that are relevant to prove material facts under the residual hearsay rule on the basis simply of their "need … plus adequate guarantees of trustworthiness." *Grotrian,* 523 F.2d at 1341 (noting that surveys are sometimes admitted on this basis). In the context of survey evidence, the interests of justice and the general purposes of the rules of evidence are generally best served by the admission of surveys that meet these two criteria. We therefore vacate and remand for reconsideration of the interest-of-justice finding following reconsideration of necessity and trustworthiness.

V. The Party Admission Theory: Admissibility of the Gengler Analysis and FasTape Survey

Schering argues that the district court should have admitted the FasTape Survey, which Pfizer commissioned, and Pfizer's internal analysis and summary of this survey (the "Gengler Analysis") as party admissions under Rule 801(d)(2). We agree.

Rule 801(d)(2) excludes from the definition of hearsay any statement that is offered against a party and is (A) the party's own statement, in either an individual or a representative capacity or (B) a statement of which the party has manifested an adoption or belief in its truth, or (C) a statement by a person authorized by the party to make a statement concerning the subject, or (D) a statement by the party's agent or servant concerning a matter within the scope of the agency or employment, made during the existence of the relationship…. Fed.R.Evid. 801(d)(2). "Admissions by a party opponent are excluded from the category of hearsay on the theory that their admissibility in evidence is the result of the adversary system, rather than satisfaction of the conditions of the hearsay rule." Fed.R.Evid. 801(d)(2) advisory committee's note (citing Edmund M. Morgan, *Basic Problems of Evidence* 265 (1962). The Advisory Committee thus recommends "generous treatment of this avenue to admissibility." *Id.*

In the present case, the district court viewed the Gengler analysis as "no more than a convenient summary of the research, not representing a conclusion by Pfizer." *Schering,* 1999 WL144921, at *7. The Gengler Analysis stated, however, that

> [flour of the top 5 messages communicated to physicians for Zyrtec are completely appropriate and relevant…. The fifth and less appropriate message *being communicated by Zyrtec representatives* concerns their claim of Zyrtec causing little or no sedation to allergic rhinitis patients. (Emphasis added).

To be able to state generally that a message is "being communicated by Zyrtec representatives" on the basis of the small number of prior statements recorded in the FasTape Survey, Gengler had to believe that this data could support an inductive inference that Zyrtec's message was being communicated more broadly. This belief in turn required reliance on the trustworthiness of the physicians' statements and on the survey methodology itself. By making this inference, Gengler thus manifested a belief in the trustworthiness of both and conceded the survey's reliability. In fact, Gengler specifically approved the FasTape Survey's methodology before the research was performed. *Pekelis* controls in these circumstances, and both the Gengler Analysis and the FasTape Survey are admissible over a hearsay objection.

CONCLUSION

For the foregoing reasons, we vacate the district court's rulings excluding the five surveys in this case. We hold that the Scott Levin Survey is admissible over a hearsay objection under Rule803(3) for the limited purpose of showing what Zyrtec representatives were implying in the detailings. We hold that the FasTape Survey is admissible both to show these implications under Rule 803(3), and as a party admission under Rule 801(d)(2) to show what the representatives were actually saying. We remand to the district court for further proceedings to determine whether any of the surveys are sufficiently trustworthy and necessary to be admitted under Rule 807 to show literal falsehoods in violation of the Settlement Agreement and Section 43(a)(2) of the Lanham Act. We express no opinion, however, as to whether there are any other grounds for excluding the above evidence, and we leave it to the district court to determine what weight to give all of the evidence admitted on remand.

B. Abandonment

1. Non-Use

Silverman v. CBS, Inc.
870 F.2d 40 (2d Cir. 1989)

NEWMAN, CIRCUIT JUDGE.

This appeal presents somewhat novel issues of both copyright and trademark law arising from the efforts of appellant Stephen M. Silverman to develop a musical based on the "Amos Andy" characters. The attempt to transport Amos, Andy, Kingfish, Algonquin J. Calhoun, and all the others from the well-known radio and television shows of earlier decades to Broadway (possibly in a cab of the Fresh Air Taxi Co.) has thus far been stymied by the assertion of copyright and trademark infringement claims by appellee CBS Inc. Silverman appeals from a judgment of the District Court for the Southern District of New York (Gerard L. Goettel, Judge) awarding CBS damages, declaratory relief, and an injunction. Because some "Amos Andy" materials are in the public domain while others remain subject to CBS copyrights, and because CBS has elected not to make commercial use of its "Amos 'n' Andy" radio and television programs, nor create new ones, since 1966, the issues primarily raised on this appeal are the extent of copyright protection available to CBS with respect to the "Amos 'n' Andy" characters and whether CBS has abandoned through non-use whatever trademarks it might have. We conclude that to a limited extent copyright infringement has occurred, that the declaratory and injunctive relief awarded CBS should be modified to avoid extension of copyright protection to public domain materials, that Silverman is entitled to limited declaratory relief, and that CBS's trademarks, if valid, have been abandoned.

Facts

The "Amos 'n' Andy" characters were created in 1928 by Freeman F. Gosden and Charles J. Correll, who wrote and produced for radio broadcasting "The Amos 'n' Andy Show." The show became one of the country's most popular radio programs. The characters in the Amos 'n' Andy programs were Black. Gosden and Correll, who were White, portrayed Amos and Andy on radio. The authors appeared in blackface in publicity photos. Black actors played the parts in the subsequent television programs.

Gosden and Correll assigned all of their rights in the "Amos 'n' Andy Show" scripts and radio programs to CBS Inc. in 1948. Gosden and Correll continued to create new

"Amos 'n' Andy" scripts, which formed the basis for CBS radio programs. The radio programs continued until 1955. Beginning in 1951 CBS also broadcast an "Amos 'n' Andy" television series. The television series was aired on CBS affiliate stations until 1953 and continued in reruns and non-network syndication until 1966. CBS has not aired or licensed for airing any of the radio or television programs since 1966.

In 1981, Silverman began writing a script for a Broadway musical based on the "Amos 'n' Andy" characters. The title of this work was originally "Amos 'n' Andy Go To The Movies." A revision was titled "Amos 'n' Andy In Hollywood," and a more extensive revision was titled "Fresh Air Taxi." Silverman sought a license to use the "Amos 'n' Andy" characters, but CBS refused.

Silverman filed this lawsuit seeking a declaration that the "Amos Andy" radio programs broadcast from March 1928 through March 1948 (the "pre-1948 radio programs") are in the public domain and that he is therefore free to make use of the content of the programs, including the characters, character names, and plots. He also sought a declaration that CBS has no rights in these programs under any body of law, including statutory and common law copyright law and trademark law. CBS asserted five counterclaims: (1) that Silverman's scripts infringed CBS's copyrights in the scripts for three post-1948 radio programs; (2) that the Silverman scripts violated section 43(a) of the Lanham Act, 15 U.S.C. §1125(a) (1982), by infringing various CBS trademarks, including "AMOS 'N' ANDY", the names of various characters such as "George ('Kingfish') Stevens," "Madame Queen," and "Lightnin'," and various phrases such as "Scuse me for protruding," "splaindat," and "Holy mackral" (perhaps Amos's best-known contribution to the language); (3) that the infringement of CBS's trademarks also violated CBS's rights under state unfair competition and anti-dilution law; (4) that Silverman had misappropriated CBS's goodwill associated with the "Amos 'n' Andy" programs and trademarks; and (5) that Silverman had obtained improper copyright registration of his first movie script, claiming it to be an original work, whereas it used protected material from scripts in which CBS held copyrights.

* * *

On the trademark side of the case, Judge Goettel ruled that the name "Amos 'n' Andy," as well as the names and appearances of "Amos 'n' Andy" characters and "other distinctive features of the ... radio and television shows" are protectable marks. *Id.* at 1356. He then set down for trial the issue of whether CBS's non-use of the marks constituted abandonment. Finally, he ruled that the issue of trademark infringement, as well as the related issues of unfair competition and dilution, were premature in the absence of a staging of Silverman's musical. *Id.* at 1357–58.

After a bench trial on the issue of abandonment, Judge Goettel concluded that CBS had not abandoned its trademarks.

Discussion

We consider first the trademark side of this case because our conclusion on the trademark issues significantly alters the context in which the copyright issues arise.

1. *Trademark Issues.* Silverman challenges the District Court's rulings that CBS has protectable trademarks in the "Amos Andy" names, characters, and other features of the radio and television programs, including phrases of dialogue, and that CBS has not abandoned these marks. We find it unnecessary to decide which features of the programs might give rise to protectable marks because we agree with Silverman that CBS has abandoned the marks.

Section 45 of the Lanham Act provides:

A mark shall be deemed to be "abandoned" —

(a) When its use has been discontinued with intent not to resume. Intent not to resume maybe inferred from circumstances. Nonuse for two[2] consecutive years shall be prima facie abandonment.

15 U.S.C. §1127 (1982). There are thus two elements for abandonment: (1) non-use and (2) intent not to resume use. Two years of non-use creates a rebuttable presumption of abandonment.

On the undisputed facts of this case, CBS made a considered decision to take the "Amos 'n' Andy" television programs off the air. It took this action in response to complaints by civil rights organizations, including the NAACP, that the programs were demeaning to Blacks. By the time the abandonment issue came before the District Court, non-use of the AMOS 'N' ANDY marks had continued for 21 years. Although CBS has no current plans to use the marks within the foreseeable future, CBS asserts that it has always intended to resume using them at some point in the future, should the social climate become more hospitable.

Ordinarily, 21 years of non-use would easily surpass the non-use requirement for finding abandonment. The District Court concluded, however, that CBS had successfully rebutted the presumption of abandonment arising from its prolonged non-use by offering a reasonable explanation for its decision to keep the programs off the air and by asserting its intention to resume use at some indefinite point in the future. This conclusion raises a question as to the proper interpretation of the statutory phrase "intent not to resume": Does the phrase mean intent *never* to resume use or does it merely mean intent not to resume use within the reasonably foreseeable future?

We conclude that the latter must be the case. The statute provides that intent not to resume may be inferred from circumstances, and two consecutive years of non-use is prima facie abandonment. Time is thereby made relevant. Indeed, if the relevant intent were intent never to resume use, it would be virtually impossible to establish such intent circumstantially. Even after prolonged non-use, and without any concrete plans to resume use, a company could almost always assert truthfully that at some point, should conditions change, it would resume use of its mark.

We do not think Congress contemplated such an unworkable standard. More likely, Congress wanted a mark to be deemed abandoned once use has been discontinued with an intent not to resume within the reasonably foreseeable future. This standard is sufficient to protect against the forfeiture of marks by proprietors who are temporarily unable to continue using them, while it also prevents warehousing of marks, which impedes commerce and competition.

We are buttressed in this conclusion by the fact that the statute requires proof of "intent not to resume," rather than "intent to abandon." The statute thus creates no state of mind element concerning the ultimate issue of abandonment. On the contrary, it avoids a subjective inquiry on this ultimate question by setting forth the circumstances under which a mark shall be "deemed" to be abandoned. Of course, one of those circumstances is intent not to resume use, which is a matter of subjective inquiry. But we think the provi-

---

2. [Editor's Note: On January 2, 1996, as a result of the TRIPS Agreement, this section of the Lanham Act was amended to read three, rather than two, years.]

sion, by introducing the two concepts of "deemed" abandonment and intent not to resume use, contemplates a distinction, and it is a distinction that turns at least in part on duration of the contemplated non-use.

Congress's choice of wording appears to have been deliberate. One early version of what became section 45 of the Lanham Act had provided that "intent to *abandon* may be inferred from the circumstances." H.R. Rep. 4744, 76th Cong., 1st Sess. (1939) (emphasis added). However, shortly thereafter a new bill modified this phrase by substituting "intent not to resume" for "intent to abandon." H.R. Rep. 6618, 76th Cong., 1st Sess. (1939). Though it has been suggested that the phrases are interchangeable, *see* Note, 56 Fordham L. Rev. 1003, 1020 n. 113 (1988), we agree with the Fifth Circuit that the phrases are better understood as having distinct meanings. We think that Congress, by speaking of "intent not to resume" rather than "intent to abandon" in this section of the Act meant to avoid the implication that intent never to resume use must be shown.

A proprietor who temporarily suspends use of a mark can rebut the presumption of abandonment by showing reasonable grounds for the suspension and plans to resume use in the reasonably foreseeable future when the conditions requiring suspension abate. But a proprietor may not protect a mark if he discontinues using it for more than 20 years and has no plans to use or permit its use in the reasonably foreseeable future. A bare assertion of possible future use is not enough.

We recognize the point, forcefully made by Judge Goettel, when he wrote:

> It would be offensive to basic precepts of fairness and justice to penalize CBS, by stripping it of its trademark rights, merely because it succumbed to societal pressures and pursued a course of conduct that it reasonably believes to be in the best interests of the community.

Silverman II, 666 F. Supp. at 581. Nonetheless, we believe that however laudable one might think CBS's motives to be, such motives cannot overcome the undisputed facts that CBS has not used its marks for more than 20 years and that, even now, it has no plans to resume their use in the reasonably foreseeable future. Though we agree with Judge Goettel that CBS should not be penalized for its worthy motive, we cannot adjust the statutory test of abandonment to reward CBS for such motive by according it protection where its own voluntary actions demonstrate that statutory protection has ceased. Moreover, we see nothing in the statute that makes the consequence of an intent not to resume use turn on the worthiness of the motive for holding such intent.

We are also mindful of the facts, relied on by the District Court, that show some minor activities by CBS regarding its properties, allegedly sufficient to rebut abandonment of the marks. These are CBS's actions in licensing the programs for limited use in connection with documentary and educational programs, challenging infringing uses brought to its attention, renewing its copyrights, and periodically reconsidering whether to resume use of the programs. But challenging infringing uses is not use, and sporadic licensing for essentially non-commercial uses of a mark is not sufficient use to forestall abandonment. Such uses do not sufficiently rekindle the public's identification of the mark with the proprietor, which is the essential condition for trademark protection, nor do they establish an intent to resume commercial use. CBS's minor activities, like worthy motives for non-use, cannot dispel the legal consequence of prolonged non-use coupled with an intent not to resume use in the reasonably foreseeable future.

Affirmed in part, vacated in part, and remanded. No costs.

———————

University Bookstore v. Wisconsin Board of Regents

33 U.S.P.Q. 2d 1385 (TTAB 1994)

HOHEIN, ADMINISTRATIVE TRADEMARK JUDGE

[The University of Wisconsin applied to register WISCONSIN BADGER and designs of the University mascot. A local bookstore in Madison, Wisconsin, opposed the registration, claiming that the University had abandoned the mark by failing to control the use and quality of the mark by numerous third parties. The bookstore even took credit for the creation of "Bucky" the Badger mascot. The TTAB rejected the opposition, held for the University.]

ABANDONMENT

Turning first to the claim of abandonment, since it is the ground common to all six oppositions, opposers essentially contend that whatever ownership interests, if any, applicant may be said to have had in the "Bucky Badger," "Bucky on W" and "WISCONSIN BADGERS" marks, such rights have been lost by applicant's failure over many years prior to January 1988 to control the nature and quality of numerous third-party uses of the marks. Applicant, while not disputing opposers' assertion that it did not actually create the marks in issue, argues that the purchasing public regards the marks as having originated with applicant inasmuch as it has adopted and continuously used them as indicia of source or origin for its goods and services. Although opposers, in particular, point to statements made prior to January 1988 by certain personnel of applicant that the marks were in the public domain and therefore were free to be used by anyone, applicant maintains that such statements, which involved only a relatively few isolated incidents, were in error and that circumstances, including its course of conduct over the years, have served to preserve the source-indicating function of each of the marks as that of signifying applicant.

As explained by Judge Nies in *Wallpaper Manufacturers, Ltd. v. Crown Wallcovering Corp.*, 680 F.2d 755, 214 U.S.P.Q. 327, 333 (CCPA 1982), maintenance of exclusivity of rights in a mark is not required in order to avoid a finding of abandonment, since "[flew longstanding trademarks could survive so rigid a standard]". Instead, so long as at least some members of the purchasing public identify applicant with each of the marks at issue, it cannot be said that applicant's course of conduct has caused any of such marks to lose its significance as a mark. 214 U.S.P.Q. at 335. In this case, as in Crown, it is necessary to remember that *(emphasis by the court)*:

> [There is a] distinction between conduct of a trademark owner which results in a loss of right to enjoin a particular use because of an affirmative *defense* available to that user and conduct which results in the loss of *all* rights of protection as a mark against use by anyone. Only when all rights of protection are extinguished is there abandonment. E. Vandenburgh, Trademark Law and Procedure 267—68 (2d Ed. 1968). While this states only a conclusion without any guides as to when all rights are deemed to have been lost, it is helpful, nevertheless, to keep the distinction in mind.

Id.

Thus, under Crown, whether any of the opposers has a right to continue to use any of the marks applicant seeks to register is not determinative of the question of abandonment; rather, the focus must be on what rights, if any, applicant has in the marks. *Id.* Moreover, as emphasized in Crown, "a mark becomes abandoned only when the mark loses its significance as an indication of origin, not the sole identification of source". 214 U.S.P.Q. at 336. Stated otherwise, in light of the pertinent change in statutory language made by the Trademark Law Revision Act of 1988, abandonment occurs only when a mark loses its significance as a mark. The court recognized, however, with respect to the obligation to police a mark, that *(footnotes omitted)*:

> Without question, distinctiveness can be lost by failing to take action against infringers. If there are numerous products in the marketplace bearing the alleged mark, purchasers may learn to ignore the "mark" as a source indication. When that occurs, the conduct of the former owner, by failing to police its mark, can be said to have caused the mark to lose its significance as a mark. However, an owner is not required to act immediately against every possibly infringing use to avoid a holding of abandonment. Such a requirement would unnecessarily clutter the courts. Some infringements are short-lived and will disappear without action by the trademark owner.... Other infringements may be characterized as "creeping," starting as a business name, and only become serious when later use is as a trademark....

214 U.S.P.Q. at 336.

Accordingly, applying the relevant law to the material facts not genuinely in dispute, we find that applicant has not abandoned the marks which it seeks to register. By way of background, it is clear that the "Bucky Badger" figure was created in 1940 by Arthur C. Evans, an artist with the firm then known as the Anson W. Thompson Company, which was requested by Brown's to produce, for sale by Brown's, a sheet of decals which included mascots designed and intended to represent applicant. Decals were then a very popular item with college students and the particular set commissioned by Brown's, which is reproduced below in reduced size, included the drawing of a belligerent "Bucky Badger" — standing upright with chest thrust outward, wearing a ribbed letterman's *W* sweater and boxing gloves, and featuring a determined upright stance, a no-nonsense stride and, perhaps most notably, a scowling facial expression — which became the standard representation:

Picture 9.2   "Bucky Badger"
Copyright University of Wisconsin-Madison.

Brown's has continuously sold decals depicting "Bucky" since 1940 and, later on, UBS likewise sold a version of such decals. Applicant's earliest use of the "Bucky Badger" figure it seeks to register occurred in 1948, when "Bucky" appeared on the front cover of the University's 1948 FOOTBALL FACTS AND CENTENNIAL SPORTS REVIEW. Although the "Bucky Badger" figure also eventually came to signify applicant's educational services, the earliest documented use of "Bucky" in such capacity is an appearance on the front cover of a 1957–58 Freshman Course Guide, which was edited by the Curriculum Committee of the University's student association and was published through the courtesy of the University Co-op, as UBS (which changed its name in 1964) was then known. Insofar as use of the "Bucky Badger" mascot on clothing is concerned, both UBS and Brown's were selling apparel which was so imprinted by the early 1950s and have continued to do so along with many other members of WMF. Marketing of such clothing by applicant did not occur until, at the earliest, sometime in 1983. With respect to use of the "Bucky on IV" mark, the record reveals that Brown's sold clothing imprinted therewith during the 1950s and continued to do so through the 1960s. Other members of WMF, but not UBS, have also sold T-shirts, sweatshirts and/or caps imprinted with the "Bucky on W" mark. Actual use thereof by applicant, for both imprinted clothing and its athletic entertainment services, first occurred about 1983 as a variation of its licensed athletic department logo. As to the"WISCONSIN BADGERS" mark, it is plain from the record that the words "BADGER" and "BADGERS" have long been associated with applicant. For example, the former word has been continuously used as the title of the University's yearbook since about 1889 and the latter term has been continuously used, first in reference to applicant's football team and later to refer as well to its other athletic teams, since 1893. While the phrase "WISCONSIN BADGERS" has long been used as a nickname for applicant's athletic teams and their fans, including members of the student body and faculty involved with the University's educational services, the earliest documented reference to applicant's athletic teams as the "WISCONSIN BADGERS" appears in a 1945 newspaper article. By the late 1980s, such usage was quite prevalent. The record further discloses that Brown's, since as early as 1955, and UBS, since the early 1960s, have continuously sold clothing bearing the mark "WISCONSIN BADGERS" and that third parties, including certain other members of WMF, have sold and/or continue to sell such imprinted apparel during the period from 1945 to the present. By contrast, it was not until the early 1980s that applicant itself first made actual use of the "WISCONSIN BADGERS" mark on imprinted clothing.

While opposers are consequently correct that in most instances, applicant has not been the first user of the subject marks for the goods and services for which registration is sought, it is critical to keep in mind that none of the opposers, or any third party, has ever used such marks as its own mark to identify and distinguish the particular goods and services involved in these proceedings. Opposers have admitted, in their responses to applicant's requests for admissions, that they have never made use of the marks applicant seeks to register as their marks. Instead, it is manifest from the record that opposers, and third parties alike, have merely sold and occasionally advertised items of apparel and other merchandise which have been imprinted with the marks.

Such sales and advertising by opposers and various third parties for many years prior to applicant's institution of a formal licensing program in January 1988 simply reflect the fact that applicant, over the years, tolerated sales and advertising of goods, including clothing, bearing the marks it presently seeks to register. Applicant, like numerous other colleges and universities, permitted others to sell imprinted merchandise as expressions of community support and goodwill. Advertising of merchandise featuring various indicia associated with applicant, including the marks at issue herein, frequently coincided with events sponsored by applicant, such as athletic events and alumni gatherings.

Thus, rather than constituting uncontrolled use by opposers and third parties which resulted in the marks losing all source indicating significance, the reality of the situation which existed for many years may best be characterized as that of a royalty-free, nonexclusive, implied license to use marks which, particularly in and around the University's Madison campus, principally signified applicant in the mind of the consuming public and have continued to do so. Although there is evidence that, chiefly among tourists and summer session students from outside the State of Wisconsin, the marks sought to be registered by applicant identify the State of Wisconsin instead of or in addition to the University, it is undisputed that, to a significant portion of the relevant public, the subject marks identify applicant as the primary source of its educational and entertainment services and as the secondary source of the apparel imprinted with such marks. Except for one minor instance, there is nothing in the record which even suggests that the nature and quality of the imprinted apparel sold by opposers and others was anything less than that of at least merchantable quality. While it is also the case that, by and large, applicant had no formal system of quality control over the subject marks before January 1988, it must be remembered that "the inference of abandonment is not drawn ... [where] satisfactory quality was maintained, and, hence, no deception of purchasers occurred." *Stockpot, Inc. v. Stock Pot Restaurant, Inc.*, 220 U.S.P.Q. 52, 59 (TTAB 1983), *aff'd*, 737 F.2d 1576, 222 U.S.P.Q. 665 (Fed. Cir. 1984). Therefore, even without, essentially, a formal system of quality control over the clothing and other imprinted merchandise sold by opposers and numerous third parties, the subject marks were not abandoned by applicant since the quality of the apparel imprinted with such marks remained at an acceptable level in virtually all instances.

Furthermore, while it is true that, as to the "Bucky Badger" figure and the terms "BADGER"and/or "BADGERS," "Bucky" and such words are in a sense ubiquitous, especially in and around the State of Wisconsin, due in large part to the facts that the badger *(taxidea taxus)* is the Wisconsin state animal and that Wisconsin is nicknamed the "Badger State," the third-party uses of "Bucky" and the terms "BADGER" and/or "BADGERS" shown on the record with respect to various diverse and distinctly different businesses located in Madison and other localities in the State of Wisconsin simply do not demonstrate that applicant has abandoned the marks it desires to register. Rather, and not surprisingly, that certain third parties, particularly those operating in and around Madison, are using the "Bucky Badger" image and/or the designation "BADGER" in connection with such disparate businesses as a laundromat, a bowling alley, a dental practice, and a restaurant/bar and social club clearly reflect an effort by those establishments to appeal to students at the University and thereby solicit their patronage. Use by other third parties of the "Bucky Badger" figure and/or the term "BADGER," in conjunction with such vastly different commercial enterprises as a fence company, a trucking firm, a bus company, a locksmith and security business, an automobile parts wholesaler, an industrial sand and limestone producer, a radiator repair shop, a snack food wholesaler, a food canning company, a medical supply firm, a self-storage facility, a balloon delivery service, a wholesale food distributor and a moving company, is plainly meant to emphasize or underscore that those firms are based in Madison or otherwise are located in the State of Wisconsin.

Opposers, in stressing that such uncontrolled uses by third parties amount to a forfeiture of any rights applicant may have had in the subject marks, are basically contending that applicant must maintain a right in gross in each mark. However, as noted previously, exclusivity of rights is not required as a matter of law in order for applicant to avoid a finding of abandonment. Even in instances where, arguably, applicant and others are each using the "Bucky Badger" figure and/or the words "BADGER" and "BAD-GERS," such as the use thereof by the Badger Conference and Niagara High School and the use of "Bucky" by groups of cross-country runners, Vietnam veterans and firefighters, the activities of these third parties are sufficiently different and distinct in nature from the university level educational and entertainment services rendered by applicant so as to preclude any inference of abandonment of the subject marks by applicant. Consequently, while a number of third parties, as well as applicant, use the image of "Bucky Badger" and/or the words "BADGER" or "BADGERS" in connection with their activities and the promotion thereof, the fact that such indicia have been diluted and are accordingly weak in terms of the scope of protection to which they would be entitled does not mean, in the case of both the uses thereof made by applicant, and those by its nonexclusive, implied licensees which inured to applicant's benefit, that the marks applicant seeks to register have lost their significance as marks. *See* 2 J. McCarthy, McCarthy on Trademarks & Unfair Competition, §17.05 (3d ed. 1994).

Furthermore, as to applicant's actions and inactions with respect to investigation of third-party uses and enforcement of its claimed rights in the marks at issue, suffice it to say that it simply was not necessary, as noted earlier in this opinion, that applicant act against every use by nonaffiliated entities in order to avoid the risk of abandonment of the marks. Such uses, which applicant does not dispute, are simply not inconsistent or otherwise at odds with the subject marks maintaining their significance as marks identifying and distinguishing applicant's goods and services since none of the third-party users has been shown by opposers to offer goods or services that the relevant purchasing public would be likely to associate with or attribute to the University or, for that matter, to even colleges and universities in general. In short, while demonstrating that the "Bucky Badger" figure and the words "BADGER" and "BADGERS" are weak in the sense that they have been diluted by their use over many years on a variety of distinctly different goods and services, the evidence herein fails to establish, or even to raise a genuine issue, that the subject marks have lost their significance as marks for the particular goods and services for which applicant seeks registration.

We emphasize that our interest is limited to protecting these marks when they imply obvious reference to the University of Wisconsin-Madison.... The coverage of the licensing program will only extend into areas in which the UW-Madison has a legitimate proprietary interest, and not into areas that would subject the program to bona fide defenses in a litigation context....

We have no desire to claim rights to any symbols, logos, or slogans which are not associated with the UW-Madison. We believe that it is relatively easy to distinguish between a design that refers to the State of Wisconsin and one that refers specifically to the UW-Madison. Color, graphics, geographic area and intent of the seller all must be taken into consideration. For example, use of the word "badger" in many Wisconsin state contexts would obviously not be considered a proprietary interest of the UW-Madison, notwithstanding our proprietary interest in the "badger" mark in a UW-Madison context.

Finally, opposers urge that there has been no fundamental change in the market for merchandise imprinted with the marks at issue which would justify applicant's adoption of its formal licensing program and excuse its asserted delay in claiming enforceable rights after many years of essentially regarding the marks as public property. Aside from the fact that, as discussed above, the supposition concerning applicant's alleged delay and its belief that the marks were in the public domain do not entitle opposers to relief on their theory of abandonment, the record is clear that applicant had legitimate reasons for adopting a formal licensing program and including therein the subject marks. Not only was applicant increasingly concerned with the prospect of additional embarrassing, obscene or other inappropriate uses of the marks and potential product liability problems if the marks were used in connection with dangerous, unsafe or unauthorized products or events, but the entire nature of the market for merchandise imprinted with college and university indicia underwent a major change starting at about the end of the 1970s. While it is undisputed that, unlike the situation in *Helpingstine*, applicant has experienced only a steady rather than a sudden or sharp increase in the growth of sales of merchandise imprinted with indicia of the University, the market as a whole for merchandise, including apparel, bearing major college and university insignia increased dramatically during the late 1970s and continued to grow appreciably throughout the 1980s. The substantial growth in the popularity of such items, and the resultant need by the colleges and universities affected thereby for tighter control over their names and other identifying symbols, caused applicant and other similarly situated institutions of higher learning to recognize that the protection and enforcement mechanisms offered by formal licensing programs were necessary in order to avoid the problems brought about by the fundamental change in the market for imprinted collegiate merchandise. Many of the producers of such goods likewise realized that to preserve the value or desirability of their merchandise, a formal system of licensing and enforcement, of the type provided by CCI/ICE, worked to their advantage and did so in spite of the higher prices caused by the imposition of licensing fees. Thus, rather than being merely a brazen attempt by applicant, as opposers insist, to bail out the deficit in its athletic department by depriving retailers of their accustomed profits on products imprinted with the subject marks, it is plain that applicant was simply acting within its rights inasmuch as the marks signified the University and continue to do so to a significant portion of the purchasers of such merchandise. We also note in this regard that, significantly, the record plainly shows that no other college or university uses such marks.

In summary, not only is it the case that none of the opposers, or any third party, has ever used the marks at issue as its own mark for the particular goods and services set forth in the applications involved in these proceedings, but the use thereby was tantamount to a royalty-free, nonexclusive, implied license from applicant which inured to applicant's benefit. Applicant tolerated uses of the marks, when their use in advertising and on clothing and other types of imprinted merchandise were plainly in reference to the University, as expressions of support for its athletic and academic programs by the business community. With but one inconsequential exception, the record is devoid of any evidence which even raises an inference that the quality of merchandise imprinted with the subject marks has ever been anything less than that of at least merchantable quality. Similarly, except for a few occasional and transitory incidents, clothing and other items bearing the marks at issue have reflected applicant's standard that such merchandise be in good taste. Applicant, in effect, has maintained adequate control over the nature and quality of the goods and services sold under the marks, both prior to and after the commencement of its formal licensing program with CCI/ICE, and has policed its marks in accordance with due regard for the scope of protection to which they are entitled.

Consequently, while many third parties use or have used the "Bucky Badger" image and the words "BADGER" and/or "BADGERS" in connection with a wide variety of diverse businesses and activities which are distinctly different from the goods and services for which applicant seeks registration, such evidence demonstrates only that the marks are diluted and therefore weak. No other college or university uses the marks at issue and the evidence of third-party use, including that by entities at the high school level as well as various professional and social organizations, does not amount to proof that the marks have been abandoned in the sense that they have lost their significance as marks. In fact, although some members of the relevant purchasing public, mainly tourists and summer students attending the University from outside the State of Wisconsin, regard the subject marks as identifying the State of Wisconsin rather than or in addition to the University, there simply is no genuine issue that to a significant portion of the relevant purchasing public, the marks identify applicant as the primary source of its educational and entertainment services and as the secondary source of the apparel imprinted with such marks. This is particularly so among purchasers residing within the State of Wisconsin and is especially true the closer one gets to the area in and around Madison, where the University has its campus. Opposers essentially concede that such is the case by admitting, on the 93rd (and notably last) page of their initial brief, that "[t]he most the University has established in these proceedings is that some people associate the Marks with it". Plainly, in these circumstances, the marks have not lost all significance as marks for applicant's goods and services and therefore, as a matter of law, have not been abandoned.

Birch Publications, Inc., et al. v. RMZ of St. Cloud, Inc.

683 N.W.2d 869 (Minn. App. 2004)

HUDSON, JUDGE

FACTS

Ruth Zulkosky and three others organized appellants RMZ of St. Cloud, Inc. (RMZ), in late 1998 to publish a business-telephone and internet directory. RMZ published a telephone directory known as "The MIDbook" in 1999 and 2000....

RMZ experienced financial difficulties, and in July 2000, Zulkosky asked Harold Anderson for financial help, and Anderson agreed to help. In order to publish a directory in 2001 and to provide a vehicle through which Anderson could provide financial assistance, Anderson created respondent Birch Publications, Inc. (Birch). Anderson also invested cash in Birch to fund its initial business operations, and Birch purchased some of RMZ's assets, which was memorialized in a bill of sale.

On September 20, 2000, RMZ filed a certificate of assumed name for "The MIDbook" with the Minnesota Secretary of State. On November 10, 2000, Birch filed a certificate of assumed name for "The MIDbook" with the Minnesota Secretary of State. Birch published the certificate in the St. Cloud Times on April 27, 2001.

An attorney for RMZ prepared an assignment of the trademark name, but the discussions broke down before the assignment occurred.

On March 2, 2001, Zulkosky drafted a letter to the Yellow Pages Publishers Association (YPPA), which stated that "the Corporation that presently owns the MIDbook directory has changed effective October 1, 2000, from Quest [RMZ] ... to Birch Publications." RMZ contends that the letter was written so Birch could have permission to publish the 2001 directory, and Zulkosky testified she should have said Birch had permission to use the name rather than stating that the ownership had changed.

In September 2002, Birch underwent a staff reorganization and terminated several of their employees, including Zulkosky. On October 3, 2002, Zulkosky sent a letter to Birch's CEO, Beverly Berg, which stated that RMZ was withdrawing its permission to use the "MIDbook" name. Birch contends that both RMZ and Birch began to sell advertising for a directory in the late fall of 2002 using the "MIDbook" name.

In November 2002, Birch and Anderson commenced an action against RMZ and Zulkosky, seeking a temporary and permanent injunction to prevent RMZ from using the trademark or tradename "MIDbook" in any business related to the publication of a business-telephone directory.

ANALYSIS
I

The trial court found that RMZ abandoned the use of the trademark to Birch, but RMZ contends that it did not abandon the MIDbook trademark because Birch did not establish that RMZ intended not to resume the use of the trademark. Birch contends that the trial court correctly found that RMZ abandoned the use of the trademark to Birch. Birch notes it hired Zulkosky, and there is no evidence that she was acting in any capacity other than as a director or employee of Birch. Birch further contends that RMZ abandoned the MIDbook trademark through non-use and declared its intention not to resume use through various actions and statements, such as Zulkosky's letter to the YPPA.

Under the Lanham Trademark Act, a trademark is abandoned when "its use has been discontinued with intent not to resume such use." 15 US. C. § 1127 (2002). A party claiming that a trademark has been abandoned must show "non-use of the name by the legal owner and no intent by that person or entity to resume use in the reasonably foreseeable future." *Emergency One, Inc. v. Am. FireEagle, Ltd.,* 228 F.3d 531, 535 (4th Cir. 2000). Mere non-use is not prima facie evidence of abandonment unless the trademark has not been used for three consecutive years. *See* 15 U.S.C. § 1127. Having "intent to resume' requires the trademark owner to have plans to resume commercial use of the trademark." *Hiland Potato Chip Co. v. Culbro Snack Foods, Inc.,* 720 F.2d 981, 984 (8th Cir. 1983) (quoting *Exxon Corp. v. Humble Exploration Co., Inc.,* 695 F.2d 96, 102–03 (5th Cir. 1983)). The Lanham Trademark Act does not permit a license for a trademark owner to merely have "an intent not to abandon," which would allow a trademark owner to protect a trademark with neither commercial use nor plans to resume commercial use. *Id.*

Here, the record shows that Zulkosky and RMZ ceased producing directories and RMZ ceased being a viable business sometime in 2001; thus, Zulkosky and RMZ ceased using the trademark in a commercial manner (i.e., to sell directories). Likewise, nothing in the record indicates that they had immediate plans to resume commercial use of the trademark. In addition, RMZ allowed Birch to publicly assume use of the trademark to sell directories, and Zulkosky voiced no objection when Birch filed its assumed name registration with the Minnesota Secretary of State and then published notice of that filing in the St. Cloud Times. Zulkosky testified that she should have said Birch had permission to use the name.

Although Zulkosky claims now that Birch merely had permission to use the name, we cannot ignore the fact that Zulkosky chose to write the letter in a manner that clearly states that the corporation that "owns" the MIDbook directory has changed. Moreover, even if the YPPA suggested that Zulkosky use the ownership language in the letter, as Zulkosky claims, she did not inform Birch that the letter she wrote to the YPPA merely gave Birch permission to use the trademark; nor did she give Birch written permission to use the trademark. Zulkosky's silence is telling.

Zulkosky also asserts that she hoped to revive RMZ as a viable business at some later date, but her stated hope is weak evidence of intent not to abandon. The owner of a trademark cannot defeat an abandonment claim by asserting a vague, subjective intent to resume use of a trademark at some unspecified future date. *See Silverman v. C.B.S., Inc.,* 870 F.2d 40, 47 (2nd Cir. 1989). The actual conduct of the parties suggests that Zulkosky had no immediate intention to revive RMZ. Rather, it appears the parties intended for Zulkosky to have a management role in Birch and that she would have the opportunity to acquire an ownership interest in Birch. As the trial court noted, "The new entity was producing the same product, under the same manager, but with Mr. Anderson being the majority shareholder." The trial court correctly concluded that Zulkosky" was using the trademark every day in her role at Birch, but RMZ Publications was no longer using [the trademark]."

We conclude that the trial court's findings were not clearly erroneous and that the trial court did not err as a matter of law in concluding that RMZ abandoned use of the trademark.

II

RMZ further argues that the trial court erred by finding that RMZ negligently abandoned the MlDbook trademark name and was estopped from denying the transfer of the trademark to Birch. RMZ contends that the trial court failed to consider all of the evidence presented at trial and instead relied solely on the letter Zulkosky wrote to the YPPA. Birch contends that the trial court correctly found that the conduct of the parties supports the estoppel claim. In support of its position, Birch notes that it reasonably relied on the words, actions, and silence of Zulkosky and contends that it acquired RMZ's business and the MlDbook name.

A party seeking to invoke the doctrine of equitable estoppel has the burden of proving three elements: (1) that the promise or inducement was made; (2) that it has reasonably relied upon the promise; and (3) that it will be harmed if estoppel is not applied. *Hydra-Mac, Inc. v. Onan Corp.,* 450 N W.2d 913, 919 (Minn. 1990). An equitable-estoppel claim arises when

> one by his acts or representations, or by his silence when he ought to speak, intentionally or through culpable negligence, induces another to believe certain facts to exist, and such other rightfully acts on the belief so induced in such manner that if the former is permitted to deny the existence of such facts it will prejudice the latter.

Transamerica Ins. Group v. Paul, 267 N W 2d 180, 183 (Minn. 1978) (quotations omitted). A plaintiff may establish an estoppel claim by showing that the defendant "through his language or conduct, induced the plaintiff to rely, in good faith, on this language or conduct to his injury, detriment or prejudice." *Semler Constr., Inc. v. City of* Hanover, 667 N W. 2d 457, 466 (Minn. App. 2003), *review denied* (Minn. Oct. 29, 2003) (citation omitted).

Here, there is considerable evidence that Zulkosky's conduct, words, and silence when she should have spoken, induced Anderson and Birch to make a substantial investment of time and money to create a viable business using the MlDbook name. First, Anderson created Birch to keep the underlying business of RMZ alive using the MlDbook name. Anderson invested thousands of dollars to create Birch, buy RMZ's office equipment, take over RMZ's lease, hire RMZ employees, and fund Birch's cash shortfalls. Second, Anderson rejected Zulkosky's proposal that he buy an interest in RMZ. Anderson's assistant participated in the initial meetings between Zulkosky and Anderson, and she testified that Anderson would only help RMZ by creating "a new company using the MlDbook name." Third, Zulkosky voiced no objection when Birch filed its assumed-name registration with the Minnesota Secretary of State and then published notice of that filing in the St. Cloud Times. Finally, Zulkosky wrote the letter to the Yellow Pages Publishers Association, which stated that "the Corporation that presently owns the MlDbook directory has changed effective October 1, 2000, from Quest [RMZ] to Birch Publications." The trial court was correct when it noted "that letter does not discuss that the trademark was by permission or by license, but was now owned by Birch." Based on all of the above, the first element of equitable estoppel has been satisfied because Zulkosky's conduct, words, and silence when she should have spoken induced Anderson and Birch to make a substantial investment of time and money to create a viable business using the MlDbook name.

Based on the facts described above, the trial court properly concluded that Anderson and Birch reasonably, and in good faith, relied on Zulkosky's conduct, words, and silence when she should have spoken. As the trial court correctly noted "Anderson clearly relied both upon [Zulkosky's] presence and the trademark use when making his investment in Birch. Officers of Plaintiff Birch Publications relied upon this continuing belief when pouring business efforts and goodwill into the trademark." Accordingly, the second element of equitable estoppel has been satisfied because Birch reasonably, and in good faith, relied on Zulkosky's inducement.

Finally, Birch and Anderson will be harmed if Birch loses the opportunity to continue to use the name MlDbook in the operation of the business. Birch believed that they had full ownership of the name MlDbook for two years, and during that time Birch added value to, commercially used, and poured business efforts and goodwill into the trademark.

DECISION

The trial court's findings were not clearly erroneous, and the trial court did not err as a matter of law in concluding that RMZ abandoned use of the trademark and that RMZ is estopped from denying the transfer of the trademark to Birch.

Affirmed.

Notes

1. Problem: One radio station, formerly known as "the Breeze," announces that it will change its name and no longer use "the Breeze" appellation. They run a series of advertisements for a month before making the change so that listeners will all know of the change. After the change is made, a competitor radio station changes its name to "The Breeze is Back." Is this abandonment or infringement? *See Cumulus Media, Inc. v. Clear Channel Communications, Inc.*, 304 F.3d 1167 (11th Cir. 2002) ("finding no abandonment because while such an announcement [of intent to change names] is the type of circumstance from which intent not to resume may be inferred … it does not alone serve to make a prima facie showing of abandonment. A defendant must also introduce evidence of non-use").

2. Trademark holders should build a case for resumption of use if they ever cease use of a mark. This will allow them to avoid a claim that they intended not to resume such use as contemplated by the Lanham Act. 15 U.S.C. 1127. *See* Christopher T. Micheletti, *Preventing Loss of Trademark Rights: Quantitative and Qualitative Assessments of "Use" and their Impact on Abandonment Determinations*, 94 Trademark Rep. 634 (2004). Is it ethical to "build a case for resumption" when no real intent for resumption exists?

3. When a licensor of a trademark files for bankruptcy protection, the effect on the licensee is that all trademark rights are terminated and it must cease use. *See,* Intellectual Property Bankruptcy Protection Act, 11 U.S.C. Sections 101 and 365(n). No other intellectual property is affected by the bankruptcy of a licensor. Patents, copyrights and trade

secret licenses continue without any impact. *See*, Ashley H. Wilkes, *In Re Gucci: The Lack of Goodwill in Matters Regarding Bankruptcy, Trademarks, and High Fashion*, 23 EMORY BANKR. DEV. J. 647 (2007). Why should trademarks be treated differently than other intellectual properties? Is this further evidence that trademarks themselves are not subject to property ownership?

4. The *Birch Publications* case, *supra,* is not only about abandonment of a trademark but also transfers of trademarks. An assignment in gross is "a sale of a trade name or mark divorced from its goodwill." *Marshak v Green*, 746 F.2d 927, 929 (2d Cir. 1984). What is it about *Birch Publications* that caused the court to believe that there was no transfer of the trade name and therefore it was abandoned?

5. In August of 2006, the PTO cancelled the trademark HAVANA CLUB as used on rum and "held" by a Cuban company. The PTO held that a trade embargo foreclosed the Cuban company's ability to sell rum in the United States and therefore the mark had been abandoned, even though it was in use in other countries in the world. *See 72* BNA's Patent, Trademark and Copyright Journal 395. This is just one more attempt at restricting the sale of rum in the United States by a Cuban company. This dispute has a long and tortured history. The mark was originally used by the Arechabala family on or in connection with the sale of rum in Cuba. HAVANA CLUB came to enjoy significant goodwill world wide. In 1960 it was nationalized by the Cuban government. A Cuban company, Pernod, was authorized to distribute HAVANA CLUB rum world wide. It has done so except in the United States. Although Pernod was able to obtain a registration in the United States under Section 44 of the Lanham Act, it had not been able to import rum because of the Cuban embargo. To make matters more interesting, Arechabala licensed to Bicardi the rights to the mark in the United States. Section 211(a) of the 1998 Omnibus Appropriations Act prohibits any transactions or payments for a trademark originally held by another but later nationalized without the express consent of the original owner(legislation that was drafted exclusively with Bicardi in mind). Arechabala would not consent to the nationalization. Therefore, the US. Court of Appeals for the Second Circuit upheld Bicardi's rights in the mark. *See,* Havana Club Holding SA v. Galleon A=SA, 103 F.3d 116 (2nd Cir. 2000). By cancelling that registration originally obtained by Pernod in 1976, the PTO opened the door to Bicardi's use of the mark on rum. Bicardi immediately announced that it would relaunch a rum bearing the HAVANA CLUB mark. What would you do?

---

2. Inappropriate Use

a. Assignment in Gross

Marshak v. Green
746 F.2d 927 (2d Cir. 1984)

POLLACK, DISTRICT JUDGE:

David Rick, the appellant, manages and promotes musical groups for entertainment under the registered trade name, "VITO AND THE SALUTATIONS". Shortly before the entry of the order complained of on this appeal, Rick was preparing to proceed to trial of his pending suit for infringement of his trade name by a competitor musical group. It was at that point that Larry Marshak, the appellee, holder of an unsatisfied monetary judgment procured three years earlier in this suit against David Rick, obtained *ex parte,* in the Court below, an Order of Attachment and Sale of Rick's trade name. The Order of the District Court directed the United States Marshal "to attach whatever proprietary interest the judgment debtor, David Rick, may have or claim to have in the registered name VITO AND THE SALUTATIONS and to sell same at public auction forthwith to satisfy plaintiff's [Marshak's] judgment against said defendant [Rick], to the extent of $17,683, plus accrued interest...." By an amendment to the initial order, the Court directed one day's advertising notice in a newspaper of general circulation in New York City and that such sale may take place at the offices of the attorneys for the judgment creditor.

The sale was advertised and the Marshal auctioned the appellant's trade name to the plaintiff, and he bought it in for the nominal sum of $100. In fact, no money was received by the Marshal.

Prior to the sale, the defendant, having been apprised of plaintiff's proceedings, moved the Court for a stay of the attachment, execution and sale. In his supporting affidavit he notified the Court of his pending infringement suit against his competitors and of the imminence of its trial. He asserted that the competitive group now represented by Marcus, the attorney who had obtained the money judgment against Rick in 1981, was attempting to effectuate a judicial sale of his rights to the trade name to reap an unfair advantage in the impending infringement trial. Rick's ownership of the trade name had been made an issue in the infringement suit. Rick claimed that Marcus, the attorney for the defendants in the infringement suit had placed the collection of the judgment with the attorneys who had obtained the order below, and that this creates a conflict of interest on the part of Marcus, to the prejudice of Rick's rights in the infringement suit. He urged, moreover, that his right to use the trade name "cannot be the subject of a forced sale."

Rick requested of the Court below protection by a stay of the execution on "that which belongs only to me."

Rick's application herein for a stay of the sale was denied and the Court ordered that the sale of the appellant's interest in the trade name may go forward, but that the purchaser must be given notice that the validity of the trade name was now the subject of litigation before another Judge of the same Court.

On this appeal, the judgment debtor contends that a trade name or mark per se is not a type of property which can be attached or sold at execution auction and that the order directing the same and the action taken thereunder were invalid.

Although no case has been found precisely such as this in which a Federal Court has confronted the issue of whether a trade name by itself can be subjected to a forced sale, courts have held that registered trade names or marks may not be validly assigned in gross. A sale of a trade name or mark divorced from its goodwill is characterized as an "assignment in gross."

A trade name or mark is merely a symbol of goodwill; it has no independent significance apart from the goodwill it symbolizes. "A trademark only gives the right to prohibit the use of it so far as to protect the owner's goodwill." *Prestonettes, Inc. v. Coty* (1924) 264 U.S. 359, 68 L. Ed. 731, 44 S. Ct. 350; a trademark cannot be sold or assigned apart from to goodwill it symbolizes, Lanham Act, § 10, 15 U.S.C. S. § 1060. There are no rights in a trademark apart from the business with which the mark has been associated; they are inseparable. Use of the mark by the assignee in connection with a different goodwill and different product would result in a fraud on the purchasing public who reasonably assume that the mark signifies the same thing, whether used by one person or another. "The consumers might buy a product thinking it to be of one quality or having certain characteristics and could find only too late to be another. To say that this would be remedied by the public soon losing faith in the product fails to give the consumer the protection it initially deserves." *Pepsico, Inc. v. Grapette Co.,* 416 F.2d 285, 289 (8th Cir. 1969).

In a case which touches the issue present herein, *Ward-Chandler Bldg. Co. v. Caldwell,* 8 Cal. App. 2d 375, 47 P.2d 758, 760 (1935), a judgment creditor attempted to force the sale of a trademark and goodwill of the debtor's beauty parlor. The attempt was turned aside. The Court there held that a judgment creditor could not force the sale of the trademark and goodwill of the debtor's beauty parlor. "The reason for this is that if the bare right of user could be transferred the name or mark would no longer serve to point out and protect the business with which it has become identified, or to secure the public against deception, but would tend to give a different business the benefit of the reputation established by the business to which the name had previously been applied." *Id.* at 760.

It has been pointed out that in the case of a service mark, confusion of the public and consumers would result if an assignee offered a service different from that offered by the assign or of the mark. *See Money Store v. Harris Corp. Finance, Inc.,* 689 F.2d 666 at 678 (7th Cir. 1982).

Exceptions do exist. The courts have upheld such assignments if they find that the assignee is producing a product or performing a service substantially similar to that of the assignor and that the consumers would not be deceived or harmed.

Courts have also upheld such assignments if there is a continuity of management. For example, in *Marshak v. Green,* 505 F. Supp. 1054 (S.D.N.Y. 1981), defendant unsuccessfully claimed that the assignment of the service mark, "The Drifters," to plaintiff was an invalid assignment in gross. The plaintiff had been the manager of the group prior to the assignment and continued in that capacity after the assignment. The Court found that the plaintiff had promised to protect the mark from infringement and had continued to provide the same singing style. "The essence of what [plaintiff] acquired was the right to inform the public that [he] is in possession of the special experience and skill symbolized by the name of the original concern, and of the sole authority to market its services." *Id.* at 1061.

There was no evidence that this case fits into either of the above exceptions. Entertainment services are unique to the performers. Moreover, there is neither continuity of management nor quality and style of music. If another group advertised themselves as VITO AND THE SALUTATIONS, the public could be confused into thinking that they were about to watch the group identified by the registered trade name.

The appellee obliquely suggested that it was not attaching the trademark per se, but rather the appellant's "… *claim* to a proprietary interest in the trade name which formed the subject matter of the *Rick v. Balsamo* litigation [the case about to go to trial]." However, the order of the District Court was that the Marshal should sell whatever proprietary interest the judgment debtor may have or claim to have in the trade name and not Rick's interest in a cause of action.

The Federal Rules of Civil Procedure, Rule 69(a) provides: "The procedure on execution … shall be in accordance with the practice and procedure of the state in which the district court is held," except to the extent that a United States statute governs. Those courts which have considered the issue have determined that state law also determines the type of property which can be subject to execution.

In New York, a money judgment may be enforced against any debt, which is past due or which is yet to become due, or upon an assignable cause of action. N.Y.C.P.L.R. §5201(a). The same statute permits enforcement of a money judgment against any property which could be assigned or transferred, whether or not it is vested. N.Y.C.P.L.R. §5201(b). However, a trade name in gross is not "property" within the meaning of the statute. *Cf. Port Chester Electrical Construction Corp. v. Atlas,* 40 N.Y.2d 652, 389 N.Y.S.2d 327, 357 N.E.2d 983 (N.Y. 1976) (creditor can enforce debtor's contractual claims to reimbursement which are due), with *Glenmore Distilleries Co. v. Seideman,* 267 F. Supp. 915, 918 (E.D.N.Y. 1967) (a claim in quantum meruit " ... being only inchoate, uncertain, and contested, has no present value ..." and is not due certainly or on demand.)

Accordingly, the appellee was not entitled to an order directing a levy of execution and sale of the appellant's registered trademark. The order appealed from is reversed and the purported sale is set aside.

Note

1. A major American manufacturer of hair care products wants to sell its products in Japan. The manufacturer finds a distributor in Japan but there is mutual distrust between the parties. Under such circumstances, the American company would usually create a distribution agreement with language that expressly controls ownership and registration rights of the trademarks. Instead of this normal practice, the American manufacturer creates a trust with a United States bank. The exclusive *res* of the trust is the American manufacturer's trademark rights in Japan. Neither the bank nor the manufacturer exercise control over the Japanese distributor for 15 years. When the Japanese distributor changes the trademark slightly without permission from the manufacturer, the American manufacturer sues for trademark infringement in the United States. Who prevails? Who is the correct plaintiff? Haven't trademark rights in Japan been abandoned be the creation of the trust which treats the trademarks as an in gross transfer? *See, e.g., Alberto-Culver Co. v. Sunstar, Inc.,* No. 0105825,2001 WL1249055 (N.D. Ill. Oct. 17, 2001). *But see,* Irene Calboli, *Trademark Assignment "With Goodwill": A Concept whose Time has Gone,* 57 FLA. L. REv. 771 (2005).

---

b. Naked Licenses/Lack of Quality Control
Clark Yocum v. Warren Covington
216 U.S.P. Q. (BNA) 210 (TTAB 1982)

OPINION BY SKOLER, MEMBER:

A petition has been filed by Clark Yocum to cancel the registration of the service mark "PIED PIPERS" issued to Warren Covington, doing business as the Warren Covington Orchestra, for "entertainment service, namely providing live singing."

As grounds for cancellation, petitioner asserts (i) ownership and prior use of the "PIED PIPERS" mark for the services of a four member vocal group originally formed in 1940, and (ii) fraudulent application for and procurement of respondent's registration based on knowledge of the existence of petitioner's group and of petitioner's use and right to use of the "PIED PIPERS" mark at the time of respondent's application for registration in 1973.

In his answer to the petition for cancellation, registrant denied the salient allegations of the petition and asserted, as affirmative defenses, (i) abandonment by petitioner of any rights he may have had in "PIED PIPERS" as a service mark, (ii) laches in pursuing petitioner's rights to protection, thereby barring him from maintaining this proceeding, (iii) knowing acquiescence in respondent's use of the mark, and (iv) "unclean hands" in maintaining this proceeding in order to "punish" registrant for seeking to recover a disputed debt with a third party who was financially associated with petitioner in this proceeding.

* * *

Petitioner in this proceeding is a musician (guitarist and vocalist) who joined a vocal group called the "PIED PIPERS" which originated in California as an 8-person aggregation and then became associated with the renowned Tommy Dorsey Orchestra as a 4-member group (one female and three male voices) in late 1939. That 4-person group, with some replacements, continued in Mr. Dorsey's employ until November of 1942, participating in live performances and making a number of "hit" recordings, frequently in conjunction with and as backup to Dorsey's then star vocalist, Frank Sinatra.

Petitioner Yocum joined the Dorsey orchestra as a guitarist in April of 1940 and by autumn of that year had become one of the "PIED PIPERS" male vocalists (replacing singer Billy Wilson) after the original 4-voice group had made two or three recordings, including the famed "I'll Never Smile Again". With the accession of petitioner, the group then consisted of Jo Stafford, Charles Lowry, John Huddleston and Yocum until the break with Dorsey in 1942. Throughout this period, the vocalists were paid by, booked by and appeared as a featured part of the Tommy Dorsey organization, apparently as employees of Mr. Dorsey. Thereafter, i.e., following the amicable November 1942 departure from the Dorsey Orchestra, the group continued to operate and perform as a unit under the name "PIED PIPERS", undertaking radio shows and guest appearances at dance engagements and concerts, and making records (including the hits "Dream", "Mamselle" and "Atchison, Topeka & the Santa Fe") through a series of contracts with Capitol Records, Inc. which ran from late 1943 to about 1950. During this period, the breakaway group of Stafford, Lowry, Huddleston, and Yocum was altered somewhat by the departure of Stafford and Huddleston and the addition of singers June Hutton and Hal Hopper in 1944. It was the Hutton-Lowry-Hopper-Yocum combination that entered into an agreement, alleged and relied on by petitioner Yocum, to the effect that each member would have an equal one-fourth interest in the group, such interest to revert to the remaining members on the demise of any member and with any replacement members to serve as employees rather than joint owners of the group and its trade name.

It is this agreement which is the basis for petitioner's assertion, as sole survivor of the group, of 100% title to the "PIED PIPERS" trade name and service mark. That group was eventually incorporated in 1947, allegedly for tax purposes and at least in part to protect the trade name, with the members becoming employees of the corporation. The evidentiary record is devoid, however, of any incorporation papers, stockholders' agreements, partnership pacts or other documents corroborating or confirming the precise features of this "PIED PIPERS" ownership and succession agreement or, for that matter, evidencing transfer of the service mark into or out of the corporation during its brief life as a California corporation and eventual dissolution for non-payment of franchise taxes some two to three years after organization (the record is not clear on exact dates).

After the demise of the corporation, petitioner's "PIED PIPERS" group (again with occasional changes in participating vocalists) continued to make tours and appearances (1963–66, both domestic and overseas appearances, including tours with the then "Tommy Dorsey Orchestra"),to undertake recording assignments and to do film, television and radio shows using the "PIED PIPERS" name until 1967. At this point, it appeared that Yocum was no longer physically capable of performing with a singing group. Notwithstanding, it is clear that he continued to claim ownership of the "PIED PIPERS" name, to receive royalties from previous recordings as to which he was a performer, and to seek suitable employment for a "PIED PIPERS" singing group in the capacity akin to owner-manager or licensor. These efforts, by and large, were patently unsuccessful during an era when public interest in big band sounds, both instrumental and vocal, was languishing, at least until the late 1970's when a licensing arrangement for the "PIED PIPERS" was made by petitioner with Dick Castle which appears to have enjoyed some success and economic viability. Respondent Covington, a trombonist with a number of major dance bands (Vincent Lopez, Horace Heidt, Les Brown, Gene Krupa) and studio orchestras, signed a contract after Tommy Dorsey's death to lead the Dorsey orchestra in 1958 (which he undertook for some three and one half years). He was selected for this assignment by Mr. Dorsey's widow, Jane Dorsey, who signed the contract as president of State Amusement Corporation. This relationship was amicably terminated and Covington thereupon formed the Warren Covington Orchestra in 1964 which he has led to date as a "big band" or studio orchestra. In 1970 pursuant to a paid assignment from RCA Records, respondent appeared as orchestra leader with an ad hoc studio group called the "PIED PIPERS" which was organized by former member Jo Stafford to produce a recorded album of some of the big band hits of Tommy Dorsey days featuring the Pied Pipers. In 1973 Covington organized his own "PIED PIPERS" group to enhance his orchestra which group (also, presumably, with changes in vocalists from time-to-time) has remained intact and continues to perform with Covington, sometimes in conjunction with the Covington Orchestra and sometimes as a hired vocal group apart from that orchestra.

After adopting the "PIED PIPERS" name in 1973, Covington retained legal assistance and applied for registration of the service mark "PIED PIPERS", alleging first use in January of 1973. Registration issued in October of 1974. The record establishes continuous use of that service mark by registrant up to the present time, mostly for tours and live concert appearances.

The issues before the Board are whether petitioner has demonstrated (i) prior ownership and continuing use of the mark "PIED PIPERS", or (ii) fraudulent procurement by respondent of his registration and, if petitioner succeeds in one of these issues, (iii) whether any of registrant's affirmative defenses preclude the granting of cancellation pursuant to this petition. The conclusions of the Board are that petitioner has failed to fully meet his statutory burden of proof on these issues and, therefore, his cancellation petition must fail.

As regards prior ownership and use, the Board finds that: (a) petitioner has established no use or ownership rights in the "PIED PIPERS" name from the time he joined the group until it left the Dorsey Orchestra (1940–1942); (b) petitioner has failed to make a clear showing of title to and use of the name by virtue of an alleged agreement between certain members of the "PIED PIPERS" made after leaving the Dorsey Orchestra until dissolution of the corporation which was established to handle the engagements and business of the group (1943–1950); (c) petitioner has, however, demonstrated valid service mark and trade name use of "PIED PIPERS" either as sole or joint owner thereof, following dissolution of the corporation and until petitioner was forced, for reasons of health and physical incapacity, to discontinue his participation as a performer with the group (1950–1966); and (d) after petitioner discontinued singing and until the time of respondent's adoption of the mark and application for registration (1967–1973), there were two instances of uncontrolled licensing by petitioner which produced a break in the chain of petitioner's continuous use necessary to prove priority over respondent and caused the mark to lose trademark significance during that period.

As regards petitioner's fraud allegations and mindful of the heavy burden which must be met in challenging a registration on this ground, the Board finds these to be not adequately supported by the record before it. First, since we find that it is respondent, not petitioner, who has superior rights in the mark "PIED PIPERS", the oath in the application which matured into respondent's registration was not in fact false. Further, even if we had found that petitioner had superior rights and that the oath was false, the evidence of record would not be sufficient to persuade us that the oath was made with fraudulent intent. Although registrant may have been aware of petitioner's status as a member of the "PIED PIPERS" group in earlier years and even petitioner's claims to rights in such name (and the record is speculative on these points), petitioner's admittedly minimal level of commercial activity with his "PIED PIPERS" group and the lack of trade visibility thereof in the 6 years preceding registrant's adoption and use of the "PIED PIPERS" mark made it plausible and understandable for respondent to assume when he sought registration (as he has asserted) that the once famous "PIED PIPERS" name was not currently in trade use and was therefore subject to appropriation by one seeking to recapture and market the nostalgia of Dorsey days and the sweet vocal sounds that accompanied those days, regardless of whether such assumption was correct.

The reasons for the foregoing conclusions are detailed below.

Petitioner's Rights during Dorsey Days

Petitioner was not an original member of the 8-vocalist or 4-vocalist "PIED PIPERS" group, although he joined the latter shortly after it came under the wing of the Dorsey Orchestra. Petitioner was an employee of Tommy Dorsey, and title to the "PIED PIPERS" mark, if anything, remained in Mr. Dorsey during the period (the record being silent as to whether the prior members who joined Dorsey in 1939 had either retained or made an explicit transfer of trade name rights to Mr. Dorsey). It is clear, however, that it was the Dorsey organization that used the mark during this period.

Rights after Dorsey Break-Away until Dissolution of Corporation

From Thanksgiving of 1942, when the then 4-member "PIED PIPERS" group began using the name on its own, until dissolution of the corporation which was established by the group in 1947 to protect the name and manage bookings, petitioner asserts ownership of the mark by virtue of an agreement, allegedly in writing (although petitioner introduced no documents nor even collateral written references), under which petitioner emerged as sole owner of the name because of his survivorship of the four members of the group who allegedly entered into that agreement. Petitioner asserts that the agreement arose out of the "partnership papers" executed concurrently with the corporation papers by which the four incorporating members (Hutton, Lowry, Huddleston, and Yocum) explicitly agreed to freeze ownership in those individuals with neither heirs nor replacements participating and rights passing only to survivors. The Board, however, is unable to find on the evidence presented that use of the mark during this period evolved into the 100% ownership status claimed by petitioner because of the striking lack of corroboration of the agreement and several evidentiary facts inconsistent therewith: (i) in 1952, Charles Lowry, one of the alleged parties to the agreement asserted by petitioner, entered into an exclusive agency contract for representation of a "PIED PIPERS" group involving parties other than the Hutton-Lowry-Hopper-Yocum combination (thus suggesting non-recognition of petitioner's alleged agreement by one of the original parties to it); (ii) formation of a corporation by the Hutton-Lowry-Hopper-Yocum team, especially for the protective purposes alleged by petitioner, would normally imply ownership of the mark by the business entity and not the individual members or stockholders thereof, and here there is no countervailing evidence to show either a license by the incorporators to the corporation (with retention of ultimate trade name ownership) or to suggest, after the corporate dissolution, a transfer of the trade name back to the petitioner or anyone else, *see Giammarese v. Delfino*, 197 U.S.P.Q. 162, 163 (N.D. Ill. 1977) (trade name normally resides in business entity and not individual members thereof); and (iii) in 1970, original member Jo Stafford put together an ad hoc "PIED PIPERS" group to make a recording with RCA Records, again suggesting unawareness of the existence of prior or continuing rights in the mark, including those of petitioner. Thus, not only are petitioner's allegations of a survivorship-type succession agreement under which he has succeeded to sole ownership of the name unsubstantiated, but successive history tends to throw doubt on the existence thereof, at least in the precise form alleged.

Petitioner's Rights after Corporate Dissolution and until Withdrawal as a Performing Member

Contrary to the Board's conclusions as to earlier periods, the Board finds that at least for the extensive period from 1950 to 1967, petitioner has established valid and prior use of the "PIED PIPERS" name for vocal group entertainment services (which probably existed as well in the preceding period if one ignores petitioner's pleaded ownership and succession agreement). Whether petitioner's rights were sole or joint, or 100% or 50% or 25%, is not clear but during this period his use of the "PIED PIPERS" service mark was well-established by the record. Live performances were documented and continuing recording activities were established under the Capital Records and other recording company contracts. Moreover, as one of the continuing members of this group (and, at times, apparently the sole continuing member), it is clear that Yocum rose to a position of leadership and at least a quasi-managerial position for the group, his name appearing more frequently than others as a signatory to documents or correspondent member in connection with recording and performance contracts, royalty arrangements and other business transactions. In this regard, it is not essential that Yocum, as petitioner, has been a sole owner or user, as alleged, rather than a joint owner and user of the mark, in order for him to maintain this proceeding as a party who would suffer damage by continuance of the registration of a junior user (as he claims respondent to be). Petitioner, if his claims of priority and a continuing use were fully established, would be damaged by the instant registration in either event and he would not need to show sole or exclusive ownership rights as against other parties.

Petitioner's Rights and Use after Withdrawal as a Performer

Although the Board finds that the record established a valid and continuing prior use by petitioner (alone or with others) for at least the 17-year period from 1950–1967, the picture becomes more murky after petitioner discontinued activity as a performer. This is not by virtue of his inability to continue singing, because it does appear that petitioner continued to assert rights to the name, to try to activate other vocalists to perform as "PIED PIPERS" and to attempt to obtain recording and performance contracts with petitioner acting in a managerial and owner capacity. The problem arises from two actions on petitioner's part which can only be characterized as unsupervised "licensing in gross", i.e., agreements to allow use of the name without adequate supervision and quality control, and which led to an interruption of the continuous use that petitioner must show to establish priority over registrant. The first of the two incidents was petitioner's intrusion into a recording session in 1970 of an ad hoc "PIED PIPERS" group (the Jo Stafford-

RCA Records special for Reader's Digest previously referred to) with a claim of illegal use of petitioner's "PIED PIPERS" mark. This resulted in payments by RCA Records of $300 and $400 to petitioner to settle his claims of name ownership but no more than that. Petitioner's own testimony is informative on this incident:

> In respect to Miss Jo Stafford because of her being an original member, I said well, give me some loot and use the name. He [producer of the album who talked to petitioner] recognized this and did pay me for the sides that were being done by the so-called Pied Pipers. That can be verified with monies I received. (Yocum deposition, 5-20-80, p. 60)

In subsequent questioning, petitioner admitted that he made no inquiry of what was being recorded, what arrangements were being used, and made no request to monitor the sessions. Petitioner explains that by virtue of his late notice of the RCA recording project, he could do nothing but acquiesce and did not want to hurt Miss Stafford, so that exercising a normal mark owner's supervisory role was not feasible on this occasion. An isolated incident of this kind might well be so regarded. However, during the 1967–1973 period petitioner entered into another uncontrolled licensing arrangement without such pressures. This was the July 1967 agreement with Lee Gotch, a former participant in petitioner's "PIED PIPERS" combinations (said to have joined the group in1952 or thereabouts). The 1-page agreement contains no hint of supervision, quality control or performance standards, its primary and virtually only provision, so far as petitioner was concerned, being an agreement to pay petitioner 5% of the gross income of Gotch's group in return for allowing him to use the "PIED PIPERS" name "as purporting to be the name of a vocal group you are about to form". The only explicit recapture conditions were Gotch's failure to adhere to the agreement (i.e., his 5% "commission" obligation to Yocum) and inability to obtain employment for Gotch's group for 6 consecutive months (whereupon Yocum could rescind).

The Board finds, therefore, that in the six years preceding respondent's adoption, use and registration of the mark, petitioner engaged in inadequately controlled licensing, thereby working an "abandonment" that negated such priority of use as petitioner may have established in earlier years and divested the "PIED PIPERS" mark of origin—indicating significance in petitioner's hands. The definition of abandonment in the Trademark Act (Section 45) reads: "A mark shall be deemed to be abandoned ... (b) when any course of conduct of the registrant, including acts of omission as well as commission, causes the mark to lose its significance as an indication of origin." Although not dealing with a registered mark in the case of petitioner's use of "PIED PIPERS", we believe that the operative principles of the Act apply to petitioner's situation. As one commentator has characterized the pertinent law:

> Abandonment because of uncontrolled licensing is purely an involuntary forfeiture of trademark rights, for the mark owner probably has no subjective intent to abandon the mark. Uncontrolled licensing causes a symbol to lose its meaning as a trademark....

> A finding of uncontrolled licensing may result in several possible effects: abandonment of all rights in the mark, cancellation of a registration of the mark, and a break in a chain of continuous use necessary to prove priority of use over another.... A mark can become abandoned by any act or omission which causes the mark to lose its significance as a trademark." J. T. McCarthy, Trademark sand Unfair Competition, §18.15 at p. 636 (1973).

The involuntary forfeiture having taken place, it is clear that respondent in 1973 could legitimately adopt and use the "PIED PIPERS" service mark, as indeed it did.

The Board has no reason to disbelieve petitioner's continued assertions that he never intended to give up the "PIED PIPERS" mark nor his hopes that the malaise of public interest in "big band"vocal music of the sort that brought earlier fame to the various Pied Piper singers would end and reacceptance would permit a return of public popularity, acceptance and commercial appetite. Indeed, this is what, in fact, appears to have happened with respect to respondent's adoption and successful use of the mark starting in 1973 and petitioner's 1978 launching through an "assignment"agreement with musician Lee Castle (nearly identical in its essential terms to the unrestricted sale of a trade name, as was found with respect to the Gotch agreement) of a competing "PIED PIPERS" aggregation that appears to have achieved some commercial success. However, while lack of intent to abandon would be relevant to voluntary relinquishment of the mark, it is not a sufficient defense against applicant's naked licensing activity.

For the foregoing reasons, the Board concludes that petitioner has not met his burden in establishing either prior and continuing rights on his part or fraudulent application behavior on respondent's part that would justify the cancellation of respondent's registration of the "PIED PIPERS" mark. Having so decided, the Board will not address in detail respondent's affirmative defenses of laches and "unclean hands", noting only that we do not believe that these are clearly established by the record, as is required of those who advance such contentions.

Decision: The petition to cancel is dismissed and respondent's registration shall remain in force.

———————

Kentucky Fried Chicken Corp. v. Diversified Packaging Corp.
549 F.2d 368 (5th Cir. 1977)

GOLDBERG, CIRCUIT JUDGE

This case presents us with something mundane, something novel, and something bizarre. The mundane includes commercial law issues now well delimited by precedent. The novel aspects of the case center on intriguing and difficult interrelationships between trademark and antitrust concepts. And the bizarre element is the facially implausible— some might say unappetizing—contention that the man whose chicken is "finger-lickin' good" has unclean hands.

Kentucky Fried Chicken Corporation, a franchisor of fast-food restaurants, brought this action claiming that defendants were infringing its trademarks and engaging in unfair competition by their manner of selling boxes and other supplies to Kentucky Fried franchisees. Defendants placed Kentucky Fried's trademarks on the supplies without Kentucky Fried's consent, and they allegedly misled franchisees with respect to the supplies' source and quality. Defendants counterclaimed, asserting that Kentucky Fried's franchise agreements, which required franchisees to buy supplies from approved sources, constituted an illegal tying arrangement. The district court, in a penetrating opinion reprinted at 376 F. Supp. 1136 (S.D. Fla.1974), ruled in Kentucky Fried's favor on every issue and enjoined defendants' activities. Although some of the issues are not without difficulty, and although we find that franchisors must walk a narrow path when including in their franchise agreements clauses requiring franchisees to buy supplies from approved sources, we affirm.

I. Facts

Colonel Harland Sanders founded the Kentucky Fried Chicken business in the early 1950s. The Colonel prepared chicken in accordance with his own secret recipe, and among the

Colonel's achievements has been to convince much of the American public that his product bears a close resemblance to the southern fried chicken that preceded peanuts as the south's most famous cuisine. The Colonel no longer owns the business, having transferred it in five different segments. The plaintiff, Kentucky Fried Chicken Corporation, now conducts the business in 47 states, and four unrelated entities conduct the business in the other three states.

Although Kentucky Fried owns some retail stores, its primary manner of conducting business, and the one of importance here, is franchising local outlets for its product. The franchise agreements require franchisees to purchase various supplies and equipment from Kentucky Fried or from sources it approves in writing. The agreements provide that such approval "shall not be unreasonably withheld." Before purchasing supplies from a source not previously approved, a franchisee must submit a written request for approval, and Kentucky Fried may require that samples from the supplier be submitted for testing. Of crucial importance is the fact that Kentucky Fried has never refused a request to approve a supplier.

The supplies that are subject to the approved-source requirement include those around which this litigation revolves: three sizes of carry-out chicken boxes, napkins, towelettes, and plastic eating utensils technically known as "sporks." Kentucky Fried sells these items to its franchisees, but under the franchise agreement the franchisees may also purchase any or all of these supplies from other approved sources. There are nine independent approved sources of cartons and a tenth that is a subsidiary of Kentucky Fried.

The specifications for these supplies require, among other things, that they bear various combinations of Kentucky Fried's trademarks. The marks, now widely known to the American public, include (1) "it's finger-lickin' good," (2) "Colonel Sanders' Recipe," (3) the portrait of Harland Sanders, (4) "Kentucky Fried Chicken," and (5) "Colonel Sanders' Recipe, Kentucky Fried Chicken."

Upon its formation in 1972, defendant Diversified Container Corporation (Container) began using Kentucky Fried's marks without its consent. Container used the marks on chicken cartons, napkins and towelettes that it advertised and sold to Kentucky Fried franchisees. Unlike other suppliers who sought and received approval, Container never requested that Kentucky Fried approve it as a source of these products, and in important respects Container's products failed to meet Kentucky Fried's specifications.[3]

Container garnered buyers for its low quality imitations of Kentucky Fried's supplies by making inaccurate and misleading statements. Container's advertisements invited franchisees to "buy direct and save" and represented that Container's products met "all standards." Container affixed Kentucky Fried's trademarks to the shipping boxes in which it delivered chicken cartons to franchisees. And when asked by franchisees whether Container was an "approved supplier" of cartons, Container employees evaded the question and said that Container sold "approved boxes."

Kentucky Fried brought this suit to enjoin Container's activities, relying upon the related theories of unfair competition and trademark infringement. Kentucky Fried did not seek damages. Defendants counterclaimed seeking treble damages for purported antitrust violations. The case was tried to the court, which resolved all claims in Kentucky Fried's favor.

---

3. Container's cartons utilized thinner cardboard than the approved product, thus making them less easy to keep closed properly and less resistant to leaking grease (or, as Kentucky Fried prefers to say, leaking "shortening"). Container's napkins were much smaller than the approved product and were made from a less satisfactory grade of paper.

On this appeal the central issues are whether the district court correctly held defendants liable on the unfair competition and trademark infringement theories and whether the court correctly held that Kentucky Fried's franchise arrangements were not shown to violate the antitrust laws. We must also address defendants' contentions that the district court should have granted a new trial on the basis of evidence allegedly discovered after trial, that the district court lacked subject matter jurisdiction, and that the district court erred in allowing Kentucky Fried to amend its reply to defendants' counterclaim. We find a kernel of truth in all Kentucky Fried's contentions and therefore affirm.

* * *

A. Forfeiture

Courts have long imposed upon trademark licensors a duty to oversee the quality of licensees' products. The rationale for this requirement is that marks are treated by purchasers as an indication that the trademark owner is associated with the product. Customers rely upon the owner's reputation when they select the trademarked goods. If a trademark owner allows licensees to depart from its quality standards, the public will be misled, and the trademark will cease to have utility as an informational device. A trademark owner who allows this to occur loses its right to use the mark.

Container argues that Kentucky Fried has forfeited its marks by inadequately controlling quality in the 47 states for which it owns the marks and by failing to control quality at all in the other three states. With respect to the 47 states in which Kentucky Fried owns the trademarks, however, the record belies Container's assertion that Kentucky Fried's program for controlling quality is a sham.[4] Retention of a trademark requires only minimal quality control, for in this context we do not sit to assess the quality of products sold on the open market. We must determine whether Kentucky Fried has abandoned quality control; the consuming public must be the judge of whether the quality control efforts have been ineffectual. We find that Kentucky Fried has sufficiently overseen the operations of its franchisees. Container has failed to carry the heavy burden placed on a party seeking to establish a forfeiture. *See American Foods, Inc. v. Golden Flake, In.,* 312 F.2d 619, 625 (5th Cir.1963).

We also find unpersuasive Container's contention based on Kentucky Fried's lack of any control at all over Kentucky Fried Chicken outlets in the other three states. Kentucky Fried does not own the marks there; Colonel Sanders conveyed the trademark rights to others before selling the remaining business to Kentucky Fried's predecessors. The trademark owners in those three states therefore are not Kentucky Fried's licensees, as Container erroneously contends, but rather concurrent owners. Concurrent ownership of marks in separate geographical territories is clearly permissible. Kentucky Fried Chicken customers in 47 states buy the product of plaintiff Kentucky Fried Chicken Corporation, backed by its reputation. Kentucky Fried Chicken customers in Florida, one of the remaining states, buy the product of the Florida owner, backed by its reputation. That many consumers are undoubtedly oblivious to the corporate structures does not undermine the trademark system; Florida customers will associate the trademarks with the Florida product, and national customers will associate the marks with the national product. That an occasional purchaser will travel between geographical districts is not a problem sufficient to justify outlawing concurrent trademark ownership.

---

4. We find unpersuasive Container's argument that Kentucky Fried's delay in detecting the use of Container's inferior products indicates a lack of quality control. That Container's deviousness succeeded for a time does not preclude Kentucky Fried from taking steps to protect its rights, now that its quality control program has located the culprit.

We conclude that Kentucky Fried has not forfeited its trademarks through unrestrained licensing. The marks are valid.

———————

Note

The quality control requirement should be abandoned in the context of business format franchising. The quality control requirement unjustly and illogically forces inconsistent treatment of licensing and non-licensing trademark owners. Moreover, imposition of the requirement creates a number of practical problems for both trademark owners and courts and ultimately results in two deceptive trademarks which may confuse and mislead the public. *See*, Michelle S. Friedman, *Naked Trademark Licenses in Business Format Franchising: The Quality Control Requirement and the Role of Local Culture*, 10 J. Tech. L. & Pol'y, 354, 376 (2005). Do you agree? If quality control is so important, why is it not uniformly required around the world?

Some countries, such as Japan, rarely enforce quality control of licensees. *See also*, Rudolph J. Kuss *The Naked Licensing Doctrine Exposed: How Courts Interpret the Lanham Act to Require Licensors to Police their Licensees and Why this Requirement Conflicts with Modern Licensing Realities and the Goals of Trademark Law*, 9 Marq. Intell. Prop. L. Rev. 361 (2005).

———————

c. Failure to Police

Wallpaper Mfrs., Ltd. v. Crown Wallcovering Corp.

680 F.2d 755 (CCAP 1982)

Nies, Judge

* * *

Policing One's Mark

Without question, distinctiveness can be lost by failing to take action against infringers. If there are numerous products in the marketplace bearing the alleged mark, purchasers may learn to ignore the "mark" as a source identification. When that occurs, the conduct of the former owner, by failing to police its mark, can be said to have caused the mark to lose its significance as a mark. However, an owner is not required to act immediately against every possibly infringing use to avoid a holding of abandonment. Such a requirement would unnecessarily clutter the courts. Some infringements are short-lived and will disappear without action by the trademark owner. In the case of a mark temporarily not in use or only used to a limited extent, a company may be hard pressed to extend its financial resources to fight an infringer when it has little or no current market under its mark. Frequently one cannot determine with any certainty that one has priority over another's use. To charge another with infringement under such circumstances can be disastrous. Other infringements may be characterized as "creeping," starting as a business name, and only become serious when later use is as a trademark.

———————

Note

The notion of denying trademark rights to a party who fails to police that mark makes good sense for several reasons. First, if trademarks are to play their intended function, reducing transaction costs so goods and services can be located easily by consumers, there must be exclusivity. If there are multiple firms making use of the same or similar marks, the inherent purpose of protecting trademarks is nullified. Second, by forcing trademark holders to police its marks, we create a system where holders are provided an incentive to establish that they have a continuing interest in a mark and that, therefore, exclusivity can be maintained, contributing to the purpose of trademark protection. Third, invalidating marks for a failure to police also clears up the Principle Register and prevents "dead wood," marks that no one has any interest in, from cluttering up the system. However, the negative side of the failure to police doctrine is that it requires or encourages mark holders to pursue expensive letter writing campaigns and law suits to control how society uses language. *See,* Deven R. Desai and Sandra L. Rierson, *Confronting the Genericism Conundrum,* 28 Cardozo L. Rev. 1789 (2007).

Chapter X

Section 43(a)

A. Unregistered "Marks"

Apart from available state law claims, the owner of an unregistered mark may enforce rights federally under Section 43(a) of the Lanham Act against one who used that mark in a manner which may cause confusion as to the origin or sponsorship of goods or services. Moreover, Section 43(a) also provides remedies where the conduct by another misrepresents the nature, characteristics, qualities, or geographic origin of that person's or another person's goods or services.

Section 43(a) is most often used to prevent use of unregistered trade dress by a third party. Trade dress is variously defined. The definition has evolved somewhat over the years. Trade dress can be the packaging in which a good is sold (product packaging trade dress). It can also be the shape of the good itself (configuration or design trade dress). Additionally, some courts have defined trade dress as the overall business impression of some commercial enterprise.

The only meaningful limitations placed on the trade dress right are that the mark is actually operating to identify source and that it is not functional. Although Section 43(a) can be used to protect any unregistered trademark as well, we focus here on trade dress.

---

15 U.S.C. §1125, Lanham Act §43

(a) Civil action

(1) Any person who, on or in connection with any goods or services, or any container for goods, uses in commerce any word, term, name, symbol, or device, or any combination thereof, or any false designation of origin, false or misleading description of fact, or false or misleading representation of fact, which—

> (A) is likely to cause confusion, or to cause mistake, or to deceive as to the affiliation, connection, or association of such person with another person, or as to the origin, sponsorship, or approval of his or her goods, services, or commercial activities by another person, …

Two Pesos, Inc. v. Taco Cabana, Inc.

505 U.S. 763 (1992)

Justice White delivered the opinion of the Court.

The issue in this case is whether the trade dress[1] of a restaurant may be protected under §43(a) of the Trademark Act of 1946 (Lanham Act), 60 Stat. 441, 15 U.S.C. §1125(a) (1982 ed.), based on a finding of inherent distinctiveness, without proof that the trade dress has secondary meaning.

I

Respondent Taco Cabana, Inc., operates a chain of fast-food restaurants in Texas. The restaurants serve Mexican food. The first Taco Cabana restaurant was opened in San Antonio in September 1978, and five more restaurants had been opened in San Antonio by 1985. Taco Cabana describes its Mexican trade dress as

> "a festive eating atmosphere having interior dining and patio areas decorated with artifacts, bright colors, paintings and murals. The patio includes interior and exterior areas with the interior patio capable of being sealed off from the outside patio by overhead garage doors. The stepped exterior of the building is a festive and vivid color scheme using top border paint and neon stripes. Bright awnings and umbrellas continue the theme." 932 F.2d 1113, 1117 (CA5 1991).

In December 1985, a Two Pesos, Inc., restaurant was opened in Houston. Two Pesos adopted a motif very similar to the foregoing description of Taco Cabana's trade dress. Two Pesos restaurants expanded rapidly in Houston and other markets, but did not enter San Antonio. In 1986, Taco Cabana entered the Houston and Austin markets and expanded into other Texas cities, including Dallas and El Paso where Two Pesos was also doing business.

In 1987, Taco Cabana sued Two Pesos in the United States District Court for the Southern District of Texas for trade dress infringement under §43(a) of the Lanham Act, 15 U.S.C. §1125(a) (1982 ed.), and for theft of trade secrets under Texas common law. The case was tried to a jury, which was instructed to return its verdict in the form of answers to five questions propounded by the trial judge. The jury's answers were: Taco Cabana has a trade dress; taken as a whole, the trade dress is nonfunctional; the trade dress is inherently distinctive;[2] the trade dress has not acquired a secondary meaning in the Texas market; and the alleged infringement creates a likelihood of confusion on the part of ordinary customers as to the source or association of the restaurant's goods or services. Because, as the jury was told, Taco Cabana's trade dress was protected if it either was inherently dis-

---

1. The District Court instructed the jury: "'Trade dress' is the total image of the business. Taco Cabana's trade dress may include the shape and general appearance of the exterior of the restaurant, the identifying sign, the interior kitchen floor plan, the decor, the menu, the equipment used to serve food, the servers' uniforms and other features reflecting on the total image of the restaurant." 1 App. 83–84. The Court of Appeals accepted this definition and quoted from *Blue Bell Bio-Medical v. Cin-Bad, Inc.*, 864 F.2d 1253, 1256 (5th Cir. 1989): "The 'trade dress' of a product is essentially its total image and overall appearance." *See* 932 F.2d 1113, 1118 (5th Cir. 1991). It "involves the total image of a product and may include features such as size, shape, color or color combinations, texture, graphics, or even particular sales techniques." *John H. Harland Co. v. Clarke Checks, Inc.*, 711 F.2d 966, 980 (11th Cir. 1983). Restatement (Third) of Unfair Competition §16, Comment *a* (Tent. Draft No. 2, Mar. 23, 1990).

2. The instructions were that, to be found inherently distinctive, the trade dress must not be descriptive.

Picture 10.1   Taco Cabana Restaurant
[Copyright 1992. Taco Cabana 1992 Annual Report.
Reprinted with permission of Taco Cabana.]

Picture 10.2   Two Pesos Restaurant

tinctive or had acquired a secondary meaning, judgment was entered awarding damages to Taco Cabana. In the course of calculating damages, the trial court held that Two Pesos had intentionally and deliberately infringed Taco Cabana's trade dress.

The Court of Appeals ruled that the instructions adequately stated the applicable law and that the evidence supported the jury's findings. In particular, the Court of Appeals rejected petitioner's argument that a finding of no secondary meaning contradicted a finding of inherent distinctiveness.

In so holding, the court below followed precedent in the Fifth Circuit. In *Chevron Chemical Co. v. Voluntary Purchasing Groups, Inc.*, 659 F.2d 695, 702 (5th Cir. 1981), the court noted that trademark law requires a demonstration of secondary meaning only when the claimed trademark is not sufficiently distinctive of itself to identify the producer; the court held that the same principles should apply to protection of trade dresses. The Court of Appeals noted that this approach conflicts with decisions of other courts, particularly the holding of the Court of Appeals for the Second Circuit in *Vibrant Sales, Inc. v. New Body Boutique, Inc.*, 652 F.2d 299 (1981), *cert. denied,* 455 U.S. 909, 71 L. Ed. 2d 448, 102 S. Ct. 1257 (1982), that §43(a) protects unregistered trademarks or designs only where secondary meaning is shown. *Chevron, supra,* at 702. We granted certiorari to resolve the conflict among the Courts of Appeals on the question whether trade dress that is inherently distinctive is protectible under §43(a) without a showing that it has acquired secondary meaning. 502 U.S. 1071 (1992). We find that it is, and we therefore affirm.

II

The Lanham Act was intended to make "actionable the deceptive and misleading use of marks" and "to protect persons engaged in … commerce against unfair competition." §45, 15 U.S.C. §1127. Section 43(a) "prohibits a broader range of practices than does §32," which applies to registered marks, *Inwood Laboratories, Inc. v. Ives Laboratories, Inc.,* 456 U.S. 844, 858, 72 L. Ed. 2d 606, 102 S. Ct. 2182 (1982), but it is common ground that §§43(a) protects qualifying unregistered trademarks and that the general principles qualifying a mark for registration under §§2 of the Lanham Act are for the most part applicable in determining whether an unregistered mark is entitled to protection under §§43(a).

* * *

Petitioner argues that the jury's finding that the trade dress has not acquired a secondary meaning shows conclusively that the trade dress is not inherently distinctive. Brief for Petitioner 9. The Court of Appeals' disposition of this issue was sound:

> "Two Pesos' argument—that the jury finding of inherent distinctiveness contradicts its finding of no secondary meaning in the Texas market—ignores the law in this circuit. While the necessarily imperfect (and often prohibitively difficult) methods for assessing secondary meaning address the empirical question of current consumer association, the legal recognition of an inherently distinctive trademark or trade dress acknowledges the owner's legitimate proprietary interest in its unique and valuable informational device, regardless of whether substantial consumer association yet bestows the additional empirical protection of secondary meaning." 932 F.2d at 1120, n.7.

Although petitioner makes the above argument, it appears to concede elsewhere in its brief that it is possible for a trade dress, even a restaurant trade dress, to be inherently distinctive and thus eligible for protection under §43(a). Brief for Petitioner 10–11, 17–18; Reply Brief for Petitioner 10–14. Recognizing that a general requirement of secondary meaning imposes "an unfair prospect of theft [or] financial loss" on the developer of fanciful or arbitrary trade dress at the outset of its use, petitioner suggests that such trade dress should receive limited protection without proof of secondary meaning. *Id.,* at 10. Petitioner argues that such protection should be only temporary and subject to defeasance when over time the dress has failed to acquire a secondary meaning. This approach is also vulnerable for the reasons given by the Court of Appeals. If temporary protection is available from the earliest use of the trade dress, it must be because it is neither functional nor descriptive, but an inherently distinctive dress that is capable of identifying a particular source of the product. Such a trade dress, or mark, is not subject to copying by concerns that have an equal opportunity to choose their own inherently distinctive trade dress. To terminate protection for failure to gain secondary meaning over some unspecified time could not be based on the failure of the dress to retain its fanciful, arbitrary, or suggestive nature, but on the failure of the user of the dress to be successful enough in the marketplace. This is not a valid basis to find a dress or mark ineligible for protection. The user of such a trade dress should be able to maintain what competitive position it has and continue to seek wider identification among potential customers.

This brings us to the line of decisions by the Court of Appeals for the Second Circuit that would find protection for trade dress unavailable absent proof of secondary meaning, a position that petitioner concedes would have to be modified if the temporary protection that it suggests is to be recognized. Brief for Petitioner 10–14. In *Vibrant Sales, Inc. v. New Body Boutique, Inc.*, 652 F.2d 299 (1981), the plaintiff claimed protection under §43(a) for a product whose features the defendant had allegedly copied. The Court of Appeals held that unregistered marks did not enjoy the "presumptive source association" enjoyed by registered marks and hence could not qualify for protection under §43(a) without proof of secondary meaning. *Id.*, at 303, 304. The court's rationale seemingly denied protection for unregistered, but inherently distinctive, marks of all kinds, whether the claimed mark used distinctive words or symbols or distinctive product design. The court thus did not accept the arguments that an unregistered mark was capable of identifying a source and that copying such a mark could be making any kind of a false statement or representation under §43(a).

This holding is in considerable tension with the provisions of the Lanham Act. If a verbal or symbolic mark or the features of a product design may be registered under §2, it necessarily is a mark "by which the goods of the applicant may be distinguished from the goods of others," 60 Stat. 428, and must be registered unless otherwise disqualified. Since §2 requires secondary meaning only as a condition to registering descriptive marks, there are plainly marks that are registrable without showing secondary meaning. These same marks, even if not registered, remain inherently capable of distinguishing the goods of the users of these marks. Furthermore, the copier of such a mark may be seen as falsely claiming that his products may for some reason be thought of as originating from the plaintiff.

Some years after *Vibrant*, the Second Circuit announced in *Thompson Medical Co. v. Pfizer Inc.*, 753 F.2d 208 (1985), that in deciding whether an unregistered mark is eligible for protection under §43(a), it would follow the classification of marks set out by Judge Friendly in *Abercrombie & Fitch*, 537 F.2d at 9. Hence, if an unregistered mark is deemed merely descriptive, which the verbal mark before the court proved to be, proof of secondary meaning is required; however, "suggestive marks are eligible for protection without any proof of secondary meaning, since the connection between the mark and the source is presumed." 753 F.2d at 216. The Second Circuit has nevertheless continued to deny protection for trade dress under §43(a) absent proof of secondary meaning, despite the fact that §§43(a) provides no basis for distinguishing between trademark and trade dress.

The Fifth Circuit was quite right in *Chevron*, and in this case, to follow the *Abercrombie* classifications consistently and to inquire whether trade dress for which protection is claimed under §43(a) is inherently distinctive. If it is, it is capable of identifying products or services as coming from a specific source and secondary meaning is not required. This is the rule generally applicable to trademarks, and the protection of trademarks and trade dress under §43(a) serves the same statutory purpose of preventing deception and unfair competition. There is no persuasive reason to apply different analysis to the two. The "proposition that secondary meaning must be shown even if the trade dress is a distinctive, identifying mark, [is] wrong, for the reasons explained by Judge Rubin for the Fifth Circuit in *Chevron*." *Blau Plumbing, Inc. v. S. O. S. Fix-It, Inc.*, 781 F.2d 604, 608 (CA7 1986). The Court of Appeals for the Eleventh Circuit also follows *Chevron, Ambrit, Inc. v. Kraft, Inc.*, 805 F.2d 974, 979 (1986), and the Court of Appeals for the Ninth Circuit appears to think that proof of secondary meaning is superfluous if a trade dress is inherently distinctive, *Fuddruckers, Inc. v. Doc's B. R. Others, Inc.*, 826 F.2d 837, 843 (1987).

It would be a different matter if there were textual basis in §43(a) for treating inherently distinctive verbal or symbolic trademarks differently from inherently distinctive trade dress. But there is none. The section does not mention trademarks or trade dress, whether they be called generic, descriptive, suggestive, arbitrary, fanciful, or functional. Nor does the concept of secondary meaning appear in the text of §43(a). Where secondary meaning does appear in the statute, 15 U.S.C. §1052 (1982 ed.), it is a requirement that applies only to merely descriptive marks and not to inherently distinctive ones. We see no basis for requiring secondary meaning for inherently distinctive trade dress protection under §43(a) but not for other distinctive words, symbols, or devices capable of identifying a producer's product.

Engrafting onto §43(a) a requirement of secondary meaning for inherently distinctive trade dress also would undermine the purposes of the Lanham Act. Protection of trade dress, no less than of trademarks, serves the Act's purpose to "secure to the owner of the mark the good-will of his business and to protect the ability of consumers to distinguish among competing producers. National protection of trademarks is desirable, Congress concluded, because trademarks foster competition and the maintenance of quality by securing to the producer the benefits of good reputation." *Park 'N Fly*, 469 U.S. at 198, citing S. Rep. No. 1333, 79th Cong., 2d Sess., 3–5 (1946) (citations omitted). By making more difficult the identification of a producer with its product, a secondary meaning requirement for a nondescriptive trade dress would hinder improving or maintaining the producer's competitive position.

Suggestions that under the Fifth Circuit's law, the initial user of any shape or design would cut off competition from products of like design and shape are not persuasive. Only nonfunctional, distinctive trade dress is protected under §43(a). The Fifth Circuit holds that a design is legally functional, and thus unprotectible, if it is one of a limited number of equally efficient options available to competitors and free competition would be unduly hindered by according the design trademark protection. This serves to assure that competition will not be stifled by the exhaustion of a limited number of trade dresses.

On the other hand, adding a secondary meaning requirement could have anticompetitive effects, creating particular burdens on the startup of small companies. It would present special difficulties for a business, such as respondent, that seeks to start a new product in a limited area and then expand into new markets. Denying protection for inherently distinctive nonfunctional trade dress until after secondary meaning has been established would allow a competitor, which has not adopted a distinctive trade dress of its own, to appropriate the originator's dress in other markets and to deter the originator from expanding into and competing in these areas.

As noted above, petitioner concedes that protecting an inherently distinctive trade dress from its inception may be critical to new entrants to the market and that withholding protection until secondary meaning has been established would be contrary to the goals of the Lanham Act. Petitioner specifically suggests, however, that the solution is to dispense with the requirement of secondary meaning for a reasonable, but brief, period at the outset of the use of a trade dress. Reply Brief for Petitioner 11–12. If §43(a) does not require secondary meaning at the outset of a business' adoption of trade dress, there is no basis in the statute to support the suggestion that such a requirement comes into being after some unspecified time.

III

We agree with the Court of Appeals that proof of secondary meaning is not required to prevail on a claim under §43(a) of the Lanham Act where the trade dress at issue is inherently distinctive, and accordingly the judgment of that court is affirmed.

It is so ordered.

CONCUR BY: Stevens; Scalia; Thomas

* * *

Justice Stevens, concurring in the judgment.

As the Court notes in its opinion, the text of §43(a) of the Lanham Act, 15 U.S.C. §1125(a) (1982 ed.), "does not mention trademarks or trade dress." Nevertheless, the Court interprets this section as having created a federal cause of action for infringement of an unregistered trademark or trade dress and concludes that such a mark or dress should receive essentially the same protection as those that are registered. Although I agree with the Court's conclusion, I think it is important to recognize that the meaning of the text has been transformed by the federal courts over the past few decades. I agree with this transformation, even though it marks a departure from the original text, because it is consistent with the purposes of the statute and has recently been endorsed by Congress.

I

It is appropriate to begin with the relevant text of §43(a). Section 43(a)[3] provides a federal remedy for using either "a false designation of origin" or a "false description or representation" in connection with any goods or services. The full text of the section makes it clear that the word "origin" refers to the geographic location in which the goods originated, and in fact, the phrase "false designation of origin" was understood to be limited to false advertising of geographic origin. For example, the "false designation of origin" language contained in the statute makes it unlawful to represent that California oranges came from Florida, or vice versa.

For a number of years after the 1946 enactment of the Lanham Act, a "false description or representation," like "a false designation of origin," was construed narrowly. The phrase encompassed two kinds of wrongs: false advertising and the common-law tort of "passing off." False advertising meant representing that goods or services possessed characteristics that they did not actually have and passing off meant representing one's goods as those of another. Neither "secondary meaning" nor "inherent distinctiveness" had anything to do with false advertising, but proof of secondary meaning was an element of the common-law passing-off cause of action. *See, e. g., G. & C. Merriam Co. v. Saalfield*, 198 F. 369, 372 (6th Cir. 1912) ("The ultimate offense always is that defendant has passed off his goods as and for those of the complainant").

II

Over time, the Circuits have expanded the categories of "false designation of origin" and "false description or representation." One treatise identified the Court of Appeals for the Sixth Circuit as the first to broaden the meaning of "origin" to include "origin of source or manufacture" in addition to geographic origin. Another early case, described as unique

---

3. Section 43(a) replaced and extended the coverage of §3 of the Trademark Act of 1920, 41 Stat. 534, as amended. Section 3 was destined for oblivion largely because it referred only to false designation of origin, was limited to articles of merchandise, thus excluding services, and required a showing that the use of the false designation of origin occurred "willfully and with intent to deceive." *Ibid.* As a result, "almost no reported decision can be found in which relief was granted to either a United States or foreign party based on this newly created remedy." Derenberg, *Federal Unfair Competition Law at the End of the First Decade of the Lanham Act: Prologue or Epilogue?*, 32 N. Y. U. L. Rev. 1029, 1034 (1957).

among the Circuit cases because it was so "forward-looking," interpreted the "false description or representation" language to mean more than mere "palming off." *L'Aiglon Apparel, Inc. v. Lana Lobell, Inc.*, 214 F.2d 649 (3rd Cir. 1954). The court explained: "We find nothing in the legislative history of the Lanham Act to justify the view that [§43(a)] is merely declarative of existing law.... It seems to us that Congress has defined a statutory civil wrong of false representation of goods in commerce and has given a broad class of suitors injured or likely to be injured by such wrong the right to relief in the federal courts." *Id.*, at 651. Judge Clark, writing a concurrence in 1956, presciently observed: "Indeed, there is indication here and elsewhere that the bar has not yet realized the potential impact of this statutory provision [§43(a)]." *Maternally Yours, Inc. v. Your Maternity Shop, Inc.*, 234 F.2d 538, 546 (2nd Cir.). Although some have criticized the expansion as unwise, it is now "a firmly embedded reality. The United States Trade Association Trademark Review Commission noted this transformation with approval: "Section 43(a) is an enigma, but a very popular one. Narrowly drawn and intended to reach false designations or representations as to the geographical origin of products, the section has been widely interpreted to create, in essence, a federal law of unfair competition.... It has definitely eliminated a gap in unfair competition law, and its vitality is showing no signs of age."

Today, it is less significant whether the infringement falls under "false designation of origin" or "false description or representation" because in either case §43(a) may be invoked. The federal courts are in agreement that §43(a) creates a federal cause of action for trademark and trade dress infringement claims. 1 J. Gilson, Trademark Protection and Practice §2.13, p. 2-178 (1991). They are also in agreement that the test for liability is likelihood of confusion: "Under the Lanham Act [§43(a)], the ultimate test is whether the public is likely to be deceived or confused by the similarity of the marks.... Whether we call the violation infringement, unfair competition or false designation of origin, the test is identical — is there a 'likelihood of confusion?'" *ew West Corp. v. NYM Co. of California, Inc.*, 595 F.2d 1194, 1201 (9th Cir. 1979) (footnote omitted). And the Circuits are in general agreement, with perhaps the exception of the Second Circuit, that secondary meaning need not be established once there is a finding of inherent distinctiveness in order to establish a trade dress violation under §43(a).

III

Even though the lower courts' expansion of the categories contained in §43(a) is unsupported by the text of the Act, I am persuaded that it is consistent with the general purposes of the Act. For example, Congressman Lanham, the bill's sponsor, stated: "The purpose of [the Act] is to protect legitimate business and the consumers of the country." 92 Cong. Rec. 7524 (1946). One way of accomplishing these dual goals was by creating uniform legal rights and remedies that were appropriate for a national economy. Although the protection of trademarks had once been "entirely a State matter," the result of such a piecemeal approach was that there were almost "as many different varieties of common law as there are States" so that a person's right to a trademark "in one State may differ widely from the rights which [that person] enjoys in another." H. R. Rep. No. 944, 76th Cong., 1st Sess., 4 (1939). The House Committee on Trademarks and Patents, recognizing that "trade is no longer local, but ... national," saw the need for "national legislation along national lines [to] secure to the owners of trademarks in interstate commerce definite rights." *Ibid.*

Congress has revisited this statute from time to time, and has accepted the "judicial legislation" that has created this federal cause of action. Recently, for example, in the Trademark Law Revision Act of 1988, 102 Stat. 3935, Congress codified the judicial interpretation of §43(a), giving its *imprimatur* to a growing body of case law from the Circuits that had expanded the section beyond its original language.

* * *

IV

In light of the consensus among the Courts of Appeals that have actually addressed the question, and the steps on the part of Congress to codify that consensus, stare decisis concerns persuade me to join the Court's conclusion that secondary meaning is not required to establish a trade dress violation under §43(a) once inherent distinctiveness has been established. Accordingly, I concur in the judgment, but not in the opinion, of the Court.

JUSTICE THOMAS, CONCURRING IN THE JUDGMENT.

Both the Court and JUSTICE STEVENS decide today that the principles that qualify a mark for registration under §2 of the Lanham Act apply as well to determining whether an unregistered mark is entitled to protection under §43(a). The Court terms that view "common ground," though it fails to explain why that might be so, and JUSTICE STEVENS decides that the view among the Courts of Appeals is textually insupportable, but worthy nonetheless of adherence. [Citation omitted.] (STEVENS, J., concurring in judgment). I see no need in answering the question presented either to move back and forth among the different sections of the Lanham Act or to adopt what may or may not be a misconstruction of the statute for reasons akin to *stare decisis*. I would rely, instead, on the language of §43(a).

Section 43(a) made actionable (before being amended) "any false description or representation, including words or other symbols tending falsely to describe or represent," when "used in connection with any goods or services." 15 U.S.C. §1125(a) (1982 ed.). This language codified, among other things, the related common-law torts of technical trademark infringement and passing off, *see Inwood Laboratories, Inc. v. Ives Laboratories, Inc.*, 456 U.S. 844, 861, n.2, 72 L. Ed. 2d 606, 102 S. Ct. 2182 (1982) (WHITE, J., concurring in result); *Chevron Chemical Co. v. Voluntary Purchasing Groups, Inc.*, 659 F.2d 695, 701 (5th Cir. 1981), *cert. denied*, 457 U.S. 1126, 73 L. Ed. 2d 1342, 102 S. Ct. 2947 (1982), which were causes of action for false descriptions or representations concerning a good's or service's source of production, *see, e. g., Yale Electric Corp. v. Robertson*, 26 F.2d 972, 973 (2d Cir. 1928); *American Washboard Co. v. Saginaw Mfg. Co.*, 103 F. 281, 284–286 (6th Cir. 1900).

At common law, words or symbols that were arbitrary, fanciful, or suggestive (called "inherently distinctive" words or symbols, or "trademarks") were presumed to represent the source of a product, and the first user of a trademark could sue to protect it without having to show that the word or symbol represented the product's source in fact. *See, e. g., Heublein v. Adams*, 125 F. 782, 784 (CC Mass. 1903). That presumption did not attach to personal or geographic names or to words or symbols that only described a product (called "trade names"), and the user of a personal or geographic name or of a descriptive word or symbol could obtain relief only if he first showed that his trade name did in fact represent not just the product, but a producer (that the good or service had developed "secondary meaning"). *See, e. g., Lorence Mfg. Co. v. J.C. Dowd & Co.*, 178 F. 73, 74–75 (2d Cir. 1910). Trade dress, which consists not of words or symbols, but of a product's packaging (or "image," more broadly), seems at common law to have been thought incapable ever of being inherently distinctive, perhaps on the theory that the number of ways to package a product is finite. Thus, a user of trade dress would always have had to show secondary meaning in order to obtain protection.

Over time, judges have come to conclude that packages or images may be as arbitrary, fanciful, or suggestive as words or symbols, their numbers limited only by the human imagination. *See, e.g., AmBrit, Inc. v. Kraft, Inc.*, 812 F.2d 1531, 1536 (11th Cir. 1986) ("square size, bright coloring, pebbled texture, polar bear and sunburst images" of the package of the "Klondike" ice cream bar held inherently distinctive), *cert. denied*, 481 U.S. 1041, 95 L. Ed. 2d 822, 107 S. Ct. 1983 (1987); *see also* Third Restatement §§13, 16. A particular trade dress, then, is now considered as fully capable as a particular trademark of serving as a "representation or designation" of source under §43(a). As a result, the first user of an arbitrary package, like the first user of an arbitrary word, should be entitled to the presumption that his package represents him without having to show that it does so in fact. This rule follows, in my view, from the language of §43(a), and this rule applies under that section without regard to the rules that apply under the sections of the Lanham Act that deal with registration.

Because the Court reaches the same conclusion for different reasons, I join its judgment.

Note

See also Dillon, Joan L. & Michael Landau, Two Pesos v. Taco Cabana: *Still More Interesting for What it Did Not Decide*, 94 Trademark Rep. 944 (2004)

B. Inherently Distinctive Trade Dress

Wal-Mart Stores, Inc. v. Samara Brothers, Inc.
529 U.S. 205 (2000)

SCALIA, J.

In this case, we decide under what circumstances a product's design is distinctive, and therefore protectible, in an action for infringement of unregistered trade dress under §43(a) of the Trademark Act of 1946 (Lanham Act), 60 Stat. 441, as amended, 15 U.S.C. §1125(a).

I

Respondent Samara Brothers, Inc., designs and manufactures children's clothing. Its primary product is a line of spring/summer one-piece seersucker outfits decorated with appliques of hearts, flowers, fruits, and the like. A number of chain stores, including JCPenney, sell this line of clothing under contract with Samara.

Petitioner Wal-Mart Stores, Inc., is one of the nation's best known retailers, selling among other things children's clothing. In 1995, Wal-Mart contracted with one of its suppliers, Judy-Philippine, Inc., to manufacture a line of children's outfits for sale in the 1996 spring/summer season. Wal-Mart sent Judy-Philippine photographs of a number of garments from Samara's line, on which Judy-Philippine's garments were to be based; Judy-Philippine duly copied, with only minor modifications, 16 of Samara's garments, many of which contained copyrighted elements. In 1996, Wal-Mart briskly sold the so-called knockoffs, generating more than $1.15 million in gross profits.

In June 1996, a buyer for JCPenney called a representative at Samara to complain that she had seen Samara garments on sale at Wal-Mart for a lower price than JCPenney was allowed to charge under its contract with Samara. The Samara representative told the buyer that Samara did not supply its clothing to Wal-Mart. Their suspicions aroused, however, Samara officials launched an investigation, which disclosed that Wal-Mart and several other major retailers—Kmart, Caldor, Hills, and Goody's—were selling the knockoffs of Samara's outfits produced by Judy-Philippine.

After sending cease-and-desist letters, Samara brought this action in the United States District Court for the Southern District of New York against Wal-Mart, Judy-Philippine, Kmart, Caldor, Hills, and Goody's for copyright infringement under federal law, consumer fraud and unfair competition under New York law, and—most relevant for our purposes—infringement of unregistered trade dress under §43(a) of the Lanham Act, 15 U.S.C. §1125(a). All of the defendants except Wal-Mart settled before trial.

After a week long trial, the jury found in favor of Samara on all of its claims. Wal-Mart then renewed a motion for judgment as a matter of law, claiming, *inter alia*, that there was insufficient evidence to support a conclusion that Samara's clothing designs could be legally protected as distinctive trade dress for purposes of §43(a). The District Court denied the motion, 969 F. Supp. 895 (SDNY 1997), and awarded Samara damages, interest, costs, and fees totaling almost $1.6 million, together with injunctive relief, *see* App. to Pet. for Cert. 56–58. The Second Circuit affirmed the denial of the motion for judgment as a matter of law, 165 F.3d 120 (1998), and we granted certiorari, 528 U.S. 808, 120 S. Ct. 308, 145 L. Ed. 2d 35 (1999).

* * *

In evaluating the distinctiveness of a mark under §2 (and therefore, by analogy, under §43(a)), courts have held that a mark can be distinctive in one of two ways. First, a mark is inherently distinctive if "[its] intrinsic nature serves to identify a particular source." *Ibid.* In the context of word marks, courts have applied the now-classic test originally formulated by Judge Friendly, in which word marks that are "arbitrary" ("Camel" cigarettes), "fanciful" ("Kodak" film), or "suggestive" ("Tide" laundry detergent) are held to be inherently distinctive. *See Abercrombie & Fitch Co.* v. *Hunting World, Inc.*, 537 F.2d 4, 10–11 (2d Cir. 1976). Second, a mark has acquired distinctiveness, even if it is not inherently distinctive, if it has developed secondary meaning, which occurs when, "in the minds of the public, the primary significance of a [mark] is to identify the source of the product rather than the product itself." *Inwood Laboratories, Inc.* v. *Ives Laboratories, Inc.*, 456 U.S. 844, 851, n. 11, 72 L. Ed. 2d 606, 102 S. Ct. 2182 (1982).[4]

The judicial differentiation between marks that are inherently distinctive and those that have developed secondary meaning has solid foundation in the statute itself. Section 2 requires that registration be granted to any trademark "by which the goods of the applicant may be distinguished from the goods of others"—subject to various limited exceptions. 15 U.S.C. §1052. It also provides, again with limited exceptions, that "nothing in this chapter shall prevent the registration of a mark used by the applicant which has

---

4. The phrase "secondary meaning" originally arose in the context of word marks, where it served to distinguish the source-identifying meaning from the ordinary, or "primary," meaning of the word. "Secondary meaning" has since come to refer to the acquired, source-identifying meaning of a non-word mark as well. It is often a misnomer in that context, since non-word marks ordinarily have no "primary" meaning. Clarity might well be served by using the term "acquired meaning" in both the word-mark and the non-word-mark contexts—but in this opinion we follow what has become the conventional terminology.

become distinctive of the applicant's goods in commerce"—that is, which is not inherently distinctive but has become so only through secondary meaning. §2(f), 15 U.S.C. §1052(f). Nothing in §2, however, demands the conclusion that *every* category of mark necessarily includes some marks "by which the goods of the applicant may be distinguished from the goods of others" *without* secondary meaning—that in every category some marks are inherently distinctive.

Indeed, with respect to at least one category of mark—colors—we have held that no mark can ever be inherently distinctive. *See Qualitex*, 514 U.S. at 162–163. In *Qualitex*, petitioner manufactured and sold green-gold dry-cleaning press pads. After respondent began selling pads of a similar color, petitioner brought suit under §43(a), then added a claim under §32 after obtaining registration for the color of its pads. We held that a color could be protected as a trademark, but only upon a showing of secondary meaning. Reasoning by analogy to the *Abercrombie & Fitch* test developed for word marks, we noted that a product's color is unlike a "fanciful," "arbitrary," or "suggestive" mark, since it does not "almost *automatically* tell a customer that [it] refers to a brand," *ibid.*, and does not "immediately ... signal a brand or a product 'source,'" 514 U.S. at 163. However, we noted that, "over time, customers may come to treat a particular color on a product or its packaging ... as signifying a brand." 514 U.S. at 162–163. Because a color, like a "descriptive" word mark, could eventually "come to indicate a product's origin," we concluded that it could be protected *upon a showing of secondary meaning. Ibid.*

It seems to us that design, like color, is not inherently distinctive. The attribution of inherent distinctiveness to certain categories of word marks and product packaging derives from the fact that the very purpose of attaching a particular word to a product, or encasing it in a distinctive packaging, is most often to identify the source of the product. Although the words and packaging can serve subsidiary functions—a suggestive word mark (such as "Tide" for laundry detergent), for instance, may invoke positive connotations in the consumer's mind, and a garish form of packaging (such as Tide's squat, brightly decorated plastic bottles for its liquid laundry detergent) may attract an otherwise indifferent consumer's attention on a crowded store shelf—their predominant function remains source identification. Consumers are therefore predisposed to regard those symbols as indication of the producer, which is why such symbols "almost *automatically* tell a customer that they refer to a brand," 514 U.S. at 162–163, and "immediately ... signal a brand or a product 'source,'" 514 U.S. at 163. And where it is not reasonable to assume consumer predisposition to take an affixed word or packaging as indication of source—where, for example, the affixed word is descriptive of the product ("Tasty" bread) or of a geographic origin ("Georgia" peaches)—inherent distinctiveness will not be found. That is why the statute generally excludes, from those word marks that can be registered as inherently distinctive, words that are "merely descriptive" of the goods, §2(e)(1), 15 U.S.C. §1052 (e)(1), or "primarily geographically descriptive of them," *see* §2(e)(2), 15 U.S.C. §1052(e)(2). In the case of product design, as in the case of color, we think consumer predisposition to equate the feature with the source does not exist. Consumers are aware of the reality that, almost invariably, even the most unusual of product designs—such as a cocktail shaker shaped like a penguin—is intended not to identify the source, but to render the product itself more useful or more appealing.

The fact that product design almost invariably serves purposes other than source identification not only renders inherent distinctiveness problematic; it also renders application of an inherent-distinctiveness principle more harmful to other consumer interests. Consumers should not be deprived of the benefits of competition with regard to the utilitarian and esthetic purposes that product design ordinarily serves by a rule of law that facilitates plausible threats of suit against new entrants based upon alleged inherent distinctiveness. How easy it is to mount a plausible suit depends, of course, upon the clarity of the test for inherent distinctiveness, and where product design is concerned we have little confidence that a reasonably clear test can be devised. Respondent and the United States as *amicus curiae* urge us to adopt for product design relevant portions of the test formulated by the Court of Customs and Patent Appeals for product packaging in *Seabrook Foods, Inc. v. Bar-Well Foods, Ltd.*, 568 F.2d 1342 (1977). That opinion, in determining the inherent distinctiveness of a product's packaging, considered, among other things, "whether it was a 'common' basic shape or design, whether it was unique or unusual in a particular field, [and] whether it was a mere refinement of a commonly-adopted and well-known form of ornamentation for a particular class of goods viewed by the public as a dress or ornamentation for the goods." *Id.* at 1344 (footnotes omitted). Such a test would rarely provide the basis for summary disposition of an anticompetitive strike suit. Indeed, at oral argument, counsel for the United States quite understandably would not give a definitive answer as to whether the test was met in this very case, saying only that "this is a very difficult case for that purpose."

It is true, of course, that the person seeking to exclude new entrants would have to establish the nonfunctionality of the design feature, *see* §43(a)(3), 15 U.S.C.A. §1125(a)(3) (Oct. 1999 Supp.) — a showing that may involve consideration of its esthetic appeal, *see Qualitex*, 514 U.S. at 170. Competition is deterred, however, not merely by successful suit but by the plausible threat of successful suit, and given the unlikelihood of inherently source-identifying design, the game of allowing suit based upon alleged inherent distinctiveness seems to us not worth the candle. That is especially so since the producer can ordinarily obtain protection for a design that *is* inherently source identifying (if any such exists), but that does not yet have secondary meaning, by securing a design patent or a copyright for the design — as, indeed, respondent did for certain elements of the designs in this case. The availability of these other protections greatly reduces any harm to the producer that might ensue from our conclusion that a product design cannot be protected under §43(a) without a showing of secondary meaning.

Respondent contends that our decision in *Two Pesos* forecloses a conclusion that product-design trade dress can never be inherently distinctive. In that case, we held that the trade dress of a chain of Mexican restaurants, which the plaintiff described as "a festive eating atmosphere having interior dining and patio areas decorated with artifacts, bright colors, paintings and murals," 505 U.S. at 765 (internal quotation marks and citation omitted), could be protected under §43(a) without a showing of secondary meaning, *see* 505 U.S. at 776. *Two Pesos* unquestionably establishes the legal principle that trade dress can be inherently distinctive, *see, e.g.*, 505 U.S. at 773, but it does not establish that *product-design* trade dress can be. *Two Pesos* is inapposite to our holding here because the trade dress at issue, the decor of a restaurant, seems to us not to constitute product *design*. It was either product packaging — which, as we have discussed, normally *is* taken by the consumer to indicate origin — or else some *tertium quid* that is akin to product packaging and has no bearing on the present case.

Respondent replies that this manner of distinguishing *Two Pesos* will force courts to draw difficult lines between product-design and product-packaging trade dress. There will indeed be some hard cases at the margin: a classic glass Coca-Cola bottle, for instance, may constitute packaging for those consumers who drink the Coke and then discard the bottle, but may constitute the product itself for those consumers who are bottle collectors, or part of the product itself for those consumers who buy Coke in the classic glass bottle, rather than a can, because they think it more stylish to drink from the former. We believe, however, that the frequency and the difficulty of having to distinguish between product design and product packaging will be much less than the frequency and the difficulty of having to decide when a product design is inherently distinctive. To the extent there are close cases, we believe that courts should err on the side of caution and classify ambiguous trade dress as product design, thereby requiring secondary meaning. The very closeness will suggest the existence of relatively small utility in adopting an inherent-distinctiveness principle, and relatively great consumer benefit in requiring a demonstration of secondary meaning.

* * *

We hold that, in an action for infringement of unregistered trade dress under § 43(a) of the Lanham Act, a product's design is distinctive, and therefore protectible, only upon a showing of secondary meaning. The judgment of the Second Circuit is reversed, and the case is remanded for further proceedings consistent with this opinion.

In re Joanne Slokevag
441 F.3d 957 (Fed. Cir 2006)441 F.3d 957

LOURIE, CIRCUIT JUDGE.

BACKGROUND

Slokevage filed an application to register a mark on the Principal Register for "pants, overalls, shorts, culottes, dresses, skirts." Slokevage described the mark in her application as a "configuration" that consists of a label with the words "FLASH DARE!" in a V-shaped background, and cut-out areas located on each side of the label. The cut-out areas consist of a hole in a garment and a flap attached to the garment with a closure device. This trade dress configuration is located on the rear of various garments.

DISCUSSION
I. Trade Dress and Product Design

On appeal, Slokevage argues that the Board erred in determining that the trade dress for which she seeks protection is product design and thus that it cannot be inherently distinctive. She asserts that the Board's reliance on the Supreme Court's decision in Wal-Mart to support its position that Slokevage's trade dress is product design is misplaced. In particular, she contends that Wal-Mart does not provide guidance on how to determine whether trade dress is product design. Moreover, she maintains that the trade dress at issue in Wal-Mart, which was classified as product design without explanation, is different from Slokevage's trade dress because the Wal-Mart trade dress implicated the overall appearance of the product and was a theme made up of many unique elements. Slokevage argues that her trade dress, in contrast, involves one component of a product design, which can be used with a variety of types of clothing. Slokevage further asserts that her trade dress is located on the rear hips of garments, which is a location that consumers frequently recognize as identifying the source of the garment.

Slokevage's trade dress constitutes product design and therefore cannot be inherently distinctive. The Lanham Act provides protection not only for words and symbols, but also for "trade dress," a category of trademarks that has been described as involving the "total image of a product," including "features such as size, shape, color or color combinations, texture, graphics, or even particular sales techniques." *Two Pesos, Inc. v. Taco Ca-*

bana, Inc., 505 U.S. 763, 764 n.1, 112 S. Ct. 2753, 120 L. Ed. 2d 615 (1992). The Supreme Court has recently observed that trade dress is a category that originally included only the packaging of a product, but has been expanded by courts to encompass the design of a product. *Wal-Mart*, 529 U.S. at 209. In order for an applicant to gain protection for trade dress, the trade dress must be distinctive, either inherently or by acquiring distinctiveness. *Two-Pesos*, 505 U.S. at 769. Trade dress is inherently distinctive when its "intrinsic nature serves to identify a particular source of a product," and, in contrast, acquires distinctiveness when the public comes to associate the product with its source. *Id.* at 768–769. The Supreme Court has determined that certain types of trade dress, in particular, product design and color, can never be inherently distinctive. *See Qualitex Co. v. Jacobson Prods. Co.*, 514 U.S. 159, 162, 115 S. Ct. 1300, 131 L. Ed. 2d 248 (1995) (color can never be inherently distinctive); *Wal-Mart*, 529 U.S. at 212 (product design is not inherently distinctive).

Directly relevant to our discussion of product design is the Court's discussion in Wal-Mart. That case addressed whether product design could ever be inherently distinctive and answered the question in the negative. The trade dress in Wal-Mart involved children's clothing decorated with "hearts, flowers, fruits, and the like." 529 U.S. at 207. The Court labeled that trade dress product design and ultimately concluded that product design is entitled to protection only if it has acquired distinctiveness. *Id.* at 216. The Court reasoned that "in the case of product design ... we think consumer predisposition to equate the feature with the source does not exist" and stated that "even the most unusual of product designs—such as a cocktail shaker shaped like a penguin—is intended not to identify the source, but to render the product itself more useful or more appealing." *Id.* at 213. Thus, the Court established a bright-line rule—product design cannot be inherently distinctive, and always requires proof of acquired distinctiveness to be protected. The Court did not recite the factors that distinguish between product packaging and product design trade dress, but stated that in "close cases" courts should classify the trade dress as product design. *Id.* at 215.

Both parties agree that if we determine that the trade dress at issue is product design, then it cannot be inherently distinctive under the decision in *Wal-Mart*. The issue pertinent to this appeal, however, is whether Slokevage's proposed trade dress is product design. Although the decision in *Wal-Mart* does not expressly address the issue of what constitutes product design, it is informative to this case because it provides examples of trade dress that are product design. The Court observed that a "cocktail shaker shaped like a penguin" is product design and that the trade dress at issue in that case, "a line of spring/summer one-piece seersucker outfits decorated with appliques of hearts, flowers, fruits, and the like" is product design. *Wal-Mart*, 529 U.S. at 207, 213. These examples demonstrate that product design can consist of design features incorporated into a product. Slokevage urges that her trade dress is not product design because it does not alter the entire product but is more akin to a label being placed on a garment. We do not agree. The holes and flaps portion are part of the design of the clothing—the cut-out area is not merely a design placed on top of a garment, but is a design incorporated into the garment itself. Moreover, while Slokevage urges that product design trade dress must implicate the entire product, we do not find support for that proposition. Just as the product design in *Wal-Mart* consisted of certain design features featured on clothing, Slokevage's trade dress similarly consists of design features, holes and flaps, featured in clothing, revealing the similarity between the two types of design.

In addition, the reasoning behind the Supreme Court's determination that product design cannot be inherently distinctive is also instructive to our case. The Court reasoned that, unlike a trademark whose "predominant function" remains source identification, product design often serves other functions, such as rendering the "product itself more useful or more appealing." *Wal-Mart*, 529 U.S. at 212, 213. The design at issue here can serve such utilitarian and aesthetic functions. For example, consumers may purchase Slokevage's clothing for the utilitarian purpose of wearing a garment or because they find the appearance of the garment particularly desirable. Consistent with the Supreme Court's analysis in *Wal-Mart*, in such cases when the purchase implicates a utilitarian or aesthetic purpose, rather than a source-identifying function, it is appropriate to require proof of acquired distinctiveness.

Finally, the Court in *Wal-Mart* provided guidance on how to address trade dress cases that may be difficult to classify: "To the extent that there are close cases, we believe that courts should err on the side of caution and classify ambiguous trade dress as product design, thereby requiring secondary meaning." 529 U.S. at 215. Even if this were a close case, therefore, we must follow that precedent and classify the trade dress as product design. We thus agree with the Board that Slokevage's trade dress is product design and therefore that she must prove acquired distinctiveness in order for her trade dress mark to be registered.

Notes

1. Of course, the *Wal-Mart* decision begs the question of what constitutes secondary meaning for trade dress. If the *Ambercrombie* analysis does not apply to arguably inherently distinctive trade dress, is it possible to use trademark doctrine to determine when trade dress has secondary meaning, or is this a new category of an appellation of source that requires new doctrine throughout? One court answered this question by pointing out that the factors which show trade dress has secondary meaning include the following: 1) exclusivity, length, and manner of use; 2) amount and manner of advertising; 3) amount of sales and number of customers; 4) established place in the market; 5) direct consumer testimony; 6) consumer surveys; and 7) intentional copying. *Herman Miller, Inc. v. Palazetti Imp. and Exp., Inc.*, 270 F.3d 298 (6th Cir. 2001). If this is the case, is there anything truly different in the analysis of what constitutes trade dress secondary meaning as opposed to what constitutes trademark secondary meaning? *Cf. International Kennel Club of Chicago, Inc.* (*supra* Chapter V).

2. Prior to the *Wal-Mart* decision, most courts defined trade dress as the total look of a product *and* its packaging. *See, e.g., John H. Harland Co. v. Clarke Checks, Inc.*, 711 F. 2d 966 (11th Cir. 1983). Will even the definition of trade dress change in light of the *Wal-Mart* case? *See* Ingrida Karins Berzins, *The Emerging Circuit Split Over Secondary Meaning in Trade Dress Law*, 152 U. Pa. L. Rev. 1661 (2004).

3. In *Wal-Mart*, do you agree that "the Court's holding that product designs are not inherently distinctive was made with little, if any, legal support and seems at odds with actual experience"? Joseph J. Ferretti, *Product Design Trade Dress Hits the Wall … Mart: Wal-Mart v. Samara Bros.*, 42 Idea 417, 450 (2002).

4. With its decision in *Taco Cabana* in 1992, the Supreme Court threw the door wide open for litigants to claim a wide range of product design trademarks. The Court chose to close this door but not overrule *Taco Cabana* in *Wal-Mart Stores, Inc.* However, is *Taco Cabana* still applicable law? After the decision in *Wal-Mart* what sort of trade dress would ever satisfy the "tertium quid" standard? If nothing would, why not just overrule *Taco*

Cabana? If the Supreme Court's intent was to signal a change in policy where they will now strictly scrutinize claims to trade dress protection while in the *Taco Cabana* era they did not, would overruling *Taco Cabana* be more intellectually honest? Besides, why the abrupt change after only eight years? What is the Supreme Court afraid of? *See also*, Lars Smith, *Trade Distinctiveness: Solving Scalia's Tertium Quid Trade Dress Conundrum*, 2005 Mich. St. L. Rev. 243 (2005) (Arguing that it is impossible to have inherently distinctive trade dress and therefore courts should focus on the distinctiveness of a trade dress rather than creating new categories); S. Lloyd Smith, *Wal-Mart v. Samara Brothers and its Progeny*, 94 Trademark Rep. 1037 (2004).

5. In the *Joanne Slokevag* case, how did the court decide if the design was product design or not? How did this decision align with the Supreme Court's decision in *Wal-Mart*?

C. Functional Trade Dress

TrafFix Devices, Inc. v. Marketing Displays, Inc.
532 U.S. 23 (2001)

Justice Kennedy delivered the opinion of the Court.

Temporary road signs with warnings like "Road Work Ahead" or "Left Shoulder Closed" must withstand strong gusts of wind. An inventor named Robert Sarkisian obtained two utility patents for a mechanism built upon two springs (the dual-spring design) to keep these and other outdoor signs upright despite adverse wind conditions. The holder of the now-expired Sarkisian patents, respondent Marketing Displays, Inc. (MDI), established a successful business in the manufacture and sale of sign stands incorporating the patented feature. MDI's stands for road signs were recognizable to buyers and users (it says) because the dual-spring design was visible near the base of the sign.

This litigation followed after the patents expired and a competitor, TrafFix Devices, Inc., sold sign stands with a visible spring mechanism that looked like MDI's. MDI and TrafFix products looked alike because they were. When TrafFix started in business, it sent an MDI product abroad to have it reverse engineered, that is to say copied. Complicating matters, TrafFix marketed its sign stands under a name similar to MDI's. MDI used the name "WindMaster," while TrafFix, its new competitor, used "WindBuster."

MDI brought suit under the Trademark Act of 1964 (Lanham Act), 60 Stat. 427, as amended, 15 U.S.C. §1051 *et seq.*, against TrafFix for trademark infringement (based on the similar names), trade dress infringement (based on the copied dual-spring design) and unfair competition. TrafFix counterclaimed on antitrust theories. After the United States District Court for the Eastern District of Michigan considered cross-motions for summary judgment, MDI prevailed on its trademark claim for the confusing similarity of names and was held not liable on the antitrust counterclaim; and those two rulings, affirmed by the Court of Appeals, are not before us.

I

We are concerned with the trade dress question. The District Court ruled against MDI on its trade dress claim. 971 F. Supp. 262 (ED Mich. 1997). After determining that the one element of MDI's trade dress at issue was the dual-spring design, *id.* at 265, it held that "no reasonable trier of fact could determine that MDI has established secondary meaning" in its alleged trade dress, *id.* at 269. In other words, consumers did not associate the look of the dual-spring design with MDI. As a second, independent reason to grant summary judgment in favor of TrafFix, the District Court determined the dual-spring design was functional. On this rationale secondary meaning is irrelevant because there can be no trade dress protection in any event. In ruling on the functional aspect of the design, the District Court noted that Sixth Circuit precedent indicated that the burden was on MDI to prove that its trade dress was nonfunctional, and not on TrafFix to show that it was functional (a rule since adopted by Congress, *see* 15 U.S.C. §1125(a)(3) (1994 ed., Supp. V)), and then went on to consider MDI's arguments that the dual-spring design was subject to trade dress protection. Finding none of MDI's contentions persuasive, the District Court concluded MDI had not "proffered sufficient evidence which would enable a reasonable trier of fact to find that MDI's vertical dual-spring design is *non-functional.*" *Id.* at 276. Summary judgment was entered against MDI on its trade dress claims.

The Court of Appeals for the Sixth Circuit reversed the trade dress ruling. 200 F.3d 929 (1999). The Court of Appeals held the District Court had erred in ruling MDI failed to show a genuine issue of material fact regarding whether it had secondary meaning in its alleged trade dress, 200 F.3d at 938, and had erred further in determining that MDI could not prevail in any event because the alleged trade dress was in fact a functional product configuration, 200 F.3d at 940. The Court of Appeals suggested the District Court committed legal error by looking only to the dual-spring design when evaluating MDI's trade dress. Basic to its reasoning was the Court of Appeals' observation that it took "little imagination to conceive of a hidden dual-spring mechanism or a tri or quad-spring mechanism that might avoid infringing [MDI's] trade dress." *Ibid.* The Court of Appeals explained that "if TrafFix or another competitor chooses to use [MDI's] dual-spring design, then it will have to find *some other way* to set its sign apart to avoid infringing [MDI's] trade dress." *Ibid.* It was not sufficient, according to the Court of Appeals, that allowing exclusive use of a particular feature such as the dual-spring design in the guise of trade dress would "hinder competition somewhat." Rather, "exclusive use of a feature must 'put competitors at a *significant* non-reputation-related disadvantage' before trade dress protection is denied on functionality grounds." *Ibid.* (quoting *Qualitex Co. v. Jacobson Products Co.*, 514 U.S. 159, 165, 131 L. Ed. 2d 248, 115 S. Ct. 1300 (1995)). In its criticism of the District Court's ruling on the trade dress question, the Court of Appeals took note of a split among Courts of Appeals in various other Circuits on the issue whether the existence of an expired utility patent forecloses the possibility of the patentee's claiming trade dress protection in the product's design. 200 F.3d at 939. *Compare Sunbeam Products, Inc. v. West Bend Co.*, 123 F.3d 246 (CA5 1997) (holding that trade dress protection is not foreclosed), *Thomas & Betts Corp. v. Panduit Corp.*, 138 F.3d 277 (CA7 1998) (same), and *Midwest Industries, Inc. v. Karavan Trailers, Inc.*, 175 F.3d 1356 (CA Fed 1999) (same), with *Vornado Air Circulation Systems, Inc. v. Duracraft Corp.*, 58 F.3d 1498, 1500 (CA10 1995) ("Where a product configuration is a significant inventive component of an invention covered by a utility patent ... it cannot receive trade dress protection"). To resolve the conflict, we granted certiorari. 530 U.S. 1260 (2000).

II

It is well established that trade dress can be protected under federal law. The design or packaging of a product may acquire a distinctiveness which serves to identify the product with its manufacturer or source; and a design or package which acquires this secondary meaning, assuming other requisites are met, is a trade dress which may not be used in a manner likely to cause confusion as to the origin, sponsorship, or approval of the goods. In these respects protection for trade dress exists to promote competition. As we explained just last Term, *see Wal-Mart Stores, Inc. v. Samara Brothers, Inc.,* 529 U.S. 205, 146 L. Ed. 2d 182, 120 S. Ct. 1339 (2000), various Courts of Appeals have allowed claims of trade dress infringement relying on the general provision of the Lanham Act which provides a cause of action to one who is injured when a person uses "any word, term name, symbol, or device, or any combination thereof … which is likely to cause confusion … as to the origin, sponsorship, or approval of his or her goods." 15 U.S.C. §1125(a)(1)(A). Congress confirmed this statutory protection for trade dress by amending the Lanham Act to recognize the concept. Title 15 U.S.C. §1125(a)(3) (1994 ed., Supp. V) provides: "In a civil action for trade dress infringement under this chapter for trade dress not registered on the principal register, the person who asserts trade dress protection has the burden of proving that the matter sought to be protected is not functional." This burden of proof gives force to the well-established rule that trade dress protection may not be claimed for product features that are functional. *Qualitex,* 514 U.S. at 164–165; *Two Pesos, Inc. v. Taco Cabana, Inc.,* 505 U.S. 763, 775, 120 L. Ed. 2d 615, 112 S. Ct. 2753 (1992). And in *Wal-Mart, supra,* we were careful to caution against misuse or over-extension of trade dress. We noted that "product design almost invariably serves purposes other than source identification." 529 U.S. at 213.

Trade dress protection must subsist with the recognition that in many instances there is no prohibition against copying goods and products. In general, unless an intellectual property right such as a patent or copyright protects an item, it will be subject to copying. As the Court has explained, copying is not always discouraged or disfavored by the laws which preserve our competitive economy. *Bonito Boats, Inc. v. Thunder Craft Boats, Inc.,* 489 U.S. 141, 160, 103 L. Ed. 2d 118, 109 S. Ct. 971 (1989). Allowing competitors to copy will have salutary effects in many instances. "Reverse engineering of chemical and mechanical articles in the public domain often leads to significant advances in technology." *Ibid.*

The principal question in this case is the effect of an expired patent on a claim of trade dress infringement. A prior patent, we conclude, has vital significance in resolving the trade dress claim. A utility patent is strong evidence that the features therein claimed are functional. If trade dress protection is sought for those features the strong evidence of functionality based on the previous patent adds great weight to the statutory presumption that features are deemed functional until proved otherwise by the party seeking trade dress protection. Where the expired patent claimed the features in question, one who seeks to establish trade dress protection must carry the heavy burden of showing that the feature is not functional, for instance by showing that it is merely an ornamental, incidental, or arbitrary aspect of the device.

In the case before us, the central advance claimed in the expired utility patents (the Sarkisian patents) is the dual-spring design; and the dual-spring design is the essential feature of the trade dress MDI now seeks to establish and to protect. The rule we have explained bars the trade dress claim, for MDI did not, and cannot, carry the burden of overcoming the strong evidentiary inference of functionality based on the disclosure of the dual-spring design in the claims of the expired patents.

The dual springs shown in the Sarkisian patents were well apart (at either end of a frame for holding a rectangular sign when one full side is the base) while the dual springs at issue here are close together (in a frame designed to hold a sign by one of its corners). As the District Court recognized, this makes little difference. The point is that the springs are necessary to the operation of the device. The fact that the springs in this very different-looking device fall within the claims of the patents is illustrated by MDI's own position in earlier litigation. In the late 1970's, MDI engaged in a long-running intellectual property battle with a company known as Winn-Proof. Although the precise claims of the Sarkisian patents cover sign stands with springs "spaced apart," U.S. Patent No. 3,646,696, col. 4; U.S. Patent No. 3,662,482, col. 4, the Winn-Proof sign stands (with springs much like the sign stands at issue here) were found to infringe the patents by the United States District Court for the District of Oregon, and the Court of Appeals for the Ninth Circuit affirmed the judgment. *Sarkisian v. Winn-Proof Corp.*, 697 F.2d 1313 (1983). Although the Winn-Proof traffic sign stand (with dual springs close together) did not appear, then, to infringe the literal terms of the patent claims (which called for "spaced apart" springs), the Winn-Proof sign stand was found to infringe the patents under the doctrine of equivalents, which allows a finding of patent infringement even when the accused product does not fall within the literal terms of the claims. 697 F.2d at 1321–1322; *see generally Warner-Jenkinson Co. v. Hilton Davis Chemical Co.*, 520 U.S. 17, 137 L. Ed. 2d 146, 117 S. Ct. 1040 (1997). In light of this past ruling—a ruling procured at MDI's own insistence—it must be concluded the products here at issue would have been covered by the claims of the expired patents.

The rationale for the rule that the disclosure of a feature in the claims of a utility patent constitutes strong evidence of functionality is well illustrated in this case. The dual-spring design serves the important purpose of keeping the sign upright even in heavy wind conditions; and, as confirmed by the statements in the expired patents, it does so in a unique and useful manner. As the specification of one of the patents recites, prior art "devices, in practice, will topple under the force of a strong wind." U.S. Patent No. 3,662,482, col. 1. The dual-spring design allows sign stands to resist toppling in strong winds. Using a dual-spring design rather than a single spring achieves important operational advantages. For example, the specifications of the patents note that the "use of a pair of springs ... as opposed to the use of a single spring to support the frame structure prevents canting or twisting of the sign around a vertical axis," and that, if not prevented, twisting "may cause damage to the spring structure and may result in tipping of the device." U.S. Patent No. 3,646,696, col. 3. In the course of patent prosecution, it was said that "the use of a pair of spring connections as opposed to a single spring connection ... forms an important part of this combination" because it "forces the sign frame to tip along the longitudinal axis of the elongated ground-engaging members." App. 218. The dual-spring design affects the cost of the device as well; it was acknowledged that the device "could use three springs but this would unnecessarily increase the cost of the device." App. 217. These statements made in the patent applications and in the course of procuring the patents demonstrate the functionality of the design. MDI does not assert that any of these representations are mistaken or inaccurate, and this is further strong evidence of the functionality of the dual-spring design.

III

In finding for MDI on the trade dress issue the Court of Appeals gave insufficient recognition to the importance of the expired utility patents, and their evidentiary significance, in establishing the functionality of the device. The error likely was caused by its misinterpretation of trade dress principles in other respects. As we have noted, even if there has been no previous utility patent the party asserting trade dress has the burden to establish the nonfunctionality of alleged trade dress features. MDI could not meet this burden. Discussing trademarks, we have said "'in general terms, a product feature is functional,' and cannot serve as a trademark, 'if it is essential to the use or purpose of the article or if it affects the cost or quality of the article.'" *Qualitex*, 514 U.S. at 165 (quoting *Inwood Laboratories, Inc. v. Ives Laboratories, Inc.*, 456 U.S. 844, 850, n. 10, 72 L. Ed. 2d 606, 102 S. Ct. 2182 (1982)). Expanding upon the meaning of this phrase, we have observed that a functional feature is one the "exclusive use of [which] would put competitors at a significant non-reputation-related disadvantage." 514 U.S. at 165. The Court of Appeals in the instant case seemed to interpret this language to mean that a necessary test for functionality is "whether the particular product configuration is a competitive necessity." 200 F.3d at 940. *See also Vornado*, 58 F.3d at 1507 ("Functionality, by contrast, has been defined both by our circuit, and more recently by the Supreme Court, in terms of competitive need"). This was incorrect as a comprehensive definition. As explained in *Qualitex, supra,* and *Inwood, supra,* a feature is also functional when it is essential to the use or purpose of the device or when it affects the cost or quality of the device. The *Qualitex* decision did not purport to displace this traditional rule. Instead, it quoted the rule as *Inwood* had set it forth. It is proper to inquire into a "significant non-reputation-related disadvantage" in cases of aesthetic functionality, the question involved in *Qualitex*. Where the design is functional under the *Inwood* formulation there is no need to proceed further to consider if there is a competitive necessity for the feature. In *Qualitex*, by contrast, aesthetic functionality was the central question, there having been no indication that the green-gold color of the laundry press pad had any bearing on the use or purpose of the product or its cost or quality.

The Court has allowed trade dress protection to certain product features that are inherently distinctive. *Two Pesos,* 505 U.S. at 774. In *Two Pesos*, however, the Court at the outset made the explicit analytic assumption that the trade dress features in question (decorations and other features to evoke a Mexican theme in a restaurant) were not functional. 505 U.S. at 767, n. 6. The trade dress in those cases did not bar competitors from copying functional product design features. In the instant case, beyond serving the purpose of informing consumers that the sign stands are made by MDI (assuming it does so), the dual-spring design provides a unique and useful mechanism to resist the force of the wind. Functionality having been established, whether MDI's dual-spring design has acquired secondary meaning need not be considered.

There is no need, furthermore, to engage, as did the Court of Appeals, in speculation about other design possibilities, such as using three or four springs which might serve the same purpose. 200 F.3d at 940. Here, the functionality of the spring design means that competitors need not explore whether other spring juxtapositions might be used. The dual-spring design is not an arbitrary flourish in the configuration of MDI's product; it is the reason the device works. Other designs need not be attempted.

Because the dual-spring design is functional, it is unnecessary for competitors to explore designs to hide the springs, say by using a box or framework to cover them, as suggested by the Court of Appeals. *Ibid.* The dual-spring design assures the user the device will work. If buyers are assured the product serves its purpose by seeing the operative mechanism that in itself serves an important market need. It would be at cross-purposes to those objectives, and something of a paradox, were we to require the manufacturer to conceal the very item the user seeks.

In a case where a manufacturer seeks to protect arbitrary, incidental, or ornamental aspects of features of a product found in the patent claims, such as arbitrary curves in the legs or an ornamental pattern painted on the springs, a different result might obtain. There the manufacturer could perhaps prove that those aspects do not serve a purpose within the terms of the utility patent. The inquiry into whether such features, asserted to be trade dress, are functional by reason of their inclusion in the claims of an expired utility patent could be aided by going beyond the claims and examining the patent and its prosecution history to see if the feature in question is shown as a useful part of the invention. No such claim is made here, however. MDI in essence seeks protection for the dual-spring design alone. The asserted trade dress consists simply of the dual-spring design, four legs, a base, an upright, and a sign. MDI has pointed to nothing arbitrary about the components of its device or the way they are assembled. The Lanham Act does not exist to reward manufacturers for their innovation in creating a particular device; that is the purpose of the patent law and its period of exclusivity. The Lanham Act, furthermore, does not protect trade dress in a functional design simply because an investment has been made to encourage the public to associate a particular functional feature with a single manufacturer or seller. The Court of Appeals erred in viewing MDI as possessing the right to exclude competitors from using a design identical to MDI's and to require those competitors to adopt a different design simply to avoid copying it. MDI cannot gain the exclusive right to produce sign stands using the dual-spring design by asserting that consumers associate it with the look of the invention itself. Whether a utility patent has expired or there has been no utility patent at all, a product design which has a particular appearance may be functional because it is "essential to the use or purpose of the article" or "affects the cost or quality of the article." *Inwood*, 456 U.S. at 850, n. 10.

TrafFix and some of its *amici* argue that the Patent Clause of the Constitution, Art. I, §8, cl. 8, of its own force, prohibits the holder of an expired utility patent from claiming trade dress protection. Brief for Petitioner 33–36; Brief for Panduit Corp. as *Amicus Curiae* 3; Brief for Malla Pollack as *Amicus Curiae* 2. We need not resolve this question. If, despite the rule that functional features may not be the subject of trade dress protection, a case arises in which trade dress becomes the practical equivalent of an expired utility patent, that will be time enough to consider the matter. The judgment of the Court of Appeals is reversed, and the case is remanded for further proceedings consistent with this opinion.

It is so ordered.

Tie Tech, Inc. v. Kinedyne Corporation
296 F.3d 778 (9th Cir. 2002)

McKEOWN, CIRCUIT JUDGE:

This case concerns the validity of a product configuration trademark for the SAFECUT tm "web-cutter" device. The issue presented is whether summary judgment was appropriate on grounds that the design is functional and therefore not protectible as a trademark. Underlying this question is the evidentiary role of a trademark registration in such a proceeding. We affirm the district court's grant of summary judgment against the trademark holder because the product design is not fanciful, but instead wholly functional, and consequently cannot have trademark significance.

BACKGROUND

Tie Tech makes and markets "wheelchair securement systems" for private and public vehicles. One of its products, the SAFECUT "web-cutter," is used in emergencies to facilitate the quick release of individuals from their securement systems. Tie Tech, which designed and marketed this cutter beginning in the 1980's, describes its product as "a hand-held, well-balanced webbing cutter" that is "made of durable polycarbonate." An advertising image portrays the SAFECUT device in action: a hand is gripping the device with four fingers fitted through an enclosed oval opening; an elongated prong of plastic guides the webbing towards a recessed cutting blade. Tie Tech offered the following depiction of the device:

In 1998, the Patent and Trademark Office (PTO) registered "the entire configuration and arbitrary embellishment" of the SAFECUT device as a trademark on its primary register. Specifically excepted from this trademark were the scalloped "finger indentations" on the handle which the examiner had previously concluded to be functional, thus precluding registration of those aspects of the design. Tie Tech achieved this result not without considerable struggle. The examiner originally rejected the application because, among other grounds, he concluded that the entire configuration was functional in design. After an appeal to the Trademark Trial and Appeal Board (TTAB), however, the application was remanded for further reconsideration, and the examiner without explanation limited his conclusions about functionality to the finger indentations on the handle and the shape of the partially concealed blade.

Kinedyne is a competitor of Tie Tech in the web-cutter market. As late as June 1999, Kinedyne was selling its own distinctive web-cutter. After some of Kinedyne's customers expressed dissatisfaction with Kinedyne's original cutter, one of its sales representatives requested a cutter similar to the SAFECUT design. According to Kinedyne's regional director, he understood that the representative wanted a SAFECUT-styled design because Kinedyne's then-current design "did not meet [unspecified] states' satisfaction."

In response to the special request, Kinedyne redesigned its web-cutter. The resulting Kinedyne cutter is virtually indistinguishable from the SAFECUT — save the color, the manufacturer's name embossed in the polycarbonate frame, and the absence of the scalloped finger indentations in the handle, the most noticeable difference.

Upon discovery of Kinedyne's new cutter, Tie Tech sued Kinedyne for trademark infringement under the Lanham Act, 15 U.S.C. §1114, as well as for unfair competition and consumer protection claims under Washington state law. Kinedyne moved for summary judgment, arguing that, as a consequence of its functionality, the design mark was invalid pursuant to 15 U.S.C. §1115(b)(8). The district court agreed and granted summary judgment for Kinedyne.

DISCUSSION

The principal issue in this case is whether the district court properly concluded, as a matter of law, that Tie Tech's product configuration is functional and thus unprotectible. Tie Tech's appeal is two-fold. It first argues that the mere fact of trademark registration alone should have been sufficient to create a material issue of fact and defeat summary judgment. In the alternative, Tie Tech argues that it presented sufficient evidence beyond its registration of non-functionality to warrant reversal. We address each contention in turn, recognizing that at the summary judgment stage our charge "is not [ourselves] to weigh the evidence and determine the truth of the matter but to determine whether there is a genuine issue for trial." *Anderson v. Liberty Lobby, Inc.*, 477 U.S. 242, 249, 91 L. Ed. 2d 202, 106 S. Ct. 2505 (1986).

As "prima facie evidence of validity," the registration certificate is simply evidence that "in the judgment of the law, is sufficient to establish a given fact, or the group or chain of facts constituting the party's claim, and which *if not rebutted or contradicted*, will remain sufficient." BLACK'S LAW DICTIONARY 1190 (6th ed. 1990) (emphasis added).

The cases often refer interchangeably to "prima facie evidence" of validity and "presumption of validity." We note that from an evidentiary viewpoint, establishment of a prima facie case is often seen as creating a presumption. For example, in the Title VII context, "establishment of a prima facie case in effect creates a presumption that the employer unlawfully discriminated against the employee." 1 JACK B. WEINSTEIN & MARGARET A. BERGER, WEINSTEIN'S FEDERAL EVIDENCE §301.29[1][a] (Joseph M. McLaughlin, ed., 2d ed. 1997). Thus, while we prefer to use the statutory language because it more precisely conveys the evidentiary nature of the registration, we acknowledge the interchangeability of the terms in practice.

* * *

In trademark terms, the registration is not absolute but is subject to rebuttal. In essence, the registration discharges the plaintiff's original common law burden of proving validity in an infringement action. *Vuitton et Fils S.A. v. J. Young Enters., Inc.*, 644 F.2d 769, 775 (9th Cir. 1981); *see also* 15 U.S.C. §1125(a)(3) (in absence of registered mark, plaintiff has burden of proving non-functionality).

Terminology with respect to the invalidity defense based on functionality is likewise not wholly consistent. The cases variously refer to the defendant as having the burden of proof or having assumed a shifting burden of production. This mixing and matching of terms has engendered some confusion in the analysis. For example, in *Vuitton* we held that the "registration ... shifts the burden of proof from the plaintiff, who would have to establish his right to exclusive use in a common law infringement action, to the defendant, who must introduce sufficient evidence to rebut the presumption of plaintiff's right to such protected use." *Id.* at 775. In contrast, the Seventh Circuit concluded that "the presumption really serves only to shift the burden of production to the defendant." *Liquid Controls*, 802 F.2d at 938.

Although the description of the burden shifting is different in these two cases, the result is the same. Overall, the plaintiff retains the ultimate burden of persuasion in a trademark infringement action, namely proof of infringement. A necessary concomitant to proving infringement is, of course, having a valid trademark; there can be no infringement of an invalid mark. Validity, then, is a threshold issue. On this point, the plaintiff in an infringement action with a registered mark is given the prima facie or presumptive advantage on the issue of validity, thus shifting the burden of production to the defendant to prove otherwise—in our case, to provide evidence of functionality. Or, to put it as we did in *Vuitton*, the defendant then bears the burden with respect to invalidity. Once the presumption of validity is overcome, however, the mark's registration is merely evidence "of registration," nothing more. This approach can be characterized as rebutting the prima facie case or "piercing the presumption."

Of course, at the summary judgment stage, all "inferences from the facts must be drawn most favorably to the nonmoving party." *Vuitton*, 644 F.2d at 776. We also recognize that functionality is generally viewed as an intensely factual issue. *Id.* at 775. Nonetheless, assuming the defendant can demonstrate through law, undisputed facts, or a combination thereof that the mark is invalid, the evidentiary bubble bursts and the plaintiff cannot survive summary judgment. In the face of sufficient and undisputed facts demonstrating functionality, as in our case, the registration loses its evidentiary significance.

Under Tie Tech's theory, on the other hand, a defendant in a trademark infringement action could never prevail at the summary judgment stage on an invalidity defense because the registration itself would always raise a material issue of fact. This approach not only inflates the evidentiary value of a trademark registration, but ignores situations where functionality can be determined as a matter of law based on undisputed facts.

In support of its position, Tie Tech points to *America Online, Inc. v. AT&T Corp.*, 243 F.3d 812, (4th Cir. 2001), where the Fourth Circuit discussed the evidentiary value of the registration:

> Although evidence rebutting the presumption may neutralize the presumption itself—i.e., that the burden of proof on the fact giving rise to the presumption has been met without rebutting evidence—it does not eliminate from the case the evidence itself that gave rise to the presumption. Thus, through the certificate of registration, the Commissioner introduces his opinion that the application of the registrant was sufficient to demonstrate a valid mark.

Id. at 818 (internal citations omitted). Although the court did not elaborate on its reasoning, the key to its decision appears to be the conclusion that a mark's registration should be treated as something of an expert's affidavit on its validity.[5]

Despite this interpretation of the certificate's evidentiary value, the *America Online* court further determined that summary judgment was inappropriate because the record contained other material evidence regarding the mark's validity beyond the certificate of registration. *Id.* Thus, the factual scenario in *America Online* is similar to that of *Vuitton* where we concluded that summary judgment was inappropriate when the plaintiff presented evidence beyond the registration that "if accepted by the trier of fact, would defeat the claim that the Vuitton design is functional." 644 F.2d at 776. Nothing was remarkable about either case—disputed issues of material fact precluded summary judgment.

Because there were genuine issues of material fact raised by the trademark holder's "other evidence," we cannot speculate as to the reach of the Fourth Circuit's analysis. But we need not reconcile the approach in *America Online* and our own because Tie Tech's case presents a decidedly different evidentiary landscape.

What Tie Tech fails to recognize is that we need not weigh any evidence, make any credibility determinations, or otherwise engage in duties appropriate for a fact finder where, as is the case here, there are no disputed material facts. Rather, upon a motion for summary judgment, it is for the court in the first instance to resolve issues of materiality "independent of and separate from the question of the incorporation of the evidentiary standard." *Anderson*, 477 U.S. at 248.

As the discussion below illuminates, Kinedyne has not only presented evidence of functionality sufficient to overcome the evidence of prima facie validity, but Tie Tech has also failed to raise a material issue of fact. By relying primarily on the same evidence offered by Kinedyne or on evidence that Kinedyne does not dispute, Tie Tech demonstrates that at least in this case, the issue is ultimately one of law, and thus properly disposed of at the summary judgment stage. *See id.* ("Only disputes over facts that might affect the outcome of the suit under the governing law will properly preclude the entry of summary judgment."). We turn now to the legal analysis of the functionality defense.

II. FUNCTIONALITY ANALYSIS

Although the Lanham Act prohibits registration of a mark that "comprises any matter that, as a whole, is functional," 15 U.S.C. §1052(e)(5), both parties recognize that not all aspects of functionality are precluded from protection. De jure, or legal, functional-

---

5. We acknowledge, as one commentator notes, that the Fourth Circuit has taken a "decidedly different view" from the Seventh Circuit on the registration's evidentiary significance. *See* 2 J. THOMAS MCCARTHY, MCCARTHY ON TRADEMARKS AND UNFAIR COMPETITION §12:60 (4th ed. 2002).

ity must be distinguished from de facto functionality which still may support trademark protection. *Clamp*, 870 F.2d at 515.

"De jure functionality ... means that the product is in its particular shape because it works better in this shape.... Before an overall product configuration can be recognized as a trademark, the entire design must be arbitrary or non de jure functional." *Textron, Inc. v. U.S. Int'l Trade Comm'n*, 753 F.2d 1019, 1025 (Fed. Cir. 1985) (quoted in *Leatherman Tool Group, Inc. v. Cooper Indus., Inc.*, 199 F.3d 1009, 1012 (9th Cir. 1999)). Thus, for example, even though a bottle is a de facto functional holder of liquid, the bottle's configuration may still qualify for trademark protection if its physical details are nonfunctional and have acquired secondary meaning. *Id.; see also In re Morton-Norwich Prods., Inc.*, 671 F.2d 1332 (C.C.P.A. 1982) (holding that configuration of "Glass Plus" spray-bottle warranted trademark protection).

Here, Kinedyne has identified three aspects of the SAFECUT's configuration — ones it incorporated into its own cutter — that it believes are de jure functional, thus precluding trademark protection: the fully enclosed handle; the rounded edges; and the prong which guides the webbing to the recessed blade. Importantly, Tie Tech has not disputed, either before the trial court or on appeal, the following factual assertions made by Kinedyne:

1. The handle design allowing the hand to pass through permits a secure grip;

2. The rounded edges prevent snagging, and help guide material to the blade; and

3. The prong serves both to guide the webbing or belting onto the cutting blade and to reduce the chance of accidental cuts or injuries.

Rather, by focusing primarily on the shape of the SAFECUT's handle, Tie Tech points to evidence in the record that other alternative designs are available which adequately get the job done.

To begin, there is nothing inherently wrong with Kinedyne's interest in copying the SAFECUT's configuration: "The requirement of nonfunctionality is based 'on the judicial theory that *there exists a fundamental right to compete through imitation of a competitor's product*, which right can only be *temporarily* denied by the patent or copyright laws.'" *Clamp*, 870 F.2d at 516 (quoting *Morton-Norwich*, 671 F.2d at 1336 (emphasis added)). Consequently, as early as *Vuitton*, we characterized the distinction between "features which constitute the actual benefit that the consumer wishes to purchase," which do not engender trademark protection, "as distinguished from an assurance that a particular entity made, sponsored, or endorsed a product," which, if incorporated into the product's design by virtue of arbitrary embellishment, does have trademark significance. 644 F.2d at 774 (internal quotations and citations omitted); *see also Qualitex Co. v. Jacobson Prods. Co.*, 514 U.S. 159, 164, 131 L. Ed. 2d 248, 115 S. Ct. 1300 (1995) ("The functionality doctrine prevents trademark law, which seeks to promote competition by protecting a firm's reputation, from instead inhibiting legitimate competition by allowing a producer to control a useful product feature.").

Unfortunately for Tie Tech, it has not pointed to any evidence of distinctiveness of the SAFECUT design other than those elements essential to its effective use. Instead, Tie Tech suggests something different when it claims that it "is not asking that Kinedyne be barred from having a webcutter with an enclosed blade, a slot and prong to guide the webbing into the blade, or even an opening through which the user can put their [sic] hand," but instead that Kinedyne should "be barred from arranging those elements into a shape that mimics that of the SAFECUT tm." In other words, Tie Tech argues that the overall appearance of its cutter, and not its separate functional parts, is what deserves protection as a nonfunctional aspect of its configuration. This cannot be the case. Where the plaintiff only offers evidence that "the whole is nothing other than the assemblage of functional parts," our court has already foreclosed this argument, holding that "it is semantic trickery to say that there is still some sort of separate 'overall appearance' which is non-functional." *Leatherman*, 199 F.3d at 1013.

Likewise, Tie Tech's evidence of alternative designs fails to raise a material factual issue under *Leatherman*. As was the case with the pocket tool at issue in *Leatherman*, Tie Tech has presented evidence that there are other webcutters with a variety of appearances and features that effectively cut webbing. In particular, Tie Tech cites to a trade journal which evaluated several webcutters including the SAFECUT and another, the Ortho, which is strikingly similar to Kinedyne's original cutter and is described in the article as "the simplest design—a rectangle with rounded corners [that] several testers found … cut the webbing faster than any of the other products." As for the SAFECUT, its shape was "lauded immediately"; one tester was quoted as saying "I like the grip…. It seems like a natural shape." Narrowing their preferences down to the Ortho and the SAFECUT, the article's testers

> split on their ultimate preference in web cutters. But all present agreed that either of the two finalists—Ortho's Web Cutter or Tie Tech's Safecut—admirably did the job. They both ripped through the test webbing in a single motion. *It simply came down to personal preference.* (Emphasis added).

This evidence certainly supports Tie Tech's contention that adequate alternative designs exist which "admirably" do the job, but to Tie Tech's detriment, it goes further. Because the product review not only demonstrates that a design such as the Ortho may be "highly functional and useful," it also undisputedly shows that the Ortho does not "offer *exactly* the same features as [the SAFECUT]," in particular the secured-grip handle, and thus fails as matter of law to support Tie Tech's interest in precluding competition by means of trademark protection. *Id*. at 1013–14 (emphasis in original).

In *Leatherman* we held that a product's manufacturer "does not have rights under trade dress law to compel its competitors to resort to alternative designs which have a different set of advantages and disadvantages. Such is the realm of patent law." *Id*. at 1014 n.7. Here, Tie Tech does not dispute that some customers may prefer a specific functional aspect of the SAFECUT, namely its closed-grip handle, even though other functional designs may ultimately get the job done just as well. As *Leatherman* reminds us, though, a customer's preference for a particular functional aspect of a product is wholly distinct from a customer's desire to be assured "that a particular entity made, sponsored, or endorsed a product." *Id*. at 1012 (quoting *Vuitton*, 644 F.2d at 774). Whereas the latter concern encompasses the realm of trademark protection, the former does not. We therefore conclude on this record that the district court appropriately granted summary judgment in favor of Kinedyne.

AFFIRMED.

Global Mfg. Group, LLC v. Gadget Universe.com
417 F. Supp. 2d 1161 (S.D. CA 2006)

Burns, District Judge.

Factual Background

The upright motorized scooter concept for pedestrians entered the market with wide spread public attention in 2001 when Dean Kamen of Segway LLC introduced its Segway

[R] Human Transporter product. Designed as an alternative to the traditional wheelchair, the Segway scooter operates on a battery rather than fuel, and enables a single rider to travel up to 12 miles per hour on sidewalks. The Segway design has only two wheels, and its gyroscope technology enables the rider to stand up and not lose his balance. That scooter sells for $ 5,000.

James Wang, the president and owner of Plaintiff GMG, admired the Segway product, and decided to create a simplified, less expensive product. In 2003, he developed his competing upright scooter. The first public disclosure of the "Q Electric Chariot" occurred in October 2003, when Wal-Mart carried the product on its website; however, the major advertising campaign began in January 2004, when Plaintiff exhibited the scooter at several trade shows. The Q scooter was different than the Segway because it had four wheels for stability and did not have the gyroscope balancing system. It sells for approximately $ 1,000, and is carried at store fronts, such as Target and Pep Boys, and on the Internet. The scooter has a unique steering system which the rider can operate either by turning the handle bar for sharp turns *or* by leaning your body weight into the desired direction for a more gradual turn. The Q Electric Chariot also differs from the Segway because it can be converted to carry cargo by attaching a cargo rack to the motorized scooter.

Since mid-2004, Gadget has offered a Rietti Civic Mover Electric Scooter for sale on Internet websites for $ 700. Like the plaintiff's Q, the Rietti has two large front wheels and two smaller back wheels to provide stability. *Id.*

In June 2005, the PTO issued a utility patent on the Q Electric Chariot on its seven claims regarding the steering method and the conversion to a cargo rack. A few weeks later, in July 2005, the PTO issued a design patent for the ornamental design.

In this action, GMG alleges that defendants have infringed upon Plaintiff's intellectual property rights in the Q electric chariot. This motion, however, concerns only GMG's second cause of action for trade dress infringement, and is brought only by Defendant Global.

Discussion

"Trade dress may be protected if it is nonfunctional and has acquired secondary meaning and if its imitation creates a likelihood of consumer confusion." *Fuddruckers, Inc. v. Doc's B.R. Others, Inc.*, 826 F.2d 837, 842. (9th Cir. 1987), *cited with approval in Two Pesos, Inc. v. Taco Cabana, Inc.*, 505 U.S. 763, 769–70, 773–74, 112 S. Ct. 2753, 120 L. Ed. 2d 615 (1992). Plaintiff bears the burden of proving three elements of its trade dress infringement claim: (1) non-functionality; (2) secondary meaning; and (3) likelihood of confusion. *Disc Golf Ass'n, Inc. v. Champion Discs, Inc.*, 158 F.3d 1002, 1005 (9th Cir. 1998).

. . .

A. Functionality

The Lanham Act expressly states that in trade dress actions when the plaintiff has not registered the trade dress, "the person who asserts trade dress protection has the burden of proving that the matter sought to be protected is not functional." *Traffix Devices, Inc. v. Marketing Displays, Inc.*, 532 U.S. 23, 29, 121 S. Ct. 1255, 149 L. Ed. 2d 164 (2001) (quoting *15 U.S.C. § 1125(a)(3)*). Functionality is a question of fact, but is subject to resolution on a summary judgment motion. *Disc Golf*, 158 F.3d at 1006.

"The physical details and design of a product maybe protected under the trademark laws only if they are nonfunctional." *Clamp Mfg. Co. v. Enco Mfg. Co., Inc.*, 870 F.2d 512, 515 (9th Cir. 1989). "The requirement of nonfunctionality is based on the judicial theory that there exists a fundamental right to compete through imitation of a competitor's prod-uct, which right can only be *temporarily* denied by the patent or copyright laws.'" *Id. at 516* (quoting *In re Morton-Norwich Prod., Inc., 671 F.2d 1332, 1336 (C.C.P.A. 1982)).* When a product is useful, trademark protection cannot be used to extend the life of the useful invention by protecting the design from competition. "If the utilitarian aspects of the product *are its essence, only* patent law protects *its configuration* from use by com-petitors." *Id.* (emphasis added). "For an overall product configuration to be recognized as a trademark, the entire design must be nonfunctional." *Clamp, 870 F.2d at 516.*

Several factors guide the decision whether a product feature is functional, including: (1) whether the design yields a utilitarian advantage; (2) whether alternative designs are available thereby showing that the plaintiff's choices were arbitrary or aesthetic; (3) whether the advertising touts the utilitarian advantages of the product; and (4) whether the particular design results from a comparatively simple or inexpensive method of man-ufacture. *See Intl Jensen, Inc. v. Metrosound U.S.A., Inc., 4 F.3d 819, 823 (9th Cir. 1993).* "No one factor is dispositive; all should be weighed collectively." *Disc Golf 158 F.3d at 1006.* The judicial "inquiry is not directed at whether the individual elements are func-tional but whether the whole collection of elements taken together are functional." *Intl Jensen, 4 F.3d at 823.* Having reviewed the arguments of counsel and the exhibits presented, the Court concludes that a question of fact exists on the functionality element.

Defendant Gadget argues that the elements of Plaintiff's Q scooter are functional. De-fendant states that the addition of the two rear wheels, which distinguishes the Q from the better known Segway product (which has the gyroscope technology to provide stabil-ity with only two large wheels) serves the function of balancing the scooter for a stable ride. Defendant contends that the two smaller rear wheels also facilitate sharp turns. The rider stands on the platform and holds the handle bars to steer, thus, those features are also functional.

Defendant is correct that each of these visible features serves a function; but its observation is limited to the de facto function of the elements. "De facto functional means that the design of a product *has a function, i.e.,* a bottle of any design holds fluid." *Textron, Inc., 753 F.2d 1019, 1025* (emphasis added). Here, the handlebars and the wheels have a use-ful function in allowing the scooter to operate, and those are the reasons the consumer purchases the product. *Vuitton, 644 F.2d at 774.* But the important test is to distinguish de jure function from the aesthetic design. "De jure functionality, on the other hand, means that the product is its particular shape because it works better in this shape." *Tex-tron, 753 F.2d at 1025.* "Non-functional features are those that are arbitrarily affixed or included for aesthetic purposes." *GMC v. Let's Make a Deal, 223 F. Supp. 2d 1183, 1196 (D. Nev. 2002).* For example, the hour-glass shaped, green, fluted bottle of the Coca-Cola company is protected by trade dress. *E.g., Rock & Roll Hall of Fame & Museum, Inc. v. Gentile Prods., 134 F.3d 749, 757 (6th Cir. 1998)* (Mann, C.J., dissenting).

Plaintiff has submitted evidence to support its position that the overall design is aes-thetic, ornamental, and incidental. For example, the inventor, Wang, selected the shape and length of the platform for its visual appeal. The front view photographs of the scooter show the curved shape of the handlebars and the recessed headlight. These design elements are arbitrary and appear to have been selected on the whim of the designer. Also, there is evidence that alternative designs exist, for example, the Columbia Chariot is shaped more like a wheel barrow and comes in a choice of colors in addition to basic yellow.

Plaintiff's argument is also supported because its advertisements do not tout the func-tion of the design, but rather focus on the engineering advantages of the scooter, such as the life of the battery and the charge, the ability to carry a load up to 250 pounds, and safety features, such as turn signals and horn.

Finally, the design patent, which protects the "new, original and ornamental" appearance of the scooter, *35 U.S.C. § 171*, is evidence supporting Plaintiff's contention that the trade dress is not functional, *see Lee v. Dayton-Hudson Corp., 838 F.2d 1186, 1188–89 (Fed. Cir. 1988).* Plaintiff's design patent claims "the ornamental design for a motor driven vehicle for transporting a standing person," as illustrated in five views of the scooter. The design patent carries a presumption that it is valid. *35 U.S.C. § 282.*

Defendant Gadget places heavy emphasis on the issuance of the utility patent. A close inspection of the *claims* of the patent, however, demonstrate that the utility patent is limited to the invention of the steering method and the conversion of the scooter to carry cargo. "Claims define the scope of patent protection." *Johnson & Johnston Assocs. v. R.E. Serv. Co., 285 F.3d 1046, 1052 (Fed. Cir. 2002)* (en banc). The Court's reading of the seven *claims* of the utility patent support that limitation. That the patent generally describes the physical embodiment of the invention (such as the platform and the handlebars, and as illustrated in the figures) does not detract from this essential distinction of the purpose of utility patent. And, as noted above, the issuance of the *design* patent for the ornamental characteristics creates a presumption of validity of that design patent for those visual elements.

In sum, each party has presented persuasive evidence on the functionality element, thus, this element is not suitable for resolution by a summary judgment motion.

Notes

1. An expired patent, which discloses but does not claim a product configuration, may provide strong evidence that the disclosed feature is functional. Greenwich Industries L.P., v. Specialized Seating Inc., No. 02 C 5000, 2003 WL 21148389 (N.D. Ill. May 16, 2003).

2. *Aesthetic functionality.* Although often criticized for not providing clear direction and being a "most controversial and ill-defined concept," A. Samuel Oddi, *The Functions of "Functionality" in Trademark Law*, 22 Hous. L. Rev. 925, 963 (1985), aesthetic functionality has at times provided a rather meaningful deterrent to the unrestrained expansion of trademark rights. One court describes the current state of the law as follows:

> Courts have recognized that "the functionality doctrine may apply even to features of a product that are purely ornamental." *Knitwaves*, 71 F.3d at 1006 (citing *Wallace Int'l Silversmiths, Inc. v. Godinger Silver Art Co.*, 916 F.2d 76, 79–81 (2d Cir. 1990)). And the Supreme Court, while "cautioning against misuse or over-extension of trade dress … noted that 'product design almost invariably serves purposes other than source identification.'" *TrafFix*, 121 S. Ct. at 1260 (explaining and quoting *Samara Bros.*, 529 U.S. at 213). In *TrafFix*, the Court identified two forms of functionality. The first, traditional functionality, deems a feature functional when "'it is essential to the use or purpose of the device or when it affects the cost or quality of the device.'" *Qualitex*, 514 U.S. at 165 (quoting Inwood Labs., 456 U.S. at 850 n.10). *Qualitex* "expand[ed] upon the meaning of this phrase [by] observing that a functional feature is one the 'exclusive use of which would put competitors at a significant non-reputation-related disadvantage.'" *TrafFix*, 121 S. Ct. at 1261 (quoting *Qualitex*, 514 U.S. at 165). But the competitive disadvantage comment did not displace the tradi-

tional functionality standard from *Inwood Laboratories*. Instead it explained the policy underlying the functionality doctrine in a way readily adaptable to the problem of aesthetic functionality, the issue presented in *Qualitex*. *See Traf-Fix*, 121 S. Ct. at 1261–62. Thus, the "significant non-reputation-related disadvantage" to competitors approach is the second form of trade dress functionality.

None of the design features [symbols such as lacrosse sticks or ski patrol crosses on clothing] that Abercrombie claims as its trade dress is essential to the use or purpose of the garments, catalog, and stores they adorn. The design features surely affect the cost and quality of the garments and the design of the catalog affects its cost and aesthetics (which determines, in part, its quality as a device for selling clothing), so a jury question exists as to whether the designs are functional in the traditional sense. However, no reasonable jury could deny the existence of a "significant non-reputation-related disadvantage" that would be imposed on competitors by protecting Abercrombie's claimed trade dress. That form of functionality governs the analysis of this case.

Abercrombie & Fitch Stores, Inc. v. Am. Eagle Outfitters, Inc., 280 F.3d 619, 641 (6th Cir. 2002).

2. For a thorough discussion of aesthetic functionality, *see* Mitchell M. Wong, *The Aesthetic Functionality Doctrine and the Law of Trade Dress Protection*, 83 CORNELL L. REV. 1116 (1998).

3. After *TrafFix*, is evidence of alternative design relevant any longer? *See* Vincent N. Palladino, *Trade Dress Functionality after TrafFix: The Lower Courts Split Again*, 93 TRADEMARK REPORTER 1219 (2003). *See also*, Clifford W. Browning, *Traffix Revisited: Exposing the Design Flaw in the Functionality Doctrine*, 94 TRADEMARK REP. 1059 (2004) (trade dress has become the practical equivalent to an expired design patent and the post-*Traffix* functionality is inherently incapable of distinguishing between design patents and trade dress); Mark Alen Thurmon, *The Rise and Fall of Trademark Law's Functionality Doctrine*, 56 FLA. L. REV. 243 (2004) (proposing a limited functionality defense similar to a fair use defense instead of adopting a rule that has "confused and divided" lower courts); Tracy-Gene G. Durkin and Julie D. Shirk, *Design Patents and Trade Dress Protection: Are the Two Mutually Exclusive?* 87 J. PAT. & TRADEMARK OFF. SOC'Y 770 (2005) (as the Supreme Court has not expressly disallowed it, the two should be simultaneously pursued).

4. TrafFix stands also for the proposition that when determining whether a design is functional, that design should be considered in its entirety, not as "discrete individual design features." Harold R. Weinberg, *Trademark Law, Functional Design Features, and the Trouble with TrafFix*, 9 J. INTELL. PROP. L. 1, 60 (2001). Since *TrafFix*, apparently many courts are applying the functionality doctrine with care. *See id.* Why is this worrisome?

5. One influential scholar claims that the recent Supreme Court's interest in trademark cases is a sign that litigants should not try to mix trademark protection with any other intellectual property protections. He claims that the Supreme Court is saying a trademark is a trademark and never anything else. *See*, Sheldon Halpern, *A High Likelihood of Confusion: Wal-Mart, Traffix, Moseley, and Dastart-The Supreme Court's New Trademark Jurisprudence*, 61 N.Y.U. ANN. SURV. AM. L. 237 (2005). Do you agree? Why would it be so bad if you could just pick the type of intellectual property protection that would serve you the best? What effect would this have on innovation?

6. The Supreme Court's recent trademark cases can also be seen as a brake on the expansion of trademark law. The Supreme Court seems to think that the scope of trademark

protection is too broad. This broad scope has the effect of chilling innovation. A broad scope of trademark protection encourages companies to be overly aggressive in enforcing their trademark rights. This over-aggression results in high costs of clearance and adoption to avoid the broad swath being plowed through society by some trademark holders. That is, the Supreme Court seems to be saying that it is appropriate to have and enforce trademarks, but that enforcement should be done in a balanced manner keeping in mind that there are three entities that must always be balanced in every trademark setting: The trademark holder's investment in the mark, society's right to be free of confusion, and third parties' right to free and unburdened competition. Analogous to the trademark system, when the patent system is out of balance in favor of patentees, it has a negative effect on innovation. *See* Adam B. Jaffe & Josh Lerner, Innovation and Its Discontents (2004).

———

D. False Advertising

Section 43(a) also makes false advertising actionable. False advertising is defined below. Basically, it is the notion of making incorrect statements about your or another's products or services. The question is when does it cross the line from mere "puffery" to misrepresentation.

It should be pointed out that, although some countries prohibit it, comparative advertising alone is not a wrong addressed by the Lanham Act. Comparative advertising that is accurate is perfectly acceptable, as it assists consumers in making rational choices in the marketplace. However, misleading consumers with untrue claims regarding a competitor's goods or services should be actionable because the competitor may not know of the advertisement or may incur the costs of other advertising to overcome the false association planted in the minds of the consumers by the untrue advertising. Section 43(a) recognizes how important producer reputation is and also how fragile that reputation is in the minds of the consumers.

———

15 U.S.C. §1125, Lanham Act §43

(a) Civil action

(1) Any person who, on or in connection with any goods or services, or any container for goods, uses in commerce any word, term, name, symbol, or device, or any combination thereof, or any false designation of origin, false or misleading description of fact, or false or misleading representation of fact, which—

...

(B) in commercial advertising or promotion, misrepresents the nature, characteristics, qualities, or geographic origin of his or her or another person's goods, services, or commercial activities, shall be liable in a civil action by any person who believes that he or she is or is likely to be damaged by such act.

———

Coors Brewing Company v. Anheuser-Busch Companies, Inc.

802 F. Supp. 965 (S.D.N.Y. 1992)

Mukasey, District Judge

Plaintiff, Coors Brewing Company, sues Anheuser-Busch Companies, Inc. and D'Arcy Masius Benton & Bowles, Anheuser-Busch's advertising agency, claiming that Anheuser-Busch's recent promotional campaign violates §43(a) of the Lanham Act, New York unfair competition law, and §§349 and 350 of New York General Business Law. Plaintiff has 'sought a preliminary injunction prohibiting defendants' continued use of the advertisements at issue. For the reasons set forth below, plaintiff's application for a preliminary injunction is denied.

I.

Since 1978, Coors has been expanding from the western United States into a nationwide market. Also since 1978, Coors has marketed a reduced-calorie beer called Coors Light. Coors manufactures its line of beers, including Coors Light, using a process that the beer industry calls "high gravity brewing." During the 30 to 60 days it takes to produce the "high gravity" brew, it is cooled to about 4 to 5 degrees centigrade. When the aging process is completed, the brew is filtered to remove yeast and other microbes. The temperature of the brew then is reduced further, to approximately minus 1 degree centigrade. Finally, the high gravity brew, whose alcohol content exceeds the statutory maximum for beer, is "blended" with water.

Most Coors Light is processed fully, i.e., brewed, blended, and bottled, in Golden, Colorado. However, somewhere between 65% (plaintiff's figure) and 85% (defendants' figure) of the Coors Light supplied to the Northeast is "blended" and bottled in Virginia. Using "special insulated railcars" (Pl. Mem. at 9), plaintiff transports the high gravity brew from Colorado to Virginia, where plaintiff adds Virginia water to the brew, further filters the mixture, and then bottles it.

Defendant Anheuser-Busch produces a reduced-calorie beer called Natural Light. Like Coors Light, Natural Light is produced by a process of "high gravity" brewing. Apparently, the only material difference between the processes used to produce Coors Light and Natural Light is that Natural Light is pasteurized, a process that involves heating, whereas Coors Light is brewed at low temperatures. In addition, Natural Light apparently is processed entirely—i.e., brewed, blended, and bottled—in regional Anheuser-Busch breweries.

Defendants recently began an advertising campaign comparing Natural Light with Coors Light. That campaign includes radio, television, and point-of-sale advertisements, which, not surprisingly, promote Natural Light at the expense of Coors Light.

Defendants' 30-second television commercial consists of a series of images accompanied by the following narrative:

> This is a railroad tanker. [flash the image of a railway tanker] This is the taste of the Rockies. [flash the image of a can of Coors Light] Tanker. [image of a railway tanker] Rockies. [image of a can of Coors Light]
>
> Actually, a concentrated form of Coors Light leaves Colorado in a tanker and travels to Virginia, where local water dilutes the Rockies concentrate before it's sent to you.
>
> So what's it gonna be, the Rockies concentrate or an ice cold Natural Light that leaves our local breweries fresh and ready to drink? Like this [picture of a Natural Light delivery truck], not like this [picture of railway tanker].

So drink fresh, cold Natural Light and don't be railroaded.

The phrase "don't be railroaded" is accompanied by the image of a can of Coors Light atop a railroad car, over which is superimposed a circle with a diagonal line through its center — the international safety warning symbol.

Similarly, defendants' radio advertisements portray a dialogue between two (male) beer-drinkers. One beer-drinker asks the other, "Did you know that Coors Light ships beer concentrate in railroad tanker cars?" The first beer-drinker then continues: "Yeah, all the way from Colorado — 1,500 miles to Virginia. That's where they add local water."

In addition, defendants have been distributing printed materials to be displayed by retailers. These point-of-sale materials assert that Coors Light is made from concentrate while Natural Light is fresh. These materials also contain the logo "Don't be railroaded" above the image a Coors Light inside the international safety warning symbol.

Plaintiff argues that the Natural Light advertisements imply that "differences in production make Natural Light 'fresh' in a way in which Coors Light is not." (Compl. P 3) In other words, those advertisements imply that Natural Light is "fresher" than Coors Light because Natural Light leaves the factory ready to drink while Coors Light leaves Colorado in a "concentrate" form, which is diluted when it reaches Coors' plant in Virginia.

Plaintiff also contends that by broadcasting nationally the Natural Light advertisements, defendants lead consumers outside the Northeast to believe erroneously that their Coors Light is shipped to Virginia to be diluted before being shipped to their regional retailers.

II. Lanham Act Claims

A party seeking a preliminary injunction must prove (1) the threat of irreparable harm, and (2) either (a) likelihood of success on the merits or (b) sufficiently serious questions going to the merits to make them a fair ground for litigation and a balance of hardships tipping decidedly in the movant's favor. Covino v. Patrissi, 1992 U.S. App. LEXIS 14230, at *8–9 (2d Cir. June 17, 1992); Jackson Dairy, Inc. v. H.P. Hood & Sons, Inc., 596 F.2d 70, 72 (2d Cir. 1979).

A. Irreparable Injury

Where a comparative advertisement is found to be false or misleading, irreparable harm will be presumed. McNeilab, Inc. v. American Home Products Corp., 848 F.2d 34, 38 (2d Cir. 1988). The Second Circuit has explained that, "A misleading comparison to a specific competing product necessarily diminishes that product's value in the minds of the consumer." Id.; see also Coca-Cola Company v. Tropicana Products, Inc., 690 F.2d 312, 317 (2d Cir. 1982) ("Sales of the plaintiffs' products would probably be harmed if the competing products' advertising tended to mislead consumers in the manner alleged.").

In the case at hand, Coors and Anheuser-Busch are direct competitors in the reduced-calorie beer market. Therefore, if plaintiff can establish that the challenged advertisements either are literally false or are misleading — that is, if plaintiff can establish a likelihood of success on the merits, then irreparable injury will be presumed.

B. Likelihood of Success

Section 43(a) of the Lanham Act provides in relevant part:

> Any person who, on or in connection with any goods or services, ... uses in commerce ... any false designation of origin, false or misleading description of fact, or false or misleading representation of fact, which —

* * *

(2) in commercial advertising or promotion, misrepresents the nature, characteristics, qualities, or geographic origin of his or her or another person's goods,
services or commercial activities,

shall be liable in a civil action by any person who believes that he or she is or is
likely to be damaged by such act.

15 U.S.C. §1125(a).

The Second Circuit has held that in order to obtain injunctive relief against a false or
misleading advertising claim[6] pursuant to section 43(a) of the Lanham Act, a plaintiff
must demonstrate either: (1) that an advertisement is literally false; or (2) that the advertisement, though literally true, is likely to mislead and confuse customers.

If a plaintiff can prove that an advertising claim is literally false, "the court may enjoin
the use of the claim 'without reference to the advertisement's impact on the buying public.'" *McNeil-P.C.C.*, 938 F.2d at 1549 (quoting *Coca-Cola Co.*, 690 F.2d at 317).

However, if the plaintiff alleges that the advertising claim, despite being literally true,
is likely to mislead or confuse customers, "It is not for the judge to determine, based solely
upon his or her own intuitive reaction, whether the advertisement is deceptive." *Johnson
& Johnson * Merck*, 960 F.2d at 297. Therefore, in order to maintain a claim of implied
falsehood under §43(a), the plaintiff must prove, "by extrinsic evidence, that the challenged
commercials tend to mislead or confuse consumers." *Id.* at 297.

In other words, the plaintiff must submit consumer surveys showing that the challenged advertising claim tends to mislead or deceive consumers. Where the plaintiff fails
to "demonstrate that a statistically significant part of the commercial audience holds the
false belief allegedly communicated by the challenged advertisement, the plaintiff cannot establish that it suffered any injury as a result of the advertisement's message." *Id.* at
298. However, "The extent to which consumers are deceived need not be established to
support the finding that an advertisement tends to mislead, all that is required is a 'qualitative showing [to] establish that a not insubstantial number of consumers received a
false or misleading impression from it.'" *McNeil-P.P.C., Inc. v. Bristol-Myers Squibb Co.*,
753 F. Supp. 1206, 1211 (S.D.N.Y. 1990) (bracket in original) (quoting *McNeilab, Inc. v.
American Home Products Corp.*, 501 F. Supp. 517, 528 (S.D.N.Y.), modified on other
grounds, 501 F. Supp. 540 (S.D.N.Y. 1980)), aff'd, 938 F.2d 1544 (2d Cir. 1991).

1. Literal Falsehoods

In the case at hand, Coors contends that the challenged advertisements contain two literal falsehoods: (1) that "Coors Light is made from 'concentrate' that is 'diluted' with
water" (Pl. Mem. at 12; *see also id.* at 13, 18–19); and (2) that "Coors Light travels to Virginia 'before it's sent to you.'" (*Id.* at 13; *see also id.* at 20)

As to defendants' advertising claim that Coors Light is made from a concentrate, Coors
has failed to prove literal falsehood. The challenged commercial states that Coors Light
travels from Colorado to Virginia in "a concentrated form" and asks, "So what's it gonna
be, the Rockies concentrate or an ice cold Natural Light ... ?" Relying on 27 C.F.R. §25.11,
which provides that a "concentrate is produced from beer by the removal of water," plain-

---

6. Under §43(a), a merchant's false or misleading claim may relate either to its own product or
another's product. *See* McNeil-P.C.C., Inc. v. Bristol-Myers Squibb Co., 938 F.2d 1544, 1548 n.1 (2d
Cir. 1991).

tiff would define "concentrate" only as a substance from which water has been removed. (Pl. Mem. at 19) However, defendants proffer another, equally plausible definition of "concentrate," namely, "a concentrated substance" or "concentrated form of something." (Def. Mem. at 8) In addition, when "concentrate" is used as an adjective, it means "concentrated." In turn, "concentrated" means "(1) rich in respect to a particular or essential element: strong, undiluted; (2) intense...." WEBSTER'S THIRD NEW INTERNATIONAL DICTIONARY 469 (1986). Because the term "concentrate" is equally open to either party's definition, defendants' advertising claim that Coors Light is made from a concentrate is ambiguous at most. Therefore, the commercial's reference to concentrate is not literally false.

In addition, plaintiff argues that the commercial's claim that Coors Light is diluted is literally false. However, dilute means, inter alia, "to make thinner or more liquid by admixture (as with water); to make less concentrated: diminish the strength, activity, or flavor of...." Id. 633. It is undisputed that water is added to the "high gravity" brew — or concentrate — to produce the final product. That process makes the concentrate less concentrated. Therefore, neither is defendants' use of the term dilute literally false.

Plaintiff also challenges as literally false, except as applied to the Northeast, defendants' claim that Coors Light travels to Virginia before it is distributed to consumers. However, Anheuser-Busch "represents that the commercials will not be broadcast on any 'superstations' or other media that can be received outside of the Northeast." (Def. Mem. at 22) Therefore, this portion of plaintiff's application for injunctive relief is moot.

2. Implied Falsehoods

Plaintiff contends that by repeatedly stating that Coors Light is made from concentrate and is diluted, and by showing Coors Light being shipped from Colorado in railway cars while stating that Natural Light leaves Anheuser-Busch factories fresh and ready to drink, defendants' commercial implies three falsehoods: (1) that Natural Light is not also made by a process of "high gravity" brewing; (2) that all of the Coors Light sold in the Northeast has been "blended" with Virginia water; and (3) that there is a difference between Colorado Coors and Virginia Coors.

As discussed above, see supra pp. 6–7, a claim for implied falsehood rises or falls on a plaintiff's evidence of consumer confusion, i.e., market surveys. In the case at hand, plaintiff retained a market research and behavioral consulting firm called Leo J. Shapiro and Associates ("Shapiro") to conduct market surveys. (Johnson Aff. P 1) Philip Johnson, Shapiro's president, has submitted an affidavit setting forth the results of those surveys (Id.); he also testified — sort of — at the preliminary injunction hearing.

Between August 7 and 10, 1992, Shapiro conducted consumer surveys in shopping malls located in Boston, Philadelphia, Washington, D.C., New York, Los Angeles, and Kansas City. (Johnson PP 4, 5) In all, Shapiro interviewed 200 men and 100 women who were over 21 years old and who had consumed beer in the preceding four weeks (Id. PP 4, 6); 50 people were interviewed at each location. (Id. P 5)

Survey respondents were shown the challenged Natural Light television advertisement. (Id. P 7) After respondents had been shown the advertisement once, they were asked the following two questions:

Question 2a: Now, tell me what you recall about the commercial I just showed you?

Probe: what else was it about?

Question 2b: And, what was the central theme or message in this commercial? What were they trying to tell you?

(*Id.* P 7 and Ex. A)

The following is a list of the relevant answers elicited by Question 2a, as well as the corresponding percentages of respondents giving those answers:

-1	Coors is diluted/waterered down	32%
-2	Coors travels by tanker/railroad, not by truck	26%
-3	Coors/Coors Light is made from concentrate	20%
-4	Coors has to travel far/across the county	20%
-5	Coors not fresh/not as fresh	2%
-6	Coors is not pure/natural	1%
-7	Natural Light comes from local breweries/made close to home	12%
-8	Natural Light is fresher	11%

In answer to Question 2a's Probe—what else respondent recalled about the commercial—4% of all respondents said that "Natural Light is purer/more natural" and another 4% said that "Natural Light is not diluted/watered down." *Id.*)

Respondents gave the following relevant answers to Question 2b—what was the central theme or message of the commercial:

-1	Coors is diluted/watered down	14%
-2	Coors/Coors Light is made from a concentrate	5%
-3	Coors not fresh/not as fresh	4%
-4	Coors is not pure/natural	3%
-5	Buy Natural Light/Natural Light is better	28%
-6	Natural Light is fresher	18%
-7	Natural Light is purer/more natural	12%
-8	Natural Light not diluted/not watered down	9%
-9	Natural Light not made from concentrate	3% (*Id.* P 14)

After respondents were asked, and answered, Questions 2a and 2b, the commercial was played a second time. Respondents then were asked six more questions:

Question 4: What, if anything, did this commercial tell you about Coors Light beer?

Probe: What else?

Question 5: Based on this commercial, do you believe that Coors Light and Natural Light are made the same way, or are they made differently?

If different: In what way is Coors Light made differently than Natural Light?

Question 6: And, based on the commercial, do you believe there is any difference between Coors Light and Natural Light in terms of the freshness of the products?

If yes: In what way is Coors Light different from Natural Light in terms of freshness?

Question 7: Based on the commercial, do you believe there is any difference between Coors Light and Natural Light in terms of the purity or naturalness of the products?

If yes: In what way is Coors Light different from Natural Light in terms of purity or naturalness?

Question 8: Do you feel that seeing this commercial would encourage You to drink Coors Light beer, discourage You from drinking Coors Light beer, or would it make no difference? Why do you say that?

Probe: Why else?

Question 9: By the way, do you believe that this commercial is talking about the Coors Light beer that is available where you buy beer? Why do you say that?

(*Id.* Aff. P 8 and Ex. A)

In answer to Question 5, whether based on the commercial respondents believed that Coors Light and Natural Light were made the same way or different ways, 67% of all respondents answered that they believed the two beers were made in different ways while 21% of all respondents answered that they believed the two beers were made the same way. Of those respondents who answered that the two beers were made in different ways,[7] (i) 29% stated that they believed that "Coors is diluted/watered down/Natural Light is not," (ii) 25% stated that Coors/Coors Light made from concentrate/Natural Light is not," and (iii) 13% stated that "Coors made in two places/Natural Light from one place." (*Id.* P 16) There were at least 20 other responses specifying differences between how the two beers are made, but those responses are not relevant to the case at hand.

Based on the answers to Question 5, plaintiff argues that 67% of all respondents falsely believed, based on the commercial in question, that Natural Light and Coors Light are made differently. (*Id.*) Adding the category of respondents who said that they believed that "Coors is diluted/watered down/Natural Light is not" (29%), and the category of respondents who said that they believed that Coors/Coors Light made from concentrate/Natural Light is not" (25%), the total percentage of the 67% of respondents who had been misled by the commercial into thinking that Natural Light is not made by a process of high gravity brewing is 54%. This means that, based on plaintiff's survey, 36.18% of all respondents were misled by defendants' commercial as to the differences between how the two beers are made.

However, "The evidentiary value of a survey's results rests upon the underlying objectivity of the survey itself." Johnson and Johnson * Merck, 960 F.2d at 300 (citing *Universal City Studios, Inc. v. Nintendo Co.*, 746 F.2d 112, 118 (2d Cir. 1984)). That objectivity is measured by such factors as whether the survey was "properly 'filtered' to screen out those who got no message from the advertisement, whether the questions are directed to the real issues, and whether the questions are leading or suggestive." *Am. Home Prod. Corp. v. Johnson & Johnson*, 654 F. Supp. 568, 590 (S.D.N.Y. 1987); *see also Weight Watchers Int'l, Inc. v. Stouffer Corp.*, 744 F. Supp. 1259, 1272 (S.D.N.Y. 1990).

In the case at hand, plaintiff's reliance on the answers elicited by Question 5 is misplaced because that question is leading and thus produced unreliable results. By asking whether, "based on the commercial," the respondent believes Coors Light and Natural Light are made the same way or different ways, Question 5 assumes that the commercial conveys some message comparing how the two beers are made. But, in response to the open-ended questions—Questions 2a and 2b—a statistically insignificant percentage of

---

7. It is not clear from Johnson's affidavit whether the percentages of respondents specifying the differences between how the two beers are made refer to percentages of all 300 respondents or whether they refer to percentages of the 67% who, in answer to Question 5a, said that the two beers are made differently. However, because plaintiff bears the burden of proof and because this is plaintiff's exhibit, I have construed the ambiguity against plaintiff and assumed that the percentages of respondents specifying differences refers to percentages of 67% of all respondents.

respondents remarked on differences between the processes by which the two beers are made. This jump in the percentage of respondents whose answers indicate a mistaken belief that Natural Light is not also made by a process of high gravity brewing from between 3% and 9% to 36.18% further suggests the leading nature of Question 5.

Question 5 is leading also in that it asks whether an obviously comparative advertisement, which disparages one product and promotes another, suggests or does not suggest a difference in the way the two products are made. This inquiry in itself implies, because the advertisement invidiously compares one product with another, that the advertisement does suggest a difference in the way the two products are made.

Moreover, Question 5 failed to inform respondents that they also could respond that they did not know if the commercial implied that Coors Light and Natural Light are made by different processes. This omission further undermines the reliability of the answers elicited by Question 5. For the above reasons, I do not credit Question 5 with probative value.

By contrast, I find that the survey's open-ended questions, 2a and 2b, were generally reliable. As stated above, Questions 2a and 2b elicited answers going principally to plaintiff's claims of literal falsehood, which I have rejected. *See supra* pp. 10–11. In answer to Question 2a, the bulk of respondents remarked that Coors Light is made from concentrate (20%), is "diluted/watered down" (32%), is transported by railway tanker (26%), and travels a long distance before it reaches customers (20%).

Because Johnson lumped together the percentage of respondents who said that Coors Light is diluted and the percentage of respondents who said that Coors Light is watered down, the 32% figure is uninformative. While I have found that it is literally true that in one sense Coors Light is "diluted," Coors Light does not appear to be "watered down," in the sense of containing more water than beer should or than Natural Light does. However, because I have no way of knowing what percentage of respondents said that Coors Light is diluted and what percentage said that Coors Light is watered down, this category of responses has no probative value. *See* Darrel Huff, *How to Statisticulate, in* How to Statistics 110–20 (1954).

Apart from the answer that Coors is diluted/watered down, Question 2a elicited only two other answers — neither from a statistically significant percentage of respondents — that go to plaintiff's implied falsehood claim. First, 2% of all respondents stated that Coors is not "fresh" or not as "fresh" as Natural Light. This response is ambiguous. Johnson never questioned any of the respondents as to what they meant by "fresh"; without such information, respondents' use of that term is ambiguous and therefore unreliable. Second, 4% of all respondents stated that Natural Light is not diluted/watered down. However, as discussed below with respect to Natural Light and above with respect to Coors Light, this response is unreliable by virtue of Shapiro's having combined the percentage of respondents who said that Natural Light is not diluted and the percentage of respondents who said that Natural Light is not watered down.

Moreover, neither of the above responses is statistically significant because an answer to an open-ended question is not statistically significant unless at least 10% of all respondents give that answer.

In answer to Question 2b, the greatest percentage — 28% — of all respondents said that Natural Light is better. The second highest percentage — 18% — of respondents answered that Natural Light is "fresher." However, as with the answers to Question 2a regarding "freshness," the answers to Question 2b regarding freshness are ambiguous because respondents were never probed about what they meant by "fresh." Therefore, I cannot assign probative weight to the answers to Question 2b about Natural Light's freshness.

Similarly, I cannot find probative weight in the answers stating that Natural Light is not diluted/watered down, which were elicited by Question 2b. Although a combined total of 9% of all respondents—just below the cut-off for statistical significance with respect to open-ended questions—gave these answers, that figure's reliability is vitiated by Shapiro's combination of the percentage of respondents saying that Natural Light is not diluted with the percentage saying that Natural Light is not watered down. Although the answers stating that the commercial implied that Natural Light is not diluted evince consumer confusion, those answers stating that Natural Light is not watered down do not necessarily evince consumer confusion because there has been no claim that Natural Light is watered down.

The commercial may tend to mislead consumers only insofar as it may lead them to believe that Coors Light is watered down while Natural Light is not. However, not only did Shapiro conflate the percentage of respondents saying that Natural Light is not diluted with the percentage saying that Natural Light is not watered down, but, as discussed above, Shapiro also conflated the percentage of respondents saying that Coors Light is diluted with the percentage saying that Coors Light is watered down. Therefore, there is no way to compare the percentage of respondents saying that Coors Light is watered down with the percentage saying that Natural Light is not watered down. Moreover, there is no way to discern whether the same respondents who said that Coors Light is watered down also said that Natural Light is not watered down—the only category with respect to the "watered down" description that is meaningful to the case at hand. Accordingly, I find that the 9% of respondents saying that Natural Light is not diluted/watered down is not reliable evidence of consumer confusion as to the differences in the way Coors Light and Natural Light are made.

The one response elicited by Question 2b that is reliable and relevant to the case at hand is that "Natural Light not made from concentrate" (3%). However, as discussed above, this answer is statistically insignificant because it falls far short of the 10% cut-off for statistical significance with respect to open-ended questions. Therefore, because only 3% of all respondents remarked that Natural Light is not made from concentrate, this answer did not occur with statistically significant frequency.

Plaintiff has invited me to enjoin the advertisement at issue despite any blemishes in Shapiro's survey technique based on the "general thrust of [the] survey rather than its quantitative results." Here, the "thrust" is to be found in the "quantitative results," or it is not to be found at all. I decline to imagine "thrust" in the absence of evidence. Nor is there significance in defendants' failure to conduct a survey of their own. The burden is plaintiff's, and defendants may rely on that if they choose. Accordingly, because I have found that the results of Question 5 are unreliable and that those results of Questions 2a and 2b that support plaintiff's claims are either ambiguous or are statistically insignificant, I find that plaintiff has failed to prove that the challenged commercial is likely to mislead consumers into believing that, unlike Coors Light, Natural Light is not made by a process of "high gravity" brewing.

As to plaintiff's two remaining implied falsehood claims, that (i) all of the Coors Light sold in the Northeast has been "blended" with Virginia water, and (ii) there is a difference between Colorado Coors and Virginia Coors, plaintiff has failed to support either of these claims with any extrinsic evidence; none of the survey questions even arguably addresses these claims. Moreover, I find that plaintiff is estopped to argue the third alleged falsehood, i.e., that there is a difference between Colorado Coors and Virginia Coors. Plaintiff has promoted its beers, including Coors Light, as "the taste of the Rockies," based on use of water from the Rocky Mountains. After having advertised for years that Coors beers tasted better than other beers because Coors beers are made from Rocky Mountain water, Coors now cannot seek an equitable remedy that would prohibit defendants' hoisting Coors by its own petard.

For the above reasons, I find that plaintiff has failed to substantiate its implied falsehood claims with reliable extrinsic evidence.

Surdyk's Liquor, Inc. v. MGM Liquor Stores, Inc.
83 F. Supp. 2d 1016 (Dist. Ct. Minn. 2000)

DOTY, DISTRICT JUDGE

This matter is before the court on (1) the parties' cross-motions to supplement the record and (2) plaintiff's motion for preliminary injunction. Based on a review of the file, record, and proceedings herein, the court (1) grants the parties' cross-motions to supplement the record and (2) grants plaintiff's motion for preliminary injunction.

BACKGROUND

Plaintiff Surdyk's Liquor, Inc. ("Surdyk's") and defendant MGM Liquor Stores, Inc. ("MGM") are rival Twin Cities wine and liquor retailers. Surdyk's owns and operates a liquor store in Northeast Minneapolis. MGM is the franchisor for a chain of 36 area liquor stores operating under the name "MGM Liquor Warehouse." The individual MGM stores are owned and operated by six different franchisees. As part of the franchise relationship, defendant MGM orchestrates joint advertising campaigns when the MGM store owners decide to conduct a coordinated sale.

In the fall of 1999, MGM published a multiple-page advertising flyer for a wine and liquor sales event called the "29th Anniversary Wine, Liquor & Beer Sale." Twenty-three MGM stores were advertised as participating in the event, which was scheduled to run from September 30 through October 20, 1999. The flyer was published by the Star Tribune and circulated widely throughout the Twin Cities metropolitan region. On September 29, 1999, the day before the sale was to begin, three private investigators hired by Surdyk's visited ten different MGM stores and attempted to purchase case quantities of 18 wines advertised for sale in the Anniversary Sale flyer. The investigators found that at each of the MGM stores surveyed the wines requested were either out of stock or stocked in very small quantities. At about half of the stores, an MGM employee stated that the requested wines could be specially ordered and delivered within two days to a week.

On October 8, 1999, Surdyk's filed a complaint with the Minnesota Attorney General's Office about MGM's advertising in connection with the Anniversary Sale. On October 14, 1999, the Attorney General's Office sent a letter to MGM, reminding MGM that several Minnesota statutes prohibit false or deceptive advertising and that "the State is empowered to seek an injunction, restitution, civil penalties and attorneys' fees in the event your company violated these statutes." Letter from Erik A. Lindseth, Assistant Attorney General, to MGM (Oct. 14, 1999) (Beach Aff., Ex. C.) The letter also stated:

> The state hereby requests that you respond immediately to this complaint. In particular, please provide evidence that the wines referenced above were available during the sale, and in what quantities they were available....

> If the wines referenced above were not available at the outset of the sale or have not been available in reasonable quantities throughout the sale, the State requests

that you cease further use of your "29th Anniversary" print advertisements for the remainder of the sale, and reconsider your use of such advertisements in future sales.

Id. On October 21, 1999, MGM responded to the letter from the Attorney General's Office with the following explanation:

When MGM prepared its advertising circular (and sales of this nature are planned more than a month in advance), it listed for sale only products which appeared on price lists distributed by its suppliers. In response to your letter, MGM confirmed with its suppliers that all the wines listed in your letter were available at the time this advertising circular was prepared. It would not be unusual, however, when dealing with wines of limited availability, for there to be some wines that are not available at a subsequent date. In this case, apparently only 4 of about 1,000 wines listed in the advertisements were not available at the time checked by Surdyk's representative.

Letter from Charles S. Modell, Counsel for MGM, to Minnesota Attorney General's Office, at 2 (Oct. 21, 1999) ("MGM Letter") (Beach Aff., Ex. D).

In November 1999, MGM again prepared a multiple-page flyer to be published in local newspapers in connection with another sales event, "The Millennium Holiday Wine, Liquor & Beer Sale." The Millennium Sale involved 33 MGM stores and was scheduled to run from November 29 through December 11, 1999. On November 30, 1999, Surdyk's sent an investigator to visit a number of participating MGM stores using a list of two dozen wines and liquors. Again, the investigator found that, for the most part, the products requested were either out of stock or stocked in small quantities. Again, the employees at many of the MGM stores suggested that the items could be special ordered and delivered within two days to a week.

On November 24, 1999, Surdyk's filed a complaint in Hennepin County District Court alleging that the MGM flyers constitute false advertising in violation of section 43(a) of the federal Lanham Act (codified at 15 U.S.C. §1125(a)); the Minnesota Uniform Deceptive Trade Practices Act, Minn. Stat. §325D.44; Minn. Stat. §325F.67 (prohibiting false advertising), and Minn. Stat. §325F.69 (prohibiting consumer fraud). On December 6, 1999, MGM removed the complaint to federal court. Surdyk's now moves for a preliminary injunction. The parties also bring cross-motions to supplement the record with material not submitted to the court during briefing of the preliminary injunction motion.

DISCUSSION
A. Cross-Motions to Supplement the Record

The parties have brought cross-motions to supplement the record with affidavits from local consumers who have recently attempted to purchase wine from MGM and Surdyk's. Because the parties have adequately explained why they did not include these materials with the original motion papers, and because these materials shed helpful light on the merits of plaintiff's false advertising claim, the court will grant the cross-motions.

* * *

C. Preliminary Injunction

Surdyk's brings a motion for preliminary injunction, asking the court to enter an order halting MGM's alleged false advertising practices. In evaluating a motion for preliminary injunction, the court considers the four factors set forth by the Eighth Circuit in Dataphase Systems, Inc. v. CL Systems, Inc.: (1) the likelihood of the movant's success on the merits; (2) the threat of irreparable harm to the movant in the absence of relief; (3) the balance between that harm and the harm that the relief would cause to the other litigants; and (4) the public interest. The court weighs the four factors to determine whether injunctive relief is warranted. The plaintiff bears the burden of proof concerning each of them.

1. Lanham Act Claim: Likelihood of Success on the Merits

Surdyk's brings a claim under section 43(a) of the Lanham Act based on MGM's alleged practice of advertising for sale wines and liquors that are unavailable in the supplies advertised. Congress enacted the Lanham Act to protect persons engaged in commerce against certain forms of unfair competition, including false or deceptive advertising. *See United Industries Corp. v. Clorox Co.*, 140 F.3d 1175, 1179. Section 43(a)(1)(b) of the Lanham Act prohibits "commercial advertising or promotion [that] misrepresents the nature, characteristics, qualities, or geographic origin of [the advertiser's] or another person's goods, services, or commercial activities." As courts have noted, "whether a product is available goes directly to one of that product's characteristics." *Tire Kingdom, Inc. v. Morgan Tire & Auto, Inc.*, 915 F. Supp. 360, 368 (S.D. Fla. 1996). Further, the Federal Trade Commission ("FTC"), the administrative agency charged by Congress with preventing unfair competition, *see* 15 U.S.C. §45, 46, has promulgated a regulation stating that "no advertisement containing an offer to sell a product should be published when the offer is not a bona fide effort to sell the advertised product." 16 C.F.R. §238.1. The FTC suggests that an advertised offer will not be considered bona fide when it "fail[s] to have available at all outlets listed in the advertisement a sufficient quantity of the advertised product to meet reasonably anticipated demands, unless the advertisement clearly and adequately discloses that supply is limited and/or the merchandise is available only at designated outlets." *Id.* §238.3(c). Thus, under the plain language of the statute and the FTC's advertising regulations, MGM's alleged conduct would appear to fall squarely within the ambit of the Lanham Act.

To prevail on a false advertising claim under section 43(a), a plaintiff must prove (1) that defendant made a false statement of fact in a commercial advertisement about its own or another's product; (2) that the statement actually deceived or would tend to deceive a substantial segment of its audience; (3) that the deception is material, in that it is likely to influence the purchasing decision; (4) that defendant caused its false statement to enter interstate commerce; and (5) that the plaintiff has been or likely to be injured as a result of the false statement, either by direct diversion of sales from itself to the defendant or by a loss of good will associated with its products.

"The false statement necessary to establish a Lanham Act violation generally falls into one of two categories: (1) commercial claims that are literally false as a factual matter, and (2) claims that may be literally true or ambiguous but which implicitly convey a false impression, are misleading in context, or likely to deceive consumers." *Id.* If a plaintiff establishes that the defendant's commercial claim is literally false, the court may grant injunctive relief without considering the advertisement's actual impact on the consuming public.

a. Literal Falsity

The court's first task is to assess whether Surdyk's is likely to prove that the commercial claims contained in MGM's sale flyers are literally false. The court will discuss the standard for analyzing literal falsity before applying that standard to the facts of this case.

(1) Standard for Assessing Literal Falsity

The court's assessment of literal falsity involves a two-stage inquiry: (1) whether the challenged advertisement conveys an explicit factual message, and (2) whether that explicit factual message is false. *See* MCCARTHY ON TRADEMARKS AND UNFAIR COMPETITION §§27:55–56 (separating the falsity analysis into two stages: (1) "determining the message of the advertisement" and (2) "proving falsity"); United Industries, 140 F.3d at 1181 (approving the analytical approach of the lower court, which had "[first] determined that the ... commercial conveyed an explicit message ... and [then] found that this message was literally untrue."). The Eighth Circuit has recently discussed the considerations that should inform an analysis of literal falsity:

> In assessing whether an advertisement is literally false, a court must analyze the message conveyed within its full context. In some circumstances, even a visual image or a visual image combined with an audio component, may be literally false. The greater the degree to which a message relies upon the viewer or consumer to integrate its components and draw the apparent conclusion, however, the less likely it is that a finding of literal falsity will be supported. Commercial claims that are implicit, attenuated, or merely suggestive usually cannot fairly be characterized as literally false.

Id. at 1180–81 (citations omitted). The issue of literal falsity, including the "interpretation of [a] commercial's message," is "a classic question of fact" that is "highly dependent upon context and inference." *Id.* at 1183.

(2) MGM Advertisements

Surdyk's has directed its Lanham Act claim at the two advertising flyers published by MGM in connection with MGM's Anniversary and Millennium Sales. The two flyers employ almost identical formats. Across a multiple-page booklet, MGM individually lists the hundreds of wine, liquor, and beer products that are being offered for sale. The vast majority of the items carry the following information: a capsule editorial description; a stock item number; the ordinary retail price per bottle; the sale price per bottle; the sale price per case. Next to a few of the wines, the word "limited" appears in the space normally containing the sale price for cases. In the back of each flyer is a page of maps showing the location of participating MGM stores. The Anniversary Flyer contains the following disclaimer, which appears in fine print on the second page of the booklet:

> Traditionally, MGM Liquor Warehouse makes every effort to insure availability of all items that are on sale, throughout the sale period. However, with a sale of this size and the very limited availability of some of these outstanding wines (in some instances only a few cases), we think it's important to offer the consumer the chance to purchase these and other fine products in this 29th Anniversary Sale on a first come first served basis. Thus we may run out quickly on some items and/or vintages. Keep in mind that availability does change throughout the year, so be sure to check in with MGM periodically for availability of the world's outstanding wines. Also note that MGM Liquor Warehouse has taken the utmost care in preparing the Anniversary Sale, but we are not responsible for typographical errors. No additional discounts may be applied to sale products. All bottles are 750ml, and are packed 12 bottles to a case unless otherwise noted.

Anniversary Flyer at 2 (Beach Aff., Ex. B). The Millennium flyer contains a disclaimer with almost identical language but also adds the following parenthetical sentence to the middle of the paragraph: "Supplier shortages may also affect the availability of some products and vintages." Millennium Flyer at 2 (Beach Aff., Ex. A). The Millennium flyer also carries the following disclaiming language at the bottom of two pages: "MGM and/or our suppliers may run out without notice on some items and/or vintages." Millennium Flyer at 3, 16. Finally, both flyers attach order forms that carry similar disclaimers in very fine print at the bottom of the form, as well as a statement that customers using the form should "allow[] a minimum of 48 hours" before picking up their orders. *See* Anniversary Flyer & Millennium Flyer (attached order forms).

(3) Literal Falsity of the MGM Advertisements

The parties disagree as to the explicit message conveyed by the MGM flyers. Surdyk's contends that these flyers, on their face, represent to the buying public that MGM has the advertised products immediately available at sale price, at each participating location, by the case and by the bottle. This representation, Surdyk's argues, is false. MGM, on the other hand, contends that the flyers, on their face, merely represent that the advertised products are generally available at sale price, with no express message that MGM stores will stock either bottles or cases of the products. This representation, MGM argues, is true. Although the court believes that Surdyk's is likely to prove literal falsity under either interpretation of the MGM advertisements, the court will address each interpretation separately.

a. "Immediate Availability"

Surdyk's argues that the MGM flyers explicitly convey a message of immediate availability. The court agrees. First, the detailed listing of the wine and liquor products, complete with individual stock item numbers, signifies that MGM actually carries each of the sale items in inventory. Second, the specific listing of case sale prices next to most of the wine and liquor listings signifies that MGM has case quantities of the items in inventory. Third, the individualized store maps signify that each participating store had ready access to the inventory advertised in the flyers. Viewed together in context, then, the textual elements of the MGM flyers convey a clear message that the sales items are available at each participating MGM store for immediate purchase, in both bottle and case quantities.

This message is reinforced by the disclaimers that appear in both flyers. The disclaimers begin by stating that "MGM Liquor Warehouse makes every effort to insure availability of all items that are on sale" but warns about "the very limited availability of some of these outstanding wines (in some instances only a few cases)." The plain, ordinary meaning of "available" is "present or ready for immediate use." *See* MERRIAM-WEBSTER'S COLLEGIATE DICTIONARY, TENTH EDITION, at 79. Thus, the very use of the term "availability" in the disclaimer strongly connotes that MGM stores carries an immediately accessible quantity of almost all advertised products in stock. This understanding is underscored by other statements in the disclaimer: that "in some instances," availability is limited to "only a few cases"; that supplies are available on a "first come first serve" basis; that MGM may "run out" if the consumer does not act quickly. Each of these statements indicate that MGM has at least some case quantities in actual inventory at the beginning of the sale. Likewise, the fact that MGM specifically denominates a few wines as "limited" in the main text of the flyers suggests: (1) that MGM nonetheless has a determinate amount of those wines on hand and (2) that bottle and case quantities are not limited with respect to the hundreds of remaining advertised wines.

Thus, the court believes it likely that a factfinder would conclude that the MGM flyers convey a clear message that MGM stores stock an immediately available supply of each product advertised in the quantities advertised. The undisputed evidence demonstrates, however, that this message is false. While shopping at certain MGM stores during both the Anniversary and Millennium Sales, private investigators hired by Surdyk's discovered that a number of wines advertised in the flyers were either completely out of stock or stocked only in small bottle quantities. *See generally* Ness & Shaw Affs. & Attached Notes. Immediately prior to the commencement of the Anniversary Sale in September, investigators visited ten MGM stores with a list of 18 advertised wines, all but one of which had been advertised as available by the case. The Hilltop store stocked not a single bottle from the investigators' list. The West Bloomington, Crystal, and Maplewood stores had only one bottle from the list. The Blaine store stocked only "a couple bottles." The Eagan store had only three bottles. Stock was little better at the Coon Rapids, Brooklyn Park, and White Bear Lake stores. Only the Vadnais Heights store had a single wine available by the case. However, even this store stocked only seven of the eighteen wines on the list. Indeed, the manager at Vadnais Heights admitted to the investigator that MGM does not always stock all of the products in its advertisements.

Further, on the second day of the Millennium Sale in November, a private investigator hired by Surdyk's surveyed nine MGM stores, including several stores not surveyed during the Anniversary Sale. On this occasion, the investigator shopped using a list of two dozen wines and liquors. The results were not significantly different from those of the first investigation. Five of the wines were entirely unavailable at all nine of the stores sampled. Three stores had none of the wines and none of the liquors on the investigator's list. Only two stores, Vadnais Heights and Minnetonka, had any of the wines in case quantities. The Vadnais Heights store had one case each of three of seventeen wines requested and the Minnetonka store had only one case.

Surdyk's directs the court to an especially telling example of the disconnect between MGM's advertised availability and its actual in-store availability. On the cover of the Millennium Flyer, MGM chose to feature a popular California Chardonnay, Far Niente. The entry for Far Niente appears on page 22 of the flyer, listing Far Niente's stock item number, its comparable bottle price, and sales prices for both bottles and cases. On the second day of the Millennium Sale, however, Far Niente was entirely unavailable at the three MGM stores in Hilltop, Crystal, and Oak Park Heights. The MGM stores in Vadnais Heights, Minnetonka, Maple Grove, Plymouth, White Bear Lake, and St. Paul had only 20 bottles of Far Niente between them. Far Niente was similarly unavailable from the ten stores shopped during the Anniversary Sale.

In short, there is ample undisputed evidence that MGM stores across the Twin Cities failed to stock a number of advertised wines in case quantities or even significant bottle quantities. Because the actual inventory in these MGM stores directly contradicts MGM's advertised claims, the court concludes that Surdyk's is likely to succeed in proving that the MGM flyers are literally false.

b. "General Availability"

MGM disagrees, however, that its sale flyers convey any message about immediate availability. Rather, MGM contends, the flyers merely communicate that the sales items are generally available, without any specific message as to whether the items are actually carried on store shelves. As discussed, the court does not believe that MGM's interpretation is correct. However, even if the court were to adopt this interpretation, the record evidence strongly supports a finding of literal falsity. Surdyk's has clearly demonstrated that a number of the sales items were unavailable even from distributors during the relevant sale periods. Jim Surdyk, the owner of Surdyk's, and Mike Cords, the wine manager at Surdyk's, have submitted affidavits stating that, based on their personal experience in the wine and liquor retail industry and a perusal of the MGM Flyers, "numerous" wines and liquors advertised by MGM "were not available in Twin Cities distribution channels, and not in the case lots advertised." Cord Aff. at P 3; *see also* Surdyk Aff. P 5. Further, the private investigation conducted by Surdyk's confirms that several products were completely unavailable in case quantities from any of the MGM stores shopped during the Anniversary and Millennium Sales. This evidence of persistent retail unavailability strongly supports the inference that these products were not available at the wholesale level either.

Indeed, the evidence of distributor unavailability for certain advertised wines goes well beyond the testimony of Surdyk's employees and investigators. As MGM itself admitted in its letter to the Minnesota Attorney General, four of the wines advertised in the Anniversary flyer were not available from distributors during the sale period. *See* MGM Letter at 2. In the same letter, MGM acknowledged that "it would not be unusual, ... when dealing with wines of limited availability, for there to be some wines that are not available [from distributors] at a [date] subsequent [to the publication of the sale flyer]." *Id.* Further, Mark Jenkins, an MGM customer, has submitted an affidavit describing his efforts to obtain three bottles of Domaine Chandon Fleur de Vigne, an item advertised for sale on the second page of the Millennium flyer. *See generally* Jenkins Aff. After traveling to MGM's Woodbury store during the sale and asking to purchase the wine, Jenkins was told by a salesperson that "Fleur de Vigne is a special order item" and informed that it would take two to three days for an order to arrive. *Id.* at P 10. A week later, having heard nothing from MGM, Jenkins called to inquire about the status of the wine. He was told by the Woodbury store manager that the "[MGM] distributor was out of stock" until the next week. *Id.* at 13. Jenkins twice followed up with calls to MGM, but each time was told that the distributor remained out of stock. Jenkins's experience obviously calls into doubt the accuracy of MGM's claims about distributor availability.

In response to this evidence, MGM offers virtually identical affidavits from three MGM employees averring that, prior to each sale, MGM "personally contacted MGM's wholesale suppliers and distributors..., in order to confirm that all of the wines listed in the advertisement would be available from our suppliers and distributors at the beginning of the sale." Mills Aff. PP 3, 5 (confirming wine supply); Hanson Aff. PP 3, 5 (confirming liquor supply); Raney Aff. PP 3, 5 (confirming beer supply). Notably absent from these affidavits, however, is any specific mention of when these suppliers were contacted and what quantity of merchandise MGM was able to confirm as available. These affidavits also appear to partially contradict another statement by MGM that it confirmed supplier availability only after the Anniversary Sale was finished. *See* MGM Letter at 2 ("In response to your letter, MGM confirmed with its suppliers that all the wines listed were available [from distributors]." (emphasis added)). Further, the affidavits describe only half-hearted attempts to confirm availability in the first place: MGM merely "informed our suppliers and distributors which wines we planned to list in the advertisement, and asked them to contact [MGM] if any of the proposed products would not be available." Mills Aff. P 5; Hanson Aff. P 5; Raney Aff. P 5. While MGM argues that its efforts were adequate to the task of ensuring availability, the record evidence clearly indicates otherwise.

Indeed, MGM's passive relationship with its suppliers highlights the fundamental problem with its conduct in this case. In its motion papers and at oral argument, MGM has repeatedly acknowledged that it has no control over the stock or inventory control procedures of any MGM franchisee. MGM has also acknowledged the unique supply difficulties associated with the wine business:

In the case of wines, you are not dealing with a product that is manufactured in unlimited quantities. New wines represent an agricultural product whose supply is limited by matters beyond anyone's control, including the size and quality of the annual grape crop. Older wines are obviously limited to the number of bottles previously produced. Supplies are therefore always limited, and it is impossible to know in advance when a wholesaler's demand will exceed supply.

MGM Letter, at 2. Yet in spite of the inherently uncertain nature of wholesale wine supply and MGM's passive, decentralized approach to inventory control, MGM has twice orchestrated advertising campaigns that belie these business realities and the availability problems they inevitably create. While MGM and its franchisees may manage their inventory in any way they like, they may not misrepresent the actual nature of that inventory to the buying public. Because there is strong evidence that just such a misrepresentation has occurred, the court concludes that Surdyk's is likely to succeed on the issue of literal falsity.

* * *

Note

If claims by one advertiser are shown to be literally false, the plaintiff need not show that the statements were material to consumers in purchasing decisions. The mere fact that they are literally false is enough to warrant an injunction. *See, e.g., Pizza Hut, Inc. v. Papa John's Int'l, Inc.*, 227 F.3d 489 (5th Cir. 2000). Why shouldn't the plaintiff have to demonstrate that the literally false statement mattered to anyone? Christopher C. Colson, *NOTE: Pizza Hut, Inc. v. Papa John's International, Inc.-Creating Conflict and Uncertainty in Lanham Act False Advertising Claims*, 41 BRANDEIS L. J. 333 (2002) (The materiality requirement was defined as "actual reliance" in reviewed case; this misstates the private plaintiff's responsibility in proving false advertising claims and assuring the market is free of such claims).

E. Outer Limits of Claims under §43(a)

Dastar Corp. v. Twentieth Century Fox Film Corp.
539 U.S. 23 (2003)

SCALIA, J.

In this case, we are asked to decide whether §43(a) of the Lanham Act, 15 U.S.C. §1125(a), prevents the unaccredited copying of a work, and if so, whether a court may double a profit award under §1117(a), in order to deter future infringing conduct.

I

In 1948, three and a half years after the German surrender at Reims, General Dwight D. Eisenhower completed Crusade in Europe, his written account of the allied campaign in Europe during World War II. Doubleday published the book, registered it with the

Copyright Office in 1948, and granted exclusive television rights to an affiliate of respondent Twentieth Century Fox Film Corporation (Fox). Fox, in turn, arranged for Time, Inc., to produce a television series, also called Crusade in Europe, based on the book, and Time assigned its copyright in the series to Fox. The television series, consisting of 26 episodes, was first broadcast in 1949. It combined a soundtrack based on a narration of the book with film footage from the United States Army, Navy, and Coast Guard, the British Ministry of Information and War Office, the National Film Board of Canada, and unidentified "Newsreel Pool Cameramen." In 1975, Doubleday renewed the copyright on the book as the "'proprietor of copyright in a work made for hire.'" App. to Pet for Cert. 9a. Fox, however, did not renew the copyright on the Crusade television series, which expired in 1977, leaving the television series in the public domain.

In 1988, Fox reacquired the television rights in General Eisenhower's book, including the exclusive right to distribute the Crusade television series on video and to sub-license others to do so. Respondents SFM Entertainment and New Line Home Video, Inc., in turn, acquired from Fox the exclusive rights to distribute Crusade on video. SFM obtained the negatives of the original television series, restored them, and repackaged the series on videotape; New Line distributed the videotapes.

Enter petitioner Dastar. In 1995, Dastar decided to expand its product line from music compact discs to videos. Anticipating renewed interest in World War II on the 50th anniversary of the war's end, Dastar released a video set entitled World War II Campaigns in Europe. To make Campaigns, Dastar purchased eight beta cam tapes of the *original* version of the Crusade television series, which is in the public domain, copied them, and then edited the series. Dastar's Campaigns series is slightly more than half as long as the original Crusade television series. Dastar substituted a new opening sequence, credit page, and final closing for those of the Crusade television series; inserted new chapter-title sequences and narrated chapter introductions; moved the "recap" in the Crusade television series to the beginning and retitled it as a "preview"; and removed references to and images of the book. Dastar created new packaging for its Campaigns series and (as already noted) a new title.

Dastar manufactured and sold the Campaigns video set as its own product. The advertising states: "Produced and Distributed by: *Entertainment Distributing*" (which is owned by Dastar), and makes no reference to the Crusade television series. Similarly, the screen credits state "DASTAR CORP presents" and "an ENTERTAINMENT DISTRIBUTING Production," and list as executive producer, producer, and associate producer, employees of Dastar. Supp. App. 2–3, 30. The Campaigns videos themselves also make no reference to the Crusade television series, New Line's Crusade videotapes, or the book. Dastar sells its Campaigns videos to Sam's Club, Costco, Best Buy, and other retailers and mail-order companies for $25 per set, substantially less than New Line's video set.

In 1998, respondents Fox, SFM, and New Line brought this action alleging that Dastar's sale of its Campaigns video set infringes Doubleday's copyright in General Eisenhower's book and, thus, their exclusive television rights in the book. Respondents later amended their complaint to add claims that Dastar's sale of Campaigns "without proper credit" to the Crusade television series constitutes "reverse passing off" in violation of §43(a) of the Lanham Act, 15 U.S.C. §1125(a), and in violation of state unfair-competition law. App. to Pet. for Cert. 31a. On cross-motions for summary judgment, the District Court found for respondents on all three counts, *id.*, at 54a–55a, treating its resolution of the Lanham Act claim as controlling on the state-law unfair-competition claim because "the ultimate test under both is whether the public is likely to be deceived or confused," *id.*, at 54a. The court awarded Dastar's profits to respondents and doubled them pursuant to §35 of the Lanham Act, 15 U.S.C. §1117(a), to deter future infringing conduct by petitioner.

The Court of Appeals for the Ninth Circuit affirmed the judgment for respondents on the Lanham Act claim, but reversed as to the copyright claim and remanded. 34 Fed. Appx. 312, 316 (2002). (It said nothing with regard to the state-law claim.) With respect to the Lanham Act claim, the Court of Appeals reasoned that "Dastar copied substantially the entire *Crusade in Europe* series created by Twentieth Century Fox, labeled the resulting product with a different name and marketed it without attribution to Fox [,and] therefore committed a 'bodily appropriation' of Fox's series." *Id.*, at 314. It concluded that "Dastar's 'bodily appropriation' of Fox's original [television] series is sufficient to establish the reverse passing off." *Ibid.* The court also affirmed the District Court's award under the Lanham Act of twice Dastar's profits. We granted certiorari.

II

* * *

Thus, as it comes to us, the gravamen of respondents' claim is that, in marketing and selling Campaigns as its own product without acknowledging its nearly wholesale reliance on the Crusade television series, Dastar has made a "false designation of origin, false or misleading description of fact, or false or misleading representation of fact, which ... is likely to cause confusion ... as to the origin ... of his or her goods." That claim would undoubtedly be sustained if Dastar had bought some of New Line's Crusade videotapes and merely repackaged them as its own. Dastar's alleged wrongdoing, however, is vastly different: it took a creative work in the public domain—the Crusade television series—copied it, made modifications (arguably minor), and produced its very own series of videotapes. If "origin" refers only to the manufacturer or producer of the physical "goods" that are made available to the public (in this case the videotapes), Dastar was the origin. If, however, "origin" includes the creator of the underlying work that Dastar copied, then someone else (perhaps Fox) was the origin of Dastar's product. At bottom, we must decide what §43(a)(1)(A) of the Lanham Act means by the "origin" of "goods."

III

The dictionary definition of "origin" is "the fact or process of coming into being from a source," and "that from which anything primarily proceeds; source." Webster's New International Dictionary 1720–1721 (2d ed. 1949). And the dictionary definition of "goods" (as relevant here) is "wares; merchandise." *Id.*, at 1079. We think the most natural understanding of the "origin" of "goods"—the source of wares—is the producer of the tangible product sold in the marketplace, in this case the physical Campaigns videotape sold by Dastar. The concept might be stretched (as it was under the original version of §43(a)) to include not only the actual producer, but also the trademark owner who commissioned or assumed responsibility for ("stood behind") production of the physical product. But as used in the Lanham Act, the phrase "origin of goods" is in our view incapable of connoting the person or entity that originated the ideas or communications that "goods" embody or contain. Such an extension would not only stretch the text, but it would be out of accord with the history and purpose of the Lanham Act and inconsistent with precedent.

Section 43(a) of the Lanham Act prohibits actions like trademark infringement that deceive consumers and impair a producer's goodwill. It forbids, for example, the Coca-Cola Company's passing off its product as Pepsi-Cola or reverse passing off Pepsi-Cola as its product. But the brand-loyal consumer who prefers the drink that the Coca-Cola Company or PepsiCo sells, while he believes that that company produced (or at least stands behind the production of) that product, surely does not necessarily believe that that company was the "origin" of the drink in the sense that it was the very first to devise the formula. The consumer who buys a branded product does not automatically assume that the brand-name company is the same entity that came up with the idea for the product, or designed the product—and typically does not care whether it is. The words of the Lanham Act should not be stretched to cover matters that are typically of no consequence to purchasers.

It could be argued, perhaps, that the reality of purchaser concern is different for what might be called a communicative product—one that is valued not primarily for its physical qualities, such as a hammer, but for the intellectual content that it conveys, such as a book or, as here, a video. The purchaser of a novel is interested not merely, if at all, in the identity of the producer of the physical tome (the publisher), but also, and indeed primarily, in the identity of the creator of the story it conveys (the author). And the author, of course, has at least as much interest in avoiding passing-off (or reverse passing-off) of his creation as does the publisher. For such a communicative product (the argument goes) "origin of goods" in §43(a) must be deemed to include not merely the producer of the physical item (the publishing house Farrar, Straus and Giroux, or the video producer Dastar) but also the creator of the content that the physical item conveys (the author Tom Wolfe, or—assertedly—respondents).

The problem with this argument according special treatment to communicative products is that it causes the Lanham Act to conflict with the law of copyright, which addresses that subject specifically. The right to copy, and to copy without attribution, once a copyright has expired, like "the right to make [an article whose patent has expired]—including the right to make it in precisely the shape it carried when patented—passes to the public." *Sears, Roebuck & Co. v. Stiffel Co.*, 376 U.S. 225, 230, 11 L. Ed. 2d 661, 84 S. Ct. 784, 1964 Dec. Comm'r Pat. 425 (1964); *see also Kellogg Co.* v. *National Biscuit Co.*, 305 U.S. 111, 121–122, 83 L. Ed. 73, 59 S. Ct. 109, 1939 Dec. Comm'r Pat. 850 (1938). "In general, unless an intellectual property right such as a patent or copyright protects an item, it will be subject to copying." *TrafFix Devices, Inc.* v. *Marketing Displays, Inc.*, 532 U.S. 23, 29, 149 L. Ed. 2d 164, 121 S. Ct. 1255 (2001). The rights of a patentee or copyright holder are part of a "carefully crafted bargain," *Bonito Boats, Inc.* v. *Thunder Craft Boats, Inc.*, 489 U.S. 141, 150–151, 103 L. Ed. 2d 118, 109 S. Ct. 971 (1989), under which, once the patent or copyright monopoly has expired, the public may use the invention or work at will and without attribution. Thus, in construing the Lanham Act, we have been "careful to caution against misuse or over-extension" of trademark and related protections into areas traditionally occupied by patent or copyright. *TrafFix*, 532 U.S., at 29. "The Lanham Act," we have said, "does not exist to reward manufacturers for their innovation in creating a particular device; that is the purpose of the patent law and its period of exclusivity." *Id.*, at 34. Federal trademark law "has no necessary relation to invention or discovery," *Trade-Mark Cases*, 100 U.S. 82, 94, 25 L. Ed. 550, 1879 Dec. Comm'r Pat. 619 (1879), but rather, by preventing competitors from copying "a source-identifying mark," "reduces the customer's costs of shopping and making purchasing decisions," and "helps assure a producer that it (and not an imitating competitor) will reap the financial, reputation-related rewards associated with a desirable product," *Qualitex Co.* v. *Jacobson Products Co.*, 514 U.S. 159, 163–164, 131 L. Ed. 2d 248, 115 S. Ct. 1300 (1995) (internal quotation marks and citation omitted). Assuming for the sake of argument that Dastar's representation of itself as the "Producer" of its videos amounted to a representation that it originated the creative work conveyed by the videos, allowing a cause of action under §43(a) for that representation would create a species of mutant copyright law that limits the public's "federal right to 'copy and to use,'" expired copyrights, *Bonito Boats, supra*, at 165.

When Congress has wished to create such an addition to the law of copyright, it has done so with much more specificity than the Lanham Act's ambiguous use of "origin." The

Visual Artists Rights Act of 1990, §603(a), 104 Stat. 5128, provides that the author of an artistic work "shall have the right ... to claim authorship of that work." 17 U.S.C. §106A(a)(1)(A). That express right of attribution is carefully limited and focused: It attaches only to specified "works of visual art," §101, is personal to the artist, §§106A(b) and (e), and endures only for "the life of the author," at §106A(d)(1). Recognizing in §43(a) a cause of action for misrepresentation of authorship of noncopyrighted works (visual or otherwise) would render these limitations superfluous. A statutory interpretation that renders another statute superfluous is of course to be avoided.

Reading "origin" in §43(a) to require attribution of uncopyrighted materials would pose serious practical problems. Without a copyrighted work as the basepoint, the word "origin" has no discernable limits. A video of the MGM film Carmen Jones, after its copyright has expired, would presumably require attribution not just to MGM, but to Oscar Hammerstein II (who wrote the musical on which the film was based), to Georges Bizet (who wrote the opera on which the musical was based), and to Prosper Merimee (who wrote the novel on which the opera was based). In many cases, figuring out who is in the line of "origin" would be no simple task. Indeed, in the present case it is far from clear that respondents have that status. Neither SFM nor New Line had anything to do with the production of the Crusade television series—they merely were licensed to distribute the video version. While Fox might have a claim to being in the line of origin, its involvement with the creation of the television series was limited at best. Time, Inc., was the principal if not the exclusive creator, albeit under arrangement with Fox. And of course it was neither Fox nor Time, Inc., that shot the film used in the Crusade television series. Rather, that footage came from the United States Army, Navy, and Coast Guard, the British Ministry of Information and War Office, the National Film Board of Canada, and unidentified "Newsreel Pool Cameramen." If anyone has a claim to being the *original* creator of the material used in both the Crusade television series and the Campaigns videotapes, it would be those groups, rather than Fox. We do not think the Lanham Act requires this search for the source of the Nile and all its tributaries.

Another practical difficulty of adopting a special definition of "origin" for communicative products is that it places the manufacturers of those products in a difficult position. On the one hand, they would face Lanham Act liability for *failing* to credit the creator of a work on which their lawful copies are based; and on the other hand they could face Lanham Act liability for *crediting* the creator if that should be regarded as implying the creator's "sponsorship or approval" of the copy, 15 U.S.C. §1125(a)(1)(A). In this case, for example, if Dastar had simply "copied [the television series] as Crusade in Europe and sold it as Crusade in Europe," without changing the title or packaging (including the original credits to Fox), it is hard to have confidence in respondents' assurance that they "would not be here on a Lanham Act cause of action."

Finally, reading §43(a) of the Lanham Act as creating a cause of action for, in effect, plagiarism—the use of otherwise unprotected works and inventions without attribution—would be hard to reconcile with our previous decisions. For example, in *Wal-Mart Stores, Inc. v. Samara Brothers, Inc.*, 529 U.S. 205, 146 L. Ed. 2d 182, 120 S. Ct. 1339 (2000), we considered whether product-design trade dress can ever be inherently distinctive. Wal-Mart produced "knockoffs" of children's clothes designed and manufactured by Samara Brothers, containing only "minor modifications" of the original designs. *Id.*, at 208. We concluded that the designs could not be protected under §43(a) without a showing that they had acquired "secondary meaning," *id.*, at 214, so that they "'identify the source of the product rather than the product itself,'" *id.*, at 211 (quoting *Inwood Laboratories, Inc. v. Ives Laboratories, Inc.*, 456 U.S. 844, 851, n. 11, 72 L. Ed. 2d 606, 102

S. Ct. 2182 (1982)). This carefully considered limitation would be entirely pointless if the "original" producer could turn around and pursue a reverse-passing-off claim under exactly the same provision of the Lanham Act. Samara would merely have had to argue that it was the "origin" of the designs that Wal-Mart was selling as its own line. It was not, because "origin of goods" in the Lanham Act referred to the producer of the clothes, and not the producer of the (potentially) copyrightable or patentable designs that the clothes embodied.

Similarly under respondents' theory, the "origin of goods" provision of §43(a) would have supported the suit that we rejected in Bonito Boats, 489 U.S. 141, 103 L. Ed. 2d 118, 109 S. Ct. 971, where the defendants had used molds to duplicate the plaintiff's unpatented boat hulls (apparently without crediting the plaintiff). And it would have supported the suit we rejected in *TrafFix*, 532 U.S. 23, 149 L. Ed. 2d 164, 121 S. Ct. 1255: The plaintiff, whose patents on flexible road signs had expired, and who could not prevail on a trade-dress claim under §43(a) because the features of the signs were functional, would have had a reverse-passing-off claim for unattributed copying of his design.

In sum, reading the phrase "origin of goods" in the Lanham Act in accordance with the Act's common-law foundations (which were *not* designed to protect originality or creativity), and in light of the copyright and patent laws (which *were*), we conclude that the phrase refers to the producer of the tangible goods that are offered for sale, and not to the author of any idea, concept, or communication embodied in those goods. Cf. 17 U.S.C. §202 (distinguishing between a copyrighted work and "any material object in which the work is embodied"). To hold otherwise would be akin to finding that §43(a) created a species of perpetual patent and copyright, which Congress may not do. *See Eldred v. Ashcroft*, 537 U.S. 186, 208, 154 L. Ed. 2d 683, 123 S. Ct. 769 (2003).

The creative talent of the sort that lay behind the Campaigns videos is not left without protection. The original film footage used in the Crusade television series could have been copyrighted, *see* 17 U.S.C. §102(a)(6), as was copyrighted (as a compilation) the Crusade television series, even though it included material from the public domain, *see* §103(a). Had Fox renewed the copyright in the Crusade television series, it would have had an easy claim of copyright infringement. And respondents' contention that Campaigns infringes Doubleday's copyright in General Eisenhower's book is still a live question on remand. If, moreover, the producer of a video that substantially copied the Crusade series were, in advertising or promotion, to give purchasers the impression that the video was quite different from that series, then one or more of the respondents might have a cause of action—not for reverse passing off under the "confusion … as to the origin" provision of §43(a)(1)(A), but for misrepresentation under the "misrepresents the nature, characteristics [or] qualities" provision of §43(a)(1)(B). For merely saying it is the producer of the video, however, no Lanham Act liability attaches to Dastar.

* * *

Because we conclude that Dastar was the "origin" of the products it sold as its own, respondents cannot prevail on their Lanham Act claim. We thus have no occasion to consider whether the Lanham Act permitted an award of double petitioner's profits. The judgment of the Court of Appeals for the Ninth Circuit is reversed, and the case is remanded for further proceedings consistent with this opinion.

It is so ordered.

ETW Corp. v. Jireh Publ.
332 F. 3d 915 (6th Cir. 2003)

GRAHAM, DISTRICT JUDGE

Plaintiff-Appellant ETW Corporation ("ETW") is the licensing agent of Eldrick "Tiger" Woods ("Woods"), one of the world's most famous professional golfers. Woods, chairman of the board of ETW, has assigned to it the exclusive right to exploit his name, image, likeness, and signature, and all other publicity rights. ETW owns a United States trademark registration for the mark "TIGER WOODS" (Registration No. 2,194,381) for use in connection with "art prints, calendars, mounted photographs, notebooks, pencils, pens, posters, trading cards, and unmounted photographs."

Defendant-Appellee Jireh Publishing, Inc. ("Jireh") of Tuscaloosa, Alabama, is the publisher of artwork created by Rick Rush ("Rush"). Rush, who refers to himself as "America's sports artist," has created paintings of famous figures in sports and famous sports events. A few examples include Michael Jordan, Mark McGuire, Coach Paul "Bear" Bryant, the Pebble Beach Golf Tournament, and the America's Cup Yacht Race. Jireh has produced and successfully marketed limited edition art prints made from Rush's paintings.

In 1998, Rush created a painting entitled *The Masters of Augusta*, which commemorates Woods's victory at the Masters Tournament in Augusta, Georgia, in 1997. At that event, Woods became the youngest player ever to win the Masters Tournament, while setting a 72-hole record for the tournament and a record 12-stroke margin of victory. In the foreground of Rush's painting are three views of Woods in different poses. In the center, he is completing the swing of a golf club, and on each side he is crouching, lining up and/or observing the progress of a putt. To the left of Woods is his caddy, Mike "Fluff" Cowan, and to his right is his final round partner's caddy. Behind these figures is the Augusta National Clubhouse. In a blue background behind the clubhouse are likenesses of famous golfers of the past looking down on Woods. These include Arnold Palmer, Sam Snead, Ben Hogan, Walter Hagen, Bobby Jones, and Jack Nicklaus. Behind them is the Masters leader board.

The limited edition prints distributed by Jireh consist of an image of Rush's painting which includes Rush's signature at the bottom right hand corner. Beneath the image of the painting, in block letters, is its title, "The Masters Of Augusta." Beneath the title, in block letters of equal height, is the artist's name, "Rick Rush," and beneath the artist's name, in smaller upper and lower case letters, is the legend "Painting America Through Sports."

As sold by Jireh, the limited edition prints are enclosed in a white envelope, accompanied with literature which includes a large photograph of Rush, a description of his art, and a narrative description of the subject painting. On the front of the envelope, Rush's name appears in block letters inside a rectangle, which includes the legend "Painting America Through Sports." Along the bottom is a large reproduction of Rush's signature two inches high and ten inches long. On the back of the envelope, under the flap, are the words "Masters of Augusta" in letters that are three-eights of an inch high, and "Tiger Woods" in letters that are one-fourth of an inch high. Woods's name also appears in the narrative description of the painting where he is mentioned twice in twenty-eight lines of text. The text also includes references to the six other famous golfers depicted in the background of the painting as well as the two caddies. Jireh published and marketed two hundred and fifty 22 1/2" x 30" serigraphs and five thousand 9" x 11" lithographs of *The Masters of Augusta* at an issuing price of $700 for the serigraphs and $100 for the lithographs.

ETW filed suit against Jireh on June 26, 1998, in the United States District Court for the Northern District of Ohio, alleging trademark infringement ...

* * *

III. Trademark Claims Under 15 U.S.C. §1125(a)
Based on the Unauthorized Use of the Likeness of Tiger Woods

* * *

ETW has registered Woods's name as a trademark, but it has not registered any image or likeness of Woods. Nevertheless, ETW claims to have trademark rights in Woods's image and likeness. Section 43 (a) of the Lanham Act provides a federal cause of action for infringement of an unregistered trademark which affords such marks essentially the same protection as those that are registered. *See* Two Pesos, Inc. v. Taco Cabana, Inc., 505 U.S. 763, 768, 120 L. Ed. 2d 615, 112 S. Ct. 2753 (1992) ("It is common ground that §43(a) protects qualifying unregistered trademarks and that the general principles qualifying a mark for registration under §2 of the Lanham Act are for the most part applicable in determining whether an unregistered mark is entitled to protection under §43(a).").

The Lanham Act defines a trademark as including "any word, name, symbol, or device, or any combination thereof" used by a person "to identify and distinguish his or her goods ... from those manufactured or sold by others and to indicate the source of the goods, even if that source is unknown." 15 U.S.C. §1127. The essence of a trademark is a designation in the form of a distinguishing name, symbol or device which is used to identify a person's goods and distinguish them from the goods of another. *See* Taco Cabana, 505 U.S. at 768 ("In order to be [protected], a mark must be capable of distinguishing the [owner's] goods from those of others."). Not every word, name, symbol or device qualifies as a protectable mark; rather, it must be proven that it performs the job of identification, *i.e.*, to identify one source and to distinguish it from other sources. If it does not do this, then it is not protectable as a trademark. *See* J. Thomas McCarthy, McCarthy on Trademarks and Unfair Competition, §3:1 (2002).

"[A] trademark, unlike a copyright or patent, is not a 'right in gross' that enables a holder to enjoin all reproductions." *Boston Athletic Ass'n v. Sullivan*, 867 F.2d 22, 35 (1st Cir. 1989) (citing *Univ. of Notre Dame du Lac v. J.C. Gourmet Food Imports Co.*, 703 F.2d 1372, 1374 (Fed. Cir. 1983)).

Here, ETW claims protection under the Lanham Act for any and all images of Tiger Woods. This is an untenable claim. ETW asks us, in effect, to constitute Woods himself as a walking, talking trademark. Images and likenesses of Woods are not protectable as a trademark because they do not perform the trademark function of designation. They do not distinguish and identify the source of goods. They cannot function as a trademark because there are undoubtedly thousands of images and likenesses of Woods taken by countless photographers, and drawn, sketched, or painted by numerous artists, which have been published in many forms of media, and sold and distributed throughout the world. No reasonable person could believe that merely because these photographs or paintings contain Woods's likeness or image, they all originated with Woods.

We hold that, as a general rule, a person's image or likeness cannot function as a trademark. Our conclusion is supported by the decisions of other courts which have addressed this issue. In *Pirone v. MacMillan, Inc.*, 894 F.2d 579 (2d Cir. 1990), the Second Circuit rejected a trademark claim asserted by the daughters of baseball legend Babe Ruth. The plaintiffs objected to the use of Ruth's likeness in three photographs which appeared in a calendar published by the defendant. The court rejected their claim, holding that "a photograph of a human being, unlike a portrait of a fanciful cartoon character, is not inherently 'distinctive' in the trademark sense of tending to indicate origin." *Id.* at 583. The court noted that Ruth "was one of the most photographed men of his generation, a larger than life hero to millions and an historical figure[.]" *Id.* The Second Circuit Court concluded that a consumer could not reasonably believe that Ruth sponsored the calendar:

> An ordinarily prudent purchaser would have no difficulty discerning that these photos are merely the subject matter of the calendar and do not in any way indicate sponsorship. No reasonable jury could find a likelihood of confusion.

Id. at 585. The court observed that "under some circumstances, a photograph of a person may be a valid trademark—if, for example, a particular photograph was consistently used on specific goods." *Id.* at 583. The court rejected plaintiffs' assertion of trademark rights in every photograph of Ruth.

In *Estate of Presley v. Russen*, 513 F. Supp. 1339, 1363–1364 (D.N.J. 1981), the court rejected a claim by the estate of Elvis Presley that his image and likeness was a valid mark. The court did find, however, as suggested by the Second Circuit in *Pirone*, that one particular image of Presley had been consistently used in the advertising and sale of Elvis Presley entertainment services to identify those services and that the image could likely be found to function as a mark.

In *Rock and Roll Hall of Fame*, the plaintiff asserted trademark rights in the design of the building which houses the Rock and Roll Hall of Fame in Cleveland, Ohio, and claimed that defendant's poster featuring a photograph of the museum against a colorful sunset was a violation of its trademark rights. 134 F.3d at 751. This court, with one judge dissenting, reversed the judgment of the district court which granted plaintiff's request for a preliminary injunction. After reviewing the evidence, the majority concluded:

> In reviewing the Museum's disparate uses of several different perspectives of its building design, we cannot conclude that they create a consistent and distinct commercial impression as an indicator of a single source of origin or sponsorship. To be more specific, we cannot conclude on this record that it is likely that the Museum has established a valid trademark in every photograph which, like Gentile's, prominently displays the front of the Museum's building.

Id. at 755. In reaching this conclusion, this court approved and followed *Pirone* and *Estate of Presley*.

Here, ETW does not claim that a particular photograph of Woods has been consistently used on specific goods. Instead, ETW's claim is identical to that of the plaintiffs in *Pirone*, a sweeping claim to trademark rights in every photograph and image of Woods. Woods, like Ruth, is one of the most photographed sports figures of his generation, but this alone does not suffice to create a trademark claim.

The district court properly granted summary judgment on ETW's claim of trademark rights in all images and likenesses of Tiger Woods.

* * *

Notes

1. Who has standing to sue under §43(a)? Competitors, for sure, but can consumers sue? Recall that under the tort of deceit in England, the tort upon which the American common law of trademarks is based, the consumer had standing to sue, not the trademark owner or competitor. *See, e.g., Ford v. Nylcare Health Plans of the Gulf Coast, Inc.,*

301 F.3d 329, 332 (5th Cir. 2003), *cert. denied sub nom, Ford v. Aetna U. S. Healthcare*, 538 U.S. 923 (2003) ("In any inquiry into Lanham Act prudential standing, the court must weigh (1) the nature of the plaintiff's alleged injury: Is the injury of a type that Congress sought to redress in providing a private remedy for violations of the [Lanham Act]?; (2) the directness or indirectness of the asserted injury; (3) the proximity or remoteness of the party to the alleged injurious conduct; (4) the speculativeness of the damages claim; and (5) the risk of duplicative damages or complexity in apportioning damages." *Procter & Gamble*, 242 F.3d at 562. Causation is undeniably relevant to at least the second, third, and fourth prongs of this test, ...) (*quoting, Proctor & Gamble v. Amway Corp.*, 242 F. 3d 539, 562 (5th Cir. 2001)).

2. In *Daystar, supra,* would the world be much different if Twentieth Century Fox prevailed? How?

3. The *ETW* case has provoked a lot of scholarship in a little time. *See, e.g.,* Michael Sloan, *NOTE: Too Famous for the Right of Publicity: ETW Corp. And the Trend Towards Diminished Protection for Top Celebrities*, 22 CARDOZO ARTS & ENT. L. J. 903 (2005) (Sixth Circuit failed to created a "coherent vision"—a better view would be to balance First Amendment Rights and publicity rights); Michael J. Breslin, *Note: ETW Corp. v. Jireh Publishing, Inc: Turning an Athlete's Publicity Over to the Public*, 11 J. INTELL. PROP. L. 369 (2004) (The court inappropriately granted First Amendment protection to artwork that exploited the commercial value of the Tiger Woods image); Barbara Solomon, *Can the Lanham Act Protect Tiger Woods? An Analysis of Whether the Lanham Act is a Proper Substitute for a Federal Right of Publicity*, 94 TRADEMARK REP. 1202 (2004) (A separate federal statute protecting the right of publicity is necessary). Why such keen interest in this case? What is the narrow holding? Is it that remarkable?

F. Section 43(b)

15 U.S.C. §1125, Lanham Act §43

(b) Importation

Any goods marked or labeled in contravention of the provisions of this section shall not be imported into the United States or admitted to entry at any customhouse of the United States. The owner, importer, or consignee of goods refused entry at any customhouse under this section may have any recourse by protest or appeal that is given under the customs revenue laws or may have the remedy given by this chapter in cases involving goods refused entry or seized.

Ross Cosmetics Distribution Ctrs. v. United States
34 U.S.P.Q.2d (BNA) 1758 (Ct. Int'l Trade 1994)

DICARLO, CHIEF JUDGE

Before the court is the remand determination of the United States Customs Service, Ruling Letter 456935 (Nov. 10, 1993), issued pursuant to the court's decision in *Ross Cosmetics Distribution Centers, Inc. v. United States*, 16 CIT, Slip Op. 93-151 (Aug. 10, 1993), modified, 16 CIT, Slip Op. 93-173 (Sept. 1, 1993). Customs' remand determination ruled that certain labels and packages of cosmetic products proposed by plaintiff for importation constitute counterfeit use of United States trademarks and, if imported, would be subject to seizure and forfeiture. Plaintiff renews its Rule 56.1 motion for judgment upon the agency record, challenging Customs decision as arbitrary, capricious, an abuse of discretion, and otherwise not in accordance with law. The court's jurisdiction in this case is provided by 28 U.S.C. §1581(h) (1988).

Background

Plaintiff, an importer of cosmetics, toiletries, and related products, requested Customs to issue a pre-importation ruling pursuant to 19 C.F.R. §177.2 (1993), regarding whether its packaging for certain bath oils and fragrance oils proposed for importation conformed with Customs-administered laws and regulations relating to trademarks, trade names, and similar intellectual property rights. Specifically, plaintiff's packages for its bath oil products GORGEOUS, LOVE BIRDS, WHISPER, OBLIVION, OSCENT, and MORNING DREAM bear language inviting customers to compare these products to the well-known products of GIORGIO, L'AIR DU TEMPS, OMBRE ROSE, OPIUM, OSCAR, and YOUTH DEW respectively. Plaintiff's products are sold at a fraction of the price of the well-known products.

Customs issued its initial ruling on June 27, 1991, Rul. Ltr. 451142. The Agency held that, because "GIORGIO," "OPIUM," and "YOUTH DEW" are trademarks registered with the United States Patent and Trademark Office (PTO) and recorded with Customs for protection against infringing importation, plaintiff's use of these marks on its packaging constituted a counterfeit use of these marks. Accordingly, plaintiff's products, if imported, would be subject to seizure and forfeiture for violation of 19 U.S.C. §1526 (1988). Customs also held in its Ruling that it was unable to issue a binding ruling regarding plaintiff's use of other marks not recorded with Customs. The Ruling stated, however, that if these marks were registered with the PTO, articles bearing such marks would be subject to seizure under 19 U.S.C. §1595a(c) (1988) for violation of 18 U.S.C. §2320 (1988). Plaintiff filed this action challenging Customs' initial ruling and seeking a judgment upon the agency record. The court issued a decision on August 10, 1993, holding that the Ruling was arbitrary, capricious, an abuse of discretion, or otherwise not in accordance with law. Ross Cosmetics, 16 CIT, Slip Op. 93-151. The court held that before Customs could conclude plaintiff's products were counterfeits, Customs must first make a finding that plaintiff's packages were "identical with or substantially indistinguishable from" the registered marks, and that Customs had failed to do so. Id. at 6–7. The court also held that the Ruling was arbitrary, because in finding that plaintiff's packages were likely to cause customer confusion, Customs simply compared plaintiff's packages to the facsimile copies of the recorded marks, rather than to the actual packages of the products, or a reasonable reproduction representing the design and color of the trademarks. Id. at 7–11. The court further held that, with respect to the unrecorded marks, Customs should investigate whether these marks are registered with the PTO. Id. at 16–17, Slip Op. 93-173 at 1. The court remanded the Ruling to Customs for redetermination.

On November 10, 1993, Customs issued its remand determination. The remand determination ruled: (1) plaintiff's products using the trademarks "OMBRE ROSE," "OPIUM," and "OSCAR" are admissible as non-infringing goods; and (2) plaintiff's products using the trademarks "GIORGIO," "YOUTH DEW," and "L'AIR DU TEMPS" are considered to infringe the rights of the respective trademark owners, and constitute a counterfeit use of these trademarks. Because "GIORGIO" and "YOUTH DEW" are recorded with Customs and "L'AIR DU TEMPS" is not, products using the trademarks "GIORGIO" and "YOUTH DEW," if imported, would be subject to seizure and forfeiture under 19 U.S.C. §1526(e), and products using the trademark "L'AIR DU TEMPS," if imported, would be subject to seizure and forfeiture under 19 U.S.C. §1595a(c) for violation of 18 U.S.C. §2320. Remand Determination, at 28.

Plaintiff now contests Customs' remand determination concerning plaintiff's use of the trademarks "GIORGIO" and "L'AIR DU TEMPS." As for "YOUTH DEW," plaintiff claims that the issue has been rendered moot by a stipulation of settlement, dated June 24, 1993, between plaintiff and the trademark owner of "YOUTH DEW," in Estee Lauder Inc. v. Apple Cosmetics Inc., No. 92 Civ. 7969 (S.D.N.Y. June 24, 1993). The stipulation provides that plaintiff "shall permanently cease and desist, directly or indirectly," from using the YOUTH DEW trademark "in comparative advertising in a manner where such trademark[] [is] substantially larger than the surrounding text or significantly set off by color or type so as to dominate the surrounding text[.]" A.R. Doc. 5 at 2. Plaintiff states that under the terms of this stipulation, it has agreed to discontinue sales of its product MORNING DREAM. Pl.'s Br. at 26.

Discussion

This court's review will be limited to that part of the remand determination challenged by plaintiff; that is, Customs' decision concerning plaintiff's use of the trademarks "GIORGIO" and "L'AIR DU TEMPS" on the proposed packaging of its products GORGEOUS and LOVE BIRDS, respectively.

1. The Products
a. "GIORGIO" v. "GORGEOUS"

The trademark "GIORGIO" is owned by Giorgio Beverly Hills, Inc., which has three valid trademark registrations with both the PTO and Customs for GIORGIO perfume and toiletry products: (1) the word mark "GIORGIO;" (2) a GIORGIO crest design; and (3) a design of alternating yellow and white vertical stripes. See A.R. Docs. 8–10. The GIORGIO packages use the stripe design as background, and bears the GIORGIO crest and the word mark "GIORGIO" in various styles and sizes. A.R. Docs. 7, 11.

The proposed package of plaintiff's product GORGEOUS invites the consumer to compare GORGEOUS to GIORGIO. The package of GORGEOUS uses diagonal yellow and white stripes as the background. A crest design appears above the name "GORGEOUS." At the top of the front panel is the language "COMPARE TO GIORGIO YOU WILL SWITCH TO…," in which the word mark "GIORGIO" is followed by the registered trademark symbol and appears in a bold and larger size print than the rest of the words. At the bottom of the front panel is a disclaimer: "OUR PRODUCTS IS IN NO MANNER ASSOCIATED WITH, OR LICENSED BY, THE MAKERS OF GIORGIO." The word mark "GIORGIO" is again followed by the registered trademark symbol. All words in the disclaimer appear to be in the same size print. A.R. Doc. 2.

b. "L'AIR DU TEMPS" v. "LOVE BIRDS"

The trademark "L'AIR DU TEMPS" is owned by Nina Ricci, S.A.R.L., and is registered with the PTO, see A.R. Doc. 15, but is not recorded with Customs. In addition to the word mark "L'AIR DU TEMPS," Nina Ricci has two valid trademark registrations with the PTO, each with a design mark of a swirled glass bottle with a closure, with one topped by one three-dimensional dove, and the second topped by two three-dimensional doves.

A.R. Docs. 16, 17. The sample box of L'AIR DU TEMPS shows a yellow background, a golden oval containing two white doves in flight in a prominent position on the front panel, a golden band across the bottom of the front panel, and the word mark "L'AIR DU TEMPS" in gold print between the oval and the band.

The proposed packaging for plaintiff's product LOVE BIRDS has a primarily yellow background with thin white stripes. The front panel of the box shows an orange oval in a prominent position and an orange band across the bottom. The orange oval contains four birds in flight and the words "LOVE BIRDS," all in gold color. At the top of the front panel is the language "COMPARE TO L'AIR DU TEMPS YOU WILL SWITCH TO...," in which the word mark "L'AIR DU TEMPS" is followed by the registered trademark symbol and appears in a bold and larger size print than the rest of the words. At the bottom of the front panel and within the orange band is a disclaimer: "OUR PRODUCTS IS IN NO MANNER ASSOCIATED WITH, OR LICENSED BY, THE MAKERS OF L'AIR DU TEMPS." The word mark "L'AIR DU TEMPS" in the disclaimer is also followed by the registered trademark symbol. All words in the disclaimer appear to be in the same size print. A.R. Doc. 2.

* * *

c. Counterfeit v. Confusingly Similar

In order to facilitate the enforcement of trademark protection at the border, Customs currently divides trademark infringement cases into two categories: those which bear a "counterfeit" mark, and those which bear a "confusingly similar" mark. Remand Determination, at 3–4. A "counterfeit" mark is defined in accordance with 15 U.S.C. §1127. A "confusingly similar" mark is defined by Customs as one "that is likely to cause confusion, or to cause mistake, or to deceive the consumer as to the origin, affiliation, or sponsorship of the goods in question." Remand Determination, at 4. This definition appears to track the language contained in section 43(a) of the Lanham Act. In addition, Customs draws a distinction between trademarks that are registered and recorded with Customs, and trademarks that are registered but not recorded with Customs. Id.

Thus, imported articles bearing "counterfeit" versions of marks recorded with Customs are subject to seizure and forfeiture under 19 U.S.C. §1526(e). Imported articles bearing "counterfeit" versions of marks not recorded with Customs are subject to seizure and forfeiture under 19 U.S.C. §1595a(c) for violation of 18 U.S.C. §2320. Remand Determination, at 4.

Imported articles bearing "confusingly similar" versions of marks recorded with Customs are ultimately subject to seizure and forfeiture under 19 U.S.C. §1595a(c) for violation of 15 U.S.C. §1124. Imported articles bearing "confusingly similar" versions of marks not recorded with Customs are currently not prohibited for importation. Id.

3. Counterfeit v. Mere Infringement

Under Customs' laws and regulations, goods that infringe upon rights of trademark owners are classified into two categories. The first category consists of counterfeit merchandise which bears "a spurious mark which is identical with, or substantially indistinguishable from, a registered mark." 15 U.S.C. §1127. Usually, "counterfeit merchandise is made so as to imitate a well-known product in all details of construction and appearance so as to deceive customers into thinking that they are getting genuine merchandise." 3 J. Thomas McCarthy, McCarthy on Trademarks and Unfair Competition §25.01[5][a] (3d ed. 1992).

The second category consists of "merely infringing" goods which are not counterfeits but bear marks likely to cause public confusion. This category includes merchandise which bears a mark that "copies or simulates" a registered mark so as to be likely to cause the public to associate the copying or simulating mark with the registered mark. *See* 15 U.S.C. §1124; 19 C.F.R. §133.21; *see also Montres Rolex, S.A. v. Snyder*, 718 F.2d 524, 527–28 (2d Cir. 1983) cert. denied 465 U.S. 1100 (1984) (distinguishing copying or simulating mark that is counterfeit mark from copying or simulating mark that is a merely infringing mark). Also included in this category is merchandise which uses any word, name, symbol, or any combination thereof, in such a manner that is likely to cause public confusion as to the origin, sponsorship, or approval of the merchandise by another person. *See* 15 U.S.C. §1125(a)(2).

The significance of the distinction between counterfeits and merely infringing goods lies in the consequences attached to the two categories. Counterfeits must be seized, and in the absence of the written consent of the trademark owner, forfeited. *See* 19 U.S.C. §1526(e); 19 C.F.R. §133.23a(b) (1993). Merely infringing goods, on the other hand, *may* be seized and forfeited for violating 15 U.S.C. §§1124 or 1125. 19 U.S.C. §1595a (c)(2)(C). Under Customs regulations, merely infringing goods may be imported if the "objectionable mark is removed or obliterated prior to importation in such a manner as to be illegible and incapable of being reconstituted." 19 C.F.R. §133.21(a), (c)(4).

4. Whether Plaintiff's Use of Registered Trademarks Constitutes Counterfeit Use

Customs determined that plaintiff's use of the word marks "GIORGIO" and "L'AIR DU TEMPS" on the packaging of its own products constituted a counterfeit use of these marks, because plaintiff applied marks "identical to the registered trademarks" to its goods without the authorization of the trademark owners. Remand Determination, at 28. The court disagrees.

It is clear that plaintiff's products are not counterfeits. Plaintiff's products GORGEOUS and LOVE BIRDS do not imitate the well-known products GIORGIO and L'AIR DU TEMPS in all details of construction and appearance. Rather, plaintiff uses the marks "GIORGIO" and "L'AIR DU TEMPS" to market its products GORGEOUS and LOVE BIRDS.

The use of another person's trademark in the context of marketing one's own product is not prohibited by law unless it creates a reasonable likelihood of confusion as to the source, identity, or sponsorship of the product. *See Saxlehner v. Wagner*, 216 U.S. 375, 380–81 (1910) (permitting seller of mineral water to use competitor's trademark denoting geographical source to truthfully state he was selling water identical in content to that of trademarked water); G.D. Searle & Co. v. Hudson Pharm. Corp., 715 F.2d 837, 842 (3d Cir. 1983) (holding manufacturer of laxative may refer to its competitor's trademark on its own product packaging to characterize its own product as "equivalent" to competitor's product); Saxony Prods., Inc. v. Guerlain, Inc., 513 F.2d 716, 722 (9th Cir. 1975) (holding Saxony may use Guerlain's trademark SHALIMAR to apprise consumers that its fragrance product is "like" or "similar" to SHALIMAR, provided such representation is truthful and that consumer confusion is not likely to result); Smith v. Chanel, Inc., 402 F.2d 562, 563 (9th Cir. 1968) (holding that perfume manufacturer who copied unpatented product sold under trademark may use trademark in his advertising to identify copied product). Customs' practice shows its acceptance of this principle.

Thus, at issue is not whether plaintiff may use the marks "GIORGIO" and "L'AIR DU TEMPS" on the packaging of its own products, but whether such use is likely to cause consumer confusion. If a likelihood of confusion exists, plaintiff's use of the marks would constitute trademark infringement, but not a counterfeit use of the marks.

In reaching the conclusion that plaintiff's use of the marks constitutes a counterfeit use, Customs misapplied 15 U.S.C. §1127, which defines a counterfeit as a spurious mark "identical with, or substantially indistinguishable from, a registered mark." According to Customs, any reference to another person's mark in the context of marketing one's own goods (whether a parallel use or comparative advertising) would constitute counterfeit use if a likelihood of confusion is found. This is because, under Customs' reasoning, the mark used in such a context would be necessarily "identical" to the registered mark. Customs' application of the statutory definition of counterfeit ignores the distinction between counterfeit and mere infringement, and therefore is not in accordance with law.

5. Whether Plaintiff's Use of Registered Trademarks Constitutes Infringement

Having held that plaintiff's use of the marks "GIORGIO" and "L'AIR DU TEMPS" does not constitute a counterfeit use, the court must now address whether such use nevertheless infringes the rights of the trademark owners.

The basic test for statutory trademark infringement is "likelihood of confusion," which has been construed by courts to mean a probability of confusion rather than a possibility of confusion. *See* 2 McCarthy on Trademarks and Unfair Competition §23.01[3][a]. In order to determine whether a likelihood of confusion exists, courts apply and balance multiple factors. *Id.* §23.03[1]. The commonly used factors include: the degree of resemblance between the conflicting marks; the similarity of the marketing methods and channels of distribution; where the goods are not directly competitive, the likelihood that the senior user will expand into the field of the junior user; the degree of distinctiveness of the mark; the characteristics of the prospective purchasers and the degree of care they exercise; the intent of the alleged infringer; and evidence of actual confusion. *Id.*

* * *

In this case, Customs applied commonly accepted factors,[8] and determined that the use of the marks "GIORGIO" and "L'AIR DU TEMPS" on the packaging of GORGEOUS and LOVE BIRDS is likely to cause confusion, and that the disclaimers on the packaging are insufficient to dispel the likelihood of confusion. Remand Determination, at 28. Plaintiff agrees that the factors Customs used to determine the likelihood of confusion are appropriate. Plaintiff asserts, however, that Customs incorrectly applied these factors to the two packages, and that Customs was arbitrary in finding the disclaimers ineffective.

Upon examining the record, which contains photocopies and samples of GIORGIO and L'AIR DU TEMPS products as well as plaintiff's proposed packaging, the court sustains Customs' finding of likelihood of confusion.

a. "GIORGIO" v. "GORGEOUS"

Applying the list of factors relevant to the determination of likelihood of confusion, Customs found the following:

(a) The word mark "GIORGIO," as used on fragrance and toiletry products, is inherently distinctive, and is therefore a strong mark entitled to a broad scope of protection. Remand Determination, at 12.

---

8. Customs applied the list of factors first enumerated in Polaroid Corp. v. Polarad Elecs. Corp., 287 F.2d 492 (2d Cir.) cert. denied, 368 U.S. 820 (1961).

(b) "GORGEOUS" and "GIORGIO" are used on identical products—perfumes and toiletries are listed in the same class (International Class-3) for the purposes of the Trademark Office. This factor enhances the likelihood of confusion. *Id.*

(c) There is a high degree of similarity between the two packages. GIORGIO is covered by a pattern of alternating vertical white and yellow stripes; GORGEOUS by a pattern of alternating diagonal white and yellow stripes, of the same width as the GIORGIO stripes. GIORGIO has the red, black, and gold GIORGIO crest; GORGEOUS a red and gold crest. On the GIORGIO packaging, the word "GIORGIO" appears slightly above the center of the front panel and in close proximity to the GIORGIO crest; on the GORGEOUS packaging, the word "GORGEOUS" also appears slightly above the center of the front panel and in close proximity to its crest. In addition, the words "GORGEOUS" and "GIORGIO" share consonants, vowels, and sounds in their pronunciation. *Id.* at 15–16.

(d) The fact that plaintiff selected and combined the three design elements utilized on GIORGIO boxes for use on its packaging (the word mark "GIORGIO," the image of a crest, and the yellow and white stripes), and the fact that the word mark "GIORGIO" appears in a prominent location on the front panel and in a darker and bigger print than the surrounding language inviting comparison, strongly suggest that plaintiff intentionally designed its packaging to be similar to GIORGIO, and thus did not develop its design in good faith. *Id.* at 14–15.

(e) Since the quality of GORGEOUS is not comparable to that of GIORGIO, GORGEOUS would be sold in discount and low-end retail stores, whereas GIORGIO is normally sold in boutiques and fine department stores. However, there is a possibility GIORGIO would be sold in the same store as GORGEOUS. Customs' survey revealed that both GIORGIO and plaintiff's products were sold by a Wal-Mart store, and that a major retail drug store chain sold both GIORGIO products and various brands of "smell-alike" products. The possibility that the two products could be sold in the same stores enhances the likelihood of confusion. *Id.* at 12–13.

(f) While a typical buyer of GIORGIO products may be expected to exercise care before purchasing because of the higher prices involved, a typical buyer of GORGEOUS would be less likely to make more than a cursory inspection of the product because low-priced items are often the subject of impulse purchasing. The nature of plaintiff's product as a target of impulse purchasing enhances the likelihood of confusion. *Id.* at 13.

On balance, Customs found the factors that enhance the likelihood of confusion outweigh the factors that diminish the likelihood of confusion. Therefore, "there is a substantial likelihood that consumers could be confused as to the source of the Ross product." *Id.* at 16.

Customs then examined whether the disclaimer used is sufficient to eliminate the confusion. Customs found that the disclaimer on the package of GORGEOUS is located at the bottom of the front panel, far from the word mark "GIORGIO" which appears in a prominent position at the top of the panel, and that the disclaimer is written in a smaller type size than any other words on the box. Customs concluded that the disclaimer could be easily overlooked by consumers and therefore is insufficient to dispel the likelihood of confusion. *Id.* at 18.

The court holds that Customs properly applied the relevant factors in determining a likelihood of confusion, and that Customs' examination of the adequacy of the disclaimer was consistent with the applicable law. Although the court may not necessarily come to the same conclusion if reviewing the case de novo, it finds there is a rational connection between the facts found and the determination made by Customs.

The court sustains Customs' finding of a likelihood of confusion with respect to plaintiff's packaging for GORGEOUS. Accordingly, packages identical to that of GORGEOUS shall be denied entry and, if imported, are subject to seizure and forfeiture under 19 U.S.C. §1595a(c).

* * *

Conclusion

For the reasons stated above, the court holds that Customs' determination that plaintiff's proposed packages of GORGEOUS and LOVE BIRDS infringe the rights of the trademark owners of "GIORGIO" and "L'AIR DU TEMPS" is not arbitrary, capricious, or an abuse of discretion, and is otherwise in accordance with law.

Further, the court holds Customs' conclusion that plaintiff's use of the trademarks "GIORGIO" and "L'AIR DU TEMPS" is a counterfeit use is not in accordance with law.

———————

Chapter XI

Dilution (Section 43(c))

A. Background

Frank Schechter, The Rational Basis of Trademark Protection
40 Harv. L. Rev. 813 (1927)*

* * *

I

The orthodox definition of "the primary and proper function of a trademark" is that given by the Supreme Court of the United States in the leading case of *Hanover Star Milling Co. v. Metcalf*: "to identify the origin or ownership of the goods to which it is affixed." The "origin or ownership" so designated by a trademark must be the "personal origin or ownership." In order to test the adequacy of this definition, which has been used by the courts practically uniformly, with but the slightest variation of language and none of meaning, it will be necessary to consider very briefly the actual usages of trade as well as certain historical data, with which the present writer has dealt more thoroughly elsewhere.

The modern trademark has two historical roots: (1) the proprietary mark, which was optionally but usually affixed to goods, by the owner, either for the benefit of illiterate clerks or in order that in case of shipwreck or piracy the goods might be identified and reclaimed by the owner. This mark was essentially a merchant's rather than a craftsman's mark and had nothing to do with the source of production of the goods in question. (2) The regulatory production mark, which was compulsorily affixed to goods by statute, administrative order or municipal or gild regulation, so that defective work might be traced to the guilty craftsman and heavily punished, or that "foreign" goods smuggled into an area over which a gild had a monopoly might be discovered and confiscated. This mark was a true mark of origin, designating as it did the actual producer of the goods.

Four hundred years ago a trademark indicated either the origin or ownership of the goods to which it was affixed. To what extent does the trademark of today really function as either? Actually, not in the least! It has been repeatedly pointed out by the very courts that insist on defining trademarks in terms of ownership or origin that, owing to the ramifications of modern trade and the national and international distribution of goods from the manufacturer through the jobber or importer and the retailer to the consumer, the source or origin of the goods bearing a well known trademark is seldom known to the

---

consumer. Over twenty years ago it was pointed out by the Circuit Court of Appeals for the Seventh Circuit that "we may safely take it for granted that not one in a thousand knowing of or desiring to purchase 'Baker's Cocoa' or 'Baker's Chocolate' know of Walter Baker & Co., Limited." The same fact has been noted concerning "Coca-Cola" and "Yorkshire Relish." With regard to the latter mark, Lord Justice Lindley said:

> "Persons may be misled and may mistake one class of goods for another, although they do not know the names of the makers of either. A person whose name is not known, but whose mark is imitated, is just as much injured in his trade as if his name was known as well as his mark. His mark, as used by him, has given a reputation to his goods. His trade depends greatly on such reputation. His mark sells his goods."[1]

A trademark may be affixed to goods by a manufacturer thousands of miles away from the consumer, or by an importer or jobber who has not manufactured but merely selected the goods and put them on the local market; or by a commission merchant who has not even selected the goods or rendered any service relating to them except to sell such as may have been sent to him by the owner. Moreover, during and since the Great War the mark of an alien enemy might be used by a purchaser from the Alien Property Custodian entirely without the consent, much less the cooperation, of the original owner of the trademark; and even though the mark may have been acquired through fraud or conspiracy of the purchaser and the Alien Property Custodian.

Discarding then the idea that a trademark or tradename informs the consumer as to the actual source or origin of goods, what does it indicate and with what result? It indicates, not that the article in question comes from a definite or particular source, the characteristics of which or the personalities connected with which a specifically known to the consumer, but merely that the goods in connection with which it is used emanate from the same — possibly anonymous — source or have reached the consumer through the same channels as certain other goods that have already given the consumer satisfaction, and that bore the same trademark. A few years ago, Judge Learned Hand wrote with regard to "Shredded Wheat Biscuit":

> "The plaintiff has at least shown that the public has become accustomed to regard its familiar wheat biscuit as emanating, if not from it by name, at least from a single, though anonymous, maker,. and the second is as good for these purposes as the first.... Though the public may, therefore, buy the biscuit because it has come to like it, the plaintiff still has a stake in that other motive for buying; i.e., that it comes from the accustomed maker."[2]

Superficially it may appear to be very fine hair-splitting to say that while the consumer does not know the specific source of a trademarked article, he nevertheless knows that two articles, bearing the same mark, emanate from a single source. However, the precise distinction is vital in the present connection, for it brings out clearly the creative and not merely symbolic nature of the modern trademark or tradename. The force of that distinction was strikingly illustrated in a very recent English case involving the application of one McDowell to register the trademark "Nuvol," which was opposed by the Standard Oil Company, owners of the well known trademark "Nujol" on medicinal oil. It was the contention of the applicant that since the Standard Oil Company did not sell "Nujol" to the English public in their own name but through The Anglo-American Company, their

1. Powell v. Birmingham Vinegar Brewery Co., Ltd., 13 Rep. Pat. Cas. 235, 250 (1896).
2. Shredded Wheat Co. v. Humphrey Cornell Co., 250 Fed. 960, 963 (2d Cir., 1918).

agents there, the British public did not know the actual source of "Nujol." Sir Duncan Kerly argued for the opponent that the fact that "Nujol" emanated from the Standard Oil Company was immaterial and that persons seeing "Nuvol" would assume that it came from the same source as "Nujol," whatever the source of "Nujol" might be. Sir Duncan's argument was pronounced as "very curious" and untenable by the lower court, but on appeal it was said by Lord Justice Warrington:

> " … The deception which I think the registration would be calculated to produce is that the two products emanate *from the same source*, and for the purposes of the present question it does not, in my opinion, matter whether the public do, or do not, know what that source is."[3]

The true functions of the trademark are, then, to identify a product as satisfactory and thereby to stimulate further purchases by the consuming public. The fact that through his trademark the manufacturer or importer may "reach over the shoulder of the retailer" and across the latter's counter straight to the consumer cannot be over-emphasized, for therein lies the key to any effective scheme of trademark protection. To describe a trademark merely as a symbol of good will, without recognizing in it an agency for the actual creation and perpetuation of good will, ignores the most potent aspect of the nature of a trademark and that phase most in need of protection. To say that a trademark "is merely the visible manifestation of the more important business goodwill, which is the 'property' to be protected against invasion" or that "the good will is the substance, the trademark merely the shadow," does not accurately state the function of a trademark today and obscures the problem of its adequate protection. The signboard of an inn in stage-coach days, when the golden lion or the golden lion or the green cockatoo actually symbolized to the hungry and wary traveler a definite smiling host, a tasty meal from a particular cook, a favorite brew and a comfortable bed, was merely "the visible manifestation" of the good will or probability of custom of the house; but today the trademark is not merely the symbol of goodwill but often the most effective agent for the creation of goodwill, imprinting upon the public mind an anonymous and impersonal guaranty of satisfaction, creating a desire for further satisfactions. The mark actually *sells* the goods. And, self-evidently, the more distinctive the mark, the more effective is its selling power.

II

The protection of trademarks originated as a police measure to prevent "the grievous deceit of the people" by the sale of defective goods, and to safeguard the collective good will and monopoly of the gild. The repression of trademark infringement came into the common law through an action of deceit and, although it is the public rather than the owner of the trademark who is actually deceived, the common law trademark action is still deceit. Equity, on the other hand, acting "in aid of" and "ancillary to" what it deemed to be a "legal right" to have a particular trademark, at first assumed jurisdiction in such cases to protect the plaintiff's "title" to trademarks, regardless of the question of deceit. Thus in the great case of *Millington v. Fox*, Lord Chancellor Cottenham stated: "Having previously come to the conclusions that there was sufficient in the case to show that the Plaintiffs had a title to the marks in question; … they undoubtedly had a right to the assistance of a court of equity to enforce that title."

However, subsequent decisions of the equity side indicated a shifting from the proprietary aspect of trademark protection to practically the same basis as that of the com-

---

3. In the Matter of McDowell's Application, *supra* note 18, at 327.

mon law—as is indicated in the oft-quoted dictum of Lord Langdale, uttered in 1842: "I think that the principle on which both the courts of law and of equity proceed is very well understood. A man is not to sell his own goods under the pretense that they are the goods of another man...."[4] Equity did not continue the unqualified protection of trademarks in aid of a definite legal right of property but acted under the doctrine of "passing off" in England, or of unfair competition in the United States, which was in itself but "a development of the law of fraud. Its aim was simply to prevent the deceitful sale or passing off of goods made by one person or firm for goods made by another."[5] Contemporary profession testimony makes this point quite clear. "The diversion of custom" is the gravamen of the action in either "passing off" or "unfair competition." The Supreme Court has held: "The essence of the wrong consists in the sale of the goods of one manufacturer or vendor for those of another.... This essential element is the same in trademark cases as in cases of unfair competition unaccompanied with trade-mark infringement."

Recent decisions both in this country and in England have extended the doctrine of "unfair competition" beyond cases where there is an actual "diversion of custom." But the process has been one of making exceptions rather than of frank recognition of the true basis of trademark protection. No necessity or justification for the protection of marks on non-competing goods is seen except (1) where, while there is no actual diversion of trade, there is a likelihood of confusion as to the source of the infringing goods; (2) where the use of the infringing mark or name may work some discredit and financial liability or other similar concrete injury on the plaintiff. Thus, a recent writer states: "Where there are no circumstances that would cause the public to think the products bearing the same name were made by the same party, no wrong is done. The classic example given in *Ainsworth v. Walmsley*: 'If he does not carry on a trade in iron, but carries on a trade in linen and stamps a lion on his linen, another person may stamp a lion on iron,'[6] is still the law."[7] This conclusion that "wrong is done" is based upon an archaic notion of the function of a trademark as solely indicating "source or origin." It assumes that "the elementary equitable principle upon which the whole law of this subject is based ... is that one may not palm off his goods as the goods of another"[8] and that the sole injury resulting from the use of the same "lion" mark on linen and iron might be a confusion as to the source of these two dissimilar products. It ignores the fact that the *creation and retention of custom*, rather than the designation of source, is the primary purpose of the trademark today, and that the preservation of the uniqueness or individuality of the trademark is of paramount importance to its owner.

The doctrine that the same trademark may be used on different classes of goods, recently restated by the Supreme Court, is said to be related to the cardinal principle that "there is no property in a trade-mark apart from the business or trade in connection with which it is employed." But why does a limitation of the protection of trademarks to goods of the same class logically and necessarily follow from the rule that there is no property in a trademark in gross? The latter rule is based upon a consideration of public policy, namely,

---

4. *Perry v. Truefitt*, 6 Beav. 66, 73 (1842), cited or quoted in, e.g., *Leather Cloth Co. v. American Leather Cloth Co.*, II H. L. Cas. 523, 538 (1865); *Reddaway v. Banham*, [1896] A. C. 199, 209; *Havana Cigar & Tobacco Factories, Ltd. v. Oddenino*, supra note 3, at 55. Ct. *McLean v. Fleming*, supra note 8, at 255; *Hanover Star Milling Co. v. Metcalf*, supra note 4, at 413–14.

5. Watkins, The Change in Trust Policy (1922) 35 Harv. Law Rev. 815, 831. *See* Coffin, Fraud as an Element of Unfair Competition (1903) 16 *ibid*. 272.

6. L. R. I Eq. 518, 524–25 (1866), evidently adopting a similar statement in *Hall v. Barrows*, 4 De G. J.& S. 150, 158 (1863).

7. Lukens, The Application of the Principles of Unfair Competition to Cases of Dissimilar Products (1927) 75 U. of Pa. L. Rev. 197, 198.

8. *Ibid*. 205.

that a man should not develop a trademark as a guaranty of the quality of his merchandise and then sell or "farm out" the use of that mark apart from his business to those who may sell a vastly inferior product under his mark.[9] This salutary principle, which has its roots, not in the common law, but in earlier "guild jurisprudence," was already enforced for precisely that reason over three hundred years ago by the cutlers of London, who, in 1624, ordained that: "No man from hensforth shall have a proper marcke vnlesse he be a forger and be able of him self to fforge & temper his stuf as a worckman sholde do."

However, this rule that a trademark must be appurtenant to a going concern should not in any way set limits to the extent of protection of such a mark when so appurtenant. Quite apart from the destruction of the uniqueness of a mark by its use on other goods, which will be discussed later on, once a mark has come to indicate to the public a constant and uniform source of satisfaction, its owner should be allowed the broadest scope possible for "the natural expansion of his trade" to other lines or fields of enterprise. This point was demonstrated with particular acuteness after the Great War in the case of such firms as The Remington Arms Company, The Winchester Repeating Arms Company and the Dupont Company, which were under the immediate necessity of transferring their activities from the manufacture of war material to peace industries of an entirely different nature but under the same trademarks and names. Under the "source or origin "theory of a function of a trademark, and the vague doctrine of "related goods," courts are still giving a most literal and rigid construction to the phrases "of the same class" or "of the same descriptive qualities." Thus bread and flour, pancake flour and syrup are in the same class, while, on the other hand, "straight" wheat flour and "prepared flours"—such as "pancake flour"—are declared not to be of the same "class of commodities." Chewing gum, held to be a "food," and chewing tobacco, held to be a "narcotic," ice cream and milk, cheese and butter are likewise found not of different classes. An equally apparent failure of the courts to keep pace with the necessities of trade and the functional development of trademarks, and a corollary to the principle that "if there is no competition, there can be no unfair competition,"[10] is the rule that a trademark or tradename is only coextensive with its use and may be used by different firms in different localities. To hold that Boston and Providence markets do not extend to Worcester, New Haven and Woonsocket, that a nationally known chain of theatres, with a branch in Boston, did not extend its market, or rather its audience, to Lynn, Lawrence, Portland or Fitchburg, or that plaintiff's stores in Northern New Jersey could not enjoin the use of plaintiff's tradename in Southern New Jersey at points twenty to thirty miles away, ignores the necessities of the chain type of organization with which the United States has been covered in recent years. Furthermore, such decisions, based upon an antiquated neighbor-hood theory of trade, fail to recognize the fact that through the existence of the telephone, the automobile, the motor bus, the high-speed interurban trolley, and the railroad, the consumer now projects his shopping far from home and comes to rely more and more upon trademarks and tradenames ~s symbols of quality and guaranties of satisfaction.

III

We have seen that the proper expansion of trademark law has been hampered by obsolete conceptions both as to the function of a trademark and as to the need for its pro-

---

9. *See* (1926) 35 Yale L. J. 496.

10. *Carroll v. Duluth Superior Milling Co.*, 232 Fed. 675, 681–82 (C. C. A. 8th, 1916); *Nat. Picture Theatres v. Foundation Film Corp.*, 266 Fed. 208, 211 (C. C. A. 2nd 1920); *Samson Cordage Works v. Puritan Cordage Mills*, 211 Fed. 603, 608 (C. C. A. 6th, 1914); *Borden Ice Cream Co. v. Borden's Condensed Milk Co.*, *supra* note 50, at 514; *Nat. Grocery Co. v. Nat. Stores Corp.*, 95 N. J. Eq. 588, 593, 123 Atl. 740, 742 (1924); *Crump Co. v. Lindsay*, 130 Va. 144, 156, 107 S. E. 679, 682 (1921).

tection. Commencing with the assumption that a trademark designates either origin or ownership—in other words, source—the law, even in its most liberal interpretation at the present time, will prevent the misuse of that mark only where there is an actual confusion created by such misuse, resulting in either diversion of trade or other concrete financial liability or injury to trade repute. However, we have intimated the possibility that the use of trademarks on entirely non-related goods may of itself concretely injure the owner of the, mark even in the absence of those elements of damage noted above. If so, what is the injury, and to what extent, if any, should the law take cognizance of such injury?

* * *

IV

From the necessities of modern trademark protection mentioned above, on the one hand, and from the decisions emphasizing the greater degree of protection to be given to coined, rather than to commonplace marks, the following principles necessarily emerge; (1) that the value of the modern trademark lies in its selling power; (2) that this selling power depends for its psychological hold upon the public, not merely upon the merit of the goods upon which it is used, but equally upon its own uniqueness and singularity; (3) that such uniqueness or singularity is vitiated or impaired by its use upon either related or non-related goods; and (4) that the degree of its protection depends in turn upon the extent to which, through the efforts or ingenuity of its owner, it is actually unique and different from other marks.

Our conclusion that the preservation of the uniqueness of a trademark should constitute the only rational basis for its protection is fortified by the doctrine that has developed within recent years in German law on this same point. In 1905 it was held by the Supreme Court at Hamburg that the owners of the "Kodak" mark for cameras were not entitled to cancel the registration of the same mark for bath tubs, the reasoning of the court being the same that would normally have been given by our own courts under similar circumstances, *viz.,* that bath tubs would not be believed by the public to have come from the Kodak Company. The application for cancellation was brought under Section 826 of the German Civil Code which provides that: "one who designedly injures another in a manner violating good morals [*gegen die guten Sitten*] is bound to indemnify the other for the injury." However, in 1924 practically the same question was submitted to another German court (the *Landesgericht* at Eiberfeld) by the owners of the well-known trademark "Odol" for mouth wash, who sought to obtain the cancellation of the registration of that same mark for various steel products. The court held that the use of the mark "Odol" even on non-competing goods was "*gegen die guten Sitten,*" pointing out that, when the public hears or reads the word "Odol," it thinks of the complainant's mouth wash, and that an article designated with the name "Odol" leads the public to assume that it is of good quality. Consequently, concludes the court, complainant has "the utmost interest in seeing that its mark is not diluted [*verwässert*]: it would lose in selling power if everyone used it as the designation of his goods":

> "The respondent has registered the mark for its steel goods for the obvious purpose of deriving from its selling power some advantage in marketing its own products. There are, of course, numerous euphonious words that the respondent could have used as the symbol of its goods; it chose the word 'Odol,' it was clear, because this mark had acquired an especially favorable prestige through the efforts of the complainant."...

> "To be sure, the parties, on account of the wholly different goods put out by them are not in actual competition. *That, however, is beside the point. The com-*

plainant has created a demand for its goods, while employing thereon a word having drawing power, for only through the year-long activity of the complainant was its selling power acquired.... Complainant's ability to compete with other manufacturers of mouth wash will be impaired if the significance of its mark is lessened."[11]

If eventually our courts squarely adopt the doctrine of the *Odol* case, which they may be circuitously approaching by their differentiation between coined and commonplace marks, it will not be the first time that they have gone to continental armories for the weapons with which to combat the commercial buccaneer. If it be objected that the *Odol* doctrine hails from a country where registration creates an "incontestable right," whereas in the United States and Great Britain registration is purely procedural and creates no rights, it should be pointed out that the *Odol* decision was based, not upon a peculiar German theory of registration, but upon broad general principles of fair trade. A further and equally groundless obstacle to so broad a protection of marks is that historical fear of monopoly which has possessed the courts ever since in the first trademark case in equity Lord Hardwicke refused injunctive relief on that account. But, as was pointed out over forty years ago by a Scotch court, "monopoly is not the thing for which the complainers contend, and which the respondents resist. On the contrary, fair trading is all for the protection of which the law is invoked."[12] The owner of a distinctive mark or name invoking the protection of equity for it, obtains thereby no monopoly of goods or services; these may be freely sold on their own merits and under their own trade symbols. All that the plaintiff in such cases asks is the preservation of a valuable, though possibly anonymous link between him and his consumer, that has been created by his ingenuity and the merit of his wares or services. "All the rest of infinity is open to defendant."[13] So limited a "monopoly" as that cannot affect legitimate competition, and is of the very essence of any rational system of individual and exclusive trade symbols.

———————

B. State Law Incorporation

Allied Maintenance Corporation v. Allied Mechanical Trades, Inc.
369 N.E.2d 1162 (Ct. Appeals NY 1977)

We are called upon today to decide whether the trade name "Allied Maintenance" is entitled to protection pursuant to section 368-d of the General Business Law—commonly referred to as the anti-dilution statute.

The plaintiff, Allied Maintenance Corporation, has been in business, in one form or another, since 1888. Throughout the many years since its inception, Allied Maintenance has concentrated the scope of its services upon the cleaning and maintenance of large office buildings. The defendant, Allied Mechanical Trades, Inc., a corporation organized in 1968 as a successor to Controlled Weather Corporation, is engaged primarily in the installation and repair of heating, ventilating and air-conditioning equipment.

———————

11. (Italics ours.) *See* Wertheimer, Broadened Protection of Names and Trade. Marks in the German Law (1925) 20 T. M. BULL. (N. S.) 76.
12. *Dunnachie & CO. v. Young & Sons,* 4 Ct. Sess. Cas. (4th series) 874, 885 (1883).
13. *Coca-Cola Co. v. Old Dominion Beverage Corp.,* 271 Fed. 600, 604 (C. C. A. 4th, 1921).

Alleging that the defendant performed maintenance services identical to those it performed, Allied Maintenance brought this action to enjoin Allied Mechanical from operating under the name "Allied" or "Allied Mechanical Trades, Inc.", or using the word "Allied" in any way in connection with its business. The trial court granted the injunction, finding that the parties were actual and potential competitors in the cleaning and maintenance industry in the metropolitan New York City area and that the auditory and visual similarity between their names created a likelihood of confusion. On this basis, the court concluded that defendant's use of the name Allied Mechanical would result in irreparable injury to plaintiff's reputation, good will, and proprietary business interests, and would thus constitute unfair competition. The Appellate Division reversed, however, finding an absence of either competition or confusion, actual or potential. The court concluded that "no user of the services of either party has been or may probably be confused or deceived by any similarity in the names of the parties." (55 AD2d 865, 866.)

In addition to the protection of trade-marks and trade names afforded by the traditional actions for trade-mark infringement and unfair competition, New York, as well as a number of other States, has adopted an anti-dilution statute. (General Business Law, §368-d.) This statute provides: "Likelihood of injury to business reputation or of dilution of the distinctive quality of a mark or trade name shall be a ground for injunctive relief in cases of infringement of a mark registered or not registered or in cases of unfair competition, *notwithstanding the absence of competition between the parties or the absence of confusion as to the source of goods or services.*" (Emphasis added.) The purpose behind the enactment of this statute was the prevention of trade-mark or trade name dilution—i.e., "the whittling away of an established trade-mark's selling power and value through its unauthorized use by others upon dissimilar products." (NY Legis Ann, 1954, p 49 [emphasis added].) In the absence of a statute of this nature, a plaintiff seeking to prohibit the use of a trade name by another would be required to frame his complaint within the strictures of an action for either trade-mark infringement or unfair competition. A brief review of the elements of these actions is useful in interpreting the legislative intent behind the enactment of section 368-d.

Historically, two causes of action have existed to protect the user of a trade-mark or trade name from its improper use by another—viz., trade-mark infringement and unfair competition. Trade-mark infringement developed as the remedy designed to protect technical trade-marks—i.e., those marks which were arbitrary, fanciful or coined. (*See* 3 Callman, Unfair Competition, Trademarks and Monopolies [3d ed], §66.1.) Trademarks such as "Kodak", "Xerox", "Exxon" and "Coke" would fall within this category. As the law evolved, the protection provided by an action for trade-mark infringement was supplemented by the formulation of a broader remedy—an action for unfair competition. (*See Dell Pub. Co. v Stanley Pub.*, 9 NY2d 126, 133.) This remedy was intended to protect nontechnical, common-law trade-marks—marks used although not registered— as well as trade names. (1 Callman, Unfair Competition, Trademarks and Monopolies [3d ed], §4.1.)

Today, in an action for trade-mark infringement brought pursuant to either New York (General Business Law, §368-b) or Federal law (Lanham Act, §32, subd [1], US Code, tit 15, §1114, subd [1]), it is necessary to show that the defendant's use of the trade-mark is likely to cause confusion, mistake or to deceive; actual confusion need not be shown. Similarly, it has been held that in an action for unfair competition a showing of a likelihood of confusion, rather than actual confusion, is all that is required to state a cause of action. Since an action for infringement as well as an action for unfair competition both require a showing that the public is likely to confuse the defendant's product or service with that of the plaintiff, relief may be difficult to secure in situations in which the parties are not in competition, nor produce similar products or perform similar services. It is for this reason that section 368-d specifically provides that an injunction may be obtained *notwithstanding the absence of competition or confusion.*

Generally, courts which have had the opportunity to interpret an anti-dilution statute have refused to apply its provisions literally. New York courts, State and Federal, have read into the statute a requirement of some showing of confusion, fraud or deception.

Judicial hesitance to enforce the literal terms of the anti-dilution statute has not been limited to New York. In Illinois, for example, some courts have gone so far as to declare the statute inapplicable where the parties are competitors and a likelihood of confusion does exist. These decisions were premised upon the belief that a plaintiff who can frame his complaint under a theory of infringement or unfair competition—albeit unsuccessfully perhaps—should not succeed under a dilution theory.

Notwithstanding the absence of judicial enthusiasm for the anti-dilution statutes, we believe that section 368-d does extend the protection afforded trade-marks and trade names beyond that provided by actions for infringement and unfair competition. The evil which the Legislature sought to remedy was not public confusion caused by similar products or services sold by competitors, but a cancer-like growth of dissimilar products or services which feeds upon the business reputation of an established distinctive trade-mark or name. Thus, it would be of no significance under our statute that Tiffany's Movie Theatre is not a competitor of, nor likely to be confused with Tiffany's Jewelry. (*See* NY Legis Ann, 1954, p 50, citing *Tiffany & Co. v Tiffany Prods.*, 147 Misc 679, affd 237 App Div 801, affd 262 NY 482.) The harm that section 368-d is designed to prevent is the gradual whittling away of a firm's distinctive trade-mark or name. It is not difficult to imagine the possible effect which the proliferation of various noncompetitive businesses utilizing the name Tiffany's would have upon the public's association of the name Tiffany's solely with fine jewelry. The ultimate effect has been appropriately termed dilution.

Although section 368-d does not require a showing of confusion or competition to obtain an injunction, it does require a "likelihood of injury to business reputation or of dilution of the *distinctive quality* of a mark or tradename." (Emphasis added.) The statute prohibits any use of a name or mark likely to dilute the *distinctive quality* of a name in use. To merit protection, the plaintiff must possess a strong mark—one which has a distinctive quality or has acquired a secondary meaning which is capable of dilution. Courts interpreting Massachusetts' anti-dilution statute—applying its terms literally—have required a showing that the trade-mark or name to be protected is either unique or has acquired a secondary meaning before issuing an injunction.

Turning to the case before us, it is quite apparent that the name "Allied" is a weak trade name. Rather than being distinctive, arbitrary, fanciful or coined, it is, in essence, generic or descriptive. Although the name "Allied" bespeaks of more originality than "maintenance", it is nevertheless a common word in English usage today. There is nothing in the name "Allied Maintenance" itself which indicates that it is an inherently strong trade name susceptible to dilution. Nor can it be said that the name Allied Maintenance has acquired a secondary meaning. Plaintiff seeks to prevent the defendant from using the word "allied" in any connection with its business. To establish secondary meaning it must be shown that through exclusive use and advertising by one entity, a name or mark has become so associated in the mind of the public with that entity or its product that it identifies the goods sold by that entity and distinguishes them from goods sold by others. A quick glance at the New York City phone directories will reveal the existence of at least 300 business entities in the metropolitan area incorporating the word "allied" in their trade name. In light of the large number of business entities using the generic term allied in their trade name, it cannot be said that the name "allied" has acquired a secondary meaning. We remain unconvinced that the public associates the word "allied" with the plaintiff's cleaning and maintenance service.

In sum, although section 368-d should be interpreted literally to effectuate its intended purpose—protection against dilution—only those trade names which are truly of *distinctive* quality or which have acquired a secondary meaning in the mind of the public should be entitled to protection under the anti-dilution statute. "Allied Maintenance" cannot be said to have attained this stature.

Accordingly, the order of the Appellate Division should be affirmed.

Cooke, J. (dissenting).

I dissent, voting for a reversal of the Appellate Division order and reinstatement of the judgment of Trial Term granting an injunction in favor of plaintiff.

The majority's analysis of section 368-d of the General Business Law, it is respectfully submitted, imposes a narrow, overly technical gloss on its terms and, in effect, dilutes the "anti-dilution" statute. For the reason that future litigants may suffer from this interpretation, a broader view is needed and, in my opinion, was intended.

In interpreting this legislation, the court should not overemphasize the importance of a memorandum in support of this statute (*see* NY Legis Ann, 1954, pp 49–51). That writing describes the author's view of the purpose of the proposed legislation and enumerates various problems in the area of dilution of a trade name or trade-mark. Dilution of a trade name through sales of dissimilar products is illustrated by somewhat fanciful examples such as "Buick aspirin tablets", "Schlitz varnish", "Kodak pianos", and "Bulova gowns" (p 49). Indeed, that dilution can occur even in the case of dissimilar products, as the memorandum notes (p 50), has long been recognized by our common law which granted the right to enjoin the use of another's name even in the absence of competition. Nevertheless, if the statute was intended to "codify the State common law concerning dilution" (NY Legis Ann, 1954, p 49; *see, also*, 3 NY Law Forum, 313, 316), there is no basis for restricting its application in the manner suggested by the majority.

Dilution does not occur only in the case of a name that is widely known. To be sure, the name Tiffany would be diluted if many noncompeting businesses used that name. However, a less well-known name can also be diluted, perhaps in a more harmful and direct manner. And dilution can occur in instances where there is competition, though in that instance a more appropriate remedy will ordinarily be found under general principles of unfair competition. The difficult case is where a specialized business, with a generic name used in other unrelated businesses, is used by a relatively small segment of the public who rely on its name. The problem occurs when that business is confronted with a newer company, bearing the same or a similar name, engaging in a field that, while perhaps noncompeting, is so closely related to that of the more established business that its customers will identify its name with the newcomer. This is such a case.

It is asserted that the legislative intent was to remedy "not public confusion caused by similar products or services sold by competitors, but a cancer-like growth of dissimilar products or services which feeds upon the business reputation of an established distinctive trade-mark or name" (p 544). It is then concluded that Allied is not sufficiently distinctive but rather is "a weak trade name" (p 545). But the terms of the statute do not require this interpretation and the protection it affords should be available to plaintiff based on the facts of this case.

While the trial court determined that plaintiff and defendant are actual and potential competitors, the Appellate Division majority found that the parties are not competitors in their own peculiar specialties nor are they likely to be. Whichever view of the facts one takes, however, it is apparent that the businesses are closely related. There is no basis in the statutory language for concluding that the enactment was not intended to provide a remedy for confusion caused by similar (though perhaps not actually competing) services such as these. The statute provides a remedy "notwithstanding the absence of competition" but does not mandate that in order to benefit from its provisions there must be no competition or dissimilar services, as urged to the contrary. Therefore, if plaintiff's name is of a distinctive quality, it is entitled to a remedy under the anti-dilution statute.

It is wrong to conclude that the name Allied Maintenance is not "an inherently strong trade name susceptible to dilution" (p 545). Of course its name is not as unique as other names held capable of dilution, but it is, to a limited audience, as distinctive as many others. The word Allied is a generic term but, as the trial court determined, that name has long been associated by the public, including customers and competitors in the building cleaning and maintenance industry, with plaintiff and its subsidiaries. Even a generic or descriptive name may acquire a secondary meaning in a given circumstance That plaintiff's name is not distinctive enough to allow it to prevent its use by others in noncompeting industries should not be a ground for allowing one in a closely related business to dilute the distinctive quality of its name in its field.

The majority opinion may be read as limiting the statute in question to the protection of only the most well-known names, such as Tiffany, of which there are few, from dilution by noncompeting products or services. The common law of the State has not so narrowed the protection afforded to less unique names and the fact that the statute operates even in the absence of competition does not, as noted, mean that it should have no effect where there is potential, if not actual, competition. A good illustration of this point is *Long's Hat Stores Corp. v Long's Clothes* (224 App Div 497). There, the plaintiff conducted a business of selling retail hats and haberdashery and, although it had discontinued its sales of clothing, it declared an intention to resume that branch of its business. The plaintiff there had developed a trade name and had a number of retail stores to which customers were attracted by the name "Long's". Some 22 years later, an individual engaged in the retail clothing business incorporated a business which maintained a retail clothing shop called "Long's Clothing". In granting an injunction to protect plaintiff's name, the Appellate Division reasoned (p 498): "In this case the plaintiff is damaged because the articles sold by the defendant are so closely related to those presently sold by the plaintiff and so identical with those which the plaintiff has sold and intends to sell in the future, that there is direct appropriation of the plaintiff's good will. In the enjoyment of its trade name the plaintiff is to be protected not only with respect to the merchandise it presently sells, but also with respect to that which the public would believe, through the deception practiced by the defendant, that the plaintiff was selling. When a trade mark has been used by the owner and by another on goods of the same class, though different in species, the question whether they are so closely related—so near akin—as to be regarded as having the "same descriptive properties' arises."' (*Rosenberg Bros. & Co. v Elliott*, 7 F. [2d] 962, 964.)"

The circumstances here are closely analogous. The name Allied, like the name Long's, is not so unique that all would know its business, but it is known to a segment of the public that makes use of the service of cleaning and maintenance of buildings. After plaintiff was in business for many years, defendant entered into a related area and, depending upon whether one accepts the view of the Appellate Division majority or the trial court, may provide in some instances the same services. The use of a name associated with a particular business by one in a closely related field is a dilution of a less well-known name and is of no less significance to the particular plaintiff than use of an extremely well-known trade name by a totally unrelated business. This is the rationale underlying the holding in Long's (*supra*), a case that has been regarded as a forerunner of the anti-dilution theory (*see* NY Legis Ann, 1954, p 50; *Tiffany & Co. v Tiffany Prods.*, 147 Misc, at p 681, *supra*). Section 368-d of the General Business Law was intended to codify cases such as *Long's* and that is why the statute should be applicable here.

Plaintiff should be granted the relief it seeks because, as a result of the similarity of names, those using defendant's services may well be confused as to the source. But the cause of action would not necessarily fail even if the two could be distinguished. Under the statute recovery is allowed even in "the absence of confusion" and, despite any suggestion to the contrary, this State's appellate courts have not expressed acceptance of any reading into the statute of a requirement of some showing of confusion).

To conclude, prior to enactment of the statute in question, in cases of this sort it was not determinative that a generic or descriptive name was so commonly used that the plaintiff could not prevent its use by unrelated businesses.... Therefore, interpreting the statute in light of the State's common law, it is submitted that under the circumstances of this case plaintiff is entitled to the relief it seeks. Accordingly, for the reasons stated, the order of the Appellate Division should be reversed.

Notes

1. Although *Allied Maintenance* is often cited as the first judicial recognition of dilution in the United States, as you can see by reading the case, the court there actually found no dilution. The dissent argues rather strenuously that to require a trademark to be famous before it is properly protected from dilution emasculates the common law of trademarks and is inconsistent with the state statute at issue there. Who is correct?

2. Although not precisely a "Kodak brand bicycle case" warned of by Schecter, *supra*, perhaps a better judicial starting point for dilution is *Instrumentalist Co. v. Marine Corps League*, 509 F. Supp. 323 (N.D. Ill. 1981). In that case, a youth charity organization in the Chicago area started using a likeness of John Philip Sousa in connection with their services. The plaintiff had been using the name and likeness for a long period in connection with its high school band awards. Although not actually pled, the court there granted the injunction based on the state dilution statute. Controversial as dilution is, it is not surprising that the poster-child case began without dilution even being pled.

Mead Data Central, Inc. v. Toyota Motor Sales, U.S.A., Inc.
875 F.2d 1026 (2d Cir. 1989)

VAN GRAAFEILAND, CIRCUIT JUDGE.

Toyota Motor Sales, U.S.A., Inc. and its parent, Toyota Motor Corporation, appeal from a judgment of the United States District Court for the Southern District of New

York (Edelstein, J.) enjoining them from using LEXUS as the name of their new luxury automobile and the division that manufactures it. The district court held that, under New York's antidilution statute, N.Y. Gen. Bus. Law §368-d, Toyota's use of LEXUS is likely to dilute the distinctive quality of LEXIS, the mark used by Mead Data Central, Inc. for its computerized legal research service. 702 F. Supp. 1031 (1988). On March 8, 1989, we entered an order of reversal, stating that an opinion would follow. This is the opinion.

THE STATUTE

Section 368-d of New York's General Business Law, which has counterparts in at least twenty other states, reads as follows:

> Likelihood of injury to business reputation or of dilution of the distinctive quality of a mark or trade name shall be a ground for injunctive relief in cases of infringement of a mark registered or not registered or in cases of unfair competition, notwithstanding the absence of competition between the parties or the absence of confusion as to the source of goods or services.

THE PARTIES AND THEIR MARKS
Mead and Lexis

Mead is a corporation organized under the laws of Delaware with its principal place of business in Miamisburg, Ohio. Since 1972, Mead has provided a computerized legal research service under the trademark LEXIS. Mead introduced evidence that its president in 1972 "came up with the name LEXIS based on Lex which was Latin for law and I S for information systems." In fact, however, the word "lexis" is centuries old. It is found in the language of ancient Greece, where it had the meaning of "phrase", "word", "speaking" or "diction." Pinkerton, *Word for Word*, 179 (1982). "Lexis" subsequently appeared in the Latin where it had a substantially similar meaning, *i.e.*, "word", "speech", or "language". Oxford Latin Dictionary (1983); Lewis and Short, *A Latin Dictionary* (1980); Lewis, *An Elementary Latin Dictionary* (1979).

Like many other Latin words, "lexis" has been incorporated bodily into the English. It can be found today in at least sixty general dictionaries or other English word books, including Webster's Ninth New Collegiate Dictionary and Webster's New World Dictionary. Moreover, its meaning has not changed significantly from that of its Latin and Greek predecessors; *e.g.*, "Vocabulary, the total set of words in a language" (American Heritage Illustrated Encyclopedic Dictionary); "A vocabulary of a language, a particular subject, occupation, or activity" (Funk & Wagnalls Standard Dictionary). The district court's finding that "to establish that LEXIS is an English word required expert testimony at trial" is clearly erroneous. Anyone with a rudimentary knowledge of English can go to a library or bookstore and find the word in one of the above-mentioned standard dictionaries.

Moreover, the record discloses that numerous other companies had adopted "Lexis" in identifying their business or its product, *e.g.*, Lexis Ltd., Lexis Computer Systems Ltd., Lexis Language and Export Information Service, Lexis Corp., Maxwell Labs Lexis 3. In sum, we reject Mead's argument that LEXIS is a coined mark which originated in the mind of its former president and, as such, is entitled per se to the greater protection that a unique mark such as "Kodak" would receive. *See Esquire, Inc. v. Esquire Slipper Mfg. Co.*, 243 F.2d 540, 543 (1st Cir. 1957); *Intercontinental Mfg. Co. v. Continental Motors Corp.*, 43 C.C.P.A. 841, 230 F.2d 621, 623, 109 U.S.P.Q. (BNA) 105 (C.C.P.A. 1956).

Nevertheless, through its extensive sales and advertising in the field of computerized legal research, Mead has made LEXIS a strong mark in that field, and the district court so found. In particular, the district court accepted studies proffered by both parties which revealed that 76 percent of attorneys associated LEXIS with specific attributes of the service provided by Mead. However, among the general adult population, LEXIS is recognized by only one percent of those surveyed, half of this one percent being attorneys or accountants. The district court therefore concluded that LEXIS is strong only within its own market.

As appears in the Addendum to this opinion, the LEXIS mark is printed in block letters with no accompanying logo.

Toyota and Lexus

Toyota Motor Corp. has for many years manufactured automobiles, which it markets in the United States through its subsidiary Toyota Motor Sales, U.S.A. On August 24, 1987 Toyota announced a new line of luxury automobiles to be called LEXUS. The cars will be manufactured by a separate LEXUS division of Toyota, and their marketing pitch will be directed to well-educated professional consumers with annual incomes in excess of $50,000. Toyota had planned to spend $18 million to $20 million for this purpose during the first nine months of 1989.

Before adopting the completely artificial name LEXUS for its new automobile, Toyota secured expert legal advice to the effect that "there is absolutely no conflict between 'LEXIS' and 'LEXUS.'" Accordingly, when Mead subsequently objected to Toyota's use of LEXUS, Toyota rejected Mead's complaints. The district court held correctly that Toyota acted without predatory intent in adopting the LEXUS mark.

The absence of predatory intent by the junior user is a relevant factor in assessing a claim under the antidilution statute, ... since relief under the statute is of equitable origin,....

Sally Gee, Inc. v. Myra Hogan, Inc., 699 F.2d 621, 626 (2d Cir. 1983) (citations omitted).

However, the district court erred in concluding that Toyota's refusal to acknowledge that its use of LEXUS might harm the LEXIS mark, deprived it of the argument that it acted in good faith. If, as we now hold, Toyota's mark did not dilute Mead's, it would be anomalous indeed to hold Toyota guilty of bad faith in proceeding in reliance on its attorney's correct advice to that effect.

The LEXUS mark is in stylized, almost script-like lettering and is accompanied by a rakish L logo. *See* Addendum.

THE LAW

The brief legislative history accompanying section 368-d describes the purpose of the statute as preventing "the whittling away of an established trade-mark's selling power and value through *its* unauthorized use by others upon dissimilar products." 1954 N.Y. Legis. Ann. 49 (emphasis supplied). If we were to interpret literally the italicized word "its", we would limit statutory violations to the unauthorized use of the identical established mark. This is what Frank Schechter, the father of the dilution theory, intended when he wrote *The Rational Basis of Trademark Protection*, 40 Harv. L. Rev. 813 (1927).

Indeed, some courts have gone so far as to hold that, although violation of an antidilution statute does not require confusion of product or source, the marks in question must be sufficiently similar that confusion may be created as between the marks themselves.

We hold only that the marks must be "very" or "substantially" similar and that, absent such similarity, there can be no viable claim of dilution.

The district court's opinion was divided into two sections. The first section dealt with Toyota's alleged violation of the Lanham Act, and the second dealt with the alleged dilution of Mead's mark under New York's antidilution statute. The district court made several findings on the issue of similarity in its Lanham Act discussion; it made none in its discussion of section 368-d. Assuming that the district court's finding of lack of physical similarity in the former discussion was intended to carry over into the latter, we would find ourselves in complete accord with it since we would make the same finding. *See* Addendum; *see also Blue Bell, Inc. v. Jaymar-Ruby, Inc.*, 497 F.2d 433, 435 (2d Cir. 1974). However, if the district court's statement in its Lanham Act discussion that "in everyday spoken English, LEXUS and LEXIS are virtually identical in pronunciation" was intended to be a finding of fact rather than a statement of opinion, we question both its accuracy and its relevance. The word LEXUS is not yet widely enough known that any definitive statement can be made concerning its pronunciation by the American public. However, the two members of this Court who concur in this opinion use "everyday spoken English", and we would not pronounce LEXUS as if it were spelled LEXIS. Although our colleague takes issue with us on this point, he does not contend that if LEXUS and LEXIS are pronounced correctly, they will sound the same. We liken LEXUS to such words as "census", "focus" and "locus", and differentiate it from such words as "axis", "aegis" and "iris". If we were to substitute the letter "i" for the letter "u" in "census", we would not pronounce it as we now do. Likewise, if we were to substitute the letter "u" for the letter "i" in "axis", we would not pronounce it as we now do. In short, we agree with the testimony of Toyota's speech expert, who testified:

> Of course, anyone can pronounce "lexis" and "lexus" the same, either both with an unstressed I or both with an unstressed U, or schwa — or with some other sound in between. But, properly, the distinction between unstressed I and unstressed U, or schwa, is a standard one in English; the distinction is there to be made in ordinary, reasonably careful speech.

In addition, we do not believe that "everyday spoken English" is the proper test to use in deciding the issue of similarity in the instant case. Under the Constitution, there is a "'commonsense' distinction between speech proposing a commercial transaction, which occurs in an area traditionally subject to government regulation, and other varieties of speech." The legitimate aim of the anti-dilution statute is to prohibit the unauthorized use of another's trademark in order to market incompatible products or services", and this constitutes a "legitimate regulation of commercial speech." *L.L. Bean, Inc. v. Drake Publishers, Inc.*, 811 F.2d 26, 32–33 (1st Cir.), *cert. denied*, 483 U.S. 1013, 107 S. Ct. 3254, 97 L. Ed. 2d 753 (1987). "Advertising is the primary means by which the connection between a name and a company is established …", *Beneficial Corp. v. Beneficial Capital Corp.*, 529 F. Supp. 445, 448 (S.D.N.Y. 1982), and oral advertising is done primarily on radio and television. When Mead's speech expert was asked whether there were instances in which LEXUS and LEXIS would be pronounced differently, he replied "Yes, although a deliberate attempt must be made to do so.… They can be pronounced distinctly but they are not when they are used in common parlance, in everyday language or speech." We take it as a given that television and radio announcers usually are more careful and precise in their diction than is the man on the street. Moreover, it is the rare television commercial that does not contain a visual reference to the mark and product, which in the instant case would be the LEXUS automobile. We conclude that in the field of commercial advertising, which is the field subject to regulation, there is no substantial similarity between Mead's mark and Toyota's.

There are additional factors that militate against a finding of dilution in the instant case. Such a finding must be based on two elements. First, plaintiff's mark must possess a distinctive quality capable of dilution. *Allied Maintenance Corp. v. Allied Mechanical Trades, Inc.*, 42 N.Y.2d 538, 545, 399 N.Y.S.2d 628, 369 N.E.2d 1162 (1977). Second, plaintiff must show a likelihood of dilution, *Sally Gee, Inc. v. Myra Hogan, Inc.*, *supra*, 699 F.2d at 625. As section 368-d expressly states, a plaintiff need not show either competition between its product or service and that of the defendant or a likelihood of confusion as to the source of the goods or services. *Allied Maintenance Corp. v. Allied Mechanical Trades, Inc.*, *supra*, 42 N.Y.2d at 543.

Distinctiveness for dilution purposes often has been equated with the strength of a mark for infringement purposes. *P.F. Cosmetique, S.A. v. Minnetonka, Inc.*, 605 F. Supp. 662, 672 (S.D.N.Y. 1985); *Allied Maintenance Corp. v. Allied Mechanical Trades, Inc.*, *supra*, 42 N.Y.2d at 545. It also has been defined as uniqueness or as having acquired a secondary meaning. Allied Maintenance, *supra*, 42 N.Y.2d at 545. A trademark has a secondary meaning if it "has become so associated in the mind of the public with that entity [Allied] or its product that it identifies the goods sold by that entity and distinguishes them from goods sold by others." *Id.* In sum, the statute protects a trademark's "selling power." *Sally Gee, Inc. v. Myra Hogan, Inc.*, *supra*, 699 F.2d at 624–25. However, the fact that a mark has selling power in a limited geographical or commercial area does not endow it with a secondary meaning for the public generally. *See Hartman v. Hallmark Cards, Inc.*, 833 F.2d 117, 121 (8th Cir. 1987); *Truck Equipment Service Co. v. Fruehauf Corp.*, 536 F.2d 1210, 1219 (8th Cir.), *cert. denied*, 429 U.S. 861, 50 L. Ed. 2d 139, 97 S. Ct. 164, 191 U.S.P.Q. (BNA) 588 (1976) (quoting *Shoppers Fair of Arkansas, Inc. v. Sanders Co.*, 328 F.2d 496, 499 (8th Cir. 1964)); *Restaurant Lutece, Inc. v. Houbigant, Inc.*, 593 F. Supp. 588, 596 (D.N.J. 1984); *Scott v. Mego International, Inc.*, 519 F. Supp. 1118, 1138 (D. Minn. 1981).

The strength and distinctiveness of LEXIS is limited to the market for its services—attorneys and accountants. Outside the market, LEXIS has very little selling power. Because only one percent of the general population associates LEXIS with the attributes of Mead's service, it cannot be said that LEXIS identifies that service to the general public and distinguishes it from others. Moreover, the bulk of Mead's advertising budget is devoted to reaching attorneys through professional journals.

This Court has defined dilution as either the blurring of a mark's product identification or the tarnishment of the affirmative associations a mark has come to convey. *Sally Gee, Inc. v. Myra Hogan, Inc.*, *supra*, 699 F.2d at 625 (quoting 3A Callman, *The Law of Unfair Competition, Trademarks and Monopolies* §84.2 at 954–55). Mead does not claim that Toyota's use of LEXUS would tarnish affirmative associations engendered by LEXIS. The question that remains, therefore, is whether LEXIS is likely to be blurred by LEXUS.

Very little attention has been given to date to the distinction between the confusion necessary for a claim of infringement and the blurring necessary for a claim of dilution. Shire, *supra*, 77 Trademark Rep. at 293. Although the antidilution statute dispenses with the requirements of competition and confusion, it does not follow that every junior use of a similar mark will dilute the senior mark in the manner contemplated by the New York Legislature.

As already stated, the brief legislative history accompanying section 368-d described the purpose of the statute as preventing "the whittling away of an established trademark's selling power and value through its unauthorized use by others upon dissimilar products." The history disclosed a need for legislation to prevent such "hypothetical anomalies" as "Dupont shoes, Buick aspirin tablets, Schlitz varnish, Kodak pianos, Bulova gowns, and so forth", and cited cases involving similarly famous marks ...

It is apparent from these references that there must be some mental association between plaintiff's and defendant's marks.

> If a reasonable buyer is not at all likely to link the two uses of the trademark in his or her own mind, even subtly or subliminally, then there can be no dilution.... Dilution theory presumes *some kind of mental association* in the reasonable buyer's mind between the two party's [sic] uses of the mark.

2 J. McCarthy, *supra*,§24.13 at 213–14.

This mental association may be created where the plaintiff's mark is very famous and therefore has a distinctive quality for a significant percentage of the defendant's market. *Sally Gee, Inc. v. Myra Hogan, Inc., supra*, 699 F.2d at 625. However, if a mark circulates only in a limited market, it is unlikely to be associated generally with the mark for a dissimilar product circulating elsewhere. As discussed above, such distinctiveness as LEXIS possesses is limited to the narrow market of attorneys and accountants. Moreover, the process which LEXIS represents is widely disparate from the product represented by LEXUS. For the general public, LEXIS has no distinctive quality that LEXUS will dilute.

The possibility that someday LEXUS may become a famous mark in the mind of the general public has little relevance in the instant dilution analysis since it is quite apparent that the general public associates nothing with LEXIS. On the other hand, the recognized sophistication of attorneys, the principal users of the service, has substantial relevance. Because of this knowledgeable sophistication, it is unlikely that, even in the market where Mead principally operates, there will be any significant amount of blurring between the LEXIS and LEXUS marks.

For all the foregoing reasons, we hold that Toyota did not violate section 368-d. We see no need therefore to discuss Toyota's remaining arguments for reversal.

C. FTDA

1. Cause of Action

15 U.S.C. §1125 (c)(1)

Subject to the principles of equity, the owner of a famous mark that is distinctive, inherently or through acquired distinctiveness, shall be entitled to an injunction against another person who, at any time after the owner's mark has become famous, commences use of a mark or trade name in commerce that is likely to cause dilution by blurring or dilution by tarnishment of the famous mark, regardless of the presence or absence of actual or likely confusion, of competition, or of actual economic injury.

---

a. Dilution by Blurring

15 U.S.C. §1125 (c)(2)(B)

(B) For purposes of paragraph (1), "dilution by blurring" is association arising from the similarity between a mark or trade name and a famous mark that impairs the distinctiveness of the famous mark. In determining whether a mark or trade name is likely to cause dilution by blurring, the court may consider all relevant factors, including the following:

(i) The degree of similarity between the mark or trade name and the famous mark.

(ii) The degree of inherent or acquired distinctiveness of the famous mark.

(iii) The extent to which the owner of the famous mark is engaging in substantially exclusive use of the mark.

(iv) The degree of recognition of the famous mark.

(v) Whether the user of the mark or trade name intended to create an association with the famous mark.

(vi) Any actual association between the mark or trade name and the famous mark.

———————

Louis Vuitton Malletier v. Haute Diggity Dog, LLC
2007 WL 3348013 (4th Cir. 2007)

* * *

Louis Vuitton Malletier S.A. ("LVM") is a well-known manufacturer of luxury luggage, leather goods, handbags, and accessories, which it markets and sells worldwide. In connection with the sale of its products, LVM has adopted trademarks and trade dress that are well recognized and have become famous and distinct. Indeed, in 2006, *BusinessWeek* ranked LOUIS VUITTON as the 17th "best brand" of all corporations in the world and the first "best brand" for any fashion business.

LVM has registered trademarks for "LOUIS VUITTON," in connection with luggage and ladies' handbags (the "LOUIS VUITTON mark"); for a stylized monogram of "LV," in connection with traveling bags and other goods (the "LV mark"); and for a monogram canvas design consisting of a canvas with repetitions of the LV mark along with four-pointed stars, four-pointed stars inset in curved diamonds, and four-pointed flowers inset in circles, in connection with traveling bags and other products (the "Monogram Canvas mark"). In 2002, LVM adopted a brightly-colored version of the Monogram Canvas mark in which the LV mark and the designs were of various colors and the background was white (the "Multicolor design"), created in collaboration with Japanese artist Takashi Murakami. For the Multicolor design, LVM obtained a copyright in 2004. In 2005, LVM adopted another design consisting of a canvas with repetitions of the LV mark and smiling cherries on a brown background (the "Cherry design").

As LVM points out, the Multicolor design and the Cherry design attracted immediate and extraordinary media attention and publicity in magazines such as *Vogue, W, Elle, Harper's Bazaar, Us Weekly, Life and Style, Travel & Leisure, People, In Style,* and *Jane.* The press published photographs showing celebrities carrying these handbags, including Jennifer Lopez, Madonna, Eve, Elizabeth Hurley, Carmen Electra, and Anna Kournikova, among others. When the Multicolor design first appeared in 2003, the magazines typically reported, "The Murakami designs for Louis Vuitton, which were the hit of the summer, came with hefty price tags and a long waiting list." *People Magazine* said, "the wait list is in the thousands." The handbags retailed in the range of $995 for a medium handbag to $4500 for a large travel bag. The medium size handbag that appears to be the model for the "Chewy Vuiton" dog toy retailed for $1190. The Cherry design appeared in 2005, and the handbags including that design were priced similarly—in the range of $995 to $2740. LVM does not currently market products using the Cherry design.

The original LOUIS VUITTON, LV, and Monogram Canvas marks, however, have been used as identifiers of LVM products continuously since 1896.

During the period 2003–2005, LVM spent more than $48 million advertising products using its marks and designs, including more than $4 million for the Multicolor design. It sells its products exclusively in LVM stores and in its own in-store boutiques that are contained within department stores such as Saks Fifth Avenue, Bloomingdale's, Neiman Marcus, and Macy's. LVM also advertises its products on the Internet through the specific websites www.louisvuitton.com and www.eluxury.com.

Although better known for its handbags and luggage, LVM also markets a limited selection of luxury pet accessories—collars, leashes, and dog carriers—which bear the Monogram Canvas mark and the Multicolor design. These items range in price from approximately $200 to $1600. LVM does not make dog toys.

Haute Diggity Dog, LLC, which is a relatively small and relatively new business located in Nevada, manufactures and sells nationally—primarily through pet stores—a line of pet chew toys and beds whose names parody elegant high-end brands of products such as perfume, cars, shoes, sparkling wine, and handbags. These include—in addition to Chewy Vuiton (LOUIS VUITTON)—Chewnel No. 5 (Chanel No. 5), Furcedes (Mercedes), Jimmy Chew (Jimmy Choo), Dog Perignonn (Dom Perignon), Sniffany & Co. (Tiffany & Co.), and Dogior (Dior). The chew toys and pet beds are plush, made of polyester, and have a shape and design that loosely imitate the signature product of the targeted brand. They are mostly distributed and sold through pet stores, although one or two Macy's stores carries Haute Diggity Dog's products. The dog toys are generally sold for less than $20, although larger versions of some of Haute Diggity Dog's plush dog beds sell for more than $100.

Haute Diggity Dog's "Chewy Vuiton" dog toys, in particular, loosely resemble miniature handbags and undisputedly evoke LVM handbags of similar shape, design, and color. In lieu of the LOUIS VUITTON mark, the dog toy uses "Chewy Vuiton"; in lieu of the LV mark, it uses "CV"; and the other symbols and colors employed are imitations, but not exact ones, of those used in the LVM Multicolor and Cherry designs.

In 2002, LVM commenced this action, naming as defendants Haute Diggity Dog; Victoria D.N. Dauernheim, the principal owner of Haute Diggity Dog; and Woofies, LLC, a retailer of Haute Diggity Dog's products, located in Asburn, Virginia, for [among other things, federal trademark dilution.] … On cross-motions for summary judgment, the district court granted Haute Diggity Dog's motion and denied LVM's motion, entering judgment in favor of Haute Diggity Dog on all of the claims. It rested its analysis on each count principally on the conclusion that Haute Diggity Dog's products amounted to a successful parody of LVM's marks, trade dress, and copyright. *See* Louis Vuitton Malletier S.A. v. Haute Diggity Dog, LLC, 464 F.Supp.2d 495 (E.D.Va.2006).

LVM appealed and now challenges, as a matter of law, virtually every ruling made by the district court.

* * *

LVM also contends that Haute Diggity Dog's advertising, sale, and distribution of the "Chewy Vuiton" dog toys dilutes its LOUIS VUITTON, LV, and Monogram Canvas marks, which are famous and distinctive, in violation of the Trademark Dilution Revision Act of 2006 ("TDRA"), 15 U.S.C.A. § 1125(c) (West Supp.2007). It argues, "Before the district court's decision, Vuitton's famous marks were unblurred by any third party trademark use." "Allowing defendants to become the first to use similar marks will obviously blur and dilute the Vuitton Marks."

Haute Diggity Dog urges that, in applying the TDRA to the circumstances before us, we reject LVM's suggestion that a parody "automatically" gives rise to "actionable dilution." Haute Diggity Dog contends that only marks that are "identical or substantially similar" can give rise to actionable dilution, and its "Chewy Vuiton" marks are not identical or sufficiently similar to LVM's marks. It also argues that "[its] spoof, like other obvious parodies," "'tends to increase public identification' of [LVM's] mark with [LVM]," *quoting Jordache*, 828 F.2d at 1490, rather than impairing its distinctiveness, as the TDRA requires.

Claims for trademark dilution are authorized by the TDRA, a relatively recent enactment, which provides in relevant part:

Subject to the principles of equity, the owner of a *famous* mark ... shall be entitled to an injunction against another person who ... commences use of a mark or trade name in commerce that is likely to cause *dilution by blurring* or *dilution by tarnishment* of the famous mark, regardless of the presence or absence of actual or likely confusion, of competition, or of actual economic injury.

15 U.S.C.A. § 1125(c)(1) (emphasis added). A mark is "famous" when it is "widely recognized by the general consuming public of the United States as a designation of source of the goods or services of the mark's owner." *Id.* § 1125(c)(2)(A). Creating causes of action for only *dilution by blurring* and *dilution by tarnishment,* the TDRA defines "dilution by blurring" as the "association arising from the similarity between a mark or trade name and a famous mark that impairs the distinctiveness of the famous mark." *Id.* § 1125(c)(2)(B).

Thus, to state a dilution claim under the TDRA, a plaintiff must show:

(1) that the plaintiff owns a famous mark that is distinctive;

(2) that the defendant has commenced using a mark in commerce that allegedly is diluting the famous mark;

(3) that a similarity between the defendant's mark and the famous mark gives rise to an association between the marks; and

(4) that the association is likely to impair the distinctiveness of the famous mark or likely to harm the reputation of the famous mark.

In the context of blurring, distinctiveness refers to the ability of the famous mark uniquely to identify a single source and thus maintain its selling power. In proving a dilution claim under the TDRA, the plaintiff need not show actual or likely confusion, the presence of competition, or actual economic injury. *See* 15 U.S.C.A. § 1125(c)(1).

The TDRA creates three defenses based on the defendant's (1) "fair use" (with exceptions); (2) "news reporting and news commentary"; and (3) "noncommercial use." *Id.* § 1125(c)(3).

A

We address first LVM's claim for dilution by blurring.

The first three elements of a trademark dilution claim are not at issue in this case. LVM owns famous marks that are distinctive; Haute Diggity Dog has commenced using "Chewy Vuiton," "CV," and designs and colors that are allegedly diluting LVM's marks; and the similarity between Haute Diggity Dog's marks and LVM's marks gives rise to an association between the marks, albeit a parody. The issue for resolution is whether the association between Haute Diggity Dog's marks and LVM's marks is likely to impair the distinctiveness of LVM's famous marks.

In deciding this issue, the district court correctly outlined the six factors to be considered in determining whether dilution by blurring has been shown. *See* 15 U.S.C.A. § 1125(c)(2)(B). But in evaluating the facts of the case, the court did not directly apply those factors it enumerated. It held simply:

[The famous mark's] strength is not likely to be blurred by a parody dog toy product. Instead of blurring Plaintiff's mark, the success of the parodic use depends upon the continued association with LOUIS VUITTON.

Louis Vuitton Malletier, 464 F.Supp.2d at 505. The amicus supporting LVM's position in this case contends that the district court, by not applying the statutory factors, misapplied the TDRA to conclude that simply because Haute Diggity Dog's product was a parody meant that "there can be no *association* with the famous mark as a matter of law." Moreover, the amicus points out correctly that to rule in favor of Haute Diggity Dog, the district court was required to find that the "association" did not impair the distinctiveness of LVM's famous mark.

LVM goes further in its own brief, however, and contends:

When a defendant uses an imitation of a famous mark in connection with related goods, a claim of parody cannot preclude liability for dilution.

* * *

The district court's opinion utterly ignores the substantial goodwill VUITTON has established in its famous marks through more than a century of *exclusive* use. Disregarding the clear Congressional mandate to protect such famous marks against dilution, the district court has granted [Haute Diggity Dog] permission to become the first company other than VUITTON to use imitations of the famous VUITTON Marks.

In short, LVM suggests that any use by a third person of an imitation of its famous marks dilutes the famous marks as a matter of law. This contention misconstrues the TDRA.

The TDRA prohibits a person from using a junior mark that is likely to dilute (by blurring) the famous mark, and blurring is defined to be an impairment to the famous mark's distinctiveness. "Distinctiveness" in turn refers to the public's recognition that the famous mark identifies a single source of the product using the famous mark.

To determine whether a junior mark is likely to dilute a famous mark through blurring, the TDRA directs the court to consider all factors relevant to the issue, including six factors that are enumerated in the statute:

(i) The degree of similarity between the mark or trade name and the famous mark.

(ii) The degree of inherent or acquired distinctiveness of the famous mark.

(iii) The extent to which the owner of the famous mark is engaging in substantially exclusive use of the mark.

(iv) The degree of recognition of the famous mark.

(v) Whether the user of the mark or trade name intended to create an association with the famous mark.

(vi) Any actual association between the mark or trade name and the famous mark.

15 U.S.C.A. § 1125(c)(2)(B). Not every factor will be relevant in every case, and not every blurring claim will require extensive discussion of the factors. But a trial court must offer a sufficient indication of which factors it has found persuasive and explain why they are persuasive so that the court's decision can be reviewed. The district court did not do this adequately in this case. Nonetheless, after we apply the factors as a matter of law, we reach the same conclusion reached by the district court.

We begin by noting that parody is not automatically a complete *defense* to a claim of dilution by blurring where the defendant uses the parody as its own designation of source, i.e., *as a trademark.* Although the TDRA does provide that fair use is a complete defense and allows that a parody can be considered fair use, it does not extend the fair use defense to parodies used as a trademark. As the statute provides:

> The following shall not be actionable as dilution by blurring or dilution by tarnishment under this subsection:
>
> (A) Any fair use ... *other than as a designation of source for the person's own goods or services,* including use in connection with ... parodying....

15 U.S.C.A. § 1125(c)(3)(A)(ii) (emphasis added). Under the statute's plain language, parodying a famous mark is protected by the fair use defense only if the parody is *not* "a designation of source for the person's own goods or services."

The TDRA, however, does not require a court to ignore the existence of a parody that is used as a trademark, and it does not preclude a court from considering parody as part of the circumstances to be considered for determining whether the plaintiff has made out a claim for dilution by blurring. Indeed, the statute permits a court to consider "all relevant factors," including the six factors supplied in § 1125(c)(2)(B).

Thus, it would appear that a defendant's use of a mark as a parody is relevant to the overall question of whether the defendant's use is likely to impair the famous mark's distinctiveness. Moreover, the fact that the defendant uses its marks as a parody is specifically relevant to several of the listed factors. For example, factor (v) (whether the defendant intended to create an association with the famous mark) and factor (vi) (whether there exists an actual association between the defendant's mark and the famous mark) directly invite inquiries into the defendant's intent in using the parody, the defendant's actual use of the parody, and the effect that its use has on the famous mark. While a parody intentionally creates an association with the famous mark in order to be a parody, it also intentionally communicates, if it is successful, that it is *not* the famous mark, but rather a satire of the famous mark. *See PETA,* 263 F.3d at 366. That the defendant is using its mark as a parody is therefore relevant in the consideration of these statutory factors.

Similarly, factors (i), (ii), and (iv) — the degree of similarity between the two marks, the degree of distinctiveness of the famous mark, and its recognizability — are directly implicated by consideration of the fact that the defendant's mark is a successful parody. Indeed, by making the famous mark an object of the parody, a successful parody might actually enhance the famous mark's distinctiveness by making it an icon. The brunt of the joke becomes yet more famous. *See Hormel Foods,* 73 F.3d at 506 (observing that a successful parody "tends to increase public identification" of the famous mark with its source); *see also Yankee Publ'g Inc. v. News Am. Publ'g Inc.,* 809 F.Supp. 267, 272–82 (S.D.N.Y.1992) (suggesting that a sufficiently obvious parody is unlikely to blur the targeted famous mark).

In sum, while a defendant's use of a parody as a mark does not support a "fair use" defense, it may be considered in determining whether the plaintiff-owner of a famous mark has proved its claim that the defendant's use of a parody mark is likely to impair the distinctiveness of the famous mark.

In the case before us, when considering factors (ii), (iii), and (iv), it is readily apparent, indeed conceded by Haute Diggity Dog, that LVM's marks are distinctive, famous, and strong. The LOUIS VUITTON mark is well known and is commonly identified as a brand of the great Parisian fashion house, Louis Vuitton Malletier. So too are its other marks and designs, which are invariably used with the LOUIS VUITTON mark. It may not be too strong to refer to these famous marks as icons of high fashion.

While the establishment of these facts satisfies essential elements of LVM's dilution claim, *see* 15 U.S.C.A. §1125(c)(1), the facts impose on LVM an increased burden to demonstrate that the distinctiveness of its famous marks is likely to be impaired by a successful parody. Even as Haute Diggity Dog's parody mimics the famous mark, it communicates simultaneously that it is not the famous mark, but is only satirizing it. *See PETA*, 263 F.3d at 366. And because the famous mark is particularly strong and distinctive, it becomes more likely that a parody will not impair the distinctiveness of the mark. In short, as Haute Diggity Dog's "Chewy Vuiton" marks are a successful parody, we conclude that they will not blur the distinctiveness of the famous mark as a unique identifier of its source.

It is important to note, however, that this might not be true if the parody is so similar to the famous mark that it likely could be construed as actual use of the famous mark itself. Factor (i) directs an inquiry into the "degree of similarity between the junior mark and the famous mark. If Haute Diggity Dog used the actual marks of LVM (as a parody or otherwise), it could dilute LVM's marks by blurring, regardless of whether Haute Diggity Dog's use was confusingly similar, whether it was in competition with LVM, or whether LVM sustained actual injury. *See* 15 U.S.C.A. §1125(c)(1). Thus, "the use of DUPONT shoes, BUICK aspirin, and KODAK pianos would be actionable" under the TDRA because the unauthorized use of the famous marks *themselves* on unrelated goods might diminish the capacity of these trademarks to distinctively identify a single source. This is true even though a consumer would be unlikely to confuse the manufacturer of KODAK film with the hypothetical producer of KODAK pianos.

But in this case, Haute Diggity Dog mimicked the famous marks; it did not come so close to them as to destroy the success of its parody and, more importantly, to diminish the LVM marks' capacity to identify a single source. Haute Diggity Dog designed a pet chew toy to imitate and suggest, but not *use,* the marks of a high-fashion LOUIS VUITTON handbag. It used "Chewy Vuiton" to mimic "LOUIS VUITTON"; it used "CV" to mimic "LV"; and it adopted *imperfectly* the items of LVM's designs. We conclude that these uses by Haute Diggity Dog were not so similar as to be likely to impair the distinctiveness of LVM's famous marks.

In a similar vein, when considering factors (v) and (vi), it becomes apparent that Haute Diggity Dog intentionally associated its marks, but only partially and certainly imperfectly, so as to convey the simultaneous message that it was not in fact a source of LVM products. Rather, as a parody, it separated itself from the LVM marks in order to make fun of them.

In sum, when considering the relevant factors to determine whether blurring is likely to occur in this case, we readily come to the conclusion, as did the district court, that LVM has failed to make out a case of trademark dilution by blurring by failing to establish that the distinctiveness of its marks was likely to be impaired by Haute Diggity Dog's marketing and sale of its "Chewy Vuiton" products.

b. Dilution by Tarnishment

15 U.S.C. § 1125 (c)(2)(C)

(C) For purposes of paragraph (1), "dilution by tarnishment" is association arising from the similarity between a mark or trade name and a famous mark that harms the reputation of the famous mark.

Louis Vuitton Malletier v. Haute Diggity Dog, LLC

2007 WL 3348013 (4th Cir. (Va.))

LVM's claim for dilution by tarnishment does not require an extended discussion. To establish its claim for dilution by tarnishment, LVM must show, in lieu of blurring, that Haute Diggity Dog's use of the "Chewy Vuiton" mark on dog toys harms the reputation of the LOUIS VUITTON mark and LVM's other marks. LVM argues that the possibility that a dog could choke on a "Chewy Vuiton" toy causes this harm. LVM has, however, provided no record support for its assertion. It relies only on speculation about whether a dog could choke on the chew toys and a logical concession that a $10 dog toy made in China was of "inferior quality" to the $1190 LOUIS VUITTON handbag. The speculation begins with LVM's assertion in its brief that "defendant Woofie's admitted that 'Chewy Vuiton' products pose a choking hazard for some dogs. Having prejudged the defendant's mark to be a parody, the district court made light of this admission in its opinion, and utterly failed to give it the weight it deserved," citing to a page in the district court's opinion where the court states:

At oral argument, plaintiff provided only a flimsy theory that a pet may some day choke on a Chewy Vuiton squeak toy and incite the wrath of a confused consumer against LOUIS VUITTON.

Louis Vuitton Malletier, 464 F.Supp.2d at 505. The court was referring to counsel's statement during oral argument that the owner of Woofie's stated that "she would not sell this product to certain types of dogs because there is a danger they would tear it open and choke on it." There is no record support, however, that any dog has choked on a pet chew toy, such as a "Chewy Vuiton" toy, or that there is any basis from which to conclude that a dog would likely choke on such a toy.

We agree with the district court that LVM failed to demonstrate a claim for dilution by tarnishment. *See Hormel Foods,* 73 F.3d at 507.

Diane Von Furstenberg Studio v. Snyder

2007 WL 2688184 (E.D.Va.) (2007)

This case arises out of alleged counterfeiting, trademark, and trade dress infringement. Plaintiff Diane Von Furstenberg Studio ("DVF") is a designer and producer of high-quality dresses and women's apparel. DVF products are identified by DVF's federally registered trademarks ("DVF Marks"). Plaintiff alleges that Defendants Catherine Snyder, d/b/a Cathy 3254, d/b/a Katrina3254@vendio.com, katrina3254@mailstep.com, d/b/a Fairfax Trading Co., and Richard Snyder (collectively "Defendants") are manufacturing, importing, distributing, and selling counterfeit DVF dresses ("Counterfeit Products") without consent or authorization, and importing, exporting, distributing, promoting, selling, and offering for sale the Counterfeit Products through an eBay account in the name of cathy3254 ("Website"). As part of its investigation, Plaintiff purchased a dress bearing DVF marks from the Website. Plaintiff identified the dress as counterfeit by the marks and label, and identified a Herndon, Virginia location as the source of the counterfeit goods. Plaintiff then filed suit and moved this Court for a temporary restraining and seizure order ("TRO"), order restraining the transfer of assets, order sealing the file, order for expedited discovery and preliminary injunction. On December 7, 2006, this Court granted the motion and issued the requested order ("the Order"). On December 8, 2006, the Order was executed upon Defendants' address in Herndon, Virginia, and Plaintiffs seized a number of dresses bearing DVF marks, along with a computer and financial records. On December 21, 2006, this Court issued a preliminary injunction against Defendants, and unsealed the case. On January 8, 2007, Defendants filed an answer to the complaint. On May 4, 2007, Defendants filed a motion to dismiss for failure to state a claim which this Court denied on June 25, 2007.

On August 15, 2007, Plaintiff filed a Motion for Summary Judgment on its claims of advertising, selling, and offering for sale counterfeit dresses and requesting a permanent injunction, statutory damages, attorneys fees, and the release of counterfeit dresses to DVF. Defendants filed an opposition to Plaintiff's Motion on September 4, 2007, alleging genuine dispute of material facts. This Motion is currently before the Court.

* * *

The Trademark Dilution Act provides that the owner of a famous mark can enjoin "another person who, at any time after the owner's mark has become famous, commences use of a mark or trade name in commerce that is likely to cause dilution by blurring or dilution by tarnishment of the famous mark." 15 USCS § 1125(c). The Fourth Circuit has defined dilution as "the lessening of the capacity of a famous mark to identify and distinguish goods or services." *CareFirst of Maryland, Inc. v. First Care*, 434 F.3d 263, 274 (4th Cir. 2006). The Supreme Court has implied that the use of an identical mark would be circumstantial evidence of actual dilution. *Moseley v. Secret Catalogue*, 537 U.S. 418, 434 (U.S.2003) (applying the previous statutory requirement of actual dilution, superceded by amendment to 15 U.S.C. § 1125(c)(1)). After its 2006 amendment, the Trademark Dilution Act requires only that the mark be "likely" to cause dilution, a standard even more easily met. 15 USCS § 1125(c).

The Plaintiff in this case argues that the DVF mark has been diluted by tarnishment, which "generally arises when the plaintiff's trademark is linked to products of shoddy quality, or is portrayed in an unwholesome or unsavory context likely to evoke unflattering thoughts about the owner's product." *Deere & Co. v. MTD Prods.*, 41 F.3d 39, 43 (2d Cir.1994). It is undisputed that Defendants chose to use Plaintiff's exact mark to capitalize on its fame, but Defendants argue that the products they sold are not of shoddy quality and thus do not tarnish Plaintiff's image. They cite to the Declaration of Colleen Collins stating that it would take a "trained eye to distinguish between the Counterfeit Dress and the DCF dress," and that ordinary consumers may not be able to distinguish them. C. Collins decl. at 4. However, Catherine Snyder also admits that dresses were returned to her by customers because of shoddy workmanship. C. Snyder depo. at 177–78.

This Court finds that there is no dispute that Defendants used the identical DVF mark on the inferior-quality dresses they sold, and that such act was likely to cause dilution of the DVF mark. Summary judgment will be granted to Plaintiff on its claims for trademark dilution.

_____

Notes

1. What is the TDRA's impact on freedom of speech? Can a college student incorporate the Wal-Mart logo into his campaign against Wal-Mart's labor practices? *See*, NOTE: Jesse A. Hofrichter, *Tool of the Trademark: Brand Criticism and Free Speech Problems with the Trademark Dilution Revision Act of 2006*, 28 Cardozo L. Rev. 1923 (2007) (arguing that the TDRA allows "elite" marks to further squelch speech).

2. The great irony is that the United States' position on dilution is, in fact, broader than required under the treaties relied on in the legislative history for the proposition that section 43(c) was mandated by United States treaty obligations. The Paris Treaty, NAFTA, and TRIPS all require contracting states to protect famous marks "from a likelihood of confusion" where section 43(c) protects famous marks regardless of confusion. *See also* S. Rep. No. 100-515, at 7–8 (1988), reprinted in 1988 U.S.C.C.A.N. 5577, 5583–84.

3. In addition to dilution by blurring or dilution by tarnishment, the Second Circuit has created "alteration dilution." In *Deere & Co. v. MTD Prods.*, 41 F.3d 39 (2d Cir. 1994), the Second Circuit affirmed a finding of dilution where MTD's advertisement depicted an animated deer (which looked identical to John Deere's famous yellow deer) to be frightened of the MTD product. There was neither blurring nor tarnishment, the court held, but it nevertheless found that MTD's ad was "likely to dilute" the famous John Deere mark by altering it. The court held that the mere act of altering the John Deere mark for MTD's comparative advertisement constituted dilution. In light of the *Victoria's Secret* case, *infra*, is this still good law?

4. The litigation between Deere and MTD has not ended. In Deere & Co. v. MTD Holdings Inc., 2004 U.S. Dist. LEXIS 2550 (S.D.N.Y. 2004), the court found John Deere's claims to its green and yellow would be functional and allow one party to quickly snap up colors hindering additional competitors from entering the marketplace.

5. Is tarnishment dilution or a separate tort? *See* David Welkowitz, Trademark Dilution: Federal, State, and International Law (2002).

_____

2. Dilution of Trade Dress

I.P. Lund Trading ApS and Kroin Inc. v. Kohler Co.
163 F.3d 27 (1st Cir. 1998)

[The plaintiff designed a faucet it called "the VOLA" to be used on bath tubs and other bathroom fixtures. Defendant or one of its licensees examined the faucets with the intent to enter a possible licensing agreement to distribute the faucets. Defendant did not enter such agreement. Instead, it manufactured and sold its own faucet that it called "Falling Water" that was allegedly confusingly similar and dilutive of plaintiff's faucet. The district court held that the plaintiff's mark was distinctive but not infringed by the defendant's faucet. The court then found that while the defendant's faucet did not infringe, it did dilute the VOLA faucet.]

* * *

VI. Dilution

Lund obtained the preliminary injunction against Kohler's distribution and promotion of the Falling Water faucet based on the district court's finding of likelihood of success under the new federal anti-dilution statute, the FTDA, which became effective in 1996. The injunction rested on the conclusion that Lund had established a likelihood of success of showing two essential elements. The first is that the "mark," that is, the VOLA product design as an identifying mark, was "famous." The second is that Kohler's Falling Water faucet "diluted" Lund's mark. Both the terms "famous" and "dilution" are terms of art given specific rigorous meanings by the FTDA.

* * *

B. Dilution

Under the FTDA, even if a mark is famous there is no relief unless that mark has been diluted. As the district court noted, there are two types of dilution recognized: blurring and tarnishing. This case involves no claim of tarnishing, an area in which Congress expressed a strong interest. Further, in light of the finding of no customer confusion, only a particular type of blurring may be involved.

The intellectual origins of the dilution doctrine are traced to a 1927 Harvard Law Review article, which urged protection against "the gradual whittling away or dispersion of the identity and hold upon the public mind of the mark or name by its use upon noncompeting goods." Schecter, The Rational Basis of Trademark Protection, 40 Harv. L. Rev. 813, 825 (1927). Although the origins of the doctrine are concerned with noncompeting goods, Congress used language in the FTDA which extends dilution protection even to competing goods. "Dilution" is defined as "the lessening of the capacity of a famous mark to identify and distinguish good or services." 15 U.S.C. §1127; *see also* H.R. Rep. No. 104-374, at 3, reprinted in 1995 U.S.C.C.A.N at 1030 (stating that dilution "applies when the unauthorized use of a famous mark reduces the public's perception that the mark signifies something unique, singular, or particular"); 3 McCarthy §24:93 ("The crux is whether this particular challenged use lessens the capacity of the famous mark to carry out its role as a trademark—namely, to identify and distinguish.").

This case differs in several respects from usual dilution cases. First, unlike most claims of dilution by tarnishment or blurring, the aspect of its product that Lund seeks to protect—the design of the VOLA faucet—likely could have been protected by a design patent. The possibility of obtaining a design patent is not dispositive of the availability of trade dress protection: more than one form of intellectual property protection may simultaneously protect particular product features. Moreover, design patent protection would not have provided protection identical to that sought here. Nevertheless, the availability of design patent protection does suggest that the claim in this case differs fundamentally from the claims the drafters of the FTDA had in mind—cases where dilution protection is the only form of protection available for a famous mark threatened by unauthorized use of the mark that lessens the mark's capacity to identify its source. Congress's intent to provide protection where none previously existed is evidenced by the House Report's statement that "[a] federal dilution statute is necessary because famous marks ordinarily are used on a nationwide basis and dilution protection is currently only available on a patch-quilt system of protection, in that only approximately 25 states have laws that prohibit trademark dilution." H.R. Rep. No. 104-374, at 3, reprinted in 1995 U.S.C.C.A.N. at 1030.

Second, Lund is seeking protection against a direct competitor. Although the FTDA states that dilution protection is available against unauthorized use of a famous mark that lessens the mark's ability "to identify and distinguish goods or services, regardless of the presence or absence of ... competition between the owner of the famous mark and other parties," 15 U.S.C. §1127 (emphasis added), dilution protection has most often been extended to non-competing uses of a mark. The FTDA recognizes the possibility that dilution may occur in some circumstances where, although some consumers are not confused as to the products' sources, a competitor's use of a mark tarnishes or blurs a senior mark. Nevertheless, such cases are likely to be exceptions to the more common cases of dilution by non-competing marks. Dilution laws are intended to address specific harms; they are not intended to serve as mere fallback protection for trademark owners unable to prove trademark infringement.

While there may be a tendency to think of dilution in terms of confusion, Congress made it clear that dilution can occur even in the absence of confusion. It is simple to see why that should be so when non-competing goods are at issue. No one would confuse Kodak pianos with Kodak film, but the use of the name on the piano could dilute its effectiveness as a mark for the film. But Congress did not say that there can be dilution without confusion only among non-competing goods. As the district court aptly noted, the analysis becomes complicated when the concept of blurring is applied to competing similar products.

We deal first with the approach taken by the district court, an approach which had support in precedent. The district court articulated the standard for determining blurring as follows: "Lund must demonstrate that 'the use of a junior mark has caused a lessening of demand for the product or services bearing the famous mark.'" *Lund I*, 11 F. Supp. 2d at 126 (quoting *Ringling Bros.-Barnum & Bailey Combined Shows, Inc. v. Utah Div. of Travel Dev.*, 955 F. Supp. 605, 616 (E.D. Va. 1997)). This, we think, is not the correct standard. As Kohler observes, demand for one product is almost always lessened whenever a competing product achieves a measurable degree of success. Further, blurring has to do with the identification of a product and that is not the same thing as a lessening of demand.

In addressing the dilution claim, the district court used the "Sweet factors," named after the six factors set forth in Judge Sweet's concurrence in *Mead Data Central, Inc. v. Toyota Motor Sales, U.S.A., Inc.*, 875 F.2d 1026, 1035 (2d Cir. 1989) (Sweet, J., concurring), which involved a claim brought under a New York dilution statute. Some district courts have used these factors to examine whether dilution exists under the FTDA.

Kohler argues that Judge Sweet's six-factor test is inappropriate in determining whether dilution has occurred for purposes of the FTDA. We agree. The Sweet factors have been criticized by both courts and commentators for introducing factors that "are the offspring of classical likelihood of confusion analysis and are not particularly relevant or helpful in resolving the issues of dilution by blurring." 3 McCarthy §24:94.1. The six Sweet factors are: "1) similarity of the marks 2) similarity of the products covered by the marks 3) sophistication of consumers 4) predatory intent 5) renown of the senior mark [and] 6) renown of the junior mark." Mead Data, 875 F.2d at 1035 (Sweet, J., concurring). McCarthy urges that only the first and fifth of Judge Sweet's factors— the similarity of the marks and the renown of the senior mark—are relevant to determining whether dilution has occurred. *See* 3 McCarthy §24:94.1; *see also Hershey Foods Corp. v. Mars, Inc.*, 998 F. Supp. 500, 520 (M.D. Pa. 1998) (stating that "whether the products are similar or not adds nothing to the analysis" because "dilution can apply to competitors"); Klieger, Trademark Dilution: The Whittling Away of the Rational

Basis for Trademark Protection, 58 U. Pitt. L. Rev. 789, 826–27 (1997) (noting that "few of these factors bear any relation to whether a particular junior use will debilitate the selling power of a mark" and that "so long as a mark qualifies for dilution protection and the senior and junior uses of the mark are not so unrelated as to foreclose the possibility of a mental connection, blurring ... is a foregone conclusion"). These criticisms are well taken.

The district court's finding of likelihood of dilution by blurring depended on its use of inappropriate Sweet factors. As McCarthy points out, use of factors such as predatory intent, similarity of products, sophistication of customers, and renown of the junior mark work directly contrary to the intent of a law whose primary purpose was to apply in cases of widely differing goods, i.e. Kodak pianos and Kodak film. *See* 3 McCarthy §24:94.1.

There are difficulties with the Sweet factors even when used with competing goods. Blurring occurs in the minds of potential customers. Predatory intent tells little about how customers in fact perceive products. That customers are sophisticated may well mean less likelihood of blurring. That customers knowingly choose to pay less to get a similar product, and trade lower price against having a product of greater fame, does not, contrary to Lund's argument, establish blurring. Indeed, the district court's findings, in the infringement context, of dissimilarity and sophistication of the customers tend to cut against any finding of blurring. "The familiar test of similarity used in the traditional likelihood of confusion test cannot be the guide [for dilution analysis], for likelihood of confusion is not the test of dilution." *Id.* §24:90.1. Instead, the inquiry is into whether target customers are likely to view the products "as essentially the same." *Id.*

There is a more fundamental problem here in attempting to apply the dilution analysis to the design itself of the competing product involved. We doubt that Congress intended the reach of the dilution concept under the FTDA to extend this far and our doubts are heightened by the presence of constitutional constraints. Where words are the marks at issue it is easy to understand that there can be blurring and tarnishment when there is a completely different product to which the words are applied. The congressional history described earlier gives such examples. What is much more difficult is to see how dilution is to be shown where some of a design is partially replicated and the result is largely dissimilar and does not create consumer confusion. If that is so, as is true here, then it is difficult to see that there has been dilution of the source signaling function of the design (even assuming that such a function has been established through secondary meaning).

Instead, it appears that an entirely different issue is at stake — not interference with the source signaling function but rather protection from an appropriation of or free riding on the investment Lund has made in its design. That investment is usually given protection by patents, which have a limited duration. *See W.T. Rogers Co.*, 778 F.2d at 348. But again, that free riding or appropriation appears to be of the beauty of the object and not of the source, and may in fact be good for consumers. As the district court observed, these sophisticated buyers know a different source is involved and are, accordingly, most likely purchasing because of the aesthetics. And even if there is some appropriation or free riding, the extent of it here is not clear. Certainly it is not plausible to think that Congress intended to protect aesthetic characteristics by simply assuming harm or damages based on the fact that the plaintiff will sell less if the defendant sells more. What is clear is that the interests here are not the interests at the core of what Congress intended to protect in the FTDA.

It is possible that Congress did not really envision protection for product design from dilution by a competing product under the FTDA, but the language it used does not permit us to exclude such protection categorically and rare cases can be imagined. But a broad reading of dilution would bring us close to the constitutional edge, and we decline to attribute such brinksmanship to Congress, and so insist on rigorous review.

Under the interpretation of the fame and dilution requirements for the FTDA set forth today, the requirements for granting the preliminary injunction have not been met.

VII. Constitutionality of the FTDA

Kohler argues that the FTDA may never constitutionally be applied to enjoin a competitor in a product design trade dress case. Kohler's constitutional challenge involves two steps. First, Kohler argues that applying the FTDA to product designs grants patent-like protections for an unlimited period of time. Second, Kohler argues that Congress's Commerce Clause power — the basis of Congress's regulation of trademarks and trade dress — cannot be used to trump the Patent Clause. Lund responds that federal anti-dilution legislation is fully consistent with Congress's Commerce Clause power, and that patent and trademark laws protect different interests and serve different goals.

The district court correctly noted that Kohler faced a "very high preliminary injunction standard on their [constitutional] claim," and that the statute was "presumptively constitutional." Lund II, 11 F. Supp. 2d at 134. The court concluded that defendant Kohler was unlikely to succeed with its argument that the FTDA is unconstitutional in all product design contexts.

Kohler's constitutional attack on application of the FTDA here is mooted by our resolution of the injunction issue. To the extent Kohler is mounting something akin to a facial attack, we think it better not to address constitutional issues in the abstract. The resolution of any conflict between the Patent Clause and the FTDA is better handled on specific facts which present the issues with clarity, and not on the basis of theoretical impacts.

VIII. Conclusion

Both the parties and the district court labored through this case without the benefit of binding precedent on a number of key and difficult issues, particularly the interpretation of the FTDA. The denial of the preliminary injunction on the infringement claim is affirmed. The grant of the injunction on the FTDA claim is vacated inasmuch as there were no findings on functionality and standards for determining both fame and dilution under the FTDA were used which are different from those announced today and the evidence does not show probability of success under those standards. The case is remanded for further proceedings not inconsistent with this opinion. No costs are awarded.

---

3. The Supreme Court's View on Dilution

Moseley v. V Secret Catalogue, Inc.

537 U.S. 418 (2003)

STEVENS, J.

In 1995 Congress amended §43 of the Trademark Act of 1946, 15 U.S.C. §1125, to provide a remedy for the "dilution of famous marks." 109 Stat. 985–986. That amendment, known as the Federal Trademark Dilution Act (FTDA), describes the factors that determine whether a mark is "distinctive and famous," and defines the term "dilution" as "the lessening of the capacity of a famous mark to identify and distinguish goods or services." The question we granted certiorari to decide is whether objective proof of actual injury to the economic value of a famous mark (as opposed to a presumption of harm arising from a subjective "likelihood of dilution" standard) is a requisite for relief under the FTDA.

I

Petitioners, Victor and Cathy Moseley, own and operate a retail store named "Victor's Little Secret" in a strip mall in Elizabethtown, Kentucky. They have no employees.

Respondents are affiliated corporations that own the VICTORIA'S SECRET trademark, and operate over 750 Victoria's Secret stores, two of which are in Louisville, Kentucky, a short drive from Elizabethtown. In 1998 they spent over $55 million advertising "the VICTORIA'S SECRET brand—one of moderately priced, high quality, attractively designed lingerie sold in a store setting designed to look like a woman's bedroom." App. 167, 170. They distribute 400 million copies of the Victoria's Secret catalog each year, including 39,000 in Elizabethtown. In 1998 their sales exceeded $1.5 billion.

In the February 12, 1998, edition of a weekly publication distributed to residents of the military installation at Fort Knox, Kentucky, petitioners advertised the "GRAND OPENING Just in time for Valentine's Day!" of their store "VICTOR'S SECRET" in nearby Elizabethtown. The ad featured "Intimate Lingerie *for every woman*"; "Romantic Lighting"; "Lycra Dresses"; "Pagers"; and "Adult Novelties/Gifts." *Id.,* at 209. An army colonel, who saw the ad and was offended by what he perceived to be an attempt to use a reputable company's trademark to promote the sale of "unwholesome, tawdry merchandise," sent a copy to respondents. *Id.,* at 210. Their counsel then wrote to petitioners stating that their choice of the name "Victor's Secret" for a store selling lingerie was likely to cause confusion with the well-known VICTORIA'S SECRET mark and, in addition, was likely to "dilute the distinctiveness" of the mark. *Id.,* at 190–191. They requested the immediate discontinuance of the use of the name "and any variations thereof." *Ibid.* In response, petitioners changed the name of their store to "Victor's Little Secret." Because that change did not satisfy respondents, they promptly filed this action in Federal District Court.

The complaint contained four separate claims: (1) for trademark infringement alleging that petitioners' use of their trade name was "likely to cause confusion and/or mistake in violation of 15 U.S.C. §1114(1)"; (2) for unfair competition alleging misrepresentation in violation of §1125(a); (3) for "federal dilution" in violation of the FTDA; and (4) for trademark infringement and unfair competition in violation of the common law of Kentucky. *Id.,* at 15, 20–23. In the dilution count, the complaint alleged that petitioners' conduct was "likely to blur and erode the distinctiveness" and "tarnish the reputation" of the VICTORIA'S SECRET trademark. *Ibid.*

After discovery the parties filed cross-motions for summary judgment. The record contained uncontradicted affidavits and deposition testimony describing the vast size of respondents' business, the value of the VICTORIA'S SECRET name, and descriptions of the items sold in the respective parties' stores. Respondents sell a "complete line of lingerie" and related items, each of which bears a VICTORIA'S SECRET label or tag.[14] Peti-

---

14. Respondents described their business as follows: "Victoria's Secret stores sell a complete line of lingerie, women's undergarments and nightwear, robes, caftans and kimonos, slippers, sachets,

tioners sell a wide variety of items, including adult videos, "adult novelties," and lingerie.[15] Victor Moseley stated in an affidavit that women's lingerie represented only about five per cent of their sales. *Id.,* at 131. In support of their motion for summary judgment, respondents submitted an affidavit by an expert in marketing who explained "the enormous value" of respondents' mark. *Id.,* at 195–205. Neither he, nor any other witness, expressed any opinion concerning the impact, if any, of petitioners' use of the name "Victor's Little Secret" on that value.

Finding that the record contained no evidence of actual confusion between the parties' marks, the District Court concluded that "no likelihood of confusion exists as a matter of law" and entered summary judgment for petitioners on the infringement and unfair competition claims. With respect to the FTDA claim, however, the court ruled for respondents.

Noting that petitioners did not challenge Victoria Secret's claim that its mark is "famous," the only question it had to decide was whether petitioners' use of their mark diluted the quality of respondents' mark. Reasoning from the premise that dilution "corrodes" a trademark either by " 'blurring its product identification or by damaging positive associations that have attached to it,' " the court first found the two marks to be sufficiently similar to cause dilution, and then found "that Defendants' mark dilutes Plaintiffs' mark because of its tarnishing effect upon the Victoria's Secret mark." It therefore enjoined petitioners "from using the mark 'Victor's Little Secret' on the basis that it causes dilution of the distinctive quality of the Victoria's Secret mark." The court did not, however, find that any "blurring" had occurred. *Ibid.*

The Court of Appeals for the Sixth Circuit affirmed. 259 F.3d 464 (2001). In a case decided shortly after the entry of the District Court's judgment in this case, the Sixth Circuit had adopted the standards for determining dilution under the FDTA that were enunciated by the Second Circuit in *Nabisco, Inc.* v. *PF Brands, Inc.,* 191 F.3d 208 (1999). *See Kellogg Co.* v. *Exxon Corp.,* 209 F.3d 562 (CA6 2000). In order to apply those standards, it was necessary to discuss two issues that the District Court had not specifically addressed—whether respondents' mark is "distinctive,"[16] and whether relief could be granted before dilution has actually occurred.[17] With respect to the first issue, the court rejected

---

lingerie bags, hanging bags, candles, soaps, cosmetic brushes, atomizers, bath products and fragrances." *Id.,* at 168.

15. In answer to an interrogatory, petitioners stated that they "sell novelty action clocks, patches, temporary tattoos, stuffed animals, coffee mugs, leather biker wallets, zippo lighters, diet formula, diet supplements, jigsaw puzzles, whyss, handcufs*[sic]*, hosiery bubble machines, greeting cards, calendars, incense burners, car air fresheners, sunglasses, ball caps, jewelry, candles, lava lamps, blacklights, fiber optic lights, rock and roll prints, lingerie, pagers, candy, adult video tapes, adult novelties, t-shirts, etc." *Id.,* at 87.

16. "It is quite clear that the statute intends distinctiveness, in addition to fame, as an essential element. The operative language defining the tort requires that 'the [junior] person's ... use ... cause dilution of the distinctive quality of the [senior] mark.' 15 U.S.C. §1125(c)(1). There can be no dilution of a mark's distinctive quality unless the mark is distinctive." *Nabisco, Inc.* v. *PF Brands, Inc.,* 191 F.3d 208, 216 (CA2 1999).

17. The Second Circuit explained why it did not believe "actual dilution" need be proved:

"Relying on a recent decision by the Fourth Circuit, Nabisco also asserts that proof of dilution under the FTDA requires proof of an 'actual, consummated harm.' *Ringling Bros.-Barnum & Bailey Combined Shows, Inc.* v. *Utah Division of Travel Dev.,* 170 F.3d 449, 464 (4th Cir. 1999). We reject the argument because we disagree with the Fourth Circuit's interpretation of the statute.

"It is not clear which of two positions the Fourth Circuit adopted by its requirement of proof of 'actual dilution.' *Id.* The narrower position would be that courts may not infer dilution from 'contextual factors (degree of mark and product similarity, etc.),' but must in-the argument that VICTORIA'S SECRET could not be distinctive because "secret" is an ordinary word used by hundreds of lingerie concerns. The court concluded that the entire mark was "arbitrary and fanciful" and therefore deserving of a high level of trademark protection. 259 F.3d at 470. On the second issue, the court relied on a distinction suggested by this sentence in the House Report: "Confusion leads to immediate injury, while dilution is an infection, which if allowed to spread, will inevitably destroy the advertising value of the mark." H. R. Rep. No. 104-374, p. 1030 (1995). This statement, coupled with the difficulty of proving actual harm, lent support to the court's ultimate conclusion that the evidence in this case sufficiently established "dilution." 259 F.3d, at 475–477. In sum, the Court of Appeals held:

> "While no consumer is likely to go to the Moseleys' store expecting to find Victoria's Secret's famed Miracle Bra, consumers who hear the name 'Victor's Little Secret' are likely automatically to think of the more famous store and link it to the Moseleys' adult-toy, gag gift, and lingerie shop. This, then, is a classic instance of dilution by tarnishing (associating the Victoria's Secret name with sex toys and lewd coffee mugs) and by blurring (linking the chain with a single, unauthorized establishment). Given this conclusion, it follows that Victoria's Secret would prevail in a dilution analysis, even without an exhaustive consideration of all ten of the *Nabisco* factors." *Id.*, at 477.

In reaching that conclusion the Court of Appeals expressly rejected the holding of the Fourth Circuit in *Ringling Bros.-Barnum & Bailey Combined Shows, Inc.* v. *Utah Div. of Travel Development,* 170 F.3d 449 (1999). In that case, which involved a claim that Utah's use on its license plates of the phrase "greatest *snow* on earth" was causing dilution of the "greatest *show* on earth," the court had concluded "that to establish dilution of a famous mark under the federal Act requires proof that (1) a defendant has made use of a junior mark sufficiently similar to the famous mark to evoke in a relevant universe of consumers a mental association of the two that (2) has caused (3) actual economic harm to the famous mark's economic value by lessening its former selling power as an advertising agent for its goods or services." *Id.*, at 461 (emphasis added). Because other Circuits have also expressed differing views about the "actual harm" issue, we granted certiorari to resolve the conflict. 535 U.S. 985 (2002).

II

Traditional trademark infringement law is a part of the broader law of unfair competition, *see Hanover Star Milling Co.* v. *Metcalf,* 240 U.S. 403, 413, 60 L. Ed. 713, 36 S. Ct. 357, 1916 Dec. Comm'r Pat. 265 (1916), that has its sources in English common law, and was largely codified in the Trademark Act of 1946 (Lanham Act). *See* B. Pattishall, D. Hilliard, & J. Welch, Trademarks and Unfair Competition 2 (4th ed. 2000) ("The United States took the [trademark and unfair competition] law of England as its own"). That law broadly prohibits uses of trademarks, trade names, and trade dress that are likely to cause confusion about the source of a product or service. *See* 15 U.S.C. §§1114, 1125(a)(1)(A). Infringement law protects consumers from being misled by the use of infringing marks and also protects producers from unfair practices by an "imitating competitor." *Qualitex Co.* v. *Jacobson Products Co.,* 514 U.S. 159, 163–164, 131 L. Ed. 2d 248, 115 S. Ct. 1300 (1995).

---

stead rely on evidence of 'actual loss of revenues' or the 'skillfully constructed consumer survey.' *Id.* at 457, 464–65. This strikes us as an arbitrary and unwarranted limitation on the methods of proof." *Nabisco,* 191 F.3d at 223.

Because respondents did not appeal the District Court's adverse judgement on counts 1, 2, and 4 of their complaint, we decide the case on the assumption that the Moseleys' use of the name "Victor's Little Secret" neither confused any consumers or potential consumers, nor was likely to do so. Moreover, the disposition of those counts also makes it appropriate to decide the case on the assumption that there was no significant competition between the adversaries in this case. Neither the absence of any likelihood of confusion nor the absence of competition, however, provides a defense to the statutory dilution claim alleged in count 3 of the complaint.

Unlike traditional infringement law, the prohibitions against trademark dilution are not the product of common-law development, and are not motivated by an interest in protecting consumers. The seminal discussion of dilution is found in Frank Schechter's 1927 law review article concluding "that the preservation of the uniqueness of a trademark should constitute the only rational basis for its protection." Rational Basis of Trademark Protection, 40 Harv. L. Rev. 813, 831. Schechter supported his conclusion by referring to a German case protecting the owner of the well-known trademark "Odol" for mouthwash from use on various noncompeting steel products. That case, and indeed the principal focus of the Schechter article, involved an established arbitrary mark that had been "added to rather than withdrawn from the human vocabulary" and an infringement that made use of the identical mark. *Id.,* at 829.

Some 20 years later Massachusetts enacted the first state statute protecting trademarks from dilution. It provided:

> "Likelihood of injury to business reputation or of dilution of the distinctive quality of a trade name or trade-mark shall be a ground for injunctive relief in cases of trade-mark infringement or unfair competition notwithstanding the absence of competition between the parties or of confusion as to the source of goods or services." 1947 Mass. Acts, p. 300, ch. 307.

Notably, that statute, unlike the "Odol" case, prohibited both the likelihood of "injury to business reputation" and "dilution." It thus expressly applied to both "tarnishment" and "blurring." At least 25 States passed similar laws in the decades before the FTDA was enacted in 1995. *See* Restatement (Third) of Unfair Competition §25, Statutory Note (1995).

III

In 1988, when Congress adopted amendments to the Lanham Act, it gave consideration to an antidilution provision. During the hearings on the 1988 amendments, objections to that provision based on a concern that it might have applied to expression protected by the First Amendment were voiced and the provision was deleted from the amendments. H. R. Rep. No. 100-1028 (1988). The bill, H. R. 1295, 104th Cong., 1st Sess., that was introduced in the House in 1995, and ultimately enacted as the FTDA, included two exceptions designed to avoid those concerns: a provision allowing "fair use" of a registered mark in comparative advertising or promotion, and the provision that noncommercial use of a mark shall not constitute dilution. *See* 15 U.S.C. §1125(c)(4).

On July 19, 1995, the Subcommittee on Courts and Intellectual Property of the House Judiciary Committee held a 1-day hearing on H. R. 1295. No opposition to the bill was voiced at the hearing and, with one minor amendment that extended protection to unregistered as well as registered marks, the subcommittee endorsed the bill and it passed the House unanimously. The committee's report stated that the "purpose of H. R. 1295 is to protect famous trademarks from subsequent uses that blur the distinctiveness of the mark or tarnish or disparage it, even in the absence of a likelihood of confusion." H. R. Rep. No. 104-374, p. 1029 (1995). As examples of dilution, it stated that "the use of DUPONT shoes, BUICK aspirin, and KODAK pianos would be actionable under this legislation." *Id.,* at 1030. In the Senate an identical bill, S. 1513, 104th Cong., 1st Sess., was introduced on December 29, 1995, and passed on the same day by voice vote without any hearings. In his explanation of the bill, Senator Hatch also stated that it was intended "to protect famous trademarks from subsequent uses that blur the distinctiveness of the mark or tarnish or disparage it," and referred to the Dupont Shoes, Buick aspirin, and Kodak piano examples, as well as to the Schechter law review article. 141 Cong. Rec. 38559–38561 (1995).

IV

The VICTORIA'S SECRET mark is unquestionably valuable and petitioners have not challenged the conclusion that it qualifies as a "famous mark" within the meaning of the statute. Moreover, as we understand their submission, petitioners do not contend that the statutory protection is confined to identical uses of famous marks, or that the statute should be construed more narrowly in a case such as this. Even if the legislative history might lend some support to such a contention, it surely is not compelled by the statutory text.

The District Court's decision in this case rested on the conclusion that the name of petitioners' store "tarnished" the reputation of respondents' mark, and the Court of Appeals relied on both "tarnishment" and "blurring" to support its affirmance. Petitioners have not disputed the relevance of tarnishment, presumably because that concept was prominent in litigation brought under state antidilution statutes and because it was mentioned in the legislative history. Whether it is actually embraced by the statutory text, however, is another matter. Indeed, the contrast between the state statutes, which expressly refer to both "injury to business reputation" and to "dilution of the distinctive quality of a trade name or trademark," and the federal statute which refers only to the latter, arguably supports a narrower reading of the FTDA. *See* Klieger, Trademark Dilution: The Whittling Away of the Rational Basis for Trademark Protection, 58 U. Pitt. L. Rev. 789, 812–813, and n. 132 (1997).

The contrast between the state statutes and the federal statute, however, sheds light on the precise question that we must decide. For those state statutes, like several provisions in the federal Lanham Act, repeatedly refer to a "likelihood" of harm, rather than to a completed harm. The relevant text of the FTDA, quoted in full in note 1, *supra,* provides that "the owner of a famous mark" is entitled to injunctive relief against another person's commercial use of a mark or trade name if that use "*causes dilution* of the distinctive quality" of the famous mark. 15 U.S.C. §1125(c)(1) (emphasis added). This text unambiguously requires a showing of actual dilution, rather than a likelihood of dilution.

This conclusion is fortified by the definition of the term "dilution" itself. That definition provides:

> "The term 'dilution' means the lessening of the capacity of a famous mark to identify and distinguish goods or services, regardless of the presence or absence of—

> "(1) competition between the owner of the famous mark and other parties, or

> "(2) likelihood of confusion, mistake, or deception." §1127.

The contrast between the initial reference to an actual "lessening of the capacity" of the mark, and the later reference to a "likelihood of confusion, mistake, or deception" in the second caveat confirms the conclusion that actual dilution must be established.

Of course, that does not mean that the consequences of dilution, such as an actual loss of sales or profits, must also be proved. To the extent that language in the Fourth Circuit's opinion in the *Ringling Bros.* case suggests otherwise, *see* 170 F.3d at 460–465, we disagree. We do agree, however, with that court's conclusion that, at least where the marks at issue are not identical, the mere fact that consumers mentally associate the junior user's mark with a famous mark is not sufficient to establish actionable dilution. As the facts of that case demonstrate, such mental association will not necessarily reduce the capacity of the famous mark to identify the goods of its owner, the statutory requirement for dilution under the FTDA. For even though Utah drivers may be reminded of the circus when they see a license plate referring to the "greatest *snow* on earth," it by no means follows that they will associate "the greatest show on earth" with skiing or snow sports, or associate it less strongly or exclusively with the circus. "Blurring" is not a necessary consequence of mental association. (Nor, for that matter, is "tarnishing.")

The record in this case establishes that an army officer who saw the advertisement of the opening of a store named "Victor's Secret" did make the mental association with "Victoria's Secret," but it also shows that he did not therefore form any different impression of the store that his wife and daughter had patronized. There is a complete absence of evidence of any lessening of the capacity of the VICTORIA'S SECRET mark to identify and distinguish goods or services sold in Victoria's Secret stores or advertised in its catalogs. The officer was offended by the ad, but it did not change his conception of Victoria's Secret. His offense was directed entirely at petitioners, not at respondents. Moreover, the expert retained by respondents had nothing to say about the impact of petitioners' name on the strength of respondents' mark.

Noting that consumer surveys and other means of demonstrating actual dilution are expensive and often unreliable, respondents and their *amici* argue that evidence of an actual "lessening of the capacity of a famous mark to identify and distinguish goods or services," §1127, may be difficult to obtain. It may well be, however, that direct evidence of dilution such as consumer surveys will not be necessary if actual dilution can reliably be proven through circumstantial evidence—the obvious case is one where the junior and senior marks are identical. Whatever difficulties of proof may be entailed, they are not an acceptable reason for dispensing with proof of an essential element of a statutory violation. The evidence in the present record is not sufficient to support the summary judgment on the dilution count. The judgment is therefore reversed, and the case is remanded for further proceedings consistent with this opinion.

It is so ordered.

Justice Kennedy, concurring.

As of this date, few courts have reviewed the statute we are considering, the Federal Trademark Dilution Act, 15 U.S.C. §1125(c), and I agree with the Court that the evidentiary showing required by the statute can be clarified on remand. The conclusion that the VICTORIA'S SECRET mark is a famous mark has not been challenged throughout the litigation, *ante*, at 6, 13, and seems not to be in question. The remaining issue is what factors are to be considered to establish dilution.

For this inquiry, considerable attention should be given, in my view, to the word "capacity" in the statutory phrase that defines dilution as "the lessening of the capacity of a famous mark to identify and distinguish goods or services." 15 U.S.C. §1127. When a competing mark is first adopted, there will be circumstances when the case can turn on the probable consequences its commercial use will have for the famous mark. In this respect, the word "capacity" imports into the dilution inquiry both the present and the potential power of the famous mark to identify and distinguish goods, and in some cases the fact that this power will be diminished could suffice to show dilution. Capacity is defined as "the power or ability to hold, receive, or accommodate." Webster's Third New International Dictionary 330 (1961); *see also* Webster's New International Dictionary 396 (2d ed. 1949) ("Power of receiving, containing, or absorbing"); 2 Oxford English Dictionary 857 (2d ed. 1989) ("Ability to receive or contain; holding power"); American Heritage Dictionary 275 (4th ed. 2000) ("The ability to receive, hold, or absorb"). If a mark will erode or lessen the power of the famous mark to give customers the assurance of quality and the full satisfaction they have in knowing they have purchased goods bearing the famous mark, the elements of dilution may be established.

Diminishment of the famous mark's capacity can be shown by the probable consequences flowing from use or adoption of the competing mark. This analysis is confirmed by the statutory authorization to obtain injunctive relief. 15 U.S.C. §1125(c)(2). The essential role of injunctive relief is to "prevent future wrong, although no right has yet been violated." *Swift & Co. v. United States,* 276 U.S. 311, 326, 72 L. Ed. 587, 48 S. Ct. 311 (1928). Equity principles encourage those who are injured to assert their rights promptly. A holder of a famous mark threatened with diminishment of the mark's capacity to serve its purpose should not be forced to wait until the damage is done and the distinctiveness of the mark has been eroded.

In this case, the District Court found that petitioners' trademark had tarnished the VICTORIA'S SECRET mark. App. to Pet. for Cert. 38a–39a. The Court of Appeals affirmed this conclusion and also found dilution by blurring. 259 F.3d 464, 477 (CA6 2001). The Court's opinion does not foreclose injunctive relief if respondents on remand present sufficient evidence of either blurring or tarnishment.

With these observations, I join the opinion of the Court.

———————

Note

1. The original FTDA was silent on whether or not dilution could be a grounds for opposing or cancelling another's trademark registration or application. The TTAB held that it could not. In 1999, Congress amended the Lanham Act to specifically allow dilution to be used as a grounds for opposing or cancelling a trademark registration or application. However, the amendment only applies to marks that were famous at the time the use commenced. *Any* trademark use prior to the petitioner's mark becoming famous will defeat a cancellation or opposition claim. *See Enterprise Rent-a-Car Co. v. Advantage Rent-a-Car Inc.,* 330 F. 3d 1333 (Fed. Cir. 2003), *cert. denied,* 1245 Ct. 958 (2003).

———————

Note on Dilution

The federal dilution cause of action under the Lanham Act is, at the time of this writing, only twelve years old; however, it has sparked significant controversy among academics and a substantial amount of litigation. An excellent treatise on the subject has also been written: David Welkowitz, TRADEMARK DILUTION: FEDERAL, STATE, AND INTERNATIONAL LAW (2002). Dilution cases now make up a substantial number of all trademark cases filed. There seems to be a bit of a boom in dilution litigation.

In adopting the FTDA, the United States Congress concluded that a nationwide, consistent scheme to protect the distinctiveness of trademarks from gradual erosion was an important objective. Some commentators, however, argue that the dilution protection contemplated in the FTDA is inconsistent with the common law origins of the United States trademark system. They argue that the common law did not protect trademarks from dilution. The legislative history to the Lanham Act itself expressly states that the statute is a codification of the common law and not an expansion of it. Therefore, the FTDA may not be consistent with the objectives of the common law of trademarks. More importantly, some commentators also argue that the FTDA grants property-like rights in trademarks that were never previously recognized by the Supreme Court. As such, the justification of dilution protection itself may be in serious question. *See, e.g.*, Kenneth L. Port, *The Unnatural Expansion of Trademark Rights: Is a Federal Dilution Statute Necessary?*, 18 SETON HALL LEG. J. 433 (1994); Kenneth L. Port, *The Congressional Expansion of American Trademark Law: A Civil Law System in the Making*, 35 WAKE FOREST L. REV. 827 (2000).

Yet, the FTDA today plays a large role in trademark litigation and it is likely to do so in the future. To be certain, the FTDA is the largest expansion of federal trademark rights since the enactment of the Lanham Act. Is it truly necessary? Are there other alternatives available to protect famous marks from use on non-competing products? Does the federal judiciary and the United States Congress share a consistent view of dilution protection?

Additionally, the Supreme Court in *Victoria's Secret* in 2003 appears to have attempted to rein in the expansion of dilution law. That is, there appears to be a serious tension between the courts and the Congress regarding the scope of the trademark right. Who is right?

Victoria's Secret held that the test for dilution is not a "likelihood of dilution," but rather "actual dilution." The Court implied that when two marks are not identical, more evidence would be required to establish dilution than merely a "mental association" by consumers. This, potentially, is a significant step in controlling the expansion of the dilution principle.

However, will dilution really now be more difficult to establish?[18]

To be sure the Ninth Circuit has implied exactly this. In vacating and remanding one finding of dilution, that court stated that *Victoria's Secret* "expanded on the requirements for a trademark dilution claim ..."[19] In at least one case, this seems to have led the court to more strict scrutiny of the dilution claim. In *Tommy Hilfiger Licensing, Inc. v. Goody's Family Clothing*,[20] in a case involving proven counterfeit sales of Tommy Hilfiger knock-off clothing, that court found that evidence of similarity to a famous Hilfiger mark, evidence of intent by the defendant to confuse, and evidence of the strength of Hilfiger's mark did not present reliable circumstantial evidence of actual dilution.

---

18. Some have argued that this will be the case in the future. Sue Ann Momta, Case Note, *Victor's Little Secret Prevails (For Now) over Victoria's Secret: The Supreme Court Requires Proof of Actual Dilution under the FTDA*, 19 SANTA CLARA COMP. & HIGH TECH. L. J. 551 (2003). Some argue that prevailing on a dilution claim is "already a difficult task". Steve Meleen, et al., *Recent Developments in Trademark Law: Elusive Dilution and Sorting the Resulting Confusion*, 11 TEX. INTELL. PROP. L. J. 351 (2003).

19. Horphag Research Ltd. V. Mario Pellegrini, 328 F.3d 1108 (9th Cir. 2003).

20. 2003 U.S. Dist. Lexis 8788 (N.D. Georgia 2003).

Therefore, on one hand, it does appear that *Victoria's Secret* has had the effect of raising the bar in establishing actionable dilution.[21] On the other hand, because Justice Stevens' opinion in *Victoria's Secret* did not articulate clear standards of what it meant by "actual proof," this may turn out to be an exercise in semantics as opposed to a change in the amount of proof required to sustain a dilution claim.

For example, in *Four Seasons Hotels & Resorts B.V. v. Four Seasons Hotels (Barbados) Ltd.*, when the defendant developer of the famous hotel chain failed to comply with quality control standards in a license agreement, the court found dilution and stated as follows:

> [Defendant's actions] diminished the capacity of the mark to distinguish the high quality of the Plaintiffs' services. In this regard, the record reflects evidence of actual harm to Four Seasons in the form of customers who complained that the Caracas hotel 'wasn't a Four Seasons'... [22]

Similarly, in *Pinehurst v. Brian Wick*,[23] the court found that the defendant's prior registration of the domain name "PinehurstResorts.com" (and related domain names) amounted to actual damage to the plaintiff because the defendant's domain name registrations prevented the plaintiff from engaging in electronic commerce using those specific domain names (even though alternatives were available) thereby diminishing the economic value of the plaintiff's mark. The court reached this conclusion as a matter of fact without any economic or statistical evidence whatsoever. Rather, the court presumed that because the defendant had registered domain names that contained the plaintiff's famous marks that some (although unquantified) actual harm was realized by the plaintiff.

Also, although Justice Stevens' opinion in *Victoria Secret's* implied that actual evidence of dilution was required when the two marks at issue were not identical, one court has held that just because the marks are identical does not excuse the plaintiff from its burden of showing actual evidence of dilution; the court expressly rejected the plaintiff's reading of *Victoria's Secret* to the contrary.[24]

Finally, the most perplexing development in light of *Victoria's Secret* is the TTAB's announced position on the matter. The TTAB has held that, although *Victoria's Secret* requires a showing of actual dilution in civil causes of action, in opposition proceedings before the Board, the standard will remain a likelihood of dilution.[25] The Board determined that if actual dilution were the standard, no oppositions could be sustained if the mark at issue was the subject of an intent-to-use application or an application under §44 of the

---

21. *See also, Reed Elsevier, Inc. V. Thelaw.net Corp.*, 269 F. Supp. 2d 942 (S.D. Ohio 2003) (rejecting defendant's motion to dismiss under Rule 12(b)(6) stating that plaintiff "in theory" had stated its cause of action but opining that, in light of *Victoria's Secret*, it is "extremely difficult to prevail on such under the Lanham Act"); *Nike Inc. V. Variety Wholesalers, Inc.*, 2003 U.S. Dist. Lexis 13310 (S.D. Georgia 2003) (dilution claim sustained because identical or nearly identical marks are at issue as required by *Victoria Secret*).

22. 267 F. Supp. 2d 1268, 1332 (S.D. Fla. 2003).

23. 256 F. Supp. 2d 424 (Mid. Dist. N.C. 2003).

24. *Savin Corp. v. Savin Group*, 2003 U.S. Dist. LEXIS 19220 (S.D.N.Y. 2003). The court held so even in light of the language from *Victoria's Secret* as follows:

> It may well be, however, that direct evidence of dilution such as consumer surveys will not be necessary if actual dilution can reliably be proven through circumstantial evidence— the obvious case is one where the junior and senior marks are identical.

537 U.S. 434.

25. *NASDAQ Stock Market, Inc, v. Antartica, S.r.l.*, 2003 T.T.A.B Lexis 391.

Lanham Act (also where use in the United States is not immediately necessary). The issue of how a mark not used in the United States (either because of the ITU application or its status under §44) could possibly become famous was not addressed.

Therefore, although we all expected the Supreme Court in *Victoria's Secret* to provide some guidance on the evasive right of trademark dilution, to overuse a cliche of the field, the Court added to, rather than subtracted from, the likelihood that trademark owners would be confused by the FTDA. Given the range of judicial opinions based on the FTDA cited in this brief note, this confusion seems to have infected the judiciary as well.

In 2006, the FTDA was amended to change the standard for dilution to a "likelihood of dilution," specifically overruling the Victoria's Secret Case. See, Trademark Dilution Revision Act, 109 P.L. 312, 120 Stat. 1730 (2006) (amending 15 U.S.C. §§ 1125(c), 1052(f) and 1127). As is made clear in the above cases, this act changed the definition of a famous mark, created explicit rights of blurring and tarnishment and did away with the notion of niche fame. As the TDRA took effect in 2006, it is difficult to state what its impact will be with any precision. One thing is for certain: the TDRA is a manifestation of the tension that has developed between the courts and Congress over the scope, nature and import of the dilution right in the United States.

---

4. Academic View of Dilution

Robert G. Bone, *A Skeptical View of the Trademark Dilution Revision Act*
11 Intell. Prop. L. Bull. 187 (2007).

The Trademark Dilution Revision Act ("TDRA"), adopted on October 6, 2006, is the result of an almost two-year campaign to overturn the Supreme Court's 2003 decision in Moseley v. V Secret Catalogue, Inc. The TDRA responds to Moseley in two ways. First, and most important, it makes clear that a plaintiff need not prove "actual dilution" to establish liability under Section 43(c), but can obtain injunctive relief by showing that a defendant's use is "likely to cause dilution." Second, it makes clear that Section 43(c) covers tarnishment as well as blurring, countering a suggestion in Moseley that the language of the statute might not include tarnishment.

The TDRA does more than address the Moseley decision. It makes clear that Section 43(c) includes descriptive marks with secondary meaning as well as inherently distinctive marks, thereby reversing a line of lower court decisions narrowly interpreting the statute. It explicitly addresses dilution for trade dress by establishing that the owner has the burden of proof on non-functionality and fame when the trade dress is unregistered. And it adds an express parody and criticism exception.

While some of its provisions are improvements, the TDRA as a whole represents a setback for American trademark law. By signaling congressional interest in shoring up dilution liability, the TDRA opens the door to more aggressive judicial application of the statute and broader interpretation. A stronger Section 43(c) threatens to sever trademark law from its policy moorings and send it in directions that risk high social costs.

This brief article argues that the problem with the TDRA, and the original Section 43(c) that it amends, is the same as the problem with dilution law more generally. Dilution, and especially dilution in its blurring form, lacks a coherent policy foundation. The lack of clear normative direction gives particularly wide latitude to industry groups to influence the legislative process in ways that serve their private interests at the expense of the public interest.

The following remarks first briefly review the principal policy arguments for dilution protection and then examine the major provisions of the TDRA in light of this policy analysis.

I. Dilution Policies

Trademarks serve as source-identifiers. When a consumer buys a tube of CREST toothpaste, for example, she relies on the CREST mark to indicate that the particular toothpaste tube comes from the same source as every other toothpaste tube labeled CREST. Because of this, she can readily access information about the toothpaste acquired through advertising, personal experience, and word of mouth. In this way, trademarks reduce consumer search costs. Moreover, by making it easier for consumers to access information about products, trademarks also make it easier for sellers to communicate information about hidden product features, which helps support incentives to maintain, and even improve, product quality.

Core trademark law secures these social benefits by protecting trademarks against uses that risk source or sponsorship confusion. Consumer confusion undermines the information transmission function of a mark by making it difficult for consumers to rely on the mark as a source-identifier and thus a symbol of brand or firm quality.

Trademark law has also manifested a concern for sellers historically, but seller harm alone was normally thought insufficient for liability in the absence of some form of consumer confusion. For example, a mark owner might complain about losing sales or suffering reputation harm, but ordinarily these harms were actionable only if they resulted from the confusion of consumers. To be sure, courts at times have been influenced to find liability by the perceived unfairness of defendant's free riding on the mark owner's goodwill, but preventing free riding has never been fully accepted as an independent ground for trademark liability.

Against this background, it is apparent why dilution has been an extremely controversial doctrine ever since Frank Schechter first introduced the idea to American trademark law in his famous 1927 article, The Rational Basis of Trademark Protection. Dilution imposes liability in the absence of any risk of consumer confusion and thus has shaky support in trademark's traditional information transmission policies. The arguments for dilution have focused historically on protecting the seller's goodwill and the mark's power to attract consumers. But this raises the critical question: Why should trademark law protect goodwill and selling power in the absence of consumer confusion?

The reasons traditionally given for protection vary with the type of dilution. There are two conventional types, both of which are actionable under Section 43(c): dilution by tarnishment, and dilution by blurring. In addition, it has been suggested that dilution might extend to preventing free riding on goodwill—dilution by free riding—although this theory has never been expressly recognized in dilution law and is not included explicitly in Section 43(c). The following discussion examines the major policy arguments for each type of dilution.

a. dilution by tarnishment

Dilution by tarnishment is the least problematic of the three types of dilution. Tarnishment refers to a use that clashes with the meanings and images the trademark owner has cultivated in the mark—or in the language of the TDRA, a use that "harms the reputation of the famous mark." An example is TIFFANY used in connection with a greasy spoon restaurant or a strip club. These associations so strongly clash with the images and feelings associated with the TIFFANY mark that consumers are likely to have difficulty evoking the mark's positive meanings in as clear and strong a way.

It is not too difficult to justify the tarnishment prong on information transmission grounds, although one must stretch the function of marks a bit to do it. The clashing associations generated by the defendant's conflicting use distort the information that the mark conveys. Moreover, in our TIFFANY strip club example, it seems reasonable to assume that the tarnishing associations would not entirely disappear over time, leaving consumers with a somewhat soured impression of the TIFFANY mark inconsistent with what the mark is supposed to convey.

The analysis is not quite this simple, however. While the argument sounds as though it is about consumer search costs, it is actually about protecting the integrity of the product itself and ensuring product diversity. The information transmission/search cost argument in its simple form assumes that a mark is distinct from the product it brands and that it conveys information about that separate product. However, the information that TIFFANY conveys, and that tarnishment harms, is not just information about a separate product; it is a large component of the product itself. Consumers do not want luxury jewelry. They want TIFFANY jewelry because of how they feel when they wear TIFFANY and because of what it says about their status and wealth. Thus, "TIFFANY jewelry" is to some extent its own product—the appearance, durability, and so on of the physical jewelry coupled with the feelings triggered and the messages conveyed by the mark itself. The latter component of the product is altered by the tarnishing use.

Trademark law is not supposed to grant exclusive rights in product features that consumers want. To be sure, it does this when it protects product design trade dress and merchandising rights, but these applications are controversial for precisely that reason. Even so, protecting TIFFANY against tarnishment fits trademark law, if somewhat awkwardly. One of the purposes of core trademark law is to support incentives to maintain and improve product quality and thus preserve a rich product diversity, and tarnishment protection does roughly the same thing. Moreover, many marks do more than convey information about a separate product. Even the CREST mark carries feelings of social confidence and cleanliness instilled by advertising and not an inherent part of the toothpaste itself. To be sure, the emotional content of the TIFFANY mark is a much larger fraction of the consumption value of TIFFANY jewelry, but the difference is, in the end, a matter of degree.

Thus, the policy case for providing some legal protection against tarnishment has weight, although it is not as strong as for confusion-based theories. Still, it is important that courts be careful about finding tarnishment. Tarnishment might produce very little consumer harm when there are relatively close substitutes for the tarnished product. Consumers unhappy with TIFFANY jewelry, for example, might just shift to another luxury brand. Moreover, famous marks often have popular meanings that extend beyond the products they brand, and those meanings invite socially valuable criticism and parody. It is important that the law carve out an exception for this type of arguably tarnishing use— just as the TDRA does—and that courts apply the exception generously.

b. dilution by blurring

Critics of dilution law focus most of their attention on dilution by blurring. Blurring refers to a use that "impairs the distinctiveness of [a] famous mark." For example, the use of TIFFANY for a luxury car is not likely to harm the reputation of TIFFANY for jewelry, but it might blur the distinctiveness of the TIFFANY mark—and especially if TIFFANY is also used for a luxury hotel, high-end restaurant, and so on.

The phenomenon of blurring is poorly understood. Unfortunately, this is an area of the law in which metaphor often substitutes for hard analysis. Nevertheless, a number of policy arguments have been offered to justify the doctrine. Some of these arguments focus on special situations, such as enjoining counterfeit goods and protecting the scarcity and exclusivity of prestige items like the ROLEX watch. The most intense debate, however, has to do with using blurring law to prevent uses of marks on unrelated products. There are three main arguments offered to support a broader doctrine: Schechter's original argument, the modern search cost argument, and the anti-free-riding argument. I shall discuss the first two here and take up the third in the following section.

1. Schechter's Argument: Protecting Selling Power

Frank Schechter, the father of American dilution law, defended a blurring theory as necessary to protect a mark's "selling power." His idea was that highly distinctive marks with strong consumer associations exert a kind of magnetic force that holds existing customers, draws in new ones, and builds goodwill, and that the law should protect the seller's interest in using marks for these purposes.

Schechter's argument continues to have enormous rhetorical appeal today, and companies invest huge sums in creating consistent brand identities on the belief that a mark has selling power. The normative question, however, is why the law should protect a mark's grip on consumers when that grip is due to factors other than information about the quality of the product (which is protected by confusion-based theories).

Schechter never addressed this question. At the time he wrote, enthusiasm for psychological advertising was nearing a peak and the practice of using psychological ads with distinctive trademarks was widespread. When he referred to a mark's "selling power," Schechter probably had in mind the emotional force of strong trademarks built up by association with psychological ads, and he seems to have assumed that the law should protect this selling power simply because private industry relied on it pervasively.

Of course, the fact a practice is widespread in an industry is not a good enough reason for the law to promote it. Private interests do not always match social interests. Moreover, today we are much more skeptical about selling power that does not have to do with product quality— irrational brand loyalty, if it exists, interferes with informed consumer choice, creates market power, and undermines efficiency. In short, protecting a mark's selling power is not by itself a good reason for protecting against blurring.

2. Search Costs

In recent years, supporters of the doctrine have developed an argument for blurring that fits the traditional information transmission function of trademarks and the related search cost rationale. According to this argument, multiple uses of the same mark on different products make it more difficult for consumers to draw an association between the mark and the plaintiff's product. The consumer must first sort among the different uses before she can make the connection, which slows her response time and increases her search costs.

This search cost argument finds some support in the cognitive psychology literature. Models of cognition suppose that the brain forms networks of association among ideas and images and that individuals retrieve particular associations by following links in the network. The more links and nodes the network has (that is, the more different products that use the same mark), the more time and effort it takes to retrieve a particular item (that is, the more time it takes consumers to isolate the correct mark-product link).

There are serious problems with this argument. For one thing, its empirical support is unconvincing. The most well known study comparing response times for undiluted and diluted marks reported about a 125 millisecond difference. As others have noted, it is difficult to see how 125 milliseconds adds much in the way of search costs. Furthermore, actual market settings often have additional cues that facilitate rapid consumer identification and retrieval and could offset some of the lag time measured in the laboratory. I suppose it might be possible that a proliferation of uses on different products could cumulatively increase search time enough to make a difference worth worrying about, but this is not at all obvious from the model or the data.

c. dilution by free riding

No dilution law expressly recognizes a cause of action simply for free riding on goodwill — and for good reason. As I, and others, have argued elsewhere, there is no persuasive economic or moral argument for trademark law to protect against free riding on goodwill. Trademark law is not about generating incentives to create new marks, and free riding by itself is perfectly acceptable on moral grounds.

Professor David Franklyn has offered the most elaborate and sophisticated defense of a remedy for free riding. Recognizing the limitations of the economic and moral arguments, he focuses on a "blended rationale" that relies on a number of different factors in addition to free riding itself, such as that the plaintiff invested a lot in creating the goodwill in its mark, that the defendant intended to and did profit substantially from its free ride, that there was no legitimate reason to use the mark, and that there were only minimal costs associated with preventing the use. He argues that these elements mutually reinforce one another to support a pragmatic judgment that as between the mark owner and the free rider, the mark owner should prevail.

There are at least three problems with Professor Franklyn's intriguing theory. First a pragmatic, all-things-considered policy judgment makes difficult policy questions too easy. For example, it is not clear from Professor Franklyn's account how combining several factors can overcome the normative deficiencies of each factor taken separately. Second, it is hard to imagine a case of free riding in which the defendant has no legitimate reason to use the mark. It is always possible to argue that use of the mark avoids duplicative investment in creating the same public associations and also benefits consumers by offering a new product with those meanings and associations attached. Third, there are always substantial costs to recognizing a dilution claim, even if only the costs of litigating the resulting lawsuits.

II. The TDRA

Even this brief overview of the policies indicates that the case for a dilution remedy — and especially for dilution by blurring and by free riding — is extremely tenuous. After the passage of the Federal Trademark Dilution Act in 1995, many courts eventually realized the problems and responded by interpreting and applying Section 43(c) narrowly. The TDRA reverses a number of these limiting interpretations and in so doing restores a broader dilution remedy that is difficult to justify on policy grounds.

Before examining the most problematic aspects of the TDRA, it is important to note two important amendments that are clearly desirable — at least as long as Congress insists on retaining some kind of dilution remedy. First, the inclusion of tarnishment makes sense. Given the stronger policy support for tarnishment than for blurring, it would be strange, indeed, if Section 43(c) protected against blurring without also protecting against tarnishment. Second, the explicit recognition of a parody exception is desirable and might even encourage judges to use the exception more aggressively.

a. likelihood of dilution

Eliminating Moseley's actual dilution requirement might appear sensible at first glance, since it codifies traditional equitable principles allowing courts to enjoin activity that threatens future harm. But the matter is not quite so simple. Preventing future harm is a good reason for injunctive relief only when the prospective harm is real and serious. In the case of dilution, however, it is unclear exactly what harm dilution creates, especially dilution by blurring, or how serious that harm actually is.

Given this uncertainty, there is a benefit to forcing plaintiffs to define the nature of the dilution risk with some care, which is exactly what the Moseley rule did. Requiring proof of actual dilution demands that judges in particular cases actually focus on the nature of the dilution, and that the parties actually debate its existence and its magnitude. Focusing attention on the dilution harm even opens up the possibility of a common law process that over time might sharpen understanding of the dilution concept and the policy reasons for protecting against it.

It is extremely unlikely that any such process will occur under the TDRA's "likelihood of dilution" rule. Given the statutory factors listed in the TDRA, a plaintiff might well prove likelihood of blurring simply by showing that its mark has strong secondary meaning and is widely recognized, that the plaintiff is the sole user of the mark, that the defendant's mark is very similar, and that consumers associate the two marks. Notice that there is no need in this analysis for the plaintiff to actually define what blurring is, determine that it actually exists, or identify any harm that it might cause. Experience with the likelihood of confusion test confirms this point—most courts tally the factors without asking about harm—as does the history of the likelihood of dilution standard under state law.

In the end, judicial determinations of likelihood of blurring will probably turn on the judges' all-things-considered moral intuitions. As experience in other areas of trademark law makes clear, these intuitive judgments are frequently unreliable. For example, a judge convinced that free riding is unfair can find likelihood of dilution without revealing her moral intuition or giving parties an opportunity to challenge it. She need only play up the factors in the balance that support her decision and downplay the factors that do not.

b. acquired as well as inherent distinctiveness

As originally conceived by Frank Schechter, the dilution theory was limited to fanciful, coined, and arbitrary marks. Schechter believed that only inherently distinctive marks were unique and distinctive enough to suffer the kind of loss in "selling power" from other uses that warranted dilution protection. For Schechter, the selling power of a descriptive mark was already diluted by the ordinary descriptive meanings it carried, and common words with descriptive meaning were likely to be used on many different products.

Congress did not expressly codify Schechter's limitation in the original Section 43(c), and many courts applied the statute to descriptive marks with strong secondary meaning just as they had done for the state anti-dilution statutes. However, the Second Circuit Court of Appeals interpreted Section 43(c) more narrowly to apply only to marks that were inherently distinctive and had acquired substantial secondary meaning. The TDRA overturns this line of precedent and makes clear that Section 43(c) covers marks that have acquired their distinctiveness through secondary meaning as well as marks that are inherently distinctive.

Whether the TDRA has it right depends on the type of dilution at stake. Tarnishment easily fits the TDRA framework. Any mark with strong secondary meaning can be tarnished whether the mark is descriptive or inherently distinctive. As for blurring, the only clearly justified application is to counterfeit goods, and those cases are also consistent with the TDRA — unless there is some reason why prestige goods would not use descriptive marks.

It is difficult to justify a dilution remedy beyond preventing tarnishment and counterfeit goods, and for that reason I would favor limiting Section 43(c) to those two types of cases. However, it appears Congress has a different view of the matter; it has chosen to extend dilution more broadly to blurring uses of marks on unrelated products. As we saw, the search cost argument, though very weak, is the only arguable policy for this extension. Yet the search cost argument does not clearly support the TDRA's application of dilution to descriptive marks.

A descriptive mark starts off with a network of associations, so consumers already face a burden sorting through the various nodes and links. This makes it unclear how much greater burden adding another node and a new link would create. Moreover, if the link that connects the mark to the plaintiff's product already stands out sharply and carries powerful product-related messages, as might be the case for descriptive marks with strong secondary meaning, consumers might have little trouble finding and following that link even when others are added to the network. Inherently distinctive marks, by contrast, start off with no network connections at all, so they might be more vulnerable to blurring (although strong secondary meaning might reduce this effect as well). If this is correct, then a blurring theory would be more appropriate for inherently distinctive than for descriptive marks.

Admittedly, this analysis is speculative. The opposite results are also possible: a descriptive mark with strong secondary meaning might be particularly sensitive to noise from other uses. In the end, firmer conclusions require a more sophisticated understanding of consumer psychology. In the face of this empirical uncertainty, I believe the better course is to choose the more restrictive alternative. Confusion-based theories already give trademarks broad protection, and it is unclear how much, if any, net benefit dilution adds. One should not expand a legal theory when the public benefits are so uncertain.

For this reason, dilution by blurring should be confined to inherently distinctive marks, contrary to the TDRA amendment. Moreover, courts should be clear that a mark actually has strong secondary meaning before giving it dilution protection.

c. dilution for trade dress

The TDRA amendment assigning the burden of proof to plaintiffs in cases with unregistered trade dress might be seen as a congressional effort to restrict the availability of dilution protection. I fear, however, that the amendment will have just the opposite effect. It sends a clear signal that Congress means to have Section 43(c) extend to trade dress, and this signal might encourage the filing of more dilution claims and perhaps also prompt broader judicial application of Section 43(c) to trade dress cases. Moreover, the elimination of Moseley's actual dilution requirement removes an impediment to weak and meritless trade dress suits by making it easier for plaintiffs to obtain preliminary injunctions and more difficult for defendants to secure summary judgments.

Before passage of the TDRA, a number of courts took a very restrictive approach to dilution protection for trade dress, especially for product design trade dress. The TDRA eases some of these limitations and opens the way for a more generous approach. This is likely to create the most serious problems for cases involving the blurring prong applied to product design. The trademark-related benefits in these cases are tenuous at best and the social costs potentially quite serious.

As for benefits, consider the effect on search costs. Every product with distinctive trade dress also has a more conventional word mark to signify source, and consumers can use that word mark as a contextual cue to help them quickly isolate the network link connecting the trade dress with the plaintiff's product. As a result, the search time benefits of prohibiting other uses of the same trade dress are likely to be even smaller than for word marks (which are very small to begin with).

Furthermore, the social costs of extending protection to trade dress are potentially very high. The main concern is that dilution law will give the trade dress owner monopoly power in the product market. The functionality doctrine is supposed to prevent this by barring trademark protection for features needed to compete. But the functionality doctrine is difficult to apply, and it is not clear how effectively it screens cases at the crucial preliminary injunction and summary judgment stages.

It is true that removing blurring protection for product design trade dress might leave some deserving cases without relief, but every legal rule has its costs. The benefits seem so uncertain and the risks so serious that an absolute bar makes sense — at least until someone is able to make a convincing demonstration that the social benefits do in fact exceed the costs.

III. Conclusion

The TDRA, on balance, expands the scope of Section 43(c) relative to pre-TDRA law, and it does so without a careful policy analysis. Expanding dilution law, even with a safe harbor for parody and criticism, risks creating high social costs without corresponding benefits. We need to take a closer look at dilution and in particular the extremely problematic blurring prong. Legal protection should be given only when it is clearly justified on policy grounds, and this means we should err on the side of a narrow statute rather than a broad one that has flimsy support.

Notes

1. The majority of academic commentators' perspective regarding dilution law is negative. The Supreme Court seems skeptical. Congress' view, expressed through the TDRA, seems to be entirely positive. Why is there such divergent views on something that appears so important? The judicial resistance is likely to continue under the TDRA. Graeme B. Dinwoodie & Mark D. Janis, *Dilution's (Still) Uncertain Future*, 105 MICH. L. REV. FIRST IMPRESSIONS 98 (2006).

2. Some academic support of federal dilution law does exist. Professor Barton Beebe argues the TDRA "represents a sensible and progressive reform of American federal antidilution protection." Barton Beebe, *A Defense of the New Federal Trademark Antidilution Law*, 16 FORDHAM INTELL. PROP., MEDIA & ENT. L.J. 1143, 1144 (2006). Another pro-dilution argument is that anti-dilution laws will protect the consumer's psychological attachment

to brand names. Shahar J. Dilbary, *Famous Trademarks and Rational Basis for Protecting "Irrational Beliefs"*, 14 Geo. Mason L. Rev. 605 (2007).

3. Japan seems to be in a similar state of confusion over its dilution laws. While Japanese trademark law is highly predictable and coherent, Japanese trademark dilution law is in disarray. Kenneth L. Port, *Trademark Dilution Law in Japan*, 4 Northwestern Journal of Technology and Intellectual Property 228 (2006).

4. What about the consumer perspective? How does the consumer factor into dilution analysis? *See, e.g.*, Jacob Jacoby, *The Psychological Foundations of Trademark Law: Secondary Meaning, Genericism, Fame, Confusion and Dilution*, 91 Trademark Rep. 1013 (2001); *Experimental Design and the Selection of Controls in Trademark and Deceptive Advertising Surveys*, 92 Trademark Rep. 890. (2002).

Chapter XII

Domain Names (Section 43(d))

A. The Problem: Cybersquatting

Cybersquatting is the practice of registering a word as a domain name in which some entity claims trademark rights. The earliest and best known examples are summarized in the article by Professor Burk below. These early cases arose at the infancy of the Internet. They are now considered some of the first instances of cybersquatting. In fact, these examples gave rise to much of the doctrine and policy that is the focus of this chapter.

Dan L. Burk, *Trademarks along the Infobahn: A First Look at the Emerging Law of Cybermarks*
1 Rich. J. L. & Tech. 1 (1995)*

* * *

MTV v. Curry

Perhaps the most notorious Internet trademark dispute to date is that involving Adam Curry and the MTV cable television channel. Curry was formerly employed as a video jockey, or "VJ" host on MTV. Curry organized an Internet site registered as "mtv.com" during his employment period, apparently with the knowledge and approval of MTV. The site was devoted to discussion of topics related to Curry's vocation, including popular culture, entertainment, and celebrities. He also established a considerable net presence by writing and circulating the "Cybersleaze Report," an electronic newsletter devoted to celebrity gossip. Curry's fame both on and off the Internet generated a high volume of traffic at the mtv.com site.

In 1993, Curry and MTV parted ways, apparently with some rancor. Among other items of dispute, MTV demanded that Curry surrender or disable the mtv.com site because it carried the designation "mtv." Curry, who had registered the site's domain name under his own name, refused to do so. The parties moved their dispute to court. Pending trial, Curry suspended his operations at mtv.com and moved to a new and equally chic site registered as "metaverse.com." The parties quietly settled the dispute on March 24, 1995, and it appears that MTV is now in control of the mtv.com domain.

Kaplan v. Princeton Review

Another Internet trademark dispute involved the Princeton Review, a purveyor of courses and materials to prepare students for standardized aptitude tests such as the SAT, LSAT, and GRE. In 1994, Princeton Review determined that its business could benefit from establishing Internet services where students could discuss test-taking strategies, acquire information and materials concerning aptitude tests, and most importantly, obtain promotional literature about Princeton Review's services. The company subsequently established such an Internet site, and registered several domain names with the InterNIC, including "princeton.com" and "review.com."

Princeton Review also registered the domain name "kaplan.com," and established an Internet site under that name. Not surprisingly, the "Stanley Kaplan Review" is Princeton Review's chief competitor in the market for standardized test preparatory courses. The chief executive of the Princeton Review cheerfully admitted that his company registered its chief rival's name in order to mock and annoy the other company. Additionally, Princeton Review hoped that cybernauts hoping to contact the Kaplan Review company would sign on to the kaplan.com site. Individuals who mistakenly did so were offered electronic materials disparaging the quality of Kaplan Review's services and extolling the comparative advantages of the Princeton Review courses.

The Kaplan Review had no on-line presence but became aware of the rogue Internet site in relatively short order. Kaplan Review demanded that Princeton Review cease using the Kaplan name in conjunction with the site. Princeton Review offered to surrender the domain name in exchange for a case of beer—either domestic or imported. Kaplan Review declined the settlement, opting instead to pursue a legal remedy. The President of Princeton Review quipped in response that his rivals had "no sense of humor, no vision, and no beer." A lawsuit was initially filed but the dispute was subsequently removed to binding arbitration. The arbitrators determined that Princeton Review should surrender the site to Kaplan Review. Princeton Review did so, but vowed to register instead the domain name "kraplan.com," which, like the kaplan.com during Princeton Review's control, would be devoted to comparative advertising disparaging Princeton's competitor.

McDonald's v. Quittner

The most recent Internet trademark dispute was created by a magazine writer attempting to generate material for his column on the Internet. In the course of writing about businesses that fail to register their names as Internet domains, writer Joshua Quittner reviewed the list of registered domain names and noted that no one had registered the name of "McDonald's," the renowned fast food chain. Quittner then contacted McDonald's corporation to get a statement regarding their failure to protect their famous name. No statement appeared forthcoming, so Quittner generated the story by registering "McDonalds.com" himself, activating the site, and circulating his new e-mail address as "ronald@mcdonalds.com." Some messages urged him to use the site to promote vegetarianism, other messages urged him to offer the domain name back to McDonald's in return for an exorbitant price.

Quittner did indeed offer the name back to McDonald's in one of his magazine columns, but not in exchange for money. In a manner reminiscent of the Princeton Review, he instead offered to surrender the domain name if McDonald's corporation would underwrite some Internet equipment for a grade school. This and other provoking articles caught the corporation's attention; they responded not by funding grade school computer access, but by pressuring the InterNIC to revoke Quittner's registration of the name.

Although the registry had stayed out of previous disputes such as the Adam Curry litigation, sticking tenaciously to its "first-come, first-served" policy, it wavered before this new corporate threat. InterNIC first resisted McDonalds' demands, then eventually agreed to revoke the registration, then changed its mind again, leaving the registration with Quittner. McDonald's ultimately agreed to donate $3,500 to purchase the equipment.

* * *

Notes

1. The act of "squatting" is not a bad thing in American jurisprudence but apparently "cybersquatting" is. *See, e.g.*, Brian Gardiner, Comment, *Squatters' Rights And Adverse Possession: A Search for Equitable Application of Property Laws*, 8 IND. INT'L & COMP. L. REV. 119 (1997); Kenneth L. Port, *Trademark Monopolies in the Blue Nowhere*, 28 WM. MITCHELL L. REV. 1091 (2002). Is cyberspace some form of precious real estate that requires special protections? Or is it precisely because cyberspace is not literal "space" that we need different rules? Have we taken the property metaphor too far?

2. Recall *AP v. INS*, *supra*, Chapter 1. Can you make an analogy between the hot news exception and the protection against cybersquatters? Who needs to be protected? Against whom is the protection desired? What is the cost of the protection?

3. One important question to keep in mind throughout these materials is whether or not trademark law "works differently in cyberspace." David Yan, *Note: Virtual Reality: Can We Ride Trademark Law to Surf Cyberspace?*, 10 FORDHAM I. P., MEDIA & ENT. L. J. 773, 775 (2000).

B. Introduction to the Current Domain Name System

Image Online Design, Inc. v. Core Association and Ken Stubbs
120 F. Supp. 2d 870 (C. D. Cal. 2000)

KELLEHER, D. J.

* * *

A. The Evolution of the Domain Name System

When a person or entity seeks to maintain an Internet web site, that party must reserve a location, called an Internet Protocol ("IP") Address. Because a random numeric address is difficult to remember, alphanumeric domain names are used. In order for a user to access the web site, the user enters the alphanumeric domain name[1] combination that

---

1. An alphanumeric domain name usually consists of two levels: a Second Level Domain and a Top Level Domain. For example, in the United States Courts' website, "http://www.uscourts.gov," the Second Level Domain is "uscourts" and the generic Top Level Domain is ".gov." The "http://" refers to the protocol used to transfer information, and the "www" simply refers to the World Wide Web.

corresponds to the assigned IP Address and is routed to the host computer. Up until very recently, an independent organization called Network Solutions, Inc. ("NSI") had the exclusive responsibility to perform the "translation" function of converting the user's alphanumeric domain name into the appropriate IP Address.

In 1993, the National Science Foundation awarded a five-year cooperative agreement to NSI, under which NSI was to serve as the exclusive provider of domain name registration services for those using the nonmilitary Top Level Domain ("TLD") names — .com, .net, .org, .edu and .gov.[2]

The International Ad Hoc Committee ("IAHC") was formed in 1996 and was charged with the task of developing administrative and management enhancements for the domain name system. In its Final Report, the IAHC called for the creation of seven new generic TLDs ("gTLDs") — .firm, .store,[3] .web, .arts, .rec, .info, and .nom.[4] The Final Report also recommended that second level domain names within the new gTLDs be distributed and administered by different, competing, registrars dispersed throughout the world, rather than just by NSI.

In response to the IAHC's Final Report, the United States Department of Commerce ("DOC") issued its own recommendations.[5] The White Paper set forth the DOC's recommendations as to how technical management of Internet domain names should develop once NSI's contract expired. The DOC sought to remedy the "widespread dissatisfaction" with the manner in which the domain name system had been run. It based this asserted dissatisfaction on (i) increased trademark disputes; (ii) growing commercial interest in the Internet and the attendant calls for a stronger management structure; (iii) international concerns that the United States government retained too much control over the domain name registration; and (iv) the absence of competition in the field of domain name registrars.

Because the United States government had been involved in the early development of the internet, many parts of the domain name system were either performed outright by U.S. government agencies, or pursuant to contracts with such agencies, including NSI's registrar activities. The DOC White Paper encouraged the ending of U.S. government in-

---

2. There are actually two types of TLDs: generic and country code. All country code TLDs are two letters, e.g. .ca for Canada and .tm for Turkmenistan. The seven generic TLDs currently used are .com, .org, .net, .gov, .edu, .mil and .int. In this order, the terms "TLD" and "gTLD" (generic Top Level Domain) will be used interchangeably.

3. This recommendation was later changed to .shop.

4. Although the IAHC has been disbanded, its Final Report may still be found at http://www.iahc.org/draft-iahc-recommend-OO.html. The recommended gTLDs would be used for the following types of entities:
    .firm for businesses, or firms
    .store for businesses offering goods to purchase
    .web for entities emphasizing activities related to the World Wide Web
    .arts for entities emphasizing cultural and entertainment activities
    .rec for entities emphasizing recreation/entertainment activities
    .info for entities providing information services
    .nom for those wishing individual or personal nomenclature

5. See "Management of Internet Names and Addresses" (the "DOC White Paper"). The DOC White Paper is a statement of policy from the United States Department of Commerce regarding the domain name system, and is available at http://www.ntia.doc.gov/ntiahome/domainname/6_5_98 dns.htm. The DOC White Paper was the successor to an earlier document entitled "A Proposal To Improve Technical Management of Internet Names and Addresses" (the "DOC Green Paper"), which is still available at http://www.ntia.doc.gov/ntiahome/domainname/dnsdrft.htm.

volvement, but was concerned with how the removal would be implemented. The DOC White Paper made numerous suggestions as to how the U.S. government removal would be implemented, as well as recommendations for how increased Internet activity could be encouraged while ensuring that trademark rights were protected.

One such recommendation was the formation of a private corporation with oversight capabilities. In 1998, the Internet Corporation for Assigned Names and Numbers ("ICANN") was formed. ICANN is a non-profit, private California corporation created expressly to assume responsibility for the IP address space allocation, protocol parameter assignment, domain name system management, and root server system management functions previously performed under U.S. Government contracts.

In November 1998, the DOC entered into a Memorandum of Understanding with ICANN to develop a plan for the management of the domain name system (the "ICANN MoU"). Under the ICANN MoU, ICANN and the DOC attempt to jointly design, develop and test the procedures used to carry out domain name system management functions without interrupting the functional operation of the Internet. Of specific relevance for this case, ICANN and DOC agreed to oversee the development of a policy for determining the circumstances under which new gTLDs would be added to the root system and to collaborate in the development of a plan for the introduction of competition in domain name registration services, including the development of accreditation procedures for new domain name registrars and the selection of third parties to participate in a test of the competitive domain name registration system.

In November 1999, ICANN and DOC arrived at an agreement regarding accreditation guidelines for the appointment of the companies that would participate in the testing of the new competitive domain name registration system. These new companies share registration functions for the popular .com, .net, and .org gTLDs. One of these agreements, which was arrived at through a consensus-based process, is a registry agreement under which NSI will operate the registry for the .com, .net, and .org gTLDs. All ICANN-accredited registrars are to have equal access to this registry operated by NSI. The terms of the registrars' access to the registry, including how the registrars are to place and renew registrations, are governed by the revised NSI-Registrar License and Agreement. As of the date this Order, there are currently forty-two companies listed on ICANN's web site as "accredited, and currently operational" registrars.

————————

Wayde Brooks, *Wrestling over the World Wide Web: ICANN's Uniform Dispute Resolution Policy for Domain Name Disputes*
22 Hamline J. Pub. L. & Pol'y 297 (2001)*

* * *

II. BACKGROUND TO THE PRESENT: INTERNET BASICS

In 1965, researchers used an ordinary telephone line to connect a computer in California with a computer at the Massachusetts Institute of Technology. Before this time, computers were solitary, unable to share programming or data with another computer. To allow computers to share information computer scientists developed "packet switching," an entirely new way of transmitting data over telephone lines.

————————

An investigation of technologies that could interconnect these network "packets," began as a small research program funded by the U.S. Department of Defense (D.o.D.) in the 1969 known as ARAPNET. ARAPNET was named after the Defense Advanced Research Projects Unit and connected computers at various universities and government installations. The original purpose of this U.S. Department of Defense network was to insure that its computer network would survive and continue to function in the event of an enemy attack. By automatically rerouting information around destroyed or damaged portions of the network, the system as a whole would continue to function.

* * *

III. THE DOMAIN NAME GAME

Everyone reading this paper has had some exposure to the Internet.... Nearly everyone in the industrialized world recognizes the phrase, "www.(fill in this blank).com." It is this "blank" that is at the heart of the domain name. A domain name is the Internet equivalent of a telephone number, street address, or ham radio call sign. In explanation,

> a domain name is an easy-to-remember replacement for an internet address. When an individual or corporation registers for a domain name, it is actually assigned an Internet Protocol (IP) address such as 169.229.97.112.... Because IP addresses are difficult to remember, Internet users substitute unique "domain names" as pseudonyms for the computer's real identification number. When a domain name is entered into a computer it is automatically converted into the numbered address, which contacts the appropriate site.[1]

These "user-friendly" addresses are referred to as Uniform Resource Locators (URL's).

* * *

A. Importance of Domain Names

Millions of web sites have been created by businesses and individuals to sell products and services, as well as provide information to web users. Internet domain names, unlike telephone numbers, convey meaning independent of their true function, which is to identify a particular site in "cyberspace" and facilitate a web or e-mail user's ability to find that site on the Internet. A domain name registered to a person or business matching that party's well known trademark or company moniker will be much easier to remember and easier to grasp intuitively. These characteristics in a domain name will result in a greater number of users visiting that particular web site for the desired reasons.

The use of a recognizable company trademark or name is enhanced by the "search and locate" nature of the Internet. If Internet users know the domain name or address of a desired Internet site, they can contact that site easily.

Even without the address, a user can use a "search engine," which is a web based program that looks for sites based upon their textual content using key words and phrases selected by the web user. This search typically produces a list of web sites that the user can then access via a hypertext link as desired.... Domain names have become the "dot. com" brands associated with a particular service, product, or idea.

---

1. Rebecca W. Gol, *Playing the Name Game: A Glimpse at the Future of the Internet Domain Name System*, 51 FED. COMM. L. J. 403, 406 (1999).

B. Domain Name Issues

Domain name disputes can be categorized into four basic types of conflict. The first category arises from the conflict between trademark law and the methods by which domain names are allocated. This domain name piracy or "cybersquatting" occurs when a party registers a domain name which is the name of a well known product or company with the intent to extort money from the original trademark holder rather than use it for trade themselves. A variation on this theme is registering a famous trademark as a domain name—not with the intent to sell it—but to capitalize on the notoriety of the famous mark to sell their own unrelated product, service, or idea.

Even the government has suffered from the confusion sown by these "reverse cyber pirates." "Whitehouse.gov" is the official U.S. government web site of the President. "Whitehouse.com" is a pornographic site that had featured "pictures" of Bill and Hillary Clinton in bondage attire. Traditional claims of dilution of trademark collide with First Amendment issues and the situation worsens when there are multiple forums and choice of law issues with which to deal, as well.

The second area of conflict in domain name disputes revolves around two or more parties with legitimate claims to use a mark as their domain name. Lawsuits simply underscore the inability of the domain name system to accommodate more than one legitimate claimant to a domain name. Because, under the current domain name system, there are simply not enough names to accommodate all of the legitimate users of a particular trademark. For example, there may be 100 users that have legitimate claims to the name "United," but there can only be one "United.com," one "United.org," and one "United.net."

One excellent example of this problem occurred in the dispute over the domain name "gateway.com." Several years before Gateway 2000, a world renown, multi-million dollar computer manufacturer, tried to reserve the domain name in question a much smaller and less well known company known as Gateway.com Inc. reserved "gateway. com," as its Internet address. Larger, well-known Gateway 2000 sued in federal court to evict smaller, more obscure Gateway.com Inc. Ultimately Gateway 2000 lost because the court found that Gateway.com Inc. had legitimate reasons for holding the domain name. Mr. Clegg, the owner of Gateway.com Inc., innocently chose the domain name more than six years ago, long before domain names had the value equated with them today.

A third and growing area of conflict in domain name disputes is called "reverse domain name hijacking." In this instance, legitimate trademark holders attempt to "recapture" existing valuable domain names from legitimate users for their own use. "Crew.com" was such a disputed domain name. This case, which was resolved using the Uniform Dispute Resolution Policy of the newly formed ICANN, is given as an example of a blatant case of "reverse domain name hijacking."

With the simplified process provided by the UDRP, reverse domain name hijacking may increase. ICANN approved arbitrators have on occasion remarked that a complainant filings under UDRP bordered on harassment and were "an abuse of the administrative proceeding."

The fourth type of conflict common to domain name disputes is one of priority. This occurs when two parties want a particular domain name but neither has any trademark rights in the name at issue. Assuming both parties have a legitimate desire, who decides which party gets the domain name and how? What if one party speculates in "Domain Name Futures"? Does it matter how the speculating party discovered the "need" of a starting company to be met by the domain name it holds? What if the parties had extremely similar domain names, such as "rocket.com" and "rockets.com?"

I

Many existing domain names are set to expire as the original contracts under which they were issued is typically for two years. The agreement required by the White Paper between NSI and ICANN "expressly anticipates policies prohibiting the warehousing or speculation of domain names." Many of the older domain names set to expire are more valuable than those currently available as they are typically shorter and encompass common words or phrases that are not presently available. With conflicts in priority between potential domain name owners, it is clear that a greater likelihood of confusion will occur among Web users. A system which encourages such conflicts is in "violation of the fundamental tenant[s] of trademark law."

* * *

IV. ICANN AND DOMAIN NAME DISPUTES

One of the first substantive acts of ICANN was the adoption of a uniform dispute resolution policy (UDRP) in October 1999. The UDRP differs from NSI's dispute-resolution policy in three main characteristics. First, trademark owners are no longer able to place a hold on domain names during any dispute-resolution process. Second, the trademark owner cannot invoke the UDRP proceedings unless the domain name is being held in "bad faith." The third and most significant change with the UDRP is a mandatory administrative dispute resolution proceeding for the disputes that do involve "bad faith" domain name holders. It is this third item which introduced arbitration as the preferred and "official" method of resolving domain name disputes.

The dispute resolution procedure will be handled online, costs approximately $1,000 and typically takes less than forty-five days to reach resolution. In order to invoke this proceeding, the registered trademark owner must make a preliminary showing of bad faith on the part of the domain name holder and, in most cases, pay the entire fees for the proceeding. Either party may dispute the ruling in court following the decision. These URDP proceedings provide a quick and relatively inexpensive opportunity for the trademark owner to challenge the abusive ownership of a domain name when compared to traditional litigation.

The UDRP had three main objectives. One was to eliminate the multitude of jurisdictions involved and laws applied to domain name disputes. Another objective was to reduce the cost of resolving domain name disputes. Cybersquatting was so inexpensive for bad actors to initiate that it could proliferate nearly unchecked, as Mr. Toeppen had demonstrated. Further, given the minuscule initial investment, cybersquatting could reap great returns. Due to the exorbitant costs in litigating, many instances of cybersquatting went unchallenged. On the other hand, legitimate domain name holders might not be able to defend their interests if challenged in the courts because of those same exorbitant litigation costs.

Third, the application of the UDRP was intended to be extremely restricted because of the objections that would inevitably arise when replacing national law with a global one. The UDRP "was supposed to be aimed at the most egregious types of cybersquatting, leaving other disputes to the courts."[2] Hardly the "ultimate arbiter of name rights on the global Internet," the UDRP was to be a quick, easy, and cheap method to handle the simplest — and, it was hoped, a majority — of domain name disputes.[3]

---

2. Dr. Milton Mueller, *Rough Justice — An Analysis of ICANN's Uniform Dispute Resolution Policy: Section 1: Disputes over Domain Names: 6 Years and Counting*, http://dcc.syr.edu/roughjustice.htm viewed March 28, 2001.

3. *Id.*

In order to achieve these three goals of the UDRP, ICANN leveraged "the centralized and monopolistic nature" of the TLDs.[4] Without ICANN approval, no one can sell domain name registrations in the generic top level domains. To complete ICANN's implementation of UDRP, all registrants are contractually bound to arbitration under the UDRP as an inescapable part of the registration contract with these ICANN approved domain name "providers."

———————

Notes

1. If I start a computer business company named "207.46.244.188" should I anticipate any problems? What if I registered the domain name <207dot46dot244dot188.com>? [Try entering these numbers in an internet browser bar].

2. ICANN is a private, nonprofit company administering domain name policy. What would have happened if the Department of Commerce never relinquished control? Does ICANN alleviate concerns about hegemony in Internet domain name administration?

3. Brooks points out that the UDRP may increase instances of reverse domain name hijacking, but does not directly address whether the UDRP will ease issues regarding priority. Of the triptych present in unfair competition law (i.e. the business, the customer, and the market itself), which stands to benefit most, according to Brooks' observations? He also refers to "domain name futures." Which group in the triptych would you say has interest in these?

4. How should one determine priority under trademark law? Is there a problem concerning priority in the context of the Internet? What if you registered a domain name and did not use it for anything other than a domain name? Would you have common-law trademark rights? Could an Article III court determine this for you?

5. Brooks also mentions that cybersquatting is inexpensive and provides great returns. Why?

6. These issues are presented to encourage the reader to examine the assumptions underpinning the UDRP and whether these are antithetical to the common law. On the other hand, does cybersquatting (and its "dangers") require a different policy?

———————

C. The Domain Name Registration Process

ICANN Information*

http://www.icann.org/general/

What is ICANN?

The Internet Corporation for Assigned Names and Numbers (ICANN) is an internationally organized, non-profit corporation that has responsibility for Internet Protocol

———————

4. *Id.*

* The following material from the ICANN web site is subject to copyright and is used with permission of ICANN. Neither the author nor this book itself is sponsored by ICANN.

(IP) address space allocation, protocol identifier assignment, generic (gTLD) and country code (ccTLD) Top-Level Domain name system management, and root server system management functions. These services were originally performed under U.S. Government contract by the Internet Assigned Numbers Authority (IANA) and other entities. ICANN now performs the IANA function.

As a private-public partnership, ICANN is dedicated to preserving the operational stability of the Internet; to promoting competition; to achieving broad representation of global Internet communities; and to developing policy appropriate to its mission through bottom-up, consensus-based processes.

What is the Domain Name System?

The Domain Name System (DNS) helps users find their way around the Internet. Every computer on the Internet has a unique address called its "IP address" (Internet Protocol address). Because IP addresses (which are strings of numbers) are hard to remember, the DNS allows a familiar string of letters (the "domain name") to be used instead. So rather than typing "192.0.34.65," you can type "www.icann.org."

What is ICANN's Role?

ICANN is responsible for coordinating the management of the technical elements of the DNS to ensure universal resolvability so that all users of the Internet can find all valid addresses. It does this by overseeing the distribution of unique technical identifiers used in the Internet's operations, and delegation of Top-Level Domain names (such as .com, .info, etc.).

Other issues of concern to Internet users, such as the rules for financial transactions, Internet content control, unsolicited commercial email (spam), and data protection are outside the range of ICANN~Rs mission of technical coordination.

Ensuring predictable results from any place on the Internet is called "universal resolvability." It is a critical design feature of the Domain Name System, one that makes the Internet the helpful, global resource that it is today. Without it, the same domain name might map to different Internet locations under different circumstances, which would only cause confusion.

How does ICANN work?

Within ICANN's structure, governments and international treaty organizations work in partnership with businesses, organizations, and skilled individuals involved in building and sustaining the global Internet. Innovation and continuing growth of the Internet bring forth new challenges for maintaining stability. Working collectively, ICANN's participants address those issues that directly concern ICANN's mission of technical coordination. Consistent with the principle of maximum self-regulation in the high-tech economy, ICANN is perhaps the foremost example of collaboration by the various constituents of the Internet community.

ICANN is governed by an internationally diverse Board of Directors overseeing the policy development process. ICANN's President directs an international staff, working from three continents, who ensure that ICANN meets its operational commitment to the Internet community.

Designed to respond to the demands of rapidly changing technologies and economies, the flexible, readily implemented policy development process originates in the three Supporting Organizations. Advisory Committees from individual user organizations, and technical communities work with the Supporting Organizations to create appropriate and effective policies. Over eighty governments closely advise the Board of Directors via the Governmental Advisory Committee.

ICANN's Board has included citizens of Australia, Brazil, Bulgaria, Canada, China, France, Germany, Ghana, Japan, Kenya, Korea, Mexico, the Netherlands, Portugal, Senegal, Spain, the United Kingdom, and the United States.

ICANN's Accomplishments
Among ICANN's recent accomplishments:

ICANN established market competition for generic domain name (gTLD) registrations resulting in a lowering of domain name costs by 80% and saving consumers and businesses over US$1 billion annually in domain registration fees.

ICANN implemented a Uniform Domain Name Dispute Resolution Policy (UDRP), which has been used to resolve more than 5000 disputes over the rights to domain names. The UDRP is designed to be efficient and cost effective.

Working in coordination with the appropriate technical communities and stakeholders, ICANN adopted guidelines for the deployment of Internationalized Domain Names (IDN), opening the way for registration of domains in hundreds of the world's languages.

ICANN's Ongoing Work

In 2000, ICANN introduced seven new gTLDs: .aero, .biz, .coop, .info, .museum, .name, and .pro. The ICANN community is currently exploring possibilities to add additional gTLDs.

In response to community concerns over privacy and accessibility, ICANN is hosting several workshops regarding Whois, the public database of domain name registrations.

With the deployment of IPv6, the new IP address numbering protocol, global network interoperability continues to be a primary mission for ICANN.

ICANN Welcomes Participation

Participation in ICANN is open to all who have an interest in global Internet policy as it relates to ICANN's mission of technical coordination. ICANN provides many online forums which are accessible through ICANN's website, and the Supporting Organizations and Advisory Committees have active mailing lists for participants. Additionally, ICANN holds public meetings throughout the year. Recent meetings have been held in Bucharest, Montreal, Shanghai, Rio de Janeiro, and Accra.

Notes

1. What legal rights does a registrant obtain by registering a domain name?

2. When a domain name is registered, the Registrar relies on the information provided by the registrant. Should the Registrar independently check the legitimacy of the registration? Should the Registrar be liable for contributory infringement if the registered domain name is a trademark of a third party? *See* Lockheed Martin v. Network Solutions, Inc. *See supra* Chapter VII.

3. If someone registers a domain name that is identical or confusingly similar to your trademark and does so with bad faith, she may be a cybersquatter. What if she just fools the registrar into changing the registration into her name? Is she a cybersquatter? A squatter? Or just a genius? What law applies? The ACPA? Property law? Tort law? Or do you take the law into your own hands, offer a large reward, and, in effect, send bounty hunters after the holder of your domain name? *See* Kremen v. Cohen, 337 F. 3d 1024 (9th Cir. 2003) (conversion of a domain name registrant by a con man who sent a forged letter to the registrar).

4. The seven original gTLDs (.com, .edu, .gov, .int, .mil, .net, and .org) were created in the 1980s. In 2000, ICANN created seven new TLDs. Four of those new TLDs (.biz, .info, .name, and .pro) are unsponsored. The other three TLDs are sponsored (.aero, .coop, and .museum). An unsponsored gTLD is governed by the ICANN processes for dispute resolution while a sponsored gTLD is not. A sponsored gTLD serves a narrower community and that sponsor is responsible for its administration.

On March 19, 2004, ICANN announced ten new sponsored TLDs as follows:

.asia
.cat
.jobs
.mail
.mobi
.post
.tel
.travel
.xxx

http://www.icann.org/announcements/announcement-19mar04.htm

5. There is currently an interesting discussion taking place about the likelihood of non-ASCII letters being adopted at TLDs. For instance, currently all TLDs have to be in ASCII letters and or 0–9 numerical numbers. However, many societies do not write in ASCII format. Chinese characters, Japanese kanji, katakana or hiragana, Russian Cyrillic letters, etc. cannot be used. However, many of these societies would like to see them adopted. Should they? What is the chief impediment? http://www.icann.org/committees/idn/non-ascii-tld-paper-13jun02.htm.

6. *VeriSign*. After some debate, ICANN is finally allowing, for a one-year trial period, the reservation of expiring domain names. For domain names that end in .com and .net, a customer can now hire VeriSign (or other registrars) to reserve a domain name for their use and registration. Paragraph 4(b)(ii) of the UDRP states as follows:

b. Evidence of Registration and Use in Bad Faith. For the purposes of Paragraph 4(a)(iii), the following circumstances, in particular but without limitation, if found by the Panel to be present, shall be evidence of the registration and use of a domain name in bad faith:

…

(ii) you have registered the domain name in order to prevent the owner of the trademark or service mark from reflecting the mark in a corresponding domain name, provided that you have engaged in a pattern of such conduct; …

Isn't this scheme to reserve marks in violation of Paragraph 4(b)(ii)? Who may be violating 4(b)(ii), the registree or the registrar?

———————

D. Legal Protections of Domain Names

1. Infringement

Intermatic v. Toeppen

947 F. Supp. 1227 (N.D. Ill. 1996)

DENLOW, MAGISTRATE JUDGE

Welcome to cyberspace! This case presents the Court with the increasingly important issue of whether and how federal and state trademark laws apply to govern names selected by users for their Internet website. As the Internet grows in prominence as a venue for business, the courts will be called upon to apply traditional legal principles to new avenues of commerce. This is such a case.

Plaintiff Intermatic Incorporated ("Intermatic"), brings this action in seven counts [including federal trademark infringement].... Toeppen denies that his conduct is unlawful.

Intermatic and Toeppen have filed cross-motions for summary judgment on all seven counts. The Court held extensive oral argument on August 29, 1996 and has reviewed the briefs, stipulations, affidavits and exhibits submitted by the parties. For the reasons set forth below, the Court recommends that Intermatic's motion for summary judgment be granted as to counts III and IV (the "Dilution counts") and be denied as to the remaining counts [including the trademark infringement count]. The Court recommends that Toeppen's motion be denied as to all counts.

I. BACKGROUND FACTS
A. The Parties.

Intermatic is a Delaware corporation having a place of business in Spring Grove, Illinois. Intermatic has been doing business under the name INTERMATIC since 1941. Intermatic has 37 offices throughout the United States and has been in business in Illinois since 1892. Intermatic is a manufacturer and distributor of a wide variety of electrical and electronic products, including computerized and programmable timers and other devices which are sold under the name and trademark INTERMATIC.

Intermatic's sales and advertising of INTERMATIC labeled products have been continuous since the 1940's. In the last 8 years, its sales in the U.S. have exceeded $850 million. *Id.* Intermatic's products prominently bear the INTERMATIC name and trademark, and well over 100 million units have been installed in homes and businesses throughout the United States.

Advertising and promotional expenditures for products bearing the INTERMATIC mark for the last 8 years have exceeded $16 million. Intermatic's co-op advertising consists of approximately 700 print ads per year, with each displaying the INTERMATIC mark. Intermatic also advertises and promotes its INTERMATIC products, mark and name by way of trade shows throughout the United States, magazines, point-of-purchase displays, brochures, radio, and television.

Defendant Toeppen resides in Champaign, Illinois, where he operates an Internet service provider business known as Net66. Toeppen has registered approximately 240 Internet domain names without seeking the permission from any entity that has previously used the names he registered, because he contends that no permission was or is necessary.

Among the domain names which he has registered are the following well known business names:

deltaairlines.com   greatamerica.com
britishairways.com   neiman-marcus.com
crateandbarrel.com   northwest airlines.com
ramadainn.com   ussteel.com
eddiebauer.com   unionpacific.com

One of Toeppen's business objectives is to profit by the resale or licensing of these domain names, presumably to the entities who conduct business under these names.

B. Intermatic's Trademarks.

Intermatic owns five incontestable trademark registrations issued by the U.S. Patent and Trademark Office for its INTERMATIC mark. Intermatic is the exclusive owner of the INTERMATIC trademark and trade name, and there are no known third party uses of INTERMATIC in the U.S. Prior to registering the intermatic.com domain name, Toeppen had never used the term intermatic for any purpose.

* * *

D. The Dispute.

In December of 1995, Toeppen applied for registration of the domain name http: www.intermatic.com ("intermatic.com") and NSI registered the domain name to Toeppen's domain name servers. A given domain name, the exact alphanumeric combination in the same network and using the same suffix, can only be registered to one entity. Intermatic subsequently attempted to register the same domain name and was prevented from registering "intermatic.com" as its domain name because of Toeppen's prior registration of that domain name.

Intermatic also became aware that Toeppen was using the mark "Intermatic" in connection with the sale of a computer software program. Upon discovery of Toeppen's prior registration and use of the Intermatic mark, Intermatic made a written demand on Toeppen that he relinquish or assign the "intermatic.com" domain name registration and discontinue use of the Intermatic mark. Toeppen agreed to discontinue using the Intermatic mark for his software product but refused to give up the "intermatic.com" domain name registration. In response to a formal request by Intermatic, NSI put Toeppen's registration on hold in April of 1996.

As long as Mr. Toeppen is allowed to retain the "intermatic.com" registration, Intermatic will be unable to acquire "intermatic.com" as an Internet domain name or use "intermatic.com" as an e-mail address on the Internet. However, Intermatic is technically capable of establishing its web page at another domain name, including, for example, "intermatic-inc.com" and it is technically capable of establishing at any available domain name a web page featuring the INTERMATIC mark and any other Internet-related marketing or business information. To date, Intermatic has not chosen to reserve any other domain name or to take any other action to establish a presence on the Internet. However, some of its distributors have placed Intermatic information on the Internet.

Until NSI placed the intermatic.com domain name on hold, Toeppen maintained intermatic.com as an active domain name on the Internet. Although he initially set up a web page regarding a software program he was developing and intended to call "Intermatic," Toeppen removed that page (which was available for less than a week) and dropped the proposed name for his software in response to demand from Intermatic. No software programs were ever sold. He then instituted as a web page a map of Champaign-Urbana, the community where Toeppen resides.

When Toeppen became aware of lntermatic's efforts to have the intermatic.com domain name placed on hold, he changed the web page associated with intermatic.com to bear the caption "Champaign-Urbana Map Page/has Moved To www.c-u.com." Toeppen moved the map and put the forwarding address on the intermatic.com page so that Internet users could update relevant hyperlinks before the NSI freeze simply locked them out of the page, as is now the case. Presently, entering intermatic.com will return a message that there is no functional domain name server at that domain name.

At no time did Toeppen use intermatic.com in connection with the sale of any available goods or services. At no time has Toeppen advertised the intermatic.com domain name in association with any goods or services. Presently, the intermatic.com domain name is not available for use by any party. Toeppen did not seek permission from Intermatic to use the intermatic.com domain name because he believes that no permission was or is necessary. Intermatic disagrees. This litigation ensued.

* * *

III. LEGAL DISCUSSION

This case involves a dispute over the ownership of a highly prized Internet address. The issue is whether the owner of the Intermatic trademark may preclude the use of the trademark as an Internet domain name by defendant Toeppen, who had made no prior use of the Intermatic name prior to registering it as an Internet domain name. This case does not involve competing claims to the same name by parties who have actively used the same name in their business, such as the use of the term "United" by United Airlines, United Van Lines, United Mineworkers Union and the United Way.

Toeppen is what is commonly referred to as a cyber-squatter. Miller, Cyber Squatters Give Carl's Jr., Others Net Loss, *Los Angeles Times*, 1996 WL 11004750. These individuals attempt to profit from the Internet by reserving and later reselling or licensing domain names back to the companies that spent millions of dollars developing the goodwill of the trademark. While many may find patently offensive the practice of reserving the name or mark of a federally registered trademark as a domain name and then attempting to sell the name back to the holder of the trademark, others may view it as a service. Regardless of one's views as to the morality of such conduct, the legal issue is whether such conduct is illegal. Cybersquatters such as Toeppen contend that because they were the first to register the domain name through NSI it is theirs. Intermatic argues that it is entitled to protect its valuable trademark by preventing Toeppen from using "intermatic.com" as a domain name.

The practical effect of Toeppen's conduct is to enjoin Intermatic from using its trademark as its domain name on the Internet. Unlike the typical trademark dispute, where both parties are using the name simultaneously and arguing whether confusion exists, the current configuration of the Internet allows only one party to use the "intermatic.com" domain name. Because the Internet assigns the top-level domain name .com to commercial and non-commercial users, there does not currently appear to be a way in which both Intermatic and Toeppen can both use the intermatic.com name.

Congress and the states have been slow to respond to the activities of the cybersquatters. Some commentators take an extremely dim view of their activities. As one commentator has noted: "There is no doubt that some of these pirates, if not most, anticipated a lottery-like bonanza, selling the domain registration to the trademark owner or canceling it in return for a huge amount of money." 1 Gilson, Trademark Protection and Practice, § 5.11[4], p. 5-237 (1996). "Dozens of companies, including Taco Bell, MTV, Kentucky Fried Chicken and others have had to cajole, pay thousands of dollars or even sue to gain the rights to domain names that match trademarks they have spent millions of dollars cultivating and protecting." Miller, Cyber Squatters Give Carl's Jr., Others Net Loss, *Los Angeles Times*, 1996 WL 11004750. However, becoming rich does not make one's activity necessarily illegal. Speculation and arbitrage have a long history in this country.

* * *

IV. INTERMATIC'S TRADEMARK INFRINGEMENT AND UNFAIR COMPETITION CLAIMS—LIKELIHOOD OF CONFUSION.

Our discussion begins with an analysis of Intermatic's trademark and unfair competition claims. Intermatic asserts that it is entitled to summary judgment on all counts by showing the likelihood of confusion resulting from Toeppen's use of Intermatic's trademark as a domain name. In order to prevail under the federal trademark infringement claim … Intermatic need only prove that: 1) it owns prior rights in the INTERMATIC mark; and 2) Toeppen's use of "intermatic.com" is likely to cause consumer confusion, deception or mistake. *Dorr-Oliver, Inc. v. Fluid-Quip, Inc.*, 94 F.3d 376 (7th Cir. 1996).

Intermatic's name and prior rights over Toeppen to use the INTERMATIC name are clear. Intermatic's first use of the INTERMATIC name and mark predates Toeppen's first use of "intermatic.com" by more than fifty years. Also, it is undisputed that Intermatic holds a valid registration for the trademark INTERMATIC.

The Seventh Circuit has held that the following seven factors should be weighed to determine if there is a likelihood of confusion: 1) the degree of similarity between the marks in appearance and suggestion; 2) the similarity of products or services for which the name is used; 3) the area and manner of concurrent use; 4) the degree of care likely to be exercised by consumers; 5) the strength of the complainant's mark; 6) actual confusion; and 7) an intent on the part of the alleged infringer to palm off his products as those of another. *Forum Corp. of North Am. v. Forum Ltd.*, 903 F.2d 434, 439 (7th Cir. 1990). The test is not whether the public would confuse the marks, but whether the viewer of an accused mark would be likely to associate the product or service with which it is connected with the source of products or services with which an earlier mark is connected. *Nike, Inc. v. "Just Did It" Enterprises*, 6 F.3d 1225, 1228–29 (7th Cir. 1993)....

1. Similarity of Marks

In this case, Toeppen's use of "intermatic.com" is similar to the federally registered name and mark of INTERMATIC because it contains the term "intermatic." Each of the five registered INTERMATIC trademarks contain the Intermatic name.

2. Similarity of Products or Services

There is no similarity between the products and services that Toeppen and Intermatic provide. Toeppen's web page contained a map of the city of Urbana, whereas Intermatic's web page would presumably contain product information or catalogs of the various Intermatic products. At the present time, Intermatic has chosen to await the outcome of this litigation before initiating its own Internet web page. More importantly though, Toeppen is willing to be enjoined from using the web site for the sale of any product or service thereby guaranteeing that his use would be entirely dissimilar from Intermatic's use.

3. The Area and Manner of Use

This factor requires the Court to "consider whether there is a relationship in use, promotion, distribution, or sales between the goods or services of the parties." *Forum Corp. of North Am. v. Forum, Ltd.*, 903 F.2d 434,442 (7th Cir. 1990). Also, a trademark protects the owner against not only its use upon the articles to which he has applied it but also upon such other articles as might naturally be supposed to come from him. *Nike, Inc. v. "Just Did It" Enterprises*, 6 F.3d 1225, 1228–29 (7th Cir. 1993). Toeppen will not be selling any goods or services through the intermatic.com domain.

Both parties are attempting to establish a presence on the Internet through the creation of a web page. The distribution channel in this case is cyberspace. As consumers "surf the net" they seek out information on a plethora of subjects or companies. Companies around the globe are scrambling to establish their presence on the Internet. It is axiomatic that companies seek to register their trademarks as domain names so that consumers can easily find information about them or their products and services. However, at the present time, there is no area and manner of concurrent use. There is no bar to Intermatic setting up a web page under a name other than intermatic.com. Because Intermatic has not set up its own web page, it is unable to demonstrate any relationship in use, promotion, distribution or sales between the goods or services of the parties.

4. Degree of Care Likely To Be Exercised By Consumers

The record contains no information regarding consumer behavior on the Internet. The Court finds that the degree of care to be exercised by consumers raises a question of fact. The consumers in this case are individuals that log onto the Internet to seek information, products, or services. There has been no evidence presented as to the degree of care that could be expected among the average Internet user. The Court cannot simply infer what degree of care would be used by consumers. Because this matter is before the Court on summary judgment, the Court infers that a fact question exists as to whether a web surfer who logged onto the intermatic.com web page and found a map of Urbana, Illinois would associate that page with Intermatic. *Nike, Inc. v. "Just Did It" Enterprises*, 6 F.3d 1225, 1230–1 (7th Cir. 1993). Thus, the Court finds that a fact question exists on this issue.

5. Strength of Intermatic's Mark

Toeppen does not contest the fact that Intermatic's mark is strong. The Court finds that the mark is strong and entitled to broad protection as a matter of law. As the Seventh Circuit noted in *Polaroid Corp. v. Polaraid Inc.*, 319 F.2d 830, 831 (7th Cir. 1963), a trademark or trade name that is a coined or invented word which has never been used as a trade name or trademark by any other entity acquires the status of a famous-brand trademark. The following language from Polaroid is applicable to the case at bar: "in the instant case plaintiffs trademark and trade name was original—it was coined and invented—and was a strong name exclusively appropriated by plaintiff. It was a name which through much effort and the expenditure of large amounts of money had acquired a widespread reputation and much good will, which plaintiff should not be required to share with defendant." *Id.* at 837.

6. Actual Confusion

There has been no evidence presented of actual confusion. Intermatic states that the use of the "intermatic.com" domain name in and of itself would cause confusion. However, this is a question of fact to be determined. *Nike, Inc. v. "Just Did It" Enterprises*, 6 F.3d 1225, 1231 (7th Cir. 1993).

7. Toeppen's Intent

Intermatic argues that Toeppen's registration of more than 200 domain names is indicia of willful intent. However, Toeppen argues that he was motivated in part to test the legality of arbitraging domain names. This is a relatively new area of law and Toeppen is free to test the waters. There has been no evidence that Toeppen intended to pass off any of his products or services as Intermatic's. Neither the software nor the map of Urbana are in anyway similar to Intermatic's products. He immediately ceased to market the software under the Intermatic name when contacted by Intermatic's counsel. Whether Toeppen's registration of several domain names is sufficient to rise to the level of willful intent is also a question of fact. *Id.* at 1231–32.

Therefore the Court recommends that since there are questions of fact as to a likelihood of confusion, the [plaintiff's motion for summary judgment for trademark infringement] should be denied.

Notes

1. Notice that even though Toeppen admitted to registering domain names and arbitraging them for profit and even though Toeppen had no prior legitimate commercial interest in the trademark INTERMATIC, the magistrate still recommended that summary judgment be denied on this trademark count. The magistrate did find in favor of Intermatic, however, regarding the trademark dilution claim and ordered the domain name transferred. The magistrate's recommendation was adopted by the court. *Intermatic Inc. v. Toeppen*, 947 F. Supp. 1227 (N.D. Ill. 1996).

2. Intermatic is illustrative of why trademark holders began to demand broader trademark protections to prevent conduct such as Toeppen's. Can you clearly articulate the harm that trademark holders would suffer if the Toeppens of the world were allowed to register domain names and then arbitrage them for profit? What, precisely, is the harm? If trademark law did not develop to protect trademark owners other than allow them the cause of action as described in Intermatic for trademark infringement, what would have been the likely result regarding the conduct of trademark claimants?

3. The magistrate judge states, "While many may find patently offensive the practice of reserving the name or mark of a federally registered trademark as a domain name and then attempting to sell the name back to the holder of the trademark, others may view it as a service. Regardless of one's views as to the morality of such conduct, the legal issue is whether such conduct is illegal." What is his point? Is he advocating for positivism? Or is he just being strict in his paternalism (i.e. "the law is the law")? Could he have as easily applied the Seventh Circuit's test to the domain name to find what "the law" was (i.e. whether or not the use infringed on the rights of a holder of the mark)?

The magistrate judge finds a likelihood of confusion applying the Seventh Circuit's factors as determined in *Forum Corp.*, *supra*. He applies the factors "Area and Manner of Use" and "Degree of Care Likely to be Exercised By Consumers" to the Internet. He states "it is axiomatic that companies seek to register their trademarks as domain names so that consumers can easily find information about them … [h]owever, at the present time, there is no area and manner of concurrent use." Additionally he says "the degree of care to be exercised by consumers raises a question of fact.... There has been no evidence presented as to the degree of care that could be expected among the average Internet user. The Court cannot simply infer [that]." What is the lesson to be drawn from these pronouncements?

———————

E. Dilution

Panavision, Int'l, L.P. v. Toeppen
141 F. 3d 1316 (9th Cir. 1998)

THOMPSON, C. J.

[As part of his larger scheme to register trademarks claimed by others as domain names, Toeppen also registered <panavision.com>. Panavision sued under the California Dilution Act and under the FTDA. Discussion regarding the California act has been omitted without further indication.]

* * *

B. Trademark Dilution Claims

The Federal Trademark Dilution Act provides:

The owner of a famous mark shall be entitled.... to an injunction against another person's commercial use in commerce of a mark or trade name, if such use begins after the mark has become famous and causes dilution of the distinctive quality of the mark.... 15 U.S.C. §1125(c).

... The protection extends only to strong and well recognized marks. Panavision' s state law dilution claim is subject to the same analysis as its federal claim.

In order to prove a violation of the Federal Trademark Dilution Act, a plaintiff must show that (1) the mark is famous; (2) the defendant is making a commercial use of the mark in commerce; (3) the defendant's use began after the mark became famous; and (4) the defendant's use of the mark dilutes the quality of the mark by diminishing the capacity of the mark to identify and distinguish goods and services. 15 U.S.C. §1125(c).

Toeppen does not challenge the district court's determination that Panavision's trademark is famous, that his alleged use began after the mark became famous, or that the use was in commerce. Toeppen challenges the district court's determination that he made "commercial use" of the mark and that this use caused "dilution" in the quality of the mark.

1. Commercial Use

Toeppen argues that his use of Panavision's trademarks simply as his domain names cannot constitute a commercial use under the Act. Case law supports this argument.

Developing this argument, Toeppen contends that a domain name is simply an address used to locate a web page. He asserts that entering a domain name on a computer allows a user to access a web page, but a domain name is not associated with information on a web page. If a user were to type Panavision.com as a domain name, the computer screen would display Toeppen's web page with aerial views of Pana, Illinois. The screen would not provide any information about "Panavision," other than a "location window" which displays the domain name. Toeppen argues that a user who types in Panavision.com, but who sees no reference to the plaintiff Panavision on Toeppen's web page, is not likely to conclude the web page is related in any way to the plaintiff, Panavision.

Toeppen's argument misstates his use of the Panavision mark. His use is not as benign as he suggests. Toeppen's "business" is to register trademarks as domain names and then sell them to the rightful trademark owners. He "acts as a 'spoiler,' preventing Panavision and others from doing business on the Internet under their trademarked names unless they pay his fee." *Panavision*, 938 F. Supp. at 621. This is a commercial use.

As the district court found, Toeppen traded on the value of Panavision's marks. So long as he held the Internet registrations, he curtailed Panavision's exploitation of the value of its trademarks on the Internet, a value which Toeppen then used when he attempted to sell the Panavision.com domain name to Panavision.

In a nearly identical case involving Toeppen and Intermatic Inc., a federal district court in Illinois held that Toeppen's conduct violated the Federal Trademark Dilution Act. *Intermatic*, 947 F. Supp. 1227 at 1241. There, Intermatic sued Toeppen for registering its trademark on the Internet as Toeppen's domain name, intermatic.com. It was "conceded that one of Toeppen's intended uses for registering the Intermatic mark was to eventually sell it back to Intermatic or to some other party." *Id.* at 1239. The court found that "Toeppen's intention to arbitrage the 'intermatic.com' domain name constituted a commercial use." *Id.*

Toeppen's reliance on *Holiday Inns, Inc. v. 800 Reservation, Inc.*, 86 F.3d 619 (6th Cir. 1996), cert. denied, 136 L. Ed. 2d 715, 117 S. Ct. 770 (1997) is misplaced. In *Holiday Inns*, the Sixth Circuit held that a company's use of the most commonly misdialed number for Holiday Inns' 1-800 reservation number was not trademark infringement.

Holiday Inns is distinguishable. There, the defendant did not use Holiday Inns' trademark. Rather, the defendant selected the most commonly misdialed telephone number for Holiday Inns and attempted to capitalize on consumer confusion.

A telephone number, moreover, is distinguishable from a domain name because a domain name is associated with a word or phrase. A domain name is similar to a "vanity number" that identifies its source. Using *Holiday Inns* as an example, when a customer dials the vanity number "1-800-Holiday," she expects to contact Holiday Inns because the number is associated with that company's trademark. A user would have the same expectation typing the domain name HolidayInns.com. The user would expect to retrieve Holiday Inns' web page.

Toeppen made a commercial use of Panavision's trademarks. It does not matter that he did not attach the marks to a product. Toeppen's commercial use was his attempt to sell the trademarks themselves. Under the Federal Trademark Dilution Act and the California Anti-dilution statute, this was sufficient commercial use.

2. Dilution

"Dilution" is defined as "the lessening of the capacity of a famous mark to identify and distinguish goods or services, regardless of the presence or absence of (1) competition between the owner of the famous mark and other parties, or (2) likelihood of confusion, mistake or deception." 15 U.S.C. §1127.

Trademark dilution on the Internet was a matter of Congressional concern. Senator Patrick Leahy (D-Vt.) stated:

> It is my hope that this anti-dilution statute can help stem the use of deceptive Internet addresses taken by those who are choosing marks that are associated with the products and reputations of others.

141 Congo Rec. §19312-01 (daily ed. Dec. 29, 1995) (statement of Sen. Leahy).

To find dilution, a court need not rely on the traditional definitions such as "blurring" and "tarnishment."[1] Indeed, in concluding that Toeppen's use of Panavision's trademarks diluted the marks, the district court noted that Toeppen's conduct varied from the two standard dilution theories of blurring and tarnishment. *Panavision*, 945 F. Supp. at 1304. The court found that Toeppen's conduct diminished "the capacity of the Panavision marks to identify and distinguish Panavision's goods and services on the Internet." *Id.*

This view is also supported by *Teletech*. There, TeleTech Customer Care Management Inc., ("TCCM"), sought a preliminary injunction against Tele-Tech Company for use of TCCM's registered service mark, "TeleTech," as an Internet domain name. *Teletech*, 977 F. Supp. at 1410. The district court issued an injunction, finding that TCCM had demonstrated a likelihood of success on the merits on its trademark dilution claim. *Id.* at 1412. The court found that TCCM had invested great resources in promoting its servicemark and Teletech's registration of the domain name teletech.com on the Internet would most likely dilute TCCM's mark. *Id.* at 1413.

Toeppen argues he is not diluting the capacity of the Panavision marks to identify goods or services. He contends that even though Panavision cannot use Panavision.com and Panaflex.com as its domain name addresses, it can still promote its goods and services on the Internet simply by using some other "address" and then creating its own web page using its trademarks.

We reject Toeppen's premise that a domain name is nothing more than an address. A significant purpose of a domain name is to identify the entity that owns the web site. "A customer who is unsure about a company's domain name will often guess that the domain name is also the company's name." *Cardservice Int'l v. McGee*, 950 F. Supp. 737,741 (B.D. Va. 1997). "[A] domain name mirroring a corporate name may be a valuable corporate asset, as it facilitates communication with a customer base." *MTV Networks, Inc. v. Curry*, 867 F. Supp. 202, 203–204 n.2 (S.D.N.Y. 1994).

Using a company's name or trademark as a domain name is also the easiest way to locate that company's web site. Use of a "search engine" can turn up hundreds of web sites, and there is nothing equivalent to a phone book or directory assistance for the Internet. *See Cardservice*, 950 F. Supp. at 741.

Moreover, potential customers of Panavision will be discouraged if they cannot find its web page by typing in "Panavision.com," but instead are forced to wade through hundreds of web sites. This dilutes the value of Panavision's trademark. We echo the words

---

1. Blurring occurs when a defendant uses a plaintiffs trademark to identify the defendant's goods or services, creating the possibility that the mark will lose its ability to serve as a unique identifier of the plaintiffs product. *Ringling Bros.-Barnum& Bailey, Combined Shows, Inc. v. B.E. Windows, Corp.*, 937 F. Supp. 204, 209 (S.D.N.Y. 1996) (citing *Deere& Co. v. MTD Prods., Inc.*, 41 F.3d 39, 43 (2d. Cir. 1994)); Thomas McCarthy, *McCarthy on Trademarks and Unfair Competition,*§24:68 at 24–111 (4th ed. 1997); *see also Ringling Bros.-Barnum & Bailey Combined Shows, Inc. v. Utah Div. of Travel Development*, 955 F. Supp. 605, 614–15 (E.D. Va. 1997) (discussing the inadequacies of current definitions of blurring and determining that blurring requires consumers to mistakenly associate a defendant's mark with a plaintiff's famous trademark).

Tarnishment occurs when a famous mark is improperly associated with an inferior or offensive product or service. *McCarthy,*§24:104 at 24–172 to 173; *Ringling Bros.*, 937 F. Supp. at 209 (citing *Hormel Foods Corp. v. Jim Henson Prods., Inc.*, 73 F.3d 497, 506 (2d. Cir. 1996)).

of Judge Lechner, quoting Judge Wood: "Prospective users of plaintiff's services who mistakenly access defendant's web site may fail to continue to search for plaintiff's own home page, due to anger, frustration or the belief that plaintiff's home page does not exist." *Jews for Jesus v. Brodsky*, 993 F. Supp. 282 (D.N.J. 1998).

Toeppen's use of Panavision.com also puts Panavision's name and reputation at his mercy. *See Intermatic*, 947 F. Supp. at 1240 ("If Toeppen were allowed to use 'intermatic.com,' Intermatic's name and reputation would be at Toeppen's mercy and could be associated with an unimaginable amount of messages on Toeppen's web page.").

We conclude that Toeppen's registration of Panavision's trademarks as his domain names on the Internet diluted those marks within the meaning of the Federal Trademark Dilution Act, 15 U.S.C. §1125(c), and the California Anti-dilution statute, Cal.Bus. & Prof. Code §14330.

III CONCLUSION

Toeppen engaged in a scheme to register Panavision's trademarks as his domain names on the Internet and then to extort money from Panavision by trading on the value of those names. Toeppen's actions were aimed at Panavision in California and the brunt of the harm was felt in California. The district court properly exercised personal jurisdiction over Toeppen.

We also affirm the district court's summary judgment in favor of Panavision under the Federal Trademark Dilution Act, 15 U.S.C. §1125(c), and the California Anti-dilution statute, Cal.Bus. & Prof. Code §14330. Toeppen made commercial use of Panavision's trademarks and his conduct diluted those marks.

Bosley Medical Institute, Inc. v. Kremer
403 F.3d 672 (9th Cir. 2005)

SILVERMAN, CIRCUIT JUDGE:

I. Background

[Bosley Medical owns the trademark to BOSLEY MEDICAL and has used such mark since 1992 in relation to surgical hair transplants services. Michael Kremer is a dissatisfied customer of Bosley Medical. Due to his dissatisfaction Kremer purchased www.BosleyMedical.com. After registering the domain name Kremer delivered a letter to Bosley stating:

> "Let me know if you want to discuss this. Once it is spread over the internet it will have a snowball effect and be too late to stop. M. Kremer [phone number]. P.S. I always follow through on my promises."

Kremer began to use www.BosleyMedical.com in 2001. This website contains critical information of Bosley Medical. The website produces no income and there are no links to Bosley's competitors.]

. . .

Ruling that Kremer's use of "Bosley Medical" in the domain name was noncommercial and unlikely to cause confusion, the district court entered summary judgment for

Kremer on the federal claims and dismissed the state law claims under California's anti-SLAPP [Strategic Lawsuit Against Public Participation] statute. Bosley now appeals.

III. Analysis
A. Trademark Infringement and Dilution Claims

The Trademark Act of 1946 ("Lanham Act") prohibits uses of trademarks, trade names, and trade dress that are likely to cause confusion about the source of a product or service. *See* 15 U.S.C. §§ 1114, *1125(a)*. In 1996, Congress amended *§ 43 of the Lanham Act* to provide a remedy for the dilution of a famous mark. *See* 15 U.S.C. § 1125 (c)....

Infringement claims are subject to a commercial use requirement. The infringement section of the Lanham Act, 15 U.S.C. § 1114, states that any person who "uses in commerce any reproduction, counterfeit, copy, or colorable imitation of a registered mark in connection with the sale, offering for sale, distribution, or advertising of any goods or services on or in connection with which such use is likely to cause confusion, or to cause mistake, or to deceive ..." can be held liable for such use. 15 U.S.C. § 1114(1)(a)....

In 1996, Congress expanded the scope of federal trademark law when it enacted the Federal Trademark Dilution Act ("FTDA"). The FTDA allows the "owner of a famous mark" to obtain "an injunction against another person's *commercial use in commerce* of a mark or trade name...." 15 U.S.C. § 1125(c)(1) (emphasis added). While the meaning of the term "commercial use in commerce" is not entirely clear, we have interpreted the language to be roughly analogous to the "in connection with" sale of goods and services requirement of the infringement statute. *See Mattel, Inc. v. MCA Records, Inc.*, 296 F.3d 894, 903 (9th Cir. 2002).

...

The Supreme Court has made it clear that trademark infringement law prevents only unauthorized uses of a trademark in connection with a commercial transaction in which the trademark is being used to confuse potential consumers. *See Prestonettes, Inc. v. Coty*, 264 U.S. 359, 368, 68 L. Ed. 731, 44 S. Ct. 350, 1924 Dec. Comm'r Pat. 508 (1924)....

As a matter of *First Amendment* law, commercial speech may be regulated in ways that would be impermissible if the same regulation were applied to noncommercial expressions. *Florida Bar v. Went For It, Inc.*, 515 U.S. 618, 623, 132 L. Ed. 2d 541, 115 S. Ct. 2371 (1995). "The *First Amendment* may offer little protection for a competitor who labels its commercial good with a confusingly similar mark, but trademark rights do not entitle the owner to quash an unauthorized use of the mark by another who is communicating ideas or expressing points of view." *Mattel*, 296 F.3d at 900 (internal quotation marks and citations omitted).

The district court ruled that Kremer's use of Bosley's mark was noncommercial. To reach that conclusion, the court focused on the "use in commerce" language rather than the "use in connection with the sale of goods" clause. This approach is erroneous. "Use in commerce" is simply a jurisdictional predicate to any law passed by Congress under the *Commerce Clause*. *See Steele v. Bulova Watch Co.*, 344 U.S. 15 U.S.C. § 1127 states that "unless the contrary is plainly apparent from the context ... the word 'commerce' means all commerce which may lawfully be regulated by Congress." Therefore, the district court should have determined instead whether Kremer's use was "in connection with a sale of goods or services" rather than a "use in commerce." ... The question before us, then, boils down to whether Kremer's use of Bosley Medical as his domain name was "in connection with a sale of goods or services." If it was not, then Kremer's use was "noncommercial" and did not violate the Lanham Act.

Bosley argues that it has met the commercial use requirement in three ways. First, it argues that a mark used in an otherwise noncommercial website or as a domain name for an otherwise noncommercial website is nonetheless used in connection with goods and services where a user can click on a link available on that website to reach a commercial site. *Nissan Motor Co. v. Nissan Computer Corp.*, 378 F.3d 1002 (9th Cir. 2004). However, Bosley's reliance on *Nissan* is unfounded.

The defendant in *Nissan* placed links to other commercial businesses directly on their website. 319 F.3d at 772–73. Kremer's website contains no commercial links, but rather contains links to a discussion group, which in turn contains advertising.... At no time did Kremer's BosleyMedical.com site offer for sale any product or service or contain paid advertisements from any other commercial entity.

Bosley's second argument that Kremer's website satisfies the "in connection with the sale of goods or services" requirement of the Lanham Act is that Kremer created his website to enable an extortion scheme in an attempt to profit from registering BosleyMedical.com. In *Panavision International, L.P. v. Toeppen*, 141 F.3d 1316 (9th Cir. 1998), this court held that a defendant's "commercial use was his attempt to sell the trademarks themselves." *Id.* at 1325.

However, in this case, there is no evidence that Kremer was trying to sell the domain name itself. The letter delivered by Kremer to Bosley's headquarters is a threat to expose negative information about Bosley on the Internet, but it makes no reference whatsoever to ransoming Bosley's trademark or to Kremer's use of the mark as a domain name.

Bosley's third and final argument that it satisfied the commercial use requirement of the Lanham Act is that Kremer's use of Bosley's trademark was in connection with *Bosley's* goods and services. In other words, Kremer used the mark "in connection with goods and services" because he prevented users from obtaining the plaintiff's goods and services. *See People for the Ethical Treatment of Animals v. Doughney*, 263 F.3d 359 (4th Cir. 2001) ("PETA"). In *PETA*, defendants created a site that promoted ideas antithetical to those of the PETA group. *Id.* at 362–63. The Fourth Circuit held that the defendant's parody site, though not having a commercial purpose and not selling any goods or services, violated the Lanham Act because it "prevented users from obtaining or using PETA's goods or services." *Id.* at 365.

However, in *PETA*, the defendant's website "provided links to more than 30 commercial operations offering goods and services." *Id.* at 366. To the extent that the *PETA* court held that the Lanham Act's commercial use requirement is satisfied because the defendant's use of the plaintiff's mark as the domain name may deter customers from reaching the plaintiff's site itself, we respectfully disagree with that rationale. While it is true that www.BosleyMedical.com is not sponsored by Bosley Medical, it is just as true that it is *about* Bosley Medical. The *PETA* approach would place most critical, otherwise protected consumer commentary under the restrictions of the Lanham Act. Other courts have also rejected this theory as over-expansive.

The Second Circuit held in *United We Stand America, Inc. v. United We Stand, America New York, Inc.*, 128 F.3d 86, 90 (2d Cir. 1997), that the "use in connection with the sale of goods and services" requirement of the Lanham Act does not require any actual *sale* of goods and services. Thus, the appropriate inquiry is whether Kremer offers *competing* services to the public. Kremer is not Bosley's competitor; he is their critic. His use of the Bosley mark is not in connection with a sale of goods or services — it is in connection with the expression of his opinion *about* Bosley's goods and services.

The dangers that the Lanham Act was designed to address are simply not at issue in this case. The Lanham Act, expressly enacted to be applied in commercial contexts, does not prohibit all unauthorized uses of a trademark.... Any harm to Bosley arises not from a competitor's sale of a similar product under Bosley's mark, but from Kremer's criticism of their services. Bosley cannot use the Lanham Act either as a shield from Kremer's criticism, or as a sword to shut Kremer up.

IV. Conclusion

We affirm the district court's entry of summary judgment in favor of Kremer with respect to the infringement and dilution claims.

———————

Notes

1. In *Panavison*, the judge discussed consumer discouragement caused by wading through "hundreds of web sites." The judge claimed that this dilutes the value of Panavision's trademark. Remember the issues raised in the previous case. If the magistrate judge in *Intermatic v. Toeppen, supra,* couldn't determine confusion partially because he could not determine the consumer's bearing toward the use of marks in domain names, why can Judge Thompson conclude that discouragement is dilution? He cites two cases to conclude, as a matter of law, that, when searching for a famous mark, multiple hits create "anger," "frustration," and are "likely to deter web [consumers]." Is dilution more likely on less sophisticated search engines? Are neophytes offered greater protections? Has the judge taken judicial notice here? If he has, of what?

2. The *Kremer* case states that the domain name analysis was not a "use in commerce" but a "use in connection with the sale of goods." What is the difference between the two and how does this relate to domain names?

3. What is needed for a domain name to be used in connection with the sale of goods?

———————

F. Anticybersquatting Consumer Protection Act (ACPA)

1. Cause of Action

15 U.S.C. §1125, Lanham Act §43

(d) Cyberpiracy prevention.

(1) (A) A person shall be liable in a civil action by the owner or a mark, including a personal name which is protected as a mark under this section, if, without regard to the goods or services of the parties, that person—

(i) has a bad faith intent to profit from that mark, including a personal name which is protected as a mark under this section; and

(ii) registers, traffics in, or uses a domain name that—

(I) in the case of a mark that is distinctive at the time of registration of the domain name, is identical or confusingly similar to that mark;

(II) in the case of a famous mark that is famous at the time of registration of the domain name, is identical or confusingly similar to or dilutive of that mark; or

    (III) is a trademark, word, or name protected by reason of section 706 of title 18, United States Code, or section 220506 of title 36, United States Code.

(B)(i) In determining whether a person has a bad faith intent described under subparagraph (A), a court may consider factors such as, but not limited to—

    (I) the trademark or other intellectual property rights of the person, if any, in the domain name;

    (II) the extent to which the domain name consists of the legal name of the person or a name that is otherwise commonly used to identify that person;

    (III) the person's prior use, if any, of the domain name in connection with the bona fide offering of any goods or services;

    (IV) the person's bona fide noncommercial or fair use of the mark in a site accessible under the domain name;

    (V) the person's intent to divert consumers from the mark owner's online location to a site accessible under the domain name that could harm the goodwill represented by the mark, either for commercial gain or with the intent to tarnish or disparage the mark, by creating a likelihood of confusion as to the source, sponsorship, affiliation, or endorsement of the site;

    (VI) the person's offer to transfer, sell, or otherwise assign the domain name to the mark owner or any third party for financial gain without having used, or having an intent to use, the domain name in the bona fide offering of any goods or services, or the person's prior conduct indicating a pattern of such conduct;

    (VII) the person's provision of material and misleading false contact information when applying for the registration of the domain name, the person's intentional failure to maintain accurate contact information, or the person's prior conduct indicating a pattern of such conduct;

    (VIII) the person's registration or acquisition of multiple domain names which the person knows are identical or confusingly similar to marks of others that are distinctive at the time of registration of such domain names, or dilutive of famous marks of others that are famous at the time of registration of such domain names, without regard to the goods or services of the parties; and

    (IX) the extent to which the mark incorporated in the person's domain name registration is or is not distinctive and famous within the meaning of subsection (c)(1) of section 43 [sub §(c)(1) of this section].

    (ii) Bad faith intent described under subparagraph (A) shall not be found in any case in which the court determines that the person believed and had reasonable grounds to believe that the use of the domain name was a fair use or otherwise lawful.

(C) In any civil action involving the registration, trafficking, or use of a domain name under this paragraph, a court may order the forfeiture or cancellation of the domain name or the transfer of the domain name to the owner of the mark.

(D) A person shall be liable for using a domain name under subparagraph (A) only if that person is the domain name registrant or that registrant's authorized licensee.

(E) As used in this paragraph, the term "traffics in" refers to transactions that include, but are not limited to, sales, purchases, loans, pledges, licenses, exchanges of currency, and any other transfer for consideration or receipt in exchange for consideration.

(2)(A) The owner of a mark may file an in rem civil action against a domain name in the judicial district in which the domain name registrar, domain name registry, or other domain name authority that registered or assigned the domain name is located if—

> (i) the domain name violates any right of the owner of a mark registered in the Patent and Trademark Office, or protected under subsection (a) or (c); and

> (ii) the court finds that the owner—

>> (I) is not able to obtain in personam jurisdiction over a person who would have been a defendant in a civil action under paragraph (1); or

>> (II) through due diligence was not able to find a person who would have been a defendant in a civil action under paragraph (1) by—

>>> (aa) sending a notice of the alleged violation and intent to proceed under this paragraph to the registrant of the domain name at the postal and e-mail address provided by the registrant to the registrar; and

>>> (bb) publishing notice of the action as the court may direct promptly after filing the action.

(B) The actions under subparagraph (A)(ii) shall constitute service of process.

(C) In an in rem action under this paragraph, a domain name shall be deemed to have its situs in the judicial district in which—

> (i) the domain name registrar, registry, or other domain name authority that registered or assigned the domain name is located; or

> (ii) documents sufficient to establish control and authority regarding the disposition of the registration and use of the domain name are deposited with the court.

(D)(i) The remedies in an in rem action under this paragraph shall be limited to a court order for the forfeiture or cancellation of the domain name or the transfer of the domain name to the owner of the mark. Upon receipt of written notification of a filed, stamped copy of a complaint filed by the owner of a mark in a United States district court under this paragraph, the domain name registrar, domain name registry, or other domain name authority shall—

> (I) expeditiously deposit with the court documents sufficient to establish the court's control and authority regarding the disposition of the registration and use of the domain name to the court; and

> (II) not transfer, suspend, or otherwise modify the domain name during the pendency of the action, except upon order of the court.

> (ii) The domain name registrar or registry or other domain name authority shall not be liable for injunctive or monetary relief under this paragraph except in the case of bad faith or reckless disregard, which includes a willful failure to comply with any such court order.

(3) The civil action established under paragraph (1) and the in rem action established under paragraph (2), and any remedy available under either such action, shall be in addition to any other civil action or remedy otherwise applicable.

(4) The in rem jurisdiction established under paragraph (2) shall be in addition to any other jurisdiction that otherwise exists, whether in rem or in personam.

———————

Sporty's Farm L.L.C. v. Sportsman's Market, Inc.
202 F.3d 489 (2d Cir. 2000)

CALABRESI, C. J.

* * *

Sportsman's is a mail order catalog company that is quite well-known among pilots and aviation enthusiasts for selling products tailored to their needs. In recent years, Sportsman's has expanded its catalog business well beyond the aviation market into that for tools and home accessories. The company annually distributes approximately 18 million catalogs nationwide, and has yearly revenues of about $50 million. Aviation sales account for about 60% of Sportsman's revenue, while non-aviation sales comprise the remaining 40%.

In the 1960s, Sportsman's began using the logo *"sporty"* to identify its catalogs and products. In 1985, Sportsman's registered the trademark *sporty's* with the United States Patent and Trademark Office. Since then, Sportsman's has complied with all statutory requirements to preserve its interest in the *sporty's* mark. *Sporty's* appears on the cover of all Sportsman's catalogs; Sportsman's international toll free number is 1-800-4*sportys*; and one of Sportsman's domestic toll free phone numbers is 1-800-*Sportys*. Sportsman's spends about $10 million per year advertising its sporty's logo.

Omega is a mail order catalog company that sells mainly scientific process measurement and control instruments. In late 1994 or early 1995, the owners of Omega, Arthur and Betty Hollander, decided to enter the aviation catalog business and, for that purpose, formed a wholly-owned subsidiary called Pilot's Depot, LLC ("Pilot's Depot"). Shortly thereafter, Omega registered the domain name sportys.com with NSI. Arthur Hollander was a pilot who received Sportsman's catalogs and thus was aware of the *sporty's* trademark.

In January 1996, nine months after registering sportys.com, Omega formed another wholly-owned subsidiary called Sporty's Farm and sold it the rights to sportys.com for $16,200. Sporty's Farm grows and sells Christmas trees, and soon began advertising its Christmas trees on a sportys.com web page. When asked how the name Sporty's Farm was selected for Omega's Christmas tree subsidiary, Ralph S. Michael, the CEO of Omega and manager of Sporty's Farm, explained, as summarized by the district court, that

> in his own mind and among his family, he always thought of and referred to the Pennsylvania land where Sporty's Farm now operates as *Spotty's farm*. The origin of the name ... derived from a childhood memory he had of his uncle's farm in upstate New York. As a youngster, Michael owned a dog named Spotty. Because the dog strayed, his uncle took him to his upstate farm. Michael thereafter referred to the farm as Spotty's farm. The name Sporty's Farm was ... a subsequent derivation.

Joint Appendix ("JA") at 277 (emphasis added). There is, however, no evidence in the record that Hollander was considering starting a Christmas tree business when he registered sportys.com or that Hollander was ever acquainted with Michael's dog Spotty.

In March 1996, Sportsman's discovered that Omega had registered sportys.com as a domain name. Thereafter, and before Sportsman's could take any action, Sporty's Farm brought this declaratory action seeking the right to continue its use of sportys.com. Sportsman's counterclaimed and also sued Omega as a third-party defendant for, *inter alia*, (1) trademark infringement, (2) trademark dilution pursuant to the FTDA, and (3) unfair

competition under state law. Both sides sought injunctive relief to force the other to relinquish its claims to sportys.com. While this litigation was ongoing, Sportsman's used
"sportys-catalogs.com" as its primary domain name.

After a bench trial, the court rejected Sportsman's trademark infringement claim and
all related claims that are based on a "likelihood of [consumer] confusion" since "the parties operate wholly unrelated businesses [and t]herefore, confusion in the marketplace is
not likely to develop." *Id.* at 282–83. But on Sportsman's trademark dilution action, where
a likelihood of confusion was not necessary, the district court found for Sportsman's. The
court concluded (1) that *sporty's* was a famous mark entitled to protection under the
FTDA since "the '*Sporty's*' mark enjoys general name recognition in the consuming public," *id.* at 288, and (2) that Sporty's Farm and Omega had diluted *sporty's* because "registration of the 'sportys.com' domain name effectively compromises Sportsman's Market's
ability to identify and distinguish its goods on the Internet.... [by] preclud[ing] Sportsman's Market from using its 'unique identifier,'" *id.* at 289. The court also held, however,
that Sportsman's could only get injunctive relief and was not entitled to "punitive damages ... profits, and attorney's fees and costs" pursuant to the FTDA since Sporty Farm
and Omega's conduct did not constitute willful dilution under the FTDA. *Id.* at 292–93.

Finally, the district court ruled that, although Sporty's Farm had violated the FTDA,
its conduct did not constitute a violation of CUTPA. This conclusion was based on the
district court's finding that Sportsman's had failed to show by a preponderance of the evidence (1) that Sporty's Farm and Omega's "conduct was immoral, unethical, oppressive,
or unscrupulous," and (2) that Sportsman's "suffered a substantial injury sufficient to establish a CUTPA claim." *Id.* at 291–92.

The district court then issued an injunction forcing Sporty's Farm to relinquish all
rights to sportys.com. And Sportsman's subsequently acquired the domain name. Both
Sporty's Farm and Sportsman's appeal. Specifically, Sporty's Farm appeals the judgment
insofar as the district court granted an injunction in favor of Sportsman's for the use of
the domain name. Sportsman's, on the other hand, in addition to urging this court to
affirm the district court's injunction, cross-appeals, quite correctly as a procedural matter, the district court's denial of damages under both the FTDA and CUPTA. *See* 16A
Charles Alan Wright et al., *Federal Practice and Procedure* §3974.4 (3d ed. 1999) ("[A]
cross-appeal is required to support modification of the judgment....").

* * *

A. Application of the ACPA to this Case

The first issue before us is whether the ACPA governs this case. The district court based
its holding on the FTDA since the ACPA had not been passed when it made its decision.
Because the ACPA became law while this case was pending before us, we must decide
how its passage affects this case. As a general rule, we apply the law that exists at the time
of the appeal.

But even if a new law controls, the question remains whether in such circumstances it
is more appropriate for the appellate court to apply it directly or, instead, to remand to the
district court to enable that court to consider the effect of the new law. We therefore asked
for additional briefing from the parties regarding the applicability of the ACPA to the case
before us. After receiving those briefs and fully considering the arguments there made, we
think it is clear that the new law was adopted specifically to provide courts with a prefer-
able alternative to stretching federal dilution law when dealing with cybersquatting cases.
Indeed, the new law constitutes a particularly good fit with this case. Moreover, the find-

ings of the district court, together with the rest of the record, enable us to apply the new law to the case before us without difficulty. Accordingly, we will do so and forego a remand.

B. "Distinctive" or "Famous"

Under the new Act, we must first determine whether *sporty's* is a distinctive or famous mark and thus entitled to the ACPA's protection. *See* 15 U.S.C. §§1125(d)(1) (A)(ii)(I), (II). The district court concluded that *sporty's* is both distinctive and famous. We agree that *sporty's* is a "distinctive" mark. As a result, and without casting any doubt on the district court's holding in this respect, we need not, and hence do not, decide whether *sporty's* is also a "famous" mark.[2]

Distinctiveness refers to inherent qualities of a mark and is a completely different concept from fame. A mark may be distinctive before it has been used—when its fame is nonexistent. By the same token, even a famous mark may be so ordinary, or descriptive as to be notable for its lack of distinctiveness. *See Nabisco, Inc. v. PF Brands, Inc.*, 191 F.3d 208, 215–26 (2d Cir. 1999). We have no doubt that *sporty's*, as used in connection with Sportsman's catalogue of merchandise and advertising, is inherently distinctive. Furthermore, Sportsman's filed an affidavit under 15 U.S.C. §1065 that rendered its registration of the *sporty's* mark incontestable, which entitles Sportsman's "to a presumption that its registered trademark is inherently distinctive." Equine Technologies, Inc. v. Equitechnology, Inc., 68 F.3d 542, 545 (1st Cir. 1995). We therefore conclude that, *for* the purposes of §1125(d)(I)(A)(ii)(I), the *sporty's* mark is distinctive.

C. "Identical and Confusingly Similar"

The next question is whether domain name sportys.com is "identical or confusingly similar to" the *sporty's* mark.[3] 15 U.S.C. §1125 (d)(l)(A)(ii)(I). As we noted above, apostrophes cannot be used in domain names. As a result, the secondary domain name in this case (sportys) is indistinguishable from the Sportsman's trademark (sporty's). We therefore conclude that, although the domain name sportys.com is not precisely identical to the *sporty's* mark, it is certainly "confusingly similar" to the protected mark under §1125(d)(1)(A)(ii)(I).

D. "Bad Faith Intent to Profit"

We next turn to the issue of whether Sporty's Farm acted with a "bad faith intent to profit" from the mark *sporty's* when it registered the domain name sportys.com. 15

---

2. In most respects, *sporty's* meets the rigorous criteria laid out in §1125(c)(1), requiring both fame and distinctiveness for protection under the FTDA. *See Nabisco Brands, Inc., v. PF Brands, Inc.,* 191 F.3d 208,216 (2d Cir. 1999). The mark (1) is sufficiently distinctive (as we discuss in the text), (2) has been used by Sportsman's for an extended period of time, (3) has had millions of dollars in advertising spent on it, (4) is used nationwide, and (5) is traded in a wide variety of retail channels. *See* 15 U.S.C. §1125(c)(1)(A)-(E). Moreover, the record does not indicate that anyone else besides Sportsman's uses *sporty's*, and the mark is, of course, registered with federal authorities. *See id.* at §1125(c)(1)(G)-(H).

More vexing is the question posed by the criterion that focuses on "the degree of recognition of the mark in the trading areas and channels of trade used by the marks' owner and the person against whom the injunction is sought." *Id.* at § 1125(c)(I)(F). Sporty's Farm contends that, although *sporty's* is a very well-known mark in the pilot and aviation niche market, Sportsman's did not (and could not) prove that the mark was well-known to *Sporty's Farm's* customers. We need not reach this question, as we would have had to do under the FTDA, since the ACPA provides protection not only to famous marks but also to distinctive marks regardless of fame.

3. We note that "confusingly similar" is a different standard from the "likelihood of confusion" standard for trademark infringement adopted by this court in *Polaroid Corp. v. PolaradElectronics Corp.*, 287 F.2d 492 (2d Cir. 1961). *See Wella Corp. v. Wella Graphics, Inc.,* 37 F.3d 46,48 (2d Cir. 1994).

U.S.C. §1125(d)(1)(A)(i). The statute lists nine factors to assist courts in determining when a defendant has acted with a bad faith intent to profit from the use of a mark. But we are not limited to considering just the listed factors when making our determination of whether the statutory criterion has been met. The factors are, instead, expressly described as indicia that "may" be considered along with other facts. *Id.* §1125(d)(1)(B)(i).

We hold that there is more than enough evidence in the record below of "bad faith intent to profit" on the part of Sporty's Farm (as that term is defined in the statute), so that "no reasonable factfinder could return a verdict against" Sportsman's. *Norville v. Staten Island Univ. Hosp.*, 196 F.3d 89, 95 (2d Cir. 1999). First, it is clear that neither Sporty's Farm nor Omega had any intellectual property rights in sportys.com at the time Omega registered the domain name. *See id.* §1125(d)(1)(B)(i)(I). Sporty's Farm was not formed until nine months after the domain name was registered, and it did not begin operations or obtain the domain name from Omega until after this lawsuit was filed. Second, the domain name does not consist of the legal name of the party that registered it, Omega. *See id.* §1125(d)(1)(B)(i)(II). Moreover, although the domain name does include part of the name of Sporty's Farm, that entity did not exist at the time the domain name was registered.

The third factor, the prior use of the domain name in connection with the bona fide offering of any goods or services, also cuts against Sporty's Farm since it did not use the site until after this litigation began, undermining its claim that the offering of Christmas trees on the site was in good faith. *See id.* §1125(d)(1)(B)(i)(III). Further weighing in favor of a conclusion that Sporty's Farm had the requisite statutory bad faith intent, as a matter of law, are the following: (1) Sporty's Farm does not claim that its use of the domain name was "noncommercial" or a "fair use of the mark," *see id.* §1125(d)(1)(B)(i)(IV), (2) Omega sold the mark to Sporty's Farm under suspicious circumstances, *see Sporty's Farm v. Sportsman's Market*, No. 96CV0756 (D. Conn. Mar. 13, 1998), *reprinted in* Joint Appendix at A277 (describing the circumstances of the transfer of sportys.com); 15 U.S.C. §1125(d)(1)(B)(i)(VI), and, (3) as we discussed above, the *sporty's* mark is undoubtedly distinctive, *see id.* §1125(d)(1)(B)(i)(IX).

The most important grounds for our holding that Sporty's Farm acted with a bad faith intent, however, are the unique circumstances of this case, which do not fit neatly into the specific factors enumerated by Congress but may nevertheless be considered under the statute. We know from the record and from the district court's findings that Omega planned to enter into direct competition with Sportsman's in the pilot and aviation consumer market. As recipients of Sportsman's catalogs, Omega's owners, the Hollanders, were fully aware that *sporty's* was a very strong mark for consumers of those products. It cannot be doubted, as the court found below, that Omega registered sportys.com for the primary purpose of keeping Sportsman's from using that domain name. Several months later, and after this lawsuit was filed, Omega created another company in an unrelated business that received the name Sporty's Farm so that it could (1) use the sportys.com domain name in some commercial fashion, (2) keep the name away from Sportsman's, and (3) protect itself in the event that Sportsman's brought an infringement claim alleging that a "likelihood of confusion" had been created by Omega's version of cybersquatting. Finally, the explanation given for Sporty's Farm's desire to use the domain name, based on the existence of the dog Spotty, is more amusing than credible. Given these facts and the district court's grant of an equitable injunction under the FTDA, there is ample and overwhelming evidence that, as a matter of law, Sporty's Farm's acted with a "bad faith intent to profit" from the domain name sportys.com as those terms are used in the ACPA.

E. Remedy

Based on the foregoing, we hold that under §1125(d)(1)(A), Sporty's Farm violated Sportsman's statutory rights by its use of the sportys.com domain name. The question that remains is what remedy is Sportsman's entitled to. The Act permits a court to "order the forfeiture or cancellation of the domain name or the transfer of the domain name to the owner of the mark," §1125(d)(1)(C) for any "domain name registered before, on, or after the date of the enactment of [the] Act," Pub. L. No. 106-113, §3010. That is precisely what the district court did here, albeit under the pre-existing law, when it directed a) Omega and Sporty's Farm to release their interest in sportys.com and to transfer the name to Sportsman's, and b) permanently enjoined those entities from taking any action to prevent and/or hinder Sportsman's from obtaining the domain name. That relief remains appropriate under the ACPA. We therefore affirm the district court's grant of injunctive relief.

We must also determine, however, if Sportsman's is entitled to damages either under the ACPA or pre-existing law. Under the ACPA, damages are unavailable to Sportsman's since sportys.com was registered and used by Sporty's Farm prior to the passage of the new law. *See id.* (stating that damages can be awarded for violations of the Act but that they are not "available with respect to the registration, trafficking, or use of a domain name that occurs before the date of the enactment of this Act.").

But Sportsman's might, nonetheless, be eligible for damages under the FTDA since there is nothing in the ACPA that precludes, in cybersquatting cases, the award of damages under any pre-existing law. *See* 15 U.S.C §1125(d)(3) (providing that any remedies created by the new act are "in addition to any other civil action or remedy otherwise applicable"). Under the FTDA, "the owner of the famous mark shall be entitled only to injunctive relief unless the person against whom the injunction is sought *willfully* intended to trade on the owner's reputation or to cause dilution of the famous mark." *Id.* §1125(c)(2) (emphasis added). Accordingly, where willful intent to dilute is demonstrated, the owner of the famous mark is—subject to the principles of equity—entitled to recover (1) damages (2) the dilutor's profits, and (3) costs. *See id.; see also id.* §1117(a) (specifying remedies).

We conclude, however, that damages are not available to Sportsman's under the FTDA. The district court found that Sporty's Farm did not act willfully. We review such findings of "willfulness" by a district court for clear error. Thus, even assuming the sporty's mark to be famous, we cannot say that the district court clearly erred when it found that Sporty's Farm's actions were not willful. To be sure, that question is a very close one, for the facts make clear that, as a Sportsman's customer, Arthur Hollander (Omega's owner) was aware of the significance of the *sporty's* logo. And the idea of creating a Christmas tree business named Sporty's Farm, allegedly in honor of Spotty the dog, and of giving that business the sportys.com domain name seems to have occurred to Omega only several months after it had registered the name. Nevertheless, given the uncertain state of the law at the time that Sporty's Farm and Omega acted, we cannot say that the district court clearly erred in finding that their behavior did not amount to willful dilution. It follows that Sportsman's is not entitled to damages under the FTDA.

Note

1. A law student recognizes that her law school has not registered a likely domain name for the school. The student registers a common abbreviation for that law school and posts

that student's view of the law school on the web page. Some of this information is simply information; some of the information is critical of the school. The law school sues the student under the ACPA. Who ought to prevail? *See* Adam Liptak, *Welcome to Our Law School, Young Man. We'll See You in Court*, N.Y. TIMES, May 6, 2002, at A12 (describing the plight of Douglas Dorhauer, a law student at Louisiana State University Law School when he registered <www.lsulaw.com>.

---

2. Bad Faith

15 U.S.C. §1125 (d)(l)(B)(i)

Virtual Works, Inc. v. Volkswagen of America, Inc.

238 F. 3d 264 (4th Cir. 2001)

WILKINSON, C. J.

Volkswagen challenges Virtual Works, Inc.'s use of the domain name vw.net under the 1999 Anticybersquatting Consumer Protection Act (ACPA). Volkswagen claims that Virtual Works registered vw.net with the purpose of one day selling it to Volkswagen. The district court agreed, holding that Virtual Works had a bad faith intent to profit from the vw.net domain name and that its use of vw.net diluted and infringed upon the VW mark. *Virtual Works, Inc. v. Network Solutions, Inc.*, 106 F. Supp. 2d 845 (E.D. Va. 2000). The district court therefore ordered Virtual Works to relinquish to Volkswagen the rights to vw.net. Because the district court did not err in holding that Virtual Works violated the ACPA, we affirm the judgment.

I.

* * *

At the time Virtual Works registered *vw.net*, two of its principals, Christopher Grimes and James Anderson, were aware that some Internet users might think that *vw.net* was affiliated with Volkswagen. According to Grimes, he and Anderson "talked about Volkswagen and decided that [they] would use the domain name for [the] company, but if Volkswagen offered to work out a deal for services or products, that [they] would sell it to [Volkswagen] for a lot of money." When Virtual Works registered vw.net, many other domain names were available for its use. For instance, *vwi.net, vwi.org, virtualworks.net*, and *virtualworks.org*, were still available.

Virtual Works used the *vw.net* domain name for approximately two years as a part of its ISP business. In December 1998, various Volkswagen dealerships contacted Virtual Works and expressed an interest in purchasing the rights to the vw.net domain name. Virtual Works, in turn, called Volkswagen, offering to sell vw.net. The terms of Virtual Works' offer, however, were somewhat unusual. Anderson left a voice mail message for Linda Scipione in Volkswagen's trademark department. In the message, Anderson stated that he owned the rights to vw.net. He also said that unless Volkswagen bought the rights to *vw.net*, Virtual Works would sell the domain name to the highest bidder. Anderson gave Volkswagen twenty-four hours to respond.

In response to what it perceived as a threat to the VW mark, Volkswagen invoked NSI's dispute resolution procedure. NSI in turn told Virtual Works that Virtual Works would lose the vw.net domain name unless it filed a declaratory judgment action against

Volkswagen. Virtual Works complied. Volkswagen subsequently counterclaimed, alleging trademark dilution, infringement, and cybersquatting under the ACPA. 15 U.S.C. §1125(d). The district court granted Volkswagen's motion for summary judgment on its cybersquatting, dilution, and infringement counterclaims and dismissed Virtual Works' cross-motions on the same. Accordingly, the district court ordered Virtual Works to relinquish to Volkswagen the rights to the *vw.net* domain name. Virtual Works appeals.

II.

A.

The ACPA was enacted in 1999 in response to concerns over the proliferation of cybersquatting—the Internet version of a land grab. According to the Senate Report accompanying the Act: "Trademark owners are facing a new form of piracy on the Internet caused by acts of 'cybersquatting,' which refers to the deliberate, bad-faith, and abusive registration of Internet domain names in violation of the rights of trademark owners." S. Rep. No. 106-140, at 4. (1999). Cybersquatting is the practice of registering "well-known brand names as Internet domain names" in order to force the rightful owners of the marks "to pay for the right to engage in electronic commerce under their own brand name." *Id.* at 5. *See also* H.R. Rep. No. 106-412, at 5–7 (1999). Cybersquatting is profitable because while it is inexpensive for a cybersquatter to register the mark of an established company as a domain name, such companies are often vulnerable to being forced into paying substantial sums to get their names back. *Sporty's Farm, L.L.C. v. Sportsman's Market, Inc.*, 202 F.3d 489, 493 (2d Cir. 2000).

Congress viewed the practice of cybersquatting as harmful because it threatened "the continued growth and vitality of the Internet as a platform" for "communication, electronic commerce, education, entertainment, and countless other yet-to-be-determined uses." S. Rep. No. 106-140, at 8. New legislation was required to address this situation because then-current law did not expressly prohibit the act of cybersquatting and cybersquatters had started to take the necessary precautions to insulate themselves from liability under the Federal Trademark Dilution Act. *Id.* at 7. Accordingly, Congress passed, and the President signed, the ACPA in 1999. Pub. L. No. 106-113, 113 Stat. 1536 (codified at 15 U.S.C. §1125(d)).

B.

* * *

In addition to listing these nine factors, the Act contains a safe harbor. The safe harbor provision states that bad faith intent "shall not be found in any case in which the court determines that the person believed and had reasonable grounds to believe that the use of the domain name was fair use or otherwise lawful." 15 U.S.C. §1125(d)(1)(B)(ii).

A court is not limited to considering these nine factors when determining the presence or absence of bad faith. 15 U.S.C. §l125(d)(1)(B)(i). The Second Circuit, in the first court of appeals case addressing the ACPA, noted that the most important grounds for finding bad faith "are the unique circumstances of the case, which do not fit neatly into the specific factors enumerated by Congress but may nevertheless be considered under the statute." *Sporty's Farm*, 202 F.3d at 499.

The remedies available under the ACPA depend on when the unlawful activity took place. A person who unlawfully registers, traffics in, or uses a domain name after the ACPA's date of enactment, November 29, 1999, can be liable for monetary damages under 15 U.S.C.

§1117(d) and can have the domain name transferred to the owner of the mark or canceled under 15 U.S.C. §1125(d)(2)(D)(i). The only remedy available for ACPA violations that occurred before November 29, 1999, however, is to have the domain name transferred to the owner of the mark or canceled. Anticybersquatting Consumer Protection Act, Pub. L. No. 106-113, §3010, 113 Stat. 1536. Since Virtual Works' alleged cybersquatting occurred before the ACPA's date of enactment, Volkswagen sought only the right to use *vw.net* for itself.

III.

Having discussed the statutory purpose and framework of the ACPA, we must now determine whether Virtual Works violated the Act. The district court found that a number of the ACPA's nine bad faith factors supported Volkswagen's claim that Virtual Works' registration of *vw.net* constituted cybersquatting under the Act. *Virtual Works*, 106 F. Supp. 2d at 848. With respect to the first and second factors, for example, the district court held that Virtual Works had no right to or interest in the VW mark and that Virtual Works had never been referred to or done business under the name VW. *Id.* at 847. With respect to the fifth factor, the district court held that the disparaging comments posted by Virtual Works harmed the goodwill of the VW mark. *Id.* Finally, the district court found that, under the ninth factor, the famousness of the VW mark also favored Volkswagen. *Id.* The district court thus granted summary judgment to Volkswagen, which we review de novo.

A.

The first inquiry under the ACPA is whether Virtual Works acted with a bad faith intent to profit from a protected mark. 15 U.S.C. §1125(d)(I)(A)(i). Virtual Works claims that the district court erred in holding that it did. We need not, however, march through the nine factors seriatim because the ACPA itself notes that use of the listed criteria is permissive. As the Second Circuit noted in *Sporty's Farms*, the factors are "expressly described as indicia that 'may' be considered along with other facts." 202 F.3d at 498 (citing 15 U.S.C. §1125(d)(1)(B)(i)).

We are mindful that the instant case comes to us on summary judgment and involves a contested determination of Virtual Works' intent. Unfortunately for Virtual Works, however, there is both circumstantial and direct evidence establishing bad faith. The following uncontested facts all provide circumstantial evidence of Virtual Works' bad faith with respect to the VW mark: 1) the famousness of the VW mark; 2) the similarity of *vw.net* to the VW mark; 3) the admission that Virtual Works never once did business as VW nor identified itself as such; and 4) the availability of *vwi.org* and *vwi.net* at the time Virtual Works registered *vw.net*. Notably, either of these domain names would have satisfied Virtual Works' own stated criterion of registering a domain name that used only two or three letters and would have eliminated any risk of confusion with respect to the VW mark.

We consider such circumstantial factors cautiously, however. We do not suggest that these four facts would alone resolve the question of Virtual Works' intent on summary judgment. The fact that a domain resembles a famous trademark, for example, hardly in and of itself establishes bad faith. Moreover, domain names that are abbreviations of a company's formal name are quite common. To view the use of such names as tantamount to bad faith would chill Internet entrepreneurship with the prospect of endless litigation.

Volkswagen, however, points to direct evidence regarding Virtual Works' intent—the statements made at registration. Grimes' deposition reveals that when registering *vw.net*, he and Anderson specifically acknowledged that *vw.net* might be confused with Volkswagen by some Internet users. They nevertheless decided to register the address for their own use, but left open the possibility of one day selling the site to Volkswagen "for a lot of money." Volkswagen claims that this is sufficient to establish bad faith registration in violation of the ACPA.

Viewing the facts in the light most favorable to Virtual Works, as we must on summary judgment, the statement at registration establishes that Virtual Works had a dual purpose in selecting *vw.net*. Contrary to Virtual Works' claim, the fact that it used *vw.net* for two years as a part of an ISP business is not dispositive of the question of intent. Virtual Works chose *vw.net* over other domain names not just because "vw" reflected the company's own initials, but also because it foresaw the ability to profit from the natural association of *vw.net* with the VW mark. Indeed, it is obvious even to a casual observer that the similarity between *vw.net* and the VW mark is overwhelming.

Moreover, the facts in the summary judgment record affirmatively support the claim that Virtual Works had a bad faith intent to profit when it attempted to sell *vw.net* to Volkswagen. It is true that a mere offer to sell a domain name is not itself evidence of unlawful trafficking. H.R. Conf. Rep. No. 106-464, at 111 (1999). The ACPA was not enacted to put an end to the sale of all domain names. This case, however, involves much more than a plain vanilla offer to sell a domain name.

Indeed, the second piece of direct evidence regarding Virtual Works' intent is the terms of its offer to Volkswagen. Virtual Works told Volkswagen that *vw.net* would be sold to the highest bidder if Volkswagen did not make an offer within twenty-four hours. Virtual Works also stated that others would jump at the chance to own a valuable domain name like *vw.net* because Internet users would instinctively associate the site with Volkswagen. Virtual Works knew, both when it registered *vw.net* and when it offered to sell the site, that consumers would associate *vw.net* with Volkswagen. It sought to maximize the advantage of this association by threatening to auction off the site. And it hoped that in an effort to protect its mark, Volkswagen would respond with a hefty offer of its own.

Likewise, Virtual Works cannot take refuge in the ACPA's safe harbor provision. The safe harbor is only available when the defendant both "believed and had reasonable grounds to believe that the use of the domain name was fair use or otherwise lawful." 15 U.S.C. §1125(d)(1)(B)(ii). The openly admitted hope of profiting from consumer confusion of *vw.net* with the VW mark disqualifies Virtual Works from the ACPA's safe harbor. A defendant who acts even partially in bad faith in registering a domain name is not, as a matter of law, entitled to benefit from the Act's safe harbor provision. Virtual Works knew it was registering a domain name bearing strong resemblance to a federally protected trademark. And it did so, at least in part, with the idea of selling the site "for a lot of money" to the mark's owner.

Just as we are reluctant to interpret the ACPA's liability provisions in an overly aggressive manner, we decline to construe the safe harbor so broadly as to undermine the rest of the statute. All but the most blatant cybersquatters will be able to put forth at least some lawful motives for their behavior. To hold that all such individuals may qualify for the safe harbor would frustrate Congress' purpose by artificially limiting the statute's reach. We do not think Congress intended the safe harbor to protect defendants operating, at least in part, with unlawful intent.

The ACPA allows a court to view the totality of the circumstances in making the bad faith determination. 15 U.S.C. §1125(d)(1)(B)(i). Here, that means looking at the purely circumstantial indicia of bad faith, as well as the direct evidence of the statements made at the time of registration and the direct evidence regarding terms of the sale. Whether our decision would be the same in the absence of any particular piece of evidence is a question we need not address. Viewed in its totality, the evidence establishes that at the time Virtual Works proposed to sell *vw.net* to Volkswagen, it was motivated by a bad faith intent to profit from the famousness of the VW mark. This is the sort of misconduct that Congress sought to discourage.

B.

The second inquiry under the ACPA is whether Virtual Works 1) registered, trafficked in, or used a domain name; 2) that is identical or confusingly similar to a distinctive mark; or 3) is identical, confusingly similar to, or dilutive of a famous mark. 15 U.S.C. §1125(d)(1)(A)(ii). There is no dispute that Virtual Works registered, trafficked in, and used *vw.net*. There is also no dispute that the VW mark is famous. The sole point of contention is whether *vw.net* is identical, confusingly similar to, or dilutive of Volkswagen's famous VW mark.

Virtual Works claims it is not similar because there is a distinction between the.*net* and.*com* TLD. According to Virtual Works, Volkswagen could not have registered *vw.net* in October of 1996 because it is an automaker and not an Internet service provider. This claim, however, is unavailing in light of the fact that NSI stopped enforcing the .*com/.net* distinction over a year before Virtual Works registered *vw.net*. The claim is also undermined by Virtual Works' admission that at the time of registration it was aware of the potential confusion with the VW mark, and by its statement to Volkswagen that users would instinctively use the *vw.net* address to link to Volkswagen's web site. *Cf. Shade's Landing, Inc. v. Williams*, 76 F. Supp. 2d 983, 990 (D. Minn. 1999) ("Because all domain names include one of these extensions, the distinction between a domain name ending with '.com' and the same name ending with '.net' is not highly significant."). The district court was correct, therefore, in holding that *vw.net* is confusingly similar to the famous VW mark.

IV.

The remedy that Volkswagen sought in district court was the right to use *vw.net* for itself. The ACPA allows a court to order "the transfer of the domain name to the owner of the mark" if the Act is violated. 15 U.S.C. §1125(d)(2)(D)(i). Because Virtual Works' violation of the ACPA supports the remedy Volkswagen seeks, we need not address Volkswagen's claims of trademark infringement or dilution.

The ACPA was not enacted to give companies the right to fence off every possible combination of letters that bears any similarity to a protected mark. Rather, it was enacted to prevent the expropriation of protected marks in cyberspace and to abate the consumer confusion resulting therefrom. The resolution of this case turns on the unique facts and circumstances which it presents. Ultimately, we believe the evidence is sufficient to establish that, as a matter of law, Virtual Works attempted to profit in bad faith from Volkswagen's famous mark. 15 U.S.C. §1125(d)(1)(A). The district court thus did not err in ordering Virtual Works to turn over *vw.net* to Volkswagen. For the foregoing reasons, we affirm the judgment.

AFFIRMED

Coca-Cola Company v. Purdy

382 F.3d 774 (8th Cir 2004)

MURPHY, CIRCUIT JUDGE.

II.

In early July 2002 Purdy began registering Internet domain names which incorporated distinctive, famous, and protected marks owned by the plaintiffs. The domain names he registered included drinkcoke.org, mycoca-cola.com, mymcdonalds.com, mypepsi.org, and my-washingtonpost.com. The latter name was almost exactly identical to one which the Washington Post had used to operate an interactive online news service (mywashingtonpost.com), the only distinguishing detail being Purdy's addition of a hyphen.

Purdy typically linked the domain names to the website abortionismurder.com which contains antiabortion commentary and graphic images of aborted and dismembered fetuses. It also contains multiple "What Can I Do?" links to a website where a visitor can purchase hats, shirts, neckties, and license plates with antiabortion themes and make donations using a credit card or bank account number. The content available at abortionismurder.com contained no references to plaintiffs, their products, or their alleged positions on abortion.

Counsel for the Washington Post entities sent a cease and desist letter to Purdy on July 8, 2002, and it persuaded his Internet service provider (ISP) to stop hosting the website at my-washingtonpost.com. Counsel for McDonald's and Pepsi contacted Purdy and his domain name registrars with similar requests around this time.

Although Purdy now claims that he targeted all of the plaintiffs because of stands they had taken in the abortion debate, it appears from the record that he initially used many of the marks only because they would attract unwitting Internet users to his antiabortion message.

III.

Purdy appeals from the district court's preliminary injunction (including its order for relief on July 23 as amended on September 5, 2002).

A.

In determining whether to grant a preliminary injunction a court considers (1) the probability of the movant's success on the merits; (2) the threat of irreparable harm to the movant; (3) the balance between this harm and the injury that granting the injunction will inflict on other interested parties; and (4) whether the issuance of the preliminary injunction is in the public interest. *See Dataphase Sys., Inc. v. C L Sys., Inc.*, 640 F.2d 109, 114 (8th Cir. 1981) (en banc). A district court has broad discretion when ruling on preliminary injunction requests, and we will reverse only for clearly erroneous factual determinations, an error of law, or an abuse of discretion. *United Indus. Corp. v. Clorox Co.*, 140 F.3d 1175, 1179 (8th Cir. 1998).

The district court found that plaintiffs had demonstrated a strong probability of success on the merits of their claim under the Anticybersquatting Consumer Protection Act, 15 U.S.C. § 1125(d). The ACPA provides in relevant part that

> A person shall be liable in a civil action by the owner of a mark ... if, without
> regard to the goods or services of the parties, that person (i) has a bad faith in-

tent to profit from that mark ... and (ii) registers, traffics in, or uses a domain name that—

(I) in the case of a mark that is distinctive at the time of registration of the domain name, is identical or confusingly similar to that mark; [or]

(II) in the case of a famous mark that is famous at the time of registration of the domain name, is identical or confusingly similar to or dilutive of that mark ...

15 U.S.C. § 1125(d)(1)(A).

The question under the ACPA is not whether the domain names which Purdy registered are likely to be confused with a plaintiff's domain name, but whether they are identical or confusingly similar to a plaintiff's mark. *See* 15 U.S.C. § 1125(d)(1)(A)(ii). It is the challenged domain name and the plaintiff's mark which are to be compared. *See* 4 McCarthy § 25:78. The inquiry under the ACPA is thus narrower than the traditional multifactor likelihood of confusion test for trademark infringement. *Northern Light Tech., Inc. v. Northern Lights Club*, 236 F.3d 57, 66 (1st Cir. 2001) (quotations omitted). The fact that confusion about a website's source or sponsorship could be resolved by visiting the website is not relevant to whether the domain name itself is identical or confusingly similar to a plaintiff's mark.

Many of Purdy's domain names differ from plaintiffs' marks only by the addition of generic terms like "my," "says," or "drink" or by the addition of a top level domain suffix. Even if Internet users were seldom to come upon mywashingtonpost.com, mymcdonalds.com or drinkcoke.org, for example, we see no error in the district court's findings that the relevant second level domains (mywashingtonpost, mymcdonalds, and drinkcoke) are confusingly similar to the Washington Post, Coke, and McDonald's marks. *See* 4 McCarthy § 25:78 (fordtrucks.com would be confusingly similar to the "Ford" mark of Ford Motor Co.). The washingtonpost.cc, washingtonpost.ws, and wpni.org domain names differ from the Washington Post and WPNI marks only in that they include a top level domain suffix. They are thus confusingly similar, if not identical, to the Post entities' marks. *See Sporty's Farm*, 202 F.3d at 497–98 (second level domain name "sportys" in sportys.com indistinguishable from Sporty's mark). Moreover, the record indicates that Purdy intended to capitalize on the similarity between his domain names and plaintiffs' marks to attract unwitting Internet users to antiabortion websites, and intentional infringers are likely to succeed in creating confusion. *See Sara Lee Corp. v. Kayser-Roth Corp.*, 81 F.3d 455, 466 (4th Cir. 1996).

He reported that he had been "checking out your web pages and I came by [drinkcoke.org]." He complained that the website had Coca-Cola's logo "all over it" and the content had shocked him. "I am a Coke drinker myself, a fan i may say ... I always have some in the fridge and I was drinking [one] right now! but I got to admit, I cant finish it after i seen this page" [sic].

Our analysis begins with the statute itself, which provides nine nonexclusive factors for courts to consider in determining whether a person has acted with bad faith intent:

(I) the trademark or other intellectual property rights of the person, if any, in the domain name;

(II) the extent to which the domain name consists of the legal name of the person or a name that is otherwise commonly used to identify that person;

(III) the person's prior use, if any, of the domain name in connection with the bona fide offering of any goods or services;

(IV) the person's bona fide noncommercial or fair use of the mark in a site accessible under the domain name;

(V) the person's intent to divert consumers from the mark owner's online location to a site accessible under the domain name that could harm the goodwill represented by the mark, either for commercial gain or with the intent to tarnish or disparage the mark, by creating a likelihood of confusion as to the source, sponsorship, affiliation, or endorsement of the site;

(VI) the person's offer to transfer, sell, or otherwise assign the domain name to the mark owner or any third party for financial gain without having used, or having an intent to use, the domain name in the bona fide offering of any goods or services, or the person's prior conduct indicating a pattern of such conduct;

(VII) the person's provision of material and misleading false contact information when applying for the registration of the domain name, the person's intentional failure to maintain accurate contact information, or the person's prior conduct indicating a pattern of such conduct;

(VIII) the person's registration or acquisition of multiple domain names which the person knows are identical or confusingly similar to marks of others that are distinctive at the time of registration of such domain names, or dilutive of famous marks of others that are famous at the time of registration of such domain names, without regard to the goods or services of the parties; and (IX) the extent to which the mark incorporated in the person's domain name registration is or is not distinctive and famous within the meaning of subsection (c)(1) of this section.

15 U.S.C. § 1125(d)(1)(B)(i). The first four factors have been seen as reasons why a defendant might in good faith have registered a domain name incorporating someone else's mark, and the other five are indicia of bad faith intent. *See Lucas Nursery & Landscaping, Inc. v. Grosse*, 359 F.3d 806, 809–10 (6th Cir. 2004).

The first four statutory factors do not appear to weigh against a finding that Purdy had a bad faith intent. He has no legal rights in any of the marks that his domain names incorporate. *See* 15 U.S.C. § 1125(d)(1)(B)(i)(I). He is not known by any of the names, and he has never previously used any of them in the offering of goods or services. *See id.* at (II)–(III). While the evidence suggests that Purdy has made some noncommercial or fair use of the plaintiffs' marks in critical commentary sites accessible under the domain names, prior to the filing of this lawsuit he principally attached the names to antiabortion websites that made no mention of plaintiffs whatsoever. *See id.* at (IV). These websites can not be considered to be completely noncommercial since they directly solicited monetary contributions and offered various antiabortion merchandise for sale. *See id.* Even after Purdy attached the domain names to his own critical commentary sites, he continued to provide links to sites that solicit funds for the antiabortion movement and sell merchandise. Such use of the domain names would apparently profit the organizations of Purdy's choice, and nothing in the ACPA suggests that Congress intended to allow cybersquatters to escape the reach of the act by channeling profits to third parties. These factors support the district court's finding that plaintiffs were likely to establish Purdy's bad faith intent to profit from the marks.

Many of the remaining statutory bad faith factors also weigh in favor of the district court's finding that plaintiffs would likely prove that Purdy acted with a bad faith intent to profit. The record contains evidence that Purdy registered multiple domain names knowing that they were identical or confusingly similar to plaintiffs' indisputably famous and distinctive marks. *See* 15 U.S.C. § 1125(d)(1)(B)(i)(VIII) & *(IX)*. It appears that he registered many of these domain names not because of stands the plaintiffs had taken on abortion, but rather to divert Internet users to websites that could tarnish and disparage their marks by creating initial confusion as to the sponsorship of the attached websites and implying that their owners have taken positions on a hotly contested issue. *See id.* at (V).

Furthermore, the record shows that just days after Purdy began registering and using the domain names at issue in this case, he apparently offered to stop using the Washington Post domain names in exchange for space on the editorial page in that newspaper. A proposal to exchange domain names for valuable consideration is not insignificant in respect to the issue of bad faith intent to profit. *See id.* at (VI). Although nothing in the record places a monetary value on access to space in a leading national newspaper like the Washington Post, that value could be significant to an advocate. Profit includes an attempt to procure an "advantageous gain or return." *See* American Heritage College Dictionary 1092 (3d ed. 1993). The statutory factors are nonexclusive, and other conduct of Purdy, such as trying to force a settlement of this action by threatening to publish private emails of WPNI employees received at wpni.org, is also suggestive of bad faith.

At this stage it appears that at least eight of the nine statutory factors weigh in favor of the district court's finding that plaintiffs would likely establish that Purdy acted with a bad faith intent to profit. The district court did not err here in finding it likely that plaintiffs would prove that Purdy and his associates had registered and used domain names with a bad faith intent to profit from their marks in violation of the ACPA.

Purdy argues that his belief that his conduct was protected by the *First Amendment* brings him within the ACPA "safe harbor" provision. Under that provision "bad faith intent … shall not be found in any case in which the court determines that the person believed and had reasonable grounds to believe that the use of the domain name was a fair use or otherwise lawful." 15 U.S.C. §1125(d)(1)(B)(ii). As plaintiffs point out, the record here contains considerable evidence that Purdy lacked reasonable grounds to believe that his continued use of the domain names in question was lawful. He continued to register and use domain names in the face of repeated complaints and warnings from the plaintiffs that such conduct was unlawful and even after the district court issued preliminary injunctive relief. Given the extensive evidence of bad faith in the record, we conclude that Purdy lacked reasonable grounds to believe that his conduct was lawful, and he is not entitled to benefit from the safe harbor provision. *See PETA*, 263 F.3d at 369 (citing *Virtual Works*, 238 F.3d at 270).

In sum, the record supports the district court's findings that Purdy registered and used domain names that are identical or confusingly similar to plaintiffs' marks with a bad faith intent to profit as defined by the ACPA. This conduct was not protected by the *First Amendment*, and Purdy is not entitled to the benefit of the safe harbor provision. The district court did not err in concluding that the plaintiffs have demonstrated a strong probability of success on the merits of their ACPA claim. *See Dataphase*, 640 F.2d at 114.

Nissan Motor Co. v. Nissan Computer Corporation
378 F.3d 1002 (9 Cir. 2004)378 F.3d 1002 (9 Cir. 2004)

RYMER, CIRCUIT JUDGE.

The plaintiff is the world famous Japanese automobile manufacturer. It has had at least one trademark registration in the United States since 1959. The defendant is an individual whose real name is Uzi Nissan. Uzi Nissan was born in Jerusalem-Israel. His family name is Nissan. Nissan is a biblical term identifying the seventh month in the Hebrew calendar. The term Nissan also is Arabic for the month of April. Uzi Nissan has used his name in connection with various businesses since 1980. The defendant registered Internet domain names "nissan.com" and "nissan.net" in May of 1994 and March of 1996, respectively. The defendant use these domain names for several years operating web sites and providing computer-related information and services. It became known as Nissan Computers. In 1999 Nissan Motors objected to these registrations. They entered negotiations with Uzi Nissan but these negotiations broke off after Uzi Nissan insisted on millions of dollars and that this amount be paid off in monthly installments in perpetuity. Negotiations broke off and Nissan filed suit under the ACPA.]

II

D

Nissan Computer seeks relief from the provision of the permanent injunction that restrains it from placing links on nissan.com and nissan.net to other websites containing disparaging remarks or negative commentary about Nissan Motor. It contends that such speech is non-commercial, thus not diluting under the FTDA. Nissan Computer also maintains that the disclaimer ordered in the preliminary injunction is sufficient to assure there is no dilution. Finally, it submits that the injunction does not control the uses of the domain names but instead, prohibits a particular type of content posted at the website.

Nissan Motor argues that we need not revisit Nissan Computer's *First Amendment* challenge to the permanent injunction because we already considered and rejected it by denying Nissan Computer's motion to stay. We disagree, as the standards for a stay differ from the review on the merits that is now before us. Beyond this, Nissan Motor defends the injunction as narrowly tailored, arguing that it restricts use of just two websites identical to the NISSAN mark. These restrictions, in its view, constitute regulation of nothing more than non-expressive trademark-equivalent domain names that do not express or communicate any views at all. For this reason, Nissan Motor asks us to hold that the *First Amendment* is not implicated because it is only when a trademark is used as part of a communicative message and not as a source identifier (which is what a domain name functions as in cyberspace) that the *First Amendment* is implicated. We disagree with this as well.

Prohibiting Nissan Computer from placing links to other sites with disparaging commentary goes beyond control of the Nissan name as a source identifier. The injunction does not enjoin use of nissan.com, but enjoins certain content on the nissan.com website. Thus, it is not the source identifier that is controlled, but the communicative message that is constrained. Consequently, the *First Amendment* is implicated.

The prohibited use of the mark is a content-based restriction because the purpose behind it is to control the message and it is not "justified without reference to the content of the regulated speech." *See, e.g., Ward v. Rock Against Racism*, 491 U.S. 781, 791, 105 L. Ed. 2d 661, 109 S. Ct. 2746 (1989) (citation and quotation omitted). "Content-based regulations pass constitutional muster only if they are the least restrictive means to further a compelling interest." *S.O.C., Inc. v. County of Clark*, 152 F.3d 1136, 1145 (9th Cir. 1998) (citing *Sable Communications of Cal. v. F.C.C.*, 492 U.S. 115, 126, 106 L. Ed. 2d 93, 109 S. Ct. 2829 (1989)). As a content-based restriction, the injunction is presumptively invalid, *see R.A.V. v. City of St. Paul*, 505 U.S. 377, 382, 120 L. Ed. 2d 305, 112 S. Ct. 2538 (1992), and not subject to a "time, place, and manner" analysis, *see Reno v. ACLU*, 521 U.S. 844, 879, 138 L. Ed. 2d 874, 117 S. Ct. 2329 (1997). Thus, it is immaterial whether there are alternative places on the web that negative commentary about Nissan Motor can be posted. The injunction is also viewpoint based because it only prohibits *disparaging* remarks and *negative* commentary. *See R.A.V.*, 505 U.S. at 391.

The FTDA anticipates the constitutional problem where the speech is not commercial but is potentially dilutive by including an exception for noncommercial use of a mark. *See* 15 U.S.C. §1125(c)(4)(B). So, the relevant question is whether linking to sites that contain disparaging comments about Nissan Motor on the nissan.com website is commercial.

"Although the boundary between commercial and non-commercial speech has yet to be clearly delineated, the core notion of commercial speech is that it does no more than propose a commercial transaction." *Mattel*, 296 F.3d at 906 (quoting *Hoffman v. Capital Cities/ABC, Inc.*, 255 F.3d 1180, 1184 (9th Cir. 2001)) (quotation marks omitted). "If speech is not 'purely commercial'—that is, if it does more than propose a commercial transaction—then it is entitled to full *First Amendment* protection." *Id.* Negative commentary about Nissan Motor does more than propose a commercial transaction and is, therefore, non-commercial.

We are persuaded by the Fourth Circuit's reasoning in a similar case involving negative material about Skippy Peanut Butter posted on skippy.com, a website hosted by the owner of the trademark SKIPPY for a cartoon comic strip. CPC, which makes Skippy Peanut Butter, successfully sought an injunction that ordered removal of the material. The court of appeals reversed. *CPC Int'l, Inc. v. Skippy Inc.*, 214 F.3d 456, 461–63 (4th Cir. 2000). Recognizing that criticism was vexing to CPC, the court emphasized how important it is that "trade-marks not be 'transformed from rights against unfair competition to rights to control language.'" *Id.* at 462 (quoting Mark A. Lemley, *The Modern Lanham Act and the Death of Common Sense*, 108 Yale L.J. 1687, 1710–11 (1999)). It held that speech critical of CPC was informational, not commercial speech. Likewise here, links to negative commentary about Nissan Motor, and about this litigation, reflect a point of view that we believe is protected.

Therefore, we conclude that the permanent injunction violates the *First Amendment* to the extent that it enjoins the placing of links on nissan.com to sites with disparaging comments about Nissan Motor.

V

Conclusion

Having held that the first use of a mark for purposes of the Federal Trademark Dilution Act is that use which is arguably offending, and such use in this case occurred when NISSAN was used in "Nissan Computer" in commerce, we must reverse and remand the partial summary judgment on dilution for the district court to consider the fame of the NISSAN mark as of 1991. On remand, it must also consider whether Nissan Computer "actually diluted" the NISSAN mark as required by *Moseley*. Injunctive relief may not restrain Nissan Computer from placing links on nissan.com and nissan.net to other sites that post negative commentary about Nissan Motor; to this extent, the relief granted is overbroad, reaches non-commercial speech, and runs afoul of the FTDA and the *First Amendment*. On all other issues, we affirm.

Notes

1. "The ACPA was intended to combat cybersquatting, not trademark infringement." *Nissan, supra.* How should the court consider the ACPA in regards to the Lanham Act?

How should the court determine if a claim brought under the ACPA is a trademark claim? As a standing requirement? Or as part of its analysis of the ACPA's scope?

2. "The inquiry under the statutory indicia of bad faith for the ACPA.... is different from the trademark infringement analysis of initial interest confusion." *Nissan, supra.* How should the court treat the provisions touching upon trademark law under the ACPA if the ACPA is not intended to combat trademark infringement? *See, e.g.,* 15 U.S.C. §§1125(d)(I)(A)(ii) & 1125(d)(I)(B)(i)(I). Has the ACPA created a property right in a trademark? *See* Smith v. City of Artesia, 772 P.2d 373, 375 (N.M. Ct. App. 1989) *cert. denied,* 772 P.2d 352 (N.M. 1989).

---

3. *In Rem* Jurisdiction: 15 U.S.C. §1125(d)(2)(A)

Harrods Limited v. Sixty Internet Domain Names
302 F.3d 214 (4th Cir. 2002)

MICHAEL, C. J.

This case involves a dispute over Internet domain names between two companies named "Harrods," both with legitimate rights to the "Harrods" name in different parts of the world. The plaintiff, Harrods Limited ("Harrods UK"), is the owner of the well-known Harrods of London department store. The defendants are 60 Internet domain names ("Domain Names" or "Names") registered in Herndon, Virginia, by Harrods (Buenos Aires) Limited ("Harrods BA "). Harrods BA, once affiliated with Harrods UK, is now a completely separate corporate entity that until recently operated a "Harrods" department store in Buenos Aires, Argentina. Harrods UK sued the 60 Domain Names under 15 U.S.C. §1125(d)(2), the in rem provision of the recently enacted Anticybersquatting Consumer Protection Act (ACPA), Pub. L. No. 106-113, 113 Stat. 1501A-545 (codified in scattered sections of 15 U.S.C.) (1999). Harrods UK alleged that the Domain Names infringed and diluted its American "Harrods" trademark and that Harrods BA registered the Names in bad faith as prohibited by 15 U.S.C. §1125(d)(1). The district court dismissed the infringement and dilution claims, holding that in rem actions could only be maintained for bad faith registration claims under §1125(d)(l). As discovery was just beginning, the district court granted summary judgment to six of the Domain Names on Harrods UK's bad faith registration claim. After full discovery and a bench trial, the court awarded judgment to Harrods UK against the remaining 54 Domain Names and ordered those names to be transferred to Harrods UK. Both sides now appeal. For the reasons that follow, we affirm the judgment as to the 54 Domain Names, reverse the dismissal of Harrods UK's infringement and dilution claims, reverse the grant of summary judgment to the six Domain Names, and remand for further proceedings.

* * *

The final issue we must consider before reaching the question of bad faith is the scope of the in rem provision of the ACPA, 15 U.S.C. §1125(d)(2). Harrods UK argues that §1125(d)(2) provides for in rem jurisdiction against domain names for traditional infringement and dilution claims under §1114, 1125(a) & (c) as well as for claims of bad faith registration with the intent to profit under §1125(d)(1). The Domain Names argue that the district court correctly limited the scope of the in rem provision to claims under §1125(d)(1) for bad faith registration of a domain name with the intent to profit. This argument has not yet been settled by any federal circuit court. Only a handful of district courts have considered the issue, and most of them agree with the district court here that §1125(d)(2) applies only to violations of §1125(d)(1), bad faith registration with intent to profit. At least one district court and two commentators have endorsed the contrary view that §1125(d)(2) authorizes an in rem action for the violation of several substantive provisions of federal trademark law. While we consider this to be a close question of statutory interpretation, we ultimately conclude that 1125(d)(2) is not limited to violations of §1125(d)(1); it also authorizes in rem actions for certain federal infringement and dilution claims.

We begin our analysis with the text of the statute. Section 1125(d)(2)(A) provides that the "owner of a mark" may file an in rem action against a domain name if:

(i) the domain name violates any right of the owner of a mark registered in the Patent and Trademark Office, or protected under subsection (a) [infringement] or (c) [dilution]; and

(ii) … the owner—

(I) is not able to obtain in personam jurisdiction over a person who would have been a defendant in a civil action under paragraph (1) [§1125(d)(1)]; or

(II) through due diligence was not able to find a person who would have been a defendant in a civil action under paragraph (1).…

15 U.S.C. §1125 (d)(2)(A). We start with the first clause, subsection (d)(2)(A)(i), which provides that an in rem action is available if "(i) the domain name violates *any right* of the owner of a mark registered in the Patent and Trademark Office, or protected under subsection (a) or (c)." 15 U.S.C. §1125(d)(2)(A)(i) (emphasis added). The broad language "any right of the owner of a mark" does not look like it is limited to the rights guaranteed by subsection (d)(l), but appears to include any right a trademark owner has with respect to the mark. This language, by itself, would include rights under §1125(d)(1), and it would also include, for example, rights under §1125(a) against trademark infringement and rights under §1125(c) against trademark dilution. If Congress had intended for subsection (d)(2) to provide in rem jurisdiction only for subsection (d)(1) claims, it could easily have said so directly. For example, Congress could have said that an in rem action is available if "the domain name violates subsection (d)(l)." Again, if the first key phrase Congress gave us—"any right of the owner of a mark"—is considered in isolation, it would authorize the in rem pursuit of any of the actions that could be brought in personam under U.S. trademark law, including infringement (subsection (a)), dilution (subsection (c)), and cybersquatting (subsection (d)(1)). *See* 4 McCarthy §25:79, at 25–290; Jennings, *supra*, at 664.

Of course, subsection (d)(2)(A)(i) does not create a claim for the owner of *any* mark, but rather for the owner of "a mark registered in the Patent and Trademark Office [PTO], or protected under subsection (a) or (c)." Thus, to understand the scope of subsection (d)(2)(A)(i), we must also consider the implications of this additional language. Generally speaking, trademark protection is a common law right that arises from the use of a mark to identify the source of certain goods or services. *Brittingham v. Jenkins*, 914 F.2d 447,452 (4th Cir. 1990); 3 McCarthy §19:3. By its terms, subsection (d)(2)(A)(i) does not provide an in rem action for the owner of *any* type of mark protected under trademark law, but only for the owner of a mark that is either (1) registered in the PTO or (2) protected under §1125(a) or (c).

According to the Domain Names, the problem with interpreting subsection (d)(2) as covering more than just bad faith claims under subsection (d)(l) is that subsection (d)(2)(A)(ii) conditions the availability of in rem jurisdiction on proof that the plaintiff is unable to find or obtain personal jurisdiction over the "person who would have been a defendant in a civil action [for bad faith registration] under paragraph (1)," that is, §1125(d)(l). As the district court explained, "because Congress chose to include in the *in rem* action the definition of potential defendants used in paragraph (I), we must therefore conclude that Congress intended for the 'bad faith intent to profit' element to be part of any in rem action." *Harrods Ltd. v. Sixty Internet Domain Names*, 110 F. Supp. 2d 420, 426 (E.D. Va. 2000).

If the only way to understand the phrase "a person who would have been a defendant in a civil action under paragraph (1)" was as a reference to subsection (d)(1)'s bad faith requirement, we would be forced to confront the tension between this language and subsection (d)(2)(A)(i)'s broad language of "any right of the owner of a mark." However, the phrase "a person who would have been a defendant in a civil action under paragraph (1)" can fairly be understood as a shorthand reference to the current registrant of the domain name. *See* 4 McCarthy §25:79, at 25–290 (This reference to paragraph (1) "does not add an extra element" to subsection (d)(2), but simply "defines the proper defendant in an in rem proceeding as the present domain name registrant."). This reading avoids tension with subsection (d)(2)(A)(i)'s reference to "any right of the owner of a mark," which does not appear to be limited to rights protected by subsection (d)(1).

The Domain Names do not give up easily. They point to other legislative history that describes the general purpose of the ACPA in terms of outlawing "cybersquatting," which is always discussed as bad faith registration with intent to profit. For example, the Senate Judiciary Committee report on the ACPA opens by explaining that "the purpose of the bill" is to protect consumers and businesses by "prohibiting the bad-faith and abusive registration of distinctive marks as Internet domain names with the intent to profit from the goodwill associated with such marks—a practice commonly referred to as 'cybersquatting.'" Sen. Rep. No. 106-140, at 4 (1999). *See also* H.R. Rep. No. 106-412, at 6. As the district court explained, this might suggest that the entire bill, including both subsection (d)(1) and subsection (d)(2), is aimed solely at bad faith registration with the intent to profit. *See Harrods*, 110 F. Supp. 2d at 426; *see also CNN*, 177 F. Supp. 2d at 523 ("The ACPA's purpose is ... to deter, prohibit and remedy 'cyberpiracy,' which is defined in the legislative history as the *bad faith* registration or use of a domain name ... [and] this purpose is given proper effect by resolving the ambiguity in favor of requiring bad faith in ACPA in rem actions.").

This reading of the language describing the general purpose of the ACPA is trumped, however, by the language Congress used when it discussed the purpose of subsection (d)(2) specifically. The Senate Report states that the in rem jurisdiction provision "allows a mark owner to seek the forfeiture, cancellation, or transfer of an infringing domain name by filing an in rem action against the name itself, provided the domain name itself *violates substantive Federal trademark law*." Sen. Rep. No. 106-140, at 10 (emphasis added). *See also* H.R. Rep. No. 106-412, at 14 (containing a statement that is nearly verbatim). Later on, the Senate Report notes that the in rem provision allows trademark owners to "proceed against the domain names themselves, provided they are, in fact, *infringing or diluting under the Trademark Act*." Sen. Rep. No.1 06-140, at 11 (emphasis added). Elsewhere, the in rem provision is described as authorizing an injunction against a domain name "provided the mark owner can show that the domain name itself violates substantive federal trademark law (i.e., that the domain name violates the rights of the registrant of a mark registered in the Patent and Trademark Office, or section 43(a) or (c) of the Trademark Act)." 145 Congo Rec. S14,714 (daily ed. Nov. 17, 1999). This language from the legislative history is not framed in terms of subsection (d)(I) or bad faith; it does not say the in rem action is available if the domain name violates the substantive cybersquatting provision of the ACPA. Rather, it says the in rem action is available for domain names that violate "substantive Federal trademark law" or which are "infringing or diluting under the Trademark Act." Sen. Rep. No. 106-140, at 10–11. Thus, when the legislative history addresses subsection (d)(2) specifically, it speaks in terms of violations of trademark law generally and of subsections (a) and (c); it does not repeat the references to bad faith registration that appear elsewhere. Just like the text of subsection (d)(2)(A)(i), this language in the legislative history suggests that the in rem action is available to enforce several of the substantive provisions of Federal trademark law.

On balance, we are left with the following. On its face, subsection (d)(2)(A)(i) provides an in rem action for the violation of "any right" of a trademark owner, not just rights provided by subsection (d)(1). Moreover, subsection (d)(2)(A)(i) authorizes in rem jurisdiction for marks "protected under subsection (a) or (c)," the very subsections underlying two of the claims that were dismissed by the district court as outside the scope of subsection (d)(2). While subsection (d)(2)(A)(ii) provides that the in rem action is available only if the plaintiff is unable to find or obtain personal jurisdiction over the "person who would have been a defendant in a civil action under paragraph (1)," we believe this language is best understood as a shorthand reference to the current registrant of the domain name, who would be the defendant in any trademark action involving a domain name. Finally, the legislative history of the ACPA specifically discussing the in rem provision speaks in terms of domain names that violate "substantive Federal trademark law" or that are "infringing or diluting under the Trademark Act." Sen. Rep. No. 106-140, at 10–11. This reinforces the language of subsection (d)(2)(A)(i), which suggests that the in rem provision is not limited to bad faith claims under subsection (d)(l). Thus, we conclude that the best interpretation of §1125(d)(2) is that the in rem provision not only covers bad faith claims under §1125(d)(1), but also covers infringement claims under §1114 and §1125(a) and dilution claims under §1125(c).

In light of this conclusion, we reverse the district court's dismissal of Harrods UK's claims for infringement and dilution and remand for further proceedings on those claims. However, the district court need not consider Harrods UK's infringement and dilution claims as against the 54 Domain Names because we affirm the court's order requiring the transfer of the 54 Names to Harrods UK. Transfer or cancellation of the defendant domain names is the only remedy available under §1125(d)(2)'s in rem provision, so Harrods UK could gain no additional relief if the court considered and ruled on its infringement and dilution claims against the 54 Names. Thus, on remand the district court need only consider Harrods UK's infringement and dilution claims against the six Argentina Names.

Caesars World, Inc. v. Caesars-palace.com
112 F. Supp. 2d 505 (E.D. Va. 2000)

BRINKEMA, D. J.

Before the Court is the June 27, 2000 Report and Recommendation ("Report") by a magistrate judge recommending that plaintiff Caesars World, Inc.'s Motion for a Finding of Contempt and for Sanctions Against Caesarcasino.com be granted, and that sanctions be entered against defendant and its attorneys, as well as default judgment against Caesarcasino.com in favor of plaintiff. Caesars World, Inc. ("Caesar's World") and defendant Caesarcasino.com have timely filed objections to the Report and Recommendation. On August 11, 2000, we heard oral argument on the objections and ordered that a ruling on the Report be held in abeyance, pending an eleven day opportunity during which defendant and its lawyers could file a new answer and discovery responses. Below is a further clarification of the rationale behind our August 11, 2000 Order.

I. PROCEDURAL BACKGROUND

On April 19, 1999, plaintiff Caesars World filed a complaint in this court alleging trademark violations against numerous Internet domain names, including defendant Caesarcasino.com. With leave of court, plaintiff amended its complaint on January 7, 2000, to include claims under the newly-enacted Anti-Cybersquatting Consumer Protection Act ("ACPA"). 15 U.S.C. §1125. On March 23, 2000, attorneys James W. Pravel, as local counsel, and Paul Michael DeCicco and Darren J. Quinn, filed Caesar casino.com's Answer to Plaintiff's Second Amended Complaint.

* * *

II. DISCUSSION

The essence of Caesarcasino.com's objections to plaintiff's discovery requests is that Caesarcasino.com, as a domain name, cannot be subject to discovery as a person or entity would be. For purposes of its discovery requests, plaintiff defined Caesarcasino.com as: "Caesarcasino.com as well as the registrant of Caesarcasino.com and any person having any ownership interest or control over Caesarcasino.com, including without limitation, NIC Holdings, Ltd." Defendant's response to each interrogatory, request for admission and document request, after the two Court orders, was: "No response to plaintiff's discovery has been or will be made by the sponsor of the litigation for defendant Internet domain name Caesarcasino.com."

Counsel for Caesarcasino.com maintains that if plaintiff wished to obtain discovery from the "sponsor of the litigation," such as the registrant of the domain name, it had to use third-party discovery devices. The magistrate judge rejected that argument:

> Someone or something (the "sponsor"), asserting the right or duty to speak on behalf of the domain name, voluntarily hired counsel and filed an answer in this court on behalf of Caesarcasino.com, presumably to preserve or claim rights to that Internet domain name. He/she/it may not have that right without being subject to discovery.

Because the ACPA is a relatively new statute, employing unfamiliar concepts of *in rem* jurisdiction, the confusion underlying this dispute is understandable. Although counsel on both sides concede that the defendant in this action is a domain name, Caesarcasino.com, it is also undeniable that a person or entity hired counsel to file an answer and various pleadings on behalf of the domain name. The ACPA does not address discovery matters arising from the new causes of action it created, and we therefore find it necessary to review traditional *in rem* jurisprudence to resolve this issue.

* * *

Applying established *in rem* concepts and procedures to the instant case, the answer should have been filed on behalf of a claimant or claimants seeking to assert their interests in the domain name. Although the *res* is the nominal defendant in an *in rem* action, the purpose of the adjudication is to determine the interests of certain persons to that *res.* Obviously, as an inanimate thing, the domain name could not and did not hire attorneys to file an answer. As claimants, the persons or entities filing the answer have reciprocal duties to engage in discovery, just as the claimant in an *in rem* admiralty action must file an answer and respond to any interrogatories served with the complaint within twenty days of filing a claim.

The ACPA does not specify a procedure for claimants in an *in rem* action. Moreover, knowledge of analogous *in rem* procedures is not widespread. Therefore, we do not find that counsel was totally unreasonable in their approach to the discovery requests. As they explain in their pleadings, counsel were motivated, at least in part, by a desire not to subject the "sponsors of the litigation" to *in personam* jurisdiction. We have recently addressed that issue and determined that *in personam* jurisdiction cannot be based merely on an appearance in an *in rem* action. Due to this confusion, the Court did not impose sanctions on August 11, 2000, but rather, permitted the "sponsors of the litigation" to come forward as claimants in this case within eleven days, by filing an amended answer or proper claim and complete responses to the outstanding discovery requests. The issue of sanctions was held in abeyance until the eleven days elapsed.

III. CONCLUSION

Because an adequate amended answer and discovery responses have been filed, our Order of August 11, 2000, has been satisfied and the Report will be dismissed by an appropriate order.

————————

Notes

1. The ACPA provides for *in rem* jurisdiction regarding a domain name only in the judicial district where the domain name registrar, registry, or other domain name authority that registered the domain name is located. 15 U.S.C. §1125(d)(2)(A). Therefore, when Mattel Inc. filed an *in rem* action under the ACPA against a multitude of domain names in the Souther District of New York, the case was properly dismissed when the domain names at issue were registered with a registrar located in Baltimore. Mattel, Inc. v. Barbie-Club.com, 310 F.3d 293 (2d Cir. 2002).

2. In 1996, one commentator claimed that trademark law was "lost in cyberspace." Kenneth Sutherlin Dueker, *Trademark Law Lost in Cyberspace: Trademark Protection for Internet Addresses,* 9 Harv. J.L. & Tech. 483, 511 (1996). Just five years later, another commentator claimed that "trademark law is no 'longer lost in cyberspace.'" Traditional causes of action such as trademark infringement, unfair competition, and dilution have been tested in domain name disputes. Internal regulation and creative administration have made it more difficult to cybersquat. All these devices act as a compass, steering trademark law towards its nexus with the Internet." Sanjeev Dave, *Trademark Law Lost in Cyberspace: Had Progress Been Made?,* 12 J. Contmp. Legal Issues 506 (2001). After studying the above material, with whom do you agree?

3. Do you have any procedural or constitutional concerns regarding *in rem* jurisdiction over domain names? Remember, the trademark Coca Cola, worth millions of dollars, is not property, according to traditional Anglo-American trademark jurisprudence; however, <franksautobody.com>, worth virtually nothing, is property. Can you explain the difference? Did it necessarily have to develop in this manner? Andrew J. Grotto, *Due*

Process and In Rem Jurisdiction Under the Anti-Cybersquatting Consumer Protection Act, 2 COLUM. SCI. & TECH. L. REV. 3 (2001).

4. In the district court opinion from the *Porsche.net* case, *supra*, the court stated as follows:

> [T]o construe the Trademark Dilution Act so as to permit *in rem* actions against allegedly diluting marks would needlessly call the constitutionality of the statute into doubt.

Porsche Cars North America, Inc. v. Porsch.com, et al., 51 F. Supp. 2d 707, 712 (E.D. Va. 1999).

If it would be unconstitutional to recognize *in rem* jurisdiction under 43(c) of the Lanham Act (the provision regarding trademark dilution), why would it not be unconstitutional to recognize *in rem* jurisdiction under 43(d) of the Lanham Act (the provision regarding domain names)?

5. If a foreign registrar refuses to comply with a United States' court ordered transfer or cancellation of a domain name, the court can order the United States registry to disable the infringing domain name. Global Santave Corp. v. globalsantafe.com, 250 F. Supp. 2d 610 (E.D. Va.2003).

6. Although parody is a defense to actions under the ACPA as in infringement or dilution, the parody must be real and simultaneous and not prevent consumers of the trademark subject of the parody from actually reaching the target site. Therefore, when Doughney, an energetic cybersquatter, registered peta.org, and claimed that a non-profit organization called "People Eating Tasty Animals" owned the registration, the People for the Ethical Treatment of Animals were not amused. They sued Doughney under the ACPA and other causes of action and prevailed because Doughney's parody blocked bona fide consumers from reaching the People for the Ethical Treatment of Animals' web site. People for the Ethical Treatment of Animals v. Doughney, 263 F.3d 359 (4th Cir. 2003). The lame attempt at humor notwithstanding, do you agree with this outcome?

7. Many argue that the Internet has transformed traditional trademark doctrine. Trademark law is "inimical to, 'property rights in gross.'" Uli Widmaier, *Use, Liability and the Structure of Trademark Law*, 33 Hoftsra L. Rev. 603, 709 (2004). The concern is that the scope of trademark law has been made to broaden significantly in or to keep up with the pace of technological change. *Id.* Is this broadening of trademark law worrisome? Should the law dictate technology or should technology dictate law?

———

4. Statutory Damages under the ACPA

15 U.S.C. §1117, Lanham Act §35

d) In a case involving a violation of section 43(d)(1) [15 USCS §1125(d)(1)], the plaintiff may elect, at any time before final judgment is rendered by the trial court, to recover, instead of actual damages and profits, an award of statutory damages in the amount of not less than $1,000 and not more than $100,000 per domain name, as the court considers just.

———

E. & J. Gallo Winery v. Spider Webs, Ltd.

286 F.3d 270 (2003)

JOLLY, C. J.

* * *

Ernest & Julio Gallo Winery ("Gallo") registered the trademark "Ernest & Julio Gallo" on October 20, 1964 with the United States Patent and Trademark Office, as Registration Number 778,837. Gallo has registered a number of other trademarks, as well as internet domain names, but had not registered the domain name at issue here. It is no surprise to us that Gallo has sold more than four billion bottles of wine and has spent more than $500 million promoting its brands. On the other hand, the individual defendants, brothers Steve and Pierce Thumann, and their father, Fred Thumann, trustee, run a family-owned prehanging millwork business named Doortown, Inc. In June 1999, they created Spider Webs Ltd. as a limited partnership. According to Steve Thumann, Spider Webs's [sic] business plan is to develop internet address names. It has registered more than 2000 internet domain names through Network Solutions, Inc., one of the companies responsible for the registration of internet domain names. Approximately 300 of these contained names that could be associated with existing businesses, including "ernestandjuliogallo.com," "firestonetires.com," "bridgestonetires.com," "bluecross-blueshield.com," "oreocookies.com," "avoncosmetics.com," and others. As the trial court found, because internet domain names cannot contain ampersands or spaces, and because all internet domain names must end in a top-level domain such as ".com," ".org," ".net," etc., "ernestandjuliogallo.com" is effectively the same thing as "Ernest & Julio Gallo." *E. & J. Gallo Winery v. Spider Webs Ltd.*, 129 F. Supp. 2d 1033, 1041 (S.D. Tex. 2001). Spider Webs sells some of the names it has registered on its web site and on the internet auction site Ebay (and apparently has refused to accept any bids of less than $10,000), although it has not yet offered "ernestandjuliogallo.com" for sale. Steve Thumann admitted in his deposition that "ernestandjuliogallo.com" is valuable because of the goodwill that Gallo had developed in its name, and that when they registered this domain name they "hoped that Gallo would contact us and we could assist them in some way." However, Spider Webs did not initiate any contact with Gallo, nor did it attempt to sell the domain name to Gallo.

Approximately six months after Gallo brought this lawsuit, Spider Webs published a website at "ernestandjuliogallo.com" that discussed the lawsuit, the risks associated with alcohol use, and alleged misrepresentations by corporations. It contained a picture of the upper half of a wine bottle with the words "Whiney Winery" ("the Whiney Winery website"). It had links to a number of other pages on the site, including: an Alcohol Awareness page that discussed the dangers of alcohol; an "Our Mission" page that was critical of corporate America; a "Press Release" about the lawsuit; and a letter from a Gallo lawyer. Although the first page contained a disclaimer that stated "This Site Is Not Affiliated With Ernest & Julio Gallo (R) Wineries," none of the other linked pages did. As of the date of the trial court's opinion, typing in "www.ernestandjuliogallo.com" as the address on a web browser led a user to a website entitled "SpinTopic." Spider Webs states that the SpinTopic website is owned by it and is a noncommercial, nonprofit, consumer information site.

II

After the defendants registered the domain name, Gallo sent a letter to Spider Webs, requesting that they release or transfer to Gallo the domain name, but Spider Webs refused to do so. On February 11, 2000, Gallo filed suit against Spider Webs Ltd., Steve

Thumann, Pierce Thumann, and Fred Thumann, Trustee (collectively, "Spider Webs"), alleging violations of the Anti-Cybersquatting Consumer Protection Act ("ACPA"), 15 U.S.C. §1125(d), trademark dilution under federal and Texas law, *see* Texas Anti-Dilution Statute, Tex. Bus. & Com. Code §16.29, trademark infringement under federal and Texas law, and unfair competition under federal and Texas law. Approximately six months later, Spider Webs published the Whiney Winery website at "ernestandjuliogallo.com." On August 31, 2000, Gallo moved for partial summary judgment on its claims of violations of the Texas Anti-Dilution Statute and the ACPA. The magistrate judge granted summary judgment to Gallo on these claims, holding that under the Texas ADS Gallo owned a distinctive mark and Spider Webs's actions created a likelihood of dilution of that mark, thereby violating the ADS. *E. & J. Gallo*, 129 F. Supp. 2d at 1037–42. The trial court further held that the ACPA was constitutional, that Spider Webs had registered the domain name in bad faith under the ACPA's standard, that Spider Webs's use was not a fair use, and therefore Spider Webs had violated the ACPA. *Id.* at 1042–48. The court ordered the defendants to transfer the domain name to Gallo within ten days from the entry of judgment, as allowed by the ACPA, *see* 15 U.S.C. §1125(d)(1)(C), and entered a permanent injunction under the ADS restraining them "from using the Internet domain name 'ERNESTANDJULIOGALLO.COM,' registering any domain name that contains the word 'Gallo,' and registering any Internet domain name that contains the words 'Ernest' and 'Julio' in combination." *Id.* at 1048. The court also awarded Gallo $25,000 in statutory damages under the ACPA, plus post-judgment interest and costs. The court granted Gallo's unopposed motion to dismiss the rest of its claims, without prejudice. Spider Webs moved for a new trial, which the magistrate judge denied. Spider Webs then filed this appeal.

* * *

IV

Spider Webs also argues that the trial court should not have awarded Gallo $25,000 in statutory damages under the ACPA because Gallo did not suffer any actual injury. We review a trial court's award of damages for clear error.

The United States trademark laws provide that:

> In a case involving a violation of section 1125(d)(1) of this title [the ACPA], the plaintiff may elect, at any time before final judgment is rendered by the trial court, to recover, instead of actual damages and profits, an award of statutory damages in the amount of not less than $1,000 and not more than $100,000 per domain name, as the court considers just.

15 U.S.C. §1117(d). Spider Webs notes that under the ACPA and applicable portions of §1117, damages "shall not be available with respect to the registration, trafficking, or use of the domain name that occurs before the date of the enactment of this Act [November 29, 1999]." 1999 Acts, P.L. 106-113, §3010, 113 Stat. 1536. They argue that because they registered the domain name prior to enactment of the ACPA, they cannot be liable. However, the evidence before the trial court demonstrated that Spider Webs "used" the domain name at least since August 15, 2000, when it hosted the "Whiney Winery" website at the domain name. Therefore, although Spider Webs registered the domain name before the effective date of the ACPA, because they *used* the domain name after this date, they can be held liable for statutory damages for this use.

In *Shields*, the Third Circuit affirmed an award of statutory damages of $10,000 per infringing domain name for the five infringing domain names in that case. *Id.* The defendant in *Shields* stated that he only used the infringing names for sixty days, but the Third

Circuit noted that there was no requirement that the court consider the duration of the infringement when calculating statutory damages, and that the court could award damages as it considered "just" under the statute. *Id.* at 487. These considerations indicate that the award of damages here was not in clear error.

The statutory damages provisions in the ACPA, which is relatively new, are akin to the statutory damages provisions of the copyright laws. In copyright law, the Supreme Court has said that the "statutory [damages] rule, formulated after long experience, not merely compels restitution of profit and reparation for injury but also is designed to discourage wrongful conduct." F.W. Woolworth Co. v. Contemporary Arts, Inc., 344 U.S. 228, 233 (1952). In this case, although Gallo did not present evidence that it actually lost any business due to Spider Webs's actions, the trial court found that Spider Webs's actions put Gallo "at risk of losing business and of having its business reputation tarnished." *E. & J. Gallo Winery*, 129 F. Supp. 2d at 1048. The award of $25,000 in statutory damages in response to the defendants' conduct is not clear error.

* * *

Notes

1. 15 U.S.C. §1117(d) allows for statutory damages as described in the principal case above. However, earlier in that same section of the Lanham Act, it states as follows:

> If the court shall find that the amount of the recovery based on profits is either inadequate or excessive the court may in its discretion enter judgment for such sum as the court shall find to be just, according to the circumstances of the case. Such sum in either of the above circumstances shall constitute compensation and not a penalty.

15 U.S.C. §1117.

This provision is often cited for the justification for denying punitive damages in all trademark infringement or dilution causes of action. *See* Chapter 13 (D)(3), *infra*. Given this, are the statutory damages contemplated in subsection (d) consistent with the main remedy provisions of the Lanham Act? If not, why?

2. Are statutory damages awarded for violation of §43(d) of the Lanham Act a matter for the judge or for the jury? The statute reads "as the court considers just." This might imply that it is a matter of law to be determined by the judge. However, in *Feltner v. Columbia Pictures TV, Inc.*, 523 U.S. 340 (1998), the Supreme Court held that although Section 504 of the Copyright Act provides for statutory damages and uses precisely the same language of "as the court considers just" that this is not a question of equity for the judge, but rather a question of fact for the jury because of the Seventh Amendment's guarantees to a jury trial. If someone challenges a judge's determination under §1117(d) of the Lanham Act, how should an appellate court rule? A claim for money damages is said to be a legal remedy and creates a right to a jury trial. *Dairy Queen, Inc. v. Wood*, 369 U.S. 469 (1962); however, a claim for an injunction is said to be an equitable right and does not create a right to a jury trial. *Gucci Am., v. Accents*, 994 F. Supp. 538 (S.D.N.Y. 1998). In most trademark cases only an injunction is requested. Therefore, most trademark cases are tried by a judge and not a jury. *See* Mark A. Thurmon, *Ending the Seventh Amendment Confusion: A Critical Analysis of the Right to a Jury Trial in Trademark Cases*, 11 Texas Intell. Prop. L. J. 1 (2002).

G. Administrative Dispute Resolution of Domain Names: The Uniform Domain Name Dispute Resolution Policy (UDRP)

1. Uniform Domain Name Dispute Resolution Policy: Purpose, Representations, Cancellations, Transfers and Changes, UDRP Paragraphs 1–4 http://www.icann.org//udrp/policy.htm

1. Purpose. This Uniform Domain Name Dispute Resolution Policy (the "Policy") has been adopted by the Internet Corporation for Assigned Names and Numbers ("ICANN'), is incorporated by reference into your Registration Agreement, and sets forth the terms and conditions in connection with a dispute between you and any party other than us (the registrar) over the registration and use of an Internet domain name registered by you. Proceedings under Paragraph 4 of this Policy will be conducted according to the Rules for Uniform Domain Name Dispute Resolution Policy (the "Rules of Procedure"), which are available at www.icann.org/udrp/udrp-rules-24oct99.htm, and the selected administrative-dispute-resolution service provider's supplemental rules.

2. Your Representations. By applying to register a domain name, or by asking us to maintain or renew a domain name registration, you hereby represent and warrant to us that (a) the statements that you made in your Registration Agreement are complete and accurate; (b) to your knowledge, the registration of the domain name will not infringe upon or otherwise violate the rights of any third party; (c) you are not registering the domain name for an unlawful purpose; and (d) you will not knowingly use the domain name in violation of any applicable laws or regulations. It is your responsibility to determine whether your domain name registration infringes or violates someone else's rights.

3. Cancellations, Transfers, and Changes. We will cancel, transfer or otherwise make changes to domain name registrations under the following circumstances:

a. subject to the provisions of Paragraph 8, our receipt of written or appropriate electronic instructions from you or your authorized agent to take such action;

b. our receipt of an order from a court or arbitral tribunal, in each case of competent jurisdiction, requiring such action; and/or

c. our receipt of a decision of an Administrative Panel requiring such action in any administrative proceeding to which you were a party and which was conducted under this Policy or a later version of this Policy adopted by ICANN. (*See* Paragraph 4(i) and (k) below.)

We may also cancel, transfer or otherwise make changes to a domain name registration in accordance with the terms of your Registration Agreement or other legal requirements.

4. Mandatory Administrative Proceeding.

This Paragraph sets forth the type of disputes for which you are required to submit to a mandatory administrative proceeding. These proceedings will be conducted before one of the administrative-dispute-resolution service providers listed at www.icann.org/udrp/ap-proved-providers.htm (each, a "Provider").

a. Applicable Disputes. You are required to submit to a mandatory administrative proceeding in the event that a third party (a "complainant") asserts to the applicable Provider, in compliance with the Rules of Procedure, that

(i) your domain name is identical or confusingly similar to a trademark or service mark in which the complainant has rights; and

(ii) you have no rights or legitimate interests in respect of the domain name; and

(iii) your domain name has been registered and is being used in bad faith.

In the administrative proceeding, the complainant must prove that each of these three elements are present.

b. Evidence of Registration and Use in Bad Faith. For the purposes of Paragraph 4(a)(iii), the following circumstances, in particular but without limitation, if found by the Panel to be present, shall be evidence of the registration and use of a domain name in bad faith:

(i) circumstances indicating that you have registered or you have acquired the domain name primarily for the purpose of selling, renting, or otherwise transferring the domain name registration to the complainant who is the owner of the trademark or service mark or to a competitor of that complainant, for valuable consideration in excess of your documented out-of-pocket costs directly related to the domain name; or

(ii) you have registered the domain name in order to prevent the owner of the trademark or service mark from reflecting the mark in a corresponding domain name, provided that you have engaged in a pattern of such conduct; or

(iii) you have registered the domain name primarily for the purpose of disrupting the business of a competitor; or

(iv) by using the domain name, you have intentionally attempted to attract, for commercial gain, Internet users to your web site or other on-line location, by creating a likelihood of confusion with the complainant's mark as to the source, sponsorship, affiliation, or endorsement of your web site or location or of a product or service on your web site or location.

c. How to Demonstrate Your Rights to and Legitimate Interests in the Domain Name in Responding to a Complaint. When you receive a complaint, you should refer to Paragraph 5 of the Rules of Procedure in determining how your response should be prepared. Any of the following circumstances, in particular but without limitation, if found by the Panel to be proved based on its evaluation of all evidence presented, shall demonstrate your rights or legitimate interests to the domain name for purposes of Paragraph 4(a)(ii):

(i) before any notice to you of the dispute, your use of, or demonstrable preparations to use, the domain name or a name corresponding to the domain name in connection with a bona fide offering of goods or services; or

(ii) you (as an individual, business, or other organization) have been commonly known by the domain name, even if you have acquired no trademark or service mark rights; or

(iii) you are making a legitimate noncommercial or fair use of the domain name, without intent for commercial gain to misleadingly divert consumers or to tarnish the trademark or service mark at issue.

———————

Telstra Corporation Limited v. Nuclear Marshmallows

WIPO Case No. D2000-0003 (Feb. 18, 2000)

[The Complainant, Telstra Corporation Limited, the largest telecommunications provider in Australia and registered trademark owner of over 50 variations of the Telstra mark, filed a complaint with the WIPO Center regarding the registration of the domain name <telstra.org>, an inactive web address. The Complainant operates five websites with the Telstra mark: <telstra.net>, <telstra.com.au>, <telstra-inc.com>, and <telstrainc.com>. The panel had difficulty locating the Respondent, Nuclear Marshmallows, because it was an unregistered business. The Complainant made several unsuccessful attempts to contact the Respondent based on the Registrar's information. The contact information changed during the Complainant's attempts. The new contact information revealed an address unassociated with the Respondent. The Complainant moved for a default hearing based on the complaint.]

* * *

6.Parties' Contentions
The Complaint

6.1 The Complainant contends that each of the three elements specified in paragraph 4(a) of the Uniform Policy are applicable to this dispute. In relation to element (i), the Complaint contends that the relevant part of the domain name in issue is <telstra>, and that this is clearly identical with or confusingly similar to the various trademarks for the word <TELSTRA> which are registered and owned by the Complainant.

6.2 In relation to element (ii), the Complaint contends that the word <TELSTRA> is an invented word, and as such is not one traders would legitimately choose unless seeking to create an impression of an association with the Complainant. The Complaint further contends that it has not licensed or otherwise permitted the Respondent to use any of its trademarks, nor has it licensed or otherwise permitted the Respondent to apply for or use any domain name incorporating any of those marks. Accordingly, the Complainant contends that the Respondent has no rights or legitimate interests in respect of the domain name in issue.

6.3 In relation to element (iii), the Complainant contends that evidence of bad faith registration and use is established by the following circumstances. First, the Respondent is in breach of the relevant Australian business names registration legislation, by virtue of its failure to register its trading name, Nuclear Marshmallows, as a business name. Secondly, the Respondent has provided false address information for the purposes of its domain name registration, in breach of the Respondent's warranty under paragraph 2(a) of the Uniform Policy. Thirdly, the trademark <TELSTRA> is one of the best known trademarks in Australia, and it is inconceivable that the person or persons behind the Respondent would not be aware of this fact. Fourthly, by virtue of the wide spread use and reputation of the trademark <TELSTRA>, members of the public in Australia would believe that the entity owning the domain name <telstra.org> was the Complainant or in some way associated with the Complainant. Fifthly, any realistic use of the domain name must misrepresent an association with the Complainant and its goodwill, resulting in passing off, breaches of Australian consumer protection legislation, and trademark infringements.

The Response

6.4 The Respondent did not file a Response to the Complaint.

7.   Findings and Conclusions

Identical or Confusingly Similar Domain Name

7.1 The domain name in issue is <telstra.org>. The relevant part of this domain name is <telstra>. The Administrative Panel finds that this part of the domain name is identical to the numerous trademark registrations of the word <TELSTRA> held by the Complainant. In addition, the Administrative Panel finds that the whole of the domain name is confusingly similar to those trademark registrations.

Respondent's Rights or Legitimate Interests in the Domain Name

7.2 The Respondent has not provided evidence of circumstances of the type specified in paragraph 4(c) of the Uniform Policy, or of any other circumstances giving rise to a right to or legitimate interest in the domain name. In light of (i) the fact that the Complainant has not licensed or otherwise permitted the Respondent to use any of its trademarks or to apply for or use any domain name incorporating any of those marks, and (ii) the fact that the word <TELSTRA> appears to be an invented word, and as such is not one traders would legitimately choose unless seeking to create an impression of an association with the Complainant, the Administrative Panel finds that the Respondent has no rights or legitimate interests in the domain name.

Domain Name Registered and Used in Bad Faith

7.3 It is less clear cut whether the Complainant has proved the third element in paragraph 4(a) of the Uniform Policy, namely that the domain name "has been registered and is being used in bad faith" by Respondent. The Administrative Panel notes two things about this provision. First, the provision contains the conjunction "and" rather than "or". Secondly, the provision refers to both the past tense ("has been registered") and the present tense ("is being used").

7.4 The significance of the use of the conjunction "and" is that paragraph 4(a)(iii) requires the Complainant to prove use in bad faith as well as registration in bad faith.

* * *

7.7 Has the Complainant proved that the domain name "has been registered in bad faith" by the Respondent? In light of the facts established in paragraphs 4.6 to 4.8, the Administrative Panel finds that the Respondent does not conduct any legitimate commercial or non-commercial business activity in Australia. In light of the facts established in paragraphs 4.6 to 4.8, the Administrative Panel further finds that the Respondent has taken deliberate steps to ensure that its true identity cannot be determined and communication with it cannot be made. Given the Complainant's numerous trademark registrations for, and its wide reputation in, the word <TELSTRA>, as evidenced by the facts established in paragraphs 4.2 to 4.5, it is not possible to conceive of a plausible circumstance in which the Respondent could legitimately use the domain name <telstra.org>. It is also not possible to conceive of a plausible situation in which the Respondent would have been unaware of this fact at the time of registration. These findings, together with the finding in paragraph 7.2 that the Respondent has no rights or interests in the domain name, lead the Administrative Panel to conclude that the domain name <telstra.org> has been registered by the Respondent in bad faith.

7.8 Has the Complainant proved the additional requirement that the domain name "is being used in bad faith" by the Respondent? The domain name <telstra.org> does not resolve to a web site or other on-line presence. There is no evidence that a web site or other on-line presence is in the process of being established which will use the domain name. There is no evidence of advertising, promotion or display to the public of the domain name. Finally, there is no evidence that the Respondent has offered to sell, rent or otherwise transfer the domain name to the Complainant, a competitor of the Complainant, or any other person. In short, there is no positive action being undertaken by the Respondent in relation to the domain name.

7.9 This fact does not, however, resolve the question. As discussed in paragraph 7.6, the relevant issue is not whether the Respondent is undertaking a positive action in bad faith in relation to the domain name, but instead whether, in all the circumstances of the case, it can be said that the Respondent is acting in bad faith. The distinction between undertaking a positive action in bad faith and acting in bad faith may seem a rather fine distinction, but it is an important one. The significance of the distinction is that the concept of a domain name "being used in bad faith" is not limited to positive action; inaction is within the concept. That is to say, it is possible, in certain circumstances, for inactivity by the Respondent to amount to the domain name being used in bad faith.

7.10 This understanding of paragraph 4(a)(iii) is supported by the actual provisions of the Uniform Policy. Paragraph 4(b) of the Uniform Policy identifies, without limitation, circumstances that "shall be evidence of the registration and use of a domain name in bad faith", for the purposes of paragraph 4(a)(iii). Only one of these circumstances (paragraph 4(b)(iv)), by necessity, involves a positive action post-registration undertaken in relation to the domain name (using the name to attract customers to a web site or other on-line location). The other three circumstances contemplate either a positive action or inaction in relation to the domain name. That is to say, the circumstances identified in paragraphs 4(b)(1), (ii) and (iii) can be found in a situation involving a passive holding of the domain name registration. Of course, these three paragraphs require additional facts (an intention to sell, rent or transfer the registration, for paragraph 4(b)(i); a pattern of conduct preventing a trade mark owner's use of the registration, for paragraph 4(b)(ii); the primary purpose of disrupting the business of a competitor, for paragraph 4(b)(iii)). Nevertheless, the point is that paragraph 4(b) recognizes that inaction (e.g. passive holding) in relation to a domain name registration can, in certain circumstances, constitute a domain name being used in bad faith. Furthermore, it must be recalled that the circumstances identified in paragraph 4(b) are "without limitation" — that is, paragraph 4(b) expressly recognizes that *other* circumstances can be evidence that a domain name was registered and is being used in bad faith.

7.11 The question that then arises is what circumstances of inaction (passive holding) other than those identified in paragraphs 4(b)(i), (ii) and (iii) can constitute a domain name being used in bad faith? This question cannot be answered in the abstract; the question can only be answered in respect of the particular facts of a specific case. That is to say, in considering whether the passive holding of a domain name, following a bad faith registration of it, satisfies the requirements of paragraph 4(a)(iii), the Administrative Panel must give close attention to all the circumstances of the Respondent's behavior. A remedy can be obtained under the Uniform Policy only if those circumstances show that the Respondent's passive holding amounts to acting in bad faith.

7.12 The Administrative Panel has considered whether, in the circumstances of this particular Complaint, the passive holding of the domain name by the Respondent amounts to the Respondent acting in bad faith. It concludes that it does. The particular circumstances of this case which lead to this conclusion are:

 (i) the Complainant's trademark has a strong reputation and is widely known, as evidenced by its substantial use in Australia and in other countries,

 (ii) the Respondent has provided no evidence whatsoever of any actual or contemplated good faith use by it of the domain name,

(iii) the Respondent has taken active steps to conceal its true identity, by operating under a name that is not a registered business name,

(iv) the Respondent has actively provided, and failed to correct, false contact details, in breach of its registration agreement, and

(v) taking into account all of the above, it is not possible to conceive of any plausible actual or contemplated active use of the domain name by the Respondent that would not be illegitimate, such as by being a passing off, an infringement of consumer protection legislation, or an infringement of the Complainant's rights under trademark law.

In light of these particular circumstances, the Administrative Panel concludes that the Respondent's passive holding of the domain name in this particular case satisfies the requirement of paragraph 4(a)(iii) that the domain name "is being used in bad faith" by Respondent.

8. Decision

8.1 The Administrative Panel decides that the Complainant has proven each of the three elements in paragraph 4(a) of the Uniform Policy. Accordingly, the Administrative Panel requires that the domain name <telstra.org> be transferred to the Complainant.

Andrew F. Christie Presiding Panelist

_____

Notes

1. UDRP proceedings are not "arbitrations" under the Federal Arbitration Act and therefore not subject to deferential review. *See* Dluhos v. Strasberg, 321 F.3d 365 (3d Cir. 2003).

2. Since the inception of the UDRP, over 15,551 domain name cases have been decided under dispute resolution policies. Under the policy, the case is always initiated by the owner claiming superior rights and the majority of these actions favor the trademark owner. Is there a bias towards trademark owners? Should a trademark owner be favored? *See* Elizabeth Thrornburg, *Fast, Cheap, and Out of Control: Lessons from the ICANN Dispute Resolution Process*, 6 J. SMALL & EMERGING BUS. L. 191, 196 (2002).

3. Many have addressed whether the UDRP is fair. *See, e.g.,* Orion Armon, *Is This as Good as It Gets? An Appraisal of ICANN's Uniform Domain Name Resolution Policy (UDRP) Three Years After Implementation*, 22 REV. LITIG. 99 (2003); Benjamin G. Davis, *Une Magouille Planetaire: The UDRP Is an International Scam*, 72 MISS. L.J. 815 (2002); John Magee, *Domain Name Disputes: An Assessment of the UDRP as Against Traditional Litigation*, 2003 U. ILL J.L. TECH & POL'Y 203 (2003). What are the implications if it is not fair? Does anyone really seem to mind?

4. WIPO reports that the number of cybersquatting disputes filed with the World Intellectual Property Organization increased by 1/4 in 2006 over 2005. It quotes Francis Gurry, WIPO Deputy Directory General, who oversees WIPO's dispute resolution work, as saying that domain names have become a commodity and the enforcement of rights in and to these commodities continues to be a great challenge. *See Cybersquatting Remains on the Rise with further Risk to Trademarks from New Registration Practices*, htttp://www.wipo.int/pressroom/en/aticles/2007/article_0014.html. Are you as nervous for the future as Francis Gurry? Do you anticipate creativity or doom?

_____

1. Identical or Confusingly Similar Mark: UDRP §4(a)(i)

4(a). Applicable Disputes. You are required to submit to a mandatory administrative proceeding in the event that a third party (a "complainant") asserts to the applicable Provider, in compliance with the Rules of Procedure, that

> (i) your domain name is identical or confusingly similar to a trademark or service mark in which the complainant has rights; …

Motorola, Inc. v. Newgate Internet, Inc.
WIPO Case No. D2000-0079 (April 14, 2000)

[The trademark TALKABOUT, a registered trademark with the USPTO, has been in use by Motorola or its predecessor since 1981. The domain name at issue was <talkabout.com>. Although Conner F. Ryan Company (CFR), a predecessor of the Respondent, NewGate Internet, Inc, originally registered the domain name and was originally licensed to sell TalkAbout products, neither party was authorized to use the trademark. Respondent informed Complainant on August 27, 1998, that it planned to use the domain name as an adult sex site. On September 2, 1998, Respondent informed complainant that it would transfer the domain name for a fee exceeding registration costs.]

* * *

It is clear that the domain name <talkabout.com> is identical or confusingly similar to the trademark registered and used by complainant, TALKABOUT. Respondent disputes this similarity by arguing that there is no actual confusion because the string Talk-About can be found in many sites on the Net. This maybe true, but is irrelevant, since paragraph 4(a)(1) of the Policy requires only that the domain name be identical or confusingly similar to a mark, which is the case here, quite independently from whether or not any actual confusion or likelihood of confusion is present.

Respondent and its predecessor CFR have claimed that they were acting "with Motorola's sanction and blessing", but they have presented no evidence to this effect. Nor have they presented any evidence that they had a trademark or common law use of the mark prior to Motorola's adoption and use of the TALKABOUT trademark. Their actions were in violation of Motorola's intellectual property rights and caused actual confusion among customers. Thus it cannot be said that the respondent or its predecessor CFR had or have a legitimate interest in respect of the domain name. Respondent argues that CFR had the right to resell Motorola's products. This assertion is not disputed by Motorola, but is irrelevant, since the right to resell products does not create the right to use a mark more extensively than required to advertise and sell the product. The use of a mark as a domain name clearly goes further than what is required merely to resell products.

* * *

This panel need not consider whether or not CFR's use of the disputed domain name was "bona fide", because it suffices to consider the respondent's subsequent use. The respondent stated that it wished to use the domain name for an adult sex site. While (as the respondent correctly points out) many adult sex sites are perfectly legal and constitute bona fide offerings of goods or services, the use of somebody else's trademark as a domain name (or even as a meta-tag) clearly does not constitute a "bona fide" offering of goods or services when the web site owner has no registered or common law rights to the mark, since the only reason to use the trademark as a domain name or meta-tag is to attract customers who were not looking for an adult sex site, but were instead looking for the products or services associated with the trademark. Such use of a trademark can create customer confusion or dilution of the mark, which is precisely what trademark laws are meant to prevent. And actions that create, or tend to create, violations of the law can hardly be considered to be "bona fide".

7. Decision

For all of the foregoing reasons, the Panel decides that the domain name registered by respondent is identical or confusingly similar to the trademark in which the complainant has rights, and that the respondent has no rights or legitimate interests in respect of the domain name, and that the respondent's domain name has been registered and is being used in bad faith. Accordingly, pursuant to Paragraph 4(i) of the Policy, the Panel requires that the registration of the domain name <talkabout.com> be transferred to the complainant.

Richard Hill Presiding Panelist, Clark W. Lackert Panelist

[Dissent by Paul Michael DeCicco omitted]

Note

1. The UDRP Panels originally looked toward trademark law measures to determine likelihood of confusion. *See* Wal-Mart Stores, Inc. v. Walsucks and Walmarket Puerto Rico, *infra* Chapter XII.G.3.d (applying the test for confusion from AMF Inc, v. Sleekcraft Boats, 599 F. 2d 341 (9th Cir. 1979)). But they now assert that, in the UDRP context, the test is more simple. *See, e.g.,* Pearl Jam v. Phoebe's Fantasy Playhouse, Nat. Arb. Forum FA 226451 (Mar. 5, 2004) ("[M]any cases have established that the test of confusing similarity under the Policy is confined to a comparison of the disputed domain name and the trademark alone, independent of the other marketing and use factors, such as the '*Sleekcraft* factors' [citation omitted] usually considered in trademark infringement or unfair competition cases."). Why the apparent change in direction?

----

2. Legitimate Interests: UDRP §4(a)(ii)

4(a) Applicable Disputes. You are required to submit to a mandatory administrative proceeding in the event that a third party (a "complainant") asserts to the applicable Provider, in compliance with the Rules of Procedure, that....

(ii) you have no rights or legitimate interests in respect of the domain name;

Paragraph 4(a)(ii) requires the Complainant to prove that the Respondent has no rights to or legitimate interests in the Domain Names. Once a Complainant establishes a prima facie showing that none of the three circumstances establishing legitimate interests or rights apply, the burden of production on this factor shifts to the Respondent to rebut the showing. The burden of proof, however, remains with Complainant to prove each of the three elements of Paragraph 4(a).

———

Volvo Trademark Holding AD v. e-motordealer Ltd.
WIPO Case No. D2002-0036 (March 22, 2002)

[The Complainant, a Swedish company selling automobiles and parts, is the owner of the registered trademark Volvo and operates numerous companies under the Volvo mark including a financial services company that offers insurance. The Respondent, e-motordealer Ltd., a new company originated to "provide a one-stop shop for all the consumer's motoring needs from sale of the car through to servicing, parts, finance and insurance through the franchised dealer network," registered <Volvoinsurance.com> on November 28, 2001. The panel concluded that the domain name <Volvoinsurance.com> is confusingly similar to the Complainant's mark.]

* * *

Respondent's Rights or Legitimate Interests in the Domain Name: Policy 4(a)(ii)

It is first convenient to recall that, according to paragraph 4(c) of the Policy, a Respondent may establish its rights or legitimate interests in the Domain Name, among other circumstances, by showing any of the following elements:

"(i) before any notice to you [Respondent] of the dispute, your use of, or demonstrable preparations to use, the Domain Name or a name corresponding to the Domain Name in connection with a bona fide offering of goods or services; *or*

(ii) you [Respondent] (as an individual, business, or other organization) have been commonly known by the Domain Name, even if you have acquired no trade mark or service mark rights; *or*

(iii) you [Respondent] are making a legitimate noncommercial or fair use of the Domain Name, without intent for commercial gain to misleadingly divert consumers or to tarnish the trade mark or service mark at issue."

Complainant contends that Respondent has no rights or legitimate interest in the Domain Name <Volvoinsurance.com> based on Complainant's continuous and long prior use of its mark VOLVO and its trade name VOLVO INSURANCE.

Respondent claims that Complainant does not have the legal right to be the sole provider of insurances for owners of Volvo Cars. Respondent asserts to have no intention to pass off as an insurance company that is part of or authorized by Complainant and holds that it has registered the Domain Name at issue for the purpose of supplying competitive quotations to Volvo drivers by providing a platform for many different insurance suppliers "to ensure the customer gets the best deal".

* * *

While the Panel is satisfied that Respondent, prior to any notice of this dispute, seems to demonstrably have started preparing an offering of goods and services, it is hard to draw a bona fide connection of this to the use of the Domain Name at issue. As shown by the search for "volvo insurance" on the Altavista search engine and by Respondent's claim that in the UK alone, there are over 200 insurance companies that provide insurance cover on Volvo cars, it is clear that the described goods and services can be and currently are marketed and sold without using a Domain Name incorporating the mark of Complainant. Respondent refers to *DaimlerChrysler A.G. v. Donald Drummonds*, WIPO Case No. D2001-0160 where the Domain Name <mer-

cedesshop.com> was found to be descriptive of the business conducted there. Respondent claims the same to be the case for this proceeding. Quoting from this Case, Respondent asserts that "in conducting the planned business it would be difficult if not impossible to altogether avoid use of the word VOLVO". The Panel disagrees. This proceeding is only concerned with the use of the word VOLVO in a Domain Name. In view of the available technology of using META-tags to increase the number of hits on search engines, there is no need for Respondent to include the protected trademark VOLVO, or any other car manufacturers' protected trademarks, in the domain name in order to carry out its business. Even if the domain name did not include the component VOLVO, Respondent's web page could be found on the Internet. Avoiding Complainant's mark in the Domain Name, therefore, would be easy and would constitute no impediment to Respondent's business.

*　*　*

Finally, in WIPO Case No. D2001-0160 mentioned above and quoted in the Response, the Domain Name at issue was <mercedesshop.com> and it was held that "under the present facts, if the Panel were to find for the Complainant, the majority can conceive of no case in which a legitimate competitor in the sale of parts and after-market accessories could ever register a domain name descriptive of that business." This Panel again disagrees. It does not see a vested right of anybody, particularly not of a competitor, to incorporate a famous trademark in its domain name in a manner confusing or diverting Internet users. As mentioned above, Respondent is not prevented from using the word or syllable VOLVO as a META tag on search engines in order to be visible on the Internet, nor is it prevented to use the term in a non-trademark sense on its webpage. It could even use the word or syllable VOLVO in the Domain Name, but, in view of the wording of paragraph 4(c)(iii) of the Policy, only in a *non-confusing and non-diverting manner*. By allowing the use of misleading and diverting domain names, Respondent could get a free ride and could bank on the goodwill created by the trademark holder with great investments and over a long period of time. Had Respondent registered a non-confusing domain name, identifying the trademark to belong to someone else, such as for instance: <insuranceforvolvos.com> or <Volvoinsurance broker.com> (which examples do not imply or even clearly exclude ownership, affiliation, endorsement or support by the trade mark holder), the Panel would could have taken a different view as to their admissibility. By contrast, the Domain Name chosen by Respondent at first sight appears to be one of Complainant's and it is only upon arriving at and studying the web page that the (intended) disclaimer can be seen. At that point, the consumer has already been diverted and mislead, attracted by the false impression created by the misleading Domain Name. The Policy wants to avoid this.

In the light of the above, the Panel finds that Respondent's intended use of the Domain Name does not represent a legitimate noncommercial or fair use of the Domain Name. The very composition of the Domain Name is suitable to mislead and divert consumers, at the same time tarnishing the trademark of Complainant. Thus, Complainant has fulfilled its burden of proof under paragraph 4(a)(ii) of the Policy.

*　*　*

7. Decision

In view of the circumstances and facts discussed above, the Panelist decides that the disputed Domain Name is identical and confusingly similar to the registered trade mark in which the Complainant has rights, that the Respondent has no rights or legitimate interests in respect of the Domain Name, and that the Respondent's Domain Name has been registered and is being used in bad faith.

Accordingly, pursuant to paragraph 4(i) of the Policy, the Panelist requires that the disputed Domain Name <Volvoinsurance.com> shall be transferred to the Complainant.

---

3. Registration and Use in Bad Faith: UDRP §4(a)(iii) and §4(b)

4(a). Applicable Disputes. You are required to submit to a mandatory administrative proceeding in the event that a third party (a "complainant") asserts to the applicable Provider, in compliance with the Rules of Procedure, that ...

(iii) your domain name has been registered and is being used in bad faith.

4(b). Evidence of Registration and Use in Bad Faith. For the purposes of Paragraph 4(a)(iii), the following circumstances, in particular but without limitation, if found by the Panel to be present, shall be evidence of the registration and use of a domain name in bad faith:

(i) circumstances indicating that you have registered or you have acquired the domain name primarily for the purpose of selling, renting, or otherwise transferring the domain name registration to the complainant who is the owner of the trademark or service mark or to a competitor of that complainant, for valuable consideration in excess of your documented out-of-pocket costs directly related to the domain name; or

(ii) you have registered the domain name in order to prevent the owner of the trademark or service mark from reflecting the mark in a corresponding domain name, provided that you have engaged in a pattern of such conduct; or

(iii) you have registered the domain name primarily for the purpose of disrupting the business of a competitor; or

(iv) by using the domain name, you have intentionally attempted to attract, for commercial gain, Internet users to your web site or other on-line location, by creating a likelihood of confusion with the complainant's mark as to the source, sponsorship, affiliation, or endorsement of your web site or location or of a product or service on your web site or location.

Recordati S.Pa. v. Domain Name Clearing Company
WIPO Case No. D2000-0194 (July 21, 2000)

[The Complainant, owner of the U.S. trademark in Recordati since 1960, is an Italian based pharmaceutical company. The Respondent, Domain Name Clearing Company, contended that the domain name in question, <recordati.com>, was an intentional misspelling of Recorditi, an Italian restaurant. The Respondent stated that the domain name was on hold and that the site was not used to make any connection to the Complainant. The panel concluded that the domain name <recordati.com> was confusingly similar to the Complainant's trademark and that the Respondent had no legitimate interests in the domain name.]

* * *

Paragraph 4(b) is not limiting as to the circumstances which may constitute evidence of bad faith and circumstances other than those enumerated in subparagraphs (i) to (iv) of Paragraph 4(b) may constitute registration and use of a domain name in bad faith.

"Bad faith" is defined in Black's Law Dictionary 7th edition at page 134 as: "1. Dishonesty of belief or purpose …". In *Halsey v. Brotherhood* (1881), 19 Ch. D. 386 Lord Coleridge L.C.J. in determining whether there was evidence of *mala fides* stated that the task of the Court was to consider "whether there is anything to show that what the defendant stated was stated without reasonable and probable cause".

Findings:

* * *

There is no evidence that the Respondent has offered to sell the registered domain name to the Complainant, thus the circumstances of s. 4(b)(i) are not met. There is no evidence that the Respondent Domain Name Clearing Company, LLC has engaged in a pattern of conduct of registering domain names in order to prevent the owner of a trademark from reflecting the trademark in a corresponding domain name, thus the circumstances of 4(b)(ii) are not met. There is no evidence that the Respondent is a competitor of the Complainant, thus the circumstances of 4(b)(iii) are not met.

Subsections 4(b)(i), 4(b)(ii) and 4(b)(iii) are examples of circumstances which, if found by the panel, shall be evidence of the registration and use of a domain name in bad faith.

The Complainant has established that the Respondent registered the domain name "recordati.com" on March 20, 1997, and did not set up a web site utilizing the domain name prior to December 11, 1998, when the domain name was placed on "hold" at the request of the Complainant.

Has the Complainant established on a balance of probabilities that the Respondent has registered and is involved in dealing with the registered domain name "recordati.com" in bad faith? The Complainant stated that the word "recordati" is not a word known in the English language. The Respondent does not deny that "recordati" is not a word in the English language but states that "recordati" is an intentional misspelling of "ricordati" which roughly translated means "remember", suggesting "nostalgia". There is no statement by the Respondent of why Respondent registered recordati.com as the phonetic equivalent of the Italian word "ricordati".

* * *

The Respondent did not commence commercial use of the domain name during the period between registration of the domain name on March 20, 1997, and the date on which the domain name was placed on "hold" on December 11, 1998. Since the registered domain name in dispute has been placed on hold the registered domain name has been renewed by the Respondent.

* * *

As found above "use in bad faith" in subsection 4(a)(iii) does not refer to "use in commerce" in the trademark sense of use but refers in the broad sense to a pattern of conduct respecting the registered domain name in dispute. Other panelists have held that passive holding of the domain name, without use in commerce, may support a holding of use in bad faith. Telstra Corporation Limited v. Nuclear Marshmallows, Case No. D2000-0003.

On a balance of probabilities, I find that the domain name "recordati.com" was registered and is being used in bad faith.

7. Decision

In the Complaint, the Complainant requested that in accordance with Paragraph 4(c)(i) of the Uniform Domain Name Dispute Resolution Policy, the Administrative Panel issue a decision that the disputed domain name be cancelled or transferred to Complainant. The Complainant having proved each of the three elements set out in paragraph 4(a)(i)(ii) and (iii) of the Uniform Domain Name Dispute Resolution Policy is entitled to a decision in favor of the Complainant. The Panel requires that the domain name recordati.com be transferred to Recordati Industria Chimica e Farmaceutica S.p.A.

Ross Carson, Panelist

Dated: July 21,2000

Notes

1. Is the standard for "bad faith" under the UDRP identical to the standard for "bad faith" under the ACPA?

2. Except in cases involving "abusive registrations"—having bad-faith intent to profit commercially from others' trademarks (e.g., cybersquatting and cyberpiracy), the adopted policy leaves the resolution of disputes to the courts (or arbitrators where agreed by the parties) and calls for registrars not to disturb a registration until those courts decide. The adopted policy establishes a streamlined, inexpensive administrative dispute-resolution procedure intended only for the relatively narrow class of cases of "abusive registrations." Thus, the fact that the policy's administrative dispute-resolution procedure does not extend to cases where a registered domain name is subject to a legitimate dispute (and may ultimately be found to violate the challenger's trademark) is a feature of the policy, not a flaw. ICANN, "Second Staff Report on Implementation Documents for the Uniform Dispute Resolution Policy," October 24, 1999 at http://www. icann.org/udrp/udrp-second-staff-report-24oct99.

3. Reconsider the cases raised by the Burk article at the beginning of this Chapter. Would any of them qualify for the safe harbor in UDRP policy?

H. Other Cybersquatting Issues

1. Typosquatting

Disney Enterprises, Inc. v. John Zuccarini,
Cupcake City and Cupcake Patrol
WIPO Case No. D2001-0489 (June 19, 2001)

[The Complainant, Disney Enterprises, owns over 50 trademarks as well as several domain names that incorporate the Disney name. The Respondents, John Zuccarini, Cupcake City and Cupcake Patrol a/k/a John Zuccarini, registered the following disputed domain names: <disneychanel.com>, <disneywallpaper.com>, <disneywold.com>, <disneywolrd.com>, <disneyworl.com>, and <walddisney.com>.]

* * *

"Cyberflying"

* * *

Thus a quick-witted respondent might seek to escape the jurisdiction of the panel by transferring the domain name to a new holder or to a new registrar after receipt of the copy of the complaint but before the formal commencement of the proceeding. Both situations arose in *British Broadcasting Corporation v. Data Art Corporation/Stoneybrook* (WIPO Case D2000-0683) [<bbcnews.com>] …

In that case, the transferee of the domain name was an associate of the respondent who had knowledge of the complaint before the transfer took place. The panel held that neither the change of registrant nor of registrar affected the proceedings. In the event, the new registrar was directed to transfer the domain name <bbcnews.com> to the BBC.

In this case, after receiving the complaint, Mr. Zuccarini transferred three of the Disputed Domain Names to a different registrar and into his own name. The panel finds these circumstances identical to those in the BBC case and that neither the change of registrant nor of registrar affects these proceedings.

Identity/confusing similarity

* * *

The Respondents argue that a domain name is an Internet Protocol ("IP") address. It is not. An IP address is a series of four one-to-three digit numbers separated by periods, e.g., 203.123.3.5. A domain name, by contrast, is a textual (or conceivably graphical) construct, such as <zuccarini.com>, which is translated by the domain name system (DNS) into a numerical IP address. The Respondents did not purchase or obtain IP addresses, they registered domain names. As textual constructs, domain names that incorporate well-known trademarks can be readily confused with those marks.

Each of the Disputed Domain Names incorporates the whole of the famous mark DISNEY. Six of the seven have DISNEY at the beginning of the name. The other precedes the mark DISNEY with the word WALD, a slight mis-spelling of the well-known abbreviation of the Complainant's founder's first name WALT, as in the Complainant's registered trademark WALT DISNEY.

Of the six beginning with the trademark DISNEY, four include slight mis-spellings of the word WORLD, a generic word famously associated with the Complainant's mark in the expression WALT DISNEY WORLD, sometimes referred to simply as DISNEY WORLD. The fifth follows the word DISNEY with the word CHANEL, a slight misspelling of the word CHANNEL, as in the Complainant's registered trademark DISNEY CHANNEL. The sixth follows the trademark DISNEY with the generic word WALLPAPER. All seven, of course, end in <.com>.

It has been decided in many cases under the Policy that "essential" or "virtual" identity is sufficient for the purposes of the Policy.

* * *

The test of confusing similarity under the Policy, unlike trademark infringement or unfair competition cases, is confined to a consideration of the Disputed Domain Name and the trademark…. In *Microsoft Corporation v. Microsofcom a.k.a. Tarek Ahmed* (WIPO case No. D2000-0548) contributing factors to the likelihood of confusion were held to be the visual similarity between the domain name and the complainant's mark and the mark being strong and immediately recognizable.

Here the mark DISNEY is indisputably strong and immediately recognizable around the world and the Panel has no hesitation in finding that each of the Disputed Domain Names is confusingly similar to the Complainant's famous mark DISNEY. In addition, the domain name <walddisney.com> is confusingly similar to the Complainant's registered trademark WALT DISNEY and the domain name <disneychanel.com> is confusingly similar to the Complainant's registered trademark DISNEY CHANNEL.

* * *

Mr. Zuccarini has admitted, under oath, both in deposition and trial testimony, as reported by the Court in *Joseph C. Shields. individuallv and t/a The Joe Cartoon Co. v. John Zuccarini, individually and t/a Cupcake City,* 89 F. Supp.2d 634.639 (US Dist. Ct. E.D. Pennsylvania 2000) that he registered variations of thousands of domain names *because they are confusingly similar to others' famous marks or personal names*—and thus are likely misspellings of these names—in an effort to divert Internet traffic to his sites. [emphasis added].

Although the domain name <disneywallpaper.com> has no misspelling, it includes a generic word likely to be typed by Internet users expecting, by so doing, to download the Complainant's "wallpaper" for their computers, as they can from the Complainant's website at <disney.com>.

The Complainant has established this element.

Illegitimacy

Having argued in relation to the issue of identity/confusing similarity that Mr. Zuccarini purchased "a particular numerical IP address", the Respondents argue in relation to the issue of legitimacy that Mr. Zuccarini purchased "the subject domain names" through a legitimate registration process. That registration process required the Respondents to agree, as a condition of registration, to be bound by the Policy for the resolution of disputes such as the present. Accordingly, the fact of registration is no evidence of legitimacy.

The Complainant has never authorized the Respondents to utilize any of its marks, nor does the Complainant have any relationship or association with the Respondents. Any use to which the Respondents might put of any of the DISNEY marks, including in connection with the services listed in the corresponding registrations, would violate the Complainant's trademark rights. The Respondents are not now and have never been known by the mark DISNEY nor by any of the Disputed Domain Names.

The Respondents' mousetrap, automatically springs upon Internet users who gain access to five of the seven Disputed Domain Names, and from which there is virtually no escape without generating "click through" revenue for the Respondents, depends for its success upon misleadingly attracting Internet users to the Respondents' sites for the Respondents' commercial gain. This use of these five Disputed Domain Names cannot constitute legitimate noncommercial or fair use within paragraph 4(c)(iii) of the Policy.

With respect to the two domain names <disneywallpaper.com> and <disney chanel.com>, which the Response says are not being used, cases under the Policy have found absence of rights or legitimate interests in domain names which have not been used. In *State Farm Mutual Automobile Insurance Company v. Rocky E. Faw* (NAF case FA94971) the respondent was found to have no legitimate interests in respect of the domain name where he had not used nor developed the domain name for a legitimate non-commercial or fair purpose and was not using the domain name in connection with a bona fide offering of goods or services ... The same considerations apply in this case and lead the Panel to the same conclusion.

The Panel finds that the Respondents have no rights or legitimate interests in any of the Disputed Domain Names within paragraph 4(a)(ii) of the Policy.

Bad Faith

The Complainant contends that the Respondents' bad faith is established under paragraphs 4(b)(ii) and 4(b)(iv) of the Policy, citing in relation to 4(b)(ii) (inter alia) cases brought against Mr. Zuccarini in which such a finding was made but in which he did not file a response. The learned Panelists in those cases were, in the absence of a response, entitled to accept the uncontradicted contentions of the Complainants: *Reuters Limited v. Global Net 2000, Inc.*(WIPO Case No. D2000-0441).

The Response filed in this case states that the Respondent [sic] operates "a business of registering 'generic' terms on the Internet for the purpose of providing click thru traffic to his customers." Leaving aside for a moment the reference to generic names, the Panel accepts that the Respondents' purpose in registering domain names which incorporate the well-known trademarks of others, including five of the Disputed Domain Names, is to generate click-thru traffic revenue.

As to paragraph 4(b)(iv) of the Policy, the Response states: "a visitor to any of the subject domains will be directed to Respondent Cupcake Party's site containing advertising programs". The Panel is satisfied that the Respondents chose and have been using the Disputed Domain Names (other than <disneychanel.com> and <walddisney.com>) in an attempt intentionally to attract Internet users, for commercial gain, to the Respondents' Cupcake Party site, where they are introduced to various advertisements, some of which have nothing to do with the Complainant's business and some of which promote music lyrics, very much a part of the Complainant's business.

* * *

To the extent to which the Respondents' site does not promote activities, goods or services associated with the Complainant, some Internet visitors may not be confused in this way, since the Respondents' business depends on trapping for commercial gain unsuspecting and inadvertent visitors, the more astute of whom may realize immediately upon their arrival at the Respondents' site that they are not at their intended destination.

Less astute visitors however, believing that they are about to visit a site associated with the Complainant, may continue for some time in that belief even though the products and services advertised to them are wholly different from those of the Complainant. In relation to these visitors the Respondents' conduct constitutes evidence of bad faith registration and use within paragraph 4(b)(iv) of the Policy.

In any event, "*the fallacy in respondent's contention is that while under traditional trademark law the similarity or nonsimilarity of the products may be considered, this is not a factor under the Policy*". *General Mills, Inc. v. John Zuccarini* [Nat. Ar. Borum FA 97050 (May 30, 2001)].

The Panel notes that the circumstances specified in paragraph 4(b) of the Policy are not exhaustive. It is open to a complainant to establish and for a Panel to find bad faith registration and use within paragraph 4(a)(iii) in other circumstances. The Complainant has contended that such findings should be made in this case.

As to registration, in *SportSoft Golf, Inc. v. Hale Irwin's Golfers' Passport* (NAF case FA94956) a finding of bad faith was made where the respondent "knew or should have known" of the registration and use of the trademark prior to registering the domain name.

Here the Respondents undoubtedly knew of the famous DISNEY mark before registering the Disputed Domain Names, all of which wholly incorporate that mark. For this reason the Panel unhesitatingly finds all the Disputed Domain Names were registered in bad faith, within the meaning of paragraph 4(a)(iii) of the Policy.

As to use, the Complainant's DISNEY mark is not generic, as the Respondents appear to assert. It is highly distinctive and unquestionably famous. It is the goodwill of the DISNEY mark "the attractive force that brings in custom" which Mr. Zuccarini misappropriates when he attracts into his mousetrap Internet users who, in relation to five of the seven Disputed Domain Names, spell the mark correctly but inadvertently misspell words commonly associated with it. The success of the Respondent's mousetrap is borne out by the *Shields* case, in which the Court noted "[Mr. Zuccarini's] click-based revenue now approaches $1 million per year." *Id* at 639.

The Panel finds the Respondents are using these five domain names in bad faith.

As to the remaining domain names, <disneywallpaper.com> and <disneychanel.com>, the Respondents say these are not in use. They submit that, for this reason, no finding of bad faith can be made, citing *DBB, Inc., v. Spotlight Magazine, INC.,* 86 F.Supp.2d 176, 185, 186 (D. WDNY 2000), which involved the expression "use in commerce", defined in the Lanham Act as, inter alia, use of a trademark "on services when it is used or displayed in the sale or advertising of services and the services are rendered in commerce". No such requirement in relation to the concept of "use" is contained in the Policy.

In many cases under the Policy, inaction (passive holding) has been found to be within the concept of "use." ...

Here the Panel takes into account the nature of the Respondents' business as described in the Response and as found by the Panel; the absence of any explanation from the Respondents as to why these domain names have not been used and the significant periods of time during which they have remained inactive. The Panel finds both are being used in bad faith within the meaning of paragraph 4(a)(iii) of the Policy.

Thus the Panel finds that all the Disputed Domain Names were registered and are being used in bad faith.

* * *

7. Decision

Pursuant to paragraphs 4(i) of the Policy and 15 of the Rules, the Panel directs that the following domain names be transferred to the Complainant:

<disneychanel.com>
<disneywallpaper.com>
<disneywold.com>
<disneywolrd.com>
<disneyword.com>
<disneyworl.com>
<walddisney.com>

Alan L. Limbury, Esq., Presiding Panelist
Peter L. Michaelson, Esq. Panelist

Gordon Harris, Esq. Panelist

Notes

1. Typosquatting has been enjoined under the ACPA as well. *See* Shields v. Zuccarini, 254 F. 3d 476 (3d Cir. 2001).

2. In *Playboy Enterprises v. Movie Name Company*, WIPO Case No. D2001-1201 (Feb. 26, 2002), respondent claimed in its response, as part of its defense, that no one would arrive at the disputed domain name by mistyping. Unfortunately for the respondent, it mistyped two of the sixteen disputed domain names in its heading.

3. This case makes a distinction between famous marks and generic marks. Would the result change if the domain name incorporated a trademark that could be considered generic? *See* Dial-A-Mattress Operating Corp. v. Ultimate Search, WIPO Case No. D2001-0764 (Sept. 26, 2001).

4. This case presents several cybersquatting issues:

   a. Mousetrapping, as described in the case, occurs when an internet user cannot exit a website without clicking a series of advertisement or pop-up ads. *See* Office-Max, Inc. v. Zuccarini, WIPO Case No. D2002-0354 (July 18, 2002).

   b. Cyberflying is transferring a disputed domain name once a complaint is filed prior to proceedings. For a detailed discussion on cyberflying *See* ABB Asea Brown Boveri Ltd v. Bienen & Bienen Enter., WIPO Case No. D2002-0718 (Sept. 29, 2002).

   c. This case makes a distinction between typosquatting and cybersquatting. Compare this case result to *PlasmaNet, Inc. v. John Zuccarini*, WIPO Case No. D2002-11 01 (Feb. 11, 2003). Zuccarini is the Respondent in both cases. The Panel refused to infer bad faith registration. What is the difference in the Panels' conclusions? Is prior behavior sufficient to establish a prima facie case for bad faith registration?

5. Is John Zuccarini also Peter Carrington? In domain name arbitration, the parties do not have equitable rights to discovery. As such, how can they resolve issues of material fact? One Panel found that John Zuccarini was also Peter Carrington. *See* Microsoft Corp. v. Party Night, Inc., WIPO D2003-0501 (Aug. 18, 2003). Another Panel did not find that John Zuccarini was Peter Carrington. *See* Yahoo! Inc. v. Peter Carrington, Nat. Arb. Forum FA 184899 (Oct. 20, 2003).

---

2. Reverse Domain Name Hijacking

To find that a party had engaged in reverse domain name highjacking ... a Respondent must show knowledge on the part of Complainant or Respondent's right or legitimate interest in respect of the domain name at issue and evidence of harassment or similar conduct by the Complainant in the face of such knowledge.

[handwritten note: Not permissible under the policy]

Goldline International, Inc. v. Gold Line
WIPO Case No. D2000-1151 (Jan. 8, 2001)

[The Complainant, GOLDLINE INTERNATIONAL, whose main industry involves the goods and services related to coins and precious metals registered its trademark with the United States PTO. The Respondent, Loren C. Stocker, a/k/a Gold Line Internet, operated several businesses under registered trademarks, including the disputed domain name <goldline.com>.]

* * *

7. Reverse Domain Name Hijacking

Respondent has asked the Panel to make a finding of attempted reverse domain name hijacking. Rule 1 defines reverse domain name hijacking as "using the Policy in bad faith to attempt to deprive a registered domain-name holder of a domain name." *See also* Rule 15(e). To prevail on such a claim, Respondent must show that Complainant knew of Respondent's unassailable right or legitimate interest in the disputed domain name or the clear lack of bad faith registration and use, and nevertheless brought the Complaint in bad faith.

Instructive is the Panel's decision in *Smart Design LLC v. Hughes*, Case No. D2000-0993 (WIPO October 18, 2000), in which the Panel found attempted reverse domain name hijacking in a similar, though not identical, situation, in which the domain name reflected a mark that was likely to have multiple legitimate uses. Taking account of the complainant's delay in bringing its claim and apparent initial acknowledgment that the respondent was the bona fide owner of the domain name, the Panel ruled that it was unreasonable for the complainant to have brought the complaint given the objective unlikelihood of success. In other words, bad faith was found to encompass both malicious intent and recklessness or knowing disregard of the likelihood that the respondent possessed legitimate interests. *Cf. Loblaws, Inc. v. Presidentchoice.inc/Presidentchoice.com*, Case Nos. AF-0170a to -0170c (eResolution, June 7, 2000) (suggesting that, "in a case where the trademark, although a well-known supermarket brand, is a common English phrase used as a mark by other businesses, the failure to conduct a cursory investigation seems especially unreasonable," though declining to find bad faith because the Policy was so new).

Under these standards, Complainant's actions in this case constitute bad faith. Prior to filing its Complaint, Complainant had to know that Complainant's mark was limited to a narrow field, and that Respondent's registration and use of the domain name could not, under any fair interpretation of the facts, constitute bad faith. Not only would a reasonable investigation have revealed these weaknesses in any potential ICANN complaint, but also, Respondent put Complainant on express notice of these facts and that any further attempt to prosecute this matter would be abusive and would constitute reverse domain name "hijack[ing]." Complaint, Annex 2. Complainant's decision to file its Complaint in the face of those facts was in bad faith. Accordingly, the Panel finds that Complainant has engaged in Reverse Domain Name Hijacking.

8. Decision

Complainant has failed utterly to establish two of the three elements of the Policy: that Respondent lacks legitimate rights or interests in the domain name "goldline.com", and that Respondent registered and is using the domain name in bad faith. The Panel therefore denies the Complainant's request that the domain name be transferred from Respondent to Complainant and declares that the Complaint was brought in bad faith and thus constitutes Reverse Domain Name Hijacking.

———————

Note

1. GOLDLINE was a registered trademark with the USPTO. How would the case differ if trademark rights were recognized under common law rights? Under the UDRP for purposes of the §4(a)(i) requirement of establishing trademark rights recognizing common law rights? What constitutes a common law trademark right? How can a complainant prove that his common law trademark right is superior to the legitimate rights of a respondent? *See* Supremo n.v./s.a v. Rao Tella, WIPO Case No. D2001-1357 (Feb. 15, 2002).

---

3. John Jacob Jingle Heimer Schmidt, His Name Is My Domain Name, Too: Using One's Own "Famous Name"

[handwritten: Common law rights in his name · Lanham Act]

Bruce Springsteen v. Jeff Burgar and Bruce Springsteen Club
WIPO Case No. D2000-1532 (Jan. 25, 2001)

* * *

[The Complainant, Bruce Springsteen, a well-known American musician, claimed common law trademark rights in his name based on his celebrated musical career. The Respondents, Bruce Springsteen Club and Jeff Burgar, appearing *pro se,* registered the disputed domain name <brucespringsteen.com> in November 2000. The site directed internet users to <www.celebrity1000.com>, a portal to over 200 other sites.]

* * *

Panel's Findings

* * *

The first question to be considered is whether the domain name at issue is identical or confusingly similar to trade marks or service marks in which the Complainant has rights.

It is common ground that there is no registered trade mark in the name "Bruce Springsteen". In most jurisdictions where trade marks are filed it would be impossible to obtain a registration of a name of that nature. Accordingly, Mr. Springsteen must rely on common law rights to satisfy this element of the three part test.

It appears to be an established principle from cases such as Jeanette Winterson, Julia Roberts, and Sade that in the case of very well known celebrities, their names can acquire a distinctive secondary meaning giving rise to rights equating to unregistered trade marks, notwithstanding the non-registerability of the name itself. It should be noted that no evidence has been given of the name "Bruce Springsteen" having acquired a secondary meaning; in other words a recognition that the name should be associated with activities beyond the primary activities of Mr. Springsteen as a composer, performer and recorder of popular music.

In the view of this Panel, it is by no means clear from the UDRP that it was intended to protect proper names of this nature. As it is possible to decide the case on other grounds, however, the Panel will proceed on the assumption that the name Bruce Springsteen is protected under the policy; it then follows that the domain name at issue is identical to that name.

It is a clearly established principal that the suffix ".com" does not carry the domain name away from identicality or substantial similarity.

The second limb of the test requires the Complainant to show that the domain name owner has no rights or legitimate interests in respect of the domain name. The way in which the UDRP is written clearly requires the Complainant to demonstrate this, and the mere assertion that the Respondent has no such rights does not constitute proof, although the panel is free to make reasonable inferences. That said, a Respondent would be well advised to proffer some evidence to the contrary in the face of such an allegation. Paragraph 4 (c) of the UDRP sets out specific circumstances to assist the Respondent in demonstrating that he or she has legitimate rights or legitimate interests in the domain name. The circumstances are stated to be non-exclusive, but are helpful in considering this issue.

Dealing with each in turn as follows:

(i) The first circumstance is that, before any notice of the dispute to the Respondent, the Respondent had shown demonstrable preparations to use the domain name in connection with a bona fide offering of goods or services. In this case, there is no suggestion that the domain name <brucespringsteen.com> had in fact been used in this way prior to notification of the complaint. Instead, the domain name resolved to another web site belonging to Mr. Burgar, namely "celebrity1000.com".

(ii) The second circumstance is that the Respondent has "been commonly known by the domain name, even if he has acquired no trade mark or service mark rights". This is much more problematic. Mr. Burgar would say that the domain name at issue was registered in the name of "Bruce Springsteen Club" and consequently that the proprietor of the domain name has "been commonly known by the domain name" as required in the UDRP. The question in this case involves the meaning of the words "commonly" and "known by" ...

(iii) It is hard to say that the mere use of the name "Bruce Springsteen Club" can give rise to an impression in the minds of internet users that the proprietor was effectively "known as" Bruce Springsteen. It is even more remote that it could be said that the proprietor was "commonly" recognised [sic] in that fashion. Accordingly the Panel finds that this circumstance in paragraph 4(c) is not met.

The third circumstance is that the Respondent is "making a legitimate non-commercial or fair use of the domain name, without intent for commercial gain to misleadingly divert customers or to tarnish the trade mark or service mark at issue".

There are a number of concepts contained within this "circumstance" which make it a complex issue to resolve. For example, at what point does use of a domain name become "commercial" or alternatively what amounts to "fair use" since those concepts appear to be in the alternative.

An internet search using the words "Bruce Springsteen" gives rise to literally thousands of hits. It is perfectly apparent to any internet user that not all of those hits are "official" or "authorised" [sic] sites. The user will browse from one search result to another to find the information and material which he or she is looking for in relation to a search item, in this case the celebrity singer Bruce Springsteen. It is therefore hard to see how it can be said that the registration of the domain name at issue can be "misleading" in its diversion of consumers to the "celebrity1000.com" website.

There have been examples in other cases of blatant attempts, for example, by the use of minor spelling discrepancies to entrap internet users onto sites which have absolutely no connection whatsoever with the name which is being used in its original or slightly altered form. In this case, the internet user, coming upon the "celebrity1000.com" website would perhaps be unsurprised to have arrived there via a search under the name "Bruce Springsteen". If the internet user wished to stay longer at the site he or she could do so, or otherwise they could clearly return to their search results to find more instructed material concerning Bruce Springsteen himself.

Accordingly, it is hard to infer from the conduct of the Respondent in this case an intent, for commercial gain, to misleadingly divert consumers. There is certainly no question of the common law rights of Mr. Springsteen being "tarnished" by association with the "celebrity1000.com" website. The Panelists' own search of that site indicates no links which would have that effect, for example connections to sites containing pornographic or other regrettable material.

Accordingly the Panel finds that Bruce Springsteen has not satisfied the second limb of the three part test in the UDRP.

Moving on to the question of bad faith, once again the UDRP contains helpful guidance as to how the Complainant may seek to demonstrate bad faith on the part of the Registrant. The four, non-exclusive, circumstances are set out in paragraph 4(b) of the UDRP, and can be dealt with as follows:

(i) The first circumstance is that there is evidence that the Registrant obtained the domain name primarily for the purpose of selling, renting or otherwise transferring it to the Complainant or to a competitor. This can be dealt with swiftly. There is simply no evidence put forward by the Complainant that there has been any attempt by Mr. Burgar to sell the domain name, either directly or indirectly.

(ii) The second circumstance is that the Registrant obtained the domain name in order to prevent the owner of the trade mark or service mark from reflecting that mark in a corresponding domain name, provided that there has been a pattern of such conduct. In this case, Bruce Springsteen's representatives point to the many other celebrity domain names registered by Mr. Burgar as evidence that he has indulged in a pattern of this conduct.

However, Mr. Burgar is clearly experienced in the ways of the internet. When he registered the domain name at issue in 1996, he would have been well aware that if he had wanted to block the activities of Bruce Springsteen or his record company in order to extract a large payment, or for whatever other reason there may be in creating such a blockage, he could, at nominal cost, have also registered the domain names <brucespringsteen.net> and <brucespringsteen.org>. He did not do so, and indeed subsequently in 1998 Mr. Springsteen's record company registered the name <brucespringsteen.net> which has been used as the host site for the official Bruce Springsteen website since that time. It appears in the top five items in a search on the internet under the name "Bruce Springsteen".

It is trite to say that, by registering the domain name at issue, the Registrant has clearly prevented Bruce Springsteen from owning that name himself. However, that does not have the effect required in paragraph 4(b)(ii) of the UDRP. That paragraph indicates that the registration should have the effect of preventing the owner of a trade mark or service mark from reflecting the mark "in a corresponding domain name". In these circumstances what is meant by the word "corresponding"? Nothing that has been done by Mr. Burgar has prevented Bruce Springsteen's official website at <brucespringsteen.net> being registered and used in his direct interests. That is surely a "corresponding domain name" for these purposes, as the expression "corresponding domain name" clearly refers back to the words "trade mark or service mark" rather than the domain name at issue referred to in the first line of paragraph 4(b)(ii).

It is perhaps pertinent to observe that the so-called "official" site at <brucespringsteen.net> was registered in 1998. It seems unlikely that, at that time, the existence of the domain name at issue did not become apparent. Whilst this is pure surmise, and consequently in no way relevant to the findings of the Panel, it might be thought that the alleged "blocking" effect of the domain name at issue might have given rise to a complaint at that time, if only in correspondence.

This Panel believes that previous Panels have all too readily concluded that the mere registration of the mark, and indeed other marks of a similar nature, is evidence of an attempt to prevent the legitimate owner of registered or common law trade mark rights from obtaining a "corresponding domain name". This is an issue which should be looked at more closely, and for the purposes of this complaint, the Panel finds that the "circumstance" in paragraph 4(b)(ii) does not arise for the purpose of demonstrating bad faith on the part of the Registrant.

[(iii)] The third circumstance is that the Registrant has obtained the domain name "primarily for the purpose of disrupting the business of a competitor". This can be dealt with very swiftly as there is no suggestion that that is the case in the present complaint.

[(iv)] The fourth circumstance is that, by using the domain name, the Registrant has "intentionally attempted to attract, for commercial gain, internet users to his website or other online location, by creating a likelihood of confusion with the Complainant's mark as to the source, sponsorship, affiliation or endorsement of the web site or location or of a product or a service on the website or location".

Once again, this sub-paragraph contains a number of concepts which render it complex to analyze and apply. However, the key issue appears to be the requirement that the use of the domain name must "create a likelihood of confusion with the Complainant's mark". As indicated above, a simple search under the name "Bruce Springsteen" on the internet gives rise to many thousands of hits. As also indicated above, even a relatively unsophisticated user would be clearly aware that not all of those hits would be directly associated in an official and authorised capacity with Bruce Springsteen himself, or his agents or record company. The nature of an internet search does not reveal the exact notation of the domain name. Accordingly, the search result may read "Bruce Springsteen-discography", but will not give the user the exact address. That only arises on a screen once the user has gone to that address. The relevance of this is that it is relatively unlikely that any user would seek to go straight to the internet and open the site <brucespringsteen.com> in the optimistic hope of reaching the official Bruce Springsteen website. If anyone sufficiently sophisticated in the use of the internet were to do that, they would very soon realize that the site they reached was not the official site, and consequently would move on, probably to conduct a fuller search.

Accordingly, it is hard to see that there is any likelihood of confusion can arise in these circumstances.

The name of the Registrant is not shown in an internet search, accordingly the fact that the Registrant in this case is "Bruce Springsteen Club" would not have the effect of giving rise to the sort of confusion which might satisfy the test under paragraph 4(b)(iv).

The Panel therefore finds that none of the circumstances in paragraph 4(b) of the UDRP are met in this case.

Paragraph 4(b) makes it quite clear that the four "circumstances" are non-exclusive. In this case, the Complainant has urged the Panel to find bad faith on the grounds of the use of the "fictitious" name "Bruce Springsteen Club" as the Registrant. It may be that there is some element of bad faith in the conduct of Mr. Burgar in registering in the name of "Bruce Springsteen Club". However, on reflection, the Panel does not believe that it is sufficient to satisfy the necessary burden under the UDRP.

* * *

There have been a number of cases concerning celebrity names, some of which were referred to in this case. Many of those decisions are flawed in some way or another.

The case of *Jeannete Winterson v. Mark Hogarth* (WIPO case number D2000-0235) has been credited with establishing the principle that common law rights can arise in a proper name. The case is also notable for an erroneous interpretation of the third requirement, namely the demonstration of bad faith. There is an indication in the case that the burden falls on the Registrant to demonstrate that the domain name at issue has been used in good faith. That is clearly not the case, and that confusion appears to have knocked on into other cases, for example the Julia Roberts case. The burden is clearly with the Complainant to demonstrate that bad faith has been shown.

In the case of *Julia Fiona Roberts v. Russell Boyd* (WIPO case number D2000-0210) the question of "permission" arises. In relation to the question of "rights or legitimate interests" it is stated that "Respondent has no relationship with or permission from Complainant for the use of her name or mark". As indicated above, that is simply irrelevant. It is perfectly clear from general principles protecting registered and unregistered trade marks the world over, and indeed from the UDRP, that whilst permission might be conclusive against an allegation of infringement if it can be shown to have been granted, the absence of permission is not conclusive that an infringement has occurred, nor is it conclusive proof that the alleged infringer has no rights of his or her own.

Further, in the Julia Roberts case, there is a suggestion that the registration of the domain name <juliaroberts.com> "necessarily prevented the Complainant from using the disputed domain name". As indicated above, that is not sufficient to meet the criteria required under the URDP for the relevant circumstance in paragraph 4(b).

The case of *Daniel C. Marino v. Video Images Productions*(WIPO case number D2000-0598) contains a passage highlighted when annexed to the complaint in this case in the following terms:

"in fact, in light of the uniqueness of the name <danmarino.com>, which is virtually identical to the Complainant's personal name and common law trade mark, it would be extremely difficult to foresee any justifiable use that the Respondent could claim. On the contrary, selecting this name gives rise to the impression of an association with the Complainant which is not based in fact."

This Panel contends that that assertion is erroneous. For all the reasons set out above, the users of the internet do not expect all sites bearing the name of celebrities or famous historical figures or politicians, to be authorised [sic] or in some way connected with the figure themselves. The internet is an instrument for purveying information, comment, and opinion on a wide range of issues and topics. It is a valuable source of information in many fields, and any attempt to curtail its use should be strongly discouraged. Users fully expect domain names incorporating the names of well known figures in any walk of life to exist independently of any connection with the figure themselves, but having been placed there by admirers or critics as the case may be.

Accordingly, in all the circumstances the Panel does not believe that Bruce Springsteen has met the necessary criteria to sustain a complaint under the UDRP.

7. Decision

In light of the foregoing, the Panel decides that although the domain name at issue is identical to the un-registered trade mark of the Complainant, the Registrant has demonstrated that he has some rights or legitimate interests in respect of the domain name, and the Complainant has failed to demonstrate that the domain name was registered and has been used in bad faith.

Accordingly, the Panel orders that the registration of the domain name be left as it stands.

Gordon D. Harris, Presiding Panelist

A. Michael Froomkin, Panelist

Dissent

Paragraph 4(a)(i) of the UDRP requires a Complainant to show the existence of "a trade mark or service mark in which Complainant has rights." The majority has presumed (and should have concluded) that the personal name "Bruce Springsteen" has acquired distinctive secondary meaning giving rise to common law trademark rights in the "famous, almost legendary, recording artist and composer, Bruce Springsteen."

The majority notes that no evidence was presented to establish secondary meaning. Complainant alleges in paragraph 14 of the Complaint, without contradiction by the Respondent, that:

Complainant is an internationally renowned and critically acclaimed composer, lyricist, recording artist, singer, musician and performer. He has been a professional singer and musician since 1964. His first album, "Greetings from Asbury Park N.J." was released to the public in 1972. Since that time, millions of copies of his recordings have been sold throughout the world. He has received numerous awards recognizing the quality of his compositions and recordings, including multiple Grammies and an Oscar. As a result of the foregoing, Complainant's name has acquired secondary meaning, has come to be recognized by the general public as indicating an association with the Complainant, and is the source of enormous goodwill towards the Complainant. Accordingly, Complainant has common law trademark rights in his name.

In addition, the majority later notes that "an internet search using the words 'Bruce Springsteen' gives rise to literally thousands of hits. Therefore, secondary meaning has been adequately shown.

Regardless of commentary that personal names (presumably without secondary meaning) are not protected, the language of paragraph 4(a)(i) does not exclude any specific type of common law trademarks from protection. The majority further concludes that the disputed domain name is identical with the common law mark. Therefore, Complainant has met the requirements of paragraph 4(a)(I).

* * *

The Dissenting Panelist would rule that Complainant has met his burden and that the disputed domain name should be transferred.

Richard W. Page, Dissenting Panelist

Gordon Sumner, p/k/a Sting v. Michael Urvan

Case No. D2000-0596

1. The Parties

1.1 The Complainant is Gordon Sumner, professionally known as "Sting", a citizen of the United Kingdom who maintains a residence in the United States. The Respondent is Michael Urvan, of Marietta, Georgia, United States of America.

2. The Domain Names and Registrar

2.1 The domain name the subject of this Complaint is "sting.com".

2.2 The Registrar of this domain name is Network Solutions, Inc of Herndon, Virginia, USA ("Registrar").

4. Factual Background

Complainant's Activities and Trademarks

4.1 In his Complaint, the Complainant asserted the following in relation to his activities and trademarks. The Complainant is a world famous musician, recording and performing artist who has, for over twenty years, rendered high-quality musical services under his name, trademark and service mark STING. Since at least as early as 1978, the Complainant has exclusively and continuously used the STING mark in connection with approximately twenty record albums, almost all of which have gone multi-platinum in the United States and enjoyed great commercial success worldwide. The Complainant has also used the STING mark in connection with innumerable world-wide concert tours involving venues with significant capacities, the majority of which sell out. The STING mark is internationally known and famous as a result of the Complainant's extensive, high-profile, and overwhelmingly commercially successful activities in the music industry. The Complainant is the owner of the STING mark as a trademark and service mark. The name STING has become synonymous in the minds of the public with the Complainant and his activities in the music industry, and serves as a symbol of the goodwill and excellent reputation associated with Sting. The STING mark is famous and entitled to the widest scope of protection afforded by law, including protection against dilution.

4.2 In his Response, the Respondent asserted that there are 20 trademark registrations of the word STING in the US, but none of them are registered by the Complainant. The word STING is a common word in the English language, and so registration of it as a domain name is not a violation of the Uniform Policy. The Respondent is not a competitor of the Complainant and the Respondent does not attempt to cause any confusion with him.

Respondent's Activities

4.3 The Complainant asserted the following in relation to the Respondent's activities and use of the domain name. Until the Respondent was contacted by a representative of the Complainant, the Respondent made no use of the domain name. After being contacted by a representative of the Complainant, Respondent linked the domain name to another site called "GunBroker.Com", which is a site that facilitates "person to person" selling of guns. During or about February of 2000, and again during or about May of 2000, the Respondent offered to sell the domain name to the Complainant for $25,000.00. Since offering to sell the domain name to the Complainant for $25,000.00, the Respondent has frequently changed the web site identified by the domain name, usually with an "under construction" message, and in some cases providing a link to a third-party operated unauthorized web site relating to the Complainant.

4.4 In his Response, the Respondent asserted that he has been using the nickname "Sting" and more recently "=Sting=" publicly on the Internet for at least 8 years. The Respondent registered the domain name in July 1995, approximately 5 years before this dispute was commenced. The Respondent did not register the domain name to sell it, nor did he register the domain to hold it hostage for any reason. The Respondent engaged in work on the web site to which he intended the domain name "sting.com" to resolve, prior to any notification of this dispute. The Respondent did not point the domain name "sting.com" to the "GunBroker.com" website—this occurred for a short time as a result of an error on the part of the Respondent's web service provider. The Complainant's assertion that the Respondent initiated contact with the Complainant is false—the first contact was initiated by the Complainant on May 16, 2000.

5. Parties' Contentions

The Complaint

5.1 The Complainant contends that each of the three elements specified in paragraph 4(a) of the Uniform Policy are applicable to the domain name the subject of this dispute.

5.2 In relation to element (i) of paragraph 4(a) of the Uniform Policy, the Complainant contends that the domain name is identical in its substantive part to the Complainant's unregistered trademark and service mark STING.

5.3 In relation to element (ii) of paragraph 4(a) of the Uniform Policy, the Complaint contends that the Respondent has no rights or legitimate interests in respect of the domain name in issue.

5.4 In relation to element (iii) of paragraph 4(a) of the Uniform Policy, the Complainant contends that evidence of bad faith registration and use is established by the following circumstances. First, the Respondent offered to sell the domain name to the Complainant for $25,000, an activity which corresponds to that listed in paragraph 4(b)(i) of the Policy as evidence of bad faith registration and use of a domain name. Secondly, the Respondent has used the domain name mark to link to the "GunBrokers.com" web site, and as such is intentionally attempting to attract, for commercial gain, Internet users to an online location by creating a likelihood of confusion with the STING mark as to source, sponsorship, affiliation, or endorsement, being an activity which corresponds to that listed in paragraph 4(b)(iv) of the Policy as evidence of bad faith registration and use of a domain name. In addition, that site is personally offensive to the Complainant and contrary to his established reputation, and tarnishes the STING mark in violation of 15 U.S.C. §1125(c). Thirdly, because the Complainant's STING mark has a strong reputation and is world famous, the Respondent can make no good faith use of the domain name, and "it is not possible to conceive of any plausible actual or contemplated active use of the [D]omain [N]ame by the Respondent that would not be illegitimate, such as by being a passing off, an infringement of consumer protection legislation, or an infringement of the Complainant's rights under trademark law".

The Response

5.5 The Respondent denies that each of the three elements specified in paragraph 4(a) of the Uniform Policy are applicable to the domain name the subject of this dispute.

5.6 In relation to element (i) of paragraph 4(a) of the Uniform Policy, the Respondent admits that he registered that domain name "sting.com", and that the domain name is identical to the STING mark. However, the Respondent challenges the Complainant's claim to owning the STING mark, and the Complainant's claim that the STING mark is world famous and exclusively associated with the Complainant and so entitled to protection against dilution. In particular, the Respondent contends that the trademark STING has been the subject of 20 registrations in the United States, none of which have been granted to the Complainant. A list purporting to be a printout from an internet search of the United States Patent and Trademark Office database of trademark registrations for the word STING is Exhibit J to the Response.

5.7 In relation to element (ii) of paragraph 4(a) of the Uniform Policy, the Respondent contends that his use of the nickname "Sting" and more recently "=Sting=" publicly on the Internet for at least 8 years has given him a legitimate interest in the domain name. The Respondent provided documentary evidence in Exhibits A, C, D, E and H to the Response, showing that for some years prior to this dispute he has used the domain name to point to a web site for email purposes, he has used the nickname "sting" or "=sting=" with global internet gaming services, and he has had in development a web site intended to be located at the URL http://www.sting.com.

5.8 In relation to element (iii) of paragraph 4(a) of the Uniform Policy, the Respondent contends that his activities since registration of the domain name demonstrate that he did not register and has not been using the domain name in bad faith. In particular, the Respondent denies the Complainant's contention that the Respondent offered to sell the domain name to the Complainant for a sum greater than out of pocket expenses. Rather, the Respondent contends that it was the Complainant, through his attorney, who contacted him in relation to the domain name. The Respondent provides in Exhibit B to the Response a copy of an email from the Complainant's attorney to him of May 17, 2000, initiating contact. The Respondent admits that upon solicitation from the Complainant's attorney he did make an offer to sell the domain name, but contends that this does not demonstrate his primary purpose in registering the domain name was to sell it to the Complainant.

5.9 In relation to the use of the domain name to point to the "GunBrokers.com" web site, the Respondent contends that because this occurred due to a mistake by his web service provider, it is not evidence of bad faith use by him. Exhibit I of the Response contains a copy of a letter purporting to be from the Respondent's web service provider explaining how this mistake occurred. In addition, the Respondent contends that he had no knowledge of the Complainant's distaste for a web site selling guns.

5.10 The Respondent makes the further contention that it cannot be said he has engaged in a pattern of conduct of preventing trademark owners from reflecting their trademark in a corresponding domain name, because the other two domain names the Respondent owns have not been offered for sale to anyone.

6. Discussion and Findings

Domain Name Identical or Confusingly Similar to Complainant's Mark

6.1 The relevant part of the domain name "sting.com" is "sting". The Complainant asserts, the Respondent admits, and this Administrative Panel finds, that the domain name is identical to the word STING.

6.2 The Complainant is not the owner of a trademark or service mark registration for the word STING. It is, however, clear that the Uniform Policy is not limited to a "registered" mark; an unregistered, or common law, mark is sufficient for the purposes of paragraph 4(a)(i). The Complainant did not provide any documentary evidence in support of his assertion that he is the owner of the unregistered trademark and/or service mark STING. However, the Uniform Policy is not limited to trademarks or service marks "owned" by the Complainant; it is sufficient for the purposes of paragraph 4(a)(i) that there be a trademark or service mark "in which the Complainant has rights". The Complainant asserted, and this Administrative Panel through the equivalent of taking judicial notice finds, that the Complainant is a world famous entertainer who is known by the name STING.

6.3 The question that arises is whether being known under a particular name is the same as having rights in that name as a "trademark or service mark". The answer to this question is not straightforward. On the one hand, there are a number of cases under the Uniform Policy in which the Panel has treated the name of a famous or at least widely known person as constituting an unregistered trademark or service mark sufficient for the purposes of paragraph 4(a)(i) (eg. *Julia Fiona Roberts v Russell Boyd* WIPO Case No. D2000-0210; *Jeannette Winterson v Mark Hogarth* WIPO Case No. D2000-0235; *Steven Rattner v BuyThisDomainName (John Pepin)* WIPO Case No. D2000-0402).

6.4 On the other hand, the *Report of the WIPO Internet Domain Name Process* of April 30, 1999, on which ICANN based the Uniform Policy, at paragraphs 165–168, states as follows (footnote citations deleted, emphasis added):

The preponderance of views, however, was in favor of restricting the scope of the procedure, at least initially, in order to deal first with the most offensive forms of predatory practices and to establish the procedure on a sound footing. Two limitations on the scope of the procedure were, as indicated above, favored by these commentators. The first limitation would confine the availability of the procedure to cases of deliberate, bad faith abusive registrations. The definition of such abusive registrations is discussed in the next section. The second limitation would define abusive registration by reference only to trademarks and service marks. *Thus, registrations that violate trade names, geographical indications or personality rights would not be considered to fall within the definition of abusive registration for the purposes of the administrative procedure.* Those in favor of this form of limitation pointed out that the violation of trademarks (and service marks) was the most common form of abuse and that the law with respect to trade names, geographical indications and personality rights is less evenly harmonized throughout the world, although international norms do exist requiring the protection of trade names and geographical indications. We are persuaded by the wisdom of proceeding firmly but cautiously and of tackling, at the first stage, problems which all agree require a solution.... [W]e consider that it is premature to extend the notion of abusive registration beyond the violation of trademarks and service marks at this stage. After experience has been gained with the operation of the administrative procedure and time has allowed for an assessment of its efficacy and of the problems, if any, which remain outstanding, the question of extending the notion of abusive registration to other intellectual property rights can always be re-visited.

It is clear from this statement that personality rights were not intended to be made subject to the proposed dispute resolution procedure. In adopting the procedure proposed in the WIPO Report, ICANN did not vary this limitation on its application. It must be concluded, therefore, that ICANN did not intend the procedure to apply to personality rights.

6.5 In the opinion of this Administrative Panel, it is doubtful whether the Uniform Policy is applicable to this dispute. Although it is accepted that the Complainant is world famous under the name STING, it does not follow that he has rights in STING *as a trademark or service mark*. Unlike the personal names in issue in the cases *Julia Fiona Roberts v Russell Boyd, Jeannette Winterson v. Mark Hogarth*, and *Steven Rattner v BuyThisDomainName (John Pepin)*, the personal name in this case is also a common word in the English language, with a number of different meanings. The following are the entries for "sting" from *Merriam-Webster's Collegiate Dictionary*:

sting vb stung ; sting.ing [ME, fr. OE stingan; akin to ON stinga to sting and prob. to Gk stachys spike of grain, stochos target, aim] vt (bef. 12c) 1: to prick painfully: as a: to pierce or wound with a poisonous or irritating process b: to affect with sharp quick pain or smart "hail stung their faces" 2: to cause to suffer acutely "stung with remorse" 3: overcharge, cheat ~ vi 1: to wound one with or as if with a sting 2: to feel a keen burning pain or smart; also: to cause such pain— sting.ing.ly adv

sting n (bef. 12c) 1 a: the act of stinging; specif: the thrust of a stinger into the flesh b: a wound or pain caused by or as if by stinging 2: stinger 2 3: a sharp or stinging element, force, or quality 4: an elaborate confidence game; specif: such a game worked by undercover police in order to trap criminals

6.6 In light of the fact that the word "sting" is in common usage in the English language, with a number of meanings, this case can be distinguished from the other cases cited above in which the Complainants' personal name was found also to be an unregistered trademark or service mark to which the Uniform Policy applies. This Administrative Panel is inclined to the view, therefore, that the Complainant's name STING is not a trademark or service mark within the scope of paragraph 4(a)(i) of the Uniform Policy. However, it is not necessary to reach a formal decision on this issue, because this Administrative Panel finds against the Complainant on other grounds, namely that the requirement of paragraph 4(a)(iii) is not met, as discussed below.

Respondent's Rights or Legitimate Interests in the Domain Name

6.7 The Respondent provided evidence of circumstances of the type specified in paragraph 4(c) of the Uniform Policy as giving rise to a right to or legitimate interest in the domain name. In particular, the Respondent provided in Exhibit C of the Response copies of various email communications to him prior to the commencement of this dispute, showing that the "UserName", the "nickname", the "Screen Name", or the "Account PIC" under which the Respondent had registered for global internet gaming services consisted of or included the word "sting". In Exhibit D to the Response, the Respondent provided copies of web page printouts from The Champions League of Quake, a service which monitors Quake servers and keeps track of the scores of registered players of this game. Those printouts show that the Respondent played this game using the player names "sting" or "=sting=". In addition, the Respondent provided evidence in Exhibit E to the Response of preparations by him to establish a web site at the URL http://www.sting.com.

6.8 Although this evidence is not irrelevant to the issue of whether or not the Respondent has a right to or a legitimate interest in the domain name, it is certainly at the weaker end of the spectrum of such evidence. The Respondent's use of the name "sting" or "=sting=" for gaming does not establish that he has been "commonly known" by the domain name as contemplated by paragraph 4(c)(ii). The word is undistinctive, and most likely is used by numerous people in cyberspace. In practice, this word provides the Respondent with anonymity rather than with a name by which he is commonly known. The Respondent's evidence of his preparations to establish a web site at the URL http://www.sting.com does not establish the circumstances contemplated by paragraph 4(c)(i), because there is no evidence that this proposed use of the domain name is in connection with a bona fide offering of goods or services.

6.9 In short, a more substantive use of the word "sting" than that proven by the Respondent is required to show a right or legitimate interest in the domain name "sting.com" (although this proven use is relevant to the issue of bad faith). On balance, therefore, this Administrative Panel finds that the Respondent does not have a right to or a legitimate interest in the domain name, in the sense in which that concept is used in paragraph 4(a)(ii) of the Uniform Policy.

Domain Name Registered and Used in Bad Faith

6.10 The Complainant has not satisfied this Administrative Panel that the Respondent registered and is using the domain name in bad faith. The Complainant asserted that the Respondent offered to sell the domain name to the Complainant for $25,000, but the Complainant provided no evidence in support of this assertion. In particular, the Complainant provided no evidence of the Respondent's alleged communications with the Complainant on this issue. The Respondent admitted that he offered to sell the domain name to the Complainant, but only after the Complainant solicited that offer. (The Respondent did not specify the price at which he offered to sell the domain name, but he did not dispute the Complainant's assertion of $25,000, so this Administrative Panel assumes the offered price was for that amount, or at least for an amount in excess of the Respondent's out-of-pocket expenses.) Although this evidence is *consistent* with the Complainant's contention that the Respondent acquired the domain name primarily for the purpose of selling it to the Complainant, as required by paragraph 4(b)(i), this evidence does not *prove* that. This evidence is equally consistent with the Respondent's contention that he acquired the domain name five years ago in good faith. In the absence of any evidence whatsoever from the Complainant going to the assertion of the Respondent's offer to sell the domain name, this Administrative Panel finds that the Complainant has not met the burden of proof on this issue.

6.11 This Administrative Panel does not accept the Complainant's contention that the linking of the domain name to the "GunBroker.com" web site constituted intentionally attempting to attract, for commercial gain, Internet users to an on-line location by creating a likelihood of confusion with the STING mark as to source, sponsorship, affiliation, or endorsement, and so constitutes an activity which corresponds to that listed in paragraph 4(b)(iv) of the Uniform Policy as evidence of bad faith registration and use of the domain name. Again, the Complainant provided no evidence in support of this contention. In particular, the Complainant provided no evidence as to the contents of the "GunBroker.com" site, and thus no evidence establishing that a likelihood of confusion with the STING mark was created as to source, sponsorship, affiliation or endorsement of the site. The Respondent admitted that the domain name did point to the "GunBroker.com" site for a period of time, but provided evidence to the effect that this was due to an error on the part of the Respondent's web service provider. The evidence is therefore consistent with the Respondent's contention that there was no intentional attempt to attract internet users for commercial gain. Once again, the Complainant has failed to satisfy its burden of proof on this point.

6.12 Finally, this Administrative Panel does not accept the Complainant's contention that "it is not possible to conceive of any plausible actual or contemplated active use of the [D]omain [N]ame by the Respondent that would not be illegitimate, such as by being a passing off, an infringement of consumer protection legislation, or an infringement of the Complainant's rights under trademark law". The words in quotation marks come from *Telstra Corporation Limited v Nuclear Marshmallows* WIPO Case No. D2000-0003. In the *Telstra* case, the trademark in question was an invented word. In this case the mark in question is a common word in the English language, with a number of meanings. Unlike the situation in the *Telstra* case, therefore, it is far from inconceivable that there is a plausible legitimate use to which the Respondent could put the domain name. The Respondent has asserted a legitimate use to which he has put, and intends to put, the domain name. Whilst the evidence provided in support of this assertion is not particularly strong, it is at least consistent with that assertion, and with his overall contention that he did not register and has not been using the domain name in bad faith. The Complainant has thus failed to satisfy the burden of proof on this point.

7. Decision

7.1 This Administrative Panel decides that the Complainant has not proven each of the three elements in paragraph 4(a) of the Uniform Policy in relation to the domain name the subject of the Complaint.

7.2 Pursuant to paragraph 4(i) of the Uniform Policy and paragraph 15 of the Uniform Rules, this Administrative Panel denies the request that the Registrar, Network Solutions, Inc, be required either to transfer to the Complainant, Gordon Sumner, p/k/a Sting, or to cancel, the domain name "sting.com".

> Andrew F. Christie
>
> Sole Panelist
>
> Dated: July 24, 2000

Notes

1. Anna Nicole Smith, recently deceased, filed under the UDRP complaining that the domain name <annanicolesmith.com> should be transferred to her. She did not prevail. The Panel stated that famous name cases "require a clear showing of high commercial value and significant recognition of the name as solely that of the performer. The *Humphrey Bogart* case [*Bogart, Inc. v. Humphrey Bogart Club*, Nat. Arb. Forum FA 162770 (Aug. 4, 2003)] cited by Complainant is a prime example of the type of case that would be expected to prevail, since virtually no one familiar with the movie industry would fail to recognize his name as that of the famous movie star. The Panel does not believe Complainant's name has yet reached that level of fame." Yet the Panel grudgingly conceded that Anna Nicole Smith did have rights in her name: "However, for the sake of careful consideration and fairness to Complainant, the Panel will assume that the Complainant has minimally prevailed on this requirement and will base its decision on the other two legs of the UDRP."

2. If your actual name is similar to a famous trademark, can you use your name as a domain name? Microsoft succeeded in convincing a teenager, named Mike Rowe, to give up the domain name mikerowesoft.com. If pursued under the UDRP, would Microsoft prevail? Should they?

3. Why did Bruce Springsteen prevail where Sting failed in enforcing domain name rights? Is it fair to performers that have names that are common words like Sting, Prince or Madonna? Aren't these words arbitrary marks and far from generic?

---

4. Your Trademark Sucks.com: Free Speech or Bad Faith?

Wal-Mart Stores, Inc. v. Walsucks and Walmarket Puerto Rico

WIPO Case No. D2000-0477 (July 20, 2000)

[The Complainant, Wal-Mart Stores, Inc., a registered trademark owner, is an internationally known discount retail store. The Respondents, Walsucks and Walmarket Puerto

[handwritten margin note: There is no 1st Amendment; no free speech]

Rico a/k/a Kenneth Harvey, registered the following disputed domain names: <wal-martcanadasucks.com>, <wal-martcanadasucks.com>, <walmartuksucks.com>, <wal-martpuertorico.com> and <walmartpuertoricosucks.com>. According to the Respondent's response, the Respondent is a domain name consultant, author and promoter of free-speech. The Respondent initiated contact with the Complainant to discuss available do-main names that incorporated the Wal-Mart trademark.]

* * *

6. Discussion and Findings

* * *

In an earlier administrative proceeding initiated by Complainant against Respondent, *Wal-Mart Stores, Inc. v. Walmarket Canada*, Case No. D2000-0150, dated May 2, 2000, the panelist determined that Complainant has rights in the trademark "Wal-Mart". This Panel adopts that determination, and finds that Complainant has rights in the trademark "Wal-Mart" within the meaning of paragraph 4(a) of the Policy.

In *Wal-Mart Stores, Inc. v. Walmarket,* the panelist determined that the "Wal-Mart" trademark is well-recognized in the United States, Canada and other countries *(id.)*. This Panel adopts that determination, and finds that the "Wal-Mart" mark is well-known in the sense of Article 6*bis* of the Paris Convention for the Protection of In-dustrial Property.

* * *

Respondent has registered the domain names "walmartcanadasucks.com", "wal-mart-canadasucks.com", "walmartuksucks.com" and "walmartpuertoricosucks.com". These do-main names share common characteristics. In each case, Complainant's "Wal-Mart" trademark is followed with an indication of place (Canada, Canada, UK and Puerto Rico, respectively). In *Wal-Mart v. Walmarket Canada,* it was determined that "walmart-canada.com" and "Wal-Mart" are confusingly similar …

Respondent has appended the term "-sucks" to domain names that are, in the absence of that term, confusingly similar to Complainant's mark. The addition of the pejorative verb "sucks" is tantamount to creating the phrase "Wal-Mart Canada sucks" (and com-parable phrases with Respondent's other "-sucks" formative domain names). The elimi-nation of the spacing between the terms of the phrase is dictated by technical factors, and by the common practice of domain name registrants. The addition of a common or generic term following a trademark does not create a new or different mark in which Re-spondent has rights.

* * *

The question whether a domain name and a trademark are confusingly similar in-volves the application of a multi factored test exemplified in the decision of the U.S. Court of Appeals for the Ninth Circuit in *AMF Inc. v. Sleekcraft Boats,* 599 F.2d 341 (9th Cir. 1979). The *Sleekcraft* factors are directed to whether there is a "likelihood of confu-sion" between two marks. While developed in the context of comparing two trademarks, the *Sleekcraft* factors have more recently been employed by the federal courts to com-pare domain names to trademarks, and domain names to domain names. The *Sleekcraft* factors were, for example, employed by the federal district court in *Bally Total Fitness* discussed *infra.* The *Sleekcraft* factors were relied upon by the Court of Appeals for the Ninth Circuit in *Brookfield Communications v. West Coast Entertainment,* 174 F.3d 1036, 1053–61 (9th Cir. 1999).

In *Sleekcraft,* the Court of Appeals for the Ninth Circuit enumerated eight factors to be weighed on the question of likelihood of confusion. These are: (1) strength of the mark; (2) proximity of the goods; (3) similarity of the marks; (4) evidence of actual confusion; (5) marketing channels used; (6) type of goods and the degree of care likely to be exercised by the purchaser; (7) defendant's intent in selecting the mark; and (8) likelihood of expansion of the product lines [footnote 8].

In the present case, two factors (weighed along with other *Sleekcraft* factors) compel a determination that Respondent's disputed domain names are confusingly similar to Complainant's mark—that is, that there is a likelihood of confusion on the part of Internet users. First, beyond doubt, Complainant's "Wal-Mart" trademark is a very strong mark, well known throughout the United States, Canada, and other parts of the world.

Second, and most compelling, is Respondent's intent in selecting the disputed domain names. As discussed below (in connection with whether Respondent establishes legitimate interests), Respondent registered the names in order to extract payment from Complainant by threatening to disrupt its business. The evidence of Respondent's pattern of conduct and bad faith is clear.

In *Brookfield Communications,* the Court of Appeals for the Ninth Circuit elaborated on the question of intent, stating:

We thus turn to intent. "The law has long been established that if an infringer 'adopts' his designation with the intent of deriving benefit from the reputation of the trade-mark or trade name, its intent may be sufficient to justify the inference that there are confusing similarities.'" *Pacific Telesis v. International Telesis Comms.,* 994 F.2d 1364, 1369 (9th Cir. 1993) (quoting Restatement of Torts, §729, Comment on Clause (b)f(1938)). An inference of confusion has similarly been deemed appropriate where a mark is adopted with the intent to deceive the public. *See Gallo,* 967 F.2d at 1293 (citing *Sleekcraft,* 599 F.2d at 354)....

This factor favors the plaintiff where the alleged infringer adopted his mark with knowledge, actual or constructive, that it was another's trademark. Nor did West Coast register its domain name for the specific purpose of subsequently selling the domain name to the trademark owner.

The internet is made useful to a worldwide public through the operation of search engines. When an internet user enters a word or combination of words into a search engine, the engine identifies web sites of potential relevance by canvassing domain names, metatags and (potentially) other web page codes. By using Complainant's "Wal-Mart" mark in its domain name, Respondent makes it likely that internet users entering "Wal-Mart" into a search engine will find its "walmartcanadasucks.com" and other "walmart"-formative web sites. Respondent's domain names are sufficiently similar to Complainant's mark (reflecting the third *Sleekcraft* factor) that internet search engine results will list Respondent's domain names and web sites when searching Complainant's mark.

Internet users with search engine results listing Respondent's domains are likely to be puzzled or surprised by the coupling of Complainant's mark with the pejorative verb "sucks". Such users, including potential customers of Complainant, are not likely to conclude that Complainant is the sponsor of the identified websites. However, it is likely (given the relative ease by which websites can be entered) that such users will choose to visit the sites, if only to satisfy their curiosity. Respondent will have accomplished his objective of diverting potential customers of Complainant to his websites by the use of domain names that are similar to Complainant's trademark.

The Panel is satisfied that in the application of the multifactored *Sleekcraft* test, the disputed domain names are confusingly similar to Complainant's trademark in the sense of paragraph 4(a)(i) of the Policy. The Panel emphasizes that Respondent's bad faith in registering and using the names is a critical factor in this analysis. The evidence on the record of this proceeding makes clear that Respondent registered the names for bad faith commercial purposes-that is, to threaten Complainant's business and demand payment as a "domain name consultant" while publicly purporting to engage in "free speech" critique of Complainant.

Respondent argues that addition of the word "sucks" to the base names "walmart-canada", "wal-martcanada", "walmartuk" and "walmartpuertorico" causes such names to lose their confusing similarity with Complainant's "Wal-Mart" trademark. Respondent contends that because an internet user or consumer viewing a "-sucks" formative domain name would assume that Complainant is not the sponsor of or associated with a website identified by such address, Respondent's "-sucks" formative marks cannot be confusingly similar to Complainant's mark.

In support of this argument, Respondent refers to *Lucent Technologies, Inc. v. Lucentsucks.com,* 95 F. Supp. 2d 528 (E.D.Vir. 2000). It is first important to note that the observations made by Judge Brinkema in the *Lucentsucks.com* opinion regarding the issue of confusing similarity are in the nature of dicta, since the court dismissed the action against defendant for lack of jurisdiction. Judge Brinkema's opinion in *Lucentsucky.com,* and one decision on which she relies, *Bally Total Fitness v. Faber,* 29 F. Supp. 2d 1161 (C.D. Cal. 1998), each lend some support to Respondent's position. However, both cases are distinguishable.

In *Bally,* the court granted summary judgment in favor of a defendant that used the "Bally" trademark on a web page, appending the word "sucks", to create a "ballysucks" web page. In that case, "ballysucks.com" was *not* registered and was *not* used as a second-level domain name. The principal issue was whether the defendant could lawfully express itself on its web page using the trademark "Bally" in combination with the word "sucks". The court held that since the "ballysucks" web page was devoted to critical commentary regarding Bally, and the defendant did not have a commercial purpose in maintaining the site, the defendant had a valid free speech interest in using Bally's mark.

The court observed that even a "ballysucks.com" domain name *might* not constitute trademark infringement (" … even if Faber did use the mark as part of a larger domain name, such as "ballysucks.com", this would not necessarily be a violation as a matter of law." 29 F. Supp., at 1165). It made this observation in the context of applying the *Sleekcraft* factors. In *Bally,* the court found the defendant's intent in establishing its "ballysucks" web page was to criticize the trademark holder, and this factor weighed heavily in favor of the defendant. In the present proceeding, Respondent's intent is different.

In *Lucentsucks.com,* the court observed that "Defendant argues persuasively that the average consumer would not confuse lucentsucks.com with a web site sponsored by plaintiff". However, the court did not undertake any particularized analysis of the disputed domain name as compared with the plaintiff's trademark. Moreover, the court observed that: "A successful showing that lucentsucks.com is effective parody and/or a cite [sic] for critical commentary would seriously undermine the requisite elements for the causes of action at issue in this case." No such showing had been made by the defendant in *Lucentsucks.com.* The court was speaking in the abstract — and in dicta — about a future case in which the trademark issues would be fully litigated. Even so, the court indicated that the defendant's intent in registering and using the disputed domain name would be an important element in determining whether cybersquatting had occurred. The Panel does not consider *Lucentsucks.com* to stand for the proposition that "-sucks" formative domain names are immune as a matter of law from scrutiny as being confusingly similar to trademarks to which they are appended. Each case must be considered on its merits.

The Panel is *not* making any determination regarding the registrants and users of other "-sucks" formative domain names (such as "walmartsucks.com"). The record of this proceeding evidences that Respondent did *not* register "walmartcanadasucks.com" and his other "-sucks" names in order to express opinions or to seek the expression of opinion of others. The record indicates that his intention was to extract money from Complainant. An application of the *Sleekcraft* factors in another context involving Complainant's mark and the word "sucks" might produce a different result than that reached here. The Panel notes that use of a domain name confusingly similar to a mark may be justified by fair use or legitimate noncommercial use considerations, and that this may in other cases permit the use of "-sucks" formative names in free expression forums.

Complainant has met the burden of proving that Respondent is the registrant of domain names that are identical or confusingly similar to a trademark in which Complainant has rights, and it has thus established the first of the three elements necessary to a finding that Respondent has engaged in abusive domain name registration.

The second element of a claim of abusive domain registration is that the Respondent has no rights or legitimate interests in respect of the domain name (Policy, para. 4(a)(ii)).

* * *

Complainant and Respondent are in disagreement as to whether the "www.walmart-canadasucks.com" website posted content before the initiation of this proceeding. Paragraph 4(c)(iii) of the Policy requires that a Respondent be "making" legitimate use of a disputed name to come within its express terms. Respondent registered the disputed domain names almost immediately following a decision against him in *Wal-Mart v. Walmarket Canada,* and Complainant initiated this proceeding shortly following his registration of the names. The Panel accepts that domain name registrants cannot always be expected to make immediate legitimate use of names since preparation is needed to launch websites. Some period reasonable under the particular circumstances must therefore be allowed between the time of registration of a domain name and the commencement of its legitimate use. Evidence of preparation to make legitimate use, appropriate to the context, should be accepted as giving rise to legitimate interests (for a reasonable period). The Panel agrees with Respondent that if trademark holders could force the transfer of confusingly similar "freedom of expression" names immediately upon their registration, this might chill legitimate protest or criticism activities on the Internet. The Panel does not therefore regard as determinative whether Respondent had posted expressive content prior to Complainant's initiation of this proceeding, and need not attempt to resolve the factual dispute as to precisely when Respondent posted content.

Neither does the Panel regard as determinative whether Respondent had posted some sufficient quantum of "free expression" prior to Complainant's initiation of this action. For purposes of deciding this proceeding, the Panel need not explore the content of Respondent's website, nor the relevance of the quantum of expression on his website. The Panel does not question the right of Internet users to post expressive content, while recognizing that there are certain accepted constraints on expression established by laws against libel and related causes of action.

Respondent initiated his dealings with Complainant by offering to sell it a domain name in which it had rights. His e-mail of February 3, 2000, prior to Complainant's initiation of the proceeding in *Wal-Mart v. Walmarket Canada* stated:

> "This is to let you know that www.Wal-MartCanada.com ... is up for auction at GreatDomains.com. I am the owner. Perhaps certain executives within your company might be interested in purchasing it. Thanks for passing this along to the appropriate individuals. Kindest regards, Kenneth J. Harvey."

Coincident with initiation of the proceeding in *Wal-Mart v. Walmarket Canada,* Respondent sent the following message to Complainant:

> "As a gesture of good will, I would like to point out that 'Wal-MartCanada.net' and 'Wal-MartCanada.org' remain unregistered. I suggest you inform Wal-Mart so that they might register those specific domain names before they are snatched up by roaming marauders."

On May 2, 2000, the panelist decided *Wal-Mart v. Walmarket Canada* against Respondent.

Between May 13 and 17, 2000, Respondent registered the disputed domain names.

On June 3, 2000, subsequent to the May 31,2000, initiation of this proceeding, Respondent sent the following message to Complainant:

> "Some time ago, before the original dispute over 'walmartcanada.com' was filed with WIPO by Mary Jane Saunders, I informed Ms. Saunders that other variations of Wal-Mart Canada domain names were available. I informed her that 'Wal-MartCanada.net' and 'Wal-MartCanada.org' were available for purchase and that she should inform executives at Wal-Mart so that they might purchase them. I refrained from buying them. Some time later, these names were—indeed—purchased by Wal-Mart. I passed on this information to Ms. Saunders in my capacity as a domain name consultant.
>
> Therefore, I would like to receive compensation for this consultation.
>
> Also, through my purchase of' 'walmartcanada.com' and 'walmartcanada-sucks.com' and other names that I presently hold, I have intentionally highlighted the fact that Wal-Mart does not hold rights to basic Internet domain names that other large corporations have purchased (in their names) years ago. This was made blatantly obvious by my prompting Wal-Mart to purchase every conceivable combination of name on their domain name buying spree from May 12th to May 16th. Again, I wish to be compensated for this pivotal role I played in protecting Wal-Mart from future difficulties.
>
> For your information, as of this morning, there are several other essential and blatantly-fundamental Wal-Mart dot-com, dot-net and dot-org names available for purchase that Wal-Mart does not own. I am not interested in buying them, as I am growing tired of this dispute and would like to bring it to an end. For an additional domain name consulting fee, I would gladly inform Wal-Mart of the important names left hanging for others to purchase at their will.
>
> If you wish to discuss this via telephone, my number is: 709-528-1996. I look forward to hearing from you.
>
> Sincerely,
>
> Kenneth J. Harvey"

Respondent has in his own words characterized himself as a "domain name consultant" who is acting in Complainant's interests, and who is seeking compensation for "the pivotal role [he has] played in protecting Wal-Mart from future difficulties". In his own words, he registered "walmartcanadasucks.com" and "other names that [he] presently holds" to "intentionally highlight[ed][sic] the fact that Wal-Mart does not hold rights to basic Internet domain names that other large corporations have purchased (in their names) years ago". Subsequent to the initiation of this proceeding—and subsequent to his claimed development of the "walmartcanadasucks.com" web site—he has demanded payment for "consulting services" from Complainant.

* * *

Respondent's claim to a "freedom of expression" interest in establishing the "walmartcanadasucks.com" and "walmartuksucks.com" web sites is contradicted by his own words. A demand for payment from the potential and actual subject of critical sites is fundamentally inconsistent with the right of free expression. It is as if a newspaper were to approach the potential subject of an adverse investigative report to propose that for an appropriate fee the report could be avoided. This would not be characterized as "free speech" activity. It would rather be characterized as "extortion".

Respondent has evidenced that his intention in establishing multiple versions of similar web sites is commercial—as an element of his domain name consultancy services. The Panel determines that Respondent's intention for registering "wal-martcanadasucks.com", "wal-martcanadasucks.com", "walmartuksucks.com", "walmartpuertorico.com" and "walmartpuertoricosucks.com" is commercial, and not within the scope of fair use or legitimate noncommercial use permitted by paragraph 4(c)(iii) of the Policy.

Respondent has registered and used the disputed domain names for a commercial purpose that is not within the boundaries of fair use. He has failed to establish rights or legitimate interests in the disputed domain names. Complainant has thus established the second element necessary to prevail on a claim of abusive domain name registration.

* * *

Respondent registered the disputed domain names, and demanded consulting fees from Complainant as compensation for his actions. Implicit in such demand is that Respondent would forego using the disputed domain names, or would transfer them to Complainant, if his consulting demands were met. Complainant would not reasonably be expected to pay a consultant to disparage its mark. The Panel determines that Respondent registered the disputed domain names for the purpose of selling or otherwise transferring rights in them to the Complainant for consideration in excess of his out-of-pocket costs directly related to the names. This constitutes bad faith within the meaning of paragraph 4(b)(i) of the Policy.

Respondent has threatened to disrupt Complainant's business if his consulting demands are not met. Respondent is not a competitor of Complainant. However, the list of bad faith factors in paragraph 4(b) of the Policy is illustrative, not exclusive. The Panel determines that Respondent's threats to disrupt Complainant's business constitute bad faith within the meaning of paragraph 4(a)(iii) of the Policy.

Respondent is intentionally using certain of the disputed domain names to attract Internet users to his websites. These domain names have been determined to be confusingly similar to Complainant's mark. Respondent acted for commercial gain, i.e., to extract consulting fees from Complainant by threatening to disrupt its business. The Panel determines that this activity constitutes bad faith within the meaning of paragraph 4(b)(iv) of the Policy.

Complainant has established the third and final element necessary for a finding that the Respondent has engaged in abusive domain name registration.

The Panel will therefore request the registrar to transfer the domain names "wal-mart-canadasucks.com", "wal-martcanadasucks.com", "walmartuksucks.com", "walmartpuertorico.com" and "walmartpuertoricosucks.com" to the Complainant.

The Panel stresses that this decision does not address legitimate freedom of expression sites established by parties critical of trademark holders. The Panel is aware that there are numerous web sites identified by "-sucks" formative domain names, including "walmartsucks.com". The Panel anticipates that Respondent (and others) may choose to characterize this decision as seeking to stifle freedom of expression on the Internet by ordering the transfer of "-sucks" formative names. Certain trademark holders might choose to characterize this decision as supporting action against "-sucks" formative domain names in other contexts. The Panel intends this decision to serve neither of these aims. This decision is directed to a blatant case of abuse of the domain name registration process—no more, no less.

7. Decision

Based on its finding that the Respondents, Walsucks and Walmarket Puerto Rico, have engaged in abusive registration of the domain names "wal-martcanadasucks.com", "wal-martcanadasucks.com", "walmartuksucks.com", "walmartpuertorico.com" and "walmartpuertoricosucks.com" within the meaning of paragraph 4(a) of the Policy, the Panel orders that the domain names "wal-martcanadasucks.com", "wal-martcanadasucks.com", "walmartuksucks.com", "walmartpuertorico.com" and "walmartpuertoricosucks.com" be transferred to the Complainant, Wal-Mart Stores, Inc.

Frederick M. Abbott Sole Panelist

[Handwritten annotations: "hugup on 'each ot' 'sucks' implied free speech body which is" ; "Single panelist boy's on crack"]

Wal-Mart Stores, Inc. v.
Wallmartcanadasucks.com and Kenneth J. Harvey
Case No. D2000-1104 (Nov. 23, 2000)

[The Complainant, Wal-Mart Stores, Inc., a registered trademark, uses its famous mark extensively throughout the world and owns retail stores in the following countries: Argentina, Brazil, Canada, China, Germany, Indonesia, Korea, Mexico, Puerto Rico, the United Kingdom, and the United States. The Respondent, Kenneth J. Harvey, registered the disputed domain name <wallmartcanadasucks.com> after losing two previous cases to Complainant.]

* * *

This case involves a much narrower question than the questions in the earlier cases: whether a domain name including the suffix "sucks" is confusingly similar to the text string to which "sucks" is appended, or, alternatively, whether a criticism or parody privilege extends to the use of the suffix "sucks." As sole panelist, I conclude that a domain name including the word "sucks" cannot be confusingly similar, and that a privilege for criticism and parody reinforces that conclusion.

* * *

6. Analysis
A. Introduction

The Respondent hardly appears with clean hands. He has been found in the past to be a Cybersquatter with respect to this complainant. His correspondence with the com-plaintiff could support an inference, as complainant suggests, of extortion — "pay me or I will continue to use the Web to disparage and embarrass you." In Panel Decision No. D2000-0477, the Respondent was found to have violated the UDRP on facts involving use of the suffix "sucks" in a domain name.

But distasteful conduct should not stampede UDRP decision makers into an unwarranted expansion of the domain name dispute process. The UDRP has a narrow scope. It is meant to protect against trademark infringement, not to provide a general remedy for all misconduct involving domain names. Posting defamatory material on a Web site would not justify revocation of a domain name under the UDRP. Posting indecent material on a Web site would not justify domain name revocation under the UDRP. While a domain name registrar may be privileged to revoke a domain name for "illegal use" under § 2 of the Registration Agreement, whether a use is illegal in general is beyond the subject matter jurisdiction of an administrative panel under the UDRP.

"Bad faith" under the UDRP is a term of art. It does not reach every use of a domain name that might constitute bad faith in the ordinary sense of term.

Disciplined construction of the UDRP is appropriate for another reason. The Policy should not be used to shut down robust debate and criticism. Allowing trademark owners to shut down sites that obviously are aimed at criticism of the trademark holder does just that.

The Respondent may be acting unfairly. He may be engaged in unwarranted disparagement. He may be acting childishly. He may be retaliating for having lost earlier Cybersquatting cases. But this does not necessarily mean that he may be forced to transfer the accused domain name to the complainant under the UDRP, considering the purpose.

The remainder of this panel decision reviews the rules of decision to be applied to this dispute, and separately analyzes the likelihood of confusion, treatment of parody and criticism under the Lanham Act, considers the implications of Panel Decision No. D2000-0477 for this case, explores the relationship between the legitimacy of Respondent interests and the content of the accused Web site, evaluates the evidence of solicitation of payment for the accused domain name, and presents factual findings and conclusions.

* * *

C. Likelihood of confusion

The ICANN Policy and the ACPA have a similar requirement that a complainant must show that the accused domain name is identical or confusingly similar to the complainant's trademark.

Bad faith, no matter how egregious, cannot supply a likelihood of confusion where it does not otherwise exist. Suppose the owner of the trademark Acmebytes registers and uses the domain name Acmebytes.com. Suppose further that the proprietor is named Agnes. If someone registers the domain name "agnesisawitch.com" and offers to surrender it in exchange for the payment of money, the bad faith elements of the ICANN Policy no doubt would be satisfied. But Agnesisawitch.com is not confusingly similar to Acmebytes.com and the presence of bad faith cannot make it so.

Two lines of authority are pertinent to this dispute. The first involves application of factors for determining likelihood of confusion under the Lanham Act to a Web page using the word "sucks" to signify criticism. The second involves the treatment of parody and criticism under the ACPA and the Lanham Act more generally.

* * *

Applying the *Bally* analysis to the instant case, I conclude that wallmartcanadasucks.com is not identical or similar to Wal-Mart's marks. They serve fundamentally different purposes. Wal-Mart's domain names serve as commercial advertisements and indications of sources of products and services. wallmartcanadasucks.com is criticism. As in *Bally*, a reasonably prudent user would not mistake the wallmartcanadasucks.com site for any of Wal-Mart's official sites. As in *Bally*, the primary purpose of the accused site is criticism, not promotion of goods related to Wal-Mart goods. Thus the information disseminated through the sites of Respondent and complainant are not related. As in *Bally*, prohibiting the Respondent from using wallmartcanadasucks.com and variants on the name would effectively isolate him from Internet users he wishes to reach in connection with his criticism of Wal-Mart. As in *Bally*, the Respondent cannot exercise his right to publish critical commentary about Wal-Mart without making reference to Wal-Mart. As in *Bally*, there is little likelihood that Wal-Mart will extend its business to operate an official anti Wal-Mart site. The *Bally* analysis, therefore, is strong authority for finding no likelihood of confusion.

2. Parody and criticism under the Lanham Act

A number of cases decided under the ACPA and, more generally, under the Lanham Act, have considered special treatment for accused domain names and marks that are used for parody or criticism.

"In general, a reference to a copyrighted work or trademark maybe permissible if the use is purely for parodic purposes. To the extent the original work must be referenced in order to accomplish the parody, that reference is acceptable."

* * *

Trademark law more generally recognizes a privilege for use of marks for parodic or critical purposes. Often, such a purpose influences the likelihood of confusion analysis.

The Restatement recognizes the special position that criticism occupies in trademark law:

"One who uses a designation that resembles the trademark, trade name collective mark or certification mark of another, not in a manner that is likely to associate the other's mark with the goods, services, or business of the actor, but rather to comment on, criticize, ridicule, parody, or disparage the other or the other's goods, services business, or mark, is subject to liability without proof of the likelihood of confusion only if the actor's conduct meets the requirements of a cause of action for defamation, invasion of privacy, or injurious falsehood."

In *Charles Atlas, Ltd.* v. *DC Comics, Inc.*, [112 F.Supp.2d 330 (S.D.N.Y. 2000)]. the district court granted summary judgment for the defendant, finding that a comic book parody of the plaintiffs advertisements for body-building courses was protected by the First Amendment and thus not infringing or diluting. It found that "The likelihood of confusion is ... slim, and is clearly outweighed by the public interest in parodic expression." [*Id.*] A threshold question was "whether defendant used the mark for an expressive purpose, or to create an incorrect association in order to confuse the public." [*Id.*] "[E]ven if plaintiff suffered some trademark [infringement], defendants' rights under the First Amendment to use plaintiffs mark to communicate the message might prevail over plaintiff's rights under the trademark law." (Footnote 26)

In domain name disputes it is critical whether the accused domain name itself signifies parodic or critical purposes, as opposed to imitation of trademark.

* * *

D. Panel Decision No. D2000-0477
[Wal-Mart Stores, Inc. v. Walsucks and Walmarket Puerto Rico]

In Panel Decision No.D2000-0477, Professor Frederick M. Abbott found "The record of this proceeding evidences that Respondent did *not* register "walmartcanadasucks.com" and his other "-sucks" names in order to express opinions or to seek the expression of opinion of others. The record indicates that his intention was to extract money from Complainant. An application of the *Sleekcraft* factors in another context involving Complainant's mark and the word "sucks" might produce a different result than that reached here. The Panel notes that use of a domain name confusingly similar to a mark may be justified by fair use or legitimate noncommercial use considerations, and that this may in other cases permit the use of "-sucks" formative names in free expression forums."

The analysis in Case No. D2000-0477 concentrated on distinguishing the Lucent sucks and Bally sucks cases. It did not consider more broadly the law relating to critical or parodic uses of domain names and trademarks. Professor Abbott distinguishes Bally on the grounds that it did not involve using ballysucks as a domain name, but rather the word ballysucks on a Web page accessible under a different domain name. This distinction does not dilute the effect of the Bally court's analysis of the relationship between parody or criticism and trademark infringement.

Professor Abbott did not find that use of a "sucks" domain name never would be permissible, but he declined to find a general immunity for use of the "sucks" suffix. On the record before him, which included use of several domain names not involving the suffix "sucks," and which were likely to create consumer confusion, he extended his finding of bad faith, associated with these confusingly similar domain names, to the domain name including "sucks."

This case involves only one domain name, which includes "sucks." I do not see how a domain name including "sucks" ever can be confusingly similar to a trademark to which "sucks" is appended. But whether or not a per se privilege for use of "sucks" is appropriate, the record in this case does not support a finding that the ICANN Policy has been violated.

E. Content of wallmartcanadasucks site and legitimacy of Respondent interests

The complainant must establish that the Respondent "has no rights or legitimate interests in respect of the domain name." Whether the complainant can establish this element depends on the legitimacy of the contents of Respondent's Web site accessible through wallmartcanadasucks.com and the use of that domain name as a means of accessing that Web site.

The accused Web site contains little criticism of Wal-Mart products or practices other than its efforts to control use of its name in Web domain names. This supports an inference that the Web site is closely related to earlier Cybersquatting cases involving this Respondent, rather than the kind of criticism of an enterprise that friends of the Internet might be comfortable in encouraging.

8. Conclusions

* * *

4. On the record in this case, the Respondent has not registered or acquired the domain name primarily for the purpose of selling, renting, or otherwise transferring the

domain name registration to the complainant or a competitor, for valuable consideration in excess of the Respondent's documented out-of-pocket costs directly related to the
domain name. Preceding cases involved a request for consulting services, but even in
those cases there was no explicit demand for payment in exchange for accused domain
names; at most, an inference could be drawn of the relationship between the request for
payment and the registration of disputed domain names. In this case, there is no request
for payment of any kind linked to the accused domain name.

5. The Respondent has not registered the domain name in order to prevent the owner
of the trademark or service mark from reflecting the mark in a corresponding domain name.
There is no likelihood of the complainant registering the accused domain name for any
purpose except to preclude domain names that evidence criticism of the Complainant.

6. The Respondent has not registered the domain name primarily for the purpose
of disrupting the business of a competitor. The Respondent and Complainant are not
competitors.

7. By using the domain name wallmartcanadasucks, the Respondent has not intentionally attempted to attract, for commercial gain, Internet users to its web site or other
on-line location, by creating a likelihood of confusion with the Complainant's mark as
to the source, sponsorship, affiliation, or endorsement of the respondent's web site or location of a product or service on the Respondent's web site or location. There is no likelihood of confusion between wallmartcanadasucks and Wal-Mart's products and services.

8. Accordingly, the complainant has not established the elements of a violation of the
ICANN Policy.

Henry H. Perritt, Jr. Sole Panelist

Note

1. Would the *Wal-Mart v. Walsucks* decision have been different if only the <wal-
sucks.com> name was in dispute?

I. Relationship between the ACPA and the UDRP

Sallen v. Corinthians Licenciamentos Ltda
273 F.3d 14 (1st Cir. 2001)

Lynch, C. J.

This case raises important issues about the relationship between the Anticybersquatting Consumer Protection Act ("ACPA") and the World Intellectual Property Organization ("WIPO") dispute resolution procedures under the Uniform Domain Name Dispute
Resolution Policy ("UDRP"). This is a dispute between Jay D. Sallen, a resident of Brook-
line, Massachusetts, and Corinthians Licenciamentos LTDA ("CL"), a Brazilian corporation, over Sallen's registration and use of the domain name corinthians.com. We are asked
to determine whether Sallen, a domain name registrant who has lost the use of a domain
name in a WIPO dispute resolution proceeding that declared him a cybersquatter under

the UDRP, may bring an action in federal court seeking (1) a declaration that he is not in violation of the ACPA; (2) a declaration that he is not required to transfer the domain name to CL; and (3) such relief as necessary to effectuate these ends.[4] The district court held that federal courts lack jurisdiction over such claims. For the reasons that follow, we reverse the district court and hold that there is federal jurisdiction over such claims.

I. This is a case in the new territory of cybersquatting (also known as "cyberpiracy" or "domain name hijacking"), an Internet phenomenon whereby individuals register Internet domain names in violation of the rights of trademark owners. S.Rep. No. 106-140, at 4 (1999). Alternatively, the case may be viewed as possibly one of "reverse domain name hijacking," whereby trademark owners abusively assert their trademark rights to strip domain names from rightful owners. *See* UDRP Rule 1, *at* http://www.icann.org/udrp/udrp-rules-24Oct99.htm (Oct. 24, 1999) (defining "reverse domain name hijacking"). Cybersquatters often register domain names incorporating the trademarks of others, with the intent of selling the domain names back to the trademark owners at a profit....

CL asserts that it has rights in Brazil to the name "Corinthiao," the Portuguese equivalent of "Corinthians," which is the name of a soccer team popular in Brazil. in the district court, and before this court, CL argued that a WIPO panel properly found that Sallen was a cybersquatter under the UDRP. The UDRP applies to Sallen because its terms are incorporated into his domain name registration agreement—a private contract. CL says that federal courts do not have jurisdiction to revisit the issue of whether Sallen is a cybersquatter as determined under that contract. Further, CL says, federal courts lack jurisdiction over Sallen's suit under the ACPA because CL has disclaimed any intent to sue Sallen under the ACPA. If Sallen cannot reasonably fear a lawsuit under the ACPA, so the argument goes, then there is no Article III case or controversy. CL insists that its victory under the UDRP is unrelated to, and unaffected by, any cause of action under the ACPA. Even if Sallen had an affirmative right under the ACPA to use corinthians.com, it says, he has contractually waived that right by agreeing to the UDRP's different legal standard in his domain name registration agreement.

Sallen unsuccessfully defended his registration and use of corinthians.com in a WIPO dispute resolution proceeding initiated by CL. WIPO Arbitration and Mediation Center Administrative Panel Decision, *Corinthians Licenciamentos LTDA v. Sallen*, No. D2000-0461 (July 17, 2000) (Bianchi, Sole Panelist), *at* http://arbiter.wipo.int/domains/decisions/html/2000/d2000-0461.html. Sallen then filed a complaint in federal court against CL seeking a declaration that his registration and use of corinthians.com is not unlawful under the ACPA. He relied on both 15 U.S.C. §1114(2)(D)(v) and the declaratory judgment statute, 28 U.S.C. §2201. Section 1114(2)(D)(v) states:

> A domain name registrant whose domain name has been suspended, disabled, or transferred under a policy described under clause (ii)(II) may, upon notice to the mark owner, file a civil action to establish that the registration or use of the domain name by such registrant is not unlawful under this chapter. The court may grant injunctive relief to the domain name registrant, including the reacti-

---

4. Sallen's initiation of these proceedings in the district court stayed the WIPO panel's order to transfer the domain name to CL. *See* UDRP ¶4(k), at http://www.icann.org/udrp/udrp-policy-24Oct99.htm (Oct. 24, 1999). After the district court dismissed Sallen's suit, however, the domain name was transferred to CL, possibly wrongfully in light of the pendency of this appeal. If the complaint were reinstated, the logic of Sallen's position is that Sallen would seek leave to amend his complaint to request an injunction returning the domain name.

vation of the domain name or transfer of the domain name to the domain name registrant

15 U.S.C. § 1114(2)(D)(v) (2000).

Sallen asserts that (1) this provision of the ACPA creates an explicit cause of action for a declaration that a registrant who has lost a domain name under the UDRP has lawfully registered and used that domain name; (2) this declaration overrides the WIPO panel's decision to the contrary; and (3) federal courts may order the domain name reactivated or transferred back to the aggrieved registrant. Sallen's position is that, despite the terms of his domain name registration agreement, and despite the WIPO panel's interpretation of those terms, he is entitled to retain registration and use of corinthians.com if his registration and use of the domain name is consistent with the ACPA.

This case raises an issue of first impression, requiring us to determine whether a domain name registrant, who has lost in a WIPO-adjudicated UDRP proceeding, may bring an action in federal court under §1114(2)(D)(v) seeking to override the result of the earlier WIPO proceeding by having his status as a nonviolator of the ACPA declared and by getting an injunction forcing a transfer of the disputed domain name back to him. The answer to this question turns on the relationship between the ACPA, in particular § 1114(2)(D)(v), and decisions of administrative dispute resolution panels contractually empowered to adjudicate domain name disputes under the UDRP.

The district court dismissed Sallen's complaint on the grounds that no actual controversy existed between the parties since CL never claimed that Sallen violated the ACPA. We hold that, although CL represented that it had "no intent to sue [Sallen] under the ACPA for his past activities in connection with corinthians.com," an actual controversy did exist between the parties concerning rights to corinthians.com, and that the district court incorrectly dismissed Sallen's complaint. Section 1114(2)(D)(v) grants domain name registrants who have lost domain names under administrative panel decisions applying the UDRP an affirmative cause of action in federal court for a declaration of nonviolation of the ACPA and for the return of the wrongfully transferred domain names. Accordingly, we reverse and remand to the district court.

* * *

Since the UDRP cannot confer federal jurisdiction where none exists, the remaining question is whether Congress has, in fact, provided a cause of action to override UDRP decisions. Under § 1114(2)(D)(v), Congress has provided registrants such as Sallen with an affirmative cause of action to recover domain names lost in UDRP proceedings. The statute clearly states that a registrant whose domain name has been "suspended, disabled, or transferred" may sue for a declaration that the registrant is not in violation of the Act and for an injunction returning the domain name. 15 U.S.C. § 1114(2)(D)(v). Sallen is a registrant. His domain name has been transferred. Now he simply seeks the declaration and injunction that the statutory provision makes available. Congress's authorization of the federal courts to "grant injunctive relief to the domain name registrant, including the reactivation of the domain name or transfer of the domain name to the domain name registrant," provides Sallen with an explicit cause of action to redress his loss of corinthians.com under the UDRP. *Cf. PHC, Inc. v. Pioneer Healthcare, Inc.*, 75 F.3d 75, 79 (1st Cir.1996) (holding that federal jurisdiction clearly exists over plaintiffs request for a declaration that it was not violating defendant's trademark rights and that it was entitled to maintain its trademark registration).

That a declaration of compliance with the ACPA trumps the panel's finding of non-compliance with the UDRP is further supported by the overlap between the two provisions. In the WIPO proceeding, the panel found that corinthians.com was confusingly similar to CL's trademark, that Sallen had no rights or legitimate interests in corinthians.com, and that the domain name was registered and being used in bad faith. Sallen argues that, under U.S. law, none of these claims is legally supported.

Although CL recognizes overlap between the UDRP and the ACPA, it argues that WIPO proceedings determine whether a registrant's use of a domain name is in accordance with the UDRP, not whether there has been a violation of a U.S. law. But a WIPO panel's application of the UDRP requires it to resolve issues of U.S. law in some cases and, in these cases, a federal court's declaration of a UDRP participant's rights directly impacts the decision issued by the WIPO panel. For instance, the panel found that Sallen had "no rights to or legitimate interests in the domain name at issue." The panel concluded that publishing quotes from the Bible before CL filed its complaint but after Sallen had notice that there was a dispute brewing was insufficient to constitute a right or legitimate interest. A finding by a federal court that Sallen was within his rights when he used corinthians.com to post Biblical quotes would directly undercut the panel's conclusion.

Similarly, the panel, taking into consideration Sallen's "lack of rights or interests in the domain name," found that Sallen had registered and used corinthians.com in bad faith. Again, Sallen asserts that he had no bad faith intent because he believed, and had reasonable grounds to believe, that his use of corinthians.com was fair or otherwise lawful under 15 U.S.C. §1125(d)(1)(B)(ii). A finding by a federal court that Sallen was within his rights would necessarily undermine the panel's conclusion that he used the domain name in bad faith.

More generally, a court's §1114(2)(D)(v) decision that a party is not a cybersquatter under the ACPA, and that a party has a right to use a domain name, necessarily negates a WIPO decision that a party is a cybersquatter under the UDRP. The conclusion that a federal court's interpretation of the ACPA supplants a WIPO panel's interpretation of the UDRP is further reinforced by the fact that WIPO does not create new law—it applies existing law. In fact, the application of the "lowest common denominator of internationally agreed and accepted principles concerning the abuse of trademarks," rather than the creation of new law, is part of the UDRP's fundamental structure.

CL claims that it does not contest any of Sallen's ACPA cybersquatting arguments, but instead defends WIPO's decision that Sallen violated the UDRP's contractual prohibition on cybersquatting. As CL understands the law, Sallen has waived his rights under the ACPA by agreeing to different standards under the UDRP. But §1114(2)(D)(v) provides disappointed administrative dispute resolution participants with a chance to have any unfavorable UDRP decision reviewed in a U.S. court. We think this provision means that a federal court's decision that Sallen was in compliance with the ACPA necessarily contradicts the WIPO panel's finding that Sallen lacked a legitimate interest in corinthians.com. Congress has defined in the ACPA what it means to lack a legitimate interest in a domain name under U.S. law. For that reason, should a federal court declare that Sallen is in compliance with the ACPA, that declaration would undercut the rationale of the WIPO panel decision.

We would not lightly assume that Congress enacted the ACPA, but intended all domain name registrants to be governed by a different standard, administered by international dispute resolution panels, with no eventual recourse to whatever affirmative protections the U.S. law might provide. A contextual understanding of §1114(2)(D)(v) supports reading the provision to include complaints such as Sallen's. Section 1114(2) addresses limitations on liability of potential defendants in trademark infringement actions. Section 1114(2)(A) creates the "innocent infringer" exception and §1114(2)(B) creates a limitation on liability of advertisers. Section 1114(2)(D), added to the Lanham Act by the ACPA, creates, among other things, an exception to liability for domain name registrars that transfer or revoke domain names from registrants pursuant to a policy by the registrar prohibiting registration of domain names that are "identical to, confusingly similar to, or dilutive of another's mark." §1114(2)(D)(ii)(II). Section 1114(2)(D)(ii)(I) also creates an exception to liability for domain name registrars that transfer or revoke domain names from registrants pursuant to a court order. The purpose of subsections (D)(i)–(ii) is "to encourage domain name registrars ... to work with trademark owners to prevent cybersquatting through a limited exemption from liability for domain name registrars ... that suspend, cancel, or transfer domain names pursuant to a court order or in the implementation of a reasonable policy prohibiting cybersquatting." H.R. Conf. Rep. No. 106-464, at 116 (1999). Subsections (D)(i)–(ii) are, on this reading, quite favorable to trademark holders because they encourage domain name registrars to cooperate with trademark holders' attempts to assert their trademark rights.

Subsection (D)(iv) then provides that if a registrar suspends or transfers a registrant's domain name based on a knowing misrepresentation by another person that "a domain name is identical to, confusingly similar to, or dilutive of a mark," then the person making the misrepresentation is liable to the registrant. This provision states that "[t]he court may also grant injunctive relief to the domain name registrant, including the reactivation of the domain name or transfer of the domain name to the domain name registrant." This subsection, in contrast to subsections (D)(i)–(ii), "protects the rights of domain name registrants against overreaching trademark owners." H.R. Conf. Rep. No.106-464, at 117. Although subsections (D)(i)–(ii) encourage enforcement of policies against cybersquatting by facilitating cooperation between registrars and trademark owners, subsection (D)(iv) provides a counterweight to ensure that this cooperation does not result in reverse domain name hijacking, whereby trademark holders abuse anticybersquatting provisions to take domain names from rightful, noninfringing registrants.

Subsection (D)(v), similar to subsection (D)(iv), also acts as a counterweight to offset potential overreaching by trademark holders. Subsection (D)(v) was viewed as an "additional protection" to subsection (D)(iv), designed to aid registrants who lose their domain names to overzealous trademark holders. *Id.* The similarity of subsections (D)(iv) and (v) is reinforced by their parallel structure. They use the exact same language, stating that "[t]he court may grant injunctive relief to the domain name registrant, including the reactivation of the domain name or transfer of the domain name to the domain name registrant." Viewed in context, and with the structure of the statute in mind, subsection (D)(v) is best understood to provide domain name holders with a cause of action to rectify reverse domain name hijacking by trademark holders using the UDRP process to require registrants to transfer domain names originally held by rightful users under U.S. law.

The legislative history also supports the proposition that §1114(2)(D)(v) was intended to provide registrants in Sallen's position with a cause of action. Senator Hatch, discussing §1114(2)(D)(v), which he offered as an amendment to the bill that was enacted as the ACPA, explained that

> a domain name registrant whose name is suspended in an extra-judicial dispute resolution procedure can seek a declaratory judgment that his use of the name was, in fact, lawful under the Trademark Act. This clarification is consistent with other provisions of the reported bill that seek to protect domain name registrants against overreaching trademark owners.

145 Congo Rec. S10, 516 (1999). This provision, along with others added by the Hatch-Leahy amendments, was understood by Senator Hatch to "balance the rights of trademark owners with the interests of Internet users" and to "preserv[e] the rights of Internet users to engage in protected expression online and to make lawful uses of others' trademarks in cyberspace." *Id.* at S10, 515. Subsection (D)(v) is best understood as creating a protection for registrants to counteract abusive behavior by trademark holders. And this abusive behavior is best understood to include administrative dispute resolution proceedings under the UDRP where those proceedings are intended, as Sallen has asserted, to strip a domain name from a registrant who has lawfully registered and used that domain name.

* * *

III.
Discussion
A. Trademark Infringement

Except for the use of PEI's protected terms in the wallpaper of Welles' website, we conclude that Welles' uses of PEI's trademarks are permissible, nominative uses. They imply no current sponsorship or endorsement by PEI. Instead, they serve to identify Welles as a past PEI "Playmate of the Year."[5]

We articulated the test for a permissible, nominative use in *New Kids On The Block v. New America Publishing, Inc.*[6] The band, New Kids On The Block, claimed trademark infringement arising from the use of their trademarked name by several newspapers. The newspapers had conducted polls asking which member of the band New Kids On The Block was the best and most popular. The papers' use of the trademarked term did not fall within the traditional fair use doctrine. Unlike a traditional fair use scenario, the defendant newspaper was using the trademarked term to describe not its own product, but the plaintiffs. Thus, the factors used to evaluate fair use were inapplicable. The use was nonetheless permissible, we concluded, based on its nominative nature.

Note

1. The relationship between the UDRP and the ACPA has attracted some attention from the courts. In *Stenzel v. Pifer*, 82 U.S.P.Q.2D (BNA) 1372 (WD Wash. 2006), the court states as follows:

> The Sallen Court stated that, in this section of the ACPA, "Congress has provided a cause of action to recover domain names lost in UDRP proceedings." 273 F.3d at 27. The Court noted that findings by a district court could undermine an arbitration panel's decision and that "a court's §1114(2)(D)(v) decision that a party is not a cybersquatter under the ACPA, and that a party has a right to use a domain name, necessarily negates a WIPO decision that a party is a cybersquatter under the UDRP." *Id.* at 28. Thus, courts have recognized that an action based on §1114(2)(D)(v) may negate a UDRP decision.

---

5. *See* New Kids on the Block v. New America Publ'g, Inc., 971 F.2d 302,306 (9th Cir. 1992) (describing a nominative use as one that "does not imply sponsorship or endorsement of the product because the mark is used only to describe the thing, rather than to identify its source").
6. 971 F.2d 302 (9th Cir. 1992).

If the Article III style courts can "negate" a UDRP decision, why would anyone file a UDRP complaint? Should UDRP decisions have some binding effect on Article III style courts?

———————

J. Nominative Use (Meta Tags)

Playboy Enterprises v. Welles

279 F.3d 796 (9th Cir. 2002), aff'd, 30 Fed. Appx. 734 (9th Cir. 2002)

NELSON, C.J.

Playboy Enterprises, Inc. (PEI), appeals the district court's grant of summary judgment as to its claims of trademark infringement, unfair competition, and breach of contract against Terri Welles; Terri Welles, Inc.; Pippi, Inc.; and Welles' current and former "webmasters," Steven Huntington and Michael Mihalko....

I.
Background

Terri Welles was on the cover of Playboy in 1981 and was chosen to be the Playboy Playmate of the Year for 1981. Her use of the title "Playboy Playmate of the Year 1981," and her use of other trademarked terms on her website are at issue in this suit. During the relevant time period, Welles' website offered information about and free photos of Welles, advertised photos for sale, advertised memberships in her photo club, and promoted her services as a spokesperson. A biographical section described Welles' selection as Playmate of the Year in 1981 and her years modeling for PEI. After the lawsuit began, Welles included discussions of the suit and criticism of PEI on her website and included a note disclaiming any association with PEI.[7]

PEI complains of four different uses of its trademarked terms on Welles' website: (1) the terms "Playboy "and "Playmate" in the metatags of the website;[8] (2) the phrase "Playmate of the Year 1981" on the masthead of the website; (3) the phrases "Playboy Playmate of the Year 1981" and "Playmate of the Year 1981" on various banner ads, which maybe transferred to other websites; and (4) the repeated use of the abbreviation "PMOY '81" as the watermark on the pages of the website.[9] PEI claimed that these uses of its marks constituted trademark infringement, dilution, false designation of origin, and unfair competition. The district court granted defendants' motion for summary judgment. PEI appeals the grant of summary judgment on its infringement and dilution claims. We affirm in part and reverse in part.

* * *

We adopted the following test for nominative use:

———————

7. The disclaimer reads as follows:" This site is neither endorsed, nor sponsored, nor affiliated with Playboy Enterprises, Inc. PLAYBOY(r) PLAYMATE OF THE YEAR (r) AND PLAYMATE OF THE MONTH(r) are registered trademarks of Playboy Enterprises, Inc."

8. Metatags are hidden code used by some search engines to determine the content of web sites in order to direct searchers to relevant sites.

9. PEI claims that "PMOY" is an unregistered trademark of PEI, standing for "Playmate of the Year."

First, the product or service in question must be one not readily identifiable without use of the trademark; second, only so much of the mark or marks may be used as is reasonably necessary to identify the product or service; and third, the user must do nothing that would, in conjunction with the mark, suggest sponsorship or endorsement by the trademark holder.

We noted in *New Kids* that a nominative use may also be a commercial one.

In cases in which the defendant raises a nominative use defense, the above three-factor test should be applied instead of the test for likelihood of confusion set forth in *Sleekcraft*. The three-factor test better evaluates the likelihood of confusion in nominative use cases. When a defendant uses a trademark nominally, the trademark will be identical to the plaintiff's mark, at least in terms of the words in question. Thus, application of the *Sleekcraft* test, which focuses on the similarity of the mark used by the plaintiff and the defendant, would lead to the incorrect conclusion that virtually all nominative uses are confusing. The three-factor test—with its requirements that the defendant use marks only when no descriptive substitute exists, use no more of the mark than necessary, and do nothing to suggest sponsorship or endorsement by the mark holder—better addresses concerns regarding the likelihood of confusion in nominative use cases.

We group the uses of PEI's trademarked terms into three for the purpose of applying the test for nominative use. First, we analyze Welles' use of the terms in headlines and banner advertisements. We conclude that those uses are clearly nominative. Second, we analyze the use of the terms in the metatags for Welles' website, which we conclude are nominative as well. Finally, we analyze the terms as used in the wallpaper of the website. We conclude that this use is not nominative and remand for a determination of whether it infringes on a PEI trademark.

1. Headlines and banner advertisements.

To satisfy the first part of the test for nominative use, "the product or service in question[.]" This situation arises "when a trademark also describes a person, a place or an attribute of a product" and there is no descriptive substitute for the trademark. In such a circumstance, allowing the trademark holder exclusive rights would allow the language to "be depleted in much the same way as if generic words were protectable." In *New Kids*, we gave the example of the trademarked term, "Chicago Bulls." We explained that "one might refer to the 'two-time world champions' or 'the professional basketball team from Chicago,' but it's far simpler (and more likely to be understood) to refer to the Chicago Bulls." Moreover, such a use of the trademark would "not imply sponsorship or endorsement of the product because the mark is used only to describe the thing, rather than to identify its source." Thus, we concluded, such uses must be excepted from trademark infringement law.

The district court properly identified Welles' situation as one which must also be excepted. No descriptive substitute exists for PEI's trademarks in this context. The court explained:

> [T]here is no other way that Ms. Welles can identify or describe herself and her services without venturing into absurd descriptive phrases. To describe herself as the "nude model selected by Mr. Hefner's magazine as its number-one prototypical woman for the year 1981" would be impractical as well as ineffectual in identifying Terri Welles to the public.

We agree. Just as the newspapers in *New Kids* could only identify the band clearly by using its trademarked name, so can Welles only identify herself clearly by using PEI's trademarked title.

The second part of the nominative use test requires that "only so much of the mark or marks may be used as is reasonably necessary to identify the product or service[.]" *New Kids* provided the following examples to explain this element: "[A] soft drink competitor would be entitled to compare its product to Coca-Cola or Coke, but would not be entitled to use Coca-Cola's distinctive lettering." Similarly, in a past case, an auto shop was allowed to use the trademarked term "Volkswagen" on a sign describing the cars it repaired, in part because the shop "did not use Volkswagen's distinctive lettering style or color scheme, nor did he display the encircled 'VW' emblem." Welles' banner advertisements and headlines satisfy this element because they use only the trademarked words, not the font or symbols associated with the trademarks.

The third element requires that the user do "nothing that would, in conjunction with the mark, suggest sponsorship or endorsement by the trademark holder." As to this element, we conclude that aside from the wallpaper, which we address separately, Welles does nothing in conjunction with her use of the marks to suggest sponsorship or endorsement by PEI. The marks are clearly used to describe the title she received from PEI in 1981, a title that helps describe who she is. It would be unreasonable to assume that the Chicago Bulls sponsored a website of Michael Jordan's simply because his name appeared with the appellation "former Chicago Bull." Similarly, in this case, it would be unreasonable to assume that PEI currently sponsors or endorses someone who describes herself as a "Playboy Playmate of the Year in 1981." The designation of the year, in our case, serves the same function as the "former" in our example. It shows that any sponsorship or endorsement occurred in the past.

In addition to doing nothing in conjunction with her use of the marks to suggest sponsorship or endorsement by PEI, Welles affirmatively disavows any sponsorship or endorsement. Her site contains a clear statement disclaiming any connection to PEI. Moreover, the text of the site describes her ongoing legal battles with the company.

For the foregoing reasons, we conclude that Welles' use of PEI's marks in her headlines and banner advertisements is a nominative use excepted from the law of trademark infringement.

2. Metatags

Welles includes the terms "playboy" and "playmate" in her metatags. Metatags describe the contents of a website using keywords. Some search engines search metatags to identify websites relevant to a search. Thus, when an internet searcher enters "playboy" or "playmate" into a search engine that uses metatags, the results will include Welles' site. Because Welles' metatags do not repeat the terms extensively, her site will not be at the top of the list of search results. Applying the three-factor test for nominative use, we conclude that the use of the trademarked terms in Welles' metatags is nominative.

As we discussed above with regard to the headlines and banner advertisements, Welles has no practical way of describing herself without using trademarked terms. In the context of metatags, we conclude that she has no practical way of identifying the content of her website without referring to PEI's trademarks.

A large portion of Welles' web site discusses her association with Playboy over the years. Thus, the trademarked terms accurately describe the contents of Welles' website, in addition to describing Welles. Forcing Welles and others to use absurd turns of phrase in their metatags, such as those necessary to identify Welles, would be particularly damaging in the internet search context. Searchers would have a much more difficult time locating relevant websites if they could do so only by correctly guessing the long phrases necessary to substitute for trademarks. We can hardly expect someone searching for Welles' site to imagine the same phrase proposed by the district court to describe Welles without referring to Playboy—"the nude model selected by Mr. Hefner's organization.... Yet if someone could not remember her name, that is what they would have to do. Similarly, someone searching for critiques of Playboy on the internet would have a difficult time if internet sites could not list the object of their critique in their metatags.

There is simply no descriptive substitute for the trademarks used in Welles' metatags. Precluding their use would have the unwanted effect of hindering the free flow of information on the internet, something which is certainly not a goal of trademark law. Accordingly, the use of trademarked terms in the metatags meets the first part of the test for nominative use.

We conclude that the metatags satisfy the second and third elements of the test as well. The metatags use only so much of the marks as reasonably necessary[10] and nothing is done in conjunction with them to suggest sponsorship or endorsement by the trademark holder. We note that our decision might differ if the metatags listed the trademarked term so repeatedly that Welles' site would regularly appear above PEI's in searches for one of the trademarked terms.[11]

* * *

IV.
Conclusion

For the foregoing reasons, we affirm the district court's grant of summary judgment as to PEI's claims for trademark infringement and trademark dilution, with the sole exception of the use of the abbreviation "PMOY." We reverse as to the abbreviation and remand for consideration of whether it merits protection under either an infringement or a dilution theory. We also affirm as to PEI's claims for breach of contract. In a separate memorandum disposition, we resolve the issues raised by Welles' cross-appeal.

AFFIRMED in part, REVERSED and REMANDED in part.

————————

Promatek Indus., Ltd v. Equitrac Corp.
300 F.3d 808 (7th Cir. 2002)

WILLIAMS, CIRCUIT JUDGE

[P]lacing a competitor's trademark in a metatag creates a likelihood of confusion. In *Brookfield Communications*, the court found that although consumers are not confused when they reach a competitor's website, there is nevertheless initial interest confusion.

————————

10. It is hard to imagine how a metatag could use more of a mark than the words contained in it, but we recently learned that some search engines are now using pictures. Searching for symbols, such as the Playboy bunny, cannot be far behind. That problem does not arise in this case, however, and we need not address it.

11. PEI asserts that it introduced evidence showing that Welles' site has been listed before PEI's on occasion. However, an examination of the evidence PEI cites shows that Welles' site, although sometimes ranked highly, was still listed below PEI's in search results.

174 F.3d at 1062. This is true in this case, because by Equitrac's placing the term Copi-track in its metatag, consumers are diverted to its website and Equitrac reaps the good-will Promatek developed in the Copitrak mark. *Id.* That consumers who are misled to Equitrac's website are only briefly confused is of little or no consequence. In fact, "that confusion as to the source of a product or service is eventually dispelled does not elimi-nate the trademark infringement which has already occurred." *Forum Corp. of N. Am. v. Forum, Ltd.*, 903 F.2d 434, 442 n.2 (7th Cir. 1990). What is important is not the duration of the confusion, it is the misappropriation of Promatek's goodwill. Equitrac cannot un-ring the bell. As the court in *Brookfield* explained, "using another's trademark in one's metatags is much like posting a sign with another's trademark in front of one's store." *Brookfield*, 174 F.3d at 1064. Customers believing they are entering the first store rather than the second are still likely to mill around before they leave. The same theory is true for websites. Consumers who are directed to Equitrac's webpage are likely to learn more about Equitrac and its products before beginning a new search for Promatek and Copi-trak. Therefore, given the likelihood of initial consumer confusion, the district court was correct in finding Promatek could succeed on the merits.

Note

1. *Adwords.* Is using adwords by an Internet search engine trademark "use in com-merce" under the Lanham Act? At least one court has said no. Rescuecom Corp. v. Google, Inc., 456 F. Supp. 2d 393 (N.D.N.Y. 2006). Google had sold sponsor link space to com-petitors of Rescuecom that would appear when a user searched "Rescuecom" on Google. Or, you might say, when someone googled "Rescuecom." The court held that this was not use contemplated by the Lanham Act. If this stands, do you see how this may change the trademark landscape rather seriously? Or, would you argue that it should be changed? *See*, Stacy L. Dogan and Mark A. Lemley, *Grounding Trademark Law through Trademark Use*, 92 Iowa L. Rev. 1669 (2007).

K. Pop-Up Advertising

U-Haul International, Inc. v. WhenU.com, Inc.
279 F. Supp. 2d 723 (E.D. Vir. 2003)

Lee, J.

THIS MATTER is before the Court on the Plaintiff U-Haul International, Inc.'s, ("U-Haul") and the Defendants WhenU.com, Inc.'s, ("WhenU") and Avi Naider's motions for summary judgment on all remaining counts of the First Amended Complaint: Counts I, II, III, IV, and V. This case involves pop-up advertising and Plaintiff U-Haul's claim that Defendant WhenU's pop-up advertising infringes upon U-Haul's trademark, constitutes copyright infringement, and amounts to unfair competition. U-Haul complains that WhenU's pop-up advertisements, which crowd the computer user's screen and block out U-Haul's website display, in effect, infringe on U-Haul's registered trademark and alter U-Haul's copyrighted advertisements. The issue presented is whether WhenU's computer software, which presents pop-up advertising when the individual computer user searches for goods and services on the Internet, is a form of trademark or copyright infringement or unfair competition. Because the computer software at issue does not copy or use U-Haul's trademark or copyright material the Court concludes that WhenU's pop-up advertising does not constitute trademark or copyright infringement or unfair competition; therefore, the Court grants WhenU's motion for summary judgment.

The Court acknowledges that this case is an attempt by a trademark owner and copyright holder to limit annoying pop-up advertising from blotting out its website on the individual computer user's screen. The average computer user who conducts a web search for the U-Haul website would expect the U-Haul website to appear on their computer screen; however, in this case, the computer screen fills with the advertisement of a U-Haul competitor. The user must then click and close the pop-up advertisement window in order to get to their destination, the U-Haul website. While at first blush this detour in the user's web search seems like a siphon-off of a business opportunity, the fact is that the computer user consented to this detour when the user downloaded WhenU's computer software from the Internet. In other words, the user deliberately or unwittingly downloaded the pop-up advertisement software. The foregoing explanation makes it clear that under the circumstances, while pop-up advertising may crowd out the U-Haul's advertisement screen through a separate window, this act is not trademark or copyright infringement, or unfair competition.

Computer users, like this trial judge, may wonder what we have done to warrant the punishment of seizure of our computer screens by pop-up advertisements for secret web cameras, insurance, travel values, and fad diets. Did we unwittingly sign up for incessant advertisements that require us to click, click, and click again in order to return to our Internet work? The Court, in this opinion, attempts to answer this question; we have invited these pop-up advertisements by downloading free screen savers and other free software from the Internet.

Despite U-Haul's plea, the Court, upon review of the applicable law, concludes that, while pop-up advertisements seize the user's computer screen with a window of advertisement, blocking out the object of your search and your document, requiring you to click several times to clear your computer screen, these advertisements do not consist [of] trademark or copyright infringement, or unfair competition. WhenU's pop-up advertisement software resides in individual computers as a result of the invitation and consent of the individual computer user, and, thus, the advertisements do not use, alter or interfere with U-Haul's trademarks and copyrights. Alas, we computer users must endure pop-up advertising along with her ugly brother unsolicited bulk email, "spam", as a burden of using the Internet.

* * *

B. Analysis
1. Trademark Infringement, Unfair Competition, and Trademark Dilution

The Court grants Defendants' motion for summary judgment on Plaintiff's trademark claims because Plaintiff fails to show how a pop-up advertisement appearing in a separate window on an individual's computer obstructing U-Haul's advertisement is a "use" of U-Haul's trademarks in commerce.

U-Haul contends that the fact that WhenU's pop-up ads appear on the same screen as U-Haul's website and logo is enough to constitute a "use in commerce" under the Lanham Act. U-Haul further argues that WhenU's use of U-Haul's trademark "U-Haul" as part of the process by which its pop-up advertisements are triggered constitutes "use in commerce."*(Id.* at 13.) U-Haul also contends that When-U's popup scheme interferes with the use of U-Haul's Web site by its customers and dealers.*(Id.* at 14.) As discussed below, however, WhenU's pop-up advertisements do not constitute "use in commerce" of U-Haul's trademarks for four reasons.

First, U-Haul relies on the premise that WhenU's pop-up ads are framed by the U-Haul website; in other words, the argument is that WhenU's ads appear as a single visual presentation as part of U-Haul's website. This position, however, is untenable. When a WhenU ad appears on a user's computer screen, it opens in a WhenU-branded window that is separate and distinct from the window in which the U-Haul website appears. It is important to note that in the Microsoft Windows environment, each program that the user launches generally appears on a separate window on the user's computer screen. In addition, the computer user may have multiple windows open at once; and in many instances, a separate window may pop-up on the user's screen notifying the user of an event: incoming e-mail, completion of a task by the computer, an appointment, etc.

Second, "use" is not established merely because trademarks are simultaneously visible to a consumer. Such comparative advertising does not violate trademark law, even when the advertising makes use of a competitor's trademark.... Thus, the appearance of WhenU's ads on a user's computer screen at the same time as the U-Haul web page is a result of how applications operate in the Windows environment and does not consist "use" pursuant to the Lanham Act.

Third, WhenU's inclusion of the U-Haul uniform resource locator ("URL") and "U-Haul" in its directory incorporated into the SaveNow program does not constitute "use" under the Lanham Act. WhenU does not sell the U-Haul URL to its customers. Nor, does WhenU display the U-Haul URL or the words "U-Haul" to the computer user when the ad pops-up. U-Haul fails to adduce any evidence that WhenU uses U-Haul's trademarks to identify the source of its goods or services. WhenU does not place the U-Haul trademarks in commerce; the SaveNow program merely uses the U-Haul URL and "U-Haul". Likewise in the instant case, WhenU's incorporation of U-Haul's URL and "U-Haul" in the SaveNow program is not a trademark use because WhenU merely uses the marks for the "pure machine-linking function" and in no way advertises or promotes U-Haul's web address or any other U-Haul trademark.

Fourth, WhenU's pop-up scheme does not interfere with the use of U-Haul's web site by its customers and dealers because the SaveNow program does not interact with U-Haul's computer servers or systems and the SaveNow program is a user-installed program where the user has made a conscious decision to install the program. U-Haul cites several cases for the proposition that interference with a Web page constitutes a use in commerce; however, Plaintiff's reliance on these cases is misplaced. The cases address situations where the defendants prevented or hindered Internet users from accessing plaintiffs' services....

In this instance, WhenU is not cybersquatting on U-Haul's trademark which serves as its domain name on the Internet. Nor, is a computer user taken to a WhenU website when the user searches for U-Haul's domain name. Furthermore, the SaveNow program does not hinder or impede Internet users from accessing U-Haul's web site in such a manner that WhenU "uses" U-Haul's trademarks. The SaveNow program resides within the user's computer and does not interact or communicate with U-Haul's website, its computer servers, or its computer systems. Further, the SaveNow program does not change the underlying appearance of the U-Haul website. In addition, the SaveNow program is installed by the computer user who can decline to accept the licensing agreement or decline to download the program. Thus, the user controls the computer display the moment the WhenU ad pops up, and the user may also have other programs with pop-up windows notifying the user of an event within the computer system. The SaveNow program is, therefore, no different than an e-mail system that pops a window up when the registered user receives a new e-mail message.

In sum, U-haul fails to establish that WhenU uses U-Haul's trademarks in commerce in violation of the Lanham Act because (1) WhenU's pop-up window is separate and distinct from U-Haul's web site, (2) WhenU does not advertise or promote U-Haul's trademarks through the use of U-Haul's URL or "U-Haul" in its SaveNow directory, and (3) the SaveNow program does not hinder or impede Internet users from accessing U-Haul's web site in such a manner that WhenU "uses" U-Haul's trademarks. Therefore, WhenU is entitled to summary judgment on U-Haul's claims of trademark infringement and unfair competition.

———————

1-800 Contacts, Inc., v. WhenU.Com, Inc.
414 F.3d 400 (2ndCir. 2005)

JOHN M. WALKER, JR., C. J.

BACKGROUND

[WhenU provides a free software called "SaveNow" that downloads pop-up advertisements related to the users internet activities. SaveNow uses keywords typed by the user to identify the ads that pertain to the user's activities. The advertisements appears in a separate screen from the user's activities.

The SaveNow user who accesses the 1-800 Contacts website will receive a SaveNow pop-up. If the user does not wish to see the SaveNow pop-up there is a visible button to close the window. If the user wishes to view the advertisement and clicks on the SaveNow pop-up, the main browser (the one with the 1-800 Contacts website) will be navigated away.

1-800 Contacts alleges that WhenU conducts infringes 1-800 Contacts trademarks by making SaveNow advertisements available. 1-800 alleges that the advertisements and pop-ups change 1-800's website and covers the trademarks.]

DISCUSSION
II. "Use" Under the Lanham Act

The Lanham Act defines "use in commerce," in relevant part, as follows:

.... For purposes of this Chapter, a mark shall be deemed to be in use in commerce-

(1) on goods when—

(A) it is placed in any manner on the goods or their containers or the displays associated therewith or on the tags or labels affixed thereto, or if the nature of the goods makes such placement impracticable, then on documents associated with the goods or their sale, and

(B) the goods are sold or transported in commerce, and

(2) on services when it is used or displayed in the sale or advertising of services and the services are rendered in commerce....

15 U.S.C. § 1127.

In issuing the preliminary injunction, the district court held that WhenU use[s] [1-800]'s mark in two ways. First, in causing pop-up advertisements for Defendant Vision Direct to appear when SaveNow users have specifically attempted to access [1-800]'s website— on which Plaintiff's trademark appears— [WhenU is] displaying Plaintiff's mark "in the ... advertising of" Defendant Vision Direct's services ... [and, t]hus, ... [is] "using" Plaintiff's marks that appear on Plaintiff's website.

Second, Defendant WhenU.com includes Plaintiff's [website address], trademark,] in the proprietary WhenU.com directory of terms that triggers pop-up advertisements on SaveNow users' computers. In so doing, Defendant WhenU.com "uses" Plaintiff's mark ... to advertise and publicize companies that are in direct competition with Plaintiff.

1-800 Contacts, 309 F. Supp. 2d at 489.

Prior to the district court's decision, two other courts had addressed the issue of "use" as it applies to WhenU's specific activities and reached the opposite conclusion. In *Wells Fargo & Co. v. WhenU.com, Inc.*, 293 F. Supp. 2d 734 (E.D. Mich. 2003), the district court denied Wells Fargo's motion for a preliminary injunction after finding that WhenU's inclusion of plaintiff Wells Fargo's trademarked website address in WhenU's proprietary directory of keywords was not "use" for purposes of the Lanham Act, and that WhenU did not alter or interfere with Wells Fargo's website in any manner. *Id. at 757–61.* The district court in *U-Haul International, Inc. v. WhenU.com, Inc.*, 279 F. Supp. 2d 723 (E.D. Va. 2003), employing a very similar analysis, granted summary judgment in favor of WhenU after concluding that WhenU's inclusion of U-Haul's trademarked website address in the SaveNow directory was not actionable because it was for a "pure machine-linking function" that was not "use" under the Lanham Act. *Id.* at 728 (internal quotation marks omitted).

In the case before us, the district court's consideration of these two comprehensive decisions on the precise issue at hand was confined to a footnote in which it cited the cases, summarized their holdings in parentheticals, and concluded, without discussion, that it "disagree[d] with, and [was] not bound by these findings." *1-800 Contacts*, 309 F. Supp. 2d at 490 n.43. Unlike the district court, we find the thorough analyses set forth in both *U-Haul* and *Wells Fargo* to be persuasive and compelling.

A. The SaveNow Directory

The district court held that WhenU's inclusion of 1-800's website address in the SaveNow directory constitutes a prohibited "use" of 1-800's trademark. *Id.* at 489. We disagree.

At the outset, we note that WhenU does not "use" 1-800's trademark in the manner ordinarily at issue in an infringement claim: it does not "place" 1-800 trademarks on any goods or services in order to pass them off as emanating from or authorized by 1-800. *See U-Haul*, 279 F. Supp. 2d at 728. The fact is that WhenU does not reproduce or display 1-800's trademarks at all, nor does it cause the trademarks to be displayed to a C-user. Rather, WhenU reproduces 1-800's website address, identical, to 1-800's 1-800 CONTACTS trademark. *See 1-800 Contacts*, 309 F. Supp. 2d at 478–79.

The district court found that the differences between 1-800's trademarks and the website address utilized by WhenU were insignificant because they were limited to the addition of the "www." and ".com" and the omission of the hyphen and a space. *See id.* We conclude that, to the contrary, the differences between the marks are quite significant because they transform 1-800's trademark—which is entitled to protection under the Lanham Act— into a word combination that functions more or less like a public key to 1-800's website.

Moreover, it is plain that WhenU is using 1-800's website address precisely because it is a website address, rather than because it bears any resemblance to 1-800's trademark, because the only place WhenU reproduces the address is in the SaveNow directory. Although the directory resides in the C-user's computer, it is inaccessible to both the C-user and the general public. *See id.* at 476 (noting that directory is scrambled to preclude access). Thus, the appearance of 1-800's website address in the directory does not create a possibility of visual confusion with 1-800's mark. More important, a WhenU pop-up ad cannot be triggered by a C-user's input of the 1-800 trademark or the appearance of that trademark on a webpage accessed by the c-user. Rather, in order for WhenU to capitalize on the fame and recognition of 1-800's trademark — the improper motivation both 1-800 and the district court ascribe to WhenU — it would have needed to put the actual trademark on the list.

In contrast to some of its competitors, moreover, WhenU does not disclose the proprietary contents of the SaveNow directory to its advertising clients nor does it permit these clients to request or purchase specified keywords to add to the directory. *See GEICO v. Google, Inc.*, 330 F. Supp. 2d 700, 703–04 (E.D. Va. 2004).

A company's internal utilization of a trademark in a way that does not communicate it to the public is analogous to a individual's private thoughts about a trademark. Such conduct simply does not violate the Lanham Act, which is concerned with the use of trademarks in connection with the sale of goods or services in a manner likely to lead to consumer confusion as to the source of such goods or services. *See* 15 U.S.C. § 1127; *see also* Louis Altman, 4 Callmann on Unfair Competition, Trademarks and Monopolies § 22:25 n.1 (4th ed. 2004).

Accordingly, we conclude that WhenU's inclusion of the 1-800 website address in its SaveNow directory does not infringe on 1-800's trademark.

B. The Pop-up Advertisements

The primary issue to be resolved by this appeal is whether the placement of pop-up ads on a C-user's screen contemporaneously with either the 1-800 website or a list of search results obtained by the C-user's input of the 1-800 website address constitutes "use" under the Lanham Act, 15 U.S.C. §§ 1114(1), *1125(a)*. The district court reasoned that WhenU, by "causing pop-up advertisements for Defendant Vision Direct to appear when SaveNow users have specifically attempted to access [1-800]'s website, ... [is] displaying [1-800]'s mark in the ... advertising of ... Vision Direct's services." *1-800 Contacts*, 309 F. Supp. 2d at 489.

The fatal flaw with this holding is that WhenU's pop-up ads do not display the 1-800 trademark. As we explained above, the WhenU pop-up ads appear in a separate window that is prominently branded with the WhenU mark; they have absolutely no tangible effect on the appearance or functionality of the 1-800 website.

More important, the appearance of WhenU's pop-up ad is not contingent upon or related to 1-800's trademark, the trademark's appearance on 1-800's website, or the mark's similarity to 1-800's website address. Rather, the contemporaneous display of the ads and trademarks is the result of the happenstance that 1-800 chose to use a mark similar to its trademark as the address to its web page and to place its trademark on its website. The pop-up ad, which is triggered by the C-user's input of 1-800's website address, would appear even if 1-800's trademarks were not displayed on its website. A pop-up ad could also appear if the C-user typed the 1-800 website address, not as an address, but as a search term in the browser's search engine, and then accessed 1-800's website by using the hyperlink that appeared in the list of search results.

In addition, 1-800's website address is not the only term in the SaveNow directory that could trigger a Vision Direct ad to "pop up" on 1-800's website. For example, an ad could be triggered if a C-user searched for "contacts" or "eye care," both terms contained in the directory, and then clicked on the listed hyperlink to 1-800's website.

Exemplifying the conceptual difficulty that inheres in this issue, the district court's decision suggests that the crux of WhenU's wrongdoing—and the primary basis for the district court's finding of "use"—is WhenU's alleged effort to capitalize on a C-user's specific attempt to access the 1-800 website. As the court explained it,

WhenU.com is doing far more than merely "displaying" Plaintiff's mark. WhenU's advertisements are delivered to a SaveNow user when the user directly accesses Plaintiff's website—thus allowing Defendant Vision Direct to profit from the goodwill and reputation in Plaintiff's website that led the user to access Plaintiff's website in the first place.

1-800 Contacts, 309 F. Supp. 2d at 490. Absent improper use of 1-800's trademark, however, such conduct does not violate the Lanham Act. *See TrafFix Devices, Inc. v. Mktg. Displays, Inc.*, 532 U.S. 23, 29, 149 L. Ed. 2d 164, 121 S. Ct. 1255 (2001). Indeed, it is routine for vendors to seek specific "product placement" in retail stores precisely to capitalize on their competitors' name recognition. WhenU employs this same marketing strategy by informing C-users who have sought out a specific trademarked product about available coupons, discounts, or alternative products that may be of interest to them.

In addition, unlike several other internet advertising companies, WhenU does not "sell" keyword trademarks to its customers or otherwise manipulate which category-related advertisement will pop up in response to any particular terms on the internal directory. In other words, WhenU does not link trademarks to any particular competitor's ads, and a customer cannot pay to have its pop-up ad appear on any specific website or in connection with any particular trademark. *See id.* at 704. Instead, the SaveNow directory terms trigger categorical associations (e.g., www.1800Contacts.com might trigger the category of "eye care"), at which point, the software will randomly select one of the pop-up ads contained in the eye-care category to send to the C-user's desktop.

Perhaps because ultimately 1-800 is unable to explain precisely how WhenU "uses" its trademark, it resorts to bootstrapping a finding of "use" by alleging other elements of a trademark claim. For example, 1-800 invariably refers to WhenU's pop-up ads as "unauthorized" in an effort, it would seem, to establish by sheer force of repetition the element of unauthorized use of a trademark. Not surprisingly, 1-800 cites no legal authority for the proposition that advertisements, software applications, or any other visual image that can appear on a C-user's computer screen must be authorized by the owner of any website that will appear contemporaneously with that image. The fact is that WhenU does not need 1-800's authorization to display a separate window containing an ad any more than Corel would need authorization from Microsoft to display its WordPerfect word-processor in a window contemporaneously with a Word word-processing window. Moreover, contrary to 1-800's repeated admonitions, WhenU's pop-up ads are authorized—if unwittingly—by the C-user who has downloaded the SaveNow software.

CONCLUSION

For the foregoing reasons, we reverse the district court's entry of a preliminary injunction and remand with instructions to (1) dismiss with prejudice 1-800's trademark infringement claims against WhenU, and (2) proceed with 1-800's remaining claims.

Note

Judge Clean uses Tidy brand detergent because it is the only one that does not bother his skin. He is such a clean freak that he has Tidy's website book-marked. He recently downloaded some software that asked if he would allow an advertising plug-in to install on his computer. He agreed. This morning, while surfing the Tidy website, a pop-up came up on his computer for Surf detergent. He promptly closed it, and then walked to the supermarket. He proceeded to the aisle that has Tidy and right next to it on the shelf was Surf. Being a man of only one detergent his whole life, he found himself purchasing another—Surf. He immediately went home to wash his robe. And the next day, he broke out all over and was in horrible pain. Is Judge Clean the victim of an offense? What is it and who is to blame? Was the result initial interest confusion or something greater?

L. "Key Word Density"

J.K. Harris & Co., LLC v. Kassel
253 F. Supp. 2d 1120 (N.D. Cal. 2003)

WILKEN, D.J.

Plaintiff J.K. Harris & Company, LLC moved for a temporary restraining order (TRO) and then a preliminary injunction enjoining Defendants from 1) using the trade name "J.K. Harris" on Defendants' "taxes. com" web site; 2) publishing defamatory, untrue or misleading information about Plaintiff; 3) using HTML code and computer programming techniques to divert Internet users looking for Plaintiff's web site to Defendants' web site; and 4) using any editorial position at Internet directories to promote Defendants' business and interfere with Plaintiff's business. The Court granted Plaintiffs request for a TRO and then, in an Order dated March 22, 2002, the Court granted in part and denied in part Plaintiff's motion for a preliminary injunction. The Court enjoined Plaintiff from "using more of Plaintiff's trade name than is reasonably necessary to identify that it is Plaintiff's services being described" and from making or disseminating certain identified allegedly false statements. March 22, 2002 Order at 21–22. Defendants then requested that they and amicus curie the Electronic Frontier Foundation (EFF) be granted leave to file a motion for reconsideration. The Court granted Defendants' request as to the issues raised by EFF's brief in support of Defendants' request for reconsideration. After considering all of the papers filed by the parties and by the amicus curie, the Court now GRANTS Defendants' motion for reconsideration....

BACKGROUND
A. The Parties

Plaintiff claims to be the largest tax representation and negotiation company in the United States. It specializes in negotiating with the IRS to eliminate or reduce assessed tax liability and to work out favorable payment terms. Defendants are direct competitors with Plaintiff in the business of tax representation.

B. Facts Relevant to False Representation Claims

Both Plaintiff and Defendants advertise their services on the Internet. Plaintiff's universal resource locator (URL) is www.jkharris.com. Defendants' URL is www.taxes.com. Defendants have published on their web site unfavorable information about Plaintiff. Prior to the issuance of the temporary restraining order in this case, Defendants' web site contained a page entitled "JK Harris Employees Tell of Wrongdoing While Complaints Pile Up." On this page, Defendants describe a federal investigation of Plaintiff, criticize Plaintiff's business practices, and republish anonymous statements about Plaintiff from individuals identified as former customers or former employees of Plaintiff. Defendants also solicit information critical of Plaintiff for publication on their web site. Plaintiff contends that numerous statements attributable both to Defendants and to those anonymously contributing to Defendants' web site are false and misleading.

C. Facts Relevant to Consumer Confusion Claim

Many consumers looking for services on the Internet use a "search engine" to identify the URL of the company they are seeking. When a user enters a name into a search engine, the search engine provides a list of web sites that contain that name and, presumably, the information sought by the user. Plaintiff alleges that Defendants have manipulated the web site architecture of taxes.com so that when a consumer searches for Plaintiff's web site, Defendants' web site is among those web sites displayed. Specifically, Plaintiff contends that this was done by a) "creating keyword density" using Plaintiff's trade name and permutations thereof; b) creating "header Tags" and "underline Tags" around sentences that use Plaintiffs trade name; c) using Plaintiff's trade name as a "keyword" in numerous areas of the web site; d) using various "hot links" to web sites with information about Plaintiff.

On October 23 and 24, 2001, Plaintiff conducted a series of searches for the name "JK Harris" on eleven different Internet search engines. In one of eleven searches, Defendants' web site was the first one listed. On most of the searches, a link to Defendants' web site under the title "Complaints about JK Harris Pile Up" was listed among the first ten links. On March 11, 2002, Plaintiff conducted an identical search. Defendants' web site appeared among the first ten web sites listed on all eleven search engines.

D. Editor Position

Defendant Kassel is an editor of the Open Directory Project (ODP). The ODP produces a comprehensive directory of web sites by relying on numerous volunteer editors who rank and decide which web sites are useful resources for the web public.

*　*　*

Discussion
A. Lanham Act

Section 43 of the Lanham Act provides:

> Any person who, on or in connection with any goods or services, or any container for goods, uses in commerce any word, term, name, symbol or device, or any combination thereof, of any false designation of origin, false or misleading description of fact, or false or misleading representation of fact, which (A) is likely to cause confusion or to cause mistake or to deceive as to the affiliation, connection or association of such person with another person, or as to the origin, sponsorship, or approval of his or her goods, services, or commercial activities by

another person … shall be liable in a civil action by any person who believes that he or she is or is likely to be damaged by such act.

15 U.S.C. § 1125.

1. Initial Interest Confusion

The Ninth Circuit has held that "initial interest confusion" is actionable under section 43 of the Lanham Act. Initial interest confusion "occurs when a consumer is lured to a product by its similarity to a known mark, even though the consumer realizes the true identity and origin of the product before consummating a purchase." *Eli Lilly & Co. v. Natural Answers, Inc.*, 233 F.3d 456, 464 (7th Cir. 2000); *see also Brookfield Communications, Inc. v. West Coast Entm't Corp.*, 174 F.3d 1036, 1062 (9th Cir. 1999).

In *Brookfield Communications*, the court enjoined the defendant from using the plaintiff's trademarked term in its HTML code. Although HTML code is not visible to consumers and, therefore, is not likely to cause consumer confusion, the use of trademarked terms in a web site's hidden code "will still result in what is known as initial interest confusion." *Brookfield Communications*, 174 F.3d at 1062. The court reasoned that

> Web surfers looking for Brookfield's "MovieBuff" products who are taken by a search engine to "westcoastvideo.com" will find a database similar enough to "MovieBuff" such that a sizeable number of consumers who were originally looking for Brookfield's product will simply decide to utilize West Coast's offerings instead. Although there is no source confusion in the sense that consumers know they are patronizing West Coast rather than Brookfield, there is nevertheless initial interest confusion in the sense that, by using "moviebuff.com" or "MovieBuff" to divert people looking for "MovieBuff" to its web site, West Coast improperly benefits from the goodwill that Brookfield developed in its mark.

Id.

Plaintiff here alleges that Defendants have constructed the taxes.com web site so that web surfers searching for Plaintiff's web site will be referred to Defendants' web site as well. Plaintiff alleges that Defendants have accomplished this purpose by applying a "strategic combination of computer programming techniques," including excessive uses of Plaintiff's trade name, the use of "header tags" and "underline tags" around sentences containing Plaintiff's trade name, and the use of larger fonts and strategic placement of sentences containing Plaintiff's trade name on Defendants' web site.

The alleged result of Defendants' conduct is that web users who search for Plaintiff's trade name are simultaneously given an opportunity to visit Defendants' web site by clicking on a link that stated, prior to the issuance of the TRO in this action, "Complaints about JK Harris Pile Up." A reasonable consumer would not believe that Plaintiff is the sponsor of this negative publicity, but might choose to investigate these charges by visiting Defendants' web site before securing Plaintiff's tax representation services. Once at www.taxes.com, potential consumers are provided with what Plaintiff alleges are false and misleading comments about Plaintiff's services. Web users might then decide that because of the negative comments about Plaintiff they should secure tax representation services from Defendants, or, they might simply decide that the services offered by Plaintiff and Defendants are sufficiently similar that "it is not worth the trouble" of returning to Plaintiff's web site. *Id.* at 1064.

In this way, Plaintiff alleges that its potential customers may be diverted to Defendants' services. As was the case in *Brookfield Communications*, consumers will immediately realize that they are not patronizing Plaintiff. Nevertheless, the alleged use of Plaintiff's trademark in the HTML code and in the content of Defendants' web site allows Defendants initially to divert Plaintiff's potential consumers to its web site.

Defendants contend that their intent is not to confuse customers, but to warn them about business practices which Defendants contend are harmful to consumers. Defendants argue that their use of Plaintiff's trademark for this purpose is "nominative" use and, therefore, permissible.

* * *

Plaintiffs request for an order enjoining Defendants from using the trade name "J.K. Harris" on their web site or in the HTML code for their web site must be evaluated pursuant to the *New Kids on the Block* three part test.

Defendants' use of the trade name J.K. Harris satisfies all three prongs of the *New Kids on the Block test*. The first prong is met because, like the singing group New Kids on the Block and the company Playboy Enterprises, the tax representation service J.K. Harris is simply "not readily identifiable without use of the mark." *New Kids on the Block*, 971 F.2d at 308. The third prong is met because it is clear from the context of Defendants' web site that Plaintiff has not sponsored or endorsed the information provided there.

While it is a closer question, the second prong of the New Kids on the Block test is also met. That prong requires that "only so much of the mark or marks be used as is reasonably necessary to identify the product or services." 971 F.2d at 308. This requirement derives from a concern that a defendant's use of the plaintiff's mark not exceed its legitimate referential purpose. What is reasonably necessary to identify the plaintiff's products or services differs from case to case. Here, there is no allegation that Defendants used anything other than J.K. Harris's trade name. Rather, Plaintiff complains that Defendants' web pages used its trade name frequently and in a manner designed to call attention to that name, for example by placing it at the beginning of a web page or underlining it. While the evidence submitted to the Court demonstrates that Defendants' web site does contain frequent references to J.K. Harris, these references are not gratuitous; rather, Defendants' web site refers to J.K. Harris by name in order to make statements about it. This referential use of Plaintiff's trade mark is exactly what the nominative fair use doctrine is designed to allow. Similarly, while the evidence submitted to the Court demonstrates that Defendants often made the J.K. Harris name visually obvious, this is not unreasonable, because criticizing J.K. Harris was one of the primary objectives of the web pages. Thus, Defendants' referential use of the J.K. Harris trade name, even though frequent and obvious, satisfies the second prong of the *New Kids on the Block* Test, in that "only so much of the mark or marks [are] used as is reasonably necessary to identify the product or services." *New Kids on the Block*, 971 F.2d at 308.

Because Defendants' use of the J.K. Harris trade name satisfies all three prongs of the *New Kids on the Block* test, Plaintiff has not demonstrated a probability of success on the merits. Therefore, Plaintiff is not entitled to a preliminary injunction limiting Defendants' use of the J.K. Harris trade name.

[The court enjoined the defendant's use of false statements in its web site but held in favor of the defendant regarding keyword density.]

Note

1. Another form of initial interest confusion is banner advertisements keyed to a trademark. When users search a specific term, such as "playboy," other advertisements which

are keyed to those search terms are displayed. This form of banner-keyed advertising may also amount to infringement resulting from the initial confusion created on the part of the user. *See, e.g.,* Playboy Enter. Inc. v. Nestsape Communications Corp, 2004 U.S. App. LEXIS 442 (9th Cir. 2004).

Chapter XIII

International Influences and Harmonization

A. Paris Convention

Paris Convention for the Protection of Industrial Property:

Article 4A(1): Any person who has duly filed an application for ... a trademark, in one of the countries of the Union, or his successors in title, shall enjoy, for the purpose of filing in the other countries, a [six month] right of priority ...

15 U.S.C. §1126 (d), Lanham Act §44(d):

An application for registration of a mark under section 1051, 1053, 1054, or 1091 of this title or under subsection (e) of this section, filed by a person described in subsection (b) of this section who has previously duly filed an application for registration of the same mark in one of the countries described in subsection (b) of this section shall be accorded the same force and effect as would be accorded to the same application if filed in the United States on the same date on which the application was first filed in such foreign country: Provided, That—

(1) the application in the United States is filed within six months from the date on which the application was first filed in the foreign country....

SCM Corp. v. Langis Foods, Ltd.
539 F. 2d 196 (D.C. Cir. 1976)

McGowan, J.

This case presents the issue whether a corporate foreign national, which has applied for a trademark registration in its home country, has priority in registering that trademark in the United States over a domestic corporation when: (1) the foreign national filed a trademark application in its home country without prior use of the trademark in any country; (2) the foreign national subsequently filed a timely application to register the trademark in the United States based upon the earlier application in its home country; (3) the foreign national used the trademark in its home country, but not in the United States prior to filing its United States application; and (4) the domestic corporation used the trademark in the United States *after* the foreign national's home country application was filed but *before* the foreign national's United States application was filed. The District Court concluded that the domestic corporation was entitled to registration of the trademark. 376 F. Supp. 962 (1974). For the reasons set forth below, we reverse.

I

On March 28, 1969, appellant Langis Foods, a Canadian corporation, filed applications to register three trademarks in Canada—APPLE TREE, ORANGE TREE, and LEMON TREE.[1] Shortly thereafter, on May 15, 1969, Langis used these marks in Canada.[2] Appellee SCM Corporation, a domestic corporation, apparently started to use the LEMON TREE trademark in this country on the same day. Both Langis and SCM subsequently applied to the United States Patent Office to register these trademarks: SCM's application, filed on June 18, 1969, requested registration of the LEMON TREE trademark; Langis's application, filed on September 19, 1969, requested registration of three trademarks—LEMON TREE, ORANGE TREE, and APPLE TREE. While these applications were pending in the Patent Office, SCM began using the marks ORANGE TREE and LIME TREE in the United States in June of 1970, and on July 22 of that year applied to the Patent Office to register those marks.

In August of 1971, the Patent Office published Langis's trademarks APPLE TREE and ORANGE TREE in its "Official Gazette" for purposes of opposition. Two months later, the Office issued a registration to Langis for the trademark LEMON TREE. SCM Corporation then instituted oppositions to the APPLE TREE and ORANGE TREE applications, and also filed a petition to cancel the LEMON TREE registration. On May 7, 1973, the Trademark Trial and Appeal Board denied the petition to cancel and dismissed the oppositions on the ground that, pursuant to section 44(d) of the Trademark Act of 1946, "[Langis] is entitled herein as a matter of right to rely upon the filing dates of its Canadian applications, i.e., March 28, 1969, and hence that it possesses superior rights in its marks as against [SCM]." 177 U.S.P.Q. at 719.

SCM then filed a complaint in the District Court seeking to have the LEMON TREE registration canceled and the APPLE TREE and ORANGE TREE registrations denied. The District Court granted SCM's motion for summary judgment on the ground that "prior right in a trademark in the United States depends on priority of use in the United States and is not affected by priority of use in a foreign country." 376 F. Supp. at 967. Since Langis used the marks in Canada but not in the United States, the court canceled the LEMON TREE registration and remanded the proceedings opposing ORANGE TREE and APPLE TREE to the Board. This appeal is taken from that final order.

II

Appellee SCM directs our attention to section 2(d) of the Trademark Act of 1946 (Lanham Act), 15 U.S.C. § 1052(d) (Supp. IV, 1974), which appears to preclude registration of the disputed trademarks by Langis. That section provides that "no trade-mark ... shall be refused registration on the principal register on account of its nature *unless* it—(d) Consists of or comprises a mark which so resembles ... a mark or trade name *previously used*

---

1. The trademarks were to cover dry crystals which, when mixed with water, would produce a fruit beverage. 376 F. Supp. at 964.

2. Canada, unlike the United States, authorizes an applicant to seek registration of a "proposed trademark" before the mark is actually used. § 16(e), Trade Marks Act, Can. Rev. Stat. ch. T-10 (1970). Canadian registration is granted only if a declaration is filed alleging that use of the trademark in Canada has commenced. *Id.* § 39(2); *see* Murrow, *The Concept of "Use" in Canadian Trademark Law*, 65 T.M. REP. 223, 224–25 (1975); Brief for Appellant at 4 n.2. *See generally* Robinson, *The Canadian Trade Marks Act of 1954: A Review of Some of Its Features*, 49 T.M. Rep. 792 (1959).

in the United States by another and not abandoned as to be likely, when applied to the goods of the applicant, to cause confusion, or to cause mistake, or to deceive...." *Id.* (emphasis added). Langis has admitted that SCM was the first to use the marks in the United States, and nowhere suggests that SCM has abandoned them. Therefore, SCM argues, section 2(d) is "*in haec verba* a complete bar to Langis obtaining or maintaining registrations for its marks." Brief at 8 (footnote omitted).

This argument must, however, be evaluated in light of legislative attempts to reconcile differences between the American and foreign systems of trademark registration. In the United States, federal registration under the Lanham Act is generally based upon first use. E.g., §1051(a)(1) (Supp. IV, 1974), 1127 (1970). Canada, however, employs a system which allows registration of a trademark without prior use. *See* note 2 *supra*. Certain provisions of the Lanham Act were designed to provide some protection to trademarks already registered elsewhere by foreign nationals, and Langis relies for protection specifically on section 44(d), which provides in relevant part that a trademark registration application filed by a foreign national "shall be accorded the same force and effect as would be accorded to the same application if filed in the United States on the same date on which the application was first filed in [the] foreign country...." *Id.* § 1126(d) (1970).

Both SCM and Langis recognize that section 44(d) protects trademarks first registered in a foreign country, and the dispute in this case goes only to the precise scope of that statutory protection. SCM contends that section 44(d) gives a foreign applicant a *constructive filing date* in the United States as of the date of the foreign filing; the filing date is important because the party with the later filing date bears the burden of proving that it possesses the prior right to the mark. SCM would concede that it had the burden of proof in this proceeding with respect to the right to register LEMON TREE since its actual filing date was subsequent to Langis's "constructive filing date" of March 28, 1969. The District Court accepted this view of section 44(d), and since Langis admitted that it had not used the mark in the United States, granted summary judgment for SCM. 376 F. Supp. at 967–68.

Appellant Langis offers a second and, in our view, more plausible interpretation of section 44(d). Langis suggests that section 44(d) grants a foreign applicant which has used the trademark in its home country *after* the foreign filing but *prior* to the actual United States filing a *constructive use date* as of the date of the foreign filing. Under this view, Langis would have priority since its constructive use date of March 28, 1969 preceded SCM's actual use date of May 15, 1969.

We think the structure of the Lanham Act reinforces Langis's interpretation of section 44(d). In the first place, section 1 of the Act, 15 U.S.C. § 1051(a)(1) (Supp. IV, 1974), requires an applicant for registration to indicate the date the trademark was first used in commerce in the United States; but foreign nationals applying pursuant to section 44(d) are exempted from that requirement, *id.* § 1126(d)(2) (1970). Moreover, the 1946 Act deals specifically with the protection to be accorded to rights acquired by third parties, and it expressly protects only those "rights acquired by third parties before the date of the filing of the first application in the foreign country...." *Id.* § 1126(d)(3). The Lanham Act also provides that nothing in section 44(d) "shall entitle the owner of a registration granted under ... section [44] to sue for acts committed prior to the date on which his mark was registered in this country unless the registration is based on use in commerce." *Id.* § 1126(d)(4) (emphasis added). The clear implication is that section 44 recognizes a registration based on something other than "use in commerce," namely, a foreign registration. *See id.* § 1126(e).

Finally, there is section 44(b) of the Act, which provides:

> Any person whose country of origin is a party to any convention or treaty relating to trademarks, trade or commercial names, or the repression of unfair competition, to which the United States is also a party, or extends reciprocal rights to nationals of the United States by law, *shall be entitled to the benefits of this section under the conditions expressed herein to the extent necessary to give effect to any provision of such convention, treaty or reciprocal law, in addition to the rights to which any owner of a mark is otherwise entitled by this chapter.*

Id. § 1126(b) (1970) (emphasis added); *see id.* § 1126(c), (e). This intent to give effect to the provisions of applicable treaties and conventions concerning trademarks is further evidenced in section 45 of the Act, which declares that the intent of Congress in enacting the 1946 Act was "to provide rights and remedies stipulated by treaties and conventions respecting trade-marks...." *Id.* § 1127. An examination of the relevant international treaty—the International Convention for the Protection of Industrial Property (the Paris Union Treaty)—resolves whatever doubt we may have concerning the reach of section 44(d).

As revised in London in 1934, Article 4 of the Paris Union Treaty provides:

> A. (1) Any person who has duly applied for ... the registration of a ... trade mark in one of the countries of the Union ... shall enjoy for the purposes of registration in other countries a right of priority during the periods hereinafter stated [six months for trademarks].

> (2) Any filing having the value of a formal national filing by virtue of the internal law of each country of the Union or of international treaties concluded among several countries of the Union shall be recognized as giving rise to a right of priority.

> B. Consequently, *subsequent filing in one of the other countries of the Union before the expiration of these periods shall not be invalidated through any acts accomplished in the interval, as, for instance, by another filing, ... or by use of the trade mark, and these facts cannot give rise to any right of third parties or any personal possession. The rights acquired by third parties before the day of the first application on which priority is based shall be reserved by the internal legislation of each country of the Union.*

53 Stat. 1748, T.S. 941 (emphasis added). This revised version clearly provides that an intervening use during the priority period cannot give rise to rights on the part of third parties. The only rights of third parties specifically protected are "[those] rights acquired by third parties *before* the day of the first application on which priority is based." Thus, to the extent that the property rights in this case depend on the Paris Union Treaty, Article 4 reinforces our conclusion that a foreign applicant's mark must be protected in this country from the date of the foreign application even as against an intervening first use by another in the United States

III

Our holding in this case is that section 44(d) of the Trademark Act of 1946, which implements Article 4 of the Paris Union Treaty, accorded appellant Langis a "right to priority" for the six months following the filing of its Canadian application for registration, that is to say, from March 28, 1969 to September 27, 1969; and that an intervening use in the United States during that period cannot invalidate Langis's right to registration in this country pursuant to an application filed on September 19, 1969. We recognize that section 2(d), ... prohibits registration of a trademark "previously used in the United States by another," 15 U.S.C. § 1052(d) (Supp. IV, 1974), but we cannot read that section in isolation from the context of the rest of the statute. Our task is to endeavor to harmonize and give full effect to both sections 2(d) and 44(d). We need only interpret the word "previously" in section 2(d) to mean "before the filing date in the Convention country" in order to give meaning to both statutory provisions. As our earlier discussion indicates, both the structure of the Act and its legislative history support such an interpretation.

Since in our view Langis is entitled to a valid federal trademark registration, we reverse the decision of the District Court and remand the case with directions to dismiss the complaint.

It is so ordered.

B. TRIPs Agreement

The Trade Related Intellectual Property Aspects of the Uruguay Round of the General Agreement on Tariffs and Trade signed in Marakesh in 1994 (TRIPs Agreement) is arguably the most significant development in international intellectual property law in the last century. In addition to setting out minimum standards for intellectual property protection, for the first time, an international treaty regarding intellectual property also provided for enforcement measures.

Under TRIPs, one country can "sue" another country before a World Trade Organization panel. If successful, the panel can issue specific trade sanctions and all member countries may impose trade sanctions against the offending nation until it is in compliance.

TRIPs requires member nations to provide a minimum level of trademark protection. It also creates an enforcement regime. Finally, TRIPs provides for dispute settlement mechanisms previously lacking in the international field.

Specifically, Article 16.1 of TRIPs requires countries to grant mark owners the exclusive right to use on or in connection with the sale of goods which are the same as or similar to those claimed in the identification of goods in their registration where a competing use would cause a likelihood of confusion.

Additionally, Article 16.2 requires members nations to cancel registrations for famous marks and provide for effective remedies to prevent the use of famous marks.

Consider the following reading from Professor Reichman.

J.H. Reichman, *Universal Minimum Standards of Intellectual Property Protection under the TRIPS Component of the WTO Agreement*
29 Int'l. Law. 345 (1995)*

* * *

A. LOGIC OF THE TRIPS AGREEMENT

Among the many causes of the drive to overcome preexisting territorial limitations on intellectual property rights, two merit attention here. First, the growing capacity of man-

---

ufacturers in developing countries to penetrate distant markets for traditional industrial products has forced the developed countries to rely more heavily on their comparative advantages in the production of intellectual goods than in the past. Second, the rise of knowledge-based industries radically altered the nature of competition and disrupted the equilibrium that had resulted from more traditional comparative advantages. Not only is the cost of research and development often disproportionately higher than in the past, but the resulting innovation embodied in today's high-tech products has increasingly become more vulnerable to free-riding appropriators. Market access for developing countries thus constituted a bargaining chip to be exchanged for greater protection of intellectual goods within a restructured global marketplace.

In response to these challenges, the TRIPS Agreement mandates mostly time-tested, basic norms of international intellectual property law as enshrined in the Paris Convention for the Protection of Industrial Property, last revised in 1967, and the Berne Convention for the Protection of Literary and Artistic Works, last revised in 1971, or in certain domestic institutions, such as laws protecting confidential information, that all developed legal systems recognize in one form or another. It also leaves notable gaps and loopholes that will offset some of the gains accruing from the exercise, especially with respect to nontraditional objects of intellectual property protection. In this respect, "both the strengths and weaknesses of the TRIPS Agreement stem from its essentially backwards-looking character." To the extent that the TRIPS Agreement significantly elevates the level of protection beyond that found in existing conventions, as certainly occurs with respect to patents, for example, the developing countries are usually afforded safeguards that few would have predicted at the outset of the negotiations. Nevertheless, both developed and developing countries guarantee that detailed "enforcement procedures as specified in this [Agreement] are available under their national laws," and they all become liable to dispute-settlement machinery for claims of nullification and impairment of benefits that can lead to cross-sectoral trade sanctions.

B. BASIC PRINCIPLES

Perhaps the most important "basic principle" that applies virtually across the board is that of national treatment of (that is, nondiscrimination against) foreign rights holders. This principle of equal treatment under the domestic laws is then carried over to relations between states in the most-favored-nation (MFN) provisions of article 4. The latter article ostensibly prevents one member country from offering a better intellectual property deal than is required by international law to nationals of a second member country and then denying similar advantages to the nationals of other member countries.

Taken together, the national treatment and MFN provisions attempt to rectify the damage that some states recently inflicted on the international intellectual property system by unilaterally asserting claims of material reciprocity with respect to hybrid legal regimes falling in the penumbra between the Paris and Berne Conventions. In practice, however, certain express limitations could diminish the effectiveness of these basic requirements. For example, while the national treatment and MFN clauses both apply "with regard to the protection of intellectual property," it turns out that, for purposes of the TRIPS Agreement, the term "intellectual property" refers only to seven of the eight subject-matter categories enumerated in sections 1 through 7 of part II. These include (1) copyrights and related rights; (2) trademarks and (3) geographical indications; (4) industrial designs; (5) patents; (6) integrated circuit designs; and (7) trade secrets or confidential information. As regards neighboring rights covered by the International Convention for the Protection of Performers, Producers of Phonograms and Broadcasting Organizations

(Rome Convention), national treatment and the MFN clause apply only to those rights that the TRIPS Agreement selectively provides, but not to rights generally flowing from that Convention.

The precise mesh of these provisions remains to be seen, but the following overall framework seems plausible. First, international intellectual property treaties existing at the time that the TRIPS Agreement takes effect are generally immunized from the MFN clause (but not the national treatment clause except as expressly provided) under a grandfather provision within the TRIPS Agreement, which only this Agreement can override. Second, existing and future agreements establishing "customs unions and free-trade areas" of a regional character may, to varying degrees, be immunized from applying MFN treatment, and possibly national treatment, to some non-TRIPS-man-dated intellectual property measures affecting intra-regional adherents, at least inso-far as past practice under article XXIV of the General Agreement on Tariffs and Trade is carried over to the WTO Agreement and applied to intellectual property rights. Third, states otherwise contemplating unilateral measures to protect intellectual prop-erty rights in the future must generally weigh the costs and benefits of nonreciproc-ity with respect to other WTO member countries, unless the measures contemplated fall outside the seven categories of "intellectual property" recognized by the TRIPS Agreement and outside the residual national treatment clauses of the Paris and Berne Conventions.

Whether any specific measures that were arguably not cognizable under existing con-ventions, such as the European Union's proposed regime to protect electronic data bases or certain levies for private copying of audio and visual recordings like those imple-mented in France, may escape the MFN and national treatment clauses of the TRIPS Agreement will thus depend on a variety of factors. These include evolving state prac-tice with respect to regional trade agreements and the extent to which decision makers interpret "intellectual property" as narrowly defining the seven categories of subject mat-ter to be protected or as broadly defining certain modalities of protection. It may also de-pend on who interprets these clauses, given the uncertain jurisdictional and substantive powers of the WTO panels to be established under binding dispute-resolution proce-dures set out in the TRIPS Agreement. In any event, the drafters seem to have built in some incentives for states contemplating new protectionist measures to seek to address their needs within the framework of ongoing multilateral discussions affecting barriers to trade in general.

Beyond these equal-treatment obligations, states must accord to the nationals of other member states those international minimum standards of intellectual property protection that are comprised within "the treatment provided for in this [TRIPS] Agree-ment." One component of this "TRIPS treatment" consists of the basic substantive pro-visions of the Paris Convention for the Protection of Industrial Property, of the Berne Convention for the Protection of Literary and Artistic Works, and of the Treaty on In-tellectual Property in Respect of Integrated Circuits (IPIC Treaty). The other component consists of minimum standards that the TRIPS Agreement applies irrespective of pre-existing international norms and sometimes at the expense of those norms. In either case, the relevant standards "are integral parts of this WTO Agreement, binding on all members."

The member states have also agreed to recognize certain fundamental objectives and principles, such as the "promotion of technological innovation" and the legitimacy of public interest exceptions to intellectual property rights generally. These provisions, of capital importance for developing countries, are discussed below.

* * *

B. TRADEMARKS, GEOGRAPHICAL INDICATIONS OF ORIGIN, AND ANTICOUNTERFEITING MEASURES

From the international legal standpoint, a formal consensus to regulate both trademarks and geographical indications has long existed under the Paris Convention. For example, this Convention established basic international minimum standards governing priority rights and the imposition of compulsory licenses, and it mandated the independence of marks for purposes of domestic adjudication. In addition, the Paris Convention sets out general provisions concerning the protection of well-known marks; the assignment of marks; the duty of all member countries to protect the integrity of marks registered as such in other member countries; the duty to protect service marks, collective marks, and trade names; and it purports to recognize even a duty to seize imported goods unlawfully bearing trademarks or other false indications of source.

In retrospect, the weakness of the international regime governing trademark protection derived only in part from the failure of key developing countries to adhere to the Paris Convention (or to its later versions), and mainly from the lax enforcement of existing norms that state practice tolerated. For example, states could usually discharge their obligations by enacting the pertinent legislation, without regard to the level of protection actually provided, so long as they respected national treatment. Nor would a state whose judicial or administrative apparatus failed to repress traffic in goods bearing counterfeit marks necessarily violate the Convention, notwithstanding formal commitments to the contrary in articles 9(1) and 10*ter*.

The TRIPS Agreement breaks with this tradition. It augments the minimum standards of protection for trademarks generally and initiates action to establish tough standards for geographic indications of origin. Above all, this Agreement appears to mandate strict enforcement of both old and new substantive norms, and it establishes the necessary legal machinery for this purpose.

1. Trademarks

Besides requiring all WTO member countries to comply with the relevant international minimum standards already set out in the Paris Convention, the TRIPS Agreement establishes a universally valid legal definition of a trademark. It then invests owners of registered marks with the exclusive right to prevent third parties from using similar marks for goods or services when such use would produce a "likelihood of confusion." The trademark owner's exclusive right must last at least seven years after initial registration or after each renewal of registration, and the principle of indefinitely renewable registrations is established for trademarks, but not apparently for service marks.

While states may continue to condition registration—but not the filing of an application for registration—on actual use of a given trademark, cancellation requires "an uninterrupted period of at least three years of non-use," and government actions that hinder such use will not constitute legally valid excuses. Member states can no longer require foreign trademark owners to couple their marks with the indigenous marks of local firms. Nor can they impose compulsory licenses or deny the principle of free assignability of marks with, or without, the business to which they pertain.

Finally, the protection of well-known marks under article 6*bis* of the Paris Convention has been strengthened in at least two ways. First, that article now applies expressly to services. Second, the same provision extends even to dissimilar goods or services when use of a registered mark would likely indicate a harmful connection between those dissimilar goods or services and the owner of the registered mark. Whether U.S. compliance with this provision will require the enactment of a federal dilution statute remains to be seen. In any event, owners of well-known marks will benefit more from the anticounterfeiting measures discussed below than from this back-handed foray into the still controversial theory of dilution.

2. Geographical Indications of Source

Geographical indications identify a good as originating in a particular region, locality, or territory "where a given quality, reputation or other characteristic of the good is essentially attributable to its geographical origin." Article 22 of the TRIPS Agreement appears to institute relatively strong protection against misleading and certain unfair uses of such indications, and article 23 appears to confer even stronger protection for geographical indications pertaining to wines and spirits, which are exempted from the likelihood of confusion test. However, three grandfather clauses retard the attainment of these goals. One such clause exempts those who have already used geographical indications of wines and spirits for at least ten years. A second and broader grandfather clause exempts acquired rights pertaining to trademarks already "applied for or registered in good faith" or to marks "acquired through use in good faith." A third clause exempts geographical indications that have become generic or customary terms in the territories of member states.

The stage has, therefore, been set for mandatory future negotiations "aimed at increasing the protection of individual geographical indications." Given the economic logic of trade negotiations, further progress in this area will probably require offsetting forms of trade compensation for the adversely affected states.

3. Anticounterfeiting Measures

The TRIPS Agreement requires members to provide detailed enforcement procedures, and these procedures must afford rights holders the possibility of obtaining injunctions and provisional measures to prevent infringements. The Agreement also fulfills an earlier goal of the Paris Convention by instituting "Special Requirements Related to Border Control Measures." These provisions enable rights holders to take legal action to require the domestic customs authorities to suspend the release of imported goods into free circulation whenever the complainants have valid grounds for suspecting that the items in question are "counterfeit trademark or pirated copyright goods." For this purpose, "counterfeit trademark goods" are defined as goods or packaging that bear unauthorized trademarks identical or similar to registered marks for such goods; and "pirated copyright goods" are defined as "unauthorized direct copies of protected Articles the making of which would have infringed either copyright law or related rights laws in the country of importation." The seizure provisions would thus apply to sound recordings protected only under a neighboring rights law as well as to more traditional literary and artistic works.

The imposition of border controls to repress imports of counterfeit goods represents one of the most overdue and promising results of the TRIPS exercise, provided that states implement these measures in a genuinely nondiscriminatory fashion and do not erect disguised barriers to trade. However, such measures will succeed only so long as the participating states enforce them vigilantly, and no weak links appear in the chain. To this end, both developed and developing countries will have to curb powerful vested interests.

* * *

Kenneth L. Port, *Trademark Harmonization: Norms, Names and Nonsense*

2 Marq. Intel. Prop. L. Rev. 33 (1998)

* * *

Objectives of Harmonization

Perhaps the most vexing problem in trademark harmonization is the failure to arrive at a workable definition of the word "harmonization." A complete review of the discourse on harmonization of law is beyond the scope of this Comment; however, there is clearly a range of perspectives on precisely what is meant by the term "harmonization." In fact, the objectives of the various perspectives seem to dictate the definition of the term. Therefore, in trademark harmonization, the first question that must be answered is "why do it?" The following might be possible reasons:

> 1. To make all trademark law in the world uniform so that trademark owners know the bounds of protection anywhere in the world by understanding the laws of one country, thereby allowing trademark owners a higher degree of confidence in the worldwide market;

> 2. To "provide an approximation of different rules in order to minimize any conflict that their differences might generate ... not necessarily imply[ing the] replication of rules";[1]

> 3. To create a relationship between things that implies the creation of accord or consonance.

The fact that this provisional determination of objectives appears to be skipped completely by some or glossed over by others seems to imply that we are operating on the presumption that harmonization of trademark laws is, like oatmeal, just the right thing to do. This type of reasoning may work in arguments about nutritious meals, but my curiosity is left unsatisfied. It seems to me that the first step is to articulate goals and objectives, and next, articulate methodologies for satisfying those objectives. It seems that the trademark harmonization debate is focused on methodologies while there has been very little systematic critique of its objectives. It appears that some might be following the erroneous belief that "the greater the intellectual property protection, the greater the progress."

There also appears to be a practical misunderstanding among the advocates of trademark harmonization. It is rather clear that trademark owners appear to believe that the objective of harmonization is No. 1 above, the drafters of the treaties (World Intellectual Property Organization and national governmental agencies) believe the objective is No. 2 above, and many scholars believe the objective is No. 3 above. This disparity leads to disappointment among trademark owners because they perceive the results as frustrating their preferred objectives. Therefore, a more thorough job ought to be done to present the precise objectives of international harmonization of trademark laws and work towards satisfying those objectives rather than satisfying new objectives created after the utopian objectives are not attained.

---

1. Stephen Zamora, *NAFTA and the Harmonization of Domestic Legal Systems: The Side Effects of Free Trade*, 12 Ariz. J. Int'l & Comp. Law 401, 427 (1995).

III.
Names and Norms

Territorial theories of sovereignty severely restrict the notion of one global legal system of trademark law to mirror the one global market place. Markets for goods and services are now worldwide in scope. Unless serious modifications are made to the Internet—such as imposing new domain name addresses which block access to individuals in foreign countries—the Internet will continue to know no boundaries. If some of the proponents of the Internet are correct, in just a few years, much of our purchasing of goods and services will transpire on the Internet via "virtual corporations" and new conflicts will arise to claim tax revenue raised by cyber sales. Therefore, trademark law should be positioned to respond to this reality in a proactive manner rather than in a reactive manner. Certainly, computer technology and use is changing so rapidly that it is difficult yet imperative to predict what trademark jurisprudence will require in the future because rational trademark jurisprudence is so important to international commerce.

However, if we are to reform the territorial theory of sovereignty, it must be replaced with something. Currently, the only recognized alternative to the territorial theory is the universality theory of sovereignty. Taking the argument to its logical extreme, I am not sure I like what I contemplate. It is axiomatic to say that it is very difficult to find common ground between the Civil Law jurisdictions and the Common Law jurisdictions on the issue of the creation of trademark rights. The creation of trademark rights is essentially synonymous with the definition of the right itself. Therefore, on a basic level, the two major legal systems in the world do not share a conceptual understanding of the trademark right itself nor how it originates. Civil Law systems emphasize registration as the key in legitimately protecting identifiers of source or origin; Common Law systems emphasize use as the key in legitimately protecting identifiers of source or origin. Although easily stated, this has some broad ramifications. Regardless of one's view of the conceptual justification for sovereignty, this fact is what keeps the nations of the world apart on trademark rights.

In October of 1994, the United States signed the Trademark Law Treaty (TLT). The TLT essentially defines the maximum procedures any signatory State may require in the trademark application process. The objective of the drafters was to harmonize procedures of trademark application in the various States and not to deal with substantive law (including the definition of the trademark right) at all. At the time of this writing, the TLT had not yet been ratified by Congress. Although most of the provisions of the TLT are consistent with the Lanham Act (and that may be why the United States supported it), there are two specific amendments that would need to be done to the Lanham Act to comply with the terms of the TLT.

First, Section 10 of the Lanham Act would have to be amended to clarify that documents filed with the Patent and Trademark Office (PTO) pursuant to the requirements of TLT Article 11 would be "recorded" for the purposes of Section 10. Currently, the PTO requires that a complete copy of the assignment document be filed for recording. Under the TLT, specifically Article 11(b)(2), only an extract from the assignment document need be recorded as evidence of the change in ownership. To mandate that PTO policy changes in this regard change, an amendment to Section 10 of the Lanham Act would be necessary in order to allow an assignee to file a mere extract of the assignment document rather than the entire document.

Second, Section 9 of the Lanham Act would have to be amended to delete the requirement of continued use as the basis for renewing a registration. Article 13 of the TLT specifically prohibits any member from requiring proof of use as an element necessary for the renewal of a registration. In order to accommodate this provision, Sections 8 and 9 of the Lanham Act would both need to be amended. One proposal under consideration is to allow trademark renewals to issue without proof of continued use but amend Section 8 to require that Continuing Use Affidavits be filed not only between the fifth and sixth years of registration, but also between the ninth and tenth year, nineteenth and twentieth year, etc.

Although not Earth-shattering in their magnitude, these required changes actually are manifestations of the larger issue: in "harmonizing" trademark laws, whose "harmony" should prevail? Should it be the Civil Law understanding of the trademark right or the Common Law understanding? In the TLT, it is rather clear that the Civil Law vision prevails because countries that emphasize use are required to de-emphasize use as a basis for registration and renewal of the trademark right.

The tension between the Civil Law understanding of the trademark right and the Common Law understanding is easily perceivable in just these two rather simple changes needed to comply with the TLT. Although the United States is apparently willing to comply with the TLT and give up the requirement that the renewal applicant prove its continued use of the mark in commerce and thereby amend Section 9 of the Lanham Act; the United States is, in fact, not entirely willing to give in on the notion that rights in the United States are based on use. Therefore, the United States appears to be in search for a creative way to comply with the specific wording of the TLT, but also not change the basic premise upon which trademark rights in the United States are based. To change without changing may be the diplomat's best friend, but how will this impact the cynic's view of international law. If you can change without changing, is it really meaningful? Is it really worth all of the time and effort?

In no way do I mean to be interpreted as being xenophobic nor ultra-nationalistic. At this point, I only intend to remind readers that there are two conceptual justifications of the trademark right recognized by industrialized nations today: base the protection on use or base the protection on registration. It seems to me that attempts at "harmonizing" the laws to date have favored the Civil Law perspective over the Common Law perspective.

This brings us back to the definition of "harmonization" and its objectives and perhaps the exact opposite side of this issue. Cynically stated, perhaps a fourth objective should be to "make everyone else in the world change their trademark law so that the United States will be proven to be the "right' system and will not have to spend time, money, energy changing its laws." In fact, I think this perspective at least subconsciously effects most of the trademark treaty drafters, American and European alike. I do not mean to imply that it is necessarily intentional. That would impugn the individual persons engaged in the effort and challenge their credibility. I intend no such unseemly charge. Rather, it seems that because the world is bifurcated along these lines, individuals doing the actual drafting would naturally have biases and values that would be evident in their drafting of the treaties. In fact, the Madrid Agreement is rather biased in its approach to these issues. So biased, in fact, that all applications filed under the Madrid Agreement have to be in French.

On the other hand, I do specifically mean to state that when the TLT or other trademark law treaties are debated before the United States Congress for ratification, the analysis will focus on xenophobic perceptions and will attempt to modify the world outlook to be more like ours rather than the converse. This competitive attitude, of course, completely defeats the purpose of harmonization, yet it appears to prevail.

If this polarization is based merely on xenophobia, it is, naturally inappropriate. If, on the other hand, there is more to this—enough to keep the two sides apart—then study and analysis is needed to understand the underlying cause. Most importantly, ignoring the reasons for this polarization will most likely doom any attempts to "harmonize" the two perspectives.

Regardless of the definition of harmonization or its objectives, to be effective harmonization must take into consideration the fact that various cultures perceive "law" in different and sometimes inconsistent ways. Most Americans view law as a rigid, legal-rational concept where penalties are applied to violators and if penalties are not applied to violators the underlying legitimacy of the law itself as law is challenged. Other cultures, such as Japan, perceive law as more of a standard or aspiration that is to be striven for. Violation of the "law" in this case may result in penalty, but the penalty itself is less severe than might be expected because a lenient penalty is much more likely to result in compliance in the future than a harsh one. Therefore, strict and rigid application of penalties in such cultures may actually have the opposite intended effect.

This is applicable in trademark law harmonization as well. What will the result of the Madrid Protocol or the Trademark Law Treaty be on the individual legal cultures and social cultures in the various signatory as well as non-signatory States?. Indeed, in my mind, it is the principal unanswered question in the debate on trademark harmonization today.

It seems paradoxical to, on one hand, argue that the world market on the Internet for goods and services has become one and it no longer recognizes national boundaries and that therefore a one, unitary, harmonized trademark legal regime is necessary. And then, on the other hand, to ignore the effect that such a regime might have on indigenous legal and social cultures of the world. If the market for goods and services has become so unified that a unitary trademark system is necessary, does that mean that a unified world legal and social culture must also follow? And, perhaps equally importantly, does that culture have to be American or even European, for that matter?

Because each country has its own unique legal culture, it is rather optimistic to presume that the exact language of any treaty will be interpreted and applied the same in all countries. Therefore, in order to achieve harmonization on something other than theoretical grounds, the application of the laws must be harmonized in each jurisdiction as well. As the United States' response to the TLT as described above demonstrates, each country will interpret treaties according to their own legal culture and to suit their own political ends. As Justice Scalia unfortunately once observed, representing how Americans generally perceive the role of international law, "we must always remember it is the U.S. Constitution which we are espousing." In other words, there is a rather vocal contingency of Americans who are currently not persuaded that international law is legitimately law in the first place. Although it may not be truly necessary to respond to Scalia-esque attacks on the validity of international law, it would add to its practical significance to trademark owners and its overall legitimacy if something other than theoretical objectives (perhaps Objective No. 3 above) was achieved.

Therefore, harmonizing trademark law by agreeing on one or two treaties is simply not enough to effect the perceived needed change regardless of the objectives one pursues. The application of those treaties at home must also be harmonized or they will be rendered rather banal in their reality. The best example of this is here in the United States itself where we can agree to scrap our adherence to use as a requirement for renewal of a trademark registration in Section 9 of the Lanham Act but simultaneously religiously adhere to use as a requirement for maintenance of the trademark registration in Section 8 of the Lanham Act and still perceive ourselves as being in complete compliance with the Trademark Law Treaty. If that is, in fact, possible, I ponder whether it was all worth it.

Of course, it may also be paradoxical but also axiomatic that this "wiggle room" assures that more countries will actually sign and then ratify treaties in the first place. If the treaty allows for each country to define for itself when it is in compliance, more countries will ratify treaties and the legitimacy of international law will be maintained because more countries will be playing by the same apparent rules and in compliance with those rules. Circular as that might be, that is basically the argument. To be sure, a flexible treaty is much more likely to be signed and ratified in the United States as well as other countries than a rigid one that demands strict compliance. However, this ability to "interpret" the treaty also provides a mechanism by which countries can avoid strict compliance or interpret anew precisely what was intended by the treaty.

In other words, to achieve its highest subscription rate, treaties must be flexible in nature and therefore many, including the Trademark Law Treaty and the Madrid Protocol, are flexible. Notice that the Madrid Agreement is not flexible. This might explain why it is undersubscribed. However, this itself ensures that the words on the page may be harmonized but that outcomes will probably not be, as these precise words are applied in various countries in order to reach different, if not inconsistent outcomes.

Therefore, in order to have harmonized outcomes, the legal cultures of the various States must also be harmonized. This, I think, is where the alternatives to the territorial theory of sovereignty in international trademark law find their largest conceptual hurdle. Harmonizing substantive trademark law is one thing, actually harmonizing its application among participating and non-participating States raises entirely new issues.

The first issue is defining or agreeing whose legal culture is the "correct" culture. Answering this question is, of course, impossible. The answer will be whatever country is the politically, economically, or militarily dominant one. However, the fact that one country may be politically, economically and/or militarily dominant does not in and of itself mean that its legal culture as it interprets international trademark laws is normatively the correct one.

In 1982 the political scientist Emily S. Rosenberg argued that much of American foreign aid before World War II was motivated by American cultural expansionism. Her well respected argument was that if a country received American aid, it also received American values, and American notions of democracy and Christianity. Rosenberg argued that foreign aid was not separable from values. If you received American foreign aid, you likely also received American values. I would extend that to say that interpretation and application of laws are not separable from the values of the drafters. It appears to me that if we attempt to harmonize legal cultures around the world just so that one trademark law applies equally and consistently around the world, we are risking the same type of cultural expansionism the Rosenberg identified in the pre-WWII era.

To me, there are two real problems with this. First, it creates the danger of one legal culture dominating others and dictating how others should be. It also makes for a less diverse world and therefore a much less interesting place to be. I will admit that, as a Comparativist, this view is self-serving. However, it is precisely these distinct legal cultures that make the world so interesting. It would be a shame to obliterate that just to satisfy the complaints of trademark owners.

That is, my primary concern is that universality theories of sovereignty as applied in international trademark law harmonization would lead to (or at least suggest) a homogeneous world culture.

* * *

Note

Should there be a new round of TRIPs negotiations? TRIPs is considered a treaty that codifies the least common denominator of trademark law. Many countries had to significantly amend their trademark laws to come into compliance with the treaty, but most of the developed countries had to do very little. Should we now push for a new treaty on trademarks? Should we now come to a conclusion about how trademarks are secured in any given country? That is, should we finally choose if it will a use-based system or a registration-based system for the world's individual countries? What of a truly international system where one registration in the world protects marks in all countries of the world notwithstanding any registration fraud in these other countries? Is that ever going to be possible? Is that ever going to be desirable?

C. Madrid Protocol

The so-called "Madrid System" provides a mechanism by which trademarks can simultaneously be registered in multiple countries. Two different international treaties constitute the Madrid System: the Madrid Agreement Concerning the International Registration of Marks ("Madrid Agreement") which took effect in 1891 and the Protocol Relating to the Madrid Agreement ("Madrid Protocol") which took effect in 1996.

The United States never ratified the Madrid Agreement and therefore American trademark users cannot take advantage of its procedures. The Madrid Protocol was ratified by the United States and took effect on November 2, 2003.

Under the Madrid Agreement, trademark applicants file an application with their home patent office. This office becomes known as the "Office of Origin". After a brief procedural review, the Office of Origin forwards the application on to WIPO. WIPO then issues an "international registration." Of course, this international registration is not what the title implies. Rather, this document is forwarded to each individual country where the applicant desires trademark rights. Each individual patent office retains final jurisdiction over the registrability of each trademark. Although WIPO retains a searchable database of all so-called international registrations, they have no substantive value in and of themselves. Each patent office retains the sovereign right to grant or deny a trademark application.

The principal justification for the Madrid Agreement is that applicants would recognize a significant savings in both time and money over filing individually in each country without the international registration. To file in most countries, each applicant needs (or at least it is highly recommended that they employ) a local counsel. Local counsels can be expensive and difficult to manage from afar. Various horror stories are told of local counsel who register trademarks in their name rather than their client's name. In Civil Law systems, trademark rights subsist in the entity that registered the mark, not who used the mark first. Although all Civil Law countries have procedures to recover a trademark registered by another through fraud, it is time consuming and expensive. Therefore, an international trademark registration system is clearly needed.

The Madrid Agreement is largely seen as a failure, however, because after more than 100 years, only 52 countries have joined. The United States and Japan refused to join.

The United States objected to the Madrid Agreement for several reasons. First, all communications, applications, and responses under the Madrid Agreement have to be in French. The English language is not allowed. When the United States is the Office of Origin, this would mean that the USPTO would have to be communicating with WIPO in French. This was perceived as too much of a burden for the USPTO.

Second, the United States objected to the concept of "central attack" under the Madrid Agreement. Under central attack, if the trademark registration in the Original Office is cancelled for any reason in the first five years of registration, the international registration and any rights derived therefrom are extinguished. This means that if a trademark registration with the Office of Origin of France, for example, is registered under the Madrid Agreement also in Luxemburg, if the trademark is cancelled in France, the Luxemburg registration is also cancelled. This concern over the central attack was a primary objection of both the United States and Japan.

Several other procedural objections raised by the most developed nations of the world, and the fact that only 52 countries had ratified the Madrid Agreement after over a 100 years, led to the related, but separate, agreement known as the Madrid Protocol.

The Madrid Protocol retains the basic system of the Madrid Agreement. That is, trademark applications are filed with one specific patent or trademark office, those applications are forwarded on to WIPO and then to the countries designated by the trademark applicant. That is, the basic notion of territoriality is preserved. Each trademark application is reviewed by each patent or trademark office and each registration exists pursuant to the laws of each individual country.

The Madrid Protocol was responsive to the primary issues raised above. First, all documents may be filed in either French or English. Second, the concept of central attack was revised. Under the Madrid Protocol, if a registrant's trademark is cancelled in the Office of Origin in the first five years of registration, other registrations obtained based on the international registration are not automatically cancelled. Rather, under the Madrid Protocol, such marks may be "transformed" to local, domestic registrations and remain in full force and effect. Finally, the Madrid Agreement required trademark users to obtain an actual registration before the international registration would issue. The Madrid Protocol now allows for the issuance of the international registration based on the application in the Office of Origin rather than the registration.

The Madrid Protocol became effective in the United States on November 2, 2003. As such, it is too early to tell the long-term effect of the Protocol. It appears that the Madrid Protocol may have the effect of saving trademark applicants some money.

As of this writing, there were 75 Contracting Parties, or member nations, to the Protocol. See http://www.wipo.int/treaties/en/ShowResults.jsp?lang=en&treaty_id=8. Although proponents of the Madrid Protocol continually point to the cost savings that the system will provide, this may not necessarily be the result in many cases. The cost saving will occur only if there is a flawless prosecution in each country's national office. If an objection is raised or an opposition filed, then the cost savings will be quickly lost, and conceivably a company may have to pay more money to protect its mark in that country than if they had just filed through that country's national system.

Compare the numbers. Filing one international application with the USPTO through the Madrid Protocol, designating France, England, Japan, and Australia would cost $1,356 for the most basic trademark available. The cost of filing individually in each of those countries would be approximately $6,287. Calculating the fees for foreign trademark protection in individual countries is intensely complicated, especially when you have to factor in professional fees. Although this figure contemplates miscellaneous foreseeable costs (translation, courier, etc.), it does not include the anticipated costs (hidden fees, fee differences from firm to firm, dealing with other PTO inquiries, etc.) of the domestic lawyer's work as an intermediary; which are, of course, inestimable and could potentially be immense. Without calculating the domestic lawyer's fees, the Protocol filing would produce a cost saving of $4,931.

What if the international registration or application fails? If a domestic company still wants to take advantage of those foreign markets after its application through the Protocol is rejected, it would then have to file individual applications in each of the four countries. This would result not only in a loss of $1,356 that was already spent on the Protocol filling, but it would also mean that the company would be forced to expend an additional $6,287 to secure the foreign trademark protection it desires. That would mean that the company would have to spend $7,643 minimum.

Therefore, on one hand, filing under the Protocol appears to result in a significant savings. However, practitioners report that, on average, approximately 50% of initial trademark applications are initially rejected by respective patent or trademark offices (depending upon the country). These rejections may be for rather simple, procedural reasons or for more substantive reasons. Regardless of the reason, if initially rejected, the trademark applicant even if filed originally under the Madrid Protocol will still have to hire local counsel to respond to the office action. Taking this into consideration, it remains to be seen whether or not a trademark applicant will recognize an aggregate savings of time and money, or whether or not the Madrid Protocol will actually add to the cost of registering a mark in numerous countries.

One aspect of the Madrid Protocol where real savings may be realized is in the renewal process. To renew a trademark filed under the Protocol, an applicant need only request a renewal of the International Registration. If the International Registration is renewed, all trademarks in all jurisdictions are renewed.

The real question for the Madrid Protocol is not really whether or not it will be a huge financial and time savings to trademark applicants. The real question is whether or not the Madrid Protocol is a stepping stone to a true international trademark registration system based on universality (where the entire world is considered one jurisdiction with all rights in all countries stemming from one registration). The current system based on territoriality may have reached its limit with the Madrid Protocol. What would you recommend as the next step? Consider the following excerpts of a paper submitted to my International and Comparative Intellectual Property Law class.

Experience with the Madrid Protocol
Adam Kibort and Paul Godfread

I. Introduction

For a majority of countries currently participating in the Madrid System, refusals to register or even office actions are less common than one might think. "During the first two years following the implementation of the Madrid Protocol on April 1, 1996, France accepted 96% of international registrations designating it, Germany 76%, Norway 74%, the Russian Federation 66% and Switzerland 81%. The highest rate of refusals comes from Spain, which refuses 51% of registrations designating it. An international registration designates on average 12 countries with over 40% of international registrations receiving no refusals at all." Although these numbers seem promising, they may be deceiving. The numbers are more likely the result of lenient examination processes on the part of the target countries. The U.S., for example, has more stringent examination requirements that a trademark applicant must meet. That is, the USPTO requires a narrow description of goods and services to receive protection. Many European countries permit broader descriptions of goods and services and provide applicants greater worldwide coverage. Because the U.S. is an anomaly in terms of its common law system, requirements such as use or bona fide intent to use the trademark in commerce would not present problems for civil law systems.

II. Experiences with the Madrid System

The remainder of this paper will focus on the experiences of other countries with the Madrid System, as well as the experiences of the U.S. since its accession Nov. 2, 2003.

WIPO Information from 2006

Through the Madrid System (Agreement and Protocol), WIPO received 36,471 trademark applications in 2006. In the same year, 37,224 trademark registrations and 15,205 trademark renewals were recorded in the International Trademark Register. The largest user of the Madrid System was Germany with 6,552 international applications (18.0% share of Madrid applications), followed by France with 3,148 (10.7%), the United States with 3,148 (8.6%), and Italy with 3,086 (8.5%).

These statistics are not all that surprising, considering both Germany and France are original members of the 1891 Madrid Agreement. However, the gap between these two countries and other economically significant countries is still wide, but narrowing each year.

Economically Developed Countries

Country	1999	2000	2001	2002	2003	2004	2005	2006
Germany	5,841	6,049	5,753	5,158	4,999	4,753	5,845	6,049
France	3,776	3,950	3,689	3,406	3,281	2,959	3,706	3,916
UK	296	457	561	622	599	722	980	1,098
Japan	N.A.	144	261	240	314	465	890	938
Australia	N.A.	N.A.	31	224	262	469	846	1,068[2]

The top twenty filers of international trademark applications under the Madrid system in 2006 were Lidl (Germany), Novartis (Switzerland), Janssen Pharmaceutica (Belgium), Henkel (Germany), Nestlé (Switzerland), Siemens (Germany), Aldi (Germany), Unilever (Netherlands), Bosch (Germany), Plus (Germany), Beiersdorf (Germany), TUI (Germany), Biofarma (France), L'Oréal (France), Philips (Netherlands), Sony Ericsson Mobile Communications (Sweden), Boehringer Ingelheim (Germany), Abercrombie & Fitch Trading Co. (USA) (the first American company to ever feature in the top 20), Coscentra (Netherlands) and Hofer (Austria).

Source: http://www.wipo.int/pressroom/en/articles/2007/article_0017.html

The United Kingdom, which joined the Madrid System in 1996, has not been a heavy user of the System. Similarly, Japan, which joined the Protocol in 2000, has not enjoyed much success with Madrid Protocol applications—instead, trademark filers tend to be more cautious about abandoning national filings in favor of Protocol filings. Furthermore, ac-

---

2. WIPO Gazette of International Marks; Statistical Supplement for 2006. Found at http://www.wipo.int/export/sites/www/madrid/en/statistics/pdf/summary2006.pdf.

cording to the Japan Patent Office, it does not appear that Japanese trademark owners have been quick to jump on board the Protocol System and register their marks internationally. This seems strange considering Japan's strong presence in the global marketplace and world economy.

Japan registrations in specific countries based on the Madrid Protocol are as follows:

Country	2000	2001	2002	2003	2004	2005	2006
Australia	N.A.	9	95	99	205	295	350
France	491	933	869	845	916	1,155	1,233
UK	114	289	266	250	352	458	508[3]

U.S. Experience

Prospects for growth of the Madrid system are promising, owing to the fact that the United States, the country with the largest trademark activity in the world, is now a member of the Madrid Protocol. However, examining the USPTO data, it appears that U.S. companies are slow to embrace the Madrid system. Since joining the Madrid system in 2003, U.S applications have grown and it is now the third largest user of the Madrid system. However, it is still represents a small portion of all U.S. trademarks. In fiscal year 2006, the USPTO received 275,790 trademark applications and granted 147,118 registrations. The 3,148 applications WIPO received with the United States as the country of origin is a small fraction by comparison.[4]

Madrid Applications Report

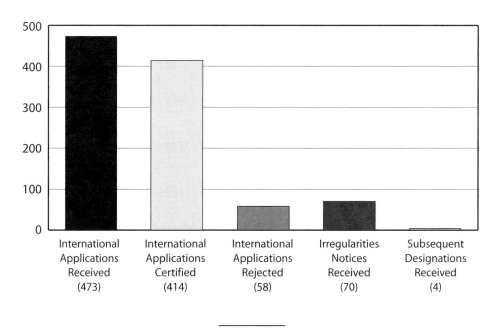

| International Applications Received (473) | International Applications Certified (414) | International Applications Rejected (58) | Irregularities Notices Received (70) | Subsequent Designations Received (4) |

---

3. Japan Patent Office Annual Report, http://www.jpo.go.jp/cgi/linke.cgi?url=/shiryou_e/toukei_e/annual_re_st2003.htm.

Updated Source: Japan Patent Office Annual Report, 2007 Statistical Data http://www.jpo.go.jp/shiryou_e/toushin_e/kenkyukai_e/pdf/annual_report2007/part5.pdf.

4. http://www.uspto.gov/web/offices/com/annual/2006/50300_workloadtables.html.
http://www.wipo.int/export/sites/www/madrid/en/statistics/pdf/summary2006.pdf.

D. Extraterritoriality

Steele v. Bulova Watch Co.
344 U.S. 280 (1952)

MR. JUSTICE CLARK delivered the opinion of the Court.

The issue is whether a United States District Court has jurisdiction to award relief to an American corporation against acts of trade-mark infringement and unfair competition consummated in a foreign country by a citizen and resident of the United States. Bulova Watch Company, Inc., a New York corporation, sued Steele, petitioner here, in the United States District Court for the Western District of Texas. The gist of its complaint charged that "Bulova," a trade-mark properly registered under the laws of the United States, had long designated the watches produced and nationally advertised and sold by the Bulova Watch Company; and that petitioner, a United States citizen residing in San Antonio, Texas, conducted a watch business in Mexico City where, without Bulova's authorization and with the purpose of deceiving the buying public, he stamped the name "Bulova" on watches there assembled and sold. Basing its prayer on these asserted violations of the trade-mark laws of the United States, Bulova requested injunctive and monetary relief. Personally served with process in San Antonio, petitioner answered by challenging the court's jurisdiction over the subject matter of the suit and by interposing several defenses, including his due registration in Mexico of the mark "Bulova" and the pendency of Mexican legal proceedings thereon, to the merits of Bulova's claim. The trial judge, having initially reserved disposition of the jurisdictional issue until a hearing on the merits, interrupted the presentation of evidence and dismissed the complaint "with prejudice," on the ground that the court lacked jurisdiction over the cause. This decision rested on the court's findings that petitioner had committed no illegal acts within the United States. With one judge dissenting, the Court of Appeals reversed; it held that the pleadings and evidence disclosed a cause of action within the reach of the Lanham Trade-Mark Act of 1946, 15 U. S. C. § 1051 *et seq*. The dissenting judge thought that "since the conduct complained of substantially related solely to acts done and trade carried on under full authority of Mexican law, and were confined to and affected only that Nation's internal commerce, [the District Court] was without jurisdiction to enjoin such conduct." We granted certiorari, 343 U.S. 962.

[1]

Petitioner concedes, as he must, that Congress in prescribing standards of conduct for American citizens may project the impact of its laws beyond the territorial boundaries of the United States. Resolution of the jurisdictional issue in this case therefore depends on construction of exercised congressional power, not the limitations upon that power itself. And since we do not pass on the merits of Bulova's claim, we need not now explore every facet of this complex and controversial Act.

The Lanham Act, on which Bulova posited its claims to relief, confers broad jurisdictional powers upon the courts of the United States. The statute's expressed intent is "to regulate commerce within the control of Congress by making actionable the deceptive and misleading use of marks in such commerce; to protect registered marks used in such commerce from interference by State, or territorial legislation; to protect persons engaged in such commerce against unfair competition; to prevent fraud and deception in such commerce by the use of reproductions, copies, counterfeits, or colorable imitations of registered marks; and to provide rights and remedies stipulated by treaties and conventions respecting trade-marks, trade names, and unfair competition entered into between the United States and foreign nations." § 45, 15 U.S.C. § 1127. To that end, § 32 (1) holds liable in a civil action by a trade-mark registrant "any person who shall, in commerce," infringe a registered trade-mark in a manner there detailed. "Commerce" is defined as "all commerce which may lawfully be regulated by Congress." § 45, 15 U. S. C. § 1127. The district courts of the United States are granted jurisdiction over all actions "arising under" the Act, § 39, 15 U.S.C. § 1121, and can award relief which may include injunctions, "according to the principles of equity," to prevent the violation of any registrant's rights. § 34, 15 U.S.C. § 1116.

The record reveals the following significant facts which for purposes of a dismissal must be taken as true: Bulova Watch Company, one of the largest watch manufacturers in the world, advertised and distributed "Bulova" watches in the United States and foreign countries. Since 1929, its aural and visual advertising, in Spanish and English, has penetrated Mexico. Petitioner, long a resident of San Antonio, first entered the watch business there in 1922, and in 1926 learned of the trade-mark "Bulova." He subsequently transferred his business to Mexico City and, discovering that "Bulova" had not been registered in Mexico, in 1933 procured the Mexican registration of that mark. Assembling Swiss watch movements and dials and cases imported from that country and the United States, petitioner in Mexico City stamped his watches with "Bulova" and sold them as such. As a result of the distribution of spurious "Bulovas," Bulova Watch Company's Texas sales representative received numerous complaints from retail jewelers in the Mexican border area whose customers brought in for repair defective "Bulovas" which upon inspection often turned out not to be products of that company. Moreover, subsequent to our grant of certiorari in this case the prolonged litigation in the courts of Mexico has come to an end. On October 6, 1952, the Supreme Court of Mexico rendered a judgment upholding an administrative ruling which had nullified petitioner's Mexican registration of "Bulova."

On the facts in the record we agree with the Court of Appeals that petitioner's activities, when viewed as a whole, fall within the jurisdictional scope of the Lanham Act. This Court has often stated that the legislation of Congress will not extend beyond the boundaries of the United States unless a contrary legislative intent appears. The question thus is "whether Congress intended to make the law applicable" to the facts of this case. *Ibid*. For "the United States is not debarred by any rule of international law from governing the conduct of its own citizens upon the high seas or even in foreign countries when the rights of other nations or their nationals are not infringed. With respect to such an exercise of authority there is no question of international law, but solely of the purport of the municipal law which establishes the duty of the citizen in relation to his own government." *Skiriotes* v. *Florida*, 313 U.S. 69, 73 (1941). As MR. JUSTICE MINTON, then sitting on the Court of Appeals, applied the principle in a case involving unfair methods of competition: "Congress has the power to prevent unfair trade practices in foreign commerce by citizens of the United States, although some of the acts are done outside the territorial limits of the United States." *Branch* v. *Federal Trade Commission*, 141 F.2d 31, 35 (1944). Nor has this Court in tracing the commerce scope of statutes differentiated between enforcement of legislative policy by the Government itself or by private litigants proceeding under a statutory right. The public policy subserved is the same in each case. In the light of the broad jurisdictional grant in the Lanham Act, we deem its scope to encompass petitioner's activities here. His operations and their effects were not confined within the territorial limits of a foreign nation. He bought component parts of his wares in the United States, and spurious "Bulovas" filtered through the Mexican border into this country; his competing goods could well reflect adversely on Bulova Watch Company's trade reputation in markets cultivated by advertising here as well as abroad. Under similar factual circumstances, courts of the United States have awarded relief to registered trademark owners, even prior to the advent of the broadened commerce provisions of the Lanham Act. Even when most jealously read, that Act's sweeping reach into "all commerce which may lawfully be regulated by Congress" does not constrict prior law or deprive courts of jurisdiction previously exercised. We do not deem material that petitioner affixed the mark "Bulova" in Mexico City rather than here, or that his purchases in the United States when viewed in isolation do not violate any of our laws. They were essential steps in the course of business consummated abroad; acts in themselves legal lose that character when they become part of an unlawful scheme."In such a case it is not material that the source of the forbidden effects upon … commerce arises in one phase or another of that program." *Mandeville Island Farms* v. *American Crystal Sugar Co.*, 334 U.S. 219, 237 (1948). In sum, we do not think that petitioner by so simple a device can evade the thrust of the laws of the United States in a privileged sanctuary beyond our borders.

American Banana Co. v. *United Fruit Co.*, 213 U.S. 347 (1909), compels nothing to the contrary. This Court there upheld a Court of Appeals' affirmance of the trial court's dismissal of a private damage action predicated on alleged violations of the Sherman Act. The complaint, in substance, charged United Fruit Company with monopolization of the banana import trade between Central America and the United States, and with the instigation of Costa Rican governmental authorities to seize plaintiff's plantation and produce in Panama. The Court of Appeals reasoned that plaintiff had shown no damage from the asserted monopoly and could not found liability on the seizure, a sovereign act of another nation. This Court agreed that a violation of American laws could not be grounded on a foreign nation's sovereign acts. Viewed in its context, the holding in that case was not meant to confer blanket immunity on trade practices which radiate unlawful consequences here, merely because they were initiated or consummated outside the territorial limits of the United States. Unlawful effects in this country, absent in the posture of the *Banana* case before us, are often decisive; this Court held as much in *Thomsen* v. *Cayser*, 243 U.S. 66 (1917), and United States v. *Sisal Sales Corp.*, 274 U.S. 268 (1927). As in *Sisal*, the crux of the complaint here is "not merely of something done by another government at the instigation of private parties;" petitioner by his "own deliberate acts, here and elsewhere, … brought about forbidden results within the United States." 274 U.S., at 276. And, unlike the *Banana* case, whatever rights Mexico once conferred on petitioner its courts now have decided to take away.

Nor do we doubt the District Court's jurisdiction to award appropriate injunctive relief if warranted by the facts after trial. 15 U. S. C. §§ 1116, 1121. Mexico's courts have nullified the Mexican registration of "Bulova"; there is thus no conflict which might afford petitioner a pretext that such relief would impugn foreign law. The question, therefore, whether a valid foreign registration would affect either the power to enjoin or the propriety of its exercise is not before us. Where, as here, there can be no interference with the sovereignty of another nation, the District Court in exercising its equity powers may command persons properly before it to cease or perform acts outside its territorial jurisdiction

Affirmed.

MR. JUSTICE BLACK took no part in the decision of this case.

DISSENT BY: MR. JUSTICE REED

DISSENT: MR. JUSTICE REED, with whom MR. JUSTICE DOUGLAS joins, dissenting.

The purpose of the Lanham Act is to prevent deceptive and misleading use of trademarks. § 45, 15 U. S. C. § 1127. To further that purpose the Act makes liable in an action by the registered holder of the trade-mark "any person who shall, in commerce," infringe such trade-mark. § 32 (1), 15 U. S. C. § 1114. "Commerce" is defined as being "all commerce which may lawfully be regulated by Congress." § 45, 15 U. S. C. § 1127.

The Court's opinion bases jurisdiction on the Lanham Act. In the instant case the only alleged acts of infringement occurred in Mexico. The acts complained of were the stamping of the name "Bulova" on watches and the subsequent sale of the watches. There were purchases of assembly material in this country by petitioners. Purchasers from petitioners in Mexico brought the assembled watches into the United States. Assuming that Congress has the power to control acts of our citizens throughout the world, the question presented is one of statutory construction: Whether Congress intended the Act to apply to the conduct here exposed.

"The canon of construction which teaches that legislation of Congress, unless a contrary intent appears, is meant to apply only within the territorial jurisdiction of the United States, *Blackmer v. United States*, [284 U.S. 421], 437, is a valid approach whereby unexpressed congressional intent may be ascertained." *Foley Bros., Inc. v. Filardo*, 336 U.S. 281, 285. Utilizing this approach, does such a contrary intent appear in the Lanham Act? If it does, it appears only in broad and general terms, *i. e.*, "to regulate commerce within the control of Congress...." § 45, 15 U. S. C. § 1127. Language of such nonexplicit scope was considered by the Court in construing the Sherman Act in *American Banana Co. v. United Fruit Co.*, 213 U.S. 347, 357. "Words having universal scope, such as 'Every contract in restraint of trade,' 'Every person who shall monopolize,' etc., will be taken as a matter of course to mean only every one subject to such legislation, not all that the legislator subsequently may be able to catch." The *American Banana Co.* case confined the Sherman Act in its "operation and effect to the territorial limits over which the lawmaker has general and legitimate power." 213 U.S., at 357. This was held to be true as to acts outside the United States, although the parties were all corporate citizens of the United States subject to process of the federal courts.

The generally phrased congressional intent in the Lanham Act is to be compared with the language of the Fair Labor Standards Act which we construed in *Vermilya-Brown Co. v. Connell*, 335 U.S. 377. There we held that by explicitly stating that the Act covered "possessions" of the United States, Congress had intended that the Act was to be in effect in all "possessions" and was not to be applied merely in those areas under the territorial jurisdiction or sovereignty of the United States.

There are, of course, cases in which a statement of specific contrary intent will not be deemed so necessary. Where the case involves the construction of a criminal statute "enacted because of the right of the Government to defend itself against obstruction, or fraud ... committed by its own citizens," it is not necessary for Congress to make specific provisions that the law "shall include the high seas and foreign countries." *United States v. Bowman*, 260 U.S. 94, 98. This is also true when it is a question of the sovereign power of the United States to require the response of a nonresident citizen. *Blackmer v. United States*, 284 U.S. 421. A similar situation is met where a statute is applied to acts committed by citizens in areas subject to the laws of no sovereign. *See Skiriotes v. Florida*, 313 U.S. 69; *Old Dominion S. S. Co. v. Gilmore*, 207 U.S. 398.

In the instant case none of these exceptional considerations come into play. Petitioner's buying of unfinished watches in the United States is not an illegal commercial act. Nor can it be said that petitioners were engaging in illegal acts in commerce when the finished watches bearing the Mexican trade-mark were purchased from them and brought into the United States by such purchasers, all without collusion between petitioner and the purchaser. The stamping of the Bulova trade-mark, done in Mexico, is not an act "within the control of Congress." It should not be utilized as a basis for action against petitioner. The Lanham Act, like the Sherman Act, should be construed to apply only to acts done within the sovereignty of the United States. While we do not condone the piratic use of trade-marks, neither do we believe that Congress intended to make such use actionable irrespective of the place it occurred. Such extensions of power bring our legislation into conflict with the laws and practices of other nations, fully capable of punishing infractions of their own laws, and should require specific words to reach acts done within the territorial limits of other sovereignties.

Cecil McBee v. Delica Co., Ltd.
417 F.3d 107 (1st Cir. 2005)

LYNCH, CIRCUIT JUDGE.

It has long been settled that the Lanham Act can, in appropriate cases, be applied extraterritorially. *See Steele v. Bulova Watch Co.*, 344 U.S. 280, 97 L. Ed. 319, 73 S. Ct. 252, 1953 Dec. Comm'r Pat. 424 (1952). This case, dismissed for lack of subject matter jurisdiction, requires us, as a matter of first impression for this circuit, to lay out a framework for determining when such extraterritorial use of the Lanham Act is proper.

In doing so, we choose not to adopt the formulations used by various other circuits. *See, e.g., Reebok Int'l, Ltd. v. Marnatech Enters.*, 970 F.2d 552, 554–57 (9th Cir. 1992); *Vanity Fair Mills v. T. Eaton Co.*, 234 F.2d 633, 642–43 (2d Cir. 1956). The best-known test, the *Vanity Fair* test, asks (1) whether the defendant is an American citizen, (2) whether the defendant's actions have a substantial effect on United States commerce, and (3) whether relief would create a conflict with foreign law. 234 F.2d at 642–43. These three prongs are given an uncertain weight. Based on *Steele* and subsequent Supreme Court case law, we disaggregate the three prongs of the *Vanity Fair* test, identify the different types of "extraterritorial" application questions, and isolate the factors pertinent to subject matter jurisdiction.

Our framework asks first whether the defendant is an American citizen; that inquiry is different because a separate constitutional basis for jurisdiction exists for control of activities, even foreign activities, of an American citizen. Further, when the Lanham Act plaintiff seeks to enjoin sales in the United States, there is no question of extraterritorial application; the court has subject matter jurisdiction.

In order for a plaintiff to reach foreign activities of foreign defendants in American courts, however, we adopt a separate test. We hold that subject matter jurisdiction under the Lanham Act is proper only if the complained—of activities have a substantial effect on United States commerce, viewed in light of the purposes of the Lanham Act. If this "substantial effects" question is answered in the negative, then the court lacks jurisdiction over the defendant's extraterritorial acts; if it is answered in the affirmative, then the court possesses subject matter jurisdiction.

We reject the notion that a comity analysis is part of subject matter jurisdiction. Comity considerations, including potential conflicts with foreign trademark law, are properly treated as questions of whether a court should, in its discretion, decline to exercise subject matter jurisdiction that it already possesses. Our approach to each of these issues is in harmony with the analogous rules for extraterritorial application of the antitrust laws.

See Hartford Fire Ins. Co. v. California, 509 U.S. 764, 795–99, 125 L. Ed. 2d 612, 113 S. Ct. 2891 (1993).

The plaintiff, Cecil McBee, an American citizen and resident, seeks to hold the defendant, Delica Co., Ltd. (Delica), responsible for its activities in Japan said to harm McBee's reputation in both Japan and the United States and for Delica's purported activities in the United States. McBee is a well-known American jazz musician; Delica is a Japanese corporation that adopted the name "Cecil McBee" for its adolescent female clothing line. McBee sued for false endorsement and dilution under the Lanham Act. The district court dismissed all of McBee's Lanham Act claims, concluding that it lacked subject matter jurisdiction. *See McBee v. Delica Co.*, 2004 U.S. Dist. LEXIS 23414, No. 02-198-P-C, 2004 WL 2674360 (D. Me. Nov. 19, 2004) (unpublished).

We affirm, albeit on different reasoning. We conclude that the court lacked jurisdiction over McBee's claims seeking (1) an injunction in the United States barring access to Delica's Internet website, which is written in Japanese, and (2) damages for harm to McBee due to Delica's sales in Japan. McBee has made no showing that Delica's activities had a substantial effect on United States commerce. As to McBee's claim for (3) an injunction barring Delica from selling its goods in the United States, we hold that the district court had jurisdiction but conclude that this claim is without merit because the only sales Delica has made into the United States were induced by McBee for purposes of this litigation, and there is no showing that Delica plans on selling into the United States again.

III.

A. Framework for Assessing Extraterritorial Use of the Lanham Act

By extraterritorial application of the Lanham Act, we mean application of the Act to activity (such as sales) of a defendant outside of the territorial boundaries of the United States. In addressing extraterritorial application of the Lanham Act, we face issues of Congressional intent to legislate extraterritorially, undergirded by issues of Congressional power to legislate extraterritorially. Usually in addressing questions of extraterritoriality, the Supreme Court has discussed Congressional intent, doing so by employing various presumptions designed to avoid unnecessary international conflict.

The parties characterize the extraterritoriality issue as, at least in part, one of subject matter jurisdiction under the Act, and it is often viewed that way.

The Supreme Court has long since made it clear that the Lanham Act could sometimes be used to reach extraterritorial conduct, but it has never laid down a precise test for when such reach would be appropriate. *Steele v. Bulova Watch Co.*, 344 U.S. 280, 97 L. Ed. 319, 73 S. Ct. 252, 1953 Dec. Comm'r Pat. 424 (1952); *see also Arabian Am. Oil Co.*, 499 U.S. at 252–53 (distinguishing *Steele*). The circuit courts have established a variety of tests for determining when extraterritorial application of the Lanham Act is appropriate, treating different factual contexts as all subject to the same set of criteria. *See Vanity Fair Mills v. T. Eaton Co.*, 234 F.2d 633, 642 (2d Cir. 1956); *see also Int'l Cafe, S.A.L., v. Hard Rock Cafe Int'l (U.S.A.), Inc.*, 252 F.3d 1274, 1278–79 (11th Cir. 2001) (applying *Vanity Fair*); *Nintendo of Am., Ltd., v. Aeropower Co.*, 34 F.3d 246, 250–51 (4th Cir. 1994) (adopting the *Vanity Fair* test, although requiring a "significant effect" rather than a "substantial effect" on United States commerce); *Reebok Int'l, Ltd. v. Marnatech Enters., Inc.*, 970 F.2d 552, 554–57 (9th Cir. 1992) (applying the jurisdictional "rule of reason" from *Timberlane Lumber Co. v. Bank of Am.*, 549 F.2d 597 (9th Cir. 1977): plaintiff must show (1) some effect on United States commerce, (2) an effect that is sufficiently great to be a cognizable injury to plaintiff under the Lanham Act, and (3) the interests and links to American commerce must be sufficiently strong in relation to those of other nations to justify, in terms of comity, an extraterritorial application of the act); *Am. Rice, Inc. v. Ark. Rice Growers Coop. Ass'n*, 701 F.2d 408, 414 & n. 8 (5th Cir. 1983) (modifying *Vanity Fair*'s first prong to require only "some effect" on United States commerce). This court has not previously addressed the question.

Steele found that there was Lanham Act jurisdiction over a defendant, selling watches in Mexico, who was a United States citizen and whose "operations and their effects were not confined within the territorial limits of a foreign nation." 344 U.S. at 286. Defendant made no sales within the United States. The Court held that the Lanham Act conferred broad jurisdiction in that its purpose was to regulate "commerce within the control of Congress." 15 U.S.C. § 1127. The Act prohibits the use of certain infringing marks "in commerce." 15 U.S.C. § 1114(1); *Id.* § 1125(a). Importantly, commerce is defined in the Act as "all commerce which may lawfully be regulated by Congress." *Id.* § 1127.

The *Steele* Court did not define the outer limits of Congressional power because it was clear that the facts presented a case within those limits. The *Steele* Court explicitly and implicitly relied on two different aspects of Congressional power to reach this conclusion. First, it explicitly relied on the power of Congress to regulate "the conduct of its own citizens," even extraterritorial conduct. Steele, 344 U.S. at 285–86. This doctrine is based on an idea that Congressional power over American citizens is a matter of domestic law that raises no serious international concerns, even when the citizen is located abroad. Second, Steele also implicitly appears to rely on Congressional power over foreign commerce, although the Foreign Commerce clause is not cited—the Court noted that the defendant's actions had an impact on the plaintiff's reputation, and thus on commerce within the United States. *See* 344 U.S. at 286–87, 288. The Steele Court concluded that an American citizen could not evade the thrust of the laws of the United States by moving his operations to a "privileged sanctuary" beyond our borders. *Id.* at 287.

For purposes of determining subject matter jurisdiction, we think certain distinctions are important at the outset. The reach of the Lanham Act depends on context; the nature of the analysis of the jurisdictional question may vary with that context. Steele addressed the pertinent Lanham Act jurisdictional analysis when an American citizen is the defendant. In such cases, the domestic effect of the international activities may be of lesser importance and a lesser showing of domestic effects may be all that is needed. We do not explore this further because our case does not involve an American citizen as the alleged infringer.

When the purported infringer is not an American citizen, and the alleged illegal activities occur outside the United States, then the analysis is different, and appears to rest solely on the foreign commerce power. Yet it is beyond much doubt that the Lanham Act can be applied against foreign corporations or individuals in appropriate cases; no court has ever suggested that the foreign citizenship of a defendant is always fatal. Some academics have criticized treating the Lanham Act differently from patent and copyright law, which generally are not applied extraterritorially. *See* C. Bradley, Extraterritorial Application of U.S. Intellectual Property Law, 37 Va. J. Int'l L. 505 (1997); *but see* R. Schechter, Comment, The Case For Limited Extraterritorial Reach of the Lanham Act, 37 Va. J. Int'l L. 619 (1997). Nonetheless, the Supreme Court recently reaffirmed the Steele approach to extraterritorial jurisdiction under the Lanham Act by distinguishing it in Arabian American Oil Co. *See* 499 U.S. at 252–53. The question becomes one of articulating a test for Lanham Act jurisdiction over foreign infringing activities by foreign defendants.

The decisions of the Supreme Court in the antitrust context seem useful to us as a guide. The Court has written in this area, on the issue of extraterritorial application, far more recently than it has written on the Lanham Act, and thus the decisions reflect more recent evolutions in terms of legal analysis of extraterritorial activity. As the Court noted in *Steele*, Lanham Act violations abroad often radiate unlawful consequences into the United States, *see* 344 U.S. at 288; *see also Schecter, supra*, at 629–30. One can easily imagine a variety of harms to American commerce arising from wholly foreign activities by foreign defendants. There could be harm caused by false endorsements, passing off, or product disparagement, or confusion over sponsorship affecting American commerce and causing loss of American sales. Further, global piracy of American goods is a major problem for American companies: annual losses from unauthorized use of United States trademarks, according to one commentator, now amount to $ 200 billion annually. *See Schecter, supra*, at 634. In both the antitrust and the Lanham Act areas, there is a risk that absent a certain degree of extraterritorial enforcement, violators will either take advantage of international coordination problems or hide in countries without efficacious antitrust or trademark laws, thereby avoiding legal authority.

In *Hartford Fire Ins. Co. v. California*, 509 U.S. 764, 125 L. Ed. 2d 612, 113 S. Ct. 2891 (1993), the Supreme Court addressed the issue of when a United States court could assert jurisdiction over Sherman Act claims brought against foreign defendants for a conspiracy that occurred abroad to raise reinsurance prices. It held that jurisdiction over foreign conduct existed under the antitrust laws if that conduct "was meant to produce and did in fact produce some substantial effect in the United States." *Id.* at 796. The *Hartford Fire* Court also held that comity considerations, such as whether relief ordered by an American court would conflict with foreign law, were properly understood not as questions of whether a United States court possessed subject matter jurisdiction, but instead as issues of whether such a court should decline to exercise the jurisdiction that it possessed. *See id.* at 797–98.

The framework stated in *Hartford Fire* guides our analysis of the Lanham Act jurisdictional question for foreign activities of foreign defendants. We hold that the Lanham Act grants subject matter jurisdiction over extraterritorial conduct by foreign defendants only where the conduct has a substantial effect on United States commerce. Absent a showing of such a substantial effect, at least as to foreign defendants, the court lacks jurisdiction over the Lanham Act claim. Congress has little reason to assert jurisdiction over foreign defendants who are engaging in activities that have no substantial effect on the United States, and courts, absent an express statement from Congress, have no good reason to go further in such situations.

The substantial effects test requires that there be evidence of impacts within the United States, and these impacts must be of a sufficient character and magnitude to give the United States a reasonably strong interest in the litigation. The "substantial effects" test must be applied in light of the core purposes of the Lanham Act, which are both to protect the ability of American consumers to avoid confusion and to help assure a trademark's owner that it will reap the financial and reputational rewards associated with having a desirable name or product. The goal of the jurisdictional test is to ensure that the United States has a sufficient interest in the litigation, as measured by the interests protected by the Lanham Act, to assert jurisdiction.

Of course, the *Vanity Fair* test includes a "substantial effects" inquiry as part of its three-part test. We differ from the *Vanity Fair* court in that we disaggregate the elements of its test: we first ask whether the defendant is an American citizen, and if he is not, then we use the substantial effects test as the sole touchstone to determine jurisdiction.

If the substantial effects test is met, then the court should proceed, in appropriate cases, to consider comity. We also transplant for Lanham Act purposes *Hartford Fire*'s holding that comity considerations are properly analyzed not as questions of whether there is subject matter jurisdiction, but as prudential questions of whether that jurisdiction should be exercised. Our analysis differs again from *Vanity Fair* on this point. *See Vanity Fair*, 234 F.2d at 642. *Vanity Fair* and other cases have considered as part of the basic jurisdictional analysis whether the defendant acted under color of protection of the trademark laws of his own country. We disagree and do not see why the scope of Congressional intent and power to create jurisdiction under the Lanham Act should turn on the existence and meaning of foreign law.

Congress could, of course, preclude the exercise of such Lanham Act jurisdiction by statute or by ratified treaty. Or it could by statute define limits in Lanham Act jurisdiction in such international cases, as it has chosen to do in the antitrust area. *See* 15 U.S.C. § 6a. It has not done so.

[The court affirmed the judgment for Delica and concluded that there were no merits to Cecil McBee's claims of trademark infringement or dilution in the United States and that it had no subject matter jurisdiction over claims of conduct in Japan.]

Notes

1. Is the *Steele* case decided correctly? Should United States courts be able to sanction conduct that occurred outside of the United States territory? *See* Curtis A. Bradley, *Territorial Intellectual Property Rights in an Age of Globalism*, 37 Va. J. Int'l L. 505 (1997); Roger E. Schechter, *The Case for Limited Extraterritorial Reach of the Lanham Act*, 37 Va. J. Int'l L. 619 (1997).

2. For the view that the domain name protection system in the United States amounts to an extraterritorial application of United States law, *see* Xuan-Thao N. Nguyen, *The Digital Trademark Right: A Troubling New Extraterritorial Reach of United States Law*, 81 N.C.L. Rev. 483 (2003). What is the price for comity under the UDRP?

3. Some have argued that we should adopt a standard as in antitrust law and enforce trademark law extraterritorially with some regularity. *See* Gary Feldon, *COMMENT: The Antitrust Model of Extraterritorial Trademark Jurisdiction: Analysis and Predictions after F. Hoffmann-LA Rouch*, 20 Emory Int'l L. Rev. 651 (2006). If so, we should expect all nations to enforce their trademark extraterritorially to assure those that sell goods and services in their country do not violate their trademark law. The United States has an established office of many attorneys who live and work full-time in Tokyo, Japan assuring that producers of products sold into the United States market do not violate the United States antitrust laws. What would the effect be if the Japanese government set up an office in Washington, D.C. with the express purpose of assuring that goods and services sold into the Japanese market complied with Japanese trademark law? Does this all go beyond comity?

4. The claim of trademark infringement in Japan was summarized by the court as follows:

> On February 28, 2002, the Japanese Patent Office ruled Delica's trademark in Japan invalid. However, Delica appealed to the Tokyo High Court, which on December 26, 2002, vacated the decision of the Japanese Patent Office. On remand, the Japanese Patent Office found for Delica and reinstated Delica's registration

of the "Cecil McBee" trademark. McBee appealed that ruling to the Tokyo High Court and lost; the trademark reinstatement has become final. The Japanese courts' rationale for finding in favor of Delica was (1) while Japanese law protects a person's full name from exploitation, McBee's full name, including his middle name, was "Cecil Leroy McBee," and thus the "Cecil McBee" line of products was not an exact copy of McBee's full name; and (2) McBee received no protection for the abbreviated version of his name, "Cecil McBee," because the name had not received sufficient recognition in general Japanese society.

Cecil McBee v. Delica Co., Ltd.,417 F.3d 107, 113 (1st Cir. 2005).

Therefore, McBee is completely without redress. Is that an appropriate outcome?

Chapter XIV

Remedies

A. Injunctions

15 U.S.C. §1116, Lanham Act §34

(a) Jurisdiction; service

The several courts vested with jurisdiction of civil actions arising under this chapter shall have power to grant injunctions, according to the principles of equity and upon such terms as the court may deem reasonable, to prevent the violation of any right of the registrant of a mark registered in the Patent and Trademark Office or to prevent a violation under subsection (a), (c), or (d) of section 1125 of this title.

...

Firma Melodiya v. ZYX Music GmbH
882 F. Supp. 1306 (S.D.N.Y. 1995)

CHIN, J.

Plaintiffs Firma Melodiya ("Melodiya") and BMG Music ("BMG") commenced this action on September 19, 1994, alleging that defendants' unauthorized manufacture, distribution and sale of Melodiya's recordings in the United States constituted federal and state copyright and trademark infringement, unfair competition, trademark dilution, false advertising and deceptive acts and practices under federal and New York state law. Subsequently, plaintiffs moved for a preliminary injunction against ZYX Music GmbH and ZYX Music Distribution Ltd. (collectively, "ZYX" or the "ZYX Defendants"), PG Records Pty. Ltd., Melodiya Australia Pty. Ltd., Unidata Solutions Pty. Ltd., HDA Entertainment Group Ptd. and Philip Allwood (collectively, the "Allwood Defendants"). A hearing was held on the preliminary injunction motion at which all parties presented witnesses and exhibits. Memoranda of law and numerous affidavits were filed prior to the hearing, and the parties were given the opportunity to submit post-hearing briefs. For the reasons stated below, plaintiffs' motion is granted. My findings of fact and conclusions of law follow.

[The Court concluded that the defendants had begun marketing compact discs in the United States containing copies of the plaintiff's master recordings and bearing the plaintiff's trademarks. The defendant alleged that it had purchased a license for this activity but the plaintiff proved that the licenses were forged.]

* * *

DISCUSSION
I. Plaintiffs' Motion for Preliminary Injunction
A. Standards for Preliminary Injunction

To succeed on their motion for a preliminary injunction, plaintiffs must demonstrate irreparable harm and either 1) likelihood of success on the merits, or 2) serious questions on the merits to make them fair ground for litigation with the balance of hardships tipping decidedly in their favor. With respect to plaintiffs' trademark infringement claims, irreparable harm may be presumed upon a showing that plaintiffs' trademark is protectible and that a likelihood of confusion exists as to the ownership or source of goods in question. Proof of confusion also serves as evidence of likelihood of success on the merits in the preliminary injunction context since an essential element of any trademark infringement claim is a likelihood of confusion as to the source of a product arising from the unauthorized use or copy of a trademark.

B. Presumed Irreparable Harm
1. Protectible Mark

The first inquiry is whether Melodiya's trademarks are entitled to protection. [The Court concluded that the MELODIYA marks were suggestive and strong.]

* * *

2. Consumer Confusion

Since I have determined that Melodiya's trademarks are suggestive and entitled to protection, the next inquiry is whether ZYX's products create a likelihood of consumer confusion as to the source or ownership of the Melodiya Recordings. Plaintiffs argue that there is a likelihood of confusion since defendants claim entitlement to Melodiya's trademarks through the U.S. Addendum, which plaintiffs allege is forged. ZYX acknowledges that "the use of the Melodiya name and logo on [its] CDs is required pursuant to the 1987 Agreement." (ZYX Mem. at 40). Defendants argue, however, that the U.S. Addendum is genuine and entitles them to use those marks. Based upon the evidence presented at the hearing, I find that plaintiffs have shown that the Addendum is a forgery and that any rights claimed by defendants to exploit the Melodiya catalogue are illusory. Accordingly, plaintiffs have demonstrated a likelihood of confusion as to the source or sponsorship of the Melodiya Recordings.

Three MezhKniga officials, Nikolai Minaev, Igor Preferansky, and Alexander Belostotsky, affirmed, either through testimony or in sworn statements, that MezhKniga never gave the Allwood Defendants any rights to distribute Melodiya recordings in the United States. Mr. Minaev, the MezhKniga official who Allwood claims signed the U.S. Addendum, testified that he never signed the Addendum and that the Addendum was a forgery. Mr. Minaev made three further observations. First, the Addendum listed, in handwriting, three disparate territories: the United States, Japan and Europe. Mr. Minaev's territory was Australia, while other officials had authorization for the United States and Europe, and it would have been "impossible" to mix all three territories in one document. In addition, the Allwood Defendants could not be the "second buyer" of the Melodiya Recordings in Japan as indicated on the Addendum, since the Japan territory already had four buyers. Finally, Mr. Minaev testified that the other signature on the U.S. Addendum, purportedly Mr. Fomichev's, was also a forgery. Mr. Minaev was credible, and I accept his testimony.

Mr. Minaev's testimony that the U.S. Addendum is a forgery was corroborated by Igor Preferansky, a MezhKniga director and MezhKniga's representative in the United States from 1985 to 1989, and Alexander Belostotsky who, from 1966, was MezhKniga's Deputy General Director and the second senior official with deal-making authority for the United States. Mr. Preferansky confirmed in his affirmation and at the hearing that he met with Philip Allwood in September 1988 in Washington, D.C. to discuss the possible exploitation of the Melodiya Recordings in the United States, a proposal that was ultimately rejected by MezhKniga. Mr. Preferansky also stated that the U.S. Addendum seemed "suspicious" since the territories were handwritten, which was unusual for MezhKniga. Finally, he testified that he was first shown the U.S. Addendum in July 1994 in Moscow and that a search through MezhKniga's files by his employees failed to uncover a copy of the Addendum or any similar document. I find that Mr. Preferansky also was credible, and I accept his testimony.

Mr. Belostotsky stated in his affidavit that MezhKniga never granted the Allwood Defendants any rights to distribute the Melodiya Recordings outside of Hong Kong, Australia and New Zealand. He also affirmed that he did not sign the U.S. Addendum and, indeed, did not see it until July or August 1994.

Additional evidence of forgery came from plaintiffs' handwriting expert, Gus Lesnevich. Mr. Lesnevich compared a facsimile and photocopy of the U.S. Addendum against twenty known and undisputed samples of Mr. Minaev's signature taken at approximately the same time as the disputed signature and noted numerous drastic discrepancies between the disputed and genuine signatures, including differences in the initial writing movements and the final stroke. Based on this analysis, Mr. Lesnevich testified that the signature on the U.S. Addendum, purported to be Mr. Minaev's signature, was a "poorly simulated signature, modeled after a genuine signature."

Mr. Lesnevich reached a similar conclusion with respect to the signature on the U.S. Addendum purported to be Mr. Fomichev's signature. He compared the Addendum to two known examples of Mr. Fomichev's signature and noted at least 9 differences between the signatures, including differences in the starting stroke, "O" shape, and size and shape of the loops on the "F," and concluded that Mr. Fomichev's signature was also a forgery. I find Mr. Lesnevich's conclusions to be logical and well-based, and his testimony is accepted.

Most damaging perhaps to defendants' position is the report of the Allwood Defendants' own handwriting expert, Leonard Timewell. Mr. Timewell compared Mr. Minaev's signature on 14 undisputed samples against the U.S. Addendum and concluded that the disputed signature was "simulated." He also declared, however, that he could not eliminate the possibility that the disputed signature on the Addendum was written by Mr. Minaev for the purpose of later repudiation. I reject this conclusion since there is absolutely no evidence in the record to support such a finding. Finally, Mr. Timewell stated that he could not reach a definitive conclusion as to Mr. Fomichev's signature, but noted that there appeared to be pronounced differences. Mr. Timewell did qualify his conclusion by stating that severe limitations were placed on the accuracy of his assessment since the Addendum was only a photocopy.

In an attempt to support their position that the Addendum is genuine, defendants submitted an affidavit dated July 14, 1994 of Igor Pleschenko, who has been an Assistant to the Trade Representative of the Russian Federation in Australia since 1994 and who was previously an employee of MezhKniga. Mr. Pleschenko stated in his affidavit that MezhKniga had granted the Allwood Defendants the right to sell Melodiya recordings in the United States. I do not give any weight to this statement, however, for two reasons: 1) Mr. Pleschenko submitted a letter on August 10, 1994, withdrawing his affidavit and declaring it "null and void" because he had no personal knowledge of the information contained in the affidavit and had merely been relying on Allwood's representations; and 2) Mr. Pleschenko's duties with MezhKniga did not involve the licensing of Melodiya recordings during the time in question.

Based on all of the above evidence, I find that the U.S. Addendum is a forgery; consequently, it is invalid. As the ZYX Defendants concede that their right to distribute the Melodiya Recordings derive from the Addendum, I find that there is a likelihood of confusion as to the source or sponsorship of the Melodiya Recordings. *See* Church of Scientology, 794 F.2d at 41 (district court's finding of likelihood of confusion affirmed where defendant, a former licensee of plaintiff, continued to use plaintiff's trademark after the license terminated).

Since Melodiya's trademarks are entitled to protection and plaintiffs have shown a likelihood of consumer confusion, irreparable harm must be presumed.

C. Actual Irreparable Harm

Plaintiffs maintain that they will suffer actual irreparable harm if a preliminary injunction is not issued, due primarily to the inferior quality of the ZYX products, the discounted prices charged by ZYX, and the unique character of the classical music customer base. Based on the evidence presented at the hearing, I find that plaintiffs have demonstrated actual irreparable harm.

The evidence presented at the hearing reveals that the disc packaging on ZYX's compact discs is not up to industry standards, for several reasons. First, the liner notes, which are important to a sophisticated consumer's appreciation of classical music, in many instances did not discuss the music on the particular compact disc but instead referred to unrelated compositions. In addition, the artwork on the labels routinely bore no relationship either to the composer or the compositions and was generally of inferior quality. Furthermore, most of the discs failed to note total playing time, which in most instances was far less than the 60 (or more) minutes generally contained in classical music compact discs. Finally, BMG's executive producer, James Pfeiffer, testified that, based on his analysis of 26 ZYX compact discs containing the Melodiya Recordings (some of which were provided by ZYX and some of which were purchased randomly in New York stores), the quality of the ZYX discs as a whole ranged from moderate to inferior. Mr. Pfeiffer also noted that while some of the inferior sonic quality could be attributed to the original recording, quality digital remastering could have improved the sonic quality.

In contrast, examination of BMG's anticipated product, including liner notes, packaging artwork, and a fully remastered compact disc (which contained the same recording as one of the ZYX discs provided to the Court (Pl. Exh. 30)), reveals that the BMG product will undoubtedly be of a higher quality. The liner notes for BMG's anticipated releases of Melodiya's recordings refer to the music contained on the disc, are much longer than ZYX's liner notes (24 pages in one instance) and written in three languages. In addition, the artwork for the disc labels are reproductions of original art bearing some relationship to the music on the disc. Finally, Mr. Pfeiffer testified that the anticipated BMG product had a longer playing time than most of ZYX's compact discs and that the music had a lower "hiss" level, reflecting an earlier recording and providing better texture to allow a fuller appreciation of the music.

I find, based on the evidence presented, that the ZYX discs are of somewhat inferior quality due primarily to the substandard packaging, the erroneous liner notes and the shortened playing time. Accordingly, plaintiffs would suffer irreparable damage to their reputation, particularly in light of BMG's anticipated release of Melodiya recordings.

I also find that plaintiffs will be damaged by ZYX's discount, or cut-rate, price for its compact discs. ZYX is selling its discs at a discount price of $5.99, which is at the low-end of the range of prices for compact discs. BMG, on the other hand, anticipates selling its compact discs for $11.99, double the price of the ZYX discs. ZYX's continued sale at a discount rate makes it more difficult for BMG to later release the same recordings at a higher price.

Finally, the limited customer base for classical music contributes to the injury suffered by BMG, since it is unlikely that a classical music consumer would purchase the same recording twice.

D. Likelihood of Success on the Merits

Since plaintiffs have shown that they would suffer irreparable harm by ZYX's continued distribution of the Melodiya Recordings, I now must determine whether plaintiffs demonstrated a likelihood of success on the merits.

1. Trademark Claims

To succeed on a claim of trademark infringement, plaintiffs must show that a likelihood of confusion as to the source or sponsorship of the Melodiya Recordings exists due to defendants' unauthorized use of the Melodiya trademarks. I find that plaintiffs have met their burden of demonstrating a likelihood of success on the merits. As discussed more fully above, plaintiffs have shown that the document upon which defendants base their rights to distribute the Melodiya Recordings in the United States is, in fact, a forgery. Since the Allwood Defendants granted a license to ZYX to distribute the Melodiya Recordings in the United States based on the U.S. Addendum and ZYX concedes it is required by that license to display Melodiya's trademarks, plaintiffs have demonstrated a likelihood of success on their claim of trademark infringement. *See* Hasbro, Inc. v. Lanard Toys, Ltd., 858 F.2d 70, 73 (2d Cir. 1988); Church of Scientology Int'l v. Elmira Mission of the Church of Scientology, 794 F.2d at 41 (likelihood of success on the merits established where former licensee admitted using licensor's trademarks and licensor proved licensee did not have authority to use those marks). I reach the same conclusion with respect to plaintiffs' claim of trademark dilution under New York state law. *See* Saban Entertainment, Inc. v. 222 World Corp., 865 F. Supp. 1047 (S.D.N.Y. 1994).

2. Common Law Claims

Although plaintiffs have withdrawn their federal statutory copyright claim as a basis for preliminary injunctive relief, defendants may still be enjoined from distributing their unauthorized copies of Melodiya's master recordings under the theories of common law copyright infringement and unfair competition. Defendants do not deny that they are distributing copies of Melodiya's master recordings but rather claim, on the basis of the U.S. Addendum, entitlement to do so. Their claim of entitlement, however, is based on a document that I have now found to be a forgery. Hence, defendants' claim of entitlement falls by the wayside, and they have no right to copy or distribute the Melodiya Recordings. Plaintiffs have therefore demonstrated a likelihood of success on their common law claims of copyright infringement and unfair competition.

Note

1. Although much is made of trademark litigation, in actuality, a small fraction of all trademark cases make it to a final decision on the merits. In civil cases terminated in the 12-month period ending on March 31, 2002, 1.4% of all cases terminated were done on a trial on the merits. There were a total of 47 cases so terminated, 24 by a bench trial and 23 by a jury trial.

Completed Trademark Cases in U.S. District Courts FY1997–FY2002

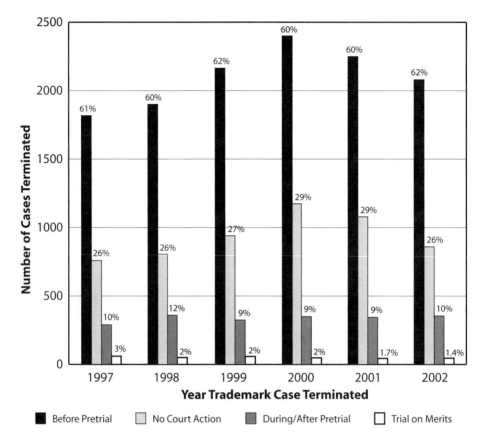

See http://www.uscourts.gov/caseload2002/tables/c04mar02.pdf.

B. Disclaimers

Home Box Office, Inc. v. Showtime/The Movie Channel Inc.
832 F.2d 1311 (2d Cir. 1987)

LUMBARD, CIRCUIT JUDGE:

Plaintiff Home Box Office (HBO) appeals from an order of the Southern District of New York by Judge Richard J. Daronco denying a motion brought by HBO for a preliminary injunction and instead granting a limited injunction. HBO began this action by seeking an injunction against defendant Showtime to prevent Showtime from using certain slogans in an advertising and promotional campaign for Showtime's cable television services. On July 15, 1987 following a hearing, the district court enjoined Showtime from using the contested slogans unless they were accompanied by disclaimers adequate to avoid confusing consumers. In that order, the district court specifically exempted certain promotional materials that Showtime presented to the court at the hearing. 665 F. Supp. 1079.

HBO contends that the district court erred by (1) considering Showtime's proposed amended advertisements at the preliminary injunction hearing instead of those originally submitted by the parties as the basis for the injunction, (2) denying HBO's motion for preliminary injunction, (3) ruling on Showtime's proposed advertisements when HBO did not have notice of, or the opportunity to be heard concerning those advertisements and by assigning HBO the burden of proof and (4) incorrectly applying the test for a preliminary injunction. Showtime cross-appeals, requesting that this court reverse the district court's grant of the preliminary injunction. We affirm the district court's issuance of a preliminary injunction order but vacate the portions of the order specifically exempting the promotional material presented by Showtime at the preliminary injunction hearing and making disclaimers an acceptable alteration of the promotional materials which would allow Showtime to continue using the slogan.

I.

HBO and Showtime are competitors in the subscription television field. Both programming services offer a variety of movies, concerts, sporting events and other programs. Both sell their television services primarily to cable operators who then sell them to consumer subscribers.

HBO identifies its service through its federally registered servicemark and trademark "HBO" which appears at the beginning of each program. HBO frequently promotes its companion "Cinemax" television service in tandem with its "HBO" service with slogans such as "HBO & CINEMAX." Showtime also frequently promotes its companion service, "The Movie Channel," along with its "Showtime" service with slogans such as "SHOWTIME/THE MOVIE CHANNEL."

At the National Cable Television Association Convention held in Las Vegas on May 17–20, 1987 (an industry trade show), Showtime launched a new advertising and promotional campaign using a new slogan as its theme. The primary slogan used was "SHOWTIME & HBO. It's Not Either/Or Anymore." (the "slogan"); the related slogans were: "THE MOVIE CHANNEL & HBO. Together is Better.", "Why SHOWTIME & HBO make such a perfect pair.", and "Play the Showtime PERFECT (HBO, Showtime) PAIR Instant Winner Game." The slogan was featured on a number of materials displayed or distributed at or near the Convention site. The materials included an outdoor highway billboard and a hot air balloon located outside the Convention Center; a rolling billboard that was driven around the Convention area; promotional videotapes played in public at the Las Vegas airport and in Convention hotel rooms; signs located in Showtime's Convention booth; promotional pens, tote bags, sunglasses, buttons and cookies distributed at Showtime's booth and/or to the hotel rooms of Convention attendees; advertisements that were distributed at the Convention and which appeared in trade publications at or about the time of the Convention; packages of promotional material distributed to Showtime's cable affiliates at or about the time of the Convention; game cards; and a brochure emphasizing the value of subscribing to both HBO and Showtime. Some, but not all, of these materials contained disclaimers stating that HBO and Showtime were unrelated services.

HBO brought this action on June 30, 1987 for (1) the wrongful use in commerce of false designations of origin, false descriptions and false representations under 15 U.S.C. §1125(a) [Lanham Act §43(a)], (2) service mark infringement under 15 U.S.C. §1114(1) [Lanham Act §32(1)]; for service mark and trade name infringement and unfair competition at common law; and for violation of the New York Anti-Dilution Statute, New York General Business Law §368-d. HBO's motion for preliminary injunction was designed to prevent Showtime from using the slogan and the related slogans in any future promotional materials.

HBO maintains that the slogan is confusing because it suggests that HBO and Showtime have merged or are engaged in a cooperative promotional campaign. To prove this, HBO produced evidence in the district court which tended to show that the slogan was the source of confusion because some observers perceived it to be part of a joint promotional campaign. The evidence presented by HBO included the promotional materials or representations of the materials used by Showtime at the Convention, a *Boston Globe* article that described the confusion caused by the slogan at the Convention among members of the cable television trade and a consumer reaction study in four cities that tested reactions to the videotaped commercial and the billboard that Showtime used at the Convention.

Showtime maintains that it adopted the slogan and undertook the related promotional campaign to educate consumers that Showtime has exclusive movies that are not available from HBO. Showtime asserts that its goal in using the slogan was to differentiate the two services and to convince consumers to subscribe to its service as well as to HBO. Showtime thus emphasizes that it sought to inform the public that Showtime and HBO are different, not to suggest any link between the services. It points to the disclaimers of any link between HBO and Showtime, and especially to the new promotional materials presented to the district court at the preliminary injunction hearing that featured disclaimers more prominently than did the materials that Showtime displayed and distributed at the Convention.

HBO also applied for a temporary restraining order on June 30, 1987. The parties agreed to a consent order at a pretrial meeting on July 1 and began settlement negotiations. No agreement was reached, however, and on July 15, the district court held a preliminary injunction hearing. At that hearing, Showtime presented mock-ups of revised promotional materials and a modified videotape commercial. HBO objected to the district court's consideration of the modified materials on several grounds, including the grounds that it had not been accorded adequate notice of the new promotional materials and that Showtime was seeking an advisory opinion. The court overruled the objection and admitted the proposed materials into evidence.

Although finding that the slogan was not "patently false," Judge Daranco credited the results of HBO's study and found that, if used alone without "adequate disclaiming information appropriate to the selected medium," it was ambiguous and likely to confuse and mislead consumers. Based on its findings, the district court enjoined Showtime from using the slogan and the related slogans "unless a prominent disclaimer, appropriate to the selected medium accompanies their use." The court thus enjoined the materials used at the Convention and any other materials not featuring an adequate disclaimer but it specifically exempted the materials presented at the hearing from the terms of the order. This court granted HBO's motion to hear this appeal on an expedited basis.

II.

* * *

Although we agree with the district court's application of the likelihood of confusion standard to Showtime's promotional materials, our view of the proper role of disclaimers in trademark infringement cases is somewhat different. Although we have found disclaimers to be adequate in certain cases, each case must be judged by considering the circumstances of the relevant business and its consumers. We have found the use of disclaimers to be an adequate remedy when they are sufficient to avoid substantially the risk of consumer confusion. In many circumstances a disclaimer can avoid the problem of objectionable infringement by significantly reducing or eliminating consumer confusion by making clear the source of a product. *See Soltex Polymer Corporation v. Fortex Industries, Inc.*, 832 F.2d 1325 (2d Cir. 1987) (minimal to moderate amount of consumer confusion found by district court could be cured effectively through the use of a disclaimer). We believe, however, that the record before us is not sufficient to support a finding that the disclaimers proposed by Showtime will be effective in substantially reducing consumer confusion. In fact, our examination of some of the promotional materials first submitted to the district court by Showtime as exhibits at the preliminary injunction hearing indicates to us that some of the potentially confusing statements are not effectively disclaimed because the disclaiming information does not appear in sufficiently close proximity to the infringing statements. As an example, we find Showtime's use of disclaimers to be especially problematic in the case of one of the multiple panel brochures submitted to the district court which had an infringing use on its back panel and a disclaimer only appearing on an inside panel. In addition, we believe that the district court should not have received or reviewed the revised promotional materials that Showtime presented at the hearing because this process did not provide sufficient notice to HBO or an adequate opportunity to be heard on the proposed disclaimers.

Requiring infringing users such as Showtime to demonstrate the effectiveness of proposed disclaimers is supported by cases from other circuits in which the use of a disclaimer by an infringing user has been found not to be sufficient to avoid consumer confusion in the marketplace. In addition, we note that there is a body of academic literature that questions the effectiveness of disclaimers in preventing consumer confusion as to the source of a product. *See* Jacoby & Raskoff, *Disclaimers as a Remedy for Trademark Infringement Litigation: More Trouble Than They Are Worth?*, 76 Trademark Rept. 35 (1986); Radin, *Disclaimers as a Remedy for Trademark Infringement: Inadequacies and Alternatives*, 76 Trademark Rept. 59 (1986); 2 H. Nims, *Unfair Competition and Trademarks* §§ 366f, 379a (4th ed. 1947).

These authors have concluded that disclaimers are frequently not effective. One discussion concluded that disclaimers, especially those (like the disclaimers in question in this case) which employ brief negator words such as "no" or "not," are generally ineffective. *See* Jacoby & Raskopf, *supra* at 54. This conclusion was based on a study of the effect of disclaimers on football jerseys, an example of the effect of corrective advertising, and a generalized framework involving behavioral science research. The authors recommended that courts should consider the effectiveness of a proposed disclaimer more carefully and "whenever disclaimers are considered, empirical studies should be used to evaluate their likely impact. At the very least, no disclaimer should issue without a full hearing regarding its likely effectiveness." *Id.* at 57–58 (citations omitted), *see also Radin, supra* at 72. Radin also advocates the use of other methods either to make a disclaimer more effective or wholly unnecessary; the primary method he advocates is altering the context in which the infringing use occurs to make consumer confusion less likely. *Id.* at 71.

Although it is conceivable that a disclaimer could alleviate the likelihood of confusion that the district court found in this case, the court did not have before it sufficient evidence regarding the revised promotional materials to decide that their disclaimers rendered them significantly less likely to confuse consumers and so that they might be exempted from the injunction. This is especially so as HBO had no opportunity to consider the proposed disclaimers and produce evidence as it had with respect to the slogans and disclaimers that Showtime used at the Convention.

In further proceedings before the district court, Showtime should be free to apply for relief from the injunction, on the basis of its use of disclaimers or otherwise, after it gives adequate notice to HBO.

Upon such an application there would be a heavy burden on Showtime to come forward with evidence sufficient to demonstrate that any proposed materials would significantly reduce the likelihood of consumer confusion. *Accord Charles of the Ritz Group Ltd. v. Quality King Distributors, Inc.*, 832 F.2d 1317 (2d Cir. 1987). We do not believe that Showtime, at any point in this litigation, has met this burden and until it satisfies the district court on the basis of proper showing, it may not use HBO's trademark in its slogan or the related slogans.

We appreciate that this assignment of the burden of proof, unlike the method utilized by the district court, might make it significantly more difficult for Showtime ever to use these slogans. Nevertheless, we believe that it is an appropriate allocation of burdens between these parties for several reasons. First, it acknowledges that by granting the preliminary injunction, the district court found that HBO had adequately proved that the slogan as Showtime first employed it was likely to cause consumer confusion. Second, it recognizes that by using the slogans as they were presented at the Convention, Showtime was infringing on HBO's trademark and, therefore, that Showtime has no right to use the mark unless and until it can demonstrate that, because of some change in the slogan or the context in which it is presented, its use will no longer constitute an infringement. Third, it alleviates the unnecessary hardship that could be imposed on HBO if it repeatedly had to catch up with Showtime's use of its trademark by adequately demonstrating that each new permutation of the slogan and its context was likely to mislead consumers. Fourth, and finally, it is the allocation of the burden of proof which best accords with our interpretation of the Lanham Act as a means of protecting trademark holders and the public from confusion as to the source and promotion of products.

We affirm the district court's issuance of a preliminary injunction but vacate that portion of the order which allowed Showtime to continue using the slogan if it utilizes an appropriate disclaimer and that portion which exempted the revised promotional materials presented to the district court at the hearing conducted before the district court on July 15, 1987. We deny Showtime's cross appeal. This case is remanded for further proceedings consistent with this opinion.

C. Recalls and Destruction

Kiki Undies Corp. v. Promenade Hosiery Mills, Inc.

308 F. Supp. 489 (S.D.N.Y. 1969), *cert. denied*, 396 U.S. 1054 (1970)

MacMahon, J.

Ordered, adjudged and decreed:

1. That the plaintiff, Kiki Undies Corp., has used and is using, in connection with its manufacture, sale and distribution of ladies' wearing apparel and garments in commerce,

the following trademarks: KIKI, KIKI KONTROL; KIKI MAGIC; KIKI SATINETTE and KIKI DELUXE.

2. That the plaintiff duly applied for and registered said trademarks on the Principal Register of the United States Patent Office. That United States Principal Register Trademark Registrations Nos. 709,385 for KIKI; 767,232 for KIKI KONTROL; 767,242 for KIKI MAGIC; 774,624 for KIKI SATINETTE and 818,716 for KIKI DELUXE were duly and legally issued and are valid; and that plaintiff, Kiki Undies Corp., has been and is the lawful owner of all right, title and interest in and to each of said registrations.

3. That defendant, Promenade Hosiery Mills, Inc. (now by change of name Promenade Mills, Inc.) has infringed the aforesaid registered trademarks by using the term Kiki as a trademark, without consent, in commerce in connection with the selling, offering for sale, distributing and advertising ladies' wearing apparel and garments.

4. That a Writ of Perpetual Injunction (attached hereto as an Exhibit to this Interlocutory Judgment) issue out of and under the seal of this Court directed to the said defendant, Promenade Hosiery Mills, Inc., its successors, assigns, officers, agents, attorneys, employees, associates and privies, enjoining and restraining them and each of them from directly or indirectly infringing the aforesaid registered trademarks.

* * *

WRIT OF PERPETUAL INJUNCTION

Promenade Hosiery Mills, Inc. (now by change of name Promenade Mills, Inc. and hereinafter called defendant), its successors or assigns, its officers, agents, servants, employees, attorneys and all other persons in active concert or participation with it or any of them who receive actual notice or knowledge of this Injunction by personal service or otherwise, are perpetually ordered and are perpetually restrained and enjoined as follows:

ENJOINED FROM:

(a) Using the term Kiki, however spelled, whether capitalized, abbreviated, printed or stylized, with or without a hyphen, whether used alone or in combination with any other word or words, whether used in caption, text or otherwise, or orally, or any reproduction, counterfeit, copy or colorable imitation thereof in connection with the sale, offering for sale, distribution or advertising of any goods or services or in connection with which such use is likely to cause confusion, or to cause mistake, or to deceive;

(b) Applying the term Kiki (as defined in paragraph (a)) or any reproduction, counterfeit, copy or colorable imitation thereof to labels, signs, prints, packages, wrappers, receptacles or advertisements intended to be used, or capable of being used, or used in connection with the sale, offering for sale, distribution, or advertising of goods or services on or in connection with which such use is likely to cause confusion, or to cause mistake, or to deceive;

(c) Using the term Kiki (as defined in paragraph (a)) on or in connection with the sale, offering for sale, distribution or advertising of leotards, tights, pantyhose, hosiery, headbands, and the like.

(d) Using the term Kiki (as defined in paragraph (a)) on or in connection with any ladies' garments or ladies' wearing apparel product.

(e) Disparaging or derogating the term Kiki (as defined in paragraph (a)) as a trademark of the plaintiff, or suggesting to anyone that plaintiff does not own it.

(f) Making, having made for it, selling, distributing or disposing of in any manner any advertising or promotional material including ad mats, racks, rack headers, point of sale devices, catalogs, letters or sales brochures using the term Kiki (as defined in paragraph (a)) for or in connection with any of the goods listed in paragraph (c) above, or any ladies' wear garments or ladies' wearing apparel, or any goods on which use of the term Kiki would be likely to cause confusion, mistake, or to deceive.

(g) Filling any order or advising others of any order which specifies any of the goods listed in paragraph (c) above, or any other goods sold, offered for sale, distributed or advertised by defendant or plaintiff or any ladies' wear goods or ladies' garments and which order uses the term Kiki (as defined in paragraph (a)) in relation to said goods.

(h) Inducing or encouraging any third party to use the term (as defined in paragraph (a)) on or in connection with the sale, offering for sale, distribution or advertising of any product listed in paragraph (c) or any ladies' wear product or ladies' garment.

(i) Aiding, abetting, encouraging or inducing another to do any of the acts herein enjoined.

ORDERED TO:

(j) Use best efforts to avoid making any financial or other contribution, directly or indirectly, toward any advertisement, publicity or other form of public announcement which contains the term Kiki (as defined in paragraph (a)) for any of the goods listed in paragraph (c) above, or for any other ladies' wear goods or ladies' garments, or in any way inducing anyone to create, publish, issue, purchase, sell, use or contribute toward such an advertisement.

(k) Respond to each order, letter, or inquiry which specifies any of the goods listed in paragraph (c) above, or any other goods sold, offered for sale, distributed or advertised by defendant or plaintiff or any ladies' wear goods and which uses the term Kiki (as defined in paragraph (a)) in relation to said goods, by mailing in reply, registered or certified mail, return receipt requested, to the originator of said order, letter or inquiry, a letter in the form annexed hereto as Exhibit A[omitted]. A copy of each such letter shall be mailed simultaneously with the original or ribbon copy to the plaintiff, and upon receiving the signed U.S. Mail Receipt indicating delivery, the defendant shall mail, within two business days, said receipt to the plaintiff.

(l) Deliver up to plaintiff, at plaintiff's place of business, within thirty (30) days after service of this Injunction all backing sheets, labels, signs, prints, packages, wrappers, receptacles, letterheads, order forms, billheads, displays, ad mats, racks, rack headers, point of sale devices, catalogs, brochures and any other promotional advertising or other matter in its possession, custody or control on which the said term Kiki (as defined in paragraph (a)) appears for products sold, offered for sale, distributed or advertised by defendant including plates, molds and matrixes for making same.

(m) Exercise its best efforts to withdraw from its customers, retailers and all others all of the materials specified in the above paragraph (l) hereof, including offering reimbursement for same, and deliver the same to plaintiff, at plaintiff's place of business, for destruction. This shall be a continuing effort. If a violation of this paragraph shall come to the attention of plaintiff, plaintiff shall call defendant's attention to such violation; and defendant shall take affirmative action to obtain cessation of such violation and shall advise plaintiff of what action it has taken.

(n) File with the Court and serve on plaintiff within thirty (30) days after service of this Injunction a report in writing, under oath, setting forth in detail the manner and form in which defendant has complied with this Injunction by that date, and again within six (6) months after such service a final report shall be filed and served setting forth in detail the manner and form in which defendant has fully complied with this Injunction.

* * *

D. Monetary Relief

15 U.S.C. §1117, Lanham Act §35

When a violation of any right of the registrant of a mark registered in the Patent and Trademark Office, a violation under section 1125(a), (c), or (d) of this title, or a willful violation under section 1125(c) of this title, shall have been established in any civil action arising under this chapter, the plaintiff shall be entitled, subject to the provisions of sections 1111 and 1114 of this title, and subject to the principles of equity, to recover (1) defendant's profits, (2) any damages sustained by the plaintiff, and (3) the costs of the action. The court shall assess such profits and damages or cause the same to be assessed under its direction. In assessing profits the plaintiff shall be required to prove defendant's sales only; defendant must prove all elements of cost or deduction claimed. In assessing damages the court may enter judgment, according to the circumstances of the case, for any sum above the amount found as actual damages, not exceeding three times such amount....

1. Recovery of Defendant's Profits (Accounting)

George Basch Co. v. Blue Coral, Inc.

968 F.2d 1532 (2d Cir. 1992), cert. denied, 506 U.S. 991

WALKER, J.

Along with several issues regarding the particulars of injunctive relief, this case presents the general question of whether, in an action for trade dress infringement, a plaintiff may recover a defendant's profits without establishing that the defendant engaged in deliberately deceptive conduct. The district court concluded that bad faith was not a necessary predicate for an accounting. We disagree. Accordingly, we hold that in order to justify an award of profits, a plaintiff must establish that the defendant engaged in willful deception.

BACKGROUND

The George Basch Co., Inc., ("Basch") manufactures and distributes NEVR-DULL, a cotton wadding metal polish. NEVR-DULL is packaged in a five ounce cylindrical metal can, about 3-1/2 inches high by 3-1/2 inches in diameter, and navy blue in color. Along with a product description and directions, the product's name is printed on the can in white block lettering. On either side of the product's name there are two red and white icons that depict what the product may be used for: the radiator grill of a car, silverware, a brass lamp, and a motor boat on a trailer.

Appellants, Blue Coral, Inc., its subsidiary Simoniz Canada Ltd., and their mutual president, Michael Moshontz (hereafter collectively referred to as "Blue Coral") manufacture and distribute a line of automotive wheel cleaning and polishing products. In both the United States and Canada, Blue Coral markets these products under the trademark ESPREE. In 1987, Blue Coral approached Basch with respect to becoming Basch's exclusive NEVR-DULL distributor in Canada. By agreement of the parties, effective July 28, 1987, Blue Coral became NEVR-DULL's exclusive Canadian distributor. NEVR-DULL was not sold under the ESPREE mark, and its Canadian trade dress remained substantially the same as the United States' version, with the exception that the French language was employed on the front of the can.

In April 1988, Blue Coral asked Basch to produce a wadding metal polish for Blue Coral to market in the United States. Blue Coral intended to add the polish to its line of ESPREE products. The parties negotiated through August of that year, at which time they ended their talks unsuccessfully due to an impasse regarding price. Blue Coral ultimately contracted with another manufacturer of metal polish.

On July 25, 1988, Blue Coral introduced EVER BRITE—the new ESPREE wadding metal polish—into the United States market. EVER BRITE was packaged in the same size cylindrical metal can used by Basch to package NEVR-DULL. The base color of the EVER BRITE can was black. On its front appeared an angled silver grid-like background. Superimposed over the center of the grid, also on an angle, were large white block letters which read "EVER BRITE." Five different types of wheel faces were depicted in the upper right hand corner of the grid. To the right of the wheel faces appeared six red and white icons that represented silverware, chrome wheels, brassware, brass beds, copperware, and car bumpers and trim.

Relations between Basch and Blue Coral turned bleak. In March 1989, Basch terminated Blue Coral's Canadian distributorship. Approximately one year later, Blue Coral introduced EVER BRITE into the Canadian market. Blue Coral's Canadian trade dress was also substantially the same as its United States' version—merely substituting French print in some places on the can where English had been used, and placing a hyphen between EVER and BRITE where none had been before.

On March 7, 1989, Basch brought this action in the United States District Court for the Eastern District of New York, Non. Jacob Mishler, *Judge.* In its complaint, Basch alleged trade dress infringement in violation of § 43(a) of the Lanham Act, *see* 15 U.S.C. § 1125(a), unfair competition under New York law, misappropriation of confidential business information, tortious interference with business relations, and violation of the New York General Business Law, §§ 349(h) and 368(d). Blue Coral moved for summary judgment on all claims. The district court granted summary judgment for Blue Coral on the § 349(h) New York General Business Law count, but denied summary judgment on Basch's other claims.

The action was tried to a jury in July 1991. The district court directed a verdict in favor of Blue Coral with respect to Basch's claim for misappropriation of confidential business information. The court also ruled that, as a matter of law, Basch was precluded from receiving damages on its trade dress infringement claim because it had failed to produce any evidence regarding actual consumer confusion or that Blue Coral acted with intent to deceive the public.

The district court concluded, however, that despite Basch's failure to introduce evidence on either of these points, Basch could recover Blue Coral's profits if it succeeded on its trade dress infringement claim. The case was submitted to the jury by special verdict. The jury exonerated Blue Coral on the tortious interference count, but found against it on Basch's trade dress infringement claim. Accordingly, it awarded Basch $200,000 in Blue Coral's profits, allegedly stemming from Blue Coral's wrongful use of its EVER BRITE trade dress.

Blue Coral timely moved for judgment n.o.v. In its motion, Blue Coral argued that: (1) Basch had failed to prove that its NEVR-DULL trade dress enjoyed secondary meaning; (2) since Basch had not shown actual consumer confusion, or deceptive conduct on Blue Coral's part, Basch could not recover any of Blue Coral's profits; (3) it was for the district judge sitting as a court in equity, and not the jury, to make an award of profits; and (4) in any event, the $200,000 award was grossly in excess of its actual profits.

The district court denied Blue Coral's motion, and entered its judgment which included the $200,000 jury award. The judgment also contained an injunction allowing Blue Coral to sell off its remaining inventory of infringing cans, but prohibiting any future use of the existing trade dress in the United States market. The district court also denied Basch's application for attorney fees. This appeal followed.

DISCUSSION
I. BLUE CORAL'S APPEAL

* * *

B. Grounds for Awarding Profits

We turn now to the issue of whether the district court correctly authorized an award of Blue Coral's profits. Section 35(a) of the Lanham Act generally provides that a successful plaintiff under the act shall be entitled, "subject to the principles of equity, to recover (1) defendant's profits, (2) any damages sustained by the plaintiff, and (3) costs of the action." 15 U.S.C. §1117(a). Clearly, the statute's invocation of equitable principles as guideposts in the assessment of monetary relief vests the district court with some degree of discretion in shaping that relief. *See id.*, (both damage and profit awards may be assessed "according to the circumstances of the case"). Nevertheless, that discretion must operate within legally defined parameters.

For example, it is well settled that in order for a Lanham Act plaintiff to receive an award of damages the plaintiff must prove either "'actual consumer confusion or deception resulting from the violation,'" *Getty Petroleum Corp. v. Island Transportation Corp.,* 878 F.2d 650, 655 (2d Cir. 1989) (quoting *PPX Enterprises, Inc. v. Audiofidelity Enterprises, Inc.,* 818 F.2d 266, 271 (2d Cir. 1987)), or that the defendant's actions were intentionally deceptive thus giving rise to a rebuttable presumption of consumer confusion. Here, Basch failed to present any evidence regarding consumer confusion or intentional deception. Accordingly, prior to the jury's deliberation, the district court correctly decided that damages were not an available form of relief. Basch does not appeal from this ruling.

However, with respect to authorizing an award of Blue Coral's profits, the district judge concluded that §35(a) affords a wider degree of equitable latitude. In denying its j.n.o.v. motion, the district court rejected Blue Coral's position that, absent a finding of defendant's willfully deceptive conduct, a court may not award profits. Rather, it relied upon contrary dictum in *Louis Vuitton S.A. v. Lee,* 875 F.2d 584, 588–89 (7th Cir. 1989), in determining that a Lanham Act plaintiff may be entitled to the profits of an innocent infringer, i.e., one who inadvertently misappropriates the plaintiff's trade dress. To the extent that the cases are ambiguous as to whether deceptive conduct is a necessary basis for an accounting, we take this opportunity to clarify the law.

The rule in this circuit has been that an accounting for profits is normally available "only if the 'defendant is unjustly enriched, if the plaintiff sustained damages from the infringement, or if the accounting is necessary to deter a willful infringer from doing so again.'" *Burndy Corp. v. Teledyne Industries, Inc.*, 748 F.2d 767, 772 (2d Cir. 1984) (quoting *W.E. Bassett Co. v. Revlon, Inc.*, 435 F.2d 656, 664 (2d Cir. 1970)). Courts have interpreted the rule to describe three categorically distinct rationales.

Thus, the fact that willfulness expressly defines the third rationale (deterrence) may suggest that the element of intentional misconduct is unnecessary in order to require an accounting based upon a theory of unjust enrichment or damages. However, the broad language contained in *Burndy Corp. and W.E. Bassett Co.* is in no way dispositive on this point. Indeed, a closer investigation into the law's historical development strongly supports our present conclusion that, under any theory, a finding of defendant's willful deceptiveness is a prerequisite for awarding profits.

Unjust Enrichment: The fact that an accounting may proceed on a theory of unjust enrichment is largely a result of legal institutional evolution. Prior to the fusion of law and equity under the Federal Rules of Civil Procedure, *see* Fed. R. Civ. P. 2., courts of law were the sole dispensary of damages, while the chancellor issued specific relief. However, in order to avoid piecemeal litigation, once a court of equity took jurisdiction over a case it would do complete justice—even if that entailed granting a monetary award. This resulted in the development of parallel remedial schemes.

Long ago, the Supreme Court explained the origin of profit awards in trademark infringement suits:

> The infringer is required in equity to account for and yield up his gains to the true owner [of the mark], upon a principle analogous to that which charges a trustee with the profits acquired by the wrongful use of the property of the *cestui que trust.* Not that equity assumes jurisdiction upon the ground that a trust exists.... The jurisdiction must be rested upon some other equitable ground—in ordinary cases, as in the present, the right to an injunction—but the court of equity, having acquired jurisdiction upon such a ground, retains it for the purpose of administering complete relief, rather than send the injured party to a court of law for his damages. And profits are then allowed as an equitable measure of compensation, on the theory of a trust *ex maleficio.*

Hamilton-Brown Shoe Co. v. Wolf Brothers & Co., 240 U.S. 251, 259, 60 L. Ed. 629, 36 S. Ct. 269 (1916).

Thus, a defendant who is liable in a trademark or trade dress infringement action may be deemed to hold its profits in constructive trust for the injured plaintiff. However, this results only "when the defendant's sales 'were attributable to its infringing use' of the plaintiff's" mark, *Burndy Corp.*, 748 F.2d at 772 (quoting *W.E. Bassett Co.*, 435 F.2d at 664), and when the infringing use was at the plaintiff's expense. *Id.* at 773. In other words, a defendant becomes accountable for its profits when the plaintiff can show that, were it not for defendant's infringement, the defendant's sales would otherwise have gone to the plaintiff. *Id.* at 772.

At bottom, this is simply another way of formulating the element of consumer confusion required to justify a damage award under the Lanham Act. As such, it follows that a profits award, premised upon a theory of unjust enrichment, requires a showing of actual consumer confusion—or at least proof of deceptive intent so as to raise the rebuttable presumption of consumer confusion. *See Resource Developers*, 926 F.2d at 140; *PPX Enterprises*, 818 F.2d at 273.

Moreover, the doctrine of constructive trust has traditionally been invoked to defeat those gains accrued by wrongdoers as a result of fraud. *See Latham v. Father Divine*, 299 N.Y. 22, 26–27, 85 N.E.2d 168, 170 (1949) ("A constructive trust will be erected whenever necessary to satisfy the demands of justice.... Its applicability is limited only by the inventiveness of men who find new ways to enrich themselves by grasping what should not belong to them."); *Restatement of Restitution,* § 160 cmt. d (1937); *cf Robert Stigwood Group Ltd. v. O'Reilly*, 530 F.2d 1096, 1100–1101 & n.9 (2d Cir.), *cert. denied,* 429 U.S. 848, 50 L. Ed. 2d 121, 97 S. Ct. 135 (1976) (recognizing that imposition of a constructive trust over defendant's profits may be an available remedy for willful copyright infringement).

The rationale underlying the Supreme Court's holding in *Hamilton Shoe Co.* reflects this purpose. There, the Court upheld a profits award for trademark infringement where the "imitation of complainant's mark was fraudulent, [and] the profits included in the decree [were] confined to such as accrued to the defendant through its persistence in the unlawful simulation...." 240 U.S. at 261. Thus, it would seem that for the defendant's enrichment to be "unjust" in terms of warranting an accounting, it must be the fruit of willful deception. *See El Greco Leather Products Co. v. Shoe World Inc.*, 726 F. Supp. 25, 29–30 (E.D.N.Y. 1989).

Where Plaintiff Sustains Damages: Historically, an award of defendant's profits has also served as a rough proxy measure of plaintiff's damages. Due to the inherent difficulty in isolating the causation behind diverted sales and injured reputation, damages from trademark or trade dress infringement are often hard to establish. Recognizing this, the Supreme Court has stated that, "infringement and damage having been found, the Act requires the trademark owner to prove only the sales of articles bearing the infringing mark." *Mishawaka Mfg. Co.*, 316 U.S. at 206.

Under this rule, profits from defendant's proven sales are awarded to the plaintiff unless the defendant can show "that the infringement had no relationship" to those earnings. *Id.* This shifts the burden of proving economic injury off the innocent party, and places the hardship of disproving economic gain onto the infringer. Of course, this "does not stand for the proposition that an accounting will be ordered merely because there has been an infringement." *Champion Plug Co.*, 331 U.S. at 131. Rather, in order to award profits there must first he "a basis for finding damage." *Id.*; *Mishawaka Mfg. Co.*, 316 U.S. at 206. While a plaintiff who seeks the defendant's profits may be relieved of certain evidentiary requirements otherwise carried by those trying to prove damages, a plaintiff must nevertheless establish its general right to damages before defendant's profits are recoverable.

Thus, under the "damage" theory of profits, a plaintiff typically has been required to show consumer confusion resulting from the infringement. *Cf. Perfect Fit Indus., Inc. v. Acme Quilting Co.*, 618 F.2d 950, 955 (2d Cir.), *cert. denied,* 459 U.S. 832, 74 L. Ed. 2d 71, 103 S. Ct. 73 (1980) (New York law of unfair competition); *G.H. Mumm Champagne v. Eastern Wine Corp.*, 142 F.2d 499, 501 (2d Cir.), *cert. denied,* 323 U.S. 715, 65 S. Ct. 41, 89 L. Ed. 575 (1944) (L. Hand, J.). Whether a plaintiff also had to show willfully deceptive conduct on the part of the defendant is not so clear. While some courts "rejected good faith as a defense to an accounting for profits," *Burger King Corp. v. Mason*, 855 F.2d 779, 781 (11th Cir. 1988) (citing *Wolfe v. National Lead Co.*, 272 F.2d 867, 871 (9th Cir. 1959), *cert. denied,* 362 U.S. 950, 4 L. Ed. 2d 868, 80 S. Ct. 860 (1960)), others have concluded that a defendant's bad faith is the touchstone of accounting liability. *Cf. Champion Plug Co.*, 331 U.S. at 131 (accounting was unavailable where "there had been no showing of fraud or palming off"); *Carl Zeiss Stiftung v. Veb Carl Zeiss Jena*, 433 F.2d 686, 706–08 (2d Cir. 1970) (discussing monetary awards which are inclusive of both damages and profits).

Deterrence: Finally, we have held that a court may award a defendant's profits solely upon a finding that the defendant fraudulently used the plaintiff's mark. *See Monsanto Chemical Co. v. Perfect Fit Mfg. Co.,* 349 F.2d 389, 396 (2d Cir. 1965), *cert. denied,* 383 U.S. 942, 86 S. Ct. 1195, 16 L. Ed. 2d 206 (1966). The rationale underlying this holding is not compensatory in nature, but rather seeks to protect the public at large. By awarding the profits of a bad faith infringer to the rightful owner of a mark, we promote the secondary effect of deterring public fraud regarding the source and quality of consumer goods and services. *Id.*; *W.E. Bassett Co.,* 435 F.2d at 664.

* * *

Although these three theories address slightly different concerns, they do share common ground. In varying degrees, a finding of defendant's intentional deceptiveness has always been an important consideration in determining whether an accounting was an appropriate remedy. In view of this, the American Law Institute has recently concluded that a finding of willful infringement is the necessary catalyst for the disgorgement of ill-gotten profits. *See Restatement,* § 37(1)(a) ("One ... is liable for the net profits earned on profitable transactions resulting from [the infringement], if, but only if, the actor engaged in conduct with the intention of causing confusion or deception ...").

We agree with the position set forth in § 37 of the *Restatement* and therefore hold that, under § 35(a) of the Lanham Act, a plaintiff must prove that an infringer acted with willful deception before the infringer's profits are recoverable by way of an accounting. Along with the *Restatement's* drafters, we believe that this requirement is necessary to avoid the conceivably draconian impact that a profits remedy might have in some cases. While damages directly measure the plaintiff's loss, *defendant's* profits measure the defendant's gain. Thus, an accounting may overcompensate for a plaintiff's actual injury and create a windfall judgment at the defendant's expense. *See Restatement,* § 37 at cmt. e. Of course, this is not to be confused with *plaintiff's* lost profits, which have been traditionally compensable as an element of plaintiff's damages.

So as to limit what may be an undue windfall to the plaintiff, and prevent the potentially inequitable treatment of an "innocent" or "good faith" infringer, most courts require proof of intentional misconduct before allowing a plaintiff to recover the defendant's profits. We underscore that in the absence of such a showing, a plaintiff is not foreclosed from receiving monetary relief. Upon proof of actual consumer confusion, a plaintiff may still obtain damages—which, in turn, may be inclusive of plaintiff's own lost profits.

Neither *Burndy Corp.* or *W.E. Bassett Co.* rejects the notion that willful deceptiveness is a necessary predicate for an award of defendant's profits. *See El Greco Leather Products Co.,* 726 F. Supp. at 29. To the contrary, both cases reflect the centrality of this factor. For example, defendant's profits were denied in *Burndy Corp.* because the plaintiff failed to establish that its own sales were diverted as a result of the infringement and that the defendant acted willfully. This finding precluded *both* unjust enrichment and deterrence as available grounds for relief. *See* 748 F.2d at 773. On the other hand, an accounting was ordered in *W.E. Bassett Co.* solely because the defendant had "deliberately and fraudulently infringed Bassett's mark." 435 F.2d at 664. Finally, to the extent that these cases suggest that a defendant's profits are recoverable whenever a plaintiff may obtain damages, we conclude that the language of *Burndy Corp.* and *W.E. Bassett Co.* was simply imprecise on this point, and we reject such a reading. *Cf. Carl Zeiss Stiftung,* 433 F.2d at 706–08.

Having stated that a finding of willful deceptiveness is necessary in order to warrant an accounting for profits, we note that it may not be sufficient. *See Springs Mills, Inc. v. Ultracashmere House, Ltd.,* 724 F.2d 352, 356 (2d Cir. 1983) ("an accounting may be appropriate whenever an infringer's conduct is willful"). While under certain circumstances, the egregiousness of the fraud may, of its own, justify an accounting, *see W.E. Bassett Co.,* 435 F.2d at 664, generally, there are other factors to be considered. Among these are such familiar concerns as: (1) the degree of certainty that the defendant benefited from the unlawful conduct; (2) availability and adequacy of other remedies; (3) the role of a particular defendant in effectuating the infringement; (4) plaintiff's laches; and (5) plaintiff's unclean hands. *See generally Restatement,* § 37(2) at cmt. f & cases cited in the reporter's notes. The district court's discretion lies in assessing the relative importance of these factors and determining whether, on the whole, the equities weigh in favor of an accounting. As the Lanham Act dictates, every award is "subject to equitable principles" and should be determined "according to the circumstances of the case." 15 U.S.C. § 1117.

In light of the foregoing legal analysis, the district court's error becomes apparent. To begin with, the district judge concluded that an accounting was warranted in order to prevent Blue Coral's unjust enrichment. However, as stated earlier, Basch produced no evidence to suggest that the infringement caused any sales diversion. As a result, there is nothing to suggest that Blue Coral's EVER BRITE sales were at Basch's expense. It follows that "an accounting based on unjust enrichment is precluded." *Burndy Corp.,* 748 F.2d at 773.

Secondly, even if Basch had shown loss of sales, it still would not have been entitled to an accounting for profits under a theory of unjust enrichment—or any other theory. The jury made no finding to the effect that Blue Coral was a bad faith infringer. Indeed, one reason why the judge refused to let the jury assess damages was the fact that Basch failed to present any evidence regarding bad faith infringement. Nevertheless, Basch argues that the court's jury instruction on liability—which suggested that the jury consider whether Blue Coral intended "to benefit" from Basch's NEVR-DULL trade dress— taken in conjunction with the special verdict finding that Blue Coral "intended to imitate Basch's NEVR-DULL trade dress," results in a constructive finding that Blue Coral engaged in intentionally deceptive conduct. We disagree.

There is an "essential distinction ... between a deliberate attempt to deceive and a deliberate attempt to compete. Absent confusion, imitation of certain successful features in another's product is not unlawful and to that extent a 'free ride' is permitted." *Norwich Pharmaceutical Co. v. Sterling Drug, Inc.,* 271 F.2d 569, 572 (2d Cir. 1959) (citation omitted). Of course, even when a likelihood of confusion does arise, that does not inexorably lead to the conclusion that the defendant acted with deliberate deceit. Depending upon the circumstances, consumer confusion might as easily result from an innocent competitor who inadvertently crosses the line between a "free ride" and liability, as it could from a defendant's intentionally fraudulent conduct.

In this regard, we note that the jury specifically found that "the acts of [Blue Coral] in violation of Basch's rights [were not] done wantonly and maliciously and in reckless disregard of Basch's rights." This conclusion is buttressed by the fact this is not a case of a counterfeit trade dress from which a jury might infer that Blue Coral "intended to deceive the public concerning the origin of the goods." *WSM, Inc. v. Tennessee Sales Co.,* 709 F.2d 1084, 1087 (6th Cir. 1983). Thus, we find no merit in Basch's contention that the jury effectively concluded that Blue Coral acted with wrongful intent.

Accordingly, we reverse the district court's denial of Blue Coral's j.n.o.v. motion, insofar as it related to the availability of an accounting in this case, and we vacate the jury's profits award. Because we hold that an accounting was not available in this case, we need not reach the issue of whether it was appropriate for the jury to calculate profits.

* * *

---

2. Recovery of Plaintiff's Actual Damages

Brunswick v. Spinit
832 F.2d 513 (1987)

[Appellant is a fishing reel manufacturer. Appellee is a former employee of Appellant and now a competing fishing reel manufacturer. The court below found the Appellee had copied one of the Appellant's fishing reels in violation of Section 43(a) of the Lanham Act and the Oklahoma Fair Trade Practices Act. The lower court issued an injunction and recall but refused to issue any monetary damages.]

* * *

Although damages may be awarded for a violation of section 43(a), the award is distinguishable from injunctive relief, because plaintiff bears a greater burden of proof of entitlement. Likelihood of confusion is insufficient; to recover damages plaintiff must prove it has been damaged by actual consumer confusion or deception resulting from the violation. Schutt Mfg. Co., 673 F.2d at 206; *see also Quabaug Rubber Co.*, 567 F.2d at 161–62. Actual consumer confusion may be shown by direct evidence, a diversion of sales or direct testimony from the public, or by circumstantial evidence such as consumer surveys.

> Although the quantum of damages, as distinguished from entitlement, must be demonstrated with specificity, courts may engage in "some degree of speculation in computing the *amount* of damages, particularly when the inability to compute them is attributable to the defendant's wrongdoing."

PPX Enters. Inc., 818 F.2d at 271 (citations omitted) (quoting *Burndy Corp.*, 748 F.2d at 771).

The district court found that there was actual confusion among consumers and retailers, Amended Findings of Fact and Conclusions of Law, record, vol. 1, at 490, and that Zebco and Spinit sell reels in the same marketing channels, in direct competition with each other. *Id.* Those findings support the court's determination that Brunswick established a legal basis for the recovery of damages, indicating that actual consumer confusion resulted from Spinit's violation of section 43(a). Nevertheless, by adding that Brunswick did not establish clear proof of damages, the court implies that Brunswick presented insufficient proof of actual damages. The court more likely meant that, although Brunswick established entitlement to damages, it failed to show that it suffered damages in fact.

Brunswick submitted evidence that in the fiscal year ending July 1983 sales of all Zebco spin-cast products dropped off by five percent, record, vol. 10, at 14, sales of spin-cast reels generally had decreased by six percent due to the recession. *Id.* at 15. Sales for the Zebco 33, however, dropped sixteen percent. *Id.* Spinit introduced testimony that the introduction of other new reels on the market might have contributed to the decrease in Zebco's sales. However, in light of the trial court's finding of actual confusion and direct competition between the reels, we are not persuaded that other reels were the sole cause of the substantial reduction in the sale of the Zebco 33. Thus, the evidence does not indicate that Brunswick failed to show it suffered any actual damages.

A defendant whose wrongful conduct has caused the difficulty in assessing damages cannot complain that the damages are somewhat speculative. *Eastman Kodak Co. v. Southern Photo Materials Co.*, 273 U.S. 359, 379, 71 L. Ed. 684, 47 S. Ct. 400 (1927). *See also DeVries v. Starr*, 393 F.2d 9, 20–21 (10th Cir. 1968). Evidence of the amount of damages may be circumstantial and inexact. *Eastman Kodak Co.*, 273 U.S. at 379.

> In a case such as this, where the wrong is of such a nature as to preclude exact ascertainment of the amount of damages, plaintiff may recover upon a showing of the extent of the damages as a matter of just and reasonable inference, although the result may be only an approximation.

Bangor Punta Operations, Inc., 543 F.2d at 1110–11 (quoting *Kestenbaum v. Falstaff Brewing Corp.*, 514 F.2d 690, 698 (5th Cir. 1975), *cert. denied*, 424 U.S. 943, 47 L. Ed. 2d 349, 96 S. Ct. 1412 (1976)).

Brunswick bases its claim for damages on the theory that Zebco lost one sale of a Model 33 as a result of each Spinit SR 210 reel sold. While this court does not necessarily believe that each Spinit sale resulted in a corresponding loss of sale by Zebco, the theory provides an upper range for an award of damages. The district court may also look to the difference in the decline of Model 33 sales as compared with the decline in sales of Zebco's other spin-cast reels. Those items of evidence provide the court a broad basis from which it may arrive at a fair, if not precise, amount with which to compensate Brunswick for wrongful infringement. We reverse the trial court's finding on damages and remand for findings of the amount of damages due.

Brunswick also appeals from the trial court's denial of its motion for post-trial discovery. After trial but before final judgment, Spinit continued to sell SR 210 reels. Brunswick moved for permission to discover the number of reels sold and the profits earned by Spinit during that period.

"Trademark infringement is a continuous wrong and, as such, gives rise to a claim for relief so long as the infringement persists." *James Burrough Ltd. v. Sign of the Beefeater, Inc.*, 572 F.2d 574, 578 (7th Cir. 1978). *See also* 4 Callmann, Unfair Competition Trademarks and Monopolies, § 22.50 at 260 (4th ed. 1983) [Callmann]. Thus, Brunswick is entitled to damages until the time the wrongful infringement ceased. The trial court had jurisdiction to award damages up to the date of final judgment, *see Rea v. Ford Motor Co.*, 560 F.2d 554, 557 (3d Cir.), *cert. denied*, 434 U.S. 923, 54 L. Ed. 2d 281, 98 S. Ct. 401 (1977), and it could permit discovery to determine those damages until the same date. Brunswick is, therefore, entitled to reasonable discovery, consistent with the trial court's determination of damages, to ascertain the amount of damages suffered after the end of trial and before final judgment.

* * *

Note

1. What elements of trademark remedies are appropriate for a judge or for the jury? *See* Mark A. Thurmon, *Ending the Seventh Amendment Confusion: A Critical Analysis of the Right to a Jury Trial in Trademark Cases*, 11 TEX. INTELL. PROP. L. J. 1 (2002).

3. Punitive Damages

15 U.S.C. §1117(a), Lanham Act §35(a)

… If the court shall find that the amount of the recovery based on profits is either inadequate or excessive the court may in its discretion enter judgment for such sum as the court shall find to be just, according to the circumstances of the case. Such sum in either of the above circumstances shall constitute compensation and not a penalty …

Getty Petroleum Corp. v. Bartco Petroleum Corp.

858 F.2d 103 (2d Cir. 1988), *cert. denied*, 490 U.S. 1006 (1989)

* * *

CARDAMONE, J.

B. § 35 and Punitive Damages

Having overcome both initial obstacles, we turn to consider the central issue presented—whether the district court erred when it found that § 35 of the Lanham Act authorized the jury to award punitive damages against the defendants for willful infringement of the "Getty" mark. To decide this question requires an examination of the Lanham Act's language, its legislative history, and relevant case law.

I. Statutory Language

Analysis commences with § 35's plain language. "Statutory construction must begin with the language employed by Congress and the assumption that the ordinary meaning of that language accurately expresses the legislative purpose." *Park 'N Fly, Inc. v. Dollar Park and Fly, Inc.*, 469 U.S. 189, 194, 83 L. Ed. 2d 582, 105 S. Ct. 658 (1985) (construing Lanham Act provision). Moreover, "absent a clearly expressed legislative intention to the contrary, that language must ordinarily be regarded as conclusive." *Consumer Prod. Safety Comm'n v. GTE Sylvania, Inc.*, 447 U.S. 102, 108, 64 L. Ed. 2d 766, 100 S. Ct. 2051 (1980).

Section 35 of the Lanham Act provides

> When a violation of any right of the registrant of a mark registered in the Patent and Trademark Office shall have been established in any civil action arising under this chapter, the plaintiff shall be entitled, … subject to the principles of equity, to recover (1) defendant's profits, (2) any damages sustained by the plaintiff, and (3) the costs of the action.… In assessing damages the court may enter judgment, according to the circumstances of the case, for any sum above the amount found as actual damages, not exceeding three times such amount. If the court shall find that the amount of the recovery based on profits is either inadequate or excessive the court may in its discretion enter judgment for such sum as the court shall find to be just, according to the circumstances of the case. Such sum in either of the above circumstances shall constitute compensation and not a penalty. The court in exceptional cases may award reasonable attorney fees to the prevailing party.

15 U.S.C. § 1117(a) (Supp. IV 1986).

As can be seen, three nonexclusive monetary remedies are provided: recovery of defendant's profits, of any damages sustained by plaintiff, or of the costs of the action. Unlimited enhancement or reduction of an award based on defendant's profits is permitted in order to correct inadequacy or excessiveness. Where—as here—the recovery is based on the plaintiff's damages, the court—not the jury—may enhance the award up to three times the amount of actual damages. Such enhancement functions as "compensation *and not a penalty*." (emphasis supplied).

No mention of punitive damages is made in this comprehensive statutory recovery scheme for infringement of a registered mark. Drawing from the statute's plain language, it is apparent that Congress did not allow for punitive damages as a remedy for holders of infringed marks. Nevertheless, the legislative history must be carefully plumbed to see if a congressional purpose contrary to that reading of the statutory language may be ascertained.

2. Legislative History

The legislation ultimately enacted as the Lanham Act or Trademark Act of 1946, Pub. L. No. 79-489, 60 Stat. 427 (1946) (codified as amended at 15 U.S.C. §§ 1051–1127 (1982 & Supp. IV 1986)), was conceived at a 1920 meeting of the American Bar Association's Patent Section. *See* J. McCarthy, 1 *Trademarks and Unfair Competition* § 5:4 (2d ed. 1984). In 1921 an A.B.A. committee formed by the Patent Section returned a draft of the bill—proposed to Congress first as the "Ernst Bill," then as the "Vestal Bill"—designed to revise the already inadequate Trademark Act of 1905, Pub. L. No. 58-84, 33 Stat. 724 (1905) (1905 Act). Both of these bills were the subject of congressional hearings and revisions until 1937. *See* 1 J. McCarthy, *supra*, at § 5:4; Koelemay, *Monetary Relief for Trademark Infringement Under the Lanham Act,* 72 Trademark Rep. 458, 481 (1982). In 1938, Congressman Lanham introduced a new bill largely based on the notes of A.B.A. trademark committee member Edward Rogers. *See* Rogers, *The Lanham Act & the Social Function of Trademarks*, 14 Law & Contemp. Probs. 173, 180 (1949). After a number of revisions, a draft finally met with the approval of both Houses of Congress and the Lanham Act was signed into law on July 5, 1946.

(a) The 1905 Act

A brief review of the background of the 1905 Act is helpful. Consistent with the merger of law and equity, § 35 of the Lanham Act, currently 15 U.S.C. § 1117(a), incorporated § 16 from the 1905 Act, 33 Stat. 728 (remedy at law for registered trademark infringement), as well as § 19, 33 Stat. 729 (remedy in equity). Both § 16 and § 19 of the 1905 Act gave the district court discretion to increase an award of actual damages up to three times its amount. In addition § 19 allowed for recovery in equity based on an infringer's profits. Section 35 of the Lanham Act echoes these earlier recovery provisions. Significantly, neither § 16 nor § 19 contained provisions for punitive damages.

Although the patent law models for the 1905 Act authorized increased damages as a punitive concept, *see* Koelemay, *supra*, at 479–80, there is evidence that the 1905 Act's discretionary enhancement provision was remedial rather than punitive in nature. As the House Report on the 1905 Act explains, enhancement was partly justified by the difficulty of proving actual damages. The provision was

> new in the law of trade-marks. Similar provisions exist in the copyright and patent laws.... The difficulty of proving exact damages in cases of this character is well understood.... The Government, which has made provision for the registration of trade-marks, should accord to the owners thereof ... full and complete redress for violation of their rights.

H.R. Rep. No. 3147, 58th Cong., 3d Sess. 9 (1904); *see* S. Rep. No. 3278, 58th Cong., 3d Sess. 10 (1905) (same language).

The 1905 Act's enhancement provision—substantially repeated in § 35 of the Lanham Act—was included to enable courts to redress fully plaintiffs whose actual damages were difficult to prove. When the enhancement provisions of the 1905 Act were transported into § 35 of the Lanham Act they carried with them the same conceptual baggage, that is to say, of being remedial and not punitive in nature. Further, at the time of the Lanham Act's passage, there were no reported cases in which judges had exercised their discretionary power to increase actual damages under § 16 or § 19 of the 1905 Act. *See* 2 J. McCarthy, *supra*, at § 30:28(B). Thus, the 1905 Act's language, history, and judicial construction give no affirmative indication that when Congress enacted § 35 of the Lanham Act—basing its recovery scheme in part on the 1905 Act—it aimed to furnish punitive damages as a remedy.

(b) § 35 of the Lanham Act

The drafters of § 35 of the Lanham Act embellished upon the 1905 Act's recovery provisions in two significant ways. First, added to the provisions for increasing recovery was the caveat that a court's enhancement of a damage award or adjustment of profits awarded "shall constitute compensation and not a penalty." Second, all monetary recovery under § 35 is "subject to the principles of equity." The legislative history of these two embellishments argues strongly that it was Congress' purpose to preclude punitive damages as a remedy for trademark infringement.

The "compensation and not a penalty" clause borrows language from the Copyright Act of 1909, Pub. L. No. 60-349; § 25(b), 35 Stat. 1075, 1081 (1909), allowing for recovery of actual damages and actual profits from an infringer, in lieu of which a court could assess such sums, within limits, as appeared to be just so long as the discretionary award was "not . . . regarded as a penalty." That phrase of the Copyright Act codified the Supreme Court's result in *Brady v. Daly*, 175 U.S. 148, 44 L. Ed. 109, 20 S. Ct. 62 (1899); *see* Koelemay, *supra*, at 521–23. The Court held in *Brady* that the imposition by statute of a mandatory minimum award for copyright infringement constituted neither penalty nor forfeiture. 175 U.S. at 154–55; *see L.A. Westermann Co. v. Dispatch Printing Co.*, 249 U.S. 100, 107-09, 63 L. Ed. 499, 39 S. Ct. 194 (1919). The minimum recovery, the Court continued, "does not change the character of the statute and render it a penal instead of a remedial one." *Brady*, 175 U.S. at 154. A.B.A. committee member Rogers referred to the *Brady* decision during joint hearings on the trademark bill in response to an inquiry on the effect of the "compensation and not a penalty" clause. *Registration of Trade-marks: Joint* Hearings on S. 2679 Before the House and Senate Comms. on Patents, 68th Cong., 2d Sess. 48 (1925) [hereinafter *1925 Hearings*]; *see* Koelemay, *supra*, at 523 & n.385. Hence, the 1909 Copyright Act's damages provision was construed at the time the Lanham Act was under consideration as a compensatory measure and not as a punitive measure. *See* Koelemay, *supra*, at 523; *see also Davilla v. Brunswick-Balke Collender Co.*, 94 F.2d 567, 570 (2d Cir.), *cert. denied*, 304 U.S. 572, 58 S. Ct. 1040, 82 L. Ed. 1536 (1938).

During the 1925 joint hearings on the draft of an early trademark bill, Rogers contrasted the 1905 Act's treble damages provision with a proposed provision that would give courts discretion to raise or lower awards of damages and profits

> [The 1905 Act's trebling provision] seems to me to be useless, and anything more than proper compensation, an artificial increase, is in the nature of a penalty. So it seems to us better to give the court discretion to award the damages which under all the circumstances of the case seemed to be just, rather than arbitrarily fix treble damages. . . .

1925 Hearings, supra, at 48 (testimony of Edward Rogers).

Concern that a trial court's discretion to increase a monetary award might serve as a punitive instead of remedial function was again manifested during hearings in 1941 before the Subcommittee on Trademarks of the House Committee on Patents. When the discussion focused on the provision for adjusting inadequate or excessive recovery based on profits, Mr. Fenning (of the United States Patent Quarterly) worried aloud that despite the "compensation and not a penalty" clause and the requirement that courts consider the circumstances of each case, the provision might allow unlimited recovery. Under this provision, he stated, "if [a judge] thinks the [infringer] has done a bad thing, the court can fine him in any sum he wants to." *Trade-marks: Hearings on H.R. 102, H.R. 5461, and S. 895 Before the Subcomm. on Trade-marks of the House Comm. on Patents*, 77th Cong., 1st Sess. 203 (1941) [hereinafter *1941 Hearings*]. Representative Lanham agreed, stating that "there should be some limitation." *Id.* But Rogers emphasized that the provision to increase or decrease recovery based on an infringer's profits was simply a recognition of the problems of proof facing plaintiffs and that if the amount proven is inadequate, "a reasonable sum in the way of ordinary damages ought to be awarded." *Id.* at 205. Reacting to the suggestion that a plaintiff receive as recovery of defendant's profits an amount exceeding defendant's total sales, Rogers further stated, "You are going to have a penalty there, and you do not want to do it." *Id.* Thus, Congress' insertion of the "compensation and not a penalty clause" supports a reading of § 35 that would preclude punitive damages.

The Lanham Act's second embellishment on the recovery provisions of the 1905 Act is the requirement that all monetary recovery under § 35 be "subject to the principles of equity." This language was added in the final draft of the Lanham bill introduced in 1945 and enacted in 1946. H.R. 1654, 79th Cong., 2d Sess. (1946); *see* Koelemay, *supra*, at 485. The only explanation for the phrase is found in a 1941 letter to Representative Lanham. *See* Koelemay, *supra*, at 485. "It seems clear," the letter explains, "that the normal principles of equity in respect of allowance of and defenses to an accounting of profits and the recovery of damages are not affected by this bill." *1941 Hearings, supra*, at 228 (letter from Milton Handler). Therefore, the writer recommends inserting "according to the principles of equity" in the first sentence of what became § 35 in order "to effectuate the intentions of the draftsmen." *Id.* Although this letter, in suggesting the addition of the words "according to the principles of equity," obviously does not evince a congressional purpose with respect to punitive damages, it is at least plain that absent express statutory authority, punitive damages are not ordinarily recoverable in equity. *See* Koelemay, *supra*, at 520; *see also Coca-Cola Co. v. Dixi-Cola Labs.*, 155 F.2d 59, 63 (4th Cir.), *cert. denied*, 329 U.S. 773, 67 S. Ct. 192, 91 L. Ed. 665 (1946). *Cf. Livingston v. Woodworth*, 56 U.S. (15 How.) 546, 559–60, 14 L. Ed. 809 (1854) (reversing punitive award for patent infringement because award based on "chastisement" was contrary to "well-established rules of equity jurisprudence").

Some years ago we construed § 35's phrase "subject to the principles of equity" to preclude any monetary relief "'where an injunction will satisfy the equities of the case' and where 'there has been no showing of fraud or palming off.'" *Carl Zeiss Stiftung v. VEB Carl Zeiss Jena*, 433 F.2d 686, 706–07 (2d Cir. 1970) (quoting *Champion Spark Plug Co. v. Sanders*, 331 U.S. 125, 131, 91 L. Ed. 1386, 67 S. Ct. 1136 (1947)), *cert. denied*, 403 U.S. 905, 91 S. Ct. 2205, 29 L. Ed. 2d 680 (1971). Thus, making recovery under § 35 subject to principles of equity scarcely can be used to support the imposition of punitive damages. Review of § 35 of the Lanham Act's legislative history consequently does not raise any doubt regarding our earlier conclusion based on reading the plain language of the Act. Neither the Lanham Act's antecedent—the 1905 Act—nor its embellishments in the context of monetary recovery evidence any congressional purpose to authorize punitive damages.

3. Relevant Caselaw

We conclude analysis of § 35 of the Lanham Act with a review of relevant caselaw. Although not on all fours with the instant matter, the Supreme Court's reasoning in *Fleischmann Distilling Corp. v. Maier Brewing Co.*, 386 U.S. 714, 18 L. Ed. 2d 475, 87 S. Ct. 1404 (1967), sheds considerable light on the availability of punitive damages under § 35. In *Fleischmann*, the Court ruled that federal courts lacked power to award reasonable attorney fees even when a plaintiff established deliberate infringement of its trademark because at that time § 35's enumeration of available compensatory remedies did not include such an award. *Id.* at 721. Eight years later Congress amended § 35 by adding that "The court in exceptional cases may award reasonable attorney fees to the prevailing party." Pub. L. No. 93-600, 88 Stat. 1955 (1975), *reprinted in* 1974 U.S. Code Cong. & Admin. News 2260 (codified at 15 U.S.C. § 1117(a) (Supp. IV 1986)).

The reasoning of *Fleischmann* began with recognition of the general rule that "attorney's fees are not ordinarily recoverable". *Id.* at 717. Exceptions to the so-called "American" rule, the Court explained, were not developed in the context of statutory causes of action—such as trademark actions under the Lanham Act—"for which the legislature had prescribed intricate remedies." *Id.* at 719 (noting Lanham Act's provisions for injunctive relief and compensatory relief measured by defendant's profits, plaintiff's damages, and costs of the action). "When a cause of action has been created by a statute which expressly provides the remedies for vindication of the cause," the Court continued, "other remedies should not readily be implied." *Id.* at 720. Because several attempts to provide for recovery of attorney fees in the Lanham Act had failed, the Court concluded that "Congress intended § 35 of the Lanham Act to mark the boundaries of the power to award monetary relief in cases arising under the Act. A judicially created compensatory remedy in addition to the express statutory remedies is inappropriate in this context." *Id.* at 721.

Even though *Fleischmann's* holding ruled out a different compensatory remedy—attorney fees—than the one under consideration, the same reasoning, we think, bars a separate recovery of punitive damages for infringement. *See* Koelemay, *supra*, at 519 & n.354 (holding in *Fleischmann* "would seem by clear analogy to foreclose an implied remedy of punitive damages"); *see also* 2 J. McCarthy, *supra*, at § 30:29(B). Further, to imply a punitive damages award for trademark infringement would inappropriately add a remedy Congress could have—but did not—include in its intricate and comprehensive recovery scheme. Instead, it intended § 35 to "mark the boundaries of the power to award monetary relief in cases arising under the Act" and, as discussed above, such monetary relief was meant to be remedial, not punitive, in nature.

Decisions from sister circuits support the view that *Fleischmann* bars an award of punitive damages under § 35. *See Metric & Multistandard Components Corp. v. Metric's, Inc.*, 635 F.2d 710, 715–16 (8th Cir. 1980) (rejecting plaintiff's argument for common law remedies for violations of § 43(a) of the Lanham Act: *Fleischmann* is "broad enough to suggest that section 35 is the exclusive provision for monetary damages for the entire Act"); *Electronics Corp. v. Honeywell, Inc.*, 487 F.2d 513 (1st Cir. 1973) (per curiam) (upholding district court holding that plaintiff not entitled to punitive damages under the Lanham Act based on *Fleischmann*, its reading of § 35, and the absence of judicial authority for such award), *aff'g* 358 F. Supp. 1230 (D. Mass. 1973), *cert. denied*, 415 U.S. 960, 94 S. Ct. 1491, 39 L. Ed. 2d 575 (1974); *see also Caesars World, Inc. v. Venus Lounge, Inc.*, 520 F.2d 269, 274 (3d Cir. 1975) (striking an award of punitive damages in reliance on district court's holding in *Electronics*).

We are unpersuaded by the district court's reference to two other circuits as having approved punitive damages as a Lanham Act remedy. Neither of those decisions discusses the availability of punitive damages under § 35 and, in fact, the punitive damages awards in both cases were authorized under state law. *Transgo, Inc. v. Ajac Transmission Parts Corp.*, 768 F.2d 1001, 1024 (9th Cir. 1985) (California law authorized punitive damages), *cert. denied*, 474 U.S. 1059, 88 L. Ed. 2d 778, 106 S. Ct. 802 (1986); *Big O Tire Dealers, Inc. v. Goodyear Tire & Rubber Co.*, 561 F.2d 1365, 1374–76 (10th Cir. 1977) (Colorado law allows such damages), *cert. dismissed*, 434 U.S. 1052, 98 S. Ct. 905, 54 L. Ed. 2d 805 (1978).

Finally, plaintiff's argument, relying on *Quaker State Oil Ref. Corp. v. Kooltone, Inc.*, 649 F.2d 94 (2d Cir. 1981), that we have already approved recovery of punitive damages under § 35 is misplaced. In *Quaker State*, the district court did not question its power to award punitive damages for federal trademark infringement, and appellants failed to challenge that power on appeal. In disagreeing with appellants' argument that "the trial judge erred in submitting to the jury the issue of punitive damages, because appellants were ... given no notice that Quaker State sought such damages," *id.* at 95, we rested our decision affirming the imposition of punitive damages on a reading of the complaint and appellants' failure to object to the jury instruction, *id.* at 95–96, thus assuming *sub silentio* the availability of punitive damages. This kind of assumption has no precedential value, as we shall explain.

Recently, we reaffirmed the precept that not every aspect of each opinion has precedential force. In *Korwek v. Hunt*, 827 F.2d 874, 877 (2d Cir. 1987), for example, we stated that in a previous opinion, "neither the district court nor this Court addressed [the question currently appealed]. The issue never was briefed, argued, or decided." The earlier panel had assumed *sub silentio* a resolution of the issue. In *Korwek* we noted that a *sub silentio* holding is "'not binding precedent.'" *Id.* (quoting *Brooks v. Flagg Bros.*, 553 F.2d 764, 774 (2d Cir. 1977), *rev'd on other grounds*, 436 U.S. 149, 56 L. Ed. 2d 185, 98 S. Ct. 1729 (1978)). Thus, inasmuch as the punitive damages issue was not briefed, argued or addressed by the *Quaker State* panel, we are not constrained by it to affirm the instant award.

In sum, we hold that § 35 of the Lanham Act does not authorize an additional award of punitive damages for willful infringement of a registered trademark. So long as its purpose is to compensate a plaintiff for its actual injuries — even though the award is designed to deter wrongful conduct — the Lanham Act remains remedial. Obviously such ruling should not be read as an incentive for deliberate trademark infringement. To the extent that deterrence of willful infringement is needed, the statutorily provided remedies of § 35 are sufficient: a district court is empowered to enhance a monetary recovery of damages or profits, *e.g., Deering, Milliken & Co. v. Gilbert*, 269 F.2d 191, 194 (2d Cir. 1959), or to award plaintiff a full accounting of an infringer's profits, *e.g., Springs Mills, Inc. v. Ultracashmere House, Ltd.*, 724 F.2d 352, 356 (2d Cir. 1983); *W.E. Bassett Co. v. Revlon, Inc.*, 435 F.2d 656, 664 (2d Cir. 1970).

* * *

Notes

1. Although the general rule is that punitive damages are not available in federal trademark litigation, creative plaintiffs and sympathetic courts have realized that although Section 35 precludes punitive damage awards, many states do not have such provisions

in their state trademark laws. Therefore, it is common to grant an injunction under the Lanham Act and punitive damages under state common law.

2. Regardless, punitive damage awards must not be excessive. Appellate courts are to review jury awards of punitive damages under the de novo standard. *Cooper Industries v. Leatherman Tool*, 532 U.S. 424 (2001). Punitive damages are not to exceed constitutional standards; however, precisely what those standards are is difficult to articulate. In the *Leatherman Tool* case, on remand, the 9th Circuit found that the previous punitive damages of $4.5 million had to be reduced to $500,000 even though the court recognized that no formula existed in determining when punitive damages were constitutional. *Leatherman Tool Group, Inc. v. Cooper Indus., Inc.*, 285 F.3d 1146 (9th Cir. 2002).

---

4. Attorneys' Fees

15 U.S.C. §1117(a), Lanham Act §35(a)

… The court in exceptional cases may award reasonable attorney fees to the prevailing party.…

Quaker State Oil Refining Corp. v. Kooltone, Inc.
649 F.2d 94 (2d Cir. 1981)

PER CURIAM:

Kooltone, Inc., Therm-X Industries, Inc., and Therm-X Chemical and Oil Corp. appeal from a judgment of the United States District Court for the Eastern District of New York after a jury trial before George C. Pratt, J. Quaker State Oil Refining Corporation sued appellants for, inter alia, trademark infringement, unfair competition by means of simulation of trade dress, false description of the nature and quality of their merchandise, and dilution of trademark value. The gravamen of the complaint was that appellants had imitated characteristics of the cans in which Quaker State sold its brand of motor oil, misleading potential Quaker State customers and injuring Quaker State's business and reputation. Appellants filed a counter-claim against Quaker State alleging violation of the antitrust laws, unfair competition and malicious prosecution, but these were dismissed either before trial or before the case was submitted to the jury. The jury then made detailed findings, in a special verdict, under which Quaker State was awarded $30,000 in appellants' profits to be returned, $2 in compensatory damages, and $55,000 in punitive damages. Quaker State later moved for attorney's fees, which Judge Pratt granted in the sum of $50,000.

* * *

Appellants further argue that Judge Pratt erred in awarding attorney's fees to Quaker State, contending that this was not an "exceptional case ( )" justifying such an award under 15 U.S.C. §1117. Appellants concede, as they must, that their infringement was found to be "deliberate and willful" by the jury, but they assert that this finding is per se insufficient to warrant award of attorney's fees. This is incorrect. Under §1117, trial judges are given considerable discretion in awarding reasonable attorney's fees; we have no doubt that Judge Pratt exercised his discretion properly.

Appellants also argue that the trial judge erred in submitting to the jury the issue of punitive damages, because appellants were allegedly given no notice that Quaker State sought such damages. It is true that plaintiff's complaint did not specifically mention punitive damages, although it did seek "such other and further relief as the nature of the case may require" Moreover, the complaint did make clear that more than single compensatory damages was sought. And finally, appellants failed to object specifically to the instruction on punitive damages after the judge gave it. Under the circumstances, we find that appellants had sufficient notice of their vulnerability to an award of punitive damages.

Appellants advance other grounds for reversal of the judgment rendered below, but they are all without merit. Accordingly, we affirm the judgment of the district court.

WSM, Inc. v. Wheeler Media Services, Inc.
810 F.2d 113 (6th Cir. 1987)

ENGEL, CIRCUIT JUDGE.

Defendants appeal an order of the United States District Court for the Middle District of Tennessee awarding plaintiff $35,785.79 in attorney fees under the "exceptional cases" provision of section 35 of the Lanham Act, 15 U.S.C. § 1117(a). The district judge held that plaintiff was entitled to the fees because defendants unnecessarily prolonged the litigation after September 27, 1982. We reverse.

The underlying controversy concerned the right to use the service mark "The Nashville Network." The defendants reserved the corporate name "Nashville Network, Inc." with the Tennessee Secretary of State in October 1980, and incorporated the "Nashville Network, Inc." under that name in September 1981. The defendants also registered the trademark with the Secretary of State in September 1981. However, the defendants never used the mark in the sense of having provided services under the mark, a circumstance which was later to be their undoing. Plaintiff, which is part of Opry Land, Inc., an entertainment corporation that owns the Grand Ole' Opry, claimed that it owned the mark and that defendants were liable for infringement and unfair competition.

In a memorandum filed October 3, 1983 the district judge found that plaintiff was the owner of the mark in dispute and on this basis granted plaintiff partial summary judgment. The judge noted that while plaintiff also claimed infringement and unfair competition by defendants, those claims were not before the court at that time. The court later granted plaintiff summary judgment on those claims in a Memorandum filed May 29, 1984. At the same time, the district court denied plaintiff's request for attorney fees:

> WSM also seeks an award of attorney fees from the point in time when the defendants knew that they did not own the mark. WSM contends that this point in time is September 17, 1982, when defendants were apprised that the character of their use as set out in defendants' depositions would not, as a matter of law support defendants' claim of ownership. This Court does not agree. Given the admissions of the defendants and the undisputed evidence on the issue of likelihood of confusion, this Court initially favored the imposition of attorney fees on the defendants. Nevertheless, the plaintiff's concession that the defendants' selection of the mark was without knowledge of WSM's use convinces this Court that the defendants' acts of infringement were not malicious, fraudulent, deliberate or willful so as to make this an exceptional case to justify requiring the defendants to bear the plaintiff's attorney fees. 15 U.S.C. § 1117.

Plaintiff moved for reconsideration of the denial of attorney fees, and on June 27, 1984 the court decided to grant plaintiff the fees it had incurred after September 17, 1982. The court stated:

> The Court awarded defendants' profits to WSM. The Court declined to exercise its discretion to declare the case an exceptional one under 15 U.S.C. § 1117 because of the innocent adoption of the term by the defendants.
>
> WSM now moves for reconsideration and for further monetary award equal to WSM's attorney fees after September 17, 1982 for the award of defendants' profits. The court deems the plaintiff's motion unopposed due to the defendants' failure to respond. Local Rule 8(b)(3).
>
> WSM contends that defendants' innocent adoption should be a shield against an award of attorney fees *only* until such time as that innocence was dissipated. There can be no doubt that by September 17, 1982, defendants knew the ultimate outcome of the case. Defendants had admitted that WSM had used the mark; had admitted that defendants had not used the mark; had asserted a likelihood of confusion; and had been fully apprised of the law.

On January 18, 1985 the court set the fees and stated that they were incurred after September 27, 1982. September 17, 1982 was the date of a letter from plaintiff to defendants in which plaintiff offered to settle the litigation. Plaintiff proposed foregoing any claims for damages or attorney fees if defendants would abandon their claim of rights to the disputed mark by September 27, 1982. This letter was apparently the basis for the district court's grant of attorney fees. The seeming discrepancy between the court's first order setting September 17 as the date on which defendant should have stopped litigating, and the second order setting September 27 as the date is undoubtedly related to the fact that plaintiff's September 17 letter gave defendant 10 days in which to desist.

First, we reject appellant's argument that section 1117 only authorizes an award of attorney fees in cases involving registered trademarks. Without deciding whether this case might in any event involve a registered trademark since plaintiff brought suit upon that theory originally, we believe, with the Eleventh Circuit in *Rickard v. Auto Publisher, Inc.*, 735 F.2d 450 (11th Cir. 1984), that all of the section 1117 remedies, including attorney's fees, apply to actions brought pursuant to 1125(a).

The district judge applied two different standards in deciding the attorney fees question. In his May 29, 1984 Memorandum he asked whether defendants' use was "malicious, fraudulent, deliberate or willful," but in his June 27, 1984 Memorandum he applied a more lenient standard. This inconsistency is understandable in light of the uncertainty in the law governing attorney fees in trademark cases.

Conflicting views on the proper standard in these cases are presented in *Noxell Corp. v. Firehouse No. 1 Bar-B-Que Restaurant*, 248 U.S. App. D.C. 329, 771 F.2d 521 (D.C. Cir. 1985). A majority held that the enactment of section 1117 by Congress indicated a desire to allow attorney fees to be recovered by prevailing parties in "exceptional" circumstances and that such exceptional circumstances were not limited by those in which a party "acted in bad faith, vexatiously, wantonly, or for oppressive reasons." *Id.* at 526 (quoting *Alyeska Pipeline Service Co. v. Wilderness Society*, 421 U.S. 240, 258–59, 44 L. Ed. 2d 141, 95 S. Ct. 1612 (1975)). Observing that this traditional "bad faith" exception to the American rule already allowed awards of attorney fees, the majority concluded: "Something less than 'bad faith,' we believe, suffices to mark a case as 'exceptional.'... We think 'exceptional,' as Congress used the word in section 35 of the Lanham Act, is most reasonably read to mean what the word is generally understood to indicate—uncommon, not run-of-the-mine." *Id.*

The dissent expressed the opinion that Congress enacted section 1117 because it was dissatisfied with the decision of the Supreme Court in *Fleischmann Distilling Co. v. Maier Brewing Co.*, 386 U.S. 714, 87 S. Ct. 1404, 18 L. Ed. 2d 475 (1967). Since that decision placed in doubt whether the traditional bad faith exception to the American rule was available under the Lanham Act, the dissent reasoned that the Congress intended only to reaffirm the bad faith exception to the American rule. In reviewing other cases that had dealt with the "exceptional case" rule, the dissent observed:

> These cases do not support an award of attorneys' fees merely upon a showing of innocent or careless judgment. Fairly read, they permit fee awards only if a litigant acts in bad faith or asserts claims so frivolous that the litigant could not have had a bona fide belief in their merit.

Noxell, 771 F.2d at 532 (footnote omitted).

We need not decide which of the two views in *Noxell* is to be preferred for we conclude that the circumstances here were not exceptional under either view. The district judge's original opinion expressly found that the defendant's conduct was not "malicious, fraudulent, deliberate or willful" even if one assumes that standard for an exceptional case under 15 U.S.C. §1117. We agree with this view of the facts in the record and do not read the trial judge's later determination to be a departure from that view.

Even applying the more lenient test of the majority in *Noxell*, we believe that test has not been met and that therefore it was an abuse of discretion to allow attorney fees under that or any other available standard. We conclude that there was justification for defendants to continue litigation after September 1982. First, at that time plaintiff's ownership of the mark was still in question. As the district court stated in its Memorandum of October 3, 1983, under section 35 of the Lanham Act ownership of a mark is established "when it is '(a) on goods ... *and* (b) on services when it is used or displayed in the sale or advertising of services *and* the services are rendered in commerce.'" App. 296 (quoting 15 U.S.C. §1127) (emphasis in Memorandum).

The great bulk of evidence which sought to establish the plaintiff's use was forthcoming only after September 1982. At the earliest, plaintiff affirmatively proved its own prior use of the trademark on October 28, 1982 in an affidavit in support of its motion for summary judgment on the issue of ownership. The affidavit stated:

> WSM has produced hundreds of hours of television entertainment programming; has executed hundreds of contracts with artists, writers and various other independent entertainment production personnel; has solicited and contracted with cable system operators; and has provided its services and facilities for the production of television shows which have been broadcast nationwide; all using the mark, THE NASHVILLE NETWORK.

All but one of the exhibits attached to the affidavit were advertisements of plaintiff's services or announcements of plaintiff's plan to start broadcasting a cable television network under the trademark in the future, but they contained no evidence of services rendered. One of the exhibits, however, was a newspaper article announcing that a show would be taped the following week "at the Nashville Network television studio" and that the show would "air on the Nashville Network." Although it can be argued that this announcement of the prospective taping was evidence of services rendered, the district court did not rely on it in finding that plaintiff owned the trademark. Rather, the court relied on evidence that the plaintiff filed on February 25, 1983. The September 17, 1982 letter, which the district court apparently thought apprised defendants of the futility of litigation, did not assert that plaintiff had used the mark.

Rather, the letter merely asserted that the defendants had not used it. This does not establish ownership.

Another indication that defendants' continuation of litigation was reasonable is that nearly six months after September 1982 the district judge was still seriously uncertain of his jurisdiction. In an order of March 14, 1983 he noted:

> Although both parties agree that the sole issue presented in the above-styled case is the ownership of the service mark The Nashville Network, the Court *sua sponte* raises the issue of whether this Court has jurisdiction under either 28 U.S.C. § 1332 or § 1338. Both parties should be cognizant of the general rule that in a trademark infringement action a federal district court has jurisdiction over an action arising under the Lanham Act, 15 U.S.C. § 1121 and 28 U.S.C. § 1338, only if the plaintiff has a registered mark.... Absent federal registration, jurisdiction of this Court over common law trademarks or other trademarks not registered exist [sic] only if there is a complete diversity of citizenship even if in determining common law rights the court refers to the federal statute.

The court thereupon ordered the exchange of briefs covering this subject. In his October 3, 1983 Memorandum the district judge concluded that he had jurisdiction, but he laid the blame for his original uncertainty upon the plaintiff:

> the jurisdictional basis for this action has been unnecessarily encumbered due to the plaintiff's over-simplification of the issues presented in this case. The plaintiff contends that because there are no issues of confusion this Court can enter final judgment in favor of either party by determining the question of ownership of the mark THE NASHVILLE NETWORK. Initially assuming this to be true, this Court like the Court in *Rare Earth, Inc. v. Hoorelbeke*, 401 F. Supp. 26, 37 n. 20 (S.D.N.Y. 1975), "entertained lingering doubts" about its subject matter jurisdiction to dispose of this case on the single issue of ownership without any determination of the trademark infringement and unfair competition claims. These doubts existed because of the generally accepted rule that a federal court lacks jurisdiction to make a declaration of ownership of a common law trademark absent federal registration of the mark or diversity of citizenship between the parties....

In addition to the two specific issues that were unclear as of September 1982, we observe that the record as a whole does not indicate that the litigation in the district court was uncommon or exceptional or that the defendants' ultimate defeat was clearer than in most trademark cases.

Accordingly, the judgment of the district court from which appeal is taken is REVERSED and the case REMANDED for further proceedings consistent with this opinion.

———————

Notes

1. Courts will sometimes, based on the "totality of the circumstances" award attorneys' fees even absent bad faith. For example, failure to conduct a survey, in itself, may not usually be grounds to award attorneys' fees, but when considered in the totality of the circumstances, it may support an award of attorneys' fees. *See, e.g., Tamko Roofing Products, Inc. v. Ideal Roofing Co.*, 282 F.3d 23 (1st Cir. 2002) (failure to conduct a survey coupled with continued use of mark after enjoined from doing so supported finding of attorneys'

fees). In fact, most recently courts seem to no longer require a separate showing of bad faith to warrant an award of attorneys' fees if the infringement was willful or deliberate. *See Earth-quake Sound Corp. v. Bumper Industries*, 352 F.3d 1210 (9th Cir. 2003).

2. When appropriate, attorneys' fees are awarded to the prevailing party, not just the plaintiff. Therefore, when the charity that had an exclusive license from the estate to the post-mortem right of publicity and other intellectual property rights in and to Princess Diana's likeness sued the Franklin Mint, a company that produced and sold trinkets and dolls bearing the name and image of Princess Diana (and many others), the court found for the defendant and awarded $2 million in attorneys' fees to the defendant because the cause of action brought by the charity was "absurd."

Appendix

Lanham Act, U.S.C. §15

§ 1051. Application for registration; verification

(a) Application for use of trademark

(1) The owner of a trademark used in commerce may request registration of its trademark on the principal register hereby established by paying the prescribed fee and filing in the Patent and Trademark Office an application and a verified statement, in such form as may be prescribed by the Director, and such number of specimens or facsimiles of the mark as used as may be required by the Director.

(2) The application shall include specification of the applicant's domicile and citizenship, the date of the applicant's first use of the mark, the date of the applicant's first use of the mark in commerce, the goods in connection with which the mark is used, and a drawing of the mark.

(3) The statement shall be verified by the applicant and specify that—

(A) the person making the verification believes that he or she, or the juristic person in whose behalf he or she makes the verification, to be the owner of the mark sought to be registered;

(B) to the best of the verifier's knowledge and belief, the facts recited in the application are accurate;

(C) the mark is in use in commerce; and

(D) to the best of the verifier's knowledge and belief, no other person has the right to use such mark in commerce either in the identical form thereof or in such near resemblance thereto as to be likely, when used on or in connection with the goods of such other person, to cause confusion, or to cause mistake, or to deceive, except that, in the case of every application claiming concurrent use, the applicant shall—

(i) state exceptions to the claim of exclusive use; and

(ii) shall specify, to the extent of the verifier's knowledge—

(I) any concurrent use by others;

(II) the goods on or in connection with which and the areas in which each concurrent use exists;

(III) the periods of each use; and

(IV) the goods and area for which the applicant desires registration.

(4) The applicant shall comply with such rules or regulations as may be prescribed by the Director. The Director shall promulgate rules prescribing the requirements for the application and for obtaining a filing date herein.

(b) Application for bona fide intention to use trademark

(1) A person who has a bona fide intention, under circumstances showing the good faith of such person, to use a trademark in commerce may request registration of its trademark on the principal register hereby established by paying the prescribed fee and filing in the Patent and Trademark Office an application and a verified statement, in such form as may be prescribed by the Director.

(2) The application shall include specification of the applicant's domicile and citizenship, the goods in connection with which the applicant has a bona fide intention to use the mark, and a drawing of the mark.

(3) The statement shall be verified by the applicant and specify—

(A) that the person making the verification believes that he or she, or the juristic person in whose behalf he or she makes the verification, to be entitled to use the mark in commerce;

(B) the applicant's bona fide intention to use the mark in commerce;

(C) that, to the best of the verifier's knowledge and belief, the facts recited in the application are accurate; and

(D) that, to the best of the verifier's knowledge and belief, no other person has the right to use such mark in commerce either in the identical form thereof or in such near resemblance thereto as to be likely, when used on or in connection with the goods of such other person, to cause confusion, or to cause mistake, or to deceive.

Except for applications filed pursuant section 1126 of this title, no mark shall be registered until the applicant has met the requirements of subsections (c) and (d) of this section.

(4) The applicant shall comply with such rules or regulations as may be prescribed by the Director. The Director shall promulgate rules prescribing the requirements for the application and for obtaining a filing date herein.

(c) Amendment of application under subsection (b) to conform to requirements of subsection (a)

At any time during examination of an application filed under subsection (b) of this section, an applicant who has made use of the mark in commerce may claim the benefits of such use for purposes of this chapter, by amending his or her application to bring it into conformity with the requirements of subsection (a) of this section.

(d) Verified statement that trademark is used in commerce

(1) Within six months after the date on which the notice of allowance with respect to a mark is issued under section 1063(b)(2) of this title to an applicant under subsection (b) of this section, the applicant shall file in the Patent and Trademark Office, together with such number of specimens or facsimiles of the mark as used in commerce as may be required by the Director and payment of the prescribed fee, a verified statement that the mark is in use in commerce and specifying the date of the applicant's first use of the mark in commerce and those goods or services specified in the notice of allowance on or in connection with which the mark is used in commerce. Subject to examination and acceptance of the statement of use, the mark shall be registered in the Patent and Trademark Office, a certificate of registration shall be issued for those goods or services recited in the statement of use for which the mark is entitled to registration, and notice of registration shall be published in the Official Gazette of the Patent and Trademark Office. Such examination may include an examination of the factors set forth in subsections (a) through (e) of section 1052 of this title. The notice of registration shall specify the goods or services for which the mark is registered.

(2) The Director shall extend, for one additional 6-month period, the time for filing the statement of use under paragraph (1), upon written request of the applicant before the expiration of the 6-month period provided in paragraph (1). In addition to an extension under the preceding sentence, the Director may, upon a showing of good cause by the applicant, further extend the time for filing the statement of use under paragraph (1) for periods aggregating not more than 24 months, pursuant to written request of the applicant made before the expiration of the last extension granted under this paragraph. Any request for an extension under this paragraph shall be accompanied by a verified statement that the applicant has a continued bona fide intention to use the mark in commerce and specifying those goods or services identified in the notice of allowance on or in connection with which the applicant has a continued bona fide intention to use the mark in commerce. Any request for an extension under this paragraph shall be accompanied by payment of the prescribed fee. The Director shall issue regulations setting forth guidelines for determining what constitutes good cause for purposes of this paragraph.

(3) The Director shall notify any applicant who files a statement of use of the acceptance or refusal thereof and, if the statement of use is refused, the reasons for the refusal. An applicant may amend the statement of use.

(4) The failure to timely file a verified statement of use under paragraph (1) or an extension request under paragraph (2) shall result in abandonment of the application, unless it can be shown to the satisfaction of the Director that the delay in responding was unintentional, in which case the time for filing may be extended, but for a period not to exceed the period specified in paragraphs (1) and (2) for filing a statement of use.

(e) Designation of resident for service of process and notices

If the applicant is not domiciled in the United States the applicant may designate, by a document filed in the United States Patent and Trademark Office, the name and address of a person resident in the United States on whom may be served notices or process in proceedings affecting the mark. Such notices or process may be served upon the person so designated by leaving with that person or mailing to that person a copy thereof at the address specified in the last designation so filed. If the person so designated cannot be found at the address given in the last designation, or if the registrant does not designate by a document filed in the United States Patent and Trademark Office the name and address of a person resident in the United States on whom may be served notices or process in proceedings affecting the mark, such notices or process may be served on the Director.

§ 1052. Trademarks registrable on principal register; concurrent registration

No trademark by which the goods of the applicant may be distinguished from the goods of others shall be refused registration on the principal register on account of its nature unless it—

(a) Consists of or comprises immoral, deceptive, or scandalous matter; or matter which may disparage or falsely suggest a connection with persons, living or dead, institutions, beliefs, or national symbols, or bring them into contempt, or disrepute; or a geographical indication which, when used on or in connection with wines or spirits, identifies a place other than the origin of the goods and is first used on or in connection with wines or spirits by the applicant on or after one year after the date on which the WTO Agreement (as defined in section 3501(9) of Title 19)) enters into force with respect to the United States.

(b) Consists of or comprises the flag or coat of arms or other insignia of the United States, or of any State or municipality, or of any foreign nation, or any simulation thereof.

(c) Consists of or comprises a name, portrait, or signature identifying a particular living individual except by his written consent, or the name, signature, or portrait of a deceased President of the United States during the life of his widow, if any, except by the written consent of the widow.

(d) Consists of or comprises a mark which so resembles a mark registered in the Patent and Trademark Office, or a mark or trade name previously used in the United States by another and not abandoned, as to be likely, when used on or in connection with the goods of the applicant, to cause confusion, or to cause mistake, or to deceive: *Provided,* That if the Director determines that confusion, mistake, or deception is not likely to result from the continued use by more than one person of the same or similar marks under conditions and limitations as to the mode or place of use of the marks or the goods on or in connection with which such marks are used, concurrent registrations may be issued to such persons when they have become entitled to use such marks as a result of their concurrent lawful use in commerce prior to (1) the earliest of the filing dates of the applications pending or of any registration issued under this chapter; (2) July 5, 1947, in the case of registrations previously issued under the Act of March 3, 1881, or February 20, 1905, and continuing in full force and effect on that date; or (3) July 5, 1947, in the case of applications filed under the Act of February 20, 1905, and registered after July 5, 1947. Use prior to the filing date of any pending application or a registration shall not be required when the owner of such application or registration consents to the grant of a concurrent registration to the applicant. Concurrent registrations may also be issued by the Director when a court of competent jurisdiction has finally determined that more than one person is entitled to use the same or similar marks in commerce. In issuing concurrent registrations, the Director shall prescribe conditions and limitations as to the mode or place of use of the mark or the goods on or in connection with which such mark is registered to the respective persons.

(e) Consists of a mark which (1) when used on or in connection with the goods of the applicant is merely descriptive or deceptively misdescriptive of them, (2) when used on or in connection with the goods of the applicant is primarily geographically descriptive of them, except as indications of regional origin may be registrable under section 1054 of this title, (3) when used on or in connection with the goods of the applicant is primarily geographically deceptively misdescriptive of them, (4) is primarily merely a surname, or (5) comprises any matter that, as a whole, is functional.

(f) Except as expressly excluded in subsections (a), (b), (c), (d), (e)(3), and (e)(5) of this section, nothing in this chapter shall prevent the registration of a mark used by the applicant which has become distinctive of the applicant's goods in commerce. The Director may accept as prima facie evidence that the mark has become distinctive, as used on or in connection with the applicant's goods in commerce, proof of substantially exclusive and continuous use thereof as a mark by the applicant in commerce for the five years before the date on which the claim of distinctiveness is made. Nothing in this section shall prevent the registration of a mark which, when used on or in connection with the goods of the applicant, is primarily geographically deceptively misdescriptive of them, and which became distinctive of the applicant's goods in commerce before December 8, 1993.

A mark which would be likely to cause dilution by blurring or dilution by tarnishment under section 1125(c) of this title, may be refused registration only pursuant to a proceeding brought under section 1063 of this title. A registration for a mark which would be likely to cause dilution by blurring or dilution by tarnishment under section 1125(c) of this title, may be canceled pursuant to a proceeding brought under either section 1064 of this title or section 1092 of this title.

§ 1053. Service marks registrable

Subject to the provisions relating to the registration of trademarks, so far as they are applicable, service marks shall be registrable, in the same manner and with the same effect as are trademarks, and when registered they shall be entitled to the protection provided in this chapter in the case of trademarks. Applications and procedure under this section shall conform as nearly as practicable to those prescribed for the registration of trademarks.

§ 1054. Collective marks and certification marks registrable

Subject to the provisions relating to the registration of trademarks, so far as they are applicable, collective and certification marks, including indications of regional origin, shall be registrable under this chapter, in the same manner and with the same effect as are trademarks, by persons, and nations, States, municipalities, and the like, exercising legitimate control over the use of the marks sought to be registered, even though not possessing an industrial or commercial establishment, and when registered they shall be entitled to the protection provided in this chapter in the case of trademarks, except in the case of certification marks when used so as to represent falsely that the owner or a user thereof makes or sells the goods or performs the services on or in connection with which such mark is used. Applications and procedure under this section shall conform as nearly as practicable to those prescribed for the registration of trademarks.

§ 1055. Use by related companies affecting validity and registration

Where a registered mark or a mark sought to be registered is or may be used legitimately by related companies, such use shall inure to the benefit of the registrant or applicant for registration, and such use shall not affect the validity of such mark or of its registration, provided such mark is not used in such manner as to deceive the public. If first use of a mark by a person is controlled by the registrant or applicant for registration of the mark with respect to the nature and quality of the goods or services, such first use shall inure to the benefit of the registrant or applicant, as the case may be.

§ 1056. Disclaimer of unregistrable matter

(a) Compulsory and voluntary disclaimers

The Director may require the applicant to disclaim an unregistrable component of a mark otherwise registrable. An applicant may voluntarily disclaim a component of a mark sought to be registered.

(b) Prejudice of rights

No disclaimer, including those made under subsection (e) of section 1057 of this title, shall prejudice or affect the applicant's or registrant's rights then existing or thereafter arising in the disclaimed matter, or his right of registration on another application if the disclaimed matter be or shall have become distinctive of his goods or services.

§ 1057. Certificates of registration

(a) Issuance and form

Certificates of registration of marks registered upon the principal register shall be issued in the name of the United States of America, under the seal of the Patent and Trademark Office, and shall be signed by the Director or have his signature placed thereon, and a record thereof shall be kept in the Patent and Trademark Office. The registration shall reproduce the mark, and state that the mark is registered on the principal register under this chapter, the date of the first use of the mark, the date of the first use of the mark in commerce, the particular goods or services for which it is registered, the number and date of the registration, the term thereof, the date on which the application for registration was received in the Patent and Trademark Office, and any conditions and limitations that may be imposed in the registration.

(b) Certificate as prima facie evidence

A certificate of registration of a mark upon the principal register provided by this chapter shall be prima facie evidence of the validity of the registered mark and of the registration of the mark, of the registrant's ownership of the mark, and of the registrant's exclusive right to use the registered mark in commerce on or in connection with the goods or services specified in the certificate, subject to any conditions or limitations stated in the certificate.

(c) Application to register mark considered constructive use

Contingent on the registration of a mark on the principal register provided by this chapter, the filing of the application to register such mark shall constitute constructive use of the mark, conferring a right of priority, nationwide in effect, on or in connection with the goods or services specified in the registration against any other person except for a person whose mark has not been abandoned and who, prior to such filing—

(1) has used the mark;

(2) has filed an application to register the mark which is pending or has resulted in registration of the mark; or

(3) has filed a foreign application to register the mark on the basis of which he or she has acquired a right of priority, and timely files an application under section 1126(d) of this title to register the mark which is pending or has resulted in registration of the mark.

(d) Issuance to assignee

A certificate of registration of a mark may be issued to the assignee of the applicant, but the assignment must first be recorded in the Patent and Trademark Office. In case of change of ownership the Director shall, at the request of the owner and upon a proper showing and the payment of the prescribed fee, issue to such assignee a new certificate of registration of the said mark in the name of such assignee, and for the unexpired part of the original period.

(e) Surrender, cancellation, or amendment by registrant

Upon application of the registrant the Director may permit any registration to be surrendered for cancellation, and upon cancellation appropriate entry shall be made in the records of the Patent and Trademark Office. Upon application of the registrant and payment of the prescribed fee, the Director for good cause may permit any registration to be amended or to be disclaimed in part: *Provided,* That the amendment or disclaimer does not alter materially the character of the mark. Appropriate entry shall be made in the records of the Patent and Trademark Office and upon the certificate of registration or, if said certificate is lost or destroyed, upon a certified copy thereof.

(f) Copies of Patent and Trademark Office records as evidence

Copies of any records, books, papers, or drawings belonging to the Patent and Trademark Office relating to marks, and copies of registrations, when authenticated by the seal of the Patent and Trademark Office and certified by the Director, or in his name by an employee of the Office duly designated by the Director, shall be evidence in all cases wherein the originals would be evidence; and any person making application therefor and paying the prescribed fee shall have such copies.

(g) Correction of Patent and Trademark Office mistake

Whenever a material mistake in a registration, incurred through the fault of the Patent and Trademark Office, is clearly disclosed by the records of the Office a certificate stating the fact and nature of such mistake, shall be issued without charge and recorded and a printed copy thereof shall be attached to each printed copy of the registration certificate and such corrected registration shall thereafter have the same effect as if the same had been originally issued in such corrected form, or in the discretion of the Director a new certificate of registration may be issued without charge. All certificates of correction heretofore issued in accordance with the rules of the Patent and Trademark Office and the registrations to which they are attached shall have the same force and effect as if such certificates and their issue had been specifically authorized by statute.

(h) Correction of applicant's mistake

Whenever a mistake has been made in a registration and a showing has been made that such mistake occurred in good faith through the fault of the applicant, the Director is authorized to issue a certificate of correction or, in his discretion, a new certificate upon the payment of the prescribed fee: *Provided,* That the correction does not involve such changes in the registration as to require republication of the mark.

§ 1058. Duration

(a) In general

Each registration shall remain in force for 10 years, except that the registration of any mark shall be canceled by the Director for failure to comply with the provisions of subsection (b) of this section, upon the expiration of the following time periods, as applicable:

(1) For registrations issued pursuant to the provisions of this chapter, at the end of 6 years following the date of registration.

(2) For registrations published under the provisions of section 1062(c) of this title, at the end of 6 years following the date of publication under such section.

(3) For all registrations, at the end of each successive 10-year period following the date of registration.

(b) Affidavit of continuing use

During the 1-year period immediately preceding the end of the applicable time period set forth in subsection (a) of this section, the owner of the registration shall pay the prescribed fee and file in the patent and trademark office—

(1) an affidavit setting forth those goods or services recited in the registration on or in connection with which the mark is in use in commerce and such number of specimens or facsimiles showing current use of the mark as may be required by the Director; or

(2) an affidavit setting forth those goods or services recited in the registration on or in connection with which the mark is not in use in commerce and showing that any such nonuse is due to special circumstances which excuse such nonuse and is not due to any intention to abandon the mark.

(c) Grace period for submissions; deficiency

(1) The owner of the registration may make the submissions required under this section within a grace period of 6 months after the end of the applicable time period set forth in subsection (a) of this section. Such submission is required to be accompanied by a surcharge prescribed by the Director.

(2) If any submission filed under this section is deficient, the deficiency may be corrected after the statutory time period and within the time prescribed after notification of the

deficiency. Such submission is required to be accompanied by a surcharge prescribed by the Director.

(d) Notice of affidavit requirement

Special notice of the requirement for affidavits under this section shall be attached to each certificate of registration and notice of publication under section 1062(c) of this title.

(e) Notification of acceptance or refusal of affidavits

The Director shall notify any owner who files 1 of the affidavits required by this section of the Commissioner's acceptance or refusal thereof and, in the case of a refusal, the reasons therefor.

(f) Designation of resident for service of process and notices

If the registrant is not domiciled in the United States, the registrant may designate, by a document filed in the United States Patent and Trademark Office, the name and address of a person resident in the United States on whom may be served notices or process in proceedings affecting the mark. Such notices or process may be served upon the person so designated by leaving with that person or mailing to that person a copy thereof at the address specified in the last designation so filed. If the person so designated cannot be found at the address given in the last designation, or if the registrant does not designate by a document filed in the United States Patent and Trademark Office the name and address of a person resident in the United States on whom may be served notices or process in proceedings affecting the mark, such notices or process may be served on the Director.

§ 1059. Renewal of registration

(a) Period of renewal; time for renewal

Subject to the provisions of section 1058 of this title, each registration may be renewed for periods of 10 years at the end of each successive 10-year period following the date of registration upon payment of the prescribed fee and the filing of a written application, in such form as may be prescribed by the Director. Such application may be made at any time within 1 year before the end of each successive 10-year period for which the registration was issued or renewed, or it may be made within a grace period of 6 months after the end of each successive 10-year period, upon payment of a fee and surcharge prescribed therefor. If any application filed under this section is deficient, the deficiency may be corrected within the time prescribed after notification of the deficiency, upon payment of a surcharge prescribed therefor.

(b) Notification of refusal of renewal

If the Director refuses to renew the registration, the Director shall notify the registrant of the Commissioner's refusal and the reasons therefor.

(c) Designation of resident for service of process and notices

If the registrant is not domiciled in the United States the registrant may designate, by a document filed in the United States Patent and Trademark Office, the name and address of a person resident in the United States on whom may be served notices or process in proceedings affecting the mark. Such notices or process may be served upon the person so designated by leaving with that person or mailing to that person a copy thereof at the address specified in the last designation so filed. If the person so designated cannot be found at the address given in the last designation, or if the registrant does not designate by a document filed in the United States Patent and Trademark Office the name and address of a person resident in the United States on whom may be served notices or process in proceedings affecting the mark, such notices or process may be served on the Director.

§ 1060. Assignment

(a)(1) A registered mark or a mark for which an application to register has been filed shall be assignable with the good will of the business in which the mark is used, or with that part of the good will of the business connected with the use of and symbolized by the mark. Notwithstanding the preceding sentence, no application to register a mark under section 1051(b) of this title shall be assignable prior to the filing of an amendment under section 1051(c) of this title to bring the application into conformity with section 1051(a) of this title or the filing of the verified statement of use under section 1051(d) of this title, except for an assignment to a successor to the business of the applicant, or portion thereof, to which the mark pertains, if that business is ongoing and existing.

(2) In any assignment authorized by this section, it shall not be necessary to include the good will of the business connected with the use of and symbolized by any other mark used in the business or by the name or style under which the business is conducted.

(3) Assignments shall be by instruments in writing duly executed. Acknowledgment shall be prima facie evidence of the execution of an assignment, and when the prescribed information reporting the assignment is recorded in the United States Patent and Trademark Office, the record shall be prima facie evidence of execution.

(4) An assignment shall be void against any subsequent purchaser for valuable consideration without notice, unless the prescribed information reporting the assignment is recorded in the United States Patent and Trademark Office within 3 months after the date of the assignment or prior to the subsequent purchase.

(5) The United States Patent and Trademark Office shall maintain a record of information on assignments, in such form as may be prescribed by the Director.

(b) An assignee not domiciled in the United States may designate by a document filed in the United States Patent and Trademark Office the name and address of a person resident in the United States on whom may be served notices or process in proceedings affecting the mark. Such notices or process may be served upon the person so designated by leaving with that person or mailing to that person a copy thereof at the address specified in the last designation so filed. If the person so designated cannot be found at the address given in the last designation, or if the assignee does not designate by a document filed in the United States Patent and Trademark Office the name and address of a person resident in the United States on whom may be served notices or process in proceedings affecting the mark, such notices or process may be served upon the Director.

§ 1061. Execution of acknowledgments and verifications

Acknowledgments and verifications required under this chapter may be made before any person within the United States authorized by law to administer oaths, or, when made in a foreign country, before any diplomatic or consular officer of the United States or before any official authorized to administer oaths in the foreign country concerned whose authority is proved by a certificate of a diplomatic or consular officer of the United States, or apostille of an official designated by a foreign country which, by treaty or convention, accords like effect to apostilles of designated officials in the United States, and shall be valid if they comply with the laws of the state or country where made.

§ 1062. Publication

(a) Examination and publication

Upon the filing of an application for registration and payment of the prescribed fee, the Director shall refer the application to the examiner in charge of the registration of marks, who shall cause an examination to be made and, if on such examination it shall appear that the applicant is entitled to registration, or would be entitled to registration upon the acceptance of the statement of use required by section 1051(d) of this title, the Director shall cause the mark to be published in the Official Gazette of the Patent and Trademark Office: *Provided,* That in the case of an applicant claiming concurrent use, or in the case of an application to be placed in an interference as provided for in section 1066 of this title the mark, if otherwise registrable, may be published subject to the determination of the rights of the parties to such proceedings.

(b) Refusal of registration; amendment of application; abandonment

If the applicant is found not entitled to registration, the examiner shall advise the applicant thereof and of the reasons therefor. The applicant shall have a period of six months in which to reply or amend his application, which shall then be reexamined. This procedure may be repeated until (1) the examiner finally refuses registration of the mark or (2) the applicant fails for a period of six months to reply or amend or appeal, whereupon the application shall be deemed to have been abandoned, unless it can be shown to the satisfaction of the Director that the delay in responding was unintentional, whereupon such time may be extended.

(c) Republication of marks registered under prior acts

A registrant of a mark registered under the provisions of the Act of March 3, 1881, or the Act of February 20, 1905, may, at any time prior to the expiration of the registration thereof, upon the payment of the prescribed fee file with the Director an affidavit setting forth those goods stated in the registration on which said mark is in use in commerce and that the registrant claims the benefits of this chapter for said mark. The Director shall publish notice thereof with a reproduction of said mark in the Official Gazette, and notify the registrant of such publication and of the requirement for the affidavit of use or nonuse as provided for in subsection (b) of section 1058 of this title. Marks published under this subsection shall not be subject to the provisions of section 1063 of this title.

§ 1063. Opposition to registration

(a) Any person who believes that he would be damaged by the registration of a mark upon the principal register, including the registration of any mark which would be likely to cause dilution by blurring or dilution by tarnishment under section 1125(c) of this title, may, upon payment of the prescribed fee, file an opposition in the Patent and Trademark Office, stating the grounds therefor, within thirty days after the publication under subsection (a) of section 1062 of this title of the mark sought to be registered. Upon written request prior to the expiration of the thirty-day period, the time for filing opposition shall be extended for an additional thirty days, and further extensions of time for filing opposition may be granted by the Director for good cause when requested prior to the expiration of an extension. The Director shall notify the applicant of each extension of the time for filing opposition. An opposition may be amended under such conditions as may be prescribed by the Director.

(b) Unless registration is successfully opposed—

(1) a mark entitled to registration on the principal register based on an application filed under section 1051(a) of this title or pursuant to section 1126 of this title shall be registered in the Patent and Trademark Office, a certificate of registration shall be issued, and notice of the registration shall be published in the Official Gazette of the Patent and Trademark Office; or

(2) a notice of allowance shall be issued to the applicant if the applicant applied for registration under section 1051(b) of this title.

§ 1064. Cancellation of registration

A petition to cancel a registration of a mark, stating the grounds relied upon, may, upon payment of the prescribed fee, be filed as follows by any person who believes that he is or will be damaged, including as a result of a likelihood of dilution by blurring or dilution by tarnishment under section 1125(c) of this title, by the registration of a mark on the principal register established by this chapter, or under the Act of March 3, 1881, or the Act of February 20, 1905:

(1) Within five years from the date of the registration of the mark under this chapter.

(2) Within five years from the date of publication under section 1062(c) of this title of a mark registered under the Act of March 3, 1881, or the Act of February 20, 1905.

(3) At any time if the registered mark becomes the generic name for the goods or services, or a portion thereof, for which it is registered, or is functional, or has been abandoned, or its registration was obtained fraudulently or contrary to the provisions of section 1054 of this title or of subsection (a), (b), or (c) of section 1052 of this title for a registration under this chapter, or contrary to similar prohibitory provisions of such prior Acts for a registration under such Acts, or if the registered mark is being used by, or with the permission of, the registrant so as to misrepresent the source of the goods or services on or in connection with which the mark is used. If the registered mark becomes the generic name for less than all of the goods or services for which it is registered, a petition to cancel the registration for only those goods or services may be filed. A registered mark shall not be deemed to be the generic name of goods or services solely because such mark is also used as a name of or to identify a unique product or service. The primary significance of the registered mark to the relevant public rather than purchaser motivation shall be the test for determining whether the registered mark has become the generic name of goods or services on or in connection with which it has been used.

(4) At any time if the mark is registered under the Act of March 3, 1881, or the Act of February 20, 1905, and has not been published under the provisions of subsection (c) of section 1062 of this title.

(5) At any time in the case of a certification mark on the ground that the registrant (A) does not control, or is not able legitimately to exercise control over, the use of such mark, or (B) engages in the production or marketing of any goods or services to which the certification mark is applied, or (C) permits the use of the certification mark for purposes other than to certify, or (D) discriminately refuses to certify or to continue to certify the goods or services of any person who maintains the standards or conditions which such mark certifies:

Provided, That the Federal Trade Commission may apply to cancel on the grounds specified in paragraphs (3) and (5) of this section any mark registered on the principal register established by this chapter, and the prescribed fee shall not be required.

Nothing in paragraph (5) shall be deemed to prohibit the registrant from using its certification mark in advertising or promoting recognition of the certification program or of the goods or services meeting the certification standards of the registrant. Such uses of the certification mark shall not be grounds for cancellation under paragraph (5), so long as the registrant does not itself produce, manufacture, or sell any of the certified goods or services to which its identical certification mark is applied.

§ 1065. Incontestability of right to use mark under certain conditions

Except on a ground for which application to cancel may be filed at any time under paragraphs (3) and (5) of section 1064 of this title, and except to the extent, if any, to which the use of a mark registered on the principal register infringes a valid right acquired under the law of any State or Territory by use of a mark or trade name continuing from a date prior to the date of registration under this chapter of such registered mark, the right of the registrant to use such registered mark in commerce for the goods or services on or in connection with which such registered mark has been in continuous use for five consecutive years subsequent to the date of such registration and is still in use in commerce, shall be incontestable: *Provided,* That—

(1) there has been no final decision adverse to registrant's claim of ownership of such mark for such goods or services, or to registrant's right to register the same or to keep the same on the register; and

(2) there is no proceeding involving said rights pending in the Patent and Trademark Office or in a court and not finally disposed of; and

(3) an affidavit is filed with the Director within one year after the expiration of any such five-year period setting forth those goods or services stated in the registration on or in connection with which such mark has been in continuous use for such five consecutive years and is still in use in commerce, and other matters specified in paragraphs (1) and (2) of this section; and

(4) no incontestable right shall be acquired in a mark which is the generic name for the goods or services or a portion thereof, for which it is registered.

Subject to the conditions above specified in this section, the incontestable right with reference to a mark registered under this chapter shall apply to a mark registered under the Act of March 3, 1881, or the Act of February 20, 1905, upon the filing of the required affidavit with the Director within one year after the expiration of any period of five consecutive years after the date of publication of a mark under the provisions of subsection (c) of section 1062 of this title.

The Director shall notify any registrant who files the above-prescribed affidavit of the filing thereof.

§ 1066. Interference; declaration by Director

Upon petition showing extraordinary circumstances, the Director may declare that an interference exists when application is made for the registration of a mark which so resembles a mark previously registered by another, or for the registration of which another has previously made application, as to be likely when used on or in connection with the goods or services of the applicant to cause confusion or mistake or to deceive. No interference shall be declared between an application and the registration of a mark the right to the use of which has become incontestable.

§ 1067. Interference, opposition, and proceedings for concurrent use registration or for cancellation; notice; Trademark Trial and Appeal Board

(a) In every case of interference, opposition to registration, application to register as a lawful concurrent user, or application to cancel the registration of a mark, the Director shall give notice to all parties and shall direct a Trademark Trial and Appeal Board to determine and decide the respective rights of registration.

(b) The Trademark Trial and Appeal Board shall include the Director, the Commissioner for Patents, the Commissioner for Trademarks, and administrative trademark judges who are appointed by the Director.

§ 1068. Action of Director in interference, opposition, and proceedings for concurrent use registration or for cancellation

In such proceedings the Director may refuse to register the opposed mark, may cancel the registration, in whole or in part, may modify the application or registration by limiting the goods or services specified therein, may otherwise restrict or rectify with respect to the register the registration of a registered mark, may refuse to register any or all of several interfering marks, or may register the mark or marks for the person or persons entitled thereto, as the rights of the parties under this chapter may be established in the proceedings: *Provided,* That in the case of the registration of any mark based on concurrent use, the Director shall determine and fix the conditions and limitations provided for in subsection (d) of section 1052 of this title. However, no final judgment shall be entered in favor of an applicant under section 1051(b) of this title before the mark is registered, if such applicant cannot prevail without establishing constructive use pursuant to section 1057(c) of this title.

§ 1069. Application of equitable principles in inter partes proceedings

In all inter partes proceedings equitable principles of laches, estoppel, and acquiescence, where applicable may be considered and applied.

§ 1070. Appeals to Trademark Trial and Appeal Board from decisions of examiners

An appeal may be taken to the Trademark Trial and Appeal Board from any final decision of the examiner in charge of the registration of marks upon the payment of the prescribed fee.

§ 1071. Appeal to courts

(a) Persons entitled to appeal; United States Court of Appeals for the Federal Circuit; waiver of civil action; election of civil action by adverse party; procedure

(1) An applicant for registration of a mark, party to an interference proceeding, party to an opposition proceeding, party to an application to register as a lawful concurrent user, party to a cancellation proceeding, a registrant who has filed an affidavit as provided in section 1058 of this title, or an applicant for renewal, who is dissatisfied with the decision of the Director or Trademark Trial and Appeal Board, may appeal to the United States Court of Appeals for the Federal Circuit thereby waiving his right to proceed under subsection (b) of this section: *Provided,* That such appeal shall be dismissed if any adverse party to the proceeding, other than the Director, shall, within twenty days after the appellant has filed notice of appeal according to paragraph (2) of this section, files notice with the Director that he elects to have all further proceedings conducted as provided in subsection (b) of this section. Thereupon the appellant shall have thirty days thereafter within which to file a civil action under subsection (b) of this section, in default of which the decision appealed from shall govern the further proceedings in the case.

(2) When an appeal is taken to the United States Court of Appeals for the Federal Circuit, the appellant shall file in the Patent and Trademark Office a written notice of appeal directed to the Director, within such time after the date of the decision from which the appeal is taken as the Director prescribes, but in no case less than 60 days after that date.

(3) The Director shall transmit to the United States Court of Appeals for the Federal Circuit a certified list of the documents comprising the record in the Patent and Trademark Office. The court may request that the Director forward the original or certified copies of such documents during pendency of the appeal. In an ex parte case, the Director shall submit to that court a brief explaining the grounds for the decision of the Patent and Trademark Office, addressing all the issues involved in the appeal. The court shall, before

hearing an appeal, give notice of the time and place of the hearing to the Director and the parties in the appeal.

(4) The United States Court of Appeals for the Federal Circuit shall review the decision from which the appeal is taken on the record before the Patent and Trademark Office. Upon its determination the court shall issue its mandate and opinion to the Director, which shall be entered of record in the Patent and Trademark Office and shall govern the further proceedings in the case. However, no final judgment shall be entered in favor of an applicant under section 1051(b) of this title before the mark is registered, if such applicant cannot prevail without establishing constructive use pursuant to section 1057(c) of this title.

(b) Civil action; persons entitled to; jurisdiction of court; status of Director; procedure

(1) Whenever a person authorized by subsection (a) of this section to appeal to the United States Court of Appeals for the Federal Circuit is dissatisfied with the decision of the Director or Trademark Trial and Appeal Board, said person may, unless appeal has been taken to said United States Court of Appeals for the Federal Circuit, have remedy by a civil action if commenced within such time after such decision, not less than sixty days, as the Director appoints or as provided in subsection (a) of this section. The court may adjudge that an applicant is entitled to a registration upon the application involved, that a registration involved should be canceled, or such other matter as the issues in the proceeding require, as the facts in the case may appear. Such adjudication shall authorize the Director to take any necessary action, upon compliance with the requirements of law. However, no final judgment shall be entered in favor of an applicant under section1051(b) of this title before the mark is registered, if such applicant cannot prevail without establishing constructive use pursuant to section 1057(c) of this title.

(2) The Director shall not be made a party to an inter partes proceeding under this subsection, but he shall be notified of the filing of the complaint by the clerk of the court in which it is filed and shall have the right to intervene in the action.

(3) In any case where there is no adverse party, a copy of the complaint shall be served on the Director, and, unless the court finds the expenses to be unreasonable, all the expenses of the proceeding shall be paid by the party bringing the case, whether the final decision is in favor of such party or not. In suits brought hereunder, the record in the Patent and Trademark Office shall be admitted on motion of any party, upon such terms and conditions as to costs, expenses, and the further cross-examination of the witnesses as the court imposes, without prejudice to the right of any party to take further testimony. The testimony and exhibits of the record in the Patent and Trademark Office, when admitted, shall have the same effect as if originally taken and produced in the suit.

(4) Where there is an adverse party, such suit may be instituted against the party in interest as shown by the records of the Patent and Trademark Office at the time of the decision complained of, but any party in interest may become a party to the action. If there be adverse parties residing in a plurality of districts not embraced within the same State, or an adverse party residing in a foreign country, the United States District Court for the District of Columbia shall have jurisdiction and may issue summons against the adverse parties directed to the marshal of any district in which any adverse party resides. Summons against adverse parties residing in foreign countries may be served by publication or otherwise as the court directs.

§ 1072. Registration as constructive notice of claim of ownership

Registration of a mark on the principal register provided by this chapter or under the Act of March 3, 1881, or the Act of February 20, 1905, shall be constructive notice of the registrant's claim of ownership thereof.

§ 1091. Supplemental register

(a) Marks registerable

In addition to the principal register, the Director shall keep a continuation of the register provided in paragraph (b) of section 1 of the Act of March 19, 1920, entitled "An Act to give effect to certain provisions of the convention for the protection of trademarks and commercial names, made and signed in the city of Buenos Aires, in the Argentine Republic, August 20, 1910, and for other purposes", to be called the supplemental register. All marks capable of distinguishing applicant's goods or services and not registrable on the principal register provided in this chapter, except those declared to be unregistrable under subsection (a), (b), (c), (d), and (e)(3) of section 1052 of this title, which are in lawful use in commerce by the owner thereof, on or in connection with any goods or services may be registered on the supplemental register upon the payment of the prescribed fee and compliance with the provisions of subsections (a) and (e) of section 1051 of this title so far as they are applicable. Nothing in this section shall prevent the registration on the supplemental register of a mark, capable of distinguishing the applicant's goods or services and not registrable on the principal register under this chapter, that is declared to be unregistrable under section 1052(e) (3) of this title, if such mark has been in lawful use in commerce by the owner thereof, on or in connection with any goods or services, since before December 8, 1993.

(b) Application and proceedings for registration

Upon the filing of an application for registration on the supplemental register and payment of the prescribed fee the Director shall refer the application to the examiner in charge of the registration of marks, who shall cause an examination to be made and if on such examination it shall appear that the applicant is entitled to registration, the registration shall be granted. If the applicant is found not entitled to registration the provisions of subsection (b) of section 1062 of this title shall apply.

(c) Nature of mark

For the purposes of registration on the supplemental register, a mark may consist of any trademark, symbol, label, package, configuration of goods, name, word, slogan, phrase, surname, geographical name, numeral, device, any matter that as a whole is not functional, or any combination of any of the foregoing, but such mark must be capable of distinguishing the applicant's goods or services.

§ 1092. Publication; not subject to opposition; cancellation

Marks for the supplemental register shall not be published for or be subject to opposition, but shall be published on registration in the Official Gazette of the Patent and Trademark Office. Whenever any person believes that such person is or will be damaged by the registration of a mark on the supplemental register—

(1) for which the effective filing date is after the date on which such person's mark became famous and which would be likely to cause dilution by blurring or dilution by tarnishment under section 1125(c) of this title; or

(2) on grounds other than dilution by blurring or dilution by tarnishment, such person may at any time, upon payment of the prescribed fee and the filing of a petition stating the ground therefor, apply to the Director to cancel such registration.

The Director shall refer such application to the Trademark Trial and Appeal Board which shall give notice thereof to the registrant. If it is found after a hearing before the Board that the registrant is not entitled to registration, or that the mark has been abandoned, the registration shall be canceled by the Director. However, no final judgment shall be entered in favor of an applicant under section 1051(b) of this title before the mark is registered, if such applicant cannot prevail without establishing constructive use pursuant to section 1057(c) of this title.

§ 1093. Registration certificates for marks on principal and supplemental registers to be different

The certificates of registration for marks registered on the supplemental register shall be conspicuously different from certificates issued for marks registered on the principal register.

§ 1094. Provisions of chapter applicable to registrations on supplemental register

The provisions of this chapter shall govern so far as applicable applications for registration and registrations on the supplemental register as well as those on the principal register, but applications for and registrations on the supplemental register shall not be subject to or receive the advantages of sections 1051(b), 1052(e), 1052(f), 1057 (b), 1057(c), 1062(a), 1063 to 1068, inclusive, 1072, 1115 and 1124 of this title.

§ 1095. Registration on principal register not precluded

Registration of a mark on the supplemental register, or under the Act of March 19, 1920, shall not preclude registration by the registrant on the principal register established by this chapter. Registration of a mark on the supplemental register shall not constitute an admission that the mark has not acquired distinctiveness.

§ 1096. Registration on supplemental register not used to stop importations

Registration on the supplemental register or under the Act of March 19, 1920, shall not be filed in the Department of the Treasury or be used to stop importations.

§ 1111. Notice of registration; display with mark; recovery of profits and damages in infringement suit

Notwithstanding the provisions of section 1072 of this title, a registrant of a mark registered in the Patent and Trademark Office, may give notice that his mark is registered by displaying with the mark the words "Registered in U.S. Patent and Trademark Office" or "Reg. U.S. Pat. & Tm. Off." or the letter R enclosed within a circle, thus ®; and in any suit for infringement under this chapter by such a registrant failing to give such notice of registration, no profits and no damages shall be recovered under the provisions of this chapter unless the defendant had actual notice of the registration.

§ 1112. Classification of goods and services; registration in plurality of classes

The Director may establish a classification of goods and services, for convenience of Patent and Trademark Office administration, but not to limit or extend the applicant's or registrant's rights. The applicant may apply to register a mark for any or all of the goods or services on or in connection with which he or she is using or has a bona fide intention to use the mark in commerce: *Provided,* That if the Director by regulation permits the filing of an application for the registration of a mark for goods or services which fall within a plurality of classes, a fee equaling the sum of the fees for filing an application in each class shall be paid, and the Director may issue a single certificate of registration for such mark.

§ 1113. Fees

(a) Applications; services; materials

The Director shall establish fees for the filing and processing of an application for the registration of a trademark or other mark and for all other services performed by and materials furnished by the Patent and Trademark Office related to trademarks and other marks. Fees established under this subsection may be adjusted by the Director once each year to reflect, in the aggregate, any fluctuations during the preceding 12 months in the Consumer Price Index, as determined by the Secretary of Labor. Changes of less than 1 percent may be ignored. No fee established under this section shall take effect until at least 30 days after notice of the fee has been published in the Federal Register and in the Official Gazette of the Patent and Trademark Office.

(b) Waiver; Indian products

The Director may waive the payment of any fee for any service or material related to trademarks or other marks in connection with an occasional request made by a department or agency of the Government, or any officer thereof. The Indian Arts and Crafts Board will not be charged any fee to register Government trademarks of genuineness and quality for Indian products or for products of particular Indian tribes and groups.

§ 1114. Remedies; infringement; innocent infringement by printers and publishers

(1) Any person who shall, without the consent of the registrant—

(a) use in commerce any reproduction, counterfeit, copy, or colorable imitation of a registered mark in connection with the sale, offering for sale, distribution, or advertising of any goods or services on or in connection with which such use is likely to cause confusion, or to cause mistake, or to deceive; or

(b) reproduce, counterfeit, copy, or colorably imitate a registered mark and apply such reproduction, counterfeit, copy, or colorable imitation to labels, signs, prints, packages, wrappers, receptacles or advertisements intended to be used in commerce upon or in connection with the sale, offering for sale, distribution, or advertising of goods or services on or in connection with which such use is likely to cause confusion, or to cause mistake, or to deceive,

shall be liable in a civil action by the registrant for the remedies hereinafter provided. Under subsection (b) hereof, the registrant shall not be entitled to recover profits or damages unless the acts have been committed with knowledge that such imitation is intended to be used to cause confusion, or to cause mistake, or to deceive.

As used in this paragraph, the term "any person" includes the United States, all agencies and instrumentalities thereof, and all individuals, firms, corporations, or other persons acting for the United States and with the authorization and consent of the United States, and any State, any instrumentality of a State, and any officer or employee of a State or instrumentality of a State acting in his or her official capacity. The United States, all agencies and instrumentalities thereof, and all individuals, firms, corporations, other persons acting for the United States and with the authorization and consent of the United States, and any State, and any such instrumentality, officer, or employee, shall be subject to the provisions of this chapter in the same manner and to the same extent as any nongovernmental entity.

(2) Notwithstanding any other provision of this chapter, the remedies given to the owner of a right infringed under this chapter or to a person bringing an action under section 1125(a) or (d) of this title shall be limited as follows:

(A) Where an infringer or violator is engaged solely in the business of printing the mark or violating matter for others and establishes that he or she was an innocent infringer or innocent violator, the owner of the right infringed or person bringing the action under section 1125(a) of this title shall be entitled as against such infringer or violator only to an injunction against future printing.

(B) Where the infringement or violation complained of is contained in or is part of paid advertising matter in a newspaper, magazine, or other similar periodical or in an electronic communication as defined in section 2510(12) of Title 18, the remedies of the owner of the right infringed or person bringing the action under section 1125(a) of this title as against the publisher or distributor of such newspaper, magazine, or other similar periodical or electronic communication shall be limited to an injunction against the presentation of such advertising matter in future issues of such newspapers, magazines, or other similar periodicals or in future transmissions of such electronic communications. The limitations of this subparagraph shall apply only to innocent infringers and innocent violators.

(C) Injunctive relief shall not be available to the owner of the right infringed or person bringing the action under section 1125(a) of this title with respect to an issue of a newspaper, magazine, or other similar periodical or an electronic communication containing infringing matter or violating matter where restraining the dissemination of such infringing matter or violating matter in any particular issue of such periodical or in an electronic communication would delay the delivery of such issue or transmission of such electronic communication after the regular time for such delivery or transmission, and such delay would be due to the method by which publication and distribution of such periodical or transmission of such electronic communication is customarily conducted in accordance with sound business practice, and not due to any method or device adopted to evade this section or to prevent or delay the issuance of an injunction or restraining order with respect to such infringing matter or violating matter.

(D)(i)(I) A domain name registrar, a domain name registry, or other domain name registration authority that takes any action described under clause (ii) affecting a domain name shall not be liable for monetary relief or, except as provided in subclause (II), for injunctive relief, to any person for such action, regardless of whether the domain name is finally determined to infringe or dilute the mark.

(II) A domain name registrar, domain name registry, or other domain name registration authority described in subclause (I) may be subject to injunctive relief only if such registrar, registry, or other registration authority has—

(aa) not expeditiously deposited with a court, in which an action has been filed regarding the disposition of the domain name, documents sufficient for the court to establish the court's control and authority regarding the disposition of the registration and use of the domain name;

(bb) transferred, suspended, or otherwise modified the domain name during the pendency of the action, except upon order of the court; or

(cc) willfully failed to comply with any such court order.

(ii) An action referred to under clause (i)(I) is any action of refusing to register, removing from registration, transferring, temporarily disabling, or permanently canceling a domain name—

(I) in compliance with a court order under section 1125(d) of this title; or

(II) in the implementation of a reasonable policy by such registrar, registry, or authority prohibiting the registration of a domain name that is identical to, confusingly similar to, or dilutive of another's mark.

(iii) A domain name registrar, a domain name registry, or other domain name registration authority shall not be liable for damages under this section for the registration or maintenance of a domain name for another absent a showing of bad faith intent to profit from such registration or maintenance of the domain name.

(iv) If a registrar, registry, or other registration authority takes an action described under clause (ii) based on a knowing and material misrepresentation by any other person that a domain name is identical to, confusingly similar to, or dilutive of a mark, the person making the knowing and material misrepresentation shall be liable for any damages, including costs and attorney's fees, incurred by the domain name registrant as a result of such action. The court may also grant injunctive relief to the domain name registrant, including the reactivation of the domain name or the transfer of the domain name to the domain name registrant.

(v) A domain name registrant whose domain name has been suspended, disabled, or transferred under a policy described under clause (ii)(II) may, upon notice to the mark owner, file a civil action to establish that the registration or use of the domain name by such registrant is not unlawful under this chapter. The court may grant injunctive relief to the domain name registrant, including the reactivation of the domain name or transfer of the domain name to the domain name registrant.

(E) As used in this paragraph—

(i) the term "violator" means a person who violates section 1125(a) of this title; and

(ii) the term "violating matter" means matter that is the subject of a violation under section 1125(a) of this title.

(3)(A) Any person who engages in the conduct described in paragraph (11) of section 110 of Title 17, and who complies with the requirements set forth in that paragraph is not liable on account of such conduct for a violation of any right under this chapter. This subparagraph does not preclude liability, nor shall it be construed to restrict the defenses or limitations on rights granted under this chapter, of a person for conduct not described in paragraph (11) of section 110 of Title 17, even if that person also engages in conduct described in paragraph (11) of section 110 of such title.

(B) A manufacturer, licensee, or licensor of technology that enables the making of limited portions of audio or video content of a motion picture imperceptible as described in subparagraph (A) is not liable on account of such manufacture or license for a violation of any right under this chapter, if such manufacturer, licensee, or licensor ensures that the technology provides a clear and conspicuous notice at the beginning of each performance that the performance of the motion picture is altered from the performance intended by the director or copyright holder of the motion picture. The limitations on liability in subparagraph (A) and this subparagraph shall not apply to a manufacturer, licensee, or licensor of technology that fails to comply with this paragraph.

(C) The requirement under subparagraph (B) to provide notice shall apply only with respect to technology manufactured after the end of the 180-day period beginning on April 27, 2005.

(D) Any failure by a manufacturer, licensee, or licensor of technology to qualify for the exemption under subparagraphs (A) and (B) shall not be construed to create an inference that any such party that engages in conduct described in paragraph (11) of section 110 of Title 17 is liable for trademark infringement by reason of such conduct.

§1115. Registration on principal register as evidence of exclusive right to use mark; defenses

(a) Evidentiary value; defenses

Any registration issued under the Act of March 3, 1881, or the Act of February 20, 1905, or of a mark registered on the principal register provided by this chapter and owned by a party to an action shall be admissible in evidence and shall be prima facie evidence of the validity of the registered mark and of the registration of the mark, of the registrant's ownership of the mark, and of the registrant's exclusive right to use the registered mark in commerce on or in connection with the goods or services specified in the registration subject to any conditions or limitations stated therein, but shall not preclude another person from proving any legal or equitable defense or defect, including those set forth in subsection (b) of this section, which might have been asserted if such mark had not been registered.

(b) Incontestability; defenses

To the extent that the right to use the registered mark has become incontestable under section 1065 of this title, the registration shall be conclusive evidence of the validity of the registered mark and of the registration of the mark, of the registrant's ownership of the mark, and of the registrant's exclusive right to use the registered mark in commerce. Such conclusive evidence shall relate to the exclusive right to use the mark on or in connection with the goods or services specified in the affidavit filed under the provisions of section 1065 of this title, or in the renewal application filed under the provisions of section 1059 of this title if the goods or services specified in the renewal are fewer in number, subject to any conditions or limitations in the registration or in such affidavit or renewal application. Such conclusive evidence of the right to use the registered mark shall be subject to proof of infringement as defined in section 1114 of this title, and shall be subject to the following defenses or defects:

(1) That the registration or the incontestable right to use the mark was obtained fraudulently; or

(2) That the mark has been abandoned by the registrant; or

(3) That the registered mark is being used by or with the permission of the registrant or a person in privity with the registrant, so as to misrepresent the source of the goods or services on or in connection with which the mark is used; or

(4) That the use of the name, term, or device charged to be an infringement is a use, otherwise than as a mark, of the party's individual name in his own business, or of the individual name of anyone in privity with such party, or of a term or device which is descriptive of and used fairly and in good faith only to describe the goods or services of such party, or their geographic origin; or

(5) That the mark whose use by a party is charged as an infringement was adopted without knowledge of the registrant's prior use and has been continuously used by such party or those in privity with him from a date prior to (A) the date of constructive use of the mark established pursuant to section 1057(c) of this title, (B) the registration of the mark under this chapter if the application for registration is filed before the effective date of the Trademark Law Revision Act of 1988, or (C) publication of the registered mark under subsection (c) of section 1062 of this title: *Provided, however,* That this defense or defect shall apply only for the area in which such continuous prior use is proved; or

(6) That the mark whose use is charged as an infringement was registered and used prior to the registration under this chapter or publication under subsection (c) of section 1062 of this title of the registered mark of the registrant, and not abandoned: *Provided, however,* That this defense or defect shall apply only for the area in which the mark was used prior to such registration or such publication of the registrant's mark; or

(7) That the mark has been or is being used to violate the antitrust laws of the United States; or

(8) That the mark is functional; or

(9) That equitable principles, including laches, estoppel, and acquiescence, are applicable.

§ 1116. Injunctive relief

(a) Jurisdiction; service

The several courts vested with jurisdiction of civil actions arising under this chapter shall have power to grant injunctions, according to the principles of equity and upon such terms as the court may deem reasonable, to prevent the violation of any right of the registrant of a mark registered in the Patent and Trademark Office or to prevent a violation under subsection (a), (c), or (d) of section 1125 of this title. Any such injunction may include a provision directing the defendant to file with the court and serve on the plaintiff within thirty days after the service on the defendant of such injunction, or such extended period as the court may direct, a report in writing under oath setting forth in detail the manner and form in which the defendant has complied with the injunction. Any such injunction granted upon hearing, after notice to the defendant, by any district court of the United States, may be served on the parties against whom such injunction is granted anywhere in the United States where they may be found, and shall be operative and may be enforced by proceedings to punish for contempt, or otherwise, by the court by which such injunction was granted, or by any other United States district court in whose jurisdiction the defendant may be found.

(b) Transfer of certified copies of court papers

The said courts shall have jurisdiction to enforce said injunction, as provided in this chapter, as fully as if the injunction had been granted by the district court in which it is sought to be enforced. The clerk of the court or judge granting the injunction shall, when required to do so by the court before which application to enforce said injunction is made, transfer without delay to said court a certified copy of all papers on file in his office upon which said injunction was granted.

(c) Notice to Director

It shall be the duty of the clerks of such courts within one month after the filing of any action, suit, or proceeding involving a mark registered under the provisions of this chapter to give notice thereof in writing to the Director setting forth in order so far as known the names and addresses of the litigants and the designating number or numbers of the registration or registrations upon which the action, suit, or proceeding has been brought, and in the event any other registration be subsequently included in the action, suit, or proceeding by amendment, answer, or other pleading, the clerk shall give like notice thereof to the Director, and within one month after the judgment is entered or an appeal is taken the clerk of the court shall give notice thereof to the Director, and it shall be the duty of the Director on receipt of such notice forthwith to endorse the same upon the file wrapper of the said registration or registrations and to incorporate the same as a part of the contents of said file wrapper.

(d) Civil actions arising out of use of counterfeit marks

(1)(A) In the case of a civil action arising under section 1114(1)(a) of this title or section 220506 of Title 36 with respect to a violation that consists of using a counterfeit mark in connection with the sale, offering for sale, or distribution of goods or services, the court may, upon ex parte application, grant an order under subsection (a) of this section pursuant to this subsection providing for the seizure of goods and counterfeit marks involved in such violation and the means of making such marks, and records documenting the manufacture, sale, or receipt of things involved in such violation.

(B) As used in this subsection the term "counterfeit mark" means—

(i) a counterfeit of a mark that is registered on the principal register in the United States Patent and Trademark Office for such goods or services sold, offered for sale, or distributed and that is in use, whether or not the person against whom relief is sought knew such mark was so registered; or

(ii) a spurious designation that is identical with, or substantially indistinguishable from, a designation as to which the remedies of this chapter are made available by reason of section 220506 of Title 36;

but such term does not include any mark or designation used on or in connection with goods or services of which the manufacture or producer was, at the time of the manufacture or production in question authorized to use the mark or designation for the type of goods or services so manufactured or produced, by the holder of the right to use such mark or designation.

(2) The court shall not receive an application under this subsection unless the applicant has given such notice of the application as is reasonable under the circumstances to the United States attorney for the judicial district in which such order is sought. Such attorney may participate in the proceedings arising under such application if such proceedings may affect evidence of an offense against the United States. The court may deny such application if the court determines that the public interest in a potential prosecution so requires.

(3) The application for an order under this subsection shall—

(A) be based on an affidavit or the verified complaint establishing facts sufficient to support the findings of fact and conclusions of law required for such order; and

(B) contain the additional information required by paragraph (5) of this subsection to be set forth in such order.

(4) The court shall not grant such an application unless—

(A) the person obtaining an order under this subsection provides the security determined adequate by the court for the payment of such damages as any person may be entitled to recover as a result of a wrongful seizure or wrongful attempted seizure under this subsection; and

(B) the court finds that it clearly appears from specific facts that—

(i) an order other than an ex parte seizure order is not adequate to achieve the purposes of section 1114 of this title;

(ii) the applicant has not publicized the requested seizure;

(iii) the applicant is likely to succeed in showing that the person against whom seizure would be ordered used a counterfeit mark in connection with the sale, offering for sale, or distribution of goods or services;

(iv) an immediate and irreparable injury will occur if such seizure is not ordered;

(v) the matter to be seized will be located at the place identified in the application;

(vi) the harm to the applicant of denying the application outweighs the harm to the legitimate interests of the person against whom seizure would be ordered of granting the application; and

(vii) the person against whom seizure would be ordered, or persons acting in concert with such person, would destroy, move, hide, or otherwise make such matter inaccessible to the court, if the applicant were to proceed on notice to such person.

(5) An order under this subsection shall set forth—

(A) the findings of fact and conclusions of law required for the order;

(B) a particular description of the matter to be seized, and a description of each place at which such matter is to be seized;

(C) the time period, which shall end not later than seven days after the date on which such order is issued, during which the seizure is to be made;

(D) the amount of security required to be provided under this subsection; and

(E) a date for the hearing required under paragraph (10) of this subsection.

(6) The court shall take appropriate action to protect the person against whom an order under this subsection is directed from publicity, by or at the behest of the plaintiff, about such order and any seizure under such order.

(7) Any materials seized under this subsection shall be taken into the custody of the court. The court shall enter an appropriate protective order with respect to discovery by the applicant of any records that have been seized. The protective order shall provide for appropriate procedures to assure that confidential information contained in such records is not improperly disclosed to the applicant.

(8) An order under this subsection, together with the supporting documents, shall be sealed until the person against whom the order is directed has an opportunity to contest such order, except that any person against whom such order is issued shall have access to such order and supporting documents after the seizure has been carried out.

(9) The court shall order that service of a copy of the order under this subsection shall be made by a Federal law enforcement officer (such as a United States marshal or an officer or agent of the United States Customs Service, Secret Service, Federal Bureau of Investigation, or Post Office) or may be made by a State or local law enforcement officer, who, upon making service, shall carry out the seizure under the order. The court shall issue orders, when appropriate, to protect the defendant from undue damage from the disclosure of trade secrets or other confidential information during the course of the seizure, including, when appropriate, orders restricting the access of the applicant (or any agent or employee of the applicant) to such secrets or information.

(10)(A) The court shall hold a hearing, unless waived by all the parties, on the date set by the court in the order of seizure. That date shall be not sooner than ten days after the order is issued and not later than fifteen days after the order is issued, unless the applicant for the order shows good cause for another date or unless the party against whom such order is directed consents to another date for such hearing. At such hearing the party obtaining the order shall have the burden to prove that the facts supporting findings of fact and conclusions of law necessary to support such order are still in effect. If that party fails to meet that burden, the seizure order shall be dissolved or modified appropriately.

(B) In connection with a hearing under this paragraph, the court may make such orders modifying the time limits for discovery under the Rules of Civil Procedure as may be necessary to prevent the frustration of the purposes of such hearing.

(11) A person who suffers damage by reason of a wrongful seizure under this subsection has a cause of action against the applicant for the order under which such seizure was made, and shall be entitled to recover such relief as may be appropriate, including damages for lost profits, cost of materials, loss of good will, and punitive damages in instances where the seizure was sought in bad faith, and, unless the court finds extenuating circumstances, to recover a reasonable attorney's fee. The court in its discretion

may award prejudgment interest on relief recovered under this paragraph, at an annual interest rate established under section 6621(a)(2) of Title 26, commencing on the date of service of the claimant's pleading setting forth the claim under this paragraph and ending on the date such recovery is granted, or for such shorter time as the court deems appropriate.

§ 1117. Recovery for violation of rights

(a) Profits; damages and costs; attorney fees

When a violation of any right of the registrant of a mark registered in the Patent and Trademark Office, a violation under section 1125(a) or (d) of this title, or a willful violation under section 1125(c) of this title, shall have been established in any civil action arising under this chapter, the plaintiff shall be entitled, subject to the provisions of sections 1111 and 1114 of this title, and subject to the principles of equity, to recover (1) defendant's profits, (2) any damages sustained by the plaintiff, and (3) the costs of the action. The court shall assess such profits and damages or cause the same to be assessed under its direction. In assessing profits the plaintiff shall be required to prove defendant's sales only; defendant must prove all elements of cost or deduction claimed. In assessing damages the court may enter judgment, according to the circumstances of the case, for any sum above the amount found as actual damages, not exceeding three times such amount. If the court shall find that the amount of the recovery based on profits is either inadequate or excessive the court may in its discretion enter judgment for such sum as the court shall find to be just, according to the circumstances of the case. Such sum in either of the above circumstances shall constitute compensation and not a penalty. The court in exceptional cases may award reasonable attorney fees to the prevailing party.

(b) Treble damages for use of counterfeit mark

In assessing damages under subsection (a) of this section, the court shall, unless the court finds extenuating circumstances, enter judgment for three times such profits or damages, whichever is greater, together with a reasonable attorney's fee, in the case of any violation of section 1114(1)(a) of this title or section 220506 of Title 36 that consists of intentionally using a mark or designation, knowing such mark or designation is a counterfeit mark (as defined in section 1116(d) of this title), in connection with the sale, offering for sale, or distribution of goods or services. In such cases, the court may in its discretion award prejudgment interest on such amount at an annual interest rate established under section 6621(a)(2) of Title 26, commencing on the date of the service of the claimant's pleadings setting forth the claim for such entry and ending on the date such entry is made, or for such shorter time as the court deems appropriate.

(c) Statutory damages for use of counterfeit marks

In a case involving the use of a counterfeit mark (as defined in section 1116(d) of this title) in connection with the sale, offering for sale, or distribution of goods or services, the plaintiff may elect, at any time before final judgment is rendered by the trial court, to recover, instead of actual damages and profits under subsection (a) of this section, an award of statutory damages for any such use in connection with the sale, offering for sale, or distribution of goods or services in the amount of—

(1) not less than $500 or more than $100,000 per counterfeit mark per type of goods or services sold, offered for sale, or distributed, as the court considers just; or

(2) if the court finds that the use of the counterfeit mark was willful, not more than $1,000,000 per counterfeit mark per type of goods or services sold, offered for sale, or distributed, as the court considers just.

(d) Statutory damages for violation of section 1125(d)(1)

In a case involving a violation of section 1125(d)(1) of this title, the plaintiff may elect, at any time before final judgment is rendered by the trial court, to recover, instead of actual damages and profits, an award of statutory damages in the amount of not less than $1,000 and not more than $100,000 per domain name, as the court considers just.

(e) Rebuttable presumption of willful violation

In the case of a violation referred to in this section, it shall be a rebuttable presumption that the violation is willful for purposes of determining relief if the violator, or a person acting in concert with the violator, knowingly provided or knowingly caused to be provided materially false contact information to a domain name registrar, domain name registry, or other domain name registration authority in registering, maintaining, or renewing a domain name used in connection with the violation. Nothing in this subsection limits what may be considered a willful violation under this section.

§ 1118. Destruction of infringing articles

In any action arising under this chapter, in which a violation of any right of the registrant of a mark registered in the Patent and Trademark Office, a violation under section 1125(a) of this title, or a willful violation under section 1125(c) of this title, shall have been established, the court may order that all labels, signs, prints, packages, wrappers, receptacles, and advertisements in the possession of the defendant, bearing the registered mark or, in the case of a violation of section 1125(a) of this title or a willful violation under section 1125(c) of this title, the word, term, name, symbol, device, combination thereof, designation, description, or representation that is the subject of the violation, or any reproduction, counterfeit, copy, or colorable imitation thereof, and all plates, molds, matrices, and other means of making the same, shall be delivered up and destroyed. The party seeking an order under this section for destruction of articles seized under section 1116(d) of this title shall give ten days' notice to the United States attorney for the judicial district in which such order is sought (unless good cause is shown for lesser notice) and such United States attorney may, if such destruction may affect evidence of an offense against the United States, seek a hearing on such destruction or participate in any hearing otherwise to be held with respect to such destruction.

§ 1119. Power of court over registration

In any action involving a registered mark the court may determine the right to registration, order the cancelation of registrations, in whole or in part, restore canceled registrations, and otherwise rectify the register with respect to the registrations of any party to the action. Decrees and orders shall be certified by the court to the Director, who shall make appropriate entry upon the records of the Patent and Trademark Office, and shall be controlled thereby.

§ 1120. Civil liability for false or fraudulent registration

Any person who shall procure registration in the Patent and Trademark Office of a mark by a false or fraudulent declaration or representation, oral or in writing, or by any false means, shall be liable in a civil action by any person injured thereby for any damages sustained in consequence thereof.

§ 1121. Jurisdiction of Federal courts; State and local requirements that registered trademarks be altered or displayed differently; prohibition

(a) The district and territorial courts of the United States shall have original jurisdiction and the courts of appeal of the United States (other than the United States Court of Appeals for the Federal Circuit) shall have appellate jurisdiction, of all actions arising under this chapter, without regard to the amount in controversy or to diversity or lack of diversity of the citizenship of the parties.

(b) No State or other jurisdiction of the United States or any political subdivision or any agency thereof may require alteration of a registered mark, or require that additional trademarks, service marks, trade names, or corporate names that may be associated with or incorporated into the registered mark be displayed in the mark in a manner differing from the display of such additional trademarks, service marks, trade names, or corporate names contemplated by the registered mark as exhibited in the certificate of registration issued by the United States Patent and Trademark Office.

§ 1122. Liability of States, instrumentalities of States, and State officials

(a) Waiver of sovereign immunity by the United States

The United States, all agencies and instrumentalities thereof, and all individuals, firms, corporations, other persons acting for the United States and with the authorization and consent of the United States, shall not be immune from suit in Federal or State court by any person, including any governmental or nongovernmental entity, for any violation under this chapter.

(b) Waiver of sovereign immunity by States

Any State, instrumentality of a State or any officer or employee of a State or instrumentality of a State acting in his or her official capacity, shall not be immune, under the eleventh amendment of the Constitution of the United States or under any other doctrine of sovereign immunity, from suit in Federal court by any person, including any governmental or nongovernmental entity for any violation under this chapter.

(c) Remedies

In a suit described in subsection (a) or (b) of this section for a violation described therein, remedies (including remedies both at law and in equity) are available for the violation to the same extent as such remedies are available for such a violation in a suit against any person other than the United States or any agency or instrumentality thereof, or any individual, firm, corporation, or other person acting for the United States and with authorization and consent of the United States, or a State, instrumentality of a State, or officer or employee of a State or instrumentality of a State acting in his or her official capacity. Such remedies include injunctive relief under section 1116 of this title, actual damages, profits, costs and attorney's fees under section 1117 of this title, destruction of infringing articles under section 1118 of this title, the remedies provided for under sections 1114, 1119, 1120, 1124, and 1125 of this title, and for any other remedies provided under this chapter.

§ 1123. Rules and regulations for conduct of proceedings in Patent and Trademark Office

The Director shall make rules and regulations, not inconsistent with law, for the conduct of proceedings in the Patent and Trademark Office under this chapter.

§ 1124. Importation of goods bearing infringing marks or names forbidden

Except as provided in subsection (d) of section 1526 of Title 19, no article of imported merchandise which shall copy or simulate the name of any domestic manufacture, or manufacturer, or trader, or of any manufacturer or trader located in any foreign country which, by treaty, convention, or law affords similar privileges to citizens of the United States, or which shall copy or simulate a trademark registered in accordance with the provisions of this chapter or shall bear a name or mark calculated to induce the public to believe that the article is manufactured in the United States, or that it is manufactured in any foreign country or locality other than the country or locality in which it is in fact manufactured, shall be admitted to entry at any customhouse of the United States; and, in order to aid the officers of the customs in enforcing this prohibition, any domestic manufacturer or trader, and any foreign manufacturer or trader, who is entitled under the provisions of a treaty, convention, declaration, or agreement between the United States and any foreign country to the advantages afforded by law to citizens of the United States in respect to trademarks and commercial names, may require his name and residence, and the name of the locality in which his goods are manufactured, and a copy of the certificate of registration of his trademark, issued in accordance with the provisions of this chapter, to be recorded in books which shall be kept for this purpose in the Department of the Treasury, under such regulations as the Secretary of the Treasury shall prescribe, and may furnish to the Department facsimiles of his name, the name of the locality in which his goods are manufactured, or of his registered trademark, and thereupon the Secretary of the Treasury shall cause one or more copies of the same to be transmitted to each collector or other proper officer of customs.

§ 1125. False designations of origin, false descriptions, and dilution forbidden

(a) Civil action

(1) Any person who, on or in connection with any goods or services, or any container for goods, uses in commerce any word, term, name, symbol, or device, or any combination thereof, or any false designation of origin, false or misleading description of fact, or false or misleading representation of fact, which—

(A) is likely to cause confusion, or to cause mistake, or to deceive as to the affiliation, connection, or association of such person with another person, or as to the origin, sponsorship, or approval of his or her goods, services, or commercial activities by another person, or

(B) in commercial advertising or promotion, misrepresents the nature, characteristics, qualities, or geographic origin of his or her or another person's goods, services, or commercial activities,

shall be liable in a civil action by any person who believes that he or she is or is likely to be damaged by such act.

(2) As used in this subsection, the term "any person" includes any State, instrumentality of a State or employee of a State or instrumentality of a State acting in his or her official capacity. Any State, and any such instrumentality, officer, or employee, shall be subject to the provisions of this chapter in the same manner and to the same extent as any nongovernmental entity.

(3) In a civil action for trade dress infringement under this chapter for trade dress not registered on the principal register, the person who asserts trade dress protection has the burden of proving that the matter sought to be protected is not functional.

(b) Importation

Any goods marked or labeled in contravention of the provisions of this section shall not be imported into the United States or admitted to entry at any customhouse of the United States. The owner, importer, or consignee of goods refused entry at any customhouse under this section may have any recourse by protest or appeal that is given under the customs revenue laws or may have the remedy given by this chapter in cases involving goods refused entry or seized.

(c) Dilution by blurring; dilution by tarnishment

(1) Injunctive relief

Subject to the principles of equity, the owner of a famous mark that is distinctive, inherently or through acquired distinctiveness, shall be entitled to an injunction against another person who, at any time after the owner's mark has become famous, commences use of a mark or trade name in commerce that is likely to cause dilution by blurring or dilution by tarnishment of the famous mark, regardless of the presence or absence of actual or likely confusion, of competition, or of actual economic injury.

(2) Definitions

(A) For purposes of paragraph (1), a mark is famous if it is widely recognized by the general consuming public of the United States as a designation of source of the goods or services of the mark's owner. In determining whether a mark possesses the requisite degree of recognition, the court may consider all relevant factors, including the following:

(i) The duration, extent, and geographic reach of advertising and publicity of the mark, whether advertised or publicized by the owner or third parties.

(ii) The amount, volume, and geographic extent of sales of goods or services offered under the mark.

(iii) The extent of actual recognition of the mark.

(iv) Whether the mark was registered under the Act of March 3, 1881, or the Act of February 20, 1905, or on the principal register.

(B) For purposes of paragraph (1), "dilution by blurring" is association arising from the similarity between a mark or trade name and a famous mark that impairs the distinctiveness of the famous mark. In determining whether a mark or trade name is likely to cause dilution by blurring, the court may consider all relevant factors, including the following:

(i) The degree of similarity between the mark or trade name and the famous mark.

(ii) The degree of inherent or acquired distinctiveness of the famous mark.

(iii) The extent to which the owner of the famous mark is engaging in substantially exclusive use of the mark.

(iv) The degree of recognition of the famous mark.

(v) Whether the user of the mark or trade name intended to create an association with the famous mark.

(vi) Any actual association between the mark or trade name and the famous mark.

(C) For purposes of paragraph (1), "dilution by tarnishment" is association arising from the similarity between a mark or trade name and a famous mark that harms the reputation of the famous mark.

(3) Exclusions

The following shall not be actionable as dilution by blurring or dilution by tarnishment under this subsection:

(A) Any fair use, including a nominative or descriptive fair use, or facilitation of such fair use, of a famous mark by another person other than as a designation of source for the person's own goods or services, including use in connection with—

(i) advertising or promotion that permits consumers to compare goods or services; or

(ii) identifying and parodying, criticizing, or commenting upon the famous mark owner or the goods or services of the famous mark owner.

(B) All forms of news reporting and news commentary.

(C) Any noncommercial use of a mark.

(4) Burden of proof

In a civil action for trade dress dilution under this chapter for trade dress not registered on the principal register, the person who asserts trade dress protection has the burden of proving that—

(A) the claimed trade dress, taken as a whole, is not functional and is famous; and

(B) if the claimed trade dress includes any mark or marks registered on the principal register, the unregistered matter, taken as a whole, is famous separate and apart from any fame of such registered marks.

(5) Additional remedies

In an action brought under this subsection, the owner of the famous mark shall be entitled to injunctive relief as set forth in section 1116 of this title. The owner of the famous mark shall also be entitled to the remedies set forth in sections 1117(a) and 1118 of this title, subject to the discretion of the court and the principles of equity if—

(A) the mark or trade name that is likely to cause dilution by blurring or dilution by tarnishment was first used in commerce by the person against whom the injunction is sought after October 6, 2006; and

(B) in a claim arising under this subsection—

(i) by reason of dilution by blurring, the person against whom the injunction is sought willfully intended to trade on the recognition of the famous mark; or

(ii) by reason of dilution by tarnishment, the person against whom the injunction is sought willfully intended to harm the reputation of the famous mark.

(6) Ownership of valid registration a complete bar to action

The ownership by a person of a valid registration under the Act of March 3, 1881, or the Act of February 20, 1905, or on the principal register under this chapter shall be a complete bar to an action against that person, with respect to that mark, that—

(A)(i) is brought by another person under the common law or a statute of a State; and

(ii) seeks to prevent dilution by blurring or dilution by tarnishment; or

(B) asserts any claim of actual or likely damage or harm to the distinctiveness or reputation of a mark, label, or form of advertisement.

(7) Savings clause

Nothing in this subsection shall be construed to impair, modify, or supersede the applicability of the patent laws of the United States.

(d) Cyberpiracy prevention

(1)(A) A person shall be liable in a civil action by the owner of a mark, including a personal name which is protected as a mark under this section, if, without regard to the goods or services of the parties, that person

(i) has a bad faith intent to profit from that mark, including a personal name which is protected as a mark under this section; and

(ii) registers, traffics in, or uses a domain name that—

(I) in the case of a mark that is distinctive at the time of registration of the domain name, is identical or confusingly similar to that mark;

(II) in the case of a famous mark that is famous at the time of registration of the domain name, is identical or confusingly similar to or dilutive of that mark; or

(III) is a trademark, word, or name protected by reason of section 706 of Title 18 or section 220506 of Title 36.

(B)(i) In determining whether a person has a bad faith intent described under subparagraph (a), a court may consider factors such as, but not limited to

(I) the trademark or other intellectual property rights of the person, if any, in the domain name;

(II) the extent to which the domain name consists of the legal name of the person or a name that is otherwise commonly used to identify that person;

(III) the person's prior use, if any, of the domain name in connection with the bona fide offering of any goods or services;

(IV) the person's bona fide noncommercial or fair use of the mark in a site accessible under the domain name;

(V) the person's intent to divert consumers from the mark owner's online location to a site accessible under the domain name that could harm the goodwill represented by the mark, either for commercial gain or with the intent to tarnish or disparage the mark, by creating a likelihood of confusion as to the source, sponsorship, affiliation, or endorsement of the site;

(VI) the person's offer to transfer, sell, or otherwise assign the domain name to the mark owner or any third party for financial gain without having used, or having an intent to use, the domain name in the bona fide offering of any goods or services, or the person's prior conduct indicating a pattern of such conduct;

(VII) the person's provision of material and misleading false contact information when applying for the registration of the domain name, the person's intentional failure to maintain accurate contact information, or the person's prior conduct indicating a pattern of such conduct;

(VIII) the person's registration or acquisition of multiple domain names which the person knows are identical or confusingly similar to marks of others that are distinctive at the time of registration of such domain names, or dilutive of famous marks of others that are famous at the time of registration of such domain names, without regard to the goods or services of the parties; and

(IX) the extent to which the mark incorporated in the person's domain name registration is or is not distinctive and famous within the meaning of subsection (c) of this section.

(ii) Bad faith intent described under subparagraph (A) shall not be found in any case in which the court determines that the person believed and had reasonable grounds to believe that the use of the domain name was a fair use or otherwise lawful.

(C) In any civil action involving the registration, trafficking, or use of a domain name under this paragraph, a court may order the forfeiture or cancellation of the domain name or the transfer of the domain name to the owner of the mark.

(D) A person shall be liable for using a domain name under subparagraph (A) only if that person is the domain name registrant or that registrant's authorized licensee.

(E) As used in this paragraph, the term "traffics in" refers to transactions that include, but are not limited to, sales, purchases, loans, pledges, licenses, exchanges of currency, and any other transfer for consideration or receipt in exchange for consideration.

(2)(A) The owner of a mark may file an in rem civil action against a domain name in the judicial district in which the domain name registrar, domain name registry, or other domain name authority that registered or assigned the domain name is located if

(i) the domain name violates any right of the owner of a mark registered in the Patent and Trademark Office, or protected under subsection (a) or (c) of this section; and

(ii) the court finds that the owner—

(I) is not able to obtain in personam jurisdiction over a person who would have been a defendant in a civil action under paragraph (1); or

(II) through due diligence was not able to find a person who would have been a defendant in a civil action under paragraph (1) by—

(aa) sending a notice of the alleged violation and intent to proceed under this paragraph to the registrant of the domain name at the postal and e-mail address provided by the registrant to the registrar; and

(bb) publishing notice of the action as the court may direct promptly after filing the action.

(B) The actions under subparagraph (A)(ii) shall constitute service of process.

(C) In an in rem action under this paragraph, a domain name shall be deemed to have its situs in the judicial district in which

(i) the domain name registrar, registry, or other domain name authority that registered or assigned the domain name is located; or

(ii) documents sufficient to establish control and authority regarding the disposition of the registration and use of the domain name are deposited with the court.

(D)(i) The remedies in an in rem action under this paragraph shall be limited to a court order for the forfeiture or cancellation of the domain name or the transfer of the domain name to the owner of the mark. upon receipt of written notification of a filed, stamped copy of a complaint filed by the owner of a mark in a United States district court under this paragraph, the domain name registrar, domain name registry, or other domain name authority shall

(I) expeditiously deposit with the court documents sufficient to establish the court's control and authority regarding the disposition of the registration and use of the domain name to the court; and

(II) not transfer, suspend, or otherwise modify the domain name during the pendency of the action, except upon order of the court.

(ii) The domain name registrar or registry or other domain name authority shall not be liable for injunctive or monetary relief under this paragraph except in the case of bad faith or reckless disregard, which includes a willful failure to comply with any such court order.

(3) The civil action established under paragraph (1) and the in rem action established under paragraph (2), and any remedy available under either such action, shall be in addition to any other civil action or remedy otherwise applicable.

(4) The in rem jurisdiction established under paragraph (2) shall be in addition to any other jurisdiction that otherwise exists, whether in rem or in personam.

§ 1126. International conventions

(a) Register of marks communicated by international bureaus

The Director shall keep a register of all marks communicated to him by the international bureaus provided for by the conventions for the protection of industrial property, trademarks, trade and commercial names, and the repression of unfair competition to which the United States is or may become a party, and upon the payment of the fees required by such conventions and the fees required in this chapter may place the marks so communicated upon such register. This register shall show a facsimile of the mark or trade or commercial name; the name, citizenship, and address of the registrant; the number, date, and place of the first registration of the mark, including the dates on which application for such registration was filed and granted and the term of such registration; a list of goods or services to which the mark is applied as shown by the registration in the country of origin, and such other data as may be useful concerning the mark. This register shall be a continuation of the register provided in section 1(a) of the Act of March 19, 1920.

(b) Benefits of section to persons whose country of origin is party to convention or treaty

Any person whose country of origin is a party to any convention or treaty relating to trademarks, trade or commercial names, or the repression of unfair competition, to which the United States is also a party, or extends reciprocal rights to nationals of the United States by law, shall be entitled to the benefits of this section under the conditions expressed herein to the extent necessary to give effect to any provision of such convention, treaty or reciprocal law, in addition to the rights to which any owner of a mark is otherwise entitled by this chapter.

(c) Prior registration in country of origin; country of origin defined

No registration of a mark in the United States by a person described in subsection (b) of this section shall be granted until such mark has been registered in the country of origin of the applicant, unless the applicant alleges use in commerce.

For the purposes of this section, the country of origin of the applicant is the country in which he has a bona fide and effective industrial or commercial establishment, or if he has not such an establishment the country in which he is domiciled, or if he has not a domicile in any of the countries described in subsection (b) of this section, the country of which he is a national.

(d) Right of priority

An application for registration of a mark under section 1051, 1053, 1054, or 1091 of this title or under subsection (e) of this section, filed by a person described in subsection (b) of this section who has previously duly filed an application for registration of the same mark in one of the countries described in subsection (b) of this section shall be accorded the same force and effect as would be accorded to the same application if filed in the United States on the same date on which the application was first filed in such foreign country: *Provided*, That—

(1) the application in the United States is filed within six months from the date on which the application was first filed in the foreign country;

(2) the application conforms as nearly as practicable to the requirements of this chapter, including a statement that the applicant has a bona fide intention to use the mark in commerce;

(3) the rights acquired by third parties before the date of the filing of the first application in the foreign country shall in no way be affected by a registration obtained on an application filed under this subsection;

(4) nothing in this subsection shall entitle the owner of a registration granted under this section to sue for acts committed prior to the date on which his mark was registered in this country unless the registration is based on use in commerce.

In like manner and subject to the same conditions and requirements, the right provided in this section may be based upon a subsequent regularly filed application in the same foreign country, instead of the first filed foreign application: *Provided,* That any foreign application filed prior to such subsequent application has been withdrawn, abandoned, or otherwise disposed of, without having been laid open to public inspection and without leaving any rights outstanding, and has not served, nor thereafter shall serve, as a basis for claiming a right of priority.

(e) Registration on principal or supplemental register; copy of foreign registration

A mark duly registered in the country of origin of the foreign applicant may be registered on the principal register if eligible, otherwise on the supplemental register in this chapter provided. Such applicant shall submit, within such time period as may be prescribed by the Director, a true copy, a photocopy, a certification, or a certified copy of the registration in the country of origin of the applicant. The application must state the applicant's bona fide intention to use the mark in commerce, but use in commerce shall not be required prior to registration.

(f) Domestic registration independent of foreign registration

The registration of a mark under the provisions of subsections (c), (d), and (e) of this section by a person described in subsection (b) of this section shall be independent of the registration in the country of origin and the duration, validity, or transfer in the United States of such registration shall be governed by the provisions of this chapter.

(g) Trade or commercial names of foreign nationals protected without registration

Trade names or commercial names of persons described in subsection (b) of this section shall be protected without the obligation of filing or registration whether or not they form parts of marks.

(h) Protection of foreign nationals against unfair competition

Any person designated in subsection (b) of this section as entitled to the benefits and subject to the provisions of this chapter shall be entitled to effective protection against unfair competition, and the remedies provided in this chapter for infringement of marks shall be available so far as they may be appropriate in repressing acts of unfair competition.

(i) Citizens or residents of United States entitled to benefits of section

Citizens or residents of the United States shall have the same benefits as are granted by this section to persons described in subsection (b) of this section.

§ 1127. Construction and definitions; intent of chapter

In the construction of this chapter, unless the contrary is plainly apparent from the context—

The United States includes and embraces all territory which is under its jurisdiction and control.

The word "commerce" means all commerce which may lawfully be regulated by Congress.

The term "principal register" refers to the register provided for by sections 1051 to 1072 of this title, and the term "supplemental register" refers to the register provided for by sections 1091 to 1096 of this title.

The term "person" and any other word or term used to designate the applicant or other entitled to a benefit or privilege or rendered liable under the provisions of this chapter includes a juristic person as well as a natural person. The term "juristic person" includes a firm, corporation, union, association, or other organization capable of suing and being sued in a court of law.

The term "person" also includes the United States, any agency or instrumentality thereof, or any individual, firm, or corporation acting for the United States and with the authorization and consent of the United States. The United States, any agency or instrumentality thereof, and any individual, firm, or corporation acting for the United States and with the authorization and consent of the United States, shall be subject to the provisions of this chapter in the same manner and to the same extent as any nongovernmental entity.

The term "person" also includes any State, any instrumentality of a State, and any officer or employee of a State or instrumentality of a State acting in his or her official capacity. Any State, and any such instrumentality, officer, or employee, shall be subject to the provisions of this chapter in the same manner and to the same extent as any nongovernmental entity.

The terms "applicant" and "registrant" embrace the legal representatives, predecessors, successors and assigns of such applicant or registrant.

The term "Director" means the Under Secretary of Commerce for Intellectual Property and Director of the United States Patent and Trademark Office.

The term "related company" means any person whose use of a mark is controlled by the owner of the mark with respect to the nature and quality of the goods or services on or in connection with which the mark is used.

The terms "trade name" and "commercial name" mean any name used by a person to identify his or her business or vocation.

The term "trademark" includes any word, name, symbol, or device, or any combination thereof—

(1) used by a person, or

(2) which a person has a bona fide intention to use in commerce and applies to register on the principal register established by this chapter,

to identify and distinguish his or her goods, including a unique product, from those manufactured or sold by others and to indicate the source of the goods, even if that source is unknown.

The term "service mark" means any word, name, symbol, or device, or any combination thereof—

(1) used by a person, or

(2) which a person has a bona fide intention to use in commerce and applies to register on the principal register established by this chapter,

to identify and distinguish the services of one person, including a unique service, from the services of others and to indicate the source of the services, even if that source is unknown. Titles, character names, and other distinctive features of radio or television programs may be registered as service marks notwithstanding that they, or the programs, may advertise the goods of the sponsor.

The term "certification mark" means any word, name, symbol, or device, or any combination thereof—

(1) used by a person other than its owner, or

(2) which its owner has a bona fide intention to permit a person other than the owner to use in commerce and files an application to register on the principal register established by this chapter,

to certify regional or other origin, material, mode of manufacture, quality, accuracy, or other characteristics of such person's goods or services or that the work or labor on the goods or services was performed by members of a union or other organization.

The term "collective mark" means a trademark or service mark—

(1) used by the members of a cooperative, an association, or other collective group or organization, or

(2) which such cooperative, association, or other collective group or organization has a bona fide intention to use in commerce and applies to register on the principal register established by this chapter,

and includes marks indicating membership in a union, an association, or other organization.

The term "mark" includes any trademark, service mark, collective mark, or certification mark.

The term "use in commerce" means the bona fide use of a mark in the ordinary course of trade, and not made merely to reserve a right in a mark. For purposes of this chapter, a mark shall be deemed to be in use in commerce—

(1) on goods when—

(A) it is placed in any manner on the goods or their containers or the displays associated therewith or on the tags or labels affixed thereto, or if the nature of the goods makes such placement impracticable, then on documents associated with the goods or their sale, and

(B) the goods are sold or transported in commerce, and

(2) on services when it is used or displayed in the sale or advertising of services and the services are rendered in commerce, or the services are rendered in more than one State or in the United States and a foreign country and the person rendering the services is engaged in commerce in connection with the services.

A mark shall be deemed to be "abandoned" if either of the following occurs:

(1) When its use has been discontinued with intent not to resume such use. Intent not to resume may be inferred from circumstances. Nonuse for 3 consecutive years shall be prima facie evidence of abandonment. "Use" of a mark means the bona fide use of such mark made in the ordinary course of trade, and not made merely to reserve a right in a mark.

(2) When any course of conduct of the owner, including acts of omission as well as commission, causes the mark to become the generic name for the goods or services on or in connection with which it is used or otherwise to lose its significance as a mark. Purchaser motivation shall not be a test for determining abandonment under this paragraph.

The term "colorable imitation" includes any mark which so resembles a registered mark as to be likely to cause confusion or mistake or to deceive.

The term "registered mark" means a mark registered in the United States Patent and Trademark Office under this chapter or under the Act of March 3, 1881, or the Act of February 20, 1905, or the Act of March 19, 1920. The phrase "marks registered in the Patent and Trademark Office" means registered marks.

The term "Act of March 3, 1881", "Act of February 20, 1905", or "Act of March 19, 1920", means the respective Act as amended.

A "counterfeit" is a spurious mark which is identical with, or substantially indistinguishable from, a registered mark.

The term "domain name" means any alphanumeric designation which is registered with or assigned by any domain name registrar, domain name registry, or other domain name registration authority as part of an electronic address on the Internet.

The term "Internet" has the meaning given that term in section 230(f)(1) of Title 47.

Words used in the singular include the plural and vice versa.

The intent of this chapter is to regulate commerce within the control of Congress by making actionable the deceptive and misleading use of marks in such commerce; to protect registered marks used in such commerce from interference by State, or territorial legislation; to protect persons engaged in such commerce against unfair competition; to prevent fraud and deception in such commerce by the use of reproductions, copies, counterfeits, or colorable imitations of registered marks; and to provide rights and remedies stipulated by treaties and conventions respecting trademarks, trade names, and unfair competition entered into between the United States and foreign nations.

§ 1128. National Intellectual Property Law Enforcement Coordination Council

(a) Establishment

There is established the National Intellectual Property Law Enforcement Coordination Council (in this section referred to as the "Council"). The Council shall consist of the following members—

(1) The Under Secretary of Commerce for Intellectual Property and Director of the United States Patent and Trademark Office, who shall serve as co-chair of the Council.

(2) The Assistant Attorney General, Criminal Division, who shall serve as co-chair of the Council.

(3) The Under Secretary of State for Economic and Agricultural Affairs.

(4) The Ambassador, Deputy United States Trade Representative.

(5) The Commissioner of Customs.

(6) The Under Secretary of Commerce for International Trade.

(7) The Coordinator for International Intellectual Property Enforcement.

(b) Duties

The Council established in subsection (a) of this section shall coordinate domestic and international intellectual property law enforcement among federal and foreign entities.

(c) Consultation required

The Council shall consult with the Register of Copyrights on law enforcement matters relating to copyright and related rights and matters.

(d) Non-derogation

Nothing in this section shall derogate from the duties of the Secretary of State or from the duties of the United States Trade Representative as set forth in section 2171 of Title 19 or from the duties and functions of the Register of Copyrights, or otherwise alter current authorities relating to copyright matters.

(e) Report

The Council shall report annually on its coordination activities to the President, and to the Committees on Appropriations and on the Judiciary of the Senate and the House of Representatives.

(f) Funding

Notwithstanding section 1346 of Title 31, or section 610 of this Act, funds made available for fiscal year 2000 and hereafter by this or any other Act shall be available for interagency funding of the National Intellectual Property Law Enforcement Coordination Council.

§ 1129. Cyberpiracy protections for individuals

(1) In general

(A) Civil liability

Any person who registers a domain name that consists of the name of another living person, or a name substantially and confusingly similar thereto, without that person's consent, with the specific intent to profit from such name by selling the domain name for financial gain to that person or any third party, shall be liable in a civil action by such person.

(B) Exception

A person who in good faith registers a domain name consisting of the name of another living person, or a name substantially and confusingly similar thereto, shall not be liable under this paragraph if such name is used in, affiliated with, or related to a work of authorship protected under Title 17, including a work made for hire as defined in section 101 of Title 17, and if the person registering the domain name is the copyright owner or licensee of the work, the person intends to sell the domain name in conjunction with the lawful exploitation of the work, and such registration is not prohibited by a contract between the registrant and the named person. The exception under this subparagraph shall apply only to a civil action brought under paragraph (1) and shall in no manner limit the protections afforded under the Trademark Act of 1946 (15 U.S.C. 1051 et seq.) or other provision of Federal or State law.

(2) Remedies

In any civil action brought under paragraph (1), a court may award injunctive relief, including the forfeiture or cancellation of the domain name or the transfer of the domain name to the plaintiff. The court may also, in its discretion, award costs and attorneys fees to the prevailing party.

(3) Definition

In this section, the term "domain name" has the meaning given that term in section 45 of the Trademark Act of 1946 (15 U.S.C 1127).

(4) Effective date

This section shall apply to domain names registered on or after November 29, 1999.

§ 1141. Definitions

In this subchapter:

(1) Basic application

The term "basic application" means the application for the registration of a mark that has been filed with an Office of a Contracting Party and that constitutes the basis for an application for the international registration of that mark.

(2) Basic registration

The term "basic registration" means the registration of a mark that has been granted by an Office of a Contracting Party and that constitutes the basis for an application for the international registration of that mark.

(3) Contracting party

The term "Contracting Party" means any country or inter-governmental organization that is a party to the Madrid Protocol.

(4) Date of recordal

The term "date of recordal" means the date on which a request for extension of protection, filed after an international registration is granted, is recorded on the International Register.

(5) Declaration of bona fide intention to use the mark in commerce

The term "declaration of bona fide intention to use the mark in commerce" means a declaration that is signed by the applicant for, or holder of, an international registration who is seeking extension of protection of a mark to the United States and that contains a statement that—

(A) the applicant or holder has a bona fide intention to use the mark in commerce;

(B) the person making the declaration believes himself or herself, or the firm, corporation, or association in whose behalf he or she makes the declaration, to be entitled to use the mark in commerce; and

(C) no other person, firm, corporation, or association, to the best of his or her knowledge and belief, has the right to use such mark in commerce either in the identical form of the mark or in such near resemblance to the mark as to be likely, when used on or in connection with the goods of such other person, firm, corporation, or association, to cause confusion, mistake, or deception.

(6) Extension of protection

The term "extension of protection" means the protection resulting from an international registration that extends to the United States at the request of the holder of the international registration, in accordance with the Madrid Protocol.

(7) Holder of an international registration

A "holder" of an international registration is the natural or juristic person in whose name the international registration is recorded on the International Register.

(8) International application

The term "international application" means an application for international registration that is filed under the Madrid Protocol.

(9) International Bureau

The term "International Bureau" means the International Bureau of the World Intellectual Property Organization.

(10) International Register

The term "International Register" means the official collection of data concerning international registrations maintained by the International Bureau that the Madrid Protocol or its implementing regulations require or permit to be recorded.

(11) International registration

The term "international registration" means the registration of a mark granted under the Madrid Protocol.

(12) International registration date

The term "international registration date" means the date assigned to the international registration by the International Bureau.

(13) Madrid Protocol

The term "Madrid Protocol" means the Protocol Relating to the Madrid Agreement Concerning the International Registration of Marks, adopted at Madrid, Spain, on June 27, 1989.

(14) Notification of refusal

The term "notification of refusal" means the notice sent by the United States Patent and Trademark Office to the International Bureau declaring that an extension of protection cannot be granted.

(15) Office of a Contracting Party

The term "Office of a Contracting Party" means—

(A) the office, or governmental entity, of a Contracting Party that is responsible for the registration of marks; or

(B) the common office, or governmental entity, of more than 1 Contracting Party that is responsible for the registration of marks and is so recognized by the International Bureau.

(16) Office of origin

The term "office of origin" means the Office of a Contracting Party with which a basic application was filed or by which a basic registration was granted.

(17) Opposition period

The term "opposition period" means the time allowed for filing an opposition in the United States Patent and Trademark Office, including any extension of time granted under section 1063 of this title.

§ 1141a. International applications based on United States applications or registrations

(a) In general

The owner of a basic application pending before the United States Patent and Trademark Office, or the owner of a basic registration granted by the United States Patent and Trademark Office may file an international application by submitting to the United States Patent and Trademark Office a written application in such form, together with such fees, as may be prescribed by the Director.

(b) Qualified owners

A qualified owner, under subsection (a) of this section, shall—

(1) be a national of the United States;

(2) be domiciled in the United States; or

(3) have a real and effective industrial or commercial establishment in the United States.

§ 1141b. Certification of the international application

(a) Certification procedure

Upon the filing of an application for international registration and payment of the prescribed fees, the Director shall examine the international application for the purpose of certifying that the information contained in the international application corresponds to the information contained in the basic application or basic registration at the time of the certification.

(b) Transmittal

Upon examination and certification of the international application, the Director shall transmit the international application to the International Bureau.

§ 1141c. Restriction, abandonment, cancellation, or expiration of a basic application or basic registration

With respect to an international application transmitted to the International Bureau under section 1141b of this title, the Director shall notify the International Bureau whenever the basic application or basic registration which is the basis for the international application has been restricted, abandoned, or canceled, or has expired, with respect to some or all of the goods and services listed in the international registration—

(1) within 5 years after the international registration date; or

(2) more than 5 years after the international registration date if the restriction, abandonment, or cancellation of the basic application or basic registration resulted from an action that began before the end of that 5-year period.

§ 1141d. Request for extension of protection subsequent to international registration

The holder of an international registration that is based upon a basic application filed with the United States Patent and Trademark Office or a basic registration granted by the Patent and Trademark Office may request an extension of protection of its international registration by filing such a request—

(1) directly with the International Bureau; or

(2) with the United States Patent and Trademark Office for transmittal to the International Bureau, if the request is in such form, and contains such transmittal fee, as may be prescribed by the Director.

§ 1141e. Extension of protection of an international registration to the United States under the Madrid Protocol

(a) In general

Subject to the provisions of section 1141h of this title, the holder of an international registration shall be entitled to the benefits of extension of protection of that international registration to the United States to the extent necessary to give effect to any provision of the Madrid Protocol.

(b) If the United States is office of origin

Where the United States Patent and Trademark Office is the office of origin for a trademark application or registration, any international registration based on such application or registration cannot be used to obtain the benefits of the Madrid Protocol in the United States.

§ 1141f. Effect of filing a request for extension of protection of an international registration to the United States

(a) Requirement for request for extension of protection

A request for extension of protection of an international registration to the United States that the International Bureau transmits to the United States Patent and Trademark Office shall be deemed to be properly filed in the United States if such request, when received by the International Bureau, has attached to it a declaration of bona fide intention to use the mark in commerce that is verified by the applicant for, or holder of, the international registration.

(b) Effect of proper filing

Unless extension of protection is refused under section 1141h of this title, the proper filing of the request for extension of protection under subsection (a) of this section shall constitute constructive use of the mark, conferring the same rights as those specified in section 1057(c) of this title, as of the earliest of the following:

(1) The international registration date, if the request for extension of protection was filed in the international application.

(2) The date of recordal of the request for extension of protection, if the request for extension of protection was made after the international registration date.

(3) The date of priority claimed pursuant to section 1141g of this title.

§ 1141g. Right of priority for request for extension of protection to the United States

The holder of an international registration with a request for an extension of protection to the United States shall be entitled to claim a date of priority based on a right of priority within the meaning of Article 4 of the Paris Convention for the Protection of Industrial Property if—

(1) the request for extension of protection contains a claim of priority; and

(2) the date of international registration or the date of the recordal of the request for extension of protection to the United States is not later than 6 months after the date of the first regular national filing (within the meaning of Article 4(A)(3) of the Paris Convention for the Protection of Industrial Property) or a subsequent application (within the meaning of Article 4(C)(4) of the Paris Convention for the Protection of Industrial Property).

§ 1141h. Examination of and opposition to request for extension of protection; notification of refusal

(a) Examination and opposition

(1) A request for extension of protection described in section 1141f(a) of this title shall be examined as an application for registration on the Principal Register under this chapter, and if on such examination it appears that the applicant is entitled to extension of protection under this subchapter, the Director shall cause the mark to be published in the Official Gazette of the United States Patent and Trademark Office.

(2) Subject to the provisions of subsection (c) of this section, a request for extension of protection under this subchapter shall be subject to opposition under section 1063 of this title.

(3) Extension of protection shall not be refused on the ground that the mark has not been used in commerce.

(4) Extension of protection shall be refused to any mark not registrable on the Principal Register.

(b) Notification of refusal

If, a request for extension of protection is refused under subsection (a) of this section, the Director shall declare in a notification of refusal (as provided in subsection (c) of this section) that the extension of protection cannot be granted, together with a statement of all grounds on which the refusal was based.

(c) Notice to International Bureau

(1) Within 18 months after the date on which the International Bureau transmits to the Patent and Trademark Office a notification of a request for extension of protection, the Director shall transmit to the International Bureau any of the following that applies to such request:

(A) A notification of refusal based on an examination of the request for extension of protection.

(B) A notification of refusal based on the filing of an opposition to the request.

(C) A notification of the possibility that an opposition to the request may be filed after the end of that 18-month period.

(2) If the Director has sent a notification of the possibility of opposition under paragraph (1)(C), the Director shall, if applicable, transmit to the International Bureau a notification of refusal on the basis of the opposition, together with a statement of all the grounds for the opposition, within 7 months after the beginning of the opposition period or within 1 month after the end of the opposition period, whichever is earlier.

(3) If a notification of refusal of a request for extension of protection is transmitted under paragraph (1) or (2), no grounds for refusal of such request other than those set forth in such notification may be transmitted to the International Bureau by the Director after the expiration of the time periods set forth in paragraph (1) or (2), as the case may be.

(4) If a notification specified in paragraph (1) or (2) is not sent to the International Bureau within the time period set forth in such paragraph, with respect to a request for extension of protection, the request for extension of protection shall not be refused and the Director shall issue a certificate of extension of protection pursuant to the request.

(d) Designation of agent for service of process

In responding to a notification of refusal with respect to a mark, the holder of the international registration of the mark may designate, by a document filed in the United States Patent and Trademark Office, the name and address of a person residing in the United States on whom notices or process in proceedings affecting the mark may be served. Such notices or process may be served upon the person designated by leaving with that person, or mailing to that person, a copy thereof at the address specified in the last designation filed. If the person designated cannot be found at the address given in the last designation, or if the holder does not designate by a document filed in the United States Patent and Trademark Office the name and address of a person residing in the United States for service of notices or process in proceedings affecting the mark, the notice or process may be served on the Director.

§ 1141i. Effect of extension of protection

(a) Issuance of extension of protection

Unless a request for extension of protection is refused under section 1141h of this title, the Director shall issue a certificate of extension of protection pursuant to the request and shall cause notice of such certificate of extension of protection to be published in the Official Gazette of the United States Patent and Trademark Office.

(b) Effect of extension of protection

From the date on which a certificate of extension of protection is issued under subsection (a) of this section—

(1) such extension of protection shall have the same effect and validity as a registration on the Principal Register; and

(2) the holder of the international registration shall have the same rights and remedies as the owner of a registration on the Principal Register.

§ 1141j. Dependence of extension of protection to the United States on the underlying international registration

(a) Effect of cancellation of international registration

If the International Bureau notifies the United States Patent and Trademark Office of the cancellation of an international registration with respect to some or all of the goods and services listed in the international registration, the Director shall cancel any extension of protection to the United States with respect to such goods and services as of the date on which the international registration was canceled.

(b) Effect of failure to renew international registration

If the International Bureau does not renew an international registration, the corresponding extension of protection to the United States shall cease to be valid as of the date of the expiration of the international registration.

(c) Transformation of an extension of protection into a United States application

The holder of an international registration canceled in whole or in part by the International Bureau at the request of the office of origin, under article 6(4) of the Madrid Protocol, may file an application, under section 1051 or 1126 of this title, for the registration of the same mark for any of the goods and services to which the cancellation applies that were covered by an extension of protection to the United States based on that international registration. Such an application shall be treated as if it had been filed on the international registration date or the date of recordal of the request for extension of protection with the International Bureau, whichever date applies, and, if the extension of protection enjoyed priority under section 1141g of this title, shall enjoy the same priority. Such an application shall be entitled to the benefits conferred by this subsection only if the application is filed not later than 3 months after the date on which the international registration was canceled, in whole or in part, and only if the application complies with all the requirements of this chapter which apply to any application filed pursuant to sectuib 1951 or 1126 of this title.

§ 1141k. Affidavits and fees

(a) Required affidavits and fees

An extension of protection for which a certificate of extension of protection has been issued under section 1141i of this title shall remain in force for the term of the international registration upon which it is based, except that the extension of protection of any mark shall be canceled by the Director—

(1) at the end of the 6-year period beginning on the date on which the certificate of extension of protection was issued by the Director, unless within the 1-year period preceding the expiration of that 6-year period the holder of the international registration files in the Patent and Trademark Office an affidavit under subsection (b) of this section together with a fee prescribed by the Director; and

(2) at the end of the 10-year period beginning on the date on which the certificate of extension of protection was issued by the Director, and at the end of each 10-year period thereafter, unless—

(A) within the 6-month period preceding the expiration of such 10-year period the holder of the international registration files in the United States Patent and Trademark Office an affidavit under subsection (b) of this section together with a fee prescribed by the Director; or

(B) within 3 months after the expiration of such 10-year period, the holder of the international registration files in the Patent and Trademark Office an affidavit under subsection (b) of this section together with the fee described in subparagraph (A) and the surcharge prescribed by the Director.

(b) Contents of affidavit

The affidavit referred to in subsection (a) of this section shall set forth those goods or services recited in the extension of protection on or in connection with which the mark is in use in commerce and the holder of the international registration shall attach to the affidavit a specimen or facsimile showing the current use of the mark in commerce, or shall set forth that any nonuse is due to special circumstances which excuse such nonuse and is not due to any intention to abandon the mark. Special notice of the requirement for such affidavit shall be attached to each certificate of extension of protection.

(c) Notification

The Director shall notify the holder of the international registration who files 1 of the affidavits of the Director's acceptance or refusal thereof and, in case of a refusal, the reasons therefor.

(d) Service of notice or process

The holder of the international registration of the mark may designate, by a document filed in the United States Patent and Trademark Office, the name and address of a person residing in the United States on whom notices or process in proceedings affecting the mark may be served. Such notices or process may be served upon the person so designated by leaving with that person, or mailing to that person, a copy thereof at the address specified in the last designation so filed. If the person designated cannot be found at the address given in the last designation, or if the holder does not designate by a document filed in the United States Patent and Trademark Office the name and address of a person residing in the United States for service of notices or process in proceedings affecting the mark, the notice or process may be served on the Director.

§ 1141*l*. Assignment of an extension of protection

An extension of protection may be assigned, together with the goodwill associated with the mark, only to a person who is a national of, is domiciled in, or has a bona fide and effective industrial or commercial establishment either in a country that is a Contracting Party or in a country that is a member of an intergovernmental organization that is a Contracting Party.

§ 1141m. Incontestability

The period of continuous use prescribed under section 1065 of this title for a mark covered by an extension of protection issued under this subchapter may begin no earlier than the date on which the Director issues the certificate of the extension of protection under section 1141i of this title, except as provided in section 1141n of this title.

§ 1141n. Rights of extension of protection

When a United States registration and a subsequently issued certificate of extension of protection to the United States are owned by the same person, identify the same mark, and list the same goods or services, the extension of protection shall have the same rights that accrued to the registration prior to issuance of the certificate of extension of protection.

Index

Tables are indicated by a bolded **t**.

A

abandonment, 306, 309
    foreclosure through trade embargo, 371
    forfeiture, 382–383
    Lanham Act § 14, 305
    loss of rights, 357–384
    nonuse, 357–371
ACPA (Anticybersquatting Consumer Protection Act), 521–550
    bad faith intent to profit, 529–537
    Lanham Act, § 43(d), 521–523
    relationship with UDRP, 592–598
    in rem jurisdiction, 540–546
    statutory damages, 546–550
    willful cybersquatting, 524–528
acquiescence, 133–140
acquisition of rights, 165–217
Administrative Procedures Act, 240
adoption and use, 165–178
advertising, comparative, 416–425. *See also* disparaging marks
    and "alteration dilution," 474
advertising, false, 416–432
    availability of product, 425–432
    Lanham Act § 43(a)(1)(B), 416
    literal and implied, 419–425, 432
advertising, pop-up, 602–609
"advertising injury," 140
adwords, 602
aesthetic functionality, 414–415
Anticybersquatting Act, 175–178, 224
application process
    Intent to Use (ITU) system, 222 **t7.3**
    Madrid Protocol application process, 223 **t7.4**
    PTO registrations and Madrid Protocol, 221
arbitrary terms, 145–146

assignment in gross
    definition, 371
    inappropriate use, sale of trade name, 371–374
attorneys' fees
Lanham Act § 35(a), 672–677

B

bad faith intent, 526–527, 529–540
    ACPA in rem jurisdiction application, 540–546
    evidence of, in UDRP, 551
    factors, Lanham Act § 43(d), 522
    famous names, 569–581
    and likelihood of confusion, 589–590
    recovery of profits without proving deception, 657–664
    safe harbor provision, 530–531
    UDRP registration and bad faith use, 552–555, 560–562
"bait and switch" confusion, 92
"bank," 217
bankruptcy, 370–371
banner advertisements, 612–613
bargain theory, 26
Beebe, Barton, 495
blurring. *See* dilution
Bone, Robert G., 488
Brooks, Wayde, 501, 505
Burk, Dan L., 497–499

C

cancellation
    failure to file Section 8 Affidavit, 220
    Lanham Act § 14, 305
"central" attack, 630
certification mark, 307
civil law, 30–33
    civil action, Lanham Act § (a)(1)(A), 385
Coase theorem, 30–31

color, 69–77, 474
    inherently distinctive, 396
    secondary meaning, 396
commerce, rendering in, 175–178
commerce, use in. *See* use
common law, 3–6, 24
competition, unfair
    freedom to compete, 28–30
    pop-up advertising, 602–605
    rational basis of trademark protec-
        tion, 449–455
comprehensive general liability plan
  (CGL), 140
concurrent use, 193–199
    federal and state registrants, 193–196
    on the internet, 200
    of unregistered mark, 165
configuration, product. *See* product con-
    figuration
confusion. *See also* likelihood of confu-
    sion
    actual, 77, 79–80, 83–84, 513–514
    confusingly similar domain names,
        556–557, 562–567, 581–592
    confusingly similar goods *vs.* coun-
        terfeit
    Lanham Act §43(b), 441–448
    confusingly similar *vs.* identical, 526
    consumer, 41–45, 610, 646–648
    direct, 102
    "dual use" exception, 106–107
    forward, 105–106
    initial interest, 92, 101–103
    intentional, 83
    Lanham Act §2(d), 248–262
    likelihood of, 77–92, 249–253
    reverse, 102–107
    as to source, 24
Constitution, U.S. *See* U.S. Constitution
constructive trust, 661
consumer. *See* likelihood of confusion
Coombe, Rosemary, 33
counterfeit goods, 623, 645–650
    Lanham Act §43(b), 441–448
Court of Appeals 1st Circuit
    ACPA and UDRP, 592–598
    application of Lanham Act extraterri-
        torially, 638–642
    dilution of trade dress, 474–478

likelihood of confusion elements,
    89–91
parody as protected speech, 35–40
Court of Appeals 2nd Circuit
    abandonment by nonuse, 357–361
    "actual dilution," 480–481n17
    admissibility of survey evidence,
        347–357
    "alteration dilution," 474
    assignment in gross, inappropriate
        use, 371–374
    attorney's fees, 672–673
    cybersquatting, 524–528
    failure to use, 196–199
    fair use; good faith for descriptive
        purposes, 115–119
    First Amendment justification, 34–35
    genericism in foreign language, 346
    generic term (Thermos), 335–338
    hot news, 14–17
    lack of use in commerce, 166–172
    legal positivism, 17–19
    likelihood of confusion elements,
        77–80, 85–89
    limited injunction, disclaimer as
        remedy, 650–654
    New York state anti-dilution statute,
        460–465
    pop-up advertising, 605–609
    primarily merely a surname, 286–290
    product packaging as trade dress,
        55–59
    punitive damages, 666–671
    recovery of accounting profits,
        657–664
    in rem jurisdiction, domain registry
        location, 545
    "Sweet factors," dilution, 476–477
    trademark protection categories,
        141–145
Court of Appeals 3rd Circuit
    nominative fair use analysis, 127–132
Court of Appeals 4th Circuit
    ACPA in rem jurisdiction application,
        540–546
    adoption and use of word mark,
        189–192
    bad faith intent to profit, 529–534
    dilution by blurring, 466–471

dilution by tarnishment, 472
domain name parody, 546
estoppel by laches, 136–139
free imitation, 59–61
international corporation, "rendering in commerce," 175–178
Court of Appeals 5th Circuit
   failure to establish use in commerce, 180–185
   quality control requirement, 380–383
   secondary meaning, descriptive *vs.* suggestive term, 153–157
   state law *vs.* Lanham Act, xxxiii–xliii
   statutory damages for domain name infringement, 547–549
Court of Appeals 6th Circuit
   aesthetic functionality, 414–415
   reversal of attorney's fees award, 673–677
   trade dress factors, secondary meaning, 400
   unauthorized use of likeness, 438–440
Court of Appeals 7th Circuit
   geographic boundaries *vs.* concurrent use, 193–199
   incontestability, generic term, 319–321
   likelihood of confusion factors, 512–514
   metatag use in competitor's domain name, 601–602
   reverse confusion, 103–107
   secondary meaning, appellation of source, 147–153
   TTAB review process, 240–241
Court of Appeals 8th Circuit
   bad faith intent to profit, 534–537
   likelihood of confusion, 80–85
   relevant public, application of *Squirto* analysis, 95–101
Court of Appeals 9th Circuit
   ACPA and protected commercial speech on internet, 535–537
   commercial *vs.* noncommercial speech, 518–521
   domain name dilution, 515–521
   famous mark, expanded requirements, 486–487

First Amendment protection of cultural icon, 41–45
functionality of product design, 406–411
"monopoly" as generic term, 338–345
nominative fair use analysis, 124–133
nongenericness of "Yellow Cab," 345–346
primarily geographically deceptively misdescriptive, 275–277
scope of property right in trademark, 19–20
vicarious liability, 111–115
Court of Appeals 10th Circuit
   initial interest confusion, 101–103
Court of Appeals 11th Circuit
   incontestability, likelihood of confusion analysis, 321–323
Court of Appeals Federal Circuit (CAFC)
   deceptively misdescriptive geographic, 283–284
   likelihood of confusion, 248–254
   merely descriptive, 262–264
   NAFTA changes to Lanham Act, 270–275
   primarily geographically deceptively misdescriptive, 277–280
   primarily geographically descriptive, 268–270
   promotional contest as service mark, 51–55
   secondary meaning, 210–216, 299–302
   trade dress as product design, 398–400
   use in commerce requirement, 172–178
Court of Appeals of New York
   state anti dilution statute, 455–460
Court of International Trade
   counterfeit *vs.* confusingly similar goods, 441–448
cyberflying, 563–567, 567
cybergriping, 45, 47
cybermarks, 497–499
cyberpiracy prevention. *See also* bad faith intent
   Lanham Act § 43(d), 521–523

cyberpiracy prevention *(continued)*
    relationship between ACPA and
        UDRP, 592–598
cybersquatting, 224, 567. *See also* bad
  faith intent
    application of ACPA to willful,
        524–528
    case, ACPA and UDRP, 592–598
    cybermarks, 497–499
    definition, 179–180, 497, 503
    dispute over domain name, 509–514
    and "hot news," 499
    mousetrapping, 567
    statistics, WIPO filings, 555
    typosquatting, 562–567, 567
    UDRP response to, 504–505

D

D. C. Circuit Court of Appeals
    foreign national priority in registra-
        tion over US, 615–619
damages
    actual, recovery of, 664–665
    punitive
    Lanham Act §35(a), 666–671
    statutory
    Lanham Act §35(d), 546–550
damage theory of profits, 661–662
Dave, Sanjeev, 545
"dead wood," 384
deception, 248–262
deceptively misdescriptive
    Lanham Act §2(e)(1), 264–268
    plausibility, 267
    two prongs, 267
de facto functionality, 410–411
de facto secondary meaning, 162–163
defenses to infringement, 115–140
    fair use, 115–124
    invalidity, 139
    laches/acquiescense, 133–140
    nominative fair use, 124–133
de jure functionality, 409–410
Denicola, Robert C., 46
descriptiveness, 263–264
descriptive term, 143–144
destructions, 654–657
deterrence, 223, 662
dilution, 449–496. *See also* parody;
  TDRA (Trademark Dilution Revision
  Act)

actual, not likelihood, 483
by blurring, 465–471, 480–481,
    490–492, 517n1
definition, 483, 516–517
domain names, 515–521
domain names, bad faith intent to
    profit, 529–534
factors establishing, 484–485
by freeriding, 489, 492
intellectual origins of doctrine,
    449–455, 475
Lanham Act §43(c), 449–496
likelihood of, in TDRA, 493
New York state anti-dilution statute,
    455–465
by pop-up advertising, 602–609
by tarnishment, 472–474
of trade dress, 474–478
U.S. Supreme Court's view, 478–485
disclaimers, 92, 650–654
Disney
    domain name dispute, 562–567
disparaging marks, 229–239
    internet domain names as, 497–499
distinctiveness, xxxvii–xxxix, 141–147,
  176
    acquired and inherent, in TDRA,
        493–494
    definition, 526
    inherently distinctive trade dress,
        394–401
    New York state, dilution, 464
    and trade dress, 386–394
District Court Central District of California
    evolution of domain name system,
        499–501
District Court Eastern District of Virginia
    ACPA, in rem jurisdiction, 543–545
    deceptively misdescriptive, 265–268
    dilution by tarnishment; product de-
        sign trade dress, 472–474
    pop-up advertising, 602–609
District Court Eastern District of
Wisconsin
    secondary meaning, inherent distinc-
        tiveness *vs.* acquired meaning,
        157–162
District Court for District of Columbia
    "Redskins" as disparaging mark,
        229–239

District Court Northern District of California
  key word density, 609–613
District Court of Maryland
  primarily geographically deceptively misdescriptive, 280–283
District Court of Massachusetts
  prior use in "intrastate commerce," 185–189
District Court of Minnesota
  false advertising, availability of product, 425–432
District Court of Western Washington
  UDRP vs. ACPA, 597–598
District Court Southern District of California
  functionality of product feature, 411–414
District Court Southern District of New York
  aspirin as generic term, 330–334
  comparative vs. false advertising, 417–425
  injunction, marketing copies of copyrighted CDs, 645–650
  injunction, recall and destroy infringing trademarked goods, 654–657
domain names. See also ACPA (Anticybersquatting Consumer Protection Act); reverse domain name hijacking
  ACPA vs. UDRP, 592–598
  bad faith intent to profit, dilution, 529–534
  commercial use of others' domain names, 515–521, 535–539
  criticism vs. parody, 588–592
  extraterritoriality, 638–642
  famous names, 569–581
  identical vs. confusingly similar mark, 556–557
  importance of, 502
  key word density, 609–613
  Lanham Act § 43(d), 497–613
  legal protections, 509–514
  nominative use (metatags), 598–602
  pop-up advertising, 602–609
  registration process, ICANN, 505–507
  reservation for use and registration, 508

system, evolution of, 499–501
types of conflicts with, 503–504
UDRP, 550–562
"use in commerce" and, 179–180
WIPO dispute, famous vs. generic marks, 562–567
Dueker, Kenneth Sutherlin, 545
                        E
Eleventh Amendment, 139
England
  history of trademark protection in, 449–453
enrichment, unjust, 660–661
entertainment services
  abandonment, 371–380
  celebrity status trademark protection, 438–441
  injunction, marketing copies of copyrighted CDs, 645–650
  television network, limited injunction with disclaimer, 650–654
  unaccredited copying of a work, 432–437
equity principles, 306, 309
EU (European Union), 284–285
evidence, survey. See survey evidence
exclusion, right of, 25
extraterritoriality, 634–643
                        F
failure to police, 383–384
fair use, 115–124
  descriptive marks, 132
  examples of, 124, 132–133
  nominative, 124–133
  nominative, three-prong test of Ninth Circuit, 130–131
famous marks doctrine, 193, 474. See also tarnishment
  consumer discouragement, 521
  cyberpiracy prevention, 521–523
  dilution, 478–485
  expanded requirements for dilution, 485–487
famous vs. distinctive, 526
  niche fame, 488
  TRIPS Agreement, 619–623
  WIPO dispute, famous vs. generic marks, 562–567
famous names, 569–581
fanciful terms, 145–146

federal law summary, 27 **fig1.1**
First Amendment protection, 33–47
   and ACPA safe harbor provision, 537
   commercial speech, 241
   commercial *vs.* noncommercial
     speech on internet, 518–521
   "dual use" exception, 106–107
first to file system, 27
first to use system, 27, 165, 182, 192–193
foreign equivalents doctrine, 346
fraud in the procurement, 285, 309
FTDA (Federal Trademark Dilution Act),
  465–496
   adoption and history of, 485–488
   California domain name dilution
     case, 515–521
   Lanham Act § 43(c)(1) and (c)(2)(B),
     465–496
functionality, xxxv–xxxvii ,290–299
   aesthetic, 414–415
   analysis, de jure *vs.* de facto, 409–411
   defense to incontestability, 309
   definition, 293–296
   determination of, 296–298
   doctrine, 72–73
   Lanham Act § 2(e)(5), 290–299
   Lanham Act § 14(3), 305
   and trade dress in utility patent,
     403–405

G

genericide, 346
genericism
   definition, generic, 143
   definition, generic mark, 146, 312
   examples, 147
   expressive, 46
generic term, 143, 144 n3
   incontestability, 319–321
generic TLDs (gTLDs), 500, 506
   new, 507
   new (sponsored and unsponsored),
     508
   Lanham Act § 14, 325
   legal status, 339
   loss of rights, 325–357
   WIPO dispute, famous *vs.* generic
     marks, 562–567
"geographical indications," 242–243
   of source, TRIPS Agreement, 623

geographic mark. *See also* primarily geographically deceptively misdescriptive
   new interpretation of deceptively
     misdescriptive, 283–284
Godfread, Paul, 631
Gold, H. David, 283
"good-place" association, 272, 274
goods as entertainment services, 185–189
goodwill, 134, 489
Gurry, Francis, 555

H

Handler, Milton, 216
Harley engine sound, 68
harmonization
   objectives of, 624, 626–627
   of trademark law, 624–628
"hot news," 7–14
   and cybersquatting, 499
   misappropriation of state, 14–17

I

ICANN (Internet Corporation for Assigned Names and Numbers), 501,
  504–507. *See also* Uniform Dispute Resolution Policy (UDRP)
icon, parody of, 41–45
imitation, 59–61
immoral marks, 224–229
incontestability, 223–224
   defenses, 306, 309
   Lanham Act § 33(b), 306–308
   determinative factor of mark
     strength, 324
   history of and confusion about,
     310–311
   Lanham Act § 15, 305–311
   likelihood of confusion, 321–323
   offensive and defensive use, 313–315
information, misappropriation of, 7–17,
  24
infringement, 77–140
   contributory, 107–110
   defenses, 115–140
   First Amendment justification, 34–35
   initial interest confusion, 101–103
   as judicial construction, 91
   legal protections of domain names,
     509–514
   likelihood of confusion, 77–92
   relevant consuming public, 93–101

reverse confusion, 103–107
   state law, xxxiv–xxxv
initial interest confusion, 611–612. *See also* domain names
   banner advertisements, 612–613
   definition, 102
injunctions as remedy, 645–650
insurance coverage, 140
Intellectual Property Protection Restoration Act (IPPRA), 140
intent to use, 200–216
   Lanham Act § 1, 200–206
international law
   extraterritoriality, 634–643
   Japan, 20–23
   Madrid Protocol, 629–631
   Paris Convention, 615–619
   TRIPS Agreement, 619–623
"international" registration system. *See* Madrid Protocol
internet. *See also* ACPA (Anticybersquatting Consumer Protection Act); cybersquatting; domain names
   advertising banner, 612–613
   adwords, use by search engine, 602
   complaint sites, 45
   cybermarks, 497–499
   domain name disputes, 497–499
   history of, 501–502
ITU (Intent to Use) system, 201–202
   intent of, 202
   secondary meaning in the making doctrine, 210–216

J

Japan
   first-to-file or first-to-use systems, 20–23, 27
   Madrid Protocol, trademark application statistics, 632–633
   trademark dilution law, 496
   trademark infringement claim summary, 642–643
jurisdiction
   Lanham Act § 34, 645–650
   Lanham Act, foreign activities of foreign nationalists, 638–642
   in rem
   Lanham Act § 43(d)(2)(A), 540–546

   location of domain name registry, 545

K

Kibort, Adam, 631
"knock-out" search, 303

L

laches, 133–140
LaFrance, Mary, 283–284
Lanham Act. *See also* ACPA (Anticybersquatting Consumer Protection Act); Appendix for text of U.S.C. § 15
   § 1, intent to use, 200–216, 207
   § 2, scandalous marks, 224–243
   § 2(a), constitutionality of, 241
   § 2(a), self-disparaging marks and slurs, 242
   § 2(b), flag or coat of arms, 243–246
   § 2(c), names, portrait, signatures, 246–248
   § 2(d), confusion, 248–262
   § 2(e)(1), deceptively misdescriptive, 264–268
   § 2(e)(1), merely descriptive, 262–264
   § 2(e)(2), changed by NAFTA, 271–275
   § 2(e)(2), primarily geographically descriptive, 268–270
   § 2(e)(3), changed by NAFTA, 271–275
   § 2(e)(3), primarily geographically deceptively misdescriptive, 270–285
   § 2(e)(4), primarily merely a surname, 285–290
   § 2(e)(5), functionality, 290–299
   § 2(f), secondary meaning, 299–302
   § 7, constructive use confers right of priority, 200–216
   § 14, cancellation, 307–308
   § 14, genericism, 325
   § 14(1), mark cancellation, 305
   § 14(3), generic name, functional *vs.* abandoned, 305
   § 15, incontestability, 305–311
   § 32, likelihood of confusion, 77–92
   § 33(b), incontestability defenses, 306–308, 307
   § 34, jurisdiction; service, 645–650

Lanham Act *(conintued)*
§35, monetary relief, 657
§35(a), attorney fees, 672–677
§35(a), punitive damages, 666–671
§35(d), statutory damages, 546–550
§37, judicial review of validity of registration, 316
§43, applied to domain name case,
610–611
§43(a), unregistered trade dress,
385–448
§43(a)(1)(A), civil action, 385
§43(a)(1)(B), false advertising, 416
§43(b), importation, counterfeit *vs.*
confusingly similar goods,
441–448
§43(c), dilution, 449–496
§43(c)(1) and (c)(2)(B), FTDA,
465–496
§43(d), cyberpiracy prevention,
521–523
§43(d), domain names, 497–613
§43(d)(2)(A), in rem jurisdiction,
540–546
§45, service mark, 51–55
§45, "use in commerce," 165–175
definition, trademark, 3
domain names, parody and criticism
under, 590
foreign national priority in registration over US corporation,
615–619
registration, dilution used to cancel,
485
source of trademark law, 3
state law, xxxiii–xliii
token use, 179
trade dress protection, 55–59
use in commerce, pop-up advertising, 605–609
liability, vicarious, 110–115
likelihood of confusion, xxxix–xli, 19–20
domain name as criticism *vs.* parody,
588–592
Lanham Act §32, 77–92
Seventh Circuit factors, 512–514
UDRP domain name identical *vs.*
confusingly similar, 556–557
litigation, completed cases in district
courts, 650 fig.

Locke, John, 25
                    M
Madrid Agreement, 629–630
Madrid Protocol, 629–631
application process under, 223 t7.4
filing savings under, 631
Madrid applications report, 633 **fig.**
rate of refusals, statistics, 631–632
U.S. experience with, 632–633
merely descriptive, 262–264
as defense for incontestability,
311–319
Lanham Act §2(e)(1), 262–264
registration if has secondary meaning, 312
metatags, 598–602
Minnesota Court of Appeals
abandonment by nonuse, 367–370
misappropriation *vs.* protected speech,
35–40
mistake (cause), 248–262
monetary relief
Lanham Act §35, 657–677
monopoly, 170, 455. *See also* competition
mousetrapping, 567
                    N
NAFTA (North American Free Trade
Agreement), 283–284
Lanham Act §2(e)(2), 271–275
naked licenses, 374–383
names
Lanham Act §2(c), 246–248
"naming," 303
Native Americans
Offensive terms, statistics, 239
"Redskins" as disparaging trademark,
229–239
natural rights
philosophy of intellectual property,
25–26
vs. positive rights, 7–14
news
misappropriation of information,
7–17, 24
nominative use, xli–xlii ,598–600
Northern District of Illinois
domain name ownership dispute,
509–514
"intent to use" and foreign trademarks, 205–210

notice, 223

O

offensive terms (Native American), statistics, 239 **fig.**
opinion letter, 303
origin of goods, 434–436

P

packaging, product. *See* product packaging
Paris Convention (for Protection of Industrial Property), 615–619
  and TRIPS Agreement, 622
parody
  criticism *vs.*, domain name, 588–592
  defense to dilution by blurring, 470–471, 546
  protected speech, 35–40
  state of the law of, 46
Pickett, Charles, 216
pop-up advertising, 602–609
portraits
  Lanham Act § 2(c), 246–248
positive rights, 17–19, 514
  legal positivism, definition of, 26–27
  vs. natural rights, 7–14
primarily geographically deceptively misdescriptive
  changed by NAFTA, 271–275
  Lanham Act § (e)(3), 270–285
permanently denied, 273
primarily geographically descriptive
changed by NAFTA, 271–275
Lanham Act § 2(e)(2), 268–270
primarily merely a surname, 285–290
primary meaning, 151
priority, 165, 180–192. *See also* first to
use system
  domain name conflict, 503–504
  first to use requirement, 180
  nationwide, 179
  in registration, Paris Convention, 615–619
  right of, and constructive use, 200–216
product configuration, 59–61
  container as trademark, 290–298
product design. *See* trade dress
product packaging, 55–59
profits, grounds for awarding, 659–663
property

incontestability and, 323–324
  in news matter, 7–14
property rights, 6, 23–24
proprietary mark, 449
protection
  bankruptcy, effect on trademark rights, 370–371
  First Amendment justification, 33–47
  economic justification of, 30–32
  of foreign trademark, Madrid Protocol, 630–631
  national, with federal registration, 223
  "rational basis" of trademark, 449–455
  requirements of, 176
  of service mark, color, 69–77
  social justification of, 32–33
  of trade dress (restaurant), 62
  under TRIPS Agreement, 619–623
PTO (Patent and Trademark Office), 219–220, 240
public interest, 99–101, 163
punitive damages, 666–672

Q

quality control, lack of, 374–383

R

recalls, 654–657
Redskins, as disparaging trademark, 229–239
registration, 219–222
  abusive, 581–592
  advantages, 222–224
  application and registration statistics, 220 t7.1
  domain name, ICANN, 505–507
  federal, 223
  foreign national with priority in, Paris Convention, 615–619
  incontestability defenses, 306
  incontestability grounds, 307–311
registration, 219–222
  Madrid Protocol, international simultaneous, 629–631
  PTO (Patent and Trademark Office), 219–220
  refusal of offensive mark, 224–229
  registration of geographical indications, 242–243

registration *(continued)*
   statutory bars to, 224–303
   use-based trademark application
      process, 221 t7.2
regulatory production mark, 449
Reichman, J.H., 619
remedies, 645–677
   disclaimers, 650–654
   injunctions, 645–650
   monetary relief, 657–677
   recalls and destructions, 654–657
requirements, trademark
   distinctiveness, 141–147
   secondary meaning, 147–162
residual hearsay rule, 351–356
Restatement of the Law (Third), 29–30,
   107
reverse confusion, 103–107
reverse domain name hijacking, 503
   case, ACPA and UDRP, 592–598
   WIPO, bad faith use of mark,
      567–568
review, PTO decisions, 240
review, TTAB, 240–241
reward theory, 26
Rosenberg, Emily S., 628
                        S
scandalous marks
   Lanham Act § 2, 224–243
scent marks, 63–66
Schechter, Frank, 449, 491
searches, 303–304
secondary meaning
   acquired, 147
   "de facto," 162–163
   definition, 395n4
   factors, 400
   Intent to Use (ITU) system, 210–216
   Lanham Act § 2(f), 299–302
   Lanham Act § 43(a), 386–390
   in the making doctrine, 216
   New York state and dilution, 464
   primary meaning, definition, 151
   service mark, color, 73
self-disparaging marks
   Lanham Act § 2(a), 242
service marks
   definition, xxxv ,52
   Lanham Act § 45, 51–55

reversal of attorney's fees award,
   673–677
sound, Harley engine, 68
sound, ship's bell, 66–68
signatures
   Lanham Act § 2(c), 246–248
Smith, Anna Nicole, 581
sounds, 66–68
source
   appellation of, *vs.* primary meaning,
      147–153
   "dual use" exception, 106–107
   "geographic indications," under
      TRIPS Agreement, 623
   inherently distinctive trade dress as,
      59–61
   misrepresentation of, 306
sovereign immunity, 139
sovereignty theories, 625–626
speech, protected
   abusive registrations, 581–592
   commercial *vs.* noncommercial
      speech on the internet, 518–521,
      535–537
   "intermediate scrutiny," 241
   internet "complaint" sites, 45
   parody, 35–45
   and the TDRA, 474
   trademark as, 241
Springsteen, Bruce, 569–581
state law
   misappropriation of "hot news,"
      14–17
   preemption of, by Lanham Act,
      xxxiii–xliv
Sting (Sumner, Gordon), 575–581
subject matter, 49–75
color, 69–77
   scent marks, 63–66
   service marks, 51–55
   sound, 66–68
   word marks, 49–55
"suggestive" marks, 144–145
surname, primarily merely
   Lanham Act § (e)(4), 285–290
survey evidence, 99, 156–157
   admissibility of, in general, 347–351
   brand-name survey, 342
   cost, expert witness, 347

evidentiary value of, 422–425
Gengler analysis and FasTape survey, 356
grounds for admissibility of, 347–351
grounds for inadmissibility of, 352–356
implied falsehoods, 420–425
likelihood of confusion, 260–261
motivation survey, 343–345
residual hearsay rule, 351–356
state of mind exception to admissibility, 349–351
"Thermos" survey, 336–337, 342–343
Tide survey, 345
"Sweet factors," 476–477
symbols, protection of, 46
Lanham Act § 2(b), 243–246

T

tarnishment. *See also* dilution
definition, 517n1
dilution by, 472–474, 489–490
and protected speech, 35–40
TDRA (Trademark Dilution Revision Act), 488–495
"actual" *vs.* "likely to cause" dilution, 488–489
amended FTDA, 488
dilution policies, 489
policy arguments, 491–492
tarnishment and parody exception, 493
territoriality principle, 192–193
"banking" marks, 217
extraterritoriality, 634–643
and rights, 180
territorial theories of sovereignty, 625
tertium quid, 62, 397, 400–401
thorough conviction standard, 240
3/13 policy, 219–220
token use, 179
trade dress
application of trademark continuum to, 146
awarding attorney's fees, 672–673
dilution for, in TDRA, 494–495
dilution of, 474–478

factors showing secondary meaning, 400
functional, 401–416
inherently distinctive, 394–401
judicial definition, 386n1
product configuration, 59–61
product-design *vs.* product-packaging, 397–398
product packaging, 55–59
protectible, xxxiv–xxxix
recovery of profits without proving deception, 657–664
of restaurant, 62, 386–394
unregistered
Lanham Act § 43(a), 385–448
trademarks
definition, xxxiv, 3
intellectual origins of dilution doctrine, 449–455
trademark continuum, 146
Trademark Examiners, 219–220, 242
trademark law
litigation, in district courts, 650 **fig**
source of, 3–6
US. experience with Madrid Protocol, 629–633
Trademark Law Treaty (TLT), 625–628
"Trademark Search Report," 303
TRIPS Agreement (Trade Related Intellectual Property Aspects), 619–623
basic principles, 620–621
"geographical indications," definition, 243
logic of, 619–620
trademarks protected under WTO, 622–623
TTAB (Trademark Trial and Appeal Board), 220
abandonment, 361–367, 374–380
condom flag as immoral mark, 224–229
likelihood to cause confusion, 254–262
primarily merely a surname, 285–286
priority right and constructive use, 202–205
"Redskins" as disparaging trademark, 229–239

TTAB *(continued)*
  registration refusal, flag or coat of
    arms, 224–225
  registration refusal, use of name
    without consent, 246–248
  scent mark, 63–66
  sound as service mark, 66–68
typosquatting, 562–567

U

unfair competition. *See* competition, unfair
Uniform Dispute Resolution Policy
(UDRP)
  § 4(a)(i), identical *vs.* confusingly
    similar, 556–557
  § 4(a) (ii), legitimate interests,
    557–560
  §§ 4(a) (iii) and 4(b), registration
    and use in bad faith, 560–562
  § 4 (b), domain name bad faith appli-
    cation, 571–573
  § 4(b)(ii), famous *vs.* generic,
    562–567
  ADR, domain names, 550–567
  cybersquatting, 224
  dispute resolution procedure of
    ICANN, 504–505
  domain names dispute, famous
    names, 569–581
  relationship with ACPA, 592–598
United States Patent and Trademark Office. *See* PTO (Patent and Trademark
Office)
U.S. Constitution, 3, 4–6. *See also* First
Amendment protection
U.S. Supreme Court
  application of Constitution to trade-
    mark law, 4–6
  definition, distinctive product design,
    394–401
  color, 69–74
  contributory infringement, dispens-
    ing of generic drug, 107–110
  fair use, consumer confusion,
    119–124
  famous marks, 478–485
  functionality determination, features
    vs. design in entirety, 401–406
  function, 449

  generic term, shredded wheat as,
    325–329
  incontestability, 309–310
  incontestability, merely descriptive as
    defense for, 311–319
  laches/acquiescence, 133–136
  misappropriation of information
    ("hot news"), 7–14
  property rights in intellectual prop-
    erty, 6
  public reputation, 93–95
  recent decisions, analysis of, 415–416
  trade dress of a restaurant, 62,
    386–394
  trademark infringement in foreign
    country by US citizen, 634–638
  unaccredited copying of a work,
    432–437
  word mark, Coca-Cola, 49–51
U.S.C. § 15. *See* Lanham Act
use. *See also* bad faith intent; ITU system
  actual application *vs.* ITU system ap-
    plication, 201
  and adoption, 165–178
  analogous to trademark use, 262
  in commerce, 176
    failure to establish, 180–185
    federal recognition prior to,
      201–202
    interstate, 199
    intrastate, 185–189
    Lanham Act § 45, 165–176,
      605–609
  concurrent, 193–199
  constructive, and right of priority
    Lanham Act § 7, 200–216
  constructive first, 201–202
  failure to, 196–199
  first, as defense to incontestability,
    309
  inappropriate
    assignment in gross, 371–374
    failure to police, 383–384
    naked licenses/lack of quality con-
      trol, 374–383
  intent to, 200–216
  misuse, defense to incontestability,
    309
  nonuse, 357–371

open, 183
prior, 180, 306
token, 179

V

validity
  evidentiary advantages to federal reg-
    istration, 224
  incontestable registration as proof,
    309
  judicial review, registration
    Lanham Act § 37, 316
  trademark continuum, 146

W

Wal-Mart Stores
  abusive registration, "walsucks,"
    581–592
  domain name as criticism *vs.* parody,
    588–592
web sites. *See* domain names; internet
Welkowitz, David, 485
Widmaier, Uli, 546
WIPO (World Intellectual Property Organization)
  cybersquatting statistics, 555
  domain names, abusive registrations,
    581–592
  domain names, famous names,
    569–581
  domain names, famous *vs.* generic
    marks, 562–567
  Madrid Protocol, 629
  Madrid Protocol, international appli-
    cation statistics, 632–633
  UDRP domain names, legitimate in-
    terests, 558–560
  UDRP domain names, identical *vs.*
    confusingly similar, 556–557
  UDRP domain names registration
    and bad faith use, 552–555
word marks, 49–55
  adoption and use, 189–192
  Coca-Cola as, 49–51
WTO (World Trade Organization), 243
  TRIPS Agreement, 619–623